Classic Theatre: The Humanities in Drama

Classic Theatre
the Humanities in Drama

Edited by

Sylvan Barnet, *Tufts University*

Morton Berman, *Boston University*

William Burto, *University of Lowell*

Educational Associates

a division of Little, Brown and Company   Boston

Library of Congress Catalog Card No. 75–13444

Published simultaneously in Canada by Little, Brown and Company (Canada) Limited

Manufactured in the United States of America

First printing

ACKNOWLEDGMENTS

Macbeth is reprinted from *The Tragedy of Macbeth*, edited by Sylvan Barnet, a Signet Classic Shakespeare Edition, 1963, by permission of The New American Library, Inc. *Edward the Second* is reprinted from *The Complete Plays of Christopher Marlowe*, edited by Irving Ribner, copyright © 1963 by Odyssey Press, Inc., by permission of the publisher, The Bobbs-Merrill Co., Inc. *The Duchess of Malfi* (text and notes) is reprinted from *Classics of the Renaissance Theatre: Seven English Plays*, edited by J. Dennis Huston and Alvin B. Kernan, by permission of the publishers, Harcourt Brace Jovanovich, Inc., copyright © 1969 by Harcourt Brace Jovanovich, Inc. *Paradise Restored* is reprinted by permission, © 1973 by Don Taylor. All rights of every kind reserved. Apply in advance for permission in writing from Margaret Ramsey Ltd., 14A Goodwin's Court, St. Martin's Lane, London WC₂. *She Stoops to Conquer* is reprinted from *The Genius of the Later English Theatre*, edited by Sylvan Barnet, Morton Berman, and William Burto, by permission of The New American Library, Inc. *Candide,* adapted by James McTaggart, is reprinted by permission of the author's agent. *The Rivals* is reprinted from *The Rivals*, edited by C.J.L. Price, by permission of Oxford University Press, copyright © 1968 by Oxford University Press, Oxford. *The Wild Duck* is reprinted from *Four Major Plays by Henrik Ibsen*, A New Translation with a Foreword by Rolf Fjelde, copyright © 1965 by Rolf Fjelde, by arrangement with The New American Library, Inc. New York, N.Y. *Hedda Gabler* is reprinted from *Hedda Gabler and Three Other Plays*, translated by Michael Meyer, copyright © 1961 by Michael Meyer, by permission of Doubleday and Co., Inc. The Introductory comments to *Hedda Gabler* are reprinted by permission from Sylvan Barnet, Morton Berman, and William Burto (eds.) , *Types of Drama: Plays and Essays*, pp. 178–180. Copyright © 1972 by Little, Brown and Co. *The Three Sisters* is reprinted by permission of Penguin Books Ltd. *Playboy of the Western World* is reprinted from *The Complete Works of John M. Synge*, by permission of Random House, Inc. Copyright 1907 and renewed 1935 by The Executors of the Estate of John M. Synge. *Mrs Warren's Profession* is reprinted by permission of The Society of Authors on behalf of the Bernard Shaw Estate.

Preface

This book contains thirteen plays, and we hesitate to add any words that will delay you from reading them. Still, a few remarks on the organization of the book may be useful.

In the Foreword, Joan Sullivan—producer of the television series called *Classic Theatre: The Humanities in Drama*—explains the aims of the series and the basis on which she chose these thirteen plays. On television each play is preceded by a thirty-minute preview with a distinguished scholar and with actors who performed in the production. The scholars who participate in the previews have generously contributed short, readable, and highly informative introductions to each play in this book. (There is one exception: Miss Eva Le Gallienne participated in the television preview to Ibsen's *Hedda Gabler,* but because her schedule did not allow her to write the introduction the editors have filled the gap.) These thirteen introductions, along with whatever footnotes are necessary, should increase the reader's understanding and enjoyment of the plays.

Perhaps it should be mentioned here too that the plays, covering more than three hundred years, are printed in the order in which they are shown on television. This order is nearly chronological; the few exceptions were made to serve the balance of television programming. Thus, because the producers wished the series to begin with a well-known play, Shakespeare's *Macbeth* (written about 1605–1606) precedes Marlowe's *Edward II* (written in the early 1590s). Similarly, the series concludes with Shaw's *Mrs Warren's Profession* (written in 1893), although Pinero's *Trelawny of the "Wells"*, Chekhov's *Three Sisters,* and Synge's *The Playboy of the Western World* were all written a few years later. No play, however, is very far out of its chronological place.

In addition to a short introduction to each play there is a long introduction to the entire book. It is divided into three parts: The Language of Drama, The Language of Television, and The Classic Theatre and Its Successor. The first part discusses the nature of drama—the playwright's ways of communicating a story through actors moving on a stage. The second part helps the television viewer to see the ways in which plays can be transformed by a new medium. The third part, of less immediate practical use to the reader or viewer, indicates some of the differences between "the classic theatre"—that is, the great dramatic tradition of the past—and the drama of our own time. The introduction as a whole, then, helps the reader of this book, the viewer of television plays, and the viewer of live plays of the past and of the present.

Foreword

The thirteen plays in this anthology are reprinted to complement the television series for Public Broadcasting. With ardent if not modest conviction I believe this series is the most significant presentation of theatre on any network in the history of American television.

You may ask, along with the conscientious editors of this book, "Why these particular thirteen dramas?" Since the conception of the series almost three years ago, I had a major criterion as I screened nearly one hundred dramas available for acquisition and produced over several seasons by the British Broadcasting Corporation. I endeavored to base my choices on the degree to which the intent of the dramatic literature was fulfilled through exceptional excellence of performance and presentation.

I had no preconceived idea of choosing "classic" plays which for me are simply the very best that survive. But as the choices narrowed down on the basis of merit to dramas not considered "contemporary," I also saw the opportunity to make some contribution to the revival—for a larger public than is reached by "live" theatre in this country—of a tradition of literature that eloquently and powerfully speaks to the guts and minds of humanity in any age. Thus the series became a significant, if in combination unusual, sampling of the most extraordinary dramatic literature conceived in the preceding four centuries of western culture.

Originally I hoped that all the programs would be derived from plays written for the theatre. The obvious choice to represent seventeenth-century drama was Molière, but there was no available production to consider. Thus it was I chose the television dramatization of the later years of John Milton; *Paradise Restored* is a fine period drama, and since it is set in the seventeenth century it afforded the link in continuity for the presentation of social and theatrical history.

Candide, the other deviation from theatrical literature, was originally of course a satiric tale. It provided some French representation and seemed especially important because it is the work of the man whose thought dominated eighteenth-century Europe. The other, and equally important, justification for its inclusion was that the translation and adaptation to the medium of television by its director, the late James McTaggart, are singularly brilliant.

I would like to share with you many of my experiences in developing this series, but, in Shakespeare's words, "the play's the thing." However, I invite you to watch the television previews that precede each drama; the previews, I trust, reflect the fruits of those experiences. These half-hour programs were designed to complete the theatre experience for the television viewer; they are your theatre playbill. Each program offers an intimate conversation with one of the eminent scholars who introduce the plays in this anthology. This conversation, with brief illustrative excerpts from the productions and short pictorial essays about the playwright and the social and theatrical history of his time, are the footnotes for your further enjoyment of the drama. You will also share conversations with leading players in the productions, videotaped in London settings that are historically associated with the play.

I have a strong personal commitment to good drama on television. In the pre-television rural Midwest where I grew up there was little opportunity to see performances of plays. Occasionally I would contrive to sleep over at a friend's house in the village and with a great sense of wickedness sneak off to the dilapidated town hall to see a traveling group of down-and-out ex-vaudevillian players (who would make the Telfers in *Trelawny of the "Wells"* look like superstars) stagger through a totally forgettable domestic comedy. The most adept part of their evening's performance was the selling of chinaware and boxes of cheap candy between the acts.

Today the hunger for compelling entertainment is not a result of a dearth of choices but of a saturation of repetitive, predictable, inarticulate formula dramas. I don't believe that that is an elitist remark because I don't believe writers like Shakespeare, Goldsmith, Chekhov, and Synge are playwrights who attract only elite audiences—when their plays are well-performed. But I do think a second-rate presentation is worse than none at all. This is partially so because television has caused audiences to demand sophisticated standards from any form of entertainment. And because I believe that a larger proportion of the population than is realized is looking for new alternative programming, I support the acquisition of foreign productions until we can match their quality.

There is a groundswell of distress among my colleagues (which is soon communicated to the professional critics and thus shortly to the public at large) regarding the importation of dramatic television material. I can only think that this may hasten the day when they rise to the challenge of their competition. And I can only further hope that your response as audience—in vast and vociferous numbers—will contribute to generating the consistent creation and financial support of exciting television theatre in this country.

Of all forms of communication or show business, television is the most unpredictable, gigantic, and complex *collaboration*. It's not really magic, but when it finally gets on that piece of master two-inch tape it sometimes feels like magic. The people who participated in making this series number in the hundreds: dozens of production crews, designers, editors, actors, producers, and directors across the water who produced the dramas; in Boston my very precious immediate staff—David Atwood, Elizabeth Deane, Monia Joblin, and Sarah Payne, other designers, composers, musicians, production crews, and consultants who contributed to the preview programs and the series presentation. And of great significance was the collaboration of the National Endowment For The Humanities, which on the basis of a list of the dramas and a proposal of intent accepted the request for the funding of this project, and with which the Mobil Oil Corporation joined in financing the acquisition of the plays.

We proudly offer you this feast of endeavor; this anthology is your "Encore" that you can call and recall long after the tube is dark.

Joan Sullivan
Producer, *Classic Theatre: The Humanities in Drama*
WGBH/Boston

April 1975

Contents

Contents

General Introduction

The Language of Drama

In ordinary speech, when we say that something is "dramatic" we usually mean one of two things. We may mean that it is striking, vivid: "she made a dramatic entrance." Or we may mean that there is a strong element of conflict, as when we speak of the drama of the courtroom, or the drama of a baseball game when a strong batter faces a strong pitcher in the second half of the ninth inning, with a tie score, two out, and a man on second base.

Both of these qualities—vividness and conflict—are normally present in the kind of artistic work that is known as drama. We should notice first, however, that a drama is basically a story that is intended to be performed by actors who play parts. "Drama" comes from a Greek word meaning "to do" or "to act," and a drama shows us people doing things—talking, walking, fighting, and so forth. But behind all these hundreds of actions that take about two hours on the stage, there is some unifying idea, one large action or doing. All of the bits of talking, walking, and fighting somehow hang together to tell a story, and the gist of this story can be called the "action" of the play. In this sense, our lives—though full of actions—rarely have *an* action. Every day we do many things, of course, but most of these doings are unconnected: for example, on the way to work we may happen to meet a friend on the street; this meeting may have no connection with anything that comes later in the day or in our life. In a play, however, there is, in the vocabulary of drama critics, *an* action—a unified story that is presented to us through all of the details. The parts all add up. The action of a play may be, for example, Boy Gets Girl, or it may be Man Makes a Tragic Mistake, or it may be Couple at Last Gets to Understand Each Other. Perhaps we can clarify the nature of this sort of action—a story that holds together the hundreds of little actions that the actors perform—by contrasting it with *All in the Family*. In this television program we notice two things. First, in any given thirty-minute program there is a basic situation—say the Bunkers' anniversary—but much of the program consists of conversations and happenings that really have no bearing on the end of the program. The anniversary is a sort of pretext for assembling people in the Bunkers' living room; then we get lots of funny remarks, some perhaps related to the occasion but others not; finally, the evening comes to an end, as evenings always do, but the ending is not the outcome of every-thing that has come in the previous twenty-nine minutes. In a sense, although there are plenty of laughs, nothing really happens in most episodes of *All in the Family.* Second, we notice that from one week to another there is no progress; each episode is independent, and the characters do not develop. Archie remains a bigot, Edith remains a dingbat. Three of these episodes do not make a three-act play, for the third episode has no relation to the first two. There is good entertain-ment in *All in the Family,* but from a dramatist's point of view there is no *action.*

Let us return now to drama as an action or story with a conflict. There is much to be said in favor of the old formula for writing plays: In the first act, get your hero up a tree; in the second act, throw stones at him; in the third act, get him down. (To say "get him down" does not necessarily imply a happy ending. It implies only that the story must come to an inevitable end; it does not just stop, but it comes to a completion, and of course one common kind of story—tragedy—usually ends with the death of the tragic hero. Such a hero is at last out of the tree, but at the cost of his life.) The formula, then, is this: establish a conflict and then settle it. The conflict is usually expressed on the stage by people opposed to other people, but of course an in-dividual can also be in conflict with fate, God, the laws of society, and even with himself.

A playwright tells his story chiefly through speeches. But a play-wright does not simply write speeches. A *wright* is a maker, and as a wheelwright made wheels and a shipwright made ships, so a play-wright makes plays. Though we may slip into thinking that a play is simply words when we read it in a book, the stuff of a playwright's trade is not simply words. Like a novelist, he tells a story; but unlike a novelist, he does not rely on words alone, for the words are spoken by actors moving on a stage; he relies on sights as well as sounds.

Setting

Let's begin with the stage and the setting. Because Shakespeare's *Macbeth,* of the plays in this book, is the best known and the first to be televised in *Classic Theatre: The Humanities in Drama,* we will draw most of our examples from *Macbeth,* though we will occasionally glance at other plays as well. When a production of *Macbeth* begins, we see three Witches moving about, amidst flashes of lightning, in some unattractive place. Since the Witches speak of the "fog and filthy air," we probably see them through a mist or dim light. And so from the start—even before a word is spoken—we see (from the lightning and mist) that these creatures live in violence, darkness, and contagion. What the Witches *say* is important, but at first we cannot really make much out of it, for we do not yet know who this Macbeth is whom they plan to meet. What we *see* tells us, more clearly than their words, that the Witches are forces of disorder. As the play progresses, we may note also that many scenes are set in darkness (often indicated by the presence of torches) : the heath is foggy, King Duncan arrives in the evening, Macbeth murders Duncan at night and arranges to have his friend Banquo murdered at night, Lady Macbeth (holding a candle) walks in her sleep. But the last act, except for the sleepwalking scene, is set in daylight, and this visual effect—daylight instead of darkness—tells us at least as clearly as can words that at last the forces of good are displacing the forces of evil. In short, many of the settings *say* a good deal. The fog is fog and night is night and daylight is daylight, but these things are also symbolic: the dramatist shows us things (here, visual effects) that stand for something else.

Finally, before we leave this matter of symbolic settings we should mention that they are not confined only to poetic plays but are even found in relatively realistic ones. Ibsen, for example, in a letter to a theatre director, explained that the lighting in *The Wild Duck* "has its significance; it differs from act to act and is calculated to correspond to the basic mood that characterizes each of the five acts." In the fourth act, for example, the light "begins to grow dark"; the fifth act, which completes the shattering of illusions, takes place in "a cold, gray morning light."

Costumes

Let us continue for a moment to talk about the ways in which drama says things even without words. Costumes tell us a good deal, on the stage as in life. They do not necessarily tell the truth about their wearers, but they tell us what the wearers want us to believe. If, on a street, we see someone who is wearing workman's clothes, we conclude either that he is a workman or that for some reason (say, political or sexual) he wants us to think that he is a workman; in any case the clothes make a statement, conscious or not. (In *Hedda Gabler* Ibsen tells us that Judge Brack wears clothes "which are elegant but a little too youthful for him.") In *Macbeth* the hero changes his garments from those of a warrior to those of a king, but we are often reminded that the king's clothing is not rightfully his. Late in the play one of the characters says what we have seen, or half seen:

> Now does he feel his title
> Hang loose about him, like a giant's robe
> Upon a dwarfish thief.

(V.ii.20–22)

Near the end of the play, when Macbeth fights to defend his own life, we see him again in armor and perhaps half-consciously remember the armed heroic Macbeth of the early part of the play, the valiant soldier who, by putting on "borrowed robes" (I.iii.109), unintentionally destroyed his own life. Yet another example of a costume that speaks to us is Lady Macbeth's nightgown in the sleepwalking scene (V.i.6), where she reveals her tortured thoughts; again we see the reality rather than the deceptive show of stolen royal garments. In the television production, notice how the untied laces dangling from the nightgown's cuffs help to convey a sense of Lady Macbeth's loss of self-control.

This use of symbolic costumes—costumes that are, of course, clothing, but that also speak to the audience—can be found as well in later plays. In the televised *Hedda Gabler,* Hedda at first wears a yellow-gold dress; then, from the first time that we see her brandishing a pistol, she wears a rich but smoldering grayish-brown dress trimmed with maroon; in the latter part of the play (after burning the manuscript of the man she wishes to control), she wears a low-cut black dress (Ibsen specifies black in the stage directions), which helps to convey her character as a beautiful but destructive woman. Similarly, in the televised version of Chekhov's *Three Sisters,* at the start we see Masha, one of the sisters, in a black dress. Bored and restless, she soon says that she is leaving and she puts on her hat. But then she hears Colonel Vershinin speak, and, attracted, she says that she will stay for lunch. She not only takes off her hat, but she also takes off the black jacket she has worn up to now: she is (so to speak) opening her protective shell. Still later, when her passion for Colonel Vershinin has increased, we see her dressed in scarlet; but toward the end of the play, on the day that he and the other soldiers are leaving the town and she is therefore back where she was at the start of the play, she is again dressed in black.

Gestures

Gestures, too, are part of the language of drama. Movements of the face, limbs, or body ("body language" is the new term), though silent, are eloquent. On the stage, as in real life, if we silently nod or shake our heads, we are saying something. In fact, if, for example, we hand someone money in silence, we may be expressing something (for example, resentment) more eloquently than if words accompany our gesture. Or if we sit on a couch and put our feet up on the coffee table, we are saying something very different from what we are saying if we sit upright on the couch with our feet on the floor, our ankles crossed. Dramatists—since they communicate not merely through words but through actors moving on a stage—often specify (in stage directions or in dialogue) significant gestures. When the Witches hail

Macbeth as king, his friend Banquo sees him "start" or react with a brief involuntary movement:

> Good sir, why do you start, and seem to fear
> Things that do sound so fair?
>
> (I.iii.51–52)

So, in a gesture, "brave Macbeth" (I.ii.16), "valiant Macbeth" (I.ii.24), conveys an inner state of surprise and perhaps fear. Most often, of course, gestures accompany and reinforce speech. When Lady Macbeth in the sleepwalking scene goes through the motions of washing blood off her hands, she says "Yet here's a spot" (V.i.40). In her mind her hands are not only soiled but also carry the foul smell of blood ("all the perfumes of Arabia will not sweeten this little hand"), and she probably passes a hand quickly under her nose and makes a face. In the televised version the actress prepares us for this a little earlier, when with a distraught look she places her fingers near her nose.

Under the heading of gestures we can include such large movements as running, fighting, and sitting. A reader can scarcely hope to visualize all of the action, but the playwrights sometimes provide help in the stage directions. A good example occurs in *Hedda Gabler*: Hedda is trying to take Loevborg away from Thea Elvsted. In Act Two, Ibsen tells us that Thea *"takes a chair and is about to sit down beside Loevborg,"* but Hedda, wanting Loevborg for herself, arranges the seating so that she is between Loevborg and Thea. This symbolic gesture is no less aggressive (despite Hedda's "Thea, darling") than when Hedda at the beginning of the act points a gun at Judge Brack.

Sound Effects

Dialogue is of course the chief way of telling a story in plays that are also literature, but first we should notice another sort of sound, non-verbal sound. We recall that *Macbeth* begins with *"Thunder and lightning,"* signs of disorder. Soon after we hear an owl shriek (another ill omen). A clinking of a bell is a signal that Macbeth and Lady Macbeth are preparing to murder King Duncan (see II.i.32,62); after the murder is discovered, the alarum bell is struck violently, making an appropriately "hideous" noise. Near the end of the play, when Lady Macbeth kills herself, there is a "cry within of women" (V.v.7), and in this latter part of the play there are "alarums," that is, sounds of soldiers assembling and fighting. And, once again, it is worth mentioning that realistic drama, as well as poetic, does not fail to draw on the power of sound effects: the pistol shots in *Hedda Gabler*, and the fire-bell in *Three Sisters* (ringing for the fire, of course, but also for the ruin of the sisters' lives) are perhaps the most obvious examples.

Dialogue

But of course dialogue, from the Greek word meaning "to converse," is the most persistent sound in a play. The playwright gives us not a transcript of our chaotic fragmentary sentences and "you-know-what-I-means," but coherent speeches that continuously reveal character and advance the story. Let us talk first about the relation of speech to the speaker. If we listen to the people around us, we notice that although they share many words, some use certain words and rhythms that others do not use. And of course their attitudes toward themselves and toward other people help to shape the sentences they speak: some people are curt, some are foul, some are brisk, some are leisurely, some are long-winded, and so on. In a play, too, the speakers often reveal their character through their speeches. Or at least some of the speeches help to give identity to the speakers. For example, at the beginning of *Macbeth* we hear the Three Witches:

FIRST WITCH   When shall we three meet again?
  In thunder, lightning, or in rain?
SECOND WITCH   When the hurlyburly's done,
  When the battle's lost and won.
THIRD WITCH   That will be ere the set of sun.

(I.i.1–5)

These lines rhyme, and, if we count the syllables and compare the length of these lines with the length of the lines of most of the other speakers, we find that these lines have seven or eight syllables whereas other speakers' lines usually have ten syllables and are not rhymed. We may only be half-conscious of it, but the speeches of the Witches have a distinctive quality—not surprising for unnatural creatures who speak strange prophecies and utter charms. The passage quoted a moment ago is very different from the first speeches we hear after the Witches leave the stage. The king, seeing a bleeding man, asks for news about the rebellion ("revolt"), and Malcolm, the king's son, says the bleeding man assisted him in the battle ("broil").

KING DUNCAN   What bloody man is that? He can report,
  As seemeth by his plight, of the revolt
  The newest state.
MALCOLM   This is the sergeant
  Who like a good and hardy soldier fought
  'Gainst my captivity. Hail, brave friend!
  Say to the king the knowledge of the broil
  As thou didst leave it.

(I.ii.1–7)

Now, we don't mean to suggest that every speech by a given character resembles every other speech by that character, and that every character has his own recognizable way of speaking. We mean only that, for the most part, as we hear a speech it seems appropriate to the speaker or at least does not violate our sense of the speaker. But any given character may have a range of voices, and the tragic hero notably ranges from a grand style to a direct style, sometimes within a single speech. Consider, for example, Macbeth's lines spoken soon after he kills King Duncan and looks at his bloody hands:

> Will all great Neptune's ocean wash this blood
> Clean from my hand? No; this my hand will rather
> The multitudinous seas incarnadine,
> Making the green one red.
>
> (II.ii.59–62)

The ocean is conceived of grandly as the realm of the sea god Neptune and, more simply, as "the green," and Macbeth's bloody hands will "incarnadine" it (redden it) and, again more simply, turn it "red." Immediately after this speech his wife speaks, and her language is far more ordinary than Macbeth's:

> My hands are of your color, but I shame
> To wear a heart so white. (*Knock.*) I hear a knocking
> At the south entry. Retire we to our chamber.
> A little water clears us of this deed.
>
> (II.ii.63–66)

We have only to compare Macbeth's "Neptune" and his "multitudinous seas" and "incarnadine" with Lady Macbeth's "a little water clears us of this deed" to see which of the two speakers is of a simpler nature. Lady Macbeth seems to speak common sense, and yet it turns out that her common sense is woefully inadequate for she will go mad from thinking about her crime. Though now she says, again matter-of-factly, "A little water clears us of this deed," in the sleepwalking scene ("What, will these hands ne'er be clean?") she will refute her earlier no-nonsense statement.

We cannot here try to trace Macbeth's speech—and character—through the entire play. However, it does seem fair to say that although Macbeth's language does not entirely lose its commanding richness, it does become harsher and plainer with Macbeth's growing despair. In the latter part of the play we increasingly hear this note of desperation, a "Valiant fury" (V.ii.14) if not madness, as in the speech when he determines to put on his armor ("harness") rather than yield. (Notice, by the way, how the first line suggests a distaste for light, and how the third line reminds us of the sounds that occurred the night Macbeth murdered Duncan.)

> I 'gin to be aweary of the sun,
> And wish th' estate o' th' world were now undone.

> Ring the alarum bell! Blow wind, come wrack!
> At least we'll die with harness on our back.
>
> (V.v.49–52)

The harsher, more stripped-down language that characterizes much (but not all) of Macbeth's later speeches is perhaps most clearly seen in his final words:

> Before my body
> I throw my warlike shield. Lay on, Macduff:
> And damned be him that first cries "Hold, enough!"
>
> (V.viii.32–34)

Plot and Structure

This simplification or lessening of Macbeth's language works along with the play's structure, the arrangement of scenes. At the beginning of this introduction we briefly made the point that in a good play everything is relevant to everything else, and that the end, therefore, comes inevitably out of everything that has preceded it. A playwright, we recall, makes or builds a play; indeed, Ibsen once went so far as to speak of himself as a sort of architect. We must now talk a little more about the way in which all of the parts are related to the whole. In the first half of the play, we see Macbeth rise (through a moral fall) to become king: Act Three, the middle act, begins with Banquo's summary: "Thou hast it now: King, Cawdor, Glamis, all"; and almost exactly in the middle of the play we get the banquet scene, which should be a symbol of community but instead, since the banquet is interrupted by Banquo's ghost, is a symbol of the chaos Macbeth has brought to Scotland. When Macbeth sees Banquo's ghost, perhaps his language is at its poorest: "Which of you have done this"; and (to the ghost), "Thou canst not say I did it," a pitiful, almost childish, attempt to claim he is innocent because he did not with his own hands kill Banquo. From this point onward we see two things of special interest: we see the growing strength of the forces opposing Macbeth, and we see less of Macbeth with Lady Macbeth. That is, the second half of the play shows us the good powers assembling, and it shows us Macbeth's increasing loneliness. As early as Act Three, Scene Two, he keeps from Lady Macbeth the knowledge that he plans to kill Banquo and Fleance. Later their separation will widen: the last we see of her is in the sleepwalking scene, at which Macbeth is not present. She will die offstage, denied even a final tragic speech, and Macbeth (unlike most of Shakespeare's other heroes) will die without an impressive speech and without anyone to offer him a word of consolation. In the other plays in this collection, too, one can see how episodes are arranged: in the tragedies, to isolate the tragic figures, ultimately bringing them to the final isolation, death; in the comedies, to bring the characters together, usually in marriage.

Of course we have only touched on some obvious matters of plot construction. In a well-constructed play, every scene is necessary and right, like the parts in an efficient machine. After all, if we are concerned with the mere story of *Macbeth*, and not with the complete significance of the story, we do not need the first scene (the meeting of the Three Witches) nor the second (the bleeding soldier's report of Macbeth's valor). These two scenes can be omitted and the rest of the story will still follow. But these scenes contribute a great deal. Shakespeare wished first to establish a threatening and uncertain atmosphere ("When the battle's lost and won," "Fair is foul, and foul is fair"), and then to establish a context of blood and violence ("What bloody man is that?"). The fair Macbeth becomes foul, and he will spill much blood. Notice, as another example, that we learn that the valiant Macbeth killed the treacherous foe "And fixed his head upon the battlements" (I.ii.23). At the end of the play we may recall this grisly detail, when Macbeth's own head is brought in, and order is at last restored. In short, in a well-written play, every speech and every scene are parts of the overall design.

Characters in Drama

When we see or read a play, we know that the persons represented—the characters—are fictional, and yet they behave more or less as we imagine real people might behave. They are psychologically consistent; their words and their actions are coherent. We can talk about their motivation, that is, about the forces—not only within the characters but also surrounding and influencing them—that cause the characters to speak and to act in the way that they do. As the play goes on, we increasingly feel that we know these people. How do we come to know them? Chiefly, by means of (1) what they say, (2) what they do, (3) what other characters say about them, and (4) what other characters do. The first two points do not need any further explanation, but the third and fourth points can be briefly amplified. What one character says about another is not necessarily true, but it at least gives us something to think about: for example, at the end of the play, Malcolm calls Macbeth a "butcher," and although we may not fully accept this severe judgment, we must take it into account just as we must take into account an earlier description of Macbeth as "valiant." The fourth point—what other characters do—means simply this: in a play, as in life, we compare people. Macbeth and Banquo both hear prophecies; but while Macbeth chooses to kill Duncan in order to make the prophecy come true, Banquo resists any temptation to act, and so we infer that Macbeth too could have refrained from criminal action if he had really wished to.

Now, the characters in plays are of course only airy nothings, but, if the playwright has done his job well, they have a convincing reality. We may even come to feel that we know Macbeth better than our next-door neighbor. We also feel, often, that these richly individualized characters—whether ancient Scots or nineteenth-century Russians —somehow reveal to us something about our own nature. One understands what Shaw meant when he wrote that as you watch Ibsen's *The Wild Duck* you find yourself "getting deeper and deeper into that Ekdal home, and getting deeper and deeper into your own life all the time."

Theme

What does a play add up to? Some critics argue that the concept of a theme (an underlying idea) is meaningless; they claim that a play gives us only an extremely detailed history of some imaginary people. But surely this view is desperate. We *can* say that *Macbeth* is about the self-destructiveness of destructiveness, or, to put it a little differently, that we pay for what we get. To the reply that these are mere truisms, we can counter: Yes, but the truisms are presented in such a way that they take on life and become a part of us rather than remain things of which we say, "I've heard it said, and I guess it's so." Surely a great play is not merely a detailed presentation of something that never was. That the theatre and life are closely connected is perhaps indicated by many theatrical terms that we apply to real life: people *show off, act* like big shots, *clown* around, make a *scene, play up* to someone, *play down* something, see how it *plays* in Peoria, and know that when they die it's *curtains.* If the theatre at its best did not seem an image of life, we would not so often see life as theatrical. And so we can try to talk about the theme or unifying idea of a play, just as we can try to see a unifying idea in any person's life or in any series of connected experiences. We need beware only of reducing the play to a neat moral tag, or even to the theme that we sense underlies it. That is, we must never believe that our statement of the theme is really the equivalent of the play itself. The play, we recognize, presents the theme with such detail that our statement of the theme is only a wedge that helps us to enter the play so that we may more fully possess it.

The Language of Television

"Opening-up" the Script

A playwright, writing for the theatre, cannot show us galloping horses, the waves beating on the shore, birds flying, and so forth. The best he can do (if he feels he must introduce such matters) is to have some character talk about such things, evoking through words what cannot be shown. And so, for example, in *Macbeth* King Duncan and Banquo describe the fragrant air surrounding Macbeth's castle and the martlets (swallows) that have without fear built their nests in the castle's various kinds of niches (jutty, frieze, buttress, coign of vantage) .

KING DUNCAN   This castle hath a pleasant seat; the air
  Nimbly and sweetly recommends itself
  Unto our gentle senses.
BANQUO   This guest of summer,
  The temple-haunting martlet, does approve
  By his loved mansionry that the heaven's breath
  Smells wooingly here. No jutty, frieze,
  Buttress, nor coign of vantage, but this bird
  Hath made his pendent bed and procreant cradle.

                        (I.vi.1–8)

But writers of television plays, or adapters of classic plays for tele-vision, can, if they wish, give us abundant exterior scenes, shot on location. It is commonly held that a television version of a play should "open up" the play, that is, should take advantage of the medium's ability to show the audience scenes that a playwright cannot show. When, for example, Duncan and Banquo speak of the air and the birds, should television merely show us Duncan and Banquo, or should it show us, as it easily can, the things they are talking about? There is no easy answer. To photograph a stage production is, in a way, to be faithful to the original playwright, but the result may be lifeless. After all, a television production is not a live production; we see two-dimensional figures on glass, not living people moving in space, and so some additional sense of the real world may be called for. On the other hand, if a script is "opened up," it is at some cost: the precious time that is taken to show clouds in the sky or riders in a wood or waves on the shore or whatever the setting is may require that speeches be deleted in order to accommodate the play to the time allotted for the television broadcast. Moreover, even if words are spoken at the same time as we see the images, as they can easily be in Duncan's and Banquo's speech about Macbeth's castle, we may feel that the emphasis is wrong; we should be hearing Shakespeare's words, not looking at birds. In the speech just quoted, for example, perhaps we should not be distracted from the suggestions of heavenly grace implicit in "temple" and "heaven's breath," or from the suggestions of fertility in "loved," "wooingly," "bed," and "procreant cradle."

What is needed, then, is not an all-embracing formula (open it up, or, alternatively, stick to the script) but a tactful response to each play, indeed to each scene and each speech. The televised adaptations of the eleven stage plays in this book (the two additional plays, *Para-dise Restored* and *Candide,* were originally written for television) respond sensitively to the plays themselves. For example, the television version of Marlowe's *Edward II* is a film of a performance in a theatre; we see no scenes that the theatre audience did not see. We never, so to speak, get a breath of fresh air, and for this oppressive play that treat-ment is appropriate. Indeed one can argue that most plays—comedies as well as tragedies—give a sense of people confined within tight limits. Because comic lovers as well as tragic heroes usually are continuously subjected to the pressure of the people immediately around them, a sense of the open spaces and rich abundance of the outside world may be destructive to a play. But the televised version of Goldsmith's charming *She Stoops to Conquer* is twice opened up effectively, once at the beginning, when we see riders looking for the house in which they will be guests, and again toward the end, when we see galloping horses pulling a coach, vividly showing us a zany coach ride that Goldsmith could only describe through the mouths of his characters. These additional scenes are attractive, and though some dialogue has indeed been deleted to make room for them, only a purist would insist that the changes are at odds with Goldsmith's play. Similarly, in the adaptation of Synge's *The Playboy of the Western World,* we get some beautiful landscape shots and even a glimpse of a mule-race along the sands, delightful scenes for which we can only be grateful. But in the adaptation of Ibsen's *The Wild Duck* we never get out of doors. We do, however, actually see the captured birds and rabbits that the characters so often talk about as they peer into a loft at the rear of the set. To show us the contents of this room is surely not to do any violence to the play; our experience of the televised version of *The Wild Duck* remains close to a theatre-goer's experience of the play. Similarly, in *Macbeth* we see on television something very close to a stage production. Thus, in the speech about Macbeth's castle we do not see the castle or the birds; we see the speakers looking upward, some sky (studio sky, to be sure) behind them, and the words thus can have their full effect. Even in the scenes of magic where, for example, the Witches disappear, or the ghost of Banquo disappears, we almost never get any tricky effects impossible on the stage but possible on television. True, in the episode with the three apparitions and the show of eight kings (IV.i.) we get a sort of magic, double-exposure effect, but it is no more magical than what a playhouse can achieve with lights and a scrim (translucent curtain) .

Shots

Faithful as a television production may try to be, however, it is inevitably different from a production in a playhouse. After all, when you go to the theatre you see the entire play from a single seat, a single angle, and though your eye focuses now here and now there, your relation to the actors and to the scene is largely fixed. But a television adaptation does not give us a photographed version of the theatre-goer's view: the screen is far too small, and television technology is far too poor, to show us simultaneously all the characters on the stage. Because distant objects cannot be seen clearly on a television screen, television usually brings us closer to the characters than we can get in a theatre. Of course we sometimes get a long shot or establishing shot

—these are necessary to give us both a sense of place and a feeling for the alliances characters form when they are onstage. (For example, in Chekhov's *Three Sisters* there are scenes of a number of people at a dining table and one or two people sitting apart.) Moreover, plays often move toward a "big" climax involving perhaps half a dozen people—again we must see their relationships—but because the television screen is small and the definition relatively poor, these scenes are difficult to present effectively. But most often we get medium shots (say, from waist to the top of the head) and close-ups (say, of a chest, neck, and head). The close-up is the chief compensation for the limitations of the long shot. (Sometimes, of course, it is not merely a compensation but an advantage: it works especially well for soliloquies [speeches spoken by an actor alone on the stage] and for asides [speeches uttered by a character but not heard by the other characters], perhaps because we are used to characters on television who address us directly, giving us the news or selling pills.) Finally, we have the tight close-up—say, from chin to forehead. It is especially useful in showing a single character at a moment of intense passion, say Macbeth when in a soliloquy he contemplates murdering Duncan, a "horrid deed" (I.vii.24) that will offend all heaven and earth. We get tight close-ups, too, when Macbeth tells his wife, immediately after the murder, that he thought he heard a voice cry "Sleep no more!" (II.ii.34), and when he learns that Fleance has escaped the hired murderers: "Then comes my fit again" (III.iv.22). Similarly, in Ibsen's *Hedda Gabler,* when Hedda tells Loevborg why she asked him questions about his most private behavior, we see her from chin to forehead; that is, we get *un*naturally close to her as she reveals her deepest, most secret feelings. And, near the end of the same play, when Judge Brack has the pleasure of shattering Hedda's illusions about Loevborg's death, we get an enormous, almost monstrous close-up of Brack's complacent yet threatening face.

Put it this way: the camera necessarily editorializes. In *Macbeth,* Duncan names his eldest son, Malcolm, as heir to the throne (I.iv.38–39), thereby apparently making it impossible for Macbeth to succeed legitimately to the throne. As Duncan makes his announcement, the camera shows Banquo looking at Macbeth, and then Macbeth looking away. All of the characters depart, but the camera, focusing on the throne from which Duncan has just risen, wordlessly tells us that Macbeth's thoughts are still dwelling on the throne. By showing us one object and not another, or one character and not another, the camera controls our responses to the play. Another clear example occurs when Macbeth, now the king, puts the crown on the table, dissatisfiedly saying, "To be thus is nothing" (III.i.48). He has the crown, but he does not feel like a king. He walks to the far end of the table, so that we see the crown very near to us and, far behind it, Macbeth. It is the camera work as much as the gestures that gives us the sense of Macbeth's remoteness from true possession of the crown. But even when it is less ingenious, there is always camera work, always a selection of a particular shot. Usually, of course, the camera shows the speaker, but if it feels that the words are less important than the hearer's response to them, it may give us a *reaction shot,* showing the hearer only, or emphasizing the hearer. In *Macbeth,* when Lennox talks about the "unruly night" (just before the murder becomes publicly known), the camera gives us a close-up of Macbeth's face, and we see Lennox only vaguely at the rear. The camera, in effect, is offering a comment: Lennox's words are less important than is Macbeth's reaction to them.

Two other points about camera shots should be made: the angle of the camera "says" something, and so too does the sharpness of the focus. First, let us consider angles. If the camera is low, close to the ground, and looking up toward the actors (a low angle shot), it tends to give them added power or dignity. When we first see Macbeth as king (III.i), he is on a platform above camera level and above Banquo, and thus he seems to dominate. He courteously reminds Banquo of the feast, but the camera angle guides the viewer to see Macbeth as a threat to Banquo: Macbeth is, literally, looking down on him. Less conspicuously, in the scene near the end of the play when Macduff reveals that he was not "of woman born" (and thus can defeat Macbeth), the camera is slightly below Macduff, thereby giving him dignity. Conversely, if the camera is high, looking down on the actors (a high angle shot), it tends to dwarf them, making them vulnerable or pitiful. When Lady Macbeth calls upon the spirits to "unsex" her (I.v.45) and prepare her to do an unnatural deed, the camera pulls back and up, from a close-up to a high angle, and we get a sort of unnatural or heaven's-eye view of her. Near the end of the play, we get a similar shot of Macbeth as he speaks the famous lines beginning "Tomorrow and tomorrow and tomorrow." When he gets to "Life's but a walking shadow, a poor player" (V.v.24), the camera pulls back and up, so that by the end of the speech, when Macbeth says that life is "full of sound and fury,/Signifying nothing," we are above him; he looks up, defiantly but impotently shouting his denunciation at whatever spiritual powers there are, and at us.

Next, let us turn to matters of focus. The camera can, of course, by looking elsewhere simply not record certain things; it can also, if it wishes, record them out of focus, for some special effect. When Macbeth is "rapt" (I.iii.128–142), the camera focuses on Macbeth in the foreground and gives us a rather blurry picture of Banquo, Ross, and Angus at the rear, thereby visually communicating Macbeth's entranced condition. Another example: in Shaw's *Mrs Warren's Profession,* when Sir George Crofts destroys Vivie's illusions about her mother's business enterprises, we get a close-up of Vivie's face with Crofts's just behind it. Both faces could have been in focus, but

Crofts's face goes out of focus, so (1) we concentrate on Vivie's re-action, and (2) we get an indication of the turmoil in Vivie's mind as the world around her fades. But when Crofts mentions that Mrs. Warren's dirty money supported Vivie's education, Vivie suddenly becomes interested in what Crofts is saying, and his face snaps back into focus.

Does all of this mean that television necessarily distorts the plays it claims to present? Not really. It offers an interpretation, and an interpretation is what every stage performance—and every armchair reading—offers. There is no such thing as a pure, perfect performance of the play-in-itself. In a stage production the director and the actors must choose how to say certain speeches, how to interpret certain characters, how much to cut, where to put the intermission, and so on. When we see a good performance we feel that we now have a better grasp of the play, or at least of certain parts of it. Similarly, a tele-vision production can help us to see, and to feel, the power of scenes that, when we read, we too easily let our eyes slide over. The final test of any performance—either live or televised—is this: does it move us to turn back to the printed page, and, if so, do we feel that the text supports the offered interpretation. In short, does the performance legitimately increase our interest in the play; and does the play— whether seen in a theatre or on a television screen or read in a book— deepen our interest in and our understanding of life. For all works of drama, finally, are about ways of living, and despite all of the nasty (and often true) things said about the false worlds that television frequently presents in its serials, game shows, and advertisements, it is surely evident from *Classic Theatre: The Humanities in Drama* that television can also give us a sense of life at its fullest and most intense.

The Classic Theatre and Its Successor

The Classic Theatre

First, it must be pointed out that of the thirteen plays in this book, two were written for television: one of these is an adaptation of Vol-taire's prose-fiction, *Candide,* and the other is a play about the life of the English poet, John Milton. It must also be pointed out that there is no ancient Greek or Roman play, and thus, in one sense, the word "classic" (Greek or Roman) does not apply. The eleven remaining plays, however, are classic in two senses: they are part of the enduring repertoire of drama, and—however different each is from the others— they more or less share certain ideas about the nature of drama and the nature of life. For example, by and large they assume that people are responsible for their actions, or, to put it a little differently, that people are not simply bundles of random impulses but creatures who can achieve a coherent personality and are accountable for their actions. To take an obvious example, it is clear that (despite the stimulus provided by the Witches) Macbeth is responsible for the murder of King Duncan, and it is equally obvious that his act is reprehensible.

The Successors

Among the most recent of these dramatists, Ibsen and Chekhov exerted an especially large influence well into the middle of the twentieth century. Arthur Miller, for example, was deeply influenced by Ibsen's "problem plays," and Lillian Hellman was influenced by both Ibsen and Chekhov. But the new plays that are vital today hold few of the assumptions of the plays of the classic tradition: the most vital theatre in the second half of the twentieth century is a fairly unified body of drama neatly labeled the Theatre of the Absurd, whose major writers are Beckett, Genet, Ionesco, Pinter, and Albee. Perhaps by talking briefly about this body of new drama we can help to get a sense of what the classic theatre is, or was. (Because earlier pages of this introduction and the introductions to each play taken as a whole will help the reader to come to some idea of the coherence of the earlier drama, it seems reasonable here to discuss indirectly the classic theatre by directly discussing its successor.) The new dramatists of the 1950s and 1960s seem to have responded to the call of Antonin Artaud (1896–1948), a French man of the theatre who during his lifetime exerted almost no influence. In "No More Masterpieces" Artaud said that respect for the traditional or classic theatre stifled new creativity; the dramatists of the future would have to discard "civilized" concepts of cause-and-effect, of coherent personality, of meaningful words. For Artaud, "story-telling psychology" (that is, the classic theatre's presentation of coherent characters whose actions make an understandable story) claims to explain everything, but is essentially untrue and has impoverished the theatre and life. "Both the theatre and we ourselves have had enough of psychology."[1]

Diminution of Man

These new writers differ among themselves, of course, and each of them differs even from play to play, but they are all preoccupied with the loneliness of man in an unintelligible world. The tragic plays of the classic theatre, too, were concerned with loneliness, but generally speaking by the end of the play the hero, though isolated from his fellows, had at least come to understand himself. And in the comedies of the classic theatre (here best exemplified by *She Stoops to Conquer* and *The Rivals*), the usual happy ending consisted of marriage following upon the elimination of all obstacles that had separated the young lovers. But behind the contemporary vision of

---

1 *The Theatre and Its Double,* p. 77. Translated from the French by Mary Caroline Richards. Copyright © 1958 by Grove Press, Inc.

unintelligible loneliness are some two hundred years of thinking that have conspired to make it difficult to think either of happy endings or of heroes confronting a mysterious but coherent cosmic order. Man, Ionesco says in *Notes and Counter Notes,* is "cut off from his religious and metaphysical roots."[2] This introduction is not the place to try to recount a century or two of mankind's history, but we can mention a few of the developments in thinking that served to cut man off from his religious roots. Darwin's *The Origin of Species* (1859) seemed, in the popular phrase, to record man's progress "Up from apes," but more closely read, it reduced man to the product of "accidental variations" and left God out of the picture, substituting a barbaric struggle for existence for a cosmic order. Karl Marx, studying the evolution of societies, at about the same time was attributing man's sense of alienation to economic forces, thereby implying that man had no identity he could properly call his own. Moreover, Marxist thinking, like Darwinian thinking, suggested that a man could not do anything of really great importance, nor could he be blamed for his misfortunes. At the end of the nineteenth century, and in the early twentieth century, Freud turned to the forces within man's mind. Ironically, Freud's effort to chart man's unconscious drives and anarchic impulses in order to help him to know himself induced a profound distrust of the self: we can scarcely be confident of our behavior, for we know that apparently heroic behavior has unconscious unheroic motives rooted in the experiences of infancy. In this view, tragic heroes are men with complexes, and religious codes are only wishful thinking.

Dissolution of Character and Plot

The result of such developments in thought seems to be that a "tragic sense" in the twentieth century commonly means a despairing or deeply uncertain view, something very different from what it meant in Greece and in Elizabethan England where, if tragedy showed man suffering greatly, it also showed his heroism. This uncertainty extends even to character or identity. We have already mentioned in the section on the language of drama that readers and spectators can talk about the unified or at least intelligible personalities of figures in plays. In fact, many of the characters in the plays of the classic theatre are subtle variations of stock characters, such as the irritable father, the passionate young lover, and so on. But for a century or so, even the idea of character—in life, not just in drama—has been questioned. In 1888, in the preface to his play *Miss Julie,* August Strindberg (anticipating Artaud) called attention to the new sense of the instability of character:

---

2 From *Notes and Counter Notes: Writings on the Theatre* by Eugene Ionesco, p. 257. Translated from the French by Donald Watson. Copyright © 1964 by Grove Press, Inc.

I have made the people in my play fairly "characterless." The middle-class conception of a fixed character was transferred to the stage, where the middle class has always ruled. A character there came to mean an actor who was always one and the same, always drunk, always comic or always melancholy, and who needed to be characterized only by some physical defect such as a club foot, a wooden leg, or a red nose, or by the repetition of some such phrase as, "That's capital," or "Barkis is willin'." . . . Since the persons in my play are modern characters, living in a transitional era more hurried and hysterical than the previous one at least, I have depicted them as more unstable, as torn and divided, a mixture of the old and the new.

In 1902, in his preface to *A Dream Play* (a play that Artaud later staged), Strindberg is more explicit: "Anything may happen, anything seems possible and probable. . . . The characters split, double, multiply, vanish, solidify, blur, clarify." His view of the fluidity of character —the characterlessness of character, one might say—has continued and is apparent in much of the Theatre of the Absurd. Ionesco, in *Fragments of a Journal,* says "I often find it quite impossible to hold an opinion about a fact, a thing or a person."[3] In *Notes and Counter Notes* Ionesco said that "chance formed us," and that we would be different if we had different experiences; characteristically a few years later he said that he was no longer sure that he believed in chance.

Along with the sense of characterlessness, or at least of the mystery of character, there developed in the drama (and in the underground film and the novel) a sense of plotlessness, or fundamental untruthfulness of the traditional plot that moved by cause and effect. In plays of the classic theatre we see one action causing the next: Macbeth, for example, kills King Duncan and almost immediately finds that his action brings sleepless nights upon him. Later he finds that his action brings about the loss of "Honor, love, obedience, troops of friends," and brings him "curses." Even in Chekhov's *Three Sisters,* the play in this book in which cause and effect are least obvious, we see the sister-in-law step by step take over the sisters' house. But in the new drama there is little interest in cause and effect. "Plots," Ionesco has said in *Conversations,* "are never interesting," and again he has said that a play should be able to stop at any point; it ends only because "the audience has to go home to bed . . . It's true for real life. Why should it be different for art?"[4] Ionesco has treated his own plots very casually, allowing directors to make "all the cuts

3 From *Fragments of a Journal* by Eugene Ionesco, p. 131. Translated from the French by Jean Stewart. Copyright © 1968 by Faber and Faber Ltd.
4 From *Conversations with Eugene Ionesco* by Claude Bonnefoy, p. 82. Translated from the French by Jan Dawson. Holt, Rinehart and Winston, 1970. Copyright © 1966 by Editions Pierre Belfond. English translation copyright © 1970 by Faber and Faber Ltd.

needed" and suggesting that endings other than those he wrote are possibilities. After all, in a meaningless world one can hardly take a dramatic plot seriously. In Ionesco's play *Victims of Duty* a character defends a new kind of irrational drama: "The theater of my dreams would be irrationalist . . . The contemporary theatre doesn't reflect the cultural tone of our period, it's not in harmony with the general drift of the other manifestations of the modern spirit. . . . We'll get rid of the principle of identity and unity of character. . . . Personality doesn't exist."[5] A policeman-psychologist (a materialist who demands law and order) offers an old-fashioned view: "I don't believe in the absurd, everything hangs together, everything can be comprehended . . . thanks to the achievements of human thought and science";[6] but he is murdered by the irrationalist.

Not surprisingly, the finest play of this new drama, Samuel Beckett's *Waiting for Godot,* ends—as the first act ended—without anything ending. Throughout the play two tramps (representations of man separated from society) have been waiting for Godot. But Godot never arrives.

VLADIMIR   Well? Shall we go?
ESTRAGON   Yes, let's go.
They do not move.
Curtain.[7]

To bring an action to completion, to establish a conflict and then settle it, as drama of the classical tradition did, is to imply an orderly (even if mysterious) world of cause and effect, of beginnings and endings, but for the dramatists of the absurd, there is no such order. At best it is *Hamlet* as seen by Tom Stoppard's Rosencrantz and Guildenstern: they are supposed to do a job they don't understand, and, instead of order or a pattern, they encounter only "Incidents! All we get is incidents! Dear God, is it too much to expect a little sustained action?"[8] Well, yes; today it is too much to expect. If we remember the classic formula—Get your hero up a tree, throw stones at him, then get him down—we can say that the new drama begins with the hero up a tree, and leaves him there.

In "No More Masterpieces" Antonin Artaud says, "Masterpieces of the past are good for the past: they are not good for us. We have the right to say what has been said and even what has not been said in a

5 From *Amédée, The New Tenant, Victims of Duty* by Eugene Ionesco, pp. 157–158. Translated from the French by Donald Watson. Grove Press. Copyright © 1958 by John Calder (Publishers) Limited.
6 Ibid., p. 159.
7 From *Waiting for Godot* by Samuel Beckett, p. 61. Translated from the French by the author. Copyright © 1954 by Grove Press, Inc.
8 From *Rosencrantz and Guildenstern Are Dead* by Tom Stoppard, p. 118. Grove Press. Copyright © 1967 by Tom Stoppard.

way that belongs to us."[9] Of course, and the new drama has already produced several pieces that surely will become classics in the sense of enduring works of art. But just as one can conjecture that such a play as Beckett's *Waiting for Godot* will for centuries hold the attention of readers and viewers, so one must grant that the best plays of the past continue to interest and to delight. Life has not utterly changed, and the work of the best writers of the past can invigorate us by bringing us into contact with ideas and emotions that perhaps we otherwise neglect. These televised plays of the classic theatre, then, are not only revivals of a drama of the past; they may help to be revivals of the people who see and read them.

Sylvan Barnet
Tufts University

Morton Berman
Boston University

William Burto
University of Lowell

---

9 *The Theatre and Its Double,* p. 74.

Classic Theatre: The Humanities in Drama

Macbeth

William Shakespeare   edited by Sylvan Barnet

Introductory Comments

S. Schoenbaum*   *Northwestern University*

Written in 1606, *Macbeth* marked the end of the great sequence of tragedies that included *Hamlet, Othello,* and *King Lear. Macbeth* is the most concentrated of the plays—namely 2,113 lines long, one-half the length of *Hamlet*—but its brevity does not mean that it is one of Shakespeare's less difficult plays. On the contrary, *Macbeth* derives its dramatic power from its complex imagery and compression of language. Despite its shortness, it has a relatively large number of scenes, twenty-eight. These scenes are not, for the most part, elaborately constructed, as are those depicting the blinding of Gloucester in *King Lear* and the play-within-the-play in *Hamlet.* In *Macbeth* the emphasis is on swiftness and movement, and the speed of the play's forward propulsion, both intellectual and poetic, makes it especially difficult for those unfamiliar with the language of Shakespeare. For this reason a closer observation of the play will be instructive.

Macbeth illustrates Shakespeare's fascination with the criminal mind. We see this fascination also in the characters of Claudius in *Hamlet,* Iago in *Othello,* and Edmund in *King Lear.* It is only in *Macbeth,* however, that the protagonist is a villain. We sense that in this play Shakespeare is going to look more closely at villainy and the consequences of murder.

Macbeth's crimes—and they are many—are those of a brutal despot. His first victim is Duncan, who is not only his king, but also his kinsman and guest. We are reminded of Dante, who in the first part of *The Divine Comedy* pays special attention to the hierarchy of sin. In his *Inferno* there are nine circles of hell. In the upper circles the punishments are not terribly severe. But lower and lower, below the burning fires (which our imagination usually associates with hell), comes ice. The crimes of ice are calculated crimes—crimes of cold blood. Among those sinners in the frigid ninth circle are Judas, Brutus, and Cassius: Judas who betrayed the church, and

---

* Adapted by Raphael Sagalyn from a lecture.

Brutus and Cassius who lifted daggers against their empire. The basest crimes, then, are those committed against benefactors (or hosts), kinsmen, and country. In slaying Duncan, Macbeth is simultaneously guilty of all three of these crimes. If he were to have a place in Dante's hell, it would be there at the bottom.

This allusion to the topography of hell is not unsubstantiated in the play. The brief appearance of the Porter, answering the banging on the castle gate, clearly associates Macbeth's home with hell, for the scene is indebted to medieval plays on the theme known as "The Harrowing of Hell," in which the gates of hell were battered. Note that the Porter speaks of the "porter of hell gate," and he asks "Who's there, i' th' name of Beelzebub?" His words "this place is too cold for hell" make the parallel especially revealing.

Another allusion comes when Macbeth begins his famous soliloquy:

If it were done when 'tis done, then 'twere well
It were done quickly.

This crucial speech, in which Macbeth wrestles with the consequences of murdering Duncan, is delivered just before the banquet at Macbeth's castle, which Duncan will attend. We are reminded of an even more famous passage from the New Testament, the Gospel According to St. John, Chapter 17. It is the scene of the Last Supper and Jesus has determined that Judas is to betray him. Jesus tells him: "That thou doest, do quickly." Judas, like Macbeth, absents himself before the meal is over. We see, then, that this scene in *Macbeth* is the last supper of King Duncan, who will be betrayed by his subject Macbeth.

Yet as loathsome as Macbeth's deeds are, he somehow remains within our bounds of human sympathy. We are told that in battle he is "valor's minion" (or favorite) and a brave and worthy soldier. We retain this noble view of Macbeth—or at least a semblance of it— even when he makes the descent from nobleman to tyrant. Macbeth holds our sympathy as well because he recognizes the consequences of his crimes. Shortly after the murder of Duncan, we hear Macbeth voice sentiments that cloak him in moral virtue:

Had I but died an hour before this chance,
I had lived a blessèd time; for from this instant
There's nothing serious in mortality:
All is but toys.

These lines, spoken in the company of Banquo, Lennox, and others, are deceitfully intended to impress the onlookers in the aftermath of the murder, but they reveal a profound truth about Macbeth's character. Had he died before he killed Duncan, his life would have been (so far as we can tell) happy and virtuous; but he kills Duncan and thus destroys what remains of his own life. Throughout the latter part of the play Macbeth realizes the enormity of his deed. He cannot freely give up the crown, but neither can he deceive himself.

Macbeth was written a few years after the accession of James I of England, a Scot who reigned from 1603 to 1625. He took a special interest in demonology, on which he fancied himself an authority. (He wrote a treatise on the subject.) In the witches' prophetic spectacle of the eight kings the last to appear is King James. To insist—as some scholars do—that *Macbeth* was especially written for the king's entertainment is perhaps to press a claim too far, but the Scottish setting and the use of witchcraft to enhance the theme do reflect a professional dramatist's willingness to cater to popular interests —when those interests coincide with his own artistic purposes. The three witches, certainly, are a powerful thematic device.

We meet them in the very first scene of the play. They are waiting for Macbeth amid thunder and lightning, lending an air of foreboding to this character we have yet to meet. They announce in unison:

Fair is foul, and foul is fair.
Hover through the fog and filthy air.

But then, in the next scene, we hear Macbeth lauded as the king's "valiant cousin" and as a "worthy gentleman." The ambiguity between these two associations makes us curious as to what kind of man this "brave Macbeth" really is. We get a clue in Scene Three when Macbeth, making his first entrance, repeats almost verbatim the witches' weather report:

So foul and fair a day I have not seen.

Already, at this early stage of the play, we are aware of Macbeth's close alliance with the supernatural influence of the witches.

Clothing is a pattern of imagery that helps identify Macbeth's character. Students who have read the play are surely familiar with his famous question:

Why do you dress me
In borrowed robes?

What does this image "borrowed robes" mean? The following references will help us to understand. First, Banquo inquires about the garments worn by the witches, who are about to announce Macbeth's accession to the throne:

What are these
So withered and so wild in their attire,
That look not like th' inhabitants o' th' earth,
And yet are on 't?

Later, Banquo describes Macbeth's "fears" and "imaginings" of his rise to the throne in this way:

> New honors come upon him,
> Like our strange garments, cleave not to their mold
> But with the aid of use.

The imagery of "borrowed robes" is now clear: Macbeth is a man who is unsuited for his kingly role. In the final act another example of the clothing imagery appears and is wholly consistent with what we have learned to be true about Macbeth. Angus, a nobleman, says:

> Those he commands move only in command,
> Nothing in love. Now does he feel his title
> Hang loose about him, like a giant's robe
> Upon a dwarfish thief.

When Macbeth dies, he dies friendless, without love. Through allusion and through imagery we learn that this man is no king at all; he is a ruthless tyrant whose bond is not with the people who serve him, but with a dark and icy underworld. In this short and powerful play, Macbeth makes a tragic descent from a "worthy gentleman" to an "abhorrèd tyrant" and, finally, to a "dead butcher." And what do we learn to be the consequences of such deeds as those committed by Macbeth? Near the end of the play Macbeth, ruminating on the death of his wife, says:

> She should have died hereafter;
> There would have been a time for such a word.

"She should have died hereafter"—the line resonates. Does it say that Lady Macbeth should have died later, after the din of battle had subsided? Or that, like all mortals, she had to die someday? Or that she should have died at a time when death had significance? The line may have one or more of these meanings. What is certain is that for Macbeth life has become

> . . . a tale
> Told by an idiot, full of sound and fury
> Signifying nothing.

William Shakespeare (1564–1616) was born in Stratford, England, into a middle-class family. Almost nothing is known of his early years except that he married in 1582 and had a child in 1583. At an unknown date he went to London. His earliest publication was his long narrative erotic poem *Venus and Adonis* (1593), followed by another long poem, *The Rape of Lucrece*, which was published the next year, when several of his plays also first saw print. In the next

7

few years he probably wrote most of his sonnets, though they were not published until 1609. But Shakespeare's non-dramatic poetry apparently was written in his spare time; probably beginning in the late 1580s. And certainly by the early 1590s, he was connected with the theatre, as both actor and playwright. In 1594 he was one of the charter members of the company that was to build, own, and act in the Globe Theatre. He continued to write plays (thirty-seven are usually attributed to him) until about 1613, when he left London and went back to Stratford, where he died, a prosperous citizen of his native town.

The Tragedy of Macbeth   *William Shakespeare*

[DRAMATIS PERSONAE

DUNCAN   *King of Scotland*

MALCOLM
DONALBAIN   *his sons*

MACBETH
BANQUO
MACDUFF
LENNOX
ROSS   *noblemen of Scotland*
MENTEITH
ANGUS
CAITHNESS

FLEANCE   *son to Banquo*

SIWARD, EARL OF NORTHUMBERLAND   *general of the English forces*

YOUNG SIWARD   *his son*

SEYTON   *an officer attending on Macbeth*

SON TO MACDUFF

AN ENGLISH DOCTOR

A SCOTTISH DOCTOR

A PORTER

AN OLD MAN

THREE MURDERERS

LADY MACBETH

LADY MACDUFF

A GENTLEWOMAN   *attending on Lady Macbeth*

HECATE

WITCHES

APPARITIONS

LORDS, OFFICERS, SOLDIERS, ATTENDANTS, AND MESSENGERS

Act One

SCENE ONE   [*An open place.*]

Thunder and lightning. Enter THREE
WITCHES.

FIRST WITCH   When shall we three meet
again?
In thunder, lightning, or in rain?
SECOND WITCH   When the hurlyburly's
done,
When the battle's lost and won.
THIRD WITCH   That will be ere the set of
5   sun.
FIRST WITCH   Where the place?
SECOND WITCH   Upon the heath.
THIRD WITCH   There to meet with Mac-
beth.
FIRST WITCH   I come, Graymalkin.°¹
SECOND WITCH   Paddock° calls.
THIRD WITCH   Anon!°
10 ALL   Fair is foul, and foul is fair.
Hover through the fog and filthy air.
Exeunt.

SCENE TWO   [*A camp.*]

Alarum within.° Enter KING [DUNCAN],
MALCOLM, DONALBAIN, LENNOX, *with* AT-
TENDANTS, *meeting a bleeding* CAPTAIN.

KING DUNCAN   What bloody man is that?
He can report,
As seemeth by his plight, of the revolt
The newest state.
MALCOLM   This is the sergeant°
Who like a good and hardy soldier fought

'Gainst my captivity. Hail, brave friend!   5
Say to the king the knowledge of the
broil°
As thou didst leave it.
CAPTAIN   Doubtful it stood,
As two spent swimmers, that do cling to-
gether
And choke their art.° The merciless Mac-
donwald—
Worthy to be a rebel for to that   10
The multiplying villainies of nature
Do swarm upon him—from the Western
Isles°
Of kerns and gallowglasses° is supplied;
And Fortune, on his damnèd quarrel°
smiling,
Showed like a rebel's whore:° but all's too
weak: 15
For brave Macbeth—well he deserves that
name—
Disdaining Fortune, with his brandished
steel,
Which smoked with bloody execution,
Like valor's minion° carved out his pas-
sage
Till he faced the slave;   20
Which nev'r shook hands, nor bade fare-
well to him,
Till he unseamed him from the nave to
th' chops,°
And fixed his head upon our battlements.
KING DUNCAN   O valiant cousin! Worthy
gentleman!
CAPTAIN   As whence the sun 'gins his re-
flection°   25
Shipwracking storms and direful thunders
break,

1 The degree sign (°) indicates a footnote, which
is keyed to the text by line number. Text references
are printed in bold type; the annotation follows in
roman type.
I.i. 8 **Graymalkin** (the witch's attendant spirit, a
gray cat). 9 **Paddock** toad. **Anon** at once.
I.ii.sd **Alarum within** trumpet call offstage. 3 **sergeant** i.e., officer (he is called, perhaps with no in-
consistency in Shakespeare's day, a captain in the
s.d. and speech prefixes). **Sergeant** is trisyllabic.

6 **broil** quarrel. 9 **choke their art** hamper each
other's doings. 12 **Western Isles** Hebrides. 13 **Of
kerns and gallowglasses** with lightly armed Irish
foot soldiers and heavily armed ones. 14 **damned
quarrel** accursed cause. 15 **Showed like a rebel's
whore** i.e., falsely appeared to favor Macdonwald.
19 **minion** (trisyllabic) favorite. 22 **nave to th'
chops** navel to the jaws. 25 **reflection** (four syllables; the ending—**ion** here and often elsewhere in
the play—is disyllabic).

So from that spring whence comfort
seemed to come
Discomfort swells. Mark, King of Scotland, mark:
No sooner justice had, with valor armed,
30 Compelled these skipping kerns to trust
their heels
But the Norweyan lord, surveying vantage,°
With furbished arms and new supplies of
men,
Began a fresh assault.

KING DUNCAN   Dismayed not this
Our captains, Macbeth and Banquo?

CAPTAIN   Yes;
35 As sparrows eagles, or the hare the lion.
If I say sooth,° I must report they were
As cannons overcharged with double
cracks;°
So they doubly redoubled strokes upon
the foe.
Except° they meant to bathe in reeking
wounds,
40 Or memorize another Golgotha,°
I cannot tell—
But I am faint; my gashes cry for help.

KING DUNCAN So well thy words become
thee as thy wounds;
They smack of honor both. Go get him
surgeons.

[*Exit* CAPTAIN, *attended.*]

Enter ROSS *and* ANGUS.

Who comes here?
45 MALCOLM   The worthy Thane° of Ross.

LENNOX What a haste looks through his
eyes! So should he look
That seems to° speak things strange.

ROSS   God save the King!

KING DUNCAN Whence cam'st thou, worthy
Thane?

ROSS   From Fife, great King;

Where the Norweyan banners flout the
sky
And fan our people cold.   50
Norway° himself, with terrible numbers,
Assisted by that most disloyal traitor
The Thane of Cawdor, began a dismal°
conflict;
Till that Bellona's bridegroom, lapped in
proof,°
Confronted him with self-comparisons,°   55
Point against point, rebellious arm
'gainst arm,
Curbing his lavish° spirit: and, to con-
clude,
The victory fell on us.

KING DUNCAN   Great happiness!

ROSS   That now
Sweno, the Norways' king, craves compo-
sition;°
Nor would we deign him burial of his
men   60
Till he disbursèd, at Saint Colme's Inch,°
Ten thousand dollars° to our general use.

KING DUNCAN No more that Thane of
Cawdor shall deceive
Our bosom interest:° go pronounce his
present° death,
And with his former title greet Macbeth.   65

ROSS I'll see it done.

KING DUNCAN What he hath lost, noble
Macbeth hath won.

Exeunt.

SCENE THREE   [*A heath.*]

Thunder. Enter the THREE WITCHES.

FIRST WITCH Where hast thou been, sister?

SECOND WITCH Killing swine.

THIRD WITCH Sister, where thou?

---

31 **surveying vantage** seeing an opportunity. 36
sooth truth. 37 **cracks** explosives. 39 **Except** unless.
40 **memorize another Golgotha** make the place as
memorable as Golgotha, "the place of the skull."
45 **Thane** (a Scottish title of nobility). 47 **seems
to** seems about to.

51 **Norway** the King of Norway. 53 **dismal** threatening. 54 **Bellona's . . . proof** the mate of the goddess of war, clad in tested (proved) armor. 55 **self-
comparisons** counter-movements. 57 **lavish** insolent.
59 **composition** terms of peace. 61 **Inch** island. 62
dollars (Spanish and Dutch currency). 64 **Our
bosom interest** my (plural of royalty) heart's trust.
present immediate.

FIRST WITCH   A sailor's wife had chestnuts in her lap,
And mounched, and mounched, and mounched. "Give me," quoth I.
5
"Aroint thee,° witch!" the rump-fed ronyon° cries.
Her husband's to Aleppo gone, master o' th' Tiger:
But in a sieve I'll thither sail,
And, like a rat without a tail,
10
I'll do, I'll do, and I'll do.
SECOND WITCH   I'll give thee a wind.
FIRST WITCH   Th' art kind.
THIRD WITCH   And I another.
FIRST WITCH   I myself have all the other;
15
And the very ports they blow,°
All the quarters that they know
I' th' shipman's card.°
I'll drain him dry as hay:
Sleep shall neither night nor day
20
Hang upon his penthouse lid;°
He shall live a man forbid:°
Weary sev'nights nine times nine
Shall he dwindle, peak,° and pine:
Though his bark cannot be lost,
25
Yet it shall be tempest-tossed.
Look what I have.
SECOND WITCH   Show me, show me.
FIRST WITCH   Here I have a pilot's thumb,
Wracked as homeward he did come.

Drum within.

30
THIRD WITCH   A drum, a drum!
Macbeth doth come.
ALL   The weïrd° sisters, hand in hand,
Posters° of the sea and land,
Thus do go about, about:
35
Thrice to thine, and thrice to mine,
And thrice again, to make up nine.
Peace! The charm's wound up.

Enter MACBETH *and* BANQUO.

MACBETH   So foul and fair a day I have not seen.

BANQUO   How far is 't called to Forres? What are these
So withered, and so wild in their attire,   40
That look not like th' inhabitants o' th' earth,
And yet are on 't? Live you, or are you aught
That man may question?° You seem to understand me,
By each at once her choppy° finger laying
Upon her skinny lips. You should be women,   45
And yet your beards forbid me to interpret
That you are so.
MACBETH   Speak, if you can: what are you?
FIRST WITCH   All hail, Macbeth! Hail to thee, Thane of Glamis!
SECOND WITCH   All hail, Macbeth! Hail to thee, Thane of Cawdor!
THIRD WITCH   All hail, Macbeth, that shalt be King hereafter!   50
BANQUO   Good sir, why do you start, and seem to fear
Things that do sound so fair? I' th' name of truth,
Are ye fantastical,° or that indeed
Which outwardly ye show? My noble partner
You greet with present grace° and great prediction   55
Of noble having° and of royal hope,
That he seems rapt withal:° to me you speak not.
If you can look into the seeds of time,
And say which grain will grow and which will not,
Speak then to me, who neither beg nor fear   60
Your favors nor your hate.
FIRST WITCH   Hail!
SECOND WITCH   Hail!
THIRD WITCH   Hail!
FIRST WITCH   Lesser than Macbeth, and greater.   65

I.iii. 6 **Aroint thee** begone. **rump-fed ronyon** fat-rumped scabby creature. 15 **ports they blow** harbors to which the winds blow (?). 17 **card** compass card. 20 **penthouse lid** eyelid (the figure is of a lean-to). 21 **forbid** cursed. 23 **peak** waste away. 32 **weird** destiny-serving (?). 33 **Posters** swift travelers.

43 **question** talk to. 44 **choppy** chapped. 53 **fantastical** imaginary. 55 **grace** honor. 56 **having** possession. 57 **rapt withal** entranced by it.

SECOND WITCH Not so happy,° yet much happier.

THIRD WITCH Thou shalt get° kings, though thou be none.

So all hail, Macbeth and Banquo!

FIRST WITCH Banquo and Macbeth, all hail!

MACBETH Stay, you imperfect° speakers,
70 tell me more:

By Sinel's° death I know I am Thane of Glamis;

But how of Cawdor? The Thane of Cawdor lives,

A prosperous gentleman; and to be King Stands not within the prospect of belief,

No more than to be Cawdor. Say from
75 whence

You owe° this strange intelligence?° Or why

Upon this blasted heath you stop our way

With such prophetic greeting? Speak, I charge you.

WITCHES vanish.

BANQUO The earth hath bubbles as the water has,

And these are of them. Whither are they
80 vanished?

MACBETH Into the air, and what seemed corporal° melted

As breath into the wind. Would they had stayed!

BANQUO Were such things here as we do speak about?

Or have we eaten on the insane° root
85 That takes the reason prisoner?

MACBETH Your children shall be kings.

BANQUO   You shall be King.

MACBETH And Thane of Cawdor too. Went it not so?

BANQUO To th' selfsame tune and words. Who's here?

Enter ROSS *and* ANGUS.

ROSS The King hath happily received, Macbeth,

The news of thy success; and when he reads°
90 Thy personal venture in the rebels' fight,

His wonders and his praises do contend

Which should be thine or his.° Silenced with that,

In viewing o'er the rest o' th' selfsame day,

He finds thee in the stout Norweyan ranks,
95 Nothing afeard of what thyself didst make,

Strange images of death. As thick as tale Came post with post,° and every one did bear

Thy praises in his kingdom's great defense,

And poured them down before him.

ANGUS   We are sent
100 To give thee, from our royal master, thanks;

Only to herald thee into his sight, Not pay thee.

ROSS And for an earnest° of a greater honor,

He bade me, from him, call thee Thane of Cawdor;
105 In which addition,° hail, most worthy Thane!

For it is thine.

BANQUO What, can the devil speak true?

MACBETH The Thane of Cawdor lives: why do you dress me
In borrowed robes?

ANGUS   Who was the thane lives yet,
110 But under heavy judgment bears that life

Which he deserves to lose. Whether he was combined°

With those of Norway, or did line° the rebel

With hidden help and vantage,° or that with both

---

66 **happy** fortunate. 67 **get** beget. 70 **imperfect** incomplete. 71 **Sinel** (Macbeth's father). 76 **owe** own, have. **intelligence** information. 81 **corporal** corporeal. 84 **insane** insanity-producing.

90 **reads** considers. 92–93 **His wonders . . . his** i.e., Duncan's speechless admiration, appropriate to him, contends with his desire to praise you (?). 97–98 **As thick . . . post** as fast as could be counted came messenger after messenger. 104 **earnest** pledge. 106 **addition** title. 111 **combined** allied. 112 **line** support. 113 **vantage** opportunity.

He labored in his country's wrack,° I know not;

But treasons capital, confessed and proved, 115

Have overthrown him.

MACBETH   [*Aside*] Glamis, and Thane of Cawdor:

The greatest is behind.° [*To* ROSS *and* ANGUS] Thanks for your pains.

[*Aside to* BANQUO] Do you not hope your children shall be kings,

When those that gave the Thane of Cawdor to me

Promised no less to them?

BANQUO [*Aside to* MACBETH] That, trusted home,° 120

Might yet enkindle you unto the crown,

Besides the Thane of Cawdor. But 'tis strange:

And oftentimes, to win us to our harm,

The instruments of darkness tell us truths,

Win us with honest trifles, to betray's 125

In deepest consequence.°

Cousins,° a word, I pray you.

MACBETH   [*Aside*] Two truths are told,

As happy prologues to the swelling° act

Of the imperial theme.—I thank you, gentlemen.—

[*Aside*] This supernatural soliciting° 130

Cannot be ill, cannot be good. If ill,

Why hath it given me earnest of success,

Commencing in a truth? I am Thane of Cawdor:

If good, why do I yield to that suggestion

Whose horrid image doth unfix my hair 135

And make my seated° heart knock at my ribs,

Against the use of nature?° Present fears

Are less than horrible imaginings.

My thought, whose murder yet is but fantastical,°

Shakes so my single° state of man that function 140

Is smothered in surmise, and nothing is

But what is not.

BANQUO   Look, how our partner's rapt.

MACBETH [*Aside*] If chance will have me King, why, chance may crown me,

Without my stir.

BANQUO   New honors come upon him,

Like our strange° garments, cleave not to their mold 145

But with the aid of use.

MACBETH   [*Aside*] Come what come may

Time and the hour runs through the roughest day.

BANQUO Worthy Macbeth, we stay upon your leisure.°

MACBETH Give me your favor.° My dull brain was wrought

With things forgotten. Kind gentlemen, your pains 150

Are registered where every day I turn

The leaf to read them. Let us toward the King.

[*Aside to* BANQUO] Think upon what hath chanced, and at more time,

The interim having weighed it,° let us speak

Our free hearts° each to other.

BANQUO   Very gladly. 155

MACBETH Till then, enough. Come, friends.

Exeunt.

SCENE FOUR   [*Forres. The palace.*]

Flourish.° Enter KING [DUNCAN], LENNOX, MALCOLM, DONALBAIN, *and* ATTENDANTS.

KING DUNCAN   Is execution done on Cawdor? Are not

Those in commission° yet returned?

---

114 **wrack** ruin. 117 **behind** i.e., to follow. 120 **home** all the way. 126 **In deepest consequence** in the most significant sequel. 127 **Cousins** i.e., fellow noblemen. 128 **swelling** stately. 130 **soliciting** inviting. 136 **seated** fixed. 137 **Against the use of nature** contrary to my natural way. 139 **fantastical** imaginary.

140 **single** unaided, weak (or "entire"?). 145 **strange** new. 148 **stay upon your leisure** await your convenience. 149 **favor** pardon. 154 **The interim having weighed it** i.e., when we have had time to think. 155 **Our free hearts** our minds freely. I.iv.sd **Flourish** fanfare. 2 **in commission** i.e., commissioned to oversee the execution.

MALCOLM   My liege,
They are not yet come back. But I have
  spoke
With one that saw him die, who did re-
  port
That very frankly he confessed his trea-
5   sons,
Implored your Highness' pardon and set
  forth
A deep repentance: nothing in his life
Became him like the leaving it. He died
As one that had been studied° in his
  death,
To throw away the dearest thing he
10   owed°
As 'twere a careless° trifle.

KING DUNCAN   There's no art
To find the mind's construction in the
  face:
He was a gentleman on whom I built
An absolute trust.

Enter MACBETH, BANQUO, ROSS, *and*
ANGUS.

         O worthiest cousin!
15 The sin of my ingratitude even now
Was heavy on me: thou art so far before,
That swiftest wing of recompense is slow
To overtake thee. Would thou hadst less
  deserved,
That the proportion° both of thanks and
  payment
Might have been mine! Only I have left
20   to say,
More is thy due than more than all can
  pay.

MACBETH   The service and the loyalty I
  owe,
In doing it, pays itself.° Your Highness'
  part
Is to receive our duties: and our duties
Are to your throne and state children
25   and servants;
Which do but what they should, by doing
  every thing

Safe toward° your love and honor.

KING DUNCAN   Welcome hither.
I have begun to plant thee, and will
  labor
To make thee full of growing. Noble
  Banquo,
That hast no less deserved, nor must be
  known   *30*
No less to have done so, let me enfold
  thee
And hold thee to my heart.

BANQUO   There if I grow,
The harvest is your own.

KING DUNCAN   My plenteous joys,
Wanton° in fullness, seek to hide them-
  selves
In drops of sorrow. Sons, kinsmen, thanes,   *35*
And you whose places are the nearest,
  know,
We will establish our estate° upon
Our eldest, Malcolm, whom we name
  hereafter
The Prince of Cumberland: which honor
  must
Not unaccompanied invest him only,   *40*
But signs of nobleness, like stars, shall
  shine
On all deservers. From hence to Inver-
  ness,
And bind us further to you.

MACBETH   The rest is labor, which is not
  used for you.°
I'll be myself the harbinger, and make
  joyful   *45*
The hearing of my wife with your approach;
So, humbly take my leave.

KING DUNCAN   My worthy Cawdor!

MACBETH [*Aside*] The Prince of Cumberland! That is a step
On which I must fall down, or else o'er-
  leap,
For in my way it lies. Stars, hide your
  fires;   *50*
Let not light see my black and deep desires:

---

9 **studied** rehearsed. 10 **owed** owned. 11 **careless**
uncared-for. 19 **proportion** preponderance. 23 **pays
itself** is its own reward. 27 **Safe toward** safeguard-
ing (?).

34 **Wanton** unrestrained. 37 **establish our estate**
settle the succession. 44 **The rest . . . you** i.e., repose is laborious when not employed for you.

The eye wink at the hand;° yet let that be
Which the eye fears, when it is done, to see.

Exit.

KING DUNCAN True, worthy Banquo; he is full so valiant,
55 And in his commendations° I am fed;
It is a banquet to me. Let's after him,
Whose care is gone before to bid us welcome.
It is a peerless kinsman. *Flourish. Exeunt.*

SCENE FIVE [*Inverness.* MACBETH'*s castle.*]

Enter MACBETH'*s wife, alone, with a letter.*

LADY MACBETH [*Reads*] "They met me in the day of success; and I have learned by the perfect'st report they have more in them than mortal knowledge. When I
5 burned in desire to question them further, they made themselves air, into which they vanished. Whiles I stood rapt in the wonder of it, came missives° from the King, who all-hailed me 'Thane of
10 Cawdor'; by which title, before, these weïrd sisters saluted me, and referred me to the coming on of time, with 'Hail, King that shalt be!' This have I thought good to deliver thee,° my dearest partner
15 of greatness, that thou mightst not lose the dues of rejoicing, by being ignorant of what greatness is promised thee. Lay it to thy heart, and farewell."

Glamis thou art, and Cawdor, and shalt be
What thou art promised. Yet do I fear
20 thy nature;
It is too full o' th' milk of human kindness°

To catch the nearest way. Thou wouldst be great,
Art not without ambition, but without
The illness° should attend it. What thou wouldst highly,
That wouldst thou holily; wouldst not play false, 25
And yet wouldst wrongly win. Thou'dst have, great Glamis,
That which cries "Thus thou must do" if thou have it;
And that which rather thou dost fear to do
Than wishest should be undone. Hie thee hither,
That I may pour my spirits in thine ear, 30
And chastise with the valor of my tongue
All that impedes thee from the golden round°
Which fate and metaphysical° aid doth seem
To have thee crowned withal.°

Enter MESSENGER.

       What is your tidings?
MESSENGER The King comes here tonight.
LADY MACBETH   Thou'rt mad to say it! 35
Is not thy master with him, who, were 't so,
Would have informed for preparation?
MESSENGER So please you, it is true. Our thane is coming.
One of my fellows had the speed of him,°
Who, almost dead for breath, had scarcely more 40
Than would make up his message.
LADY MACBETH   Give him tending;
He brings great news.   *Exit* MESSENGER.
      The raven himself is hoarse
That croaks the fatal entrance of Duncan
Under my battlements. Come, you spirits
That tend on mortal° thoughts, unsex me here, 45
And fill me, from the crown to the toe, top-full
Of direst cruelty! Make thick my blood,

52 **wink at the hand** i.e., be blind to the hand's deed. 55 **his commendations** commendations of him. I.v. 8 **missives** messengers. 14 **deliver thee** report to you. 21 **milk of human kindness** i.e., gentle quality of human nature.

24 **illness** wickedness. 32 **round** crown. 33 **metaphysical** supernatural. 34 **withal** with. 39 **had the speed of him** outdistanced him. 45 **mortal** deadly.

Stop up th' access and passage to remorse,°
That no compunctious visitings of na-
ture°
50 Shake my fell° purpose, nor keep peace
between
Th' effect° and it! Come to my woman's
breasts,
And take my milk for° gall, you murd'-
ring ministers,°
Wherever in your sightless° substances
You wait on° nature's mischief! Come,
thick night,
And pall° thee in the dunnest° smoke of
55 hell,
That my keen knife see not the wound it
makes,
Nor heaven peep through the blanket of
the dark,
To cry "Hold, hold!"

Enter MACBETH.

     Great Glamis! Worthy Cawdor!
Greater than both, by the all-hail here-
after!°
60 Thy letters have transported me beyond
This ignorant° present, and I feel now
The future in the instant.°

MACBETH   My dearest love,
Duncan comes here tonight.

LADY MACBETH   And when goes hence?

MACBETH Tomorrow, as he purposes.

LADY MACBETH   O, never
65 Shall sun that morrow see!
Your face, my Thane, is as a book where
men
May read strange matters. To beguile
the time,°
Look like the time; bear welcome in your
eye,
Your hand, your tongue: look like th'
innocent flower,

But be the serpent under 't. He that's
coming   70
Must be provided for: and you shall put
This night's great business into my
dispatch;°
Which shall to all our nights and days to
come
Give solely sovereign sway and master-
dom.

MACBETH We will speak further.

LADY MACBETH   Only look up clear.° 75
To alter favor ever is to fear.°
Leave all the rest to me.   *Exeunt.*

SCENE SIX   [*Before* MACBETH's *castle.*]

Hautboys° and torches. Enter KING [DUN-
CAN], MALCOLM, DONALBAIN, BANQUO,
LENNOX, MACDUFF, ROSS, ANGUS, *and* AT-
TENDANTS.

KING DUNCAN This castle hath a pleasant
seat;° the air
Nimbly and sweetly recommends itself
Unto our gentle° senses.

BANQUO   This guest of summer,
The temple-haunting martlet,° does
approve°
By his loved mansionry° that the heaven's
breath   5
Smells wooingly here. No jutty,° frieze,
Buttress, nor coign of vantage,° but this
bird
Hath made his pendent bed and procre-
ant° cradle.
Where they most breed and haunt,° I
have observed
The air is delicate.

Enter LADY [MACBETH].

KING DUNCAN   See, see, our honored
hostess!   10

---

48 **remorse** compassion. 49 **compunctious visitings
of nature** natural feelings of compassion. 50 **fell**
savage. 51 **effect** fulfillment. 52 **for** in exchange
for. 52 **ministers** agents. 53 **sightless** invisible. 54
wait on assist. 55 **pall** enshroud. **dunnest** darkest.
59 **all-hail hereafter** the third all-hail (?) the all-
hail of the future (?). 61 **ignorant** unknowing. 62
instant present. 67 **To beguile the time** i.e., to deceive people of the day.

72 **dispatch** management. 75 **look up clear** appear
undisturbed. 76 **To alter . . . fear** to show a disturbed face is dangerous.
I.vi.sd **Hautboys** oboes. 1 **seat** site. 3 **gentle** soothed.
4 **temple-haunting martlet** martin (swift) nesting in
churches. **approve** prove. 5 **mansionry** nests. 6 **jutty**
projection. 7 **coign of vantage** advantageous corner.
8 **procreant** breeding. 9 **haunt** visit.

The love that follows us sometime is our trouble,
Which still we thank as love.° Herein I teach you
How you shall bid God 'ield° us for your pains
And thank us for your trouble.

LADY MACBETH   All our service
In every point twice done, and then done
15 double,
Were poor and single business° to contend
Against those honors deep and broad wherewith
Your Majesty loads our house: for those of old,
And the late dignities heaped up to them,
We rest your hermits.°

KING DUNCAN   Where's the Thane of
20 Cawdor?
We coursed° him at the heels, and had a purpose
To be his purveyor:° but he rides well,
And his great love, sharp as his spur, hath holp° him
To his home before us. Fair and noble hostess,
We are your guest tonight.

25 LADY MACBETH   Your servants ever
Have theirs, themselves, and what is theirs, in compt,°
To make their audit at your Highness' pleasure,
Still° to return your own.

KING DUNCAN   Give me your hand.
Conduct me to mine host: we love him highly,
And shall continue our graces towards
30 him.
By your leave, hostess.   *Exeunt.*

Hautboys. Torches. Enter a Sewer,° and diverse Servants with dishes and service over the stage. Then enter MACBETH.

MACBETH If it were done° when 'tis done, then 'twere well
It were done quickly. If th' assassination
Could trammel up° the consequence, and catch,
With his surcease,° success;° that but this blow
Might be the be-all and the end-all—here, 5
But here, upon this bank and shoal of time,
We'd jump° the life to come. But in these cases
We still° have judgment here; that we but teach
Bloody instructions, which, being taught, return
To plague th' inventor: this even-handed° justice 10
Commends° th' ingredients of our poisoned chalice
To our own lips. He's here in double trust:
First, as I am his kinsman and his subject,
Strong both against the deed; then, as his host,
Who should against his murderer shut the door, 15
Not bear the knife myself. Besides, this Duncan
Hath borne his faculties° so meek, hath been
So clear° in his great office, that his virtues
Will plead like angels trumpet-tongued against
The deep damnation of his taking-off; 20
And pity, like a naked newborn babe,

11–12 **The love . . . love** the love offered me sometimes inconveniences me, but still I value it as love. 13 **'ield** reward. 16 **single business** feeble service. 20 **your hermits** dependents bound to pray for you. 21 **coursed** pursued. 22 **purveyor** advance-supply officer. 23 **holp** helped. 26 **Have theirs . . . compt** have their dependents, themselves, and their possessions in trust. 28 **Still** always.

I.vii.sd **Sewer** chief butler. 1 **done** over and done with. 3 **trammel up** catch in a net. 4 **his surcease** Duncan's death (?) the consequence's cessation (?). **success** what follows. 7 **jump** risk. 8 **still** always. 10 **even-handed** impartial. 11 **Commends** offers. 17 **faculties** powers. 18 **clear** spotless.

Striding° the blast, or heaven's cherubin horsed
Upon the sightless couriers° of the air,
Shall blow the horrid deed in every eye,
That° tears shall drown the wind. I have
25 no spur
To prick the sides of my intent, but only
Vaulting ambition, which o'erleaps itself
And falls on th' other——

Enter LADY [MACBETH].

       How now! What news?
LADY MACBETH He has almost supped.
Why have you left the chamber?
MACBETH Hath he asked for me?
30 LADY MACBETH   Know you not he has?
MACBETH We will proceed no further in this business:
He hath honored me of late, and I have bought°
Golden opinions from all sorts of people,
Which would be worn now in their newest gloss,
Not cast aside so soon.
35 LADY MACBETH   Was the hope drunk
Wherein you dressed yourself? Hath it slept since?
And wakes it now, to look so green° and pale
At what it did so freely? From this time
Such I account thy love. Art thou afeard
To be the same in thine own act and
40 valor
As thou art in desire? Wouldst thou have that
Which thou esteem'st the ornament of life,
And live a coward in thine own esteem,
Letting "I dare not" wait upon° "I would,"
Like the poor cat° i' th' adage?
45 MACBETH   Prithee, peace!
I dare do all that may become a man;
Who dares do more is none.

LADY MACBETH   What beast was 't then
That made you break° this enterprise to me?
When you durst do it, then you were a man;
And to be more than what you were, you would
50 Be so much more the man. Nor time nor place
Did then adhere,° and yet you would make both.
They have made themselves, and that their° fitness now
Does unmake you. I have given suck, and know
55 How tender 'tis to love the babe that milks me:
I would, while it was smiling in my face,
Have plucked my nipple from his boneless gums,
And dashed the brains out, had I so sworn as you
Have done to this.
MACBETH   If we should fail?
LADY MACBETH   We fail?
But° screw your courage to the sticking-place,°
60 And we'll not fail. When Duncan is asleep—
Whereto the rather shall his day's hard journey
Soundly invite him—his two chamberlains
Will I with wine and wassail° so convince°
65 That memory, the warder° of the brain,
Shall be a fume, and the receipt of reason
A limbeck only:° when in swinish sleep
Their drenchèd natures lies° as in a death,
What cannot you and I perform upon

---

48 **break** broach. 52 **adhere** suit. 53 **that their** their very. 60 **But** only. **sticking-place** notch (holding the bowstring of a taut crossbow). 64 **wassail** carousing. **convince** overpower. 65 **warder** guard. 66–67 **receipt . . . only** i.e., the receptacle (**receipt**), which should collect the distillate of thought—reason—will be a mere vessel (**limbeck**) of undistilled liquids. 68 **lies** lie.

22 **Striding** bestriding. 23 **sightless couriers** invisible coursers (i.e., the winds). 25 **That** so that. 32 **bought** acquired. 37 **green** sickly. 44 **wait upon** follow. 45 **cat** (who wants fish but fears to wet its paws).

Th' unguarded Duncan, what not put
70 upon
His spongy° officers, who shall bear the
  guilt
Of our great quell°
MACBETH Bring forth men-children only;
For thy undaunted mettle° should
  compose
Nothing but males. Will it not be
  received,
When we have marked with blood those
75 sleepy two
Of his own chamber, and used their very
  daggers,
That they have done 't?
LADY MACBETH   Who dares receive it
  other,°
As we shall make our griefs and clamor
  roar
Upon his death?
MACBETH   I am settled, and bend up
80 Each corporal agent to this terrible feat.
Away, and mock the time° with fairest
  show:
False face must hide what the false heart
  doth know.

  Exeunt.

Act Two

SCENE ONE [*Inverness. Court of* MAC-
BETH's *castle.*]

Enter BANQUO, *and* FLEANCE, *with a torch
before him.*

BANQUO How goes the night, boy?
FLEANCE The moon is down; I have not
  heard the clock.
BANQUO And she goes down at twelve.
FLEANCE   I take 't, 'tis later, sir.
BANQUO Hold, take my sword. There's
  husbandry° in heaven.
  Their candles are all out. Take thee that
5 too.

A heavy summons° lies like lead upon
  me,
And yet I would not sleep. Merciful
  powers,
Restrain in me the cursèd thoughts that
  nature
Gives way to in repose!

Enter MACBETH, *and a Servant with a
torch.*

                    Give me my sword!
Who's there?   10
MACBETH A friend.
BANQUO What, sir, not yet at rest? The
  King's a-bed:
He hath been in unusual pleasure, and
Sent forth great largess to your offices:°
This diamond he greets your wife withal, 15
By the name of most kind hostess; and
  shut up°
In measureless content.
MACBETH   Being unprepared,
Our will became the servant to defect,°
Which else should free have wrought.
BANQUO   All's well.
I dreamt last night of the three weïrd
  sisters: 20
To you they have showed some truth.
MACBETH   I think not of them.
Yet, when we can entreat an hour to
  serve,
We would spend it in some words upon
  that business,
If you would grant the time.
BANQUO   At your kind'st leisure.
MACBETH If you shall cleave to my con-
  sent, when 'tis,°   25
It shall make honor for you.
BANQUO   So° I lose none
In seeking to augment it, but still keep
My bosom franchised° and allegiance
  clear,°
I shall be counseled.

71 **spongy** sodden. 72 **quell** killing. 73 **mettle** substance. 77 **other** otherwise. 81 **mock the time** beguile the world.
II.i. 4 **husbandry** frugality.

6 **summons** call (to sleep). 14 **largess to your offices**
gifts to your servants' quarters. 16 **shut up** concluded. 18 **Our . . . defect** our good will was
hampered by our deficient preparations. 25 **cleave
. . . 'tis** join my cause, when the time comes. 26
So provided that. 28 **franchised** free (from guilt).
28 **clear** spotless.

MACBETH   Good repose the while!
30 BANQUO Thanks, sir. The like to you!

Exit BANQUO [*with* FLEANCE].

MACBETH Go bid thy mistress, when my
drink is ready,
She strike upon the bell. Get thee to bed.

Exit [*Servant*].

Is this a dagger which I see before me,
The handle toward my hand? Come, let
me clutch thee.
35 I have thee not, and yet I see thee still.
Art thou not, fatal vision, sensible°
To feeling as to sight, or art thou but
A dagger of the mind, a false creation,
Proceeding from the heat-oppressèd
brain?
40 I see thee yet, in form as palpable
As this which now I draw.
Thou marshal'st me the way that I was
going;
And such an instrument I was to use.
Mine eyes are made the fools o' th' other
senses,
45 Or else worth all the rest. I see thee still;
And on thy blade and dudgeon° gouts° of
blood,
Which was not so before. There's no such
thing.
It is the bloody business which informs°
Thus to mine eyes. Now o'er the one half-
world
Nature seems dead, and wicked dreams
50 abuse°
The curtained sleep; witchcraft celebrates
Pale Hecate's offerings;° and withered
murder,
Alarumed° by his sentinel, the wolf,
Whose howl's his watch, thus with his
stealthy pace,
With Tarquin's° ravishing strides,
55   towards his design

Moves like a ghost. Thou sure and firm-
set earth,
Hear not my steps, which way they walk,
for fear
Thy very stones prate of my whereabout,
And take the present horror from the
time,
Which now suits with it.° Whiles I threat,
he lives: 60
Words to the heat of deeds too cold
breath gives.

A bell rings.

I go, and it is done: the bell invites me.
Hear it not, Duncan, for it is a knell
That summons thee to heaven, or to hell.

Exit.

SCENE TWO [MACBETH's *castle.*]

Enter LADY [MACBETH].

LADY MACBETH That which hath made
them drunk hath made me bold;
What hath quenched them hath given
me fire. Hark! Peace!
It was the owl that shrieked, the fatal
bellman,
Which gives the stern'st good-night.° He
is about it.
The doors are open, and the surfeited
grooms   5
Do mock their charge with snores. I have
drugged their possets,°
That death and nature° do contend
about them,
Whether they live or die.
MACBETH [*Within*]   Who's
there? What, ho?
LADY MACBETH Alack, I am afraid they
have awaked

---

36 **sensible** perceptible. 46 **dudgeon** wooden hilt.
gouts large drops. 48 **informs** gives shape (?). 50
abuse deceive. 52 **Hecate's offerings** offerings to
Hecate (goddess of sorcery). 53 **Alarumed** called to
action. 55 **Tarquin** (Roman tyrant who ravished
Lucrece).

59–60 **take . . . it** remove (by noise) the horrible
silence attendant on this moment and suitable to
it (?).
II.ii. 3–4 **bellman . . . good-night** i.e., the owl's call,
portending death, is like the town crier's call to a
condemned man. 6 **possets** (bedtime drinks). 7 **nature** natural vitality.

And 'tis not done! Th' attempt and not
the deed
Confounds° us. Hark! I laid their daggers ready;
He could not miss 'em. Had he not resembled
My father as he slept, I had done't.

Enter MACBETH.

             My husband!
MACBETH   I have done the deed. Didst
thou not hear a noise?
LADY MACBETH   I heard the owl scream
and the crickets cry.
Did not you speak?
MACBETH   When?
LADY MACBETH   Now.
MACBETH   As I descended?
LADY MACBETH   Ay.
MACBETH   Hark!
Who lies i' th' second chamber?
LADY MACBETH   Donalbain.
MACBETH   This is a sorry° sight.
LADY MACBETH   A foolish thought, to say
a sorry sight.
MACBETH   There's one did laugh in 's
sleep, and one cried "Murder!"
That they did wake each other. I stood
and heard them.
But they did say their prayers, and ad-
dressed them
Again to sleep.
LADY MACBETH   There are two lodged to-
gether.
MACBETH   One cried "God bless us!" and
"Amen" the other,
As they had seen me with these hang-
man's° hands:
List'ning their fear, I could not say
"Amen,"
When they did say "God bless us!"
LADY MACBETH   Consider it not so deeply.
MACBETH   But wherefore could not I pro-
nounce "Amen"?
I had most need of blessing, and "Amen"
Stuck in my throat.

LADY MACBETH   These deeds must not be
thought
After these ways; so, it will make us mad.
MACBETH   Methought I heard a voice cry
"Sleep no more!
Macbeth does murder sleep"—the inno-
cent sleep,
Sleep that knits up the raveled sleave° of
care,
The death of each day's life, sore labor's
bath,
Balm of hurt minds, great nature's sec-
ond course,°
Chief nourisher in life's feast——
LADY MACBETH   What do you mean?
MACBETH   Still it cried "Sleep no more!"
to all the house:
"Glamis hath murdered sleep, and there-
fore Cawdor
Shall sleep no more: Macbeth shall sleep
no more."
LADY MACBETH   Who was it that thus
cried? Why, worthy Thane,
You do unbend° your noble strength, to
think
So brainsickly of things. Go get some
water,
And wash this filthy witness° from your
hand.
Why did you bring these daggers from
the place?
They must lie there: go carry them, and
smear
The sleepy grooms with blood.
MACBETH   I'll go no more.
I am afraid to think what I have done;
Look on 't again I dare not.
LADY MACBETH   Infirm of purpose!
Give me the daggers. The sleeping and
the dead
Are but as pictures. 'Tis the eye of child-
hood
That fears a painted° devil. If he do
bleed,

11 **Confounds** ruins. 20 **sorry** miserable. 27 **hang-man's** executioner's (i.e., bloody).

36 **knits up the raveled sleave** straightens out the tangled skein. 38 **second course** i.e., sleep (the less substantial first course is food). 44 **unbend** relax. 46 **witness** evidence. 54 **painted** depicted.

55   I'll gild° the faces of the grooms withal,
     For it must seem their guilt.

     Exit. Knock within.

     MACBETH   Whence is that knocking?
     How is 't with me, when every noise ap-
     palls me?
     What hands are here? Ha! They pluck
     out mine eyes!
     Will all great Neptune's ocean wash this
     blood
     Clean from my hand? No; this my hand
60   will rather
     The multitudinous seas incarnadine,°
     Making the green one red.°

     Enter LADY [MACBETH].

     LADY MACBETH My hands are of your
     color, but I shame
     To wear a heart so white. (*Knock.*) I
     hear a knocking
     At the south entry. Retire we to our
65   chamber.
     A little water clears us of this deed:
     How easy is it then! Your constancy
     Hath left you unattended.° (*Knock.*)
     Hark! more knocking.
     Get on your nightgown,° lest occasion
     call us
70   And show us to be watchers.° Be not lost
     So poorly° in your thoughts.
     MACBETH   To know my deed, 'twere best
     not know myself. (*Knock.*)
     Wake Duncan with thy knocking! I
     would thou couldst!   *Exeunt.*

     SCENE THREE   [MACBETH's *castle.*]

     Enter a PORTER. *Knocking within.*

     PORTER   Here's a knocking indeed! If a
     man were porter of hell gate, he should

have old° turning the key. (*Knock.*)
Knock, knock, knock! Who's there, i' th'
name of Beelzebub? Here's a farmer, that   5
hanged himself on th' expectation of
plenty.° Come in time! Have napkins
enow° about you; here you'll sweat for 't.
(*Knock.*) Knock, knock! Who's there, in
th' other devil's name? Faith, here's an   10
equivocator,° that could swear in both
the scales against either scale; who committed treason enough for God's sake, yet
could not equivocate to heaven. O, come
in, equivocator. (*Knock.*) Knock, knock,   15
knock! Who's there? Faith, here's an English tailor come hither for stealing out of
a French hose:° come in, tailor. Here you
may roast your goose.° (*Knock.*) Knock,
knock; never at quiet! What are you? But   20
this place is too cold for hell. I'll devil-
porter it no further. I had thought to
have let in some of all professions that
go the primrose way to th' everlasting
bonfire. (*Knock.*) Anon, anon! [*Opens an*   25
entrance.] I pray you, remember the
porter.

     Enter MACDUFF *and* LENNOX.

MACDUFF   Was it so late, friend, ere you
went to bed, That you do lie so late?
PORTER   Faith, sir, we were carousing till   30
the second cock:° and drink, sir, is a
great provoker of three things.
MACDUFF   What three things does drink
especially provoke?
PORTER   Marry, sir, nose-painting, sleep,   35
and urine. Lechery, sir, it provokes and
unprovokes; it provokes the desire, but it
takes away the performance: therefore
much drink may be said to be an equivocator with lechery: it makes him and it   40
mars him; it sets him on and it takes him

---

55 **gild** paint. 61 **incarnadine** redden. 62 **the green one red** (perhaps "the green one" means "the ocean," but perhaps "one" here means "totally," "uniformly"). 67–68 **Your . . . unattended** your firmness has deserted you. 69 **nightgown** dressing-gown. 70 **watchers** i.e., up late. 71 **poorly** weakly.

II.iii. 2–3 **should have old** would certainly have plenty of. 5–7 **farmer . . . plenty** (the farmer hoarded so he could later sell high, but when it looked as though there would be a crop surplus he hanged himself). 8 **enow** enough. 11 **equivocator** i.e., Jesuit (who allegedly employed deceptive speech to further God's ends). 18 **French hose** tight-fitting hose. 19 **goose** pressing iron. 31 **second cock** (about 3 A.M.).

off; it persuades him and disheartens
him; makes him stand to and not stand
to; in conclusion, equivocates him in a
45 sleep, and giving him the lie, leaves him.
MACDUFF I believe drink gave thee the
lie° last night.
PORTER That it did, sir, i' the very throat
on me: but I requited him for his lie,
50 and, I think, being too strong for him,
though he took up my legs sometime, yet
I make a shift to cast° him.
MACDUFF Is thy master stirring?

Enter MACBETH.

Our knocking has awaked him; here he
comes.
LENNOX Good morrow, noble sir.
55 MACBETH   Good morrow, both.
MACDUFF Is the king stirring, worthy
Thane?
MACBETH   Not yet.
MACDUFF He did command me to call
timely° on him:
I have almost slipped° the hour.
MACBETH   I'll bring you to him.
MACDUFF I know this is a joyful trouble
to you;
60 But yet 'tis one.
MACBETH The labor we delight in physics
pain.°
This is the door.
MACDUFF   I'll make so bold to call,
For 'tis my limited service.°

Exit MACDUFF.

LENNOX Goes the king hence today?
MACBETH   He does: he did appoint so.
LENNOX The night has been unruly.
65 Where we lay,
Our chimneys were blown down, and, as
they say,
Lamentings heard i' th' air, strange
screams of death,

And prophesying with accents terrible
Of dire combustion° and confused events
New hatched to th' woeful time: the ob-
scure bird°   70
Clamored the livelong night. Some say,
the earth
Was feverous and did shake.
MACBETH   'Twas a rough night.
LENNOX My young remembrance cannot
parallel
A fellow to it.

Enter MACDUFF.

MACDUFF O horror, horror, horror!
Tongue nor heart   75
Cannot conceive nor name thee.
MACBETH AND LENNOX What's the matter?
MACDUFF Confusion° now hath made his
masterpiece.
Most sacrilegious murder hath broke ope
The Lord's anointed temple, and stole
thence   80
The life o' th' building.
MACBETH   What is 't you say? The life?
LENNOX Mean you his Majesty?
MACDUFF Approach the chamber, and de-
stroy your sight
With a new Gorgon:° do not bid me
speak;
See, and then speak yourselves. Awake,
awake!   85

Exeunt MACBETH *and* LENNOX.

Ring the alarum bell. Murder and Trea-
son!
Banquo and Donalbain! Malcolm!
Awake!
Shake off this downy sleep, death's coun-
terfeit,°
And look on death itself! Up, up, and see
The great doom's image!° Malcolm!
Banquo!   90
As from your graves rise up, and walk
like sprites,°

46–47 **gave thee the lie** called you a liar (with a pun
on "stretched you out"). 52 **cast** (with a pun on
"cast," meaning "vomit"). 57 **timely** early. 58
slipped let slip. 61 **The labor . . . pain** labor that
gives us pleasure cures discomfort. 63 **limited
service** appointed duty.

69 **combustion** tumult. 70 **obscure bird** bird of
darkness, i.e., the owl. 78 **Confusion** destruction.
84 **Gorgon** (creature capable of turning beholders
to stone). 88 **counterfeit** imitation. 90 **great doom's
image** likeness of Judgment Day. 91 **sprites** spirits.

To countenance° this horror. Ring the bell.

Bell rings. Enter LADY [MACBETH].

LADY MACBETH What's the business,
That such a hideous trumpet calls to parley
The sleepers of the house? Speak, speak!
95 MACDUFF   O gentle lady,
'Tis not for you to hear what I can speak:
The repetition,° in a woman's ear,
Would murder as it fell.

Enter BANQUO.

              O Banquo, Banquo!
Our royal master's murdered.
LADY MACBETH   Woe, alas!
What, in our house?
100 BANQUO   Too cruel anywhere.
Dear Duff, I prithee, contradict thyself,
And say it is not so.

Enter MACBETH, LENNOX, *and* ROSS.

MACBETH Had I but died an hour before this chance,
I had lived a blessèd time; for from this instant
105 There's nothing serious in mortality:°
All is but toys.° Renown and grace is dead,
The wine of life is drawn, and the mere lees°
Is left this vault° to brag of.

Enter MALCOLM *and* DONALBAIN.

DONALBAIN What is amiss?
MACBETH   You are, and do not know 't.
The spring, the head, the fountain of your blood
110 Is stopped; the very source of it is stopped.
MACDUFF Your royal father's murdered.
MALCOLM   O, by whom?
LENNOX Those of his chamber, as it seemed, had done 't:

Their hands and faces were all badged° with blood;
So were their daggers, which unwiped we found   115
Upon their pillows. They stared, and were distracted.
No man's life was to be trusted with them.
MACBETH O, yet I do repent me of my fury,
That I did kill them.
MACDUFF   Wherefore did you so?
MACBETH Who can be wise, amazed,° temp'rate and furious,   120
Loyal and neutral, in a moment? No man.
The expedition° of my violent love
Outrun the pauser, reason. Here lay Duncan,
His silver skin laced with his golden blood,
And his gashed stabs looked like a breach in nature   125
For ruin's wasteful entrance: there, the murderers,
Steeped in the colors of their trade, their daggers
Unmannerly breeched with gore.° Who could refrain,°
That had a heart to love, and in that heart
Courage to make 's love known?
LADY MACBETH   Help me hence, ho!   130
MACDUFF Look to° the lady.
MALCOLM [*Aside to* DONALBAIN] Why do we hold our tongues,
That most may claim this argument for ours?°
DONALBAIN [*Aside to* MALCOLM] What should be spoken here,
Where our fate, hid in an auger-hole,°   135
May rush, and seize us? Let's away:
Our tears are not yet brewed.
MALCOLM [*Aside to* DONALBAIN] Nor our strong sorrow

114 **badged** marked. 120 **amazed** bewildered. 122 **expedition** haste. 128 **Unmannerly breeched with gore** covered with unseemly breeches of blood. **refrain** check oneself. 131 **Look to** look after. 133 **That most . . . ours?** who are the most concerned with this topic. 135 **auger-hole** i.e., unsuspected place.

92 **countenance** be in keeping with. 97 **repetition** report. 105 **serious in mortality** worthwhile in mortal life. 106 **toys** trifles. 107 **lees** dregs. 108 **vault** (1) wine vault (2) earth, with the sky as roof (?).

Upon the foot of motion.°
BANQUO   Look to the lady.

[LADY MACBETH *is carried out.*]

And when we have our naked frailties
140 hid,°
That suffer in exposure, let us meet
And question° this most bloody piece of work,
To know it further. Fears and scruples°
shake us.
In the great hand of God I stand, and thence
145 Against the undivulged pretense° I fight
Of treasonous malice.
MACDUFF   And so do I.
ALL   So all.
MACBETH Let's briefly° put on manly readiness,
And meet i' th' hall together.
ALL   Well contented.

Exeunt [all but MALCOLM *and*
DONALBAIN].

MALCOLM What will you do? Let's not
consort with them.
150 To show an unfelt sorrow is an office°
Which the false man does easy. I'll to England.
DONALBAIN To Ireland, I; our separated fortune
Shall keep us both the safer. Where we are
There's daggers in men's smiles; the near in blood,
The nearer bloody.
MALCOLM   This murderous shaft
155 that's shot
Hath not yet lighted, and our safest way
Is to avoid the aim. Therefore to horse;
And let us not be dainty of° leave-taking,
But shift away. There's warrant° in that theft

Which steals itself° when there's no
mercy left.   160
Exeunt.

SCENE FOUR [*Outside* MACBETH'*s castle.*]

Enter ROSS *with an* OLD MAN.

OLD MAN Threescore and ten I can re-
member well:
Within the volume of which time I have seen
Hours dreadful and things strange, but this sore° night
Hath trifled former knowings.°
ROSS   Ha, good father,
Thou seest the heavens, as troubled with man's act,   5
Threatens his bloody stage. By th' clock 'tis day,
And yet dark night strangles the travel-ing lamp:°
Is 't night's predominance,° or the day's shame,
That darkness does the face of earth en-tomb,
When living light should kiss it?
OLD MAN   'Tis unnatural,   10
Even like the deed that's done. On Tues-day last
A falcon, tow'ring in her pride of place,°
Was by a mousing° owl hawked at and killed.
ROSS And Duncan's horses—a thing most strange and certain—
Beauteous and swift, the minions° of their race,   15
Turned wild in nature, broke their stalls, flung out,°
Contending 'gainst obedience, as they would make
War with mankind.
OLD MAN 'Tis said they eat° each other.

137–139 **Our tears . . . motion** i.e., we have not yet had time for tears nor to express our sorrows in action (?). 140 **naked frailties hid** poor bodies clothed. 142 **question** discuss. 143 **scruples** sus-picions. 145 **undivulged pretense** hidden purpose. 147 **briefly** quickly. 150 **office** function. 158 **dainty of** fussy about. 159 **warrant** justification.

160 **steals itself** steals oneself away.
II.iv. 3 **sore** grievous. 4 **trifled former knowings** made trifles of former experiences. 7 **traveling lamp** i.e., the sun. 8 **predominance** astrological suprem-acy. 12 **tow'ring . . . place** soaring at her summit. 13 **mousing** i.e., normally mouse-eating. 15 **minions** darlings. 16 **flung out** lunged wildly. 18 **eat** ate.

ROSS They did so, to th' amazement of mine eyes,
That looked upon 't.

Enter MACDUFF.

20   Here comes the good Macduff.
How goes the world, sir, now?
MACDUFF   Why, see you not?
ROSS Is 't known who did this more than bloody deed?
MACDUFF Those that Macbeth hath slain.
ROSS   Alas, the day!
What good could they pretend?°
MACDUFF   They were suborned:°
Malcolm and Donalbain, the king's two
25 sons,
Are stol'n away and fled, which puts upon them
Suspicion of the deed.
ROSS   'Gainst nature still.
Thriftless° ambition, that will ravin up°
Thine own life's means! Then 'tis most like
30 The sovereignty will fall upon Macbeth.
MACDUFF He is already named,° and gone to Scone
To be invested.°
ROSS   Where is Duncan's body?
MACDUFF Carried to Colmekill,
The sacred storehouse of his predecessors
And guardian of their bones.
35 ROSS   Will you to Scone?
MACDUFF No, cousin, I'll to Fife.
ROSS   Well, I will thither.
MACDUFF Well, may you see things well done there. Adieu,
Lest our old robes sit easier than our new!
ROSS Farewell, father.
OLD MAN God's benison° go with you,
40   and with those
That would make good of bad, and friends of foes!

Exeunt omnes.

Act Three

SCENE ONE [*Forres. The palace.*]

Enter BANQUO.

BANQUO Thou hast it now: King, Cawdor, Glamis, all,
As the weïrd women promised, and I fear
Thou play'dst most foully for 't. Yet it was said
It should not stand° in thy posterity,
But that myself should be the root and father   5
Of many kings. If there come truth from them—
As upon thee, Macbeth, their speeches shine—
Why, by the verities on thee made good,
May they not be my oracles as well
And set me up in hope? But hush, no more!   10

Sennet° sounded. Enter MACBETH *as*
KING, LADY [MACBETH], LENNOX, ROSS,
LORDS, *and* ATTENDANTS

MACBETH Here's our chief guest.
LADY MACBETH If he had been forgotten,
It had been as a gap in our great feast,
And all-thing° unbecoming.
MACBETH Tonight we hold a solemn° supper, sir,
And I'll request your presence.
BANQUO   Let your Highness   15
Command upon me, to the which my duties
Are with a most indissoluble tie
For ever knit.
MACBETH Ride you this afternoon?
BANQUO   Ay, my good lord.
MACBETH We should have else desired your good advice   20
(Which still° hath been both grave and prosperous°)

24 **pretend** hope for. **suborned** bribed. 28 **Thriftless** wasteful. **ravin up** greedily devour. 31 **named** elected. 32 **invested** installed as king. 40 **benison** blessing.

III.i.4 **stand** continue. sd **Sennet** trumpet call. 13 **all-thing** altogether. 14 **solemn** ceremonious. 21 **still** always. **grave and prosperous** weighty and profitable.

28

In this day's council; but we'll take to-
morrow.
Is 't far you ride?
BANQUO   As far, my lord, as will fill up
the time
'Twixt this and supper. Go not my horse
25   the better,°
I must become a borrower of the night
For a dark hour or twain.
MACBETH   Fail not our feast.
BANQUO   My lord, I will not.
MACBETH   We hear our bloody cousins are
bestowed°
30   In England and in Ireland, not confessing
Their cruel parricide, filling their hearers
With strange invention.° But of that to-
morrow,
When therewithal we shall have cause of
state
Craving us jointly.° Hie you to horse.
Adieu,
Till you return at night. Goes Fleance
35   with you?
BANQUO   Ay, my good lord: our time does
call upon 's.
MACBETH   I wish your horses swift and
sure of foot,
And so I do commend you to their backs.
Farewell.   *Exit* BANQUO.
40   Let every man be master of his time
Till seven at night. To make society
The sweeter welcome, we will keep ourself
Till supper-time alone. While° then, God
be with you!

Exeunt LORDS [*and all but* MACBETH *and
a* SERVANT].

Sirrah,° a word with you: attend° those
men
45   Our pleasure?
ATTENDANT   They are, my lord, without°
the palace gate.
MACBETH   Bring them before us.

Exit SERVANT.

To be thus is nothing, but° to be safely
thus—
Our fears in° Banquo stick deep,
And in his royalty of nature reigns that   50
Which would° be feared. 'Tis much he
dares;
And, to° that dauntless temper° of his
mind,
He hath a wisdom that doth guide his
valor
To act in safety. There is none but he
Whose being I do fear: and under him   55
My genius is rebuked,° as it is said
Mark Antony's was by Cæsar. He chid
the sisters,
When first they put the name of King
upon me,
And bade them speak to him; then proph-
etlike
They hailed him father to a line of kings.   60
Upon my head they placed a fruitless
crown
And put a barren scepter in my gripe,°
Thence to be wrenched with an unlineal
hand,
No son of mine succeeding. If 't be so,
For Banquo's issue have I filed° my
mind;   65
For them the gracious Duncan have I
murdered;
Put rancors° in the vessel of my peace
Only for them, and mine eternal jewel°
Given to the common enemy of man,°
To make them kings, the seeds of Ban-
quo kings!   70
Rather than so, come, fate, into the list,°
And champion me to th' utterance!°
Who's there?

Enter SERVANT *and* TWO MURDERERS.

Now go to the door, and stay there till we
call.

---

25 **Go . . . better** unless my horse goes better
than I expect. 29 **are bestowed** have taken refuge.
32 **invention** lies. 33–34 **cause . . . jointly** matters
of state demanding our joint attention. 43 **While**
until. 44 **Sirrah** (common address to an inferior).
attend await. 46 **without** outside.

48 **but** unless. 49 **in** about. 51 **would** must. 52 **to**
added to. **temper** quality. 56 **genius is rebuked**
guardian spirit is cowed. 62 **gripe** grasp. 65 **filed**
defiled. 67 **rancors** bitter enmities. 68 **eternal jewel**
i.e., soul. 69 **common enemy of man** i.e., the Devil.
71 **lists** lists. 72 **champion me to th' utterance** fight
against me to the death.

Exit SERVANT.

Was it not yesterday we spoke together?

MURDERERS   It was, so please your Highness.

75 MACBETH   Well then, now
Have you considered of my speeches?
Know
That it was he in the times past, which
held you
So under fortune,° which you thought
had been
Our innocent self: this I made good to
you
In our last conference; passed in proba-
80   tion° with you,
How you were born in hand,° how
crossed;° the instruments,°
Who wrought with them, and all things
else that might
To half a soul° and to a notion° crazed
Say "Thus did Banquo."

FIRST MURDERER   You made it known to us.

MACBETH   I did so; and went further,
85   which is now
Our point of second meeting. Do you find
Your patience so predominant in your
nature,
That you can let this go? Are you so
gospeled,°
To pray for this good man and for his
issue,
Whose heavy hand hath bowed you to
90   the grave
And beggared yours for ever?

FIRST MURDERER   We are men, my liege.

MACBETH   Ay, in the catalogue ye go for°
men;
As hounds and greyhounds, mongrels,
spaniels, curs,
Shoughs, water-rugs° and demi-wolves, are
clept°

All by the name of dogs: the valued file° 95
Distinguishes the swift, the slow, the
subtle,
The housekeeper,° the hunter, every one
According to the gift which bounteous
nature
Hath in him closed,° whereby he does
receive
Particular addition, from the bill°   100
That writes them all alike: and so of
men.
Now if you have a station in the file,
Not i' th' worst rank of manhood, say 't,
And I will put that business in your
bosoms
Whose execution takes your enemy off,   105
Grapples you to the heart and love of us,
Who wear our health but sickly in his
life,°
Which in his death were perfect.

SECOND MURDERER   I am one, my liege,
Whom the vile blows and buffets of the
world
Hath so incensed that I am reckless what 110
I do to spite the world.

FIRST MURDERER   And I another
So weary with disasters, tugged with for-
tune,
That I would set° my life on any chance,
To mend it or be rid on 't.

MACBETH   Both of you
Know Banquo was your enemy.

BOTH MURDERERS   True, my lord. 115

MACBETH   So is he mine, and in such
bloody distance°
That every minute of his being thrusts
Against my near'st of life:° and though I
could
With barefaced power sweep him from
my sight
And bid my will avouch° it, yet I must
not,   120

77–78 **held . . . fortune** kept you from good fortune (?). 80 **passed in probation** reviewed the
proofs. 81 **borne in hand** deceived. **crossed**
thwarted. **instruments** tools. 83 **half a soul** a half-
wit. **notion** mind. 88 **gospeled** i.e., made meek by
the gospel. 92 **go for** pass as. 94 **Shoughs, water-
rugs** shaggy dogs, long-haired water dogs. **clept**
called.

95 **valued file** classification by valuable traits. 97
housekeeper watchdog. 99 **closed** enclosed. 100
Particular addition, from the bill special distinction
in opposition to the list. 107 **wear . . . life** have
only imperfect health while he lives. 113 **set**
risk. 116 **distance** quarrel. 118 **near'st of life** most
vital spot. 120 **avouch** justify.

For° certain friends that are both his and mine,

Whose loves I may not drop, but wail his fall°

Who I myself struck down: and thence it is

That I to your assistance do make love,

Masking the business from the common eye

125 For sundry weighty reasons.

SECOND MURDERER   We shall, my lord,

Perform what you command us.

FIRST MURDERER   Though our lives——

MACBETH   Your spirits shine through you.

Within this hour at most

I will advise you where to plant yourselves,

Acquaint you with the perfect spy° o' th'

130 time,

The moment on 't;° for 't must be done tonight,

And something° from the palace; always thought°

That I require a clearness:° and with him—

To leave no rubs° nor botches in the work—

135 Fleance his son, that keeps him company,

Whose absence is no less material to me

Than is his father's, must embrace the fate

Of that dark hour. Resolve yourselves apart:°

I'll come to you anon.

MURDERERS   We are resolved, my lord.

MACBETH   I'll call upon you straight.°

140 Abide within.

It is concluded: Banquo, thy soul's flight,

If it find heaven, must find it out tonight.

Exeunt.

---

121 **For** because of. 122 **wail his fall** bewail his death. 130 **perfect spy** exact information (?) (**spy** literally means "observation"; apparently Macbeth already has the Third Murderer in mind). 131 **on 't** of it. 132 **something** some distance. **thought** remembered. 133 **clearness** freedom from suspicion. 134 **rubs** flaws. 138 **Resolve yourselves apart** decide by yourself. 140 **straight** immediately.

SCENE TWO   [*The palace.*]

Enter MACBETH'S LADY *and a* SERVANT.

LADY MACBETH   Is Banquo gone from court?

SERVANT   Ay, madam, but returns again tonight.

LADY MACBETH   Say to the King, I would attend his leisure

For a few words.

SERVANT   Madam, I will.   *Exit.*

LADY MACBETH   Nought's had, all's spent,

Where our desire is got without content: 5

'Tis safer to be that which we destroy

Than by destruction dwell in doubtful joy.

Enter MACBETH.

How now, my lord! Why do you keep alone,

Of sorriest° fancies your companions making,

Using those thoughts which should indeed have died   10

With them they think on? Things without° all remedy

Should be without regard: what's done is done.

MACBETH   We have scorched° the snake, not killed it:

She'll close° and be herself, whilst our poor malice°

Remains in danger of her former tooth.   15

But let the frame of things disjoint,° both the worlds° suffer,

Ere we will eat our meal in fear, and sleep

In the affliction of these terrible dreams

That shake us nightly: better be with the dead,

Whom we, to gain our peace, have sent to peace,   20

III.ii. 9 **sorriest** most despicable. 11 **without** beyond. 13 **scorched** slashed, scored. 14 **close** heal. **poor malice** feeble enmity. 16 **frame of things disjoint** universe collapse. **both the worlds** heaven and earth (?).

Than on the torture° of the mind to lie
In restless ecstasy.° Duncan is in his grave;
After life's fitful fever he sleeps well.
Treason has done his° worst: nor steel,
nor poison,

25 Malice domestic,° foreign levy, nothing,
Can touch him further.

LADY MACBETH   Come on.
Gentle my lord, sleek° o'er your rugged°
looks;
Be bright and jovial among your guests
tonight.

MACBETH So shall I, love; and so, I pray,
be you:

30 Let your remembrance apply to Banquo;°
Present him eminence,° both with eye
and tongue:
Unsafe the while, that we must lave°
Our honors in these flattering streams
And make our faces vizards° to our
hearts,
Disguising what they are.

35 LADY MACBETH   You must leave this.

MACBETH O, full of scorpions is my mind,
dear wife!
Thou know'st that Banquo, and his
Fleance, lives.

LADY MACBETH But in them nature's
copy's° not eterne.

MACBETH There's comfort yet; they are
assailable.
Then be thou jocund. Ere the bat hath

40 flown
His cloistered flight, ere to black Hecate's
summons
The shard-borne° beetle with his drowsy
hums
Hath rung night's yawning peal, there
shall be done
A deed of dreadful note.

LADY MACBETH   What's to be done?

MACBETH Be innocent of the knowledge,
dearest chuck,°   45
Till thou applaud the deed. Come,
seeling° night,
Scarf up° the tender eye of pitiful day,
And with thy bloody and invisible hand
Cancel and tear to pieces that great bond°
Which keeps me pale! Light thickens,
and the crow   50
Makes wing to th' rooky° wood.
Good things of day begin to droop and
drowse,
Whiles night's black agents to their preys
do rouse.
Thou marvel'st at my words: but hold
thee still;
Things bad begun make strong them-
selves by ill: 55
So, prithee, go with me.   *Exeunt.*

SCENE THREE   [*Near the palace.*]

Enter THREE MURDERERS.

FIRST MURDERER But who did bid thee
join with us?

THIRD MURDERER   Macbeth.

SECOND MURDERER He needs not our mis-
trust; since he delivers
Our offices and what we have to do
To the direction just.°

FIRST MURDERER   Then stand with us.
The west yet glimmers with some streaks
of day.   5
Now spurs the lated° traveler apace
To gain the timely inn, and near ap-
proaches
The subject of our watch.

THIRD MURDERER   Hark! I hear horses.

BANQUO (*Within*) Give us a light there,
ho!

---

21 **torture** i.e., rack. 22 **ecstasy** frenzy. 24 **his** its. 25 **Malice domestic** civil war. 27 **sleek** smooth. **rugged** furrowed. 30 **Let . . . Banquo** focus your thoughts on Banquo. 31 **Present him eminence** honor him. 32 **Unsafe . . . lave** i.e., you and I are unsafe because we must dip. 34 **vizards** masks. 38 **nature's copy** nature's lease (?) imitation (i.e., a son) made by nature (?). 42 **shard-borne** borne on scaly wings (?) dung-bred (?).

45 **chuck** chick (a term of endearment). 46 **seeling** eye-closing. 47 **Scarf up** blindfold. 49 **bond** i.e., between Banquo and fate (?) Banquo's lease on life (?) Macbeth's link to humanity (?). 51 **rooky** full of rooks.
III.iii. 2–4 **He needs . . . just** we need not mistrust him (i.e., the Third Murderer) since he describes our duties according to our exact directions. 6 **lated** belated.

SECOND MURDERER   Then 'tis he. The rest
10 That are within the note of expectation°
Already are i' th' court.
FIRST MURDERER   His horses go about.
THIRD MURDERER   Almost a mile: but he
does usually—
So all men do—from hence to th' palace
gate
Make it their walk.

Enter BANQUO *and* FLEANCE, *with a torch.*

SECOND MURDERER   A light, a light!
THIRD MURDERER   'Tis he.
15 FIRST MURDERER   Stand to 't.
BANQUO   It will be rain tonight.
FIRST MURDERER   Let it come down.

[*They set upon* BANQUO.]

BANQUO   O, treachery! Fly, good Fleance,
fly, fly, fly!

[*Exit* FLEANCE.]

Thou mayst revenge. O slave! [*Dies.*]
THIRD MURDERER   Who did strike out the
light?
FIRST MURDERER   Was 't not the way?°
THIRD MURDERER   There's but one down;
20 the son is fled.
SECOND MURDERER   We have lost best half
of our affair.
FIRST MURDERER   Well, let's away and say
how much is done.
Exeunt.

SCENE FOUR   [*The palace.*]

Banquet prepared. Enter MACBETH, LADY
[MACBETH], ROSS, LENNOX, LORDS, *and*
ATTENDANTS.

MACBETH   You know your own degrees;°
sit down:
At first and last, the hearty welcome.
LORDS   Thanks to your Majesty.

MACBETH   Ourself will mingle with so-
ciety°
And play the humble host.   5
Our hostess keeps her state,° but in best
time
We will require° her welcome.
LADY MACBETH   Pronounce it for me, sir,
to all our friends,
For my heart speaks they are welcome.

Enter FIRST MURDERER.

MACBETH   See, they encounter° thee with
their hearts' thanks.   10
Both sides are even: here I'll sit i' th'
midst:
Be large in mirth; anon we'll drink a
measure°
The table round. [*Goes to* MURDERER]
There's blood upon thy face.
MURDERER   'Tis Banquo's then.
MACBETH   'Tis better thee without than
he within.°   15
Is he dispatched?
MURDERER   My lord, his throat is cut; that
I did for him.
MACBETH   Thou art the best o' th' cut-
throats.
Yet he's good that did the like for
Fleance;
If thou didst it, thou art the nonpareil.   20
MURDERER   Most royal sir, Fleance is
'scaped.
MACBETH   [*Aside*] Then comes my fit again:
I had else been perfect,
Whole as the marble, founded° as the
rock,
As broad and general as the casing° air:
But now I am cabined, cribbed,° con-
fined, bound in   25
To saucy° doubts and fears.—But
Banquo's safe?
MURDERER   Ay, my good lord: safe in a
ditch he bides,

---

4 **society** the company. 6 **keeps her state** remains
seated in her chair of state. 7 **require** request. 10
encounter meet. 12 **measure** goblet. 15 **thee without**
than he within outside you than inside him. 23
founded firmly based. 24 **broad . . . casing** uncon-
fined as the surrounding. 25 **cribbed** penned up.
26 **saucy** insolent.

---

10 **within the note of expectation** on the list of
expected guests. 19 **way** i.e., thing to do.
III.iv. 1 **degrees** ranks.

With twenty trenchèd° gashes on his head,
The least a death to nature.

MACBETH   Thanks for that.
[*Aside*] There the grown serpent lies; the
30   worm° that's fled
Hath nature that in time will venom breed,
No teeth for th' present. Get thee gone. Tomorrow
We'll hear ourselves° again.

     Exit MURDERER.

LADY MACBETH   My royal lord,
You do not give the cheer.° The feast is sold
That is not often vouched, while 'tis
35   a-making,
'Tis given with welcome. To feed were best at home;°
From thence, the sauce to meat° is ceremony;
Meeting were bare without it.

     Enter the Ghost of Banquo, and sits in
     MACBETH's *place.*

MACBETH   Sweet remembrancer!°
Now good digestion wait on appetite,
40 And health on both!

LENNOX   May 't please your Highness sit.

MACBETH   Here had we now our country's honor roofed,°
Were the graced person of our Banquo present—
Who may I rather challenge for unkindness
Than pity for mischance!°

45 ROSS   His absence, sir,
Lays blame upon his promise. Please 't your Highness
To grace us with your royal company?

MACBETH   The table's full.

LENNOX   Here is a place reserved, sir.

MACBETH   Where?

LENNOX   Here, my good lord. What is 't
that moves your Highness?   50

MACBETH   Which of you have done this?

LORDS   What, my good lord?

MACBETH   Thou canst not say I did it. Never shake
Thy gory locks at me.

ROSS   Gentlemen, rise, his Highness is not well.

LADY MACBETH   Sit, worthy friends. My
lord is often thus,   55
And hath been from his youth. Pray you, keep seat.
The fit is momentary; upon a thought°
He will again be well. If much you note him,
You shall offend him and extend his passion.°
Feed, and regard him not.—Are you a man?   60

MACBETH   Ay, and a bold one, that dare look on that
Which might appall the devil.

LADY MACBETH   O proper stuff!
This is the very painting of your fear.
This is the air-drawn dagger which, you said,
Led you to Duncan. O, these flaws° and starts,   65
Impostors to° true fear, would well become
A woman's story at a winter's fire,
Authorized° by her grandam. Shame itself!
Why do you make such faces? When all's done,
You look but on a stool.

MACBETH   Prithee, see there!   70
Behold! Look! Lo! How say you?
Why, what care I? If thou canst nod, speak too.
If charnel houses° and our graves must send

---

28 **trenchèd** trench-like. 30 **worm** serpent. 33 **hear ourselves** talk it over. 34 **the cheer** a sense of cordiality. 34–36 **The feast . . . home** i.e., the feast seems sold (not given) during which the host fails to welcome the guests. Mere eating is best done at home. 37 **meat** food. 38 **remembrancer** reminder. 42 **our country's honor roofed** our nobility under one roof. 44–45 **Who . . . mischance** whom I hope I may reprove because he is unkind rather than pity because he has encountered an accident.

57 **upon a thought** as quick as thought. 59 **extend his passion** lengthen his fit. 65 **flaws** gusts, outbursts. 66 **to** compared with. 68 **Authorized** vouched for. 73 **charnel houses** vaults containing bones.

75   Those that we bury back, our monuments
Shall be the maws of kites.°

[Exit Ghost.]

LADY MACBETH   What, quite unmanned in folly?

MACBETH   If I stand here, I saw him.

LADY MACBETH   Fie, for shame!

MACBETH   Blood hath been shed ere now, i' th' olden time,
Ere humane statute purged the gentle weal;°
Ay, and since too, murders have been per-
80   formed
Too terrible for the ear. The times has been
That, when the brains were out, the man would die,
And there an end; but now they rise again,
With twenty mortal murders on their crowns,°
And push us from our stools. This is
85   more strange
Than such a murder is.

LADY MACBETH   My worthy lord,
Your noble friends do lack you.

MACBETH   I do forget.
Do not muse at me, my most worthy friends;
I have a strange infirmity, which is noth-
ing
To those that know me. Come, love and
90   health to all!
Then I'll sit down. Give me some wine, fill full.

Enter Ghost.

I drink to th' general joy o' th' whole table,
And to our dear friend Banquo, whom we miss;
Would he were here! To all and him we thirst,°

And all to all.°

LORDS   Our duties, and the pledge.   95

MACBETH   Avaunt! and quit my sight! Let the earth hide thee!
Thy bones are marrowless, thy blood is cold;
Thou hast no speculation° in those eyes
Which thou dost glare with.

LADY MACBETH   Think of this, good peers, 100
But as a thing of custom; 'tis no other.
Only it spoils the pleasure of the time.

MACBETH   What man dare, I dare.
Approach thou like the rugged Russian bear,
The armed rhinoceros, or th' Hyrcan° tiger;   105
Take any shape but that, and my firm nerves°
Shall never tremble. Or be alive again,
And dare me to the desert° with thy sword.
If trembling I inhabit then, protest me
The baby of a girl.° Hence, horrible shadow!   110
Unreal mock'ry, hence!   *[Exit Ghost.]*
                Why, so: being gone,
I am a man again. Pray you, sit still.

LADY MACBETH   You have displaced the mirth, broke the good meeting,
With most admired° disorder.

MACBETH   Can such things be,
And overcome us° like a summer's cloud, 115
Without our special wonder? You make me strange
Even to the disposition that I owe,°
When now I think you can behold such sights,
And keep the natural ruby of your cheeks,
When mine is blanched with fear.

ROSS   What sights, my lord? 120

LADY MACBETH   I pray you, speak not: he grows worse and worse;

74–75 **our . . . kites** our tombs shall be the bellies of rapacious birds. 79 **purged the gentle weal** i.e., cleansed the state and made it gentle. 84 **mortal murders on their crowns** deadly wounds on their heads. 94 **thirst** desire to drink.

95 **all to all** everything to everybody (?) let everybody drink to everybody (?). 98 **speculation** sight. 105 **Hyrcan** of Hyrcania (near the Caspian Sea). 106 **nerves** sinews. 108 **the desert** a lonely place. 109–110 **If . . . girl** if then I tremble, proclaim me a baby girl. 114 **admired** amazing. 115 **overcome us** come over us. 116–117 **You . . . owe** i.e., you make me wonder what my nature is.

Question enrages him: at once, good night.
Stand not upon the order of your going,°
But go at once.

LENNOX   Good night; and better health
Attend his Majesty!

125 LADY MACBETH   A kind good night to all!
Exeunt Lords.

MACBETH   It will have blood, they say:
blood will have blood.
Stones have been known to move and trees to speak;
Augures and understood relations° have
By maggot-pies and choughs and rooks brought forth°

130 The secret'st man of blood. What is the night?°

LADY MACBETH   Almost at odds° with morning, which is which.

MACBETH   How say'st thou, that Macduff denies his person
At our great bidding?

LADY MACBETH   Did you send to him, sir?

MACBETH   I hear it by the way,° but I will send:
There's not a one of them but in his
135 house
I keep a servant fee'd.° I will tomorrow,
And betimes° I will, to the weïrd sisters:
More shall they speak, for now I am bent° to know
By the worst means the worst. For mine own good
140 All causes° shall give way. I am in blood
Stepped in so far that, should I wade no more,
Returning were as tedious as go o'er.
Strange things I have in head that will to hand,
Which must be acted ere they may be scanned.°

LADY MACBETH   You lack the season of all natures,° sleep.   *145*

MACBETH   Come, we'll to sleep. My strange and self-abuse°
Is the initiate fear that wants hard use.°
We are yet but young in deed.   *Exeunt.*

SCENE FIVE   [*A Witches' haunt.*]

Thunder. Enter the THREE WITCHES, *meeting* HECATE.

FIRST WITCH   Why, how now, Hecate! you look angerly.

HECATE   Have I not reason, beldams° as you are,
Saucy and overbold? How did you dare
To trade and traffic with Macbeth
In riddles and affairs of death;   *5*
And I, the mistress of your charms,
The close contriver° of all harms,
Was never called to bear my part,
Or show the glory of our art?
And, which is worse, all you have done   *10*
Hath been but for a wayward son,
Spiteful and wrathful; who, as others do,
Loves for his own ends, not for you.
But make amends now: get you gone,
And at the pit of Acheron°   *15*
Meet me i' th' morning: thither he
Will come to know his destiny.
Your vessels and your spells provide,
Your charms and everything beside.
I am for th' air; this night I'll spend   *20*
Unto a dismal and a fatal end:
Great business must be wrought ere noon.
Upon the corner of the moon
There hangs a vap'rous drop profound;°
I'll catch it ere it come to ground: *25*
And that distilled by magic sleights°
Shall raise such artificial sprites°

---

123 **Stand . . . going** do not insist on departing in your order of rank. 128 **Augures and understood relations** auguries and comprehended reports. 129 **By . . . forth** by magpies, choughs, and rooks (telltale birds) revealed. 130 **What is the night** what time of night is it. 131 **at odds** striving. 134 **by the way** incidentally. 136 **fee'd** i.e., paid to spy. 137 **betimes** quickly. 138 **bent** determined. 140 **causes** considerations. 144 **may be scanned** can be examined.

145 **season of all natures** seasoning (preservative) of all living creatures. 146 **My strange and self-abuse** my strange delusion. 147 **initiate . . . use** beginner's fear that lacks hardening practice.
III.v. 2 **beldams** hags. 7 **close contriver** secret inventor. 15 **Acheron** (river of Hades). 24 **profound** heavy. 26 **sleights** arts. 27 **artificial sprites** spirits created by magic arts (?) artful (cunning) spirits (?).

As by the strength of their illusion
Shall draw him on to his confusion.°
30 He shall spurn fate, scorn death, and bear
His hopes 'bove wisdom, grace, and fear:
And you all know security°
Is mortals' chiefest enemy.

Music and a song.

Hark! I am called; my little spirit, see,
35 Sits in a foggy cloud and stays for me.

[Exit.]

Sing within, "Come away, come away,"
&c.

FIRST WITCH   Come, let's make haste; she'll
soon be back again.   *Exeunt.*

SCENE SIX   *[The palace.]*

Enter LENNOX *and another* LORD.

LENNOX   My former speeches have but hit
your thoughts,°
Which can interpret farther. Only I say
Things have been strangely borne.° The
gracious Duncan
Was pitied of Macbeth: marry, he was
dead.
And the right-valiant Banquo walked too
5   late;
Whom, you may say, if 't please you,
Fleance killed,
For Fleance fled. Men must not walk too
late.
Who cannot want the thought,° how
monstrous
It was for Malcolm and for Donalbain
To kill their gracious father? Damnèd
10   fact!°
How it did grieve Macbeth! Did he not
straight,
In pious rage, the two delinquents tear,

That were the slaves of drink and thralls°
of sleep?
Was not that nobly done? Ay, and wisely
too;
For 'twould have angered any heart alive   *15*
To hear the men deny 't. So that I say
He has borne° all things well: and I do
think
That, had he Duncan's sons under his
key—
As, an 't° please heaven, he shall not—
they should find
What 'twere to kill a father. So should
Fleance.   *20*
But, peace! for from broad words,° and
'cause he failed
His presence at the tyrant's feast, I hear,
Macduff lives in disgrace. Sir, can you
tell
Where he bestows himself?
LORD   The son of Duncan,
From whom this tyrant holds the due of
birth,°   *25*
Lives in the English court, and is received
Of the most pious Edward° with such
grace
That the malevolence of fortune nothing
Takes from his high respect.° Thither
Macduff
Is gone to pray the holy King, upon his
aid°   *30*
To wake Northumberland° and warlike
Siward;
That by the help of these, with Him
above
To ratify the work, we may again
Give to our tables meat, sleep to our
nights,
Free from our feasts and banquets bloody
knives,   *35*
Do faithful homage and receive free°
honors:

29 **confusion** ruin. 32 **security** overconfidence.
III.vi. 1 **My . . . thoughts** i.e., my recent words
have only coincided with what you have in your
mind. 3 **borne** managed. 8 **cannot want the thought**
can fail to think. 10 **fact** evil deed.

13 **thralls** slaves. 17 **borne** managed. 19 **an 't** if it.
21 **for from broad words** because of frank talk. 25
due of birth birthright. 27 **Edward** Edward the
Confessor (reigned 1042–1066). 28–29 **nothing . . .
respect** does not diminish the high respect in
which he is held. 30 **upon his aid** to aid him
(Malcolm). 31 **To wake Northumberland** i.e., to
arouse the people in an English county near Scotland. 36 **free** freely granted.

All which we pine for now. And this re-
port
Hath so exasperate the King that he
Prepares for some attempt of war.

LENNOX   Sent he to Macduff?

LORD   He did: and with an absolute "Sir,
40   not I,"
The cloudy° messenger turns me his back,
And hums, as who should say "You'll
rue the time
That clogs° me with this answer."

LENNOX   And that well might
Advise him to a caution, t' hold what
distance
45   His wisdom can provide. Some holy angel
Fly to the court of England and unfold
His message ere he come, that a swift
blessing
May soon return to this our suffering
country
Under a hand accursed!

LORD   I'll send my prayers with him.

Exeunt.

Act Four

SCENE ONE   [*A Witches' haunt.*]

Thunder. Enter the THREE WITCHES.

FIRST WITCH   Thrice the brinded° cat hath
mewed.

SECOND WITCH   Thrice and once the hedge-
pig° whined.

THIRD WITCH   Harpier° cries. 'Tis time, 'tis
time.

FIRST WITCH   Round about the caldron go:
5   In the poisoned entrails throw.
Toad, that under cold stone
Days and nights has thirty-one
Swelt'red venom sleeping got,°
Boil thou first i' th' charmèd pot.

10 ALL   Double, double, toil and trouble;
Fire burn and caldron bubble.

SECOND WITCH   Fillet° of a fenny° snake,
In the caldron boil and bake;
Eye of newt and toe of frog,
Wool of bat and tongue of dog,   15
Adder's fork° and blindworm's° sting,
Lizard's leg and howlet's° wing,
For a charm of pow'rful trouble,
Like a hell-broth boil and bubble.

ALL   Double, double, toil and trouble;   20
Fire burn and caldron bubble.

THIRD WITCH   Scale of dragon, tooth of
wolf,
Witch's mummy,° maw and gulf°
Of the ravined° salt-sea shark,
Root of hemlock digged i' th' dark,   25
Liver of blaspheming Jew,
Gall of goat, and slips of yew
Slivered in the moon's eclipse,
Nose of Turk and Tartar's lips,
Finger of birth-strangled babe   30
Ditch-delivered by a drab,°
Make the gruel thick and slab:°
Add thereto a tiger's chaudron,°
For th' ingredience of our caldron.

ALL   Double, double, toil and trouble;   35
Fire burn and caldron bubble.

SECOND WITCH   Cool it with a baboon's
blood,
Then the charm is firm and good.

Enter HECATE *and the other* THREE
WITCHES.

HECATE   O, well done! I commend your
pains;
And every one shall share i' th' gains: 40
And now about the caldron sing,
Like elves and fairies in a ring,
Enchanting all that you put in.

Music and a song: "Black Spirits," &c.

[*Exeunt* HECATE *and the other* THREE
WITCHES.]

SECOND WITCH   By the pricking of my
thumbs,

---

41 **cloudy** disturbed. 43 **clogs** burdens.
IV.i. 1 **brinded** brindled. 2. **hedge-pig** hedgehog.
3 **Harpier** (an attendant spirit, like Graymalkin and
Paddock in I.i). 8 **Swelt'red venom sleeping got**
venom sweated out while sleeping.

12 **Fillet** slice. **fenny** from a swamp. 16 **fork** forked
tongue. **blindworm** (a legless lizard). 17 **howlet**
owlet. 23 **Witch's mummy** mummified flesh of a
witch. **maw and gulf** stomach and gullet. 24 **ravined**
ravenous. 31 **Ditch-delivered by a drab** born in a
ditch of a harlot. 32 **slab** viscous. 33 **chaudron** entrails.

45 Something wicked this way comes:
    Open, locks,
    Whoever knocks!

Enter MACBETH.

MACBETH How now, you secret, black, and
    midnight hags!
    What is 't you do?
ALL   A deed without a name.
MACBETH I conjure you, by that which
50   you profess,
    Howe'er you come to know it, answer me:
    Though you untie the winds and let them
    fight
    Against the churches; though the yesty°
    waves
    Confound° and swallow navigation up;
    Though bladed corn be lodged° and trees
55   blown down;
    Though castles topple on their warders'
    heads;
    Though palaces and pyramids do slope°
    Their heads to their foundations; though
    the treasure
    Of nature's germens° tumble all together,
60   Even till destruction sicken,° answer me
    To what I ask you.
FIRST WITCH   Speak.
SECOND WITCH   Demand.
THIRD WITCH   We'll answer.
FIRST WITCH Say, if th' hadst rather hear
    it from our mouths,
    Or from our masters?
MACBETH   Call 'em, let me see 'em.
FIRST WITCH Pour in sow's blood, that
    hath eaten
65   Her nine farrow;° grease that's sweaten°
    From the murderer's gibbet throw
    Into the flame.
ALL   Come, high or low,
    Thyself and office° deftly show!

Thunder. FIRST APPARITION: *an Armed*
Head.

MACBETH Tell me, thou unknown
    power——

FIRST WITCH   He knows my thought:
    Hear his speech, but say thou nought.   70
FIRST APPARITION Macbeth! Macbeth!
    Macbeth! Beware Macduff!
    Beware the Thane of Fife. Dismiss me:
    enough.
    He descends.
MACBETH Whate'er thou art, for thy good
    caution thanks:
    Thou hast harped° my fear aright. But
    one word more——
FIRST WITCH He will not be commanded.
    Here's another,   75
    More potent than the first.

Thunder. SECOND APPARITION: *a Bloody*
Child.

SECOND APPARITION Macbeth! Macbeth!
    Macbeth!
MACBETH Had I three ears, I'd hear thee.
SECOND APPARITION Be bloody, bold, and
    resolute! Laugh to scorn
    The pow'r of man, for none of woman
    born   80
    Shall harm Macbeth.   *Descends.*
MACBETH Then live, Macduff: what need
    I fear of thee?
    But yet I'll make assurance double sure,
    And take a bond of fate.° Thou shalt not
    live;
    That I may tell pale-hearted fear it lies, 85
    And sleep in spite of thunder.

Thunder. THIRD APPARITION: *a Child*
Crowned, with a tree in his hand.

                            What is this,
    That rises like the issue° of a king,
    And wears upon his baby-brow the round
    And top of sovereignty?°
ALL   Listen, but speak not to 't.
THIRD APPARITION Be lion-mettled, proud,
    and take no care   90
    Who chafes, who frets, or where conspirers
    are:
    Macbeth shall never vanquished be until

---

53 **yesty** foamy. 54 **Confound** destroy. 55 **bladed corn be lodged** grain in the ear be beaten down. 57 **slope** bend. 59 **nature's germens** seeds of all life. 60 **sicken** i.e., sicken at its own work. 65 **farrow** young pigs. **sweaten** sweated. 68 **office** function.

74 **harped** hit upon, struck the note of. 84 **take a bond of fate** get a guarantee from fate (i.e., he will kill Macduff and thus will compel fate to keep its word). 87 **issue** offspring. 88–89 **round/And top of sovereignty** i.e., crown.

Great Birnam Wood to high Dunsinane Hill
Shall come against him.   *Descends.*
MACBETH   That will never be.
95   Who can impress° the forest, bid the tree
Unfix his earth-bound root? Sweet bode-ments,° good!
Rebellious dead,° rise never, till the Wood
Of Birnam rise, and our high-placed Mac-beth
Shall live the lease of nature,° pay his breath
To time and mortal custom.° Yet my
100   heart
Throbs to know one thing. Tell me, if your art
Can tell so much: shall Banquo's issue ever
Reign in this kingdom?
ALL   Seek to know no more.
MACBETH   I will be satisfied.° Deny me this,
And an eternal curse fall on you! Let me
105   know.
Why sinks that caldron? And what noise°
is this?

Hautboys.

FIRST WITCH   Show!
SECOND WITCH   Show!
THIRD WITCH   Show!
110   ALL   Show his eyes, and grieve his heart;
Come like shadows, so depart!

A show of eight Kings and BANQUO, *last
[King] with a glass° in his hand.*

MACBETH   Thou art too like the spirit of
Banquo. Down!
Thy crown does sear mine eyelids. And thy hair,
Thou other gold-bound brow, is like the first.
115   A third is like the former. Filthy hags!

Why do you show me this? A fourth!
Start,° eyes!
What, will the line stretch out to th' crack
of doom?°
Another yet! A seventh! I'll see no more.
And yet the eighth appears, who bears a glass
Which shows me many more; and some I
see   *120*
That twofold balls and treble scepters°
carry:
Horrible sight! Now I see 'tis true;
For the blood-boltered° Banquo smiles
upon me,
And points at them for his. What, is this
so?
FIRST WITCH   Ay, sir, all this is so. But why *125*
Stands Macbeth thus amazedly?
Come, sisters, cheer we up his sprites,°
And show the best of our delights:
I'll charm the air to give a sound,
While you perform your antic round,°   *130*
That this great king may kindly say
Our duties did his welcome pay.

Music. The WITCHES *dance, and vanish.*

MACBETH   Where are they? Gone? Let this
pernicious hour
Stand aye accursèd in the calendar!
Come in, without there!

Enter LENNOX.

LENNOX   What's your Grace's will? *135*
MACBETH   Saw you the weird sisters?
LENNOX   No, my lord.
MACBETH   Came they not by you?
LENNOX   No indeed, my lord.
MACBETH   Infected be the air whereon they
ride,
And damned all those that trust them! I
did hear
The galloping of horse.° Who was't came
by?   *140*
LENNOX   'Tis two or three, my lord, that
bring you word

---

95 **impress** conscript. 96 **bodements** prophecies. 97 **Rebellious dead** (perhaps a reference to Banquo; but perhaps a misprint for "rebellion's head"). 99 **lease of nature** natural lifespan. 100 **mortal custom** natural death. 104 **satisfied** i.e., fully informed. 106 **noise** music. IV.sd **glass** mirror.   116 **Start** i.e., from the sockets. 117 **crack of doom** blast (of a trumpet?) at doomsday. 121 **twofold balls and treble scepters** (coronation emblems). 123 **blood-boltered** matted with blood. 127 **sprites** spirits. 130 **antic round** grotesque circular dance. 140 **horse** horses (or "horsemen")

Macduff is fled to England.
MACBETH   Fled to England?
LENNOX Ay, my good lord.
MACBETH [*Aside*] Time, thou anticipat'st°
my dread exploits.
145 The flighty purpose never is o'ertook
Unless the deed go with it.° From this
moment
The very firstlings of my heart° shall be
The firstlings of my hand. And even now,
To crown my thoughts with acts, be it
thought and done:
150 The castle of Macduff I will surprise;°
Seize upon Fife; give to th' edge o' th'
sword
His wife, his babes, and all unfortunate
souls
That trace him in his line.° No boasting
like a fool;
This deed I'll do before this purpose cool:
But no more sights!—Where are these
155 gentlemen?
Come, bring me where they are.   *Exeunt.*

SCENE TWO [MACDUFF'S *castle.*]

Enter MACDUFF'S *wife, her* SON, *and* ROSS.

LADY MACDUFF What had he done, to
make him fly the land?
ROSS You must have patience, madam.
LADY MACDUFF   He had none:
His flight was madness. When our actions
do not,
Our fears do make us traitors.
ROSS   You know not
5 Whether it was his wisdom or his fear.
LADY MACDUFF Wisdom! To leave his wife,
to leave his babes,
His mansion and his titles,° in a place
From whence himself does fly? He loves us
not;

He wants the natural touch:° for the poor
wren,
The most diminutive of birds, will fight,   10
Her young ones in her nest, against the
owl.
All is the fear and nothing is the love;
As little is the wisdom, where the flight
So runs against all reason.
ROSS   My dearest coz,°
I pray you, school° yourself. But, for your
husband,   15
He is noble, wise, judicious, and best
knows
The fits o' th' season.° I dare not speak
much further:
But cruel are the times, when we are
traitors
And do not know ourselves; when we hold
rumor
From what we fear,° yet know not what
we fear,   20
But float upon a wild and violent sea
Each way and move. I take my leave of
you.
Shall not be long but I'll be here again.
Things at the worst will cease,° or else
climb upward
To what they were before. My pretty
cousin,   25
Blessing upon you!
LADY MACDUFF Fathered he is, and yet
he's fatherless.
ROSS I am so much a fool, should I stay
longer,
It would be my disgrace° and your discom-
fort.
I take my leave at once.   *Exit* ROSS.
LADY MACDUFF Sirrah,° your father's dead: 30
And what will you do now? How will you
live?
SON As birds do, mother.

---

144 **anticipat'st** foretold. 145–146 **The flighty . . .
it** the fleeting plan is never fulfilled unless an
action accompanies it. 147 **firstlings of my heart**
i.e., first thoughts, impulses. 150 **surprise** attack
suddenly. 153 **trace him in his line** are of his
lineage.
IV.ii. 7 **titles** possessions.

9 **wants the natural touch** i.e., lacks natural affection for his wife and children. 14 **coz** cousin. 15
school control. 17 **fits o' th' season** disorders of the
time. 19–20 **hold rumor/From what we fear** believe
rumors because we fear. 24 **cease** i.e., cease worsen-
ing. 29 **It would be my disgrace** i.e., I would weep.
30 **Sirrah** (here an affectionate address to a child).

LADY MACDUFF   What, with worms and flies?

SON   With what I get, I mean; and so do they.

LADY MACDUFF   Poor bird! thou'dst never fear the net nor lime,°

35   The pitfall nor the gin.°

SON   Why should I, mother? Poor birds they are not set for.
My father is not dead, for all your saying.

LADY MACDUFF   Yes, he is dead: how wilt thou do for a father?

SON   Nay, how will you do for a husband?

LADY MACDUFF   Why, I can buy me twenty

40   at any market.

SON   Then you'll buy 'em to sell° again.

LADY MACDUFF   Thou speak'st with all thy wit, and yet, i' faith,
With wit enough for thee.°

SON   Was my father a traitor, mother?

45   LADY MACDUFF   Ay, that he was.

SON   What is a traitor?

LADY MACDUFF   Why, one that swears and lies.°

SON   And be all traitors that do so?

LADY MACDUFF   Every one that does so is a traitor, and must be hanged.

SON   And must they all be hanged that

50   swear and lie?

LADY MACDUFF   Every one.

SON   Who must hang them?

LADY MACDUFF   Why, the honest men.

SON   Then the liars and swearers are fools;

55   for there are liars and swearers enow° to beat the honest men and hang up them.

LADY MACDUFF   Now, God help thee, poor monkey! But how wilt thou do for a father?

60   SON   If he were dead, you'd weep for him. If you would not, it were a good sign that I should quickly have a new father.

LADY MACDUFF   Poor prattler, how thou talk'st!

Enter a MESSENGER.

Messenger   Bless you, fair dame! I am not to you known,
Though in your state of honor I am perfect.°   65

I doubt° some danger does approach you nearly:
If you will take a homely° man's advice,
Be not found here; hence, with your little ones.
To fright you thus, methinks I am too savage;
To do worse to you were fell° cruelty,   70
Which is too nigh your person. Heaven preserve you!
I dare abide no longer.   *Exit* MESSENGER.

LADY MACDUFF   Whither should I fly?
I have done no harm. But I remember now
I am in this earthly world, where to do harm
Is often laudable, to do good sometime   75
Accounted dangerous folly. Why then, alas,
Do I put up that womanly defense,
To say I have done no harm?—What are these faces?

Enter MURDERERS.

MURDERER   Where is your husband?

LADY MACDUFF   I hope, in no place so unsanctified   80
Where such as thou mayst find him.

MURDERER   He's a traitor.

SON   Thou li'st, thou shag-eared° villain!

MURDERER   What, you egg!

[*Stabbing him.*]

Young fry° of treachery!

SON   He has killed me, mother:
Run away, I pray you!

[*Dies.*]
Exit [LADY MACDUFF], *crying "Murder!"*
[*followed by* MURDERERS].

---

34 **lime** birdlime (smeared on branches to catch birds). 35 **gin** trap. 41 **sell** betray. 43 **for thee** i.e., for a child. 47 **swears and lies** i.e., takes an oath and breaks it. 55 **enow** enough.

65 **in . . . perfect** I am fully informed of your honorable rank. 66 **doubt** fear. 67 **homely** plain. 70 **fell** fierce. 82 **shag-eared** hairy-eared (?), with shaggy hair hanging over the ears (?). 83 **fry** spawn.

SCENE THREE   [*England. Before the King's palace.*]

Enter MALCOLM *and* MACDUFF.

MALCOLM Let us seek out some desolate shade, and there
Weep our sad bosoms empty.

MACDUFF   Let us rather
Hold fast the mortal° sword, and like good men
Bestride our down-fall'n birthdom.° Each new morn
New widows howl, new orphans cry, new
5   sorrows
Strike heaven on the face, that° it re-sounds
As if it felt with Scotland and yelled out
Like syllable of dolor.°

MALCOLM   What I believe, I'll wail;
What know, believe; and what I can re-dress,
10   As I shall find the time to friend,° I will.
What you have spoke, it may be so per-chance.
This tyrant, whose sole° name blisters our tongues,
Was once thought honest:° you have loved him well;
He hath not touched you yet. I am young; but something
You may deserve of him through me;° and
15   wisdom°
To offer up a weak, poor, innocent lamb
T' appease an angry god.

MACDUFF   I am not treacherous.

MALCOLM   But Macbeth is.
A good and virtuous nature may recoil
In° an imperial charge. But I shall crave
20   your pardon;
That which you are, my thoughts cannot transpose:°

Angels are bright still, though the bright-est° fell:
Though all things foul would wear° the brows of grace,
Yet grace must still look so.°

MACDUFF   I have lost my hopes.

MALCOLM   Perchance even there where I
did find my doubts.   25
Why in that rawness° left you wife and child,
Those precious motives, those strong knots of love,
Without leave-taking? I pray you,
Let not my jealousies° be your dishonors,
But mine own safeties. You may be rightly just°   30
Whatever I shall think.

MACDUFF   Bleed, bleed, poor country:
Great tyranny, lay thou thy basis° sure,
For goodness dare not check° thee: wear thou thy wrongs;
The title is affeered.° Fare thee well, lord:
I would not be the villain that thou think'st   35
For the whole space that's in the tyrant's grasp
And the rich East to boot.

MALCOLM   Be not offended:
I speak not as in absolute fear of you.
I think our country sinks beneath the yoke;
It weeps, it bleeds, and each new day a gash   40
Is added to her wounds. I think withal°
There would be hands uplifted in my right;°
And here from gracious England° have I offer
Of goodly thousands: but, for° all this,
When I shall tread upon the tyrant's head,   45
Or wear it on my sword, yet my poor country

IV.iii. 3 **mortal** deadly. 4 **Bestride our down-fall'n birthdom** protectively stand over our native land. 6 **that** so that. 8 **Like syllable of dolor** similar sound of grief. 10 **to friend** friendly, propitious. 12 **sole** very. 13 **honest** good. 15 **deserve of him through me** i.e., earn by betraying me to Macbeth. **wisdom** it may be wise. 19–20 **recoil/In** give way under. 21 **transpose** transform.

22 **the brightest** i.e., Lucifer. 23 **would wear** desire to wear. 24 **so** i.e., like itself. 26 **rawness** unprotected condition. 29 **jealousies** suspicions. 30 **rightly just** perfectly honorable. 32 **basis** foundation. 33 **check** restrain. 34 **affeered** legally confirmed. 41 **withal** moreover. 42 **in my right** on behalf of my claim. 43 **England** i.e., the King of England. 44 **for** despite.

Shall have more vices than it had before,
More suffer, and more sundry ways than ever,
By him that shall succeed.
MACDUFF   What should he be?
MALCOLM   It is myself I mean, in whom I know
50   All the particulars° of vice so grafted°
That, when they shall be opened,° black Macbeth
Will seem as pure as snow, and the poor state
Esteem him as a lamb, being compared
With my confineless harms.°
55   MACDUFF   Not in the legions
Of horrid hell can come a devil more damned
In evils to top Macbeth.
MALCOLM   I grant him bloody,
Luxurious,° avaricious, false, deceitful,
Sudden,° malicious, smacking of every sin
That has a name: but there's no bottom, none,
60   In my voluptuousness:° your wives, your daughters,
Your matrons and your maids, could not fill up
The cistern of my lust, and my desire
All continent° impediments would o'erbear,
65   That did oppose my will. Better Macbeth
Than such an one to reign.
MACDUFF   Boundless intemperance
In nature° is a tyranny; it hath been
Th' untimely emptying of the happy throne,
And fall of many kings. But fear not yet
70   To take upon you what is yours: you may
Convey° your pleasures in a spacious plenty,
And yet seem cold, the time° you may so hoodwink.

We have willing dames enough. There cannot be
That vulture in you, to devour so many
As will to greatness dedicate themselves,   75
Finding it so inclined.
MALCOLM   With this there grows
In my most ill-composed affection° such
A stanchless° avarice that, were I King,
I should cut off the nobles for their lands,
Desire his jewels and this other's house: 80
And my more-having would be as a sauce
To make me hunger more, that I should forge
Quarrels unjust against the good and loyal,
Destroying them for wealth.
MACDUFF   This avarice
Sticks deeper, grows with more pernicious root   85
Than summer-seeming° lust, and it hath been
The sword of our slain kings.° Yet do not fear.
Scotland hath foisons to fill up your will
Of your mere own.° All these are portable,°
With other graces weighed.   90
MALCOLM   But I have none: the king-becoming graces,
As justice, verity, temp'rance, stableness,
Bounty, perseverance, mercy, lowliness,
Devotion, patience, courage, fortitude,
I have no relish of° them, but abound   95
In the division of each several crime,°
Acting it many ways. Nay, had I pow'r, I should
Pour the sweet milk of concord into hell,
Uproar° the universal peace, confound
All unity on earth.
MACDUFF   O Scotland, Scotland!   100

---

51 **particulars** special kinds. **grafted** engrafted. 52 **opened** in bloom, i.e., revealed. 55 **confineless harms** unbounded evils. 58 **Luxurious** lecherous. 59 **Sudden** violent. 61 **voluptuousness** lust. 64 **continent** restraining. 67 **In nature** in man's nature. 71 **Convey** secretly manage. 72 **time** age, i.e., people.

77 **ill-composed affection** evilly compounded character. 78 **stanchless** never-ending. 86 **summer-seeming** befitting summer, i.e., youthful (?) transitory (?). 87 **sword of our slain kings** i.e., the cause of death to our kings. 88–89 **foisons . . . own** enough abundance of your own to satisfy your covetousness. 89 **portable** bearable. 95 **relish of** taste for (?) trace of (?). 96 **division of each several crime** variations of each kind of crime. 99 **Uproar** put into a tumult.

MALCOLM   If such a one be fit to govern, speak:
I am as I have spoken.

MACDUFF   Fit to govern!
No, not to live. O nation miserable!
With an untitled tyrant bloody-sceptered,
When shalt thou see thy wholesome
105   days again,
Since that the truest issue of thy throne
By his own interdiction° stands accursed,
And does blaspheme his breed?° Thy royal father
Was a most sainted king: the queen that bore thee,
110   Oft'ner upon her knees than on her feet,
Died° every day she lived. Fare thee well!
These evils thou repeat'st upon thyself
Hath banished me from Scotland. O my breast,
Thy hope ends here!

MALCOLM   Macduff, this noble passion,
115   Child of integrity, hath from my soul
Wiped the black scruples,° reconciled my thoughts
To thy good truth and honor. Devilish Macbeth
By many of these trains° hath sought to win me
Into his power; and modest wisdom° plucks me
From over-credulous haste: but God
120   above
Deal between thee and me! For even now
I put myself to° thy direction, and
Unspeak mine own detraction; here abjure
The taints and blames I laid upon myself,
125   For° strangers to my nature. I am yet
Unknown to woman, never was forsworn,
Scarcely have coveted what was mine own,
At no time broke my faith, would not betray
The devil to his fellow, and delight

No less in truth than life. My first false speaking   130
Was this upon myself. What I am truly,
Is thine and my poor country's to command:
Whither indeed, before thy here-approach,
Old Siward, with ten thousand warlike men,
Already at a point,° was setting forth.   135
Now we'll together, and the chance of goodness
Be like our warranted quarrel!° Why are you silent?

MACDUFF   Such welcome and unwelcome things at once
'Tis hard to reconcile.

Enter a DOCTOR.

MALCOLM   Well, more anon. Comes the King forth, I pray you?   140

DOCTOR   Ay, sir. There are a crew of wretched souls
That stay° his cure: their malady convinces
The great assay of art;° but at his touch,
Such sanctity hath heaven given his hand,
They presently amend.°

MALCOLM   I thank you, doctor.   145

Exit [DOCTOR].

MACDUFF   What's the disease he means?

MALCOLM   'Tis called the evil:°
A most miraculous work in this good King,
Which often since my here-remain in England
I have seen him do. How he solicits heaven,
Himself best knows: but strangely-visited° people,   150
All swoll'n and ulcerous, pitiful to the eye,
The mere° despair of surgery, he cures,

135 **at a point** prepared. 136–137 **the chance . . . quarrel** i.e., may our chance of success equal the justice of our cause. 142 **stay** await. 142–143 **convinces/The great assay of art** i.e., defies the efforts of medical science. 145 **presently amend** immediately recover. 146 **evil** (scrofula, called "the king's evil" because it could allegedly be cured by the king's touch). 150 **strangely-visited** oddly afflicted. 152 **mere** utter.

107 **interdiction** curse, exclusion. 108 **breed** ancestry. 111 **Died** i.e., prepared for heaven. 116 **scruples** suspicions. 118 **trains** plots. 119 **modest wisdom** i.e., prudence. 122 **to** under. 125 **For** as.

Hanging a golden stamp° about their necks,
Put on with holy prayers: and 'tis spoken,
155 To the succeeding royalty he leaves
The healing benediction. With this strange virtue°
He hath a heavenly gift of prophecy,
And sundry blessings hang about his throne
That speak° him full of grace.

Enter ROSS.

MACDUFF   See, who comes here?
MALCOLM   My countryman; but yet I
160 know him not.
MACDUFF   My ever gentle° cousin, welcome hither.
MALCOLM   I know him now: good God, betimes° remove
The means that makes us strangers!
ROSS   Sir, amen.
MACDUFF   Stands Scotland where it did?
ROSS   Alas, poor country!
165 Almost afraid to know itself! It cannot
Be called our mother but our grave, where nothing°
But who knows nothing is once seen to smile;
Where sighs and groans, and shrieks that rent the air,
Are made, not marked;° where violent sorrow seems
170 A modern ecstasy.° The dead man's knell
Is there scarce asked for who, and good men's lives
Expire before the flowers in their caps,
Dying or ere they sicken.
MACDUFF   O, relation
Too nice,° and yet too true!
MALCOLM   What's the newest grief?
ROSS   That of an hour's age doth hiss the
175 speaker;°
Each minute teems° a new one.

MACDUFF   How does my wife?
ROSS   Why, well.
MACDUFF   And all my children?
ROSS   Well too.
MACDUFF   The tyrant has not battered at their peace?
ROSS   No; they were well at peace when I did leave 'em.
MACDUFF   Be not a niggard of your speech: how goes 't?   180
ROSS   When I came hither to transport the tidings,
Which I have heavily° borne, there ran a rumor
Of many worthy fellows that were out;°
Which was to my belief witnessed° the rather,
For that I saw the tyrant's power° afoot.   185
Now is the time of help. Your eye in Scotland
Would create soldiers, make our women fight,
To doff their dire distresses.
MALCOLM   Be 't their comfort
We are coming thither. Gracious England hath
Lent us good Siward and ten thousand men;   190
An older and a better soldier none
That Christendom gives out.°
ROSS   Would I could answer
This comfort with the like! But I have words
That would° be howled out in the desert air,
Where hearing should not latch° them.
MACDUFF   What concern they?   195
The general cause or is it a fee-grief
Due to some single breast?°
ROSS   No mind that's honest
But in it shares some woe, though the main part
Pertains to you alone.
MACDUFF   If it be mine,

153 **stamp** coin. 156 **virtue** power. 159 **speak** proclaim. 161 **gentle** noble. 162 **betimes** quickly. 166 **nothing** no one. 169 **marked** noticed. 170 **modern ecstasy** i.e., ordinary emotion. 173–174 **relation/Too nice** tale too accurate. 175 **That . . . speaker** i.e., the report of the grief of an hour ago is hissed as stale news. 176 **teems** gives birth to.

182 **heavily** sadly. 183 **out** i.e., up in arms. 184 **witnessed** attested. 185 **power** army. 192 **gives out** reports. 194 **would** should. 195 **latch** catch. 196–197 **fee-grief/Due to some single breast** i.e., a personal grief belonging to an individual.

200 Keep it not from me, quickly let me have it.

ROSS Let not your ears despise my tongue for ever,
Which shall possess them with the heaviest sound
That ever yet they heard.

MACDUFF   Humh! I guess at it.

ROSS Your castle is surprised;° your wife and babes
Savagely slaughtered. To relate the manner,
205 Were, on the quarry° of these murdered deer,
To add the death of you.

MALCOLM   Merciful heaven!
What, man! Ne'er pull your hat upon your brows;
Give sorrow words. The grief that does not speak
Whispers the o'er-fraught heart,° and bids
210 it break.

MACDUFF My children too?

ROSS   Wife, children, servants, all
That could be found.

MACDUFF   And I must be from thence!
My wife killed too?

ROSS   I have said.

MALCOLM   Be comforted.
Let's make us med'cines of our great revenge,
215 To cure this deadly grief.

MACDUFF He has no children. All my pretty ones?
Did you say all? O hell-kite!° All?
What, all my pretty chickens and their dam
At one fell swoop?

MALCOLM Dispute° it like a man.
220 MACDUFF   I shall do so;
But I must also feel it as a man.
I cannot but remember such things were,
That were most precious to me. Did heaven look on,

And would not take their part? Sinful Macduff,
They were all struck for thee! Naught° 225
that I am,
Not for their own demerits but for mine
Fell slaughter on their souls. Heaven rest them now!

MALCOLM Be this the whetstone of your sword. Let grief
Convert to anger; blunt not the heart, enrage it.

MACDUFF O, I could play the woman with mine eyes, 230
And braggart with my tongue! But, gentle heavens,
Cut short all intermission;° front to front°
Bring thou this fiend of Scotland and myself;
Within my sword's length set him. If he 'scape,
Heaven forgive him too!

MALCOLM   This time goes manly. 235
Come, go we to the King. Our power is ready;
Our lack is nothing but our leave.° Macbeth
Is ripe for shaking, and the pow'rs above
Put on their instruments.° Receive what cheer you may.
The night is long that never finds the day. 240

Exeunt.

Act Five

SCENE ONE [*Dunsinane. In the castle.*]

Enter a DOCTOR OF PHYSIC *and a* WAITING-GENTLEWOMAN.

DOCTOR I have two nights watched with you, but can perceive no truth in your report. When was it she last walked?

GENTLEWOMAN Since his Majesty went into the field, I have seen her rise from 5

204 **surprised** suddenly attacked. 206 **quarry** heap of slaughtered game. 210 **Whispers the o'er-fraught heart** whispers to the overburdened heart. 217 **hell-kite** hellish bird of prey. 220 **Dispute** counter.

225 **Naught** wicked. 232 **intermission** interval. **front to front** forehead to forehead i.e., face to face. 237 **Our lack is nothing but our leave** i.e., we need only to take our leave. 239 **Put on their instruments** arm themselves (?) urge us, their agents, onward (?).

her bed, throw her nightgown upon her, unlock her closet,° take forth paper, fold it, write upon 't, read it, afterwards seal it, and again return to bed; yet all this while in a most fast sleep.

DOCTOR   A great perturbation in nature, to receive at once the benefit of sleep and do the effects of watching!° In this slumb'ry agitation, besides her walking and other actual performances,° what, at any time, have you heard her say?

GENTLEWOMAN   That, sir, which I will not report after her.

DOCTOR   You may to me, and 'tis most meet° you should.

GENTLEWOMAN   Neither to you nor anyone, having no witness to confirm my speech.

Enter LADY [MACBETH], *with a taper.*

Lo you, here she comes! This is her very guise,° and, upon my life, fast asleep! Observe her; stand close.°

DOCTOR   How came she by that light?

GENTLEWOMAN   Why, it stood by her. She has light by her continually. 'Tis her command.

DOCTOR   You see, her eyes are open.

GENTLEWOMAN   Ay, but their sense° are shut.

DOCTOR   What is it she does now? Look, how she rubs her hands.

GENTLEWOMAN   It is an accustomed action with her, to seem thus washing her hands: I have known her continue in this a quarter of an hour.

LADY MACBETH   Yet here's a spot.

DOCTOR   Hark! she speaks. I will set down what comes from her, to satisfy° my remembrance the more strongly.

LADY MACBETH   Out, damned spot! Out, I say! One: two: why, then 'tis time to do 't. Hell is murky. Fie, my lord, fie! A soldier, and afeard? What need we fear who knows it, when none can call our pow'r to ac-

compt?° Yet who would have thought the old man to have had so much blood in him?

DOCTOR   Do you mark that?

LADY MACBETH   The Thane of Fife had a wife. Where is she now? What, will these hands ne'er be clean? No more o' that, my lord, no more o' that! You mar all with this starting.

DOCTOR   Go to,° go to! You have known what you should not.

GENTLEWOMAN   She has spoke what she should not, I am sure of that. Heaven knows what she has known.

LADY MACBETH   Here's the smell of the blood still. All the perfumes of Arabia will not sweeten this little hand. Oh, oh, oh!

DOCTOR   What a sigh is there! The heart is sorely charged.°

GENTLEWOMAN   I would not have such a heart in my bosom for the dignity° of the whole body.

DOCTOR   Well, well, well——

GENTLEWOMAN   Pray God it be, sir.

DOCTOR   This disease is beyond my practice.° Yet I have known those which have walked in their sleep who have died holily in their beds.

LADY MACBETH   Wash your hands; put on your nightgown; look not so pale! I tell you yet again, Banquo's buried. He cannot come out on 's° grave.

DOCTOR   Even so?

LADY MACBETH   To bed, to bed! There's knocking at the gate. Come, come, come, come, give me your hand! What's done cannot be undone. To bed, to bed, to bed!

Exit LADY [MACBETH].

DOCTOR   Will she go now to bed?

GENTLEWOMAN   Directly.

DOCTOR   Foul whisp'rings are abroad. Unnatural deeds

Do breed unnatural troubles. Infected minds

V.i. 7 **closet** chest. 13 **effects of watching** deeds of one awake. 15 **actual performance** deeds. 20 **meet** suitable. 25 **guise** custom. 26 **close** hidden. 32 **sense** i.e., powers of sight. 42 **satisfy** confirm.

48–49 **to accompt** into account. 58 **Go to** (an exclamation). 67 **charged** burdened. 69 **dignity** worth, rank. 73–74 **practice** professional skill. 80 **on 's** of his.

To their deaf pillows will discharge their
90 secrets.
More needs she the divine than the physi-
cian.
God, God forgive us all! Look after her;
Remove from her the means of all an-
noyance,°
And still° keep eyes upon her. So good
night.
My mind she has mated° and amazed my
95 sight:
I think, but dare not speak.
GENTLEWOMAN   Good night, good doctor.

Exeunt.

SCENE TWO [*The country near Dunsinane.*]

Drum and colors. Enter MENTEITH, CAITH-
NESS, ANGUS, LENNOX, SOLDIERS.

MENTEITH   The English pow'r° is near, led
on by Malcolm,
His uncle Siward and the good Macduff.
Revenges burn in them; for their dear°
causes
Would to the bleeding and the grim alarm
Excite the mortified man.°
5 ANGUS   Near Birnam Wood
Shall we well meet them; that way are they
coming.
CAITHNESS   Who knows if Donalbain be
with his brother?
LENNOX   For certain, sir, he is not. I have a
file°
Of all the gentry: there is Siward's son,
And many unrough° youths that even
10 now
Protest° their first of manhood.
MENTEITH   What does the tyrant?
CAITHNESS   Great Dunsinane he strongly
fortifies.
Some say he's mad; others, that lesser hate
him,

Do call it valiant fury: but, for certain,
He cannot buckle his distempered° cause   15
Within the belt of rule.°
ANGUS   Now does he feel
His secret murders sticking on his hands;
Now minutely revolts upbraid° his faith-
breach.
Those he commands move only in com-
mand,
Nothing in love. Now does he feel his title   20
Hang loose about him, like a giant's robe
Upon a dwarfish thief.
MENTEITH   Who then shall blame
His pestered° senses to recoil and start,
When all that is within him does con-
demn
Itself for being there?
CAITHNESS.   Well, march we on,   25
To give obedience where 'tis truly owed.
Meet we the med'cine° of the sickly weal,°
And with him pour we, in our country's
purge,
Each drop of us.°
LENNOX   Or so much as it needs
To dew° the sovereign° flower and drown
the weeds.   30
Make we our march towards Birnam.

Exeunt, marching.

SCENE THREE [*Dunsinane. In the castle.*]

Enter MACBETH, DOCTOR, *and* ATTENDANTS.

MACBETH   Bring me no more reports; let
them fly all!
Till Birnam Wood remove to Dunsinane
I cannot taint° with fear. What's the boy
Malcolm?
Was he not born of woman? The spirits
that know
All mortal consequences° have pro-
nounced me thus: 5

15 **distempered** swollen by dropsy. 16 **rule** self-
control. 18 **minutely revolts upbraid** rebellions
every minute rebuke. 23 **pestered** tormented. 27
med'cine i.e., Malcolm. **weal** commonwealth. 29
Each drop of us i.e., every last drop of our blood
(?). 30 **dew** bedew, water (and thus make grow).
sovereign (1) royal (2) remedial.
V.iii. 3 **taint** become infected. 5 **mortal consequences** future human events.

93 **annoyance** injury. 94 **still** continuously. 95 **mated**
baffled.
V.ii. 1 **pow'r** army. 3 **dear** heartfelt. 4–5 **Would
. . . man** i.e., would incite a dead man (or "a paralyzed man") to join the bloody and grim call to
battle. 8 **file** list. 10 **unrough** i.e., beardless. 11 **Protest** assert.

"Fear not, Macbeth; no man that's born
of woman
Shall e'er have power upon thee." Then
fly, false thanes,
And mingle with the English epicures.
The mind I sway° by and the heart I bear
Shall never sag with doubt nor shake with
10   fear.

Enter SERVANT.

The devil damn thee black, thou cream-
faced loon!°
Where got'st thou that goose look?
SERVANT   There is ten thousand——
MACBETH   Geese, villain?
SERVANT   Soldiers, sir.
MACBETH   Go prick thy face and over-red°
thy fear,
Thou lily-livered boy. What soldiers,
15   patch?°
Death of° thy soul! Those linen° cheeks
of thine
Are counselors to fear. What soldiers,
whey-face?
SERVANT   The English force, so please you.
MACBETH   Take thy face hence.

[*Exit Servant.*]

                          Seyton!—I am sick at heart,
When I behold—Seyton, I say!—This
20   push°
Will cheer me ever, or disseat° me now.
I have lived long enough. My way of life
Is fall'n into the sear,° the yellow leaf,
And that which should accompany old
age,
As honor, love, obedience, troops of
25   friends,
I must not look to have; but, in their
stead,
Curses not loud but deep, mouth-honor,
breath,
Which the poor heart would fain deny,
and dare not.
Seyton!

Enter SEYTON.

SEYTON   What's your gracious pleasure?
MACBETH   What news more?   30
SEYTON   All is confirmed, my lord, which
was reported.
MACBETH   I'll fight, till from my bones my
flesh be hacked.
Give me my armor.
SEYTON   'Tis not needed yet.
MACBETH   I'll put it on.
Send out moe° horses, skirr° the country
round.   35
Hang those that talk of fear. Give me
mine armor.
How does your patient, doctor?
DOCTOR   Not so sick, my lord,
As she is troubled with thick-coming
fancies
That keep her from her rest.
MACBETH   Cure her of that.
Canst thou not minister to a mind dis-
eased,   40
Pluck from the memory a rooted sorrow,
Raze out° the written troubles of the
brain,
And with some sweet oblivious° antidote
Cleanse the stuffed bosom of that perilous
stuff
Which weighs upon the heart?
DOCTOR   Therein the patient   45
Must minister to himself.
MACBETH   Throw physic° to the dogs, I'll
none of it.
Come, put mine armor on. Give me my
staff.
Seyton, send out.—Doctor, the thanes fly
from me.—
Come, sir, dispatch.° If thou couldst, doc-
tor, cast   50
The water° of my land, find her disease
And purge it to a sound and pristine
health,
I would applaud thee to the very echo,
That should applaud again.—Pull 't off,
I say.—

9 **sway** move. 11 **loon** fool. 14 **over-red** cover with red. 15 **patch** fool. 16 **of** upon. **linen** i.e., pale. 20 **push** effort. 21 **disseat** i.e., unthrone (with word-play on "cheer," pronounced "chair"). 23 **sear** withered.

35 **moe** more. **skirr** scour. 42 **Raze out** erase. 43 **oblivious** causing forgetfulness. 47 **physic** medical science. 50 **dispatch** hurry. 50–51 **cast/The water** analyze the urine.

55 What rhubarb, senna, or what purgative drug,
Would scour these English hence? Hear'st thou of them?

DOCTOR Ay, my good lord; your royal preparation
Makes us hear something.

MACBETH   Bring it° after me.
I will not be afraid of death and bane°
60 Till Birnam Forest come to Dunsinane.

DOCTOR [*Aside*] Were I from Dunsinane away and clear,
Profit again should hardly draw me here.

Exeunt.

SCENE FOUR   [*Country near Birnam Wood.*]

Drum and colors. Enter MALCOLM, SI-
WARD, MACDUFF, SIWARD'S SON, MENTEITH,
CAITHNESS, ANGUS, *and* SOLDIERS, *march-
ing.*

MALCOLM Cousins, I hope the days are near at hand
That chambers will be safe.°

MENTEITH   We doubt it nothing.°

SIWARD What wood is this before us?

MENTEITH   The Wood of Birnam.

MALCOLM Let every soldier hew him down a bough
And bear 't before him. Thereby shall we
5 shadow
The numbers of our host, and make dis-
covery°
Err in report of us.

SOLDIERS   It shall be done.

SIWARD We learn no other but° the confident tyrant
Keeps still in Dunsinane, and will en-
dure°
Our setting down before 't.

10 MALCOLM   'Tis his main hope,
For where there is advantage to be given°

Both more and less° have given him the revolt,
And none serve with him but constrainèd things
Whose hearts are absent too.

MACDUFF   Let our just censures
Attend the true event,° and put we on   15
Industrious soldiership.

SIWARD   The time approaches,
That will with due decision make us know
What we shall say we have and what we owe.°
Thoughts speculative their unsure hopes relate,
But certain issue strokes must arbitrate:°   20
Towards which advance the war.°

Exeunt, marching.

SCENE FIVE   [*Dunsinane. Within the castle.*]

Enter MACBETH, SEYTON, *and* SOLDIERS,
with drum and colors.

MACBETH Hang out our banners on the outward walls.
The cry is still "They come!" Our castle's strength
Will laugh a siege to scorn. Here let them lie
Till famine and the ague° eat them up.
Were they not forced° with those that should be ours,   5
We might have met them dareful,° beard to beard,
And beat them backward home.

A cry within of women.

            What is that noise?

SEYTON It is the cry of women, my good lord.   [*Exit.*]

---

58 **it** i.e., the armor. 59 **bane** destruction.
V.iv. 2 **That chambers will be safe** i.e., that a man will be safe in his bedroom. **nothing** not at all. 6 **discovery** reconnaissance. 8 **no other but** nothing but that. 9 **endure** allow. 11 **advantage to be given** afforded an opportunity.

12 **more and less** high and low. 14–15 **just cen-
sures/Attend the true event** true judgment await the actual outcome. 18 **owe** own (the contrast is between "what we shall say we have" and "what we shall really have"). 20 **certain issue strokes must arbitrate** the definite outcome must be decided by battle. 21 **war** army.
V.v. 4 **ague** fever. 5 **forced** reinforced. 6 **met them dareful** i.e., met them in the battlefield boldly.

MACBETH   I have almost forgot the taste of fears:
The time has been, my senses would have cooled
To hear a night-shriek, and my fell° of hair
Would at a dismal treatise° rouse and stir
As life were in 't. I have supped full with horrors.
Direness, familiar to my slaughterous thoughts,
Cannot once start° me.

[*Enter* SEYTON.]

Wherefore was that cry?
SEYTON   The Queen, my lord, is dead.
MACBETH   She should° have died hereafter;
There would have been a time for such a word.°
Tomorrow, and tomorrow, and tomorrow
Creeps in this petty pace from day to day,
To the last syllable of recorded time;
And all our yesterdays have lighted fools
The way to dusty death. Out, out, brief candle!
Life's but a walking shadow, a poor player
That struts and frets his hour upon the stage
And then is heard no more. It is a tale
Told by an idiot, full of sound and fury
Signifying nothing.

Enter a MESSENGER.

Thou com'st to use thy tongue; thy story quickly!
MESSENGER   Gracious my lord,
I should report that which I say I saw,
But know not how to do 't.
MACBETH   Well, say, sir.
MESSENGER   As I did stand my watch upon the hill,
I looked toward Birnam, and anon, methought,
The wood began to move.
MACBETH   Liar and slave!
MESSENGER   Let me endure your wrath, if 't be not so.

Within this three mile may you see it coming;
I say a moving grove.
MACBETH   If thou speak'st false,
Upon the next tree shalt thou hang alive,
Till famine cling° thee. If thy speech be sooth,°
I care not if thou dost for me as much.
I pull in resolution,° and begin
To doubt° th' equivocation of the fiend
That lies like truth: "Fear not, till Birnam Wood
Do come to Dunsinane!" And now a wood
Comes towards Dunsinane. Arm, arm, and out!
If this which he avouches° does appear,
There is nor flying hence nor tarrying here.
I 'gin to be aweary of the sun,
And wish th' estate° o' th' world were now undone.
Ring the alarum bell! Blow wind, come wrack!
At least we'll die with harness° on our back.

Exeunt.

SCENE SIX   [*Dunsinane. Before the castle.*]

Drum and colors. Enter MALCOLM, SIWARD, MACDUFF, *and their army, with boughs.*

MALCOLM   Now near enough. Your leavy° screens throw down,
And show like those you are. You, worthy uncle,
Shall, with my cousin, your right noble son,
Lead our first battle.° Worthy Macduff and we°
Shall take upon 's what else remains to do,
According to our order.°

40 **cling** wither. **sooth** truth. 42 **pull in resolution** restrain confidence. 43 **doubt** suspect. 47 **avouches** asserts. 50 **th' estate** the orderly condition. 52 **harness** armor.
V.vi. 1 **leavy** leafy. 4 **battle** battalion. **we** (Malcolm uses the royal "we"). 6 **order** plan.

11 **fell** pelt. 12 **treatise** story. 15 **start** startle. 17 **should** inevitably would (?). 18 **word** message.

SIWARD   Fare you well.
Do we° but find the tyrant's power° to-
night,
Let us be beaten, if we cannot fight.
MACDUFF   Make all our trumpets speak;
give them all breath,
Those clamorous harbingers of blood and
10   death.

Exeunt. Alarums continued.

SCENE SEVEN   [*Another part of the field.*]

Enter MACBETH.

MACBETH   They have tied me to a stake; I
cannot fly,
But bearlike I must fight the course.°
What's he
That was not born of woman? Such a one
Am I to fear, or none.

Enter YOUNG SIWARD.

YOUNG SIWARD   What is thy name?
5   MACBETH   Thou'lt be afraid to hear it.
YOUNG SIWARD   No; though thou call'st thy-
self a hotter name
Than any is in hell.
MACBETH   My name's Macbeth.
YOUNG SIWARD   The devil himself could
not pronounce a title
More hateful to mine ear.
MACBETH   No, nor more fearful.
YOUNG SIWARD   Thou liest, abhorred ty-
10   rant; with my sword
I'll prove the lie thou speak'st.

Fight, and YOUNG SIWARD *slain.*

MACBETH   Thou wast born of woman.
But swords I smile at, weapons laugh to
scorn,

Brandished by man that's of a woman
born.

Exit.

Alarums. Enter MACDUFF.

MACDUFF   That way the noise is. Tyrant,
show they face!
If thou be'st slain and with no stroke of   15
mine,
My wife and children's ghosts will haunt
me still.
I cannot strike at wretched kerns,° whose
arms
Are hired to bear their staves.° Either
thou, Macbeth,
Or else my sword, with an unbattered
edge,
I sheathe again undeeded.° There thou   20
shouldst be;
By this great clatter, one of greatest note
Seems bruited.° Let me find him, Fortune!
And more I beg not.   *Exit. Alarums.*

Enter MALCOLM *and* SIWARD.

SIWARD   This way, my lord. The castle's
gently rend'red:°
The tyrant's people on both sides do fight;   25
The noble thanes do bravely in the war;
The day almost itself professes° yours,
And little is to do.
MALCOLM   We have met with foes
That strike beside us.°
SIWARD   Enter, sir, the castle.

Exeunt. Alarum.

[SCENE EIGHT   *Another part of the field.*]

Enter MACBETH.

MACBETH   Why should I play the Roman
fool, and die

---

7 **Do we** if we do. **power** forces.
V.vii. 2 **course** bout, round (he has in mind an attack of dogs or men upon a bear chained to a
stake).

17 **kerns** foot soldiers (contemptuous). 18 **staves**
spears. 20 **undeeded** i.e., having done nothing. 22
bruited reported. 24 **gently rend'red** surrendered
without a struggle. 27 **itself professes** declares itself.
29 **beside us** i.e., deliberately miss us (?) as our
comrades (?).

On mine own sword? Whiles I see lives,° the gashes
Do better upon them.

Enter MACBETH.

MACDUFF   Turn, hell-hound, turn!
MACBETH   Of all men else I have avoided thee.
But get thee back! My soul is too much
5   charged°
With blood of thine already.
MACDUFF   I have no words:
My voice is in my sword, thou bloodier villain
Than terms can give thee out!°

Fight. Alarum.

MACBETH   Thou losest labor:
As easy mayst thou the intrenchant° air
With thy keen sword impress° as make
10   me bleed:
Let fall thy blade on vulnerable crests;
I bear a charmèd life, which must not yield
To one of woman born.
MACDUFF   Despair° thy charm,
And let the angel° whom thou still hast served
Tell thee, Macduff was from his mother's
15   womb
Untimely ripped.
MACBETH   Accursèd be that tongue that tells me so,
For it hath cowed my better part of man!°
And be these juggling fiends no more believed,
20   That palter° with us in a double sense;
That keep the word of promise to our ear,
And break it to our hope. I'll not fight with thee.
MACDUFF   Then yield thee, coward,
And live to be the show and gaze o' th' time:°

We'll have thee, as our rarer monsters° are,   25
Painted upon a pole,° and underwrit,
"Here may you see the tyrant."
MACBETH   I will not yield,
To kiss the ground before young Malcolm's feet,
And to be baited° with the rabble's curse.
Though Birnam Wood be come to Dunsinane,   30
And thou opposed, being of no woman born,
Yet I will try the last. Before my body
I throw my warlike shield. Lay on, Macduff;
And damned be him that first cries "Hold, enough!"   *Exeunt, fighting. Alarums.*
[Re-]enter fighting, and MACBETH *slain.*
[Exit MACDUFF, *with* MACBETH.] *Retreat and flourish.*° *Enter, with drum and colors,* MALCOLM, SIWARD, ROSS, THANES, *and* SOLDIERS.

MALCOLM   I would the friends we miss were safe arrived.   35
SIWARD   Some must go off;° and yet, by these I see,
So great a day as this is cheaply bought.
MALCOLM   Macduff is missing, and your noble son.
ROSS   Your son, my lord, has paid a soldier's debt:
He only lived but till he was a man;   40
The which no sooner had his prowess confirmed
In the unshrinking station° where he fought,
But like a man he died.
SIWARD   Then he is dead?
ROSS   Ay, and brought off the field. Your cause of sorrow
Must not be measured by his worth, for then   45
It hath no end.

SIWARD   Had he his hurts before?

ROSS   Ay, on the front.

SIWARD   Why then, God's soldier be he!
Had I as many sons as I have hairs,
I would not wish them to a fairer death:
And so his knell is knolled.

50 MALCOLM   He's worth more sorrow,
And that I'll spend for him.

SIWARD   He's worth no more:
They say he parted well and paid his
  score:°
And so God be with him! Here comes
  newer comfort.

Enter MACDUFF, *with* MACBETH's *head.*

MACDUFF   Hail, King! for so thou art: be-
  hold, where stands
Th' usurper's cursèd head. The time is
55 free.°
I see thee compassed° with thy kingdom's
  pearl,
That speak my salutation in their minds,
Whose voices I desire aloud with mine:
Hail, King of Scotland!

ALL   Hail, King of Scotland!

Flourish.

MALCOLM   We shall not spend a large ex-
60   pense of time

Before we reckon with your several loves,°
And make us even with you. My thanes
  and kinsmen,
Henceforth be earls, the first that ever
  Scotland
In such an honor named. What's more to
  do,
Which would be planted newly with the
  time°—   65
As calling home our exiled friends abroad
That fled the snares of watchful tyranny,
Producing forth the cruel ministers°
Of this dead butcher and his fiendlike
  queen,
Who, as 'tis thought, by self and violent°
  hands   70
Took off her life—this, and what needful
  else
That calls upon us,° by the grace of Grace
We will perform in measure, time, and
  place:°
So thanks to all at once and to each one,
Whom we invite to see us crowned at
  Scone.   75

Flourish. Exeunt Omnes.

61 **reckon with your several loves** reward the devotion of each of you. 64–65 **What's more . . . time**
i.e., what else must be done which should be newly
established in this age. 68 **ministers** agents. 70 **self
and violent** her own violent. 72 **calls upon us** demands my attention. 73 **in measure, time and place**
fittingly, at the appropriate time and place.

52 **parted well and paid his score** departed well
and settled his account. 55 **The time is free** the
world is liberated. 56 **compassed** surrounded.

Edward II

Christopher Marlowe   edited by Irving Ribner

Introductory Comments

Clifford Leech

Marlowe's age was one of great enterprise, ambition, and splendid literature, but it was not the "merry England" of legend. It was a time of violence in the streets (in which Marlowe was more than once involved), of appalling savagery in its mode of inflicting capital punishment, and of torture. Both Shakespeare and Marlowe freely presented violence in their plays, but they saw it for the foul thing it was and is. They also had a strong wish to relate the past to the present, and *Edward II,* written on an English historical theme, reflects that wish.

Edward I, the father of Edward II, was a major conqueror. He subdued Wales and he made a temporary conquest of Scotland. Indeed, he dreamed of a United Kingdom long before it came into being. His son, the central figure in Marlowe's play, lost his father's gains in Scotland at the disastrous battle of Bannockburn (1314), which is referred to in the satirical Scots ballad quoted in the play (II.ii.). In Edward II's reign not only did the dream of a United Kingdom evaporate but England itself fell apart. Because of his infatuation with the obscure Frenchman Gaveston, Edward's barons turned against him, forced him to abdicate, and then murdered him in the most brutal way imaginable. Edward's queen, the sister of the French king, became the mistress of Mortimer and fully acquiesced in Edward's murder.

Among Marlowe's plays, *Tamburlaine, Doctor Faustus,* and *Edward II* are deservedly the best known. Faustus operates on a cosmic scale, as did Tamburlaine; *Edward II* is at face value a small story of English humiliation. The resemblance to Shakespeare's *Henry VI* is obvious enough: after the triumph of Agincourt, England lost France and split apart through quarrels among the great lords.

But there is an important difference. In Shakespeare's *Henry VI* the central theme seems to be the welfare of the kingdom; Marlowe's *Edward II,* however, concerns itself less with England as a national entity than with personal relations. There are four main characters:

Edward, Gaveston, Mortimer, and Isabella. The way in which these people have an impact on one another provides the impetus for the working out of events. The barons, without Mortimer, would have been more manageable, but Mortimer resents the favors shown to Gaveston, a mere upstart (see I.iv.). Mortimer is not avid for personal power when he first appears in the play, but circumstances force him into prominence; this makes him very different from Tamburlaine and Faustus. When he finds himself in power, he is corrupted, and willingly accepts the dreadful manner of Edward's killing. Isabella, though attached to Mortimer, does not plan infidelity until Edward finally repudiates her at Tynemouth (II.iv.), and even then she determines to have one more try at reconciliation. She is a sensual, passionate woman, who by her very nature wants a man at her side. And Mortimer is there. There is an interesting parallel here to the way in which Edward turns to the younger Spencer as soon as Gaveston is dead. So Isabella becomes Mortimer's mistress and his accomplice in the final phase of the play. The reader or spectator may ask how it comes about that she can subscribe to her husband's murder, but perhaps Isabella's response indicates Marlowe's recognition that a woman's love can grow rancid if it is tried too hard.

Yet at the center is of course the homosexual love of Gaveston and Edward. Gaveston does seem to be fond of Edward, but he is also the opportunist who will trade on Edward's love for him. In the first scene he plans to set himself up as the court pornographer, and he encourages Edward in his actions against the barons and, particularly dangerously, against the church. But Edward shows excessive pride always, particularly in his delight in bestowing honors for favors received. He even gives Gaveston the title of "Lord of Man" (I.i.). Historically there was no such title, but there is appropriateness in the ambiguous use of "Man" here, meaning both the island and the king himself. The king, after all, is emblematic of "man," and the upstart has become his "Lord."

Although Edward is a strange tragic figure for Marlowe, we have to remember two things. After the two "world tragedies" of *Tamburlaine* and *Faustus,* Marlowe seems to have turned to the tragedies of personal life within a society, here and in *The Jew of Malta* and *The Massacre at Paris* (which concerns itself with French history, particularly with the massacre of the Huguenots that took place not long before the play was written). More importantly, in *Edward II* Marlowe is concerned with the way in which a personally "insignificant" man, so different from Tamburlaine or Faustus, can achieve tragic stature through extreme suffering. There is no scene in the whole of Elizabethan or Jacobean drama more horrifying than the scene of Edward's murder. It has of course a direct reference to the homosexual practice that Edward has enjoyed with Gaveston, and no one can see it or read it or think about it without anguish. When we see anyone die, it is an anguishing experience, and he or she becomes at that moment a tragic figure. Edward, for all his weakness, comes out as our master when he dies so terribly.

The play on English historical themes enjoyed a short-lived popularity. Apart from eccentric examples—the most splendid being John Ford's *Perkin Warbeck* of about 1630—the genre lasted not much more than ten years. But Marlowe gave us the one play of the 1590s that ranks with Shakespeare's series, though it is done in a different mode. Shakespeare's way was to use plot, sub-plot, and counter-plot. Marlowe follows a simple action through to the end. And he did not say at all firmly: "It will be all right: justice will be done. The accession of Edward III will put things in order." He offers only the formal display of Edward II's body and Mortimer's head. There is not much consolation to be got from that.

Edward II is highly personal, but Marlowe did not know he was soon to be killed. Though it was surely one of his last plays, it cannot be regarded as any sort of a "testament," as can Shakespeare's *The Tempest*. But here, unlike in *Tamburlaine* and *Faustus*, he centered on a man born to greatness, experiencing arrogance and insecurity, and then given over to humiliation and grim murder.

Edward II was first printed in 1594. We have no record of contemporary reactions to it. But it has come in a major way to the twentieth-century theatre. The version of Bertolt Brecht and Lion Feuchtwanger, so often played by undergraduates in our time, misses the wide sweep of Marlowe's action and softens the grimness of the original. But Marlowe's play is still much with us. This is not simply because of a more tolerant attitude to homosexuality. It is also, I think, because we have become more deeply aware of how much cruelty man can inflict on man.

Christopher Marlowe (1564–1593) was born the same year as Shakespeare. He went to Cambridge and obtained his B.A. and M.A., but he disappeared for a time, apparently doing secret service work on behalf of the Privy Council, which interceded for him on the occasion of his candidature for the M.A. degree. Apparently the university was dubious because of Marlowe's frequent absence from Cambridge and the rumor that he was planning to enter the English College at Rheims, which trained men for the priesthood that was surreptitiously serving in England in the interest of the Roman church. The Privy Council was able to assure the university that Marlowe had been working in the English government's interest.

After leaving Cambridge Marlowe spent most of his few remaining years in London, during which time he wrote six plays. Probably while still at Cambridge he did translations of Ovid's *Elegies* and the first book of Lucan's *Pharsalia,* and of the story of Dido, based closely on Vergil's *Aeneid* but presented in ironic terms. In London he achieved an extraordinary success with two plays about Tamburlaine, the Mongol conqueror. Marlowe died at the age of twenty-nine, stabbed, in alleged self-defense, in a tavern in Deptford (southeast London today).

The Troublesome Reign and Lamentable Death of Edward the Second   Christopher Marlowe

KING EDWARD THE SECOND

PRINCE EDWARD   *his Son, afterwards* KING EDWARD THE THIRD

EARL OF KENT   *Brother of King Edward the Second*

GAVESTON

WARWICK

LANCASTER

PEMBROKE

ARUNDEL

LEICESTER

BERKELEY

MORTIMER SENIOR

MORTIMER JUNIOR   *his Nephew*

SPENCER SENIOR

SPENCER JUNIOR   *his Son*

ARCHBISHOP OF CANTERBURY

BISHOP OF COVENTRY

BISHOP OF WINCHESTER

BALDOCK

BEAUMONT

TRUSSEL

GURNEY

MATREVIS

LIGHTBORN

SIR JOHN OF HAINAULT

LEVUNE

RICE AP HOWELL

ABBOT, MONKS, HERALD, LORDS, POOR MEN, JAMES, MOWER, CHAMPION,
    MESSENGERS, SOLDIERS, AND ATTENDANTS

QUEEN ISABELLA   *Wife of King Edward the Second*

NIECE TO KING EDWARD THE SECOND   *daughter of the Duke of Gloucester*

LADIES

THE SCENE *England, France.*

Act One

SCENE ONE

Enter GAVESTON, *reading on a letter that was brought him from the king.*

GAVESTON My father is deceased. Come, Gaveston,°
And share the kingdom with thy dearest friend.
Ah, words that make me surfeit with delight!
What greater bliss can hap to Gaveston
5 Than live and be the favorite of a king?
Sweet prince, I come; these, these thy amorous lines
Might have enforced me to have swum from France,°
And, like Leander,° gasped upon the sand,
So thou wouldst smile and take me in thy arms.
10 The sight of London to my exiled eyes
Is as Elysium to a new-come soul;
Not that I love the city or the men,
But that it harbors him I hold so dear,
The king, upon whose bosom let me die,°
15 And with the world be still at enmity.
What need the arctic people love starlight,
To whom the sun shines both by day and night?
Farewell base stooping to the lordly peers.
My knee shall bow to none but to the king.
20 As for the multitude that are but sparks,
Raked up in embers of their poverty——°

I.i. 1 **Gaveston** Son of a Gascon knight in the service of King Edward I, he had been brought up as a childhood friend of Edward II. 7 **France** Gaveston had been banished to his native Gascony by King Edward I. The young Edward II's first act upon becoming king was to call his friend home in 1307. 8 **Leander** hero of the Greek love story who nightly swam the Hellespont to be with his beloved Hero; he finally drowned. Marlowe retold the story in his poem *Hero and Leander.* 14 **die** swoon with joy. There is little justification for the emendation, 'lie' adopted by some modern editors. 20–21 **sparks . . . poverty** Fires were kept alive overnight by raking ashes over the live embers.

Tanti;° I'll fawn first on the wind
That glanceth at my lips and flieth away.
But how now, what are these?

Enter three POOR MEN.

POOR MEN Such as desire your worship's service. 25
GAVESTON What canst thou do?
FIRST POOR MAN I can ride.
GAVESTON But I have no horses. What art thou?
SECOND POOR MAN A traveler.
GAVESTON Let me see—thou wouldst do well 30
To wait at my trencher° and tell me lies at dinner time,
And as I like your discoursing, I'll have you.
And what art thou?
THIRD POOR MAN A soldier, that hath served against the Scot.
GAVESTON Why, there are hospitals° for such as you. 35
I have no war, and therefore, sir, be gone.
THIRD POOR MAN Farewell, and perish by a soldier's hand,
That wouldst reward them with an hospital.
GAVESTON Ay, ay, these words of his move me as much
As if a goose should play the porpentine° 40
And dart her plumes, thinking to pierce my breast.
But yet it is no pain to speak men fair.
I'll flatter these and make them live in hope. [*Aside.*]
You know that I came lately out of France,
And yet I have not viewed my lord the king. 45
If I speed well, I'll entertain you all.

---

22 **Tanti** So much for that (an expression of contempt). 31 **trencher** a flat wooden dish on which food was served. 35 **hospitals** homes for disabled soldiers. 40 **porpentine** porcupine (supposed in popular superstition to be able to dart its quills).

POOR MEN   We thank your worship.

GAVESTON   I have some business; leave me to myself.

POOR MEN   We will wait here about the court.

Exeunt [POOR MEN].

50 GAVESTON   Do. These are not men for me.
I must have wanton° poets, pleasant wits,
Musicians, that with touching of a string
May draw the pliant king which way I please.
Music and poetry is his delight;
Therefore I'll have Italian masks° by
55 night,
Sweet speeches, comedies, and pleasing shows;
And in the day, when he shall walk abroad,
Like sylvan nymphs my pages shall be clad.
My men, like satyrs grazing° on the lawns,
Shall with their goat-feet dance an antic
60 hay.°
Sometime a lovely boy in Dian's° shape,
With hair that gilds the water as it glides,
Crownets° of pearl about his naked arms,
And in his sportful hands an olive tree,
To hide those parts which men delight to
65 see,
Shall bathe him in a spring; and there, hard by,
One like Actæon° peeping through the grove,
Shall by the angry goddess be transformed,

And running in the likeness of an hart,
By yelping hounds pulled down, and
seem to die—   70
Such things as these best please his majesty.
My lord! Here comes the king and the nobles
From the parliament. I'll stand aside.

[*He retires.*]

Enter KING [EDWARD], LANCASTER, MORTIMER SENIOR, MORTIMER JUNIOR, EDMUND,° EARL OF KENT, GUY, EARL OF WARWICK, [*and others*].

KING EDWARD   Lancaster!

LANCASTER   My lord.   75

GAVESTON   That Earl of Lancaster do I abhor. [*Aside.*]

KING EDWARD   Will you not grant me this?
In spite of them
I'll have my will, and these two Mortimers,
That cross me thus, shall know I am displeased. [*Aside.*]

MORTIMER SENIOR   If you love us, my lord,
hate Gaveston.   80

GAVESTON   That villain Mortimer! I'll be his death. [*Aside.*]

MORTIMER JUNIOR   Mine uncle here, this earl, and I myself
Were sworn to your father at his death,
That he should ne'er return into the realm.
And know, my lord, ere I will break my
oath,   85
This sword of mine, that should offend your foes,
Shall sleep within the scabbard at thy need,
And underneath thy banners march who will,
For Mortimer will hang his armor up.

51 **wanton** amorous. 55 **Italian masks** elaborate Elizabethan entertainments involving disguises, thought in the sixteenth century to have come from Italy, but actually of obscure origins, although certainly influenced by Italian customs. Marlowe here is anachronistic, since there were no masks in Edward's time. 59 **grazing** strolling. 60 **antic hay** an old-fashioned dance. 61 **Dian** the Greek goddess of chastity and the hunt (to be portrayed by a boy, as were all women's parts in Elizabethan entertainments). 63 **Crownets** bracelets. 67 **Actæon** a hunter, in Greek mythology, transformed by Diana into a stag after having seen her bathing, and then killed by his own hounds. The story is in Ovid's *Metamorphoses*.

sd **Edmund** an anachronism, since Edmund of Woodstock. Earl of Kent, Edward's half-brother, was not born until 1301, and thus was only six years old at the time of Gaveston's recall in 1307. The Mortimers, similarly, had no actual part in the opposition to Gaveston. Thomas, Earl of Lancaster, grandson of Henry III, was a powerful opponent of Gaveston, the Spencers, and Edward II.

90   GAVESTON   *Mort Dieu!* [*Aside.*]

KING EDWARD   Well, Mortimer, I'll make
thee rue these words.

Beseems it thee to contradict thy king?

Frown'st thou thereat, aspiring Lancaster?

The sword shall plane the furrows of thy
brows,

95   And hew these knees that now are grown
so stiff.

I will have Gaveston, and you shall know

What danger 'tis to stand against your
king.

GAVESTON   Well done, Ned! [*Aside.*]

LANCASTER   My lord, why do you thus incense your peers,

100   That naturally would love and honor you

But for that base and obscure Gaveston?

Four earldoms have I besides Lancaster—

Derby, Salisbury, Lincoln, Leicester;

These will I sell to give my soldiers pay,

105   Ere Gaveston shall stay within the realm;

Therefore, if he be come, expel him
straight.

KENT   Barons and earls, your pride hath
made me mute,

But now I'll speak, and to the proof,° I
hope.

I do remember in my father's days,

Lord Percy of the north, being highly

110   moved,

Braved° Mowbery in presence of the king;

For which, had not his highness loved him
well,

He should have lost his head; but with his
look

The undaunted spirit of Percy was ap-
peased,

115   And Mowbery and he were reconciled.

Yet dare you brave the king unto his face?

Brother, revenge it, and let these their
heads

Preach upon poles for trespass of their
tongues.

WARWICK   O, our heads!

KING EDWARD   Ay, yours; and therefore I

120   would wish you grant——

WARWICK   Bridle thy anger, gentle Mortimer.

MORTIMER JUNIOR   I cannot, nor I will
not; I must speak.

Cousin,° our hands I hope shall fence our
heads

And strike off his that makes you threaten
us.

Come, uncle, let us leave the brainsick
king   125

And henceforth parley with our naked
swords.

MORTIMER SENIOR   Wiltshire hath men
enough to save our heads.

WARWICK   All Warwickshire will love him
for my sake.

LANCASTER   And northward Gaveston hath
many friends.

Adieu, my lord, and either change your
mind,   130

Or look to see the throne, where you
should sit,

To float in blood, and at thy wanton°
head

The glozing° head of thy base minion°
thrown.

Exeunt [*all but* KING EDWARD, KENT, GAV-
ESTON *and* ATTENDANTS].

KING EDWARD   I cannot brook these haughty
menaces.

Am I a king, and must be overruled?   135

Brother, display my ensigns in the field;

I'll bandy° with the barons and the earls,

And either die or live with Gaveston.

GAVESTON   I can no longer keep me from
my lord.

[*He comes forward.*]

KING EDWARD   What, Gaveston! Welcome!
Kiss not my hand;   140

Embrace me, Gaveston, as I do thee.

Why shouldst thou kneel? Knowest thou
not who I am?

Thy friend, thyself, another Gaveston!

---

108 **to the proof** irrefutably. 111 **Braved** challenged.

123 **Cousin** any relative outside the immediate
family. Mortimer was very distantly related to the
king. 132 **wanton** irresponsible. 133 **glozing** flattering. **minion** favorite. 137 **bandy** exchange blows.

Not Hylas was more mourned of Hercules°

Than thou hast been of me since thy
145   exile.

GAVESTON   And since I went from hence, no soul in hell
Hath felt more torment than poor Gaveston.

KING EDWARD   I know it. Brother, welcome home my friend.
Now let the treacherous Mortimers conspire,
150   And that high minded Earl of Lancaster!
I have my wish in that I joy thy sight,
And sooner shall the sea o'erwhelm my land,
Than bear the ship that shall transport thee hence.
I here create thee Lord High Chamberlain,
155   Chief Secretary to the state and me,
Earl of Cornwall, King and Lord of Man.°

GAVESTON   My lord, these titles far exceed my worth.

KENT   Brother, the least of these may well suffice
For one of greater birth than Gaveston.

KING EDWARD   Cease, brother, for I cannot
160   brook these words.
Thy worth, sweet friend, is far above my gifts;
Therefore, to equal it, receive my heart.
If for these dignities thou be envied,
I'll give thee more; for but to honor thee,
165   Is Edward pleased with kingly regiment.
Fearst thou thy person? Thou shalt have a guard.
Wantest thou gold? Go to my treasury.
Wouldst thou be loved and feared? Receive my seal;
Save or condemn, and in our name command

---

144 **Hylas . . . Hercules** Hylas was a youth who accompanied Hercules with Jason on the quest for the golden fleece and was carried off by Nymphs when he went ashore at Nysia to draw water. Hercules mourned and searched for him but could find only an echo. 156 **King and Lord of Man** Rulers of the Isle of Man, between England and Ireland, had certain sovereign rights and were called kings.

Whatso thy mind affects or fancy likes.   *170*

GAVESTON   It shall suffice me to enjoy your love,
Which whiles I have, I think myself as great
As Caesar riding in the Roman street,
With captive kings at his triumphant car.

Enter the BISHOP OF COVENTRY.

KING EDWARD   Whither goes my lord of Coventry so fast?   *175*

COVENTRY   To celebrate your father's exequies.
But is that wicked Gaveston returned?

KING EDWARD   Ay, priest, and lives to be revenged on thee,
That wert the only cause of his exile.

GAVESTON   'Tis true, and but for reverence of these robes,   *180*
Thou shouldst not plod one foot beyond this place.

COVENTRY   I did no more than I was bound to do;
And, Gaveston, unless thou be reclaimed,
As then I did incense the parliament,
So will I now, and thou shalt back to France.   *185*

GAVESTON   Saving your reverence, you must pardon me.

KING EDWARD   Throw off his golden mitre, rend his stole,
And in the channel° christen him anew.

KENT   Ah, brother, lay not violent hands on him,
For he'll complain unto the see of Rome.   *190*

GAVESTON   Let him complain unto the see of hell;
I'll be revenged on him for my exile.

KING EDWARD   No, spare his life, but seize upon his goods.
Be thou lord bishop and receive his rents,
And make him serve thee as thy chaplain.   *195*
I give him thee—here, use him as thou wilt.

GAVESTON   He shall to prison and there die in bolts.

---

188 **channel** open gutter through which sewage flowed.

KING EDWARD   Ay, to the Tower, the Fleet,° or where thou wilt.

COVENTRY   For this offence, be thou accursed of God!

KING EDWARD   Who's there? Convey this
200 priest to the Tower.

COVENTRY   True, true.

KING EDWARD   But in the meantime, Gaveston, away,
And take possession of his house and goods.
Come, follow me, and thou shalt have my guard
205 To see it done and bring thee safe again.

GAVESTON   What should a priest do with so fair a house?
A prison may beseem his holiness.

[*Exeunt.*]

SCENE TWO

Enter both the MORTIMERS, WARWICK *and* LANCASTER.

WARWICK°   'Tis true, the bishop is in the Tower,
And goods and body given to Gaveston.

LANCASTER   What! Will they tyrannise upon the church?
Ah, wicked king! Accursèd Gaveston!
This ground, which is corrupted with
5   their steps,
Shall be their timeless° sepulcher or mine.

MORTIMER JUNIOR   Well, let that peevish Frenchman guard him sure;
Unless his breast be sword-proof he shall die.

MORTIMER SENIOR   How now! Why droops the Earl of Lancaster?

MORTIMER JUNIOR   Wherefore is Guy of
10   Warwick discontent?

LANCASTER   That villain Gaveston is made an earl.

MORTIMER SENIOR   An earl!

WARWICK   Ay, and besides Lord Chamberlain of the realm,
And Secretary too, and Lord of Man.

MORTIMER SENIOR   We may not, nor we   15
will not suffer this.

MORTIMER JUNIOR   Why post we not from hence to levy men?

LANCASTER   'My Lord of Cornwall,' now at every word!
And happy is the man whom he vouchsafes,
For vailing of his bonnet,° one good look.
Thus, arm in arm, the king and he doth   20
march.
Nay more, the guard upon his lordship waits,
And all the court begins to flatter him.

WARWICK   Thus leaning on the shoulder of the king,
He nods, and scorns, and smiles at those that pass.

MORTIMER SENIOR   Doth no man take exceptions at° the slave?   25

LANCASTER   All stomach° him, but none dare speak a word.

MORTIMER JUNIOR   Ah, that bewrays° their baseness, Lancaster!
Were all the earls and barons of my mind,
We'll hale him from the bosom of the king,
And at the court gate hang the peasant   30
up,
Who, swoll'n with venom of ambitious pride,
Will be the ruin of the realm and us.

Enter the [ARCH]BISHOP OF CANTERBURY
[*and an* ATTENDANT].

WARWICK   Here comes my lord of Canterbury's grace.

LANCASTER   His countenance bewrays he is displeased.

CANTERBURY   First were his sacred garments rent and torn,   35

___

198 **Fleet** a London prison.
I.ii. 1 **Warwick** Guy, Earl of Warwick, historically was the most persistent foe of Gaveston and Edward II. 6 **timeless** premature.

19 **vailing of his bonnet** lifting his hat. 25 **take exceptions at** object to. 26 **stomach** are angry at (the stomach was regarded as the producer of choler, and therefore the seat of anger). 27 **bewrays** reveals.

Then laid they violent hands upon him; next
Himself imprisoned, and his goods asseized.°
This certify the Pope; away, take horse.

[*Exit* ATTENDANT.]

LANCASTER   My lord, will you take arms against the king?
CANTERBURY   What need I? God himself is

40   up in arms,
When violence is offered to the church.
MORTIMER JUNIOR   Then will you join with us that be his peers,
To banish or behead that Gaveston?
CANTERBURY   What else, my lords? For it concerns me near;

45   The bishopric of Coventry is his.

Enter QUEEN [ISABELLA].°

MORTIMER JUNIOR   Madam, whither walks your majesty so fast?
QUEEN ISABELLA   Unto the forest,° gentle Mortimer,
To live in grief and baleful discontent,
For now my lord the king regards me not,

50   But dotes upon the love of Gaveston.
He claps his cheeks and hangs about his neck,
Smiles in his face and whispers in his ears,
And when I come, he frowns, as who should say,
'Go whither thou wilt, seeing I have Gaveston.'
MORTIMER SENIOR   Is it not strange that he

55   is thus bewitched?
MORTIMER JUNIOR   Madam, return unto the court again.
That sly inveigling Frenchman we'll exile
Or lose our lives; and yet, ere that day come,
The king shall lose his crown, for we have power,

And courage too, to be revenged at full.   60
CANTERBURY   But yet lift not your swords against the king.
LANCASTER   No, but we'll lift Gaveston from hence.
WARWICK   And war must be the means, or he'll stay still.
QUEEN ISABELLA   Then let him stay; for rather than my lord
Shall be oppressed by civil mutinies,   65
I will endure a melancholy life,
And let him frolic with his minion.
CANTERBURY   My lords, to ease all this, but hear me speak:
We and the rest that are his counselors
Will meet and with a general consent   70
Confirm his banishment with our hands and seals.
LANCASTER   What we confirm the king will frustrate.
MORTIMER JUNIOR   Then may we lawfully revolt from him.
WARWICK   But say, my lord, where shall this meeting be?
CANTERBURY   At the New Temple.°   75
MORTIMER JUNIOR   Content.
CANTERBURY   And, in the meantime, I'll entreat you all
To cross to Lambeth° and there stay with me.
LANCASTER   Come then, let's away.
MORTIMER JUNIOR   Madam, farewell.   80
QUEEN ISABELLA   Farewell, sweet Mortimer, and for my sake
Forbear to levy arms against the king.
MORTIMER JUNIOR   Ay, if words will serve; if not, I must.

[*Exeunt.*]

SCENE THREE

Enter GAVESTON *and the* EARL OF KENT.

GAVESTON   Edmund, the mighty prince of Lancaster,

---

37 **asseized** taken possession of. sd **Queen Isabella** Daughter of King Philip the Fair of France, she was born in 1292 and married king Edward in 1308. Her affair with Mortimer occurred much later. 47 **forest** wilderness (the queen is speaking figuratively).

75 **New Temple** house founded by the Knights Templar. 78 **Lambeth** a palace held by the Archbishops of Canterbury since 1179.

That hath more earldoms than an ass can
    bear,
And both the Mortimers, two goodly men,
With Guy of Warwick, that redoubted
    knight,
Are gone towards Lambeth. There let
5   them remain.

[*Exeunt.*]

SCENE FOUR

Enter [LANCASTER, WARWICK, PEMBROKE,
MORTIMER SENIOR, MORTIMER JUNIOR, *the*
ARCHBISHOP OF CANTERBURY *and* ATTEND-
ANTS].

LANCASTER   Here is the form of Gaveston's
    exile;
May it please your lordship to subscribe
    your name.
CANTERBURY   Give me the paper.

[*He subscribes, as do the others after
him.*]

LANCASTER   Quick, quick, my lord; I long
    to write my name.
WARWICK   But I long more to see him
5   banished hence.
MORTIMER JUNIOR   The name of Mortimer
    shall fright the king,
Unless he be declined from that base
    peasant.

Enter KING [EDWARD, KENT,] *and* GAVES-
TON.

KING EDWARD   What? Are you moved that
    Gaveston sits here?
It is our pleasure; we will have it so.
LANCASTER   Your grace doth well to place
10   him by your side,
For nowhere else the new earl is so safe.
MORTIMER SENIOR   What man of noble
    birth can brook this sight?
Quam male conveniunt!°
See what a scornful look the peasant casts.

PEMBROKE   Can kingly lions fawn on
    creeping ants?   *15*
WARWICK   Ignoble vassal, that like Phaeton
Aspir'st unto the guidance of the sun.
MORTIMER JUNIOR   Their downfall is at
    hand, their forces down.
We will not thus be faced and over-
    peered.°
KING EDWARD   Lay hands on that traitor
    Mortimer!   *20*
MORTIMER SENIOR   Lay hands on that trai-
    tor Gaveston!
KENT   Is this the duty that you owe your
    king?
WARWICK   Ye know our duties; let him
    know his peers.
KING EDWARD   Whither will you bear him?
    Stay, or ye shall die.
MORTIMER SENIOR   We are no traitors;
    therefore threaten not.   *25*
GAVESTON   No, threaten not, my lord, but
    pay them home!
Were I a king——
MORTIMER JUNIOR   Thou villain,° where-
    fore talks thou of a king,
That hardly art a gentleman by birth?
KING EDWARD   Were he a peasant, being my
    minion,   *30*
I'll make the proudest of you stoop to
    him.
LANCASTER   My lord, you may not thus dis-
    parage° us.
Away, I say, with hateful Gaveston!
MORTIMER SENIOR   And with the Earl of
    Kent that favors him.

[*Attendants remove* KENT *and* GAVESTON.]

KING EDWARD   Nay, then lay violent hands
    upon your king.   *35*
Here, Mortimer, sit thou in Edward's
    throne.
Warwick and Lancaster, wear you my
    crown.
Was ever king thus over-ruled as I?

___

I.iv. 13 **Quam male conveniunt.** How badly they
suit one another.

19 **faced and over-peered** bullied and looked down
upon (with a probable pun on 'peer'). 28 **villain**
(1) scoundrel (2) peasant bound to the land. 32
disparage vilify.

LANCASTER Learn then to rule us better and the realm.

MORTIMER JUNIOR What we have done,
40　our heart-blood shall maintain.

WARWICK Think you that we can brook this upstart pride?

KING EDWARD Anger and wrathful fury stops my speech.

CANTERBURY Why are you moved? Be patient, my lord,
And see what we your counselors have done.

MORTIMER JUNIOR My lords, now let us all
45　be resolute,
And either have our wills or lose our lives.

KING EDWARD Meet you for this, proud overdaring peers?
Ere my sweet Gaveston shall part from me,
This isle shall fleet° upon the ocean
50　And wander to the unfrequented Inde.°

CANTERBURY You know that I am legate to the Pope;
On your allegiance to the see of Rome,
Subscribe as we have done to his exile.

MORTIMER JUNIOR Curse him if he refuse, and then may we
55　Depose him and elect another king.

KING EDWARD Ay, there it goes! But yet I will not yield;
Curse me, depose me, do the worst you can.

LANCASTER Then linger not, my lord, but do it straight.

CANTERBURY Remember how the bishop was abused.
Either banish him that was the curse
60　thereof,
Or I will presently discharge these lords
Of duty and allegiance due to thee.

KING EDWARD It boots° me not to threat; I must speak fair.
The legate of the Pope will be obeyed. [*Aside.*]
My lord, you shall be Chancellor of the
65　realm,
Thou, Lancaster, High Admiral of our fleet;

Young Mortimer and his uncle shall be earls,
And you, Lord Warwick, President of the North,
And thou of Wales. If this content you not,
Make several kingdoms of this monarchy　70
And share it equally amongst you all,
So I may have some nook or corner left
To frolic with my dearest Gaveston.

CANTERBURY Nothing shall alter us; we are resolved.

LANCASTER Come, come, subscribe.　　　　　75

MORTIMER JUNIOR Why should you love him whom the world hates so?

KING EDWARD Because he loves me more than all the world.
Ah, none but rude and savage-minded men
Would seek the ruin of my Gaveston;
You that be noble-born should pity him.　80

WARWICK You that are princely-born should shake him off.
For shame subscribe, and let the lown° depart.

MORTIMER SENIOR Urge him, my lord.

CANTERBURY Are you content to banish him the realm?

KING EDWARD I see I must, and therefore am content.　　　　　　　　　　　　85
Instead of ink I'll write it with my tears.

He [subscribes].

MORTIMER JUNIOR The king is love-sick for his minion.

KING EDWARD 'Tis done, and now, accursèd hand, fall off!

LANCASTER Give it me; I'll have it published in the streets.

MORTIMER JUNIOR I'll see him presently dispatched away.　　　　　　　　90

CANTERBURY Now is my heart at ease.

WARWICK　　　　　　　　　And so is mine.

PEMBROKE This will be good news to the common sort.

MORTIMER SENIOR Be it or no, he shall not linger here.

Exeunt [all except KING EDWARD].

---

49 **fleet** float. 50 **Inde** India. 63 **boots** avails.

82 **lown** peasant.

KING EDWARD   How fast they run to banish him I love.

They would not stir, were it to do me
95 good.

Why should a king be subject to a priest?

Proud Rome, that hatchest such imperial grooms,

For these thy superstitious taper-lights,

Wherewith thy antichristian churches blaze,

100 I'll fire thy crazèd° buildings and enforce

The papal towers to kiss the lowly ground.

With slaughtered priests may Tiber's channel swell,

And banks raised higher with their sepulchers.

As for the peers that back the clergy thus,

105 If I be king, not one of them shall live.

Enter GAVESTON.

GAVESTON   My lord, I hear it whispered everywhere

That I am banished and must fly the land.

KING EDWARD   'Tis true, sweet Gaveston—O, were it false!

The legate of the Pope will have it so,

And thou must hence, or I shall be de-
110 posed.

But I will reign to be revenged of them,

And therefore, sweet friend, take it patiently.

Live where thou wilt, I'll send thee gold enough;

And long thou shalt not stay, or if thou dost,

I'll come to thee; my love shall ne'er de-
115 cline.

GAVESTON   Is all my hope turned to this hell of grief?

KING EDWARD   Rend not my heart with thy too-piercing words.

Thou from this land, I from myself am banished.

GAVESTON   To go from hence grieves not poor Gaveston,

But to forsake you, in whose gracious
120 looks

The blessedness of Gaveston remains;

For nowhere else seeks he felicity.

KING EDWARD   And only this torments my wretched soul,

That, whether I will or no, thou must depart.

Be governor of Ireland in my stead,   *125*

And there abide till fortune call thee home.

Here take my picture, and let me wear thine;

[They exchange pictures.]

O, might I keep thee here as I do this,

Happy were I, but now most miserable.

GAVESTON   'Tis something to be pitied of a king.   *130*

KING EDWARD   Thou shalt not hence; I'll hide thee, Gaveston.

GAVESTON   I shall be found, and then 'twill grieve me more.

KING EDWARD   Kind words and mutual talk makes our grief greater;

Therefore, with dumb embracement, let us part—

Stay, Gaveston, I cannot leave thee thus.   *135*

GAVESTON   For every look my lord drops down a tear;

Seeing I must go, do not renew my sorrow.

KING EDWARD   The time is little that thou hast to stay,

And therefore give me leave to look my fill.

But come, sweet friend, I'll bear° thee on thy way.   *140*

GAVESTON   The peers will frown.

KING EDWARD   I pass° not for their anger. Come, let's go.

O that we might as well return as go.

Enter QUEEN ISABELLA.

QUEEN ISABELLA   Whither goes my lord?

KING EDWARD   Fawn not on me, French strumpet; get thee gone.   *145*

QUEEN ISABELLA   On whom but on my husband should I fawn?

GAVESTON   On Mortimer, with whom, ungentle queen—

100 **crazèd** ruined.

140 **bear** accompany. 142 **pass** care.

I say no more; judge you the rest, my lord.

QUEEN ISABELLA   In saying this, thou wrong'st me, Gaveston.

150   Is't not enough that thou corrupts my lord
And art a bawd to his affections,°
But thou must call mine honor thus in question?

GAVESTON   I mean not so; your grace must pardon me.

KING EDWARD   Thou art too familiar with that Mortimer,
155   And by thy means is Gaveston exiled.
But I would wish thee reconcile the lords,
Or thou shalt ne'er be reconciled to me.

QUEEN ISABELLA   Your highness knows it lies not in my power.

KING EDWARD   Away then; touch me not. Come, Gaveston.

QUEEN ISABELLA   Villain, 'tis thou that
160   robb'st me of my lord.

GAVESTON   Madam, 'tis you that rob me of my lord.

KING EDWARD   Speak not unto her; let her droop and pine.

QUEEN ISABELLA   Wherein, my lord, have I deserved these words?
Witness the tears that Isabella sheds,
Witness this heart, that sighing for thee
165   breaks,
How dear my lord is to poor Isabel.

KING EDWARD   And witness heaven how dear thou art to me.
There weep; for till my Gaveston be repealed,
Assure thyself thou com'st not in my sight.

Exeunt [KING] EDWARD *and* GAVESTON.

QUEEN ISABELLA   O miserable and dis-
170   tressèd queen!
Would, when I left sweet France and was embarked,
That charming° Circes,° walking on the waves,
Had changed my shape, or at the marriage-day

The cup of Hymen° had been full of poison,
Or with those arms that twined about my neck   175
I had been stifled, and not lived to see
The king my lord thus to abandon me.
Like frantic Juno will I fill the earth
With ghastly murmur of my sighs and cries,
For never doted Jove on Ganymede°   180
So much as he on cursèd Gaveston.
But that will more exasperate his wrath;
I must entreat him, I must speak him fair,
And be a means to call home Gaveston.
And yet he'll ever dote on Gaveston,   185
And so am I for ever miserable.

Enter [LANCASTER, WARWICK, PEMBROKE,°
MORTIMER SENIOR, *and* MORTIMER JUNIOR].

LANCASTER   Look where the sister of the king of France
Sits wringing of her hands and beats her breast.

WARWICK   The king, I fear, hath ill entreated° her.

PEMBROKE   Hard is the heart that injures such a saint.   190

MORTIMER JUNIOR   I know 'tis 'long of° Gaveston she weeps.

MORTIMER SENIOR   Why? He is gone.

MORTIMER JUNIOR   Madam, how fares your grace?

QUEEN ISABELLA   Ah, Mortimer! Now breaks the king's hate forth,
And he confesseth that he loves me not.

MORTIMER JUNIOR   Cry quittance, madam, then, and love not him.   195

QUEEN ISABELLA   No, rather will I die a thousand deaths,

---

151 **affections** idle inclinations. 172 **charming** having power to enchant. **Circes** variant of Circe, the enchantress of Homer's *Odyssey*.

174 **Hymen** Greek god of marriage. 178–180 **Juno . . . Ganymede** Juno, queen of the gods, was enraged when her husband, Jove, carried off the handsome boy, Ganymede to be his cup-bearer and favorite. The story is told in Ovid's *Metamorphoses*. sd **Pembroke** Aymer de Valence, at first opposed Edward and Gaveston, but joined the king's party after a quarrel with Lancaster and Warwick. He died in 1324, while serving as the king's envoy in France. 189 **entreated** treated. 191 **'long of** because of.

And yet I love in vain; he'll ne'er love me.

LANCASTER   Fear ye not, madam; now his minion's gone,

His wanton humor will be quickly left.

200 QUEEN ISABELLA   O never, Lancaster! I am enjoined

To sue unto you all for his repeal.

This wills my lord, and this must I perform,

Or else be banished from his highness' presence.

LANCASTER   For his repeal, madam? He comes not back,

205 Unless the sea cast up his shipwrack body.

WARWICK   And to behold so sweet a sight as that,

There's none here but would run his horse to death.

MORTIMER JUNIOR   But, madam, would you have us call him home?

QUEEN ISABELLA   Ay, Mortimer, for till he be restored,

The angry king hath banished me the
210 court;

And therefore, as thou lovest and tender'st me,

Be thou my advocate unto these peers.

MORTIMER JUNIOR   What, would ye have me plead for Gaveston?

MORTIMER SENIOR   Plead for him he that will; I am resolved.

LANCASTER   And so am I, my lord. Dissuade
215 the queen.

QUEEN ISABELLA   O Lancaster, let him dissuade the king,

For 'tis against my will he should return.

WARWICK   Then speak not for him; let the peasant go.

QUEEN ISABELLA   'Tis for myself I speak, and not for him.

PEMBROKE   No speaking will prevail, and
220 therefore cease.

MORTIMER JUNIOR   Fair queen, forbear to angle for the fish

Which, being caught, strikes him that takes it dead.

I mean that vile torpedo,° Gaveston,

That now, I hope, floats on the Irish seas.

QUEEN ISABELLA   Sweet Mortimer, sit down
by me awhile,   225

And I will tell thee reasons of such weight

As thou wilt soon subscribe to his repeal.

MORTIMER JUNIOR   It is impossible, but speak your mind.

QUEEN ISABELLA   Then thus, but none shall hear it but ourselves.

[*She talks to* MORTIMER JUNIOR *apart.*]

LANCASTER   My lords, albeit the queen win Mortimer,   230

Will you be resolute and hold with me?

MORTIMER SENIOR   Not I, against my nephew.

PEMBROKE   Fear not, the queen's words cannot alter him.

WARWICK   No? Do but mark how earnestly she pleads.

LANCASTER   And see how coldly his looks make denial.   235

WARWICK   She smiles; now for my life his mind is changed.

LANCASTER   I'll rather lose his friendship, I, than grant.

MORTIMER JUNIOR   Well, of necessity it must be so.

My lords, that I abhor base Gaveston,

I hope your honors make no question,   240

And therefore, though I plead for his repeal,

'Tis not for his sake, but for our avail;

Nay for the realm's behoof, and for the king's.

LANCASTER   Fie, Mortimer, dishonor not thyself!

Can this be true, 'twas good to banish him?   245

And is this true, to call him home again?

Such reasons make white black and dark night day.

MORTIMER JUNIOR   My lord of Lancaster, mark the respect.°

LANCASTER   In no respect can contraries be true.

QUEEN ISABELLA   Yet, good my lord, hear what he can allege.   250

---

223 **torpedo** cramp-fish or electric ray.   248 **respect** consideration of a special situation.

WARWICK All that he speaks is nothing; we are resolved.

MORTIMER JUNIOR Do you not wish that Gaveston were dead?

PEMBROKE I would he were.

MORTIMER JUNIOR Why then, my lord, give me but leave to speak.

MORTIMER SENIOR But, nephew, do not
255 play the sophister.°

MORTIMER JUNIOR This which I urge is of a burning zeal
    To mend the king and do our country good.
    Know you not Gaveston hath store of gold,
    Which may in Ireland purchase him such friends
260 As he will front the mightiest of us all?
    And whereas he shall live and be beloved,
    'Tis hard for us to work his overthrow.

WARWICK Mark you but that, my lord of Lancaster.

MORTIMER JUNIOR But were he here, detested as he is,
    How easily might some base slave be sub-
265 orned
    To greet his lordship with a poniard,
    And none so much as blame the mur-
    derer,
    But rather praise him for that brave at-
    tempt
    And in the chronicle enrol his name
    For purging of the realm of such a plague.

270 PEMBROKE He saith true.

LANCASTER Ay, but how chance this was not done before?

MORTIMER JUNIOR Because, my lords, it was not thought upon.
    Nay, more, when he shall know it lies in us
    To banish him and then to call him
275 home,
    'Twill make him vail the top-flag of his pride,
    And fear to offend the meanest nobleman.

MORTIMER SENIOR But how if he do not, nephew?

MORTIMER JUNIOR Then may we with some color° rise in arms;
    For howsoever we have borne it out,   280
    'Tis treason to be up against the king;
    So shall we have the people of our side,
    Which for his father's sake lean to the king,
    But cannot brook a night-grown mush-
    rump,°
    Such a one as my lord of Cornwall is,   285
    Should bear us down of the nobility.
    And when the commons and the nobles join,
    'Tis not the king can buckler° Gaveston.
    We'll pull him from the strongest hold he hath.
    My lords, if to perform this I be slack,   290
    Think me as base a groom as Gaveston.

LANCASTER On that condition, Lancaster will grant.

WARWICK And so will Pembroke and I.

MORTIMER SENIOR   And I.

MORTIMER JUNIOR In this I count me highly gratified,
    And Mortimer will rest at your com-
    mand.   295

QUEEN ISABELLA And when this favor Isa-
    bel forgets,
    Then let her live abandoned and forlorn.
    But see, in happy time, my lord the king,
    Having brought the Earl of Cornwall on his way,
    Is new returned. This news will glad him much,   300
    Yet not so much as me. I love him more
    Than he can Gaveston; would he loved me
    But half so much, then were I treble-
    blessed!

Enter KING EDWARD, *mourning.*

KING EDWARD He's gone, and for his ab-
    sence thus I mourn.
    Did never sorrow go so near my heart   305
    As doth the want of my sweet Gaveston;

---

255 **play the sophister** use false arguments.

279 **color** pretext, excuse. 284 **mushrump** mush-room (one of many variant forms). 288 **buckler** protect (literally with a shield).

And could my crown's revenue bring him
 back,
I would freely give it to his enemies
And think I gained, having bought so dear
 a friend.
QUEEN ISABELLA Hark, how he harps upon
310 his minion.
KING EDWARD My heart is as an anvil unto
 sorrow,
Which beats upon it like the Cyclops'
 hammers
And with the noise turns up my giddy
 brain
And makes me frantic for my Gaveston.
Ah, had some bloodless Fury rose from
315 hell
And with my kingly scepter struck me
 dead,
When I was forced to leave my Gaveston.
LANCASTER *Diablo!* What passions call you
 these?
QUEEN ISABELLA My gracious lord, I come
 to bring you news.
KING EDWARD That you have parlèd with
320 your Mortimer.
QUEEN ISABELLA That Gaveston, my lord,
 shall be repealed.
KING EDWARD Repealed? The news is too
 sweet to be true.
QUEEN ISABELLA But will you love me, if
 you find it so?
KING EDWARD If it be so, what will not
 Edward do?
QUEEN ISABELLA For Gaveston, but not for
325 Isabel.
KING EDWARD For thee, fair queen, if thou
 lovest Gaveston;
I'll hang a golden tongue about thy neck,
Seeing thou hast pleaded with so good suc-
 cess.
QUEEN ISABELLA No other jewels hang
 about my neck
Than these,° my lord; nor let me have
330 more wealth
Than I may fetch from this rich treasury.
O how a kiss revives poor Isabel!
KING EDWARD Once more receive my hand,
 and let this be

330 **these** i.e., Edward's arms.

A second marriage 'twixt thyself and me.
QUEEN ISABELLA And may it prove more
 happy than the first.   335
My gentle lord, bespeak these nobles fair,
That wait attendance for a gracious look
And on their knees salute your majesty.
KING EDWARD Courageous Lancaster, em-
 brace thy king.
And, as gross vapors perish by the sun,   340
Even so let hatred with thy sovereign's
 smile.
Live thou with me as my companion.
LANCASTER This salutation overjoys my
 heart.
KING EDWARD Warwick shall be my chiefest
 counselor.
These silver hairs will more adorn my
 court   345
Than gaudy silks or rich embroidery.
Chide me, sweet Warwick, if I go astray.
WARWICK Slay me, my lord, when I offend
 your grace.
KING EDWARD In solemn triumphs and in
 public shows,
Pembroke shall bear the sword before the
 king.   350
PEMBROKE And with this sword Pembroke
 will fight for you.
KING EDWARD But wherefore walks young
 Mortimer aside?
Be thou commander of our royal fleet;
Or, if that lofty office like thee not,
I make thee here Lord Marshal of the
 realm.   355
MORTIMER JUNIOR My lord, I'll marshal so
 your enemies,
As England shall be quiet and you safe.
KING EDWARD And as for you, Lord Morti-
 mer of Chirke,°
Whose great achievements in our foreign
 war
Deserves no common place, nor mean re-
 ward,   360
Be you the general of the levied troops
That now are ready to assail the Scots.
MORTIMER SENIOR In this your grace hath
 highly honored me,

358 **Chirke** border city between Shropshire and
Wales, of which the elder Mortimer was lord.

For with my nature war doth best agree.

QUEEN ISABELLA   Now is the king of Eng-
365   land rich and strong,
Having the love of his renownèd peers.

KING EDWARD   Ay, Isabel, ne'er was my
heart so light.
Clerk of the crown, direct our warrant
forth
For Gaveston to Ireland.

[*Enter* BEAUMONT.]

Beaumont, fly
370   As fast as Iris or Jove's Mercury.°

BEAUMONT   It shall be done, my gracious
lord.

[*Exit.*]

KING EDWARD   Lord Mortimer, we leave
you to your charge.
Now let us in and feast it royally.
Against° our friend the Earl of Cornwall
comes,
375   We'll have a general tilt and tournament,
And then his marriage shall be solem-
nized;
For wot you not that I have made him
sure
Unto our cousin, the Earl of Gloucester's
heir?°

LANCASTER   Such news we hear, my lord.

KING EDWARD   That day, if not for him, yet
380   for my sake,
Who in the triumph will be challenger,
Spare for no cost; we will requite your
love.

WARWICK   In this or ought your highness
shall command us.

KING EDWARD   Thanks, gentle Warwick.
Come, let's in and revel.

Exeunt all except the MORTIMERS.

MORTIMER SENIOR   Nephew, I must to Scot-
385   land; thou stayest here.

Leave now to oppose thyself against the
king.
Thou seest by nature he is mild and calm,
And, seeing his mind so dotes on Gaves-
ton,
Let him without controlment have his
will.
The mightiest kings have had their min-
ions.   390
Great Alexander loved Hephaestion;°
The conquering Hercules for Hylas°
wept,
And for Patroclus° stern Achilles
drooped.
And not kings only, but the wisest men:
The Roman Tully° loved Octavius,   395
Grave Socrates, wild Alcibiades.°
Then let his grace, whose youth is flexible
And promiseth as much as we can wish,
Freely enjoy that vain, light-headed earl,
For riper years will wean him from such
toys.°   400

MORTIMER JUNIOR   Uncle, his wanton hu-
mor grieves not me;
But this I scorn, that one so basely born
Should by his sovereign's favor grow so
pert
And riot it with the treasure of the
realm.
While soldiers mutiny for want of pay,   405
He wears a lord's revenue on his back,
And, Midas-like,° he jets° it in the court
With base outlandish cullions° at his
heels,
Whose proud fantastic liveries make such
show,

370 **Iris . . . Mercury** Iris was the messenger of
Juno, as Mercury was that of Jove. 374 **Against** in
preparation for the time when. **Earl of Cornwall**
i.e., Gaveston. 378 **Earl . . . heir** Gilbert de Clare,
eighth Earl of Gloucester, was married to King Edward's sister. Their daughter, Margaret, became
the wife of Gaveston.

391 **Hephaestion** the close friend and companion
of Alexander the Great. 392 **Hylas** See note I.i. 144.
393 **Patroclus** the friend of Achilles, whose slaying
by Hector finally aroused Achilles to action and
brought an end to the Trojan war. 395 **Tully** Marcus Tullius Cicero, the great Roman orator and
statesman. He had no relation to the Emperor
Augustus Caesar (Octavius) comparable to that of
Gaveston to Edward. 396 **Alcibiades** a somewhat
rakish young man of noble birth and good looks
befriended by the Greek philosopher, Socrates.
400 **toys** foolish pastimes. 407 **Midas-like** like
Midas, the mythical king endowed by Dionysius
with the power to turn all he touched to gold. **jets
it** struts. 408 **outlandish cullions** foreign scoundrels.

410 As if that Proteus,° god of shapes, ap-
      peared.
    I have not seen a dapper Jack so brisk.
    He wears a short Italian hooded cloak,
    Larded with pearl, and in his Tuscan
      cap
    A jewel of more value than the crown.
415 While others walk below, the king and he
    From out a window laugh at such as we,
    And flout our train, and jest at our attire.
    Uncle, 'tis this that makes me impatient.
    MORTIMER SENIOR But, nephew, now you
      see the king is changed.
    MORTIMER JUNIOR Then so am I, and live
420   to do him service.
    But whiles I have a sword, a hand, a
      heart,
    I will not yield to any such upstart.
    You know my mind; come, uncle, let's
      away.

    Exeunt.

Act Two

SCENE ONE

Enter SPENCER [JUNIOR]° *and* BALDOCK.°

BALDOCK Spencer,
    Seeing that our lord th' Earl of Glouces-
      ter's dead,
    Which of the nobles dost thou mean to
      serve?
SPENCER JUNIOR Not Mortimer, nor any
    of his side,
5   Because the king and he are enemies.
    Baldock, learn this of me: a factious lord
    Shall hardly do himself good, much less
      us,
    But he that hath the favor of a king

May with one word advance us while we
    live.
The liberal Earl of Cornwall is the man 10
On whose good fortune Spencer's hope
    depends.
BALDOCK What, mean you then to be his
    follower?
SPENCER JUNIOR No, his companion, for
    he loves me well
And would have once preferred me to
    the king.
BALDOCK But he is banished; there's small
    hope of him. 15
SPENCER JUNIOR Ay, for a while; but,
    Baldock, mark the end.
A friend of mine told me in secrecy
That he's repealed and sent for back
    again,
And even now a post came from the
    court
With letters to our lady from the king, 20
And as she read she smiled, which makes
    me think
It is about her lover Gaveston.
BALDOCK 'Tis like enough, for since he
    was exiled
She neither walks abroad nor comes in
    sight.
But I had thought the match had been
    broke off 25
And that his banishment had changed
    her mind.
SPENCER JUNIOR Our lady's first love is
    not wavering;
My life for thine she will have Gaveston.
BALDOCK Then hope I by her means to be
    preferred,
Having read unto her since she was a 30
    child.
SPENCER JUNIOR Then, Baldock, you must
    cast the scholar off
And learn to court it like a gentleman.
'Tis not a black coat° and a little band,
A velvet-caped cloak, faced before with
    serge,
And smelling to a nosegay all the day, 35
Or holding of a napkin in your hand,

---

410 **Proteus** a sea deity who changed his shape
whenever men tried to restrain him.
II.i. sd **Spencer Junior** Hugh le Despenser, who
married the elder sister of Gaveston's wife, daughter
of the Earl of Gloucester. Always a strong partisan
of King Edward, he was executed at Hereford in
November, 1326, one month after the execution of
his father. **Baldock** Robert of Baldock, keeper of
the king's privy seal, fled with King Edward, was
captured in November, 1326, and died the following year.

33 **black coat** the traditional garb of the scholar.

Or saying a long grace at a table's end,
Or making low legs to a nobleman,
Or looking downward with your eyelids
close,
And saying, 'Truly, an't may please your
40   honor,'
Can get you any favor with great men;
You must be proud, bold, pleasant, reso-
lute,
And now and then stab, as occasion
serves.

BALDOCK Spencer, thou knowest I hate
such formal toys
45 And use them but of mere hypocrisy.
Mine old lord whiles he lived was so
precise
That he would take exceptions at my
buttons,
And being like pin's heads, blame me for
the bigness;
Which made me curate-like in mine attire,
50 Though inwardly licentious enough
And apt for any kind of villainy.
I am none of these common pedants, I,
That cannot speak without *propterea
quod.*

SPENCER JUNIOR But one of those that
saith *quandoquidem*°
55 And hath a special gift to form a verb.°

BALDOCK Leave off this jesting, here my
lady comes.

Enter the KING'S NIECE.

NIECE The grief for his exile was not so
much
As is the joy of his returning home.
This letter came from my sweet Gaveston.
What needst thou, love, thus to excuse
60 thyself?
I know thou couldst not come and visit
me.
'I will not long be from thee, though I
die.' [*She reads.*]
This argues the entire love of my lord.

'When I forsake thee, death seize on my
heart.' [*She reads.*]
But rest thee here where Gaveston shall
sleep.   65

[*She places the letter in her bosom.*]

Now to the letter of my lord the king.
He wills me to repair unto the court
And meet my Gaveston. Why do I stay,
Seeing that he talks thus of my marriage
day?
Who's there? Baldock!   70
See that my coach° be ready; I must
hence.

BALDOCK It shall be done, madam.

NIECE And meet me at the park-pale
presently.

Exit [BALDOCK].

Spencer, stay you and bear me company,
For I have joyful news to tell thee of.   75
My lord of Cornwall is a-coming over
And will be at the court as soon as we.

SPENCER JUNIOR I knew the king would
have him home again.

NIECE If all things sort out as I hope they
will,
Thy service, Spencer, shall be thought
upon.   80

SPENCER JUNIOR I humbly thank your
ladyship.

NIECE Come, lead the way; I long till I
am there.

[*Exeunt.*]

SCENE TWO

Enter [KING] EDWARD, QUEEN [ISABELLA],
LANCASTER, MORTIMER [JUNIOR], WAR-
WICK, PEMBROKE, KENT [*and*] ATTENDANTS.

KING EDWARD The wind is good; I wonder
why he stays;
I fear me he is wracked° upon the sea.

53–54 **propterea quod … quandoquidem** Both
are terms meaning 'because' and used in formal
rhetoric. 55 **form a verb** use language eloquently.

71 **coach** an anachronism, since coaches were not
introduced into England until the middle of the
sixteenth century. II.ii. 2 **wracked** shipwrecked.

QUEEN ISABELLA Look, Lancaster, how passionate he is,
And still his mind runs on his minion.
5 LANCASTER My lord——
KING EDWARD How now! What news? Is Gaveston arrived?
MORTIMER JUNIOR Nothing but Gaveston! What means your grace?
You have matters of more weight to think upon;
The king of France sets foot in Normandy.
KING EDWARD A trifle! We'll expel him
10   when we please.
But tell me, Mortimer, what's thy device°
Against the stately triumph we decreed?
MORTIMER JUNIOR A homely one, my lord, not worth the telling.
KING EDWARD Prithee let me know it.
MORTIMER JUNIOR But seeing you are so
15   desirous, thus it is:
A lofty cedar tree, fair flourishing,
On whose top-branches kingly eagles perch,
And by the bark a canker° creeps me up
And gets unto the highest bough of all;
20   The motto, *Æque tandem*.°
KING EDWARD And what is yours, my lord of Lancaster?
LANCASTER My lord, mine's more obscure than Mortimer's.
Pliny° reports there is a flying fish
Which all the other fishes deadly hate,
And therefore, being pursued, it takes the
25   air.
No sooner is it up, but there's a fowl
That seizeth it; this fish, my lord, I bear;
The motto this: *Undique mors est*.°
KING EDWARD Proud Mortimer! Ungentle Lancaster!

Is this the love you bear your sovereign? 30
Is this the fruit your reconcilement bears?
Can you in words make show of amity,
And in your shields display your rancorous minds?
What call you this but private libelling
Against the Earl of Cornwall and my brother? 35
QUEEN ISABELLA Sweet husband, be content; they all love you.
KING EDWARD They love me not that hate my Gaveston.
I am that cedar, shake me not too much;
And you the eagles; soar ye ne'er so high,
I have the jesses° that will pull you down; 40
And *Æque tandem* shall that canker cry
Unto the proudest peer of Britainy.
Though thou compar'st him to a flying fish,
And threatenest death whether he rise or fall,
'Tis not the hugest monster of the sea, 45
Nor foulest harpy,° that shall swallow him.
MORTIMER JUNIOR If in his absence thus he favors him,
What will he do whenas he shall be present?
LANCASTER That shall we see; look where his lordship comes.

Enter GAVESTON.

KING EDWARD My Gaveston! 50
Welcome to Tynemouth! Welcome to thy friend!
Thy absence made me droop and pine away;
For, as the lovers of fair Danaë,°
When she was locked up in a brazen tower,
Desired her more and waxed outrageous, 55
So did it sure with me. And now thy sight

---

11 **device** a painting on a shield, accompanied by a motto. 18 **canker** canker-worm, a striped green caterpillar which destroys plants. 20 **Æque tandem** equally at last (the sense being that Gaveston, the canker, will finally reach the top of the tree and be equal with the eagle, Edward). 23 **Pliny** Gaius Plinius Secundus, or Pliny the Elder, Roman author of the *Naturalis Historia*. Actually there is no such account in Pliny, although there is a description similar to Marlowe's in Sir John Hawkins' account of his second voyage to Guiana, published in 1565. 28 **Undique mors est** Death is on all sides.

40 **jesses** short straps, usually of leather, tied to the legs of trained hawks and used to control them. 46 **harpy** legendary bird with the head of a woman. 53 **Danaë** legendary Greek heroine who, although locked up in a tower by her father, was wooed by Zeus in the form of a shower of gold. Greek mythology does not record that she had other lovers.

Is sweeter far than was thy parting hence
Bitter and irksome to my sobbing heart.

GAVESTON   Sweet lord and king, your
speech preventeth mine,

60   Yet have I words left to express my joy.
The shepherd nipped with biting winter's
rage
Frolics not more to see the painted°
spring,
Than I do to behold your majesty.

KING EDWARD   Will none of you salute my
Gaveston?

LANCASTER   Salute him? Yes. Welcome

65   Lord Chamberlain.

MORTIMER JUNIOR   Welcome is the good
Earl of Cornwall.

WARWICK   Welcome, Lord Governor of the
Isle of Man.

PEMBROKE   Welcome, Master Secretary.

KENT   Brother, do you hear them?

KING EDWARD   Still will these earls and bar-

70   ons use me thus?

GAVESTON   My lord, I cannot brook these
injuries.

QUEEN ISABELLA   Ay me, poor soul, when
these begin to jar.

[*Aside.*]

KING EDWARD   Return it to their throats;
I'll be thy warrant.

GAVESTON   Base, leaden earls, that glory in
your birth,

75   Go sit at home and eat your tenants' beef,
And come not here to scoff at Gaveston,
Whose mounting thoughts did never creep
so low
As to bestow a look on such as you.

LANCASTER   Yet I disdain not to do this for
you.

[*He draws his sword.*]

KING EDWARD   Treason, treason! Where's

80   the traitor?

PEMBROKE   Here! Here!

KING EDWARD   Convey hence Gaveston;
they'll murder him.

GAVESTON   The life of thee shall salve this
foul disgrace.

MORTIMER JUNIOR   Villain, thy life unless
I miss mine aim.

[*He wounds* GAVESTON.]

QUEEN ISABELLA   Ah, furious Mortimer,
what hast thou done?   85

MORTIMER JUNIOR   No more than I would
answer, were he slain.

[*Exit* GAVESTON *with* ATTENDANTS.]

KING EDWARD   Yes, more than thou canst
answer, though he live.
Dear shall you both aby° this riotous
deed.
Out of my presence; come not near the
court.

MORTIMER JUNIOR   I'll not be barred the
court for Gaveston.   90

LANCASTER   We'll hale him by the ears
unto the block.

KING EDWARD   Look to your own heads; his
is sure enough.

WARWICK   Look to your own crown, if you
back him thus.

KENT   Warwick, these words do ill beseem
thy years.

KING EDWARD   Nay, all of them conspire to
cross me thus,   95
But if I live, I'll tread upon their heads
That think with high looks thus to tread
me down.
Come, Edmund, let's away and levy men;
'Tis war that must abate these barons'
pride.

Exit KING [EDWARD *with* QUEEN ISABELLA
and KENT].

WARWICK   Let's to our castles, for the king
is moved.   100

MORTIMER JUNIOR   Moved may he be, and
perish in his wrath!

LANCASTER   Cousin, it is no dealing with
him now.
He means to make us stoop by force of
arms,
And therefore let us jointly here protest°
To prosecute that Gaveston to the death. 105

---

62 **painted** adorned with flowers.

88 **aby** pay for. 104 **protest** vow.

MORTIMER JUNIOR By heaven, the abject villain shall not live.

WARWICK I'll have his blood or die in seeking it.

PEMBROKE The like oath Pembroke takes.

LANCASTER And so doth Lancaster.
Now send our heralds to defy° the king,
And make the people swear to put him
110 down.

Enter a MESSENGER.

MORTIMER JUNIOR Letters? From whence?

MESSENGER From Scotland, my lord.

[*He gives letters to* MORTIMER, *who reads.*]

LANCASTER Why, how now, cousin, how fares all our friends?

MORTIMER JUNIOR My uncle's taken prisoner by the Scots.°

LANCASTER We'll have him ransomed, man; be of good cheer.

MORTIMER JUNIOR They rate his ransom
115 at five thousand pound.
Who should defray the money but the king,
Seeing he is taken prisoner in his wars?
I'll to the king.

LANCASTER Do, cousin, and I'll bear thee company.

WARWICK Meantime, my lord of Pem-
120 broke and myself
Will to Newcastle here and gather head.°

MORTIMER JUNIOR About it then, and we will follow you.

LANCASTER Be resolute and full of secrecy.

WARWICK I warrant you.

[*Exeunt all but* MORTIMER JUNIOR *and* LANCASTER.]

MORTIMER JUNIOR Cousin, and if he will
125 not ransom him,
I'll thunder such a peal into his ears
As never subject did unto his king.

LANCASTER Content, I'll bear my part.
Holla! Who's there?

[*Enter a* GUARD.]

MORTIMER JUNIOR Ay, marry, such a guard as this doth well.

LANCASTER Lead on the way.   130

GUARD Whither will your lordships?

MORTIMER JUNIOR Whither else but to the king?

GUARD His highness is disposed to be alone.

LANCASTER Why, so he may, but we will speak to him.

GUARD You may not in, my lord.   135

MORTIMER JUNIOR May we not?

[*Enter* KING EDWARD *and* KENT.]

KING EDWARD How now! What noise is this?
Who have we there? Is't you?
[*Going.*]

MORTIMER JUNIOR Nay, stay, my lord, I come to bring you news;
Mine uncle's taken prisoner by the Scots. 140

KING EDWARD Then ransom him.

LANCASTER 'Twas in your wars; you should ransom him.

MORTIMER JUNIOR And you shall ransom him, or else——

KENT What, Mortimer! You will not threaten him?

KING EDWARD Quiet yourself; you shall have the broad seal   145
To gather for him throughout the realm.°

LANCASTER Your minion Gaveston hath taught you this.

MORTIMER JUNIOR My lord, the family of the Mortimers
Are not so poor, but, would they sell their land,
Would levy men enough to anger you.   150
We never beg, but use such prayers as these.
[*He grasps his sword.*]

KING EDWARD Shall I still be haunted° thus?

---

109 **defy** renounce allegiance to. 113 **uncle's . . . Scots** There is no historical basis for this episode. 121 **gather head** raise an army.

145–146 **broad seal . . . realm** royal license to collect alms (as a beggar) for him. The king is being contemptuous and insulting. 152 **haunted** pursued.

MORTIMER JUNIOR Nay, now you are here alone, I'll speak my mind.

LANCASTER And so will I, and then, my lord, farewell.

MORTIMER JUNIOR The idle triumphs,
155 masks, lascivious shows,
And prodigal gifts bestowed on Gaveston,
Have drawn thy treasure dry and made thee weak,
The murmuring commons overstretchèd hath.

LANCASTER Look for rebellion; look to be deposed.
160 Thy garrisons are beaten out of France,
And, lame and poor, lie groaning at the gates.
The wild O'Neil,° with swarms of Irish kerns,°
Lives uncontrolled within the English pale.
Unto the walls of York the Scots made road
165 And unresisted drave away rich spoils.

MORTIMER JUNIOR The haughty Dane commands the narrow seas,
While in the harbor ride thy ships unrigged.

LANCASTER What foreign prince sends thee ambassadors?

MORTIMER JUNIOR Who loves thee, but a sort of flatterers?

LANCASTER Thy gentle queen, sole sister to
170 Valois,°
Complains that thou hast left her all forlorn.

MORTIMER JUNIOR Thy court is naked, being bereft of those
That makes a king seem glorious to the world;
I mean the peers, whom thou shouldst dearly love.
175 Libels are cast again thee in the street,
Ballads and rhymes made of thy overthrow.

LANCASTER The Northern borderers, seeing their houses burnt,
Their wives and children slain, run up and down,
Cursing the name of thee and Gaveston.

MORTIMER JUNIOR When wert thou in the field with banner spread? 180
But once, and then thy soldiers marched like players,
With garish robes, not armor, and thyself,
Bedaubed with gold, rode laughing at the rest,
Nodding and shaking of thy spangled crest,
Where women's favors hung like labels° down. 185

LANCASTER And thereof came it that the fleering° Scots,
To England's high disgrace, have made this jig:°

Maids of England, sore may you mourn,
For your lemans° you have lost at Bannocksbourn,°
With a heave and a ho! 190
What weeneth the King of England,
So soon to have won Scotland?
With a rombelow!°

MORTIMER JUNIOR Wigmore° shall fly° to set my uncle free.

LANCASTER And when 'tis gone, our swords shall purchase more. 195
If ye be moved, revenge it as you can.
Look next to see us with our ensigns spread.

[*Exit with* MORTIMER JUNIOR.]

KING EDWARD My swelling heart for very anger breaks.
How oft have I been baited by these peers,
And dare not be revenged, for their power is great! 200

185 **labels** pieces of parchment used to affix seals to documents. 186 **fleering** jeering. 187 **jig** mocking song. 189 **lemans** sweethearts. **Bannocksbourn** battle against the Scots, fought on June 21, 1314, in which the English suffered a crushing defeat. 193 **rombelow** a meaningless term used in refrains. 194 **Wigmore** Mortimer Junior's estate. **shall fly** i.e., will be sold.

162 **O'Neil** Shane O'Neil was an Irish leader of Marlowe's own day. **kerns** foot-soldiers. 170 **Valois** Queen Isabella's brothers actually were not of the house of Valois, although her cousin, Philip of Valois, did eventually become king of France.

Yet, shall the crowing of these cockerels°
Affright a lion? Edward, unfold thy paws,
And let their lives' blood slake thy fury's
    hunger.
If I be cruel and grow tyrannous,
Now let them thank themselves and rue
205 too late.
KENT   My lord, I see your love to Gaveston
Will be the ruin of the realm and you,
For now the wrathful nobles threaten
    wars,
And therefore, brother, banish him for
    ever.
KING EDWARD   Art thou an enemy to my
210 Gaveston?
KENT   Ay, and it grieves me that I favored
    him.
KING EDWARD   Traitor, begone! Whine
    thou with Mortimer.
KENT   So will I, rather than with Gaves-
    ton.
KING EDWARD   Out of my sight, and trouble
    me no more.
KENT   No marvel though thou scorn thy
215 noble peers,
When I thy brother am rejected thus.
KING EDWARD   Away!

    Exit [KENT].

Poor Gaveston, that hast no friend but
    me,
Do what they can, we'll live in Tyne-
    mouth here,
220 And so I walk with him about the walls,
What care I though the earls begirt us
    round?
Here comes she that's cause of all these
    jars.

    Enter QUEEN [ISABELLA, *with the* KING'S
    NIECE, *two*] LADIES, [GAVESTON,] BALDOCK,
    and SPENCER [JUNIOR].

QUEEN ISABELLA   My lord, 'tis thought the
    earls are up in arms.
KING EDWARD   Ay, and 'tis likewise thought
    you favor 'em.
QUEEN ISABELLA   Thus do you still suspect
225 me without cause?

201 **cockerels** young roosters.

NIECE   Sweet uncle, speak more kindly to
    the queen.
GAVESTON   My lord, dissemble with her;
    speak her fair.

    [*Aside to* KING EDWARD.]

KING EDWARD   Pardon me, sweet, I forgot
    myself.
QUEEN ISABELLA   Your pardon is quickly
    got of Isabel.
KING EDWARD   The younger Mortimer is
    grown so brave   230
That to my face he threatens civil wars.
GAVESTON   Why do you not commit him
    to the Tower?
KING EDWARD   I dare not, for the people
    love him well.
GAVESTON   Why, then we'll have him
    privily made away.
KING EDWARD   Would Lancaster and he
    had both caroused   235
A bowl of poison to each other's health.
But let them go, and tell me what are
    these.
NIECE   Two of my father's servants whilst
    he lived.
May't please your grace to entertain them
    now?
KING EDWARD   Tell me, where wast thou
    born? What is thine arms?   240
BALDOCK   My name is Baldock, and my
    gentry
I fetched from Oxford, not from heraldry.
KING EDWARD   The fitter art thou, Baldock,
    for my turn.
Wait on me, and I'll see thou shalt not
    want.
BALDOCK   I humbly thank your majesty.   245
KING EDWARD   Knowest thou him, Gaves-
    ton?
GAVESTON   Ay, my lord;
His name is Spencer; he is well allied.
For my sake, let him wait upon your
    grace.
Scarce shall you find a man of more desert.
KING EDWARD   Then, Spencer, wait upon
    me; for his sake   250
I'll grace thee with a higher style ere long.
SPENCER JUNIOR   No greater titles happen
    unto me

Than to be favored of your majesty.

KING EDWARD   Cousin, this day shall be your marriage feast.

And, Gaveston, think that I love thee
255 well,

To wed thee to our niece, the only heir

Unto the Earl of Gloucester late deceased.

GAVESTON   I know, my lord, many will stomach° me,

But I respect neither their love nor hate.

KING EDWARD   The headstrong barons shall
260 not limit me;

He that I list to favor shall be great.

Come, let's away; and when the marriage ends,

Have at the rebels and their 'complices.

Exeunt.

SCENE THREE

Enter LANCASTER, MORTIMER [JUNIOR,]
WARWICK, PEMBROKE, KENT [*and others*].

KENT   My lords, of love to this our native land

I come to join with you and leave the king,

And in your quarrel and the realm's be-hoof

Will be the first that shall adventure life.

LANCASTER   I fear me you are sent of
5 policy,°

To undermine us with a show of love.

WARWICK   He is your brother; therefore have we cause

To cast° the worst and doubt of your re-volt.

KENT   Mine honor shall be hostage of my truth;

10 If that will not suffice, farewell, my lords.

MORTIMER JUNIOR   Stay, Edmund; never was Plantagenet

False of his word, and therefore trust we thee.

PEMBROKE   But what's the reason you should leave him now?

KENT   I have informed the Earl of Lan-caster.

LANCASTER   And it sufficeth. Now, my lords, know this,   15

That Gaveston is secretly arrived

And here in Tynemouth frolics with the king.

Let us with these our followers scale the walls

And suddenly surprise them unawares.

MORTIMER JUNIOR   I'll give the onset.

WARWICK   And I'll follow thee.   20

MORTIMER JUNIOR   This tottered° ensign of my ancestors,

Which swept the desert shore of that Dead Sea

Whereof we got the name of Mortimer,

Will I advance upon these castle walls.

Drums, strike alarum, raise them from their sport,   25

And ring aloud the knell of Gaveston.

LANCASTER   None be so hardy as to touch the king,

But neither spare you Gaveston nor his friends.

Exeunt.

SCENE FOUR

Enter KING [EDWARD] *and* SPENCER [JUNIOR].

KING EDWARD   O tell me, Spencer, where is Gaveston?

SPENCER JUNIOR   I fear me he is slain, my gracious lord.

KING EDWARD   No, here he comes. Now let them spoil and kill.

[*Enter*] *to them* [QUEEN ISABELLA, *the* KING'S NIECE,] GAVESTON, [*and* OTHERS].

Fly, fly, my lords, the earls have got the hold;

Take shipping and away to Scarborough;   5

258 **stomach** take offense at.
II.iii. 5 **policy** political deception. 8 **cast** anticipate.

21 **tottered** tattered.

84

Spencer and I will post away by land.

GAVESTON   O stay, my lord, they will not
injure you.

KING EDWARD   I will not trust them. Gaveston, away.

GAVESTON   Farewell, my lord.

10   KING EDWARD   Lady, farewell.

NIECE   Farewell, sweet uncle, till we meet
again.

KING EDWARD   Farewell, sweet Gaveston,
and farewell, niece.

QUEEN ISABELLA   No farewell to poor
Isabel thy queen?

KING EDWARD   Yes, yes, for Mortimer, your
lover's sake.

QUEEN ISABELLA   Heavens can witness I
15   love none but you.

Exeunt [all but QUEEN] ISABELLA.

From my embracements thus he breaks
away.

O that mine arms could close this isle
about,

That I might pull him to me where I
would,

Or that these tears that drizzle from mine
eyes

20   Had power to mollify his stony heart,

That when I had him we might never
part.

Enter [LANCASTER, WARWICK, MORTIMER
JUNIOR, *and* OTHERS]. *Alarums [within].*

LANCASTER   I wonder how he 'scaped?

MORTIMER JUNIOR   Who's this? The
queen!

QUEEN ISABELLA   Ay, Mortimer, the miserable queen,

Whose pining heart her inward sighs have
blasted,

And body with continual mourning
25   wasted.

These hands are tired with haling of my
lord

From Gaveston, from wicked Gaveston,

And all in vain, for when I speak him fair,

He turns away and smiles upon his
minion.

MORTIMER JUNIOR   Cease to lament, and
30   tell us where's the king?

QUEEN ISABELLA   What would you with the
king? Is't him you seek?

LANCASTER   No madam, but that cursèd
Gaveston.

Far be it from the thought of Lancaster

To offer violence to his sovereign.

We would but rid the realm of Gaveston.   *35*

Tell us where he remains, and he shall
die.

QUEEN ISABELLA   He's gone by water unto
Scarborough;

Pursue him quickly, and he cannot 'scape;

The king hath left him, and his train is
small.

WARWICK   Forslow° no time. Sweet Lancaster, let's march.   *40*

MORTIMER JUNIOR   How comes it that the
king and he is parted?

QUEEN ISABELLA   That this your army, going several ways,

Might be of lesser force, and with the
power

That he intendeth persently to raise,

Be easily suppressed; and therefore be
gone.   *45*

MORTIMER JUNIOR   Here in the river rides
a Flemish hoy;°

Let's all aboard and follow him amain.

LANCASTER   The wind that bears him
hence will fill our sails.

Come, come aboard; 'tis but an hour's
sailing.

MORTIMER JUNIOR   Madam, stay you
within this castle here.   *50*

QUEEN ISABELLA   No, Mortimer, I'll to my
lord the king.

MORTIMER JUNIOR   Nay, rather sail with us
to Scarborough.

QUEEN ISABELLA   You know the king is so
suspicious,

As if he hear I have but talked with you,

Mine honor will be called in question;   *55*

And therefore, gentle Mortimer, be gone.

MORTIMER JUNIOR   Madam, I cannot stay
to answer you,

But think of Mortimer as he deserves.

II.iv.   40 **Forslow** waste.   46 **Flemish hoy** a small
fishing vessel used in the North Sea.

[*Exeunt all but* QUEEN ISABELLA.]

QUEEN ISABELLA   So well hast thou de-
    served, sweet Mortimer,
60   As Isabel could live with thee forever.
    In vain I look for love at Edward's hand,
    Whose eyes are fixed on none but Gaves-
        ton;
    Yet once more I'll importune him with
        prayers.
    If he be strange and not regard my words,
65   My son and I will over into France
    And to the king my brother there com-
        plain
    How Gaveston hath robbed me of his love.
    But yet I hope my sorrows will have end,
    And Gaveston this blessèd day be slain.

    Exit.

    SCENE FIVE

    Enter GAVESTON, *pursued.*

GAVESTON   Yet, lusty lords, I have escaped
    your hands,
    Your threats, your 'larums,° and your hot
        pursuits;
    And though divorcèd from King Edward's
        eyes,
    Yet liveth Pierce of Gaveston unsurprised,
    Breathing, in hope—*malgrado*° all your
5   beards,
    That muster rebels thus against your
        king—
    To see his royal sovereign once again.

    Enter [WARWICK, LANCASTER, PEMBROKE,
    MORTIMER JUNIOR, SOLDIERS, JAMES, *and
    other* ATTENDANTS *of* PEMBROKE].

WARWICK   Upon him, soldiers; take away
    his weapons.
MORTIMER JUNIOR   Thou proud disturber
    of thy country's peace,
    Corrupter of thy king, cause of these
10   broils,
    Base flatterer, yield! And were it not for
        shame,

Shame and dishonor to a soldier's name,
    Upon my weapon's point here shouldst
        thou fall
    And welter in thy gore.
LANCASTER   Monster of men,
    That, like the Greekish strumpet,°
        trained° to arms   15
    And bloody wars so many valiant knights,
    Look for no other fortune, wretch, than
        death.
    King Edward is not here to buckler° thee.
WARWICK   Lancaster, why talk'st thou to
    the slave?
    Go, soldiers, take him hence, for, by my
        sword,   20
    His head shall off. Gaveston, short warn-
        ing
    Shall serve thy turn. It is our country's
        cause
    That here severely we will execute
    Upon thy person. Hang him at a bough.
GAVESTON   My lord——   25
WARWICK   Soldiers, have him away.
    But for thou wert the favorite of a king,
    Thou shalt have so much honor° at our
        hands.
GAVESTON   I thank you all, my lords. Then
    I perceive
    That heading is one, and hanging is the
        other,   30
    And death is all.

    Enter EARL OF ARUNDEL.°

LANCASTER   How now, my lord of
    Arundel?
ARUNDEL   My lords, King Edward greets
    you all by me.
WARWICK   Arundel, say your message.
ARUNDEL   His majesty,
    Hearing that you had taken Gaveston,   35
    Entreateth you by me, yet but he may
    See him before he dies; for why,° he says,

---

15 **Greekish strumpet** Helen of Troy. **trained** enticed. 18 **buckler** See note I.iv. 288. 28 **so much
honor** Gentlemen were beheaded, hanging being
reserved for common thieves. sd **Arundel** Edmund
Fitzalan, Earl of Arundel, at first opposed King
Edward, but later joined the king's part and was
executed by Mortimer in November, 1326. 37 **for
why** because.

II.v. 2 **'larums** alarms. 5 **malgrado** in spite of.

And sends you word, he knows that die he
   shall;
And if you gratify his grace so far,
40 He will be mindful of the courtesy.
WARWICK How now?
GAVESTON Renownèd Edward, how thy
   name
Revives poor Gaveston.
WARWICK   No, it needeth not.
Arundel, we will gratify the king
In other matters; he must pardon us in
   this.
45 Soldiers, away with him.
GAVESTON Why, my lord of Warwick,
Will not these delays beget my hopes?
I know it, lords, it is this life you aim at;
Yet grant King Edward this.
MORTIMER JUNIOR   Shalt thou appoint
What we shall grant? Soldiers, away with
50 him.
Thus we'll gratify the king;
We'll send his head by thee; let him be-
   stow
His tears on that, for that is all he gets
Of Gaveston, or else his senseless trunk.
LANCASTER Not so, my lord, lest he bestow
55 more cost
In burying him than he hath ever earned.
ARUNDEL My lords, it is his majesty's re-
   quest,
And in the honor of a king he swears,
He will but talk with him and send him
   back.
WARWICK When, can you tell? Arundel,
60 no; we wot
He that the care of realm remits°
And drives his nobles to these exigents
For Gaveston, will, if he sees him once,
Violate any promise to possess him.
ARUNDEL Then if you will not trust his
65 grace in keep,
My lords, I will be pledge for his return.
MORTIMER JUNIOR It is honorable in thee
   to offer this,
But for we know thou art a noble gentle-
   man,
We will not wrong thee so, to make away
70 A true man for a thief.

61 **remits** abandons.

GAVESTON How mean'st thou, Mortimer?
   That is over-base.
MORTIMER JUNIOR Away, base groom, rob-
   ber of king's renown.
Question with thy companions and thy
   mates.
PEMBROKE My lord Mortimer, and you,
   my lords, each one,
To gratify the king's request therein,   75
Touching the sending of this Gaveston,
Because his majesty so earnestly
Desires to see the man before his death,
I will upon mine honor undertake
To carry him and bring him back again; 80
Provided this, that you my lord of Arun-
   del
Will join with me.
WARWICK   Pembroke, what wilt thou do?
Cause yet more bloodshed? Is it not
   enough
That we have taken him, but must we now
Leave him on 'had I wist,' and let him
   go?   85
PEMBROKE My lords, I will not over-woo
   your honors,
But if you dare trust Pembroke with the
   prisoner,
Upon mine oath, I will return him back.
ARUNDEL My lord of Lancaster, what say
   you in this?
LANCASTER Why, I say, let him go on
   Pembroke's word.   90
PEMBROKE And you, Lord Mortimer?
MORTIMER JUNIOR How say you, my lord
   of Warwick?
WARWICK Nay, do your pleasures; I know
   how 'twill prove.
PEMBROKE Then give him me.
GAVESTON   Sweet sovereign, yet I come
To see thee ere I die.
WARWICK   Yet not perhaps,   95
If Warwick's wit and policy prevail.
   [*Aside.*]
MORTIMER JUNIOR My lord of Pembroke,
   we deliver him you;
Return him on your honor. Sound, away!

Exeunt [*all except*] PEMBROKE, [ARUNDEL,]
GAVESTON, [JAMES, *and other* ATTENDANTS
of PEMBROKE].

PEMBROKE   My lord, you shall go with me.
100   My house is not far hence, out of the way
A little, but our men shall go along.
We that have pretty wenches to our wives,
Sir, must not come so near and balk their lips.
ARUNDEL   'Tis very kindly spoke, my lord of Pembroke.
105   Your honor hath an adamant° of power
To draw a prince.
PEMBROKE   So, my lord. Come hither, James.
I do commit this Gaveston to thee.
Be thou this night his keeper; in the morning
We will discharge thee of thy charge. Be gone.
GAVESTON   Unhappy Gaveston, whither
110   goest thou now?

Exit [PEMBROKE *with* ATTENDANTS].

HORSE-BOY   My lord, we'll quickly be at Cobham.

Exeunt.

Act Three

SCENE ONE

Enter GAVESTON *mourning,* [JAMES, *and others of*] *the Earl of Pembroke's Men.*

GAVESTON   O treacherous Warwick, thus to wrong thy friend.
JAMES   I see it is your life these arms pursue.
GAVESTON   Weaponless must I fall, and die in bands?°
O, must this day be period of my life?
5   Center of all my bliss!° And ye be men,
Speed to the king.

Enter WARWICK *and his company* [*of Soldiers*].

WARWICK   My lord of Pembroke's men,

---

105 **adamant** magnet.
III.i. 3 **bands** bondage. 5 **Center . . . bliss** i.e., the day of his reunion with the king, which was to be the firm center of his happiness, as the middle of the earth was considered to be the center of the universe.

Strive no longer; I will have that Gaveston.
JAMES   Your lordship doth dishonor to yourself,
And wrong our lord, your honorable friend.
WARWICK   No, James, it is my country's cause I follow.   10
Go, take the villain; soldiers, come away.
We'll make quick work. Commend me to your master,
My friend, and tell him that I watched it well.
Come, let thy shadow° parley with King Edward.
GAVESTON   Treacherous earl, shall I not see the king?   15
WARWICK   The king of heaven perhaps, no other king.
Away!

Exeunt WARWICK *and his Men with* GAVESTON.

JAMES   Come, fellows, it booted not° for us to strive;
We will in haste go certify our lord.

Exeunt.

SCENE TWO

Enter KING EDWARD *and* SPENCER [JUNIOR, BALDOCK, *and* NOBLES *of the King's side, and Soldiers*] *with drums and fifes.*

KING EDWARD   I long to hear an answer from the barons
Touching my friend, my dearest Gaveston.
Ah, Spencer, not the riches of my realm
Can ransom him; ah, he is marked to die.
I know the malice of the younger Mortimer.   5
Warwick I know is rough, and Lancaster
Inexorable, and I shall never see
My lovely Pierce, my Gaveston again.
The barons overbear me with their pride.
SPENCER JUNIOR   Were I King Edward, England's sovereign,   10

---

14 **shadow** ghost. 18 **booted not** was of no avail.

Son to the lovely Eleanor of Spain,
Great Edward Longshanks'° issue, would
    I bear
These braves,° this rage, and suffer un-
    controlled
These barons thus to beard me in my
    land,
In mine own realm? My lord, pardon my
15   speech.
Did you retain your father's magnanimity,
Did you regard the honor of your name,
You would not suffer thus your majesty
Be counterbuffed of your nobility.
Strike off their heads, and let them preach
20   on poles.°
No doubt, such lessons they will teach the
    rest,
As by their preachments° they will profit
    much
And learn obedience to their lawful king.
KING EDWARD   Yea, gentle Spencer, we have
    been too mild,
Too kind to them; but now have drawn
25   our sword,
And if they send me not my Gaveston,
We'll steel it on their crest and poll their
    tops.°
BALDOCK   This haught resolve becomes
    your majesty,
Not to be tied to their affection,°
As though your highness were a school-
30   boy still,
And must be awed and governed like a
    child.

Enter SPENCER SENIOR° *with his trun-
cheon and Soldiers.*

SPENCER SENIOR   Long live my sovereign,
    the noble Edward,
In peace triumphant, fortunate in wars!
KING EDWARD   Welcome, old man. Com'st
    thou in Edward's aid?

Then tell thy prince of whence and what
    thou art.   35
SPENCER SENIOR   Lo, with a band of bow-
    men and of pikes,
Brown bills° and targeteers, four hundred
    strong,
Sworn to defend King Edward's royal
    right,
I come in person to your majesty,
Spencer, the father of Hugh Spencer there,   40
Bound to your highness everlastingly,
For favors done, in him, unto us all.
KING EDWARD   Thy father, Spencer?
SPENCER JUNIOR   True, and it like your
    grace,
That pours, in lieu of all your goodness
    shown,
His life, my lord, before your princely
    feet.   45
KING EDWARD   Welcome ten thousand
    times, old man, again.
Spencer, this love, this kindness to thy
    king,
Argues thy noble mind and disposition.
Spencer, I here create thee Earl of Wilt-
    shire,°
And daily will enrich thee with our favor,   50
That as the sunshine shall reflect o'er thee.
Beside, the more to manifest our love,
Because we hear Lord Bruce doth sell his
    land
And that the Mortimers are in hand
    withal,
Thou shalt have crowns of us t'outbid the
    barons.   55
And, Spencer, spare them not, but lay it
    on.
Soldiers, a largess, and thrice welcome all.
SPENCER JUNIOR   My lord, here comes the
    queen.

Enter QUEEN [ISABELLA] *and her son,*
[PRINCE EDWARD,] *and* LEVUNE, *a Frenchman.*

KING EDWARD   Madam, what news?
QUEEN ISABELLA   News of dishonor, lord,
    and discontent.

III.ii. 12 **Edward Longshanks** King Edward I. 13
braves insults. 20 **poles** The heads of traitors were
placed on poles and exhibited on London bridge.
22 **preachments** sermons. 27 **poll their tops** behead
them (as the tops of trees are trimmed). 29 **their
affection** what they affect, or desire. sd **Spencer
Senior** Hugh le Despenser, a strong supporter of
Edward II, executed at Bristol in 1326.

37 **Brown bills** bronzed halberds. 49 **Spencer . . .
Wiltshire** Young Spencer historically was never Earl
of Wiltshire. This is Marlowe's invention.

Our friend Levune, faithful and full of
60　trust,
Informeth us by letters and by words
That Lord Valois our brother, king of
France,
Because your highness hath been slack in
homage,
Hath seizèd Normandy into his hands.
65　These be the letters, this the messenger.
KING EDWARD　Welcome, Levune. Tush,
Sib,° if this be all,
Valois and I will soon be friends again.
But to my Gaveston; shall I never see,
Never behold thee now? Madam, in this
matter
70　We will employ you and your little son;
You shall go parley with the king of
France.
Boy, see you bear you bravely to the king,
And do your message with a majesty.
PRINCE EDWARD　Commit not to my youth
things of more weight
75　Than fits a prince so young as I to bear,
And fear not, lord and father, heaven's
great beams
On Atlas'° shoulder shall not lie more
safe
Than shall your charge committed to my
trust.
QUEEN ISABELLA　Ah, boy, this towardness
makes thy mother fear
Thou art not marked to many days on
80　earth.
KING EDWARD　Madam, we will that you
with speed be shipped,
And this our son; Levune shall follow
you
With all the haste we can dispatch him
hence.
Choose of our lords to bear you company,
And go in peace; leave us in wars at
85　home.
QUEEN ISABELLA　Unnatural wars, where
subjects brave their king;
God end them once! My lord, I take my
leave
To make my preparation for France.

66 **Sib** wife. 77 **Atlas** the Titan of Greek mythology condemned by Zeus to bear the heavens upon his shoulders.

[*Exit with* PRINCE EDWARD.]

Enter ARUNDEL.

KING EDWARD　What, Lord Arundel, dost
thou come alone?
ARUNDEL　Yea, my good lord, for Gaveston
is dead.　　　　　　　　　　　　　　90
KING EDWARD　Ah, traitors! Have they put
my friend to death?
Tell me, Arundel, died he ere thou cam'st,
Or didst thou see my friend to take his
death?
ARUNDEL　Neither, my lord, for as he was
surprised,
Begirt with weapons and with enemies
round,　　　　　　　　　　　　　　95
I did you highness' message to them all,
Demanding him of them, entreating
rather,
And said, upon the honor of my name,
That I would undertake to carry him
Unto your highness and to bring him back.　100
KING EDWARD　And tell me, would the reb-
els deny me that?
SPENCER JUNIOR　Proud recreants.
KING EDWARD　　Yea, Spencer, traitors all.
ARUNDEL　I found them at the first inex-
orable.
The Earl of Warwick would not bide the
hearing,
Mortimer hardly; Pembroke and Lan-
caster　　　　　　　　　　　　　　105
Spake least. And when they flatly had
denied,
Refusing to receive me pledge for him,
The Earl of Pembroke mildly thus be-
spake:
'My lords, because our sovereign sends for
him
And promiseth he shall be safe returned,　110
I will this undertake, to have him hence
And see him re-delivered to your hands.'
KING EDWARD　Well, and how fortunes that
he came not?
SPENCER JUNIOR　Some treason or some vil-
lainy was cause.
ARUNDEL　The Earl of Warwick seized him
on his way;　　　　　　　　　　　　115
For being delivered unto Pembroke's men,

Their lord rode home thinking his pris-
oner safe;
But ere he came, Warwick in ambush lay,
And bare him to his death, and in a
trench
Strake° off his head, and marched unto
120   the camp.
SPENCER JUNIOR   A bloody part, flatly
against law of arms.
KING EDWARD   O shall I speak, or shall I
sigh and die!
SPENCER JUNIOR   My lord, refer your ven-
geance to the sword
Upon these barons; hearten up your men;
Let them not unrevenged murder your
125   friends.
Advance your standard, Edward, in the
field,
And march to fire them from their start-
ing holes.°
KING EDWARD   By earth, the common
mother of us all,   *He kneels.*
By heaven, and all the moving orbs
thereof,
By this right hand, and by my father's
130   sword,
And all the honors 'longing° to my crown,
I will have heads and lives for him as
many
As I have manors, castles, towns, and
towers.

[*He rises.*]

Treacherous Warwick! Traitorous Mortimer!
135 If I be England's king, in lakes of gore
Your headless trunks, your bodies will I
trail,
That you may drink your fill, and quaff
in blood,
And stain my royal standard with the
same,
That so my bloody colors may suggest
140 Remembrance of revenge immortally
On your accursèd traitorous progeny,
You villains that have slain my Gaveston!

And in this place of honor and of trust,
Spencer, sweet Spencer, I adopt thee here,
And merely of our love we do create thee *145*
Earl of Gloucester° and Lord Chamber-
lain,
Despite of times, despite of enemies.
SPENCER JUNIOR   My lord, here's a messen-
ger from the barons
Desires access unto your majesty.
KING EDWARD   Admit him near.   *150*

Enter the HERALD *from the Barons, with
his coat of arms.*

HERALD   Long live King Edward, Eng-
land's lawful lord.
KING EDWARD   So wish not they, I wis, that
sent thee hither.
Thou com'st from Mortimer and his
'complices;
A ranker rout of rebels never was.
Well, say thy message.   *155*
HERALD   The barons up in arms by me
salute
Your highness with long life and hap-
piness,
And bid me say, as plainer° to your grace,
That if without effusion of blood
You will this grief have ease and remedy, *160*
That from your princely person you re-
move
This Spencer, as a putrefying branch
That deads the royal vine, whose golden
leaves
Empale your princely head, your diadem,
Whose brightness such pernicious upstarts
dim,   *165*
Say they; and lovingly advise your grace
To cherish virtue and nobility,
And have old servitors in high esteem,
And shake off smooth dissembling flat-
terers.
This granted, they, their honors, and their
lives,   *170*
Are to your highness vowed and conse-
crate.

---

120 **Strake** struck. 127 **starting holes** holes in which
wild animals might take refuge from hunters usually to be driven out by fire. 131 **'longing** belonging.

146 **Earl of Gloucester** Being married to the Earl
of Gloucester's daughter, young Spencer did in fact
succeed to the title following the death of his
wife's brother. 158 **plainer** complainant.

SPENCER JUNIOR   Ah, traitors, will they still display their pride?

KING EDWARD   Away, tarry no answer, but be gone.
Rebels, will they appoint their sovereign
His sports, his pleasures, and his com-
175   pany?
Yet, ere thou go, see how I do divorce

[He] embrace[s] SPENCER.

Spencer from me. Now get thee to thy lords,
And tell them I will come to chastise them
For murdering Gaveston. Hie thee, get thee gone.
Edward with fire and sword follows at thy
180   heels.

[Exit HERALD.*]*

My lord, perceive you how these rebels swell?
Soldiers, good hearts, defend your sover-
eign's right,
For now, even now, we march to make them stoop.
Away!

Exeunt. Alarums, excursions, a great fight, and a retreat [sounded within].

SCENE THREE

Enter KING *[EDWARD],* SPENCER SENIOR, SPENCER JUNIOR, *and the* NOBLEMEN *of the King's side.*

KING EDWARD   Why do we sound retreat? Upon them, lords!
This day I shall pour vengeance with my sword
On those proud rebels that are up in arms
And do confront and countermand their king.

SPENCER JUNIOR   I doubt it not, my lord,
5   right will prevail.

SPENCER SENIOR   'Tis not amiss, my liege, for either part
To breathe awhile; our men, with sweat and dust
All choked well near, begin to faint for heat,

And this retire refresheth horse and man.

SPENCER JUNIOR   Here come the rebels.   10

Enter the BARONS, MORTIMER *[JUNIOR,]* LANCASTER, WARWICK, PEMBROKE *and others.*

MORTIMER JUNIOR   Look, Lancaster, yonder is Edward
Among his flatterers.

LANCASTER   And there let him be
Till he pay dearly for their company.

WARWICK   And shall, or Warwick's sword shall smite in vain.

KING EDWARD   What, rebels, do you shrink and sound retreat?   15

MORTIMER JUNIOR   No, Edward, no; thy flatterers faint and fly.

LANCASTER   Thou'd best betimes forsake them, and their trains,
For they'll betray thee, traitors as they are.

SPENCER JUNIOR   Traitor on thy face, rebellious Lancaster!

PEMBROKE   Away, base upstart, brav'st thou nobles thus?   20

SPENCER SENIOR   A noble attempt and honorable deed,
Is it not, trow ye, to assemble aid
And levy arms against your lawful king?

KING EDWARD   For which ere long their heads shall satisfy,
T'appease the wrath of their offended king.   25

MORTIMER JUNIOR   Then, Edward, thou wilt fight it to the last
And rather bathe thy sword in subjects' blood
Than banish that pernicious company.

KING EDWARD   Ay, traitors all, rather than thus be braved,
Make England's civil towns huge heaps of stones   30
And ploughs to go about our palace gates.

WARWICK   A desperate and unnatural resolution.
Alarum to the fight! St. George° for England,

III.iii. 33 **St. George** an anachronism, since St. George was not adopted as the patron saint of England until the reign of Edward III.

And the barons' right.

KING EDWARD   Saint George for England,
35   and King Edward's right.

[*Alarums. Exeunt the two parties severally.*]

Enter [KING] EDWARD [*and his followers,*]
with the BARONS [*and* KENT,] *captives.*

KING EDWARD   Now, lusty lords, now, not
by chance of war,
But justice of the quarrel and the cause,
Vailed is your pride. Methinks you hang
the heads,
But we'll advance them, traitors. Now 'tis
time
40   To be avenged on you for all your braves
And for the murder of my dearest friend,
To whom right well you knew our soul
was knit,
Good Pierce of Gaveston, my sweet fa-
vorite.
Ah, rebels, recreants, you made him away!

KENT   Brother, in regard of thee and of thy
45   land,
Did they remove that flatterer from thy
throne.

KING EDWARD   So, sir, you have spoke;
away, avoid our presence.

[*Exit* KENT.]

Accursèd wretches, was't in regard of us,
When we had sent our messenger to re-
quest
He might be spared to come to speak with
50   us,
And Pembroke undertook for his return,
That thou, proud Warwick, watched the
prisoner,
Poor Pierce, and headed° him against law
of arms?
For which thy head shall overlook the rest,
As much as thou in rage outwent'st the
55   rest.

WARWICK   Tyrant, I scorn thy threats and
menaces;
'Tis but temporal that thou canst inflict.°

LANCASTER   The worst is death, and better
die to live
Than live in infamy under such a king.

KING EDWARD   Away with them, my lord of
Winchester!   60
These lusty leaders, Warwick and Lan-
caster,
I charge you roundly, off with both their
heads!
Away!

WARWICK   Farewell, vain world.

LANCASTER   Sweet Mortimer, farewell.   65

MORTIMER JUNIOR   England, unkind to thy
nobility,
Groan for this grief. Behold how thou art
maimed.

KING EDWARD   Go, take that haughty Mor-
timer to the Tower;
There see him safe bestowed; and for the
rest,
Do speedy execution on them all.   70
Be gone!

MORTIMER JUNIOR   What, Mortimer, can
raggèd stony walls
Immure thy virtue that aspires to heaven?
No, Edward, England's scourge, it may
not be;
Mortimer's hope surmounts his fortune
far.   75

[*Exit under guard with the other captive
Barons.*]

KING EDWARD   Sound, drums and trumpets!
March with me, my friends.
Edward this day hath crowned him king
anew.

Exit [*with all except*] SPENCER JUNIOR,
LEVUNE *and* BALDOCK.

SPENCER JUNIOR   Levune, the trust that we
repose in thee
Begets the quiet of King Edward's land.
Therefore be gone in haste, and with ad-
vice   80
Bestow that treasure on the lords of
France,
That, therewith all enchanted, like the
guard
That suffered Jove to pass in showers of
gold

53 **headed** beheaded. 57 **temporal . . . inflict** i.e.,
you can only harm my body (not my soul).

To Danaë,° all aid may be denied

85 To Isabel the queen, that now in France
Makes friends, to cross the seas with her
    young son
And step into his father's regiment.°

LEVUNE That's it these barons and the
    subtle queen
Long leveled° at.

BALDOCK   Yea, but, Levune, thou seest
These barons lay their heads on blocks

90 together;
What they intend, the hangman frustrates
    clean.

LEVUNE Have you no doubts, my lords, I'll
    clap so close°
Among the lords of France with England's
    gold,
That Isabel shall make her plaints in vain,
And France shall be obdurate with her

95 tears.

SPENCER JUNIOR Then make for France
    amain. Levune, away.
Proclaim King Edward's wars and vic-
    tories.

Exeunt.

Act Four

SCENE ONE

Enter KENT.

KENT Fair blows the wind for France.
    Blow, gentle gale,
Till Edmund be arrived for England's
    good.
Nature, yield to my country's cause in
    this.
A brother, no, a butcher of thy friends,
Proud Edward, dost thou banish me thy

5 presence?
But I'll to France and cheer the wrongèd
    queen,
And certify what Edward's looseness is.

83–84 **Jove . . . Danaë** See note II.ii. 53. 87 **regiment** royal authority. 89 **leveled** aimed. 92 **clap so
close** work so secretly.

Unnatural king, to slaughter noblemen
And cherish flatterers. Mortimer, I stay
Thy sweet escape. Stand gracious, gloomy
    night,   10
To his device.

Enter MORTIMER [JUNIOR,] *disguised.*

MORTIMER JUNIOR Holla! Who walketh
    there?
Is't you, my lord?

KENT   Mortimer, 'tis I;
But hath thy potion wrought so happily?

MORTIMER JUNIOR It hath, my lord; the   15
    warders all asleep,
I thank them, gave me leave to pass in
    peace.
But hath your grace got shipping unto
    France?

KENT Fear it not.

Exeunt.

SCENE TWO

Enter QUEEN [ISABELLA] *and her son,*
[PRINCE EDWARD].

QUEEN ISABELLA Ah, boy, our friends do
    fail us all in France.
The lords are cruel and the king unkind.
What shall we do?

PRINCE EDWARD   Madam, return to Eng-
    land
And please my father well, and then a fig
For all my uncle's friendship here in
    France.   5
I warrant you, I'll win his highness
    quickly;
'A loves me better than a thousand
    Spencers.

QUEEN ISABELLA Ah, boy, thou art de-
    ceived, at least in this,
To think that we can yet be tuned to-
    gether.
No, no, we jar too far. Unkind Valois,   10
Unhappy Isabel, when France rejects,
Whither, oh, whither dost thou bend thy
    steps?

Enter SIR JOHN OF HAINAULT.

SIR JOHN   Madam, what cheer?

QUEEN ISABELLA   Ah, good Sir John of
Hainault,°
Never so cheerless, nor so far distressed.

SIR JOHN   I hear, sweet lady, of the king's
15   unkindness,
But droop not, madam; noble minds con-
temn°
Despair. Will your grace with me to
Hainault,
And there stay time's advantage with your
son?
How say you, my lord, will you go with
your friends,
20   And share of all our fortunes equally?

PRINCE EDWARD   So pleaseth the queen, my
mother, me it likes.
The king of England, nor the court of
France,
Shall have me from my gracious mother's
side,
Till I be strong enough to break a staff;
And then have at the proudest Spencer's
25   head.

SIR JOHN   Well said, my lord.

QUEEN ISABELLA   O, my sweet heart, how
do I moan thy wrongs,
Yet triumph in the hope of thee, my joy.
Ah, sweet Sir John, even to the utmost
verge
30   Of Europe or the shore of Tanais,°
Will we with thee to Hainault, so we will.
The marquis is a noble gentleman;
His grace, I dare presume, will welcome
me.
But who are these?

Enter KENT *and* MORTIMER [JUNIOR].

KENT   Madam, long may you live,
Much happier than your friends in Eng-
35   land do.

QUEEN ISABELLA   Lord Edmund and Lord
Mortimer alive!

Welcome to France. The news was here,
my lord,
That you were dead or very near your
death.

MORTIMER JUNIOR   Lady, the last was tru-
est of the twain,
But Mortimer, reserved for better hap,   40
Hath shaken off the thraldom of the
Tower
And lives t'advance your standard, good
my lord.

PRINCE EDWARD   How mean you, and° the
king, my father, lives?
No, my Lord Mortimer, not I, I trow.

QUEEN ISABELLA   Not, son! Why not? I
would it were no worse.   45
But, gentle lords, friendless we are in
France.

MORTIMER JUNIOR   Monsieur le Grand, a
noble friend of yours,
Told us, at our arrival, all the news—
How hard the nobles, how unkind the
king
Hath showed himself. But, madam, right
makes room   50
Where weapons want; and though a
many° friends
Are made away, as Warwick, Lancaster,
And others of our party and faction,
Yet have we friends, assure your grace, in
England
Would cast up caps and clap their hands
for joy,   55
To see us there appointed for° our foes.

KENT   Would all were well and Edward
well reclaimed,
For England's honor, peace, and quietness.

MORTIMER JUNIOR   But by the sword, my
lord, it must be deserved;
The king will ne'er forsake his flatterers.   60

SIR JOHN   My lords of England, sith the
ungentle king
Of France refuseth to give aid of arms
To this distressèd queen his sister here,
Go you with her to Hainault. Doubt ye
not
We will find comfort, money, men and
friends   65

IV.ii. sd **Sir John of Hainault** uncle of the Princess
Philippa, who was to be the wife of King Edward
III. 16 **contemn** hold in contempt. 30 **Tanais** the
river Don, regarded by Elizabethans as dividing
Europe from Asia.

43 **and** if. 51 **a many** many (a common Elizabethan
usage). 56 **appointed for** ready for battle with.

Ere long, to bid the English king a base.°
How say, young prince, what think you of
the match?°
PRINCE EDWARD   I think King Edward will
outrun us all.
QUEEN ISABELLA   Nay, son, not so; and you
must not discourage
Your friends that are so forward in your
70   aid.
KENT   Sir John of Hainault, pardon us, I
pray;
These comforts that you give our woful
queen
Bind us in kindness all at your command.
QUEEN ISABELLA   Yea, gentle brother, and
the God of heaven
Prosper your happy motion, good Sir
75   John.
MORTIMER JUNIOR   This noble gentleman,
forward in arms,
Was born, I see, to be our anchor-hold.
Sir John of Hainault, be it thy renown,
That England's queen and nobles in dis-
tress
Have been by thee restored and com-
80   forted.
SIR JOHN   Madam, along, and you, my
lord, with me,
That England's peers may Hainault's wel-
come see.

[*Exeunt.*]

SCENE THREE

Enter KING [EDWARD], ARUNDEL, *the two*
SPENCERS, *with* OTHERS.

KING EDWARD   Thus after many threats of
wrathful war,
Triumpheth England's Edward with his
friends;
And triumph, Edward, with his friends
uncontrolled.

My lord of Gloucester, do you hear the
news?
SPENCER JUNIOR   What news, my lord?   5
KING EDWARD   Why, man, they say there is
great execution
Done through the realm. My lord of Arun-
del,
You have the note, have you not?
ARUNDEL   From the lieutenant of the
Tower, my lord.
KING EDWARD   I pray let us see it. [*He takes
the note.*] What have we there?   10
Read it, Spencer.

[*He hands it to*] SPENCER [JUNIOR, *who*]
reads their names.

Why so; they barked° apace a month ago.
Now, on my life, they'll neither bark nor
bite.
Now, sirs the news from France? Glouces-
ter, I trow
The lords of France love England's gold
so well   15
As Isabel gets no aid from thence.
What now remains? Have you proclaimed,
my lord,
Reward for them can bring in Mortimer?
SPENCER JUNIOR   My lord, we have; and if
he be in England,
'A will be had ere long, I doubt it not.   20
KING EDWARD   If, dost thou say? Spencer,
as true as death,
He is in England's ground; our portmas-
ters
Are not so careless of their king's com-
mand.

Enter a MESSENGER.

How now, what news with thee? From
whence come these?
MESSENGER   Letters, my lord, and tidings
forth of France;   25
To you, my lord of Gloucester, from
Levune.

[*He gives letters to* SPENCER JUNIOR.]

KING EDWARD   Read.
SPENCER JUNIOR [*reads*]   My duty to your
honor premised, &c. I have, according to

---

66 **bid . . . base** i.e., challenge the English king.
Prisoner's base was a boys' game in which a runner
was chased from base to base by another player.
To 'bid a base' is to challenge a player to a run.
67 **match** i.e., the game of prisoner's base.

IV.iii. 12 **barked** embarked.

30 instructions in that behalf, dealt with the king of France his lords, and effected that the queen, all discontented and discomforted, is gone; whither, if you ask, with Sir John of Hainault, brother to the mar-
35 quis, into Flanders. With them are gone Lord Edmund and the Lord Mortimer, having in their company divers of your nation, and others; and as constant report goeth, they intend to give King Edward
40 battle in England sooner than he can look for them. This is all the news of import. Your honor's in all service, Levune.

KING EDWARD   Ah, villains, hath that Mortimer escaped?
With him is Edmund gone associate?
And will Sir John of Hainault lead the
45 round?°
Welcome, a God's name, madam, and your son;
England shall welcome you and all your rout.
Gallop apace, bright Phœbus,° through the sky,
And dusky night, in rusty iron car,
Between you both shorten the time, I
50 pray,
That I may see that most desirèd day
When we may meet these traitors in the field.
Ah, nothing grieves me but my little boy
Is thus misled to countenance their ills.
Come, friends, to Bristow, there to make
55 us strong;
And, winds, as equal be to bring them in,
As you injurious were to bear them forth.

[*Exeunt.*]

SCENE FOUR

Enter QUEEN, [ISABELLA,] *her son,* [PRINCE EDWARD,] KENT, MORTIMER JUNIOR, *and* SIR JOHN [OF HAINAULT].

QUEEN ISABELLA   Now, lords, our loving friends and countrymen,

Welcome to England all, with prosperous winds.
Our kindest friends in Belgia° have we left,
To cope° with friends at home; a heavy case
When force to force is knit, and sword and glaive°   5
In civil broils makes kin and countrymen
Slaughter themselves in others, and their sides
With their own weapons gored. But what's the help?
Misgoverned kings are cause of all this wrack;°
And, Edward, thou art one among them all   10
Whose looseness hath betrayed thy land to spoil
And made the channels° overflow with blood.
Of thine own people patron shouldst thou be,
But thou——
MORTIMER JUNIOR   Nay, madam, if you be a warrior,   15
You must not grow so passionate in speeches.
Lords, sith that we are by sufferance of heaven
Arrived and armèd in this prince's right,
Here for our country's cause swear we to him
All homage, fealty, and forwardness;   20
And for the open wrongs and injuries
Edward hath done to us, his queen and land,
We come in arms to wreck it° with the swords,
That England's queen in peace may repossess
Her dignities and honors; and withal   25
We may remove these flatterers from the king,
That havocs° England's wealth and treasury.

45 **round** dance. 48 **Phœbus** the sun god (Apollo) who drove the chariot of the sun across the sky.

IV.iv. 3 **Belgia** the Netherlands. 4 **cope** fight. 5 **glaive** lance. 9 **wrack** disaster. 12 **channels** street gutters through which sewage flowed. 23 **wreck it** cause destruction. 27 **havocs** causes havoc with.

SIR JOHN   Sound trumpets, my lord, and
forward let us march.
Edward will think we come to flatter him.

KENT   I would he never had been flattered
30   more.

[*Exeunt.*]

SCENE FIVE

Enter KING, [EDWARD] BALDOCK, *and*
SPENCER JUNIOR, *flying about the stage.*

SPENCER JUNIOR   Fly, fly, my lord, the
queen is over-strong;
Her friends do multiply, and yours do fail.
Shape we our course to Ireland, there to
breathe.

KING EDWARD   What, was I born to fly and
run away,
And leave the Mortimers conquerors be-
5   hind?
Give me my horse, and let's r'enforce our
troops,
And in this bed of honor die with fame.

BALDOCK   O no, my lord, this princely resolution
Fits not the time; away, we are pursued.

[*Exeunt.*]

[*Enter*] KENT *alone, with a sword and
target.*

KENT   This way he fled, but I am come too
10   late.
Edward, alas, my heart relents for thee.
Proud traitor, Mortimer, why dost thou
chase
Thy lawful king, thy sovereign, with thy
sword?
Vile wretch, and why hast thou, of all un-
kind,°
Borne arms against thy brother and thy
15   king?
Rain showers of vengeance on my cursèd
head,
Thou God, to whom in justice it belongs
To punish this unnatural revolt.
Edward, this Mortimer aims at thy life.

O fly him, then! But, Edmund, calm this
rage;   20
Dissemble, or thou diest, for Mortimer
And Isabel do kiss while they conspire;
And yet she bears a face of love forsooth.
Fie on that love that hatcheth death and
hate.
Edmund, away. Bristow to Longshanks'°
blood   25
Is false; be not found single for suspect.
Proud Mortimer pries near into thy walks.

Enter QUEEN [ISABELLA], MORTIMER [JUN-
IOR], *the young* PRINCE [EDWARD], *and* SIR
JOHN OF HAINAULT.

QUEEN ISABELLA   Successful battles gives
the God of kings
To them that fight in right and fear His
wrath.
Since then successfully we have prevailed,   30
Thanks be heaven's great architect, and
you.
Ere farther we proceed, my noble lords,
We here create our well-belovèd son,
Of love and care unto his royal person,
Lord Warden of the realm, and sith the
fates   35
Have made his father so unfortunate,
Deal you, my lords, in this, my loving
lords,
As to your wisdoms fittest seems in all.

KENT   Madam, without offence, if I may
ask,
How will you deal with Edward in his
fall?   40

PRINCE EDWARD   Tell me, good uncle, what
Edward do you mean?

KENT   Nephew, your father; I dare not call
him king.

MORTIMER JUNIOR   My lord of Kent, what
needs these questions?
'Tis not in her controlment,° nor in ours,
But as the realm and parliament shall
please,   45
So shall your brother be disposèd of.
I like not this relenting mood in Edmund.
Madam, 'tis good to look to him betimes.

IV.v. 14 **unkind** contrary to nature.

25 **Longshanks** See note III.ii.12. 44 **controlment**
power.

[*Aside to* QUEEN ISABELLA.]

QUEEN ISABELLA My lord, the Mayor of
    Bristow knows our mind.
MORTIMER JUNIOR Yea, madam, and they
50 scape not easily
    That fled the field.
QUEEN ISABELLA   Baldock is with the king.
    A goodly chancellor, is he not my lord?
SIR JOHN So are the Spencers, the father
    and the son.
KENT This, Edward, is the ruin of the
    realm.

    Enter RICE AP HOWELL° *and the* MAYOR
    OF BRISTOW, *with* SPENCER SENIOR, [*pris-
    oner, and* ATTENDANTS].

RICE   God save Queen Isabel and her
55   princely son.
    Madam, the mayor and citizens of Bris-
    tow,
    In sign of love and duty to this presence,
    Present by me this traitor to the state,
    Spencer, the father to that wanton Spencer,
60 That, like the lawless Catiline° of Rome,
    Revelled in England's wealth and treas-
    ury.
QUEEN ISABELLA   We thank you all.
MORTIMER JUNIOR Your loving care in this
    Deserveth princely favors and rewards.
    But where's the king and the other Spen-
    cer fled?
RICE   Spencer the son, created Earl of
65   Gloucester,
    Is with that smooth-tongued scholar Bal-
    dock gone
    And shipped but late for Ireland with the
    king.
MORTIMER JUNIOR Some whirlwind fetch
    them back or sink them all.

    [*Aside.*]

    They shall be started° thence, I doubt it
    not.

sd **Rice ap Howell** a partisan of the barons, commissioned by Queen Isabella to stir up opposition
to King Edward in Wales and to capture him if
possible. 60 **Catiline** Lucius Sergius Catilina, a
Roman noble whose famous conspiracy was defeated largely through the efforts of Cicero. 69
started driven from hiding (a hunting term).

PRINCE EDWARD Shall I not see the king
    my father yet?   70
KENT Unhappy is Edward, chased from
    England's bounds.

    [*Aside.*]

SIR JOHN Madam, what resteth? Why
    stand ye in a muse?
QUEEN ISABELLA   I rue my lord's ill-fortune;
    but alas,
    Care of my country called me to this war.
MORTIMER JUNIOR Madam, have done
    with care and sad complaint;   75
    Your king hath wronged your country
    and himself,
    And we must seek to right it as we may.
    Meanwhile, have hence this rebel to the
    block.
    Your lordship cannot privilege your head.
SPENCER SENIOR Rebel is he that fights
    against his prince;   80
    So fought not they that fought in Ed-
    ward's right.
MORTIMER JUNIOR Take him away; he
    prates.

    [*Exeunt* ATTENDANTS *with* SPENCER SEN-
    IOR.]

                    You, Rice ap Howell,
    Shall do good service to her majesty,
    Being of countenance° in your country
    here,
    To follow these rebellious runagates.°   85
    We in meanwhile, madam, must take ad-
    vice,
    How Baldock, Spencer, and their 'com-
    plices,
    May in their fall be followed to their end.

    Exeunt.

SCENE SIX

    Enter the ABBOT, MONKS, [KING] EDWARD,
    SPENCER [JUNIOR,] *and* BALDOCK, [*the
    three latter disguised*].

ABBOT Have you no doubt, my lord; have
    you no fear;

84 **countenance** authority. 85 **runagates** runaways.

As silent and as careful will we be
To keep your royal person safe with us,
Free from suspect, and fell invasion
5 Of such as have your majesty in chase,
Yourself, and those your chosen company,
As danger of this stormy time requires.

KING EDWARD Father, thy face should harbor no deceit.

O, hadst thou ever been a king, thy heart,
10 Piercèd deeply with sense of my distress,
Could not but take compassion of my state.
Stately and proud, in riches and in train,
Whilom I was powerful and full of pomp;
But what is he whom rule and empery
15 Have not in life or death made miserable?
Come, Spencer; come, Baldock, come, sit down by me;
Make trial now of that philosophy
That in our famous nurseries of arts
Thou sucked'st from Plato and from Aristotle.
20 Father, this life contemplative is heaven.
O that I might this life in quiet lead.
But we, alas, are chased, and you, my friends,
Your lives and my dishonor they pursue.
Yet, gentle monks, for treasure, gold nor fee,
25 Do you betray us and our company.

MONKS Your grace may sit secure, if none but we
Do wot of your abode.

SPENCER JUNIOR Not one alive, but shrewdly I suspect
A gloomy fellow in a mead below.
30 'A gave a long look after us, my lord,
And all the land I know is up in arms,
Arms that pursue our lives with deadly hate.

BALDOCK We were embarked for Ireland, wretched we,
With awkward winds and sore tempests driven
35 To fall on shore, and here to pine in fear
Of Mortimer and his confederates.

KING EDWARD Mortimer! Who talks of Mortimer?
Who wounds me with the name of Mortimer,

That bloody man? Good father, on thy lap
Lay I this head, laden with mickle° care. 40
O might I never open these eyes again,
Never again lift up this drooping head,
O never more lift up this dying heart!

SPENCER JUNIOR Look up, my lord. Baldock, this drowsiness
Betides no good; here even we are betrayed. 45

Enter, with Welsh hooks,° RICE AP
HOWELL, *a* MOWER, *and the* EARL OF
LEICESTER.°

MOWER Upon my life, those be the men ye seek.

RICE Fellow, enough. My lord, I pray be short;
A fair commission warrants what we do.

LEICESTER The queen's commission, urged by Mortimer.
What cannot gallant Mortimer with the queen? 50
Alas, see where he sits, and hopes unseen
T'escape their hands that seek to reave his life.
Too true it is, *Quem dies vidit veniens superbum,*
Hunc dies vidit fugiens jacentem.°
But, Leicester, leave to grow so passionate. 55
Spencer and Baldock, by no other names,
I arrest you of high treason here.
Stand not on titles, but obey th'arrest;
'Tis in the name of Isabel the queen.
My lord, why droop you thus? 60

KING EDWARD O day! The last of all my bliss on earth,
Center of all misfortune! O my stars,
Why do you lour unkindly on a king?
Comes Leicester, then, in Isabella's name
To take my life, my company from me? 65

IV.vi. 40 **mickle** much. sd **Welsh hooks** partisans, with cross pieces below their blades. **Leicester** Henry, Earl of Leicester, younger brother to Thomas, Earl of Lancaster and, like his brother, a foe of Edward and the Spencers. 53–54 **Quem . . . jacentem** Whom the coming day (dawn) saw in his pride, the departing day (evening) saw cast down. (The lines are from Seneca's *Thyestes.*)

Here, man, rip up this panting breast of
   mine,
And take my heart in rescue of my friends.
RICE   Away with them.
SPENCER JUNIOR   It may become thee yet
To let us take our farewell of his grace.
ABBOT   My heart with pity earns° to see
70   this sight,
   A king to bear these words and proud
   commands.
KING EDWARD   Spencer, ah, sweet Spencer,
   thus then must we part.
SPENCER JUNIOR   We must, my lord, so will
   the angry heavens.
KING EDWARD   Nay, so will hell and cruel
   Mortimer;
75   The gentle heavens have not to do in this.
BALDOCK   My lord, it is in vain to grieve or
   storm.
   Here humbly of your grace we take our
   leaves.
   Our lots are cast; I fear me, so is thine.
KING EDWARD   In heaven we may, in earth
   never shall we meet.
   And, Leicester, say, what shall become of
80   us?
LEICESTER   Your majesty must go to Kil-
   lingworth.°
KING EDWARD   Must! 'Tis somewhat hard,
   when kings must go.
LEICESTER   Here is a litter ready for your
   grace,
   That waits your pleasure, and the day
   grows old.
RICE   As good be gone as stay and be be-
85   nighted.
KING EDWARD   A litter hast thou? Lay me
   in a hearse,
   And to the gates of hell convey me hence.
   Let Pluto's° bells ring out my fatal knell
   And hags howl for my death at Charon's°
   shore,
   For friends hath Edward none but these
90   and these,

And these must die under a tyrant's
   sword.
RICE   My lord, be going; care not for these,
   For we shall see them shorter by the
   heads.
KING EDWARD   Well, that shall be, shall be.
   Part we must.
   Sweet Spencer, gentle Baldock, part we
   must.   95
   Hence feignèd weeds!° Unfeignèd are my
   woes.

[*He throws off his disguise.*]

Father, farewell. Leicester, thou stay'st for
me,
And go I must. Life, farewell, with my
   friends.

Exeunt KING EDWARD *and* LEICESTER.

SPENCER JUNIOR   O, is he gone? Is noble
   Edward gone,
   Parted from hence, never to see us more?   100
   Rent,° sphere of heaven, and, fire, forsake
   thy orb!
   Earth, melt to air! Gone is my sovereign,
   Gone, gone, alas, never to make return.
BALDOCK   Spencer, I see our souls are
   fleeted hence;
   We are deprived the sunshine of our life.   105
   Make for a new life, man; throw up thy
   eyes
   And heart and hand to heaven's immortal
   throne;
   Pay nature's debt with cheerful counte-
   nance.
   Reduce we all our lessons unto this,
   To die, sweet Spencer, therefore live we
   all;   110
   Spencer, all live to die, and rise to fall.
RICE   Come, come, keep these preachments
   till you come to the place appointed. You,
   and such as you are, have made wise work
   in England. Will your lordships away?   115
MOWER   Your worship, I trust, will remem-
   ber me?
RICE   Remember thee, fellow? What else?
   Follow me to the town.

[*Exeunt.*]

70 **earns** grieves. 81 **Killingworth** Kenilworth castle.
88 **Pluto** Greek god of the underworld. 89 **Charon**
boatman who conveyed departed spirits across the
river Styx.

96 **weeds** clothes. 101 **Rent** rend.

Act Five

SCENE ONE

Enter KING [EDWARD], LEICESTER, [*the*]
BISHOP [OF WINCHESTER, *and* TRUSSEL].

LEICESTER Be patient, good my lord, cease
to lament.
Imagine Killingworth Castle were your
court
And that you lay for pleasure here a space,
Not of compulsion or necessity.
KING EDWARD Leicester, if gentle words
5   might comfort me,
Thy speeches long ago had eased my sor-
rows,
For kind and loving hast thou always
been.
The griefs of private men are soon allayed,
But not of kings. The forest deer, being
struck,
Runs to an herb° that closeth up the
10   wounds,
But when the imperial lion's flesh is gored,
He rends and tears it with his wrathful
paw,
And highly scorning that the lowly earth
Should drink his blood, mounts up into
the air.°
And so it fares with me, whose dauntless
15   mind
The ambitious Mortimer would seek to
curb,
And that unnatural queen, false Isabel,
That thus hath pent and mewed me in a
prison;
For such outrageous passions cloy my soul,
20   As with the wings of rancor and disdain
Full often am I soaring up to heaven,
To plain me° to the gods against them
both.
But when I call to mind I am a king,
Methinks I should revenge me of the
wrongs

That Mortimer and Isabel have done.   25
But what are kings when regiment° is
gone,
But perfect shadows in a sunshine day?
My nobles rule, I bear the name of king;
I wear the crown, but am controlled by
them,
By Mortimer and my unconstant queen,   30
Who spots my nuptial bed with infamy,
Whilst I am lodged within this cave of
care,
Where sorrow at my elbow still attends,
To company my heart with sad laments,
That bleeds within me for this strange ex-
change.   35
But tell me, must I now resign my crown,
To make usurping Mortimer a king?
WINCHESTER Your grace mistakes; it is for
England's good
And princely Edward's right we crave the
crown.
KING EDWARD No, 'tis for Mortimer, not
Edward's head;   40
For he's a lamb, encompassèd by wolves,
Which in a moment will abridge his life.
But if proud Mortimer do wear this
crown,
Heavens turn it to a blaze of quenchless
fire;°
Or like the snaky wreath of Tisiphon,°   45
Engirt the temples of his hateful head;
So shall not England's vine° be perishèd,
But Edward's name survives, though Ed-
ward dies.
LEICESTER My lord, why waste you thus
the time away?
They stay your answer; will you yield your
crown?   50
KING EDWARD Ah, Leicester, weigh how
hardly I can brook
To lose my crown and kingdom without
cause,
To give ambitious Mortimer my right,

V.i. 10 **herb** dittany, or Dictanum, supposed according to legend to possess healing powers known
to wild animals by instinct. 14 **mounts . . . air**
i.e., the lion. 22 **plain me** complain.

26 **regiment** rule, authority. 44 **blaze . . . fire** i.e.,
like the crown which Medea gave to Creusa, for
whom Jason had deserted her. When Creusa placed
it upon her head, it burst into flames, and although
the metal melted it could not be removed. 47 **England's vine** the symbolic vine on the English crown.

That like a mountain overwhelms my bliss,

In which extreme my mind here murdered
55   is.

But what the heavens appoint, I must obey.

Here, take my crown; the life of Edward too;

[He takes off the crown.]

Two kings in England cannot reign at once.

But stay awhile; let me be king till night,

That I may gaze upon this glittering
60   crown;

So shall my eyes receive their last content,

My head, the latest honor due to it,

And jointly both yield up their wishèd right.

Continue ever thou celestial sun;
65 Let never silent night possess this clime.

Stand still you watches of the element;°

All times and seasons, rest you at a stay,

That Edward may be still fair England's king.

But day's bright beams doth vanish fast away,
70 And needs I must resign my wishèd crown.

Inhuman creatures, nursed with tiger's milk,

Why gape you for your sovereign's overthrow?

My diadem I mean, and guiltless life.

See, monsters, see, I'll wear my crown again.

[He puts on the crown.]

75 What, fear you not the fury of your king?

But, hapless Edward, thou art fondly led;

They pass° not for thy frowns as late they did,

But seeks to make a new-elected king;

Which fills my mind with strange despairing thoughts,

Which thoughts are martyrèd with endless
80   torments,

And in this torment comfort find I none,

66 **element** sky. 77 **pass** care.

But that I feel the crown upon my head,

And therefore let me wear it yet awhile.

TRUSSEL My lord, the parliament must have present news,

And therefore say, will you resign or no?   85

The KING *rageth.*

KING EDWARD I'll not resign, but whilst I live—

Traitors, be gone, and join you with Mortimer!

Elect, conspire, install, do what you will;

Their blood and yours shall seal these treacheries.

WINCHESTER This answer we'll return, and
so farewell.   90

LEICESTER Call them again, my lord, and speak them fair,

For if they go, the prince shall lose his right.

KING EDWARD Call thou them back; I have no power to speak.

LEICESTER My lord, the king is willing to resign.

WINCHESTER If he be not, let him choose.   95

KING EDWARD O would I might, but heavens and earth conspire

To make me miserable. Here receive my crown.

Receive it? No, these innocent hands of mine

Shall not be guilty of so foul a crime.

He of you all that most desires my blood   100

And will be called the murderer of a king,

Take it. What, are you moved? Pity you me?

Then send for unrelenting Mortimer

And Isabel, whose eyes, being turned to steel,

Will sooner sparkle fire than shed a tear.   105

Yet stay, for rather than I will look on them,

Here, here! *[He gives the crown.]*
               Now, sweet God of heaven,

Make me despise this transitory pomp

And sit for aye enthronizèd in heaven.

Come, death, and with thy fingers close
my eyes,   110

Or if I live, let me forget myself.

WINCHESTER My lord——

KING EDWARD Call me not lord! Away—
out of my sight!
Ah, pardon me; grief makes me lunatic.
115 Let not that Mortimer protect my son;
More safety is there in a tiger's jaws
Than his embracements. Bear this to the
queen,
Wet with my tears, and dried again with
sighs.

[*He gives a handkerchief.*]

If with the sight thereof she be not moved,
120 Return it back and dip it in my blood.
Commend me to my son, and bid him rule
Better than I. Yet how have I transgressed,
Unless it be with too much clemency?
TRUSSEL And thus most humbly do we
take our leave.

[*Exeunt the* BISHOP OF WINCHESTER *and*
TRUSSEL *with the crown.*]

KING EDWARD Farewell; I know the next
125 news that they bring
Will be my death, and welcome shall it be.
To wretched men death is felicity.

[*Enter* BERKELEY,° *who gives a paper to*
LEICESTER.]

LEICESTER Another post. What news
brings he?
KING EDWARD Such news as I expect. Come,
Berkeley, come,
130 And tell thy message to my naked breast.
BERKELEY My lord, think not a thought so
villainous
Can harbor in a man of noble birth.
To do your highness service and devoir
And save you from your foes, Berkeley
would die.
LEICESTER My lord, the council of the
135 queen commands
That I resign my charge.
KING EDWARD And who must keep me
now? Must you, my lord?

BERKELEY Ay, my most gracious lord, so
'tis decreed.
KING EDWARD [*taking the paper*] By Mortimer, whose name is written here.
Well may I rent° his name that rends my
heart! 140

[*He tears the paper.*]

This poor revenge hath something eased
my mind.
So may his limbs be torn as is this paper.
Hear me, immortal Jove, and grant it too.
BERKELEY Your grace must hence with me
to Berkeley° straight.
KING EDWARD Whither you will; all places
are alike, 145
And every earth is fit for burial.
LEICESTER Favor him, my lord, as much as
lieth in you.
BERKELEY Even so betide my soul as I use
him.
KING EDWARD Mine enemy hath pitied my
estate,
And that's the cause that I am now re-
moved. 150
BERKELEY And thinks your grace that
Berkeley will be cruel?
KING EDWARD I know not; but of this am I
assured,
That death ends all, and I can die but
once.
Leicester, farewell.
LEICESTER Not yet, my lord; I'll bear you
on your way. 155

Exeunt.

SCENE TWO

Enter MORTIMER [JUNIOR] *and* QUEEN ISA-
BELLA.

MORTIMER JUNIOR Fair Isabel, now have
we our desire;
The proud corrupters of the light-brained
king
Have done their homage to the lofty gallows,

sd **Berkeley** Sir Thomas Berkeley, who had been
deprived of his inheritance by Spencer Junior because of his father's support of Lancaster. Berkeley
castle was restored to him by Queen Isabella after
she had captured it.

140 **rent** rend. 144 **Berkeley** Berkeley castle in
Gloucestershire.

And he himself lies in captivity.
Be ruled by me, and we will rule the
5   realm.
In any case take heed of childish fear,
For now we hold an old wolf by the ears,°
That, if he slip, will seize upon us both,
And gripe the sorer, being griped himself.
Think therefore, madam, that imports us
10   much
To erect° your son with all the speed we
may,
And that I be protector over him,
For our behoof will bear the greater sway
Whenas a king's name shall be under writ.
QUEEN ISABELLA   Sweet Mortimer, the life
15   of Isabel,
Be thou persuaded that I love thee well,
And therefore, so the prince my son be
safe,
Whom I esteem as dear as these mine eyes,
Conclude against his father what thou
wilt,
20   And I myself will willingly subscribe.
MORTIMER JUNIOR   First would I hear news
he were deposed,
And then let me alone to handle him.

Enter MESSENGER.

Letters! From whence?
MESSENGER   From Killingworth, my lord.
QUEEN ISABELLA   How fares my lord the
king?
MESSENGER   In health, madam, but full of
25   pensiveness.
QUEEN ISABELLA   Alas, poor soul, would I
could ease his grief.

[*Enter the* BISHOP OF WINCHESTER *with
the crown.*]

Thanks, gentle Winchester. Sirrah, be
gone.

[*Exit* MESSENGER.]

WINCHESTER   The king hath willingly resigned his crown.
QUEEN ISABELLA   O happy news! Send for
the prince, my son.

WINCHESTER   Further, ere this letter was
sealed, Lord Berkeley came,   30
So that he now is gone from Killingworth;
And we have heard that Edmund laid a
plot
To set his brother free; no more but so.
The lord of Berkeley is so pitiful°
As Leicester that had charge of him be-
fore.   35
QUEEN ISABELLA   Then let some other be
his guardian.
MORTIMER JUNIOR   Let me alone, here is
the privy seal.

[*Exit the* BISHOP OF WINCHESTER.]

Who's there? Call hither Gurney and
Matrevis.°

[*To* ATTENDANTS *within.*]

To dash° the heavy-headed Edmund's
drift,°
Berkeley shall be discharged, the king removed,   40
And none but we shall know where he
lieth.
QUEEN ISABELLA   But, Mortimer, as long as
he survives,
What safety rest for us or for my son?
MORTIMER JUNIOR   Speak, shall he pres-
ently° be dispatched and die?
QUEEN ISABELLA   I would he were, so it
were not by my means.   45

Enter MATREVIS *and* GURNEY.

MORTIMER JUNIOR   Enough.
Matrevis, write a letter presently
Unto the lord of Berkeley from ourself
That he resign the king to thee and
Gurney,
And when 'tis done we will subscribe our
name.   50

---

34 **pitiful** full of pity, easily moved. 38 **Gurney and
Matrevis** Thomas Gournay fled the country after
King Edward's murder, was captured at Marseilles,
and died mysteriously on his way back to England;
he was probably murdered to prevent his revealing
his accomplices. Sir John Maltravers was Edward's
jailor. 39 **dash** ruin. **drift** design or plot. 44 **presently** immediately.

V.ii. 7 **an old wolf by the ears** a popular proverb.
11 **erect** establish on the throne.

MATREVIS It shall be done, my lord. [*He writes.*]

MORTIMER JUNIOR   Gurney.

GURNEY   My lord.

MORTIMER JUNIOR As thou intendest to rise by Mortimer,
Who now makes Fortune's wheel turn as he please,
Seek all the means thou canst to make him droop,
And neither give him kind word nor good
55   look.

GURNEY I warrant you, my lord.

MORTIMER JUNIOR And this above the rest: because we hear
That Edmund casts° to work his liberty,
Remove him still from place to place by night,
60   Till at the last he come to Killingworth,
And then from thence to Berkeley back again.
And by the way, to make him fret the more,
Speak curstly° to him; and in any case
Let no man comfort him if he chance to weep,
65   But amplify his grief with bitter words.

MATREVIS Fear not, my lord, we'll do as you command.

MORTIMER JUNIOR So now away; post thitherwards amain.

QUEEN ISABELLA Whither goes this letter? To my lord the king?
Commend me humbly to his majesty,
70   And tell him that I labor all in vain
To ease his grief and work his liberty,
And bear him this as witness of my love.

[*She gives a ring.*]

MATREVIS I will, madam.

[*Exeunt* MATREVIS *and* GURNEY.]

MORTIMER JUNIOR Finely dissembled. Do so still, sweet queen.
Here comes the young prince with the
75   Earl of Kent.

QUEEN ISABELLA Something he whispers in his childish ears.

MORTIMER JUNIOR If he have such access unto the prince,
Our plots and stratagems will soon be dashed.

QUEEN ISABELLA Use Edmund friendly as if all were well.

Enter the young PRINCE [EDWARD] *and the* EARL OF KENT *talking with him.*

MORTIMER JUNIOR How fares my honorable lord of Kent?   80

KENT In health, sweet Mortimer. How fares your grace?

QUEEN ISABELLA Well, if my lord your brother were enlarged.°

KENT I hear of late he hath deposed himself.

QUEEN ISABELLA The more my grief.

MORTIMER JUNIOR And mine.   85

KENT Ah, they do dissemble. [*Aside.*]

QUEEN ISABELLA Sweet son, come hither; I must talk with thee.

MORTIMER JUNIOR Thou being his uncle and the next of blood,
Do look to be protector over the prince?

KENT Not I, my lord. Who should protect the son,   90
But she that gave him life? I mean the queen.

PRINCE EDWARD Mother, persuade me not to wear the crown.
Let him be king. I am too young to reign.

QUEEN ISABELLA But be content, seeing it his highness' pleasure.

PRINCE EDWARD Let me but see him first, and then I will.   95

KENT Ay, do, sweet nephew.

QUEEN ISABELLA Brother, you know it is impossible.

PRINCE EDWARD Why, is he dead?

QUEEN ISABELLA No, God forbid.

KENT I would those words proceeded from your heart.   100

MORTIMER JUNIOR Inconstant Edmund, dost thou favor him,
That wast a cause of his imprisonment?

KENT The more cause have I now to make amends.

58 **casts** plots. 63 **curstly** harshly.

82 **enlarged** liberated.

MORTIMER JUNIOR   I tell thee, 'tis not meet that one so false

105   Should come about the person of a prince.
My lord, he hath betrayed the king his brother,
And therefore trust him not.

PRINCE EDWARD   But he repents and sorrows for it now.

QUEEN ISABELLA   Come, son, and go with this gentle lord and me.

PRINCE EDWARD   With you I will, but not
110   with Mortimer.

MORTIMER JUNIOR   Why, youngling, 'sdain'st thou so of Mortimer?
Then I will carry thee by force away.

PRINCE EDWARD   Help, uncle Kent; Mortimer will wrong me.

QUEEN ISABELLA   Brother Edmund, strive not; we are his friends.

115   Isabel is nearer than the Earl of Kent.

KENT   Sister, Edward is my charge; redeem him.

QUEEN ISABELLA   Edward is my son, and I will keep him.

KENT   Mortimer shall know that he hath wrongèd me.
Hence will I haste to Killingworth Castle
120   And rescue agèd Edward from his foes,
To be revenged on Mortimer and thee.

Exeunt [on one side QUEEN ISABELLA, PRINCE EDWARD, and MORTIMER JUNIOR; on the other, KENT].

SCENE THREE

Enter MATREVIS and GURNEY [and SOLDIERS, with KING EDWARD].

MATREVIS   My lord, be not pensive; we are your friends.
Men are ordained to live in misery.
Therefore come; dalliance dangereth our lives.

KING EDWARD   Friends, whither must unhappy Edward go?
5   Will hateful Mortimer appoint no rest?
Must I be vexèd like the nightly bird°

Whose sight is loathsome to all winged fowls?
When will the fury of his mind assuage?
When will his heart be satisfied with blood?
If mine will serve, unbowel straight this breast,   10
And give my heart to Isabel and him;
It is the chiefest mark they level at.

GURNEY   Not so, my liege; the queen hath given this charge
To keep your grace in safety.
Your passions make your dolors to increase.   15

KING EDWARD   This usage makes my misery increase.
But can my air of life continue long
When all my senses are annoyed with stench?
Within a dungeon England's king is kept,
Where I am starved for want of sustenance.   20
My daily diet is heart-breaking sobs,
That almost rents the closet of my heart.
Thus lives old Edward not relieved by any,
And so must die, though pitièd by many.
O, water, gentle friends, to cool my thirst   25
And clear my body from foul excrements.

MATREVIS   Here's channel water,° as our charge is given.
Sit down, for we'll be barbers to your grace.

KING EDWARD   Traitors, away! What, will you murder me,
Or choke your sovereign with puddle water?   30

GURNEY   No, but wash your face and shave away your beard,
Lest you be known and so be rescuèd.

MATREVIS   Why strive you thus? Your labor is in vain.

KING EDWARD   The wren may strive against the lion's strength,
But all in vain; so vainly do I strive   35
To seek for mercy at a tyrant's hand.

V.iii. 6 **nightly bird** owl.   27 **channel** See note IV.iv.12.

They wash him with puddle water, and shave his beard away.

Immortal powers, that knows the painful cares
That waits upon my poor distressèd soul,
O level all your looks upon these daring men,
That wrongs their liege and sovereign,
40 England's king.
O Gaveston, it is for thee that I am wronged;
For me both thou and both the Spencers died,
And for your sakes a thousand wrongs I'll take.
The Spencers' ghosts, wherever they remain,
Wish well to mine; then tush, for them I'll
45 die.
MATREVIS 'Twixt theirs and yours shall be no enmity.
Come, come away. Now put the torches out;
We'll enter in by darkness to Killingworth.

Enter KENT.

GURNEY How now, who comes there?
MATREVIS Guard the king sure; it is the
50 Earl of Kent.
KING EDWARD O gentle brother, help to rescue me.
MATREVIS Keep them asunder; thrust in the king.
KENT Soldiers, let me but talk to him one word.
GURNEY Lay hands upon the earl for this assault.
KENT Lay down your weapons, traitors;
55 yield the king.
MATREVIS Edmund, yield thou thyself, or thou shalt die.
KENT Base villains, wherefore do you gripe me thus?
GURNEY Bind him and so convey him to the court.
KENT Where is the court but here? Here is the king,
60 And I will visit him. Why stay you me?

MATREVIS The court is where Lord Mortimer remains;
Thither shall your honor go; and so farewell.

Exeunt MATREVIS *and* GURNEY, *with* KING [EDWARD].

KENT O miserable is that commonweal, where lords
Keep courts, and kings are locked in prison!
SOLDIER Wherefore stay we? On, sirs, to the court. 65
KENT Ay, lead me whither you will, even to my death,
Seeing that my brother cannot be released.

Exeunt.

SCENE FOUR

Enter MORTIMER [JUNIOR] *alone.*

MORTIMER JUNIOR The king must die, or Mortimer goes down;
The commons now begin to pity him.
Yet he that is the cause of Edward's death
Is sure to pay for it when his son is of age,
And therefore will I do it cunningly. 5
This letter, written by a friend of ours,
Contains his death, yet bids them save his life.

[*He reads.*]

"*Edwardum occidere nolite timere bonum est;*
Fear not to kill the king, 'tis good he die."
But read it thus, and that's another sense: 10
"*Edwardum occidere nolite timere bonum est;*
Kill not the king, 'tis good to fear the worst."
Unpointed° as it is, thus shall it go,
That, being dead, if it chance to be found,
Matrevis and the rest may bear the blame, 15
And we be quit that caused it to be done.
Within this room is locked the messenger

V.iv. 13 **Unpointed** without punctuation.

That shall convey it and perform the rest.
And by a secret token that he bears,
Shall he be murdered when the deed is
20   done.
Lightborn,° come forth!

[*Enter* LIGHTBORN.]

Art thou as resolute as thou wast?
LIGHTBORN   What else, my lord? And far
   more resolute.
MORTIMER JUNIOR   And hast thou cast°
   how to accomplish it?
LIGHTBORN   Ay, ay, and none shall know
25   which way he died.
MORTIMER JUNIOR   But at his looks, Light-
   born, thou wilt relent.
LIGHTBORN   Relent! Ha, ha! I use much to
   relent.
MORTIMER JUNIOR   Well, do it bravely, and
   be secret.
LIGHTBORN   You shall not need to give in-
   structions;
30   'Tis not the first time I have killed a man.
I learned in Naples how to poison flowers,
To strangle with a lawn° thrust through
   the throat,
To pierce the windpipe with a needle's
   point,
Or whilst one is asleep, to take a quill
35   And blow a little powder in his ears,
Or open his mouth and pour quicksilver
   down.
But yet I have a braver way than these.
MORTIMER JUNIOR   What's that?
LIGHTBORN   Nay, you shall pardon me;
   none shall know my tricks.
MORTIMER JUNIOR   I care not how it is, so
40   it be not spied.
Deliver this to Gurney and Matrevis.
   [*He gives a letter.*]
At every ten miles' end thou hast a horse.
Take this. [*He gives money.*] Away, and
   never see me more.
LIGHTBORN   No.
45   MORTIMER JUNIOR   No,

Unless thou bring me news of Edward's
   death.
LIGHTBORN   That will I quickly do. Farewell, my lord.

[*Exit.*]

MORTIMER JUNIOR   The prince I rule, the
   queen do I command,
And with a lowly congé° to the ground,
The proudest lords salute me as I pass;   50
I seal, I cancel, I do what I will.
Feared am I more than loved; let me be
   feared,
And when I frown, make all the court
   look pale.
I view the prince with Aristarchus'° eyes,
Whose looks were as a breeching° to a boy.   55
They thrust upon me the protectorship
And sue to me for that that I desire.
While at the council-table, grave enough,
And not unlike a bashful Puritan,
First I complain of imbecility,°   60
Saying it is *onus quam gravissimum;*°
Till, being interrupted by my friends,
Suscepi that *provinciam*° as they term it;
And to conclude, I am Protector now.
Now is all sure; the queen and Mortimer   65
Shall rule the realm, the king, and none
   rule us.
Mine enemies will I plague, my friends ad-
   vance,
And what I list command who dare con-
   trol?
*Major sum quam cui possit fortuna
   nocere.*°
And that this be the coronation day,   70
It pleaseth me, and Isabel the queen.

[*Trumpets sound within.*]

The trumpets sound; I must go take my
   place.

21 **Lightborn** The name, invented by Marlowe, may be a translation of Lucifer. 24 **cast** see note at II.iii.8. 32 **lawn** thread.

49 **congé** bow. 54 **Aristarchus** Greek grammarian and schoolmaster of the second century B.C. 55 **breeching** beating. 60 **imbecility** weakness. 61 **onus quam gravissimum** a very heavy load. 63 **Suscepi that provinciam** I accepted that province (undertook the task). 69 **Major . . . nocere** I am too great for fortune to harm me.

Enter the young KING, [EDWARD III], [*the*] BISHOP [OF CANTERBURY,] CHAMPION, NOBLES, [*and*] QUEEN [ISABELLA].

CANTERBURY   Long live King Edward, by the grace of God,
King of England and lord of Ireland.

CHAMPION   If any Christian, Heathen, Turk, or Jew,
75
Dares but affirm that Edward's not true king,
And will avouch his saying with the sword,
I am the champion that will combat him.

MORTIMER JUNIOR   None comes, sound trumpets.

[*Trumpets sound.*]

KING EDWARD III   Champion, here's to thee.

[*He gives a purse.*]

QUEEN ISABELLA   Lord Mortimer, now take him to your charge.
80

Enter SOLDIERS, *with the* EARL OF KENT *prisoner.*

MORTIMER JUNIOR   What traitor have we there with blades and bills?

SOLDIER   Edmund, the Earl of Kent.

KING EDWARD III   What hath he done?

SOLDIER   'A would have taken the king away perforce,
As we were bringing him to Killingworth.

MORTIMER JUNIOR   Did you attempt his rescue, Edmund? Speak.
85

KENT   Mortimer, I did; he is our king,
And thou compell'st this prince to wear the crown.

MORTIMER JUNIOR   Strike off his head! He shall have martial law.

KENT   Strike off my head! Base traitor, I defy thee.

KING EDWARD III   My lord, he is my uncle and shall live.
90

MORTIMER JUNIOR   My lord, he is your enemy and shall die.

KENT   Stay, villains!

KING EDWARD III   Sweet mother, if I cannot pardon him,
Entreat my Lord Protector for his life.

QUEEN ISABELLA   Son, be content; I dare not speak a word.
95

KING EDWARD III   Nor I, and yet methinks I should command;
But, seeing I cannot, I'll entreat for him.
My lord, if you will let my uncle live,
I will requite it when I come to age.

MORTIMER JUNIOR   'Tis for your highness' good and for the realm's.
100
How often shall I bid you bear him hence?

KENT   Art thou king? Must I die at thy command?

MORTIMER JUNIOR   At our command. Once more away with him.

KENT   Let me but stay and speak; I will not go.
Eithr my brother or his son is king,
105
And none of both them thirst for Edmund's blood.
And therefore, soldiers, whither will you hale me?

[*Soldiers*] *hale* KENT *away, and carry him to be beheaded.*

KING EDWARD III   What safety may I look for at his hands,
If that my uncle shall be murdered thus?

QUEEN ISABELLA   Fear not, sweet boy, I'll guard thee from thy foes.
110
Had Edmund lived, he would have sought thy death.
Come, son, we'll ride a-hunting in the park.

KING EDWARD III   And shall my uncle Edmund ride with us?

QUEEN ISABELLA   He is a traitor; think not on him; come.

Exeunt.

SCENE FIVE

Enter MATREVIS *and* GURNEY.

MATREVIS   Gurney, I wonder the king dies not,
Being in a vault up to the knees in water,
To which the channels of the castle run,

From whence a damp continually ariseth,
5   That were enough to poison any man,
Much more a king brought up so tenderly.
GURNEY   And so do I, Matrevis. Yester-
night
I opened but the door to throw him meat,
And I was almost stifled with the savor.
10   MATREVIS   He hath a body able to endure
More than we can inflict, and therefore
now
Let us assail his mind another while.
GURNEY   Send for him out thence, and I
will anger him.
MATREVIS   But stay, who's this?
Enter LIGHTBORN.
LIGHTBORN   My Lord Protector
greets you.

[*He gives letter.*]

GURNEY   What's here? I know not how to
15   conster it.
MATREVIS   Gurney, it was left unpointed
for the nonce;
'*Edwardum occidere nolite timere,*'
That's his meaning.
LIGHTBORN   Know you this token? I must
have the king.

[*He gives token.*]

MATREVIS   Ay, stay awhile; thou shalt have
20   answer straight.
This villain's sent to make away the king.
[*Aside.*]
GURNEY   I thought as much.   [*Aside.*]
MATREVIS   And when the murder's done,
See how he must be handled for his labor.
Pereat iste!° Let him have the king.
[*Aside.*]
What else? Here is the key, this is the
25   lake;°
Do as you are commanded by my lord.
LIGHTBORN   I know what I must do. Get
you away.
Yet be not far off; I shall need your help.
See that in the next room I have a fire,
30   And get me a spit, and let it be red-hot.

MATREVIS   Very well.
GURNEY   Need you anything besides?
LIGHTBORN   What else? A table and a
feather-bed.
GURNEY   That's all?
LIGHTBORN   Ay, ay; so, when I call you,
bring it in.
MATREVIS   Fear not you that.   35
GURNEY   Here's a light to go into the
dungeon.

[*He gives a light, and then exits with*
MATREVIS.]

LIGHTBORN   So now
Must I about this gear.° Ne'er was there
any
So finely handled as this king shall be.
Foh, here's a place indeed, with all my
heart.   40
KING EDWARD   Who's there? What light is
that? Wherefore comes thou?
LIGHTBORN   To comfort you and bring you
joyful news.
KING EDWARD   Small comfort finds poor Ed-
ward in thy looks.
Villain, I know thou com'st to murder me.
LIGHTBORN   To murder you, my most gra-
cious lord?   45
Far is it from my heart to do you harm.
The queen sent me to see how you were
used,
For she relents at this your misery.
And what eyes can refrain from shedding
tears
To see a king in this most piteous state?   50
KING EDWARD   Weep'st thou already? List
awhile to me
And then thy heart, were it as Gurney's is,
Or as Matrevis', hewn from the Caucasus,
Yet will it melt ere I have done my tale.
This dungeon where they keep me is the
sink   55
Wherein the filth of all the castle falls.
LIGHTBORN   O villains!
KING EDWARD   And there in mire and pud-
dle have I stood

V.v. 24 **Pereat iste** Let him perish. 25 **lake** pit or
dungeon.

38 **gear** business.

This ten days' space; and, lest that I should sleep,
60   One plays continually upon a drum.
They give me bread and water, being a king;
So that, for want of sleep and sustenance,
My mind's distempered, and my body's numbed,
And whether I have limbs or no I know not.
O, would my blood dropped out from
65   every vein,
As doth this water from my tattered robes.
Tell Isabel, the queen, I looked not thus,
When for her sake I ran at tilt in France
And there unhorsed the Duke of Clere-mont.
LIGHTBORN   O speak no more, my lord; this
70   breaks my heart.
Lie on this bed, and rest yourself awhile.
KING EDWARD   These looks of thine can harbor nought but death.
I see my tragedy written in thy brows.
Yet stay awhile; forbear thy bloody hand,
75   And let me see the stroke before it comes,
That even then when I shall lose my life,
My mind may be more steadfast on my God.
LIGHTBORN   What means your highness to mistrust me thus?
KING EDWARD   What means thou to dis-semble with me thus?
LIGHTBORN   These hands were never
80   stained with innocent blood,
Nor shall they now be tainted with a king's.
KING EDWARD   Forgive my thought for hav-ing such a thought.
One jewel have I left; receive thou this.

[*He gives a jewel.*]

Still fear I, and I know not what's the cause,
85   But every joint shakes as I give it thee.
O, if thou harbor'st murder in thy heart,
Let this gift change thy mind and save thy soul.
Know that I am a king. O, at that name
I feel a hell of grief! Where is my crown?
90   Gone, gone, and do I remain alive?

LIGHTBORN   You're overwatched,° my lord; lie down and rest.
KING EDWARD   But that grief keeps me wak-ing, I should sleep;
For not these ten days have these eyes' lids closed.
Now as I speak they fall, and yet with fear
Open again. O wherefore sits thou here?   95
LIGHTBORN   If you mistrust me, I'll be gone, my lord.
KING EDWARD   No, no, for if thou mean'st to murder me,
Thou wilt return again, and therefore stay. [*He sleeps.*]
LIGHTBORN   He sleeps.
KING EDWARD [*waking*]   O let me not die
yet. Stay, O stay a while!   100
LIGHTBORN   How now, my lord?
KING EDWARD   Something still buzzeth in mine ears
And tells me if I sleep I never wake.
This fear is that which makes me tremble thus;
And therefore tell me, wherefore art thou
come?   105
LIGHTBORN   To rid thee of thy life. Ma-trevis, come!

[*Enter* MATREVIS *and* GURNEY.]

KING EDWARD   I am too weak and feeble to resist.
Assist me, sweet God, and receive my soul!
LIGHTBORN   Run for the table.
KING EDWARD   O spare me, or dispatch me
in a trice.   110

[MATREVIS *brings in a table.*]

LIGHTBORN   So, lay the table down, and stamp on it,
But not too hard, lest that you bruise his body.

[KING EDWARD *is murdered.*]

MATREVIS   I fear me that this cry will raise the town,
And therefore let us take horse and away.
LIGHTBORN   Tell me, sirs, was it not bravely
done?   115

91 **overwatched** exhausted from lack of sleep.

GURNEY Excellent well. Take this for thy reward.

GURNEY *stabs* LIGHTBORN, [*who dies*].

Come, let us cast the body in the moat,
And bear the king's to Mortimer our lord.
Away!

Exeunt [*with the bodies*].

SCENE SIX

Enter MORTIMER [JUNIOR] *and* MATREVIS.

MORTIMER JUNIOR Is't done, Matrevis, and the murderer dead?

MATREVIS Ay, my good lord; I would it were undone.

MORTIMER JUNIOR Matrevis, if thou now growest penitent
I'll be thy ghostly father;° therefore choose
5 Whether thou wilt be secret in this
Or else die by the hand of Mortimer.

MATREVIS Gurney, my lord, is fled, and will, I fear,
Betray us both; therefore let me fly.

MORTIMER JUNIOR Fly to the savages.

10 MATREVIS I humbly thank your honor.

[*Exit.*]

MORTIMER JUNIOR As for myself, I stand as Jove's huge tree,°
And others are but shrubs compared to me.
All tremble at my name, and I fear none;
Let's see who dare impeach me for his death.

Enter QUEEN [ISABELLA].

QUEEN ISABELLA Ah, Mortimer, the king
15 my son hath news
His father's dead, and we have murdered him!

MORTIMER JUNIOR What if he have? The king is yet a child.

QUEEN ISABELLA Ay, ay, but he tears his hair, and wrings his hands,

And vows to be revenged upon us both.
Into the council chamber he is gone   20
To crave the aid and succor of his peers.
Ay me, see where he comes, and they with him.
Now, Mortimer, begins our tragedy.

Enter KING [EDWARD THE THIRD,] *with the* LORDS, [*and* ATTENDANTS].

FIRST LORD Fear not, my lord; know that you are a king.

KING EDWARD III Villain!   25

MORTIMER JUNIOR How now, my lord?

KING EDWARD III Think not that I am frighted with thy words.
My father's murdered through thy treachery,
And thou shalt die, and on his mournful hearse
Thy hateful and accursed head shall lie   30
To witness to the world that by thy means
His kingly body was too soon interred.

QUEEN ISABELLA Weep not, sweet son.

KING EDWARD III Forbid me not to weep; he was my father;
And had you loved him half so well as I,   35
You could not bear his death thus patiently.
But you, I fear, conspired with Mortimer.

FIRST LORD Why speak you not unto my lord the king?

MORTIMER JUNIOR Because I think scorn to be accused.
Who is the man dare say I murdered him?   40

KING EDWARD III Traitor, in me my loving father speaks
And plainly saith, 'twas thou that murdered'st him.

MORTIMER JUNIOR But hath your grace no other proof than this?

KING EDWARD III Yes, if this be the hand of Mortimer.

[*He shows letter.*]

MORTIMER JUNIOR False Gurney hath betrayed me and himself.   45

[*Aside.*]

QUEEN ISABELLA I feared as much; murder cannot be hid.

V.vi. 4 **ghostly father** priest (who brings sacraments to one about to die). 11 **Jove's huge tree** the oak.

[*Aside.*]

MORTIMER JUNIOR 'Tis my hand; what gather you by this?

KING EDWARD III That thither thou didst send a murderer.

MORTIMER JUNIOR What murderer? Bring forth the man I sent.

KING EDWARD III Ah, Mortimer, thou
50 knowest that he is slain;
And so shalt thou be too. Why stays he here?
Bring him into a hurdle,° drag him forth;
Hang him, I say, and set his quarters up;
But bring his head back presently to me.

QUEEN ISABELLA For my sake, sweet son,
55 pity Mortimer.

MORTIMER JUNIOR Madam, entreat not; I will rather die
Than sue for life unto a paltry boy.

KING EDWARD III Hence with the traitor, with the murderer!

MORTIMER JUNIOR Base Fortune, now I see that in thy wheel
There is a point, to which when men as-
60 pire,
They tumble headlong down. That point I touched,
And, seeing there was no place to mount up higher,
Why should I grieve at my declining fall?
Farewell, fair queen; weep not for Morti-mer,
65 That scorns the world, and, as a traveler,
Goes to discover countries yet unknown.

KING EDWARD III What! Suffer you the traitor to delay?

[MORTIMER JUNIOR *is taken away by the* FIRST LORD *and* ATTENDANTS.]

QUEEN ISABELLA As thou received'st thy life from me,
Spill not the blood of gentle Mortimer!

KING EDWARD III This argues that you spilt
70 my father's blood;
Else would you not entreat for Mortimer.

QUEEN ISABELLA I spill his blood? No!

KING EDWARD III Ay, madam, you; for so the rumor runs.

QUEEN ISABELLA That rumor is untrue; for loving thee,
Is this report raised on poor Isabel. 75

KING EDWARD III I do not think her so un-natural.

SECOND LORD My lord, I fear me it will prove too true.

KING EDWARD III Mother, you are suspected for his death,
And therefore we commit you to the Tower
Till further trial may be made thereof; 80
If you be guilty, though I be your son,
Think not to find me slack or pitiful.

QUEEN ISABELLA Nay, to my death, for too long have I lived,
Whenas my son thinks to abridge my days.

KING EDWARD III Away with her. Her words enforce these tears, 85
And I shall pity her if she speak again.

QUEEN ISABELLA Shall I not mourn for my belovèd lord,
And with the rest accompany him to his grave?

SECOND LORD Thus, madam; 'tis the king's will you shall hence.

QUEEN ISABELLA He hath forgotten me; stay, I am his mother. 90

SECOND LORD That boots° not; therefore, gentle madam, go.

QUEEN ISABELLA Then come, sweet death, and rid me of this grief.

[*Exit with* SECOND LORD.]

[*Enter* FIRST LORD, *with the head of* MORTIMER JUNIOR.]

FIRST LORD My lord, here is the head of Mortimer.

KING EDWARD III Go fetch my father's hearse where it shall lie,
And bring my funeral robes.

---

52 **hurdle** cart on which condemned criminals were taken to the gallows.

91 **boots** avails.

[*Exeunt* ATTENDANTS.]

95   Accursèd head,
Could I have ruled thee then, as I do
   now,
Thou hadst not hatched this monstrous
   treachery!
Here comes the hearse; help me to mourn,
   my lords.
[*Re-enter* ATTENDANTS *with the hearse and
funeral robes.*]

Sweet father, here unto thy murdered
   ghost
I offer up this wicked traitor's head,   100
And let these tears, distilling° from mine
   eyes,
Be witness of my grief and innocency.

   [*Exeunt.*]

101 **distilling** falling slowly.

The Duchess of Malfi

John Webster   edited by J. Dennis Huston and Alvin B. Kernan

Introductory Comments

Michael Goldman   *Queens College*

The Duchess of Malfi draws us into a world that has the texture of a nightmare—a disturbing blend of sensuality, terror, physical corruption, and mystery. To its inhabitants, it is a dark world, painful and bewildering—one character calls it a "deep pit of darkness," another a "wilderness," and several liken it to hell—but it has a terrible deformed vitality, an intensity of presence like that of madness or hallucination.

The most frightening thing about a nightmare is that it attacks us from inside. Waking horrors may go away or be destroyed, but nightmares speak to us of an inexpungeable and frightening life hidden inside our skins. The world of *The Duchess of Malfi* is real in the way a nightmare is real: it releases and brings before our eyes images of violent impulses that are ordinarily suppressed. Webster has this very much in mind, as we may see from an early speech made by the Duchess. When she tries to tell her steward, Antonio, that she loves him, she finds it hard to express herself directly, and complains that:

> as a tyrant doubles with his words
> And fearfully equivocates, so we
> Are forced to express our violent passions
> In riddles and in dreams.

The play, too, expresses violent and hidden passions in the "riddles and dreams" of its complex stage poetry.

It is typical of Webster's language that sinister suggestions can appear in the most neutral or pleasant contexts. Thus the Duchess here compares herself, surprisingly, to a "tyrant." The word links her to her tyrannical brother, Ferdinand, who will later have her hunted down and murdered for marrying Antonio. Ferdinand's own violent sexual passion for his sister is expressed not only in the nightmare-like tortures he prepares for her, but in the madness that attacks him after her death. He believes himself to be a wolf, the only difference being that "A wolf's skin was hairy on the outside;/His on the inside." This sense of something horrible from inside coming out into the light and taking over the world is one of the dominant sensations of the play.

The Duchess, like many of the women depicted in the great dramatic roles of the period, is mature, passionate, and commanding. She is gifted with a deep and quick sensuality, a proud and assured authority, courage (always a hard quality to portray convincingly on stage, but absolutely central to this role), and a kind of pilgrim decency and modesty that makes her calm and Christian acceptance of death credible at the end. She is a complex figure, and when she is properly played we respond to her not only with pity, but with awe and not a little fear.

Though Webster's audience would have found the Duchess sympathetic from the start, it would also have found some aspects of her character—and especially of her marriage—disturbing. Renaissance Englishmen took disobedience to family authority far more seriously than we do, and the Duchess defies her brothers' express prohibition to marry. They also took the social hierarchy very seriously—seeing in it a reflection of the divine order of the universe—and would certainly not have approved of ladies of princely blood marrying their stewards. They would have known, too, that secret marriages were sinful and forbidden.

The play works hard to make the married couple powerfully sympathetic to us. Still, it shows the Duchess as dangerously precipitous—too casually scoffing at her brothers' threat, briskly wooing Antonio, indifferent to the niceties of religion. As we have seen, this is a risk not only physical but also spiritual. The audience would not feel that her marriage was in itself damnable, but it might well feel that, given the circumstances, the Duchess ought to worry a little more about putting her soul in jeopardy. In sum, we see her as a woman who lives by a vigorous, healthy, essentially attractive instinct—but who is forced to act it out in an essentially corrupt world, where even the healthiest desires take on a questionable taint. Her greatness is tied up with her rashness—she never hesitates, but accepts the risks and never grows corrupt. Indeed, she grows greater and purer as the play goes on, closer to heaven and our hearts.

The play's action falls into three parts. The first is a battle for the Duchess's body, and ends when Ferdinand succeeds in discovering the secret marriage and imprisoning his sister. The second is a battle for her soul in which he attempts to bring her to madness and despair. He fails when the Duchess not only keeps her sanity but meets death with Christian humility, her thoughts focused on heaven. The final phase is a battle on the Duchess's behalf—Bosola's attempt to revenge her death on Ferdinand, a revenge that both succeeds and fails.

Bosola is a remarkable creation. Webster has taken a conventional stage type of the period, the Malcontent—a savage satirist of court life whose dramatic assignment is usually to carry out a Machiavellian scheme of revenge—and created a baffled, dangerous, contradictory human being, and a richly conceived and very difficult acting part. Londoners in 1612 would have been familiar with the figure of the impoverished gentleman, the out-of-work soldier or scholar (Bosola is both), dependent for his livelihood on winning the favor of a great lord, ready to turn his hand to almost anything to gain advancement. In Bosola, Webster stresses both the harshness of the Malcontent's satirical vision and the bleak amorality of the professional spy. He also gives him a genius for cruelty.

When Bosola visits the Duchess in the guise of a bellman, he torments her for a noble purpose. His aim is to "mortify" her, in the Christian sense—to bring her to an awareness of the vanity of mortal life—so as to help prepare her to meet death in a proper frame of mind. Thus, he helps thwart Ferdinand's plot to bring her to despair and so to damnation. But we should not miss the point that Bosola succeeds in doing good only by exercising his gift for inflicting pain. Later he succeeds in killing Ferdinand, but he also kills Antonio in a grotesque accident and murders an innocent servant for little reason. His talent is for torment, whether he will or no.

The last act is a deliberate tangle of murders. With the Duchess gone, the world seems to fall apart. The tone, at times, takes on the comic savagery of caricature. Webster even introduces a comic doctor who, unlike the physician in *Macbeth,* believes he can minister to a mind diseased. His ludicrous failure with Ferdinand parallels Bosola's doomed efforts to do good.

The play ends, as tragedies of this period generally do, with a restoration of order; but it is at best a very tentative restoration. A child is brought on stage, the Duchess's eldest son by Antonio. Perhaps he will someday reign in Malfi. All around him, however, lie corpses, the remains of the play's grotesque and convulsive finale. The child is silent, and we cannot feel—nor are we meant to—anything as strong as the relief and release that mark the end of *Macbeth.* Dying, Bosola has seemed to sum things up on the side of despair by saying we are all "Like dead walls and vaulted graves/That, ruin'd, leave no echo." But his words strike another note by reminding us that, after the Duchess's death, we have heard her own voice echoing through a ruined cloister, sadly warning Antonio of the danger he faces—though he, significantly enough, cannot quite grasp her meaning.

If Webster compels us to see life as a ruin in the last act, he also compels us to remember the Duchess, and she is like the echo in the ruin—tender, enduring, very likely unavailing. Earlier, when the Duchess, imprisoned by Ferdinand and near despair, is so angry that she curses the stars, Bosola says to her, "Look you, the stars shine still," and the mood Webster leaves us with at the end of the play is like a glimpse of the stars shining still above her prison. Something not quite destroyed glimmers above the nightmare.

We know very little about *John Webster*. There is no record of his birth, though it must have been around 1580. A John Webster was admitted to the study of law in London in 1598, and since Webster's plays are full of legal allusions it is frequently assumed that this John Webster and the playwright are one and the same; but it is no more than an assumption. We do know that Webster began to be active in the London theatre around 1602 and quickly acquired at least a modest reputation. His two great plays—far superior to anything else he wrote—are *The White Devil*, first performed and published in 1612, and *The Duchess of Malfi*, written and first performed between 1612 and 1614. Later in the decade came a tragedy, *The Guise* (no copy, however, survives), and *The Devil's Law-Case* (published in 1623). Aside from this, there are several collaborations, some commemorative verses, and the posthumously published *Appius and Virginia*. Even the date of his death is conjectural. A friend, writing in 1635, refers to Webster in the past tense, and so we leave him.

The Duchess of Malfi

John Webster

[BOSOLA *gentleman of the Duchess' horse*
FERDINAND *Duke of Calabria*
CARDINAL *his brother*
ANTONIO *steward of the Duchess' household*
DELIO *his friend*
FOROBOSCO
MALATESTE *a count*
The Marquis of PESCARA
SILVIO *a lord*
CASTRUCHIO *an old lord*
RODERIGO
GRISOLAN *lords*
THE DUCHESS *sister of Ferdinand and the Cardinal*
CARIOLA *her woman*
JULIA *wife to Castruchio and mistress to the Cardinal*
The DOCTOR
COURT OFFICERS
The several madmen, including: ASTROLOGER, TAILOR, PRIEST, DOCTOR
OLD LADY
THREE YOUNG CHILDREN
TWO PILGRIMS
ATTENDANTS, LADIES, EXECUTIONERS]

Act One

SCENE ONE   [*The Duchess' palace in Amalfi*]

[*Enter* ANTONIO *and* DELIO.]

DELIO   You are welcome to your country, dear Antonio,
You have been long in France, and you return
A very formal Frenchman, in your habit.°
How do you like the French court?
ANTONIO   I admire it;
In seeking to reduce both State and peo-
5   ple
To a fixed order, their judicious king
Begins at home. Quits° first his royal palace
Of flatt'ring sycophants, of dissolute,
And infamous persons, which° he sweetly terms
10   His Master's masterpiece, the work of Heaven,
Consid'ring duly, that a prince's court
Is like a common fountain, whence should flow
Pure silver-drops in general. But if't chance
Some cursed example poison't near the head,°
15   Death and diseases through the whole land spread.
And what is't makes this blessèd government,
But a most provident council, who dare freely
Inform him° the corruption of the times?
Though some o' th' court hold it presumption
20   To instruct princes what they ought to do,
It is a noble duty to inform them

What they ought to foresee. Here comes Bosola,
The only court-gall:° yet I observe his railing
Is not for simple love of piety:
Indeed he rails at those things which he wants,   25
Would be as lecherous, covetous, or proud,
Bloody, or envious, as any man,
If he had means to be so.—Here's the Cardinal.

[*Enter* BOSOLA *and the* CARDINAL.]

BOSOLA   I do haunt you still.
CARDINAL   So.   30
BOSOLA   I have done you better service than to be slighted thus. Miserable age, where only the° reward of doing well, is the doing of it!
CARDINAL   You enforce° your merit too   35
much.
BOSOLA   I fell into the galleys in your service, where, for two years together, I wore two towels instead of a shirt, with a knot on the shoulder, after the fashion of a   40
Roman mantle. Slighted thus, I will thrive some way: blackbirds fatten best in hard weather,° why not I, in these dog days?°
CARDINAL   Would you could become honest,——   45
BOSOLA   With all your divinity, do but direct me the way to it. I have known many travel far for it, and yet return as arrant knaves, as they went forth; because they carried themselves always along with   50
them.° [*Exit* CARDINAL.] Are you gone? Some fellows, they say, are possessed with the devil, but this great fellow were able

---

23 **court-gall** both a sore spot in the court and a bitter railer against the court. 33 **only the** the only. 35 **enforce** emphasize. 42–43 **blackbirds . . . weather** It was commonly thought that blackbirds grew fat in cold weather—perhaps because their ruffled feathers made them seem heavier then. 43 **dog days** corrupt times. 49–51 **because . . . them** because they could not get away from the **evil** within themselves.

I.i. 3 **habit** dress. 7 **Quits** empties. 9 **which** modifies either the "royal palace" or the process of ridding. 14 **head** both the source of the fountain and the chief of state. 18 **Inform him** inform him about.

to possess the greatest devil, and make him
55 worse.

ANTONIO   He hath denied thee some suit?

BOSOLA   He and his brother are like plum
trees, that grow crooked over standing°
pools, they are rich, and o'erladen with
60 fruit, but none but crows, pies,° and cater-
pillars feed on them. Could I be one of
their flatt'ring panders, I would hang on
their ears like a horseleech, till I were full,
and then drop off. I pray, leave me. Who
65 would rely upon these miserable depend-
ences,° in expectation to be advanced
tomorrow? What creature ever fed worse,
than hoping Tantalus;° nor ever died any
man more fearfully, than he that hoped
70 for a pardon? There are rewards for
hawks, and dogs, when they have done us
service; but for a soldier, that hazards his
limbs in a battle, nothing but a kind of
geometry° is his last supportation.

75 DELIO   Geometry?

BOSOLA   Ay, to hang in a fair pair of slings,
take his latter swing in the world, upon an
honorable pair of crutches, from hospital
to hospital. Fare ye well sir, and yet do not
80 you scorn us; for places in the court are
but like beds in the hospital, where this
man's head lies at that man's foot, and so
lower and lower. [*Exit* BOSOLA.]

DELIO   I knew this fellow seven years in the
galleys,°
For a notorious murther, and 'twas
85 thought
The Cardinal suborned it:° he was released

By the French general, Gaston de Foix°
When he recovered Naples.

ANTONIO   'Tis great pity
He should be thus neglected: I have heard
He's very valiant. This foul melancholy   90
Will poison all his goodness; for, I'll tell
you,
If too immoderate sleep be truly said
To be an inward rust unto the soul,
It then doth follow want of action
Breeds all black malcontents, and their
close rearing,°   95
Like moths in cloth, do hurt° for want of
wearing.°

SCENE TWO

[DELIO *and* ANTONIO *pass into the inner
stage, where* CASTRUCHIO,° SILVIO, RODE-
RIGO, *and* GRISOLAN *are entering.*]

DELIO   The presence° 'gins to fill. You
promised me
To make me the partaker of the natures
Of° some of your great courtiers.

ANTONIO   The Lord Cardinal's
And other strangers', that are now in
court?
'I shall. Here comes the great Calabrian
duke.   5

[*Enter* FERDINAND *and* ATTENDANTS.]

FERDINAND   Who took the ring° oft'nest?

SILVIO   Antonio Bologna, my lord.

---

58 **standing** stagnant. 60 **pies** magpies. 66 **dependence** social inferiority that makes one dependent
upon the favors of another. 68 **Tantalus** a wrong-
doer who was punished in Hades by being set,
thirsty and hungry, in a pool of water that receded
whenever he tried to drink from it and under a
tree whose fruit he could never reach. 73–74 **kind
of geometry** hanging in a stiff, angular position. 84
seven . . . galleys This statement only appears to
contradict Bosola's complaint in lines 34–35. His
claim there that for two years—an arbitrary identi-
fication of an indefinite period of time—he has
gone without a change of clothes is presented as an
illustration of the wretched conditions imposed
upon galley slaves. 86 **suborned it** secretly induced
him to do it.

87 **Gaston de Foix** Webster is confused here, for
although Gaston de Foix was a French general who
won an important victory over the Spanish and
papal armies at Ravenna in 1512, he had nothing
to do with the conquest of Naples in 1501: at that
time he was only thirteen years old. 95 **their . . .
rearing** their self-centered, invidious brooding. 96
do hurt hurts (the verb governs "close rearing,"
but it is given a plural form because of its proximity to "moths in cloth"). **wearing** exposure to the
air (of action).
I.ii.sd **Castruchio** The name is meant to suggest
impotence. 1 **presence** presence chamber, where
nobility received official visitors. 2–3 **To . . . Of**
to tell me about the characters of. 6 **took the ring**
won at jousting (by carrying off a ring with one's
lance).

FERDINAND Our sister Duchess' great master° of her household? Give him the jewel.—When shall we leave this sportive action, and fall to action indeed?

CASTRUCHIO Methinks, my lord, you should not desire to go to war in person.

FERDINAND [*Aside*] Now for some gravity: —why, my lord?

CASTRUCHIO It is fitting a soldier arise to be a prince, but not necessary a prince descend to be a captain!

FERDINAND No?

CASTRUCHIO No, my lord, he were far better do it by a deputy.

FERDINAND Why should he not as well sleep, or eat, by a deputy? This might take idle, offensive, and base office from him, whereas the other deprives him of honor.

CASTRUCHIO Believe my experience: that realm is never long in quiet where the ruler is a soldier.

FERDINAND Thou toldst me thy wife could not endure fighting.

CASTRUCHIO True, my lord.

FERDINAND And of a jest she broke of° a captain she met full of wounds: I have forgot it.

CASTRUCHIO She told him, my lord, he was a pitiful fellow, to lie, like the children of Ismael,° all in tents.°

FERDINAND Why, there's a wit were able to undo all the chirurgeons° o' the city, for although gallants should quarrel, and had drawn their weapons, and were ready to go to it; yet her persuasions would make them put up.°

CASTRUCHIO That she would, my lord.

How do you like my Spanish jennet?°

RODERIGO He is all fire.

FERDINAND I am of Pliny's opinion.° I think he was begot by the wind; he runs as if he were ballassed° with quicksilver.°

SILVIO True, my lord, he reels from the tilt° often.

RODERIGO *and* GRISOLAN Ha, ha, ha!

FERDINAND Why do you laugh? Methinks you that are courtiers should be my touchwood:° take fire when I give fire; that is, laugh when I laugh, were the subject never so witty——

CASTRUCHIO True, my lord, I myself have heard a very good jest, and have scorned to seem to have so silly° a wit, as to understand it.

FERDINAND But I can laugh at your fool, my lord.

CASTRUCHIO He cannot speak, you know, but he makes faces; my lady cannot abide him.

FERDINAND No?

CASTRUCHIO Nor endure to be in merry company: for she says too much laughing, and too much company, fills her too full of the wrinkle.°

FERDINAND I would then have a mathematical instrument° made for her face, that she might not laugh out of compass.° I shall shortly visit you at Milan, Lord Silvio.

SILVIO Your grace shall arrive most welcome.

FERDINAND You are a good horseman, Antonio; you have excellent riders in France, what do you think of good horsemanship?

8–9 **great master** steward. 32 **broke of** told about. 36–37 **children of Ismael** Arabs. **tents** a pun, meaning both "tents" in the modern sense and also rolls of lint used for dressing wounds. 38–43 **there's . . . up** The sexual innuendoes in this speech—obvious in "drawn their weapons," "go to it," and "put up" and probable in "undo" and "persuasions"—suggest both Julia's promiscuity and Ferdinand's licentiousness. The lewdness prevalent in Ferdinand's idiom suggests powerful incestuous desires, not fully suppressed. 39 **chirurgeons** surgeons. 45 **jennet** a small Spanish horse.

47 **Pliny's opinion** In his *Natural History*, Pliny wrote that some Portuguese mares were impregnated by the West Wind. 49 **ballassed** ballasted. **quicksilver** the element mercury, noted for its mobility. 50–51 **reels . . . tilt** shies away from the ring that is the target in tilting (cf. I.ii.6). 55 **touchwood** tinder. 60 **silly** simple. 70–71 **fills . . . wrinkle** There is in this speech a sexual pun, which Castruchio, who is stupidly innocent of his wife's unfaithfulness, does not recognize. **wrinkle** both a physical and a moral blemish and, here, pudendum as well. 73 **mathematical instrument** some compass-like device for confining movement. 74 **out of compass** to excess.

ANTONIO   Nobly, my lord: as out of the Grecian horse° issued many famous
85 princes: so out of brave horsemanship, arise the first sparks of growing resolution, that raise the mind to noble action.

FERDINAND   You have bespoke it worthily.

[*Enter* DUCHESS, CARDINAL, CARIOLA,° JULIA, *and* ATTENDANTS.]

SILVIO   Your brother, the Lord Cardinal,
90 and sister Duchess.

CARDINAL   Are the galleys come about?°

GRISOLAN   They are, my lord.

FERDINAND   Here's the Lord Silvio, is come to take his leave.

95 DELIO [*Aside to* ANTONIO.]   Now sir, your promise: what's that Cardinal? I mean his temper? They say he's a brave fellow, will play his five thousand crowns at tennis, dance, court ladies, and one that hath
100 fought single combats.

ANTONIO   Some such flashes° superficially hang on him, for form; but observe his inward character: he is a melancholy churchman. The spring in his face is
105 nothing but the engend'ring of toads:° where he is jealous of any man, he lays worse plots for them, than ever was imposed on Hercules,° for he strews in his way flatterers, panders, intelligencers,
110 atheists, and a thousand such political° monsters. He should have been Pope, but instead of coming to it by the primitive decency° of the Church, he did bestow bribes, so largely and so impudently as if
115 he would have carried it away without

Heaven's knowledge. Some good he hath done——

DELIO   You have given too much of him. What's his brother?

ANTONIO   The Duke there? a most perverse and turbulent nature:
What appears in him mirth, is merely outside;   120
If he laugh heartily, it is to laugh
All honesty out of fashion.

DELIO   Twins?°

ANTONIO   In quality:
He° speaks with others' tongues, and hears men's suits
With others' ears, will seem to sleep o' th' bench
Only to entrap offenders in their answers;   125
Dooms men to death by information,°
Rewards, by hearsay.°

DELIO   Then the law to him
Is like a foul black cobweb to a spider:
He makes it his dwelling, and a prison
To entangle those shall feed him.°

ANTONIO   Most true: 130
He ne'er pays debts, unless they be shrewd turns,°
And those he will confess that he doth owe.
Last, for his brother there, the Cardinal:
They that do flatter him most say oracles°
Hang at his lips, and verily I believe them: 135
For the devil speaks in them.
But for their sister, the right noble Duchess,
You never fixed your eye on three fair medals,
Cast in one figure, of so different temper.°

84 **Grecian horse** The huge wooden horse which the Greeks secretly filled with their best and noblest soldiers and which the Trojans foolishly transported within the walls of their city. sd **Cariola** Cariola's name, like Castruchio's, is thematically appropriate. A "carriolo" was, among other things, a trundle bed, which servants like Cariola used to sleep in so that they might remain accessible to their mistresses. 91 **come about** returned to port. 101 **flashes** examples of showy behavior. 104–105 **spring . . . toads** countenance of nobility hides a vicious, scheming temperament. 108 **Hercules** a mythical hero, considered the strongest mortal, who performed twelve superhuman "labors." 110 **political** plotting. 112–113 **primitive decency** simple and straightforward honesty.

122 **Twins** Are these two brothers twins, then? 123 **He** Ferdinand. 126 **information** the testimony of informers. 126–127 **Dooms . . . hearsay** Antonio implies that Ferdinand's judgments are arbitrary and cruel, for the testimony of informers, who are paid for what they say, is hardly more reliable evidence than hearsay. When Ferdinand is their judge, men are doomed to death or rewarded indiscriminately as he chooses. 130 **those . . . him** those that he feeds upon. 131 **shrewd turns** evil doings. 134 **oracles** words of great wisdom. 138–139 **You . . . temper** You have never seen three medals depicting the same figure which are made of such different kinds of metal as these three people.

140 For her discourse, it is so full of rapture,
You only will begin, then to be sorry
When she doth end her speech; and wish,
 in wonder,
She held it less vainglory to talk much
Than your penance, to hear her.° Whilst
 she speaks,
145 She throws upon a man so sweet a look,
That it were able to raise one to a gal-
 liard°
That lay in a dead palsy; and to° dote
On that sweet countenance. But in that
 look
There speaketh so divine a continence,
150 As cuts off all lascivious and vain hope.
Her days are practiced° in such noble
 virtue,
That sure her nights, nay more, her very
 sleeps,
Are more in heaven, than other ladies'
 shrifts.°
Let all sweet ladies break their flatt'ring
 glasses,°
And dress themselves in her.°
155 DELIO   Fie, Antonio,
You play the wire-drawer° with her com-
 mendations.
ANTONIO I'll case the picture up.° Only
 thus much°—
All her particular worth grows to this
 sum:
She stains° the time past, lights the time to
 come.

141–144 **You . . . her** a deceptively difficult statement, which may be paraphrased: Just when you
have begun (to feel this rapture), you will become
sorry that she has ended her speech. And then,
under the wonder of her spell, you will wish that
she thought it more noble ("less vainglory") to talk
a great deal than she thought it discomforting to
you ("your penance") to hear her talk. 146 **galliard**
a lively dance. 147 **and to** and (it is also able to
make one). 151 **practiced** habitually spent. 153
shrifts confessions to a priest. 154 **glasses** mirrors.
155 **And . . . her** and follow her example. 156
wire-drawer one who draws out wire from metal
and, metaphorically, one who overextends the
limits of truth. 157 **I'll . . . up** put this picture of
her (that I have presented) away. **Only . . . much**
Only this will I say in summary. 159 **stains** deprives
of luster.

CARIOLA You must attend my lady, in the
 gallery,   160
Some half an hour hence.
ANTONIO   I shall.

[*Exeunt* ANTONIO *and* DELIO.]

FERDINAND Sister, I have a suit to you.°
DUCHESS   To me, sir?
FERDINAND A gentleman here: Daniel de
 Bosola,
One that was in the galleys.
DUCHESS   Yes, I know him.
FERDINAND A worthy fellow h'is. Pray let
 me entreat for   165
The provisorship of your horse.°
DUCHESS   Your knowledge of him
Commends him, and prefers him.
FERDINAND   Call him hither.

[*Exit* ATTENDANT.]

We are now upon parting.° Good Lord
 Silvio
Do us commend to all our noble friends
At the leaguer.°
SILVIO   Sir, I shall.   170
DUCHESS You are for Milan?
SILVIO   I am.
DUCHESS Bring the caroches.° We'll bring
 you down to the haven.

[*Exeunt* DUCHESS, CARIOLA, SILVIO,
CASTRUCHIO, RODERIGO, GRISOLAN, JULIA,
and ATTENDANTS.]

CARDINAL Be sure you entertain that
 Bosola
For your intelligence.° I would not be
 seen in't.
And therefore many times I have slighted
 him   175
When he did court our furtherance, as
 this morning.
FERDINAND Antonio, the great master of
 her household
Had been far fitter.

162 **a . . . you** one who has a request to make of
you. 165–166 **let . . . horse** Let me entreat you to
let him serve as your groom. 168 **upon parting** preparing to leave. 170 **leaguer** camp. 172 **caroches**
coaches. 173–174 **entertain . . . intelligence** use
Bosola to gather information secretly.

CARDINAL   You are deceived in him,
His nature is too honest for such business.—
He comes: I'll leave you.

[*Enter* BOSOLA.]

180 BOSOLA   I was lured° to you.
[*Exit* CARDINAL.]
FERDINAND   My brother here, the Cardinal, could never
Abide you.
BOSOLA   Never since he was in my debt.
FERDINAND   May be some oblique character in your face
Made him suspect you?
BOSOLA   Doth he study physiognomy?
There's no more credit to be given to th'
185   face,
Than to a sick man's urine, which some call
The physician's whore, because she cozens him.°
He did suspect me wrongfully.
FERDINAND   For that
You must give great men leave to take their times:
Distrust doth cause us seldom be° de-
190   ceived;
You see, the oft shaking of the cedar tree
Fastens it more at root.
BOSOLA   Yet take heed:
For to suspect a friend unworthily,
Instructs him the next way° to suspect you,
And prompts him to deceive you.
FERDINAND   There's gold.
195 BOSOLA   So:
What follows? Never rained such showers as these
Without thunderbolts i' th' tail of them.°

Whose throat must I cut?
FERDINAND   Your inclination to shed blood rides post°
Before my occasion to use you. I give you that°   200
To live i' th' court, here, and observe the Duchess,
To note all the particulars of her havior:
What suitors do solicit her for marriage
And whom she best affects. She's a young widow;
I would not have her marry again.
BOSOLA   No, sir?   205
FERDINAND   Do not you ask the reason, but be satisfied
I say I would not.
BOSOLA   It seems you would create me
One of your familiars.
FERDINAND   Familiar? what's that?
BOSOLA   Why, a very quaint invisible devil in flesh,
An intelligencer.
FERDINAND   Such a wind of thriving   210
thing I would wish thee; and ere long, thou mayst arrive
At a higher place° by't.
BOSOLA [*Trying to give the money back.*]
Take your devils,
Which hell calls angels:° these cursed gifts would make
You a corrupter, me an impudent traitor,   215
And should I take these they'd take me to hell.
FERDINAND   Sir, I'll take nothing from you that I have given.
There is a place that I procured for you
This morning, the provisorship o' th' horse,
Have you heard on't?
BOSOLA   No.

---

180 **lured** called, with the implicit idea of "enticed into a trap." 185–187 **There's . . . him** Most kinds of sickness would not be recognizable in a urinary analysis. 190 **seldom be** to be seldom. 194 **the . . . way** in the quickest way. 196–197 **Never . . . them** Bosola here refers to the mythical story in which Zeus transforms himself into a shower of gold in order to possess Danae, who is imprisoned in a brass tower. The obscene use of the word "tail" in this speech provides almost as good an example of

Bosola's cynicism as his bold conclusion: "Whose throat must I cut?" 199 **rides post** rides swiftly, upon horseback, changing mounts often. 200 **I . . . that** I command you. 212 **higher place** the kind of ambiguous statement that is characteristic of villains in Renaissance drama. Ferdinand may mean either a better social position or a scaffold (from which to be hanged). 214 **angels** gold coins, which derived their name from the image of the archangel Michael on them.

FERDINAND   'Tis yours; is't not worth
220   thanks?
BOSOLA   I would have you curse yourself
   now, that your bounty,
   Which makes men truly noble,° e'er
   should make
   Me a villain: oh, that to avoid ingratitude
   For the good deed you have done me, I
   must do
225   All the ill man can invent. Thus the devil
   Candies all sins o'er,° and what Heaven
   terms vild,°
   That names he complimental.°
FERDINAND   Be yourself.
   Keep your old garb of melancholy: 'twill
   express
   You envy those that stand above your
   reach,
   Yet strive not to come near 'em. This will
230   gain
   Access to private lodgings, where yourself
   May, like a politic dormouse,——
BOSOLA   As I have seen some,
   Feed in a lord's dish, half asleep, not
   seeming
   To listen to any talk, and yet these rogues
   Have cut his throat in a dream.° What's
235   my place?
   The provisorship o' th' horse? say then my
   corruption
   Grew out of horse dung. I am your crea-
   ture.
FERDINAND   Away!
BOSOLA   Let good men, for good deeds,
   covet good fame,
   Since place and riches oft are bribes of
240   shame;
   Sometimes the devil doth preach.
      Exit BOSOLA.

   [*Enter* CARDINAL, DUCHESS, *and* CARIOLA.]

CARDINAL   We are to part from you: and
   your own discretion
   Must now be your director.
FERDINAND   You are a widow:

You know already what man is; and there-
fore
Let not youth, high promotion, elo-
quence,——   245
CARDINAL   No, nor any thing without the
   addition, honor,
   Sway your high blood.
FERDINAND   Marry? they are
   most luxurious,°
   Will° wed twice.
CARDINAL   O fie!
FERDINAND   Their livers° are
   more spotted
   Than Laban's sheep.°
DUCHESS   Diamonds are of most value,
   They say, that have passed through most
   jewelers' hands.   250
FERDINAND   Whores, by that rule, are pre-
   cious.
DUCHESS   Will you hear me?
   I'll never marry——
CARDINAL   So most widows say,
   But commonly that motion° lasts no
   longer
   Than the turning of an hourglass; the
   funeral sermon
   And it, end both together.
FERDINAND   Now hear me: 255
   You live in a rank pasture; here, i' th'
   court,
   There is a kind of honeydew° that's
   deadly:
   'Twill poison your fame;° look to't; be
   not cunning,
   For they whose faces do belie their hearts
   Are witches, ere they arrive at twenty
   years,   260
   Ay, and give the devil suck.
DUCHESS   This is terrible good counsel.
FERDINAND   Hypocrisy is woven of a fine
   small thread,
   Subtler than Vulcan's engine:° yet, be-
   lieve't,

247 **luxurious** incontinent. 248 **Will** who will. **livers**
The liver was believed to be the source of passion.
249 **Laban's sheep** In Laban's flock were many
spotted sheep (Genesis 30:29–43). 253 **motion** resolution. 257 **honeydew** a sweet, sticky substance se-
creted by some plants. 258 **fame** reputation. 263
Vulcan's engine the net that Vulcan used to catch
his wife, Venus, and her paramour, Mars.

222 **Which . . . noble** because money gives man
a position of nobility in society. 226 **Candies . . .
o'er** makes sins seem tempting. **vild** vile. 227 **complimental** worthy of compliment, good. 235 **in a
dream** while he slept.

Your darkest actions, nay, your privat'st
  thoughts,
Will come to light.

265 CARDINAL   You may flatter yourself,
  And take your own choice, privately be
  married
  Under the eaves of night——

FERDINAND   Think't the best voyage
  That e'er you made; like the irregular
  crab,
  Which, though't goes backward, thinks
  that it goes right,
270 Because it goes its own way; but observe,
  Such weddings may more properly be said
  To be executed, than celebrated.

CARDINAL   The marriage night
  Is the entrance into some prison.

FERDINAND   And those joys,
  Those lustful pleasures, are like heavy
  sleeps
  Which do forerun man's mischief.°

275 CARDINAL   Fare you well.
  Wisdom begins at the end:° remember it.
  [*Exit* CARDINAL.]

DUCHESS   I think this speech between you
  both was studied,
  It came so roundly off.

FERDINAND   You are my sister,
  This was my father's poniard:° do you see,
  I'd be loath to see't look rusty,° 'cause
280   'twas his.
  I would have you to give o'er these charge-
  able° revels;
  A visor and a mask° are whispering-
  rooms°
  That were ne'er built for goodness: fare
  ye well.
  And women like that part, which, like the
  lamprey,°
  Hath ne'er a bone in't.

DUCHESS   Fie sir!

FERDINAND   Nay,   *285*
  I mean the tongue—variety of courtship—°
  What cannot a neat knave with a smooth
  tale
  Make a woman believe? Farewell, lusty
  widow.

[*Exit* FERDINAND.]

DUCHESS   Shall this move me? If all my
  royal kindred
  Lay in my way unto this marriage,   *290*
  I'd make them my low footsteps.° And
  even now,
  Even in this hate, as men in some great
  battles,
  By apprehending danger, have achiev'd
  Almost impossible actions (I have heard
  soldiers say so),
  So I, through frights and threat'nings, will
  assay   *295*
  This dangerous venture. Let old wives re-
  port
  I winked, and chose a husband. Cariola,
  To thy known secrecy I have given up
  More than my life, my fame.°

CARIOLA   Both shall be safe:
  For I'll conceal this secret from the world *300*
  As warily as those that trade in poison
  Keep poison from their children.

DUCHESS   Thy protestation
  Is ingenious° and hearty: I believe it.
  Is Antonio come?

CARIOLA   He attends you.

DUCHESS   Good, dear soul,
  Leave me; but place thyself behind the
  arras,   *305*
  Where thou mayst overhear us. Wish me
  good speed,
  For I am going into a wilderness,
  Where I shall find nor path, nor friendly
  clew°
  To be my guide.

---

275 **mischief** misfortune. 276 **Wisdom . . . end** considers the end before beginning an action. 279 **poniard** dagger. 280 **I'd . . . rusty** I would not like to see it covered with your blood ("rusty"). 281 **chargeable** expensive. 282 **visor . . . mask** part of the costume used by lords and ladies participating in the revelry of a masque. **whispering-rooms** small rooms where secret, often amorous, interviews were held. 284 **lamprey** eel-like fish.

286 **variety of courtship** (the source of) variety in courtship (because it can express love in so many different ways). (?) 291 **footsteps** steppingstones. 299 **fame** reputation. 303 **ingenious** straightforward. 308 **clew** something that helps one out of a labyrinth.

[CARIOLA *goes behind the curtain, and the* DUCHESS *draws the traverse to reveal* ANTONIO.]

              I sent for you. Sit down:
Take pen and ink, and write. Are you ready?
310 ANTONIO   Yes.
DUCHESS   What did I say?
ANTONIO   That I should write somewhat.
DUCHESS   Oh, I remember:
After these triumphs and this large expense
It's fit, like thrifty husbands,° we inquire
315 What's laid up for tomorrow.
ANTONIO   So please your beauteous excellence.
DUCHESS   Beauteous?
Indeed I thank you. I look young for your sake:
You have ta'en my cares upon you.
ANTONIO   I'll fetch your grace
The particulars of your revenue and expense.
DUCHESS   Oh, you are an upright treasurer,
320   but you mistook,°
For when I said I meant to make inquiry
What's laid up for tomorrow, I did mean
What's laid up yonder for me.
ANTONIO   Where?
DUCHESS   In heaven.
I am making my will, as 'tis fit princes should,
325 In perfect memory, and I pray, sir, tell me
Were not one better make it smiling, thus,
Than in deep groans and terrible ghastly looks,
As if the gifts we parted with procured
That violent distraction?
ANTONIO   Oh, much better.
DUCHESS   If I had a husband now, this care
330   were quit;
But I intend to make you overseer.
What good deed shall we first remember? Say.
ANTONIO   Begin with that first good deed, began i' th' world,

After man's creation, the sacrament of marriage.
I'd have you first provide for a good husband;   335
Give him all.
DUCHESS   All?
ANTONIO   Yes, your excellent self.
DUCHESS   In a winding sheet?
ANTONIO   In a couple.
DUCHESS   St. Winifred!° that were a strange will.
ANTONIO   'Twere strange
If there were no will in you to marry again.
DUCHESS   What do you think of marriage?   340
ANTONIO   I take't, as those that deny purgatory:
It locally°contains or heaven, or hell;
There's no third place in't.
DUCHESS   How do you affect° it?
ANTONIO   My banishment, feeding my melancholy,
Would often reason thus:——
DUCHESS   Pray, let's hear it.   345
ANTONIO   Say a man never marry, nor have children,
What takes that from him? only the bare name
Of being a father, or the weak delight
To see the little wanton° ride a-cock-horse
Upon a painted stick, or hear him chatter   350
Like a taught starling.
DUCHESS   Fie, fie, what's all this?
One of your eyes is bloodshot, use my ring to't.
They say 'tis very sovereign:° 'twas my wedding ring,
And I did vow never to part with it,
But to my second husband.   355
ANTONIO   You have parted with it now.
DUCHESS   Yes, to help your eyesight.
ANTONIO   You have made me stark blind.
DUCHESS   How?
ANTONIO   There is a saucy and ambitious devil

---

314 **husbands** a pun, meaning both "stewards" and "married men." 320 **mistook** misunderstood (me).

338 **St. Winifred** a Welsh saint of the seventh century who was beheaded by Caradoc ap Alauc when she rejected his amorous advances. 342 **locally** in itself. 343 **affect** feel about. 349 **wanton** fellow. 353 **sovereign** effective.

Is dancing in this circle.°
DUCHESS   Remove him.
ANTONIO   How?
DUCHESS   There needs small conjuration,°
360   when your finger
May do it: thus, is it fit?°

*[She puts the ring on his finger and] he
kneels.*

ANTONIO   What said you?
DUCHESS   Sir,
This goodly roof of yours is too low
  built;°
I cannot stand upright in't, nor discourse
Without° I raise it higher: raise yourself,
Or if you please, my hand° to help you:
365   so.

[Raises him.]

ANTONIO   Ambition, madam, is a great
  man's madness
That is not kept in chains and close-pent
  rooms,
But in fair lightsome lodgings, and is girt
With the wild noise of prattling visitants,°
370   Which makes it lunatic, beyond all cure.
Conceive not I am so stupid,° but I aim
Whereto your favors tend. But he's a fool
That, being a-cold, would thrust his hand
  i' th' fire
To warm them.
DUCHESS   So, now the ground's broke,
375   You may discover what a wealthy mine
I make you lord of.
ANTONIO   O my unworthiness!
DUCHESS   You were ill° to sell yourself.
This dark'ning of your worth is not like
  that
Which tradesmen use° i' th' city; their
  false lights

Are to rid° bad wares off. And I must tell
  you   380
If you will know where breathes a com-
  plete man,
(I speak it without flattery), turn your
  eyes
And progress through° yourself.
ANTONIO   Were there nor heaven, nor hell,
I should be honest: I have long served
  virtue,
And ne'er ta'en wages of her.
DUCHESS   Now she pays it.   385
The misery of us that are born great:
We are forced to woo, because none dare
  woo us.
And as a tyrant doubles with his words,°
And fearfully° equivocates, so we
Are forced to express our violent passions   390
In riddles and in dreams, and leave the
  path
Of simple virtue, which was never made
To seem the thing it is not. Go, go brag
You have left me heartless; mine is in your
  bosom:
I hope 'twill multiply love there. You do
  tremble: 395
Make not your heart so dead a piece of
  flesh
To fear more than to love me. Sir, be con-
  fident.
What is't distracts you? This is flesh and
  blood, sir,
'Tis not the figure cut in alabaster
Kneels at my husband's tomb.° Awake,
  awake, man!   400
I do here put off all vain ceremony,

---

380 **rid** pass. 383 **progress through** look carefully at.
388 **doubles . . . words** employs phrases with ambiguous, double meanings. 389 **fearfully** causing
fear (in others). 399–400 '**Tis . . . tomb** The whiteness of alabaster made it, like marble, suitable for
use in funeral monuments. The Duchess' reference
here is, no doubt, to a statue that marks her first
husband's tomb. But like much of the language in
this scene—with its talk of wills, winding sheets,
and wildly jabbering lunatics—the imagery looks
forward to the Duchess' future as well as backward
to her past. By the careful repetition of images
such as these, Webster skillfully outlines the hostile,
constricting world that circumscribes the lovers and
threatens their happiness.

359 **circle** the ring. 360 **small conjuration** little
magic. 361 **is it fit** Does it fit? 362 **This . . . built**
Your humble attitude makes me uncomfortable.
364 **Without** unless. 365 **my hand** (here is) my
hand. 369 **visitants** visitors. 371 **so stupid** so lunatic
(as to be ambitious). 377 **ill** ill-advised. 379 **tradesmen use** Food shops were kept dark so that buyers
could not closely examine a tradesman's wares.

And only do appear to you, a young widow
That claims you for her husband, and like a widow,
I use but half a blush in't.°

ANTONIO   Truth speak for me,
405 I will remain the constant sanctuary
Of your good name.

DUCHESS   I thank you, gentle love,
And 'cause° you shall not come to me in debt,
Being now my steward, here upon your lips
I sign your *Quietus est.*° This you should have begged now:
I have seen children oft eat sweetmeats
410 thus,
As fearful to devour them too soon.

ANTONIO   But for your brothers?

DUCHESS   Do not think of them:
All discord without° this circumference
Is only to be pitied, and not feared.
415 Yet, should they know it, time will easily
Scatter the tempest.

ANTONIO   These words should be mine,
And all the parts you have spoke, if some part of it
Would not have savored° flattery.

DUCHESS   Kneel.

[*Enter* CARIOLA.]

ANTONIO   Ha?

DUCHESS   Be not amazed; this woman's of my counsel.
I have heard lawyers say, a contract in a
420 chamber,
Per verba [de] presenti,° is absolute marriage.

Bless, Heaven, this sacred gordian,° which let violence
Never untwine.

ANTONIO   And may our sweet affections, like the spheres,
Be still° in motion.°

DUCHESS   Quick'ning,° and make 425
The like soft music.°

ANTONIO   That we may imitate the loving palms,
Best emblem of a peaceful marriage,
That ne'er bore fruit divided.°

DUCHESS   What can the Church force more?   430

ANTONIO   That Fortune may not know an accident
Either of joy or sorrow, to divide
Our fixèd wishes.

DUCHESS   How can the Church build faster?
We now are man and wife, and 'tis the Church
That must but echo this. Maid,° stand apart,   435
I now am blind.°

ANTONIO   What's your conceit° in this?

DUCHESS   I would have you lead your fortune by the hand,
Unto your marriage bed:
(You speak in me this, for we now are one)
We'll only lie, and talk together, and plot 440
T'appease my humorous° kindred; and if you please,
Like the old tale, in *Alexander and Lodowick,*°

---

404 **I . . . in't** I have been made bold by my experience. 407 **'cause** so that. 409 **Quietus est** This phrase, which was often used in account books, literally means "It is finished," and in this instance the reference is to Antonio's obligations as steward. But the word "quietus" is also associated with death (cf. *Hamlet* III.i.75), since man makes his acquittance with nature at death. Here, although the Duchess is conscious of only the first meaning, both are implicit because the marriage hastens Antonio's death. 413 **without** outside. 418 **savored** resembled. 421 **Per . . . presenti** "through words of the present (tense)": the lovers henceforth accept

each other as husband and wife, in a contract that is legally valid. 422 **gordian** a knot that cannot be untied. 424-425 **like . . . motion** Planets were thought to revolve around the earth in concentric, transparent, spherical shells. 425 **still** always. **Quick'ning** stirring to life. 426 **music** The harmonious motion of the planets in the spheres was supposed to make sweet music. 427-429 **That . . . divided** Fruit-bearing palm trees were thought to depend for their productivity upon a male palm tree. 435 **Maid** Cariola. 436 **I . . . blind** I have been made blind by love (because I have eyes only for Antonio). **conceit** meaning. 441 **humorous** volatile, subject to many humors. 442 **Alexander and Lodowick** two legendary friends so alike no one

Lay a naked sword between us, keep us chaste.

Oh, let me shroud° my blushes in your bosom,

445 Since 'tis the treasury of all my secrets.

[ANTONIO *and the* DUCHESS *begin to exit slowly.*]

CARIOLA   Whether the spirt of greatness, or of woman

Reign most in her, I know not, but it shows

A fearful madness: I owe her much of pity.

Exeunt.

Act Two

SCENE ONE   [*The* DUCHESS' *palace about a year later*]

[*Enter* BOSOLA *and* CASTRUCHIO.]

BOSOLA   You say you would fain be taken for an eminent courtier?

CASTRUCHIO   'Tis the very main° of my ambition.

5 BOSOLA   Let me see, you have a reasonable good face for't already, and your nightcap° expresses your ears sufficient largely.° I would have you learn to twirl the strings of your band° with a good grace; and in a

10 set speech, at th'end of every sentence, to hum three or four times, or blow your nose till it smart again, to recover your memory. When you come to be a president° in criminal causes, if you smile upon

15 a prisoner, hang him, but if you frown upon him and threaten him, let him be sure to scape the gallows.

CASTRUCHIO   I would be a very merry president,——

BOSOLA   Do not sup a-nights; 'twill beget 20 you an admirable wit.

CASTRUCHIO   Rather it would make me have a good stomach° to quarrel, for they say your roaring boys° eat meat seldom, and that makes them so valiant. But how 25 shall I know whether the people take me for an eminent fellow?

BOSOLA   I will teach a trick to know it: give out you lie a-dying, and if you hear the common people curse you, be sure 30 you are taken for one of the prime nightcaps.°

[*Enter* OLD LADY.]

You come from painting now?

OLD LADY   From what?

BOSOLA   Why, from your scurvy face- 35 physic.° To behold thee not painted inclines somewhat near a miracle. These, in thy face here, were deep ruts and foul sloughs° the last progress.° There was a lady in France that, having had the small- 40 pox, flayed the skin off her face, to make it more level; and whereas before she looked like a nutmeg grater,° after she resembled an abortive hedgehog.°

OLD LADY   Do you call this painting? 45

BOSOLA   No, no, but you call it careening° of an old morphewed° lady, to make her disembogue° again. There's rough-cast° phrase to your plastic.°

OLD LADY   It seems you are well acquainted 50 with my closet?°

---

23 **good stomach** predisposition. 24 **roaring boys** bullies, quarrelsome young men. 32 **nightcaps** lawyers. 36 **face-physic** a preparation that purges the face of unwanted layers of skin. 39 **sloughs** both "ditches" and "layers of dead skin." **the . . . progress** the last time a journey was made by our ruler (and by the coach of time across your face). 43 **nutmeg grater** because her face was so pock-marked. 44 **hedgehog** In flaying, the skin would be removed in strips that would roll up and stick out like spines on a hedgehog. 46 **careening** scraping. 47 **morphewed** covered with scaly skin. 48 **disembogue** set out on a journey. **rough-cast** cast in a kind of rough plaster. 48–49 **There's . . . plastic** There's language as ugly as your appearance. 49 **plastic** molding. 51 **closet** most private room.

could tell them apart; so true was Lodowick to their friendship that he married the Princess of Hungaria in Alexander's name and then every night placed a naked sword in the bed between himself and the Princess in order to keep from wronging Alexander. 444 **shroud** bury.

II.i 3 **main** goal. 7 **nightcap** the coif, a white cap worn by lawyers. **expresses . . . largely** makes your ears stick out far enough. 9 **band** white tabs that were also part of the lawyer's official costume. 14 **president** presiding judge.

BOSOLA   One would suspect it for a shop of witchcraft, to find in it the fat of serpents, spawn of snakes, Jews' spittle, and
55   their young children's ordure, and all these for the face. I would sooner eat a dead pigeon,° taken from the soles of the feet of one sick of the plague, than kiss one of you fasting.° Here are two of you,
60   whose sin of your youth is the very patrimony of the physician,° makes him renew his footcloth° with the spring, and change his high-prized° courtesan with the fall of the leaf: I do wonder you do not loathe
65   yourselves. Observe my meditation now: What thing is in this outward form of man
To be beloved? We account it ominous,
If nature do produce a colt, or lamb,
A fawn, or goat, in any limb resembling
70   A man; and fly from't as a prodigy.°
Man stands amazed to see his deformity,
In any other creature but himself.
But in our own flesh, though we bear diseases
Which have their true names only ta'en from beasts,
As the most ulcerous wolf,° and swinish
75   measle;°
Though we are eaten up of lice and worms,
And though continually we bear about us
A rotten and dead body, we delight
To hide it in rich tissue:° all our fear,
80   Nay, all our terror, is lest our physician
Should put us in the ground, to be made sweet.
Your wife's gone to Rome. You two couple,° and get you

To the wells at Lucca,° to recover° your aches.

[*Exeunt* CASTRUCHIO *and* OLD LADY.]

I have other work on foot: I observe our Duchess
Is sick a-days, she pukes, her stomach seethes,°   85
The fins° of her eyelids look most teeming blue,°
She wanes i' th' cheek, and waxes fat i' th' flank;
And, contrary to our Italian fashion,
Wears a loose-bodied gown. There's somewhat in't.
I have a trick may chance discover it,   90
A pretty one; I have bought some apricocks,°
The first our spring yields.° [*Enter* ANTONIO *and* DELIO.]
DELIO [*Aside.*]   And so long since married? You amaze me.
ANTONIO   [*Aside.*]   Let me seal your lips for ever,
For did I think that anything but th' air
Could carry these words from you, I should wish   95
You had no breath at all. [*To* BOSOLA.] Now sir, in your contemplation?°
You are studying to become a great wise fellow?
BOSOLA   Oh sir, the opinion° of wisdom is a foul tetter,° that runs all over a man's body: if simplicity direct us to have no°   100
evil, it directs us to a happy being. For the subtlest folly proceeds from the subtlest wisdom. Let me be simply honest.

---

57 **dead pigeon** Pigeons were sometimes pressed against plague sores in the hope that the poison would be drawn to the birds and out of the sores. 59 **fasting** when your stomach is empty (and your breath foul). 60–61 **whose . . . physician** whose sins of lust in your youth have infected you with syphilis, and have thus guaranteed the physician an income for life. 62 **footcloth** decorative accouterments for a horse, which advertised the eminence of the owner. 63 **high-prized** both highly prized and high-priced. 70 **prodigy** unnatural monster. 75 **wolf** ulcer. **swinish measle** leprosy. 79 **rich tissue** elaborate clothing. 82 **couple** join, both as traveling

and as sleeping companions. 83 **wells at Lucca** warm springs near Pisa. **recover** heal. 85 **seethes** is violently agitated. 86 **fins** edges. **teeming blue** the blue color characteristic of the eyelids of pregnant women. 91–92 **I . . . yields** Bosola intends to find out if the Duchess is pregnant by offering her apricots and thus appealing to the strong craving for fruit that is often demonstrated by pregnant women. 91 **apricocks** apricots. 96 **in your contemplation** (Have we interrupted you while you were rapt) in contemplation? 98 **opinion** teachings. 99 **tetter** skin disease, eczema. 100 **have no** have nothing to do with.

ANTONIO   I do understand your inside.°
105 BOSOLA   Do you so?
ANTONIO   Because you would not seem to
appear to th' world
Puffed up with your preferment, you continue
This out-of-fashion melancholy; leave it,
leave it.
BOSOLA   Give me leave to be honest in any
110 phrase, in any compliment whatsoever.
Shall I confess myself to you? I look no
higher than I can reach: they are the gods,
that must ride on winged horses; a lawyer's mule of a slow pace will both suit my
115 disposition and business. For, mark me,
when a man's mind rides faster than his
horse can gallop they quickly both tire.
ANTONIO   You would look up to heaven,
but I think
The devil, that rules i' th' air, stands in
your lights.
120 BOSOLA   Oh, sir, you are lord of the ascendant,° chief man with the Duchess: a
duke was your cousin-german,° removed.
Say you were lineally descended from
King Pippin,° or he himself, what of this?
125 Search the heads of the greatest rivers in
the world, you shall find them but bubbles
of water. Some would think the souls of
princes were brought forth by some more
weighty cause than those of meaner per-
130 sons; they are deceived; there's the same
hand to them: the like passions sway
them; the same reason that makes a vicar
go to law for a tithe pig° and undo his
neighbors, makes them° spoil a whole
135 province, and batter down goodly cities
with the cannon.

[*Enter* DUCHESS *and* LADIES.]

DUCHESS   Your arm, Antonio; do I not
grow fat?
I am exceeding short-winded. Bosola,
I would have you, sir, provide for me a
litter,

Such a one, as the Duchess of Florence
rode in.   *140*
BOSOLA   The Duchess used one, when she
was great with child.
DUCHESS   I think she did. [*To one of her
ladies.*]   Come hither, mend my ruff,°
Here. When?° Thou art such a tedious
lady; and
Thy breath smells of lemon peels;° would
thou hadst done;°
Shall I sound° under thy fingers? I am   *145*
So troubled with the mother.°
BOSOLA   [*Aside.*]   I fear too much.
DUCHESS [*To* ANTONIO.]   I have heard you
say that the French courtiers
Wear their hats on 'fore the King.
ANTONIO   I have seen it.
DUCHESS   In the presence?°
ANTONIO   Yes.
DUCHESS   Why should not we bring up that
fashion?   *150*
'Tis ceremony more than duty that con-
sists
In the removing of a piece of felt:
Be you the example to the rest o' th'
court;
Put on your hat first.
ANTONIO   You must pardon me:
I have seen, in colder countries than in
France,°   *155*
Nobles stand bare° to th' prince; and the
distinction

142 **ruff** a lace collar. 143 **When** an expression of
impatience. 144 **peels** In the first three editions of
the play, the word is spelled "pils" and "pills,"
which could mean either pills or peels. Though
the spelling becomes "peels" in the fourth edition,
we cannot know for certain whether this waiting-
woman sweetened her breath with lemon peels or
with little lemon pills. The exact particulars of
this reference, though, are not important; what
matters is its general effect: the Duchess' complaint
again draws attention to one of the corruptions of
the flesh that Bosola has just railed against. **would
. . . done** I wish you were finished. 145 **sound**
swoon. 146 **mother** the name Elizabethans gave to
a kind of hysteria that was accompanied by swelling
in the throat and choking. The pun on the obvious
meaning of "mother" is also intended, and it is
this meaning of the word that Bosola refers to in
his subsequent aside. 149 **presence** presence chamber. 155 **in . . . France** i.e. in England. 156 **bare**
bare-headed.

104 **inside** the true nature that you are covering
up. 120–121 **lord . . . ascendant** ruling power. 122
cousin-german first ("germane") cousin. 124 **King
Pippin** father of Charlemagne. 133 **tithe pig** a pig
owed to the vicar as a tithe. 34 **them** princes.

Methought showed reverently.

BOSOLA   I have a present for your grace.

DUCHESS   For me, sir?

BOSOLA   Apricocks, madam.

DUCHESS   O sir, where are they?
I have heard of none to-year.°

160 BOSOLA   [*Aside.*]   Good, her color rises.

DUCHESS   Indeed, I thank you: they are
wondrous fair ones.
What an unskillful fellow is our gardener!
We shall have none this month.

BOSOLA   Will not your grace pare them?

DUCHESS   No, they taste of musk,° me-
165   thinks; indeed they do.

BOSOLA   I know not: yet I wish your grace
had pared 'em.

DUCHESS   Why?

BOSOLA   I forgot to tell you the knave
gard'ner,
Only to raise his profit by them the
sooner,
Did ripen them in horse dung.

DUCHESS   Oh, you jest.°
[*To* ANTONIO.] You shall judge: pray
taste one.

170 ANTONIO   Indeed, madam,
I do not love the fruit.

DUCHESS   Sir, you are loath
To rob us of our dainties: 'tis a delicate
fruit,
They say they are restorative?°

BOSOLA   'Tis a pretty art,
This grafting.°

DUCHESS   'Tis so: a bett'ring of nature.

BOSOLA   To make a pippin grow upon a
175   crab,°
A damson on a blackthorn.° [*Aside.*]
How greedily she eats them!
A whirlwind strike off these bawd far-
thingales,°

For, but for that, and the loose-bodied
gown,
I should have discovered apparently°
The young springal° cutting a caper in
her belly.   *180*

DUCHESS   I thank you, Bosola: they were
right good ones,
If they do not make me sick.

ANTONIO   How now, madam?

DUCHESS   This green fruit and my stomach
are not friends.
How they swell me!

BOSOLA [*Aside.*]   Nay, you are too much
swelled already.   *185*

DUCHESS   Oh, I am in an extreme cold
sweat.

BOSOLA   I am very sorry. [*Exit.*]

DUCHESS   Lights to my chamber! O, good
Antonio,
I fear I am undone.   *Exit* DUCHESS.

DELIO   Lights there, lights!

ANTONIO   O my most trusty Delio, we are
lost:
I fear she's fall'n in labor, and there's left *190*
No time for her remove.

DELIO   Have you prepared
Those ladies to attend her? and procured
That politic° safe conveyance for the
midwife
Your Duchess plotted?°

ANTONIO   I have.

DELIO   Make use then of this forced oc-
casion:°   *195*
Give out that Bosola hath poisoned her,
With these apricocks. That will give some
color°
For her keeping close.°

ANTONIO   Fie, fie, the physicians
Will then flock to her.

DELIO   For that you may pretend
She'll use some prepared antidote of her
own,   *200*
Lest the physicians should repoison her.

160 **to-year** this year. 165 **musk** an animal secretion used in making perfume. 169 **Oh, you jest** The Duchess' unruffled reaction to Bosola's vile suggestion attests to the intensity of her desire for fruit. 173 **restorative** healthful. 174 **grafting** a double-entendre, referring to propagation both in fruit trees and in human beings (because the physical union in sexual intercourse can be considered another form of grafting). 175 **pippin, crab** different kinds of apples. 176 **damson, blackthorn** different kinds of plums. 177 **farthingales** hooped petticoats. 179 **apparently** openly manifesting itself. 180 **springal** youth. 193 **politic** secret. 194 **plotted** planned. 195 **forced occasion** circumstances forced upon us. 197 **color** reason. 198 **close** privately shut away.

ANTONIO   I am lost in amazement. I know not what to think on't.

Ex[eunt].

SCENE TWO   [*A hall in the* DUCHESS' *palace*]

[*Enter* BOSOLA *and* OLD LADY.]

BOSOLA   So, so: there's no question but her tetchiness° and most vulturous eating of the apricocks are apparent° signs of breeding—[*To the* OLD LADY.] Now?

5   OLD LADY   I am in haste, sir.

BOSOLA   There was a young waiting-woman, had a monstrous desire to see the glasshouse°——

OLD LADY   Nay, pray let me go!

10   BOSOLA   And it was only to know what strange instrument° it was, should swell up a glass to the fashion of a woman's belly.

OLD LADY   I will hear no more of the
15   glasshouse; you are still abusing women!

BOSOLA   Who, I? no, only, by the way now and then, mention your frailties. The orange tree bears ripe and green fruit and blossoms altogether. And some of
20   you give entertainment for pure love, but more, for more precious reward. The lusty spring smells well, but drooping autumn tastes well.° If we have the same golden showers that rained in the time of
25   Jupiter the Thunderer, you have the same Danaes still, to hold up their laps to receive them.° Didst thou never study the mathematics?

OLD LADY   What's that, sir?

BOSOLA   Why, to know the trick how to
30   make a many lines meet in one center.° Go, go; give your foster daughters° good counsel: tell them, that the devil takes delight to hang at a woman's girdle, like a false rusty watch, that she cannot dis-
35   cern how the time passes.°

[*Exit* OLD LADY.]

[*Enter* ANTONIO, DELIO, RODERIGO, GRISOLAN.]

ANTONIO   Shut up the court gates.

RODERIGO   Why sir? What's the danger?

ANTONIO   Shut up the posterns° presently,° and call

All the officers o' th' court.

GRISOLAN   I shall instantly.

[*Exit.*]

ANTONIO   Who keeps the key o' th' park gate?

RODERIGO   Forobosco.   40

ANTONIO   Let him bring't presently.

[*Exit* RODERIGO.]

[*Enter* SERVANTS, GRISOLAN, RODERIGO.]

FIRST SERVANT   Oh, gentlemen o' th' court, the foulest treason!

BOSOLA   [*Aside.*] If that these apricocks should be poisoned now,

Without my knowledge!

FIRST SERVANT   There was taken even now

A Switzer° in the Duchess' bedchamber.

SECOND SERVANT   A Switzer?   45

FIRST SERVANT   With a pistol in his great codpiece.°

BOSOLA   Ha, ha, ha.

II.ii 2 **tetchiness** touchiness. 3 **apparent** obvious. 8 **glasshouse** glass factory. 11 **instrument** a double-entendre. 21–23 **The . . . well** The lusty young woman and the aging whore both find something rewarding in love—one, the act itself; the other, the money she receives for it. 23–27 **If . . . them** See note to I.ii.196–197. Bosola's argument here is simply that where there are men who are willing to pay for love, there are women to sell it.

30–31 **Why . . . center** another obscene reference to the lap of a whore. 32 **foster daughters** women for whom she serves as a midwife. 36 **the . . . passes** Because the devil impassions men with desires even for women who are old, women are deluded into thinking that they have not lost the beauty of their youth (and have, consequently, not grown old). 38 **posterns** back gates. **presently** now, at this present moment. 45 **Switzer** a Swiss mercenary. 46 **With . . . codpiece** The codpiece was a baglike flap formerly worn in the front of men's breeches and since replaced by the fly. Bosola's laughter upon hearing that the pistol has been hidden in the Switzer's codpiece results from his recognition of the obvious double-entendre in

FIRST SERVANT   The codpiece was the case
  for't.
SECOND SERVANT   There was a cunning
  traitor.
Who would have searched his codpiece?
FIRST SERVANT   True, if he had kept out of
  the ladies' chambers.
And all the moulds of his buttons were
50 leaden bullets.
SECOND SERVANT   Oh wicked cannibal: a
  firelock in's codpiece?
FIRST SERVANT   'Twas a French plot, upon
  my life.
SECOND SERVANT   To see what the devil
  can do.
ANTONIO   All the officers here?
SERVANTS   We are.
ANTONIO   Gentlemen,
  We have lost much plate° you know; and
  but this evening
  Jewels, to the value of four thousand
55 ducats
  Are missing in the Duchess' cabinet.°
  Are the gates shut?
FIRST SERVANT   Yes.
ANTONIO   'Tis the Duchess' pleasure
  Each officer be locked into his chamber
  Till the sun-rising; and to send the keys
  Of all their chests, and of their outward
60 doors
  Into her bedchamber. She is very sick.
RODERIGO   At her pleasure.°
ANTONIO   She entreats you take't not ill.
  The innocent
  Shall be the more approved° by it.
BOSOLA   Gentlemen o' th' wood yard,°
65 where's your Switzer now?
FIRST SERVANT   By this hand, 'twas cred-
  ibly reported by one o' th' black guard.°

[*Exeunt* BOSOLA, RODERIGO, *and* SERVANTS.]

DELIO   How fares it with the Duchess?
ANTONIO   She's exposed
  Unto the worst of torture, pain, and fear.
70 DELIO   Speak to her all happy comfort.

"pistol"—a double-entendre that is developed by
the servants in the succeeding speeches.
54 **plate** money. 56 **in . . . cabinet** from the Duchess' chamber. 62 **At . . . pleasure** perhaps an un-
intentional pun. 64 **approved** proven good. 65 **wood**

ANTONIO   How I do play the fool with
  mine own danger!°
You are this night, dear friend, to post to
  Rome;°
My life lies in your service.
DELIO   Do not doubt me.
ANTONIO   Oh, 'tis far from me: and yet
  fear presents me
Somewhat° that looks like danger.
DELIO   Believe it, 75
'Tis but the shadow of your fear, no
  more:
How superstitiously we mind° our evils!
The throwing down salt, or crossing of a
  hare;
Bleeding at nose, the stumbling of a
  horse:
Or singing of a cricket, are of power   80
To daunt whole man in us.° Sir, fare you
  well:
I wish you all the joys of a blessèd father;
And, for my faith, lay this° unto your
  breast,
Old friends, like old swords, still are
  trusted best.   [*Exit* DELIO.]

[*Enter* CARIOLA *with a child.*]

CARIOLA   Sir, you are the happy father of
  a son: 85
Your wife commends him to you.
ANTONIO   Blessèd comfort!
For heaven's sake tend her well: I'll
  presently
Go set a figure° for's nativity.   *Exeunt.*

SCENE THREE   [*A hall in the* DUCHESS'
              palace]

[*Enter* BOSOLA *with a dark lanthorn.*°]

BOSOLA   Sure I did hear a woman shriek:
  list, ha?

---

yard place where firewood was cut. 67 **black guard**
kitchen servants. 71 **How . . . danger** What a fool
I am to increase the possibility of revealing our
secret marriage (by having a child). 72 **Rome**
where the Duchess' brothers are. 75 **Somewhat**
something. 77 **mind** notice. 81 **To . . . us** to rob
us of all our bravery. 83 **this** my faith. 88 **set a**
figure check the horoscope for.
II.iii.sd **dark lanthorn** a lantern with only one open-

And the sound came, if I received it
  right,
From the Duchess' lodgings; there's some
  stratagem
In the confining all our courtiers
To their several wards. I must have part
5   of° it,
My intelligence° will freeze else. List
  again,
It may be 'twas the melancholy bird,
Best friend of silence, and of solitariness,
The owl, that screamed so—ha!—An-
  tonio?

[*Enter* ANTONIO *with a candle, his sword
drawn.*]

ANTONIO   I heard some noise: who's there?
10   What art thou? Speak.
BOSOLA   Antonio! Put not your face nor
  body
To such a forced expression of fear—
I am Bosola, your friend.
ANTONIO   Bosola!
  [*Aside.*] This mole does undermine me
  —heard you not
A noise even now?
BOSOLA   From whence?
15 ANTONIO   From the Duchess' lodging.
BOSOLA   Not I. Did you?
ANTONIO   I did, or else I dreamed.
BOSOLA   Let's walk towards it.
ANTONIO   No. It may be 'twas
But the rising of the wind.
BOSOLA   Very likely.
Methinks 'tis very cold, and yet you sweat.
You look wildly.
20 ANTONIO   I have been setting a figure
For the Duchess' jewels.°
BOSOLA   Ah, and how
  falls your question?
Do you find it radical?°
ANTONIO   What's that to you?

'Tis rather to be questioned what design,
When all men were commanded to their
  lodgings,
Makes you a nightwalker.
BOSOLA   In sooth I'll tell you: 25
Now all the court's asleep, I thought the
  devil
Had least to do here; I came to say my
  prayers,
And if it do offend you I° do so,
You are a fine courtier.
ANTONIO   [*Aside.*] This fellow will undo
  me.
You gave the Duchess apricocks today;   30
Pray heaven they were not poisoned.
BOSOLA   Poisoned! a Spanish fig°
For the imputation!
ANTONIO   Traitors are ever confident,
Till they are discovered. There were
  jewels stol'n too,
In my conceit,° none are to be suspected   35
More than yourself.
BOSOLA   You are a false steward.
ANTONIO   Saucy slave! I'll pull thee up by
  the roots.
BOSOLA   May be the ruin will crush you to
  pieces.
ANTONIO   You are an impudent snake in-
  deed, sir,
Are you scarce warm, and do you show
  your sting?°   40
[BOSOLA° . . .
ANTONIO]   You libel well, sir.
BOSOLA   No sir, copy it out,
And I will set my hand to't.°

28 **I** that I. 32 **Spanish fig** an expression of contempt, accompanied by the obscene gesture of
thrusting the thumb between the forefinger and the
middle finger. 35 **conceit** opinion. 40 **Are . . .
sting** The reference is to the fiftieth fable of Aesop,
"The Countryman and the Snake." A villager finds
a snake almost frozen and takes it home to warm
it by the fire, but as soon as it is revived by the
heat, the serpent tries to attack the countryman's
wife and children. The reference to Bosola as
"scarce warm" here is motivated by the fact that
he has only recently been appointed to the provisorship of the Duchess' horses. 41 **Bosola** A speech
seems to be missing here. 41–42 **copy . . . to't**
Make your charges formally, and I will set my
hand to the task of answering them. (Otherwise,
be quiet.)(?)

ing, which could be closed to shut off the light
(often used by someone who wanted to move
stealthily at night). 5 **have . . . of** find out about.
6 **intelligence** information gathered as a spy. 20–
21 **I . . . jewels** I have been checking a horoscope
(to see if I can trace) the Duchess' jewels. 22 **radical**
resolvable by astrology.

ANTONIO   My nose bleeds.
One that were superstitious would count
This ominous—when it merely comes° by
chance.
Two letters, that are wrought here for my
45   name
Are drowned in blood!°
Mere accident. For you, sir, I'll take
order:°
I' th' morn you shall be safe.° [*Aside.*]
'Tis that must color
Her lying-in. [*To* BOSOLA.] Sir, this door
you pass not.
50   I do not hold it fit that you come near
The Duchess' lodgings till you have quit°
yourself;
[*Aside.*] The great are like the base; nay,
they are the same,
When they seek shameful ways to avoid
shame.   *Ex*[*it*].
BOSOLA   Antonio hereabout did drop a
paper,
Some of your help, false friend:° oh,
55   here it is.
What's here?—a child's nativity calculated?
[*Reads.*] The Duchess was delivered of a
son, 'tween the hours twelve and one, in
the night: Anno Dom: 1504.—That's this
60   year—*decimo nono Decembris,*—That's
this night—taken according to the Me-
ridian of Malfi—That's our Duchess:
happy discovery!—The Lord of the first
house,° being combust° in the ascendant,
65   signifies short life, and Mars being in a
human sign, joined to the tail of the

Dragon, in the eighth house, doth
threaten a violent death; *Caetera non
scrutantur.*°
Why now 'tis most apparent. This pre-
cise° fellow   70
Is the Duchess' bawd:° I have it to my
wish.°
This is a parcel of intelligency°
Our courtiers were cased up° for! It needs
must follow,
That I must be committed, on pretense
Of poisoning her, which I'll endure and
laugh at.   75
If one could find the father now—but
that
Time will discover. Old Castruchio
I' th' morning posts to Rome; by him I'll
send
A letter, that shall make her brothers'
galls
O'erflow their livers. This was a thrifty
way.°   80
Though lust do mask in ne'er so strange
disguise
She's oft found witty, but is never wise.
[*Exit.*]

SCENE FOUR   [*The* CARDINAL's *palace in
                 Rome*]

[*Enter* CARDINAL *and* JULIA.]

CARDINAL   Sit: thou art my best of wishes.
Prithee, tell me
What trick didst thou invent to come to
Rome
Without thy husband?
JULIA   Why, my lord, I told him
I came to visit an old anchorite°
Here, for devotion.

---

44 **merely comes** in actuality comes merely. 45–46
Two . . . blood Exactly what Antonio is referring
to here is a mystery. He may be holding two handkerchiefs, embroidered with his initials, that he has
used to absorb the blood from his nosebleed; or he
may hold two official letters that require his signa-
ture as steward and have become spotted with
blood. 47 **I'll . . . order** I'll issue an order for
your arrest. 48 **safe** in custody. 51 **quit** acquitted
yourself (of any blame for her sickness). 55 **false
friend** the dark lantern (associated with secret,
underhanded dealings proceeding under the cover
of night). 63–64 **Lord . . . house** the planet that
controls the boy's nativity. **combust** burned up by
being too near the sun (and, therefore, having lost
its power).

69 **Caetera non scrutantur** The rest (of the horoscope) remains unexamined. 70 **precise** (seemingly)
strait-laced. 71 **bawd** pander. **I . . . wish** I have
succeeded in getting what I wanted (i.e. important
secret information). 72 **parcel of intelligency** a
piece of really significant information. 73 **cased up**
ordered to keep to their quarters. 80 **thrifty way**
shrewd scheme.
II.iv. 4 **anchorite** hermit.

5 CARDINAL   Thou art a witty° false one:
I mean to him.

JULIA   You have prevailèd with me
Beyond my strongest thoughts: I would not° now
Find you inconstant.

CARDINAL   Do not put thyself
To such a voluntary torture, which proceeds
Out of your own guilt.

JULIA   How, my lord?

10 CARDINAL   You fear
My constancy, because you have approved°
Those giddy and wild turnings in yourself.

JULIA Did you e'er find them?

CARDINAL   Sooth, generally for women:
A man might strive to make glass malleable,
Ere he should make them fixed.

15 JULIA   So, my lord!——

CARDINAL We had need go borrow that fantastic glass°
Invented by Galileo the Florentine,
To view another spacious world i' th' moon,
And look to find a constant woman there.

JULIA This is very well, my lord.

20 CARDINAL   Why do you weep?
Are tears your justification? The selfsame tears
Will fall into your husband's bosom, lady,
With a loud protestation that you love him
Above the world. Come, I'll love you wisely,

25 That's jealously, since I am very certain
You cannot me make cuckold.°

JULIA   I'll go home
To my husband.

CARDINAL   You may thank me, lady,
I have taken you off your melancholy perch,

Bore you upon my fist, and showed you game,
And let you fly at it. I pray thee, kiss me.°   30
When thou wast with thy husband, thou wast watched
Like a tame elephant:° (still you are to thank me)
Thou hadst only kisses from him, and high feeding,°
But what delight was that? 'Twas just like one
That hath a little fing'ring on the lute,   35
Yet cannot tune it:° (still you are to thank me)

JULIA You told me of a piteous wound i' th' heart,
And a sick liver, when you wooed me first,
And spake like one in physic.°

CARDINAL   Who's that?

[Enter SERVANT.]

Rest firm, for my affection to thee,   40
Lightning moves slow to't.

SERVANT   Madam, a gentleman
That's come post from Malfi desires to see you.

CARDINAL Let him enter; I'll withdraw.
Exit.

SERVANT He says
Your husband, old Castruchio, is come to Rome,
Most pitifully tired with riding post.   45
[Exit SERVANT.]

[Enter DELIO.]

JULIA Signior Delio! [*Aside.*] 'Tis one of my old suitors.

DELIO I was bold to come and see you.

5 **witty** an ironic echo of the same word from the closing line of the preceding scene. 7 **I . . . not** I could not bear to. 11 **approved** given vent to. 16 **fantastic glass** telescope. 25–26 **I . . . cuckold** You cannot make me a cuckold (because I am not married to you).

28–30 **I . . . me** The Cardinal's imagery here is derived from the sport of falconry, but there are double-entendres in what he says—a habit of speech that links him psychologically with his brother. 32 **tame elephant** Elephants were tamed by being kept awake for so long that they would do anything in order to sleep. 33 **high feeding** Obscene jokes are directed at Castruchio's impotence, which makes him capable only of kissing Julia. 36 **tune it** make it play a tune. 39 **in physic** under the care of a physician.

JULIA Sir, you are welcome.

DELIO Do you lie° here?

JULIA   Sure° your own experience
Will satifsy you no; our Roman prelates
Do not keep lodging for ladies.

50   DELIO   Very well.
I have brought you no commendations
from your husband,
For I know none by him.

JULIA   I hear he's come to Rome?

DELIO I never knew man and beast, of a
horse and a knight,
So weary of each other. If he had had a
good back,
He would have undertook to have borne

55   his horse,
His breach° was so pitifully sore.

JULIA   Your laughter
Is my pity.°

DELIO   Lady, I know not whether
You want money, but I have brought you
some.

JULIA From my husband?

DELIO   No, from mine own allowance.°

JULIA I must hear the condition, ere I be

60   bound to take it.

DELIO Look on't, 'tis gold. Hath it not a
fine color?

JULIA I have a bird more beautiful.

DELIO   Try the sound on't.

JULIA A lute string far exceeds it;°
It hath no smell, like cassia° or civet;°
Nor is it physical,° though some fond°

65   doctors
Persuade us, seethe't in cullises.° I'll tell
you,

This is a creature bred by——
[*Enter* SERVANT.]

SERVANT   Your husband's come,
Hath delivered a letter to the Duke of
Calabria,
That, to my thinking, hath put him out
of his wits.
[*Exit* SERVANT.]

JULIA Sir, you hear.   70
Pray let me know your business and your
suit,
As briefly as can be.

DELIO   With good speed. I
would wish you,
At such time, as you are nonresident
With your husband, my mistress.

JULIA Sir, I'll go ask my husband if I
shall,   75
And straight return your answer. *Exit.*

DELIO   Very fine,
Is this her wit or honesty° that speaks
thus?
I heard one say the Duke was highly
moved
With a letter sent from Malfi. I do fear
Antonio is betrayed. How fearfully   80
Shows his ambition now; unfortunate
Fortune!
They pass through whirlpools, and deep
woes do shun,
Who the event weigh, ere the action's
done.   *Exit.*

SCENE FIVE   [*The same*]

[*Enter*] CARDINAL, *and* FERDINAND, *furious, with a letter.*

FERDINAND I have this night digged up a
mandrake.°

CARDINAL   Say you?

FERDINAND And I am grown mad with't.

CARDINAL What's the prodigy?°

FERDINAND Read there, a sister damned;
she's loose, i' th' hilts:°
Grown a notorious strumpet.

---

48 **lie** stay. **Sure** surely. 56 **breach** behind. 56–57
Your . . . pity Julia's answer here is purposely
ambiguous. She may be saying either "What you
laugh at, I pity," or "What you laugh at makes
my position (as Castruchio's wife) pitiful." 59
allowance income. 61–63 **Look . . . it** As Delio
proposes a liaison with her, Julia thinks about the
Cardinal, her present lover, and she unconsciously
replies to Delio's proposition by employing the same
kind of imagery (from falconry and lute-playing)
that the Cardinal has just finished using. 64 **cassia**
cinnamon. **civet** an animal secretion used in making
perfume. 65 **physical** health-restoring. **fond** foolish.
65–66 **Nor . . . cullises** Nor is it health-restoring—
though some foolish doctors argue to the contrary—
when it is boiled in a broth. 66 **cullises** broths.

77 **honesty** chastity.
II.v. 1 **mandrake** a root that was thought to induce
madness if plucked. 2 **prodigy** unnatural event.
3 **loose . . . hilts** unchaste.

CARDINAL   Speak lower.

FERDINAND   Lower?

5 Rogues do not whisper't now, but seek to
  publish't—
  As servants do the bounty of their lords—
  Aloud; and with a covetous, searching
  eye,
  To mark who note them. Oh, confusion
  seize her:
  She hath had most cunning bawds to
  serve her turn,
10 And more secure conveyances° for lust,
   Than towns of garrison,° for service.

CARDINAL   Is't possible?
Can this be certain?

FERDINAND   Rhubarb,° oh for rhubarb
To purge this choler; here's the cursèd
day°
To prompt° my memory, and here't shall
stick
Till of her bleeding heart I make a
15 sponge
To wipe it out.

CARDINAL   Why do you make yourself
So wild a tempest?

FERDINAND   Would I could be one,
That I might toss her palace 'bout her
ears,
Root up her goodly forests, blast her
meads,°
20 And lay her general territory as waste,
As she hath done her honor's.

CARDINAL   Shall our blood,
The royal blood of Aragon and Castile,
Be thus attainted?

FERDINAND   Apply desperate physic,
We must not now use balsamum,° but
fire,
The smarting cupping-glass,° for that's
25 the mean
To purge infected blood, such blood as
hers.

There is a kind of pity in mine eye;
I'll give it to my handkercher, and now
'tis here:
I'll bequeath this° to her bastard.

CARDINAL   What to do?

FERDINAND   Why, to make soft lint for his
mother's wounds,   30
When I have hewèd her to pieces.

CARDINAL   Cursed creature!
Unequal nature, to place women's hearts
So far upon the left side.°

FERDINAND   Foolish men,
That e'er will trust their honor in a bark,
Made of so slight, weak bulrush as is
woman,   35
Apt every minute to sink it!

CARDINAL   Thus ignorance, when it hath
purchased honor
It cannot wield it.

FERDINAND   Methinks I see her laughing,
Excellent hyena!° Talk to me somewhat,
quickly,
Or my imagination will carry me   40
To see her in the shameful act of sin.

CARDINAL   With whom?

FERDINAND   Happily,° with some strong-
thighed bargeman;
Or one o' th' wood yard, that can quoit
the sledge°
Or toss the bar, or else some lovely squire° 45
That carries coals up to her privy lodgings.

CARDINAL   You fly beyond your reason.

FERDINAND   Go to, mistress!°
'Tis not your whore's milk, that shall
quench my wildfire,
But your whore's blood.

---

29 **this** the handkerchief. 32–33 **to . . . side** It
was thought that only the hearts of deceitful persons were located on the left ("sinister") side.
39 **hyena** Its lechery, as well as its laughter, makes
it an appropriate image for Ferdinand to use here.
43 **Happily** probably, by hap. 43–45 **Happily . . .
squire** The violence of the Duke's rage and the
nature of his visions about the Duchess' lovers—
as powerful, physically active men—suggest an
intense sexual jealousy. 44 **quoit the sledge** throw
the hammer. 47 **mistress** Ferdinand jealously rails
against the Duchess—as if she were a mistress
who had deserted him for another lover.

---

10 **secure conveyances** secret arrangements. 11
towns of towns (have) of. 12 **Rhubarb** thought to
cure men of excessive anger by purging them of it.
13 **here's . . . day** Ferdinand refers here to the
horoscope that Bosola has enclosed. 14 **To prompt**
to keep in. 19 **meads** meadows. 24 **balsamum** healing ointment. 25 **cupping-glass** a small vacuum glass
used for drawing blood.

CARDINAL   How idly shows this rage!
50   which carries you,
   As men conveyed by witches, through the
   air
   On violent whirlwinds. This intemperate
   noise
   Fitly resembles deaf men's shrill discourse,
   Who talk aloud, thinking all other men
   To have their imperfection.
55 FERDINAND   Have not you
   My palsy?
   CARDINAL   Yes, I can be angry
   Without this rupture;° there is not in
   nature
   A thing, that makes man so deformed, so
   beastly,
   As doth intemperate anger. Chide your-
   self.
   You have diverse men, who never yet ex-
60   pressed
   Their strong desire of rest but by unrest,
   By vexing of themselves. Come, put your-
   self
   In tune.
   FERDINAND   So, I will only study° to seem
   The thing I am not. I could kill her now,
65 In you, or in myself,° for I do think
   It is some sin in us, heaven doth revenge
   By her.
   CARDINAL   Are you stark mad?
   FERDINAND   I would have their bodies
   Burnt in a coal-pit, with the ventage°
   stopped
   That their cursed smoke might not as-
   cend to heaven;
   Or dip the sheets they lie in, in pitch or
70   sulphur,
   Wrap them in't, and then light them like
   a match;
   Or else to boil their bastard to a cullis,
   And give't his lecherous father, to renew
   The sin of his back.°
   CARDINAL   I'll leave you.
   FERDINAND   Nay, I have done;

I am confident, had I been damned in
hell,   75
And should have heard of this, it would
have put me
Into a cold sweat. In, in, I'll go sleep:
Till I know who leaps my sister, I'll not
stir.
That known, I'll find scorpions to string
my whips,
And fix her in a general eclipse.°   80
Exeunt.

Act Three

SCENE ONE   [*The* DUCHESS' *palace at
            Amalfi, a few years later*

[*Enter* ANTONIO *and* DELIO.]

ANTONIO   Our noble friend, my most be-
loved Delio,
Oh, you have been a stranger long at
court,
Came you along with the Lord Ferdi-
nand?
DELIO   I did, sir, and how fares your noble
Duchess?
ANTONIO   Right fortunately well. She's an
excellent   5
Feeder of pedigrees: since you last saw
her,
She hath had two children more, a son
and daughter.
DELIO   Methinks 'twas yesterday. Let me
but wink,
And not behold your face,° which to
mine eye
Is somewhat leaner: verily I should
dream   10
It were within this half hour.
ANTONIO   You have not been in law,°
friend Delio,
Nor in prison, nor a suitor at the court,
Nor begged the reversion° of some great
man's place,

---

80 **And . . . eclipse** and cast her forever into darkness.
III.i. 8–9 **Let . . . face** It seems hardly more than
a wink's time since I last saw your face. 12 **in law**
involved in a legal case. 14 **reversion** right of succession to.

---

57 **rupture** complete lack of control. 63 **study** work.
64–65 **I could . . . myself** I could kill you, and even
myself, now. 68 **ventage** chimney. 73–74 **to . . .
back** to make him, literally, take his son back.

Nor troublèd with an old wife, which°
15 doth make
Your time so insensibly° hasten.
DELIO   Pray sir tell me,
Hath not this news arrived yet to the ear
Of the Lord Cardinal?
ANTONIO   I fear it hath;
The Lord Ferdinand, that's newly come
to court,
Doth bear himself right dangerously.
20 DELIO   Pray why?
ANTONIO   He is so quiet, that he seems to
sleep
The tempest out, as dormice do in winter;
Those houses that are haunted are most
still,
Till the devil be up.
DELIO   What say the common people?
ANTONIO   The common rabble do directly
25 say
She is a strumpet.
DELIO   And your graver heads,
Which would be politic,° what censure
they?
ANTONIO   They do observe I grow to in-
finite purchase°
The left-hand° way, and all suppose the
Duchess
Would amend it, if she could. For, say
30 they,
Great princes, though they grudge their
officers
Should have such large and unconfinèd
means
To get wealth under them, will not com-
plain
Lest thereby they should make them
odious
35 Unto the people. For other obligation
Of love, or marriage, between her and
me,
They never dream of.

[*Enter* FERDINAND, DUCHESS, *and* BOSOLA.]

DELIO   The Lord Ferdinand
Is going to bed.
FERDINAND   I'll instantly to bed,
For I am weary: I am to bespeak
A husband for you.°
DUCHESS   For me, sir! pray who is't?   40
FERDINAND   The great Count Malateste.°
DUCHESS   Fie upon him,
A count? He's a mere stick of sugar
candy,°
You may look quite thorough° him: when
I choose
A husband, I will marry for your honor.
FERDINAND   You shall do well in't. How
is't,° worthy Antonio?   45
DUCHESS   But, sir, I am to have private
conference with you,
About a scandalous report is spread
Touching mine honor.
FERDINAND   Let me be ever deaf to't:
One of Pasquil's paper bullets,° court
calumny,
A pestilent air, which princes' palaces   50
Are seldom purged of. Yet, say that it
were true,
I pour it in your bosom,° my fixed love
Would strongly excuse, extenuate, nay,
deny
Faults were they apparent in you. Go, be
safe
In your own innocency.
DUCHESS   Oh blessed comfort: 55
This deadly air is purged.
Exeunt [DUCHESS, ANTONIO, DELIO].
FERDINAND   Her guilt treads on
Hot burning cultures.° Now, Bosola,

39–40 **I am . . . you** I am to speak in favor of a prospective husband for you. 41 **Count Malateste** a name Webster chose probably for the effect of the obscene pun. 42 **He's . . . candy** He is of little worth. 43 **thorough** through. 45 **How is't** How is business? 49 **Pasquil's . . . bullets** satirical attacks. (Pasquil, or Pasquin, was the name given a statue to which Italian writers commonly affixed satires.) 52 **pour . . . bosom** I confess to you that. 57 **cultures** the iron blade in the front of a plow. In medieval England, people could demonstrate their innocence of a crime if they could walk unharmed on red-hot cultures.

15 **which** because you are not involved in any of these tedious undertakings. 16 **insensibly** exceeding the powers of the senses to record. 27 **politic** more prudent. 28 **purchase** wealth. 29 **left-hand** under-handed.

How thrives our intelligence?°°

BOSOLA   Sir, uncertainly:
'Tis rumored she hath had three bastards, but
By whom we may go read i' th' stars.

60   FERDINAND   Why some
Hold opinion all things are written there.

BOSOLA   Yes, if we could find spectacles to read them;
I do suspect, there hath been some sorcery
Used on the Duchess.

FERDINAND   Sorcery? To what purpose?

BOSOLA   To make her dote on some desert-
65   less fellow,
She shames to acknowledge.

FERDINAND   Can your faith give way
To think there's power in potions or in charms
To make us love, whether we will or no?

BOSOLA   Most certainly.

FERDINAND   Away, these are mere guller-
70   ies,° horrid things
Invented by some cheating mountebanks°
To abuse us. Do you think that herbs or charms
Can force the will? Some trials have been made
In the foolish practice. But the ingre-
dients
Were lenative poisons,° such as are of
75   force
To make the patient mad; and straight the witch
Swears, by equivocation,° they are in love.
The witchcraft lies in her° rank blood: this night
I will force confession from her. You told me
You had got, within these two days, a
80   false key°
Into her bedchamber.

BOSOLA   I have.

FERDINAND   As I would wish.°

BOSOLA   What do you intend to do?

FERDINAND   Can you guess?

BOSOLA   No.

FERDINAND   Do not ask then.
He that can compass° me, and know my drifts,°
May say he hath put a girdle 'bout the world,°   85
And sounded all her quicksands.

BOSOLA   I do not
Think so.

FERDINAND   What do you think
then, pray?

BOSOLA   That you
Are your own chronicle too much,° and grossly
Flatter yourself.

FERDINAND   Give me thy hand; I thank thee.
I never gave pension° but to flatterers   90
Till I entertainèd thee: farewell,
That friend a great man's ruin strongly checks,
Who rails into his belief° all his defects.
Exeunt.

SCENE TWO   [*The* DUCHESS' *bedchamber*]

[*Enter* DUCHESS, ANTONIO, *and* CARIOLA.]

DUCHESS   Bring me the casket hither, and the glass;°
You get no lodging here tonight, my lord.

ANTONIO   Indeed, I must persuade one.

DUCHESS   Very good:
I hope in time 'twill grow into a custom,
That noblemen shall come with cap and knee,°   5
To purchase a night's lodging of their wives.

ANTONIO   I must lie here.

---

58 **intelligence** system for spying. 60 **we . . . stars** we cannot determine by any factual evidence. 70 **gulleries** tricks. 71 **mountebanks** charlatans, pitchmen who mounted benches and peddled their wares, which were usually elixirs and cure-alls. 75 **lenative poisons** powerful drugs. 77 **by equivocation** by equating love with madness. 78 **her** the Duchess'. 80 **false key** pass key. 81 **As . . . wish** I want it.

84 **compass** comprehend. **drifts** secret schemes. 85 **put . . . world** traveled around the world (i.e. has done everything). 88 **Are . . . much** talk too much about the enormity of your deeds. 90 **pension** reward for service. 93 **belief** awareness.
III.ii. 1 **glass** mirror. 5 **with . . . knee** on bended knee, with cap in hand.

DUCHESS   Must? you are a lord of misrule.°
ANTONIO   Indeed, my rule is only in the
night.
DUCHESS   To what use will you put me?
ANTONIO   We'll sleep together.
DUCHESS   Alas, what pleasure can two lov-
10 ers find in sleep?
CARIOLA   My lord, I lie with her often,
and I know
She'll much disquiet you.
ANTONIO   See, you are complained of.
CARIOLA   For she's the sprawling'st bed-
fellow.
ANTONIO   I shall like her the better for
that.
15 CARIOLA   Sir, shall I ask you a question?
ANTONIO   I pray thee Cariola.
CARIOLA   Wherefore still, when you lie
with my lady
Do you rise° so early?
ANTONIO   Laboring men,
Count the clock oft'nest, Cariola,
Are glad when their task's ended.
20 DUCHESS   I'll stop your mouth.

[*Kisses him.*]

ANTONIO   Nay, that's but one. Venus had
two soft doves
To draw her chariot: I must have another.

[*Kisses her.*]

When wilt thou marry, Cariola?
CARIOLA   Never, my lord.
ANTONIO   O fie upon this single life: forgo
it.
We read how Daphne,° for her peevish
25 slight°
Became a fruitless bay tree; Syrinx°
turned

To the pale empty reed; Anaxarete°
Was frozen into marble: whereas those
Which married, or proved kind unto
their friends°
Were, by a gracious influence, transhaped   30
Into the olive, pomegranate, mulberry;
Became flowers, precious stones, or emi-
nent stars.
CARIOLA   This is vain poetry; but I pray
you tell me,
If there were proposed me wisdom, riches,
and beauty,
In three several young men, which should
I choose?   35
ANTONIO   'Tis a hard question. This was
Paris' case,°
And he was blind in't, and there was
great cause:
For how was't possible he could judge
right,
Having three amorous goddesses in view,
And they stark naked? 'Twas a motion   40
Were able to benight the apprehension°
Of the severest counselor of Europe.
Now I look on both your faces, so well
formed,
It puts me in mind of a question I would
ask.
CARIOLA   What is't?
ANTONIO   I do wonder why hard-
favored° ladies,   45
For the most part, keep worse-favored
waiting-women

27 **Anaxarete** a mythical Grecian queen who
scorned the advances of Iphis and stood unmoved
as he hanged himself, for which she was punished
by being turned into marble. 29 **friends** lovers.
36 **Paris' case** Paris, the handsomest of men,
was asked to judge who among the goddesses was
the fairest—Hera, Athena, or Aphrodite. Because
all three of the goddesses, who stood naked before
him, were beautiful, he could not choose a winner;
so each offered him a reward as a bribe. Hera
promised greatness, Athena offered success in war,
and Aphrodite told him that she would give him
the most beautiful woman in the world for his
wife. Finally, he judged Aphrodite the winner, and
she subsequently helped him to carry off Helen,
with disastrous consequences for himself and his
city. 40 **motion** spectacle. 41 **benight the apprehension** obscure the judgment. 45 **hard-favored** unattractive.

7 **lord of misrule** master of the court revels (which
were held at night). 18 **rise** a double-entendre. 25
Daphne a nymph who, pursued by Pan, was transformed into a bay tree at her own entreaty. **peevish
slight** foolish rejection of Pan. 26 **Syrinx** a nymph
who was changed into a reed in order to escape
Pan's pursuit.

To attend them, and cannot endure fair ones.

DUCHESS   Oh, that's soon answered.
Did you ever in your life know an ill painter
Desire to have his dwelling next door to
50   the shop
Of an excellent picture maker? 'Twould disgrace
His face-making,° and undo him. I prithee
When were we so merry? My hair tangles.

ANTONIO [*Aside to* CARIOLA.] Pray thee,
Cariola, let's steal forth° the room,
And let her talk to herself: I have diverse
55   times
Served her the like when she hath chafed extremely.
I love to see her angry—softly Cariola.

Exeunt [ANTONIO *and* CARIOLA].

DUCHESS   Doth not the color of my hair
'gin to change?
When I wax grey, I shall have all the court
Powder their hair with arras,° to be like
60   me:
You have cause to love me, I entered you into° my heart

[*Enter* FERDINAND, *unseen.*]

Before you would vouchsafe to call for the keys.
We shall one day have my brothers take°
you napping.
Methinks his presence, being now in court,
Should make you keep your own bed, but
65   you'll say
Love mixed with fear is sweetest. I'll assure you
You shall get no more children till my brothers
Consent to be your gossips.° Have you lost your tongue?

[*In the mirror she sees* FERDINAND *holding a poniard.*]

'Tis welcome:
For know, whether I am doomed to live, or die,   70
I can do both like a prince. FERDINAND
gives her a poniard.

FERDINAND   Die then, quickly.
Virtue, where art thou hid? What hideous thing
Is it, that doth eclipse thee?
DUCHESS   Pray, sir, hear me——
FERDINAND   Or is it true, thou art but a bare name,
And no essential thing?
DUCHESS   Sir——
FERDINAND   Do not speak.   75
DUCHESS   No sir:
I will plant my soul in mine ears, to hear you.°
FERDINAND   Oh most imperfect light of human reason,
That mak'st us so unhappy, to foresee
What we can least prevent. Pursue thy wishes   80
And glory in them: there's in shame no comfort,
But to be past all bounds and sense of shame.
DUCHESS   I pray sir, hear me: I am married——
FERDINAND   So!
DUCHESS   Happily,° not to your liking, but for that
Alas, your shears do come untimely now   85
To clip the bird's wings, that's already flown.
Will you see my husband?
FERDINAND   Yes, if I could change
Eyes with a basilisk.°
DUCHESS   Sure, you came hither
By his confederacy.°

52 **face-making** a pun, meaning both portrait-painting and make-up work. 54 **forth** forth from. 60 **arras** a white powder. 61 **entered . . . into** offered you. 63 **take** discover. 68 **gossips** sponsors at a baptism.

77 **I will . . . you** I will listen to you with the utmost attention. 84 **Happily** probably. 88 **basilisk** a legendary reptile that could kill with a look. 89 **By his confederacy** The Duchess remains hopeful, thinking that Ferdinand's appearance has been arranged with Antonio. But she is, of course, mistaken, and the indefiniteness of her reference in the phrase "By his confederacy" emphasizes the

FERDINAND   The howling of a wolf
Is music to thee, screech owl; prithee,
90   peace.
Whate'er thou art that hast enjoyed my
sister,
(For I am sure thou hear'st me), for
thine own sake
Let me not know thee. I came hither pre-
pared
To work thy discovery, yet am now per-
suaded
95   It would beget such violent effects
As would damn° us both. I would not for
ten millions
I had beheld thee; therefore, use all
means.
I never may have knowledge of thy name;
Enjoy thy lust still, and a wretched life,
On that condition. And for thee, vild°
100   woman,
If thou do wish thy lecher may grow old
In thy embracements, I would have thee
build
Such a room for him, as our anchorites°
To holier use inhabit. Let not the sun
Shine on him, till he's dead. Let dogs and
105   monkeys
Only converse with him, and such dumb
things
To whom nature denies use° to sound his
name.
Do not keep a paraquito, lest she learn it;
If thou do love him, cut out thine own
tongue,
Lest it bewray him.
110 DUCHESS   Why might not I marry?
I have not gone about, in this, to create
Any new world, or custom.
FERDINAND   Thou art undone:
And thou hast ta'en that massy sheet of
lead
That hid thy husband's bones, and folded
it

About my heart.
DUCHESS   Mine bleeds for't.
FERDINAND   Thine? thy heart? 115
What should I name't, unless a hollow
bullet°
Filled with unquenchable wildfire?
DUCHESS   You are in this
Too strict,° and were you not my princely
brother
I would say too willful. My reputation
Is safe.
FERDINAND Dost thou know what reputa-
tion is?   120
I'll tell thee, to small purpose, since
th'instruction
Comes now too late:
Upon a time° Reputation, Love and
Death
Would° travel o'er the world: and it was
concluded
That they should part, and take three
several ways.   125
Death told them they should find him in
great battles,
Or cities plagued with plagues. Love
gives them counsel
To inquire for him 'mongst unambitious
shepherds,
Where dow'ries were not talked of, and
sometimes
'Mongst quiet kindred, that had nothing
left   130
By their dead parents. "Stay," quoth
Reputation,
"Do not forsake me: for it is my nature,
If once I part from any man I meet,
I am never found again." And so, for
you:
You have shook hands with° Reputation, 135
And made him invisible. So fare you
well.
I will never see you more.
DUCHESS   Why should only I,
Of all the other princes of the world
Be cased up, like a holy relic? I have
youth,

magnitude of her error. It is not a "confederacy"
with Antonio that has prompted Ferdinand's appearance; instead, it is his emotional and psychological commitment to the forces of evil and destruction represented by the basilisk. 96 **damn** The
first quarto edition reads "dampe." 100 **vild** vile.
103 **anchorites** hermits. 107 **use** skill.

116 **hollow bullet** cannon ball. 118 **strict** unyielding. 123 **Upon a time** once. 124 **would** wished to.
135 **shook . . . with** parted from.

And a little beauty.

140 FERDINAND   So you have some virgins°
That are witches. I will never see thee
more.   *Exit.*

Enter [CARIOLA *and*] ANTONIO *with a
pistol.*

DUCHESS   You saw this apparition?°
ANTONIO   Yes: we are
Betrayed. How came he hither? I should
turn
This, to thee, for that.
[Points the pistol at CARIOLA.]
CARIOLA   Pray, sir, do; and when
That you have cleft my heart, you shall
145   read there
Mine innocence.
DUCHESS   That gallery° gave him en-
trance.
ANTONIO   I would this terrible thing
would come again,
That, standing on my guard, I might re-
late°
My warrantable love. Ha! what means
this?
DUCHESS   He left this with me. *She shows
the poniard.*
150 ANTONIO   And, it seems, did wish
You would use it on yourself?
DUCHESS   His action seemed
To intend so much.°
ANTONIO   This hath a handle to't
As well as a point: turn it towards him,
and
So fasten the keen edge in his rank gall.

[Knocking.]

How now? Who knocks? More earth-
quakes?°
155 DUCHESS   I stand
As if a mine, beneath my feet, were ready
To be blown up.
CARIOLA   'Tis Bosola.
DUCHESS   Away!

Oh misery, methinks unjust actions
Should wear these masks and curtains,
and not we.
You must instantly part hence: I have
fashioned it° already.   160

Ex[it] ANT[ONIO].

[Enter BOSOLA.]

BOSOLA   The Duke your brother is ta'en
up in a whirlwind;
Hath took horse, and's rid post to Rome.
DUCHESS   So late?
BOSOLA   He told me, as he mounted into
th' saddle,
You were undone.
DUCHESS   Indeed, I am very near it.
BOSOLA   What's the matter?   165
DUCHESS   Antonio, the master of our
household,
Hath dealt so falsely with me in's ac-
counts:
My brother stood engaged° with me for
money
Ta'en up of° certain Neapolitan Jews,
And Antonio lets the bonds be forfeit.   170
BOSOLA   Strange. [*Aside.*] This is cunning.
DUCHESS   And hereupon
My brother's bills at Naples are protested
Against.° Call up our officers.
BOSOLA   I shall.
Exit.

[Enter ANTONIO.]

DUCHESS   The place that you must fly to,
is Ancona.
Hire a house there. I'll send after you   175
My treasure, and my jewels. Our weak
safety
Runs upon enginous wheels:° short syl-
lables
Must stand for periods.° I must now ac-
cuse you
Of such a feignèd crime, as Tasso calls
Magnanima mensogna: a noble lie,   180

---

140 **So . . . virgins** So, you know, have some
virgins. 142 **apparition** the sudden and unexpected
appearance of Ferdinand. 146 **gallery** upstairs corridor (in this case, the upper stage). 148 **relate**
demonstrate. 152 **intend so much** imply as much.
155 **earthquakes** serious problems.

160 **fashioned it** contrived a plan. 168 **engaged** committed. 169 **Ta'en up of** borrowed from. 172–173
protested Against called in for payment. 177 **Runs
. . . wheels** depends upon speed and ingenuity.
178 **periods** well-proportioned sentences.

'Cause it must shield our honors—Hark,
they are coming.

[*Enter* BOSOLA *and* OFFICERS. *The* DUCH-
ESS *and* ANTONIO *begin their feigned dispute.*]

ANTONIO Will your grace hear me?

DUCHESS I have got well by° you: you
have yielded me
A million of loss; I am like to inherit
185   The people's curses for your stewardship.
You had the trick, in audit time, to be
sick
Till I had signed your *Quietus;* and that
cured you
Without help of a doctor. Gentlemen,
I would have this man be an example to
you all:
So shall you hold my favor. I pray let
190   him;°
For h'as done that, alas, you would not
think of;
And, because I intend to be rid of him,
I mean not to publish.° Use your fortune
elsewhere.

ANTONIO I am strongly armed to brook
my overthrow,
195   As commonly men bear with a hard year:
I will not blame the cause on't; but do
think
The necessity of my malevolent star
Procures this, not her humor.° O, the inconstant
And rotten ground of service, you may
see;
200   'Tis ev'n like him that, in a winter night,
Takes a long slumber o'er a dying fire,
As loth to part from't, yet parts thence as
cold
As when he first sat down.

DUCHESS   We do confiscate,
Towards the satisfying of your accounts,
All that you have.

205   ANTONIO I am all yours; and 'tis very fit
All mine should be so.

DUCHESS   So, sir, you have your pass.°

ANTONIO You may see, gentlemen, what
'tis to serve
A prince with body and soul.   *Exit.*

BOSOLA Here's an example for extortion:
what moisture is drawn out of the sea, 210
when foul weather comes, pours down,
and runs into the sea again.

DUCHESS I would know what are your
opinions
Of this Antonio.

SECOND OFFICER He could not abide to see 215
a pig's head gaping.° I thought your
grace would find him a Jew.°

THIRD OFFICER I would you had been his
officer, for your own sake.

FOURTH OFFICER You would have had 220
more money.

FIRST OFFICER He stopped his ears with
black wool, and to those came to him for
money said he was thick of hearing.

SECOND OFFICER Some said he was an 225
hermaphrodite,° for he could not abide a
woman.

FOURTH OFFICER How scurvy proud he
would look, when the treasury was full.
Well, let him go.   230

FIRST OFFICER Yes, and the chippings of
the butt'ry° fly after him, to scour his
gold chain.°

DUCHESS Leave us. What do you think of
these?°   *Exeunt* [OFFICERS].

BOSOLA That these are rogues, that in's
prosperity,   235

---

ess. 206 **pass** leave to go. 215–216 **He . . . gaping**
He could not stand to see people feasting on pork
(because he hated feasting in general and the
eating of pork in particular). 217 **Jew** an unusually
clever miser. 226 **hermaphrodite** an individual
having both male and female sexual characteristics.
231–232 **chippings . . . butt'ry** bread crumbs, used
for polishing gold. 233 **gold chain** steward's badge
of office. 234 **these** these officers. 235–280 **That . . .
virtue** Bosola's praise of Antonio is primarily a
clever trick: he thinks that the steward has been
acting as the Duchess' bawd, and he hopes that his
praise of him will win for himself the Duchess'
confidence. It is not, however, beyond Bosola's
power to recognize worth, even though he sees very
little of it around him, so there is just enough
honesty in his speech to make it a consummate
work of deception.

---

183 **got . . . by** had enough of. 190 **let him** let
him go. 193 **publish** publicly announce (what he
has done). 196–198 **but . . . humor** This overthrow
has been brought about by evil Fortune's unalter-
able decree, not by the capriciousness of the Duch-

But to have waited on his fortune, could
have wished

His dirty stirrup riveted through their
noses:

And followed after's° mule, like a bear in
a ring.°

Would have prostituted their daughters
to his lust;

Made their first-born intelligencers;°

240 thought none happy

But such as were born under his blessed
planet;

And wore his livery. And do these lice
drop off now?

Well, never look to have the like° again;

He hath left a sort of flatt'ring rogues behind him;

Their doom must follow. Princes pay flat-

245 terers,

In their own money. Flatterers dissemble
their vices,

And they dissemble their lies:° that's justice.

Alas, poor gentleman,——

DUCHESS   Poor! he hath amply filled his
coffers.

BOSOLA   Sure he was too honest. Pluto°

250 the god of riches,

When he's sent by Jupiter° to any man,

He goes limping, to signify that wealth

That comes on God's name, comes slowly;
but when he's sent

On the devil's errand, he rides post and
comes in by scuttles.°

Let me show you what a most unvalued°

255 jewel

You have, in a wanton humor, thrown
away

To bless the man shall° find him. He was
an excellent

Courtier, and most faithful; a soldier
that thought it

As beastly to know his own value too little,

As devilish to acknowledge it too much: 260

Both his virtue and form deserved a far
better fortune.

His discourse rather delighted to judge
itself, than show itself.°

His breast was filled with all perfection,

And yet it seemed a private whisp'ring
room:

It made so little noise of't.

DUCHESS   But he was basely descended. 265

BOSOLA   Will you make yourself a mercenary herald,

Rather to examine men's pedigrees, than
virtues?

You shall want° him:

For know an honest statesman to a
prince,

Is like a cedar, planted by a spring: 270

The spring bathes the tree's root; the
grateful tree

Rewards it with his shadow. You have
not done so;

I would sooner swim to the Bermoothas°
on

Two politicians'° rotten bladders, tied

Together with an intelligencer's heart-
string,   275

Than depend on so changeable a prince's
favor.

Fare thee well, Antonio, since the malice
of the world

Would needs down with thee, it cannot
be said yet

That any ill happened unto thee,

Considering thy fall was accompanied
with virtue.   280

DUCHESS   Oh, you render me excellent
music.

238 **after's** after Antonio's. **like . . . ring** Rings
were thrust through the noses of bears so that they
could be marched in procession before bearbaiting
events. 240 **intelligencers** spies. 243 **the like** one as
good as Antonio. 246–247 **Flatterers . . . lies** Flatterers pretend that princes do not have vices, and
princes pretend that flatterers do not lie. 250 **Pluto**
actually King of the Underworld; the god of riches
was Plutus. Webster's error in this case may, however, be intentional, for he may want to emphasize
the extent to which Bosola's thinking is dominated
by the powers of blackness. 251 **Jupiter** king of the
gods. 254 **by scuttles** runs quickly. 255 **unvalued**
invaluable.

257 **man shall** man who shall. 262 **to . . . itself**
to be sound, rather than showy. 268 **want** miss.
273 **Bermoothas** Bermuda, which was thought of as
a distant and primitive island. 274 **politicians** self-
interested schemers.

BOSOLA   Say you?

DUCHESS   This good one that you speak
of—is my husband.

BOSOLA   Do I not dream? Can this ambi-
tious age
Have so much goodness in't as to prefer
A man merely for worth, without these
285   shadows
Of wealth, and painted honors? possible?°

DUCHESS   I have had three children by
him.

BOSOLA   Fortunate lady,
For you have made your private nuptial
bed
The humble and fair seminary° of peace.
No question but many an unbeneficed°
290   scholar
Shall pray for you for this deed, and re-
joice
That some preferment in the world can
yet
Arise from merit. The virgins of your
land
That have no dowries shall hope your
example
Will raise them to rich husbands. Should
295   you want
Soldiers, 'twould make the very Turks
and Moors
Turn Christians, and serve you for this
act.
Last, the neglected poets of your time,
In honor of this trophy° of a man,
Raised by that curious engine,° your
300   white hand,
Shall thank you in your grave for't; and
make that
More reverend than all the cabinets°
Of living princes. For Antonio,
His fame shall likewise flow from many a
pen,
When heralds shall want coats, to sell to
305   men.°

DUCHESS   As I taste comfort, in this
friendly speech,
So would I find concealment°——

BOSOLA   Oh the secret of my prince,
Which I will wear on th' inside of my
heart.

DUCHESS   You shall take charge of all my
coin and jewels
And follow him, for he retires himself   310
To Ancona.

BOSOLA   So.

DUCHESS   Whither, within few days,
I mean to follow thee.

BOSOLA   Let me think:
I would wish your grace to feign a pil-
grimage
To Our Lady of Loretto, scarce seven
leagues
From fair Ancona, so may you depart   315
Your country with more honor, and your
flight
Will seem a princely progress,° retaining
Your usual train about you.

DUCHESS   Sir, your direction
Shall lead me, by the hand.

CARIOLA   In my opinion,
She were better progress to the baths at
Lucca,°   320
Or go visit the Spa°
In Germany: for, if you will believe me,
I do not like this jesting with religion,
This feigned pilgrimage.

DUCHESS   Thou art a superstitious fool!
Prepare us instantly for our departure.   325
Past sorrows, let us moderately lament
them;
For those to come, seek wisely to prevent
them.

Exit [DUCHESS *with* CARIOLA].

BOSOLA   A politician is the devil's quilted°
anvil:
He fashions all sins on him, and the
blows
Are never heard; he may work in a lady's
chamber,   330

---

286 **possible** (Is it) possible? 289 **seminary** seed bed.
290 **unbeneficed** not supported by a lord. 299
trophy prize. 300 **engine** source of power. 302 **cabi-
nets** advisors. 305 **When . . . men** when heralds no
longer shall deal in the corrupt practice of selling
coats of arms to men (i.e. when men are rewarded
for virtue rather than for bribery).

307 **concealment** secrecy. 317 **progress** official journey. 320 **Lucca** a resort near Pisa. 321 **Spa** a town
in Belgium famous for its mineral waters. 328
quilted covered with a sound-absorbing material.

As here for proof. What rests,° but I reveal
All to my lord? Oh, this base quality
Of intelligencer! Why, every quality i' th'
world
Prefers but gain, or commendation.°
335 Now for this act, I am certain to be
raised:
And men that paint weeds to the life° are
praised.   *Exit.*

SCENE THREE   [*The* CARDINAL'*s palace in
Rome*]

[*Enter*] CARDINAL, FERDINAND, MALATESTE,
PESCARA, SILVIO, DELIO.

CARDINAL   Must we turn soldier then?
MALATESTE   The Emperor,°
Hearing your worth that way, ere you at-
tained
This reverend garment, joins you in com-
mission
With the right fortunate soldier, the Mar-
quis of Pescara°
And the famous Lannoy.°
5 CARDINAL   He that had the honor
Of taking the French king° prisoner?
MALATESTE   The same.
Here's a plot° drawn for a new fortifica-
tion
At Naples.
FERDINAND   This great Count Malateste,°
I perceive

Hath got employment.
DELIO   No employment, my lord,
A marginal note in the muster book,°
that he is   10
A voluntary lord.°
FERDINAND   He's no soldier?
DELIO   He has worn gunpowder, in's hol-
low tooth,
For the toothache.
SILVIO   He comes to the leaguer° with a
full intent
To eat fresh beef, and garlic; means to
stay   15
Till the scent be gone,° and straight re-
turn to court.
DELIO   He hath read all the late service,°
As the city chronicle° relates it,
And keeps two pewterers going, only to
express
Battles in model.°
SILVIO   Then he'll fight by the book.°   20
DELIO   By the almanac, I think,
To choose good days and shun the
critical.°
That's his mistress' scarf.
SILVIO   Yes, he protests
He would do much for that taffeta,——
DELIO   I think he would run away from a
battle   25
To save it from taking° prisoner.
SILVIO   He is horribly afraid
Gunpowder will spoil the perfume
on't,——
DELIO   I saw a Dutchman break his pate°
once
For calling him pot-gun;° he made his
head
Have a bore in't, like a musket.   30

331 **rests** remains. 333–334 **Why . . . commendation** Every quality of character leads to some reward: (if the quality is evil), the reward is gain;
(if it is good), the prize is only commendation. 336
to the life so that they seem lifelike.
III.iii. 1 **Emperor** Charles V, the greatest of all
Hapsburg emperors, who ruled from 1519 to 1558.
4 **Marquis of Pescara** the soldier who commanded
the Italian army in its victory over Francis I of
France at Pavia in 1525. 5 **Lannoy** Viceroy of
Naples, one of the Italian commanders at Pavia and
a favorite of Charles V. 6 **French king** Francis I,
who would surrender his sword at Pavia only to
Lannoy. 7 **plot** diagram. 8 **Malateste** the ruling
family in Rimini, Italy, during the sixteenth century 10 **muster book** a register of the officers and
men in a military unit. 11 **voluntary lord** a lord
who volunteers for military service. 14 **leaguer**
alliance. 16 **Till . . . gone** until the good food is
eaten. 17 **all . . . service** all about the recent
military maneuvers. 18 **city chronicle** official reports
about the affairs of a city. 20 **model** miniature
reproductions (with pewter soldiers). **by the book**
according to some generally accepted treatise on
military strategy. 22 **critical** days of crisis. 26 **taking**
being taken. 28 **break his pate** strike him across
the head. 29 **pot-gun** popgun, a braggart.

SILVIO I would he had made a touchhole°
to't.°
He is indeed a guarded sumpter-cloth°
Only for the remove° of the court.

[*Enter* BOSOLA.]

PESCARA Bosola arrived? What should be
the business?
35 Some falling out amongst the cardinals?
These factions amongst great men, they
are like
Foxes when their heads are divided:°
They carry fire in their tails, and all the
country
About them goes to wrack for't.
SILVIO   What's that Bosola?
40 DELIO I knew him in Padua—a fantas-
tical° scholar, likesuch who study to
know how many knots was in Hercules'
club; of what color Achilles'° beard was,
or whether Hector° were not troubled
45 with the toothache. He hath studied himself half blear-eyed to know the true sym-
metry of Caesar's nose by a shoeing horn.°
And this he did to gain the name of a
speculative man.
50 PESCARA Mark Prince Ferdinand,
A very salamander° lives in's eye,
To mock the eager violence of fire.
SILVIO That cardinal hath made more
bad faces with his oppression than ever
55 Michael Angelo made good ones: he lifts
up's nose,° like a foul porpoise° before a
storm,——
PESCARA The Lord Ferdinand laughs.

DELIO Like a deadly cannon, that light-
ens° ere it smokes.
PESCARA These are your true pangs of
death,   60
The pangs of life, that struggle with great
statesmen,°——
DELIO In such a deformèd silence,°
witches whisper their charms.
CARDINAL [*On the other side of the stage.*]
Doth she make religion her riding hood
To keep her from the sun and tempest?°
FERDINAND   That!°
That damns her. Methinks her fault and
beauty   65
Blended together show like leprosy:
The whiter, the fouler. I make it a ques-
tion
Whether her beggarly brats were ever
christened.
CARDINAL I will instantly solicit the state
of Ancona
To have them banished.
FERDINAND [*To the* CARDINAL.]
                    You are for° Loretto? 70
I shall not be at your ceremony;° fare
you well.

---

of foul weather to come. 59 **lightens** gives off light
(of fire). 60–61 **These . . . statesmen** This passage
is confusing enough to be textually corrupt: it is
difficult to see how "The pangs of life, that struggle
with great statesmen" can be an accurate description of "true pangs of death." The general meaning
of the statement is, however, clear. The whispered
secrets between statesmen are pangs of death because they soon result in destructive actions; the
pangs of life are either the life of suffering that
comes to those who struggle against great statesmen
or, more likely, the pains that accompany the for-
mulation of the statesmen's ideas—in actuality
pangs of death because of the nature of their
results. This interpretation of Pescara's speech,
however, demands an emendation of the second
line so that it reads: "The pangs of life, that
struggles within great statesmen." But whether
there is a textual corruption in this passage or not,
its implication is that the whispered secrets between the Cardinal and Ferdinand are directed
toward evil ends. 62 **In . . . silence** in such unnatural whispers. 64 **sun . . . tempest** the Cardinal,
who theoretically represents the light of God, and
Ferdinand, whose anger is violent, like a tempest.
That That is correct! 70 **for** headed for. 71 **ceremony** his official installation as a soldier.

31 **touchhole** the vent in firearms through which
the charge was ignited. **I . . . to't** I wish he had
burst his false pride completely. 32 **guarded sump-
ter-cloth** ornamental blanket. 33 **remove** location.
37 **heads are divided** when they are tied tail to tail
(cf. Judges 15:4). 40–41 **fantastical** pursuing foolish
fantasies. 43 **Achilles** the greatest Greek warrior in
the Trojan War. 44 **Hector** the greatest Trojan
warrior. 46–47 **to . . . horn** to learn that Caesar's
nose was as symmetrical and well-tapered as a shoe-
horn. 51 **salamander** thought capable of living in
fire. 55–56 **lifts up's nose** He sniffs around for
trouble. 56 **foul porpoise** The appearance of por-
poises around a ship was believed to be a warning

[*To* BOSOLA.] Write to the Duke of Malfi,
my young nephew
She had by her first husband, and ac-
quaint him
With's mother's honesty.
BOSOLA   I will.
FERDINAND   Antonio!
75 A slave, that only smelled of ink and
counters°
And ne'er in's life looked like a gentle-
man
But in the audit time.° Go, go presently;
Draw me out an hundred and fifty of our
horse,
And meet me at the fort bridge.°
Exeunt.

SCENE FOUR [*Loretto*]

[*Enter*] TWO PILGRIMS *to the Shrine of
Our Lady of Loretto.*

FIRST PILGRIM I have not seen a goodlier
shrine than this;
Yet I have visited many.
SECOND PILGRIM The Cardinal of Aragon
Is this day to resign his cardinal's hat;°
His sister Duchess likewise is arrived
5 To pay her vow of pilgrimage. I expect
A noble ceremony.
FIRST PILGRIM No question.—They come.

*Here the ceremony of the Cardinal's in-
stallment in the habit of a soldier: performed in delivering up his cross, hat,
robes, and ring at the shrine, and invest-
ing him with sword, helmet, shield, and
spurs. Then* ANTONIO, *the* DUCHESS, *and
their children, having presented themselves at the shrine, are (by a form of
banishment in dumb show expressed
towards them by the* CARDINAL *and the
state of* ANCONA) *banished. During all
which ceremony this ditty is sung to
very solemn music, by diverse churchmen; and then exeunt.*

The author disclaims this ditty to be his.
Arms and honors deck thy story
To thy fame's eternal glory.
Adverse fortune ever fly thee;
No disastrous fate come nigh thee.   10
I alone will sing thy praises,
Whom to honor virtue raises;
And thy study that divine is,
Bent to martial discipline is.
Lay aside all those robes lie by thee,   15
Crown thy arts with arms; they'll beau-
tify thee.
O worthy of worthiest name, adorned in
this manner,
Lead bravely thy forces on, under war's
warlike banner.
O mayst thou prove fortunate in all
martial courses,
Guide thou still by skill, in arts and
forces: 20
Victory attend thee nigh, whilst fame
sings loud thy powers;
Triumphant conquest crown thy head,
and blessings pour down showers.
FIRST PILGRIM Here's a strange turn of
state: who would have thought
So great a lady would have matched her-
self
Unto so mean° a person? Yet the Cardinal 25
Bears himself much too cruel.
SECOND PILGRIM   They are banished.
FIRST PILGRIM But I would ask what
power hath this state
Of Ancona, to determine of° a free
prince?
SECOND PILGRIM They are a free state, sir,
and her brother showed
How that the Pope, forehearing of her
looseness,   30
Hath seized into th' protection of the
Church
The dukedom which she held as dow-
ager.°

75 **counters** pieces of wood or bone used in keeping
accounts. 77 **But . . . time** In audit time, the Duke
implies, Antonio made enough money to qualify
as a gentleman. 79 **fort bridge** drawbridge.
III.iv. 3 **to . . . hat** resigning his church position

(to become a soldier). 25 **mean** of a low social class.
28 **determine of** pass judgment against. 32 **dowager**
property received by a widow upon the death of
her husband.

FIRST PILGRIM   But by what justice?
SECOND PILGRIM   Sure I think by none,
Only her brother's instigation.
FIRST PILGRIM   What was it, with such
35 violence he took
Off from her finger?
SECOND PILGRIM   'Twas her wedding ring,
Which he vowed shortly he would sacrifice
To his revenge.
FIRST PILGRIM   Alas Antonio!
If that a man be thrust into a well,
No matter who sets hand to't,° his own
40 weight
Will bring him sooner to th' bottom.
Come, let's hence.
Fortune makes this conclusion general:
All things do help th'unhappy man to
fall.   *Exeunt.*

SCENE FIVE   [*Somewhere near Loretto*]

[*Enter*] ANTONIO, DUCHESS, CHILDREN,
CARIOLA, SERVANTS.

DUCHESS   Banished Ancona?
ANTONIO   Yes, you see what power
Lightens° in great men's breath.
DUCHESS   Is all our train
Shrunk to this poor remainder?
ANTONIO   These poor men,
Which have got little in your service, vow
To take your fortune.° But your wiser
5 buntings,°
Now they are fledged,° are gone.
DUCHESS   They have done wisely.
This puts me in mind of death: physicians thus,
With their hands full of money, use to
give o'er°
Their patients.
ANTONIO   Right° the fashion of the world:
From decayed fortunes every flatterer
10 shrinks;

Men cease to build where the foundation
sinks.
DUCHESS   I had a very strange dream tonight.
ANTONIO   What was't?
DUCHESS   Methought I wore my coronet of
state,
And on a sudden all the diamonds
Were changed to pearls.
ANTONIO   My interpretation 15
Is, you'll weep shortly; for to me, the
pearls
Do signify your tears.
DUCHESS   The birds that live i' th' field
On the wild benefit of nature live
Happier than we; for they may choose
their mates,
And carol their sweet pleasures to the
spring. 20

[*Enter* BOSOLA *with a letter, which he
gives to the* DUCHESS.]

BOSOLA   You are happily o'erta'en.
DUCHESS   From my brother?
BOSOLA   Yes, from the Lord Ferdinand,
your brother,
All love, and safety——
DUCHESS   Thou dost blanch mischief;
Wouldst make it white.° See, see, like to
calm weather
At sea before a tempest, false hearts speak
fair 25
To those they intend most mischief. [*She
reads*] a letter:
"Send Antonio to me; I want his head in
a business."
A politic equivocation—
He doth not want your counsel, but your
head:
That is, he cannot sleep till you be dead. 30
And here's another pitfall, that's strewed
o'er
With roses. Mark it, 'tis a cunning one:
"I stand engaged for your husband for
several debts at Naples. Let not that trou-

40 sets . . . to't gives him the initial push.
III.v. 2 **Lightens** explodes. 5 **take . . . fortune** endure your misfortune with you. **buntings** little birds. 6 **are fledged** have acquired enough feathers to fly. 8 **o'er** up. 9 **Right** such is.

23–24 **Thou . . . white** You try to cover the blackness of your evil intentions with the whiteness (of feigned friendliness).

35 ble him: I had rather have his heart than
his money."
And I believe so too.

BOSOLA   What do you believe?

DUCHESS   That he so much distrusts my
husband's love,
He will by no means believe his heart is
with him
40 Until he see it. The devil is not cunning
enough
To circumvent us in riddles.

BOSOLA   Will you reject that noble and
free league
Of amity and love which I present you?

DUCHESS   Their league is like that of some
politic° kings
Only to make themselves of strength and
45 power
To be our after-ruin. Tell them so.

BOSOLA   And what from you?

ANTONIO   Thus tell him: I will not
come.

BOSOLA   And what of this?

ANTONIO   My brothers° have dispersed
Bloodhounds abroad, which till I hear
are muzzled
50 No truce—though hatched with ne'er
such politic skill—
Is safe that hangs upon our enemies'
will.°
I'll not come at them.

BOSOLA   This proclaims your breeding.
Every small thing draws a base mind to
fear,
As the adamant° draws iron. Fare you
well, sir;
You shall shortly hear from's.   *Exit.*

55 DUCHESS   I suspect some ambush:
Therefore, by all my love, I do conjure
you
To take your eldest son and fly towards
Milan.
Let us not venture all this poor remain-
der

In one unlucky bottom.°

ANTONIO   You counsel safely.
Best of my life, farewell. Since we must
part,   60
Heaven hath a hand in't: but no other-
wise
Than as some curious artist takes in
sunder
A clock or watch, when it is out of
frame,°
To bring't in better order.

DUCHESS   I know not which is best,
To see you dead, or part with you. Fare-
well, boy,   65
Thou art happy, that thou hast not un-
derstanding
To know thy misery. For all our wit
And reading brings us to a truer sense
Of sorrow. In the eternal Church, sir,
I do hope we shall not part thus.

ANTONIO   O be of comfort,   70
Make patience a noble fortitude:
And think not how unkindly° we are
used.
Man, like to cassia,° is proved best being
bruised.

DUCHESS   Must I, like to a slave-born Rus-
sian,
Account it praise to suffer tyranny?   75
And yet, O Heaven, thy heavy hand is
in't.
I have seen my little boy oft scourge his
top,°
And compared myself to't: nought made
me e'er go right,
But Heaven's scourge stick.

ANTONIO   Do not weep:
Heaven fashioned us of nothing; and we
strive   80
To bring ourselves to nothing. Farewell,
Cariola,
And thy sweet armful.° [*To the* DUCHESS.]
If I do never see thee more,
Be a good mother to your little ones,

---

44 **politic** conniving. 48 **brothers** brothers-in-law.
49–51 **which . . . will** Until those bloodhounds are
tied up, no truce that depends on our enemies'
good will is safe for us—no matter how skillfully
couched in ambiguous language it may be. 54 **adamant** magnet.

59 **bottom** the hold of a ship (i.e. in one precarious
place). 63 **frame** order. 72 **unkindly** both evilly and
unnaturally. 73 **cassia** bark that, when pounded, is
a source of cinnamon. 77 **scourge his top** spin his
toy top. 82 **sweet armful** the babies she holds.

And save them from the tiger: fare you well.

DUCHESS   Let me look upon you once
85   more, for that speech

Came from a dying father: your kiss is colder

Than I have seen an holy anchorite

Give to a dead man's skull.

ANTONIO   My heart is turned to a heavy lump of lead,°

With which I sound my danger: fare you
90   well.

Exit [with elder SON].

DUCHESS   My laurel is all witherèd.

CARIOLA   Look, madam, what a troop of armèd men

Make° toward us.

Enter BOSOLA *with a guard[, all wearing armored masks].*

DUCHESS   O, they are very welcome:

When Fortune's wheel is overcharged with° princes,

The weight makes it move swift. I would
95   have my ruin

Be sudden. I am your adventure,° am I not?

BOSOLA   You are. You must see your husband no more,——

DUCHESS   What devil art thou, that counterfeits Heaven's thunder?

BOSOLA   Is that terrible? I would have you tell me whether

Is that note worse that° frights the silly
100   birds

Out of the corn, or that which doth allure them

To the nets? You have harkened to the last too much.

DUCHESS   O misery! like to a rusty o'ercharged cannon,

Shall I never fly in pieces? Come: to what prison?

BOSOLA   To none.

DUCHESS   Whither then?

BOSOLA   To your palace. *105*

DUCHESS   I have heard that Charon's° boat serves to convey

All o'er the dismal lake, but brings none back again.

BOSOLA   Your brothers mean you safety and pity.

DUCHESS   Pity!

With such a pity men preserve alive *110*

Pheasants and quails, when they are not fat enough

To be eaten.

BOSOLA   These are your children?

DUCHESS   Yes.

BOSOLA   Can they prattle?°

DUCHESS   No.

But I intend, since they were born accursed, *115*

Curses shall be their first language.

BOSOLA   Fie, madam!

Forget this base, low fellow.

DUCHESS   Were I a man,

I'd beat that counterfeit face° into thy other——

BOSOLA   One of no birth.

DUCHESS   Say that he was born mean:

Man is most happy, when's own actions *120*

Be arguments and examples of his virtue.

BOSOLA   A barren, beggarly virtue.

DUCHESS   I prithee, who is greatest? Can you tell?

Sad tales befit my woe: I'll tell you one.

A salmon, as she swam unto the sea, *125*

Met with a dogfish, who encounters her

With this rough language: "Why art thou so bold

To mix thyself with our high state of floods°

Being no eminent courtier, but one

That for the calmest and fresh time o' th' year *130*

---

89 **lump of lead** Sailors took depth readings by dropping heavy lumps of lead overboard. 93 **Make** The verb is plural because of its proximity to "men." 94 **overcharged with** turned over by (the weight of the princes tied to it). 96 **adventure** what you venture after. 99–100 **whether . . . worse that** which note is worse, that which.

106 **Charon** the old boatman who ferried the souls of the dead across the river Styx to Hades. 113 **prattle** talk. 118 **counterfeit face** the armored visor. 128 **high . . . floods** the deep sea (of the court's high intrigue).

Dost live in shallow rivers, rankst thyself
With silly smelts and shrimps? And dar-
est thou
Pass by our° dogship° without reverence?"
"O," quoth the salmon, "sister, be at
peace:
135 Thank Jupiter, we both have passed the
net.
Our value never can be truly known,
Till in the fisher's basket we be shown;
I' th' market then my price may be the
higher,
Even when I am nearest to the cook, and
fire."
140 So, to great men, the moral may be
stretched:
Men oft are valued high,° when th'are
most wretched.
But, come, whither you please. I am
armed 'gainst misery,
Bent to all sways of the oppressor's will.
There's no deep valley, but near some
great hill.°   *Ex[eunt]*.

Act Four

SCENE ONE [*In a prison somewhere near
Loretto*]

[*Enter* FERDINAND *and* BOSOLA.]

FERDINAND How doth our sister Duchess
bear herself
In her imprisonment?
BOSOLA   Nobly. I'll describe her:
She's sad, as one long used to't, and she
seems
Rather to welcome the end of misery
5 Than shun it—a behavior so noble,
As gives a majesty to adversity.
You may discern the shape of loveliness

More perfect in her tears, than in her
smiles.
She will muse four hours together, and
her silence,
Methinks, expresseth more than if she
spake.   10
FERDINAND Her melancholy seems to be
fortified
With a strange disdain.
BOSOLA   'Tis so, and this restraint
(Like English mastives, that grow fierce
with tying)
Makes her too passionately apprehend
Those pleasures she's kept from.
FERDINAND   Curse upon her! 15
I will no longer study in the book
Of another's heart:° inform her what I
told you.   *Exit.*

[BOSOLA *enters the* DUCHESS' *inner-stage
prison.*]

BOSOLA All comfort to, your grace;——
DUCHESS   I will have none.
'Pray thee, why dost thou wrap thy poi-
soned pills
In gold and sugar?°   20
BOSOLA Your elder brother, the Lord Fer-
dinand,
Is come to visit you, and sends you word,
'Cause once he rashly made a solemn vow
Never to see you more. He comes i' th'
night,
And prays you, gently, neither torch nor
taper   25
Shine in your chamber. He will kiss your
hand;
And reconcile himself, but, for his vow,
He dares not see you.
DUCHESS   At his pleasure.
Take hence the lights: he's come.
[*Exeunt* SERVANTS *with lights.*]

[*Enter* FERDINAND.]

FERDINAND   Where are you?
DUCHESS   Here sir.

---

133 **our** The plural was used in any address to royal
persons. **dogship** a term of abuse, satirizing such
types of formal address as "your lordship." 141
valued high judged worthy (by God). 144 **There's
. . . hill** Even in despair man finds cause for hope
—in the power of God.

IV.i. 16–17 **I . . . heart** I will no longer waste my
time trying to figure out what is in her heart. 19–
20 **why . . . sugar** Why do you cover up your
hatred and evil designs with feigned courtesy?

FERDINAND This darkness suits you well.

30 DUCHESS   I would ask your pardon.

FERDINAND You have it;
For I account it the honorabl'st revenge
Where I may kill, to pardon.° Where are
your cubs?

DUCHESS Whom?

35 FERDINAND Call them your children;
For though our national law distinguish
bastards
From true legitimate issue, compassionate
nature
Makes them all equal.

DUCHESS   Do you visit me for this?
You violate a sacrament o' th' Church°
Shall make you howl in hell for't.

40 FERDINAND   It had been well,
Could you have lived thus° always, for
indeed
You were too much i' th' light.° But no
more;
I come to seal my peace with you: here's
a hand,

Gives her a dead man's hand.

To which you have vowed much love;
the ring° upon't
You gave.

45 DUCHESS   I affectionately kiss it.

FERDINAND Pray do, and bury the print of
it in your heart.
I will leave this ring with you, for a love-
token,
And the hand, as sure as the ring. And do
not doubt
But you shall have the heart too. When
you need a friend
Send it to him that owed° it: you shall

50 see
Whether he can aid you.

DUCHESS   You are very cold.
I fear you are not well after your travel.
Ha, lights!—Oh, horrible!

FERDINAND Let her have lights enough.
[*Exit.*]

[*Enter* SERVANTS *with lights.*]

DUCHESS What witchcraft doth he practice,° that he hath left
A dead man's hand here?——   55

*Here is discovered, behind a traverse,
the artificial figures of* ANTONIO *and his
children, appearing as if they were dead.*

BOSOLA Look you, here's the piece from
which 'twas ta'en.
He doth present you this sad spectacle
That, now you know directly they are
dead,
Hereafter you may wisely cease to grieve
For that which cannot be recovered.   60

DUCHESS There is not between heaven
and earth one wish
I stay for after this. It wastes me more,
Than were't my picture, fashioned out of
wax,
Stuck with a magical needle, and then
buried
In some foul dunghill.° And yond's an
excellent property   65
For a tyrant, which I would account
mercy,——

BOSOLA What's that?

DUCHESS If they would bind me to that
lifeless trunk,°
And let me freeze to death.

BOSOLA   Come, you must live.

DUCHESS That's the greatest torture souls
feel in hell: 70
In hell that they must live, and cannot
die.
Portia,° I'll new kindle thy coals again,

54 **What . . . practice** A dead man's hand was one
of the charms used in attempts to cure madness by
witchcraft. 63–65 **my . . . dunghill** The reference
here is to the black-magic practice of putting an
evil spell on someone by sticking pins into a doll
that looks like him. By then burying the doll in a
dunghill, the magician calls upon supernatural
spirits to curse even the corpse of the intended
victim by denying it proper burial. 68 **lifeless trunk**
(the statue of) dead Antonio. 72 **Portia** Brutus'
wife, who committed suicide by swallowing red-hot
coals after she heard of her husband's death.

32–33 **For . . . pardon** For I consider it most honorable to pardon, when I could kill. 39 **sacrament
. . . Church** her marriage to Antonio, which she
believes is recognized by the eternal Church (cf.
III.v.68). 41 **thus** in darkness. 42 **too . . . light** too
conspicuous. 44 **ring** her wedding ring, which was
earlier seized by the Cardinal. 50 **owed** owned.

And revive the rare and almost dead ex-
ample
Of a loving wife.
BOSOLA   O, fie! despair? remember
You are a Christian.°
75 DUCHESS   The Church enjoins fasting:
I'll starve myself to death.
BOSOLA   Leave this vain sorrow;
Things, being at the worst, begin to
mend:
The bee when he hath shot his sting into
your hand
May then play with your eyelid.°
DUCHESS   Good comfortable° fellow,
Persuade a wretch that's broke upon the
80 wheel°
To have all his bones new set: entreat
him live,
To be executed again. Who must dis-
patch me?
I account this world a tedious theater,
For I do play a part in't 'gainst my will.
BOSOLA Come, be of comfort, I will save
85 your life.
DUCHESS Indeed, I have not leisure to
tend so small a business.
BOSOLA Now, by my life, I pity you.
DUCHESS   Thou art a fool then,
To waste thy pity on a thing so wretched
As cannot pity itself. I am full of daggers.
90 Puff! let me blow these vipers from me.

[*She turns to a* SERVANT.]

What are you?
SERVANT   One that wishes you long life.
DUCHESS I would thou wert hanged for
the horrible curse

Thou hast given me: I shall shortly
grow° one
Of the miracles of pity. I'll go pray. No,
I'll go curse.
BOSOLA   Oh fie!
DUCHESS   I could curse the stars. 95
BOSOLA Oh, fearful!
DUCHESS And those three smiling seasons
of the year
Into a Russian winter—nay, the world
To its first chaos.°
BOSOLA Look you, the stars shine still.
DUCHESS   Oh, but you must 100
Remember, my curse hath a great way to
go:
Plagues, that make lanes through largest
families,
Consume them.
BOSOLA   Fie lady!
DUCHESS   Let them° like tyrants
Never be remembered, but for the ill
they have done:
Let all the zealous prayers of mortifièd 105
Churchmen forget them,——
BOSOLA   O uncharitable!
DUCHESS Let Heaven, a little while, cease
crowning martyrs
To punish them.
Go, howl them this, and say I long to
bleed.
It is some mercy when men kill with
speed. 110
Exit [*with* SERVANTS].

[*Enter* FERDINAND.]

FERDINAND Excellent, as I would wish:
she plagued in art.°
These presentations are but framed in
wax
By the curious° master in that quality,
Vincentio Lauriola,° and she takes them
For true, substantial bodies.

75 **You . . . Christian** Suicide is forbidden by
Christianity. 78–79 **The . . . eyelid** After it has
used its stinger on your hand, the bee may sit even
on your eyelid without being able to do any harm.
79 **comfortable** free from pain. 80 **broke . . . wheel**
In Webster's time, men were tortured by being
bound to a wheel and then stretched until their
bones broke under the strain. Fortune, too, was
often thought of as a great wheel of torture, to
which all men were tied and upon which they were
eventually broken if they trusted too much in material rewards (see the Duchess' reference to this
belief at III.v.93).

93 **grow** become. 97–99 **And . . . chaos** And (I
could curse) spring, summer, and fall so that they
became one long winter; in fact, I could wish the
world restored to its original state of chaos. 103
them her brothers. 111 **she . . . art** She was tormented by these wax figures. 113 **curious** ingenious.
114 **Vincentio Lauriola** historically unidentifiable,
but here he is clearly meant to be a skillful wax-
worker.

115 BOSOLA   Why do you do this?
FERDINAND   To bring her to despair.
BOSOLA   'Faith,° end here,
And go no farther in your cruelty.
Send her a penitential garment, to put on
Next to her delicate skin, and furnish her
With beads° and prayerbooks.
120 FERDINAND   Damn her! that body of hers,
While that my blood ran pure in't, was
    more worth
Than that which thou wouldst comfort,
    called a soul.°
I will send her masques° of common
    courtesans,
Have her meat served up by bawds and
    ruffians,
And, 'cause she'll needs be° mad, I am
125   resolved
To remove forth° the common hospital
All the mad folk, and place them near
    her lodging.
There let them practice° together, sing,
    and dance,
And act their gambols to the full o' th'
    moon:°
130 If she can sleep the better for it, let her.
Your work is almost ended.
BOSOLA   Must I see her again?
FERDINAND   Yes.
BOSOLA   Never.
FERDINAND   You must.
BOSOLA   Never in mine own shape;°
That's forfeited by my intelligence°
And this last cruel lie. When you send
    me next,
The business shall be comfort.
135 FERDINAND   Very likely.°

Thy pity is nothing of kin to thee.
    Antonio
Lurks about Milan; thou shalt shortly
    thither,
To feed a fire as great as my revenge,
Which ne'er will slack till it have spent
    his fuel;
Intemperate agues make physicians cruel. 140
Exeunt.

SCENE TWO   [*The same place*].

[*Enter* DUCHESS *and* CARIOLA.]

DUCHESS   What hideous noise was that?
CARIOLA   'Tis the wild consort
Of madmen, lady, which your tyrant
    brother
Hath placed about your lodging. This
    tyranny,
I think, was never practiced till this hour.
DUCHESS   Indeed, I thank him: nothing
    but noise and folly   5
Can keep me in my right wits, whereas
    reason
And silence make me stark mad. Sit
    down.
Discourse to me some dismal tragedy.
CARIOLA   O 'twill increase your melan-
    choly.
DUCHESS   Thou art deceived;
To hear of greater grief would lessen
    mine.   10
This is a prison?
CARIOLA   Yes, but you shall live
To shake this durance° off.
DUCHESS   Thou art a fool:
The robin red-breast and the nightingale
Never live long in cages.
CARIOLA   Pray dry your eyes.
What think you of, madam?   15
DUCHESS   Of nothing:
When I muse thus, I sleep.
CARIOLA   Like a madman, with your eyes
    open?
DUCHESS   Dost thou think we shall know
    one another

---

116 **'Faith** an interjection, contracted from "in
faith." 120 **beads** rosary beads. 120–122 **that . . .
soul** There is in this declaration—because the
Duchess' body is its focus—another unconscious suggestion of Ferdinand's sexual desires for his sister.
123 **masques** courtly entertainments. 125 **needs be**
willfully continues to be. 126 **forth** from. 128 **practice** carry on their activities. 129 **full . . . moon**
the time when madmen were thought to be most
mad. 132 **in . . . shape** without being disguised.
133 **intelligence** work as a spy. 135 **Very likely** a
cynical rejoinder, because Bosola will then offer her
the "comfort" of death.

IV.ii. 12 **durance** hardship.

In th'other world?

20 CARIOLA   Yes, out of question.

DUCHESS   O, that it were possible we
might
But hold some two days' conference with
the dead:
From them I should learn somewhat I
am sure
I never shall know here. I'll tell thee a
miracle;
25 I am not mad yet, to my cause of sorrow.°
Th' heaven o'er my head seems made of
molten brass,
The earth of flaming sulphur, yet I am
not mad.
I am acquainted with sad misery,
As the tanned galley slave is with his oar.
30 Necessity makes me suffer constantly,
And custom makes it easy. Who do I look
like now?

CARIOLA   Like to your picture in the gal-
lery,
A deal of life in show,° but none in prac-
tice:°
Or rather like some reverend monument
Whose ruins are even pitied.

35 DUCHESS   Very proper:
And Fortune seems only to have her eye-
sight,°
To behold my tragedy.
How now! What noise is that? [*Enter*
SERVANT.]

SERVANT   I am come to tell you,
Your brother hath intended you some
sport.°
40 A great physician when the Pope was sick
Of a deep melancholy, presented him
With several sorts of madmen, which
wild object,
Being full of change and sport, forced
him to laugh,

And so th'imposthume° broke: the selfsame cure
The Duke intends on you.

DUCHESS   Let them come in.   45

SERVANT   There's a mad lawyer, and a
secular priest,
A doctor that hath forfeited his wits
By jealousy; an astrologian
That in his works said such a day o' th'
month
Should be the day of doom, and, failing
of't,   50
Ran mad; an English tailor, crazed i' th'
brain
With the study of new fashion; a gentle-
man usher°
Quite beside himself with care to keep in
mind
The number of his lady's salutations
Or "How do you?" she employed him in
in each morning;°   55
A farmer too, an excellent knave in
grain,°
Mad, 'cause he was hindered transporta-
tion;°
And let° one broker,° that's mad, loose to
these,
You'd think the devil were among them.

DUCHESS   Sit Cariola. Let them loose when
you please,   60
For I am chained to endure all your
tyranny.

[*Enter* MADMEN.] *Here, by a* MADMAN,
*this song is sung to a dismal kind of
music.*

O let us howl, some heavy note,
    Some deadly-doggèd howl,
Sounding as from the threat'ning throat,
    Of beasts and fatal fowl.   65

---

25 **to . . . sorrow** which is why I feel sorrow. 33
show appearance. **practice** action. 36 **Fortune . . .
eyesight** Traditionally, the goddess Fortune was
pictured as blindfolded because she distributed her
rewards so arbitrarily. Here the Duchess implies
that momentarily Fortune's blindfold has been removed so that she can see the sad results of her
handiwork. 39 **sport** entertainment.

44 **imposthume** ulcer (which caused the melancholy). 52 **usher** an attendant who walks before a
person of rank, greeting guests and introducing
strangers. 55 **How . . . morning** a double-entendre,
meaning the usher was made to serve her sexually
as well as socially. 56 **in grain** both "in the grain
trade" and "in essence (a knave)." 57 **hindered
transportation** denied export. 58 **let** turn. **broker**
pawnbroker.

As ravens, screech owls, bulls, and bears,
  We'll bell,° and bawl our parts,
Till irksome noise have cloyed your ears,
  And corrosived° your hearts.
70   At last when as our choir wants breath,
    Our bodies being blest,
  We'll sing like swans, to welcome death,
    And die in love and rest.

MAD ASTROLOGER Doomsday not come
75 yet? I'll draw it nearer by a perspective,° or make a glass that shall set all the world on fire upon an instant. I cannot sleep; my pillow is stuffed with a litter of porcupines.

80 MAD LAWYER Hell is a mere glasshouse,° where the devils are continually blowing up women's souls on hollow irons,° and the fire never goes out.

MAD PRIEST I will lie with every woman in
85 my parish the tenth night: I will tithe them over like haycocks.°

MAD DOCTOR Shall my pothecary° outgo° me, because I am a cuckold? I have found out his roguery: he makes alum° of his
90 wife's urine and sells it to Puritans, that have sore throats with over-straining.°

MAD ASTROLOGER I have skill in heraldry.

MAD LAWYER Hast?

MAD ASTROLOGER You do give for your
95 crest a woodcock's° head, with the brains picked out on't. You are a very ancient gentleman.

MAD PRIEST Greek is turned Turk;° we are only to be saved by the Helvetian
100 translation.°

MAD ASTROLOGER [*To* LAWYER.] Come on sir, I will lay the law to you.°

MAD LAWYER Oh, rather lay° a corrosive: the law will eat to the bone.

MAD PRIEST He that drinks but to satisfy 105 nature is damned.

MAD DOCTOR If I had my glass° here, I would show a sight should make all the women here call me mad doctor.

MAD ASTROLOGER [*Pointing to* PRIEST.]   110 What's he, a ropemaker?°

MAD LAWYER No, no, no, a snuffling° knave that, while he shows the tombs, will have his hand in a wench's placket.°

MAD PRIEST Woe to the caroche° that 115 brought home my wife from the masque at three o'clock in the morning; it had a large featherbed in it.

MAD DOCTOR I have pared the devil's nails° forty times, roasted them in raven's 120 eggs, and cured agues with them.

MAD PRIEST Get me three hundred milch° bats, to make possets° to procure sleep.

MAD DOCTOR All the college may throw their caps° at me; I have made a soap- 125 boiler costive:° it was my masterpiece——

Here the dance consisting of eight MAD-MEN, *with music answerable thereunto, after which* BOSOLA, *like an old man, enters.*

DUCHESS Is he mad too?

SERVANT   Pray question him; I'll leave you.

[*Exeunt* SERVANT *and* MADMEN.]

BOSOLA I am come to make thy tomb.

DUCHESS   Ha, my tomb?

---

67 **bell** bellow. 69 **corrosived** corroded. 75 **perspective** telescope. 80 **glasshouse** a factory where glass is made. 81–82 **blowing . . . irons** A sexual meaning is implicit in this statement, and in most of the lunatic raving that follows; these madmen, like Lear on the heath, are acutely conscious of the intensity of man's sexual desires. 86 **haycocks** stacks of hay, but an obscene pun is intended as well. 87 **pothecary** druggist. **outgo** get the best of. 89 **alum** an astringent formerly used to treat inflamed tissue. 91 **over-straining** singing too loudly and, also, straining too much of the life out of religion. 95 **woodcock** thought to be a stupid bird. 98 **Greek . . . Turk** The Greek text of the Bible has been made to serve nonbelievers (all non-Puritans). 99 **Helvetian translation** the translation of the Bible officially approved by the Puritans.

102 **I . . . you** I will explain the church law to you. 103 **Oh . . . lay** You might just as well apply. 107 **glass** some sort of magnifying glass. 111 **ropemaker** i.e. one who is in league with the hangman. 112 **snuffling** sanctimonious. 114 **placket** both "pocket" and "pudendum." 115 **caroche** a luxurious carriage. 119–120 **I . . . nails** I have brought the devil under my control. 122 **milch** milk-bearing. 123 **possets** a hot drink made of sweetened, spiced milk curdled with ale or wine. 124–125 **throw . . . caps** vainly seek to surpass me in skill. 125–126 **I . . . costive** I have made one who boils soap constipated (an unusual accomplishment because soap was an essential element used in manufacturing suppositories).

Thou speakst as if I lay upon my death-
bed,
Gasping for breath. Dost thou perceive
130   me sick?
    BOSOLA   Yes, and the more dangerously,
    since thy sickness is insensible.°
    DUCHESS   Thou art not mad, sure; dost
    know me?
    BOSOLA   Yes.
    DUCHESS   Who am I?
135   BOSOLA   Thou art a box of worm seed,° at
    best but° a salvatory of green mummy.°
    What's this flesh? a little cruded° milk,
    fantastical puff paste:° our bodies are
    weaker than those paper prisons boys use
140   to keep flies in, more contemptible—since
    ours is to preserve earthworms. Didst
    thou ever see a lark in a cage? such is the
    soul in the body: this world is like her
    little turf of grass° and the heaven o'er
145   our heads, like her looking glass,° only
    gives us a miserable knowledge of the
    small compass of our prison.
    DUCHESS   Am not I thy Duchess?
    BOSOLA   Thou art some great woman,
150   sure; for riot° begins to sit on thy fore-
    head (clad in grey hairs) twenty years
    sooner than on a merry milkmaid's.
    Thou sleepst worse, than if a mouse
    should be forced to take up her lodging
155   in a cat's ear. A little infant, that breeds
    its teeth, should it lie with thee, would
    cry out, as if thou wert the more unquiet
    bedfellow.°
    DUCHESS   I am Duchess of Malfi still.
160   BOSOLA   That makes thy sleeps so broken:
    Glories, like glowworms, afar off shine
    bright,

But looked to near, have neither heat nor
light.
    DUCHESS   Thou art very plain.°
    BOSOLA   My trade is to flatter the dead,
    not the living: I am a tomb-maker.
    DUCHESS   And thou comst to make my
    tomb?   165
    BOSOLA   Yes.
    DUCHESS   Let me be a little merry;
    Of what stuff wilt thou make it?
    BOSOLA   Nay, resolve me° first. Of what
    fashion?
    DUCHESS   Why, do we grow fantastical° in
    our deathbed?   170
    Do we affect fashion in the grave?
    BOSOLA   Most ambitiously. Princes'
    images on their tombs
    Do not lie as they were wont, seeming to
    pray
    Up to heaven, but with their hands un-
    der their cheeks,°
    As if they died of the toothache. They
    are not carved   175
    With their eyes fixed upon the stars; but,
    as
    Their minds were wholly bent upon the
    world,
    The selfsame way they seem to turn their
    faces.
    DUCHESS   Let me know fully therefore the
    effect
    Of this thy dismal preparation,   180
    This talk, fit for a charnel.°
    BOSOLA   Now I shall;

[*Enter* EXECUTIONERS *with*] *a coffin,
cords, and a bell.*

Here is a present from your princely
brothers,
And may it arrive welcome, for it brings
Last benefit, last sorrow.
    DUCHESS   Let me see it.
    I have so much obedience in my blood   185
    I wish it in their veins, to do them good.

---

131 **insensible** not apparent to the senses. 135 **box
. . . seed** a box of food for worms. 136 **but** only.
salvatory . . . mummy either a container for an un-
ripened mummy (because you are still alive) or an
ointment box for fresh mummia, a drug derived
from embalmed bodies. 137 **cruded** curdled. 138
puff paste a light pastry. 144, 145 **turf of grass,
looking glass** articles that were put into bird cages
in an attempt to keep the captured birds happy.
150 **riot** lines of sorrow that disturb the previous
order of beauty. 155–158 **A . . . bedfellow** You
sleep more restlessly than a baby cutting teeth.

163 **plain** plain-spoken. 169 **resolve me** Answer my
question. 170 **fantastical** obsessed by fantasies. 174
with . . . cheeks in a semirecumbent position. 181
charnel cemetery.

BOSOLA   This is your last presence chamber.

CARIOLA   O my sweet lady!

DUCHESS   Peace! it affrights not me.

BOSOLA   I am the common bellman,°

190   That usually is sent to condemned persons,

The night before they suffer.

DUCHESS   Even now thou saidst
Thou wast a tomb-maker?

BOSOLA   'Twas to bring you
By degrees to mortification.° Listen:

[*Rings the bell.*]

Hark, now every thing is still,

195   The screech owl and the whistler shrill°
Call upon our dame,° aloud,
And bid her quickly don her shroud.
Much you had of land and rent,
Your length in clay's now competent.

200   A long war disturbed your mind;
Here your perfect peace is signed.
Of what is't fools make such vain keep-
ing?
Sin° their conception, their birth, weep-
ing:
Their life, a general mist of error,

205   Their death, a hideous storm of terror.
Strew your hair with powders sweet:
Don clean linen, bathe your feet,
And, the foul fiend° more to check,
A crucifix let bless your neck.

210   'Tis now full tide 'tween night and day,
End your groan, and come away.

[EXECUTIONERS *approach.*]

CARIOLA   Hence, villains, tyrants, murderers. Alas!
What will you do with my lady? Call for
help.

---

189 **bellman** one who was supposed to drive evil
spirits away from the soul. 192–193 '**Twas . . .
mortification** It was to get you accustomed to the
idea of dying. 195 **whistler shrill** a bird whose
song was supposed to be a foreboding of evil.
196 **our dame** the Duchess. 203 **Sin** The word here
assumes the meanings of both "since" and "sin"
(which attends man's conception). 208 **foul fiend**
the devil.

DUCHESS   To whom? To our next neighbors? They are mad-folks.

BOSOLA   Remove that noise.

[EXECUTIONERS *seize* CARIOLA, *who struggles.*]

DUCHESS   Farewell, Cariola, *215*
In my last will I have not much to give:
A many hundred guests have fed upon
me;
Thine will be a poor reversion.°

CARIOLA   I will die with her.

DUCHESS   I pray thee, look thou givst my
little boy
Some syrup for his cold, and let the girl *220*
Say her prayers, ere she sleep.

[CARIOLA *is forced off.*]

       Now, what you please.
What death?

BOSOLA   Strangling. Here are your executioners.

DUCHESS   I forgive them:
The apoplexy, catarrh,° or cough o' th'
lungs   *225*
Would do as much as they do.

BOSOLA   Doth not death fright you?

DUCHESS   Who would be afraid on't?
Knowing to meet such excellent company
In th'other world.

BOSOLA   Yet, methinks,
The manner of your death should much
afflict you;   *230*
This cord should terrify you?

DUCHESS   Not a whit:
What would it pleasure me, to have my
throat cut
With diamonds? or to be smotherèd
With cassia? or to be shot to death with
pearls?
I know death hath ten thousand several
doors   *235*
For men to take their exits; and 'tis
found
They go on such strange geometrical
hinges,

---

218 **reversion** estate passed on to her. 225 **catarrh**
hemorrhage.

You may open them both ways.° Any
  way, for heaven sake,
So I were out of your whispering. Tell
  my brothers
That I perceive death, now I am well
240 awake,
Best gift is they can give, or I can take.
I would fain put off my last woman's
  fault:
I'll not be tedious to you.

EXECUTIONERS   We are ready.

DUCHESS Dispose my breath how please
  you, but my body
Bestow upon my women, will you?

245 EXECUTIONERS   Yes.

DUCHESS Pull, and pull strongly, for your
  able strength
Must pull down heaven upon me—
Yet stay, heaven-gates are not so highly
  arched
As princes' palaces: they that enter there
Must go upon their knees. [*She kneels.*]
250 Come violent death,
Serve for mandragora° to make me sleep.
Go tell my brothers, when I am laid out,
They then may feed in quiet. *They stran-*
  gle her.

BOSOLA   Where's the waiting woman?
Fetch her. Some other strangle the children.

[*Exeunt* EXECUTIONERS.]

[*Enter one with* CARIOLA.]

Look you, there sleeps your mistress.

255 CARIOLA   O you are damned
Perpetually for this. My turn is next,
Is't not so ordered?

BOSOLA   Yes, and I am glad
You are so well prepared for't.

CARIOLA   You are deceived sir,
I am not prepared for't. I will not die;
260 I will first come to my answer, and know
How I have offended.

BOSOLA   Come, dispatch her.
You kept her° counsel; now you shall
  keep ours.

CARIOLA I will not die—I must not—I
  am contracted
To a young gentleman.

EXECUTIONER [*Showing the noose.*]
          Here's your wedding ring.

CARIOLA Let me but speak with the
  Duke. I'll discover   265
Treason to his person.

BOSOLA   Delays: throttle her.

EXECUTIONER She bites and scratches.

CARIOLA   If you kill me now,
I am damned. I have not been at confes-
  sion
This two years.

BOSOLA   When!°

CARIOLA   I am quick with child.°

BOSOLA   Why then,
Your credit's saved.° Bear her into th'
  next room.   270
Let this lie still.

[EXECUTIONERS *strangle* CARIOLA *and
exeunt with her body.*]
[*Enter* FERDINAND.]

FERDINAND   Is she dead?

BOSOLA   She is what
You'd have her. But here begin your pity.

[BOSOLA *draws the traverse and*] *shows
the children strangled.*

Alas, how have these offended?

FERDINAND   The death
Of young wolves is never to be pitied.

BOSOLA Fix your eye here.

FERDINAND   Constantly.

BOSOLA   Do you not weep? 275
Other sins only speak; murther shrieks
  out:
The element of water moistens the earth,
But blood flies upwards and bedews the
  heavens.

FERDINAND Cover her face. Mine eyes dazzle:° she died young.

---

238 **You . . . ways** Death may come and get you,
or you may go to it (by committing suicide). 251
mandragora a plant formerly used as a narcotic.
262 **her** the Duchess'.

269 **When** an exclamation of impatience. **quick
. . . child** pregnant. (Criminals who were pregnant
were sometimes granted a stay of execution until
the birth of the child.) 270 **Your . . . saved** Your
reputation is saved—because your death will prevent you from bearing a bastard child. 279 **dazzle**
are dazzled.

280 BOSOLA   I think not so: her infelicity
Seemed to have years too many.

FERDINAND   She and I were twins:
And should I die this instant I had lived
Her time to a minute.

BOSOLA   It seems she was born first:
You have bloodily approved° the ancient
truth,
285 That kindred commonly do worse agree°
Than remote strangers.

FERDINAND   Let me see her face again—
Why didst not thou pity her? What an
excellent
Honest man mightst thou have been
If thou hadst borne her to some sanctu-
ary!
290 Or, bold in a good cause, opposed thyself
With thy advancèd sword above thy
head,
Between her innocence and my revenge!
I bade thee, when I was distracted of my
wits,
Go kill my dearest friend, and thou hast
done't.
295 For let me but examine well the cause.
What was the meanness of her match to
me?
Only, I must confess, I had a hope,
Had she continued widow, to have
gained
An infinite mass of treasure by her
death;°
And that was the main cause—her mar-
300 riage,
That drew a stream of gall quite through
my heart.
For thee (as we observe in tragedies
That a good actor many times is cursed
For playing a villain's part), I hate thee
for't.

284 **approved** proven. 285 **do . . . agree** differ more. 297–299 **Only . . . death** The Duke, desperately searching for the reason why he found his sister's marriage to Antonio so hateful, here presents an obvious rationalization: even if the Duchess had died without remarrying, her estate would have gone to her first son, the young Duke of Malfi (see III.iii.66). The real explanation for Ferdinand's intense jealousy of Antonio is, of course, too frightening for him to admit, or even to recognize consciously.

And, for my sake, say thou hast done
much ill, well.   305
BOSOLA   Let me quicken your memory,
for I perceive
You are falling into ingratitude. I challenge
The reward due to my service.

FERDINAND   I'll tell thee,
What I'll give thee——
BOSOLA   Do.
FERDINAND   I'll give thee a pardon
For this murther.
BOSOLA   Ha?
FERDINAND   Yes: and 'tis   310
The largest bounty I can study° to do
thee.
By what authority didst thou execute
This bloody sentence?
BOSOLA   By yours.
FERDINAND   Mine? Was I her judge?
Did any ceremonial form of law
Doom her to not-being? Did a complete
jury   315
Deliver her conviction up i' th' court?
Where shalt thou find this judgment reg-
istered
Unless in hell? See, like a bloody fool
Th' hast forfeited thy life, and thou shalt
die for't.
BOSOLA   The office of justice is perverted
quite   320
When one thief hangs another. Who shall
dare
To reveal this?
FERDINAND   Oh, I'll tell thee:
The wolf shall find her grave and scrape
it up,
Not to devour the corpse, but to discover
The horrid murther.
BOSOLA   You, not I, shall quake for't.   325
FERDINAND   Leave me.
BOSOLA   I will first receive my pension.°
FERDINAND   You are a villain.
BOSOLA   When your ingratitude
Is judge, I am so——
FERDINAND   O horror!

311 **study** consciously bring myself. 326 **pension** reward for services.

That not the fear of Him which binds the devils

330 Can prescribe man obedience.
Never look upon me more.

BOSOLA   Why fare thee well.
Your brother and yourself are worthy men;
You have a pair of hearts are hollow graves—
Rotten, and rotting others. And your vengeance,
Like two chained bullets,° still goes arm

335 in arm.
You may be brothers, for treason, like the plague,
Doth take much in a blood.° I stand like one
That long hath ta'en a sweet and golden dream:
I am angry with myself, now that I wake.

FERDINAND Get thee into some unknown
340 part o' th' world,
That I may never see thee.

BOSOLA   Let me know
Wherefore I should be thus neglected? Sir,
I served your tyranny, and rather strove
To satisfy yourself, than all the world;

345 And though I loathed the evil, yet I loved
You that did counsel it, and rather sought
To appear a true servant than an honest man.

FERDINAND I'll go hunt the badger° by owl-light:°
'Tis a deed of darkness.   *Exit.*

BOSOLA He's much distracted. Off my
350 painted honor!°
While with vain hopes our faculties we tire,
We seem to sweat in ice and freeze in fire.°

What would I do, were this to do again?
I would not change my peace of conscience
For all the wealth of Europe. She stirs;
here's life.   355
Return, fair soul, from darkness, and lead mine
Out of this sensible° hell. She's warm; she breathes:
Upon thy pale lips I will melt my heart
To store them with fresh color. Who's there?
Some cordial drink!° Alas! I dare not
call: 360
So pity would destroy pity.° Her eye opes,
And heaven in it seems to ope, that late was shut,
To take me up to mercy.

DUCHESS   Antonio!
BOSOLA Yes, madam, he is living,
The dead bodies you saw were but feigned
statues;   365
He's reconciled to your brothers: the Pope hath wrought
The atonement.

DUCHESS   Mercy.   *She dies.*
BOSOLA Oh, she's gone again: there the cords of life broke.
Oh sacred innocence, that sweetly sleeps
On turtles'° feathers, whilst a guilty con-
science   370
Is a black register, wherein is writ
All our good deeds and bad, a perspective
That shows us hell. That we cannot be suffered
To do good when we have a mind to it!   375
This is manly sorrow:
These tears, I am very certain, never grew
In my mother's milk. My estate° is sunk
Below the degree of fear: where were
These penitent fountains while she was living?
Oh, they were frozen up! Here is a sight 380

335 **chained bullets** Cannon balls were sometimes chained together to increase the extent of their destructive force. 337 **take . . . blood** runs in the blood of particular families. 348 **badger** an animal that avoided daylight. **owl-light** night. **I'll . . . owl-light** I shall henceforth carry out my activities in darkness. 350 **painted honor** false sense of importance, as a spy for Ferdinand. 352 **We . . . fire** We are always uncomfortably restless and unsatisfied.

337 **sensible** apparent to the senses. 360 **cordial drink** medicine to induce revival. 361 **So . . . pity** By pitying her and calling out for help, I would only destroy her whom I pity because Ferdinand would return and kill her. 370 **turtles** turtledoves (traditionally a symbol of love and peace). 377 **estate** condition.

As direful to my soul as is the sword
Unto a wretch hath slain his father. Come,
I'll bear thee hence,
And execute thy last will—that's deliver
385 Thy body to the reverend dispose
Of some good women: that the cruel tyrant
Shall not deny me. Then I'll post to Milan,
Where somewhat I will speedily enact
Worth my dejection.°
Exit [carrying the body].

Act Five

SCENE ONE   [*A public place in Milan*]

[*Enter* ANTONIO *and* DELIO.]

Antonio   What think you of my hope of
  reconcilement
To the Aragonian brethren?
DELIO   I misdoubt it,
For though they have sent their letters of
  safe conduct
For your repair° to Milan, they appear
But nets to entrap you. The Marquis of
5   Pescara,
Under whom you hold certain land in
  cheat,°
Much 'gainst his noble nature, hath been
  moved
To seize those lands, and some of his de-
  pendants
Are at this instant making it their suit
10 To be invested in your revenues.
I cannot think they mean well to your
  life
That do deprive you of your means of
  life,
Your living.
ANTONIO   You are still an heretic.°
To any safety I can shape myself.

DELIO   Here comes the Marquis. I will
  make myself   15
Petitioner for some part of your land,
To know whether° it is flying.°
ANTONIO   I pray do.

[*Enter* PESCARA.]

DELIO   Sir, I have a suit to you.
PESCARA   To me?
DELIO   An easy one:
There is the citadel of St. Bennet,°
With some demesnes,° of late in the pos-
  session   20
Of Antonio Bologna; please you bestow
  them on me?
PESCARA   You are my friend. But this is
  such a suit
Nor fit for me to give, nor you to take.
DELIO   No sir?
PESCARA   I will give you ample reason for't
Soon, in private. Here's the Cardinal's
  mistress.   25

[*Enter* JULIA.]

JULIA   My lord, I am grown your poor
  petitioner,
And should be an ill beggar had I not
A great man's letter here, the Cardinal's,
To court you in my favor.

[*She gives him a letter.*]

PESCARA   He entreats for you
The citadel of St. Bennet, that belonged   30
To the banished Bologna.
JULIA   Yes.
PESCARA   I could not have thought of a
  friend I could
Rather pleasure with it: 'tis yours.
JULIA   Sir, I thank you.
And he shall know how doubly I am en-
  gaged,
Both in your gift and speediness of giving, 35
Which makes your grant the greater.
Exit.

---

389 **Worth my dejection** keeping with my abase-
ment.
V.i. 4 **repair** return. 6 **in cheat** subject to return
to the lord only if the tenant dies without an heir
or if he commits a felony. 13 **heretic** skeptic.

17 **whether** The second and third quarto editions
read "whither." **it . . . flying** it is wantonly being
given away. 19 **St. Bennet** St. Benedict. 20 **demesnes**
land attached to the citadel.

ANTONIO   [*Aside.*] How they fortify
Themselves with my ruin!
DELIO   Sir, I am
Little bound to you.
PESCARA   Why?
DELIO Because you denied this suit to me,
    and gave't
To such a creature.
40 PESCARA   Do you know what it was?
It was Antonio's land—not forfeited
By course of law, but ravished from his
    throat
By the Cardinal's entreaty. It were not fit
I should bestow so main a piece of wrong
45 Upon my friend: 'tis a gratification
Only due to a strumpet; for it is injustice.
Shall I sprinkle the pure blood of in-
    nocents
To make these followers I call my friends
Look ruddier° upon me? I am glad
This land, ta'en from the owner by such
50 wrong,
Returns again unto so foul an use,
As salary for his lust. Learn, good Delio,
To ask noble things of me, and you shall
    find
I'll be a noble giver.
DELIO   You instruct me well.
ANTONIO [*Aside.*] Why, here's a man, now,
55 would fright° impudence
From sauciest beggars.
PESCARA   Prince Ferdinand's
    come to Milan
Sick, as thy give out, of an apoplexy;
But some say 'tis a frenzy. I am going
To visit him.   *Exit.*
ANTONIO   'Tis a noble old fellow.°
DELIO What course do you mean to take,
60 Antonio?
ANTONIO   This night I mean to venture all
    my fortune,
Which is no more than a poor ling'ring
life,

To the Cardinal's worst of malice.° I
    have got
Private access to his chamber, and intend
To visit him, about the mid of night,   65
As once his brother did our noble Duch-
    ess.°
It may be that the sudden apprehension
Of danger—for I'll go in mine own
    shape—,
When he shall see it fraight° with love
    and duty,
May draw the poison out of him, and
    work   70
A friendly reconcilement. If it fail,
Yet it shall rid me of this infamous call-
    ing,°
For better fall once, than be ever falling.
DELIO I'll second you in all danger; and,
    howe'er,
My life keeps rank with yours.   75
ANTONIO   You are still my loved and best
    friend.   *Exeunt.*

SCENE TWO [*The palace of the Aragonian
    brothers in Milan*]

[*Enter* PESCARA *and* DOCTOR.]

PESCARA Now, doctor, may I visit your
    patient?
DOCTOR If't please your lordship, but he's
    instantly
To take the air here in the gallery,
By my direction.
PESCARA   Pray thee, what's his disease?
DOCTOR A very pestilent disease, my lord,   5
They call lycanthropia.°
PESCARA   What's that?
I need a dictionary to't.

49 **ruddier** more glowingly. 55 **fright** drive away.
59 **old fellow** The Marquis of Pescara never actually
lived to be an "old fellow"; he died when he was
thirty-six. There is, however, a good reason why
Webster makes him old: that way he commands respect as one who has lived long enough to become
wise.

63 **To . . . malice** against the worst malice of the
Cardinal. 66 **As . . . Duchess** The reference is to
the time that Ferdinand came unexpectedly into the
Duchess' bedchamber while she was combing her
hair and readying herself for bed. Antonio does
not yet know about the murderous visit that Ferdinand made while the Duchess was in prison.
69 **fraight** abounding with. 72 **infamous calling**
life of disgrace.
V.ii. 6 **lycanthropia** a mania in which the victim
imagines himself a wolf.

DOCTOR   I'll tell you:
  In those that are possessed with't there
  o'erflows
  Such melancholy humor, they imagine
  Themselves to be transformèd into
10 wolves,
  Steal forth to churchyards in the dead of
  night,
  And dig dead bodies up: as two nights
  since
  One met the Duke, 'bout midnight in a
  lane
  Behind St. Mark's church, with the leg
  of a man
  Upon his shoulder; and he howled fear-
15 fully—
  Said he was a wolf; only the difference
  Was a wolf's skin was hairy on the out-
  side,
  His on the inside. Bade them take their
  swords,
  Rip up his flesh, and try. Straight I was
  sent for,
  And having ministered to him, found his
20 grace
  Very well recoverèd.
PESCARA   I am glad on't.
DOCTOR Yet not without some fear
  Of a relapse. If he grow to his fit again,
  I'll go a nearer way to work with him
25 Than ever Paracelsus° dreamed of. If
  They'll give me leave, I'll buffet his mad-
  ness out of him.
  Stand aside: he comes.

  [*Enter* CARDINAL, FERDINAND, MALATESTE,
  and BOSOLA, *who remains behind.*]

FERDINAND Leave me.
MALATESTE Why doth your lordship love
  this solitariness?
30 FERDINAND Eagles commonly fly alone.
  They are crows, daws,° and starlings that
  flock together. Look, what's that follows
  me?
MALATESTE Nothing, my lord.
35 FERDINAND Yes.

MALATESTE 'Tis your shadow.
FERDINAND Stay it; let it not haunt me.
MALATESTE Impossible, if you move, and
  the sun shine.
FERDINAND I will throttle it.

[*He attacks his shadow.*]

MALATESTE Oh, my lord, you are angry
  with nothing.   40
FERDINAND You are a fool. How is't possi-
  ble I should catch my shadow unless I
  fall upon't? When I go to hell, I mean to
  carry a bribe: for, look you, good gifts
  evermore make way for the worst persons.   45
PESCARA Rise, good my lord.
FERDINAND I am studying the art of patience.
PESCARA 'Tis a noble virtue——
FERDINAND To drive six snails before me,
  from this town to Moscow; neither use   50
  goad nor whip to them, but let them
  take their own time—the patient'st man
  i' th' world match me for an experiment!
  And I'll crawl after like a sheep-biter.°
CARDINAL Force him up.   55

[*They make* FERDINAND *stand up.*]

FERDINAND Use me well, you were best.°
  What I have done, I have done. I'll con-
  fess nothing.
DOCTOR Now let me come to him. Are you
  mad, my lord?
  Are you out of your princely wits?
FERDINAND   What's he?
PESCARA   Your doctor.
FERDINAND Let me have his beard sawed
  off, and his eyebrows   60
  Filed more civil.°
DOCTOR   I must do mad tricks with him,
  For that's the only way on't. I have
  brought
  Your grace a salamander's° skin, to keep
  you
  From sun-burning.

25 **Paracelsus** a German physician and alchemist
noted for his radical ways of treating diseases. 31
daws crowlike birds.

54 **sheep-biter** a sheep-stealing dog. 56 **you . . .
best** an interjectory phrase meaning "you would be
well-advised to." 60–61 **Let . . . civil** I wish his
appearance were not so hostile. 63 **salamander**
thought capable of living in fire.

FERDINAND   I have cruel sore eyes.

DOCTOR   The white of a cockatrice° egg is
65   present remedy.

FERDINAND   Let it be a new-laid one, you
were best.
Hide me from him: physicians are like
kings:
They brook no contradiction.

DOCTOR   Now he begins
To fear me; now let me alone with him.

[FERDINAND *tries to take off his gown;*
CARDINAL *seizes him.*]

70   CARDINAL   How now, put off your gown?

DOCTOR   Let me have some forty urinals
filled with rose-water: he and I'll go pelt
one another with them: now he begins to
fear me. Can you fetch a frisk,° sir?
75   [*Aside to* CARDINAL.] Let him go; let him
go upon my peril. I find by his eye, he
stands in awe of me: I'll make him as
tame as a dormouse.

[CARDINAL *releases* FERDINAND.]

FERDINAND   Can you fetch your frisks, sir!
80   I will stamp him into a cullis;° flay off his
skin, to cover one of the anatomies.° This
rogue hath set i' th' cold yonder, in
Barber-Chirurgeons' Hall.° Hence, hence!
you are all of you like beasts for sacrifice:
[*throws the* DOCTOR *down and beats him*]
85   there's nothing left of you, but tongue
and belly,° flattery and lechery.   [*Exit.*]

65 **cockatrice** a legendary monster with the head,
wings, and legs of a cock and the tail of a serpent.
Because most of its power was thought to be vested
in its eyes—its look was deadly—and because egg
whites were often used in treating sore eyes, the
white of a cockatrice's egg would theoretically be an
ideal remedy for the affliction the Duke complains
of. 74 **fetch a frisk** dance a caper. 80 **cullis** broth,
made partly by pounding fowl. 81 **anatomies** skele-
tons. 83 **Barber-Chirurgeons' Hall** the place where
barber-surgeons went to pick up corpses of executed felons, which they used for anatomical ex-
periments. 85–86 **tongue and belly** In ancient
religious ceremonies, the tongues and entrails of
sacrificial animals were left for the gods. But Ferdinand intends another meaning as well: in his despair he sees man as essentially a deceiver and a
creature of appetite; he is not a complex, integrated
human being, but only a tongue and a belly.

PESCARA   Doctor, he did not fear you
throughly.°

DOCTOR   True, I was somewhat too forward.

BOSOLA [*Aside.*]   Mercy upon me! What a
fatal judgment
Hath fall'n upon this Ferdinand!

PESCARA   Knows your grace   90
What accident hath brought unto the
Prince
This strange distraction?

CARDINAL [*Aside.*]   I must feign some-
what.° Thus they say it grew:
You have heard it rumored for these
many years,
None of our family dies but there is seen   95
The shape of an old woman, which is
given
By tradition to us to have been murdered
By her nephews, for her riches. Such a
figure
One night, as the Prince sat up late at's
book,
Appeared to him; when crying out for
help,   100
The gentlemen of's chamber found his
grace
All on a cold sweat, altered much in face
And language. Since which apparition
He hath grown worse and worse, and I
much fear
He cannot live.   105

BOSOLA   Sir, I would speak with you.

PESCARA   We'll leave your grace,
Wishing to the sick Prince, our noble
lord,
All health of mind and body.

CARDINAL   You are most welcome.

[*Exeunt* PESCARA, MALATESTE, *and* DOC-
TOR.]

Are you come? [*Aside.*] So—this fellow
must not know
By any means I had intelligence   110
In° our Duchess' death. For, though I
counseled it,

87 **throughly** completely. 93 **feign somewhat** make
up something. 110–111 **had . . . In** had a part in
the planning of.

The full of all th' engagement° seemed to grow
From Ferdinand. Now sir, how fares our sister?
I do not think but sorrow makes her look
Like to an oft-dyed garment. She shall now   115
Taste comfort from me—Why do you look so wildly?
Oh, the fortune of your master here, the Prince,
Dejects you, but be you of happy comfort:
If you'll do one thing for me I'll entreat,
Though he had a cold tombstone o'er his bones,   120
I'll make you what you would be.

BOSOLA   Anything?
Give it me in a breath,° and let me fly to't:
They that think long, small expedition win,°
For musing much o' th' end, cannot begin.

[*Enter* JULIA.]

JULIA   Sir, will you come in to supper?
CARDINAL   I am busy! Leave me!   125
JULIA [*Aside.*] What an excellent shape hath that fellow!   *Exit.*
CARDINAL   'Tis thus: Antonio lurks here in Milan;
Inquire him out, and kill him. While he lives,
Our sister cannot marry, and I have thought
Of an excellent match for her. Do this, and style me°   130
Thy advancement.
BOSOLA   But, by what means shall I find him out?
CARDINAL   There is a gentleman called Delio
Here in the camp, that hath been long approved°
His loyal friend. Set eye upon that fellow,

Follow him to mass; may be Antonio,   135
Although he do account religion
But a school-name,° for fashion of the world
May accompany him. Or else go inquire out
Delio's confessor, and see if you can bribe
Him to reveal it. There are a thousand ways   140
A man might find to trace him—as, to know°
What fellows haunt the Jews for taking up°
Great sums of money, for sure he's in want;
Or else go to th' picture makers, and learn
Who brought her picture lately.° Some of these   145
Happily may take——
BOSOLA   Well, I'll not freeze i' th' business,
I would see that wretched° thing, Antonio,
Above all sights i' th' world.
CARDINAL   Do and be happy.°
Exit.
BOSOLA   This fellow doth breed basilisks° in's eyes,
He's nothing else but murder: yet he seems   150
Not to have notice of the Duchess' death.

112 **full . . . engagement** everything to do with the deed. 122 **in a breath** quickly. 123 **small . . . win** accomplish little 130 **style me** call me the means to. 133 **hath . . . approved** has long proved to be.

137 **school-name** mere word. 141 **know** find out. 142 **for taking up** to borrow. 144-145 **Or . . . lately** The exact meaning of this passage is difficult to determine: "brought" may be a printer's misreading of "bought." If the verb is "brought," the passage is an obvious development of the Cardinal's idea that Antonio is "in want": needing cash, he has sold a miniature of the Duchess to a dealer. If, however, the verb is "bought," the "Who" governing it is ambiguous. It may refer either to "picture makers" or to Antonio, depending on whether he has sold his wife's picture to get money or bought it as a keepsake. Most modern editions emend to "bought," but because the first quarto leading seems to develop logically out of the Cardinal's thought, "brought" is here retained. 147 **wretched** an equivocation, meaning either despicable or pitiable. 148 **be happy** Be happy (in the advancement that will follow as a result of your seeing him). 149 **basilisk** a mythical monster that could kill with a look.

'Tis his cunning. I must follow his example:
There cannot be a surer way to trace,
Than that of an old fox. [*Enter* JULIA,
pointing a pistol at him.]

JULIA   So, sir, you are well met.

BOSOLA   How now?

155 JULIA   Nay, the doors are fast enough.
Now sir, I will make you confess your
treachery.

BOSOLA   Treachery?

JULIA   Yes, confess to me
Which of my women 'twas you hired to
put
Love-powder into my drink?

BOSOLA   Love-powder?

160 JULIA   Yes, when I was at Malfi—
Why should I fall in love with such a
face else?
I have already suffered for thee so much
pain,
The only remedy to do me good
Is to kill my longing.

BOSOLA   Sure, your pistol holds
Nothing but perfumes or kissing comfits.°

165   Excellent lady,
You have a pretty way on't to discover°
Your longing. Come, come, I'll disarm
you
And arm you thus—[*embraces her*] yet
this is wondrous strange.

JULIA   Compare thy form and my eyes together;

170 You'll find my love no such great miracle.
[*Kisses him.*] Now you'll say
I am a wanton. This nice° modesty in
ladies
Is but a troublesome familiar°
That haunts them.

BOSOLA   Know you me, I am a blunt soldier.°

175 JULIA   The better:
Sure, there wants fire where there are no
lively sparks

Of roughness.

BOSOLA   And I want compliment.°

JULIA   Why, ignorance
In courtship cannot make you do amiss,
If you have a heart to do well.

BOSOLA   You are very fair.

JULIA   Nay, if you lay beauty to my
charge,   180
I must plead unguilty.

BOSOLA   Your bright eyes
Carry a quiver of darts in them,° sharper
Than sunbeams.

JULIA   You will mar me with
commendation.
Put yourself to the charge of courting me,
Whereas now I woo you.   185

BOSOLA   [*Aside.*] I have it, I will work
upon this creature.
Let us grow most amorously familiar.
If the great Cardinal now should see me
thus,
Would he not count me a villain?

JULIA   No, he might count me a wanton, 190
Not lay a scruple of offense on you:
For if I see and steal a diamond,
The fault is not i' th' stone, but in me,
the thief
That purloins it. I am sudden with you:
We that are great women of pleasure, use
to cut off°   195
These uncertain wishes and unquiet long-
ings,
And in an instant join the sweet delight
And the pretty excuse together; had you
been i' th' street
Under my chamber window, even there
I should have courted you.

BOSOLA   Oh, you are an excellent lady. 200

JULIA   Bid me do somewhat for you
presently
To express I love you.

BOSOLA   I will, and if you love me,
Fail not to effect it.

---

165 **kissing comfits** breath sweeteners. 166 **discover** make known. 172 **nice** foolish. 173 **familiar** family spirit (Webster's ironic echo of the Cardinal's pre-varication, ll. 83–95). 175 **blunt soldier** a double-entendre, like most of the language in this inter-view.

177 **compliment** The homonym, "complement," is also implied. 181–182 **Your . . . them** Cupid was supposed to afflict people with love by shooting them with enchanted darts, and it was through the eyes that love was most commonly thought to enter the body. 195 **use . . . off** are in the habit of dis-pensing with.

The Cardinal is grown wondrous melancholy;

Demand the cause, let him not put you off

205 With feigned excuse; discover the main ground on't.

JULIA Why would you know this?

BOSOLA I have depended on him,
And I hear that he is fallen in some disgrace
With the Emperor. If he be, like the mice
210 That forsake falling houses,° I would shift
To other dependence.

JULIA You shall not need follow the wars:°
I'll be your maintenance.

BOSOLA And I your loyal servant;
But I cannot leave my calling.

215 JULIA Not leave an
Ungrateful general for the love of a sweet lady?
You are like some, cannot sleep in featherbeds,
But must have blocks for their pillows.

BOSOLA Will you do this?

JULIA Cunningly.

BOSOLA Tomorrow I'll expect th'intelligence.

JULIA Tomorrow!° Get you into my cab-
220 inet;°
You shall have it with you:° do not delay me—
No more than I do you. I am like one
That is condemned: I have my pardon promised,
But I would see it sealed. Go, get you in;
You shall see me wind my tongue about
225 his heart
Like a skein of silk.
[BOSOLA *withdraws behind the traverse.*]

[*Enter* CARDINAL.]

CARDINAL Where are you?
[*Enter* SERVANTS.]

SERVANTS Here.

CARDINAL Let none, upon your lives,
Have conference with the Prince Ferdinand,
Unless I know it. [*Aside.*] In this distraction
He may reveal the murther. 230
[*Exeunt* SERVANTS.]
Yond's my ling'ring consumption:
I am weary of her; and by any means
Would be quit of——

JULIA How now, my lord?
What ails you?

CARDINAL Nothing.

JULIA Oh, you are much altered:
Come, I must be your secretary,° and remove 235
This lead from off your bosom—What's the matter?

CARDINAL I may not tell you.

JULIA Are you so far in love with sorrow,
You cannot part with part of it? or think you
I cannot love your grace when you are sad,
As well as merry? or do you suspect 240
I, that have been a secret to your heart
These many winters, cannot be the same
Unto your tongue?

CARDINAL Satisfy thy longing.
The only way to make thee keep my counsel
Is not to tell thee.

JULIA Tell your echo this— 245
Or flatterers, that, like echoes, still report
What they hear, though most imperfect—
and not me;
For, if that you be true unto yourself,
I'll know.°

CARDINAL Will you rack me?°

JULIA No, judgment shall
Draw it from you. It is an equal fault 250
To tell one's secrets unto all, or none.

CARDINAL The first argues folly.

JULIA But the last, tyranny.

209–210 like . . . houses Mice were thought to desert old houses just before they fell down. 212 **follow the wars** follow after the Cardinal when he goes to war. 220 **Tomorrow** Not tomorrow, but now! **cabinet** closet. 221 **with you** at your appearance.

235 **secretary** one entrusted with secrets. 248–249 **For . . . know** for you can be true to yourself only by telling me. 249 **rack me** put me upon the rack.

CARDINAL   Very well. Why, imagine I have committed
   Some secret deed which I desire the world
   May never hear of!
255 JULIA   Therefore may not I know it?
   You have concealed for me as great a sin
   As adultery. Sir, never was occasion
   For perfect trial of my constancy
   Till now. Sir, I beseech you.
CARDINAL   You'll repent it.
JULIA   Never.
CARDINAL   It hurries thee to ruin: I'll not
260   tell thee.
   Be well advised, and think what danger 'tis
   To receive a prince's secrets. They that do,
   Had need have their breasts hooped with adamant°
   To contain them. I pray thee yet be satisfied.
265   Examine thine own frailty; 'tis more easy
   To tie knots, than unloose them. 'Tis a secret
   That, like a ling'ring poison, may chance lie
   Spread in thy veins, and kill thee seven year hence.
JULIA   Now you dally with° me.
CARDINAL   No more. Thou shalt know it.
   By my appointment,° the great Duchess
270   of Malfi
   And two of her young children, four nights since,
   Were strangled.
JULIA   Oh heaven! Sir, what have you done?
CARDINAL   How now? How settles this?
275   Think you your bosom
   Will be a grave dark and obscure enough
   For such a secret?
JULIA   You have undone yourself, sir.
CARDINAL   Why?
JULIA   It lies not in me to conceal it.
280 CARDINAL   No?
   Come, I will swear you to't upon this book.

263 **adamant** unyielding steel. 269 **dally with** make a fool of. 270 **appointment** order.

JULIA   Most religiously.
CARDINAL   Kiss it.

[*She kisses a Bible.*]

   Now you shall never utter it. Thy curiosity
   Hath undone thee: thou'rt poisoned with that book.   285
   Because I knew thou couldst not keep my counsel,
   I have bound thee to't by death.

[*Enter* BOSOLA.]

BOSOLA   For pity sake, hold.
CARDINAL   Ha, Bosola!
JULIA [*To the* CARDINAL.]   I forgive you
   This equal piece of justice you have done,
   For I betrayed your counsel to that fellow: 290
   He overheard it. That was the cause I said
   It lay not in me to conceal it.
BOSOLA   Oh foolish woman,
   Couldst not thou have poisoned him?
JULIA   'Tis weakness,
   Too much to think what should have been done. I go,
   I know not whither.   [*Dies.*]
CARDINAL   Wherefore comst thou hither?   295
BOSOLA   That I might find a great man, like yourself,
   Not out of his wits, as the Lord Ferdinand,
   To remember my service.
CARDINAL   I'll have thee hewed in pieces.
BOSOLA   Make not yourself such a promise of that life
   Which is not yours to dispose of.
CARDINAL   Who placed thee here?   300
BOSOLA   Her lust, as she intended.
CARDINAL   Very well,
   Now you know me for your fellow murderer.
BOSOLA   And wherefore should you lay fair marble colors°
   Upon your rotten purposes to° me?

303 **fair . . . colors** paint to make wood look like marble. 304 **to** toward.

305 Unless you imitate some that do plot great treasons,
And when they have done, go hide themselves i' th' graves
Of those were actors in't.

CARDINAL No more: there is a fortune attends thee.

BOSOLA Shall I go sue to Fortune any longer?
'Tis the fool's pilgrimage.

CARDINAL   I have honors in store for
310 thee.

BOSOLA There are a many ways that conduct to seeming
Honor, and some of them very dirty ones.

CARDINAL Throw to the devil
Thy melancholy. The fire burns well,
What need we keep a stirring of't, and
315 make
A greater smother?° Thou wilt kill Antonio?

BOSOLA Yes.

CARDINAL   Take up that body.

BOSOLA   I think I shall
Shortly grow the common bier for churchyards!

CARDINAL I will allow thee some dozen of attendants,
320 To aid thee in the murther.

BOSOLA Oh, by no means: physicians that apply horseleeches to any rank swelling use to cut off their tails, that the blood may run through them the faster. Let me
325 have no train° when I go to shed blood, lest it make me have a greater—when I ride to the gallows.

CARDINAL Come to me after midnight, to help to remove that body to her own
330 lodging. I'll give out she died o' th' plague; 'twill breed the less inquiry after her death.

BOSOLA Where's Castruchio her husband?

CARDINAL He's rode to Naples to take possession of Antonio's citadel.

BOSOLA Believe me, you have done a very
335 happy turn.

CARDINAL Fail not to come. There is the master key

Of our lodgings, and by that you may conceive
What trust I plant in you.   *Exit.*

BOSOLA   You shall find me ready.
Oh poor Antonio, though nothing be so needful
To thy estate, as pity, yet I find   340
Nothing so dangerous. I must look to my footing;
In such slippery ice-pavements men had need
To be frost-nailed° well: they may break their necks else.
The precedent's here afore me: how this man
Bears up in blood!° seems fearless! Why, 'tis well: 345
Security° some men call the suburbs of hell,
Only a dead wall between. Well, good Antonio,
I'll seek thee out; and all my care shall be
To put thee into safety from the reach
Of these most cruel biters, that have got 350
Some of thy blood already. It may be
I'll join with thee in a most just revenge.
The weakest arm is strong enough, that strikes
With the sword of justice. Still methinks the Duchess
Haunts me—there, there!—'tis nothing but my melancholy.   355
O penitence, let me truly taste thy cup,
That throws men down, only to raise them up.   *Exit.*

SCENE THREE   [*Somewhere near the* DUCHESS' *grave*]

[*Enter* ANTONIO *and* DELIO.] ECHO *from the* DUCHESS' *grave.*

DELIO Yond's the Cardinal's window. This fortification
Grew from the ruins of an ancient abbey.

---

343 **frost-nailed** equipped with hobnailed boots for gripping the ice. 345 **Bears . . . blood** shows his courage. 346 **Security** lack of danger.

And to yond side o' th' river lies a wall,
Piece of a cloister, which in my opinion
5   Gives the best echo that you ever heard;
So hollow, and so dismal, and withal
So plain in the distinction° of our words,
That many have supposed it is a spirit
That answers.
ANTONIO   I do love these ancient ruins:
10 We never tread upon them, but we set
Our foot upon some reverend history,
And, questionless,° here in this open court,
Which now lies naked to the injuries
Of stormy weather, some men lie interred
15 Loved the Church so well and gave so largely to't
They thought it should have canopied their bones
Till doomsday. But all things have their end:
Churches and cities, which have diseases like to men,
Must have like death that we have.
ECHO   *Like death that we have.*
DELIO   Now the echo hath caught you.
20 ANTONIO   It groaned, methought, and gave
A very deadly accent!
ECHO   *Deadly accent.*
DELIO   I told you 'twas a pretty one. You may make it
A huntsman, or a falconer, a musician,
Or a thing of sorrow.
ECHO   *A thing of sorrow.*
ANTONIO   Ay sure, that suits it best.
25 ECHO   *That suits it best.*
ANTONIO   'Tis very like my wife's voice.
ECHO   *Ay, wife's voice.*
DELIO   Come, let's walk farther from't.
I would not have you go to th' Cardinal's tonight.
Do not.
ECHO   *Do not.*
DELIO   Wisdom doth not more moderate
30 wasting sorrow

Than time.° Take time for't: be mindful of thy safety.
ECHO   *Be mindful of thy safety.*
ANTONIO   Necessity compels me:
Make scrutiny throughout the passages°
Of your own life; you'll find it impossible
To fly your fate.
ECHO   *O fly your fate.*   35
DELIO   Hark, the dead stones seem to have pity on you
And give you good counsel.
ANTONIO   Echo, I will not talk with thee,
For thou art a dead thing.
ECHO   *Thou art a dead thing.*
ANTONIO   My Duchess is asleep now,
And her little ones—I hope sweetly. Oh, heaven   40
Shall I never see her more?
ECHO   *Never see her more.*
ANTONIO   I marked not one° repetition of the Echo
But that: and, on the sudden, a clear light
Presented me a face folded in sorrow.
DELIO   Your fancy, merely.
ANTONIO   Come, I'll be out of this ague;°   45
For to live thus, is not indeed to live:
It is a mockery, and abuse of life.
I will not henceforth save myself by halves.
Lose all, or nothing.
DELIO   Your own virtue save you!
I'll fetch your eldest son, and second you.   50
It may be that the sight of his° own blood,
Spread in so sweet a figure, may beget
The more compassion.
ANTONIO   However, fare you well.
Though in our miseries Fortune hath a part
Yet in our noble sufferings she hath none.   55
Contempt of pain—that we may call our own.   *Exe[unt].*

V.iii. 7 **distinction** articulation. 12 **questionless** unquestionably. 30–31 **Wisdom . . . time** Wisdom does not alleviate the pain of consuming sorrow any better than time (?).

33 **passages** events. 42 **I . . . one** I did not notice the significance of one. 45 **ague** a sickness characterized by intermittent chills and fever. 51 **his** the Cardinal's family's.

SCENE FOUR   [*The palace of the Aragonian brothers in Milan*]

[*Enter*] CARDINAL, PESCARA, MALATESTE, RODERIGO, GRISOLAN.

CARDINAL   You shall not watch tonight by the sick Prince;
His grace is very well recovered.
MALATESTE   Good my lord, suffer us.°
CARDINAL   Oh, by no means:
The noise and change of object in his eye
Doth more distract him. I pray, all to bed;
5 And though you hear him in his violent fit,
Do not rise, I entreat you.
PESCARA   So sir, we shall not——
CARDINAL   Nay, I must have you promise
Upon your honors, for I was enjoined to't
By himself; and he seemed to urge it sensibly.°
10 PESCARA   Let our honors bind this trifle.
CARDINAL   Nor any of your followers.
PESCARA   Neither.
CARDINAL   It may be, to make trial of your promise,
When he's asleep, myself will rise, and feign
Some of his mad tricks, and cry out for help,
15 And feign myself in danger.
MALATESTE   If your throat were cutting,
I'd not come at you, now I have protested against it.
CARDINAL   Why, I thank you.
[*Withdraws.*]
GRISOLAN   'Twas a foul storm tonight.
RODERIGO   The Lord Ferdinand's chamber shook like an osier.°
20 MALATESTE   'Twas nothing but pure kindness in the devil,
To rock his own child.

Exeunt [RODERIGO, MALATESTE, PESCARA, GRISOLAN].

CARDINAL   The reason why I would not suffer these
About my brother is because at midnight
I may with better privacy convey
Julia's body to her own lodging. O, my conscience!   25
I would pray now, but the devil takes away my heart
For having any confidence in prayer.
About this hour I appointed Bosola
To fetch the body: when he hath served my turn,
He dies.   *Exit.* 30

[*Enter* BOSOLA.]

BOSOLA   Ha! 'twas the Cardinal's voice. I heard him name
Bosola, and my death—listen, I hear one's footing.

[*Enter* FERDINAND.]

FERDINAND   Strangling is a very quiet death.
BOSOLA   Nay, then, I see I must stand upon my guard.
FERDINAND   What say' to that? Whisper, softly: do you agree to't?   35
So it must be done i' th' dark: the Cardinal
Would not for a thousand pounds the doctor should see it.   *Exit.*
BOSOLA   My death is plotted; here's° the consequence of murther.°
We value not desert, nor Christian breath,
When we know black deeds must be cured with death.   40
[*Withdraws.*]

[*Enter* ANTONIO *and a* SERVANT.]

SERVANT   Here stay, sir, and be confident, I pray:
I'll fetch you a dark lanthorn. *Exit.*
ANTONIO   Could I take him
At his prayers, there were hope of pardon.
BOSOLA   Fall right my sword:

V.iv. 3 **suffer us** Allow us then to watch over him. 10 **sensibly** when he was in full possession of his senses. 19 **osier** willow tree.

38 **here's** the plotting of my death. **murther** (my doing) murder.

[*Half-crazed by fears that he will be murdered,* BOSOLA *mistakes* ANTONIO *for the Cardinal or one of the henchmen and runs him through, from behind.*]

I'll not give thee so much leisure as to
45 pray.
ANTONIO Oh, I am gone. Thou hast ended a long suit,
In a minute.
BOSOLA   What art thou?
ANTONIO   A most wretched thing,
That only have thy benefit in death,
To appear myself.° [*Enter* SERVANT *with a dark lanthorn.*]
SERVANT   Where are you sir?
ANTONIO Very near my home.° Bosola?
50 SERVANT   Oh misfortune!
BOSOLA [*To* SERVANT.] Smother thy pity, thou art dead else—Antonio!
The man I would have saved 'bove mine own life!
We are merely the stars' tennis balls, struck and banded°
Which way please them. Oh, good Antonio,
55 I'll whisper one thing in thy dying ear,
Shall make thy heart break quickly. Thy fair Duchess
And two sweet children——
ANTONIO   Their very names
Kindle a little life in me.
BOSOLA   Are murdered!
ANTONIO Some men have wished to die
60 At the hearing of sad tidings: I am glad
That I shall do't in sadness. I would not now
Wish my wounds balmed, nor healed: for I have no use
To put my life to. In all our quest of greatness,
Like wanton boys whose pastime is their care,
65 We follow after bubbles, blown in th'air.
Pleasure of life, what is't? only the good hours

Of an ague; merely a preparative to rest,
To endure vexation. I do not ask
The process of my death. Only commend me
To Delio.
BOSOLA   Break, heart!   70
ANTONIO And let my son fly the courts of princes.   [*Dies.*]
BOSOLA Thou seemst to have loved Antonio?
SERVANT   I brought him hither,
To have reconciled him to the Cardinal.
BOSOLA I do not ask thee that.
Take him up, if thou tender thine own life,   75
And bear him where the Lady Julia
Was wont to lodge. Oh, my fate moves swift.
I have this Cardinal in the forge already;
Now I'll bring him to th' hammer. (O direful misprision!°)
I will not imitate things glorious,   80
No more than base:° I'll be mine own example.
[*To the* SERVANT.] On, on! And look thou represent,° for silence,
The thing thou bearst.   *Exeunt.*

SCENE FIVE [*The same*]

[*Enter*] CARDINAL *with a book.*

CARDINAL I am puzzled in a question about hell:
He° says in hell there's one material fire,
And yet it shall not burn all men alike.
Lay him by. How tedious is a guilty conscience!
When I look into the fishponds in my garden,   5
Methinks I see a thing armed with a rake°
That seems to strike at me. Now? Art thou come?

48–49 **That . . . myself** The only benefit that I get from you in death is to be again myself (and no longer have to run and hide). 50 **home** final resting place. 53 **banded** bandied.

79 **misprision** mistake. 81 **No . . . base** any more than I will seek to copy what is base. 82 **represent** imitate.
V.v. 2 **He** the author of the book. 6 **armed . . . rake** The devil was traditionally thought to carry a fork of some sort.

[*Enter* BOSOLA *and* SERVANT, *with* AN-TONIO'*s body.*]

Thou lookst ghastly:
There sits in thy face some great deter-
mination,
Mixed with some fear.

10 BOSOLA   Thus it lightens into° action:
I am come to kill thee.
CARDINAL   Ha? Help! our guard!
BOSOLA   Thou art deceived:
They are out of thy howling.
CARDINAL   Hold, and I will faithfully di-
vide
Revenues with thee.

15 BOSOLA   Thy prayers and proffers
Are both unseasonable.
CARDINAL   Raise the watch:
We° are betrayed!
BOSOLA   I have confined your flight:
I'll suffer your retreat to Julia's chamber,
But no further.
CARDINAL   Help! We are betrayed!

[*Enter* PESCARA, MALATESTE, RODERIGO,
and GRISOLAN, *above.*]

MALATESTE   Listen.
CARDINAL   My dukedom for rescue!
RODERIGO   Fie upon his counterfeit-
20 ing.
MALATESTE   Why, 'tis not the Cardinal.
RODERIGO   Yes, yes, 'tis he:
But I'll see him hanged ere I'll go down
to him.
CARDINAL   Here's a plot upon me! I am
assaulted! I am lost,
Unless some rescue!
GRISOLAN   He doth this pretty well,
But it will not serve to laugh me° out of
25 mine honor.°
CARDINAL   The sword's at my throat!
RODERIGO   You would not bawl so
loud then.
MALATESTE   Come, come. Let's go to bed:
he told us thus much aforehand.

PESCARA   He wished you should not come
at him, but believ't,
The accent of the voice sounds not in
jest.
I'll down to him, howsoever, and with
engines°   30
Force ope the doors. [*Exit.*]
RODERIGO   Let's follow him aloof,
And note how the Cardinal will laugh at
him.   [*Exeunt above.*]
BOSOLA   There's for you first:
'Cause° you shall not unbarricade the
door
To let in rescue.   35
He kills the SERVANT.
CARDINAL   What cause hast thou to pur-
sue my life?
BOSOLA   Look there.
CARDINAL   Antonio!
BOSOLA   Slain by my hand un-
wittingly.
Pray, and be sudden:° when thou killedst
thy sister,
Thou tookst from Justice her most equal
balance,
And left her naught but her sword.
CARDINAL   O mercy!   40
[*He falls to his knees.*]
BOSOLA   Now it seems thy greatness was
only outward:
For thou fallst faster of thyself than ca-
lamity
Can drive thee. I'll not waste longer
time. There.
[*Stabs the* CARDINAL.]
CARDINAL   Thou hast hurt me.
BOSOLA   Again. [*Stabs him again.*]
CARDINAL   Shall I die like a leveret,°
Without any resistance? Help! help!
help!   45
I am slain.

[*Enter* FERDINAND.]

FERDINAND   Th'alarum?° give me a
fresh horse.
Rally the vaunt-guard,° or the day is lost.

---

10 **lightens into** shows itself as it rises to. 17 **We** The Cardinal uses the royal "we" here, perhaps in an unconscious attempt to establish his authority over Bosola, and certainly in an effort to summon others to his help. 25 **laugh me** trick me. **mine honor** my vow to him not to interfere.

30 **engines** tools. 34 **'Cause** so that. 38 **sudden** quick. 44 **leveret** small hare. 46 **alarum** the trumpet call to arms. 47 **vaunt-guard** the foremost ranks of the army.

Yield, yield! I give you the honor of arms,
Shake my sword over you. Will you yield?
CARDINAL   Help me! I am your brother.
50 FERDINAND   The devil!
My brother fight upon the adverse party!

He wounds the CARDINAL *and, in the*
scuffle, gives BOSOLA *his death wound.*

There flies your ransom.°
CARDINAL   Oh justice,
I suffer now for what hath former been:
Sorrow is held the eldest child of sin.
55 FERDINAND Now you're brave fellows.
Caesar's fortune was harder than Pompey's: Caesar died in the arms of prosperity, Pompey at the feet of disgrace. You
both died in the field; the pain's nothing.
60 Pain many times is taken away with the
apprehension of greater—as the toothache
with the sight of a barber° that comes to
pull it out: there's philosophy for you.
BOSOLA   Now my revenge is perfect.° Sink,
thou main cause
65 Of my undoing!—The last part of my life
Hath done me best service.

He kills FERDINAND.

FERDINAND   Give me some wet hay:° I am
broken winded.
I do account this world but a dog kennel:
I will vault credit, and affect high pleasures
Beyond death.°
70 BOSOLA   He seems to come to himself,
Now he's so near the bottom.
FERDINAND   My sister! oh, my sister! there's
the cause on't.
Whether we fall by ambition, blood, or
lust,
Like diamonds, we are cut with our own
dust.   [*Dies.*]
75 CARDINAL   Thou hast thy payment too.
BOSOLA   Yes, I hold my weary soul in my
teeth:

'Tis ready to part from me. I do glory
That thou, which stoodst like a huge
pyramid
Begun upon a large and ample base,
Shalt end in a little point, a kind of
nothing.   80

[*Enter* PESCARA, MALATESTE, RODERIGO,
and GRISOLAN.]

PESCARA   How now, my lord?
MALATESTE   O sad disaster!
RODERIGO   How comes this?
BOSOLA   Revenge!—for the Duchess of
Malfi, murderèd
By th'Aragonian brethren; for Antonio,
Slain by this hand; for lustful Julia,
Poisoned by this man; and lastly, for my-
self,   85
That was an actor in the main of all,
Much 'gainst mine own good nature, yet
i' th' end
Neglected.°
PESCARA   How now, my lord?
CARDINAL   Look to my brother:
He° gave us these large wounds as we
were struggling
Here i' th' rushes.° And now, I pray, let
me   90
Be laid by, and never thought of. [*Dies.*]
PESCARA   How fatally, it seems, he did
withstand°
His own rescue!
MALATESTE   Thou wretched thing of
blood,
How came Antonio by his death?
BOSOLA   In a mist—I know not how—   95
Such a mistake as I have often seen
In a play. Oh, I am gone—
We are only like dead walls or vaulted
graves
That, ruined, yield no echo. Fare you
well.

---

52 **ransom** (chance for) being ransomed. 62 **barber**
Barbers served also as surgeons at this time. 64
perfect complete. 67 **wet hay** thought to be the
best food for a broken-winded horse. 69–70 **I . . .**
death I will leap over things credited to be of
worth in this world, and I will strive after the true
pleasures that lie beyond death.

87–88 **yet . . . Neglected** "which, ultimately, I neglected." There may be a hint here, too, of Bosola's
feeling of alienation from society—his feeling that
he, as well as his own "good nature," was neglected.
89 **He** Bosola. 90 **rushes** Greens and reeds were
sometimes used to cover cold castle floors. 92 **with-**
stand offer opposition to (by counseling us against).

100 It may be pain, but no harm, to me to die
In so good a quarrel. Oh this gloomy
world,
In what a shadow or deep pit of darkness
Doth, womanish° and fearful,° mankind
live?
Let worthy minds ne'er stagger in dis-
trust
105 To suffer death or shame for what is just:
Mine is another voyage.   [*Dies.*]
PESCARA   The noble Delio, as I came to
th' palace,
Told me of Antonio's being here, and
showed me
A pretty gentleman, his son and heir.

[*Enter* DELIO *with* ANTONIO's *son.*]

MALATESTE   O, sir, you come too late.
110 DELIO   I heard so, and

Was armed° for't ere I came. Let us make
noble use
Of this great ruin, and join all our force
To establish this young hopeful gentle-
man
In's mother's right. These wretched, emi-
nent° things
Leave no more fame behind 'em, than
should one   *115*
Fall in a frost and leave his print in
snow:
As soon as the sun shines, it ever melts
Both form and matter. I have ever
thought
Nature doth nothing so great for great
men,
As when she's pleased to make them lords
of truth: *120*
Integrity of life is fame's best friend,
Which nobly, beyond death, shall crown
the end.   *Exeunt.*

103 **womanish** timorous. **fearful** both frightened
and frightening.

111 **armed** prepared. 114 **eminent** conspicuous.

Paradise Restored

a dramatization of the life of John Milton

Don Taylor

Introductory Comments

Judith A. Kates *Harvard University*

Paradise Restored is a play written for television, based on the life
and work of the seventeenth-century poet, John Milton. It interprets
what is known and conjectured about him, and tries to create for us
an understanding of some of the personal triumphs and defeats that
lie behind his epic poem on the fall of humanity, *Paradise Lost*. Most
of the play takes place toward the end of his life, around 1665, when,
blind, disillusioned, and defeated, he strove to complete the great
work for which he had strenuously prepared himself throughout his
youth. The scene is set in the country cottage to which the Milton
family moves to escape the horrors of the Great Plague and to try to
provide Milton with the peace he needs to finish his poem. There is
also a series of flashbacks sketching significant moments in the previous twenty years, the cataclysmic period of the English Revolution
in which Milton, as thinker and writer, was an active participant.

A major focus of this play is the agonizing conflict between Milton
and his daughter Mary. Since the Restoration of King Charles II to
the throne of England in 1660, Milton, who had been a passionate
opponent of monarchy and a supporter of Parliament's rebellion
against Charles's father (Charles I), has been deprived of almost all
financial support. In fact, he had barely escaped execution at the time
of the Restoration, and is forced to live in great privacy, dependent
on the women of his family for companionship and help with his
work. And that's the rub. We see from the beginning the battle of
wills between the uncompromising, austere father, demanding effort
and upright conduct of himself and everyone around him, and the
defiant daughter, unable to understand the life and ideals of a father
with whom she has not previously lived closely and longing for the
ordinary pleasures of youth.

Their struggle is exacerbated both by their personal history and by
the general condition of women at the time. Mary identifies with
her dead mother, who, according to the early biographers, struggled
bitterly with her husband during the first months of their marriage.

190

She "had been used to a great House and much Company and Joviality." But marriage to John Milton meant participating in the "philosophical Life" of one of England's greatest and most hard-working scholars, a man dedicated to books, the life of the mind and spirit, and the austerity of seventeenth-century Puritanism. She is supposed to have gone back to her family in 1642 after two months of marriage, and not to have returned until 1645. Though they then lived together and had children, it is hard to imagine them achieving the "marriage of true minds" Milton had hoped for. The play emphasizes his bitter disillusionment, and also suggests the price paid by his wife in a breaking of spirit.

In the play, this history of conflict and pain underlies the struggle between Milton and Mary, who looks so much like her mother. He sees her as the reincarnation of the spirit of pride and defiance that destroyed his home and hopes. She sees him as the tyrannical, cold, incomprehensible oppressor of both her mother and herself. She defies him by her refusal to learn or care about his beloved books. He suffers from her ignorance and inability to share in his intense mental life.

Both suffer, directly or indirectly, because of the prevailing condition of women. Milton's difficulties with his first wife, which are so much a part of the struggle with Mary, stemmed at least in part from the usual education (or lack of it) of women of his class. It would have been very hard for him to find an upper middle-class woman with anything near the education necessary to share in his scholarly interests. The notion that women "come second in God's order" (as Betty reminds Mary), when translated into inferior and limited education, meant unexpected pain for a man who longed for a union of minds and souls as well as bodies.

The play presents another side of this disparity in intellectual training through Betty's moving story about her reasons for marrying Milton. Marriage to a great scholar meant freedom to her, a chance for the "things of the spirit" within her to speak.

The play reminds us of the extraordinary idealism Milton brought to marriage, when, in the flashback, Sir Henry Vane mentions Milton's famous pamphlets on divorce. To the outrage of his contemporaries, Milton had written several works urging that divorce be permissible not only on grounds of adultery but also of mental incompatibility. For him, real marriage demanded love and a true "mixture of minds."

The flashback is presented as a series of reminiscences inspired by the visit of Milton's friend and former assistant in his post as Latin Secretary to Parliament, the poet Andrew Marvell. Several scenes show Milton's involvement in the great events of mid-seventeenth-century England. The Revolution (including the Civil War) appeared to its participants to involve both politics and religion. The political conflict resolved itself into a fundamental question: who should rule in England, the king or Parliament? The adherents of

Parliamentary rule (popularly called Roundheads), among whom were Cromwell and Milton, felt that they were fighting for the rule of law and representative government against a tyrant. King Charles and the Royalists (or Cavaliers) fought for what they considered to be a divinely ordained monarchy, answerable only to God. When the Parliamentary army under Cromwell won the war in the 1640s, they executed Charles as a tyrant, and we hear Milton's exultation. His belief that freedom was possible and that God meant people to be free determined his political choices. His positions were independent and extraordinarily liberal for his time.

Freedom of conscience was crucial to him, and this determined his position on the religious issues of the Revolution. The king's party also stood for the imposition on all English subjects of the Anglican form of worship, the religion we now call Episcopalian or Church of England. But many of the king's opponents were equally authoritarian, seeking to impose on everyone the Presbyterian form of worship and church organization. A third religious party, usually called Independents, believed that each congregation should be allowed to determine its form of worship according to the consciences of its members, that no uniformity should be imposed by government decree. In this group we find Cromwell and Milton.

Milton's vigorous writings on these political and religious subjects led the Parliamentary leaders to ask him in 1649 to become Secretary of Foreign Tongues to the Council of State. (This is represented in the scene with Sir Henry Vane.) From then until the Restoration, Milton played an active role in state affairs, never giving up his beliefs in the establishment of a just commonwealth where reason and liberty could prevail. But events forced him to despair that his ideals could ever be translated into reality. Parliament seemed to him and many others to become the instrument of economic and political dominance for one group that sought to perpetuate its power. Finally, Cromwell, pressed by the radical demands of his army for total democracy and redistribution of wealth, dissolved the Long Parliament in 1653 and established himself as Lord Protector. As we see in the play, Milton originally supported him, but then, to his total disillusionment, saw this champion of liberty become a dictator, a king in all but name. After Cromwell's death in 1658, the situation deteriorated until Parliament in 1660 recalled to the throne Charles Stuart, the son of the executed king.

To Milton, the Restoration meant that the English people had chosen slavery and rejected freedom, "bondage with ease" rather than "strenuous liberty" (*Paradise Lost*, XII). He was forcel to give up hope that he would ever see the kingdom of God on earth, a truly free community where people could choose the way to a virtuous and holy life. Yet he never gave up his faith in the potential for good within each individual. Instead, he turned back to the heroic poetic enterprise for which he had prepared himself, before his involvement in the "great deeds" of his time. *Paradise Lost* presents both the fall and defeat of humanity, and its potential triumph through faith and the struggle to live well.

In the final scenes, the play brings together these intellectual and personal conflicts. Just as Milton's ideals for a political and spiritual community had been defeated, so had his hopes for a personal communion with a loved woman. Yet there is a reconciliation of his conflicts with the women in his life, through the essential goodness of Betty. With her, he declares his belief in the paradise within ourselves, in our own hearts. The play closes with this prelude to his renewed inspiration and poetic energy, as we hear him pouring out the final lines of the poem in which Adam and Eve and all humanity are promised "a Paradise within thee, happier far."

John Milton (1608–1674) was born in London, the son of a prosperous businessman. He acquired an extraordinary education through independent study and work at Christ's College, Cambridge. He consciously prepared to be a poet, and published early works such as *Comus* and *Lycidas* in the 1630s. The outbreak of the Civil War (1639) interrupted his plans for poetry. The delay caused by his prose writings on important political and religious issues of the day and by his efforts as Latin Secretary to Parliament (1649–1659) lasted almost twenty years. During this period he also became totally blind. After the Restoration (1660) he lived privately, composing the great works that earned him a place in English poetry second only to Shakespeare's—*Paradise Lost, Paradise Regained,* and *Samson Agonistes.*

Don Taylor (1936———) was born in London. He began his career in television with the British Broadcasting Company in 1960. His talent as a director and playwright are well known in Great Britain, where his works have appeared on television and in the theatre. *Paradise Restored* appeared on BBC-TV first in 1972, and again in 1974.

Paradise Restored   *Don Taylor*

SEXTON

JOHN MILTON

ELIZABETH *his wife*

MARY *his daughter*

DEBORAH *his daughter*

ANNE *his daughter*

MARY POWELL *his first wife*

DRIVER

ANDREW MARVELL

MARY POWELL (MILTON)

SIR HENRY VANE

LADY CATHERINE RANELAGH

DR. SCROBY

JOHN BRADSHAW

OLIVER CROMWELL

DOCTOR

LAMBERT

HARRISON *2 troopers*

DINNER GUESTS AND COUNCILMEN

ONE *London street. Exterior. Dawn.*

A red cross being painted on a wooden door.[1]

Below it, newly painted and dripping, "Lord have mercie on us."

In longer shot we see a house in a small street in London, in the earliest light of dawn. Outside it stands a cart. Fifteen or twenty human bodies are lying at random in the back of the cart, covered with an assortment of improvised shrouds and blankets. We are conscious of projecting feet and dangling hands.

A large man in a black cloak is coming out of the house, carrying over his shoulder what is obviously a newly dead body, loosely wrapped in a blanket. He heaves the body into the back of the cart. A middle-aged woman is in tears at the door of the house. In the interior darkness, someone pulls her in and closes the door.

The cart begins to move away. In CU[2] we see the driver, big faced and uncouth. He holds the reins with his left hand, and rings a handbell with his right. He intones mournfully.

SEXTON Bring out your dead! Bring out your dead!

As the death cart rounds the corner, it is passed by another vehicle going the other way. This is a travelling cart, or hired coach, canvas covered. At the front sits a driver with a musket across his knees, and a pistol at his side.

TWO *The cart. Interior. Dawn.*

The inside of the cart is full of trunks and books and linen in packs. Five people are seated on benches round the sides.

JOHN MILTON sits in one corner, wrapped in a cloak. He is fifty-seven years old, but still a goodlooking man for his age, and his shoulder length hair is still more auburn than grey. His eyes are bright and clear, but their stillness reveals that they no longer see anything.

Near him sits his wife, ELIZABETH MILTON. She is twenty-six years old, dark haired, good looking in a plain and unadorned fashion, dressed with severe regard to the puritan ethic, and now wrapped up against the chill morning. She is a quiet, undemonstrative woman, placid on the surface, but with an intense inner-directed vision which her husband cannot see on her face, and is perhaps only partly aware of. In daily life she is quiet, practical, efficient, and submissive to her husband. Certainly no one but he knows anything of what goes on inside her.

Next to ELIZABETH, and half leaning on her, sits ANNE, aged nineteen. ANNE has been crippled from birth. She holds her head slightly to one side, due to a tension in the neck, and finds it difficult to keep complete control of her head movements. Her legs turn badly inward at the knees and feet, and walking is an effort, so that she looks like an old woman in motion. She is shy and quiet and says little. When she does speak, it is with some difficulty, so she avoids speech as much as she can. Her stutter, which can be very bad, is probably psychological in origin, and may be worst or easiest at moments of great tension. Her eyes are clear and bright, and suggest a trapped rather than a childish mind. She is thin and not well fleshed, but her face has a well-proportioned bone structure, and her eyes are large, and this gives her an ethereal kind of beauty. She is half asleep.

1 This script was written expressly for television production. Therefore, the stage directions include many audio and visual special effects instructions that do not appear in scripts for stage production.
2 **CU** close up.

MARY *is aged almost seventeen, and is seated on the other side of the cart. She is a sharp-faced, sharp-eyed, blonde-headed girl, with the best of the family good looks, and energetic with the awareness of her newly emergent personality. She is wide awake, shivering slightly in the cold of first light.*

DEBORAH, *who is thirteen, sits near Mary, a quiet, affectionate girl, who watches what goes on around her with the slightly awestruck detachment of someone too young to appreciate fully what is happening. In appearance she is most like her father.*

MILTON   Is it light yet Betty?

ELIZABETH   Nearly light. But the sun's not through.

MILTON   How many in the death cart today?

ELIZABETH   Perhaps ten or fifteen, God rest their souls.

MILTON   God sends his plagues on a corrupt and servile generation. When he speaks in anger, his voice is terrible.

ELIZABETH   Amen.

(She looks at MARY *and* DEBORAH.*)*

MARY *(after an insolent pause)*   Amen.

MILTON *(voice over[3])*   Oh dark, dark, dark, amid the blaze of noon,
Irrecoverably dark, total eclipse,
Without all hope of day.

ELIZABETH   There were terrible happenings last night in Bunhill Field.

MARY   There's a plague pit there, I saw them digging it.

ELIZABETH   A poor man ran and cast himself into the pit, still alive, among all the dead bodies. Then four or five others, men and women, followed his example. The night was full of crying and screaming, and they had to call out the watch.

DEBORAH   Will we be safe at Chalfont, Father?

MILTON   No man is ever safe Deb. But I am persuaded of God's providence towards us, in His providing this cottage.

DEBORAH   But they do have plague in the country too don't they?

ELIZABETH   We must trust in His mercy Deb.

MILTON *(voice over)*   Why was the sight
To such a tender ball as the eye confined
So obvious and so easy to be quenched
And not as feeling through all parts diffused
That she might look at will through every pore
Then had I not been thus exiled from light
As in the land of darkness, yet in light
To live a life half dead, a living death
And buried: but, O yet more miserable,
Myself my sepulchre, a moving grave.

THREE   *Towards the edge of London. Exterior. Morning.*

We see the cart continuing its slow progress.

FOUR   *At Turnham Green. Exterior. Morning.*

The cart now moves out onto open grass with a few trees. The sun is now out.

FIVE   *The cart. Interior. Morning.*

ELIZABETH   Are you still cold Nan? The sun's up now.

ANNE   Y . . . Y . . . *(She gives up and nods.)*

ELIZABETH   There's a long way to go yet.

*(*ANNE *snuggles into* ELIZABETH. *Across the cart,* DEBORAH *smiles faintly at* ELIZABETH, *who smiles back.)*

---

3 **Voice over** while the voice of the character is heard, his image is not seen.

SIX   *The front of the cart. Interior/Exterior. Morning.*

MARY *is sitting with the* DRIVER. *The others can be seen in the back.*

MARY   Where are we now?
DRIVER   Just crossing Turnham Green. So I'll need to keep me eyes open for highwaymen.
MARY   Are there really highwaymen?
DRIVER   Here, Putney Heath, Wimbledon Common, terrible! It's with the Army being disbanded you see. Good shots they are, some of them.

(DEBORAH *comes and sits beside* MARY.)

DEBORAH   Was our real mother as nice as Betty?
MARY   Nicer than Misses Minsnull! A thousand thousand times.
DEBORAH   Shh!
MARY   When Father said he was going to marry her I told him I didn't care, and I don't. I hate her.
DEBORAH   Mary!
MARY   It's all right, he's asleep. Our real mother was an angel.
DEBORAH   Do you really remember her?
MARY   She was warm. And she used to dance with me. I remember that.
DEBORAH   You can't really remember. You were only three.
MARY   I remember.
DEBORAH   I wish I could have seen her.
MARY   She was Mary like me, and Granny Powell says I look exactly like her. She was seventeen when she married Father and Granny Powell says I might be her ghost.

SEVEN   *The cart. Interior. Morning.*

(MILTON *wakes.*)

MILTON   Where are we Betty?
ELIZABETH   Crossing Turnham Green.
MILTON   Who's with you? Nan?
ELIZABETH   Yes, she's dozing.
MILTON   I can feel the sun.

EIGHT   *Near Chalfont. Exterior. Afternoon.*

The cart is going through fertile countryside, with low rolling hills.

NINE   *The cottage front door. Exterior. Afternoon.*

The cart is being unloaded by the driver, helped by ELIZABETH *and the girls. The cottage stands just outside a small village, rising behind to a small hill.*

TEN   *The cottage front hallway. Interior. Afternoon.*

The hallway is wide, with a fireplace, like an extra room.
    ELIZABETH *comes from the cart with some books.* ANNE *is sitting on a chair, foreground.*

ELIZABETH   Help me with the books Nan.
ANNE   I can't c . . . c . . . carry things.
ELIZABETH   You can manage a few books, if you're careful.
ANNE   No, I can't, I'll f . . . f . . . fall.
ELIZABETH   Just these small ones to begin with. Hold out your hands.

(*With great care she helps* ANNE *to get hold of a few books.* ANNE *almost whimpers with fear.*)

ELEVEN   *The Cottage, the Bottom of the stairs. Interior. Afternoon.*

MARY *is coming down the narrow stairs, and sees* ELIZABETH *with* ANNE *by the door.*

TWELVE   *The cottage front hallway. Interior. Afternoon.*

ELIZABETH   (*smiling*)   There.
ANNE   (*smiling*)   Where shall . . . I . . . ?

ELIZABETH In the study.

(ANNE *limps painfully along the passage, fighting for her balance.*)

THIRTEEN *The cottage, ground floor passage. Interior. Afternoon.*

MARY *goes along the passage at right angles to the hall, to* DEBORAH, *in the dining room.*

FOURTEEN *The cottage dining room. Interior. Afternoon.*

DEBORAH *is sorting through a pile of pewter.*

MARY She's trying to steal Nan from us now.

(*In the background* ANNE *limps into the study with the books.* ELIZABETH *follows her and we hear her talking.*)

DEBORAH Who, Betty?
MARY She's stolen our father, and now she wants Nan too.
DEBORAH Father likes her.
MARY She won't persuade me with her smiling. Nor you Deb. Promise.
DEBORAH Don't you like Father, Mary?
MARY He's old, and he's blind, and he doesn't love us.

FIFTEEN *The cottage garden. Exterior. Evening.*

MILTON *comes out of the cottage side door, on* ELIZABETH'S *arm. The sun is sinking.*

MILTON The air's good. What time is it?
ELIZABETH Towards evening.
MILTON Am I facing the sun?
ELIZABETH Yes. But it's almost behind the hill.
MILTON I thought so. Walk me into the garden for a moment.

ELIZABETH There's a tree for you to sit under in the afternoons.
MILTON Are we on a hillside?
ELIZABETH Yes, the road passes our front door then goes on over a little hill towards Beaconsfield. The hill comes right round behind the garden.
MILTON I can still remember the colours of sky and sun Betty, in spite of my long darkness. I can remember flowers too, especially the wild roses.
ELIZABETH We've reached the tree. There's a seat.

(*Without help, he feels for the seat with his hand and leg, and lowers himself into it.* ELIZABETH *sits near him.*)

MILTON Ah. Yes. I have it. It only takes me a few days to know a new place.

(*A brief moment of silence.*)

Betty.
ELIZABETH Yes?

(*He puts his hand up to her face and feels it.*)

MILTON I wish I could have seen you. I have your picture in my mind's eye. But I'm sure it isn't the same.

SIXTEEN *The cottage, by the study window. Interior. Evening.*

(MARY *and* DEBORAH *are watching* MILTON *and* ELIZABETH *through the window.*)

MARY She only married him to get his money when he dies.
DEBORAH That's wicked!
MARY Granny Powell told me that. All his money should be ours because we're his children, but she wants it all for herself. He wouldn't give Granny Powell her money either, her rightful widow's thirds, when she was starving. It was just after the war, and the Parliament stole all her lands, she told me all about it.

DEBORAH I don't believe everything Granny Powell says. I think he loves us.
MARY He doesn't love anybody.

SEVENTEEN *The cottage study. Interior. Night.*

By candlelight, MILTON *is seated in his chair, and* ELIZABETH *is reading Spenser to him. She comes to an end. He is very preoccupied.*)

ELIZABETH That's the end of the canto.
MILTON Yes . . .
ELIZABETH Shall I come to you in the morning for dictation?
MILTON No.
ELIZABETH But the book of Paradise. You were to finish it here.
MILTON A man must know what his work is, and wherein he is useful . . . When I was a young man, Betty, I studied hard, so that, as a scholar, I could offer my learning to help men towards truth, and as a poet, I could praise God's creation in song, such a song as men would not willingly let die when once they had heard it sung. When we overthrew the King, I thought it honour to postpone my plans for poetry, and put myself at the service of the Commonwealth, to justify its deeds, in the teeth of Europe; and even when blindness struck out my eyes, the Council of State made it clear to me that my services were still not unvalued. But the English people preferred slavery, and I was enslaved with the rest. Now, blind, despised, among enemies, now can I be useful to any man?
ELIZABETH The poem will justify all things.
MILTON Justify, justify! . . . Do the plague sores justify? Or do they condemn?
ELIZABETH Are not all the works of God justifiable, even His anger?
MILTON It isn't faith I lack Betty, it's energy. We had our chance of liberty and honesty towards God, and we rejected it. How can I speak to a generation already condemned, justly condemned! In the days of humiliation, silence is preferable.

(*Pause.*)

ELIZABETH I'll wait then till you call me.
MILTON I shall need to be read to. Send Mary to me at five.

EIGHTEEN *The cottage,* MILTON's *bedroom. Interior. Dawn.*

(MILTON *lies in his bed near the window. There are several bookshelves containing large volumes, and some smaller ones of poetry. There is also a writing desk, with pen and ink, an uncompleted bound manuscript, and a writing chair.*
   On another chair, MARY *sits reading aloud to* MILTON. *She reads in a dull uninvolved voice, and it is clear that she does not understand what she is saying. Her pronunciation and scansion are largely correct, but this only adds to the mechanical effect, as does the fact that she is only half awake.*)

MARY . . . ad vatis fata recurrunt
tendentemque manus et in illo tempore primum
inrita dicentem nec quicquam voce moventem
sacrilegae perimunt, perque os, pro Iuppiter! illud
auditum sixis intellectumque ferarum
sensibut in ventos anima exhalta recessit.
Te maestae volucres, Orpheu, te turba ferarum,
te rigidi silices, te carmina saepe secutae
fleverunt silvae . . .

(MARY *yawns involuntarily.* MILTON *hears her.*)

MILTON Stop.

(MARY *looks up.*)

Did you yawn?
MARY Yes.
MILTON Can you think of no comment more fitting than a yawn?

MARY I don't understand it.

MILTON I don't ask for comprehension, but I do demand respect. Do you wish to understand?

MARY No, I can't.

MILTON Then you shall remain illiterate. At the slightest sign of interest, Mary, I could have made you master of this tongue. But you prefer brute silence. So I had to content you with the mere sounds, by rote, like a talking bird.

MARY I do as you ask me Father . . . I try to pronounce correctly.

MILTON Do you know what you were reading?

MARY The poet Ovid.

MILTON His description of the death of Orpheus the singer, who could charm the very birds and stones with his music—torn to pieces by the brute women of Cicones, who could not understand his song.

MARY Shall I continue?

MILTON No. If Ovid is to be yawned at, let him rest in decent silence. Send Deb to me.

(MARY *closes the book and replaces it in the shelf, then goes into the passage.*)

NINETEEN *The cottage, the upstairs passage. Interior. Morning.*

(*She calls up the stairs to* DEBORAH, *who is still in her room.*)

MARY Deb!

DEBORAH Yes?

MARY Father wants you to read.

(MARY *goes downstairs, near to tears.*
    DEBORAH *comes down from her room, still in her nightgown, and goes in to her father.*)

TWENTY *The cottage,* MILTON's *bedroom. Interior. Morning.*

DEBORAH It's me Father.

MILTON Good morning Deb.

DEBORAH Good morning Father.

MILTON Read to me from the Testament. Judges, sixteen.

DEBORAH The Latin Testament Father?

MILTON No, the Greek. Enough Latin for one morning.

(DEBORAH *gets out a large book and begins to read in Greek, without comprehension.*)

TWENTY-ONE *The cottage, the front hall. Interior. Morning.*

(MARY *comes downstairs to* ANNE, *who is embroidering with a painful slowness, but great concentration.* MARY *sits down beside her, but doesn't pick up her own work.*)

ANNE Are you c . . . c . . . crying Mary?

MARY No. I've been reading to Father and it's made my eyes water.

ANNE I wish I c . . . c . . . could r . . . r . . . read. But it's not worth t . . . t . . . teaching a c . . . c . . . c . . . cripple, is it?

MARY You don't want to read Nan. It's silly.

ANNE And I couldn't p . . . p . . . pronounce the words p . . . p . . . properly. If I'd been the s . . . s . . . son he prayed for, I might have been a g . . . g . . . great scholar too, and he would have loved me. But even when he could still see, he could hardly bear to l . . . l . . . look at me. I remember that. I'm one of the b . . . blessings of his blindness.

(MARY *is in violent silent tears.*)

TWENTY-TWO *The cottage,* MILTON's *bedroom. Interior. Morning.*

(DEBORAH *is still reading aloud in Greek.* CU MILTON.)

MILTON (*voice over*) And Samson called unto the Lord, and said, O Lord God, remember me I pray thee, only this once O God, that I may be at once avenged of the Philistines for my two eyes.

(DEBORAH's *teeth are chattering.* MILTON *looks up.*)

MILTON   Deb? Are you shivering?
DEBORAH   I'm sorry Father.
MILTON   Are you not dressed?
DEBORAH   Not yet Father.
MILTON   My dear child . . .

(*He puts out his arms to her. She comes to him and he embraces her.*)

MILTON   You read very well Deb, and comforted me greatly. But you mustn't get cold. Go and get dressed now.
DEBORAH   Yes Father.

(*She goes.* MILTON *lies back on the bed, and presses out his hands to feel the posts. He mutters.*)

MILTON   Dear God, who heard Samson's prayer, hear mine in my darkness.

TWENTY-THREE   *The cottage dining room. Interior. Morning.*

ELIZABETH *is preparing to set for breakfast. She goes towards the hallway.*

TWENTY-FOUR   *The cottage, front hallway. Interior. Morning.*

(MARY *is still sitting with* ANNE *as* ELIZABETH *enters.*)

ELIZABETH   Come in and help me with the breakfast Mary. While we are without a servant we must all lend a hand.

(ELIZABETH *goes back to the dining room.* MARY *rises, still trying to control her tears, and follows her.* ANNE *watches, then bends her spindly fingers back to her needlework with renewed energy.*)

TWENTY-FIVE   *Cottage dining room. Interior. Morning.*

(MARY *comes in and begins to help to prepare the breakfast, which is to consist of bread and cheese and butter, with appropriate plates, knives, etc., and mugs for beer. In the centre of the table* ELIZABETH *places a piece of cold roast beef.*)

ELIZABETH   The beef is for Father, but we may have a piece when he is finished.

(MARY *says nothing.*)

Is anything wrong Mary? Have you been crying?
MARY   No.
ELIZABETH   Did you read badly?
MARY   I don't know. I yawned.
ELIZABETH   And Father was angry?
MARY   I couldn't help it. I was tired.
ELIZABETH   You must learn patience with him Mary. As he has had to learn it. Can you imagine what it must be like to live in darkness?
MARY   It's just the same when you close your eyes. It's not that bad.
ELIZABETH   And it requires great patience on his part to listen to you reading—he who is a great scholar of Latin.
MARY   We don't want to do it. He makes us!
ELIZABETH   Without us he is cut off from books, for we are too poor now to employ a secretary, as he did before the King came in. For him that is a worse torture than blindness.
MARY   I've been doing it every day since I was twelve! Since before you came!
ELIZABETH   Mary . . .
MARY   Why did you come? *We* didn't want you!
ELIZABETH   No, I know you didn't. But he did.
MARY   He can't love you. He's never even seen you, and anyway, he's too old. Granny Powell told me why you came really.

Don Taylor

ELIZABETH Why was that?
MARY (*a wicked smile*) It doesn't matter.

(ELIZABETH *stops laying the table.* MARY *continues, carving slices of beef for her father's plate.*)

ELIZABETH Mary, we must learn to live together here. I don't know what Mrs Powell has told you. I'll tell you simply that my uncle, Doctor Paget, asked me if I would like to marry Mr Milton, who was lonely, and needed a wife to organise his home, and to act as a mother to his daughters . . .

(MARY *throws down the knife.*)

MARY You're not our mother, and you never can be! She was an angel, but he hated her too, like everybody else, and drove her away!
ELIZABETH I know nothing about your mother Mary, except that she died bearing Deb; and I respect her memory, as he does. For her sake, let me love you, and let us both try to make his life as easy as we can. He is an old man, much afflicted. The plague has depressed his spirits greatly, and made him unable to complete his book of Paradise, which vexes him after so many years of labour. We must all help him till he is more himself.
MARY Let him burn it then. For all I care.

(ELIZABETH *is silent.*)

ELIZABETH Eat your breakfast Mary. I must go up and help him to dress.

(ELIZABETH *goes, and* MARY *sits and cuts herself a piece of bread and cheese. After a few seconds,* ANNE *comes in with* DEBORAH. *In silence they take their places and begin to breakfast.*)

MARY Good morning Sisters.
ANNE Good morning Mary.
DEBORAH Good morning Mary.
MARY Are we eating in silence today?
ANNE Can't we have some p . . . p . . . peace Mary?

MARY It depends at what price. I think it's time we grew up.

TWENTY-SIX *Cottage study. Interior. Day.*

Organ music. MILTON *is playing a small organ he has brought with him, with considerable skill. For the first time we see on his face a contented smile.*

TWENTY-SEVEN *Cottage ground floor passage. Interior. Day.*

MARY *is standing outside the study, plucking up courage to enter.*

TWENTY-EIGHT *Cottage study. Interior. Day.*

MARY *comes in and looks at* MILTON. *He is playing and humming in a resonant voice, and clearly hasn't heard. She stares, fascinated by his unawareness of her presence. Suddenly he stops.*

MILTON Is someone there?
MARY It's me Father.
MILTON Mary. I didn't hear you come in child. Sit down and listen to me play; and then perhaps we'll sing together before dinner. My father was a composer you know, and a good one too. Music is in our family.

(*He plays again.* MARY *is uncertain what to do.*)

When I was in Italy I met some fine musicians. (*Sadly.*) And dear Henry Lawes, who wrote this, was my friend.

(*He stops playing for a second and is abstracted. This gives* MARY *her opportunity.*)

MARY Father, I want to speak to you.
MILTON What about child?

(A half pause as MARY *plucks up her courage before blurting out.)*

MARY   I want to go to the Church in the village on Sunday.

(Pause.)

MILTON   You cannot.

MARY   Why not?

MILTON   Because I say you cannot. I am your father, and that is my word.

MARY   But that doesn't stop me wanting to go.

MILTON   *(mildly)* Mary, do you openly disobey me?

MARY   It is my right as a Christian to go to Church if my conscience tells me to.

MILTON   That is true.

MARY   And it's the law. It's the law that we should go to Church to please the King.

MILTON   To please the King! Child, do you know to whom you are talking? You are talking to the scourge of Kings, the man who defended and proclaimed Charles' execution to the whole world and set every crown in Europe trembling! My conscience is not at the King's command, and neither is yours. Your conscience is between yourself and Christ, and no power on earth can touch it.

MARY   Then you cannot command me not to go to Church father.

(Pause.)

MILTON   Quote me your texts.

MARY   My texts?

MILTON   Your decision to attend Church is doubtless the result of a thorough and diligent examination of the Word of God. You will have combed the Scriptures, and armed your conscience with the relevant verses. Let me hear them.

MARY   I have none.

MILTON   On what grounds, then, do you base your decision to attend Church?

MARY   On . . . a feeling.

MILTON   On ignorance, I think you mean. However, Mary, I am not ignorant of God's Word, and it is the duty of the wise to instruct the foolish in these matters. I find nothing in Scripture to warrant attendance to the hirelings of the English Church. You will continue with your private devotions in the usual way. Now, shall we sing? I haven't heard your voice lifted up in song since we came to Giles Chalfont.

*(*MARY, *in increasing panic, digs her heels in.)*

MARY   Father, I cannot be brushed aside like a child. I am not a child!

MILTON   Mary, you are trifling with me.

MARY   My mother was married at my age. Mistress of her own house.

MILTON   No, Mistress of *my* house Mary. That is an error you share with her. And I might be listening to her voice now, the same rebellious insolent pride that destroyed my home.

(Pause. An odd intensity of recollection comes over the old man.)

Come here . . . come here child . . .

*(*MARY *comes across to him, not very willingly. He touches her face, totally rapt in memory. He does not see her wince.)*

I've been told you look very like your mother. Is that so?

MARY   Granny Powell says I do.

MILTON   Your hair is . . . golden, I believe, but not colourless—dark, like ripe wheat.

MARY   Yes.

MILTON   And your eyes are blue, like the sky of Tuscany. A fine clear-cut nose, skin very soft and pale. Remarkable for one bred in the country.

MARY   I was bred in London.

MILTON   Yes . . . It's as though my hands remember.

*(*MARY *pushes his hands away and retreats into a corner. He is suddenly isolated, his reverie broken.)*

MILTON   Have you gone Mary?

MARY   No, I'm still here.

MILTON Why did you brush my hands away?

MARY Because I'm not my mother. You can't put *me* away because I won't do what you say!

MILTON You must do as I say Mary. It's a woman's duty to obey. And that duty is doubled in a daughter.

MARY (*very upset*) I *can't* obey you any more! I *am* going to Church. And I won't read to you again, not ever, any more, or write down your poem!

MILTON (*quietly*) Am I to live in silence now, as well as darkness Mary?

MARY (*all restraint cracking*) I don't know, I don't know, I wish you were dead, I wish I was dead and with my mother!

(*She bursts into tumultuous tears. Stumblingly he gets up, putting his hand by mistake on the keys and sounding a cluster of notes.*)

MILTON Elizabeth! Deborah! Anne! Come here!

(DEBORAH *comes in first, followed by* ANNE. *They look at the scene a little awestruck.* ELIZABETH *comes in and makes to go to* MARY.)

ELIZABETH Oh Mary, don't cry . . .

MILTON Leave her alone Betty! Deborah, Anne, are you here?

DEBORAH Yes Father.

ANNE Yes Father.

MILTON Betty, you may sit down.

(*She does so. The girls remain standing,* MARY *still sobbing bitterly.*)

MILTON You see here, wife and daughters, my undutiful daughter Mary, who exults in her father's blindness and wishes him dead.

ELIZABETH Dear Husband John . . .

MILTON Silence Betty!

(ELIZABETH *seems about to speak, but thinks better of it.*)

Let her tears be an example to all of us to preserve the rule of a Christian household in this family. Man is the servant of God, and woman is the servant of man. One Corinthians Eleven: "I would have you know that the head of every man is Christ: and the head of the woman is the man. He is the image and glory of God, but the woman is the glory of the man. Neither was the man created for the woman; but the woman for the man." That is the Scripture teaching, and who here will dare to say that it is false? Betty?

ELIZABETH No John.

MILTON Anne?

ANNE N . . . N . . . N . . . No Father.

MILTON Deborah?

DEBORAH No Father.

MILTON Mary?

(MARY *is still in tears.*)

Mary?

MARY (*screaming*) No Father No Father No Father No Father No Father No Father No Father . . . !

ELIZABETH Mary, dear Mary . . .

(ELIZABETH *goes to her to embrace her.*)

MARY Leave me alone!

(MARY *stumbles blindly from the room.* MILTON *is very shaken.*)

MILTON Elizabeth. Take me to my room.

(*She leads him out and up the stairs.* ANNE *and* DEBORAH *are alone in the shattered room.* DEBORAH *runs to* ANNE *and hugs her.*)

DEBORAH Oh Nan, poor Nan, what shall we do?

ANNE M . . . M . . . Mary will go.

TWENTY-NINE *Cottage garden. Exterior. Afternoon.*

MARY *is sitting outside the porch of the side door, topping and tailing goose-berries for a fruit tart.*
A man's voice is heard.

MARVELL Mary. Mary Milton!

(*She turns and sees a man on a horse by the gate.* ANDREW MARVELL *is forty-four years old at this time, a full-faced, large-eyed man with a generous mouth, looking somewhat world worn, nearer to the 1681 portrait than the one in the National Portrait Gallery. He is dressed in the Puritan manner, but with something of the flamboyance of one who is also a gentleman and at the centre of the restoration London world. He wears a handsome travelling cloak, a large hat with a feather, and a long black wig. He is always short of money, so he is not richly dressed, but by the side of the plain and thrifty Miltons, he looks very much the gentleman of fashion. He is armed, with a sword and a pistol.*)

MARVELL Tell your father he has a visitor: Mr Marvell, the Member for Hull.

(*He gets off his horse.* MARY *gets up and goes to the gate.*)

MARY He isn't here sir.
MARVELL Now, I heard in Oxford that Milton was staying in a little box at Giles Chalfont, to be safe from the plague. My sources are usually reliable.

(MARY *calls to* DEBORAH *in the house, and takes the horse's head.*)

MARY Deb, run down to the Inn and call an ostler for Mr Marvell's horse. Hurry!

(DEBORAH *runs out of the house and past them down the road.*)

MARVELL Good morning Deb.
DEBORAH (*running*) Good morning Sir!
MARVELL He is well I hope.
MARY Yes sir, he's gone for his walk . . . with his wife.
MARVELL (*looking doubtfully at the cottage*) Have you room for a visitor here, or shall I lodge at the Inn?
MARY I'm sure he would want you here Mr. Marvell. He'll be back quite soon.
MARVELL Do you remember me?
MARY Yes sir. You were a regular visitor.
MARVELL I've been beyond the sea for eighteen months with His Majesty's Ambassador to Russia. You were still a gawky girl when I saw you last. Now you look fit for better things than holding horses. Here, let me tie him to the fence till the ostler comes. He's an amiable beast, he won't tear up the gate post.
MARY Will you come inside sir?
MARVELL (*strolling into the garden towards the seat under the tree.* MARY *follows him*) No, I'm quite happy here in the garden till your father comes. Trees are one of the pleasanter things of life. My solitary ride was very restorative, if rather dangerous. How are you Mary? John Milton's daughter will be something of a scholar by now.
MARY No sir. I have no skill in learning.
MARVELL Well, that's of no significance neither. When I was tutor to the Lord General Fairfax's daughter, I taught her to turn a hexameter with the best of us. But she married His Grace the Duke of Buckingham, of whose exploits you may have heard. So all my earnest instruction came to nothing.

(MARY *smiles in spite of herself.*)

MARY Father will be glad to see you. He chafes at the company of women. (*Pause.*) We have not been happy here.
MARVELL Well. Perhaps a bowl or two of wine and some masculine conversation will remedy that. Your father is one of England's great ones, Mary. We cannot have him down in his dumps.

(MARY *manages a rueful smile.*)

THIRTY *Cottage dining room. Interior. Night.*

Candlelight. In the foreground, seated round the table, ELIZABETH *and* DEBORAH, *reading,* ANNE *sewing, and* MARY *making a new candle for her candlestick. In the background, we can see into the study, where* MILTON *and* MARVELL *are seated by the fire, drinking wine and talking.*

ELIZABETH (*quietly*) You can go to bed now. I shall attend to your father. He and Mr Marvell will talk many hours yet.

ANNE Goodnight mother.

(ANNE *kisses* ELIZABETH *on the cheek and goes.*)

DEBORAH Goodnight mother.

(DEBORAH *likewise.*)

MARY Goodnight.

(*A pause, and the merest brush of a kiss.* ELIZABETH *looks down sadly.*)

THIRTY-ONE *Cottage study. Interior. Night.*

(*Candlelight, firelight.* MARVELL *regularly refills his wineglass.* MILTON's *glass is empty, and he does not refill it.*)

MILTON What's the news in Parliament?

MARVELL We are to meet in Oxford in the autumn. Honourable members are currently leaving town in a great hurry.

MILTON And what will happen in the autumn?

MARVELL The war against liberty will be continued by the King's ministers. Some few of us will fight what rearguard action we can.

MILTON Has the freedom of conscience Bill any chance this session?

MARVELL I should say none, in the current atmosphere. Indeed, in October we read a Bill that will grieve you especially: a new measure to tighten the laws against unlicensed printing.

MILTON So my poem, if it ever sees the light, must be censored by my Lord Archbishop of Canterbury?

MARVELL No remedy, it must.

MILTON I would rather give it to the fire.

MARVELL Your friends would be sorry for that.

MILTON Will they ever let the notorious Milton publish again?

MARVELL Not a pamphlet, certainly. I think a poem—a non-satirical poem—might pass.

MILTON There's plenty of satire in *Paradise Lost*. We must hope the fools are too blind to spot it.

MARVELL I assure you, the Archbishop is.

(*They both smile, but* MILTON's *smile soon fades.*)

MILTON But the work isn't finished yet.

MARVELL So I understand.

MILTON It lacks little, a few hundred lines, no more. But—the Muse deserts me, as unworthy I look back upon my life, and I see all my dearest projects and innermost desires broken in pieces. The Muse abhors failure. She turns her face another way.

MARVELL Onto Mr Dryden[4] perhaps?

MILTON No, she draws the line there.

(*They both laugh.*)

MARVELL It isn't failure, though it may seem so to you. Great deeds remain great deeds. And much has been salvaged from the wreck.

MILTON My dear fellow, the Commonwealth is destroyed, its leaders dead or dishonoured, and the sons of Belial[5] ravage and swear in the streets of London, drunk more often than fed. The King spends his time in a whore's belly, and the people of God are persecuted for their faith. When we executed the first Charles, and set up the rule of the Saints, I didn't foresee this day!

MARVELL Were you there?

MILTON The King's execution? Yes.

MARVELL It was a very cold day. He died well.

MILTON He died like a tyrant, unrepentant and afraid. He was terrified anyone should touch the axe lest they should blunt the edge.

4 **Mr Dryden** John Dryden (1631–1700), English poet, dramatized Milton's *Paradise Lost* in 1677.
5 **Belial** One of the fallen angels. Puritans called Charles II's courtiers "the sons of Belial."

MARVELL He need not have feared. It took his head at a blow, like a turnip. There was a low groan in the crowd, do you remember? And then silence. Except for the birds.

MILTON Not in my heart. In my heart there was exultation, and praise of God's justice.

MARVELL The iron logic of revolution that cost a fool his head.

MILTON Was it only sixteen years ago, that day?

MARVELL Tuesday January the 30th, 1649.

MILTON I had forgotten it was a Tuesday. I was a private man still. I could still see.

THIRTY-TWO *London. The study in Milton's Barbican house. Interior. Day.*

(*A large open room, sparsely furnished, except for mountains of books, on shelves, on tables, in piles.*

MILTON, *aged forty-one, sits at a large desk, reading. He reads with his right eye only, fairly close to the page. There is a sound of a young baby crying.*)

MILTON (*calling*) Mary!

(MARY POWELL MILTON *enters, aged twenty-four, looking very like young Mary, and played by the same actress. Her hair, which is her most attractive feature, is a rich dark blonde, and her breasts and figure are fuller than young* MARY'S, *from childbirth. She has less of young* MARY'S *eagerness, as though something of her had been broken, and something calmer and more placid had grown in its place.*)

MARY POWELL Yes?

MILTON Is the child unwell?

MARY POWELL She has the colic. Nurse is with her.

MILTON Can she not be quieted? She disturbs my studies.

MARY POWELL A three-months child will cry, husband, regardless of your instructions.

MILTON At least she is whole and straight. That is a blessing.

(MILTON *returns to his studies.* MARY POWELL *is as if alone. She wanders across the room to the window in a desultory manner.*)

MARY POWELL Husband!

MILTON What is it?

MARY POWELL There's a coach outside. A very grand coach, and a gentleman descending.

(*Knocks heard below at the door.* MILTON *rises and crosses to the window.*)

MILTON Go to the door Mary, don't leave it to Jane.

(MARY POWELL *hurries out. Milton looks at the coach.*)

MILTON A coach. And an escort of horse . . . Am I to be taken to prison in luxury?

(*Past the half-protesting* MARY, SIR HENRY VANE *enters.* VANE *is thirty-six, very much the energetic Puritan politician. Twenty years of experience in politics is reflected on his face, in the subtlety of his approach to ideas, and his directness with people.*

He is one of the aristocrats of the Commonwealth Government, of ancient and noble family, so he wears his Puritanism with a pronounced dash.)

MARY POWELL John, the gentleman . . .

VANE Excuse my lack of ceremony Mr Milton, and don't let the Troopers alarm you. A member of the Government needs an escort in London at the moment.

MILTON Sir Henry Vane!

VANE Your servant sir.

MILTON Mary, you may go.

(She does so. MILTON *remains uncertain, while* VANE *walks round the room, looking at it.)*

MILTON Will you sit down sir?

VANE Thank you.

MILTON On my right side, sir, if you please. My left eye is a little obscure.

VANE A bad eye must be a handicap to a scholar.

MILTON It's nothing sir, I assure you.

(Pause. VANE *studies* MILTON.*)*

VANE Mr Milton, you have been a notorious pamphleteer.

MILTON I have done my duty as I saw it, by putting my learning at the service of the State.

VANE Your Divorce pamphlets are, one might say, infamous; though I notice your wife is with you at the moment.

MILTON I have written pamphlets on the general subject of God's Word with regard to marriage and divorce. I have written nothing about my wife.

VANE You should know sir. You also wrote this I believe?

(He throws on the table a copy of "The Tenure of Kings and Magistrates." There is a faint suggestion of fear in MILTON's *answer.)*

MILTON Yes, I did.

VANE A justification of the deposing of Kings. Again in general terms, no names mentioned. By which I gather that you are a Commonwealthsman?

MILTON I believe liberty is within our grasp, if we can learn to take it.

VANE So do I too, Mr Milton.—I have to tell you that this morning, at the meeting of the Council of State, your name was proposed for the office of Secretary of State for Foreign Languages. And that you were adopted by the Council for that post. An official messenger will visit you later this afternoon. But I wished to see you for myself, so as to be able to talk to my colleague, General Cromwell, about

you. Certainly Mr Milton, you are amazed, not surprisingly. Will you accept the post?

MILTON *(dumbstruck)* I don't know sir.

VANE Your scholarship, of course, is beyond question, and we don't doubt that you could accomplish the office of preparing our diplomatic correspondence quite adequately.

MILTON Sir. I have to tell you, I am a scholar and a poet. I am nobody's amanuensis. I have always held it as wisdom that statesmen should be advised by the wisest men of the age, and that poets and philosophers are peculiarly fitted to serve in this way. That is why I wrote my pamphlets. But I am no mere translator or scribe.

VANE Which is the precise reason, Mr Milton, for my brief visit. The Commonwealth is short of men of culture. Our enemies call us Roundheads, and think we do nothing but praise God and knock each other on the head. The exiled Royalists boast openly that we are a Government of unlettered shopkeepers, and that all the English scholars are with them in Holland.

MILTON That is a base lie!

VANE Of course it is sir, we both know it, and so do they. Nevertheless, General Cromwell and myself both feel that the time may shortly be upon us when we shall need men of literary ability. There are other ways of defending England than by the sword. Your name was mentioned, not because you can write a passable letter in Latin or French, but because *this* *(he gestures to "Tenure")* proves that you can argue, and score, and triumph in words, and we will need a man who can do that.

MILTON That is an honour I have not looked for. I have prayed to be enabled to serve the State, but I envisaged it in a private capacity. I shall ask for God's guidance.

VANE And you will need your own wits too, I assure you. God tends to leave the governing of nations to our own devices;

though he does seem to give General Cromwell fairly detailed instructions. You will have no vote in the Council, of course, but you must be at all meetings, and a wise man's voice will make itself heard without a vote. The King's head is off, Mr Milton, and the swords are back in their scabbards, but the real battle, the political battle, is joined, and still at issue.

MILTON   I shall be honoured to bear my part in it sir.

THIRTY-THREE   *London, the landing outside the study. Interior. Day.*

MARY POWELL *is listening at the door. Inside the men's voices can be heard, still in urgent discussion. Downstairs, the child begins to cry again.* MARY POWELL *has heard the important fact. Sadly, she begins to walk down the staircase. A very long shot emphasises her isolation.*

THIRTY-FOUR   *Lady Ranelagh's dining room. Interior. Day.*

(In close-up, the angry face of DR SCROBY, *a Presbyterian divine, dressed for his calling. We are at a formal dinner given by* LADY CATHERINE RANELAGH, *and at the moment all attention is focussed on the argument raging between* SCROBY *and* MILTON. SCROBY, *eating a great deal, tends to fluster and anger.* MILTON *preserves a cool disdain.* LADY RANELAGH *is an intelligent and educated thirty-six.*

The table is groaning, but MILTON *has eaten little.*

Two or three other eaters are totally absorbed in the battle between the doctor and the poet. The scene is played partly off their reactions.)

SCROBY   My Lady Ranelagh, the excellence of your table is only equalled by the wisdom of the gentlemen you invite to attend it, but in bringing Mr Milton in, you exceed the bounds of decency!

LADY RANELAGH   Mr Milton is an honoured friend of long standing, Dr Scroby. In what does he offend you?

SCROBY   In everything ma'am. Is he not a renegade from the Presbyterian party, a Divorcer, who believes in taking a new wife by the week, and who has banished his own wife to the country for the furtherance of that intention? Does he not advocate a licentious freedom to print any blasphemy or sacrilege against God's revealed truth, without restriction? Is he not now a member of that Government which has illegally murdered its anointed Sovereign, and has he not written vicious and scurrilous slanders in its defence, and against the late and saintly King?

LADY RANELAGH   Some of what *you* say is plain slander, Doctor, as I suspect you know. Mr Milton is a scholar worth your respect, and a poet.

SCROBY   We have no use for poets, ma'am. Let them go to Holland with the Cavaliers.

MILTON   Aeschylus carried his sword against the Persians, sir, and Cicero accepted a Consulship in the defence of freedom. I follow their example.

SCROBY   Freedom, sir? Not one man in a hundred sought the King's death. The Parliament had to be purged of two-thirds of its members . . .

MILTON   Of your party sir . . .

SCROBY   . . . before even a pretence of legality could be fabricated. Now, were it not for Cromwell and the Army, the young King would be back within the week!

MILTON   And the loyal Presbyterians, who took up arms against his father, would cheer him to the echo, no doubt.

SCROBY   We took up arms for law, not revolution!

MILTON   But some of us took up arms for

freedom sir, for freedom to worship God according to conscience, regardless of Bishop or Presbyter. You cannot control men's minds, and once their eyes are open you may be sure they will see.

SCROBY The people sir . . .

MILTON If the crass and slavish multitude, in ignorance and superstition, will willingly surrender our hard-won liberty to Charles Stuart, who changes his allegiance as he changes his whore, then God be praised for Oliver Cromwell and his swords, for preserving that freedom, by force of arms!

LADY RANELAGH Oliver has found his advocate, Dr Scroby. You must look to your pens.

THIRTY-FIVE *The study of Milton's London house. Interior. Night.*

MILTON *is reading at his desk, by candlelight. There are even more books than before.*

He is reading a large printed work in Latin, studying it closely with his right eye. He blinks his right eye several times, and looks up from the book.

The candle goes in and out of focus, seems to expand and contract, then settles down, haloed.

MILTON *rubs his right eye.*

The candle begins to lose focus again. MILTON *looks up, closes his right eye, feels his left.*

MILTON Dear God, let me not go blind.

THIRTY-SIX *The council chamber at Whitehall. Interior. Day.*

(An imposing room in the former royal palace. A large table, with perhaps twenty-five to thirty seated men round it, the cabinet of the Commonwealth Government. VANE *is present, seated next to* CROMWELL, *who says little and listens much.* JOHN BRADSHAW, *the Lord President, a rather prosaic lawyer of about*

forty-eight, is in the Chair. Milton is towards the far end of the table, surrounded by other secretaries taking minutes. There is a hum of general conversation. Then BRADSHAW *rises to speak. He places a copy of Salmasius's tract on the table.)*

BRADSHAW Gentlemen . . . the book we have been expecting is upon us. *The Defence of the Late King against the People of England,* by the Frenchman Salmasius —by common consent the leading scholar of Europe—suborned and hired by Charles Stuart to defame and scandalise this nation. In it, we are all branded as sacrilegious and regicides, and it has to be admitted that Salmasius has done his work well. He has hunted through the Scriptures and the Classical authors for any text or verse that he can bend against us, and the result is formidable. Measures have already been taken to prevent the importing of the book, and existing copies are already burned. But the book is at large in the capitals of Europe, and it will do us immeasurable harm if it is not answered, and in Latin too. The question is, who in England, and of our party, would dare to challenge Salmasius?

(A brief silence. VANE *makes an obviously previously discussed suggestion.)*

VANE I propose our Secretary, Mr Milton.

CROMWELL Seconded.

BRADSHAW Mr Milton, will you serve in this?

(MILTON looks haggard and ill.)

MILTON Gentlemen, I am conscious of the honour you do me in selecting me for this great task. From my youth I have burned, if not to do great deeds, at least to celebrate them. The deeds have been done for me by some who sit here. It is for me to write their celebration.

(CROMWELL nods approval to BRADSHAW.)

BRADSHAW It is proposed then, that Mr Milton do prepare something in answer to the book of Salmasius, and when he has done it, to bring it to the Council. Are we agreed?

(*They all raise their hands, some murmuring "agreed".*)

BRADSHAW   Agreed.

THIRTY-SEVEN   *Study of Milton's London house. Interior. Day.*

(MILTON *is seated in the middle of the room in a large chair, with his head bent back. A* DOCTOR *is bandaging his head. On a small table is a fearsome collection of tools, and evidence of recent bleeding.*)

MILTON   The pain in my temples is difficult to bear.
DOCTOR   The wounds I made last time are beginning to suppurate. Next time the poison can be drawn away, and with it, perhaps, that which clouds the eye.
MILTON   You have purged me daily, and cupped me and my neck is raw from your caustics. Truly, I think the remedy is worse than the disease.
DOCTOR   Perhaps, when we remove the poison . . .

(*The* DOCTOR *does not continue, and begins to collect his instruments.* MILTON *relaxes his posture, then watches the* DOCTOR.)

MILTON   Will I be blind?
DOCTOR   How is the left eye?
MILTON   Nothing. A fog. Greyness.
DOCTOR   And the right?
MILTON   Sometimes things seem very bright, like a rainbow across my vision, or a halo round lights. Sometimes everything is blurred, and sometimes I can see well enough.
DOCTOR   If you could spend, say, a year in a shaded place, the inner wounds might heal. But in that time you must read and write nothing at all.
MILTON   Not read?

DOCTOR   The alternative is total blindness, quite soon.
MILTON   Thank you.

(*The* DOCTOR *inclines his head and goes.* MILTON *gets up and goes to his desk, piled and surrounded with books, and in the middle,* SALMASIUS's *book. He looks at his desk, then walks across to the large window at the end of the room, and stands there in long shot, looking at the light.*)

THIRTY-EIGHT   *Study in Milton's London house. Interior. Night.*

(*Close-up guttering candle. Another is lit from it, and it is put out as the new candle is pressed into place, by* MARY POWELL, *now in the first months of pregnancy. She carries several candles, and begins to walk across the room to change the others, all of which are burning low. The room is now even fuller of books, in piles, on chairs, so that* MARY POWELL, *and* MILTON, *who is working at his desk, seem almost hidden among them.* MILTON *looks up at her.*)

MILTON   Mary.
MARY POWELL   Yes?
MILTON   Come and sit with me.

(*They sit together on a settle, surrounded and shadowed by skyscrapers of books.*)

MILTON   Mary, I think I shall soon be blind.
MARY POWELL   Day and night you are bent over your books . . .
MILTON   I must then write the answer to Salmasius. It is my duty.
MARY POWELL   At the price of your eyes.
MILTON   I think blindness, perhaps, was destined for me. At best, if I read nothing, live the life of a drone, I might have a few more years of this one-eyed sight.
MARY POWELL   Then do that, do it, rather than walk freely into the darkness!

MILTON   In a way, it's a little thing. Some men are called upon to die for fame. Blindness is nothing to that. And to topple the greatest scholar in Europe, and defend the honour of the English people, that's worth such eyes as I have left. Men died at Edgehill, Marston and Naseby for our freedom, while I was at home with my books. Now it's my turn, with my weapons.

(MARY POWELL *looks down, near to tears.*)

MILTON   Look at me. I must learn to study that face, so that I can remember it in my darkness.

(*He touches her face.*)

Poor Mary. God made us strange bedfellows.

MARY POWELL   I hope I have done my duty.

MILTON   I should have left you on your farm in Oxfordshire. You were a country plant, and withered in town.

(*He gets up and crosses to the door.*)

MARY POWELL   Town or country, the place is all one. I have learned to be your wife. Doubtless we shall know more in heaven.

MILTON   Assuredly, we shall.

MARY POWELL   Goodnight husband.

MILTON   Goodnight Mary.

(*She goes out.* MILTON *crosses slowly to his desk and sits, in the half light.*)

MILTON   "I must work the works of him that sent me, while it is day. The night cometh, when no man can work," saith the Evangelist John . . .

THIRTY-NINE   *The downstairs hallway of* MILTON's *London house. Interior. Day.*

(*A large wooden staircase, panelled corridor leading to other rooms.* LADY RANELAGH *has just entered and is talking to* MARY POWELL, *now very pregnant.*)

LADY RANELAGH   I have brought him the book from the printers. It looks well.

MARY POWELL   He will not see it.

(*Upstairs, we see* MILTON, *now stone blind, beginning to feel his way down the stairs.*)

MILTON   My dear Catherine, is that you? How are you? Well?

LADY RANELAGH   Well, John. And I have a sturdy book for you.

MILTON   Good, good . . .

(*His descent is agony for the watchers.*)

LADY RANELAGH   (*quietly to* MARY) Should we not help him? He will fall.

MARY POWELL   (*quietly*)   He will not be helped. He has fallen over, or bumped into, almost every object in the house. He says he must learn not to be dependent.

MILTON   Whispers, whispers! Two more steps Mary?

MARY POWELL   Three.

MILTON   Ah, three . . . Now.

LADY RANELAGH   (*giving him the book*) There it is.

MILTON   No. No. Not one letter can I see. A faint chink, like an old blind, but nothing more. It's a shame after so much work. It feels well.

LADY RANELAGH   It reads well too.

MILTON   Yes, yes, I think it will make the Frenchman jump, I think. Now, to find my way to the sitting room, and a cordial for you after your errand.

(*They watch him begin to inch his way along the passage.* MARY POWELL *turns to* LADY RANELAGH.)

MARY POWELL   I wish he could have seen the child.

FORTY   *The London house, a darkened room. Interior. Night.*

(*Solemn music. A large, darkened room, a bier, candles around it. On the bier,* MARY POWELL.)

From the darkness, MILTON, *led by* LADY RANELAGH, *both in mourning. He lets go of her hand, feels his way to the bier, feels for* MARY POWELL'S *face and lips, and kisses her.*)

MILTON (*quietly and privately*) Goodnight Mary. You precede me into the light.

(*He gets up and rejoins* LADY RANELAGH.)

How is the child?

LADY RANELAGH She will live.

MILTON I shall call her Deborah, because she brought glad tidings to a people sore oppressed. "Awake, awake, Deborah, awake, awake, utter a song!"

LADY RANELAGH Amen.

MILTON Amen. (*Very quietly.*) Thy will be done.

(LADY RANELAGH *leads him away.*)

FORTY-ONE *A gallery in the palace at Whitehall. Interior. Day.*

(VANE, MILTON *and* BRADSHAW *walking to a Council meeting,* MILTON *on* BRADSHAW'S *arm. The whole scene played walking.*)

BRADSHAW All Europe talks of the Defence of the English People. Our agents in Sweden tell us that your taunts have broken Salmasius, Queen Christina has dismissed him, and that he will never live to answer you!

MILTON I whipped him raw with the truth.

VANE We may soon be giving Europe a new topic of conversation, I fear.

BRADSHAW You fear?

VANE Today we discuss the long promised dissolution of Parliament, do we not?

BRADSHAW Oh. Yes.

MILTON This Parliament has sat for thirteen years. The voice of the people must be heard.

VANE Milton, let me tell you, as one who loves you, you often talk a great deal of nonsense. (MILTON *smiles.*) The people will have us out, the Presbyters in, and Charles back in two weeks, if we let them. The voice of *some* of the people must be heard, perhaps.

MILTON Does it matter how, so long as we select the worthiest men?

BRADSHAW I fear a dissolution. It's a leap into the dark. Better to prolong this Parliament, and be safe.

VANE We would all like to be safe. But the Army will demand a dissolution unless Cromwell keeps them in check. But will he? That's the question.

(*They have reached the chamber door.* TWO TROOPERS *stand on guard, with pikes.* VANE *goes to one of them, and taps him on the chest.*)

VANE Look at these fine fellows. Are they our guards, or are we their prisoners?

MILTON They are the right hand of God.

VANE Cromwell would agree with you. To me, they look like soldiers. Shall we go in?

(*They enter the chamber. The doors close behind them and the* TROOPERS *recross their pikes.*)

FORTY-TWO CROMWELL'S *lodgings at Whitehall. Interior. Night.*

(*This was once one of the most imposing private chambers of the royal palace, but somehow* CROMWELL *has imposed his personality on it, so that it now seems the room of a practical, God-intoxicated soldier. It is late at night.* MILTON *is seated in a chair, but* CROMWELL *is restless, and keeps moving, a man with a problem which is ultimately beyond his Resources to solve. The room shows evidence of the recent presence of many men. Begin with* CROMWELL *in close-up. He is a man with an almost brutal quality of energy, a violence of emotion which expresses itself in action, and in conviction of rightness, and with a habit of looking directly and blazingly at men, which is rather lost on a blind man, but is practised just the same, out of habit. He is fifty-four.*)

CROMWELL Soldiers, Mr Milton, under God they won the war, under God they do not intend to lose the peace. If I hadn't held them back, they would have ruled this land four years ago. At Corkbush Field, in 48, three complete regiments mutinied. They wanted freedom of conscience, they wanted it at once, they wanted votes for every man of them, and they drew themselves up there, wearing green favours and Leveller[6] pamphlets in their helmets! But God spoke to me with a voice of firmness. I rode along their front rank, plucking their favours and pamphlets to the ground; and I drew out their leader, one Robert Arnold, and I shot him in front of them. If one man there had dared to musket me, the Parliament House would have become a barracks. Four years ago, and still nothing is done, still the soldiers' demands are ignored, still I have not done that which Lambert and Harrison urge on me daily!

MILTON The Parliament has betrayed its trust. It will not reform the Church, and it greases its own palm.

CROMWELL Yes, we know they are corrupt, and some of them are whoremasters, and some of them are fools . . . It is very late, Mr Milton, near midnight I think. Till half an hour ago they were all here —the Parliamentary leaders, Sidney, Marten, Vane. But can they be trusted, what they say? . . . I sent for you here to my lodging because I have need of the cool voice of reason after so much wrangling . . . and because I do not underestimate the power of the pen. Where do you stand?

MILTON I stand for God and his people.

CROMWELL I hope we all do that . . . Are you with me and the Army, or with Vane and the Parliament?

6 The Levellers were radicals during the English Civil War.

MILTON I care for principles, my Lord General, not for parties. I care for freedom of my conscience to worship God, I care for freedom to speak and write and print; I care for freedom of the Parliament, within certain limits, and I abhor the tyranny of Kings. I think good men have the right to choose their own Government.

CROMWELL I too. But what if they choose wrong, against what God has revealed in these past wars?

MILTON Just men will not choose wrong.

CROMWELL Who are the just men?

MILTON Those who serve God.

CROMWELL But how can we see into men's hearts? I would know that trick.

MILTON By prayer.

CROMWELL Prayer is my daily relief. But it doesn't tell me who is to have the power of decision in England.

You wrote a book, I believe, some years ago, calling for an end to the licensing of printing.

MILTON It was ignored.

CROMWELL And now you are yourself one of our censors?

MILTON If we must have censors, they should be the best and learnedest men.

CROMWELL Do you suggest we should allow the printing of anything, regardless how scandalous or obscene?

MILTON Certainly I do. If it is truth, all men will profit by it. If it is evil, we will see it for what it is, and be better armed to defeat it.

CROMWELL If all men may speak, why may not all men rule too? Are you a Leveller at heart, do you call for a Democracy? I have put the Levellers in prison.

MILTON The multitude is ignorant, and easily misled. To rule is the prerogative of the wise. I am no Leveller.

CROMWELL The Parliament think they are wise. So wise that they wish to perpetuate themselves for life, and to have the choosing of the candidates for the vacant seats. The Army will not endure that.

MILTON   The Army is of God, and must be heard.

CROMWELL   We have reached a wall, Mr Milton, a wall which the people of England are afraid to cross. The Army is ready to tear it down, and enter the pleasant fields beyond. But will the people follow them through, or will they stay behind, crying for their dead King and his Ungodly son?

MILTON   Someone must be first into the breach.

CROMWELL   I have led charges of horse. I have marched and countermarched, and been wounded, and killed men, all for the love of Parliament, and the rule of law. Now, events force me to contemplate an action whose possible consequences make my hair stand on end.

MILTON   My eyes are darkened, My Lord General, and I no longer wear my sword. But my pen is at your command.

CROMWELL   Make a note of tomorrow's date, Mr Milton: April the twentieth, sixteen fifty-three. In the history of our land, it may be a day worth remembering.

FORTY-THREE   *The council chamber at Whitehall. Interior. Day.*

(*Ten or fifteen men are present, and there is uproar.* MILTON *sits quietly in his usual place.*)

BRADSHAW   Gentlemen, some order please.

VANE   Silence, in God's name! So a man may speak!

(*The noise partially stops.*)

By now you all know what happened this morning. Cromwell came with his Troopers, and dissolved the House, by force . . .

(*Uproar again.* VANE *tries to speak above and through it.*)

Now, those of us here . . . some of the Lord General's friends are noticeably ab-

sent, I see . . . we must decide on a course of action . . .

(*The chamber doors are thrown open and* CROMWELL *enters, with* LAMBERT *and* HARRISON *at either elbow. Silence.*)

CROMWELL   Gentlemen, if you are met here as private persons, you shall not be disturbed; but if as a Council of State, this is no place for you; and since you cannot but know what was done at the House this morning, so take notice that Parliament is dissolved.

BRADSHAW   Sir, we have heard what you did at the House this morning, and before many hours all England will hear of it. But you are mistaken to think that the Parliament is dissolved, for no power in England can dissolve them but themselves!

(CROMWELL *explodes into one of his towering rages.*)

CROMWELL   In God's name, gentlemen, do you wish me to bring in my Troopers?

(*Chaos. The chamber begins to empty very quickly.* VANE *walks slowly and calmly to* CROMWELL, *putting on his hat and drawing on his gloves.*)

VANE   Sir, we have worked together like brothers these ten years, but this is not honest sir, it is against morality and common honesty. You may find me at my estate in the country till the rule of law is restored. Good day sir.

(VANE *goes.*)

CROMWELL   (*bellowing*)   Oh, Sir Henry Vane, Sir Henry Vane, the lord deliver me from Sir Henry Vane!

(*Everyone has left the chamber except* CROMWELL, LAMBERT, HARRISON *and* MILTON, *who is still seated in his place.*

CROMWELL   Mr Milton, the meeting is dispersed.

MILTON   With your indulgence, Lord General, I need an arm to guide me to the gallery where my secretary is waiting.

(CROMWELL *crosses to him.*)

CROMWELL   Come sir. Let me perform one kindly deed today, so that God will not forget me in my prayers. I shall have need of him.

(*Long shot as he leads* MILTON *through the doors and* LAMBERT *and* HARRISON *close them.*)

FORTY-FOUR   *The cottage. Milton's study. Interior. Night.*

(*It is very late. The fire is burning low and the candles are beginning to gutter.* MARVELL *is pouring the last of the wine.*)

MILTON   To support Cromwell, as I did then, was not the answer, though it seemed so at the time. It seemed as though a just and Godly man with power to do so, had decided to act in the common good.

MARVELL   But if Lord Protector, why not King? Oliver was King in all but name.

MILTON   We were no nearer a free republic than when we first executed Charles. That was when the decisions should have been made. But the men of those days acted from self-interest and fear.

MARVELL   As they invariably do.

MILTON   When Cromwell was dead, and anarchy upon us, I gave the State a model for a new Commonwealth. But no one listened.

MARVELL   By writing that pamphlet when you did, you put yourself in great danger.

MILTON   I expected to die, as many of my friends died; or were dishonoured worse than by death: Cromwell and Bradshaw and Ireton dug up from their Christian graves, and hung up at Tyburn for the mob to gawp at; their rotten heads cut off and piked.

MARVELL   They put Cromwell's on a pinnacle at Westminster Hall. It's still there, what the crows have left.

MILTON   On that day I blessed my blindness. In a manner I loved the man. I did not wish to see him reduced to that extremity.

MARVELL   We had to fight hard for your life. Only one vote saved you in the House, and that after many days of lobbying. We told them, God forgive us, that the Almighty had already justly punished you with blindness, and that there was no call for the House to go further. But there were some who were determined to see you ride a cart to Tyburn.

MILTON   I meant the words I had written, and I would have stood by them on the scaffold if it had been required of me.

MARVELL   They died well, our friends: Vane with a smile on his face, Harrison praising God, as they cut out his bowels.

MILTON   When I heard of the desecration of the graves, I knew the barbarians had returned to England.

MARVELL   And yet, in a sense, we have beaten them. The King gets his own way now because his wishes and those of Parliament coincide. When they do not, we shall see him stoop.

MILTON   I'm glad we wear our slavery so comfortably.

MARVELL   It is harder for you. You had a vision of what might have been. Few of us shared it. We live from day to day.

MILTON   But what more oft in nations grown corrupt
And by their vices brought to servitude
Than to love bondage more than liberty
Bondage with ease, than strenuous liberty.

(*Pause.* MARVELL *realises this aspect cannot be pursued, compromise not being a Miltonic virtue.*)

MARVELL   I am eager for your poem. You must not keep your friends waiting.

MILTON   (*a slight smile*)   Shall we go to bed then? It must be very late.

MARVELL   Three o'clock.

MILTON   Elizabeth!

FORTY-FIVE   *Cottage dining room. Interior. Night.*

ELIZABETH *has fallen asleep over her book, her candle almost out.*

FORTY-SIX   *The cottage. Exterior. Day.*

Long shot of MARVELL *and* MILTON *and* ELIZABETH *coming out of the cottage.* DEBORAH *is standing by the gate, holding* MARVELL's *horse.*

FORTY-SEVEN   *Cottage. Milton's bedroom. Interior. Day.*

(MARY *and* ANNE *are making* MILTON's *bed. This is one of the tasks* ANNE *enjoys doing.*)

MARY   Come with me Nan, back to London.

ANNE   I c . . . c . . . can't Mary.

MARY   We can, if we want to!

ANNE   There's the p . . . p . . . plague.

MARY   I'm not frightened of the plague. Or we could go to Granny Powell's at Oxford.

ANNE   I can't Mary. I'm not l . . . l . . . like you. I have to be l . . . l . . . looked after.

MARY   I'll look after you Nan, it'll be just like it was before Betty came.

ANNE   I l . . . l . . . l . . . love Betty, Mary. She's kind to me. I don't want to go.

FORTY-EIGHT   *Cottage. Exterior. Day.*

(MARVELL *is ready to leave.*)

MILTON   Shall I see you again soon?

MARVELL   I shall hope so. Indeed I live to so little purpose on the earth, I sometimes feel I shall forget my own name, if I don't hear it often in the mouths of my friends.

(*He mounts his horse.*)

MILTON   You underrate yourself. Your satires walk the town briskly enough.

MARVELL   They are trifles I dare not name in your presence. I wrote some sweeter verses when I was a younger man. But my enemies would make hay with them, so they must never see the light. I shall tuck them with me into the tomb. Anyway, whoever heard of a poet in Parliament!

FORTY-NINE   *The cottage.* MILTON's *bedroom. Interior. Day.*

MARY   You see Nan, we could set up in a shop together. A hat shop!

ANNE   Mary, you can't even stitch a s . . . s . . . straight seam.

MARY   But you sew beautifully Nan! Anything to get away from here, and Father, and his horrible books!

ANNE   I w . . . w . . . wish I could read his b . . . books.

(MARY *is by the writing desk.*)

MARY   This is the new one, the one he has been dictating in the mornings these seven years . . . Shall I take it downstairs and burn it?

ANNE   (*genuinely horrified*) No, Mary, no!

(MARY *looks at it and puts it down with distaste.*)

MARY   All right then, if you won't come with me, I'll go alone!

(MARY *goes out.* ANNE *hobbles over to the desk, picks up the manuscript and after a second, clumsily kisses it.*)

FIFTY   *The cottage garden. Exterior. Day.*

(*We see* MARVELL *riding away.* MILTON, *led by* ELIZABETH, *crosses to his seat under the tree.* ELIZABETH *returns to the cottage, and at the door, meets* MARY *coming out.*)

MARY   Is Father asleep?

ELIZABETH   No, but he probably soon will be in this warm sun. Mr Marvell has done him good. He's almost his old self.

MARY   I must talk to him.

ELIZABETH   Mary.

MARY   What?

ELIZABETH   Have mercy.

MARY   It's nothing to do with you.

(ELIZABETH *watches anxiously as* MARY *crosses the grass to her father. He is dozing, and has not heard her. She looks at his sleeping face.*)

MARY   Father.

(*He wakes with a little start.*)

MILTON   Who is it? Betty?

MARY   It's me Father.

MILTON   Mary. Well Mary?

MARY   I want to leave you Father.

(*Having said it, there is little else to say.* MILTON, *only half awake, lets it sink in. We are conscious of a kind of weariness.*)

My mother left her home at my age, to set up her own house . . .

MILTON   Your mother was married.

MARY   I want you to give me the money for my dowry, and I shall leave you and set myself up in London.

MILTON   Your dowry . . . ? Do you know what I had with your mother for dowry, Mary?

MARY   No.

MILTON   Nothing. Powell her father promised me a thousand pounds—in addition to the three hundred he already owed me. Not one penny was paid, nor will it ever be paid if I know the Powells. Your dowry shall be the same riches your mother brought me.

(MARY *is dumbfounded.*)

MARY   But Father . . . I must have a dowry, if I am ever to marry!

MILTON   Mary, you are a child in such things, so ignorant of the world you are not fit to leave home. I have no money to give you. My estate is just enough for us to live on in this frugal manner. What the State paid me for my services was all lost when the King returned.

(MARY *is desperate.*)

MARY   It isn't true! I know you have money. I think it's all true what Granny Powell says!

MILTON   And what has that estimable gentlewoman been telling you?

(MARY *hesitates for a second, but then her panic masters her.*)

MARY   That you're keeping it all for her! For Betty! That all your money is rightfully ours, but she married you to get it from us!

(MILTON *can barely speak.*)

MILTON   Mary, leave my presence!

MARY   I shall go, even without the money! You can't stop me. You can't even see me, whether I'm here or not!

(MILTON *rises and thunders at her. He is wounded, and when he is wounded, invective always comes to his aid.*)

MILTON   Go then child, go to London, and starve in the streets, go and sell yourself in Covent Garden to the first poxed Sir Nobody who offers you the price of a mouldy loaf, go and join the gaggle of ragged whores at the playhouse back door, longing for a sight or touch of the scabbed King's handkerchief! You know nothing, you fear nothing, you love nothing, you respect nothing. I am not your father, you are not my child, leave me, leave me in peace!

(MARY, *not really understanding, but petrified by this outburst, runs out of the garden in tears.* MILTON *sinks back into the chair, trembling.* ELIZABETH *has been watching from the cottage door, and now runs after* MARY.)

FIFTY-ONE *The small hill behind the Cottage garden. Exterior. Day.*

(MARY *runs up the hill, and reaches the top exhausted, where she throws herself to the ground and sobs bitterly. A few seconds later* ELIZABETH *arrives, slowing to a walk.*)

ELIZABETH   Mary.

MARY   Go away, go away, go away!

(*After a second of indecision,* ELIZABETH *sits by her.*)

ELIZABETH   Mary, we must speak.

MARY   No, no!

ELIZABETH   You will get nothing from your father by trying to force him. Kings and Bishops and Generals could not move him.

MARY   I am his daughter!

ELIZABETH   And I am your mother, if only in law. I would like to help you.

MARY   My mother is dead, in her grave these thirteen years. If she were here, she would look after me. She wouldn't let him hate me like this!

ELIZABETH   He doesn't hate you.

MARY   He does, he does!

(MARY *coughs and blubbers tears and snot.* ELIZABETH *offers her a handkerchief. After a second,* MARY *takes it.*)

ELIZABETH   Would you like to know why I married him?

MARY   To get our money, that's why.

ELIZABETH   No, there isn't any money, to speak of . . . I was brought up in Cheshire, a long way from here, in a small town, in a good family of honest people.

MARY   I wasn't!

ELIZABETH   Hear me out Mary. By the time I was your age, I knew that Nantwich was not enough for me. My father forced no marriages upon me, but the men who asked for me filled me with despair. They talked of crops and seasons and fat cows. I am not an educated woman Mary, not much more so than you—but I knew *that* life wasn't mine, that there were things of the spirit in me, that would speak . . . But the world is not made for women. In God's order we come second.

MARY   I don't come second to anyone!

ELIZABETH   Then your likely future is what mine was: twenty-three, unmarried, the spinster at home with father . . . (*The two women exchange a look.*) But I had an uncle in London—Doctor Paget, your father's friend. He told me of Mr Milton, of his loneliness. And of course I knew his name, as the man who had written against the King. He asked me if I could care for an old blind scholar, with three difficult daughters, none too tolerant as to his temper. And I saw my chance. Not what some women would choose, perhaps, but for me, freedom. I have since come to love him, which is fortunate. My widowhood is likely to be long, if God spares me. But to have lived with such a man, even if God judges that the time must be short, is worth something.

MARY   What is it to do with me?

ELIZABETH   Only to tell you that I have been in your shoes. I have wanted to get away so much that I was almost prepared to destroy myself, as you will, if you leave here with no money.

MARY   Betty, you don't understand! Who is he? I don't know him, he isn't my father.

ELIZABETH   You are your father's daughter as well as your mother's child.

MARY   For eleven years, after my mother died, we hardly saw him. He was always on Government business, or locked in his study, or receiving great men from abroad, come to shower him with praises. We were more like the household dogs, slinking from room to room, than his children. We had to find our own way to live, with the servants, and with Granny Powell as our friend. But when you came, and Granny Powell was taken away, and we had to live daily with this blind stranger in our house, had to be meek and respectful, had to read to him in languages we didn't understand, had to listen to him haranguing us about the weakness and sinfulness of womankind, and wishing in his heart we were sons. He rejected us for eleven years. So now I reject him! I do!

ELIZABETH   Mary, he is an old man now, and the young are merciless. They can afford to be, with their energy undimmed, and everything before, not behind. Come back with me now, make your peace with him.

MARY   Submit and crawl before him!

ELIZABETH   If necessary, yes. And I promise you I shall speak with him, and make it possible for you to leave this house in an honourable manner.

MARY   Do you promise that?

ELIZABETH   Yes, I promise. I'm not your enemy. I'm almost young enough to be your friend.

(*In long shot, they both rise and begin to walk down to the cottage.*)

FIFTY-TWO   *The cottage study. Interior. Night.*

(MILTON *and* ELIZABETH *together, by candlelight. She has been reading to him, but at the moment he is abstracted in thought.*)

MILTON   Where's Mary?

ELIZABETH   I have sent her to bed. I thought it best.

MILTON   And Deborah, where is she? She always kisses me goodnight.

ELIZABETH   She was very upset, and went to bed even before her sister.

MILTON   Will she leave me too?

ELIZABETH   No. It disturbs her to see Mary in tears and you so drawn. She is a child with much love to give.

MILTON   And my misshapen Nan, was she disturbed too?

ELIZABETH   She applied herself to her embroidery.

MILTON   Bring her to me now. Let me touch her.

ELIZABETH   No. She is asleep.

MILTON   In the same house, but in darkness. All in our separate rooms.

ELIZABETH   I spoke to Mary this afternoon.

MILTON   She has said things to me no father should hear.

ELIZABETH   She wants your love. If you will not give it, she will hurt you.

MILTON   I, not give it! All I ask is obedience, which is a father's right, and God's ordinance.

ELIZABETH   If only we were all granted our rights, husband, Christ could sound for judgement.

(*Sightlessly, he looks up at her.*)

MILTON   She is full of pride. By pride our first parents fell. By pride her mother made my home into a battleground. It is very strange to hear one Mary speak, and to see the other Mary so clearly in my mind's eye.

ELIZABETH   She honours her mother's memory.

MILTON   She never knew her. She was a toddling child when God took her from me.

ELIZABETH   She speaks as if she knew her.

MILTON   She dreams of an angelic mother who could do no wrong. The reality was far otherwise.

ELIZABETH   (*tentatively*)   Was it a marriage of love, husband?

MILTON   What does that mean, a marriage of love? . . . I had spent my life in continuous study, till I was thirty. I was preparing myself for the great work I was quite sure I would do in the world. Then I went to Italy for a year, to converse with poets and philosophers at that fountainhead of European wisdom. When I returned, I decided it was time I had a wife. I had to go to Oxford for my father, to collect some money Powell owed him, and I saw his daughter there: a sharp and lively girl of seventeen, brought up on a country farm with her brothers and sisters; and I, a scholar of thirty-four, living an austere life of study, devoted to the service of God. I had read greatly of love in the poets and philosophers, and I had felt its brutal power, hard as a fist in my own breast. But I was chaste, and had remained so, in spite of the many temptations of Italy, believing that only he whose life was without spot could hope to accomplish worthy things. I brought her back to London, and it was there that we both found out who we had married. It was not as the poets had described it. It was bitter and black and full of anguish. I soon discovered that we had nothing in common but the marriage bed. She wished to have the ordering of my house, which I denied her, and within a week we were sworn enemies. I saw there could never be any true companionship and lacking that, I was condemned to grind in the mill of an undelighted and servile copulation, and to be as truly lonely as ever I had been before I met her. After six weeks we spared each other. I gave her permission to revisit her mother at Oxford. While she was there, the war between King and Parliament began, and the Powells were Royalists, of course. I didn't see Mary again for three years.

ELIZABETH   How did she come back to you?

MILTON   I never expected to see her again. But the King lost the war, and whether out of genuine repentance, or because her family, knowing their estates were forfeit to Parliament, decided they had better keep friendly with Mr Milton after all, I found her one day on her knees before me.

ELIZABETH   And you forgave her?

MILTON   She returned; and we lived as man and wife for seven years, she bearing me three daughters, and my son, who died. We made a way of living, and we cared for each other, as people do who live and bear children together. But if there is marriage in Heaven, this was not it. Something had happened to Mary while she was away. The life had gone

out of her. And I had reached for one of life's prizes, and failed to hold it.

ELIZABETH   As you speak of her, I see our Mary.

MILTON   There is a music of the spheres,[7] Betty, which only the pure in heart can hear. It is the sound of God's harmony, such music as angels make upon the battlements of Heaven. I wanted it on earth. I tried to bring it down, out of the empyrean, to sound in men's ears today, on this ground of England. I thought we would build the Holy City here, and I looked, and it was Babel. That was where Paradise was truly lost, in the hearts of men who would not reach for that which is within every man's grasp. So I am left here with my ruins. My wife, who escaped into death, my country, which preferred slavery, my children, who cannot love me, my blindness.

(After a short pause, ELIZABETH rises and begins to blow out all the candles. The fire is almost dead, so it is almost full darkness.)

MILTON   What are you doing?

ELIZABETH   Snuffing the candles.

MILTON   Why?

ELIZABETH   There. Now I am in the dark too.

MILTON   Betty?

ELIZABETH   And to be darker still, my eyes are closed, tight.

(She holds out her hand.)

ELIZABETH   Can you feel my hand?

MILTON   Yes. Yes, I have it.

ELIZABETH   Tell me, dear husband, since we are both in darkness, if Paradise is truly lost in the world, where shall we find it again?

MILTON   In our own hearts, where Orpheus is not torn, where the savage women stand spellbound by his song, and the circling planets sing in consort with all the voices of men . . . Till it

7 **Music of the spheres,** Thought to be produced by the rotation of heavenly bodies, the highest of which was called the empyrean.

comes on earth, with a sound of angel
trumpets, and the building of the city of
light, Paradise is within ourselves, to find
or be lost as each one shall choose.

ELIZABETH Amen.

MILTON Amen.

*(They sit still in the dark, holding
hands.)*

FIFTY-THREE *The cottage. Milton's bedroom. Interior. First dawn.*

*(MILTON is in bed, and ELIZABETH is just
tidying it. Candles are lighted, but the
first light of dawn is just beginning
through the window.)*

MILTON Betty, have we watched till dawn?

ELIZABETH Almost. You must rest now.

MILTON I shall sell the most part of my
library, Betty.

ELIZABETH Sell your books?

MILTON You may keep any you value, but
my heirs have no use for them, and books
are an indulgence for a blind man. With
that money, I shall send out Mary and
Nan to learn the craft of lacemaking, so
that they may live when I am gone. For
what money I have shall go to you. Will
it serve, Betty? Or will they run from me
still like a monster?

ELIZABETH Yes husband. I think it will
serve.

*(He settles down in the bed. She goes to
the window, and opens it a little, then
goes downstairs.)*

FIFTY-FOUR *The cottage. Downstairs passage and study. Interior. Dawn.*

*(She comes downstairs, opens a window
in the study, then opens the door to the
garden.*

FIFTY-FIVE *Cottage garden. Exterior.
Dawn.*

*(She stands under the porch. There is
birdsong, and the light is increasing
rapidly.)*

MILTON *(from upstairs)* Betty! Betty!

(She hurries in and up the stairs.)

FIFTY-SIX *Cottage. Milton's bedroom. Interior. Dawn.*

(MILTON is sitting up in bed.)

MILTON Get pen and ink, and the manuscript. We ended, "To bring forth fruits,
joy and eternal bliss."

(She hurries to the desk.)

ELIZABETH Yes, the speech of the Archangel Michael.

MILTON Continue from there:
"He ended, and thus Adam last replied:
How soon hath thy prediction, seer blest,
Measured this transient world, the Race
of time,
Till time stand fixed: beyond is all abyss,
Eternity, whose end no eye can reach,
Greatly instructed, I shall hence depart.
Greatly in peace of thought, and have my
fill
Of Knowledge, what this vessel can con-
tain;
Beyond which was my folly to aspire.
Henceforth I learn that to obey is best,
And love with fear the only God, to walk
As in his presence, ever to observe
His providence, and on him sole depend.
Merciful over all his works, with good
Still overcoming evil, and by small
Accomplishing great things, by things
deemed weak
Subverting worldly strong, and worldly
wise
By simply meek: that suffering for
Truth's sake
Is fortitude to highest victory,
And to the faithful Death the Gate of
Life;
Taught this by his example whom I now
Acknowledge my Redeemer ever blest."

*(He continues dictating, but sound
fades, and we hear no more)*

She Stoops to Conquer

Oliver Goldsmith

edited by Sylvan Barnet, Morton Berman, and William Burto

Introductory Comments

William W. Appleton   *Columbia University*

In Oliver Goldsmith's novel *The Vicar of Wakefield* (1766), a shabby actor touring the countryside complains that audiences go to the theatre "only to be amused." Quite obviously Goldsmith shared these audiences' feelings, and it is his antipathy to the tearful comedy then fashionable in London that perhaps best explains why he began his career as a dramatist only after he had made a name for himself as a poet, novelist, and essayist.

His views on comedy are best expressed in his short *Essay on the Theatre; or, A Comparison between Laughing and Sentimental Comedy* (1772). Reiterating his earlier observation that "amusement is the great object of the theatre," he wittily defined the present state of comedy. "It is only sufficient to raise the characters a little; to deck out the hero with a riband, or to give the heroine a title; then to put an insipid dialogue, without character or humor, into their mouths, give them mighty good hearts, very fine clothes, furnish a new set of scenes, make a pathetic scene or two, with a sprinkling of tender melancholy conversation through the whole, and there is no doubt but all the ladies will cry and all the gentlemen applaud." It was an age that wept copiously, and though Goldsmith had no aversion to such displays, in the theatre, he argued, tears belonged to the muse of tragedy.

In his first play, *The Good Natured Man* (1768), he attempted to bring back laughter to the playhouse. He pleaded for a return to nature and humor, "in whatever walk of life" they were to be found. As a result, he introduced into his comedy a scene in which his good-hearted but recklessly generous hero is arrested for debt by two oafish bailiffs. To avoid embarrassing him when a young lady unexpectedly arrives, the bailiffs boorishly attempt to pass themselves off as gentlemen. The scene seems wholly innocuous to us, but many eighteenth-century playgoers dismissed it as "low."

Goldsmith's play was not a conspicuous success, but in his subsequent comedy, *She Stoops to Conquer*, he showed himself undeterred and still in pursuit of nature and humor. Breaking with tradition, he set his scene not in London, the usual setting for comedy, but in the countryside. It was a milieu that was congenial to him and one that offered him a wide comic scope. There the hunting-fishing-shooting gentry still stuck to their traditional way of life. The squires fussed over their dogs and horses, snored through the parson's sermons, and whiled away the evenings with cribbage and claret. Their wives and daughters had their household duties and responsibilities, mending the linen and seeing to the larder, but often they were bored to distraction. During race week they might occasionally attend a neighborhood ball, a solitary fiddler scraping away while they whirled through a set of old-fashioned country dances. Otherwise there were few diversions to break the dull routine, and understandably they hungered for the society, the fashions, and the gossip of London.

In changing his setting, Goldsmith flung open the doors of comedy. He took the spectators out of the stuffy drawing rooms of the city and transported them into the invigorating air of the country. In doing so he no doubt had in mind the example of his comic predecessor, George Farquhar. Some seventy years earlier he too had ventilated English comedy by removing it from London to Shrewsbury and Lichfield. Goldsmith's debts to his predecessor, both in tone and substance, are substantial. Following Farquhar's practice, in *She Stoops to Conquer* he made use of a brace of heroes, one comic and one sentimental. Miss Hardcastle, Goldsmith's heroine, specifically compares herself to Cherry, the innkeeper's daughter in Farquhar's *The Beaux' Stratagem* (1707), and Goldsmith even flirted with the notion of entitling his own play *The Belle's Stratagem.*

But while Goldsmith was determined to bring back laughter to the theatre, his experience with *The Good Natured Man* had made him wary, and he was well aware that he was catering to a peculiar audience. Sanctimonious in public, they were uninhibited in private, and Goldsmith's brilliant portrait of the two-faced Young Marlow is a comic indictment of the hypocrisies of the age. Goldsmith was careful, however, to steer his course carefully. Like Kate Hardcastle he stooped—but not too much. He gives us only one scene, regrettably, of Tony Lumpkin and his cronies at The Three Pigeons. He does not even allow us a glimpse of Bet Bouncer, Tony's girlfriend, with her "two eyes as black as sloes, and cheeks as broad and red as a pulpit cushion." Even so, despite his compromises, his play was novel enough to cause a flutter of alarm at Covent Garden Theatre. The three principal roles—Miss Hardcastle, Tony Lumpkin, and Young Marlow—were declined by leading members of the company. Rehearsals were lackluster, and the manager openly apprehensive of failure. But in the best tradition of the theatre, the play had a triumphant success in spite of these initial difficulties, and if the actors who turned down the leading roles proved themselves embarrassingly short-sighted, subsequent generations of actors have amply atoned for them. Goldsmith's comedy, even in its most minor roles, is ideally suited to the rich character acting in which the English then and now have always excelled.

Audiences have never permitted the play to disappear from the standard repertory, and its lasting appeal requires little explanation. The action is somewhat complex but manipulated with extraordinary dexterity, and the plot moves with a speed that nears the pace of farce. The basic comic confusion—Young Marlow's mistaken assumption that Mr. Hardcastle's house is an inn—also suggests the world of farce, but curiously enough this incident has its basis in an actual event from Goldsmith's own youth.

Like his friend Dr. Johnson, Goldsmith had a healthy respect for the common reader. As a dramatist he had a similar respect for the average playgoer. He wrote for the average man, but certainly he was a far-from-average writer. His style has a deceptive simplicity. He avoids literary artifice and makes use of the most ordinary language. But in Tony Lumpkin he created one of nature's poets. He speaks as if language had just been invented. With his extraordinary zest for living, his good heart, and freshness of vision, he resembles Goldsmith himself, and it is he, above all, who keeps the play radiantly alive.

Despite the success of *She Stoops to Conquer,* Goldsmith had no imitators. It is not hard to understand why. Only a genius can manipulate the normal and the every day as effectively as he did. His career as a dramatist was unfortunately all too short. Barely a year after the production of *She Stoops to Conquer,* he died, still in his early forties. He left us only two comedies and a short farce of little consequence, but few would quarrel with the opinion that his death was a major loss to English comedy.

Oliver Goldsmith (1730?–1774), son of an Irish clergyman, was educated at Trinity College, Dublin. Later he studied medicine and traveled through Europe on foot. Settling in London in 1756, he briefly practiced medicine then turned to literature. He proved himself astonishingly versatile, equally gifted as an essayist, novelist, poet, and dramatist. Among his most celebrated works are *The Citizen of the World* (1762), *The Vicar of Wakefield* (1766), *The Deserted Village* (1770), and *She Stoops to Conquer* (1773). He was an original member of Dr. Johnson's Club. Despite Goldsmith's sometimes absurd behavior, Dr. Johnson both respected and admired him.

She Stoops to Conquer   *Oliver Goldsmith*

SIR CHARLES MARLOW

YOUNG MARLOW   *his son*

HARDCASTLE

HASTINGS

TONY LUMPKIN

DIGGORY

MRS. HARDCASTLE

MISS HARDCASTLE

MISS NEVILLE

MAID

LANDLORD, SERVANTS, *etc.*

Prologue *By David Garrick, Esq.*

Enter MR. WOODWARD,[1] *dressed in black, and holding a handkerchief to his eyes.*

Excuse me, sirs, I pray—I can't yet
  speak—
I'm crying now—and have been all the
  week!
" 'Tis not alone this mourning suit," good
  masters;
"I've that within"[2]—for which there are
  no plasters!
Pray would you know the reason why I'm
  crying?
The Comic Muse, long sick, is now
  a-dying!
And if she goes, my tears will never stop;
  For as a player, I can't squeeze out one
  drop:
I am undone, that's all—shall lose my
  bread—
  I'd rather, but that's nothing—lose my
  head.
When the sweet maid is laid upon the
  bier,
  Shuter and I shall be chief mourners
  here.
To her a mawkish drab of spurious breed,
Who deal in sentimentals will succeed!
Poor Ned and I are dead to all intents;
  We can as soon speak Greek as senti-
  ments.
Both nervous grown, to keep our spirits
  up,
  We now and then take down a hearty
  cup.
What shall we do?—If Comedy forsake
  us!
  They'll turn us out, and no one else will
  take us.

But, why can't I be moral?—Let me try—
My heart thus pressing—fixed my face
  and eye—
With a sententious look, that nothing
  means
(Faces are blocks, in sentimental scenes),
Thus I begin—"All is not gold that glit-
  ters,
  Pleasure seems sweet, but proves a glass
  of bitters.
When ign'rance enters, folly is at hand;
  Learning is better far than house and
  land.
Let not your virtue trip, who trips may
  stumble,
  And virtue is not virtue, if she tumble."
I give it up—morals won't do for me;
  To make you laugh, I must play tragedy.
One hope remains—hearing the maid was
  ill,
  A doctor comes this night to show his
  skill.
To cheer her heart, and give your muscles
  motion,
  He in five draughts prepared, presents a
  potion:
A kind of magic charm—for be assured,
  If you will swallow it, the maid is cured.
But desp'rate the doctor, and her case is,
  If you reject the dose, and make wry
  faces!
This truth he boasts, will boast it while
  he lives,
  No pois'nous drugs are mixed in what
  he gives.
Should he succeed, you'll give him his
  degree;
  If not, within he will receive no fee!
The college, you, must his pretensions
  back,
  Pronounce him regular, or dub him
  quack.

1 A popular London actor; Edward "Ned" Shuter, mentioned in the prologue, was another popular actor, of low comedy. 2 Paraphrase of *Hamlet,* I. ii. 77ff.

Act One

SCENE ONE *A chamber in an old-fashioned house.*

Enter MRS. HARDCASTLE *and* MR. HARDCASTLE.

MRS. HARDCASTLE I vow, Mr. Hardcastle, you're very particular. Is there a creature in the whole country, but ourselves, that does not take a trip to town now and then, to rub off the rust a little? There's the two Miss Hoggs, and our neighbor, Mrs. Grigsby, go to take a month's polishing every winter.

HARDCASTLE Aye, and bring back vanity and affectation to last them the whole year. I wonder why London cannot keep its own fools at home. In my time, the follies of the town crept slowly among us, but now they travel faster than a stagecoach. Its fopperies come down, not only as inside passengers, but in the very basket.[3]

MRS. HARDCASTLE Aye, *your* times were fine times, indeed; you have been telling us of *them* for many a long year. Here we live in an old rumbling mansion, that looks for all the world like an inn, but that we never see company. Our best visitors are old Mrs. Oddfish, the curate's wife, and little Cripplegate, the lame dancing master: and all our entertainment your old stories of Prince Eugene[4] and the Duke of Marlborough. I hate such old-fashioned trumpery.

HARDCASTLE And I love it. I love everything that's old: old friends, old times, old manners, old books, old wine; and, I believe, Dorothy (*taking her hand*), you'll own I have been pretty fond of an old wife.

MRS. HARDCASTLE Lord, Mr. Hardcastle, you're forever at your Dorothy's and your old wife's. You may be a Darby, but I'll be no Joan,[5] I promise you. I'm not so old as you'd make me, by more than one good year. Add twenty to twenty, and make money of that.

HARDCASTLE Let me see; twenty added to twenty makes just fifty and seven.

MRS. HARDCASTLE It's false, Mr. Hardcastle: I was but twenty when I was brought to bed of Tony, that I had by Mr. Lumpkin, my first husband; and he's not come to years of discretion yet.

HARDCASTLE Nor ever will, I dare answer for him. Aye, you have taught *him* finely!

MRS. HARDCASTLE No matter. Tony Lumpkin has a good fortune. My son is not to live by his learning. I don't think a boy wants much learning to spend fifteen hundred a year.

HARDCASTLE Learning, quotha! A mere composition of tricks and mischief!

MRS. HARDCASTLE Humor, my dear; nothing but humor. Come, Mr. Hardcastle, you must allow the boy a little humor.

HARDCASTLE I'd sooner allow him a horsepond! If burning the footmen's shoes, frightening the maids, and worrying the kittens be humor, he has it. It was but yesterday he fastened my wig to the back of my chair, and when I went to make a bow, I popped my bald head in Mrs. Frizzle's face!

MRS. HARDCASTLE And am I to blame? The poor boy was always too sickly to do any good. A school would be his death. When he comes to be a little stronger, who knows what a year or two's Latin may do for him?

HARDCASTLE Latin for him! A cat and fiddle! No, no, the alehouse and the stable are the only schools he'll ever go to.

MRS. HARDCASTLE Well, we must not snub the poor boy now, for I believe we shan't have him long among us. Anybody that looks in his face may see he's consumptive.

HARDCASTLE Aye, if growing too fat be one of the symptoms.

3 An outside compartment, usually for luggage, at the rear of a stagecoach. 4 Marlborough's ally at the Battle of Blenheim (1704).

5 In the eighteenth century, stock names for a happy couple.

MRS. HARDCASTLE   He coughs sometimes.

HARDCASTLE   Yes, when his liquor goes the wrong way.

MRS. HARDCASTLE   I'm actually afraid of his lungs.

HARDCASTLE   And truly, so am I; for he sometimes whoops like a speaking trumpet— (TONY *hallooing behind the scenes*) O, there he goes—a very consumptive figure, truly!

Enter TONY, *crossing the stage.*

MRS. HARDCASTLE   Tony, where are going, my charmer? Won't you give papa and I a little of your company, lovee?

TONY   I'm in haste, mother; I cannot stay.

MRS. HARDCASTLE   You shan't venture out this raw evening, my dear; you look most shockingly.

TONY   I can't stay, I tell you. The Three Pigeons expects me down every moment. There's some fun going forward.

HARDCASTLE   Aye; the alehouse, the old place: I thought so.

MRS. HARDCASTLE   A low, paltry set of fellows.

TONY   Not so low, neither. There's Dick Muggins, the exciseman; Jack Slang the horse doctor; Little Aminadab, that grinds the music box; and Tom Twist, that spins the pewter platter.

MRS. HARDCASTLE   Pray, my dear, disappoint them for one night at least.

TONY   As for disappointing *them,* I should not so much mind; but I can't abide to disappoint *myself.*

MRS. HARDCASTLE   (*detaining him*). You shan't go.

TONY   I will, I tell you.

MRS. HARDCASTLE   I say you shan't.

TONY   We'll see which is strongest, you or I.

Exit, hauling her out.

HARDCASTLE   *solus.*[6]

HARDCASTLE   Aye, there goes a pair that only spoil each other. But is not the whole age in a combination to drive sense and discretion out of doors? There's my pretty darling Kate; the fashions of the times have almost infected her too. By living a year or two in town, she is as fond of gauze and French frippery as the best of them.

Enter MISS HARDCASTLE.

HARDCASTLE   Blessings on my pretty innocence! Dressed out as usual, my Kate. Goodness! What a quantity of superfluous silk hast thou got about thee, girl! I could never teach the fools of this age that the indigent world could be clothed out of the trimmings of the vain.

MISS HARDCASTLE   You know our agreement, sir. You allow me the morning to receive and pay visits, and to dress in my own manner; and in the evening I put on my housewife's dress to please you.

HARDCASTLE   Well, remember, I insist on the terms of our agreement; and, by the bye, I believe I shall have occasion to try your obedience this very evening.

MISS HARDCASTLE   I protest, sir, I don't comprehend your meaning.

HARDCASTLE   Then, to be plain with you, Kate, I expect the young gentleman I have chosen to be your husband from town this very day. I have his father's letter, in which he informs me his son is set out, and that he intends to follow himself shortly after.

MISS HARDCASTLE   Indeed! I wish I had known something of this before. Bless me, how shall I behave? It's a thousand to one I shan't like him; our meeting will be so formal, and so like a thing of business, that I shall find no room for friendship or esteem.

HARDCASTLE   Depend upon it, child, I'll never control your choice; but Mr. Marlow, whom I have pitched upon, is the son of my old friend, Sir Charles Marlow, of whom you have heard me talk so often. The young gentleman has been bred a scholar, and is designed for an employment in the service of his country. I am told he's a man of an excellent understanding.

6 Alone.

MISS HARDCASTLE   Is he?

HARDCASTLE   Very generous.

MISS HARDCASTLE   I believe I shall like him.

HARDCASTLE   Young and brave.

MISS HARDCASTLE   I'm sure I shall like him.

HARDCASTLE   And very handsome.

MISS HARDCASTLE   My dear papa, say no more (*kissing his hand*). He's mine, I'll have him!

HARDCASTLE   And, to crown all, Kate, he's one of the most bashful and reserved young fellows in all the world.

MISS HARDCASTLE   Eh! you have frozen me to death again. That word "reserved" has undone all the rest of his accomplishments. A reserved lover, it is said, always makes a suspicious husband.

HARDCASTLE   On the contrary, modesty seldom resides in a breast that is not enriched with nobler virtues. It was the very feature in his character that first struck me.

MISS HARDCASTLE   He must have more striking features to catch me, I promise you. However, if he be so young, so handsome, and so everything as you mention, I believe he'll do still. I think I'll have him.

HARDCASTLE   Aye, Kate, but there is still an obstacle. It is more than an even wager, he may not have *you*.

MISS HARDCASTLE   My dear papa, why will you mortify one so? Well, if he refuses, instead of breaking my heart at his indifference, I'll only break my glass for its flattery, set my cap to some newer fashion, and look out for some less difficult admirer.

HARDCASTLE   Bravely resolved! In the meantime I'll go prepare the servants for his reception; as we seldom see company, they want as much training as a company of recruits the first day's muster.   *Exit.*

MISS HARDCASTLE (*sola*).   Lud, this news of papa's puts me all in a flutter. Young, handsome; these he put last; but I put them foremost. Sensible, good-natured; I like all that. But then reserved, and sheepish; that much against him. Yet can't he be cured of his timidity by being taught to be proud of his wife? Yes, and can't I—but I vow I'm disposing of the husband before I have secured the lover.

Enter MISS NEVILLE.

MISS HARDCASTLE   I'm glad you're come, Neville, my dear. Tell me, Constance, how do I look this evening? Is there anything whimsical about me? Is it one of my well-looking days, child? Am I in face today?

MISS NEVILLE   Perfectly, my dear. Yet, now I look again—bless me!—sure, no accident has happened among the canary birds or the goldfishes? Has your brother or the cat been meddling? Or has the last novel been too moving?

MISS HARDCASTLE   No; nothing of all this. I have been threatened—I can scarce get it out—I have been threatened with a lover.

MISS NEVILLE   And his name?

MISS HARDCASTLE   Is Marlow.

MISS NEVILLE   Indeed!

MISS HARDCASTLE   The son of Sir Charles Marlow.

MISS NEVILLE   As I live, the most intimate friend of Mr. Hastings, *my* admirer. They are never asunder. I believe you must have seen him when we lived in town.

MISS HARDCASTLE   Never.

MISS NEVILLE   He's a very singular character, I assure you. Among women of reputation and virtue, he is the modestest man alive; but his acquaintance give him a very different character among creatures of another stamp: you understand me.

MISS HARDCASTLE   An odd character, indeed. I shall never be able to manage him. What shall I do? Pshaw, think no more of him, but trust to occurrences for success. But how goes on your own affair, my dear? Has my mother been courting you for my brother Tony as usual?

MISS NEVILLE   I have just come from one of our agreeable tête-à-têtes. She has been saying a hundred tender things, and setting off her pretty monster as the very pink of perfection.

MISS HARDCASTLE And her partiality is such that she actually thinks him so. A fortune like yours is no small temptation. Besides, as she has the sole management of it, I'm not surprised to see her unwilling to let it go out of the family.

MISS NEVILLE A fortune like mine, which chiefly consists in jewels, is no such mighty temptation. But at any rate, if my dear Hastings be but constant, I make no doubt to be too hard for her at last. However, I let her suppose that I am in love with her son; and she never once dreams that my affections are fixed upon another.

MISS HARDCASTLE My good brother holds out stoutly. I could almost love him for hating you so.

MISS NEVILLE It is a good-natured creature at bottom, and I'm sure would wish to see me married to anybody but himself. But my aunt's bell rings for our afternoon's walk round the improvements. *Allons.* Courage is necessary, as our affairs are critical.

MISS HARDCASTLE "Would it were bed-time and all were well."[7]

Exeunt.

SCENE II *An alehouse room*

Several shabby fellows with punch and tobacco. TONY *at the head of the table, a little higher than the rest, a mallet in his hand.*

OMNES Hurrea! hurrea! hurrea! bravo!

FIRST FELLOW Now, gentlemen, silence for a song. The squire is going to knock himself down[8] for a song.

OMNES Aye, a song, a song.

TONY Then I'll sing you, gentlemen, a song I made upon this alehouse, the Three Pigeons.

Song

Let schoolmasters puzzle their brain

With grammar, and nonsense, and learning;
Good liquor, I stoutly maintain,
 Gives genius a better discerning.
Let them brag of their heathenish gods,
 Their Lethes, their Styxes, and Stygians;
Their Quis, and their Quaes, and their Quods,[9]
 They're all but a parcel of pigeons.
  Toroddle, toroddle, toroll!

When Methodist preachers come down,
 A-preaching that drinking is sinful,
I'll wager the rascals a crown,
 They always preach best with a skinful.
But when you come down with your pence,
 For a slice of their scurvy religion,
I'll leave it to all men of sense,
 But you, my good friend, are the pigeon.
  Toroddle, toroddle, toroll!

Then come, put the jorum[10] about,
 And let us be merry and clever,
Our hearts and our liquors are stout,
 Here's the Three Jolly Pigeons for ever.
Let some cry up woodcock or hare,
 Your bustards, your ducks, and your widgeons;
But of all the birds in the air,
 Here's a health to the Three Jolly Pigeons.
  Toroddle, toroddle, toroll!

OMNES Bravo, bravo!

FIRST FELLOW The squire has got spunk in him.

SECOND FELLOW I loves to hear him sing, bekeays he never gives us nothing that's *low.*

THIRD FELLOW O damn anything that's *low,* I cannot bear it.

FOURTH FELLOW The genteel thing is the genteel thing at any time; if so be that a

---

7 Cf. Falstaff in *1 Henry IV*, V. i. 125. 8 Tony, as chairman, is calling upon himself for a song.

9 Latin relative pronouns. 10 Drinking bowl.

gentleman bees in a concatenation accordingly.

THIRD FELLOW   I like the maxum of it, Master Muggins. What, though I am obligated to dance a bear, a man may be a gentleman for all that. May this be my poison if my bear ever dances but to the very genteelest of tunes: "Water Parted," or the minuet in *Ariadne.*

SECOND FELLOW   What a pity it is the squire is not come to his own. It would be well for all the publicans within ten miles round of him.

TONY   Ecod, and so it would, Master Slang. I'd then show what it was to keep choice of company.

SECOND FELLOW   Oh, he takes after his own father for that. To be sure, old squire Lumpkin was the finest gentleman I ever set my eyes on. For winding the straight horn, or beating a thicket for a hare, or a wench, he never had his fellow. It was a saying in the place, that he kept the best horses, dogs, and girls, in the whole county.

TONY   Ecod, and when I'm of age I'll be no bastard, I promise you. I have been thinking of Bet Bouncer and the miller's gray mare to begin with. But come, my boys, drink about and be merry, for you pay no reckoning. Well, Stingo, what's the matter?

Enter LANDLORD.

LANDLORD   There be two gentlemen in a post chaise at the door. They have lost their way upo' the forest; and they are talking something about Mr. Hardcastle.

TONY   As sure as can be, one of them must be the gentleman that's coming down to court my sister. Do they seem to be Londoners?

LANDLORD   I believe they may. They look woundily[11] like Frenchmen.

TONY   Then desire them to step this way, and I'll set them right in a twinkling. (*Exit* LANDLORD.) Gentlemen, as they mayn't be good enough company for you,

step down for a moment, and I'll be with you in the squeezing of a lemon.
  Exeunt Mob.

TONY   (*solus*)   Father-in-law has been calling me whelp and hound this half year. Now, if I pleased, I could be so revenged upon the old grumbletonian. But then I'm afraid—afraid of what? I shall soon be worth fifteen hundred a year, and let him frighten me out of *that* if he can!

Enter LANDLORD, *conducting* MARLOW *and* HASTINGS.

MARLOW   What a tedious, uncomfortable day have we had of it! We were told it was but forty miles across the country, and we have come above threescore!

HASTINGS   And all, Marlow, from that unaccountable reserve of yours that would not let us enquire more frequently on the way.

MARLOW   I own, Hastings, I am unwilling to lay myself under an obligation to everyone I meet, and often stand the chance of an unmannerly answer.

HASTINGS   At present, however, we are not likely to receive any answer.

TONY   No offense, gentlemen. But I'm told you have been enquiring for one Mr. Hardcastle in these parts. Do you know what part of the country you are in?

HASTINGS   Not in the least, sir, but should thank you for information.

TONY   Nor the way you came?

HASTINGS   No, sir; but if you can inform us——

TONY   Why, gentlemen, if you know neither the road you are going, nor where you are, nor the road you came, the first thing I have to inform you is, that—you have lost your way.

MARLOW   We wanted no ghost to tell us that.[12]

TONY   Pray, gentlemen, may I be so bold as to ask the place from whence you came?

MARLOW   That's not necessary towards directing us where we are to go.

11 Extremely.

12 Cf. Horatio in *Hamlet*, I. v. 125.

TONY No offense; but question for question is all fair, you know. Pray, gentlemen, is not this same Hardcastle a cross-grained, old-fashioned, whimsical fellow with an ugly face, a daughter, and a pretty son?

HASTINGS We have not seen the gentleman; but he has the family you mention.

TONY The daughter, a tall, trapesing, trolloping, talkative maypole—the son, a pretty, well-bred, agreeable youth, that everybody is fond of?

MARLOW Our information differs in this. The daughter is said to be well-bred, and beautiful; the son, an awkward booby, reared up and spoiled at his mother's apron string.

TONY He-he-hem!—Then, gentlemen, all I have to tell you is, that you won't reach Mr. Hardcastle's house this night, I believe.

HASTINGS Unfortunate!

TONY It's a damned long, dark, boggy, dirty, dangerous way. Stingo, tell the gentlemen the way to Mr. Hardcastle's. (*Winking upon the* LANDLORD.) Mr. Hardcastle's of Quagmire Marsh, you understand me.

LANDLORD Master Hardcastle's! Lack-a-daisy, my masters, you're come a deadly deal wrong! When you came to the bottom of the hill, you should have crossed down Squash Lane.

MARLOW Cross down Squash Lane!

LANDLORD Then you were to keep straight forward, until you came to four roads.

MARLOW Come to where four roads meet!

TONY Aye, but you must be sure to take only one of them.

MARLOW O, sir, you're facetious!

TONY Then, keeping to the right, you are to go sideways till you come upon Crack-skull Common: there you must look sharp for the track of the wheel, and go forward, till you come to Farmer Murrain's barn. Coming to the farmer's barn, you are to turn to the right, and then to the left, and then to the right about again, till you find out the old mill——

MARLOW Zounds, man! We could as soon find out the longitude!

HASTINGS What's to be done, Marlow?

MARLOW This house promises but a poor reception; though perhaps the landlord can accommodate us.

LANDLORD Alack, master, we have but one spare bed in the whole house.

TONY And to my knowledge, that's taken up by three lodgers already. (*After a pause, in which the rest seem disconcerted.*) I have hit it. Don't you think, Stingo, our landlady could accommodate the gentlemen by the fireside, with—three chairs and a bolster?

HASTINGS I hate sleeping by the fireside.

MARLOW And I detest your three chairs and a bolster.

TONY You do, do you?—then let me see— what if you go on a mile further, to the Buck's Head; the old Buck's Head on the hill, one of the best inns in the whole country?

HASTINGS Oho! so we have escaped an adventure for this night, however.

LANDLORD (*apart to* TONY) Sure, you ben't sending them to your father's as an inn, be you?

TONY Mum, you fool, you. Let *them* find that out. (*To them.*) You have only to keep on straight forward, till you come to a large old house by the roadside. You'll see a pair of large horns over the door. That's the sign. Drive up the yard, and call stoutly about you.

HASTINGS Sir, we are obliged to you. The servants can't miss the way?

TONY No, no: but I tell you, though, the landlord is rich, and going to leave off business; so he wants to be thought a gentleman, saving your presence, he! he! he! He'll be for giving you his company, and, ecod, if you mind him, he'll persuade you that his mother was an alderman, and his aunt a justice of peace!

LANDLORD A troublesome old blade, to be sure; but 'a keeps as good wines and beds as any in the whole country.

MARLOW Well, if he supplies us with these, we shall want no further connec-

tion. We are to turn to the right, did you
say?

TONY No, no; straight forward. I'll just
step myself, and show you a piece of the
way. (*To the* LANDLORD.) Mum.

LANDLORD Ah, bless your heart for a
sweet, pleasant—damned mischievous son
of a whore.   *Exeunt.*

Act Two

An old-fashioned house.

(*Enter* HARDCASTLE, *followed by three or
four awkward* SERVANTS.)

HARDCASTLE Well, I hope you're perfect
in the table exercise I have been teaching you these three days. You all know
your posts and your places, and can show
that you have been used to good company,
without ever stirring from home.

OMNES Aye, aye.

HARDCASTLE When company comes, you
are not to pop out and stare, and then
run in again, like frightened rabbits in a
warren.

OMNES No, no.

HARDCASTLE You, Diggory, whom I have
taken from the barn, are to make a show
at the side table; and you, Roger, whom
I have advanced from the plow, are to
place yourself behind *my* chair. But you're
not to stand so, with your hands in your
pockets. Take your hands from your
pockets, Roger; and from your head, you
blockhead, you. See how Diggory carries
his hands. They're a little too stiff, indeed, but that's no great matter.

DIGGORY Aye, mind how I hold them. I
learned to hold my hands this way, when
I was upon drill for the militia. And so
being upon drill——

HARDCASTLE You must not be so talkative,
Diggory. You must be all attention to the
guests. You must hear us talk, and not
think of talking; you must see us drink,
and not think of drinking; you must see
us eat, and not think of eating.

DIGGORY By the laws, your worship, that's
perfectly unpossible. Whenever Diggory
sees yeating going forward, ecod, he's always wishing for a mouthful himself.

HARDCASTLE Blockhead! Is not a bellyful
in the kitchen as good as a bellyful in the
parlor? Stay your stomach with that reflection.

DIGGORY Ecod, I thank your worship, I'll
make a shift to stay my stomach with a
slice of cold beef in the pantry.

HARDCASTLE Diggory, you are too talkative. Then, if I happen to say a good
thing, or tell a good story at table, you
must not all burst out a-laughing, as if
you made part of the company.

DIGGORY Then, ecod, your worship must
not tell the story of old Grouse in the gun
room: I can't help laughing at that—he!
he! he!—for the soul of me! We have
laughed at that these twenty years—ha!
ha! ha!

HARDCASTLE Ha! ha! ha! The story is a
good one. Well, honest Diggory, you may
laugh at that—but still remember to be
attentive. Suppose one of the company
should call for a glass of wine, how will
you behave? A glass of wine, sir, if you
please. (*To* DIGGORY.) Eh, why don't you
move?

DIGGORY Ecod, your worship, I never have
courage till I see the eatables and drink-
ables brought upo' the table, and then
I'm as bauld as a lion.

HARDCASTLE What, will nobody move?

FIRST SERVANT I'm not to leave this pleace.

SECOND SERVANT I'm sure it's no pleace of
mine.

THIRD SERVANT Nor mine, for sartain.

DIGGORY Wauns, and I'm sure it canna be
mine.

HARDCASTLE You numskulls! and so
while, like your betters, you are quarrel-
ing for places, the guests must be starved.
O, you dunces! I find I must begin all
over again.—But don't I hear a coach
drive into the yard? To your posts, you
blockheads. I'll go in the meantime and
give my old friend's son a hearty reception at the gate.   *Exit* HARDCASTLE.

DIGGORY By the elevens, my pleace is gone quite out of my head.

ROGER I know that my pleace is to be everywhere!

FIRST SERVANT Where the devil is mine?

SECOND SERVANT My pleace is to be nowhere at all; and so I'ze go about my business!

Exeunt SERVANTS, *running about as if frighted, different ways.*

Enter SERVANT *with candles, showing in* MARLOW *and* HASTINGS.

SERVANT Welcome, gentlemen, very welcome! This way.

HASTINGS After the disappointments of the day, welcome once more, Charles, to the comforts of a clean room and a good fire. Upon my word, a very well-looking house; antique but creditable.

MARLOW The usual fate of a large mansion. Having first ruined the master by good housekeeping, it at last comes to levy contributions as an inn.

HASTINGS As you say, we passengers are to be taxed to pay for all these fineries. I have often seen a good sideboard, or a marble chimney piece, though not actually put in the bill, inflame a reckoning confoundedly.

MARLOW Travelers, George, must pay in all places. The only difference is, that in good inns you pay dearly for luxuries, in bad inns, you are fleeced and starved.

HASTINGS You have lived pretty much among them. In truth, I have been often surprised that you, who have seen so much of the world, with your natural good sense, and your many opportunities, could never yet acquire a requisite share of assurance.

MARLOW The Englishman's malady. But tell me, George, where could I have learned that assurance you talk of? My life has been chiefly spent in a college or an inn, in seclusion from that lovely part of the creation that chiefly teach men confidence. I don't know that I was ever familiarly acquainted with a single modest woman—except my mother. But among females of another class, you know——

HASTINGS Aye, among them you are impudent enough of all conscience!

MARLOW They are of *us,* you know.

HASTINGS But in the company of women of reputation I never saw such an idiot, such a trembler; you look for all the world as if you wanted an opportunity of stealing out of the room.

MARLOW Why, man, that's because I *do* want to steal out of the room. Faith, I have often formed a resolution to break the ice, and rattle away at any rate. But I don't know how, a single glance from a pair of fine eyes has totally overset my resolution. An impudent fellow may counterfeit modesty, but I'll be hanged if a modest man can ever counterfeit impudence.

HASTINGS If you could but say half the fine things to them, that I have heard you lavish upon the barmaid of an inn, or even a college bed-maker——

MARLOW Why, George, I can't say fine things to them. They freeze, they petrify me. They may talk of a comet, or a burning mountain, or some such bagatelle; but to me, a modest woman, dressed out in all her finery, is the most tremendous object of the whole creation.

HASTINGS Ha! ha! ha! At this rate, man, how can you ever expect to marry?

MARLOW Never; unless, as among kings and princes, my bride were to be courted by proxy. If, indeed, like an Eastern bridegroom, one were to be introduced to a wife he never saw before, it might be endured. But to go through all the terrors of a formal courtship, together with the episode of aunts, grandmothers, and cousins, and at last to blurt out the broad staring question of, Madam, will you marry me? No, no, that's a strain much above me, I assure you!

HASTINGS I pity you. But how do you intend behaving to the lady you are come down to visit at the request of your father?

MARLOW   As I behave to all other ladies. Bow very low; answer yes, or no, to all her demands. But for the rest, I don't think I shall venture to look in her face till I see my father's again.

HASTINGS   I'm surprised that one who is so warm a friend can be so cool a lover.

MARLOW   To be explicit, my dear Hastings, my chief inducement down was to be instrumental in forwarding your happiness, not my own. Miss Neville loves you; the family don't know you; as my friend you are sure of a reception; and let honor do the rest.

HASTINGS   My dear Marlow! But I'll suppress the emotion. Were I a wretch, meanly seeking to carry off a fortune, you should be the last man in the world I would apply to for assistance. But Miss Neville's person is all I ask, and that is mine, both from her deceased father's consent, and her own inclination.

MARLOW   Happy man! You have talents and art to captivate any woman. I'm doomed to adore the sex, and yet to converse with the only part of it I despise. This stammer in my address, and this awkward unprepossessing visage of mine, can never permit me to soar above the reach of a milliner's prentice, or one of the duchesses of Drury Lane.[13] Pshaw! this fellow here to interrupt us.

Enter HARDCASTLE.

HARDCASTLE   Gentlemen, once more you are heartily welcome. Which is Mr. Marlow? Sir, you're heartily welcome. It's not my way, you see, to receive my friends with my back to the fire. I like to give them a hearty reception in the old style at my gate. I like to see their horses and trunks taken care of.

MARLOW   (*aside*)   He has got our names from the servants already. (*To him.*) We approve your caution and hospitality, sir. (*To* HASTINGS.)   I have been thinking, George, of changing our traveling dresses

in the morning. I am grown confoundedly ashamed of mine.

HARDCASTLE   I beg, Mr. Marlow, you'll use no ceremony in this house.

HASTINGS   I fancy, [Charles], you're right: the first blow is half the battle. I intend opening the campaign with the white and gold.

HARDCASTLE   Mr. Marlow—Mr. Hastings —gentlemen—pray be under no constraint in this house. This is Liberty Hall, gentlemen. You may do just as you please here.

MARLOW   Yet, George, if we open the campaign too fiercely at first, we may want ammunition before it is over. I think to reserve the embroidery to secure a retreat.

HARDCASTLE   Your talking of a retreat, Mr. Marlow, puts me in mind of the Duke of Marlborough, when we went to besiege Denain. He first summoned the garrison——

MARLOW   Don't you think the *ventre d'or* waistcoat will do with the plain brown?

HARDCASTLE   He first summoned the garrison, which might consist of about five thousand men——

HASTINGS   I think not: brown and yellow mix but very poorly.

HARDCASTLE   I say, gentlemen, as I was telling you, he summoned the garrison, which might consist of about five thousand men——

MARLOW   The girls like finery.

HARDCASTLE   Which might consist of about five thousand men, well appointed with stores, ammunition, and other implements of war. "Now," says the Duke of Marlborough to George Brooks, that stood next to him—you must have heard of George Brooks—"I'll pawn my Dukedom," says he, "but I take that garrison without spilling a drop of blood." So——

MARLOW   What, my good friend, if you gave us a glass of punch in the meantime, it would help us to carry on the siege with vigor.

HARDCASTLE   Punch, sir! (*Aside.*) This is

---

13 Women of the town.

the most unaccountable kind of modesty I ever met with.

MARLOW Yes, sir, punch! A glass of warm punch, after our journey, will be comfortable. This is Liberty Hall, you know.

HARDCASTLE Here's a cup, sir.

MARLOW (*aside*) So this fellow, in his Liberty Hall, will only let us have just what he pleases.

HARDCASTLE (*taking the cup*) I hope you'll find it to your mind. I have prepared it with my own hands, and I believe you'll own the ingredients are tolerable. Will you be so good as to pledge me, sir? Here, Mr. Marlow, here is our better acquaintance. (*Drinks.*)

MARLOW (*aside*) A very impudent fellow this! But he's a character, and I'll humor him a little. Sir, my service to you. (*Drinks.*)

HASTINGS (*aside*) I see this fellow wants to give us his company, and forgets that he's an innkeeper, before he has learned to be a gentleman.

MARLOW From the excellence of your cup, my old friend, I suppose you have a good deal of business in this part of the country. Warm work, now and then, at elections, I suppose?

HARDCASTLE No, sir, I have long given that work over. Since our betters have hit upon the expedient of electing each other, there's no business "for us that sell ale."[14]

HASTINGS So, then you have no turn for politics, I find.

HARDCASTLE Not in the least. There was a time, indeed, I fretted myself about the mistakes of government, like other people; but finding myself every day grow more angry, and the government growing no better, I left it to mend itself. Since that, I no more trouble my head about Heyder Ally or Ally Cawn than about "Ally Croaker."[15] Sir, my service to you.

HASTINGS So that with eating above stairs, and drinking below, with receiving your friends within, and amusing them without, you lead a good, pleasant, bustling life of it.

HARDCASTLE I do stir about a great deal, that's certain. Half the differences of the parish are adjusted in this very parlor.

MARLOW (*after drinking*) And you have an argument in your cup, old gentleman, better than any in Westminster Hall.[16]

HARDCASTLE Aye, young gentleman, that, and a little philosophy.

MARLOW (*aside*) Well, this is the first time I ever heard of an innkeeper's philosophy.

HASTINGS So then, like an experienced general, you attack them on every quarter. If you find their reason manageable, you attack it with your philosophy; if you find they have no reason, you attack them with this. Here's your health, my philosopher. (*Drinks.*)

HARDCASTLE Good, very good, thank you; ha! ha! Your generalship puts me in mind of Prince Eugene, when he fought the Turks at the battle of Belgrade. You shall hear——

MARLOW Instead of the battle of Belgrade, I believe it's almost time to talk about supper. What has your philosophy got in the house for supper?

HARDCASTLE For supper, sir! (*Aside.*) Was ever such a request to a man in his own house!

MARLOW Yes, sir, supper, sir; I begin to feel an appetite. I shall make devilish work tonight in the larder, I promise you.

HARDCASTLE (*aside*) Such a brazen dog sure never my eyes beheld. (*To him.*) Why, really, sir, as for supper I can't well tell. My Dorothy, and the cook-maid, settle these things between them. I leave these kind of things entirely to them.

MARLOW You do, do you?

HARDCASTLE Entirely. By the bye, I believe they are in actual consultation upon what's for supper this moment in the kitchen.

14 Ordinary people. 15 Ally and Cawn were Indian sultans; "Ally Croaker," a popular Irish song.

16 Seat of Law Courts.

MARLOW   Then I beg they'll admit *me* as one of their privy council. It's a way I have got. When I travel I always choose to regulate my own supper. Let the cook be called. No offense, I hope, sir.

HARDCASTLE   Oh no, sir, none in the least; yet, I don't know how: our Bridget, the cook-maid, is not very communicative upon these occasions. Should we send for her, she might scold us all out of the house.

HASTINGS   Let's see your list of the larder, then. I ask it as a favor. I always match my appetite to my bill of fare.

MARLOW   (*to* HARDCASTLE, *who looks at them with surprise*)   Sir, he's very right, and it's my way, too.

HARDCASTLE   Sir, you have a right to command here. Here Roger, bring us the bill of fare for tonight's supper; I believe it's drawn out. [*Exit* ROGER.] Your manner, Mr. Hastings, puts me in mind of my uncle, Colonel Wallop. It was a saying of his, that no man was sure of his supper till he had eaten it.

HASTINGS   (*aside*)   All upon the high ropes! His uncle a colonel! We shall soon hear of his mother being a justice of peace. [*Re-enter* ROGER.] But let's hear the bill of fare.

MARLOW   (*perusing*)   What's here? For the first course; for the second course; for the dessert. The devil, sir, do you think we have brought down the whole Joiners' Company, or the Corporation of Bedford, to eat up such a supper? Two or three little things, clean and comfortable, will do.

HASTINGS   But let's hear it.

MARLOW   (*reading*)   For the first course at the top, a pig, and prune sauce.

HASTINGS   Damn your pig, I say!

MARLOW   And damn your prune sauce, say I!

HARDCASTLE   And yet, gentlemen, to men that are hungry, pig with prune sauce is very good eating.

MARLOW   At the bottom a calf's tongue and brains.

HASTINGS   Let your brains be knocked out, my good sir, I don't like them.

MARLOW   Or you may clap them on a plate by themselves. I do.

HARDCASTLE   (*aside*)   Their impudence confounds me. (*To them.*) Gentlemen, you are my guests, make what alterations you please. Is there anything else you wish to retrench or alter, gentlemen?

MARLOW   Item: A pork pie, a boiled rabbit and sausages, a florentine,[17] a shaking pudding, and a dish of tiff-taff-taffety cream!

HASTINGS   Confound your made dishes; I shall be as much at a loss in this house as at a green and yellow dinner at the French ambassador's table. I'm for plain eating.

HARDCASTLE   I'm sorry, gentlemen, that I have nothing you like, but if there be anything you have a particular fancy to——

MARLOW   Why really, sir, your bill of fare is so exquisite, that any one part of it is full as good as another. Send us what you please. So much for supper. And now to see that our beds are aired, and properly taken care of.

HARDCASTLE   I entreat you'll leave all that to me. You shall not stir a step.

MARLOW   Leave that to you! I protest, sir, you must excuse me; I always look to these things myself.

HARDCASTLE   I must insist, sir, you'll make yourself easy on that head.

MARLOW   You see I'm resolved on it. (*Aside.*) A very troublesome fellow this, as ever I met with.

HARDCASTLE   Well, sir, I'm resolved at least to attend you. (*Aside.*) This may be modern modesty, but I never saw anything look so like old-fashioned impudence.

Exeunt MARLOW *and* HARDCASTLE.

HASTINGS   (*solus*)   So I find this fellow's civilities begin to grow troublesome. But who can be angry at those assiduities which are meant to please him? Ha! what do I see? Miss Neville, by all that's happy!

---

17 A baked pie.

Enter MISS NEVILLE.

MISS NEVILLE   My dear Hastings! To what unexpected good fortune, to what accident, am I to ascribe this happy meeting?

HASTINGS   Rather let me ask the same question, as I could never have hoped to meet my dearest Constance at an inn.

MISS NEVILLE   An inn! Sure you mistake; my aunt, my guardian, lives here. What could induce you to think this house an inn?

HASTINGS   My friend, Mr. Marlow, with whom I came down, and I, have been sent here as to an inn, I assure you. A young fellow, whom we accidentally met at a house hard by, directed us thither.

MISS NEVILLE   Certainly it must be one of my hopeful cousin's tricks, of whom you have heard me talk so often: ha! ha! ha!

HASTINGS   He whom your aunt intends for you? He of whom I have such just apprehensions?

MISS NEVILLE   You have nothing to fear from him, I assure you. You'd adore him if you knew how heartily he despises me. My aunt knows it, too, and has undertaken to court me for him, and actually begins to think she has made a conquest.

HASTINGS   Thou dear dissembler! You must know, my Constance, I have just seized this happy opportunity of my friend's visit here to get admittance into the family. The horses that carried us down are now fatigued with their journey, but they'll soon be refreshed; and then, if my dearest girl will trust in her faithful Hastings, we shall soon be landed in France, where even among slaves the laws of marriage are respected.

MISS NEVILLE   I have often told you that though ready to obey you, I yet should leave my little fortune behind with reluctance. The greatest part of it was left me by my uncle, the India Director, and chiefly consists in jewels. I have been for some time persuading my aunt to let me wear them. I fancy I'm very near succeeding. The instant they are put into my possession you shall find me ready to make them and myself yours.

HASTINGS   Perish the baubles! Your person is all I desire. In the meantime, my friend Marlow must not be let into his mistake. I know the strange reserve of his temper is such that, if abruptly informed of it, he would instantly quit the house before our plan was ripe for execution.

MISS NEVILLE   But how shall we keep him in the deception? Miss Hardcastle is just returned from walking; what if we still continue to deceive him?—This, this way —(*They confer.*)

Enter MARLOW.

MARLOW   The assiduities of these good people tease me beyond bearing. My host seems to think it ill manners to leave me alone, and so he claps not only himself, but his old-fashioned wife on my back. They talk of coming to sup with us, too; and then, I suppose, we are to run the gantlet through all the rest of the family. —What have we got here?—

HASTINGS   My dear Charles! Let me congratulate you!—The most fortunate accident!—Who do you think is just alighted?

MARLOW   Cannot guess.

HASTINGS   Our mistresses, boy, Miss Hardcastle and Miss Neville. Give me leave to introduce Miss Constance Neville to your acquaintance. Happening to dine in the neighborhood, they called, on their return, to take fresh horses here. Miss Hardcastle has just stepped into the next room, and will be back in an instant. Wasn't it lucky? eh!

MARLOW   (*aside*)   I have just been mortified enough of all conscience, and here comes something to complete my embarrassment.

HASTINGS   Well! but wasn't it the most fortunate thing in the world?

MARLOW   Oh! yes. Very fortunate—a most joyful encounter.—But our dresses, George, you know, are in disorder. —What if we should postpone the happiness till tomorrow?—Tomorrow at her own house.—It will be every bit as convenient—and rather more respectful. —Tomorrow let it be. (*Offering to go.*)

MISS NEVILLE   By no means, sir. Your ceremony will displease her. The disorder of your dress will show the ardor of your impatience. Besides, she knows you are in the house, and will permit you to see her.

MARLOW   Oh! the devil! how shall I support it? Hem! hem! Hastings, you must not go. You are to assist me, you know. I shall be confoundedly ridiculous. Yet, hang it! I'll take courage. Hem!

HASTINGS   Pshaw, man! it's but the first plunge, and all's over. She's but a woman, you know.

MARLOW   And of all women, she that I dread most to encounter!

Enter MISS HARDCASTLE, *as returned from walking, a bonnet, etc.*

HASTINGS (*introducing them*)   Miss Hardcastle. Mr. Marlow. I'm proud of bringing two persons of such merit together, that only want to know, to esteem each other.

MISS HARDCASTLE (*aside*)   Now, for meeting my modest gentleman with a demure face, and quite in his own manner. (*After a pause, in which he appears very uneasy and disconcerted.*) I'm glad of your safe arrival, sir—I'm told you had some accidents by the way.

MARLOW   Only a few, madam. Yes, we had some. Yes, madam, a good many accidents, but should be sorry—madam—or rather glad of any accidents—that are so agreeably concluded. Hem!

HASTINGS (*to him*)   You never spoke better in your whole life. Keep it up, and I'll insure you the victory.

MISS HARDCASTLE   I'm afraid you flatter, sir. You that have seen so much of the finest company can find little entertainment in an obscure corner of the country.

MARLOW (*gathering courage*)   I have lived, indeed, in the world, madam; but I have kept very little company. I have been but an observer upon life, madam, while others were enjoying it.

MISS NEVILLE   But that, I am told, is the way to enjoy it at last.

HASTINGS (*to him*)   Cicero never spoke better. Once more, and you are confirmed in assurance forever.

MARLOW (*to him*)   Hem! Stand by me, then, and when I'm down, throw in a word or two to set me up again.

MISS HARDCASTLE   An observer, like you, upon life, were, I fear, disagreeably employed, since you must have had much more to censure than to approve.

MARLOW   Pardon me, madam. I was always willing to be amused. The folly of most people is rather an object of mirth than uneasiness.

HASTINGS (*to him*)   Bravo, bravo. Never spoke so well in your whole life. Well, Miss Hardcastle, I see that you and Mr. Marlow are going to be very good company. I believe our being here will but embarrass the interview.

MARLOW   Not in the least, Mr. Hastings. We like your company of all things. (*To him.*) Zounds! George, sure you won't go? How can you leave us?

HASTINGS   Our presence will but spoil conversation, so we'll retire to the next room. (*To him.*) You don't consider, man, that we are to manage a little tête-à-tête of our own.

Exeunt [HASTINGS *and* MISS NEVILLE.]

MISS HARDCASTLE (*after a pause*)   But you have not been wholly an observer, I presume, sir. The ladies, I should hope, have employed some part of your addresses.

MARLOW (*relapsing into timidity*)   Pardon me, madam, I—I—I—as yet have studied —only—to—deserve them.

MISS HARDCASTLE   And that some say is the very worst way to obtain them.

MARLOW   Perhaps so, madam. But I love to converse only with the more grave and sensible part of the sex.—But I'm afraid I grow tiresome.

MISS HARDCASTLE   Not at all, sir; there is nothing I like so much as grave conversation myself; I could hear it forever. Indeed, I have often been surprised how a man of sentiment could ever admire those light airy pleasures, where nothing reaches the heart.

MARLOW It's—a disease—of the mind, madam. In the variety of tastes there must be some who, wanting a relish for—um-a-um.

MISS HARDCASTLE I understand you, sir. There must be some, who, wanting a relish for refined pleasures, pretend to despise what they are incapable of tasting.

MARLOW My meaning, madam, but infinitely better expressed. And I can't help observing—a——

MISS HARDCASTLE (*aside*) Who could ever suppose this fellow impudent upon some occasions. (*To him.*) You were going to observe, sir——

MARLOW I was observing, madam—I protest, madam, I forget what I was going to observe.

MISS HARDCASTLE (*aside*) I vow and so do I. (*To him.*) You were observing, sir, that in this age of hypocrisy—something about hypocrisy, sir.

MARLOW Yes, madam. In this age of hypocrisy, there are few who upon strict inquiry do not—a—a—a——

MISS HARDCASTLE I understand you perfectly, sir.

MARLOW (*aside*) Egad! and that's more than I do myself!

MISS HARDCASTLE You mean that in this hypocritical age there are few that do not condemn in public what they practise in private, and think they pay every debt to virtue when they praise it.

MARLOW True, madam; those who have most virtue in their mouths, have least of it in their bosoms. But I'm sure I tire you, madam.

MISS HARDCASTLE Not in the least, sir; there's something so agreeable and spirited in your manner, such life and force—pray, sir, go on.

MARLOW Yes, madam. I was saying—that there are some occasions—when a total want of courage, madam, destroys all the—and puts us—upon a—a—a——

MISS HARDCASTLE I agree with you entirely,

a want of courage upon some occasions assumes the appearance of ignorance, and betrays us when we most want to excel. I beg you'll proceed.

MARLOW Yes, madam. Morally speaking, madam—but I see Miss Neville expecting us in the next room. I would not intrude for the world.

MISS HARDCASTLE I protest, sir, I never was more agreeably entertained in all my life. Pray go on.

MARLOW Yes, madam. I was—but she beckons us to join her. Madam, shall I do myself the honor to attend you?

MISS HARDCASTLE Well then, I'll follow.

MARLOW (*aside*) This pretty smooth dialogue has done for me.   *Exit.*

MISS HARDCASTLE (*sola*) Ha! ha! ha! Was there ever such a sober, sentimental interview? I'm certain he scarce looked in my face the whole time. Yet the fellow, but for his unaccountable bashfulness, is pretty well, too. He has good sense, but then so buried in his fears, that it fatigues one more than ignorance. If I could teach him a little confidence, it would be doing somebody that I know of a piece of service. But who is that somebody?—That, faith, is a question I can scarce answer.   *Exit.*

Enter TONY *and* MISS NEVILLE, *followed by* MRS. HARDCASTLE *and* HASTINGS.

TONY What do you follow me for, cousin Con? I wonder you're not ashamed to be so very engaging.

MISS NEVILLE I hope, cousin, one may speak to one's own relations, and not be to blame.

TONY Aye, but I know what sort of a relation you want to make me, though; but it won't do. I tell you, cousin Con, it won't do; so I beg you'll keep your distance, I want no nearer relationship. (*She follows, coquetting him to the back scene.*)

MRS. HARDCASTLE Well! I vow, Mr. Hastings, you are very entertaining. There's nothing in the world I love to talk of so much as London, and the fashions, though I was never there myself.

HASTINGS Never there! You amaze me! From your air and manner, I concluded you had been bred all your life either at Ranelagh, St. James's, or Tower Wharf.[18]

MRS. HARDCASTLE Oh! sir, you're only pleased to say so. We country persons can have no manner at all. I'm in love with the town, and that serves to raise me above some of our neighboring rustics; but who can have a manner, that has never seen the Pantheon, the Grotto Gardens, the Borough, and such places where the nobility chiefly resort? All I can do is to enjoy London at second hand. I take care to know every tête-à-tête from the *Scandalous Magazine,* and have all the fashions as they come out, in a letter from the two Miss Rickets of Crooked Lane. Pray how do you like this head, Mr. Hastings?

HASTINGS Extremely elegant and *dégagée,* upon my word, madam. Your *friseur* is a Frenchman, I suppose?

MRS. HARDCASTLE I protest, I dressed it myself from a print in the *Ladies' Memorandum-book* for the last year.

HASTINGS Indeed. Such a head in a side box, at the playhouse, would draw as many gazers as my Lady Mayoress at a city ball.

MRS. HARDCASTLE I vow, since inoculation began, there is no such thing to be seen as a plain woman; so one must dress a little particular, or one may escape in the crowd.

HASTINGS But that can never be your case, madam, in any dress! (*Bowing.*)

MRS. HARDCASTLE Yet, what signifies *my* dressing when I have such a piece of antiquity by my side as Mr. Hardcastle? All I can say will never argue down a single button from his clothes. I have often wanted him to throw off his great flaxen wig, and where he was bald, to

plaster it over like my Lord Pately, with powder.

HASTINGS You are right, madam; for, as among the ladies there are none ugly, so among the men there are none old.

MRS. HARDCASTLE But what do you think his answer was? Why, with his usual Gothic vivacity, he said I only wanted him to throw off his wig to convert it into a *tête*[19] for my own wearing!

HASTINGS Intolerable! At your age you may wear what you please, and it must become you.

MRS. HARDCASTLE Pray, Mr. Hastings, what do you take to be the most fashionable age about town?

HASTINGS Some time ago forty was all the mode; but I'm told the ladies intend to bring up fifty for the ensuing winter.

MRS. HARDCASTLE Seriously? Then I shall be too young for the fashion!

HASTINGS No lady begins now to put on jewels till she's past forty. For instance, Miss there, in a polite circle would be considered as a child, as a mere maker of samplers.

MRS. HARDCASTLE And yet Mrs.[20] Niece thinks herself as much a woman, and is as fond of jewels as the oldest of us all.

HASTINGS Your niece, is she? And that young gentleman, a brother of yours, I should presume?

MRS. HARDCASTLE My son, sir. They are contracted to each other. Observe their little sports. They fall in and out ten times a day, as if they were man and wife already. (*To them.*) Well, Tony, child, what soft things are you saying to your cousin Constance this evening?

TONY I have been saying no soft things; but that it's very hard to be followed about so! Ecod! I've not a place in the house now that's left to myself but the stable.

MRS. HARDCASTLE Never mind him, Con, my dear. He's in another story behind your back.

18 Tower Wharf, and the Borough in the following speech, were unfashionable places; the other names refer to resorts of the nobility.

19 A lady's wig. 20 Mistress, applied to unmarried as well as to married women.

MISS NEVILLE   There's something generous in my cousin's manner. He falls out before faces to be forgiven in private.

TONY   That's a damned confounded—crack.[21]

MRS. HARDCASTLE   Ah! he's a sly one. Don't you think they're like each other about the mouth, Mr. Hastings? The Blenkinsop mouth to a *T*. They're of a size, too. Back to back, my pretties, that Mr. Hastings may see you. Come, Tony.

TONY   You had as good not make me, I tell you. (*Measuring.*)

MISS NEVILLE   Oh lud! he has almost cracked my head.

MRS. HARDCASTLE   Oh, the monster! For shame, Tony. You a man, and behave so!

TONY   If I'm a man, let me have my fortin. Ecod! I'll not be made a fool of no longer.

MRS. HARDCASTLE   Is this, ungrateful boy, all that I'm to get for the pains I have taken in your education? I that have rocked you in your cradle, and fed that pretty mouth with a spoon! Did not I work that waistcoat to make you genteel? Did not I prescribe for you every day, and weep while the receipt was operating?

TONY   Ecod! you had reason to weep, for you have been dosing me ever since I was born. I have gone through every receipt in *The Complete Housewife* ten times over; and you have thoughts of coursing me through Quincy[22] next spring. But, ecod! I tell you, I'll not be made a fool of no longer.

MRS. HARDCASTLE   Wasn't it all for your good, viper? Wasn't it all for your good?

TONY   I wish you'd let me and my good alone, then. Snubbing this way when I'm in spirits. If I'm to have any good, let it come of itself; not to keep dinging it, dinging it into one so.

MRS. HARDCASTLE   That's false; I never see you when you're in spirits. No, Tony, you then go to the alehouse or kennel. I'm never to be delighted with your agreeable wild notes, unfeeling monster!

TONY   Ecod! Mamma, your own notes are the wildest of the two.

MRS. HARDCASTLE   Was ever the like? But I see he wants to break my heart, I see he does.

HASTINGS   Dear Madam, permit me to lecture the young gentleman a little. I'm certain I can persuade him to his duty.

MRS. HARDCASTLE   Well, I must retire. Come, Constance, my love. You see, Mr. Hastings, the wretchedness of my situation. Was ever poor woman so plagued with a dear, sweet, pretty, provoking, undutiful boy?

Exeunt MRS. HARDCASTLE *and* MISS NEVILLE.

HASTINGS, TONY

TONY (*singing*)   "There was a young man riding by, and fain would have his will. Rang do didlo dee."
Don't mind her. Let her cry. It's the comfort of her heart. I have seen her and sister cry over a book for an hour together, and they said they liked the book the better the more it made them cry.

HASTINGS   Then you're no friend to the ladies, I find, my pretty young gentleman?

TONY   That's as I find 'um.

HASTINGS   Not to her of your mother's choosing, I dare answer! And yet she appears to me a pretty, well-tempered girl.

TONY   That's because you don't know her as well as I. Ecod! I know every inch about her; and there's not a more bitter cantankerous toad in all Christendom!

HASTINGS (*aside*)   Pretty encouragement this for a lover!

TONY   I have seen her since the height of that. She has as many tricks as a hare in a thicket, or a colt the first day's breaking.

HASTINGS   To me she appears sensible and silent.

TONY   Aye, before company. But when she's with her playmates, she's as loud as a hog in a gate.

HASTINGS   But there is a meek modesty about her that charms me.

TONY   Yes, but curb her never so little,

she kicks up, and you're flung in a ditch.

HASTINGS Well, but you must allow her a little beauty.—Yes, you must allow her some beauty.

TONY Bandbox! She's all a made-up thing, mun. Ah! could you but see Bet Bouncer of these parts, you might then talk of beauty. Ecod, she has two eyes as black as sloes, and cheeks as broad and red as a pulpit cushion. She'd make two of she.

HASTINGS Well, what say you of a friend that would take this bitter bargain off your hands?

TONY Anon?[23]

HASTINGS Would you thank him that would take Miss Neville, and leave you to happiness and your dear Betsy?

TONY Aye; but where is there such a friend, for who would take *her?*

HASTINGS I am he. If you but assist me, I'll engage to whip her off to France, and you shall never hear more of her.

TONY Assist you! Ecod, I will, to the last drop of my blood. I'll clap a pair of horses to your chaise that shall trundle you off in a twinkling, and may be get you a part of her fortin beside in jewels that you little dream of.

HASTINGS My dear squire, this looks like a lad of spirit.

TONY Come along then, and you shall see more of my spirit before you have done with me.

(*Singing.*)
We are the boys
That fears no noise
Where the thundering cannons roar.

Exeunt.

Act Three

Enter HARDCASTLE *solus.*

HARDCASTLE What could my old friend Sir Charles mean by recommending his son as the modestest young man in town? To me he appears the most impudent piece of brass that ever spoke with a tongue. He has taken possession of the easy chair by the fireside already. He took off his boots in the parlor, and desired me to see them taken care of. I'm desirous to know how his impudence affects my daughter.—She will certainly be shocked at it.

Enter MISS HARDCASTLE, *plainly dressed.*

HARDCASTLE Well, my Kate, I see you have changed your dress, as I bid you; and yet, I believe, there was no great occasion.

MISS HARDCASTLE I find such a pleasure, sir, in obeying your commands, that I take care to observe them without ever debating their propriety.

HARDCASTLE And yet, Kate, I sometimes give you some cause, particularly when I recommended my *modest* gentleman to you as a lover today.

MISS HARDCASTLE You taught me to expect something extraordinary, and I find the original exceeds the description!

HARDCASTLE I was never so surprised in my life! He has quite confounded all my faculties!

MISS HARDCASTLE I never saw anything like it: and a man of the world, too!

HARDCASTLE Aye, he learned it all abroad —what a fool was I, to think a young man could learn modesty by traveling. He might as soon learn wit at a masquerade.

MISS HARDCASTLE It seems all natural to him.

HARDCASTLE A good deal assisted by bad company and a French dancing master.

MISS HARDCASTLE Sure, you mistake papa! A French dancing master could never have taught him that timid look— that awkward address—that bashful manner——

HARDCASTLE Whose look? whose manner, child?

MISS HARDCASTLE Mr. Marlow's: his *mauvaise honte,*[24] his timidity, struck me at the first sight.

23 "What?"

24 Bashfulness.

HARDCASTLE Then your first sight deceived you; for I think him one of the most brazen first sights that ever astonished my senses!

MISS HARDCASTLE Sure, sir, you rally! I never saw anyone so modest.

HARDCASTLE And can you be serious! I never saw such a bouncing, swaggering puppy since I was born. Bully Dawson[25] was but a fool to him.

MISS HARDCASTLE Surprising! He met me with a respectful bow, a stammering voice, and a look fixed on the ground.

HARDCASTLE He met me with a loud voice, a lordly air, and a familiarity that made my blood freeze again.

MISS HARDCASTLE He treated me with diffidence and respect; censured the manners of the age; admired the prudence of girls that never laughed; tired me with apologies for being tiresome; then left the room with a bow, and "Madam, I would not for the world detain you."

HARDCASTLE He spoke to me as if he knew me all his life before; asked twenty questions, and never waited for an answer; interrupted my best remarks with some silly pun; and when I was in my best story of the Duke of Marlborough and Prince Eugene, he asked if I had not a good hand at making punch. Yes, Kate, he asked your father if he was a maker of punch!

MISS HARDCASTLE One of us must certainly be mistaken.

HARDCASTLE If he be what he has shown himself, I'm determined he shall never have my consent.

MISS HARDCASTLE And if he be the sullen thing I take him, he shall never have mine.

HARDCASTLE In one thing then we are agreed—to reject him.

MISS HARDCASTLE Yes: but upon conditions. For if you should find him less impudent, and I more presuming; if you find him more respectful, and I more importunate—I don't know—the fellow is well enough for a man. Certainly we don't meet many such at a horse race in the country.

HARDCASTLE If we should find him so— but that's impossible. The first appearance has done my business. I'm seldom deceived in that.

MISS HARDCASTLE And yet there may be many good qualities under that first appearance.

HARDCASTLE Aye, when a girl finds a fellow's outside to her taste, she then sets about guessing the rest of his furniture. With her, a smooth face stands for good sense, and a genteel figure for every virtue.

MISS HARDCASTLE I hope, sir, a conversation begun with a compliment to my good sense won't end with a sneer at my understanding?

HARDCASTLE Pardon me, Kate. But if young Mr. Brazen can find the art of reconciling contradictions, he may please us both, perhaps.

MISS HARDCASTLE And as one of us must be mistaken, what if we go to make further discoveries?

HARDCASTLE Agreed. But depend on't I'm in the right.

MISS HARDCASTLE And depend on't I'm not much in the wrong.

Exeunt.

Enter TONY, *running in with a casket.*

TONY Ecod! I have got them. Here they are. My cousin Con's necklaces, bobs and all. My mother shan't cheat the poor souls out of their fortin neither. Oh! my genius, is that you?

Enter HASTINGS.

HASTINGS My dear friend, how have you managed with your mother? I hope you have amused her with pretending love for your cousin, and that you are willing to be reconciled at last? Our horses will be refreshed in a short time, and we shall soon be ready to set off.

TONY And here's something to bear your charges by the way (*Giving the casket.*)

25 A ruffian.

Your sweetheart's jewels. Keep them, and hang those, I say, that would rob you of one of them.

HASTINGS But how have you procured them from your mother?

TONY Ask me no questions, and I'll tell you no fibs. I procured them by the rule of thumb. If I had not a key to every drawer in mother's bureau, how could I go to the alehouse so often as I do? An honest man may rob himself of his own at any time.

HASTINGS Thousands do it every day. But to be plain with you, Miss Neville is endeavoring to procure them from her aunt this very instant. If she succeeds, it will be the most delicate way at least of obtaining them.

TONY Well, keep them, till you know how it will be. But I know how it will be well enough; she'd as soon part with the only sound tooth in her head!

HASTINGS But I dread the effects of her resentment, when she finds she has lost them.

TONY Never you mind her resentment, leave *me* to manage that. I don't value her resentment the bounce of a cracker.[26] Zounds! here they are! Morrice![27] prance!

Exit HASTINGS.

TONY, MRS. HARDCASTLE, *and* MISS NEVILLE.

MRS. HARDCASTLE Indeed, Constance, you amaze me. Such a girl as you want jewels? It will be time enough for jewels, my dear, twenty years hence, when your beauty begins to want repairs.

MISS NEVILLE But what will repair beauty at forty, will certainly improve it at twenty, madam.

MRS. HARDCASTLE Yours, my dear, can admit of none. That natural blush is beyond a thousand ornaments. Besides, child, jewels are quite out at present. Don't you see half the ladies of our ac-

quaintance, my Lady Kill-daylight, and Mrs. Crump, and the rest of them, carry their jewels to town, and bring nothing but paste and marcasites[28] back?

MISS NEVILLE But who knows, madam, but somebody that shall be nameless would like me best with all my little finery about me?

MRS. HARDCASTLE Consult your glass, my dear, and then see, if with such a pair of eyes, you want any better sparklers. What do you think, Tony, my dear, does your cousin Con want any jewels, in your eyes, to set off her beauty?

TONY That's as thereafter may be.

MISS NEVILLE My dear aunt, if you knew how it would oblige me.

MRS. HARDCASTLE A parcel of old-fashioned rose and table-cut things.[29] They would make you look like the court of King Solomon at a puppet show. Besides, I believe I can't readily come at them. They may be missing, for aught I know to the contrary.

TONY (*apart to* MRS. HARDCASTLE) Then why don't you tell her so at once, as she's so longing for them. Tell her they're lost. It's the only way to quiet her. Say they're lost, and call me to bear witness.

MRS. HARDCASTLE (*apart to* TONY) You know, my dear, I'm only keeping them for you. So if I say they're gone, you'll bear me witness, will you? He! he! he!

TONY Never fear me. Ecod! I'll say I saw them taken out with my own eyes.

MISS NEVILLE I desire them but for a day, madam. Just to be permitted to show them as relics, and then they may be locked up again.

MRS. HARDCASTLE To be plain with you, my dear Constance, if I could find them, you should have them. They're missing, I assure you. Lost, for aught I know; but we must have patience wherever they are.

MISS NEVILLE I'll not believe it; this is but a shallow pretense to deny me. I know they're too valuable to be so slightly kept,

---

26 Explosion of a firecracker. 27 "Move on."

28 Ornaments of crystallized iron pyrites. 29 I.e., gems cut in a manner no longer fashionable.

and as you are to answer for the loss——

MRS. HARDCASTLE Don't be alarmed, Constance. If they be lost, I must restore an equivalent. But my son knows they are missing, and not to be found.

TONY That I can bear witness to. They are missing, and not to be found, I'll take my oath on't.

MRS. HARDCASTLE You must learn resignation, my dear; for though we lose our fortune, yet we should not lose our patience. See me, how calm I am.

MISS NEVILLE Aye, people are generally calm at the misfortunes of others.

MRS. HARDCASTLE Now, I wonder a girl of your good sense should waste a thought upon such trumpery. We shall soon find them; and, in the meantime, you shall make use of my garnets till your jewels be found.

MISS NEVILLE I detest garnets.

MRS. HARDCASTLE The most becoming things in the world to set off a clear complexion. You have often seen how well they look upon me. You *shall* have them. *Exit.*

MISS NEVILLE I dislike them of all things. You shan't stir. Was ever anything so provoking to mislay my own jewels, and force me to wear her trumpery.

TONY Don't be a fool. If she gives you the garnets, take what you can get. The jewels are your own already. I have stolen them out of her bureau, and she does not know it. Fly to your spark, he'll tell you more of the matter. Leave me to manage *her.*

MISS NEVILLE My dear cousin!

TONY Vanish. She's here, and has missed them already. [*Exit* MISS NEVILLE.] Zounds! how she fidgets and spits about like a catherine wheel!

Enter MRS. HARDCASTLE.

MRS. HARDCASTLE Confusion! thieves! robbers! We are cheated, plundered, broke open, undone!

TONY What's the matter, what's the matter, mamma? I hope nothing has happened to any of the good family!

MRS. HARDCASTLE We are robbed. My bureau has been broke open, the jewels taken out, and I'm undone!

TONY Oh! is that all! Ha! ha! ha! By the laws, I never saw it better acted in my life. Ecod, I thought you was ruined in earnest, ha, ha, ha!

MRS. HARDCASTLE Why, boy, I *am* ruined in earnest. My bureau has been broke open, and all taken away.

TONY Stick to that; ha, ha, ha! stick to that. I'll bear witness, you know, call me to bear witness.

MRS. HARDCASTLE I tell you, Tony, by all that's precious, the jewels are gone, and I shall be ruined forever.

TONY Sure I know they're gone, and I am to say so.

MRS. HARDCASTLE My dearest Tony, but hear me. They're gone, I say.

TONY By the laws, mamma, you make me for to laugh, ha! ha! I know who took them well enough, ha! ha! ha!

MRS. HARDCASTLE Was there ever such a blockhead, that can't tell the difference between jest and earnest? I tell you I'm not in jest, booby!

TONY That's right, that's right! You must be in a bitter passion, and then nobody will suspect either of us. I'll bear witness that they are gone.

MRS. HARDCASTLE Was there ever such a cross-grained brute, that won't hear me? Can you bear witness that you're no better than a fool? Was ever poor woman so beset with fools on one hand, and thieves on the other?

TONY I can bear witness to that.

MRS. HARDCASTLE Bear witness again, you blockhead you, and I'll turn you out of the room directly. My poor niece, what will become of *her?* Do you laugh, you unfeeling brute, as if you enjoyed my distress?

TONY I can bear witness to that.

MRS. HARDCASTLE Do you insult me, monster? I'll teach you to vex your mother, I will.

TONY I can bear witness to that. (*He runs off, she follows him.*)

Enter MISS HARDCASTLE *and* MAID.

MISS HARDCASTLE What an unaccountable creature is that brother of mine, to send them to the house as an inn, ha! ha! I don't wonder at his impudence.

MAID But what is more, madam, the young gentleman as you passed by in your present dress, asked me if you were the barmaid. He mistook you for the barmaid, madam!

MISS HARDCASTLE Did he? Then as I live I'm resolved to keep up the delusion. Tell me, Pimple, how do you like my present dress? Don't you think I look something like Cherry in *The Beaux' Stratagem*?[30]

MAID It's the dress, madam, that every lady wears in the country, but when she visits or receives company.

MISS HARDCASTLE And are you sure he does not remember my face or person?

MAID Certain of it.

MISS HARDCASTLE I vow, I thought so; for though we spoke for some time together, yet his fears were such, that he never once looked up during the interview. Indeed, if he had, my bonnet would have kept him from seeing me.

MAID But what do you hope from keeping him in his mistake?

MISS HARDCASTLE In the first place, I shall be *seen,* and that is no small advantage to a girl who brings her face to market. Then I shall perhaps make an acquaintance, and that's no small victory gained over one who never addresses any but the wildest of her sex. But my chief aim is to take my gentleman off his guard, and like an invisible champion of romance, examine the giant's force before I offer to combat.

MAID But you are sure you can act your part, and disguise your voice, so that he may mistake that, as he has already mistaken your person?

MISS HARDCASTLE Never fear me. I think I have got the true bar cant. Did your honor call?—Attend the Lion[31] there.—Pipes and tobacco for the Angel.—The Lamb has been outrageous this half hour.

MAID It will do, madam. But he's here.
Exit MAID.

Enter MARLOW.

MARLOW What a bawling in every part of the house; I have scarce a moment's repose. If I go to the best room, there I find my host and his story. If I fly to the gallery, there we have my hostess with her curtsy down to the ground. I have at last got a moment to myself, and now for recollection. (*Walks and muses.*)

MISS HARDCASTLE Did you call, sir? Did your honor call?

MARLOW (*musing*) As for Miss Hardcastle, she's too grave and sentimental for me.

MISS HARDCASTLE Did your honor call? (*She still places herself before him, he turning away.*)

MARLOW No, child. (*Musing.*) Besides from the glimpse I had of her, I think she squints.

MISS HARDCASTLE I'm sure, sir, I heard the bell ring.

MARLOW No, no. (*Musing.*) I have pleased my father, however, by coming down, and I'll tomorrow please myself by returning. (*Taking out his tablets,*[32] *and perusing.*)

MISS HARDCASTLE Perhaps the other gentleman called, sir?

MARLOW I tell you, no.

MISS HARDCASTLE I should be glad to know, sir. We have such a parcel of servants.

MARLOW No, no, I tell you. (*Looks full in her face.*) Yes, child, I think I did call. I wanted—I wanted—I vow, child, you are vastly handsome.

MISS HARDCASTLE O la, sir, you'll make one ashamed.

MARLOW Never saw a more sprightly,

---

30 The landlord's daughter in Farquhar's play.

31 Typical names of inn rooms. 32 Memorandum book.

malicious eye. Yes, yes, my dear, I did call. Have you got any of your—a—what d'ye call it in the house?

MISS HARDCASTLE No, sir, we have been out of that these ten days.

MARLOW One may call in this house, I find, to very little purpose. Suppose I should call for a taste, just by way of trial, of the nectar of your lips; perhaps I might be disappointed in that, too.

MISS HARDCASTLE Nectar! nectar! that's a liquor there's no call for in these parts. French, I suppose. We keep no French wines here, sir.

MARLOW Of true English growth, I assure you.

MISS HARDCASTLE Then it's odd I should not know it. We brew all sorts of wines in this house, and I have lived here these eighteen years.

MARLOW Eighteen years! Why one would think, child, you kept the bar before you were born. How old are you?

MISS HARDCASTLE O! sir, I must not tell my age. They say women and music should never be dated.

MARLOW To guess at this distance, you can't be much above forty. (*Approaching.*) Yet nearer I don't think so much. (*Approaching.*) By coming close to some women they look younger still; but when we come very close indeed—— (*Attempting to kiss her.*)

MISS HARDCASTLE Pray, sir, keep your distance. One would think you wanted to know one's age as they do horses, by mark of mouth.

MARLOW I protest, child, you use me extremely ill. If you keep me at this distance, how is it possible you and I can be ever acquainted?

MISS HARDCASTLE And who wants to be acquainted with you? I want no such acquaintance, not I. I'm sure you did not treat Miss Hardcastle that was here awhile ago in this obstropalous manner. I'll warrant me, before her you looked dashed, and kept bowing to the ground, and talked, for all the world, as if you was before a justice of peace.

MARLOW (*aside*) Egad! she has hit it, sure enough. (*To her.*) In awe of her, child? Ha! ha! ha! A mere awkward, squinting thing! No, no! I find you don't know me. I laughed, and rallied her a little; but I was unwilling to be too severe. No, I could not be too severe, curse me!

MISS HARDCASTLE Oh! then, sir, you are a favorite, I find, among the ladies?

MARLOW Yes, my dear, a great favorite. And yet, hang me, I don't see what they find in me to follow. At the Ladies' Club in town I'm called their agreeable Rattle. Rattle, child, is not my real name, but one I'm known by. My name is Solomons. Mr. Solomons, my dear, at your service. (*Offering to salute her.*)

MISS HARDCASTLE Hold, sir; you are introducing me to your club, not to yourself. And you're so great a favorite there, you say?

MARLOW Yes, my dear. There's Mrs. Mantrap, Lady Betty Blackleg, the Countess of Sligo, Mrs. Langhorns, old Miss Biddy Buckskin and your humble servant, keep up the spirit of the place.

MISS HARDCASTLE Then it's a very merry place, I suppose?

MARLOW Yes, as merry as cards, suppers, wine, and old women can make us.

MISS HARDCASTLE And their agreeable Rattle, ha! ha! ha!

MARLOW (*aside*) Egad! I don't quite like this chit. She looks knowing, methinks. You laugh, child!

MISS HARDCASTLE I can't but laugh to think what time they all have for minding their work or their family.

MARLOW (*aside*) All's well, she don't laugh at me. (*To her.*) Do you ever work, child?

MISS HARDCASTLE Aye, sure. There's not a screen or a quilt in the whole house but what can bear witness to that.

MARLOW Odso! Then you must show me your embroidery. I embroider and draw patterns myself a little. If you want a judge of your work you must apply to me. (*Seizing her hand.*)

Enter HARDCASTLE, *who stands in surprise.*

MISS HARDCASTLE   Aye, but the colors don't look well by candlelight. You shall see all in the morning. (*Struggling.*)

MARLOW   And why not now, my angel? Such beauty fires beyond the power of resistance.—Pshaw! the father here! My old luck: I never nicked seven that I did not throw ames-ace three times following.[33]

Exit MARLOW.

HARDCASTLE   So, madam. So I find *this* is your *modest* lover. This is your humble admirer that kept his eyes fixed on the ground, and only adored at humble distance. Kate, Kate, art thou not ashamed to deceive your father so?

MISS HARDCASTLE   Never trust me, dear papa, but he's still the modest man I first took him for, you'll be convinced of it as well as I.

HARDCASTLE   By the hand of my body, I believe his impudence is infectious! Didn't I see him seize your hand? Didn't I see him haul you about like a milkmaid? And now you talk of his respect and his modesty, forsooth!

MISS HARDCASTLE   But if I shortly convince you of his modesty that he has only the faults that will pass off with time, and the virtues that will improve with age, I hope you'll forgive him.

HARDCASTLE   The girl would actually make one run mad! I tell you I'll not be convinced. I am convinced. He has scarcely been three hours in the house, and he has already encroached on all my prerogatives. You may like his impudence, and call it modesty. But my son-in-law, madam, must have very different qualifications.

MISS HARDCASTLE   Sir, I ask but this night to convince you.

HARDCASTLE   You shall not have half the time, for I have thoughts of turning him out this very hour.

MISS HARDCASTLE   Give me that hour then, and I hope to satisfy you.

HARDCASTLE   Well, an hour let it be then. But I'll have no trifling with your father. All fair and open, do you mind me?

MISS HARDCASTLE   I hope, sir, you have ever found that I considered your commands as my pride; for your kindness is such, that my duty as yet has been inclination.

Act Four

Enter HASTINGS *and* MISS NEVILLE.

HASTINGS   You surprise me! Sir Charles Marlow expected here this night! Where have you had your information?

MISS NEVILLE   You may depend upon it. I just saw his letter to Mr. Hardcastle, in which he tells him he intends setting out a few hours after his son.

HASTINGS   Then, my Constance, all must be completed before he arrives. He knows me; and should he find me here, would discover my name, and perhaps my designs, to the rest of the family.

MISS NEVILLE   The jewels, I hope, are safe?

HASTINGS   Yes, yes. I have sent them to Marlow, who keeps the keys of our baggage. In the meantime, I'll go to prepare matters for our elopement. I have had the squire's promise of a fresh pair of horses; and, if I should not see him again, will write him further directions.   *Exit.*

MISS NEVILLE   Well! success attend you. In the meantime, I'll go amuse my aunt with the old pretense of a violent passion for my cousin.   *Exit.*

Enter MARLOW, *followed by* SERVANT.

MARLOW   I wonder what Hastings could mean by sending me so valuable a thing as a casket to keep for him, when he knows the only place I have is the seat of a post coach at an inn door. Have you deposited the casket with the landlady,

33 Dicing terms.

as I ordered you? Have you put it into her own hands?

SERVANT Yes, your honor.

MARLOW She said she'd keep it safe, did she?

SERVANT Yes, she said she'd keep it safe enough; she asked me how I came by it, and she said she had a great mind to make me give an account of myself.

Exit SERVANT.

MARLOW Ha! ha! ha! They're safe, however. What an unaccountable set of beings have we got amongst! This little barmaid, though, runs in my head most strangely, and drives out the absurdities of all the rest of the family. She's mine, she must be mine, or I'm greatly mistaken.

Enter HASTINGS.

HASTINGS Bless me! I quite forgot to tell her that I intended to prepare at the bottom of the garden. Marlow here, and in spirits too!

MARLOW Give me joy, George! Crown me, shadow me with laurels! Well, George, after all, we modest fellows don't want for success among the women.

HASTINGS Some women, you mean. But what success has your honor's modesty been crowned with now, that it grows so insolent upon us?

MARLOW Didn't you see the tempting, brisk, lovely little thing that runs about the house with a bunch of keys to its girdle?

HASTINGS Well! and what then?

MARLOW She's mine, you rogue you. Such fire, such motions, such eyes, such lips— but, egad! she would not let me kiss them though.

HASTINGS But are you so sure, so very sure of her?

MARLOW Why man, she talked of showing me her work above stairs and I am to improve the pattern.

HASTINGS But how can *you*, Charles, go about to rob a woman of her honor?

MARLOW Pshaw! pshaw! We all know the honor of a barmaid of an inn. I don't in-

tend to *rob* her, take my word for it; there's nothing in this house I shan't honestly *pay* for.

HASTINGS I believe the girl has virtue.

MARLOW And if she has, I should be the last man in the world that would attempt to corrupt it.

HASTINGS You have taken care, I hope, of the casket I sent you to lock up? It's in safety?

MARLOW Yes, yes. It's safe enough. I have taken care of it. But how could you think the seat of a post coach at an inn door a place of safety? Ah! numskull! I have taken better precautions for you than you did for yourself. I have——

HASTINGS What?

MARLOW I have sent it to the landlady to keep for you.

HASTINGS To the landlady!

MARLOW The landlady.

HASTINGS You did?

MARLOW I did. She's to be answerable for its forthcoming, you know.

HASTINGS Yes, she'll bring it forth with a witness.

MARLOW Wasn't I right? I believe you'll allow that I acted prudently upon this occasion?

HASTINGS (*aside*) He must not see my uneasiness.

MARLOW You seem a little disconcerted, though, methinks. Sure nothing has happened?

HASTINGS No, nothing. Never was in better spirits in all my life. And so you left it with the landlady, who, no doubt, very readily undertook the charge?

MARLOW Rather too readily. For she not only kept the casket, but, through her great precaution, was going to keep the messenger too. Ha! ha! ha!

HASTINGS He! he! he! They're safe, however.

MARLOW As a guinea in a miser's purse.

HASTINGS (*aside*) So now all hopes of fortune are at an end, and we must set off without it. (*To him.*) Well, Charles, I'll leave you to your meditations on the pretty barmaid, and, he! he! he! may you be as successful for yourself as you have been for me. *Exit.*

MARLOW Thank ye, George! I ask no more. Ha! ha! ha!

Enter HARDCASTLE.

HARDCASTLE I no longer know my own house. It's turned all topsy-turvy. His servants have got drunk already. I'll bear it no longer, and yet, from my respect for his father, I'll be calm. (*To him.*) Mr. Marlow, your servant. I'm your very humble servant. (*Bowing low.*)

MARLOW Sir, your humble servant. (*Aside.*) What's to be the wonder now?

HARDCASTLE I believe, sir, you must be sensible, sir, that no man alive ought to be more welcome than your father's son, sir. I hope you think so?

MARLOW I do, from my soul, sir. I don't want much entreaty. I generally make my father's son welcome wherever he goes.

HARDCASTLE I believe you do, from my soul, sir. But though I say nothing to your own conduct, that of your servants is insufferable. Their manner of drinking is setting a very bad example in this house, I assure you.

MARLOW I protest, my very good sir, that's no fault of mine. If they don't drink as they ought, *they* are to blame. I ordered them not to spare the cellar. I did, I assure you. (*To the side scene.*) Here, let one of my servants come up. (*To him.*) My positive directions were, that as I did not drink myself, they should make up for my deficiencies below.

HARDCASTLE Then they had your orders for what they do! I'm satisfied!

MARLOW They had, I assure you. You shall hear from one of themselves.

Enter SERVANT, *drunk.*

MARLOW You, Jeremy! Come forward, sirrah! What were my orders? Were you not told to drink freely, and call for what you thought fit, for the good of the house?

HARDCASTLE (*aside*) I begin to lose my patience.

JEREMY (*staggering forward*) Please your honor, liberty and Fleet Street[34] forever! Though I'm but a servant, I'm as good as another man. I'll drink for no man before supper, sir, dammey! Good liquor will sit upon a good supper, but a good supper will not sit upon—hiccup—upon my conscience, sir. *Exit.*

MARLOW You see, my old friend, the fellow is as drunk as he can possibly be. I don't know what you'd have more, unless you'd have the poor devil soused in a beer barrel.

HARDCASTLE Zounds! He'll drive me distracted if I contain myself any longer. Mr. Marlow, sir; I have submitted to your insolence for more than four hours, and I see no likelihood of its coming to an end. I'm now resolved to be master here, sir, and I desire that you and your drunken pack may leave my house directly.

MARLOW Leave your house!—Sure, you jest, my good friend! What, when I'm doing what I can to please you!

HARDCASTLE I tell you, sir, you don't please me; so I desire you'll leave my house.

MARLOW Sure, you cannot be serious! At this time o' night, and such a night! You only mean to banter me!

HARDCASTLE I tell you, sir, I'm serious; and, now that my passions are roused, I say this house is mine, sir; this house is mine, and I command you to leave it directly.

MARLOW Ha! ha! ha! A puddle in a storm. I shan't stir a step, I assure you. (*In a serious tone.*) This your house, fellow! It's my house. This is my house. Mine, while I choose to stay. What right have you to bid me leave this house, sir? I never met with such impudence, curse me, never in my whole life before.

HARDCASTLE Nor I, confound me if ever I did! To come to my house, to call for what he likes, to turn me out of my own chair, to insult the family, to order his

34 London street, known for taverns.

servants to get drunk, and then to tell me *This house is mine, sir.* By all that's impudent, it makes me laugh. Ha! ha! ha! Pray sir (*bantering*), as you take the house, what think you of taking the rest of the furniture? There's a pair of silver candlesticks, and there's a firescreen, and here's a pair of brazen-nosed bellows, perhaps you may take a fancy to them?

MARLOW   Bring me your bill, sir, bring me your bill, and let's make no more words about it.

HARDCASTLE   There are a set of prints, too. What think you of "The Rake's Progress"[35] for your own apartment?

MARLOW   Bring me your bill, I say; and I'll leave you and your infernal house directly.

HARDCASTLE   Then there's a mahogany table, that you may see your own face in.

MARLOW   My bill, I say.

HARDCASTLE   I had forgot the great chair, for your own particular slumbers, after a hearty meal.

MARLOW   Zounds! bring me my bill, I say, and let's hear no more on't.

HARDCASTLE   Young man, young man, from your father's letter to me, I was taught to expect a well-bred modest man as a visitor here, but now I find him no better than a coxcomb and a bully; but he will be down here presently, and shall hear more of it.   *Exit.*

MARLOW   How's this! Sure I have not mistaken the house! Everything looks like an inn. The servants cry "Coming"; the attendance is awkward; the barmaid, too, to attend us. But she's here, and will further inform me. Whither so fast, child? A word with you.

Enter MISS HARDCASTLE.

MISS HARDCASTLE   Let it be short, then. I'm in a hurry. (*Aside.*) I believe he begins to find out his mistake. But it's too soon quite to undeceive him.

MARLOW   Pray, child, answer me one ques-

tion. What are you, and what may your business in this house be?

MISS HARDCASTLE   A relation of the family, sir.

MARLOW   What, a poor relation?

MISS HARDCASTLE   Yes, sir. A poor relation appointed to keep the keys, and to see that the guests want nothing in my power to give them.

MARLOW   That is, you act as the barmaid of this inn.

MISS HARDCASTLE   Inn. O law! What brought that in your head? One of the best families in the country keep an inn! Ha, ha, ha, old Mr. Hardcastle's house an inn!

MARLOW   Mr. Hardcastle's house! Is this house Mr. Hardcastle's house, child?

MISS HARDCASTLE   Aye, sure. Whose else should it be?

MARLOW   So then all's out, and I have been damnably imposed on. O, confound my stupid head, I shall be laughed at over the whole town. I shall be stuck up in caricatura in all the print shops. "The Dullissimo Maccaroni." To mistake this house of all others for an inn, and my father's old friend for an innkeeper. What a swaggering puppy must he take me for. What a silly puppy do I find myself. There again, may I be hanged, my dear, but I mistook you for the barmaid.

MISS HARDCASTLE   Dear me! dear me! I'm sure there's nothing in my *behaviour*[36] to put me upon a level with one of that stamp.

MARLOW   Nothing, my dear, nothing. But I was in for a list of blunders, and could not help making you a subscriber. My stupidity saw everything the wrong way. I mistook your assiduity for assurance, and your simplicity for allurement. But it's over. This house I no more show my face in!

MISS HARDCASTLE   I hope, sir, I have done nothing to disoblige you. I'm sure I should be sorry to affront any gentleman

35 Hogarth's series of engravings (1735).

36 Miss Hardcastle continues to affect a vulgar speech.

who has been so polite, and said so many civil things to me. I'm sure I should be sorry (*pretending to cry*) if he left the family upon my account. I'm sure I should be sorry people said anything amiss, since I have no fortune but my character.

MARLOW (*aside*) By heaven, she weeps. This is the first mark of tenderness I ever had from a modest woman, and it touches me. (*To her.*) Excuse me, my lovely girl, you are the only part of the family I leave with reluctance. But to be plain with you, the difference of our birth, fortune and education, make an honorable connection impossible, and I can never harbor a thought of seducing simplicity that trusted in my honor, or bringing ruin upon one whose only fault was being too lovely.

MISS HARDCASTLE (*aside*) Generous man! I now begin to admire him. (*To him.*) But I'm sure my family is as good as Miss Hardcastle's, and though I'm poor, that's no great misfortune to a contented mind, and, until this moment, I never thought that it was bad to want fortune.

MARLOW And why now, my pretty simplicity?

MISS HARDCASTLE Because it puts me at a distance from one, that if I had a thousand pound I would give it all to.

MARLOW (*aside*) This simplicity bewitches me, so that if I stay I'm undone. I must make one bold effort, and leave her. (*To her.*) Your partiality in my favor, my dear, touches me most sensibly, and were I to live for myself alone, I could easily fix my choice. But I owe too much to the opinion of the world, too much to the authority of a father, so that —I can scarcely speak it—it affects me. Farewell. *Exit.*

MISS HARDCASTLE I never knew half his merit till now. He shall not go, if I have power or art to detain him. I'll still preserve the character in which I stooped to conquer, but will undeceive my papa, who, perhaps, may laugh him out of his resolution. *Exit.*

Enter TONY, MISS NEVILLE.

TONY Aye, you may steal for yourselves the next time. I have done my duty. She has got the jewels again, that's a sure thing; but she believes it was all a mistake of the servants.

MISS NEVILLE But, my dear cousin, sure, you won't forsake us in this distress. If she in the least suspects that I am going off, I shall certainly be locked up, or sent to my Aunt Pedigree's which is ten times worse.

TONY To be sure, aunts of all kinds are damned bad things. But what can I do? I have got you a pair of horses that will fly like Whistlejacket, and I'm sure you can't say but I have courted you nicely before her face. Here she comes, we must court a bit or two more, for fear she should suspect us. (*They retire, and seem to fondle.*)

Enter MRS. HARDCASTLE.

MRS. HARDCASTLE Well, I was greatly fluttered, to be sure. But my son tells me it was all a mistake of the servants. I shan't be easy, however, till they are fairly married, and then let her keep her own fortune. But what do I see? Fondling together, as I'm alive! I never saw Tony so sprightly before. Ah! have I caught you, my pretty doves? What, billing, exchanging stolen glances, and broken murmurs! Ah!

TONY As for murmurs, mother, we grumble a little now and then, to be sure. But there's no love lost between us.

MRS. HARDCASTLE A mere sprinkling, Tony, upon the flame, only to make it burn brighter.

MISS NEVILLE Cousin Tony promises to give us more of his company at home. Indeed, he shan't leave us any more. It won't leave us, cousin Tony, will it?

TONY O! it's a pretty creature. No, I'd sooner leave my horse in a pound, than leave you when you smile upon one so. Your laugh makes you so becoming.

MISS NEVILLE Agreeable cousin! Who can help admiring that natural humor, that pleasant, broad, red, thoughtless (*patting his cheek*) ah! it's a bold face.

MRS. HARDCASTLE   Pretty innocence!

TONY   I'm sure I always loved cousin Con's hazel eyes, and her pretty long fingers, that she twists this way and that, over the haspicholls,[37] like a parcel of bobbins.

MRS. HARDCASTLE   Ah, he would charm the bird from the tree. I was never so happy before. My boy takes after his father, poor Mr. Lumpkin, exactly. The jewels, my dear Con, shall be yours incontinently. You shall have them. Isn't he a sweet boy, my dear? You shall be married tomorrow, and we'll put off the rest of his education, like Dr. Drowsy's sermons, to a fitter opportunity.

Enter DIGGORY.

DIGGORY   Where's the squire? I have got a letter for your worship.

TONY   Give it to my mamma. She reads all my letters first.

DIGGORY   I had orders to deliver it into your own hands.

TONY   Who does it come from?

DIGGORY   Your worship mun ask that o' the letter itself.

TONY   I could wish to know, though. (*Turning the letter, and gazing on it.*) [*Exit* DIGGORY.]

MISS NEVILLE   (*aside*) Undone, undone. A letter to him from Hastings. I know the hand. If my aunt sees it, we are ruined forever. I'll keep her employed a little if I can. (*To* MRS. HARDCASTLE.) But I have not told you, madam, of my cousin's smart answer just now to Mr. Marlow. We so laughed. You must know, madam. This way a little, for he must not hear us. (*They confer.*)

TONY   (*still gazing*) A damned cramp piece of penmanship, as ever I saw in my life. I can read your print-hand very well. But here there are such handles, and shakes, and dashes, that one can scarce tell the head from the tail. "To Anthony Lumpkin, Esquire." It's very odd, I can

read the outside of my letters, where my own name is, well enough. But when I come to open it, it's all—buzz. That's hard, very hard; for the inside of the letter is always the cream of the correspondence.

MRS. HARDCASTLE   Ha! ha! ha! Very well, very well. And so my son was too hard for the philosopher.

MISS NEVILLE   Yes, madam; but you must hear the rest, madam. A little more this way, or he may hear us. You'll hear how he puzzled him again.

MRS. HARDCASTLE   He seems strangely puzzled now himself, methinks.

TONY   (*still gazing*) A damned up-and-down hand, as if it was disguised in liquor. (*Reading.*) "Dear Sir." Aye, that's that. Then there's an *M*, and a *T*, and an *S*, but whether the next be an "izzard"[38] or an *R*, confound me, I cannot tell.

MRS. HARDCASTLE   What's that, my dear? Can I give you any assistance?

MISS NEVILLE   Pray, aunt, let me read it. Nobody reads a cramp hand better than I (*twitching the letter from her*). Do you know who it is from?

TONY   Can't tell, except from Dick Ginger the feeder.

MISS NEVILLE   Aye, so it is. (*Pretending to read.*) Dear Squire, Hoping that you're in health, as I am at this present. The gentlemen of the Shakebag club has cut the gentleman of Goose-green quite out of feather. The odds—um—odd battle—um —long fighting—um, here, here, it's all about cocks, and fighting; it's of no consequence, here, put it up, put it up. (*Thrusting the crumpled letter upon him.*)

TONY   But I tell you, miss, it's of all the consequence in the world. I would not lose the rest of it for a guinea. Here, mother, do you make it out? Of no consequence! (*Giving* MRS. HARDCASTLE *the letter.*)

MRS. HARDCASTLE   How's this! (*Reads.*) "Dear Squire, I'm now waiting for Miss

---

37 Harpsichord.

38 The letter Z.

Neville, with a post chaise and pair, at the bottom of the garden but I find my horses yet unable to perform the journey. I expect you'll assist us with a pair of fresh horses, as you promised. Dispatch is necessary, as the hag"—aye, the hag—"your mother, will otherwise suspect us. Yours, Hastings." Grant me patience. I shall run distracted. My rage chokes me.

MISS NEVILLE   I hope, madam, you'll suspend your resentment for a few moments, and not impute to me any impertinence, or sinister design, that belongs to another.

MRS. HARDCASTLE   (*curtsying very low*) Fine spoken, madam, you are most miraculously polite and engaging, and quite the very pink of courtesy and circumspection, madam. (*Changing her tone.*) And you, you great ill-fashioned oaf, with scarce sense enough to keep your mouth shut. Were you, too, joined against me? But I'll defeat all your plots in a moment. As for you, madam, since you have got a pair of fresh horses ready, it would be cruel to disappoint them. So, if you please, instead of running away with your spark, prepare, this very moment, to run off with *me*. Your old Aunt Pedigree will keep you secure, I'll warrant me. You, too, sir, may mount your horse, and guard us upon the way. Here, Thomas, Roger, Diggory, I'll show you that I wish you better than you do yourselves.   *Exit.*

MISS NEVILLE   So now I'm completely ruined.

TONY   Aye, that's a sure thing.

MISS NEVILLE   What better could be expected from being connected with such a stupid fool, and after all the nods and signs I made him.

TONY   By the laws, miss, it was your own cleverness, and not my stupidity, that did your business. You were so nice and so busy with your Shakebags and Goosegreens, that I thought you could never be making believe.

Enter HASTINGS.

HASTINGS   So, sir, I find by my servant, that you have shown my letter, and be-

trayed us. Was this well done, young gentleman?

TONY   Here's another. Ask Miss there who betrayed you. Ecod, it was her doing, not mine.

Enter MARLOW.

MARLOW   So I have been finely used here among you. Rendered contemptible, driven into ill manners, despised, insulted, laughed at.

TONY   Here's another. We shall have old Bedlam broke loose presently.

MISS NEVILLE   And there, sir, is the gentleman to whom we all owe every obligation.

MARLOW   What can I say to him, a mere boy, an idiot, whose ignorance and age are a protection.

HASTINGS   A poor contemptible booby, that would but disgrace correction.

MISS NEVILLE   Yet with cunning and malice enough to make himself merry with all our embarrassments.

HASTINGS   An insensible cub.

MARLOW   Replete with tricks and mischief.

TONY   Baw! damme, but I'll fight you both one after the other—with baskets.

MARLOW   As for him, he's below resentment. But your conduct, Mr. Hastings, requires an explanation. You knew of my mistakes, yet would not undeceive me.

HASTINGS   Tortured as I am with my own disappointments, is this a time for explanations? It is not friendly, Mr. Marlow.

MARLOW   But, sir——

MISS NEVILLE   Mr. Marlow, we never kept on your mistake, till it was too late to undeceive you. Be pacified.

Enter SERVANT.

SERVANT   My mistress desires you'll get ready immediately, madam. The horses are putting to. Your hat and things are in the next room. We are to go thirty miles before morning.   *Exit* SERVANT.

MISS NEVILLE   Well, well; I'll come presently.

MARLOW (*to* HASTINGS) Was it well done, sir, to assist in rendering me ridiculous? To hang me out for the scorn of all my acquaintance? Depend upon it, sir, I shall expect an explanation.

HASTINGS Was it well done, sir, if you're upon that subject, to deliver what I entrusted to yourself, to the care of another, sir?

MISS NEVILLE Mr. Hastings, Mr. Marlow. Why will you increase my distress by this groundless dispute? I implore, I entreat you——

Enter SERVANT.

SERVANT Your cloak, madam. My mistress is impatient.

MISS NEVILLE I come. [*Exit* SERVANT.] Pray be pacified. If I leave you thus, I shall die with apprehension!

Enter SERVANT.

SERVANT Your fan, muff, and gloves, madam. The horses are waiting.
[*Exit* SERVANT.]

MISS NEVILLE O, Mr. Marlow! if you knew what a scene of constraint and ill-nature lies before me, I'm sure it would convert your resentment into pity.

MARLOW I'm so distracted with a variety of passions, that I don't know what I do. Forgive me, madam. George, forgive me. You know my hasty temper, and should not exasperate it.

HASTINGS The torture of my situation is my only excuse.

MISS NEVILLE Well, my dear Hastings, if you have that esteem for me that I think, that I am sure you have, your constancy for three years will but increase the happiness of our future connection. If——

MRS. HARDCASTLE (*within*) Miss Neville. Constance, why, Constance, I say!

MISS NEVILLE I'm coming. Well, constancy. Remember, constancy is the word. *Exit.*

HASTINGS My heart! How can I support this? To be so near happiness, and such happiness!

MARLOW (*to* TONY) You see now, young gentleman, the effects of your folly. What might be amusement to you, is here disappointment, and even distress.

TONY (*from a reverie*) Ecod, I have hit it. It's here. Your hands. Yours and yours, my poor Sulky. My boots there, ho! Meet me two hours hence at the bottom of the garden; and if you don't find Tony Lumpkin a more good-natur'd fellow than you thought for, I'll give you leave to take my best horse, and Bet Bouncer into the bargain. Come along. My boots, ho! *Exeunt.*

Act Five

SCENE ONE *Scene continues.*

Enter HASTINGS *and* SERVANT.

HASTINGS You saw the old lady and Miss Neville drive off, you say?

SERVANT Yes, your honor. They went off in a post coach, and the young squire went on horseback. They're thirty miles off by this time.

HASTINGS Then all my hopes are over.

SERVANT Yes, sir. Old Sir Charles is arrived. He and the old gentleman of the house have been laughing at Mr. Marlow's mistake this half hour. They are coming this way.

HASTINGS Then I must not be seen. So now to my fruitless appointment at the bottom of the garden. This is about the time. *Exit.*

Enter SIR CHARLES *and* HARDCASTLE.

HARDCASTLE Ha! ha! ha! The peremptory tone in which he sent forth his sublime commands.

SIR CHARLES And the reserve with which I suppose he treated all your advances.

HARDCASTLE And yet he might have seen something in me above a common innkeeper, too.

SIR CHARLES Yes, Dick, but he mistook you for an uncommon innkeeper, ha! ha! ha!

HARDCASTLE   Well, I'm in too good spirits to think of anything but joy. Yes, my dear friend, this union of our families will make our personal friendships hereditary; and though my daughter's fortune is but small——

SIR CHARLES   Why, Dick, will you talk of fortune to me? My son is possessed of more than a competence already, and can want nothing but a good and virtuous girl to share his happiness and increase it. If they like each other, as you say they do——

HARDCASTLE   *If,* man! I tell you they *do* like each other. My daughter as good as told me so.

SIR CHARLES   But girls are apt to flatter themselves, you know.

HARDCASTLE   I saw him grasp her hand in the warmest manner myself; and here he comes to put you out of your *ifs,* I warrant him.

Enter MARLOW.

MARLOW   I come, sir, once more, to ask pardon for my strange conduct. I can scarce reflect on my insolence without confusion.

HARDCASTLE   Tut, boy, a trifle. You take it too gravely. An hour or two's laughing with my daughter will set all to rights again. She'll never like you the worse for it.

MARLOW   Sir, I shall be always proud of her approbation.

HARDCASTLE   Approbation is but a cold word, Mr. Marlow; if I am not deceived, you have something more than approbation thereabouts. You take me?

MARLOW   Really, sir, I have not that happiness.

HARDCASTLE   Come, boy, I'm an old fellow, and know what's what, as well as you that are younger. I know what has past between you; but mum.

MARLOW   Sure, sir, nothing has passed between us but the most profound respect on my side, and the most distant reserve on hers. You don't think, sir, that my impudence has been passed upon all the rest of the family.

HARDCASTLE   Impudence! No, I don't say that—not quite impudence—though girls like to be played with, and rumpled a little too, sometimes. But she has told no tales, I assure you.

MARLOW   I never gave her the slightest cause.

HARDCASTLE   Well, well, I like modesty in its place well enough. But this is over-acting, young gentleman. You may be open. Your father and I will like you the better for it.

MARLOW   May I die, sir, if I ever——

HARDCASTLE   I tell you, she don't dislike you; and as I'm sure you like her——

MARLOW   Dear sir—I protest, sir——

HARDCASTLE   I see no reason why you should not be joined as fast as the parson can tie you.

MARLOW   But hear me, sir——

HARDCASTLE   Your father approves the match, I admire it, every moment's delay will be doing mischief; so——

MARLOW   But why won't you hear me? By all that's just and true, I never gave Miss Hardcastle the slightest mark of my attachment, or even the most distant hint to suspect me of affection. We had but one interview, and that was formal, modest, and uninteresting.

HARDCASTLE   *(aside)*   This fellow's formal, modest impudence is beyond bearing.

SIR CHARLES   And you never grasped her hand, or made any protestations!

MARLOW   As heaven is my witness, I came down in obedience to your commands. I saw the lady without emotion, and parted without reluctance. I hope you'll exact no further proofs of my duty, nor prevent me from leaving a house in which I suffer so many mortifications.   *Exit.*

SIR CHARLES   I'm astonished at the air of sincerity with which he parted.

HARDCASTLE   And I'm astonished at the deliberate intrepidity of his assurance.

SIR CHARLES   I dare pledge my life and honor upon his truth.

HARDCASTLE   *(looking out to right)*   Here

comes my daughter, and I would stake my happiness upon her veracity.

Enter MISS HARDCASTLE.

HARDCASTLE   Kate, come hither, child. Answer us sincerely, and without reserve; has Mr. Marlow made you any professions of love and affection?

MISS HARDCASTLE   The question is very abrupt, sir! But since you require unreserved sincerity, I think he has.

HARDCASTLE (*to* SIR CHARLES)   You see.

SIR CHARLES   And pray, madam, have you and my son had more than one interview?

MISS HARDCASTLE   Yes, sir, several.

HARDCASTLE (*to* SIR CHARLES)   You see.

SIR CHARLES   But did he profess any attachment?

MISS HARDCASTLE   A lasting one.

SIR CHARLES   Did he talk of love?

MISS HARDCASTLE   Much, sir.

SIR CHARLES   Amazing! And all this formally?

MISS HARDCASTLE   Formally.

HARDCASTLE   Now, my friend, I hope you are satisfied.

SIR CHARLES   And how did he behave, madam?

MISS HARDCASTLE   As most professed admirers do. Said some civil things of my face, talked much of his want of merit, and the greatness of mine; mentioned his heart, gave a short tragedy speech, and ended with pretended rapture.

SIR CHARLES   Now I'm perfectly convinced, indeed. I know his conversation among women to be modest and submissive. This forward, canting, ranting manner by no means describes him, and I am confident he never sat for the picture.

MISS HARDCASTLE   Then what, sir, if I should convince you to your face of my sincerity? If you and my papa, in about half an hour, will place yourselves behind that screen, you shall hear him declare his passion to me in person.

SIR CHARLES   Agreed. And if I find him what you describe, all my happiness in him must have an end.   *Exit.*

MISS HARDCASTLE   And if you don't find

him what I describe—I fear my happiness must never have a beginning.

Exeunt.

[SCENE TWO]   *Scene changes to the back of the garden.*

Enter HASTINGS.

HASTINGS   What an idiot am I, to wait here for a fellow, who probably takes a delight in mortifying me. He never intended to be punctual, and I'll wait no longer. What do I see? It is he, and perhaps with news of my Constance.

Enter TONY, *booted and spattered.*

HASTINGS   My honest squire! I now find you a man of your word. This looks like friendship.

TONY   Aye, I'm your friend, and the best friend you have in the world, if you knew but all. This riding by night, by the bye, is cursedly tiresome. It has shook me worse than the basket of a stagecoach.

HASTINGS   But how? Where did you leave your fellow travelers? Are they in safety? Are they housed?

TONY   Five and twenty miles in two hours and a half is no such bad driving. The poor beasts have smoked for it: rabbit me, but I'd rather ride forty miles after a fox, than ten with such varment.

HASTINGS   Well, but where have you left the ladies? I die with impatience.

TONY   Left them? Why, where should I leave them, but where I found them?

HASTINGS   This is a riddle.

TONY   Riddle me this, then. What's that goes round the house, and round the house, and never touches the house?

HASTINGS   I'm still astray.

TONY   Why, that's it, mon. I have led them astray. By jingo, there's not a pond or slough within five miles of the place but they can tell the taste of.

HASTINGS   Ha, ha, ha, I understand; you took them in a round, while they supposed themselves going forward. And so you have at last brought them home again.

TONY   You shall hear. I first took them down Feather-Bed Lane, where we stuck fast in the mud. I then rattled them crack over the stones of Up-and-Down Hill—I then introduced them to the gibbet on Heavy-Tree Heath, and from that, with a circumbendibus, I fairly lodged them in the horsepond at the bottom of the garden.

HASTINGS   But no accident, I hope.

TONY   No, no. Only mother is confoundedly frightened. She thinks herself forty miles off. She's sick of the journey, and the cattle can scarce crawl. So, if your own horses be ready, you may whip off with cousin, and I'll be bound that no soul here can budge a foot to follow you.

HASTINGS   My dear friend, how can I be grateful?

TONY   Aye, now it's dear friend, noble squire. Just now, it was all idiot, cub, and run me through the guts. Damn *your* way of fighting, I say. After we take a knock in this part of the country, we kiss and be friends. But if you had run me through the guts, then I should be dead, and you might go kiss the hangman.

HASTINGS   The rebuke is just. But I must hasten to relieve Miss Neville; if you keep the old lady employed, I promise to take care of the young one.

TONY   Never fear me. Here she comes. Vanish. [*Exit* HASTINGS.] She's got from the pond, and draggled up to the waist like a mermaid.

Enter MRS. HARDCASTLE.

MRS. HARDCASTLE   Oh, Tony, I'm killed. Shook. Battered to death. I shall never survive it. That last jolt that laid us against the quickset hedge has done my business.

TONY   Alack, mamma, it was all your own fault. You would be for running away by night, without knowing one inch of the way.

MRS. HARDCASTLE   I wish we were at home again. I never met so many accidents in so short a journey. Drenched in the mud, overturned in a ditch, stuck fast in a slough, jolted to a jelly, and at last to lose our way. Whereabouts do you think we are, Tony?

TONY   By my guess we should be upon Crackskull Common, about forty miles from home.

MRS. HARDCASTLE   O lud! O lud! the most notorious spot in all the country. We only want a robbery to make a complete night on't.

TONY   Don't be afraid, mamma, don't be afraid. Two of the five that kept here[39] are hanged, and the other three may not find us. Don't be afraid. Is that a man that's galloping behind us? No; it's only a tree. Don't be afraid.

MRS. HARDCASTLE   The fright will certainly kill me.

TONY   Do you see any thing like a black hat moving behind the thicket?

MRS. HARDCASTLE   O death!

TONY   No, it's only a cow. Don't be afraid, mamma, don't be afraid.

MRS. HARDCASTLE   As I'm alive, Tony, I see a man coming towards us. Ah! I'm sure on't. If he perceives us, we are undone.

TONY   (*aside*)   Father-in-law, by all that's unlucky, come to take one of his night walks. (*To her.*) Ah, it's a highwayman, with pistols as long as my arm. A damned ill-looking fellow.

MRS. HARDCASTLE   Good Heaven defend us! He approaches.

TONY   Do you hide yourself in that thicket and leave me to manage him. If there be any danger I'll cough and cry hem. When I cough be sure to keep close.

MRS. HARDCASTLE *hides behind a tree in the back scene.*

Enter HARDCASTLE.

HARDCASTLE   I'm mistaken, or I heard voices of people in want of help. Oh,

39 Frequented the place.

Tony, is that you? I did not expect you so soon back. Are your mother and her charge in safety?

TONY Very safe, sir, at my Aunt Pedigree's. Hem.

MRS. HARDCASTLE (*from behind*) Ah, death! I find there's danger.

HARDCASTLE Forty miles in three hours; sure, that's too much, my youngster.

TONY Stout horses and willing minds make short journeys, as they say. Hem.

MRS. HARDCASTLE (*from behind*) Sure he'll do the dear boy no harm.

HARDCASTLE But I heard a voice here; I should be glad to know from whence it came?

TONY It was I, sir, talking to myself, sir. I was saying that forty miles in four hours was very good going. Hem. As to be sure it was. Hem. I have got a sort of cold by being out in the air. We'll go in if you please. Hem.

HARDCASTLE But if you talked to yourself, you did not answer yourself. I am certain I heard two voices, and am resolved (*raising his voice*) to find the other out.

MRS. HARDCASTLE (*from behind*) Oh! he's coming to find me out. Oh!

TONY What need you go, sir, if I tell you? Hem. I'll lay down my life for the truth—hem—I'll tell you all, sir. (*Detaining him.*)

HARDCASTLE I tell you I will not be detained. I insist on seeing. It's in vain to expect I'll believe you.

MRS. HARDCASTLE (*running forward from behind*) O lud, he'll murder my poor boy, my darling. Here, good gentleman, whet your rage upon me. Take my money, my life, but spare that young gentleman, spare my child, if you have any mercy.

HARDCASTLE My wife! as I'm a Christian. From whence can she come, or what does she mean?

MRS. HARDCASTLE (*kneeling*) Take compassion on us, good Mr. Highwayman. Take our money, our watches, all we have, but spare our lives. We will never bring you to justice, indeed, we won't, good Mr. Highwayman.

HARDCASTLE I believe the woman's out of her senses. What, Dorothy, don't you know me?

MRS. HARDCASTLE Mr. Hardcastle, as I'm alive! My fears blinded me. But who, my dear, could have expected to meet you here, in this frightful place, so far from home. What has brought you to follow us?

HARDCASTLE Sure, Dorothy, you have not lost your wits. So far from home, when you are within forty yards of your own door! (*To him.*) This is one of your old tricks, you graceless rogue, you! (*To her.*) Don't you know the gate, and the mulberry tree; and don't you remember the horsepond, my dear?

MRS. HARDCASTLE Yes, I shall remember the horsepond as long as I live; I have caught my death in it. (*To* TONY.) And it is to you, you graceless varlet, I owe all this? I'll teach you to abuse your mother, I will.

TONY Ecod, mother, all the parish says you have spoiled me, and so you may take the fruits on't.

MRS. HARDCASTLE I'll spoil you, I will. *Follows him off the stage.*

HARDCASTLE There's morality, however, in his reply. *Exit.*

Enter HASTINGS *and* MISS NEVILLE.

HASTINGS My dear Constance, why will you deliberate thus? If we delay a moment, all is lost forever. Pluck up a little resolution, and we shall soon be out of the reach of her malignity.

MISS NEVILLE I find it impossible. My spirits are so sunk with the agitations I have suffered, that I am unable to face any new danger. Two or three years' patience will at last crown us with happiness.

HASTINGS Such a tedious delay is worse than inconstancy. Let us fly, my charmer. Let us date our happiness from this very moment. Perish fortune. Love and content will increase what we possess beyond a monarch's revenue. Let me prevail.

MISS NEVILLE No, Mr. Hastings, no. Prudence once more comes to my relief, and I will obey its dictates. In the moment of passion, fortune may be despised, but it ever produces a lasting repentance. I'm resolved to apply to Mr. Hardcastle's compassion and justice for redress.

HASTINGS But though he had the will, he has not the power to relieve you.

MISS NEVILLE But he has influence, and upon that I am resolved to rely.

HASTINGS I have no hopes. But since you persist, I must reluctantly obey you.

Exeunt.

SCENE THREE *Scene changes* [*the house.*]

Enter SIR CHARLES *and* MISS HARDCASTLE.

SIR CHARLES What a situation am I in. If what you say appears, I shall then find a guilty son. If what he says be true, I shall then lose one that, of all others, I most wished for a daughter.

MISS HARDCASTLE I am proud of your approbation, and, to show I merit it, if you place yourselves as I directed, you shall hear his explicit declaration. But he comes.

SIR CHARLES I'll to your father, and keep him to the appointment.

Exit SIR CHARLES.

Enter MARLOW.

MARLOW Though prepared for setting out, I come once more to take leave, nor did I, till this moment, know the pain I feel in the separation.

MISS HARDCASTLE (*in her own natural manner*) I believe sufferings cannot be very great, sir, which you can so easily remove. A day or two longer, perhaps, might lessen your uneasiness, by showing the little value of what you think proper to regret.

MARLOW (*aside*) This girl every moment improves upon me. (*To her.*) It must not be, madam. I have already trifled too long with my heart. My very pride begins to submit to my passion. The disparity of education and fortune, the anger of a parent, and the contempt of my

equals begin to lose their weight; and nothing can restore me to myself but this painful effort of resolution.

MISS HARDCASTLE Then go, sir. I'll urge nothing more to detain you. Though my family be as good as hers you came down to visit, and my education, I hope, not inferior, what are these advantages without equal affluence? I must remain contended with the slight approbation of imputed merit; I must have only the mockery of your addresses, while all your serious aims are fixed on fortune.

Enter HARDCASTLE *and* SIR CHARLES *from behind.*

SIR CHARLES Here, behind this screen.

HARDCASTLE Aye, aye, make no noise. I'll engage my Kate covers him with confusion at last.

MARLOW By heavens, madam, fortune was ever my smallest consideration. Your beauty at first caught my eye; for who could see that without emotion? But every moment that I converse with you, steals in some new grace, heightens the picture, and gives it stronger expression. What at first seemed rustic plainness, now appears refined simplicity. What seemed forward assurance, now strikes me as the result of courageous innocence and conscious virtue.

SIR CHARLES What can it mean! He amazes me!

HARDCASTLE I told you how it would be. Hush!

MARLOW I am now determined to stay, madam, and I have too good an opinion of my father's discernment, when he sees you, to doubt his approbation.

MISS HARDCASTLE No, Mr. Marlow, I will not, cannot detain you. Do you think I could suffer a connection, in which there is the smallest room for repentance? Do you think I would take the mean advantage of a transient passion, to load you with confusion? Do you think I could ever relish that happiness, which was acquired by lessening yours!

MARLOW By all that's good, I can have no

happiness but what's in your power to grant me. Nor shall I ever feel repentance, but in not having seen your merits before. I will stay, even contrary to your wishes; and though you should persist to shun me, I will make my respectful assiduities atone for the levity of my past conduct.

MISS HARDCASTLE   Sir, I must entreat you'll desist. As our acquaintance began, so let it end, in indifference. I might have given an hour or two to levity; but, seriously, Mr. Marlow, do you think I could ever submit to a connection, where *I* must appear mercenary, and *you* imprudent? Do you think, I could ever catch at the confident addresses of a secure admirer?

MARLOW   (*kneeling*)   Does this look like security? Does this look like confidence? No, madam, every moment that shows me your merit, only serves to increase my diffidence and confusion. Here let me continue——

SIR CHARLES   I can hold it no longer. Charles, Charles, how hast thou deceived me! Is this your indifference, your uninteresting conversation!

HARDCASTLE   Your cold contempt; your formal interview. What have you to say now?

MARLOW   That I'm all amazement! What can it mean?

HARDCASTLE   It means that you can say and unsay things at pleasure; that you can address a lady in private, and deny it in public; that you have one story for us, and another for my daughter!

MARLOW   Daughter! This lady your daughter!

HARDCASTLE   Yes, sir, my only daughter, my Kate; whose else should she be?

MARLOW   Oh, the devil!

MISS HARDCASTLE   Yes, sir, that very identical tall, squinting lady you were pleased to take me for. (*Curtsying.*) She that you addressed as the mild, modest, sentimental man of gravity, and the bold, forward, agreeable Rattle of the Ladies' Club: ha, ha, ha.

MARLOW   Zounds, there's no bearing this; it's worse than death.

MISS HARDCASTLE   In which of your characters, sir, will you give us leave to address you? As the faltering gentleman, with looks on the ground, that speaks just to be heard, and hates hypocrisy: or the loud, confident creature, that keeps it up with Mrs. Mantrap, and old Miss Biddy Buckskin, till three in the morning? Ha, ha, ha!

MARLOW   Oh, curse on my noisy head. I never attempted to be impudent yet, that I was not taken down. I must be gone.

HARDCASTLE   By the hand of my body, but you shall not. I see it was all a mistake, and I am rejoiced to find it. You shall not, sir, I tell you. I know she'll forgive you. Won't you forgive him, Kate? We'll all forgive you. Take courage, man. (*They retire, she tormenting him, to the back scene.*)

Enter MRS. HARDCASTLE *and* TONY.

MRS. HARDCASTLE   So, so, they're gone off. Let them go, I care not.

HARDCASTLE   Who gone?

MRS. HARDCASTLE   My dutiful niece and her gentleman, Mr. Hastings, from town. He who came down with our modest visitor here.

SIR CHARLES   Who, my honest George Hastings? As worthy a fellow as lives, and the girl could not have made a more prudent choice.

HARDCASTLE   Then, by the hand of my body, I'm proud of the connection.

MRS. HARDCASTLE   Well, if he has taken away the lady, he has not taken her fortune; that remains in this family to console us for her loss.

HARDCASTLE   Sure, Dorothy, you would not be so mercenary?

MRS. HARDCASTLE   Aye, that's my affair, not yours.

HARDCASTLE   But you know, if your son, when of age, refuses to marry his cousin, her whole fortune is then at her own disposal.

MRS. HARDCASTLE   Ah, but he's not of age, and she has not thought proper to wait for his refusal.

Enter HASTINGS *and* MISS NEVILLE.

MRS. HARDCASTLE (*aside*) What, returned so soon! I begin not to like it.

HASTINGS (*to* HARDCASTLE) For my late attempt to fly off with your niece, let my present confusion be my punishment. We are now come back, to appeal from your justice to your humanity. By her father's consent, I first paid her my addresses, and our passions were first founded in duty.

MISS NEVILLE Since his death, I have been obliged to stoop to dissimulation to avoid oppression. In an hour of levity, I was ready even to give up my fortune to secure my choice. But I'm now recovered from the delusion, and hope from your tenderness what is denied me from a nearer connection.

MRS. HARDCASTLE Pshaw, pshaw, this is all but the whining end of a modern novel.

HARDCASTLE Be it what it will, I'm glad they're come back to reclaim their due. Come hither, Tony, boy. Do you refuse this lady's hand whom I now offer you?

TONY What signifies my refusing? You know I can't refuse her till I'm of age, father.

HARDCASTLE While I thought concealing your age, boy, was likely to conduce to your improvement, I concurred with your mother's desire to keep it secret. But since I find she turns it to a wrong use, I must now declare, you have been of age these three months.

TONY Of age! Am I of age, father?

HARDCASTLE Above three months.

TONY Then you'll see the first use I'll make of my liberty. (*Taking* MISS NEVILLE'*s hand.*) Witness all men by these presents, that I, Anthony Lumpkin, Esquire of BLANK place, refuse you, Constantia Neville, spinster, of no place at all, for my true and lawful wife. So Constance Neville may marry whom she pleases and Tony Lumpkin is his own man again!

SIR CHARLES O brave squire!

HASTINGS My worthy friend!

MRS. HARDCASTLE My undutiful offspring!

MARLOW Joy, my dear George, I give you joy, sincerely. And could I prevail upon my little tyrant here to be less arbitrary, I should be the happiest man alive, if you would return me the favor.

HASTINGS (*to* MISS HARDCASTLE) Come, madam, you are now driven to the very last scene of all your contrivances. I know you like him, I'm sure he loves you, and you must and shall have him.

HARDCASTLE (*joining their hands*) And I say so, too. And Mr. Marlow, if she makes as good a wife as she has a daughter, I don't believe you'll ever repent your bargain. So now to supper. Tomorrow we shall gather all the poor of the parish about us, and the mistakes of the night shall be crowned with a merry morning; so, boy, take her; and as you have been mistaken in the mistress, my wish is, that you may never be mistaken in the wife.

Epilogue   By Dr. Goldsmith

Well, having stooped to conquer with success,

And gained a husband without aid from dress,

Still as a barmaid, I could wish it too,

As I have conquered him to conquer you:

And let me say, for all your resolution,

That pretty barmaids have done execution.

Our life is all a play, composed to please,

"We have our exits and our entrances."[40]

The first act shows the simple country maid,

Harmless and young, of everything afraid;

Blushes when hired, and with unmeaning action,

"I hopes as how to give you satisfaction."

Her second act displays a livelier scene,—

Th' unblushing barmaid of a country inn,

Who whisks about the house, at market caters,

Talks loud, coquets the guests, and scolds the waiters.

40 Cf. *As You Like It,* II, vii. 141.

Next the scene shifts to town, and there
she soars,
The chophouse toast of ogling connois-
seurs.
On squires and cits she there displays her
arts,
And on the gridiron broils her lovers'
hearts—
And as she smiles, her triumphs to com-
plete,
Even common councilmen forget to eat.
The fourth act shows her wedded to the
squire,
And madam now begins to hold it higher;
Pretends to taste, at operas cries *caro*,
And quits her "Nancy Dawson,"[41] for *Che
Faro.*[42]

Dotes upon dancing, and in all her pride,
Swims round the room, the Heinel[43] of
Cheapside:
Ogles and leers with artificial skill,
Till having lost in age the power to kill,
She sits all night at cards, and ogles at
spadille.[44]
Such, through our lives, th' eventful his-
tory—
The fifth and last act still remains for me.
The barmaid now for your protection
prays,
Turns female barrister, and pleads for
Bayes.[45]

41 A popular song. 42 An aria in Glück's opera, *Orfeo.*

43 Popular German dancer. 44 Leading trump in ombre, a card game. 45 I.e., the author (cf. Bayes in Buckingham's *The Rehearsal*).

Candide

Voltaire   translated and adapted for television by James McTaggart

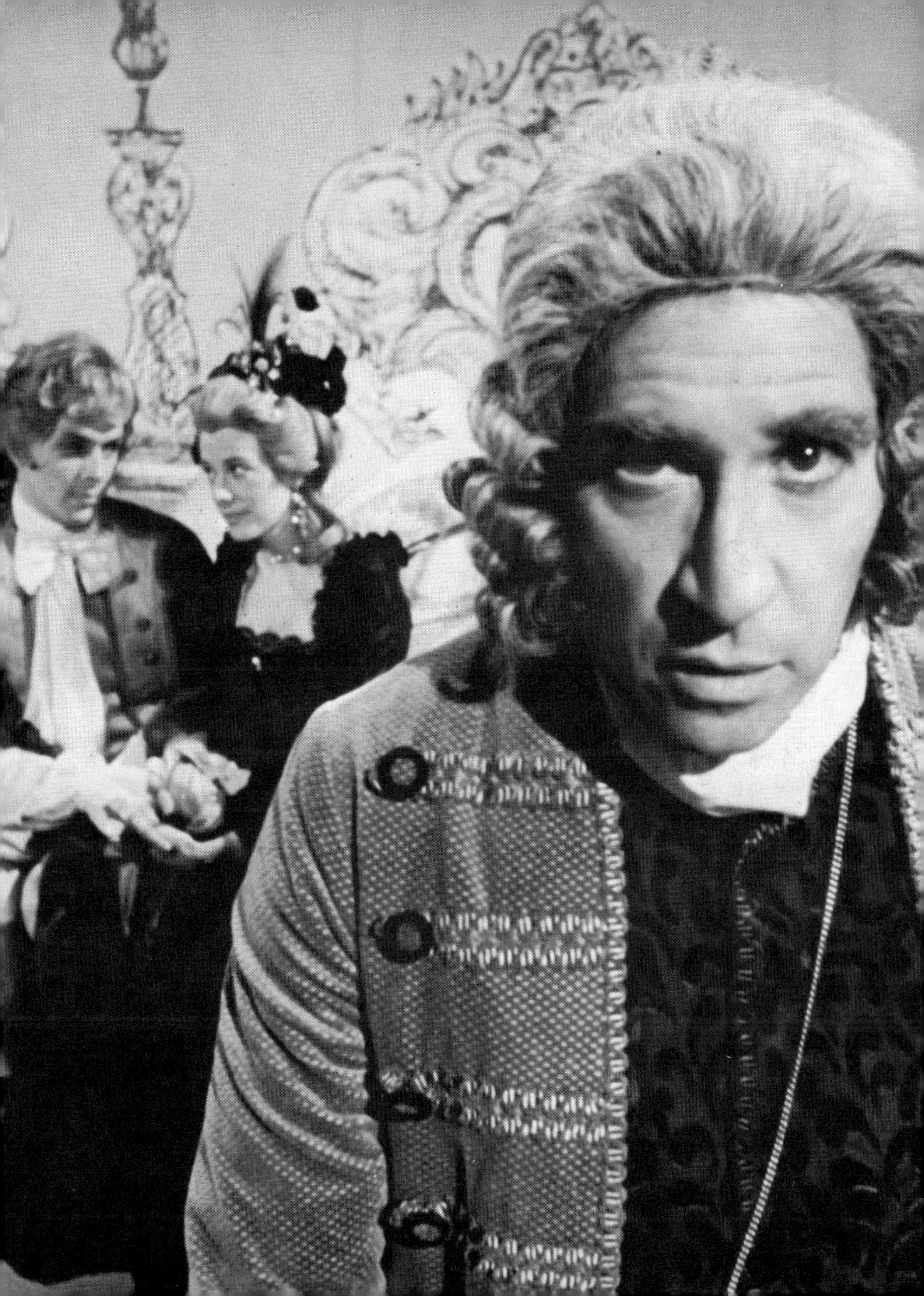

Introductory Comments

Georges May   *Yale University*

When Voltaire's slim book entitled *Candide, or Optimism* was first published in late 1758 or early 1759, it immediately became a best-seller. It has remained one ever since. Not only does it, therefore, deserve its place in the present series because it is a true classic—in that it is read in the classroom—but it has through the ages held a broad appeal, in the original French as well as in translations, for a public much larger and more diversified than that of teachers and students. It has never stopped stimulating the talent of illustrators, imitators, and adapters. Over two centuries after it was written, it has once again demonstrated, with the success of Leonard Bernstein's musical comedy, its sustained appeal and relevance.

This fortune of *Candide* is all the more surprising since the book clearly owed much if not most of its initial success to its topicality and to allusions to current events. To give a few examples, 1756 was the date of the Lisbon earthquake, of the end of the military regime of the Spanish Jesuits in Paraguay, and of the onset of the Seven Years' War; and 1757 was that of the execution of British Admiral John Byng. Similarly, most of the institutions that are satirized in *Candide*—galleys, the Inquisition, slavery, high-seas piracy—also belong to a forgotten world. Any topicality *Candide* has today must, therefore, depend entirely on the degree of erudition of its public or on learned footnotes, with which editors adorn the bottom of their pages but for which television technicians have yet to devise an appropriate substitute. Yet evidence shows that *Candide* remains enjoyable today for a non-scholarly public, as indeed it was intended to be by its author nearly 220 years ago.

This apparent paradox raises a first question, the answer to which is a simple one. All the historical events and institutions present in *Candide* are but a pretext for Voltaire to aim beyond them at the human causes that had brought them into being. These events and institutions depicted in the story being uniformly bad, it follows that their causes lie with human imperfections, foibles, and vices. Even among the few of our contemporaries who still hold to the belief in the perfectibility of man—one of the tenets of the Age of Enlightenment—there is a general consensus that no noticeable improvement has taken place since the middle of the eighteenth century. And so can be explained the continuing relevance to us of adventures taking place in a world outwardly so different from our own.

We must next ask ourselves whether Voltaire chose to single out in *Candide* all that was bad about human life simply because he was a depressive maniac, in which case of course the relevance of what he had to say would be more restricted than it seems to be. The answer is no: aside from the comic tone sustained throughout the book, and aside from the fact that Voltaire gives us the feeling that he is enjoying himself as he spins his yarn of horrors, a few truly good people— notably James and Cacambo—cross the path of the hero, who, although thrice a murderer, is a rather good man himself. The character who embodies radical pessimism, Martin, is not the author's mouthpiece. Voltaire's purpose was simply to correct what he felt was a distorted view of man and his world, which he ascribed to the philosophy of optimism made fashionable by some of Leibnitz's followers. This correction he chose to effect by means of overemphasis, not only because he disagreed strongly with their views, but because he felt they were guilty themselves of the worst kinds of overemphasis: they were exaggeratedly systematic, dogmatic, pedantic, hermetic, and bombastic. Pangloss (in Greek: all-tongue) is thus meant to ridicule not only the philosophy of systematic optimism but *any* absolute and abstruse philosophy—what is termed at the beginning of the story "metaphysico-theologo-cosmolo-nigology."

The result is that, even though the Leibnitzian philosophy of optimism has now sunk into the same oblivion as the Lisbon earthquake, the Jesuit empire, or the daughters of Pope Urban X (who never existed), we can still recognize in Pangloss the embodiment of some of the evils that beset us. We are still suffocated and intimidated by obscure, pretentious, and dogmatic philosophies, as we are still the victims of wars, diseases, and natural disasters, and as we are still oppressed by—because addicted to—fanaticism, bigotry, racism, lust, greed, power madness, lies, robberies, and other violent crimes.

If the formula adopted in *Candide* thus permits relevance to co-exist with obsolete topicality, it is because the themes lying behind the once-topical allusions are eternal ones. They are the stuff from which satire has always been made. Indeed, they are so commonplace that they invite one to ask yet another question: how is it that the story built around them is not nearly as dull and boring as such triteness should normally lead us to expect? The answer is that in any form of expressive art—literature in Voltaire's case, television in McTaggart's —themes cannot be dissociated from their expression, except by an artificial and arbitrary process of analysis. In other words, a work of art can be superbly original even when its ideological contents are of the utmost banality. Nor is banality necessarily to be disdained; it often has the uncommon merit of being true.

Voltaire, who prior to *Candide* had written many high-styled tragedies, noble epics, and scholarly historical treatises, chose to treat in this little book the most serious of themes in the most facetious of manners. Since high-sounding philosophy was one of his targets, it behooved him not to fall himself into the trap of self-seriousness. In other words, Voltaire is no more Pangloss than he is Martin.

Just as the original story's sequence of adventures and their rhythm are faithfully observed in the television production, so is the tongue-in-cheek tone of Voltaire's prose cleverly transposed, within the limitations imposed by the change in medium. This feature having primarily to do with style—that is to say with the transfer of the narrator's personality into written language—McTaggart chose to add one character to the existing cast, that of Voltaire himself, thus allowing the television viewer to hear his voice, just as the reader does in a different way.

Dealing with fundamentally serious and occasionally even tragic themes in a facetious, ironical, witty, and dead-pan manner creates a tension, a dissonance, the end product of which is humor. Convinced as he was that preaching was not the most effective means of persuasion, Voltaire resorted to humorous satire, to a lampoon instead of a sermon; but the seriousness of the intent remains unmistakable. Hence a final question: what exactly was this intent?

Voltaire was too intelligent a man simply to wish to fulminate against evil. Evil, he thought, was natural and therefore unavoidable. Moreover, since most people tend quite spontaneously to dislike evil (the Marquis de Sade, Voltaire's junior by more than half a century, was only fifteen when *Candide* was published), why bother to write one more book simply to condemn it? Voltaire's purpose was rather to show how stupid and dangerous it is to pretend that evil does not exist: stupid, because it does exist; dangerous, because ignoring it means accepting it, whereas we should fight it and whenever possible reduce it.

And so the story of *Candide* is designed to show how the experience of living in the real world necessarily opens the eyes of any reasonable human being to the presence of evil, usually though not always man-made. A blank sheet of paper at the outset (*candidus* is Latin for white), the hero learns slowly and gradually as he undergoes the ordeal of the celebrated trial-and-error method. After having had to unlearn the silly dogmas taught to him by Pangloss, he ends up reversing the roles and teaching his erstwhile master to stop talking and get down to work. For the conclusion of *Candide* is not despair. An awareness of the ridicule, the cruelty, and the absurdity of much that surrounds us is not meant to leave us wondering whether suicide is not the only acceptable and reasonable solution. Voltaire's *Candide* is not Camus' *Sisyphus*. The conclusion of *Candide* is that, by dint of hard work, man can make his world a little better for himself and for others.

As he wrote *Candide,* Voltaire, like his hero at the end of the story, was about to settle down, after an already long life of struggles and tribulations, in the countryside, not of Turkey but of Ferney. Here he would henceforth work in peace and freedom, cultivating his garden both literally—by managing a largish argicultural estate—and figuratively—by writing *Candide* and many more books yet to come. He was sixty-five and in frail health. Yet his greatest fights and greatest triumphs were still ahead of him.

A story does not have to be autobiographical in the conventional sense of the word for it to be rooted in the depth of its author's soul. All masterpieces are, and *Candide* is a masterpiece. Although Candide himself is sillier, clumsier, and especially more naïve than Voltaire ever was, and although his character is no more to be taken at face value than are his companions' and their misadventures (regardless of the fact that each of them is grounded in historical truth), the life of Candide echoes that of its author inasmuch as it leads through the same arguments to the same conclusion—in sixty-five pages, rather than sixty-five years. Because *Candide* is such a summation, and such a lucid and ironical one, its meaning and relevance have remained unabated through the ages.

François-Marie Arouet (1694–1778) was born in Paris of a well-to-do family. He first achieved fame in his twenties with verse plays and poems, and adopted in 1718 the pseudonym Voltaire. Imprisoned twice at the Bastille for irreverence, he also was forced to live in England as an exile from 1726 to 1729. Unable thereafter to recapture the good graces of the French court, he traveled for twenty-five years (1734–1759), stopping for a while in Lorraine (not yet a possession of the French Crown), in Prussia at the court of Frederick the Great, and in Geneva. Having grown very wealthy through shrewd investments, and having remained a bachelor (though not always a celibate), he never stopped writing plays, works of history, essays, and philosophical tales. In 1759 he settled in Ferney, on the French side of the Swiss border. A landed squire and the foremost European man of letters, he spent the rest of his life entertaining innumerable famous visitors, writing relentlessly, attacking all forms of tyranny and intolerance—and even correcting several gross miscarriages of justice—and exchanging letters with hundreds of correspondents throughout Europe. He died in Paris. More than 20,000 of his letters have been preserved and published. The rest of his literary output, illustrating nearly all existing genres and innovating a few, makes him one of the most productive writers ever.

James MacTaggart (1928–1974) was a television producer with the British Broadcasting Corporation for several years. His productions included Rostand's *Cyrano de Bergerac,* Shaw's *Man and Superman,* and Webster's *The Duchess of Malfi.* He translated, adapted, and directed *Candide* in 1973 and in 1974 was awarded the Desmond Davis Award for outstanding creative contribution to television.

VOLTAIRE

BARON

BARONESS

CUNEGONDE

CANDIDE

YOUNG BARON *(also* REVEREND FATHER COLONEL; CONVICT*)*

DOCTOR PANGLOSS *(also* CONVICT*)*

TWO SOLDIERS *(also* TWO LOUTS*)*

MINISTER *(also* ORATOR, MAN*)*

MINISTER'S WIFE

JAMES

MAN IN BLACK

EXECUTIONER

OLD WOMAN

DON ISSACHAR

THE GRAND INQUISITOR

CACAMBO *(also* FIRST SERVANT*)*

SHINY SOUTH AMERICAN FACE

DON FERNANDO D'IBARAA Y FIGUEORA Y MASCARENES Y LAMPOURDOS Y
　　SOUZA *(also* THE GOVERNOR*)*

VERY VERY OLD MAN

GRAND OFFICIAL

KING (OF EL DORADO)

SHIP CAPTAIN

JUDGE

MARTIN

ABBOT

MADAME LA MARQUISE

OLD CRONE

OFFICER OF THE WATCH

SIX SERVANTS *(first of which is* CACAMBO*)*

SIX KINGS *(first is* ACHMET III, *sixth is* THEODORE*)*

OVERSEER

DERVISH

OLD TURKISH GARDENER

AND A HOST OF OTHERS

This production is conceived entirely for the studio. No film or location is intended. Since the novel really takes place in the head it would be a mistake to get involved in the realities of blood and war and rapine, for these must be kept at more than arm's length or the wit of the thesis will be lost.

An extensive use of models, colour separation, and ingenuity should bring about a fast moving and entertaining production true to the spirit of the novel.

Darkness.

Music. Distant but approaching. Something bright and witty and eighteenth century.[1]

Wolfgang Amadeus Mozart would do. An oval shape appears on the screen. Pale blue. Draped around the top of it appears the name—"CANDIDE".

Then underneath it appear the words "By Voltaire," and as they do a silhouette appears in the oval and transforms it into a cameo.

And then the words and the cameo outline remove themselves, the silhouette is lit from the front and the silhouette turns to us. It speaks. And this is what it says.

VOLTAIRE   Once upon a time, in Germany, there was a castle.

(And as he says this the castle appears behind him.)

The castle of Thunder-ten-tronckh! In it lived the Baron of . . .

(Another cameo appears. Somewhere. Of the BARON.*)*

. . . Thunder-ten-tronckh.

(It becomes three dimensional and he turns and leers at us in a most distasteful way.)

He was one of the biggest barons in the country, because his castle, despite the expense, not only had a door but even windows. And his wife . . .

(And the BARON *is replaced by the* BARONESS. *She's around twenty-five stone.)*

. . . was one of the biggest baronesses in the country.

(The BARONESS *leers and gives place to* CUNEGONDE.*)*

Ah! Their daughter Cunegonde. Sweet. Seventeen. To see her was to love her. None . . .

(And CANDIDE *steps into the frame confronting* CUNEGONDE *who lowers her eyes.)*

. . . more so than this our hero: Candide himself. Just look at him. Pure simple and unspoiled. Nobody . . . *quite* knew where he came from. The older servants reckoned he was the son of the Baron's sister by a gentleman she could not possibly actually marry, he having only seventy-one quarterings on his coat of arms whereas she had no fewer than seventy-two. Think of that! Candide did. He hadn't any quarterings at all. And being madly in love with Cunegonde, who naturally had seventy-two as well, he hadn't a hope, poor thing.

*(*CANDIDE *is still gazing fervently upon* CUNEGONDE.*)*

[1] This script was written expressly for television production. Therefore, the stage directions include many audio and visual special effects instructions that do not appear in scripts for stage production.

If they stand there like that much longer
. . . Ah!

(CUNEGONDE *is hailed off and replaced by the* YOUNG BARON *who glares at* CANDIDE *who goes. The* YOUNG BARON *turns and leers at us in the style of his family.*)

The son and heir. Young Baron Thunder-ten-tronckh. Brother to the delectable Cunegonde. A chip . . . off the old Block. And now ladies and gentlemen . . .
(*The* YOUNG BARON *gives way to* PANGLOSS.)

. . . the oracle, the luminary, the paradigm . . . the Tutor of the household: The esteemed Doctor Pangloss. Propounder of the philosophy of metaphysico-theologo-cosmolo-nigology. Or, in a word, optimism. But listen for yourself.

(*The cameo shape around* PANGLOSS *wipes itself right out to the edge of the screen wiping off*[2] VOLTAIRE *and the drawing. We are in a room of the chateau sketchily suggested.* PANGLOSS *is addressing his three young charges. The* BARON *and* BARONESS *watch fondly. The pupils are probably sitting in a row. Piles of dusty and boring-looking books. An astrolabe.*)

PANGLOSS It is therefore demonstrated that things cannot be otherwise. Since everything is made for a purpose therefore everything is made for the best possible purpose. Consider. The nose was designed to support spectacles—and so we *have* spectacles. Consider. Legs were obviously developed to be covered by breeches—and so we *have* breeches. Stones were made to be trimmed and turned into castles—and so our noble Baron *has* a castle. A beautiful castle. The greatest Baron in the province must needs *have*

the best possible home. And his good lady Baroness is the best of all possible Baronesses. There is no effect without a cause, my children. Everything, everything has its Sufficient Reason. And so anyone who tells you everything is good is talking rubbish. *Rubbish!* Everything is for the best . . . in this, the best of all possible worlds.

(*Applause from the class and the* BARON *and the* BARONESS. PANGLOSS *bows.* CANDIDE *turns to camera and we go in close to him.*)

CANDIDE (*musing*) It appears to me perfectly evident that the greatest thing in the world would be to have been born Baron of Thunder-ten-tronckh. And after that to be Mademoiselle Cunegonde. And after that to see her every day. And after that to listen to Doctor Pangloss, the greatest philosopher in the land, and consequently the world.

(*And now we see a hedge in a formal garden. On our side of the hedge and looking over it is* CUNEGONDE, *deeply engrossed.* VOLTAIRE *crosses the background and his attention is drawn towards her. He goes and stands beside her and also looks. She of course does not see him since he isn't there.*

He turns to us and indicates with a jerk of the head that we should join him. We push in and look over the hedge too.

What we see, most discreetly screened by bushes but nonetheless quite unmistakable, is DOCTOR PANGLOSS *with great dexterity and gusto coupling with one of the serving maids.*

Now we look across the hedge at CUNEGONDE *and* VOLTAIRE *who is looking at her but mostly we look at* CUNEGONDE. *Her eyes are wide with interest. Her rosy lips are moist and slightly parted. She holds her breath. Probably her eyes and nostrils are dilating in time to the merry rhythm of the good doctor and the happy squeals of the serving wench.*

When CUNEGONDE *speaks it is of course to herself and in a tense whisper.*)

2 **wipes . . . off** an image on the television screen that is either part of a larger image (also on the screen) or one of two or more images appearing simultaneously on the screen which expands to cover up and remove the other image(s).

CUNEGONDE Applied physics. How interesting. There is the cause.

(*And an involuntary shiver of delight escapes her.*)

Ahhhh! And there the effect. Ohhhhhhh!

(*She cups her sweet breasts with her sweet hands.*)

I feel absolutely certain that I should benefit from an experiment like that. Perhaps . . . perhaps Monseiur Candide . . . and I . . . could find . . . a Sufficient Reason.

(*And* VOLTAIRE *shrugs as if to say, why not?*

And goodness me, here is CANDIDE *himself, we are in the castle and we see him pass behind a screen. Once there only his feet and modica of legs are seen. No sooner has he gone behind it as though to emerge at the other end when his feet stop and look, as it were. And in from the other side come the feet of* CUNEGONDE. *And they stop and look. And they approach slightly. And then a tiny lace handkerchief lands between them. And then* CANDIDE's *hand picks it up.*

And then there's a breathless pause and all four legs begin to tremble and the feet to edge even closer.

And then the BARON *comes into the foreground and stops and watches the feet for a bit. And then he looks at us as though to say Vateffer haff ve here!*

And as he goes to peer round the one end we go and peer round the other so that we see not only what he sees but the effect upon him.

What we see are CANDIDE *and* CUNEGONDE *with their eyes fixed upon each other's, their breasts heaving, their breaths breathing, their hands straying and their lips all but touching.*

And the effect upon the BARON *is very interesting. His face changes from its normal choleric red to an unusual deep purple. With a great bellow of rage he knocks over the screen, hauls* CUNEGONDE

off her friend and casts her away, and confronts the trembling CANDIDE.

He lets out one more bellow and grabs him by the scruff of the neck.

And suddenly we are looking at the drawing of the castle. And the door opens. And a tiny distant BARON VON THUNDER-TEN-TRONCKH *holds a tiny wriggling* CANDIDE *by the neck and then boots him bouncingly down the steps. Lets out one more distant tiny bellow and goes back in and slams the door.*)

PANGLOSS My Lord, never fear. All is for the best in this most beautiful of all possible castles. Things could not have been otherwise.

(VOLTAIRE *strolls in to the foreground and watches* CANDIDE *pick himself up, gently stroke his backside, and limp off.*)

VOLTAIRE And so. The adventures of Candide . . . began.

(*We said* CANDIDE *walked off but we didn't mean it. What really happens is that he walks on to the spot, so to speak, like Marcel Marceau. And the drawing, which is on a horizontal roller, moves instead. It shows the countryside and forests and things.*)

He walked and walked and *walked*. Didn't care where. He cried a lot.

(CANDIDE *cries.*)

Made accusing gestures at heaven.

(CANDIDE *makes accusing gestures at heaven.*)

For turning him out of the nicest of all possible castles and away from the most beautiful of all possible little baronesses. To which he cast back soulful sad looks.

(CANDIDE *casts back soulful sad looks.*)

It got dark.

(*It gets dark.*)

There was a rather wet thunderstorm.

(There is rather a wet thunderstorm.)

He went to sleep in a field.

(CANDIDE lies down.)

It snowed of course.

(It snows of course.)

You might say he wasn't all that happy. Well wait till you hear the rest.

(The background goes dark. VOLTAIRE takes a slight stroll probably. It gets light again. Perhaps a cock crows in a disgustingly healthy manner. Perhaps not.)

The next day Candide reached the town of Waldberghoff-trarbk-dikdorff. Not in too good a shape either.

(We mix through[3] to a perspective drawing of a very straight road stretching into the distance. And CANDIDE is limping towards us from dead centre.

He stops in foreground and looks off shot.

We jump round and look over his shoulder at what he's looking at. An inn, a table outside the door, and at the table two louts in blue uniforms . . . gorging themselves. The inn is represented sketchily by a sign or something.

CANDIDE's mouth waters. His eyes follow each forkful. His stomach rumbles. The two louts look up at the sky for signs of rain after the thunder and then realise it's CANDIDE. They gaze at him, chewingly.)

FIRST SOLDIER *(quietly)* Oi. There's a well set up young fella.
SECOND SOLDIER *(equally quietly)* Yeah. Just about the right height too.

(They rise in unison, wiping their mouths and hands and smile gaptoothed and as engagingly as is within their range. They indicate the table.)

FIRST SOLDIER Please, young sir, do us the honour of eating with us.

3 **mix through** dissolve.

(CANDIDE advances a little and they go one to either side of him.)

CANDIDE The honour is mine. But. I have no money. I couldn't pay my share.
FIRST SOLDIER Tut tut tut! A man of quality like you never pays for nuffink.

(The SECOND SOLDIER has been looking at him very closely.)

SECOND SOLDIER And pardon my observing, but aren't you five foot five or so in height?
CANDIDE Why yes.
FIRST SOLDIER Then you must eat with us.

(And they escort him to the table.)

Men of your standing——
SECOND SOLDIER ——and height——
FIRST SOLDIER ——must never be without ready money. We shall give you some. What were men made for, but to help one another.
SECOND SOLDIER Always saying it. Always.
CANDIDE And so is Maitre Pangloss.
FIRST SOLDIER Really.
CANDIDE Oh yes. And all is for the best.
SECOND SOLDIER So it is.
FIRST SOLDIER And to prove it, please accept these few coins to tide you over.

(He presses money into CANDIDE's hand and leads him over to the table where they pour wine into goblets.)

CANDIDE How can I repay you?
FIRST SOLDIER Do you not have a great affection for——
CANDIDE Oh yes! I have a great affection for Mademoiselle Cunegonde.
FIRST SOLDIER No. It was the King of the Bulgars we're asking if you don't have a great affection for.
CANDIDE Well no. I've never seen him.
SECOND SOLDIER What? But he's the most charming king.
FIRST SOLDIER Delightful. We must drink to his health.

(And suddenly they all have a goblet. The SOLDIERS raise theirs and speak in unison.)

SOLDIERS   The King of the Bulgars.

(*And* CANDIDE *raises his. And they watch him closely and with satisfaction.*)

CANDIDE   The King of the Bulgars.

(*And he's only got half a mouthful down when the* FIRST SOLDIER *snatches his goblet and the* SECOND *drops to his knees and snaps shackles on* CANDIDE'S *ankles.*)

FIRST SOLDIER   That'll do. You are now the prop, the mainstay, the defender, the *hero* of the King of the Bulgars. Congratulations!

(*And he seizes* CANDIDE *warmly by both wrists. And when he takes his hands away* CANDIDE *has handcuffs on as well.*)

Ehbout . . . TUN!

(*And the* SECOND SOLDIER *spins him round.*)

Qui . . . eck . . . MATCH!

(*And he gives* CANDIDE *a hefty thump between the shoulder blades and they step briskly off like in Commanding Officer's orderly room.*)

SECOND SOLDIER   Def doight def doight def doight def!

(*We cut back to the table.* VOLTAIRE *is sitting at it pouring himself some wine.*)

VOLTAIRE   And so Candide joined the army.

(*MS*[4] FIRST SOLDIER. *No particular backing.*)

FIRST SOLDIER   Now today we har gonna learn . . .

(*And the following are shouted as horders.*)

Le . . . eft TUN!
RI . . . ight TUN!
Slo . . . ope AMS!

4 **MS** medium (distance) shot.

Order . . . AMS!
Preeese . . . ent AMS!
Cock yore pieces!
Ta . . . ake HAIM!
FI . . . . . .

(*And he suddenly looks alarmed, doesn't finish, and ducks down out of shot. Musket shot.*
   There's a great rattle of musket fire and a singing ricochet and he comes back up again purple.)

FIRST SOLDIER   And as a reward for yore orrible hunseemly beavyar FIRTY WACKS WIV A BIG STICK!

(*And he raises a bloody great cudgel and as he crashes it down we cut back to* VOLTAIRE *quietly sipping away and we hear the distant owowowows of* CANDIDE.)

VOLTAIRE   And he'd probably have been beaten to death . . . if the Bulgars hadn't suddenly gone to war with the Abars.

(*Drums start and increase in pitch and volume as he speaks.*)

The world has never known anything as beautiful or as brilliant as those two armies. The trumpets, fifes, woodwinds, drums . . . oh and cannon, too . . .

(*And they've all joined in now and he has to shout to be heard.*)

. . . made such a harmony as Hell itself has never heard.

(*And now we see the battlefield. A table-top model, smoke and explosions and things, all done to real sound effects and the screams of the dying.*)

VOLTAIRE (*over*)   First the cannon knocked down nearly six thousand men on each side. Next the muskets rid this best of all possible worlds of nine or ten thousand arrant rogues who infected it. The bayonet was the Sufficient Reason for the removal of a few thousand more.

(And we've been tilting up from the battlefield to the cyc[5]—and there peering and looming over the horizon is a huge giant VOLTAIRE *towering over the battlefield, i.e., the actor standing at the far side of the table top.)*

Candide managed to hide quite successfully during this heroic butchery.

(And he looks down to where presumably CANDIDE *is hidden. And we see him, mixing through to his hidey-hole. I think it ought to be a pile of corpses, of various sexes, ages, and nationalities, and his sweet face should peer out at us with trembling consternation.)*

CANDIDE If this really *is* the best of all possible worlds, then I am truly fortunate to be in it and not in any of the others.

(A final corpse crashes onto the heap. The noise of battle dies. We hear a distant Te Deum. Or rather, two distant Te Deums. CANDIDE *puts his hand out and looks up as though checking the end of a rainshower. He struggles to get out of the pile.*
We return to VOLTAIRE *still huge above the battlefield, listening to the pious music with respect and satisfaction.)*

VOLTAIRE Both armies won and both gave thanks to God. The same God, of course.

   And so Candide left the army; there being no one left to restrain him.

   In the villages he saw old men dying, children with their throats cut, young girls disembowelled after meeting the needs of a platoon of heroes, and various other fruits of civilisation. Candide kept on walking. All the way to Holland. A very religious country.

(An ORATOR, *talking to a vast assembly —well, a man in a pulpit thing talking to four heads in the foreground.*
Perhaps they are dummy heads with

---

5 **cyc** cyclorama. A visual effect achieved by a white cloth, hung, stretched, and lighted behind a scene to create a feeling of infinity.

hats on and informed by cunning wires to nod or shake according to the mood of the ORATOR. *There is the suggestion of the door of a house in the background.)*

MINISTER And seventeenthly, brethren, consider Charity.

(The heads nod.)

Is there anything more important than Charity?

(They shake.)

Charity suffereth long and is kind.

(They nod.)

Charity envieth not.

(They shake.)

Charity——

(He breaks off as a hand of great dirtiness is stuck up under his nose. The nose wrinkles in disgust. He looks along the arm. So do we. On the other end of it is the pitiable CANDIDE *in rags.)*

CANDIDE Charity?

(And having caught the trick, he nods hopefully. The MINISTER *glowers, all beetley browed.)*

MINISTER Do you believe in the Cause?

CANDIDE *(modestly)* There is no Effect without the Cause.

(The MINISTER *jerks his head a couple of times as though trying to sort that one out. Some of the heads nod. He notices this and doesn't care for it.)*

MINISTER Do you believe the Pope is Antichrist?

CANDIDE I haven't heard so. But whether he is or whether he isn't, I still need something to eat.

(More heads nod. The MINISTER *gets infuriated.)*

MINISTER You . . . you . . . you don't *deserve* to eat, you don't.

(The heads shake.)

Get away from here or we'll run you in.

(The heads nod vigorously. Thus encouraged the MINISTER *gives a final great roar.)*

Go away!

*(*CANDIDE *backs away, rather surprised at the turn of events. Even more surprisingly a cascade of water falls from out the sky onto his head. He looks up. So do we. It wasn't really the sky but a first-floor window.*

At the window is an outraged lady. And in her hand she is holding and shaking the last drops out of a pot de chambre.)

MINISTER'S WIFE   Doesn't believe the Pope is Antichrist indeed. That'll show you what a good Baptist can do, my lad.

(Meanwhile on the ground. CANDIDE *has subsided onto it, a picture of abject misery. And* VOLTAIRE *is standing beside him looking up at the* WIFE.)

VOLTAIRE   Such religious zeal! Such . . . sincerity! Well, along came an Anabaptist. That's . . . a man who *hasn't* been baptised. Name of James.

(Enter JAMES. *A middle-aged manufacturer. He stops and stares at* CANDIDE. *Looks up at the sky, then takes out his handkerchief and wipes him down.)*

He was a kind man. If it had two legs, no feathers, and a soul, then it was his brother.

JAMES   My poor friend. What a way to treat . . . anybody. You will come home with me and have a bath a meal and a change of . . .

(He looks at CANDIDE's *rags and finishes rather lamely.)*

. . . and clothes.

(He tries to get CANDIDE *up but* CANDIDE *grasps his ankles and grovels engagingly.)*

CANDIDE   Maitre Pangloss *told* me that all is for the best in this world. Ah! How can I ever repay you?

JAMES   If you like you can work in my factory.

CANDIDE   *(feelingly)*   What do you make, sir?

JAMES   Cloth.

(He says this as he's holding CANDIDE's *rags and more or less getting him to his feet.)*

CANDIDE   Ah. Hollands.

JAMES   No as a matter of fact. We make Persian cloth here.

CANDIDE   How terribly interesting.

(But JAMES *has managed to lead him away.* VOLTAIRE *has remained.)*

VOLTAIRE   The very next day, Candide went for a walk.

*(*CANDIDE *immediately reappears from the side he left but now very spruce and neat in nice new clothes. As he gets under where the window is he edges out across the pavement looking up.*

He gets into fairly big close-up and we probably lose VOLTAIRE. *And then he moves on a little and then wham into the same close-up from the other direction comes the nastiest, dirtiest, smelliest, greasiest, toothlessiest, rheumiest, poxiest horror you ever did see or smell, in your life.*

Nice though he is, CANDIDE *retires a little. But the ghastly spectre follows and grasps his wrist with a filthy withered claw. It begins to cry. Not a nice sight.)*

PANGLOSS   *(for 'tis he)*   Alas! Don't you recognise your dear Pangloss?

(It's the most ridiculous question you ever heard. CANDIDE *thinks so too and peers. Of course he didn't. But it is. He's shattered.)*

CANDIDE   You? My dear Maitre! Heaven forfend! What happened to you? Why aren't you in the most beautiful of all possible castles? How is Mademoiselle Cunegonde?

PANGLOSS Dead!

(CANDIDE *faints. Just like that. He drops out the bottom of the shot and* PANGLOSS *bends down looks around after him. And we slam cut to a corner of an inn.*

They sit either side of a little table.

PANGLOSS *is whacking into great hunks of food and gulping down wine from a bottle.*

CANDIDE *sits beside him and hangs on his every word.*)

CANDIDE How . . . did she . . . ?

PANGLOSS She was disembowelled by Bulgar soldiers after as many of them as could manage raped her.

(CANDIDE *faints again. He just crashes onto the floor.*

PANGLOSS *is bending over the wine bottle and doesn't notice. He rattles on.*)

PANGLOSS They bashed in the head of the Baron, cut the Baroness to pieces, and the young baron got the same fate as his sister. Then they knocked down the castle and stole all the livestock.

(*He takes a great swig and his eyes suddenly gleam with pleasure.*)

But we were revenged. The Abars did Exactly the Same to a Bulgar castle, ho, ho! You all right?

(CANDIDE *has come round and is struggling up onto the seat again.*)

CANDIDE Yes yes. Forgive me. But how did you come to this pass? The Cause, the Effect, the Sufficient Reason for your condition?

(PANGLOSS *takes another great bite and swig and with gleaming eyes responds to the question. Albeit with self-pity.*)

PANGLOSS Love.

(CANDIDE *is taken aback. And rather apprehensive.*)

CANDIDE Love?

PANGLOSS Love. Love did it.

CANDIDE Well . . . I know my experience of love is limited to one brief kiss and a lot of kicks on the behind, but I fail . . .

PANGLOSS You remember Pacquette?

CANDIDE The chambermaid?

PANGLOSS Oh my dear Candide. In her arms I sampled the delights of paradise—which produced the torments of Hell you see written on my face.

CANDIDE But how?

PANGLOSS She had . . . an unfortunate infection; which she'd got from a Franciscan monk. A clever man who'd traced it to its source. He'd got it from an old countess, who'd got it from a captain of horse, who'd got it from a duchess, who'd got it from a page, who'd got it from a Jesuit, who'd got it, when he was a novice, in a direct line from a shipmate of Christopher Columbus. And nobody'll get it from me because I'm dying.

(*And he crams another large morsel down his maw.*)

CANDIDE Oh Pangloss! What a pedigree. The Devil himself must have sired it.

PANGLOSS Not at all not at all. It's an essential ingredient in the best of all possible worlds. Consider. If Columbus had not been there in the Americas to catch the disease, we should have neither chocolate nor cochineal!

CANDIDE Ah!

PANGLOSS Consider also. Only we have the disease at the moment. The Turks, Indians, Persians, Chinese, Siamese, Japanese know nothing about it. Yet. But there is a Sufficient Reason to suppose that they will through time. Meanwhile it's doing very well amongst us in Europe. Particularly amongst those highly trained soldiers of the various armies which decide our destiny. Be assured, if an army of thirty thousand confronts another army of thirty thousand, there will be at least twenty thousand on each side Riddled with the Pox!

CANDIDE   Isn't that marvellous? But look, we must get you cured.

PANGLOSS   Eh? How my friend? I haven't a penny to my name. Have you ever heard of anybody being cured of anything without paying?

CANDIDE   James!

PANGLOSS   Which James?

CANDIDE   Of course!

(*He snaps his fingers and stands up.*)

He'll help you.

PANGLOSS   James who?

(*And he takes another great swig as* CANDIDE *hurries off.*
And VOLTAIRE *strolls on and* PANGLOSS *and the inn disappear.*)

VOLTAIRE   So Candide begged the Anabaptist to help his old tutor in his hour of need. Which he did. And Pangloss was given treatment to cure the fruits of love. He only lost one eye and one ear in the process. And because he could write well and knew all about arithmetic, the good James made him his bookkeeper. And two months later took both the doctor and Candide with him when he made a trip on business to Lisbon.

(*We leave* VOLTAIRE *and come to the ship.*
[Note: *There are so many ships in the tale that it would be worth making a modicum of construction to represent them all. I suppose it might as well be the bit always chosen for Robinson Crusoe: the quarterdeck and poop and mizzen and bits of rigging and sail hanging down and the wheel and that.*
If we use the camera mounting which tilts on its horizontal axis we won't have to tilt the ship and it'll come in cheaper.]
When we come upon CANDIDE *and* PANGLOSS *and* JAMES *we are tilting ever so gently from side to side and they are remaining in what appears to be a true vertical by swaying gently from side to side in unison.*
Though we do not hear them we can

see that PANGLOSS—*peering round with his only eye from one to the other (his other covered by a black patch)—is laying down the law on the best of all possible worlds.*
All this is taken in swiftly. VOLTAIRE *continues.*)

The journey was pleasant. Until they came within sight of Lisbon.

(CANDIDE *raises his hand and points across* PANGLOSS *to port.*)

CANDIDE   Lisbon?

(*Instead of an answer from anyone—except perhaps God—there is the most appalling peal of thunder, everything goes black, a terrifying wind starts to scream through the rigging and terrified passengers join in.*
We have a highly psychedelic and colourful storm. Flickering and flashing and fluctuating. Lights and horrible clouds rip across the sky. The camera starts to tilt madly and as it goes right the trio rush to the left and crash into the starboard gunnel.
Then when the camera tilts to the left they go rushing over to the port gunnel on the right. (If I may remind you, we're looking aft—or backwards.) Things start to crash down onto the deck; spars and tars for example. All this seen flickeringly—like a very old colour movie. And as they rush from side to side amidst yells off of "We're sinking!" they shout at one another in a philosophical sort of way.)

JAMES   How do you reconcile this with the best of all possible worlds?

PANGLOSS   Easy. This is quite indispensable. Particular misfortunes make for the general good. This . . .

(*As the helmsman disappears overboard.*)

. . . the more particular misfortunes, the greater the general good.

(*As he says this they are careering towards the gunnel.*)

JAMES I see. But . . .

(*And he disappears over the gunnel forever.*

CANDIDE *starts to tear off clothes as though he's going to jump in to save him.*)

CANDIDE James! Master! Friend! Come back!

(*But* PANGLOSS *grapples him tight and restrains him, the two of them swaying about in the eerie flickering light.*)

PANGLOSS No No No. Do not interfere!
CANDIDE (*incredulous*) INTERFERE?!
PANGLOSS Consider. Since everything is for the best, it follows that this storm was made expressly so that the Anabaptist would be drowned in it. Otherwise it would have no meaning.

(CANDIDE *looks at him and gives up the struggle. Still yelling against the wind and the greatly increased screams of those left on board he looks deep into* PANGLOSS's *eye.*)

CANDIDE And will *we* be drowned in it?
PANGLOSS I hope not.

(*And they look down at their feet. And the flood is rising and the ship is sinking. And somebody screams "We are sinking" and really means it.*

And they are. That is to say that a goldfish tank in another part of the studio, filled with green water and agitated from the side, is on another camera which is supered[6] *on* CANDIDE *and* PANGLOSS. *And the camera is tilting relentlessly down and down and the water is creeping up and up and engulfing the ship. And huge bubbles come up and everything. And fish swim by. And we take down the lights on the ship and hold nice bright ones on* CANDIDE *and*

the good DOCTOR PANGLOSS *and they go into swimming motions and slow motions and every kind of motion imaginable and the bubbles get bigger and the screams become a sort of general uguguggle.*

And the camera on CANDIDE *and* PANGLOSS *pans*[7] *gently left and down so that they float up right and off. And on to whom under the sea should we pan but* VOLTAIRE. *Wouldn't it be nice to have his voice under-watery distortery?*)

VOLTAIRE And you could hardly be blamed for thinking that was the end of the tale. Not a bit of it. Candide and Pangloss floated ashore. Clinging to the piece of mast which is *de rigueur* on these occasions. And they walked into Lisbon.

(*And we see them walking into Lisbon. That is to say a drawing passing behind them—or a city in smoking ruins.*)

(*voice over*) Or what was left of it. The shipwreck had been caused by a tidal wave which had been caused by an earthquake which had been trying to destroy the entire city. Candide and Pangloss helped to dig survivors out of the rubble and then sat down to the best meal they could manage.

(*And there's a long table in an inn with a lot of downcast citizens picking at their food. And in the middle* PANGLOSS *and* CANDIDE. PANGLOSS, *never missing bite or sip, is by way of cheering them up.*)

PANGLOSS Cheer up. Be of good heart. Consider, my friends, if there is an earthquake in Lisbon . . . It cannot be Doing Damage Anywhere Else! Therefore your Misfortune is the Good Fortune of others.

(*This is greeted with a burst of dolorous sobbing from the grateful citizens.*)

All is for the best. Things cannot be otherwise.

---

6 **supered** one image superimposed on another.

7 **pans** moving the camera from left to right.

(And he beams around him with this unanswerable logic and comes nose to nose with a little fierce MAN IN BLACK *who sits beside him and looks at him keenly. He speaks softly and politely.)*

MAN IN BLACK I take it sir, that you do not believe in Original Sin. For if all is for the best there can be no Fall, and no Hell?

PANGLOSS I beg Your Excellency's most gracious pardon, but the Fall of Man is Necessary to the best of all possible worlds.

(The MAN IN BLACK *raises one eyebrow gently.)*

MAN IN BLACK Ah! Then you do not believe in Free Will?

*(*PANGLOSS *smiling with pleasure at having someone of calibre to argue with.)*

PANGLOSS Aha, forgive me Your Excellency but there is room for Free Will *and* Necessity. It is Necessary to *have* Free Will.

(And he gulps down some more wine and chuckles in a spluttery sort of way and looks round for applause at this penetrating aphorism but all that happens, apart from a nice smile from CANDIDE, *is that the* MAN IN BLACK *snaps his fingers and two great louts get up from the table and seize* PANGLOSS *and haul him to his feet bending his arms in a very painful manner. His exuberance dies in the circumstances.* CANDIDE *leaps to his feet.)*

CANDIDE Sir, what are you doing, sir?

MAN IN BLACK Sir, I am arresting your philosophical friend, sir.

CANDIDE And upon what authority, sir?

MAN IN BLACK Upon the Authority of The Inquisition of The Holy Mother Church, sir.

(This produces very little effect. Apart from moans, wails, renewed sobbings, muttered prayers, and crossings, freez-ings, backings away, the clatter of knives dropped on the table, the crash of goblets bouncing on the floor, and an avalanche of utensils dropped from the nerveless hands of a serving wench, nothing much happens at all.

When the new earthquake is over CANDIDE *speaks.)*

CANDIDE But he meant no harm.

(The MAN IN BLACK, *about to turn away, turns back. And his eyes suddenly burn and pierce and flay* CANDIDE *as he digests this idea. And then he speaks very quietly indeed.)*

MAN IN BLACK Why then . . . we have another log for the fire.

(And he nods and they grab CANDIDE *and* PANGLOSS *and before you can say Pope Gregory the Ninth they've marched them out. They pass behind* VOLTAIRE *and we settle on him. He clicks his tongue and shakes his head and leans across the table for a conspiratorial chat.)*

VOLTAIRE If you open your mouth here the only thing you should say is . . .

(And he leans back and shouts.)

. . . Landlord!

(And the LANDLORD *arrives at a great licking lick and slunges more vino into* VOLTAIRE's *goblet.)*

Three-quarters of Libson had disappeared taking thirty thousand of its inhabitants with it. The Church in its infinite wisdom decided that a sure remedy against a repeat performance would be to burn a few people at the stake. Pangloss was given the signal honour of joining them.

*(*PANGLOSS's *anguished and thoroughly frightened face. We come back and he's marching in procession. He's wearing a mitre and cassock adorned with flames and devils. We see flames and smoke projected onto the* Cyc.

We cut ahead to what he's staring at: three stakes and a gibbet against the dull red sky—probably a drawing, perhaps a model. It's raining too—if we can manage that as well.)

But for some reason, also given the unusual honour of being hanged rather than burned.

(PANGLOSS *again. He gulps and passes on. The air is filled with solemn religious music. Three more men pass through the shot, similarly garbed.)*

The . . . kindling, was provided by a Basque who had unpardonably married his godmother and two Portuguese who had an incurable aversion to bacon.

(*And now* CANDIDE. *His devils aren't so nasty and his flames go down not up but the garb is the same. He pauses and stares.*

The model again. The stakes now have figures and the fires are lit. A little figure is hauled wriggling up the gibbet.

The music swells. We see CANDIDE. *He is thumped forward by a huge and ugly sort of* EXECUTIONER *fellow. And they pass on. While this was going on the voice of* VOLTAIRE *continues.)*

Candide was reprieved . . . that is to say, sentenced to be flogged within an inch of his death.

(*At this point* CANDIDE *is pushed out. And who follows him in, as though walking solemnly in procession, but* VOLTAIRE. *He cocks an ear and smiles at us.)*

Remark the artistry of the ceremony: they flogged him in time to the music.

(*We listen with him. And indeed we can just hear the owowows of* CANDIDE *in a great and majestical rhythm.*

VOLTAIRE *nods agreeably with the rhythm.)*

A nicety which Candide must have appreciated at the very seat of his being.

The auto-da-fé was a great success. And that evening there was an even bigger earthquake.

(*The vast* EXECUTIONER *monster with the light of flames flickering across him as he wields the flail for the last few strokes across the bottom, so to speak, of the picture. Then stops. Then leans forward and drags* CANDIDE *up into the shot by the hair and stands him more or less up and turns him round.)*

EXECUTIONER Go in peace!

(*And with a hefty great kick he propels* CANDIDE *out of shot. And* CANDIDE *lands into another shot, onto a pile of welcoming rubble with a foot and hand sticking out, and bursts into even more tears.)*

CANDIDE Oh my dear Pangloss, greatest of all philosophers, was it *really* necessary that the good Anabaptist should be drowned? *Really* necessary that Mademoiselle Cunegonde should have her—tummy ripped open? And *really* necessary that I should see you hanged—before I could find out what it's all about? Really?

(*And engulfed in great sobs he throws himself on the heap. And a very creaky and ugly little* OLD WOMAN *creeps in and over to him.*

She taps him on the shoulder and he starts up, afraid.)

OLD WOMAN Young man. You are to come with me. I am to look after you and make you better. Give me your hand.

(*She bends and takes his hand and he gets up and she's holding the hand sticking out of the rubble.*

Now we come to a room. It's a nice room, richly furnished and with a nice big divan in the middle. A door here and there. That sort of thing.

VOLTAIRE *is sitting on the divan very relaxed and not a bit surprised to see us.)*

VOLTAIRE And that is what she did. She made him better. In a little room in the town. And three days later she brought him here, very furtively, to this charming abode just outside Lisbon.

(*He turns expectantly to the door. We follow his gaze. Obligingly it opens and the* OLD WOMAN *ushers in a heavily cloaked figure. She escorts it to the middle of the room and leaves it.*

VOLTAIRE *has now disappeared. The heavily cloaked figure waits for a bit and then peers out. It is* CANDIDE. *Looking very refreshed and nice. He removes the cloak and waits.*

Then the far door opens and he whirls round. Here comes the OLD WOMAN *again. This time with a heavily veiled female figure. Beautifully dressed, dripping with jewels, and trembling in a most intriguing fashion.*

The OLD WOMAN *brings her to* CANDIDE. *Then she indicates to him that he should lift the veil. Tentatively* CANDIDE *does so. A little, looking for encouragement from the* OLD WOMAN.

Then a little more. Then, incredulous, he whips the veil off. It is CUNEGONDE!

With a quiet little gasp he drops at her feet in a swoon. Not to be outdone she gives a little gasp and swoons too, but managing to land on the bed.

The OLD WOMAN *finds a little bottle in the recesses of her clothes and sprinkles its contents over the doting pair.*)

OLD WOMAN In the name of Our Lady of Atocha, the good Saint Anthony of Padua and the equally good Saint James of Compostella, waken up.

(*They do. And rise and gaze upon each other.*)

CANDIDE Is it really you?
CUNEGONDE Yes.
CANDIDE And you really live?
CUNEGONDE Yes.
CANDIDE So you were *not* raped, and your . . . tummy was *not* ripped open!

CUNEGONDE Oh yes. But it is not obligatory to *die* after that sort of thing.

(*More cries and sighs. The* OLD WOMAN *looks at them and heads for the door.*)

OLD WOMAN A little less noise, I think.

(*She goes.*)

CANDIDE But your father, your mother?
CUNEGONDE Dead.
CANDIDE Your brother?
CUNEGONDE Also.
CANDIDE And what are you doing in Portugal? And how did you know I was here? And what's all this about?

(*And he waves his hand around at the nice room.*)

CUNEGONDE Gently gently! Sit down and be a good boy and I'll tell you everything.
CANDIDE Everything.
CUNEGONDE Everything.

(*Holding hands and still gazing upon each other they subside and perch on the edge of the bed.*)

Well. You know about the war?
CANDIDE I know about the war.
CUNEGONDE Well. One day a great horde of Bulgars swept into our beautiful castle of Thunder-ten-tronckh. They slit my father's throat and chopped my mother into little pieces. So I fainted. Well. When I came to, I found myself being ravished by a great vulgar Bulgar.
CANDIDE Only one?

(*He seems almost disappointed that the story doesn't tally with what* PANGLOSS *told him. She looks at him curiously.*)

CUNEGONDE Isn't that enough?
CANDIDE Oh more than adequate. Go on.
CUNEGONDE Well. I scratched and bit and fought and kicked (not realising that all that was going on is perfectly *normal* in wartime, you see) and he got annoyed and stabbed me just here.

(*She rubs her left flank.*)

Still have the mark.

CANDIDE   Ah! I should like to see that.

CUNEGONDE   All in good time.

CANDIDE   Ah!

CUNEGONDE   Well. A Bulgar captain came in and saw us. The soldier didn't even get up! Naturally the captain got very angry at this lack of respect——

CANDIDE   Of course.

CUNEGONDE   ——so he killed him.

CANDIDE   On top of you?

CUNEGONDE   Yes.

CANDIDE   Tut tut. Then what happened?

CUNEGONDE   Well. The captain dressed my wound.

(*She smiles gently at this equivocal memory.*)

Then he made me a prisoner of war. In his own quarters.

CANDIDE   That was kind of him.

CUNEGONDE   Yes he was kind. And he had a nice white skin. All soft.

CANDIDE   Oh.

CUNEGONDE   Well. At the end of three months, he got bored with me and sold me to a Jewish merchant called don Issachar who was mad about women and brought me to Portugal and set me up in this house.

CANDIDE   And so . . .

CUNEGONDE   Wait, there's more. One day, at mass, the Grand Inquisitor . . .

(CANDIDE *crosses himself quickly.*)

. . . spotted me and fell madly in love with me.

CANDIDE   Of course.

(*From now he starts to caress her a little, becoming more bold as she chatters on through her story.*)

CUNEGONDE   Well. He tried to bully don Issachar into parting with me but the Jew is quite powerful at the court and wasn't having any of that. Then the Grand Inquisitor threatened him with an auto-da-fé and the Jew compromised—he has me on Mondays, Wednesdays, and the Sabbath, and the Grand Inquisitor all the other days. It's gone on for six months now and apart from arguments about which day *is* the Sabbath it's working out quite well.

CANDIDE   Oh. But how did you find me?

CUNEGONDE   Well. You know about the earthquake?

CANDIDE   I know about the earthquake.

CUNEGONDE   Well. When the Inquisitor decided to hold an auto-da-fé so that there wouldn't be another earthquake he very kindly invited me along. I had a very good seat and we all got refreshments between the mass and the executions. Well. It was bad enough watching those Jews and the Basque being burnt, but when I suddenly recognised my dear tutor Doctor Pangloss being hanged I fainted clean away, then to recover and look again and see you—stripped stark naked—well—my head reeled with horror and despair.

(*And she falls across his knees with her arms around his lower parts and he doesn't exactly cast her off.*

After a little pause she looks up very seriously.)

Though I must tell you, in all honesty, your skin is even nicer than my Bulgar Captain's.

(CANDIDE *lets out a great sigh. They kiss. They fall over sideways together on the bed.*)

Well. When they'd finished flogging you in time to the music, I sent my old serving woman to look after you. And here you are.

(CANDIDE *is just opening his mouth to say "And here I am" when somebody else says it for him.*)

SOMEBODY ELSE   And here I am.

(*This rather surprises the lovers. They stare at one another, then abruptly sit up and stare at the somebody else. It's* DON ISSACHAR, *with his back to them as he closes the door ever so carefully.*)

Candide

DON ISSACHAR (*gleefully sing-song*) I've come to exercise my rights, my little sweetheart, because it is the Sab——

(*And he turns from the door and stops in mid flight and the wind leaves his sails and the second half of the word emerges limply and falls on the floor.*)

——bath.

(*And then the wind gets back into his sails again, nay a hurricane, and he huffs and puffs at the fear-frozen lovers as they rise tentatively to their feet.*)

You little Christian Bitch! So! Is not enough I am sharing with an Inquisitor? I sharing also am with this . . .

(*And he draws a long nasty-looking dagger and advances quickly upon* CANDIDE, *shouting.*)

Dogmeat!

(*But as he gets to him* CANDIDE *whips out his even longer sword from under his cloak, holds it out vaguely, and* DON ISSACHAR *runs himself through with it.*
CUNEGONDE *lets out a bloodcurdling scream.* DON ISSACHAR *looks at them in great surprise. He drops his dagger, understandably, seizes the sword with both hands and crashes over backwards with it sticking out of his belly.*)

CANDIDE Oh dear.

CUNEGONDE Merciful heavens! A man killed. In my house. What are we going to do?

CANDIDE Now Pangloss would have given us good advice. If he hadn't been hanged.

(*The* OLD WOMAN *comes rushing in, having heard the scream.*)

OLD WOMAN What on earth . . . ? Merciful heavens. What have you done to don Issachar?

(CANDIDE *opens his mouth to speak. But somebody else speaks first.*)

ANOTHER SOMEBODY ELSE Yes. What *have* you done to don Issachar?

(*They all spin round to the man at the other door. The* OLD WOMAN *and* CUNEGONDE *drop immediately to their knees.* CANDIDE *remains rooted to the spot.*)

CUNEGONDE Oh, Monseigneur le Grand Inquisitor.

OLD WOMAN Grand Inquisitor.

CANDIDE Inquisitor!?

INQUISITOR Ah. You! You do not appear to have benefited one jot from the flogging I arranged for you. I'll have to arrange something else. A shade more permanent. Mmmm?

(*And he advances very slowly and nastily towards* CANDIDE. CANDIDE *turns straight to camera and takes us into his confidence.*)

CANDIDE Now. If this holy man calls for help, (a) he will have me very definitely burnt at the stake, and (b) he may well do as much for Cunegonde. He is my rival. I've already killed one man. In for a penny, in for a pound.

(*And he swings round and plucks the sword from the belly of* DON ISSACHAR *saying——*)

Excuse me.

(*And plunges it up to the hilt in the gut of the* GRAND INQUISITOR *saying——*)

Sorry about this. Necessity. Doctor Pangloss would have explained. If you hadn't hanged him.

(*And the* GRAND INQUISITOR *speechlessly nods his understanding and crashes onto the floor on his front with the sword sticking out his back. Only now do the* OLD WOMAN *and* CUNEGONDE *look up, and then down.* CUNEGONDE *screams of course.*)

CUNEGONDE *Another* man killed in my house! What to do what to do?

OLD WOMAN Here's what to do. Madame

will collect all her money and jewellery while Candide saddles up three good horses then we'll all ride like Hades to Cadiz. But not too fast for I have only one buttock left. The weather is very nice for this time of the year and it's pleasant to travel in the cool of the evening.

CANDIDE Excellent idea.

(*And he assists* CUNEGONDE *towards the door, talking as he does so.*)

And then what do we do?

OLD WOMAN We find a ship. We cannot stay in this country within reach of the Inquisition.

CANDIDE You're absolutely right. Let's go.

(*They go. And who is standing beside the door watching them but* VOLTAIRE. *The room disappears behind him and he strolls a little way.*)

VOLTAIRE Well. They reached Cadiz with only one minor mishap—all Cunegonde's money and jewellery disappeared. So did a Franciscan friar who happened to stay at the same inn.

(*He shrugs as though to say: Make of that what you will and what do you expect anyway? He rests his hands on the edge of some sort of table.*)

But then they actually had a stroke of good luck. The military lessons Candide had so painstakingly learnt proved very useful and he became . . .

(*He looks down. We go down or cut to* VOLTAIRE's *hand which is pointing at a toy soldier.*)

. . . a captain!

(*The soldier is facing us and he has a backdrop behind him on which is roughly painted a street and crowds of people waving flags.*
    VOLTAIRE's *forefinger and thumb take* CANDIDE *by the helmet and make him execute a crisp right turn.*)

And they gave him . . .

(*And the hand snaps its finger and immediately the soldier glides from right to left because he's on a little conveyor belt and tiny tinny martial music breaks out and the tiny painted people cheer tiny tinnily.*)

. . . a company. To command.

(*And* CANDIDE *marches out left and his company march in right: a single file of toy soldiers. And perhaps we come out wider and see* VOLTAIRE *gleefully winding the handle as he continues through the noise.*)

And they were all off to South America with plenty of guns and ammunition to point out the error of their ways to some reverend Jesuit Fathers who were preaching independence to the Indians so they could rule them for themselves.

(*The camera attaches itself to the last of the toy soldiers until it comes to a toy sailing ship. The conveyor belt, with the soldiers stuck to it, is so arranged that as they come to the edge they tilt forward one by one and appear to disappear, so to speak, into the hold of the ship.*)

So they all embarked. And so did . . .

(*And along the conveyor belt come . . .*)

. . . Mademoiselle Cunegonde, the old woman, the horses belonging to the erstwhile Grand Inquisitor of Portugal, and two valets; one of whom—Cacambo—was from South America and of whom we shall see more.

(VOLTAIRE *now leans in over the ship.*)

And off they went.

(*He takes a big breath puffs out his cheeks like a cherub zephyr on an ancient chart and blows hard.*
    The ship moves off, bumping up and down on a painted ocean.)

The voyage was perfectly normal.

(The lights grow dim on the tossing ship and lightning strikes and thunder roars and great gouts of water pour over it.)

There wasn't much room for drill, so Candide did a lot of philosophising.

(The toy ship disappears. We see the bowels of the ship. Pure Rowlandson. Soldiers and women and children crammed onto the screen in one impacted mass leaning lying sitting lounging, keening dying spitting scrounging, and all heaving about and up to the mad rhythm of the ship.
And in the middle, benign and fresh and sweatless, CANDIDE.*)*

CANDIDE Optimism, my dear friends and companions.

(He smiles sweetly around. No response —except from a loud whinnying laugh from a horse. CACAMBO *tries to look attentive.)*

CANDIDE Optimism. I feel certain the New World is that Best of all Possible Worlds mentioned by our dear Doctor Pangloss.

CUNEGONDE Perhaps. But I have suffered so much in my world that I'm no longer hopeful about anything.

OLD WOMAN Suffered! You! Suffered!

(And she cackles in a rather upsetting way.)

Dear madame. Compared with me you have not yet started.

*(*CUNEGONDE *looks a bit piqued at this and goes all prim and patronising.)*

CUNEGONDE My good woman. Unless you have been ravished by *two* Bulgars, stabbed in the . . . ah . . . *twice*, had *two* mothers and two fathers horribly murdered before your very eyes, and seen two of your lovers whipped at an auto-da-fé, then I don't think you can substantiate such a claim. Added to which I was born a baroness with seventy-two

quarterings on my coat of arms and *yet* I have . . . cooked for a Bulgar captain. So there.

OLD WOMAN Madame. You know nothing of my birth. And you'd soon change your tune if I showed you my backside.

(This not unnaturally creates a certain amount of interest amongst those gathered round. They gather closer if it is possible.
The OLD WOMAN *looks around at them.)*

OLD WOMAN My eyes . . . were not always bloodshot and rimmed with red. My nose . . . did not always touch my chin. And I have not always been a servant. Permit me to tell my tale.

*(*EVERYBODY *nods.)*

I am the daughter of Pope Urban the Tenth and The Princess of Palestrina.

(Loud gasp.
VOLTAIRE *pops in.)*

VOLTAIRE Please note the discretion: we use a fictitious name for the Pope.

OLD WOMAN Till the age of fourteen I lived in luxury and splendour. And *I* was splendid. My breasts were just forming. And what breasts! White and firm and shaped like the Venus de Medici's. And what eyes! Brilliant flashing lights which quite eclipsed the sparkling of the stars, as the local poets were always telling me. The women who dressed me and undressed me fell about in ecstasy when they beheld me from the front.

(Everybody goes "Mmmmm.")

And from behind.

(Everybody goes "Aaaaahh!"
She carries on.
But VOLTAIRE *has strolled into the foreground and now talks to us.)*

VOLTAIRE And she went on.
For two chapters and most of the Atlantic Ocean.

How she was affianced to an Italian Prince.

How the Prince was poisoned by his ex-mistress on the eve of the wedding.

How her mother took her away from it all and their ship was attacked by pirates and they were all stripped and searched for diamonds in curious places and raped and made slaves and raped again. And again.

How the pirates were in turn attacked by a gang who wanted the women badly.

How she saw her mother torn in two by over-ardent suitors.

How she nearly died of the plague while all around her did.

How she was sold over and over again and ravished at regular intervals.

And how finally, she came to lose one of her buttocks. It happened at the Siege of Azof. The soldiers, lacking their normal rations, decided to eat the women. But a pious Muslim Priest persuaded them to do it by installments, and before they could take a second helping the garrison was relieved.

And so they reached South America.

(*And there is a great crash.*

The ship shudders and everyone falls about and luggage falls down from bunks and the horses whinny and hens cackle and there is general chaos.

And a hatch opens and a SHINY SOUTH AMERICAN FACE *beams down and calls out:*)

SHINY SOUTH AMERICAN FACE   Eet's Buenos Ayres, amigos. Everybody change!

(*Now we are in a reception hall in the Spatial Palatial Genre. Or at least we see a picture of one, and that will do very well.*

In the foreground is VOLTAIRE.

In the background a magnificent figure poses, dressed magnificently and with magnificent moustachios. He is actually standing on a pedestal; there is certainly one in his head.)

VOLTAIRE   The Governor.

(*He turns away and strolls round this apparition as one would a public statue.*)

Don Fernando d'Ibaraa y Figueora y Mascarenes y Lampourdos y Souza. Proud. Haughty. As he should be with so many names. So disdainful, superior, and affected, that everyone who met him also wanted to kick him. It was young Captain Candide's duty to report immediately to the Governor.

(*As he is saying this,* CANDIDE *and* CUNEGONDE *come in and* VOLTAIRE *discreetly leaves.*

CANDIDE *bows very low.*)

CANDIDE   At your service, don Fernando d'Ibaraa y Figueora y Mascarenes y Lampourdos y Souza.

(*He stays deeply bowed throughout this. Mainly because it allows him to read off the piece of paper he is holding.*

CUNEGONDE *stands stiff and proud staring at the* GOVERNOR.

The GOVERNOR *revolves slowly towards them and then—doing! He clocks* CUNEGONDE *and is transfixed.*

VOLTAIRE *sticks his head round the edge of the frame.*)

VOLTAIRE   I omitted to tell you that don Fernando d'Ibaraa y Figueora y Mascarenes y Lampourdos y Souza was also the greatest womaniser this side of the Sierra Madre.

(*He pops out again.*

CANDIDE *straightens up and notices that the* GOVERNOR *is stepping like a man in a dream across the gap to* CUNEGONDE. *He steps so close that his magnificent moustachios are in danger of tickling her. His nostrils, if we can see them, dilate and he seems to be breathing with some difficulty.*)

DON FERNANDO   Ess thees yore wayfe? Mmmm?

(CANDIDE *turns to camera. Looking worried. Tricky, moral-wise.*)

CANDIDE I can't say it is because it isn't. Nor my sister.

(*He shrugs. Oh well. He looks sheepish and guilty.*)

We are . . . betrothed, Your Excellency.

(DON FERNANDO *leans even closer to* CUNEGONDE, *who leans back but not too far.*)

DON FERNANDO Ah ha!

(*This hardly reassures* CANDIDE. *So he burbles on brightly and placatingly.*)

CANDIDE And we'd both be very grateful, Your Excellency, if Your Excellency would deign to marry us, Your Excellency.

(DON FERNANDO'*s moustachios are now brushing* CUNEGONDE'*s lips.*)

DON FERNANDO Go and eenspect yore trooops.

(CANDIDE *stamps to attention.*)

CANDIDE At once!

(*And he bows low again, fishing for his bit of paper.*)

. . . don   Fer . . . fer . . . nando d'Ibar . . .

(DON FERNANDO *waves a hand behind his back.*)

DON FERNANDO Doan waiss my tayme, Capitano.

CANDIDE Absolutely not, Your Excellency!

(*And* CANDIDE *doubles off.*
 In a trice DON FERNANDO *whips an arm round* CUNEGONDE *and bends her into a back-breaking tango special, gloating over her bosom and the free hand rippling up and down her thighs.*)

DON FERNANDO Aye aye aye!

(*Followed by a voluble stream of Spanish endearments and sighs and protestations of intense passion and love but mostly passion. He stops.*)

CUNEGONDE Pardon?

DON FERNANDO Beloved tomorrow we weell merry . . . een thee chorch or out thee chorch, anyhow but somehow, yes?

CUNEGONDE Um . . . goodness!

DON FERNANDO You mus say yes!

(*And he straightens her up and drops to his knees and presses his face into her belly and grips her thighs and runs a spare hand up her skirt.*)

CUNEGONDE Well. I'll have to think it over.

(DON FERNANDO *leaps to his feet.*)

DON FERNANDO Feefteen meenits! No more!

CUNEGONDE Thank you.

(*She trips off.*
 He marches up and down in great agitation, twirling his moustachios, beating his forehead, moaning.
 Then he stops, grabs his manhood with both hands, and lets out a roar like a wounded bull.
 And now we are outside a door watching CUNEGONDE *and the* OLD WOMAN *whispering intensely together.*)

OLD WOMAN Mademoiselle. You have seventy-two quarterings to your coat of arms and not a hapenny to your name. You simply *must* be the wife of the greatest gentleman in South America with the magnificent moustachios. You've earned it. Marry him, *and* make Captain Candide's fortune.

CUNEGONDE And it's hardly betraying Candide, because I've been previously ravished by all sorts of people.

OLD WOMAN That's it.

CUNEGONDE Mmm.

(*Now we see* VOLTAIRE *standing in front of a drawing of Buenos Ayres looking out to sea through a telescope.*)

VOLTAIRE Meanwhile, down at the harbour. What have we here?

(*And we look through his telescope. It is another ship—though it will probably*

look remarkably like the same ship—standing in the shore.
We hear him musing.)

Portuguese . . . Man o' war . . . And *there's* the sting.

(*We see him again.*)

Officers of the Law. And a magistrate.

(*He snaps the telescope shut.*)

Poor Candide!

CANDIDE   And a magistrate?

(*He appears to be standing in the middle of a parade ground, with little tents and things in the background.*
All around we hear the crash of armed feet.
Beside him is his valet, CACAMBO. CANDIDE *is giving him a lot of attention in his head, but is watching his company marching about off camera.*)

CACAMBO   And a magistrate. All the way from Portugal. And if you don't fly this minute, Master, you'll be burning within the hour.

CANDIDE   Do you really think so? *Abowwwwwwwwt tun!*

(*And there is a great crash of feet, as they abowt tun.*)

CACAMBO   I know so, Master.

CANDIDE   Right. We'll fly. You saddle the Inquisitor's horses and we'll go to the Governor's palace for Mademoiselle Cunegonde. *Ehbowwwwwwwwt tun!*

(*Crash crash crash.*)

CACAMBO   But the magistrate's already there!

CANDIDE   Oh. What'll we do, Cacambo?

CACAMBO   Leave her and run.

CANDIDE   What? A beautiful baroness with seventy-two quarterings?

(*And he finally turns and devotes all his attention to* CACAMBO.)

What will become of her? And don Fer . . .

(*He waves his hands about to indicate the rest of the name.*)

. . . was going to marry us.

CACAMBO   Oh *she*—with respect—will manage. And *she* didn't murder the Grand Inquisitor of Portugal.

CANDIDE   True. Oh Cunegonde! Oh Cacambo! When shall I ever see her again:

(*And he breaks down and has a little weep.*)

CACAMBO   God knows.

CANDIDE   Yes I suppose he does.

CACAMBO   Come *on*, Master.

CANDIDE   Right. Just a minute.

(*And he rallies himself and turns to look back at the troops and in a sad little chokey voice says:*)

About turn.

(*Nothing.*
He looks worried.)

About turn.

(*Nothing.*
CACAMBO *grabs his hand and starts to pull him away.*)

I hope those poor fellows can swim.

(*And* CACAMBO *drags him off.*
VOLTAIRE *wanders in, backwards, from the other side, looking towards the disappearing troops.*)

VOLTAIRE   Some of them could. So Candide rode off to a new set of adventures. But where was Cacambo taking him?

CANDIDE   Cacambo. Where are you taking me? Do you know?

(*They are riding like mad, side by side, though we don't see the horses.*
Behind them are wild South American hills.)

CACAMBO   Of course. I lived many years in this country before going to Spain.

CANDIDE   Ah. Then where are we going?

CACAMBO   To the land of the Jesuit Fathers.

(*At this piece of information,* CANDIDE *reins in his horse abruptly with a great whinnying and standing up in the stirrups and that.*
And CACAMBO, *who does not, goes shooting off screen to the left.*)

CANDIDE But I came here to *fight* the Jesuit Fathers. On behalf of the King!

CACAMBO True.

(*And he rides gently back into shot.*)

And now the King would like to have you burnt at the stake.

(*Pause.*)

CANDIDE True. Let's go to the Jesuit Fathers.

(*And he rides off left.*
And CACAMBO *smiles and wheels about and follows. And I'm not joking when I say wheels. Though they might just as well be on hobby horses, or big rocking horses. Anything.*
A green and shady arbour.
CACAMBO *stands patiently while* CANDIDE *marches up and down chewing his lip and looking worried.*
Behind stand two guards; the Indians the Jesuits are inciting against Spain.)

Supposing, Cacambo, supposing the Reverend Father Colonel puts us to death?

(CACAMBO *looks at him. I mean, how do you answer a question like that? And before he can, a voice does.*)

VOICE I don't expect that will be necessary.

(*And there in the doorway is the* REVEREND FATHER COLONEL *himself. Surprisingly young and fresh and attractive and proud, dressed as a soldier on top of priest's clothing.*
The two guards cross themselves and drop to the floor and crawl and kiss his spurs muttering "Blessed Reverend Father Colonel, sir."
And the blessed REVEREND FATHER COLONEL *kicks them smartly about the ribs and, as they depart, the bottom.*)

COLONEL Get out, scum! Ingrates!

(*He turns to* CANDIDE.)

Imagine trying to build an empire out of that. Never mind. We'll do it. Whether they want it or not. Now young sir.

(*And* CANDIDE *drops to his knees indicating to* CACAMBO *to do likewise, and* CANDIDE *tries to kiss the* COLONEL's *ring, but the* COLONEL *offers him his sword in lieu and he kisses that.*)

COLONEL Please. Do not look so worried. I understand you are German. And being German are therefore not Spanish. And being not Spanish therefore I can talk to you.

(*And he helps him to his feet.*
And CANDIDE *looks at him closely, because he is beginning to feel, as we do, that we've seen the* COLONEL *somewhere before.*)

I too am German. And what part do you come from?

CANDIDE Westphalia, Reverend Father Colonel.

(*And now the* COLONEL *looks surpised and gives* CANDIDE *a closer look.*)

COLONEL Why so do I. And what part of Westphalia?

CANDIDE I was born . . .

(*And he is nearly overcome by emotion.*)

. . . in the castle of . . . Thunder-ten-tronckh.

COLONEL Heavens! So was I! Candide is it really you?

CANDIDE It's a miracle! Monsieur le Baron! Cacambo, it's the heir to Thunder-ten-tronckh! The young master.

(*And* CACAMBO *scratches his head and keeps his silence while the other two embrace and exclaim and laugh and cry.*
And eventually they simmer down and sit down if there's anything to sit on, gazing with delight into each other's eyes though it's only fair to say there's

more delight in CANDIDE's *eyes, than in the* YOUNG BARON's, *but then there would be.*)

But Pangloss told me you'd been buggered by Bulgars and then killed in a most unpleasant fashion. Oh how happy he would be if he hadn't gone and got himself hanged!

YOUNG BARON   Oh I was. Left for dead with the rest of my family.

CANDIDE   I can tell you something about that, but go on.

YOUNG BARON   Oh? Well. A priest came along and sprinkled holy water on us. Well. It was a bit salty and some got in my eye and the good father saw it flutter so they didn't bury me after all, but took me back to his order which was the Jesuits. Well. As you know, Candide, I've always been rather nice looking and the Father Superior took a fancy to me and dressed me up as a novice and took me about with him to Rome and places; and one way and another I've got on very well and here I am in charge of this post.

CANDIDE   Miraculous! Wonderful! Fate has led me straight to you to rescue me . . . and . . . listen . . . your dear sister.

YOUNG BARON   Cunegonde?   But   she was——

CANDIDE   No she wasn't. And at this very moment she is in the Governor's residence at . . . Buenos Ayres!

YOUNG BARON   Buenos Ayres! My dear Candide! We shall raise a force *now!* Ride in. And ride out with Cunegonde!

(*He turns to go to give orders.*)

CANDIDE   Oh yes! And then she and I can be married!

(*The* YOUNG BARON *stops suddenly and his shoulders look all hunchy and tense and he turns slowly to* CANDIDE *with a burning eye.*)

YOUNG BARON   What insolence is this? *You* presume to marry my sister? A bar-

oness with seventy-two quarterings on her coat of arms? *You!*

CANDIDE   Well . . . Holy Father Colonel, sir. You see I *did* rescue her from a Jew and an Inquisitor.

(*And the* YOUNG BARON *slowly moves towards him.*)

YOUNG BARON   Oh?

CANDIDE   Yes. And she *wants* to marry me.

YOUNG BARON   What's that got to do with it?

CANDIDE   (*gulping*)   And Doctor Pangloss said that all men are equal.

YOUNG BARON   We'll soon see about *that*, you cheekly little man!

(*And he's drawn his sword and on the word "that" he slaps* CANDIDE *with the flat of it across the side of his face.*

But CANDIDE *unhappily doesn't read the signals right and by the end of the speech he finds his sword up to the hilt in yet another stomach.*

The YOUNG BARON *stares at him, lets out a great sigh, and falls backwards off the sword.*

CANDIDE *is left staring at the blade. He starts to cry.*)

CANDIDE   Dear Heaven! I'm the mildest man imaginable and yet I've already killed three men. And two of them were priests!

(*Meanwhile* CACAMBO *has leapt to the entrance to the arbour and is looking anxiously out.*)

There is nothing for it but to sell our lives dear . . . sword in hand.

(CANDIDE *marches towards the entrance and* CACAMBO *places a hand on his chest and pushes him back.*)

CACAMBO   No thank you, Master. There are other things to try first.

(*And now we are outside the arbour and someone is peering into it. Danger? No it's* VOLTAIRE, *as we see when he turns round and steps back swiftly out of the way.*

    CACAMBO *strides out with great assurance, shouting.*)

Make way for the Reverend Father Colonel! Make way!

(*And the cloak and hat of the Reverend Father Colonel come tentatively to the doorway and* CANDIDE's *face peers fearfully out and then he takes a deep breath and straightens up and marches off.*)

VOLTAIRE And they *did* make way—all the way to the frontier until Candide and Cacambo were safe. Well. Safe from the Jesuits. But where to go now?

(*Somewhere.*)

CACAMBO We'll go to Cayenne.

CANDIDE And desert Mademoiselle Cunegonde? Never!

CACAMBO If we go back to Buenos Ayres they will burn you at the stake.

CANDIDE We'll go to Cayenne. How long will it take?

CACAMBO Not very.

CANDIDE Then let's go.

VOLTAIRE It took a month.

(*He takes a little stroll to get away from the arbour. And as he describes the journey we see sketchily pass behind him the terrain through which they pass but we need not see them. We can hear, however, the jungle shrieks, screams, chanting of natives, gunshots and yells of brigands, the whinny and thump of the horses falling dead, and so on. To all of which* VOLTAIRE *reacts with glinting eyes and a certain amount of relish.*)

VOLTAIRE It wasn't easy. It wasn't easy at all.
They sweated up mountains
They forced across rivers
They skidded down precipices
Were hunted by savages
Ambushed by brigands
Lived off the land

And watched their horses drop dead from fatigue.

(*He's now at a cane break or jungly bit.*)

And at the end of a month . . .

(*The jungly bit crashes open and* CANDIDE *and* CACAMBO *crash through to stand panting in the foreground. Their clothes are in shreds.*

    CACAMBO *looks a bit haunted and dirty and matted and weary and shiny and hollow eyed; but of course, as you'd expect,* CANDIDE *looks like a pantomime Robinson Crusoe—all fresh and clean and delicious.*)

. . . they *still* hadn't reached Cayenne . . . or Anywhere.

(*Their eyes scan the horizon greedily and in* CACAMBO's *case glassily.*)

CACAMBO Do you see Cayenne, Master?

CANDIDE Not a sneeze of it.

(*Then* CANDIDE's *eyes drop lower and he alerts.*)

Cacambo! Look! A little canoe moored in that river there.

CACAMBO A lil canoe!

(CANDIDE *becomes the General.*)

CANDIDE Now. It may not be entirely ethical. But my plan is to fill that little canoe with coconuts then launch it upon the bosom of the waters and see where they take us.

(*CS*[8] *of* VOLTAIRE.)

VOLTAIRE And that's just what they did. At first the voyage was pleasant enough, and a welcome rest, as they drifted through a nice assortment of scenery, sometimes wild and sometimes gentle.

(*And as he says this we pull back and lo and behold he's sitting on a pile of coconuts in the stern of the boat, munching a piece while the scenery floats past be-*

8 CS close shot.

hind. And we keep on coming out and find ourselves ahead of the boat with CACAMBO *amidships and* CANDIDE *peering ahead in the bow, both vaguely paddling.)*

But then . . .

*(*CANDIDE *alerts ahead with amazement and concern and turns quickly to* CACAMBO *whose mouth is slowly opening and we look ahead too and see [zooming in to a picture] a huge cavern into a high mountain looming up ahead, dark and yawning and threatening.*

Looking aft again the two are paddling like mad to turn the canoe to the bank and M. VOLTAIRE *has wisely disappeared but their efforts avail them not and they get wildly pitched about on the rushing waters and we look forward again and with a great whoosh! The black maw spreads out until it fills the screen and all goes black. And now we have a real psychedelic trip. Weird lights and flashes streaking past over the petrified faces, accompanied by a terrible echoing roar of water under which we imagine all sorts of unrecognizable screams and wails and moans.*

And a ghostly green VOLTAIRE *is gently superimposed transparently on all this and he speaks with a rolling echo.*

And this went on for twenty-four hours. Then suddenly . . .

(And suddenly it is. With a great crash cut VOLTAIRE *disappears, the roaring stops. And the duo are floating along peacefully in the blinking sunlight. They stare in surprise at the beautiful countryside, as we do, or at least at a drawing of it; an immense plain bordered all round by inaccessible mountains standing jaggedly into the sky.)*

CANDIDE   Look, Cacambo. It's even nicer than Westphalia. Let's moor the boat and head for that village.

(A glade.
Four or three children are playing.

They're dressed in rags. But the rags are gold brocade. They're playing Petinque.

We look closely at the balls. Surprise surprise. They're made of gold and emerald and ruby.

We cut to CANDIDE *and* CACAMBO *who are passing by but stop at this remarkable sight.)*

CACAMBO   Those must be the sons of the King of this country.

(They look away to one side as a voice calls "coooeee" and there stands a man waving to the children.)

CANDIDE   And that must be the Royal Family's tutor.

(Pleased with their lightning analysis of the situation they smile and watch the children run away and are about to move on when they notice something. The balls lying on the ground.

CANDIDE *runs to them and* CACAMBO *follows and they pick them up and run after the tutor.)*

CANDIDE   Sir! Sir! You forgot these precious playthings.

(They shove them into the man's hands. The man looks very surprised, smiles and drops them on the ground. Then he looks closely into CANDIDE'S *face, gets slightly anxious, and hurries the children away.)*

Well I never.

CACAMBO   He doesn't seem to want them.

(They look at the balls. At one another. Shrug. Pick them up. And march off.)

CANDIDE   Where on earth can we be, Cacambo?

VOLTAIRE   Where indeed?

(He's sitting at a table in an inn; sipping a delightfully coloured liqueur from a glass of crystal and gold leaf.

If we see the two young men and the two young women who are serving we will notice that they're dressed in cloth of gold. And the dishes are gold. And all sorts of things are gold or precious stones. If we happen to see any of the diners, they turn out to be perfectly ordinary humble people, despite the rich stuff of their costumes.)

A country where the princes are so well brought up they despise gold. Armed with their new wealth Candide and Cacambo came to this charming place for something to eat. And they had:
Bowls of parrot soup
A steamed eagle
Very tasty roast monkeys
A dish of buntings
Another of humming birds
Various very nice casseroles
And delicious pastries.
And then waiters kept on pouring this rather cheeky liqueur made from cane sugar.

(And now we see CANDIDE and CACAMBO suitably stuffed amidst the remains of the banquet.)

(voice over)   And they thought they could more than adequately pay for it all with two of the balls they had picked up.

(With a plonk CANDIDE drops a golden ball on the table and with another CACAMBO follows suit.
     CANDIDE gestures grandly.)

CANDIDE   Keep the change.
CACAMBO (in Spanish)   Keep the change.

(Everybody looks at them in amazement. Then someone titters. Then somebody else. And people stand up to look at them.
     CANDIDE speaks quietly to CACAMBO out of the corner of his mouth.)

CANDIDE   Have I tipped too much?

(Then everyone is roaring with laughter till the tears are coursing down their cheeks. And the two get very uncomfortable.
     At last they sober down a little and wiping the tears from his eyes the LAND-

LORD sits down beside them and speaks. In Spanish.)

What's he say what's he say?

(Not taking their eyes from the LANDLORD, CACAMBO and CANDIDE lean together and CACAMBO translates while the LANDLORD rattles on.)

CACAMBO   Sirs, we see well that you are strangers. We are not accustomed to seeing any. Forgive us for laughing when you try to pay us with the common stones of the highway.
CANDIDE   The common stones of the highway!?
CACAMBO   The common stones of the highway. Doubtless you do not have any of the money of the country, but it isn't necessary anyway. All hotels are paid for by the government.
CANDIDE   Paid for by the government?
CACAMBO   Paid for by the government. You have done badly here because this is a poor village, but elsewhere you will be received properly.

(The LANDLORD stands up and bows and everybody applauds and everybody smiles.
     CANDIDE stands up and bows back and as he straightens up he turns to camera and addresses us confidentially.)

CANDIDE   What is this country where everything is so different from anything I've seen? It's probably the land where everything comes out right. There must be one somewhere. And no matter what Pangloss said I did notice from time to time that it all came out wrong in Westphalia.

(And something is plucking at his sleeve and he turns and it's a VERY VERY OLD MAN. A VERY VERY OLD MAN who can speak his language.)

VERY VERY OLD MAN   You have come—and goodness knows *how* you have come for our mountains are in-ac-cessible—where no stranger before you has come—at least I can't remember and I'm a hundred and seventy-two next week—you have come to that land the Spaniard calls El Dorado.

CANDIDE El Dorado! Of course! El Dorado, Cacambo!

(And he picks up one of the pieces of gold.)

The Place of Gold. Men have sought it for centuries and failed. We shall be famous and rich.

VERY VERY OLD MAN Famous and rich where, young sir?

CANDIDE Why at home. In Europe.

VERY VERY OLD MAN You will never see it more.

CANDIDE } *(together)* { Beg your pardon?
CACAMBO }   { Sorry?

VERY VERY OLD MAN Our mountains are in-ac-cessible . . .

CANDIDE *(simultaneously)* In-ac-cessible yes we heard.

VERY VERY OLD MAN . . . from both sides. This is how we have retained our innocence and natural goodness. Also we are forbidden to try to leave.

CANDIDE Forbidden? And who forbids it? The King? The Law?

VERY VERY OLD MAN The consent of the people. That *is* the law.

(This is a new idea to CANDIDE. *His natural bent for philosophy makes him terribly interested.)*

CANDIDE But, venerable sir, without formal Law, how do you deal with wrong-doers?

VERY VERY OLD MAN Wrongdoers. What are wrongdoers?

CANDIDE People who . . . do wrong . . .

VERY VERY OLD MAN We have none of those.

CANDIDE . . . who *break* the Law.

VERY VERY OLD MAN But the Law *is* the collective consent of the people, so why should they dream of breaking it?

(This idea so flumboosters CANDIDE *that he can't get his metaphysical hooks into it anywhere.)*

I see our simple ideas are strange to you. We must send you to the capital where wiser men than I will explain them. And the King will wish to meet you.

(And he turns and speaks rapidly in Spanish to all the others and there is a great burst of people going to arrange things.
We return to VOLTAIRE.)

VOLTAIRE So they went to the capital. In a coach drawn by the usual form of transport: large red sheep, or llamas. And when they reached the King's palace they were welcomed by twenty beautiful young women who bathed them and dressed them and delivered them to the throne room.

(And we see the picture of a most glitteringly magnificent hall with a more glitteringly magnificent throne in the foreground, and sitting on that throne an even more glitteringly magnificent KING. *Surrounded by damsels and officials.*
And at the back of the chamber a tight little group with CANDIDE *and* CACAMBO, *dressed superbly, waiting nervously to be called. And there's lovely music and a choir of sweet maidenly voices and* CACAMBO *speaks out of the side of his mouth to a rather* GRAND OFFICIAL.)

CACAMBO What's the drill? On the knees, on the belly, hands on head, hands on bum, lick his boots or what? Eh?

GRAND OFFICIAL The custom, sir, is to embrace His Majesty and kiss him upon both cheeks.

CACAMBO Oh.

(And there's a ruddy great fanfare and CANDIDE *and* CACAMBO *march stiffly forward as everyone applauds. And they embrace the* KING *and all that. And the* KING *indicates to them that they should sit upon his left and his right and they do and the* KING *stands up.)*

KING I bid these rare strangers welcome. We shall learn much from them. Perhaps they may learn a little from us.

(He sits down and there's another ruddy great fanfare and the ladies of the court start dancing in a rather nice undulating style.

The KING *leans over to* CANDIDE.*)*

I understand you have many questions. Please begin.

*(*CANDIDE's *face lights up.)*

CANDIDE   Am I correct in thinking you have no religion in El Dorado?

(The KING's *face hardens a little but politeness overcomes his pique.)*

KING   Why of course we have. The one the true the only religion.
CANDIDE   Ah. Which one is that?
KING   Which one? How could there possibly be two? Why do you ask such strange questions?
CANDIDE   Because I see no priests.
KING   But we are all "priests." We need no one else to come between us and God.
CANDIDE   But how do you confess?
KING   Confess what?
CANDIDE   Um . . . transgressions.
KING   Transgressions. I do not know this word. Explain it to me.
CANDIDE   Well . . .

(He sighs and looks unhappy at the task before him. He is saved for the moment by the end of the first bit of the dance. The KING *rises and applauds. Everybody bows.*

At the back of the chamber a group of courtiers is bowed low. It straightens up. Between the two in the foreground and looking at us over their shoulders is VOLTAIRE *in a big gold brocade hat.)*

VOLTAIRE   They stayed a month. Partly because they weren't allowed to leave but mostly because it was the nearest place to Paradise either of them could imagine. And yet . . . and yet . . .

(The Baths.

CACAMBO *is stretched out on his front stark naked being oiled and massaged by a fair damsel who is also stark naked. Or*

as near it as the seriousness of the time slot allows.

[*Digression:* VOLTAIRE *would have been greatly amused to discover that nudity on television is not allowed with levity, but that clothes may only disappear fine by degrees and beautifully less as one approaches the centre of gravity. End of Digression.*]

Another damsel pops sweetmeats in his mouth to the rhythm of yet another who plays on the flute or something. One would like to capture something of the soft, fleshly innocence of Ingres' painting of the ladies of the harem.

We hear CANDIDE's *voice but do not yet see him.*

CANDIDE *(voice over)*   Cacambo.
CACAMBO *(lazily)*   Yes, Master.
CANDIDE *(voice over)*   Cacambo. It *is* true that the chateau where I was born was not as nice as it is here in El Dorado. But. All the same. Mademoiselle Cunegonde is not *here.*
CACAMBO *(astonished)*   You still pine for Mademoiselle Cunegonde? Now?
CANDIDE *(voice over)*   Oh yes.

(And now we see him. Surrounded by even more naked lovelies, doing even nicer things to him.)

Every moment of the day.
CACAMBO   But Mademoiselle Cunegonde is no longer *in* your castle. She's in Buenos Ayres beyond your reach. So let's stay here.

*(*CANDIDE *rises to the argument with warmth. He straightens up, shaking off the lovelies, who pout.)*

CANDIDE   No! If we stay here we'll just be like everyone else.

CACAMBO   Am I complaining?
CANDIDE   Whereas. If we leave here with only a dozen of those big sheep loaded with pebbles, we'll be richer than all the Kings of the world put together, the inquisitors wouldn't dare touch us, and we could carry off Mademoiselle Cunegonde without any trouble. What do you think?

KING   I think you are mad, Candide.

(We've jumped to him on a slam cut. He's sitting on the throne. Or something.)

Mad. However. I could not be tyrant enough to keep strangers here against their will. So be it.

CANDIDE   Oh thank you, Your Majesty.

KING   There is only one thing I should like to point out.

CANDIDE   Your mountains are inaccessible.

CACAMBO   On both sides.

KING   That is so. You must wait until my engineers construct machines to hoist you up the sheer cliffs which are ten thousand feet high.

CANDIDE   Thank you, Your Majesty.

KING   Ask for anything you want for your journey. It shall be given.

(CANDIDE and CACAMBO look at each other. CANDIDE is a little shy so CACAMBO speaks.)

CACAMBO   Your Majesty. Just a few sheep? Loaded with provisions? And some pebbles and dirt?

KING   *(smiling)*   I cannot imagine what you'll do in Europe with our yellow dust. But take as much as you like, and much good will it do you.

CACAMBO   Oh it will!

(On the right a sheer cliff [cutout] running away to distant craggy skyline [drawing]. Up behind the mountains rises the sun [Phoebus], with his bright grinning face. Which changes gradually and it's VOLTAIRE.)

VOLTAIRE/PHOEBUS   And so the ingenious engineers of El Dorado built a machine to hoist them out of the Kingdom.

(And passing jerkily up the foreground cliff go CANDIDE and CACAMBO on a platform, waving down to unseen cheering crowds like balloononauts.)

And they took with them not just a few, not just a dozen, but one hundred and two big red sheep.

(And as he says this up the cliff goes another platform [model] loaded with red sheep [toys].)

Two to ride on; twenty with provisions, thirty loaded with wonderful gifts, and fifty with gold and jewels and diamonds.

(And as he says this we mix through to the Caravanserai en route. That is, we see all the models, with models of CANDIDE and CACAMBO riding, moving along a little conveyor belt, in silhouette through silhouette trees and shrubs with a background of mountains.)

(Voice over)   And off they set. To reach the coast to charter a ship to sail to Buenos Ayres to ransom the fair Cunegonde. The first day everything went splendidly. The second day two sheep went into a bog and disappeared.

(And with two sharp cracks two of the sheep in the line disappear.)

Another two died of fatigue shortly after.

(Crack crack another two go.)

Seven or eight perished of hunger in the desert.

(Crack crack crack crack crack crack crack or crack. And as this is going on and the sheep fall down we pull back and it's a little shooting gallery with VOLTAIRE banging away like mad.)

A lot more fell down a cliff.

(And he lets rip a few more shots and puts the amazingly ahead-of-its-time repeater on the counter.)

And so on. After a hundred days they had——

CACAMBO   Exactly two left.

(We have slam cut again and CACAMBO is just returning to CANDIDE who is sitting sadly on the ground. He nods.)

CANDIDE   It's true, my friend. The riches of this world pass away. Everything fades and withers. Except virtue. And the joy of seeing Mademoiselle Cunegonde again.

CACAMBO I dare say. But we're still richer than the King of Spain will ever be.

(And he holds up a handful of sparklers.)

And we'll soon reach the coast. Come.

(And CANDIDE *springs up.)*

CANDIDE And we'll find a ship captain to take us to Buenos Ayres!

SHIP CAPTAIN Ah no no no no no no no no, no!

(We've slam cut into a tavern and the three of them are leaning over a table at one another.)

CANDIDE But why not, Captain?

SHIP CAPTAIN Because I'll be hanged. And you'll be hanged.

CANDIDE Why so?

SHIP CAPTAIN Because your Cunegonde is the favourite mistress of don Fernando D'Ibaraa y Figueora y Mascarenes y Lampourdos y Souza. That's why.

*(*CANDIDE *lets out a terrible cry as though stabbed and there is a sudden hush as all those grizzled sea dogs turn and stare. And* CANDIDE's *mouth starts to crumble round the edges and he starts to cry. The* SHIP CAPTAIN *gets up and backs away muttering "Sacramento!" or something appropriate and joins his cronies who crowd round wanting to know and the hubbub of conversation rises again.* CACAMBO *waits patiently while* CANDIDE *dries out a little then speaks through his tears.)*

CANDIDE O Pangloss Pangloss! Forgive me, dear Doctor but after this I can no longer believe in optimism.

CACAMBO What on earth is optimism?

CANDIDE It is a mania for insisting everything's fine when you know everything's awful. Look my dear friend. In our pockets we each have diamonds worth six or seven million. You're cleverer than I am so take what you've got and *you* go and get Cunegonde. I shouldn't think they'll hang you since you haven't killed an Inquisitor.

CACAMBO True. But what about you?

CANDIDE Well.

(He's just about stopped crying, by the way.)

I'll get hold of another ship and go to Venice to wait for you.

CACAMBO Right. I'll start right away.

(They both stand up and embrace, moved by parting after so many adventures.)

CANDIDE And don't forget the Old Woman.

CACAMBO Of course.

(And he goes. Watched sadly by CANDIDE.
CANDIDE *looks round then goes over to the* SHIP CAPTAIN.)*

CANDIDE How much to take me and two big red sheep to Venice?

SHIP CAPTAIN What big red sheep?

CANDIDE The ones outside the door.

(The SHIP CAPTAIN *whips the door open and sticks his head out briefly and turns back again.)*

SHIP CAPTAIN Ten thousand piastres.

CANDIDE Done.

(The SHIP CAPTAIN *turns to camera in CU[9] astonished.)*

SHIP CAPTAIN Ho ho! If he doesn't hesitate he must be rich.

(He sucks his teeth and counts his fingers. Then speaks to CANDIDE.)*

On second thoughts . . . it's twenty thousand piastres to Venice.

CANDIDE Right.

(The SHIP CAPTAIN *looks briefly to camera again.)*

9 **CU** close up.

SHIP CAPTAIN Ho ho! (*To* CANDIDE.) Ah! You mean Venice, Italy? Ah! That's thirty thousand piastres.

CANDIDE Whatever you say.

SHIP CAPTAIN (*To camera*) Carramba! Those big red sheep must be loaded with treasure! I'll take the thirty thousand for now and we'll see what's what. (*To* CANDIDE.) Meet me here at cockcrow with the money, Your Excellency, and we'll set sail.

CANDIDE Agreed.

(*The* SHIP CAPTAIN *stalks off right. We have a quick wipe through one of those farmyard dawn pictures with the cock silhouetted against the glow as the sun comes over the hill with one quick cockadoodledoooo and wipe straight back to* CANDIDE *who hasn't moved and the* SHIP CAPTAIN *marches straight in from the right again.*)

SHIP CAPTAIN Morning Your Excellency.

CANDIDE Here you are.

(*And he hands him a sack containing thirty thousand piastres.*)

We go?

SHIP CAPTAIN You remain here in comfort Your Excellency while I load the big red sheep then I'll bring the boat back for you.

CANDIDE Fine. Don't be long.

(*And the* CAPTAIN *goes again and we go with him but only as far as the door where we find* VOLTAIRE *leaning nonchalantly against the lintel, and gazing out to sea.*)

VOLTAIRE He was.

(*And he turns into the tavern to where* CANDIDE *is sitting at the table again with his back to the door and taps him on the shoulders.*

And CANDIDE *turns round and looks in the direction indicated. And we look too and see a ship in full sail putting out to sea.*

And CANDIDE *smiles and nods then gets*

the message and runs out the door shouting.)

CANDIDE No! It's not! It mustn't! It *can't* be!

VOLTAIRE It was.

(*A Law Court. Large and dark and Kafkaesque. A drawing gloomily tailing off into outer darkness. A dwarfed* CANDIDE *is looking up and shouting and banging the table at his side.*)

CANDIDE And therefore My Lord I demand that justice be done and that that perfidious Sea Captain be brought back to trial.

(*And we look up a vast wooden cliff towards the* JUDGE *whom we cannot see but after a little pause a little old wizened head peers over at us.*)

JUDGE Yeeeeeessss. I'll look into the matter should he return in the meantime that will be ten thousand piastres costs and another ten thousand for kicking up such a din in my court next case.

(*And* CANDIDE *opens his mouth to complain but nothing comes out. He's speechless.*)

(*Now we're looking at a tree or a door or anything convenient and* VOLTAIRE *with a satchel full of rolled papers over his shoulders and a hammer and nails and as he says the following he nails up a poster.*)

VOLTAIRE So Candide, having lost a fortune equal to that of at least twenty monarchs, decided to book a humble passage to Europe. And since this final misfortune had plunged him into a deep melancholy, he also decided to advertise for a suitable companion.

(*And he steps aside and lets us read the poster. Which says:*

"M. CANDIDE, NOW LODGING AT THE TAVERNA DEL SOL OFFERS PASSAGE, BOARD, AND TWO THOUSAND PIASTRES TO AN HONEST MAN TO BE HIS COMPANION TO BOR-

DEAUX—PROVIDED THAT THE SAID HONEST MAN IS THE UNLUCKIEST AND MOST MISER- ABLE IN THE PROVINCE."

Slam cut and we're looking out a window away across a flat piece of landscape. Winding back and forth across the painted plain are thousands of painted men in an exact replica of that bit where the people of Saint Petersburg come to Ivan the Awful in that Eisenstein[10] thing and the head of the line seems to be just outside the door. And it is. We hear real Russian type sobbing and pan across the closed door to where CANDIDE *is interviewing a candidate for the post.* CANDIDE *is clutching the other man and both are drenched in tears.* CANDIDE *sniffles bravely through his.)*

CANDIDE No no no my dear friend. Don't go on. You're not nearly miserable enough—Next!

(And we go back shuffling with the wretch and the door opens and surprise, in walks VOLTAIRE. *But he's not a client, he's ushering, and he brings in* MARTIN *and stands him up against the wall so we can look at him.)*

VOLTAIRE At last he chose one. Martin here. A wise man. He wasn't really worse off than anybody else, but since he was a scholar Candide thought he might be the most interesting to talk to.

(He nods politely to MARTIN *who nods a "Can I go now?" and* VOLTAIRE *nods a "yes indeed" and* MARTIN *goes off.)*

And so they set sail for Europe.

(There are MARTIN *and* CANDIDE *on yet another [same] ship.)*

(Voice over.) Passing the time in endless discussion.

CANDIDE So when you think about it, even after all that misery I do still have

10 A reference to Sergei Eisenstein's film, *Ivan the Terrible.*

quite a lot of money and I *do* hope to see Cunegonde again. So although things aren't as good as they are in El Dorado things aren't too *bad.* One may therefore detect a tendency towards The Good and so discern the hand of *God.* Wouldn't you agree, Martin?

MARTIN No.

CANDIDE Oh. Why not?

MARTIN I don't discern the hand of God much. He's outclassed in this world.

(CANDIDE looks anxiously around for nasty men in black.)

CANDIDE Hush! I've already been to one auto-da-fé. You must be possessed by the Devil.

(He crosses himself.
MARTIN *shrugs.)*

MARTIN The Devil's into everything. Why not me? I think God's given up the struggle. I've never known a country that didn't want to destroy its neighbouring country nor a family that didn't want to score off another family. All over the world the weak are exploited by the strong. A million paid assassins roam up and down Europe murdering and pillaging by numbers to earn their daily bread. And where things appear not too bad, men's hearts are eaten away by envy and greed and the worry of owning things. No sir. I do not much discern the hand of God.

CANDIDE But there is *some* good to be found.

MARTIN Where? I've never seen it.

(Suddenly there's a sound of cannon-fire, doubled and redoubled, from away across the water. And CANDIDE *whips out his telescope and we see what he sees. In the circle a ship [animation] blasting away with cannon to the left. And the circle whips to the left and we see another ship blasting away to the right.)*

CANDIDE *(Voice over.)* It's a pirate attacking a merchantman.

(The circle passes backwards and forwards from one ship to another until a shot topples the masts of one of them and there are terrible creaks and groans and screams, and the hit one begins to sink.)

(Voice over.) There are hundreds of them! Drowning! My God!

(We see CANDIDE *and* MARTIN *and* MARTIN *looks at* CANDIDE *quizzically.)*

MARTIN Your *who?*

(And still peering through the glass CANDIDE *becomes excited.)*

CANDIDE Martin! I can see one of my big red sheep! Look!

(And he hands the glass to MARTIN *who refuses it.)*

You see? God has *not* given up. He's punished that scoundrel of a ship captain who robbed me.

MARTIN Oh yes. God has punished that scoundrel. The Devil has drowned all the others.

CANDIDE If you're so pessimistic, why do you think the world was made?

*(*MARTIN *turns and looks at him with very clear eyes and a kind of gentle pity.)*

MARTIN To drive us mad.

CANDIDE Ha! I don't agree with you for a moment, Martin, but you are an interesting fellow. When we reach France I shall go overland to Venice, to wait there for Cunegonde. Will you come with me?

MARTIN You have money. I have none. I'll follow you anywhere.

CANDIDE Oh good. We shall go via Paris. We have the time.

(They stroll off across the deck still chatting.
At the foot of the mast they pass VOLTAIRE.)*

VOLTAIRE At last they reached France.

(We hear completely incomprehensible nautical suggestions and VOLTAIRE *starts to drop the sail.)*

And Paris. And immediately a spry little Abbot latched himself on like a leech.

(An insert cameo appears of the spry little ABBOT, *jiggling about in an unaccountable way and talking nineteen to the dozen though we don't hear a word.)*

Gossip, contact, guide, and provider of any pleasure . . . for a price.

(And the cameo wipes outwards and VOLTAIRE *disappears and we see why the* ABBOT *is jiggling about. He's in the back of a coach between* CANDIDE *and* MARTIN.)*

ABBOT Tomorrow my dear dear friends to the theatre there are many many wonderful wonderful plays to be seen in Paris yes and I can procure places for us. All three. In a row. Just like that. I have contacts my dear friends contacts many contacts. I am much loved.

CANDIDE How many plays have you in the French language, Monsieur?

ABBOT Ooooh about five or six thousand.

CANDIDE Oh that's a *lot.* And how many of those are really good?

ABBOT Oooooh fifteen or sixteen.

MARTIN That's a lot.

(The ABBOT *flashes him one of those sudden toothy totally meaningless smiles you get from people who want to con you and still seem nice.)*

ABBOT But tonight we'll merry merry be at the home of the beautiful Marquise de Baccarat playing cards and supping and making witty conversation with the most scintillating company in all Paris.

*(*CANDIDE *beams.*
MARTIN *nods resignedly.*
And we go slam into the most scintillating company in all Paris.
A room. Poorly lit. A table. And round it the most dreary-looking bunch of gnaw-vitals you ever did see, clutch-

ing their grubby cards, staring at one another readily, and playing (if one may use the word) like zombies.
MADAME LA MARQUISE *is seated beside the banker keeping a piercing eye on everybody with that smile again.*
Opposite her is a fifteen-year-old girl evidently expressing a naive interest in the game, but actually signalling to mama when they are cheating by winking in a variety of ways.
Dead silence.
The door opens and the ABBOT *ushers in* CANDIDE *and* MARTIN.)

Madame la Marquise I have the honour to present Monsieur Candide from Westphalia and Monsieur Martin his companion.

(Nothing.
The ABBOT *does his smile to* CANDIDE *then scuttles over to the* MARQUISE.)

CANDIDE   Even The Baroness of Thunder-ten-tronckh was more polite than this.
MARTIN   Wait.

(The ABBOT *is bending over whispering in the ear of the* MARQUISE.
She gets the message and half rises from her chair with a great beam of welcome.
MARTIN *smiles grimly.)*

Told you.
CANDIDE   Told me what?
MARTIN   Nothing.
MARQUISE   Monsieur Candide. A thousand welcomes.
MARTIN   *(aside)*   A thousand francs.
CANDIDE   Thanks.

(And he prances forward to her in the most elegant eighteenth-century Westphalian way he knows.
A flunkey closes the door. He turns round. It is VOLTAIRE.)

VOLTAIRE   They all thought he was an English Milord. So they took him for fifty thousand in the first two deals. And later.

After supper. Upstairs. He won the jackpot.

(A Bedroom.
A Bed.
The MARQUISE *is sort of insinuating herself at* CANDIDE.)

MARQUISE   You have lost much, cheri. You may still gain.
CANDIDE   Ah-ha! What shall we play at now?
MARQUISE   Are you still really madly in love with this Mademoiselle Cunegonde de Thunder-ten-tronckh you have told me about?
CANDIDE   Oh yes. Indubitably.

(And with a silvery tinkling laugh [whatever that is] she throws herself back on the bed in a décolleté sort of way.)

MARQUISE   You are so witty. You young men from Westphalia.
CANDIDE   Really?
MARQUISE   Why yes. A Frenchman would only have said, "It is true that I *did* love Mademoiselle Cunegonde; but now that I look upon you, Madame, I'm afraid I love her no longer."
CANDIDE   Really? Well. I only want to say what's right. I don't want to be witty.

(She wiggles about a bit more.)

MARQUISE   Your passion for her really began when you picked up her little handkerchief?

*(CANDIDE *has a little swoony memory.)*

CANDIDE   Oh. Yes Madame.

(And suddenly there is a long slim leg pointing straight out with an elegantly turned foot on the end of it.)

MARQUISE   Then now pick up my little garter.

(And miraculously lying on the floor is a little garter.)

CANDIDE   Anything to oblige, Madame.

(And he picks it up and brings it to the leg, standing there like a spare garter at a wedding.)

MARQUISE   And put it on for me.

(CANDIDE starts to put it on.)

On me.

CANDIDE   Oh.

(He makes a sort of movement towards her. Before he can proceed further with this disgusting spectacle which shouldn't be allowed to be seen, even by Lord Longford, a great big curtain is drawn across the ugly scene.
By the flunkey, i.e., VOLTAIRE.)

VOLTAIRE   Such scenes only take place in the diseased minds of authors who are determined to tell us the truth at all costs. Much better to leave it to *your* imagination.

(Now we are back in the coach.
MARTIN has obviously gone home.
We are left with the keen-to-know-everything ABBOT, and a very remorseful CANDIDE.)

ABBOT   What happened then my dear dear friend tell me tell me tell me.

CANDIDE   I betrayed my love.

(As far as the ABBOT is concerned this is a very kinky way of describing coitus. He manages to swallow his tendency to dribble and says with a chokey voice—)

ABBOT   I do not *quite* follow you, my dear dear friend.

CANDIDE   I should have gone to Venice; to Cunegonde.

ABBOT   She's waiting for you there?

CANDIDE   I do not know. I hope we shall meet again there. Though I am no longer worthy.

ABBOT   But she has written to say so?

CANDIDE   Written? How could she know where to find me? She has never ever written to me.

ABBOT   Ah. Oh. Mmmm.

(And he goes off into a deep think while CANDIDE has a little cry.
We look at CANDIDE's anguished face in BCU.[11] And we suddenly hear MARTIN speak:)

MARTIN   *(Voice over)*   Monsieur Candide. A letter for you.

(And a ruddy great letter is thrust under CANDIDE's face. He sits up and the camera tilts up sideways and pulls back to show him in bed, MARTIN standing beside him.
CANDIDE tears the letter open and reads.)

CANDIDE   Martin! It's from her! Cunegonde!

(His eyes are avidly scanning the paper and the first words make him go—)

Woooh! Blah blah blah left Cacambo and the old woman at Bordeaux blah blah blah I have fallen ill, in a hotel, quite close by to you come come come here is the address blah blah blah. My heart is ever yours. Cunegonde.

(He leaps out of bed.)

My clothes.

MARTIN   You're going there?

CANDIDE   Where else?

MARTIN   If you say so.

(And we are in Another Bedroom.
With a big fourposter bed.
CANDIDE approaches it tremblingly and stretches his hand out to the drawn curtains.
At his side is an OLD CRONE. Not the old woman.
In the background hovers MARTIN.)

OLD CRONE   Careful young sir, the light could kill her.

(And she goes to the side of the bed and draws out a pale hand and CANDIDE falls upon it and covers it not only with his

---

11 **BCU** big or extreme close-up.

mouth but with a lot of tears. And three or four huge diamond rings. And the pale hand he loves wiggles slightly in acknowledgement.

Then the door bursts open and in marches an OFFICER OF THE WATCH, *followed by the little* ABBOT *and a constable or three.*)

OFFICER OF THE WATCH Ha ha! Are these the two foreigners who've been behaving suspiciously?

ABBOT They are indeed officer indeed indeed they are they are. Yes.

OFFICER OF THE WATCH Thank you. Arrest them.

(*The constables whip out shackles and busy themselves clapping them on to* CANDIDE *and* MARTIN.)

CANDIDE What is the meaning of this? Eh?

(MARTIN *leans over and speaks quietly to him.*)

MARTIN I think it means that *he's* a rogue (*pointing at* OFFICER). *He's* a rogue (*pointing at* ABBOT), and *she's* an impostor (*pointing to bed*).

CANDIDE Nonsense! This is Cunegonde's right hand.

MARTIN My left foot.

(*He whips back the curtains and there is a squeal and up in the bed sits a startled and totally unknown young lady.*

The ABBOT *looks a little sheepish and draws back a little.*

CANDIDE *takes a stride towards him.*)

CANDIDE Ah-ha!

(*The* OFFICER *steps between them confronting* CANDIDE *nose to nose.*)

OFFICER OF THE WATCH Ho ho! You are still under arrest.

CANDIDE And why sir?

OFFICER OF THE WATCH Because you are foreigners, sir.

CANDIDE Is that all sir?

OFFICER OF THE WATCH It's enough, sir. There's been an attempt on the life of the King.

ENTIRE WATCH God save the King!

OFFICER OF THE WATCH And all foreigners are under suspicion. You will kindly accompany me to the dungeon. Hup two three.

(*The little* ABBOT *darts over to* CANDIDE *and nudges him. He nods at the* OFFICER *and rubs his fingertips together and winks.*

CANDIDE *looks baffled.*)

MARTIN (*quietly*) Bribe him.

CANDIDE Ah! Officer! One moment. I should like to express my appreciation for your zeal. Each of these three diamonds is worth about three thousand. Do take them.

OFFICER OF THE WATCH Why bless me sir, what a gentleman you are! I see I have been gravely mistaken in you. Release them.

(*The* WATCH *busies itself getting the shackles off again.*)

Allow me to give you safe conduct so that unpleasant incidents like this do not recur.

CANDIDE I go to Venice.

OFFICER OF THE WATCH Alas. I'm afraid that would be pushing it rather a bit. Let me take you to Dieppe. I have a brother there. If you have a diamond left for him he will look after you as I would myself.

(*Everybody bows and smiles and all the men march out leaving the* OLD CRONE *and the false Cunegonde and then the* ABBOT *scuttles back in and the young woman dives her right hand under the bedclothes but the* ABBOT *wrenches it out and twists it up behind her back and hauls off the rings and rushes out leaving the women screaming and wailing.*

[*It would tidy it up if, before they all left, while the* ABBOT *was bowing to* CANDIDE, *the* OFFICER *popped one of the*

313

diamonds into his hand . . . stretched out waiting behind his back.]

We are back on yet another [identical] ship.

CANDIDE *and* MARTIN *are looking forward.*)

CANDIDE Is that Portsmouth?

MARTIN Does it make any difference?

CANDIDE I must say I am surprised to be going to Venice from Dieppe via Portsmouth, aren't you, Martin?

MARTIN Nothing surprises me.

CANDIDE You know England. Are they as mad there as the French?

MARTIN Yes but in a different way. You know the two countries are at war just now over a few acres of Canadian snow? And that they're spending more on this glorious war than the whole of Canada is worth? It's not for me to say which country is richer in citizens who ought to be locked up. I can promise you that the English are quite remarkably dreary. And bad tempered.

CANDIDE But look, Martin. They don't *seem* bad tempered. Look, the whole quayside is thronged with people laughing and cheering.

(*And indeed we can now hear hordes of English people cheering.*

Now we see them. Or perhaps a drawing with a lot of little flags stuck in being waggled from behind.

They move to the gunnel and lean over next to a sailor.)

Excuse me, what's all this about? Is it carnival time?

(*The sailor turns and lo 'tis* VOLTAIRE.)

VOLTAIRE Sort of.

CANDIDE And what are they celebrating?

VOLTAIRE That.

(*He points.*

We see another ship. And kneeling on the deck is a very large man in the uniform of a Naval Officer. And his hands are being tied behind his back and then a blindfold will be tied over his eyes and four soldiers are priming their muskets in a very relaxed kind of way and we see all this over the following dialogue.)

CANDIDE (*voice over*) Dear God! Who's that?

VOLTAIRE A famous English Admiral.

CANDIDE Dear God! But why kill one of their own admirals?

VOLTAIRE Because *he* hasn't killed as many enemy as he should.

CANDIDE Dear God!

VOLTAIRE He yielded a battle to a French Admiral by not going close enough to him.

CANDIDE But he must have been as close to the French Admiral as the French Admiral was to him.

VOLTAIRE I couldn't argue with that. But in England it's reckoned to be a good idea to kill an Admiral from time to time to encourage the others.

(*Now the preparations are ready and the drums roll and the great crowd falls silent like when the penalty's being kicked.*

Drum stops.

Distant order of fire!

Crack crack crack crack.

It's a goal!

Immense cheer of delight as the admiral crashes over on to the deck.

Now we return to see CANDIDE *and* MARTIN *and* VOLTAIRE.

VOLTAIRE *turns away.*

CANDIDE *is obviously shattered.*)

CANDIDE Oh God! Oh Martin! *Does* the devil rule everywhere?

(MARTIN *shrugs.*)

I shall not set foot in this barbaric country. This . . . England. I'll get the captain to take us to Venice immediately —even if he cheats us like that other rogue in South America.

(*Now the whole screen is filled with a lovely painting of St. Mark's Square.*

CANDIDE *and* MARTIN *walk in and look and* CANDIDE *embraces* MARTIN *and jumps up and down with joy.*)

God be praised! Everything is as good as it possibly could be. Right! *We* find Cacambo. *He* takes us to Cunegonde. It's as simple as that.

(*He strides off.*
MARTIN *follows. With a little less exuberance.*
And on strolls VOLTAIRE.
It might be nice if the background changed according to his dialogue.)

VOLTAIRE   Well, they looked.
First they looked in all the hotels.
Then they looked in all the bars.
Then they looked in all the cafes.
Then they looked in all the churches.
Then they looked in all the brothels.
The seasons changed.

(*The seasons change. It starts to snow.*)

Every day they looked.
Every day they sent to the Rialto to enquire about arriving ships.
Every day they watched the barks arrive from the mainland.
Nothing.
Not a trace of Cacambo or Cunegonde.
Candide went into a decline.

(*We cut to* CANDIDE *declining in bed.*
MARTIN *sits resignedly beside him.*)

CANDIDE   She's dead! No doubt about it, Martin. She's dead. And I might just as well die too. Better to have stayed in El Dorado than return to this accursed Europe. You're right, Martin. Life is nothing but illusion and disaster.

(*And he dives beneath the bedclothes groaning and moaning and sighing.*
MARTIN *looks at him grimly.*
Or at least at the bottom heaving under the clothes.)

MARTIN   You really are a great big simpleton, aren't you. You really reckoned a halfbreed servant, with five or six million

in his pockets, would go to the end of the world to find your beloved and bring her back to you here in Venice? He'll go off with her himself, if he finds her. And if he doesn't, he'll go off with someone else. Forget Cacambo, Candide. And your mistress Cunegonde.

(*Renewed wails from* CANDIDE *and a very agitated heap of bedclothes.*)

Stop playing the tragic hero, and come downstairs and get some food inside you.
CANDIDE   (*muffled*)   No no no no no no No!

(*Slam cut to the dining room.*
CANDIDE *followed by* MARTIN *is just going in and catches up with a* SERVANT *carrying in food.*)

What's for supper?

(*The* SERVANT *inclines his head to* CANDIDE. *But instead of saying "boiled beef and two veg" he speaks quietly and says something quite unexpected.*)

SERVANT   Be ready to leave here with us. No messing about.

(*CANDIDE is rather startled. He looks closely into the man's face. It is . . . CACAMBO!!!!!!!!*)

CANDIDE   *Cacambo! It's you! At last!*

(*CANDIDE goes spare. His face lights up like a beacon. He embraces* CACAMBO *abruptly thereby causing two or three mince patties to roll off the tray he is carrying and go splat upon the floor.*)

Where's my darling Cunegonde? Take me to her. Now! Oh, I shall *die* with joy when I see her!

(*But* CACAMBO *bends down and starts to spoon up the patties.*
CANDIDE *bends down too, looking rapturously into his face.*
CACAMBO *speaks out of the side of his mouth with one eye on the men around the dining table and one on the patties.*)

CACAMBO She's not here she's in Constantinople.

CANDIDE Constantinople? Oh dear heaven! But were she in China I should fly to her. Come. We must go *now!*

CACAMBO No. After supper. I can't talk to you any more at the moment. I'm a slave. And my master's waiting for his supper.

(He straightens up with his salvage.
CANDIDE gets up too.)

Go and eat. But be ready to go.

(And he marches towards the table and the six men sitting round it.
Each one has a servant, so there are another five flunkeys fluttering about.
CANDIDE turns to MARTIN.)

CANDIDE You see?
MARTIN You haven't found her yet.
CANDIDE Martin you are incorrigible.
MARTIN I am also hungry.

(And they go in and sit with the six. In a profound silence. A figure comes into the foreground, watching. It turns.)

VOLTAIRE Candide tried to eat while Martin went relentlessly through the menu. And then a very strange thing happened. Or six strange things. Or the same strange thing six times.

(We jump into the table. The meal is over. Wine is being sipped. Nobody talks.
CACAMBO approaches his new master and as he pours wine into his glass, speaks. Quietly, but loud enough to be heard by the company.)

CACAMBO Sire. Your Majesty can leave when he wishes. The ship is ready.

(CACAMBO goes. General surprise.
A SECOND SERVANT goes to another of the six.)

SECOND SERVANT Sire, Your Majesty's coach is at Padua and the bark is ready.

(The master makes a sign and the SERVANT goes.
They all stare at each other with greater surprise.
A THIRD SERVANT comes to a third master.)

THIRD SERVANT You need not stay any longer, Your Majesty. I have prepared everything.

(And he clears out. Then a fourth to a fourth.)

FOURTH SERVANT Your Majesty, everything is in order for your departure.

(CANDIDE has now got over his surprise and turns to speak very quietly to MARTIN.)

CANDIDE They're taking part in a masquerade for the Carnival.

(But MARTIN is looking at them all keenly.)

MARTIN Are they?

(A FIFTH SERVANT comes to the fifth.)

FIFTH SERVANT The gondola is ordered, Your Majesty, and will be here directly.

(A SIXTH SERVANT comes up to the sixth and though he tries to speak very quietly he speaks with a certain amount of agitation and they can't help hearing them.)

SIXTH SERVANT Look, they won't give you any more credit Your Majesty nor to me neither. They're going to bung us in the clink tonight or I'm the monkey's uncle, so I'm off to fend for myself. Tata.

(And he scuttles off.
A long and deep silence ensues. They all stare at each other.
CANDIDE gets rather embarrassed and clears his throat.)

CANDIDE Gentlemen. What a strange joke! You have all decided to be Kings for the Carnival? Isn't that rather overdoing it?

(CACAMBO's *new master slowly turns his head on his neck like a Cocteau statue and fixes* CANDIDE *with a basilisk eye. Two basilisk eyes.*)

FIRST KING   I do not joke, monsieur. I am Achmet III, for many years Grand Sultan of the Ottoman Empire. I usurped my brother. His son usurped me. I am allowed to eke out my days in what was once my harem. I am also allowed, occasionally, to travel for my health's sake. And I have come to Venice for the Carnival.

(CANDIDE *is choked. Nods apologetically but can't speak.*

MARTIN *gives him a little sidelong smile. Then the man next to the* FIRST KING *speaks.*)

SECOND KING   (*he's about twenty*)   I am Ivan IV, Czar of All the Russias. I was removed from my throne before I was removed from my cradle. I was brought up in prison. Sometimes they let me travel; with two guards. And I have come to Venice for the Carnival.

(*Another silence. The atmosphere is electric, as they say. They all look at the* THIRD, *a rather beery looking gent running to fat.*)

THIRD KING   I am Charles Edward Stuart, rightful King of England, Scotland, Ireland, and Wales. Exiled like my father and my grandfather. When I claimed my throne my enemies defeated me and tore out the hearts of six hundred of my followers. I too have been in prison. And I have come to Venice for the Carnival.

(*All turn to the* FOURTH.)

FOURTH KING   I am Augustus III, Elector of Saxony and King of the Poles. Like *my* father before me I lost my inheritance in the reverses of war. And I have come to Venice for the Carnival.

(*It's plain sailing now. Nobody's going to drop the ball at this point. They all look expectantly at number* FIVE.)

FIFTH KING   I too am King of the Poles, Stanislas I. I lost my throne twice. Once to him (*and he indicates* AUGUSTUS III) and once to his father. But I have not fared so badly for at least I still rule somewhere, though it is only the Duchy of Lorraine. And I have come to Venice for the Carnival.

(*They all acknowledge his good fortune with a gracious nod of the heads and* CANDIDE *looks quite cheered up after the tales of woe. He turns eagerly to number* SIX.)

SIXTH KING   Gentlemen, I am not nearly so grand as the rest of you. But I was a King: they declared me King Theodore I of Corsica. Unfortunately the French wanted it back and I did not have the power to resist them. I fled. In London I was thrown in prison for debt. I who have sat on a throne, have also lain on straw. And it rather looks as though I'm going to get the same treatment here, though I have come, like Your Majesties, to Venice for the Carnival.

(*Murmurs of compassion all round.*

CANDIDE *turns to* MARTIN *and speaks quietly.*)

CANDIDE   Oh I wish Pangloss could have been here to see this. Oh Martin, if such things happen to monarchs, what may not happen to us?

MARTIN   There's a difference?

(CANDIDE *looks rather shocked by this but his attention is diverted down the table where the* FIRST FIVE KINGS *are gathered round poor* THEODORE.)

CANDIDE   Look they're all giving him money. How much should I give him? I don't want to seem patronising to a King.

MARTIN   I'm sure he wouldn't mind.

(*And* CANDIDE *rises, fumbling.*)

CANDIDE   Your Majesty, permit me to press upon you this tiny diamond; a bagatelle; scarcely worth a thought.

(THEODORE *whips out his Hatton Garden eyeglass and studies it.*)

SIXTH KING How much is a thought worth?

CANDIDE Oh about two thousand, not much more.

(*And* CANDIDE *bows low and* MARTIN *inclines his head and they both go away.*
And the KINGS *look at each other in astonishment.*)

FIRST KING Who is this man, not even a King, who can and does give a hundred times more than we?

FIFTH KING Makes you wonder if it's worth it.

(*But* CANDIDE *and* MARTIN *are now at the door speaking to* CACAMBO.)

CACAMBO Now. I've already arranged with the captain of the ship that's taking Achmet III back to Constantinople that he should take you two too. We're all packed so you hurry and get your things and we'll see you down at the quay.

CANDIDE Right.

CACAMBO Right.

(*And they all scamper off this way and that way.*
And then we're on a ship [yes . . . that ship] and it's night and CANDIDE *and* CACAMBO *are on the deck surrounded by luggage and* CACAMBO *comes on board and passes them and then* ACHMET III *and* CANDIDE *bow deeply and calls after the* KING.])

CANDIDE Your Majesty. I should dearly like to purchase Cacambo's freedom.

(*And* ACHMET *looks at him with a speculative eye. And smiles a little wintry smile.*)

FIRST KING I would not part with Cacambo for a king's ransom.

(*And he turns to walk on.*)

CANDIDE Two kings?

(*And* ACHMET *stops and turns and the smile is a little warmer and he inclines his head as though he'll think about it and walks on.*
CANDIDE *falls upon* CACAMBO's *neck and hugs him.*)

So that'll be all right now tell me about Cunegonde, dear Cacambo. What's she doing? Is she still beautiful? Does she still love me? Is she well? What did you do, buy a palace for her or something at Constantinople? Tell me.

CACAMBO My dear master. Cunegonde is washing dishes for an old prince who has hardly any dishes left to wash.

CANDIDE Oh!

CACAMBO But sadder than that . . .

CANDIDE Sadder than that?

CACAMBO Sadder than that is the fact that she's grown quite revoltingly ugly.

CANDIDE Ayeee!

(*And he sinks onto his luggage.*)

Ah Cunegonde!

MARTIN Shall we get off? There's still time?

(*But* CANDIDE *looks at him and rises with great dignity.*)

CANDIDE I am a man of honour, Martin. Beautiful or ugly, it is my duty to love her. Always.

(*And there are great shoutings and preparations for casting off and all that sort of stuff.*)

But how was she reduced to this? What happened to the five or six millions you went off with?

CACAMBO Well. Didn't I have to give two million to don Fernando d'Ibaraa y Figueora y Mascarenes y Lampourdos y Souza to get her away?

CANDIDE And the rest?

CACAMBO A pirate took it. Then he took Cunegonde.

CANDIDE Ah no.

CACAMBO Then he took all of us—to the Dardanelles. Cunegonde and the old woman ended up as servants and I as slave to Achmet III.

CANDIDE Well . . . I still have a few diamonds left. There shouldn't be much trouble getting her out of it. Pity she's so ugly though.

(*A map of the Eastern Mediterranean with a little drawing of their boat wiggling across it from the Adriatic down and round and up towards the Dardanelles.*

And Constantinople or Istanbul as it is sometimes called.

And VOLTAIRE *strolls in in front of it with a pointer in his hand.*)

VOLTAIRE On they sailed towards Constantinople. Here. (*And he points at it.*) And the drill was that they would then charter another boat and come along the Sea of Marmora. Here. Until they found Cunegonde and the Old Woman. Here and Here. When they reached Constantinople.

(*And the little ship sails in and disappears.*)

They had no difficulty in ransoming Cacambo from Achmet III. And they immediately set out again in a . . .

(*And the map disappears and he's standing on the poop of a little galley with several benches of decrepit rowers rowing behind him.*)

. . . galley. Rowed by convicts. Some of whom rowed better than others. And two of whom rowed very badly indeed.

(*And there are two men on one bench, one old and in a terrible state, the other younger and in a terrible state.*

Falling about on the bench and dropping the oar and banging into the CONVICTS *behind because they're coming when they're going and the ones in front because they're going when they're coming and all that sort of thing. And of course they're getting very special attention from the* OVERSEER *who rewards*

them with copious blows from a long thing.

And they wince and moan and don't look too happy at all.

This misfortune naturally brings them to the attention of the ever-compassionate CANDIDE, *who is standing on the rear deck with* MARTIN *and* CACAMBO.)

CANDIDE Look at those poor wretches, Martin. If only dear Pangloss were here he could explain it so that they wouldn't make us feel so miserable.

(*And he looks at them a little more closely with a puzzled air. And he walks along the central walk to look even more closely and* CACAMBO *and* MARTIN *follow him. And* CANDIDE *stops and speaks over his shoulder.*)

You know, Cacambo, if I hadn't had the bad luck to see Pangloss hanged, nor had the bad luck to kill the Young Baron, I might almost believe that was them sitting there, rowing so badly.

(*And* BOTH CONVICTS *let out great cries of amazement and drop the oar in earnest and the* OVERSEER *rushes up and lays into them.*)

Oh stop stop you must stop beating these poor souls!

(*And the* OLD CONVICT *rises like a spectre to his feet and reaches out a claw.*)

FIRST CONVICT What? It's Candide!

(*And the other one gets up.*)

OTHER CONVICT What? Candide?
CANDIDE What? Do I dream? Do I wake? Is it Monsieur le Baron whom I killed? Is it Maitre Pangloss whom I saw hanged?
BOTH CONVICTS It's us! It's us!

(*And* MARTIN *is peering over* CACAMBO's *shoulder.*)

MARTIN What? Is *that* the great philosopher?
CANDIDE Shipmaster. How much to ran-

som Monsieur de Thunder-ten-tronckh one of the leading barons in the Holy Roman Empire?

(*And the* YOUNG BARON *bows.*)

And Doctor Pangloss the most profound thinker in all Germany?

OVERSEER   Christian dog, if these two convicts christian dogs are really barons and thinkers that'll be fifty thousand.

CANDIDE   Done. Release them.

(*And with great shouts and exclamations* PANGLOSS *is unshackled and falls at* CANDIDE'*s feet crying.*)

PANGLOSS   Oh Candide Candide my dear dear pupil, a million thanks a thousand million thanks!

(*And the* YOUNG BARON *inclines his head through all of one-and-a-half degrees and says—*)

YOUNG BARON   I shall reply you as soon as I get the money.

(*And now we jump to a setup which looks like five-thirteenths of the last supper.*
That is to say a narrow table with CANDIDE *in the middle,* PANGLOSS *crushed up against him on his right, the* YOUNG BARON *crushed up against him on his left, and* CACAMBO *and* MARTIN *at each end.*
All eating and getting in one another's soup.
It could be in a tiny cabin. It could be on the poop, watched by the slavering galley slaves. Aucune importance.)

CANDIDE   Once again, Reverend Father, I really must apologise for running you through with my sword.

YOUNG BARON   Don't say another word; I was a little hasty myself. But doubtless you want to know by what strange chance you came to find me in the galleys.

CANDIDE   Absolutely.

YOUNG BARON   Well. I recovered. Then I was captured, and sent back to my order

in Rome. Well. I became chaplain to the French Ambassador in Constantinople. I met a very nice young page at the court —a . . . well-built young chap—you know. It was a warm evening and he expressed a desire to bathe. So . . . I took the opportunity to bathe too. Hygienic, you know. Well. *I* didn't know it's a crime punishable by death in Turkey for a Christian to be found naked with a young Turk. They beat the soles of my feet for a long time and threw me in this galley.

CANDIDE   Barbarous!

YOUNG BARON   Well *I've* never heard of a graver injustice. But what I want to know is: why's my sister in Turkey washing up dishes for a refugee Transylvanian Prince?

(CANDIDE *smiles hurriedly and changes the subject quickly by turning to* PANGLOSS.)

CANDIDE   But you, my dear tutor, what strange quirks of fortune have brought us together again?

PANGLOSS   Well.

It's true you saw me hanged. I should have burned of course but as you will remember it was pouring and they couldn't get the fire started. Now they may be absolutely red hot at burning people but when it comes to hanging the Holy Inquisition are amateurs. I don't think I could have been more badly hanged. The rope was wet and wouldn't slip, d'ye see.

Well.

They cut me down and sold me to a surgeon so that he could cut me up. He made a primary incision from me nave to me chaps and it must have brought me round because I sat up on the slab and yelled. He thought he was dissecting the Devil he did. But at last he saw reason and stitched me up and I recovered and got a job with a Venetian merchant who took me to Constantinople.

Well.

One day out of curiosity I wandered into a mosque. There was nobody there except a very old Muslim priest and a very pretty girl saying her Our Fathers.

Now her dress was cut agreeably low and she had a little nosegay nestling between her delicious tits.

It fell out.

Well.

Naturally I picked it up. And replaced it. Where it had come from. With a great deal of care. You can't rush a thing like that. The old Muslim priest didn't agree. The longer I took the more angry he got. I suppose because I was a Christian. Anyway he yelled for somebody to come and do something about it and they did. They beat the soles of my feet for a long time and threw me in this galley. On the very same bench as Monsieur le Baron here.

CANDIDE   That really is astonishing.

PANGLOSS   Yes. They whip us twenty times a day and we still haven't learned how to row.

CANDIDE   What a terrible tale. Don't you think so Baron?

YOUNG BARON   No worse than mine.

CANDIDE   Tell me, maitre. Now that you've been hanged, dissected, beaten black and blue, and made a galley slave: do you still maintain that all is for the best in the best of all possible worlds?

PANGLOSS   My beliefs have not changed by the slightest iota. Consider: when all's said and done I am a philosopher! Where would we be if philosophers went round changing their minds all the time? Ha? It wouldn't be proper.

CANDIDE   And is that the only reason your beliefs haven't changed?

PANGLOSS   Certainly not, my dear Candide. Consider: is it remotely possible that the great philosopher Leibnitz *and* I could be wrong? Eh?

(CANDIDE *shakes his head. But slowly and sadly and with none of the verve he would have shown at his last meeting with* PANGLOSS.)

CANDIDE   I see.

YOUNG BARON   Well what I don't see is how my sister comes to be out here skivvying for some broken down old aristocrat from Central Europe.

(CANDIDE *can avoid the tale no longer . . . or the fact that he bears some responsibility for the fact that the* YOUNG BARON's *precious sister has been raped from the Atlantic to the Aegean by a fornicating great pirate.*)

CANDIDE   Well.

VOLTAIRE   No point in needlessly distressing you.

(*We have slam cut away from the galley and* VOLTAIRE *is standing against a landscape, a skyline behind him with a house on the edge and two tiny silhouettes hanging out silhouette washing.*)

They sailed on. Arguing and discussing and philosophising endlessly until they came to the home of the broken down old aristocrat. That's it. And that's Cunegonde and the Old Woman hanging out the washing. And that's Candide running towards them.

(*And* VOLTAIRE *withdraws.*

And CANDIDE *is running, a tiny silhouette along the skyline, to his* CUNEGONDE, *who drops her washing and runs to him. Arms out and in slow motion like those insufferable interminable titles on the programmes of inexhaustible American lady comics.*

But what is this? As they grow closer the figure of CANDIDE *slows down. It stops. It takes three steps back.*

And now the other figure is almost upon him and . . .

Crash we are looking at a stunned mid-shot of CANDIDE *and* CUNEGONDE *hurtling past camera into his arms.*

And the other four come up beyond with the BARON *and* PANGLOSS *leading and they stop. And they take three steps back. And then she hurtles herself into their arms, while* CANDIDE *is left in the foreground stunned by a sudden attack of catalepsis.*

And then CUNEGONDE *disengages herself from the others and turns to fondle* CANDIDE *and we see why.*

And I quote directly from the book:
Her face is blackened, her eyes
Red rimmed and bloodshot,
Her bosom dried up,
Her cheeks shrivelled,
Her arms red and scaly.

So who is going to blame Candide?
And the OLD WOMAN *bursts upon them all and beside her* CUNEGONDE *is Miss World 1759.*

The men stare at them and put on ghastly smiles.

([In case you had not noticed, by the bye, CANDIDE, *our sky-blue incorruptible, has remained as fair and unblemished as the first moment we saw him.*

Time and sun and wind and starvation and rapine and buggery and other unpleasantnesses may leave their mark on others, but not on him.])

CUNEGONDE Ah Candide my love, my sweet, my white-skinned beauty, you have come to rescue us yet again. This time there can be no mistake. This time there can be no putting off. We shall be married at once!

(Moment de stupefaction.

CANDIDE *clears his throat. But before he can speak, not that he knows what he is going to say, somebody else does.)*

YOUNG BARON Never!

CANDIDE I beg your pardon?

YOUNG BARON I shall never countenance such vulgarity on her part or such insolence on yours. My sister has seventy-two quarterings on her coat of arms and she will marry none but a Baron of the Holy Roman Empire. At *least!*

*(*CUNEGONDE *throws herself at his feet and bathes his shoes with tears.)*

CUNEGONDE Oh my dear brother, please, please I love him I love him!

OLD WOMAN She loves him she loves him.

(But the YOUNG BARON *shakes his head inflexibly if you can do that.*

CANDIDE *has been staring at him.*

He does not really deep down want to marry CUNEGONDE. *But his dander is finally up.*

He walks like a hero to confront the YOUNG BARON, *stepping carefully over his intended.)*

CANDIDE You thundering great nincompoop! I have rescued you and ransomed you out of rowing in the galleys. I have rescued your sister and I will ransom her out of washing dishes. She's been raped from Europe to South America and ravished from South America to Turkey. She's ugly to boot. And now when I have the decency to make her my wife you *still* try to stop me with your stupid airs. If I don't keep a firm grip on myself I'll kill you all over again.

YOUNG BARON Go on. Kill me all over again. But while I breathe you will not marry my sister.

*(*CANDIDE *clenches his teeth and his fists and with a great effort turns away, stepping carefully over his intended and the* OLD WOMAN *who is now down comforting her sobs.*

The YOUNG BARON *cannot move since his sister's arms are round his ankles in a virtue-like grip.*

CANDIDE *goes to the other three.)*

CANDIDE What *are* we going to do with him?

MARTIN Do as he suggests. Chuck him in the sea.

PANGLOSS We could arrange a left-handed marriage.

CANDIDE Pardon?

PANGLOSS If she gives you her left hand in marriage she won't pass on rank or rights to the children. There are many precedents.

CANDIDE And what do you think, Cacambo?

Candide

CACAMBO   I think you'll get the best of all possible results . . .

PANGLOSS   Ah-ha!

CACAMBO   If we shove him back in the galleys, he's out of your way and no worse off than you found him.

CANDIDE   What a thoroughly good idea.

(And here is VOLTAIRE *again, against the landscape.*

Perhaps we see the distantiny figures march off again, but probably we do not.)

VOLTAIRE   So they did. With no fuss, a little money, and not even arousing the suspicions of his sister, they replaced the Baron in the galleys thereby having the double pleasure of putting one over on a Jesuit and punishing the arrogance of a German Baron.

(And VOLTAIRE *strolls along until he is standing in front of a little farmhouse building, bang up against it, and beside a wide-open window, which allows us to see something of the interior, but not very much.)*

So Candide married his Cunegonde and they lived . . . happy ever after?

Well.

Not quite.

They'd lost practically all their money, and with what was left they bought this place: a little market garden. To support them for the time being. Until their fortunes improved. That's what they told each other.

(During this, CANDIDE *has come moodily to the window and is staring moodily out.)*

But the days went by. And with them Cunegonde grew more shrewish and ugly.

(And CUNEGONDE *appears at the window screaming undecipherable imprecations and brandishing a cooking utensil at* CANDIDE, *who puts his hands over his ears and goes followed, by her.)*

Pangloss grew more and more filled with self-pity because he wasn't the shining light of some German university.

(And PANGLOSS *comes to the window and wilts pallidly and then gnashes his teeth and shakes his fist at heaven.)*

The Old Woman grew even uglier and nastier than Cunegonde.

(And the OLD WOMAN *appears and does to* PANGLOSS *what* CUNEGONDE *did to* CANDIDE *and* PANGLOSS *goes off and the* OLD WOMAN *spits out the window and follows him.)*

Cacambo——

(And before he can speak on, CACAMBO *rises up into the foreground humping a huge sack of vegetables and wipes the spit off his head.)*

CACAMBO   Oi! I do all the work around here and now they spit on me.

(And he struggles off.

VOLTAIRE *waves a hand after him.)*

VOLTAIRE   Cacambo.

(And MARTIN *has appeared at the window and gazes inexpressibly out while resting his elbows peaceably on the cill. I'm always amazed that's how you spell sill.)*

Only Martin seemed able to put up with life.

MARTIN   What's the point of complaining? Tell me where it's any better?

(And VOLTAIRE *looks up and shakes him by the hand.*

And CANDIDE *appears again.)*

CANDIDE   El Dorado.

(And CACAMBO *drifts back into the foreground.)*

CACAMBO   El Dorado.

(And PANGLOSS *appears.)*

PANGLOSS   El Dorado.

(And the OLD WOMAN, *calm.)*

OLD WOMAN   El Dorado.

(*And* CUNEGONDE, *quite dreamy.*)

CUNEGONDE   El Dorado.

(*And they are all jammed together sway-ing gently to the dreamy rhythm.*
And they murmur together.)

ALL   El Dorado.

MARTIN   Then lead us, Master, and we shall follow you there.

(*And* CANDIDE *smiles ruefully.*)

CANDIDE   Would that I could, Martin.

(*And they all stand there gazing out and not looking at each other and not speak-ing for ever such a long time.*
And then the OLD WOMAN *speaks:*)

OLD WOMAN   I'd like to know which is worse? To be raped a hundred times by pirates, have a buttock cut off, be whipped and hanged at an auto-da-fé, dissected, put in the galleys; in sum to go through all that we've gone through . . . or to be stuck here with nothing to do?

CANDIDE   That . . . is a very good ques-tion.

(*And* VOLTAIRE, *who has been standing there all this time strolls on and we with him.*)

VOLTAIRE   And they decided to answer it so that they would finally be at peace with the world. So they consulted the wis-est man in the land: a very famous and superior dervish.

(*And he comes to a door. It is just a freestanding door, but of a large house which does not need to be there.*
And our band of adventurers files in and CANDIDE *knocks on the door.*
VOLTAIRE *waits with interest.*
The door opens and there is the famous and superior DERVISH *in a funny hat and a long goonie.*
They bow to him and he bows back.)

CANDIDE   Reverend Father. We come to ask if you could explain to us why there is so much trouble and unhappiness in the world.

DERVISH   What does it matter, one way or the other? When His Highness the Sub-lime Porte sends a ship to Egypt does he worry whether or not the mice aboard the ship are comfortable?

PANGLOSS   Maitre, I should like, as one philosopher to another, you understand, to argue with you a little on Cause and Effect, The Best of All Possible Worlds, The Origins of Evil, The Nature of the Soul, and above all the Doctrine of Op-timism.

(*The* DERVISH *slams the door in their faces.*)

Oh.

(CANDIDE *looks thoughtful.*)

CANDIDE   Mmmm.

OLD WOMAN   Why the nasty old dervish!

CUNEGONDE   Knock on the door again, my love, and *make* him answer.

MARTIN   With respect, madame. I rather think that was his answer.

CANDIDE   Mmmmm. Let's go home. To our little market garden.

(*And they all troop out again.*
And VOLTAIRE *strolls on again.*)

VOLTAIRE   And on the way home they passed another market garden with a nice old market gardener who invited them in for refreshments.

(*And as he says this, he has arrived at another door, but simple, in a modest house which is not there either but does have an arbour of orange trees over it to shade the company.*
And our lot is sitting around a very old TURK, *who is nicely passing out the sherbet. And he is answering a question evidently put to him by* PANGLOSS.)

OLD TURKISH GARDENER (*common or market*) No sir. All I know of Constantinople is that I send the produce of my garden there to be sold.

CANDIDE   Obviously you have a great deal of land here.

OLD TURKISH GARDENER   No sir. I have precisely twenty acres.

(CACAMBO, *who knows all about it, says:*)

CACAMBO   Then you must have a lot of workers.

OLD TURKISH GARDENER   No sir. Only my family.

CANDIDE   Then how do you do it?

OLD TURKISH GARDENER   Work sir. Work. Work is the greatest thing in the world because it drives off the three greatest evils in the world: Boredom, Vice, and Poverty.

PANGLOSS   Ah! Now! If I may take you up on a——

CANDIDE   Thank you. You have been most kind. (*He stands up.*) And helpful. I should like to stay and philosophise with you——

(*The* OLD TURKISH GARDENER *leaps up startled and definitely worried.*)

OLD TURKISH GARDENER   What? Philosophise did you say?

CANDIDE   Forgive me. I did not wish to distress you. There is only one thing to be done: we must all go and work in *our* garden.

(*Outburst.*)

CUNEGONDE   I'll get sunburnt!

OLD WOMAN   I am the daughter of a Pope!

PANGLOSS   Some of us were created to work with the Mind!

CACAMBO   Good!

MARTIN   By all means. Let's work and cut out the theories. It's the only way to make life bearable.

(*And as they are all marching off, we go in on* VOLTAIRE.)

VOLTAIRE   And so they went home. And they worked in the garden.

(*And as he speaks, we see them all going about various tasks.*)

And they worked very well and very hard and the garden repaid them. And although things were not so good as in El Dorado, things were not really too bad. And sometimes Pangloss would turn to Candide and say . . .

(*And we are in the tool shed and* PANGLOSS *is sitting on a barrow munching a snack. Dressed as a peasant of course.*

And CANDIDE *is sorting something of a horticultural nature out. Dressed as a peasant of course.*)

PANGLOSS   . . . consider, my dear Candide. Everything is interconnected in this the best of all possible worlds. Look at it this way. *If* you had not been kicked out of that beautiful castle because you loved Mademoiselle Cunegonde; *if* you had not suffered at the hands of the Inquisition; *if* you had not marched across South America; *if* you had not run the Baron through; *if* you hadn't lost all those big red sheep from El Dorado . . .

CANDIDE   El Dorado.

PANGLOSS   . . . why, you would not be here amongst the candied fruit and the pistachio nuts.

(*And he munches away happily.*

And suddenly a period garden implement is shoved under his nose.)

CANDIDE   I'm sure you're absolutely right. But we must go and work in the garden.

(*And they go to work in the garden.*

And VOLTAIRE *comes in and takes up the last of the pistachio nuts.*)

VOLTAIRE
Happy ever after?
Not ever after.
Not happy.
They lived.

(*And we zoomp out and show the whole studio and every single person is marching down four abreast led by* CANDIDE *and* PANGLOSS *and* CUNEGONDE *and* MARTIN *and* CACAMBO *and everybody else.*

And they are all carrying gardening and agricultural implements and singing a great merry serious song to the words.)

We must go and work in the garden.

And the credits roll and the last is for VOLTAIRE *and, as the workers march past,* he comes towards us with his quizzical smile and then he turns into profile and the lights go down from the front and an oval cameo zoomps in around his head blocking everything out but his silhouette.

Fade out.

The Rivals

Richard Brinsley Sheridan   edited by C. J. L. Price

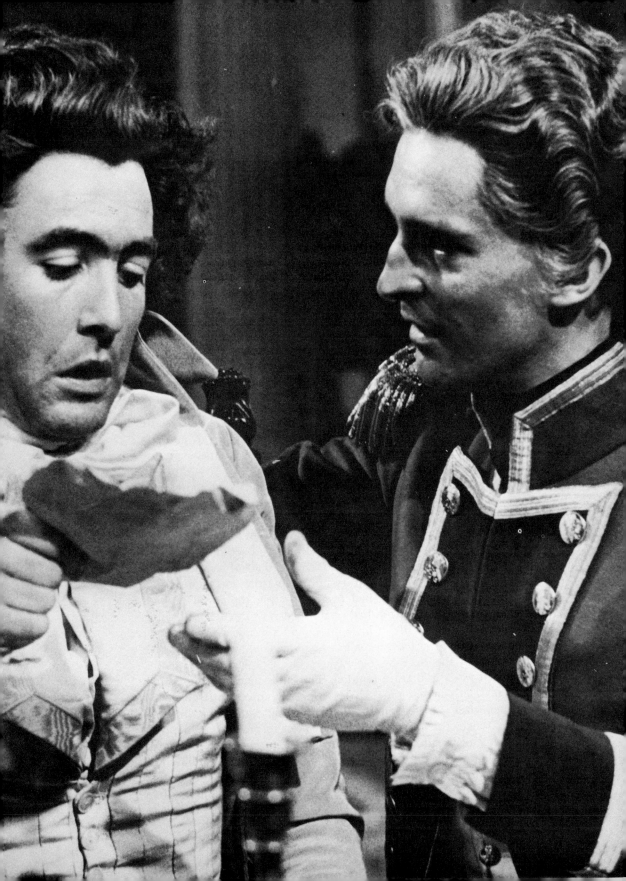

Introductory Comments

William W. Appleton   *Columbia University*

Oliver Goldsmith began his career as a dramatist too late. Richard Brinsley Sheridan abandoned playwrighting too early. He crammed almost all of his creative activity into the five-year period between 1774 and 1779, and then for more than thirty years he devoted his energies to politics. Born in Dublin, the son of an actor-manager, he was taken to England at an early age and educated at Harrow. The player's son never forgot the snubs and hardships he endured there, and these experiences doubtless contributed to his lifelong distaste for the theatre—except as a source of income. Unable to afford a university education, in 1770 he joined his family in Bath where the elder Sheridan was teaching elocution.

Good-looking and witty, young Sheridan was ideally suited to play the role of a buck-about-town, but he had one serious disadvantage— no money. In a city such as Bath, then the most fashionable resort in England, it was particularly awkward. As Sheridan's dramatic predecessor William Congreve once put it: "Don't you see how worthless great men and dull rich rogues avoid a witty man of small fortune? Why, he looks like a writ of inquiry into their titles and estates!"

For some fifty years Bath had been attracting the world of high society, ever since Beau Nash had established it as a center of fashion and codified its way of life. A little more than a hundred miles west of London, it was purportedly a spa in which one could recover from the dissipations of the city and the ravages of the spleen. In actuality, however, it was a miniature London. The amusements of the visitors were the same—masquerades, balls, concerts, and theatre-going. So were their vices—chiefly gambling and drinking. Under the direction of John Wood, the architect, Bath had been reconstructed in a Palladian style of breath-taking sweep and elegance, and at this Athens-on-the-Avon one could experience either the pleasures of London or the rigors of the cure or both.

At Bath, Sheridan met Elizabeth Linley, a beautiful and gifted young singer. Their courtship reads like a movie scenario—a flight to

France, a rival admirer, two duels, the lovers separated by disapproving parents, and finally, matrimony. Confronted with the responsibility of supporting a wife, Sheridan decided to turn dramatist. Not surprisingly, he found inspiration in his own recent adventures. Lydia Languish, the heroine of *The Rivals,* bears some resemblance to Elizabeth Linley in her addiction to the romantic world of the sentimental novel. Bob Acres, the reluctant duelist, has some affinities to Sheridan's rival, and Sheridan himself is not unlike Captain Absolute's *alter ego,* the dashing Ensign Beverley. But it was characteristic of Sheridan throughout his career to draw on his own experiences. In writing his comic opera, *The Duenna* (1775), he made use of some verses he had written to Elizabeth, and in his tragedy, *Pizarro* (1799), he interpolated passages from his own Parliamentary speeches.

He had no aversion, however, to borrowing inspiration from other sources as well. Goldsmith's *She Stoops to Conquer,* first performed in 1773, has a number of affinities to *The Rivals.* It has even been suggested that Sheridan's play might more aptly have been called *He Stoops to Conquer.* Both are comedies of double identity with contrasting pairs of lovers, and a number of characters in both have similar features. The resemblances between Mr. Hardcastle and Sir Anthony Absolute (plain-spoken fathers), Mrs. Hardcastle and Mrs. Malaprop (affected older women), and Tony Lumpkin and Bob Acres (rustic gentry), are not entirely attributable to the fact that these roles were played by the same actors. These figures are variants on more or less stock comic types. But comedy thrives on figures who are amusing largely because of their standard responses: grumpy fathers, conniving matrons, and so on.

Well aware that he was writing to please "a mixed assembly," Sheridan concocted his play to appeal to a variety of palates. In addition to the comic figures, he included Julia and Faulkland, two sentimental lovers. In most modern productions little attention is paid to these two roles, but Sheridan, like Goldsmith, was well aware that a considerable portion of his audience still favored sentimental comedy and he was not averse to catering to them.

The initial version of *The Rivals* had its first performance on January 17, 1775, at Covent Garden Theatre. It was not a success. The play was too long and several of the actors did not know their parts. Furthermore, the characterization of Sir Lucius O'Trigger gave offense. The text of this first version of the play has not survived, but contemporary criticism makes it plain that the original Sir Lucius was a quarrelsome fortune-hunter and an insult to the Irish. The play was promptly withdrawn. Sheridan was not one to waste his words or his time, so he set to work at once. He cut and tightened the script. The erring actors learned their lines properly, and the role of Sir Lucius, completely rewritten, was given to a younger, more sympathetic actor. The second version of the play, performed two weeks later, was an instantaneous success.

The Rivals has the engaging high spirits of youth. Whatever disdain the twenty-three-year-old playwright had for the theatre, he had an innate sense of the stage and the ability to manipulate stock theatrical types and situations in a masterful way. In this respect he somewhat resembles his great contemporary, the French dramatist Beaumarchais (1732–1799), whose comedy *The Barber of Seville* had its premiere in Paris a month after *The Rivals*. But Beaumarchais used these traditional materials with a difference. The resourceful Figaro is a pre-French-Revolutionary hero, Count Almaviva, the representative of a doomed aristocracy. Sheridan used his materials to no such purpose. He felt no urge to reform either comedy or society. He brought nothing new to the traditional materials of comedy, though his wit and energy made them seem new.

The Rivals is perhaps not as great a comedy as Sheridan's *The School for Scandal* (1777). Both dramatize the society of Bath but from different angles of vision. In *The School for Scandal*, Sheridan sees life there through the eyes of a sophisticated man of the world, well aware of its frauds and hypocrisies. *The Rivals* shows us Bath through the eyes of a younger man, less wise in the ways of the world. Like Goldsmith's *She Stoops to Conquer, The Rivals* relies primarily on character and situation. The laughter is robust, and if the wit is less dazzling than that in *The School for Scandal,* the play has, for many, a more lasting and broader appeal.

Richard Brinsley Sheridan (1751–1816), born in Dublin, son of an actor, was educated at Harrow. He married Elizabeth Linley after a romantic courtship. His first play, *The Rivals,* was produced in 1775 and his comic opera *The Duenna* in the same year. The following year he bought Garrick's share in Drury Lane Theatre and managed it until 1809. He was elected a Member of Parliament in 1780 and for thirty years played an active role in Whig politics. He wrote only two other plays of consequence, *The Critic* (1779) and *Pizarro* (1799). Witty, charming, and handsome, throughout his life he was plagued by debts and in later years afflicted by brain disease. He was buried in Westminster Abbey.

The Rivals   *Richard Brinsley Sheridon*

Dramatis Personae

Men

SIR ANTHONY ABSOLUTE

CAPTAIN ABSOLUTE

FAULKLAND

ACRES

SIR LUCIUS O'TRIGGER

FAG

DAVID

COACHMAN

Women

MRS. MALAPROP

LYDIA LANGUISH

JULIA

LUCY

MAID, BOY, SERVANTS, &C.

SCENE *Bath.* Time of Action, within One Day.[1]

Prologue

BY THE AUTHOR

Enter SERJEANT-AT-LAW *and* ATTORNEY *following and giving a paper*

SERJEANT   What's here—a vile cramp
hand! I cannot see
Without my spectacles.
ATTORNEY   He means his fee.[2]
. . . .[3]
—They'll either clear the sight—or serve
as blinkers.
SERJEANT   How's this?—a *poet's* brief?
ATTORNEY   Aye even so:——
SERJEANT   The deuce!—a *poet* and a *fee!*
—O ho!—
Some noble writer I suppose?—
ATTORNEY   Oh! No!
A student erring from the Temple's
bounds
Pleads to a trespass on the Muse's
grounds.
SERJEANT   Ill fare the truant who with
giddy haste
Forsakes an *orchard*—for a barren *waste!*
ATTORNEY   Nor pleads *He* worse—who
with a decent sprig
Of bays—adorns his legal waste of wig:
Full bottomed heroes thus, on signs, un-
furl
A leaf of laurel in a grove of curl!
SERJEANT   Yet tell your client that in *ad-
verse* days,
This wig—is warmer than a bush of bays:
And tell him too—how hard it is to deal
With that dread court—from whence
there's no appeal!
No tricking there—to blunt the edge of
law,

Or, damn'd in *equity,* escape by—*flaw:*—
But *judgment* given—their sentence must
remain!—
No *writ of error* lies to—*Drury-Lane!*
ATTORNEY   Do you then, sir, our student's
place supply:—
Profuse of robe, and prodigal of tie—
Do you—with all those blushing pow'rs
of face,
And wonted bashful hesitating grace
Rise in the court—and flourish on the
case.   *Exit* ATTORNEY.
SERJEANT   For practice then—suppose—
(this brief will show it)—
Me—Serjeant *Lewis*[4]—counsel for the
poet:
But first—lest partial spleen our words
pervert—
My client's *right of challenge* I'll exert.
—Above—below—in jackets silk—or flan-
nel—
Hissers of all kind I—strike off the panel.
—[*looking round*]
No!—no such thing!—no spite!—no
hoarded fury!
—I think I never faced—a milder *jury!*
Sad else our plight—where frowns are—
transportation!
A *hiss*—the *gallows!*—and a *groan*—*dam-
nation!*[5]
But from so mild a court—'tis past dis-
pute
He'll gain *some favour*—if not costs of
suit.
There's one thing only I shall mention
more—[*going*]
—This culprit—ne'er was at your bar be-
fore:

1 The first edition reads: "Time of Action, Five
Hours." 2 The opening lines are missing in the
Somerville College MS., so everything preceding
"fee" is taken from the prologue that was given on
the second night. 3 Missing. I invent the following
to suggest the sense:
    "For spectacles well suit such pretty thinkers."

4 W. T. Lewis (1748?–1811) acted the part of
Faulkland, and may have taken the Serjeant, too.
The Town and Country Magazine, Jan. 1775, suggests that Lee performed the Serjeant. A third
possibility is that the part was acted by Lee Lewes.
5 The play was nearly damned on the first night,
so Sheridan carefully revised the prologue for the
second performance.

Of all intruders should he prove the
worst,
Forgive the trespass—since it is the FIRST.

Act One

SCENE ONE   *A street in Bath.*

COACHMAN *crosses the stage.—Enter* FAG,
looking after him.

FAG   What!—Thomas!—Sure, 'tis he?—
What!—Thomas!—Thomas!

COACHMAN   Hey!—Odd's life![6]—Mr. Fag!
—give us your hand, my old fellow-
servant.

FAG   Excuse my glove, Thomas:—I'm
dev'lish glad to see you, my lad: why, my
prince of charioteers, you look as hearty!
—but who the deuce thought of seeing
you in Bath!

COACHMAN   Sure, Master, Madam Julia,
Harry, Mrs. Kate, and the postillion be
all come!

FAG   Indeed!

COACHMAN   Aye! Master thought another
fit of the gout was coming to make him a
visit:—so he'd a mind to gi't the slip, and
whip! we were all off at an hour's warning.

FAG   Aye, aye! hasty in everything, or it
would not be Sir Anthony Absolute!

COACHMAN   But tell us, Mr. Fag, how does
young master? Odd! Sir Anthony will
stare to see the Captain here!

FAG   I do not serve Captain Absolute
now.—

COACHMAN   Why sure!

FAG   At present I am employed by Ensign[7]
Beverley.

COACHMAN   I doubt, Mr. Fag, you ha'n't
changed for the better.

FAG   I have not changed, Thomas.

COACHMAN   No! why, didn't you say you
had left young master?

FAG   No.—Well, honest Thomas, I must
puzzle you no farther:—briefly then—
Capt. Absolute and Ensign Beverley are
one and the same person.

COACHMAN   The devil they are!

FAG   So it is indeed, Thomas; and the
Ensign-half of my master being on guard
at present—the *Captain* has nothing to
do with me.

COACHMAN   So, so!—What, this is some
freak, I warrant!—Do, tell us, Mr. Fag,
the meaning o't—you know I ha' trusted
you.

FAG   You'll be secret, Thomas?

COACHMAN   As a coach-horse.

FAG   Why then the cause of all this is—
LOVE,—Love, Thomas, who (as you may
get read to you) has been a masquerader
ever since the days of Jupiter.[8]

COACHMAN   Aye, aye;—I guessed there
was a lady in the case:—but pray, why
does your master pass only for *Ensign?*
—Now if he had shammed *General,* indeed—

FAG   Ah! Thomas, there lies the mystery
o' the matter.—Hark'ee, Thomas, my
master is in love with a lady of a very
singular[9] taste: a lady who likes him better as a *half-pay*[10] *Ensign* than if she knew
he was son and heir to Sir Anthony Absolute, a baronet of three thousand
a-year!

COACHMAN   That is an odd taste indeed!
—but has she got the stuff, Mr. Fag? is
she rich, hey?

FAG   Rich!—why, I believe she owns half
the stocks![11]—Z——ds![12] Thomas, she
could pay the national debt as easily as
I could my washerwoman!—She has a

---

6 Probably a corruption of "God's life," as in
"th 'slife." 7 The most junior infantry officer, who
carried the colours in battle.

8 The most powerful of the classical gods changed
himself into a bull and a swan in his pursuit of
women. One of Sheridan's earliest attempts at a
play was *Jupiter* (or *Ixion*), which he wrote in
collaboration with his friend N. B. Halhed. It
showed Jupiter coming down to earth to woo
Major Amphitryon's wife. 9 Odd. 10 Drawing half
his allowance because he was not on active service.
11 Money lent to the government. 12 A corruption
of "God's wounds."

lap-dog that eats out of gold,—she feeds her parrot with small pearls,—and all her thread-papers[13] are made of bank-notes!

COACHMAN   Bravo!—Faith!—Odd! I warrant she has a set of thousands[14] at least:—but does she draw kindly[15] with the Captain?

FAG   As fond as pigeons.[16]

COACHMAN   May one hear her name?

FAG   Miss Lydia Languish.—But there is an old tough aunt in the way;—though, by the by—she has never seen my master—for he got acquainted with Miss while on a visit in Gloucestershire.

COACHMAN   Well—I wish they were once harnessed together in matrimony.—But pray, Mr. Fag, what kind of a place is this Bath?—I ha' heard a deal of it—here's a mort[17] o'merry-making—hey?

FAG   Pretty well, Thomas, pretty well—'tis a good lounge;[18] in the morning we go to the pump-room (though neither my master nor I drink the waters); after breakfast we saunter on the parades or play a game at billiards; at night we dance: but d—n the place, I'm tired of it: their regular hours stupefy me—not a fiddle nor a card after eleven!—However, Mr. Faulkland's gentleman and I keep it up a little in private parties;—I'll introduce you there, Thomas—you'll like him much.

COACHMAN   Sure I know Mr. Du-Peigne[19] —you know his master is to marry Madam Julia.

FAG   I had forgot.—But Thomas you must polish a little—indeed you must.—Here now—this wig! what the devil do you do with a *wig*, Thomas?—none of the Lon-don whips of any degree of *ton*[20] wear *wigs* now.

COACHMAN   More's the pity! more's the pity, I say—Odd's life! when I heard how the lawyers and doctors had took to their own hair, I thought how 'twould go next:—Odd rabbit it![21] when the fashion had got foot on the Bar, I guessed 'twould mount to the Box![22]—But 'tis all out of character, believe me, Mr. Fag: and look'ee, I'll never gi' up mine—the lawyers and doctors may do as they will.

FAG   Well, Thomas, we'll not quarrel about that.

COACHMAN   Why, bless you, the gentlemen of they professions ben't all of a mind—for in our village now, tho'ff[23] *Jack Gauge*, the *exciseman*,[24] has ta'en to his carrots,[25] there's little Dick, the farrier,[26] swears he'll never forsake his *bob*,[27] tho' all the college[28] should appear with their own heads!

FAG   Indeed! well said, Dick! But hold—mark! mark! Thomas.

COACHMAN   Zooks![29] 'tis the Captain!—Is that the lady with him?

FAG   No! no! that is Madam Lucy—my master's mistress's maid.—They lodge at that house—but I must after him to tell him the news.

COACHMAN   Odd! he's giving her money!—well, Mr. Fag—

FAG   Good-bye, Thomas.—I have an appointment in Gyde's Porch[30] this evening at eight; meet me there, and we'll make a little party.

Exeunt severally.

13 Soft paper used for rolling up skeins of thread. 14 Thread-papers worth thousands. 15 The analogy is with a horse and mare pulling together in the shafts of a coach. 16 The turtle-doves of poetry and romance. 17 Dialect for "a great amount." 18 Place for relaxing. 19 He of the comb: a French valet. Cf. De-la-Grace, the dancing-master (p. 361), and La Vérole in Vanbrugh's *The Relapse* (1696).

20 Men of fashion gave up wigs, and began powdering their hair. 21 Probably a genteel way of saying "God rot it." 22 Fashion would force coachmen to follow the example of legal gentlemen. 23 Though. 24 Customs officers measured the contents of casks. "Gage, an exciseman," is a character in a later play that Sheridan had a hand in: *The Camp*, acted in 1778. 25 His own red hair. 26 Animal doctor. 27 Bob-wig: it kept close to the head and had short curls at the nape. 28 Professional institution to which doctors belong. 29 "Gadzooks!", an exclamation, though once an oath. 30 Gyde's Assembly rooms were on the Lower Walks.

SCENE TWO *A Dressing-room in* MRS. MALAPROP's *lodgings.*

LYDIA *sitting on a sofa, with a book in her hand.*—LUCY, *has just returned from a message.*

LUCY Indeed, ma'am, I traversed half the town in search of it:—I don't believe there's a circulating library[31] in Bath I ha'n't been at.

LYDIA And could you not get *The Reward of Constancy?*

LUCY No, indeed, ma'am.

LYDIA Nor *The Fatal Connexion?*

LUCY No, indeed, ma'am.

LYDIA Nor *The Mistakes of the Heart?*

LUCY Ma'am, as ill-luck would have it, Mr. Bull[32] said Miss Sukey Saunter had just fetched it away.

LYDIA Heigh-ho!—Did you inquire for *The Delicate Distress?*—

LUCY Or *The Memoirs of Lady Woodford?* Yes indeed, ma'am.—I asked everywhere for it; and I might have brought it from Mr. Frederick's,[33] but Lady Slattern Lounger, who had just sent it home, had so soiled and dog's-eared[34] it, it wa'n't fit for a Christian to read.

LYDIA Heigh-ho!—Yes, I always know when Lady Slattern has been before me. —She has a most observing thumb; and I believe cherishes her nails for the convenience of making marginal notes.— Well, child,[35] what *have* you brought me?

LUCY Oh! here, ma'am. [*Taking books from under her cloak, and from her pockets.*] This is *The Gordian Knot,*—and this *Peregrine Pickle.* Here are *The Tears of Sensibility,* and *Humphry Clinker.* This is *The Memoirs of a Lady of Quality, written by herself,*—and here the second volume of *The Sentimental Journey.*

LYDIA Heigh-ho!—What are those books by the glass?

LUCY The great one is only *The Whole Duty of Man*—where I press a few blonds,[36] ma'am.

LYDIA Very well—give me the *sal volatile.*[37]

LUCY Is it in a blue cover, ma'am?

LYDIA My smelling bottle, you simpleton!

LUCY Oh, the drops!—Here, ma'am.

LYDIA Hold!—here's some one coming— quick! see who it is.—

Exit LUCY.

Surely I heard my cousin Julia's voice!

Re-enter LUCY.

LUCY Lud! ma'am, here is Miss Melville.

LYDIA Is is possible!——

Enter JULIA.

LYDIA My dearest Julia, how delighted am I!—[*Embrace.*] How unexpected was this happiness!

JULIA True, Lydia—and our pleasure is the greater;—but what has been the matter?—you were denied to me at first!

LYDIA Ah! Julia, I have a thousand things to tell you!—but first inform me, what has conjured[38] you to Bath?—Is Sir Anthony here?

JULIA He is—we are arrived within this hour—and I suppose he will be here to wait on Mrs. Malaprop as soon as he is dressed.[39]

LYDIA Then before we are interrupted, let me impart to you some of my distress!—I know your gentle nature will sympathize with me, tho' your prudence may condemn me!—My letters have informed you of my whole connection with Beverley; —but I have lost him, Julia!—my aunt

31 A bookseller's collection lent out on payment of a fee. 32 Lewis Bull, a Bath bookseller. 33 William Frederick, another Bath bookseller. In the *Bath Journal,* 24 Sept. 1770, he said he was giving up his circulating library. 34 The top corner of the page turned down to show where the reader had stopped. 35 She appears to be only a little younger than her mistress, but Lydia shows her a kindly condescension.

36 Silk lace. 37 A solution of ammonium carbonate sometimes drunk as sal volatile or, as crystals, sniffed as smelling salts. Both were restoratives to ward off faintness or headaches. 38 Brought by magical compulsion. 39 Put on formal (as distinct from travelling) clothes.

has discovered our intercourse by a note she intercepted, and has confined me ever since!—Yet, would you believe it? she has fallen absolutely in love with a tall Irish baronet she met one night since we have been here, at Lady Macshuffle's rout.[40]

JULIA   You jest, Lydia!

LYDIA   No, upon my word.—She really carries on a kind of correspondence with him, under a feigned name though, till she chooses to be known to him;—but it is a *Delia* or a *Celia*,[41] I assure you.

JULIA   Then, surely, she is now more indulgent to her niece.

LYDIA   Quite the contrary. Since she has discovered her own frailty she is become more suspicious of mine. Then I must inform you of another plague!—That odious *Acres* is to be in Bath to-day; so that I protest I shall be teased out of all spirits!

JULIA   Come, come, Lydia, hope the best. —Sir Anthony shall use his interest with Mrs. Malaprop.

LYDIA   But you have not heard the worst. Unfortunately I had quarrelled with my poor Beverley, just before my aunt made the discovery, and I have not seen him since, to make it up.

JULIA   What was his offence?

LYDIA   Nothing at all!—But, I don't know how it was, as often as we had been together, we had never had a quarrel!— And, somehow, I was afraid he would never give me an opportunity.—So, last Thursday, I wrote a letter to myself, to inform myself that Beverley was at that time paying his addresses to another woman.—I signed it *your Friend unknown,* showed it to Beverley, charged him with his falsehood, put myself in a violent passion, and vowed I'd never see him more.

JULIA   And you let him depart so, and have not seen him since?

LYDIA   'Twas the next day my aunt found the matter out. I intended only to have teased him three days and a half, and now I've lost him for ever!

JULIA   If he is as deserving and sincere as you have represented him to me, he will never give you up so. Yet consider, Lydia, you tell me he is but an ensign, and you have thirty thousand pounds!

LYDIA   But you know I lose most of my fortune if I marry without my aunt's consent, till of age; and that is what I have determined to do, ever since I knew the penalty.—Nor could I love the man, who would wish to wait a day for the alternative.

JULIA   Nay, this is caprice!

LYDIA   What, does Julia tax me with caprice?—I thought her lover Faulkland had enured her to it.

JULIA   I do not love even *his* faults.

LYDIA   But a-propos[42]—you have sent to him, I suppose?

JULIA   Not yet, upon my word—nor has he the least idea of my being in Bath. —Sir Anthony's resolution was so sudden, I could not inform him of it.

LYDIA   Well, Julia, you are your own mistress (though under the protection of Sir Anthony), yet have you for this long year, been a slave to the caprice, the whim, the jealousy of this ungrateful Faulkland, who will ever delay assuming the right of a husband, while you suffer him to be equally imperious as a lover.

JULIA   Nay, you are wrong entirely.—We were contracted before my father's death. —That, and some consequent embarrassments, have delayed what I know to be my Faulkland's most ardent wish.—He is too generous to trifle on such a point.— And for his character, you wrong him there too.—No, Lydia, he is too proud, too noble to be jealous; if he is captious, 'tis without dissembling; if fretful, without rudeness.—Unused to the fopperies[43] of love, he is negligent of the little duties expected from a lover—but being un-

40 Party. 41 Names much used in love poetry of the previous hundred years, and so fashionable in courtship.

42 On the subject we are discussing. 43 Petty refinements.

339

hackneyed[44] in the passion, his affection is ardent and sincere; and as it engrosses his whole soul, he expects every thought and emotion of his mistress to move in unison with his.—Yet, though his pride calls for this full return—his humility makes him undervalue those qualities in him, which would entitle him to it; and not feeling why he should be loved to the degree he wishes, he still suspects that he is not loved enough.—This temper, I must own, has cost me many unhappy hours; but I have learned to think myself his debtor, for those imperfections which arise from the ardour of his attachment.

LYDIA Well, I cannot blame you for defending him.—But tell me candidly, Julia, had he never saved your life, do you think you should have been attached to him as you are?—Believe me, the rude blast that overset your boat was a prosperous gale of love to him.

JULIA Gratitude may have strengthened my attachment to Mr. Faulkland, but I loved him before he had preserved me; yet surely that alone were an obligation sufficient—

LYDIA Obligation?—Why, a water-spaniel would have done as much.—Well, I should never think of giving my heart to a man because he could swim!

JULIA Come, Lydia, you are too inconsiderate.

LYDIA Nay, I do but jest.—What's here?

Enter LUCY *in a hurry.*

LUCY O ma'am, here is Sir Anthony Absolute just come home with your aunt.

LYDIA They'll not come here.—Lucy, do you watch.

Exit LUCY.

JULIA Yet I must go.—Sir Anthony does not know I am here, and if we meet, he'll detain me, to show me the town.—I'll take another opportunity of paying my respects to Mrs. Malaprop, when she shall treat me, as long as she chooses, with her

select words so ingeniously *misapplied,*[45] without being *mispronounced.*

Re-enter LUCY.

LUCY O Lud! ma'am, they are both coming up stairs.

LYDIA Well, I'll not detain you, coz.[46]—Adieu, my dear Julia. I'm sure you are in haste to send to Faulkland.—There—through my room you'll find another stair-case.

JULIA Adieu——[*Embrace.*] *Exit* JULIA.

LYDIA Here, my dear Lucy, hide these books.—Quick, quick!—Fling *Peregrine Pickle* under the toilet—throw *Roderick Random* into the closet—put *The Innocent Adultery* into *The Whole Duty of Man*—thrust *Lord Aimworth* under the sofa—cram *Ovid* behind the bolster—there—put *The Man of Feeling* into your pocket—so, so,—now lay *Mrs. Chapone* in sight, and leave *Fordyce's Sermons* open on the table.

LUCY O burn it, ma'am! the hair-dresser has torn away[47] as far as *Proper Pride.*

LYDIA Never mind—open at *Sobriety.*—Fling me *Lord Chesterfield's Letters.*—Now for 'em.

Enter MRS. MALAPROP, *and* SIR ANTHONY ABSOLUTE.

MRS. MALAPROP There, Sir Anthony, there sits the deliberate simpleton, who wants to disgrace her family, and lavish herself on a fellow not worth a shilling!

LYDIA Madam, I thought you once——

MRS. MALAPROP You thought, miss!—I don't know any business you have to think at all.—Thought does not become a young woman. But the point we would request of you is, that you will promise to forget this fellow—to illiterate[48] him, I say, quite from your memory.

LYDIA Ah! madam! our memories are independent of our wills.—It is not so easy to forget.

MRS. MALAPROP But I say it is, miss; there

44 Not over-accustomed to.

45 The words are chosen carefully but used wrongly. 46 Cousin. 47 In making curling-papers. 48 Obliterate.

is nothing on earth so easy as to *forget,* if a person chooses to set about it.—I'm sure I have as much forgot your poor dear uncle as if he had never existed—and I thought it my duty so to do; and let me tell you, Lydia, these violent memories don't become a young woman.

SIR ANTHONY Why sure she won't pretend to remember what she's ordered not!—aye, this comes of her reading!

LYDIA What crime, madam, have I committed to be treated thus?

MRS. MALAPROP Now don't attempt to extirpate[49] yourself from the matter; you know I have proof controvertible[50] of it.—But tell me, will you promise to do as you're bid?—Will you take a husband of your friend's choosing?

LYDIA Madam, I must tell you plainly, that had I no preference for any one else, the choice you have made would be my aversion.

MRS. MALAPROP What business have you, miss, with *preference* and *aversion?* They don't become a young woman; and you ought to know, that as both always wear off, 'tis safest in matrimony to begin with a little *aversion.* I am sure I hated your poor dear uncle before marriage as if he'd been a black-a-moor[51]—and yet, miss, you are sensible what a wife I made!—and when it pleased heav'n to release me from him, 'tis unknown what tears I shed!—But suppose we were going to give you another choice, will you promise us to give up this Beverley?

LYDIA Could I belie my thoughts so far as to give that promise, my actions would certainly as far belie my words.

MRS. MALAPROP Take yourself to your room.—You are fit company for nothing but your own ill-humours.

LYDIA Willingly, ma'am—I cannot change for the worse.

Exit LYDIA.

MRS. MALAPROP There's a little intricate[52] hussy for you!

SIR ANTHONY It is not to be wondered at, ma'am—all this is the natural consequence of teaching girls to read.—Had I a thousand daughters, by heaven! I'd as soon have them taught the black art[53] as their alphabet!

MRS. MALAPROP Nay, nay, Sir Anthony, you are an absolute misanthropy.[54]

SIR ANTHONY In my way hither, Mrs. Malaprop, I observed your niece's maid coming forth from a circulating library!—She had a book in each hand—they were half-bound volumes, with marble covers![55]—From that moment I guessed how full of duty I should see her mistress!

MRS. MALAPROP Those are vile places, indeed!

SIR ANTHONY Madam! a circulating library in a town is, as an ever-green tree,[56] of diabolical knowledge!—It blossoms through the year!—And depend on it, Mrs. Malaprop, that they who are so fond of handling the leaves, will long for the fruit at last.

MRS. MALAPROP Fie, fie, Sir Anthony, you surely speak laconically![57]

SIR ANTHONY Why, Mrs. Malaprop, in moderation, now, what would you have a woman know?

MRS. MALAPROP Observe me,[58] Sir Anthony.—I would by no means wish a daughter of mine to be a progeny[59] of learning; I don't think so much learning becomes a young woman; for instance—I would never let her meddle with Greek, or Hebrew, or Algebra, or Simony, or Fluxions, or Paradoxes,[60] or such inflam-

---

49 Extricate. 50 Incontrovertible. 51 Negro. 52 Ingrate.

53 Magic or witchcraft. 54 Misanthropist. 55 Spine and corners of the cover were bound in leather, and the remainder in paper boards coloured to look like veins of marble. 56 Cf. Genesis ii. 17: "a tree of the knowledge of good and evil." 57 Ironically. 58 Mark my words. 59 Prodigy. 60 Simony is the buying and selling of church livings. Since she goes on to mention "mathematical and astronomical instruments," some vaguely scientific suggestion is probably intended. She may have meant "cyclometry, fluxions, and parallax," terms referring to the measuring of cycles, the calculus, and the difference between the true and the apparent place of a planet.

matory branches of learning—neither would it be necessary for her to handle any of your mathematical, astronomical, diabolical instruments;—but, Sir Anthony, I would send her, at nine years old, to a boarding-school, in order to learn a little ingenuity and artifice.— Then, sir, she should have a supercilious[61] knowledge in accounts;—and as she grew up, I would have her instructed in geometry,[62] that she might know something of the contagious[63] countries;—but above all, Sir Anthony, she should be mistress of orthodoxy,[64] that she might not mis-spell, and mis-pronounce words so shamefully as girls usually do; and likewise that she might reprehend[65] the true meaning of what she is saying.—This, Sir Anthony, is what I would have a woman know;—and I don't think there is a superstitious[66] article in it.

SIR ANTHONY Well, well, Mrs. Malaprop, I will dispute the point no further with you: though I must confess, that you are a truly moderate and polite arguer, for almost every third word you say is on my side of the question.—But, Mrs. Malaprop, to the more important point in debate,—you say, you have no objection to my proposal.

MRS. MALAPROP None, I assure you.—I am under no positive engagement with Mr. Acres, and as Lydia is so obstinate against him, perhaps your son may have better success.

SIR ANTHONY Well, madam, I will write for the boy directly.—He knows not a syllable of this yet, though I have for some time had the proposal in my head. He is at present with his regiment.

MRS. MALAPROP We have never seen your son, Sir Anthony; but I hope no objection on his side.

SIR ANTHONY Objection!—let him object if he dare!—No, no, Mrs. Malaprop, Jack knows that the least demur puts me in a

frenzy directly.—My process was always very simple—in their younger days, 'twas "Jack do this";—if he demurred—I knocked him down—and if he grumbled at that—I always sent him out of the room.

MRS. MALAPROP Aye, and the properest way, o' my conscience!—nothing is so conciliating[67] to young people as severity.— Well, Sir Anthony, I shall give Mr. Acres his discharge, and prepare Lydia to receive your son's invocations;[68]—and I hope you will represent *her* to the Captain as an object not altogether illegible.[69]

SIR ANTHONY Madam, I will handle the subject prudently.—Well, I must leave you—and let me beg you, Mrs. Malaprop, to enforce this matter roundly to the girl; —take my advice—keep a tight hand— if she rejects this proposal—clap her under lock and key:—and if you were just to let the servants forget to bring her dinner for three or four days, you can't conceive how she'd come about!

Exit SIR ANTHONY.

MRS. MALAPROP Well, at any rate I shall be glad to get her from under my intuition.[70]—She has somehow discovered my partiality for Sir Lucius O'Trigger—sure, Lucy can't have betrayed me!—No, the girl is such a simpleton, I should have made her confess it.—Lucy!—Lucy!— [*Calls.*] Had she been one of your artificial ones,[71] I should never have trusted her.

Enter LUCY.

LUCY Did you call, ma'am?

MRS. MALAPROP Yes, girl.—Did you see Sir Lucius while you was[72] out?

LUCY No, indeed, ma'am, not a glimpse of him.

MRS. MALAPROP You are sure, Lucy, that you never mentioned——

61 Superficial. 62 Geography. 63 Contiguous. 64 Orthography. 65 Apprehend. 66 Superfluous.

67 Constricting. 68 A possible usage, but she may mean "protestations." 69 Ineligible. 70 Tuition. 71 Artful. 72 A common usage of the day.

LUCY O Gemini![73] I'd sooner cut my tongue out.

MRS. MALAPROP Well, don't let your simplicity be imposed on.

LUCY No, ma'am.

MRS. MALAPROP So, come to me presently, and I'll give you another letter to Sir Lucius;—but mind Lucy—if ever you betray what you are intrusted with—(unless it be other people's secrets to me) you forfeit my malevolence[74] for ever:—and your being a simpleton shall be no excuse for your locality.[75]

Exit MRS. MALAPROP.

LUCY Ha! ha! ha!—So, my dear *simplicity,* let me give you a little respite—[*altering her manner*]—let girls in my station be as fond as they please of appearing expert, and knowing in their trusts;—commend me to a mask of *silliness,* and a pair of sharp eyes for my own interest under it!—Let me see to what account have I turned my *simplicity* lately—[*looks at a paper*]. For *abetting Miss Lydia Languish in a design of running away with an Ensign!—in money—sundry times—twelve pound twelve—gowns, five—hats, ruffles, caps, &c., &c.,—numberless!—From the said Ensign, within this last month, six guineas and a half.—*About a quarter's pay!—Item, *from Mrs. Malaprop, for betraying the young people to her*—when I found matters were likely to be discovered—*two guineas, and a black paduasoy.*[76]—Item, *from Mr. Acres, for carrying divers letters*—which I never delivered—*two guineas, and a pair of buckles.*—Item, *from Sir Lucius O'Trigger—three crowns—two gold pocket-pieces*[77]*—and a silver snuff-box!*—Well done, *simplicity!*—Yet I was forced to make my Hibernian[78] believe, that he was corresponding, not with the *aunt,* but

with the *niece;* for, though not over rich, I found he had too much pride and delicacy to sacrifice the feelings of a gentleman to the necessities of his fortune.

Exit.

Act Two

SCENE ONE CAPTAIN ABSOLUTE's *lodgings.*

CAPTAIN ABSOLUTE *and* FAG.

FAG Sir, while I was there Sir Anthony came in: I told him, you had sent me to inquire after his health, and to know if he was at leisure to see you.

ABSOLUTE And what did he say on hearing I was at Bath?

FAG Sir, in my life I never saw an elderly gentleman more astonished! He started back two or three paces, rapped out a dozen interjectoral[79] oaths, and asked, what the devil had brought you here!

ABSOLUTE Well, sir, and what did you say?

FAG O, I lied, sir—I forget the precise lie, but you may depend on't, he got no truth from me. Yet, with submission, for fear of blunders in future, I should be glad to fix what *has* brought us to Bath: in order that we may lie a little consistently. —Sir Anthony's servants were curious, sir, very curious indeed.

ABSOLUTE You have said nothing to them——?

FAG O, not a word, sir—not a word.— Mr. Thomas, indeed, the coachman (whom I take to be the discreetest of whips) ——

ABSOLUTE 'Sdeath![80]—you rascal! you have not trusted him!

FAG O, *no,* sir!—no—no—not a syllable, upon my veracity!—He was, indeed, a little inquisitive; but I was sly, sir—devilish sly!—My master (said I), honest Thomas (you know, sir, one says *honest* to one's

---

73 Possibly a corruption of "Jesu domine." Gemini, the twins, is a sign of the Zodiac, and a constellation. 74 Benevolence. 75 Loquacity. 76 A corded silk gown. 77 Coins carried as lucky charms. 78 Irishman.

79 Interjectional. 80 An oath, from "God's death."

inferiors) is come to Bath to *recruit*—Yes, sir—I said, to *recruit*—and whether for men, money, or constitution,[81] you know, sir, is nothing to him, nor any one else.

ABSOLUTE Well—*recruit*—will do—let it be so——

FAG O, sir, recruit will do surprisingly—indeed, to give the thing an air; I told Thomas, that your Honour had already enlisted five disbanded chairmen,[82] seven minority waiters,[83] and thirteen billiard markers.[84]

ABSOLUTE You blockhead, never say more than is necessary.

FAG I beg pardon, sir—I beg pardon—But with submission, a lie is nothing unless one supports it.—Sir, whenever I draw on my invention for a good current lie, I always forge indorsements, as well as the bill.

ABSOLUTE Well, take care you don't hurt your credit, by offering too much security.[85]—Is Mr. Faulkland returned?

FAG He is above, sir, changing his dress.

ABSOLUTE Can you tell whether he has been informed of Sir Anthony's and Miss Melville's arrival?

FAG I fancy not, sir; he has seen no one since he came in, but his gentleman, who was with him at Bristol.—I think, sir, I hear Mr. Faulkland coming down—

ABSOLUTE Go, tell him, I am here.

FAG Yes, sir—[*going*]. I beg pardon, sir, but should Sir Anthony call, you will do me the favour to remember, that we are *recruiting,* if you please.

ABSOLUTE Well, well.

FAG And in tenderness to my character, if your Honour could bring in the chairmen and waiters, I shall esteem it as an obligation;—for though I never scruple a lie to serve my master, yet it hurts one's conscience to be found out.

Exit.

ABSOLUTE Now for my whimsical friend—if he does not know that his mistress is here, I'll tease him a little before I tell him——

Enter FAULKLAND.

Faulkland, you're welcome to Bath again; you are punctual in your return.

FAULKLAND Yes; I had nothing to detain me, when I had finished the business I went on. Well, what news since I left you? How stand matters between you and Lydia?

ABSOLUTE Faith, much as they were; I have not seen her since our quarrel, however I expect to be recalled every hour.

FAULKLAND Why don't you persuade her to go off with you at once?

ABSOLUTE What, and lose two thirds of her fortune? You forget that my friend.—No, no, I could have brought her to that long ago.

FAULKLAND Nay then, you trifle too long—if you are sure of *her,* propose to the aunt *in your own character,* and write to Sir Anthony for his consent.

ABSOLUTE Softly, softly, for though I am convinced my little Lydia would elope with me as Ensign Beverley, yet am I by no means certain that she would take me with the impediment of our friends' consent, a regular humdrum wedding, and the reversion[86] of a good fortune on my side; no, no, I must prepare her gradually for the discovery, and make myself necessary to her, before I risk it.—Well, but

81 Strength. 82 The Sedan chair was made to carry one person, and was borne by two chairmen, who stood in the shafts at each end. 83 A crux. A possible meaning is that of youthful or part-time waiters. Philip B. Daghlian (in *Mod. Lang. Quart.,* vi [1945], 421-2) suggests that it alludes to Robert Mackreth, once billiard-marker and waiter at Arthur's coffee house, but M.P. for Castle Rising from 1774. 84 Men who kept the score in billiard rooms. 85 The play on words concerns crediting what Fag says and his obtaining financial credit. In making out a bill of exchange, Fag will ask a paying agent (here, his invention) to hand over something to the payee at some future date. If the payee requires the sum immediately, he may sell the bill to someone else by endorsing it, so becoming security for payment.

86 Inheritance of an estate.

Faulkland, you'll dine with us to-day at the hotel?

FAULKLAND   Indeed I cannot: I am not in spirits to be of such a party.

ABSOLUTE   By heavens! I shall forswear your company. You are the most teasing, captious, incorrigible lover!—Do love like a man!

FAULKLAND   I own I am unfit for company.

ABSOLUTE   Am not *I* a lover; aye, and a romantic one too? Yet do I carry everywhere with me such a confounded farrago[87] of doubts, fears, hopes, wishes, and all the flimsy furniture of a country miss's brain!

FAULKLAND   Ah! Jack, your heart and soul are not, like mine, fixed immutably on one only object.—You throw for a large stake, but losing—you could stake, and throw again:—but I have set my sum of happiness on this cast, and not to succeed were to be stripped of all.

ABSOLUTE   But, for heaven's sake! what grounds for apprehension can your whimsical brain conjure up at present?

FAULKLAND   What grounds for apprehension did you say? Heavens! are there not a thousand! I fear for her spirits—her health—her life.—My absence may fret her; her anxiety for my return, her fears for me, may oppress her gentle temper. And for her health—does not every hour bring me cause to be alarmed? If it rains, some shower may even then have chilled her delicate frame!—If the wind be keen, some rude blast may have affected her! The heat of noon, the dews of the evening, may endanger the life of her, for whom only I value mine. O! Jack, when delicate and feeling souls are separated, there is not a feature in the sky, not a movement of the elements, not an aspiration[88] of the breeze, but hints some cause for a lover's apprehension!

ABSOLUTE   Aye, but we may choose whether we will take the hint or not.—So then, Faulkland, if you were convinced that Julia were well and in spirits, you would be entirely content?

FAULKLAND   I should be happy beyond measure—I am anxious only for that.

ABSOLUTE   Then to cure your anxiety at once—Miss Melville is in perfect health, and is at this moment in Bath!

FAULKLAND   Nay, Jack—don't trifle with me.

ABSOLUTE   She is arrived here with my father within this hour.

FAULKLAND   Can you be serious?

ABSOLUTE   I thought you knew Sir Anthony better than to be surprised at a sudden whim of this kind.—Seriously then, it is as I tell you—upon my honour.

FAULKLAND   My dear friend!—Hollo, Du-Peigne! My hat—my dear Jack—now nothing on earth can give me a moment's uneasiness.

Enter FAG.

FAG   Sir, Mr. Acres just arrived is below.

ABSOLUTE   Stay, Faulkland, this Acres lives within a mile of Sir Anthony, and he shall tell you how your mistress has been ever since you left her.—Fag, show the gentleman up.

Exit FAG.

FAULKLAND   What, is he much acquainted in the family?

ABSOLUTE   O, very intimate: I insist on your not going: besides, his character will divert you.

FAULKLAND   Well, I should like to ask him a few questions.

ABSOLUTE   He is likewise a rival of mine—that is of my *other self's,* for he does not think his friend Capt. Absolute ever saw the lady in question;—and it is ridiculous enough to hear him complain to me of *one Beverley,* a concealed skulking rival, who——

FAULKLAND   Hush!—He's here.

Enter ACRES.

ACRES   Hah! my dear friend, noble captain, and honest Jack, how do'st thou? Just arrived faith, as you see.—Sir, your

87 Confused mixture. 88 Breath.

humble servant. Warm work on the roads Jack—Odds whips and wheels![89] I've travelled like a comet, with a tail of dust all the way as long as the Mall.[90]

ABSOLUTE   Ah! Bob, you are indeed an eccentric planet, but we know your attraction hither—Give me leave to introduce Mr. Faulkland to you; Mr. Faulkland, Mr. Acres.

ACRES   Sir, I am most heartily glad to see you: sir, I solicit your connections.[91]—Hey Jack—what this is Mr. Faulkland, who——?

ABSOLUTE   Aye, Bob, Miss Melville's Mr. Faulkland.

ACRES   Od'so! she and your father can be but just arrived before me—I suppose you have seen them.—Ah! Mr. Faulkland, you are indeed a happy man.

FAULKLAND   I have not seen Miss Melville yet, sir—I hope she enjoyed full health and spirits in Devonshire?

ACRES   Never knew her better in my life, sir—never better.—Odd's blushes and blooms! she has been as healthy as the German Spa.[92]

FAULKLAND   Indeed!—I did hear that she had been a little indisposed.

ACRES   False, false, sir—only said to vex you: quite the reverse I assure you.

FAULKLAND   There, Jack, you see she has the advantage of me; I had almost fretted myself ill.

ABSOLUTE   Now are you angry with your mistress for not having been sick.

FAULKLAND   No, no, you misunderstand me:—yet surely a little trifling indisposition is not an unnatural consequence of absence from those we love.—Now confess—isn't there something unkind in this violent, robust, unfeeling health?

ABSOLUTE   O, it was very unkind of her to be well in your absence, to be sure!

ACRES   Good apartments, Jack.

FAULKLAND   Well, sir, but you were saying that Miss Melville has been so *exceedingly* well—what, then she has been merry and gay I suppose?—Always in spirits—hey?

ACRES   Merry! Odds crickets! she has been the belle and spirit of the company wherever she has been—so lively and entertaining! so full of wit and humour!

FAULKLAND   There, Jack, there—O, by my soul! there is an innate levity in woman, that nothing can overcome.—What! happy, and I away!

ABSOLUTE   Have done:—how foolish this is! Just now you were only apprehensive for your mistress's *spirits*.

FAULKLAND   Why, Jack, have I been the joy and spirit of the company?

ABSOLUTE   No, indeed, you have not.

FAULKLAND   Have I been lively and entertaining?

ABSOLUTE   O, upon my word, I acquit you.

FAULKLAND   Have I been full of wit and humour?

ABSOLUTE   No, faith, to do you justice, you have been confoundedly stupid indeed.

ACRES   What's the matter with the gentleman?

ABSOLUTE   He is only expressing his great satisfaction at hearing that Julia has been so well and happy—that's all—hey, Faulkland?

FAULKLAND   Oh! I am rejoiced to hear it—yes, yes, she has a *happy* disposition!

ACRES   That she has indeed—then she is so accomplished—so sweet a voice—so expert at her harpsichord—such a mistress of flat and sharp, squallante, rumblante, and quiverante![93]—there was this time month—Odds minnums[94] and crotchets! how she did chirrup at Mrs. Piano's[95] concert!

FAULKLAND   There again, what say you to this? You see she has been all mirth and song—not a thought of me!

---

89 One of Acre's "oaths referential": see his speech, p. 348. 90 The fashionable walk to the north of St. James's Park. 91 Beg leave to become acquainted with you. 92 A health resort near the German border of Belgium, and celebrated for its mineral springs.

93 Acres tries to give an Italian air to the English words "squalling," "rumbling," and "quivering." 94 Minims are half the value of a semibreve, and crotchets, a quarter. 95 The musical direction for "soft" or "softly."

ABSOLUTE Pho! man, is not music the food of love?[96]

FAULKLAND Well, well, it may be so.—Pray Mr.——what's his d—d name? Do you remember what songs Miss Melville sung?

ACRES Not I, indeed.

ABSOLUTE Stay now, they were some pretty, melancholy, purling stream airs,[97] I warrant; perhaps you may recollect:—did she sing—*"When absent from my soul's delight"*?

ACRES No, that wa'n't it.

ABSOLUTE Or—*"Go, gentle gales"?*——*"Go, gentle gales!"* [*Sings.*]

ACRES O no! nothing like it.—Odds! now I recollect one of them—*"My heart's my own, my will is free."* [*Sings.*]

FAULKLAND Fool! fool that I am! to fix all my happiness on such a trifler! 'Sdeath! to make herself the pipe and ballad-monger of a circle! to soothe her light heart with catches[98] and glees![99]—What can you say to this, sir?

ABSOLUTE Why, that I should be glad to hear my mistress had been so merry, *sir.*

FAULKLAND Nay, nay, nay—I am not sorry that she has been happy—no, no, I am glad of that—I would not have had her sad or sick—yet surely a sympathetic heart would have shown itself even in the choice of a song—she might have been temperately healthy, and, somehow, plaintively gay;—but she has been dancing too, I doubt not!

ACRES What does the gentleman say about dancing?

ABSOLUTE He says the lady we speak of dances as well as she sings.

ACRES Aye truly, does she—there was at our last race-ball——

FAULKLAND Hell and the devil! There! there!—I told you so! I told you so! Oh!

she thrives in my absence!—Dancing!—but her whole feelings have been in opposition with mine!—I have been anxious, silent, pensive, sedentary—my days have been hours of care, my nights of watchfulness.—She has been all Health! Spirit! Laugh! Song! Dance!—Oh! d—n'd, d—n'd levity!

ABSOLUTE For heaven's sake! Faulkland, don't expose yourself so.—Suppose she has danced, what then?—does not the ceremony of society often oblige——

FAULKLAND Well, well, I'll contain myself—perhaps as you say—for form sake.—What, Mr. Acres, you were praising Miss Melville's manner of dancing a *minuet*—hey?

ACRES O I dare insure her for that—but what I was going to speak of was her *country-dancing:*—Odds swimmings! she has such an air with her!—

FAULKLAND Now disappointment on her!—defend this, Absolute, why don't you defend this?—Country-dances! jigs, and reels! Am I to blame now? A minuet I could have forgiven—I should not have minded that—I say I should not have regarded a minuet—but *country-dances!* Z——ds! had she made one in a cotillion[100]—I believe I could have forgiven even that—but to be monkey-led for a night!—to run the gauntlet thro' a string of amorous palming puppies![101]—to show paces like a managed[102] filly!—O Jack, there never can be but *one* man in the world, whom a truly modest and delicate woman ought to pair with in a *country-dance;* and even then, the rest of the couples should be her great uncles and aunts!

100 The minuet was a dignified dance performed in small steps, the cotillion was livelier, and country dances were boisterous. The distinctions were brought out in the *General Evening Post,* 3–5 June 1777, in a report on a ball at court: "about a dozen minuets were danced, and then the company rose to country dances and cotillons." 101 Raw, conceited fellows, anxious to get their hands on the girls. 102 Taught the "manège," stepping and moving according to the strict practice of the riding school.

96 Cf. the first line of *Twelfth Night:* "If music be the food of love, play on." 97 Gently pleasing, rippling sounds. 98 Short, amusing songs. 99 Unaccompanied part-songs.

ABSOLUTE Aye, to be sure!—grand-fathers and grand-mothers!

FAULKLAND If there be but one vicious mind in the set,[103] 'twill spread like a contagion—the action of their pulse beats to the lascivious movement of the jig—their quivering, warm-breathed sighs impregnate the very air—the atmosphere becomes electrical[104] to love, and each amorous spark darts thro'every link of the chain!—I must leave you—I own I am somewhat flurried—and that confounded looby[105] has perceived it.

[*Going.*]

ABSOLUTE Nay, but stay, Faulkland, and thank Mr. Acres for his good news.

FAULKLAND D—n his news!

Exit FAULKLAND.

ABSOLUTE Ha! ha! ha! Poor Faulkland! five minutes since—"nothing on earth could give him a moment's uneasiness!"

ACRES The gentleman wa'n't angry at my praising his mistress, was he?

ABSOLUTE A little jealous, I believe, Bob.

ACRES You don't say so? Ha! ha! jealous of me?—that's a good joke.

ABSOLUTE There's nothing strange in that, Bob; let me tell you, that sprightly grace and insinuating manner of yours will do some mischief among the girls here.

ACRES Ah! you joke—ha! ha!—mischief—ha! ha! But you know I am not my own property, my dear Lydia has forestalled me.—She could never abide me in the country, because I used to dress so badly—but odds frogs[106] and tambours![107] I sha'n't take matters so here—now ancient madam[108] has no voice in it.—I'll make my old clothes know who's master—I

shall straightway cashier[109] the hunting-frock—and render my leather breeches incapable.[110]—My hair has been in training some time.

ABSOLUTE Indeed!

ACRES Aye—and tho'ff the side-curls are a little restive, my hind-part takes to it very kindly.

ABSOLUTE O, you'll polish, I doubt not.

ACRES Absolutely I propose so.—Then if I can find out this Ensign Beverley, odds triggers and flints![111] I'll make him know the difference o't.

ABSOLUTE Spoke like a man—but pray, Bob, I observe you have got an odd kind of a new method of swearing——

ACRES Ha! ha! you've taken notice of it—'tis genteel, isn't *it?*—I didn't invent it myself, though; but a commander in our militia[112]—a great scholar, I assure you—says that there is no meaning in the common oaths, and that nothing but their antiquity makes them respectable;—because, he says, the ancients would never stick to an oath or two, but would say, by Jove! or by Bacchus! or by Mars! or by Venus! or by Pallas! according to the sentiment[113]—so that to swear with propriety, says my little major, the "oath should be an echo to the sense;"[114] and this we call the *oath referential,* or *sentimental swearing*—ha! ha! ha! 'tis genteel,[115] isn't it?

ABSOLUTE Very genteel,[116] and very new indeed—and I dare say will supplant all other figures of imprecation.

ACRES Aye, aye, the best terms will grow obsolete—Damns have had their day.

103 The number of people required for the figure of a dance. 104 "These exhalations, or subtile effluvia, constitute electricity. . . . They seem to adhere to the extremities of the bodies which they surround, and from which they recede, in the form of sparks" (*A New and Complete Dictionary of Arts and Sciences* [2nd ed., 1763], p. 1050). 105 Fool. 106 Ornamental loop or tuft or a military tunic. 107 Round frame used in embroidering. 108 His mother: "the old lady."

109 Dismiss from service. 110 Unable to give further service. 111 The trigger of a gun released the hammer which, striking the flint, produced a spark to ignite the powder. 112 Trained bands who armed themselves, for their own defence. They were under the command of the Lords-lieutenants. 113 The opinion expressed. 114 Pope, *An Essay in Criticism* (1711), lines 364–365:
"th 'Tis not enough no harshness gives offence, The sound must seem an echo to the sense." 115 Suited to a gentleman. 116 Affected.

Enter FAG.

FAG Sir, there is a gentleman below, desires to see you.—Shall I show him into the parlour?

ABSOLUTE Aye—you may.

ACRES Well, I must be gone——

ABSOLUTE Stay; who is it, Fag?

FAG Your father, sir.

ABSOLUTE You puppy, why didn't you show him up directly?

Exit FAG.

ACRES You have business with Sir Anthony.—I expect a message from Mrs. Malaprop at my lodgings—I have sent also to my dear friend, Sir Lucius O'Trigger.—Adieu, Jack, we must meet at night, when you shall give me a dozen bumpers[117] to little Lydia.

ABSOLUTE That I will, with all my heart.

Exit ACRES.

ABSOLUTE Now for a parental lecture.—I hope he has heard nothing of the business that has brought me here—I wish the gout[118] had held him fast in Devonshire, with all my soul!

Enter SIR ANTHONY.

ABSOLUTE Sir, I am delighted to see you here; and looking so well!—Your sudden arrival at Bath made me apprehensive for your health.

SIR ANTHONY Very apprehensive, I dare say, Jack.—What you are recruiting here, hey?

ABSOLUTE Yes, sir, I am on duty.

SIR ANTHONY Well, Jack, I am glad to see you, tho' I did not expect it, for I was going to write to you on a little matter of business.—Jack, I have been considering that I grow old and infirm, and shall probably not trouble you long.

ABSOLUTE Pardon me, sir, I never saw you look more strong and hearty; and I pray frequently that you may continue so.

SIR ANTHONY I hope your prayers may be heard with all my heart. Well then, Jack, I have been considering that I am so strong and hearty, I may continue to plague you a long time.—Now, Jack, I am sensible that the income of your commission[119] and what I have hitherto allowed you, is but a small pittance for a lad of your spirit.

ABSOLUTE Sir, you are very good.

SIR ANTHONY And it is my wish, while yet I live, to have my boy make some figure in the world.—I have resolved, therefore, to fix you at once in a noble independence.

ABSOLUTE Sir, your kindness overpowers me—such generosity makes the gratitude of reason more lively than the sensations even of filial affection.

SIR ANTHONY I am glad you are so sensible of my attention—and you shall be master of a large estate in a few weeks.

ABSOLUTE Let my future life, sir, speak my gratitude: I cannot express the sense I have of your munificence.——Yet, sir, I presume you would not wish me to quit the army?

SIR ANTHONY O, that shall be as your wife chooses.

ABSOLUTE My wife, sir!

SIR ANTHONY Aye, aye,—settle that between you—settle that between you.

ABSOLUTE A *wife,* sir, did you say?

SIR ANTHONY Aye, a wife—why; did not I mention her before?

ABSOLUTE Not a word of her, sir.

SIR ANTHONY Odd so!—I mus'n't forget *her,* tho'.—Yes, Jack, the independence I was talking of is by a marriage—the fortune is saddled with a wife—but I suppose that makes no difference.

ABSOLUTE Sir! sir!—you amaze me!

SIR ANTHONY Why, what the devil's the matter with the fool? Just now you were all gratitude and duty.

ABSOLUTE I was, sir,—you talked to me of

---

117 You shall drink to her, with full glass, a dozen times. 118 Painful swellings of the joints, common among the leisured classes.

119 His warrant as an ensign. *The Royal Kalendar* (1793), p. 141, notes that an ensign in the Foot Guards drew 5s. 10d. a day and 4s. 6d. subsistence, while a second lieutenant in a Foot Regiment drew 3s. 8d. and 3s. 0d. These rates were full pay.

independence and a fortune, but not a word of a wife.

SIR ANTHONY   Why—what difference does that make? Odds life, sir! if you have the estate, you must take it with the live stock[120] on it, as it stands.

ABSOLUTE   If my happiness is to be the price, I must beg leave to decline the purchase.—Pray, sir, who is the lady?

SIR ANTHONY   What's that to you, sir?—Come, give me your promise to love, and to marry her directly.

ABSOLUTE   Sure, sir, this is not very reasonable, to summon my affections for a lady I know nothing of!

SIR ANTHONY   I am sure, sir, 'tis more unreasonable in you to *object* to a lady you know nothing of.

ABSOLUTE   Then, sir, I must tell you plainly, that my inclinations are fixed on another—my heart is engaged to an angel.

SIR ANTHONY   Then pray let it send an excuse.——It is very sorry—but *business* prevents its waiting on her.

ABSOLUTE   But my vows are pledged to her.

SIR ANTHONY   Let her foreclose, Jack; let her foreclose; they are not worth redeeming:[121] besides, you have the angel's vows in exchange, I suppose; so there can be no loss there.

ABSOLUTE   You must excuse me, sir, if I tell you, once for all, that in this point I cannot obey you.

SIR ANTHONY   Harkee', Jack;—I have heard you for some time with patience—I have been cool—quite cool; but take care—you know I am compliance itself—when I am not thwarted;—no one more easily led—when I have my own way;—but don't put me in a frenzy.

ABSOLUTE   Sir, I must repeat it—in this I cannot obey you.

SIR ANTHONY   Now, d—n me! if ever I call you *Jack* again while I live!

ABSOLUTE   Nay, sir, but hear me.

SIR ANTHONY   Sir, I won't hear a word—not a word! not one word! so give me your promise by a nod—and I'll tell you what, Jack—I mean, you dog—if you don't, by——

ABSOLUTE   What, sir, promise to link myself to some mass of ugliness! to——

SIR ANTHONY   Z——ds! sirrah! the lady shall be as ugly as I choose: she shall have a hump on each shoulder; she shall be as crooked as the Crescent; her one eye shall roll like the Bull's in Cox's Museum[122]—she shall have a skin like a mummy, and the beard of a Jew—she shall be all this, sirrah!—yet I'll make you ogle her all day, and sit up all night to write sonnets on her beauty.

ABSOLUTE   This is reason and moderation indeed!

SIR ANTHONY   None of your sneering, puppy! no grinning, jackanapes![123]

ABSOLUTE   Indeed, sir, I never was in a worse humour for mirth in my life.

SIR ANTHONY   'Tis false, sir! I know you are laughing in your sleeve: I know you'll grin when I am gone, sirrah!

ABSOLUTE   Sir, I hope I know my duty better.

SIR ANTHONY   None of your passion, sir! none of your violence! if you please.—It won't do with me, I promise you.

ABSOLUTE   Indeed, sir, I never was cooler in my life.

SIR ANTHONY   'Tis a confounded lie!—I know you are in a passion in your heart; I know you are, you hypocritical young dog! But it won't do.

ABSOLUTE   Nay, sir, upon my word.

SIR ANTHONY   So you will fly out! can't you be cool, like me? What the devil good can *passion* do!—*Passion* is of no service, you impudent, insolent, over-

---

120 Living creatures: as opposed to "dead stock," furniture and equipment. 121 A "pledge" was a security given for something borrowed, and when it was not redeemed within the stated time, the lender could regard the security as his own property.

122 James Cox was a jeweller who exhibited mechanical "toys" in Spring Gardens, 1772–75. One of them was "a curious bull" and another was "a pedestal of four bulls." 123 Impertinent youngster.

bearing reprobate!—There you sneer again!—don't provoke me!—but you rely upon the mildness of my temper—you do, you dog! you play upon the meekness of my disposition! Yet take care—the patience of a saint may be overcome at last! —but mark! I give you six hours and a half to consider of this: if you then agree, without any condition, to do everything on earth that I choose, why—confound you! I may in time forgive you——If not, z——ds! don't enter the same hemisphere with me! don't dare to breathe the same air, or use the same light with me; but get an atmosphere and a sun of your own! I'll strip you of your commission; I'll lodge a five-and-threepence[124] in the hands of trustees, and you shall live on the interest.—I'll disown you, I'll disinherit you, I'll unget you! and—d——n me, if ever I call you Jack again!

Exit SIR ANTHONY.

ABSOLUTE *solus.*

ABSOLUTE   Mild, gentle, considerate father —I kiss your hands.—What a tender method of giving his opinion in these matters Sir Anthony has! I dare not trust him with the truth.—I wonder what old, wealthy hag it is that he wants to bestow on me!—yet he married himself for love! and was in his youth a bold intriguer, and a gay companion!

Enter FAG.

FAG   Assuredly, sir, our father is wrath to a degree; he comes down stairs eight or ten steps at a time—muttering, growling, and thumping the bannisters all the way: I, and the cook's dog, stand bowing at the door—rap! he gives me a stroke on the head with his cane; bids me carry that to my master; then kicking the poor turnspit[125] into the area, d—ns us all for a puppy triumvirate![126]—Upon my credit, sir, were I in your place, and found my

father such very bad company, I should certainly drop his acquaintance.
ABSOLUTE   Cease your impertinence, sir, at present.—Did you come in for nothing more?—Stand out of the way!

Pushes him aside, and exit.

FAG *solus.*

FAG   Soh! Sir Anthony trims[127] my master. He is afraid to reply to his father—then vents his spleen on poor Fag!—When one is vexed by one person, to revenge one's self on another, who happens to come in the way—is the vilest injustice! Ah! it shows the worst temper—the basest——

Enter ERRAND-BOY.

BOY   Mr. Fag! Mr. Fag! your master calls you.
FAG   Well, you little, dirty puppy, you need not bawl so!—The meanest disposition! the——
BOY   Quick, quick, Mr. Fag.
FAG   Quick! quick! you impudent jackanapes! am I to be commanded by you too? you little, impertinent, insolent, kitchen-bred——
Exit, kicking and beating him.

SCENE TWO   *The North Parade.*

Enter LUCY.

LUCY   So—I shall have another rival to add to my mistress's list—Captain Absolute.——However, I shall not enter his name till my purse has received notice in form.[128] Poor Acres is dismissed!—Well, I have done him a last friendly office, in letting him know that Beverley was here before him.—Sir Lucius is generally more punctual when he expects to hear from his *dear Dalia,* as he calls her:—I wonder he's not here!—I have a little scruple of conscience from this deceit; tho' I should not be paid so well, if my hero knew that *Delia* was near fifty, and her own mistress.

---

124 Cut him off with a quarter of a guinea.
125 Roasting spits were turned by small dogs pressing on a treadwheel. 126 Impertinent trio.

127 Scolds. 128 A bribe.

Enter SIR LUCIUS O'TRIGGER.

SIR LUCIUS Hah! my little embassadress—upon my conscience I have been looking for you; I have been on the South Parade this half-hour.

LUCY [*speaking simply*] O gemini! and I have been waiting for your worship here on the North.

SIR LUCIUS Faith!—may be that was the reason we did not meet; and it is very comical too, how you could go out and I not see you—for I was only taking a nap at the Parade Coffee-house, and I chose the *window* on purpose that I might not miss you.

LUCY My stars! Now I'd wager a sixpence I went by while you were asleep.

SIR LUCIUS Sure enough it must have been so—and I never dreamt it was so late, till I waked. Well, but my little girl, have you got nothing for me?

LUCY Yes, but I have—I've got a letter for you in my pocket.

SIR LUCIUS O faith! I guessed you weren't come empty-handed—well—let me see what the dear creature says.

LUCY There, Sir Lucius.

[*Gives him a letter.*]

SIR LUCIUS [*reads*] "Sir—there is often a sudden incentive[129] impulse in love, that has a greater induction[130] than years of domestic combination: such was the commotion I felt at the first superfluous[131] view of Sir Lucius O'Trigger."—Very pretty, upon my word. "Female punctuation[132] forbids me to say more; yet let me add, that it will give me joy infallible[133] to find Sir Lucius worthy the last criterion of my affections.—Delia." Upon my conscience! Lucy, your lady is a great mistress of language.—Faith, she's quite the queen of the dictionary!—for the devil a word dare refuse coming at her call—though one would think it was quite out of hearing.

LUCY Aye, sir, a lady of her experience——

SIR LUCIUS Experience! what, at seventeen?

LUCY O true, sir—but then she reads so—my stars! how she will read off-hand!

SIR LUCIUS Faith, she must be very deep read to write this way—though she is rather an arbitrary writer too—for here are a great many poor words pressed[134] into the service of this note, that would get their *habeas corpus*[135] from any court in Christendom.

LUCY Ah! Sir Lucius, if you were to hear how she talks of you!

SIR LUCIUS O tell her, I'll make her the best husband in the world, and Lady O'Trigger into the bargain!—But we must get the old gentlewoman's consent—and do everything fairly.

LUCY Nay, Sir Lucius, I thought you wa'n't rich enough to be so nice.[136]

SIR LUCIUS Upon my word, young woman, you have hit it:—I am so poor that I can't afford to do a dirty action.—If I did not want money I'd steal your mistress and her fortune with a great deal of pleasure.—However, my pretty girl [*gives her money*], here's a little something to buy you a ribband; and meet me in the evening, and I'll give you an answer to this. So, hussy, take a kiss before-hand, to put you in mind.   [*Kisses her.*]

LUCY O lud! Sir Lucius—I never seed such a gemman! My lady won't like you if you're so impudent.

SIR LUCIUS Faith she will, Lucy——that same——pho! what's the name of it?—*Modesty!*——is a quality in a lover more praised by the women than liked; so, if your mistress asks you whether Sir Lucius ever gave you a kiss, tell her fifty—my dear.

LUCY What, would you have me tell her a lie?

---

129 Instinctive. 130 Production. 131 Superficial.
132 Punctilio. 133 Ineffable.

134 "Impressed": forced by Press Gang into the service of army or navy. 135 A writ of *habeas corpus* ("You may have the body") requires that a detainee should be taken before a judge so that the legality of the arrest may be considered. The sense, here, is "release." 136 Scrupulous.

SIR LUCIUS Ah, then, you baggage![137] I'll make it a truth presently.

LUCY For shame now; here is some one coming.

SIR LUCIUS O faith, I'll quiet your conscience.

Sees FAG.—*Exit, humming a tune.*

Enter FAG.

FAG So, so ma'am. I humbly beg pardon.

LUCY O lud!—now, Mr. Fag—you flurry one so.

FAG Come, come, Lucy, here's no one by —so a little less simplicity, with a grain or two more sincerity, if you please.—— You play false with us, madam.—I saw you give the baronet a letter.—My master shall know this—and if he don't call him out[138]—I will.

LUCY Ha! ha! ha! you gentlemen's gentlemen are so hasty.—That letter was from Mrs. Malaprop, simpleton.—She is taken with Sir Lucius's address.[139]

FAG How! what tastes some people have! —Why, I suppose I have walked by her window an hundred times.——But what says our young lady? Any message to my master?

LUCY Sad news, Mr. Fag!—A worse rival than Acres!—Sir Anthony Absolute has proposed his son.

FAG What, Captain Absolute?

LUCY Even so.—I overheard it all.

FAG Ha! ha! ha!—very good, faith.— Good-bye, Lucy, I must away with this news.

LUCY Well—you may laugh—but it is true, I assure you. [*Going.*] But—Mr. Fag —tell your master not to be cast down by this.

FAG O he'll be so disconsolate!

LUCY And charge him not to think of quarrelling with young Absolute.

FAG Never fear!—never fear!

LUCY Be sure—bid him keep up his spirits.

FAG We will—we will.

Exeunt severally.

137 A saucy girl. 138 Challenge to a duel. 139 Bearing.

Act Three

SCENE ONE *The North Parade.*

Enter ABSOLUTE.

ABSOLUTE 'Tis just as Fag told me, indeed.—Whimsical enough, faith! My father wants to *force* me to marry the very girl I am plotting to run away with!— He must not know of my connection with her yet awhile.—He has too summary a method of proceeding in these matters. However, I'll read my recantation instantly.—My conversion is something sudden, indeed—but I can assure him it is very *sincere*.——So, so—here he comes.— He looks plaguy gruff.

[*Steps aside.*]

Enter SIR ANTHONY.

[SIR ANTHONY] No—I'll die sooner than forgive him.—*Die*, did I say? I'll live these fifty years to plague him.—At our last meeting, his impudence had almost put me out of temper.—An obstinate, passionate, self-willed boy!—Who can he take after? This is my return for getting him before all his brothers and sisters!— for putting him, at twelve years old, into a marching regiment, and allowing him fifty pounds a-year, beside his pay ever since!—But I have done with him;—he's anybody's son for me.—I never will see him more,—never—never—never—never!

ABSOLUTE Now for a penitential face.

SIR ANTHONY Fellow, get out of my way.

ABSOLUTE Sir, you see a penitent before you.

SIR ANTHONY I see an impudent scoundrel before me.

ABSOLUTE A sincere penitent.—I am come, sir, to acknowledge my error, and to submit entirely to your will.

SIR ANTHONY What's that?

ABSOLUTE I have been revolving, and reflecting, and considering on your past goodness, and kindness, and condescension[140] to me.

140 Affability.

SIR ANTHONY Well, sir?

ABSOLUTE I have been likewise weighing and balancing what you were pleased to mention concerning duty, and obedience, and authority.

SIR ANTHONY Well, puppy?

ABSOLUTE Why then, sir, the result of my reflection is—a resolution to sacrifice every inclination of my own to your satisfaction.

SIR ANTHONY Why now, you talk sense—absolute sense—I never heard anything more sensible in my life.—Confound you, you shall be *Jack* again!

ABSOLUTE I am happy in the appellation.

SIR ANTHONY Why, then, Jack, my dear Jack, I will now inform you—who the lady really is.—Nothing but your passion and violence, you silly fellow, prevented my telling you at first. Prepare, Jack, for wonder and rapture——prepare.——What think you of Miss Lydia Languish?

ABSOLUTE Languish! What, the Languishes of Worcestershire?

SIR ANTHONY Worcestershire! No. Did you never meet Mrs. Malaprop and her niece, Miss Languish, who came into our country just before you were last ordered to your regiment?

ABSOLUTE Malaprop! Languish! I don't remember ever to have heard the names before. Yet stay,—I think I do recollect something.——*Languish! Languish!* She squints, don't she?—A little, red-haired girl?

SIR ANTHONY Squints?—A red-haired girl! —Z——ds! no.

ABSOLUTE Then I must have forgot; it can't be the same person.

SIR ANTHONY Jack! Jack! what think you of blooming, love-breathing seventeen?

ABSOLUTE As to that, sir, I am quite indifferent.—If I can please you in the matter, 'tis all I desire.

SIR ANTHONY Nay, but Jack, such eyes! such eyes! so innocently wild! so bashfully irresolute! Not a glance but speaks and kindles some thought of love! Then, Jack, her cheeks, Jack! so deeply blushing at the insinuations of her tell-tale eyes!

Then, Jack, her lips!—O Jack, lips smiling at their own discretion; and if not smiling, more sweetly pouting; more lovely in sullenness!

ABSOLUTE [*aside*] That's she, indeed.—Well done, old gentleman!

SIR ANTHONY Then, Jack, her neck![141]—O Jack! Jack!

ABSOLUTE And which is to be mine, sir, the niece or the aunt?

SIR ANTHONY Why, you unfeeling, insensible puppy, I despise you! When I was of your age, such a description would have made me fly like a rocket![142] The *aunt*, indeed!—Odds life! when I ran away with your mother, I would not have touched anything old or ugly to gain an empire.

ABSOLUTE Not to please your father, sir?

SIR ANTHONY To please my father!—— Z——ds! not to please——O, my father! —Oddso!—yes—yes; if my father, indeed, had desired—that's quite another matter.—Though he wa'n't the indulgent father that I am, Jack.

ABSOLUTE I dare say not, sir.

SIR ANTHONY But, Jack, you are not sorry to find your mistress is so beautiful.

ABSOLUTE Sir, I repeat it; if I please you in this affair, 'tis all I desire. Not that I think a woman the worse for being handsome; but, sir, if you please to recollect, you before hinted something about a hump or two, one eye, and a few more graces of that kind.—Now, without being very nice, I own I should rather choose a wife of mine to have the usual number of limbs, and a limited quantity of back: and tho *one* eye may be very agreeable, yet as the prejudice has always run in favour of *two,* I would not wish to affect a singularity in that article.

SIR ANTHONY What a phlegmatic[143] sot it is! Why, sirrah, you're an anchorite![144]—a vile, insensible stock.[145]—You a soldier!—

141 Neck, shoulders, and upper part of breasts, as exposed in the fashion of the day. 142 A firework. 143 Sluggish. 144 Hermit. 145 Heavy block of wood.

you're a walking block, fit only to dust the company's regimentals on!—Odd's life! I've a great mind to marry the girl myself!

ABSOLUTE   I am entirely at your disposal, sir; if you should think of addressing Miss Languish yourself, I suppose you would have me marry the aunt; or if you should change your mind, and take the old lady—'tis the same to me—I'll marry the niece.

SIR ANTHONY   Upon my word, Jack, thou'rt either a very great hypocrite, or——but, come, I know your indifference on such a subject must be all a lie—I'm sure it must—come, now—damn your demure face!—come, confess, Jack—you have been lying—ha'n't you? You have been playing the hypocrite, hey?—I'll never forgive you, if you ha'n't been lying and playing the hypocrite.

ABSOLUTE   I'm sorry, sir, that the respect and duty which I bear to you should be so mistaken.

SIR ANTHONY   Hang your respect and duty! But, come along with me, I'll write a note to Mrs. Malaprop, and you shall visit the lady directly. Her eyes shall be the Promethean[146] torch to you—come along, I'll never forgive you if you don't come back, stark mad with rapture and impatience— if you don't, egad, I'll marry the girl myself!

Exeunt.

SCENE TWO   JULIA's *dressing-room.*

FAULKLAND *solus.*

FAULKLAND   They told me Julia would return directly; I wonder she is not yet come!—How mean does this captious, unsatisfied temper of mine appear to my cooler judgment! Yet I know not that I indulge it in any other point:—but on this one subject, and to this one subject,

146 Prometheus stole fire from heaven to animate his men of clay. Lydia's eyes shall give Jack life.

whom I think I love beyond my life, I am ever ungenerously fretful, and madly capricious!—I am conscious of it—yet I cannot correct myself! What tender, honest joy sparkled in her eyes when we met! —How delicate was the warmth of her expressions!—I was ashamed to appear less happy—though I had come resolved to wear a face of coolness and upbraiding. Sir Anthony's presence prevented my proposed expostulations:—yet I must be satisfied that she has not been so *very* happy in my absence.—She is coming!—Yes!—I know the nimbleness of her tread when she thinks her impatient Faulkland counts the moments of her stay.

Enter JULIA.

JULIA   I had not hoped to see you again so soon.

FAULKLAND   Could I, Julia, be contented with my first welcome—restrained as we were by the presence of a third person?

JULIA   O Faulkland, when your kindness can make me thus happy, let me not think that I discovered something of coldness in your first salutation.

FAULKLAND   'Twas but your fancy, Julia. —I *was* rejoiced to see you—to see you in such health.—Sure I had no cause for coldness?

JULIA   Nay then, I see you have taken something ill.—You must not conceal from me what it is.

FAULKLAND   Well then—shall I own to you that my joy at hearing of your health and arrival here, by your neighbour Acres, was somewhat damped, by his dwelling much on high spirits you had enjoyed in Devonshire—on your mirth— your singing—dancing, and I know not what!—For such is my temper, Julia, that I should regard every mirthful moment in your absence as a treason to constancy:— The mutual tear that steals down the cheek of parting lovers is a compact, that no smile shall live there till they meet again.

JULIA   Must I never cease to tax my Faulkland with this teasing minute caprice?—

Can the idle reports of a silly boor weigh in your breast against my tried affection?

FAULKLAND They have no weight with me, Julia: no, no—I am happy if you have been so—yet only say, that you did not sing with *mirth*—say that you *thought* of Faulkland in the dance.

JULIA I never can be happy in your absence.—If I wear a countenance of content, it is to show that my mind holds no doubt of my Faulkland's truth.——If I seemed sad—it were to make malice triumph, and say, that I had fixed my heart on one, who left me to lament his roving, and my own credulity.—Believe me, Faulkland, I mean not to upbraid you, when I say, that I have often dressed sorrow in smiles, lest my friends should guess whose unkindness had caused my tears.

FAULKLAND You were ever all goodness to me.—O, I am a brute when I but admit a doubt of your true constancy!

JULIA If ever, without such cause from you, as I will not suppose possible, you find my affections veering but a point,[147] may I become a proverbial scoff for levity, and base ingratitude.

FAULKLAND Ah! Julia, that last word is grating to me. I would I had no title to[148] your *gratitude!* Search your heart, Julia; perhaps what you have mistaken for love, is but the warm effusion of a too thankful heart!

JULIA For what quality must I love you?

FAULKLAND For no quality! To regard me for any quality of mind or understanding, were only to *esteem* me. And for person— I have often wished myself deformed, to be convinced that I owed no obligation *there* for any part of your affection.

JULIA Where Nature has bestowed a show of nice attention in the features of a man, he should laugh at it, as misplaced. I have seen men, who in *this* vain article perhaps might rank above you; but my heart has never asked my eyes if it were so or not.

FAULKLAND Now this is not well from *you*, Julia.—I despise person in a man.—Yet if you loved me as I wish, though I were an Æthiop,[149] you'd think none so fair.

JULIA I see you are determined to be unkind.—The *contract* which my poor father bound us in gives you more than a lover's privilege.

FAULKLAND Again, Julia, you raise ideas that feed and justify my doubts.—I would not have been more free—no—I am proud of my restraint.——Yet—yet—perhaps your high respect alone for this solemn compact has fettered your inclinations, which else had made a worthier choice.—How shall I be sure, had you remained unbound in thought and promise, that I should still have been the object of your persevering love?

JULIA Then try me now.—Let us be free as strangers as to what is past:—*my* heart will not feel more liberty!

FAULKLAND There now! so hasty, Julia! so anxious to be free!—If your love for me were fixed and ardent, you would not lose your hold, even tho' I wished it!

JULIA O, you torture me to the heart!— I cannot bear it.

FAULKLAND I do not mean to distress you. —If I loved you less, I should never give you an uneasy moment.—But hear me. —All my fretful doubts arise from this— Women are not used to weigh, and separate the motives of their affections:—the cold dictates of prudence, gratitude, or filial duty, may sometimes be mistaken for the pleadings of the heart.——I would not boast—yet let me say, that I have neither age, person, or character, to found dislike on;—my fortune such as few ladies could be charged with *indiscretion* in the match.—O Julia! when *Love* receives such countenance from *Pru-*

---

147 One of the thirty-two points of the compass, i.e. 11° 15'. 148 Claim upon.

149 Like "eremite," this word belongs to poetic language. The allusion here is to absolute contrast, as in *Romeo and Juliet*, I. v. 49 ("Like a rich jewel in an Ethiop's ear"), or *Love's Labour's Lost*, IV. iii. 116–117 ("Thou for whom Jove would swear/ Juno but an Ethiop were").

dence, nice minds will be suspicious of its *birth.*

JULIA   I know not whither your insinuations would tend:—but as they seem pressing to insult me—I will spare you the regret of having done so.—I have given you no cause for this!

Exit in tears.

FAULKLAND   In tears! Stay, Julia: stay but for a moment.——The door is fastened! —Julia;—my soul—but for one moment: —I hear her sobbing!—'Sdeath! what a brute am I to use her thus! Yet stay!— Aye—she is coming now:—how little resolution there is in woman!—How a few soft words can turn them!——No, faith! —she is *not* coming either.——Why, Julia—my love—say but that you forgive me—come but to tell me that.—Now, this is being *too* resentful:—stay! she *is* coming too—I thought she would—no *steadiness* in anything! her going away must have been a mere trick then.—She sha'n't see that I was hurt by it.—I'll affect indifference.—[*Hums a tune: then listens.*]—— No—Z——ds! she's *not* coming!—nor don't intend it, I suppose.—This is not *steadiness,* but *obstinacy!* Yet I deserve it.—What, after so long an absence, to quarrel with her tenderness!—'twas barbarous and unmanly!—I should be ashamed to see her now.—I'll wait till her just resentment is abated—and when I distress her so again, may I lose her for ever! and be linked instead to some antique virago, whose gnawing passions, and long-hoarded spleen, shall make me curse my folly half the day, and all the night!

Exit.

SCENE THREE   MRS. MALAPROP'S *lodgings.*

MRS. MALAPROP, *with a letter in her hand, and* CAPTAIN ABSOLUTE.

MRS. MALAPROP   Your being Sir Anthony's son, Captain, would itself be a sufficient accommodation;[150]—but from the ingenuity[151] of your appearance, I am convinced you deserve the character here given of you.

ABSOLUTE   Permit me to say, madam, that as I never yet have had the pleasure of seeing Miss Languish, my principal inducement in this affair at present, is the honour of being allied to Mrs. Malaprop; of whose intellectual accomplishments, elegant manners, and unaffected learning, no tongue is silent.

MRS. MALAPROP   Sir, you do me infinite honour!—I beg, Captain, you'll be seated. —[*Sit.*]—Ah! few gentlemen now-a-days know how to value the ineffectual[152] qualities in a woman!—few think how a little knowledge becomes a gentlewoman! Men have no sense now but for the worthless flower of beauty!

ABSOLUTE   It is but too true, indeed, ma'am. —Yet I fear our ladies should share the blame—they think our admiration of *beauty* so great, that knowledge in *them* would be superfluous. Thus, like garden-trees, they seldom show fruit, till time has fobbed them of the more specious blossom.—Few, like Mrs. Malaprop and the orange-tree, are rich in both at once!

MRS. MALAPROP   Sir—you overpower me with good breeding.—He is the very pine-apple[153] of politeness!—You are not ignorant, Captain, that this giddy girl has somehow contrived to fix her affections on a beggarly, strolling,[154] eaves-dropping Ensign, whom none of us have seen, and nobody knows anything of.

ABSOLUTE   O, I have heard the silly affair before.—I'm not at all prejudiced against her on *that* account.

MRS. MALAPROP   You are very good, and very considerate, Captain.—I am sure I have done everything in my power since I exploded[155] the affair! Long ago I laid my positive conjunctions[156] on her never to think on the fellow again;—I have

---

150 Recommendation. 151 Ingenuousness. 152 Intellectual. 153 Pinnacle. 154 Tramping. 155 Exposed. 156 Injunctions.

since laid Sir Anthony's preposition[157] before her;—but, I am sorry to say, she seems resolved to decline every particle[158] that I enjoin[159] her.

ABSOLUTE   It must be very distressing, indeed, ma'am.

MRS. MALAPROP   Oh! it gives me the hydrostatics[160] to such a degree!—I thought she had persisted[161] from corresponding with him; but behold this very day, I have interceded[162] another letter from the fellow! I believe I have it in my pocket.

ABSOLUTE   [aside] O the devil! my last note.

MRS. MALAPROP   Aye, here it is.

ABSOLUTE   [aside] Aye, my note, indeed! O the little traitress Lucy.

MRS. MALAPROP   There, perhaps you may know the writing.
[*Gives him the letter.*]

ABSOLUTE   I think I have seen the hand before—yes, I certainly must have seen this hand before:——

MRS. MALAPROP   Nay, but read it, Captain.

ABSOLUTE   [reads] "My soul's idol, my adored Lydia!"—Very tender, indeed!

MRS. MALAPROP   Tender! aye, and profane, too, o' my conscience!

ABSOLUTE   "I am excessively alarmed at the intelligence you send me, the more so as my new rival"——

MRS. MALAPROP   That's you, sir.

ABSOLUTE   "has universally the character of being an accomplished gentleman, and a man of honour."——Well, that's handsome enough.

MRS. MALAPROP   O, the fellow had some design in writing so.

ABSOLUTE   That he had, I'll answer for him, ma'am.

MRS. MALAPROP   But go on, sir—you'll see presently.

ABSOLUTE   "As for the old weather-beaten she-dragon who guards you"—Who can he mean by that?

MRS. MALAPROP   Me, sir—me—he means me, there—what do you think now?—But go on a little further.

ABSOLUTE   Impudent scoundrel!—"it shall go hard but I will elude her vigilance, as I am told that the same ridiculous vanity which makes her dress up her coarse features, and deck her dull chat with hard words which she don't understand"——

MRS. MALAPROP   There, sir! an attack upon my language! What do you think of that?—an aspersion upon my parts of speech! Was ever such a brute! Sure if I reprehend[163] anything in this world, it is the use of my oracular[164] tongue, and a nice derangement[165] of epitaphs![166]

ABSOLUTE   He deserves to be hanged and quartered![167] Let me see—"same ridiculous vanity"—

MRS. MALAPROP   You need not read it again, sir.

ABSOLUTE   I beg pardon, ma'am——"does also lay her open to the grossest deceptions from flattery and pretended admiration"—an impudent coxcomb![168]——"so that I have a scheme to see you shortly with the old harridan's consent, and even to make her a go-between in our interviews."—Was ever such assurance!

MRS. MALAPROP   Did you ever hear anything like it?—he'll elude my vigilance, will he?—yes, yes! ha! ha! he's very likely to enter these doors!—we'll try who can plot best!

ABSOLUTE   So we will, ma'am—so we will. Ha! ha! ha! a conceited puppy, ha! ha! ha!——Well, but Mrs. Malaprop, as the girl seems so infatuated by this fellow, suppose you were to wink at her corresponding with him for a little time—let her even plot an elopement with him—then do you connive at her escape—while I, just in the nick,[169] will have the fellow laid by the heels,[170] and fairly contrive to carry her off in his stead.

MRS. MALAPROP   I am delighted with the scheme, never was anything better perpetrated!

ABSOLUTE   But, pray, could not I see the

---

157 Proposition.   158 Article.   159 Inflict upon.   160 Hysterics. 161 Desisted. 162 Intercepted.

163 Comprehend.   164 Vernacular.   165 Arrangement. 166 Epithets. 167 Cut up into four pieces, a fate reserved for traitors. 168 Conceited ass. 169 Of time. 170 Confine or put out of action.

lady for a few minutes now?—I should like to try her temper a little.

MRS. MALAPROP Why, I don't know—I doubt she is not prepared for a visit of this kind.—There is a decorum in these matters.

ABSOLUTE O Lord! she won't mind *me*—only tell her Beverley——

MRS. MALAPROP Sir!——

ABSOLUTE [*aside*] Gently, good tongue.

MRS. MALAPROP What did you say of Beverley?

ABSOLUTE O, I was going to propose that you should tell her, by way of jest, that it was Beverley who was below—she'd come down fast enough then—ha! ha! ha!

MRS. MALAPROP 'Twould be a trick she well deserves.—Besides you know the fellow tells her he'll get my consent to see her—ha! ha!—Let him if he can, I say again.—Lydia, come down here! [*Calling.*]—He'll make me a *go-between in their interviews!*—ha! ha! ha!—Come down, I say, Lydia!—I don't wonder at your laughing, ha! ha! ha!—his impudence is truly ridiculous.

ABSOLUTE 'Tis very ridiculous, upon my soul, ma'am, ha! ha! ha!

MRS. MALAPROP The little hussy won't hear.—Well, I'll go and tell her at once who it is.—She shall know that Capt. Absolute is come to wait on her.—And I'll make her behave as becomes a young woman.

ABSOLUTE As you please, ma'am.

MRS. MALAPROP For the present, Captain, your servant. Ah! you've not done laughing yet, I see—*elude my vigilance!*—yes, yes, ha! ha! ha!   *Exit.*

ABSOLUTE Ha! ha! ha! one would think now that I might throw off all disguise at once, and seize my prize with security—but such is Lydia's caprice, that to undeceive were probably to lose her.—I'll see whether she knows me.

[*Walks aside, and seems engaged in looking at the pictures.*]

Enter LYDIA.

LYDIA What a scene am I now to go thro'! Surely nothing can be more dreadful than to be obliged to listen to the loathsome addresses of a stranger to one's heart.—I have heard of girls persecuted as I am, who have appealed in behalf of their favoured lover to the generosity of his rival: suppose I were to try it—there stands the hated rival—an officer too!—but O, how unlike my Beverley!—I wonder he don't begin—truly he seems a very negligent wooer!—quite at his ease, upon my word!—I'll speak first.—[*Aloud.*] Mr. Absolute.

ABSOLUTE Madam.

LYDIA O heav'ns! Beverley!

ABSOLUTE Hush!—hush, my life!—softly! Be not surprised!

LYDIA I am so astonished! and so terrified! and so overjoyed!—For heav'n's sake! how came you here?

ABSOLUTE Briefly—I have deceived your aunt.—I was informed that my new rival was to visit here this evening, and contriving to have him kept away, have passed myself on *her* for Capt. Absolute.

LYDIA O, charming!—And she really takes you for young Absolute?

ABSOLUTE O, she's convinced of it.

LYDIA Ha! ha! ha! I can't forbear laughing to think how her sagacity is overreached!

ABSOLUTE But we trifle with our precious moments—such another opportunity may not occur—then let me now conjure my kind, my condescending angel, to fix the time when I may rescue her from undeserved persecution, and with a licensed[171] warmth plead for my reward.

LYDIA Will you then, Beverley, consent to forfeit that portion of my paltry wealth!—that burden on the wings of love?

ABSOLUTE O, come to me—rich only thus—in loveliness.—Bring no portion to me but thy love—'twill be generous in you, Lydia—for well you know, it is the only dower your poor Beverley can repay.

171 Married.

LYDIA How persuasive are his words!—how charming will poverty be with him!

ABSOLUTE Ah! my soul, what a life will we then live! Love shall be our idol and support! We will worship him with a monastic strictness; abjuring all worldly toys, to centre every thought and action there.—Proud of calamity, we will enjoy the wreck of wealth; while the surrounding gloom of adversity shall make the flame of our pure love show doubly bright.—By heav'ns! I would fling all goods of fortune from me with a prodigal hand, to enjoy the scene where I might clasp my Lydia to my bosom, and say, the world affords no smile to me—but here. [*Embracing her.*]——[*Aside.*] If she holds out now the devil is in it!

LYDIA Now could I fly with him to the Antipodes! but my persecution is not yet come to a crisis.

Enter MRS. MALAPROP, *listening.*

MRS. MALAPROP [*aside*] I am impatient to know how the little hussy deports herself.

ABSOLUTE So pensive, Lydia!—is then your warmth abated?

MRS. MALAPROP [*aside*] Warmth abated!—So! she has been in a passion, I suppose.

LYDIA No—nor ever can while I have life.

MRS. MALAPROP [*aside*] An ill-tempered little devil!—She'll be in a passion all her life—will she?

LYDIA Think not the idle threats of my ridiculous aunt can ever have any weight with me.

MRS. MALAPROP [*aside*] Very dutiful, upon my word!

LYDIA Let her choice be *Captain Absolute,* but Beverley is mine.

MRS. MALAPROP [*aside*] I am astonished at her assurance!—to his face—this is his face!

ABSOLUTE Thus then let me enforce my suit. [*Kneeling.*]

MRS. MALAPROP [*aside*] Aye—poor young man!—down on his knees entreating for pity!—I can contain no longer.—[*Aloud.*] Why, thou vixen!—I have overheard you.

ABSOLUTE [*aside*] O, confound her vigilance!

MRS. MALAPROP Capt. *Absolute*—I know not how to apologize for her shocking rudeness.

ABSOLUTE [*aside*] So—all's safe, I find.—[*Aloud.*] I have hopes, madam, that time will bring the young lady——

MRS. MALAPROP O, there's nothing to be hoped for from her! She's as headstrong as an allegory[172] on the banks of Nile.

LYDIA Nay, madam, what do you charge me with now?

MRS. MALAPROP Why, thou unblushing rebel—didn't you tell this gentleman to his face that you loved another better?—didn't you say you never would be his?

LYDIA No, madam—I did not.

MRS. MALAPROP Good heav'ns! what assurance!—Lydia, Lydia, you ought to know that lying don't become a young woman!—Didn't you boast that *Beverley* —that stroller[173] *Beverley*—possessed your heart?—Tell me that, I say.

LYDIA 'Tis true, ma'am, and none but *Beverley*——

MRS. MALAPROP Hold;—hold, Assurance!—you shall not be so rude.

ABSOLUTE Nay, pray Mrs. Malaprop, don't stop the young lady's speech:—she's very welcome to talk thus—it does not hurt *me* in the least, I assure you.

MRS. MALAPROP You are *too* good, Captain—*too* amiably patient—but come with me, miss.—Let us see you again soon, Captain.—Remember what we have fixed.

ABSOLUTE I shall, ma'am.

MRS. MALAPROP Come, take a graceful leave of the gentleman.

LYDIA May every blessing wait on my *Beverley,* my loved *Bev*——

MRS. MALAPROP Hussy! I'll choke the word in your throat!—come along—come along.

Exeunt severally, BEVERLEY (ABSOLUTE). *kissing his hand to* LYDIA—MRS. MALAPROP *stopping her from speaking.*

---

172 Alligator. 173 Tramp or itinerant actor.

SCENE FOUR   ACRES's *lodgings.*

ACRES *and* DAVID. ACRES *has just dressed.*

ACRES   Indeed, David—do you think I become it so?

DAVID   You are quite another creature, believe me, master, by the Mass! an' we've any luck we shall see the Devon monkey-rony[174] in all the print-shops[175] in Bath!

ACRES   Dress *does* make a difference, David.

DAVID   'Tis all in all, I think.—Difference! why, an' you were to go now to Clod-Hall,[176] I am certain the old lady wouldn't know you: Master Butler wouldn't believe his own eyes, and Mrs. Pickle would cry, "Lard presarve[177] me!" —our dairy-maid would come giggling to the door, and I warrant Dolly Tester,[178] your Honour's favourite, would blush like my waistcoat.—Oons![179] I'll hold a gallon,[180] there a'n't a dog in the house but would bark, and question whether *Phyllis* would wag a hair of her tail!

ACRES   Aye, David, there's nothing like polishing.

DAVID   So I says of your Honour's boots; but the boy never heeds me!

ACRES   But, David, has Mr. De-la-Grace[181] been here? I must rub up my balancing, and chasing, and boring.[182]

DAVID   I'll call again, sir.

ACRES   Do—and see if there are any letters for me at the post-office.

DAVID   I will.—By the Mass, I can't help looking at your head!—If I hadn't been by at the cooking, I wish I may die if I should have known the dish again myself! *Exit.*

ACRES *comes forward, practising a dancing step.*

ACRES   Sink, slide—coupee![183]—Confound the first inventors of cotillons![184] say I— they are as bad as algebra to us country gentlemen.—I can walk a minuet[185] easy enough when I'm forced!—and I have been accounted a good stick in a country-dance.—Odds jigs and tabors![186]—I never valued[187] your cross-over to couple—figure in—right and left—and I'd foot it with e'er a captain in the county!—but these outlandish heathen allemandes[188] and co-tillons are quite beyond me!—I shall never prosper at 'em, that's sure.—Mine are true-born English legs—they don't understand their curst French lingo!— their *pas* this, and *pas* that, and *pas* t'other!—Damn me! my feet don't like to be called paws! no, 'tis certain I have most antigallican[189] toes!

Enter SERVANT.

SERVANT   Here is Sir Lucius O'Trigger to wait on you, sir.

ACRES   Show him in.

Enter SIR LUCIUS.

SIR LUCIUS   Mr. Acres, I am delighted to embrace you.

ACRES   My dear Sir Lucius, I kiss your hands.

SIR LUCIUS   Pray, my friend, what has brought you so suddenly to Bath?

ACRES   Faith! I have followed Cupid's Jack-a-Lantern,[190] and find myself in a quagmire at last.—In short, I have been very ill-used, Sir Lucius.—I don't choose

174 Both "monkey" and "macaroni" were used at this period for "fop." Cf. "A slim beast made for shew/Which the men call a monkey, but ladies a beau!" (Anthony Pasquin, *A Postscript to the New Bath Guide* [1790], p. 62). 175 Shops selling engraved portraits, views, and caricatures. 176 Acres's house in rural Devonshire. 177 Dialect for "Lord preserve." 178 From "tester-bed," a bed with a canopy. Dolly was clearly a chambermaid. 179 From "Zounds!": see p. 336, n. 12. 180 I'll wager a gallon of ale that the dogs will not know you. 181 See p. 337, n. 19. 182 Dance movements: "boring" is from the French "bourrée," and "chasing" from "chas-sée." "Balancing" is to move in opposite directions from one's partner.

183 Cross over. 184 See "cotillion," p. 347, n. 100. 185 See p. 347, n. 100. 186 Small drums. 187 Gave much thought to. 188 A lively German dance. 189 Hostile to everything French. 190 Ignis fatuus, a flame of marsh-gas, which misleads travellers.

to mention names, but look on me as on a very ill-used gentleman.

SIR LUCIUS   Pray, what is the case?—I ask no names.

ACRES   Mark me, Sir Lucius, I fall as deep as need be in love with a young lady—her friends take my part—I follow her to Bath—send word of my arrival, and receive answer, that the lady is to be otherwise disposed of.—This, Sir Lucius, I call being ill-used.

SIR LUCIUS   Very ill, upon my conscience. —Pray, can you divine the cause of it?

ACRES   Why, there's the matter: she has another lover, one *Beverley,* who, I am told, is now in Bath.—Odds slanders and lies! he must be at the bottom of it.

SIR LUCIUS   A rival in the case, is there?— And you think he has supplanted you unfairly?

ACRES   Unfairly!—to be sure he has.—He never could have done it fairly.

SIR LUCIUS   Then sure you know what is to be done!

ACRES   Not I, upon my soul!

SIR LUCIUS   We wear no swords here,[191] but you understand me.

ACRES   What! fight him?

SIR LUCIUS   Aye, to be sure: what can I mean else?

ACRES   But he has given me no provocation.

SIR LUCIUS   Now, I think he has given you the greatest provocation in the world.— Can a man commit a more heinous offence against another than to fall in love with the same woman? O, by my soul, it is the most unpardonable breach of friendship!

ACRES   Breach of friendship! Aye, aye: but I have no acquaintance with this man. I never saw him in my life.

SIR LUCIUS   That's no argument at all—he has the less right then to take such a liberty.

ACRES   'Gad, that's true.—I grow full of anger, Sir Lucius!—I fire apace! Odds hilts and blades![192] I find a man may have a deal of valour in him and not know it! But couldn't I contrive to have a little right of my side?

SIR LUCIUS   What the devil signifies *right* when your *honour* is concerned? Do you think *Achilles,*[193] or my little *Alexander the Great*[194] ever inquired where the right lay? No, by my soul, they drew their broadswords, and left the lazy sons of peace to settle the justice of it.

ACRES   Your words are a grenadier's[195] march to my heart! I believe courage must be catching!—I certainly do feel a kind of valour rising as it were—a kind of courage, as I may say.——Odds flints, pans,[196] and triggers! I'll challenge him directly.

SIR LUCIUS   Ah, my little friend! if we had *Blunderbuss-Hall* here—I could show you a range of ancestry, in the O'Trigger line, that would furnish the new room;[197] every one of whom had killed this man!—For though the mansion-house and dirty acres have slipt through my fingers, I thank heav'n our honour, and the family-pictures, are as fresh as ever.

ACRES   O Sir Lucius! I have had ancestors too! every man of 'em colonel or captain in the militia!—Odds balls and barrels! say no more—I'm braced for it—The thunder of your words has soured the milk of human kindness[198] in my breast! ——Z—ds! as the man in the play says, "I could do such deeds"—[199]

SIR LUCIUS   Come, come, there must be no

---

191 Beau Nash, Master of Ceremonies at Bath, forbade the wearing of swords "as they often tore the ladies' clothes."

192 Cf. Sir Joseph Wittol's oath in Congreve's *The Old Bachelor* (1693), II. i: "Gads-Daggers-Belts-Blades-and Scabbards." 193 Champion of the Greeks in the Trojan War. 194 356–323 B.C., King of Macedon: "little" is an endearment. 195 Acres seems to have connected Achilles and Alexander with the first line of "The British Grenadiers": "Some talk of Alexander, and some of Hercules." 196 Part of a gun's firelock holding the powder. 197 The Upper Assembly rooms, east of the Circus and opened in 1771. 198 From *Macbeth,* I. v. 199 Possibly misquoting Lear's "I will do such things" (II. iv).

passion at all in the case—these things should always be done civilly.

ACRES I must be in a passion, Sir Lucius —I must be in a rage.—Dear Sir Lucius, let me be in a rage, if you love me.— Come, here's pen and paper. [*Sits down to write.*] I would the ink were red!— Indite, I say indite!—How shall I begin? Odds bullets and blades! I'll write a good bold hand, however.

SIR LUCIUS Pray compose yourself.

ACRES Come—now shall I begin with an oath? Do, Sir Lucius, let me begin with a damme.

SIR LUCIUS Pho! pho! do the thing decently and like a Christian. Begin now,— "*Sir*"——

ACRES That's too civil by half.

SIR LUCIUS "*To prevent the confusion that might arise*"—

ACRES Well——

SIR LUCIUS "*From our both addressing the same lady*"——

ACRES Aye—there's the reason—"*same lady*"—Well——

SIR LUCIUS "*I shall expect the honour of your company*"——

ACRES Z——ds! I'm not asking him to dinner.

SIR LUCIUS Pray be easy.

ACRES Well then—"*honour of your company*"——

SIR LUCIUS "*To settle our pretensions*"—

ACRES Well—

SIR LUCIUS Let me see—aye, *King's-Mead-Fields* will do—"*in King's-Mead-Fields.*"

ACRES So that's done.—Well, I'll fold it up presently; my own crest—a hand and dagger shall be the seal.

SIR LUCIUS You see now this little explanation will put a stop at once to all confusion or misunderstanding that might arise between you.

ACRES Aye, we fight to prevent any misunderstanding.

SIR LUCIUS Now, I'll leave you to fix your own time.—Take my advice, and you'll decide it this evening if you can; then let the worst come of it, 'twill be off your mind to-morrow.

ACRES Very true.

SIR LUCIUS So I shall see nothing more of you, unless it be by letter, till the evening.—I would do myself the honour to carry your message; but, to tell you a secret, I believe I shall have just such another affair on my own hands. There is a gay captain here, who put a jest on me lately at the expense of my country, and I only want to fall in with the gentleman, to call him out.

ACRES By my valour, I should like to see you fight first! Odds life! I should like to see you kill him, if it was only to get a little lesson.

SIR LUCIUS I shall be very proud of instructing you.—Well for the present—but remember now, when you meet your antagonist, do everything in a mild and agreeable manner.—Let your courage be as keen, but at the same time as polished as your sword.

Exeunt severally.

Act Four

SCENE ONE ACRES's *lodgings.*

ACRES *and* DAVID

DAVID Then, by the Mass, sir! I would do no such thing—ne'er a Sir Lucius O'Trigger in the kingdom should make me fight, when I wa'n't so minded. Oons! what will the old lady say, when she hears o't!

ACRES Ah! David, if you had heard Sir Lucius!—Odds sparks and flames! he would have roused your valour.

DAVID Not he, indeed. I hates such blood-thirsty cormorants.[200] Look'ee, master, if you'd wanted a bout at boxing, quarter-staff, or short-staff,[201] I should never be the man to bid you cry off: but for your curst sharps and snaps,[202] I never knew any good come of 'em.

ACRES But my honour, David, my hon-

200 A large, greedy bird. 201 The short-staff was a cudgel, and the quarter-staff a long pole tipped with iron. 202 Sharp swords and snapping pistols.

our! I must be very careful of my honour.

DAVID Aye, by the Mass! and I would be very careful of it; and I think in return my *honour* couldn't do less than to be very careful of *me*.

ACRES Odds blades! David, no gentleman will ever risk the loss of his honour!

DAVID I say then, it would be but civil in *honour* never to risk the loss of a *gentleman*.—Look'ee, master, this *honour* seems to me to be a marvellous false friend; aye, truly, a very courtier-like servant.—Put the case, I was a gentleman (which, thank God, no one can say of me); well—my honour makes me quarrel with another gentleman of my acquaintance.—So—we fight. (Pleasant enough that.) Boh!—I kill him—(the more's my luck). Now, pray who gets the profit[203] of it?—Why, my *honour*.—But put the case that he kills me!—by the Mass! I go to the worms, and my honour whips over to my enemy!

ACRES No, David—in that case!—Odds crowns and laurels! your honour follows you to the grave.

DAVID Now, that's just the place where I could make a shift to do without it.

ACRES Z——ds, David, you're a coward! —It doesn't become my valour to listen to you.—What, shall I disgrace my ancestors?—Think of that, David—think what it would be to disgrace my ancestors!

DAVID Under favour, the surest way of not disgracing them, is to keep as long as you can out of their company. Look'ee now, master, to go to them in such haste —with an ounce of lead in your brains— I should think might as well be let alone. Our ancestors are very good kind of folks; but they are the last people I should choose to have a visiting acquaintance with.

ACRES But David, now, you don't think there is such very, very, *very* great danger, hey?—Odds life! people often fight without any mischief done!

203 Cf. Falstaff on "honour" in *King Henry IV, Pt. I, V. i.*

DAVID By the Mass, I think 'tis ten to one against you!—Oons! here to meet some lion-headed fellow, I warrant, with his d—n'd double-barrelled swords, and cut-and-thrust pistols! Lord bless us! it makes me tremble to think o't.—Those be such desperate bloody-minded weapons! Well, I never could abide 'em!—from a child I never could fancy 'em!—I suppose there's a'n't so merciless a beast in the world as your loaded pistol!

ACRES Z——ds! I *won't* be afraid!—Odds fire and fury! you shan't make me afraid! —Here is the challenge, and I have sent for my dear friend Jack Absolute to carry it for me.

DAVID Aye, i' the name of mischief, let *him* be the messenger.—For my part, I wouldn't lend a hand to it for the best horse in your stable. By the Mass! it don't look like another letter! It is, as I may say, a designing and malicious-looking letter!—and I warrant smells of gunpowder, like a soldier's pouch!—Oons! I wouldn't swear it mayn't go off!

ACRES Out, you poltroon!—You ha'n't the valour of a grasshopper.

DAVID Well, I say no more—'twill be sad news, to be sure, at Clod-Hall!—but I ha' done.—How Phyllis will howl when she hears of it!—Aye, poor bitch, she little thinks what shooting her master's going after!—And I warrant old Crop, who has carried your honour, field and road, these ten years, will curse the hour he was born.

[*Whimpering.*]

ACRES It won't do, David—I am determined to fight—so get along, you coward, while I'm in the mind.

Enter SERVANT.

SERVANT Captain Absolute, sir.

ACRES O! show him up.   *Exit* SERVANT.

DAVID Well, heaven send we be all alive this time to-morrow.

ACRES What's that!—Don't provoke me, David!

DAVID Good-bye, master. [*Whimpering.*]

ACRES Get along, you cowardly, dastardly, croaking raven.

Exit DAVID.

Enter ABSOLUTE.

ABSOLUTE What's the matter, Bob?

ACRES A vile, sheep-hearted blockhead!— If I hadn't the valour of St. George and the dragon to boot——

ABSOLUTE But what did you want with me, Bob?

ACRES O!—There——

[*Gives him the challenge.*]

ABSOLUTE *"To Ensign Beverley."* [*Aside.*] So—what's going on now? [*Aloud.*] Well, what's this?

ACRES A challenge!

ABSOLUTE Indeed!—Why, you won't fight him, will you, Bob?

ACRES 'Egad, but I will, Jack.—Sir Lucius has wrought me to it. He has left me full of rage—and I'll fight this evening, that so much good passion mayn't be wasted.

ABSOLUTE But what have I to do with this?

ACRES Why, as I think you know something of this fellow, I want you to find him out for me, and give him this mortal defiance.

ABSOLUTE Well, give it to me, and trust me he gets it.

ACRES Thank you, my dear friend, my dear Jack; but it is giving you a great deal of trouble.

ABSOLUTE Not in the least—I beg you won't mention it.—No trouble in the world, I assure you.

ACRES You are very kind.—What it is to have a friend!—You couldn't be my second—could you, Jack?

ABSOLUTE Why no, Bob—not in *this* affair—it would not be quite so proper.[204]

ACRES Well then, I must get my friend Sir Lucius. I shall have your good wishes, however, Jack.

ABSOLUTE Whenever he meets you, believe me.

SERVANT Sir Anthony Absolute is below, inquiring for the Captain.

ABSOLUTE I'll come instantly.—Well, my little hero, success attend you.   [*Going.*]

ACRES Stay—stay, Jack.—If Beverley should ask you what kind of a man your friend Acres is, do tell him I am a devil of a fellow—will you, Jack?

ABSOLUTE To be sure I shall.—I'll say you are a determined dog—hey, Bob?

ACRES Aye, do, do—and if that frightens him, 'egad, perhaps he mayn't come. So tell him I generally kill a man a week; will you, Jack?

ABSOLUTE I will, I will; I'll say you are called in the country *"Fighting Bob!"*

ACRES Right, right—'tis all to prevent mischief; for I don't want to take his life if I clear my honour.

ABSOLUTE No!—that's very kind of you.

ACRES Why, you don't wish me to kill him—do you, Jack?

ABSOLUTE No, upon my soul, I do not. —But a devil of a fellow, hey? [*Going.*]

ACRES True, true—but stay—stay, Jack— you may add that you never saw me in such a rage before—a most devouring rage!

ABSOLUTE I will, I will.

ACRES Remember, Jack—a determined dog!

ABSOLUTE Aye, aye, *"Fighting Bob!"*

Exeunt severally.

SCENE TWO MRS. MALAPROP's *lodgings.*
MRS. MALAPROP *and* LYDIA.

MRS. MALAPROP Why, thou perverse one! —tell me what you can object to him?— Isn't he a handsome man?—tell me that. —A genteel[205] man? a pretty figure of a man?

LYDIA [*aside*] She little thinks whom she

204 Because Absolute is believed to be a friend of Beverley, Acres's opponent.

205 Refined.

is praising!—[*Aloud.*] So is Beverley, ma'am.

MRS. MALAPROP   No caparisons,[206] miss, if you please!—Caparisons don't become a young woman.—No! Captain Absolute is indeed a fine gentleman!

LYDIA [*aside*]   Aye, the Captain Absolute *you* have seen.

MRS. MALAPROP   Then he's *so* well bred; —*so* full of alacrity, and adulation!—and has *so much* to say for himself:—in such good language, too!—His physiognomy[207] so grammatical!—Then his presence is so noble!—I protest, when I saw him, I thought of what Hamlet says in the play: —"Hesperian curls!—the front of *Job* himself!—an eye, like *March,* to threaten at command!—a station, like Harry Mercury, new"[208]—something about kissing— on a hill—however, the similitude[209] struck me directly.

LYDIA [*aside*]   How enraged she'll be presently when she discovers her mistake!

Enter SERVANT.

SERVANT   Sir Anthony and Captain Absolute are below, ma'am.

MRS. MALAPROP   Show them up here.

Exit SERVANT.

Now, Lydia, I insist on your behaving as becomes a young woman.—Show your good breeding at least, though you have forgot your duty.

LYDIA   Madam, I have told you my resolution!—I shall not only give him no encouragement, but I won't even speak to, or look at him.

[*Flings herself into a chair, with her face from the door.*]

Enter SIR ANTHONY *and* ABSOLUTE.

SIR ANTHONY   Here we are, Mrs. Malaprop, come to mitigate the frowns of un-

relenting beauty—and difficulty enough I had to bring this fellow.—I don't know what's the matter; but if I hadn't held him by force, he'd have given me the slip.

MRS. MALAPROP   You have infinite trouble, Sir Anthony, in the affair. I am ashamed for the cause!—[*Aside to her.*] Lydia, Lydia, rise, I beseech you!—pay your respects!

SIR ANTHONY   I hope, madam, that Miss Languish has reflected on the worth of this gentleman, and the regard due to her aunt's choice, and *my* alliance.—[*Aside to him.*] Now, Jack, speak to her!

ABSOLUTE [*aside*]   What the d——l shall I do!—[*Aloud.*] You see, sir, she won't even look at me, whilst you are here.—I knew she wouldn't!—I told you so.—Let me entreat you, sir, to leave us together!

[ABSOLUTE *seems to expostulate with his father.*]

LYDIA [*aside*]   I wonder I ha'n't heard my aunt exclaim yet! Sure she can't have looked at him!—perhaps their regimentals are alike, and she is something blind.

SIR ANTHONY   I say, sir, I won't stir a foot yet!

MRS. MALAPROP   I am sorry to say, Sir Anthony, that my affluence[210] over my niece is very small.—[*Aside to her.*] Turn round, Lydia, I blush for you!

SIR ANTHONY   May I not flatter myself that Miss Languish will assign what cause of dislike she can have to my son!—Why don't you begin, Jack?—[*Aside to him.*] Speak, you puppy—speak!

MRS. MALAPROP   It is impossible, Sir Anthony, she can have any.—She will not say she has.—[*Aside to her.*] Answer, hussy! why don't you answer?

SIR ANTHONY   Then, madam, I trust that a childish and hasty predilection will be no bar to Jack's happiness.—[*Aside to him.*] Z——ds! sirrah! why don't you speak?

LYDIA [*aside*]   I think my lover seems as little inclined to conversation as myself. —How strangely blind my aunt must be!

ABSOLUTE   Hem! hem!—madam—hem!—

206 Comparisons. 207 Phraseology. 208 From *Hamlet*, III, iv:
Hyperion's curls; the front of Jove himself;
An eye like Mars, to threaten and command;
A station like the herald Mercury
New-lighted on a heaven-kissing hill.
209 Simile.

210 Influence.

[ABSOLUTE *attempts to speak, then returns to* SIR ANTHONY.]—Faith! sir, I am so confounded!—and so—so—confused!—I told you I should be so, sir,—I knew it.—The—the—tremor of my passion entirely takes away my presence of mind.

SIR ANTHONY But it don't take away your voice, fool, does it?—Go up, and speak to her directly!

[ABSOLUTE *makes signs to* MRS. MALAPROP *to leave them together*.]

MRS. MALAPROP Sir Anthony, shall we leave them together?—[*Aside to her*.] Ah! you stubborn, little vixen!

SIR ANTHONY Not yet, ma'am, not yet!—[*Aside to him*.] What the d—l are you at? unlock your jaws, sirrah, or——

[ABSOLUTE *draws near* LYDIA.]

ABSOLUTE [*aside*] Now heav'n send she may be too sullen to look round!—I must disguise my voice.—[*Speaks in a low hoarse tone*.]——Will not Miss Languish lend an ear to the mild accents of true love?—Will not——

SIR ANTHONY What the d—l ails the fellow?—Why don't you speak out?—not stand croaking like a frog in a quinsy!—[211]

ABSOLUTE The—the—excess of my awe, and my—my—my modesty, quite choke me!

SIR ANTHONY Ah! your *modesty* again!—I'll tell you what, Jack, if you don't speak out directly, and glibly, too, I shall be in such a rage!—Mrs. Malaprop, I wish the lady would favour us with something more than a side-front!

[MRS. MALAPROP *seems to chide* LYDIA.]

ABSOLUTE So!—all will out I see!

[*Goes up to* LYDIA, *speaks softly*.]

Be not surprised, my Lydia; suppress all surprise at present.

LYDIA [*aside*] Heav'ns! 'tis Beverley's voice!—Sure he can't have imposed on Sir Anthony, too!—

[*Looks round by degrees, then starts up*.]

Is this possible!—my Beverley!—how can this be?—my Beverley?

ABSOLUTE [*aside*] Ah! 'tis all over.

SIR ANTHONY Beverley!—the devil!—Beverley!—What can the girl mean?—This is my son, Jack Absolute!

MRS. MALAPROP For shame, hussy! for shame!—your head runs so on that fellow, that you have him always in your eyes!—Beg Captain Absolute's pardon directly.

LYDIA I see no Captain Absolute, but my loved Beverley!

SIR ANTHONY Z——ds! the girl's mad!—her brain's turned by reading!

MRS. MALAPROP O' my conscience, I believe so!—What do you mean by Beverley, hussy!—You saw Captain Absolute before to-day; there he is—your husband that shall be.

LYDIA With all my soul, ma'am—when I refuse my Beverley——

SIR ANTHONY O! she's as mad as Bedlam![212]—or has this fellow been playing us a rogue's trick!—Come here, sirrah! who the d——l are you?

ABSOLUTE Faith, sir, I am not quite clear myself; but I'll endeavour to recollect.

SIR ANTHONY Are you my son, or not?—answer for your mother, you dog, if you won't for me.

MRS. MALAPROP Aye, sir, who are you? O mercy! I begin to suspect!——

ABSOLUTE [*aside*] Ye Powers of Impudence befriend me!—[*Aloud*.] Sir Anthony, most assuredly I am your wife's son; and that I sincerely believe myself to be *yours* also, I hope my duty has always shown.—Mrs. Malaprop, I am your most respectful admirer—and shall be proud to add affectionate nephew.—I need not tell my Lydia, that she sees her faithful *Beverley*, who, knowing the singular generosity of her temper, assumed that name, and a station, which has proved a test of the

211 Inflammation of the tonsils.

212 The hospital of St. Mary of Bethlehem, which was a lunatic asylum in the eighteenth century. It was close to Moorfields, London.

most disinterested love, which he now hopes to enjoy in a more elevated character.

LYDIA [*sullenly*] So!—there will be no elopement after all!

SIR ANTHONY Upon my soul, Jack, thou art a very impudent fellow![213] to do you justice, I think I never saw a piece of more consummate assurance!

ABSOLUTE O, you flatter me, sir—you compliment—'tis my *modesty* you know, sir—my *modesty* that has stood in my way.

SIR ANTHONY Well, I am glad you are not the dull, insensible varlet you pretended to be, however!—I'm glad you have made a fool of your father, you dog—I am.——So this was your *penitence,* your *duty,* and *obedience!*—I thought it was d——n'd sudden!—You *never heard their names before,* not you!—*What!* The *Languishes* of Worcestershire, hey?—*if you could please me in the affair, 'twas all you desired!*—Ah! you dissembling villain!—What!—[*pointing to* LYDIA.] she squints, don't she?—a little red-haired girl!—hey? —Why, you hypocritical young rascal—I wonder you a'n't ashamed to hold up your head!

ABSOLUTE 'Tis with difficulty, sir—I *am* confused—very much confused, as you must perceive.

MRS. MALAPROP O Lud! Sir Anthony!—a new light breaks in upon me!—hey!—how! what! Captain, did *you* write the letters then?—What!—am I to thank *you* for the elegant compilation[214] of "*an old weather-beaten she-dragon*"—hey?—O mercy! was it *you* that reflected on my parts of speech?

ABSOLUTE Dear sir! my modesty will be overpowered at last, if you don't assist me.—I shall certainly not be able to stand it!

SIR ANTHONY Come, come, Mrs. Malaprop, we must forget and forgive—Odds life! matters have taken so clever[215] a turn all

of a sudden, that I could find in my heart, to be so good-humoured! and so gallant! —hey! Mrs. Malaprop!

MRS. MALAPROP Well, Sir Anthony, since *you* desire it, we will not anticipate[216] the past;—so mind young people—our retrospection[217] will now be all to the future.

SIR ANTHONY Come, we must leave them together; Mrs. Malaprop, they long to fly into each other's arms, I warrant! [*Aside.*] —Jack—isn't the cheek as I said, hey?— and the eye, you rogue!—and the lip— hey?—Come, Mrs. Malaprop, we'll not disturb their tenderness—theirs is the time of life for happiness!——"*Youth's the season made for joy*—[*sings*]—hey! Odds life! I'm in such spirits,—I don't know what I couldn't do!—Permit me, ma'am—[*Gives his hand to* MRS. MALAPROP.] [*Sings.*] Tol-de-rol!—gad, I should like a little fooling myself—Tol-de rol! de-rol!

Exit singing, and handing MRS. MALAPROP [LYDIA *sits sullenly in her chair*].

ABSOLUTE [*aside*] So much thought bodes me no good.—[*Aloud.*] So grave, Lydia!

LYDIA Sir!

ABSOLUTE [*aside*] So!—egad! I thought as much!—That d——n'd monosyllable has froze me!—[*Aloud.*] What, Lydia, now that we are as happy in our friends' consent, as in our mutual vows——

LYDIA [*peevishly*] *Friends' consent,* indeed!

ABSOLUTE Come, come, we must lay aside some of our romance—a little *wealth* and *comfort* may be endured after all. And for your fortune, the lawyers shall make such settlements as——

LYDIA *Lawyers!*—I *hate* lawyers!

ABSOLUTE Nay then, we will not wait for their lingering forms, but instantly procure the licence, and——

LYDIA The *licence!*—I *hate* licence!

213 Cf. Lord Foppington in Vanbrugh's *The Relapse,* IV. vi: "Strike me dumb, Tam, thou art a very impudent fellow." 214 Appellation. 215 Neat.

216 Exacerbate. 217 Introspection. The line is laughable as it stands in that she says that they will foresee the past and recall the future, a hope that has all the qualities of an Irish "bull."

ABSOLUTE   O my love! be not so unkind!—
thus let me entreat——   [Kneeling.]
LYDIA   Pshaw!—what signifies kneeling,
when you know I *must have* you?
ABSOLUTE   [*rising*] Nay, madam, there
shall be no constraint upon your inclinations, I promise you.—If I have lost your
heart,—I resign the rest.—[*Aside*.] 'Gad, I
must try what a little *spirit* will do.
LYDIA   [*rising*]   Then, sir, let me tell you,
the interest you had there was acquired
by a mean, unmanly imposition, and deserves the punishment of fraud.—What,
you have been treating *me* like a *child*!—
humouring my romance! and laughing, I
suppose, at your success!
ABSOLUTE   You wrong me, Lydia, you
wrong me.—Only hear——
LYDIA   So, while *I* fondly imagined we
were deceiving my relations, and flattered
myself that I should outwit and incense
them all—behold! my hopes are to be
crushed at once, by my aunt's consent and
approbation—and *I* am myself the only
dupe at last! [*Walking about in heat.*]—
But here, sir, here is the picture—*Beverley's* picture! [*taking a miniature from her
bosom*] which I have worn, night and day,
in spite of threats and entreaties!—There,
sir [*flings it to him*]—and be assured I
throw the original from my heart as
easily.
ABSOLUTE   Nay, nay, ma'am, we will not
differ as to that.—Here [*taking out a picture*], here is Miss Lydia Languish.—
What a difference!—aye, *there* is the
heav'nly assenting smile that first gave
soul and spirit to my hopes!—those are
the lips which sealed a vow, as yet scarce
dry in Cupid's calendar!—and there, the
half resentful blush that *would* have
checked the ardour of my thanks.—Well,
all that's past!—all over indeed!—There,
madam—in *beauty*, that copy is not equal
to you, but in my mind its merit over the
original, in being still the same, is such—
that—I cannot find in my heart to part
with it.   [*Puts it up again.*]
LYDIA   [*softening*]   'Tis *your own* doing, sir
—I, I, I suppose you are perfectly satisfied.

ABSOLUTE   O, most certainly—sure now
this is much better than being in love!—
ha! ha! ha!—there's some spirit in *this*!—
What signifies breaking some scores of
solemn promises, all that's of no consequence, you know.—To be sure people
will say, that Miss didn't know her own
mind—but never mind that:—or perhaps
they may be ill-natured enough to hint,
that the gentleman grew tired of the lady
and forsook her—but don't let that fret
you.
LYDIA   There's no bearing his insolence.
[*Bursts into tears.*]

   Enter MRS. MALAPROP *and* SIR ANTHONY.

MRS. MALAPROP   [*entering*]   Come, we must
interrupt your billing and cooing for a
while.
LYDIA   This is worse than your treachery
and deceit, you base ingrate!   [*Sobbing.*]
SIR ANTHONY   What the devil's the matter
now!—Z——ds! Mrs. Malaprop, this is
the *oddest billing* and *cooing* I ever
heard!—but what the deuce is the meaning of it?—I'm quite astonished!
ABSOLUTE   Ask the lady, sir.
MRS. MALAPROP   O mercy!—I'm quite
analysed,[218] for my part!—why, Lydia,
what is the reason of this?
LYDIA   Ask the gentleman, ma'am.
SIR ANTHONY   Z——ds! I shall be in a
frenzy!—why, Jack, you are not come out
to be any one else, are you?
MRS. MALAPROP   Aye, sir, there's no more
trick, is there?—you are not like Cer-
berus,[219] *three* gentlemen at once, are you?
ABSOLUTE   You'll not let me speak—I say
the lady can account for this much better
than I can.
LYDIA   Ma'am, you once commanded me
never to think of Beverley again—there is
the man—I now obey you:—for, from
this moment, I renounce him for ever.

   Exit LYDIA.

MRS. MALAPROP   O mercy! and miracles!
what a turn here is!—why sure, Captain,

218 Paralysed. 219 Pluto's three-headed dog, who
guarded the entrance to Hades.

you haven't behaved disrespectfully to my niece?

SIR ANTHONY Ha! ha! ha!—ha! ha! ha!—now I see it—ha! ha! ha!—now I see it—you have been too lively, Jack.

ABSOLUTE Nay, sir, upon my word——

SIR ANTHONY Come, no lying, Jack—I'm sure 'twas so.

MRS. MALAPROP O Lud! Sir Anthony!—O fie, Captain!

ABSOLUTE Upon my soul, ma'am——

SIR ANTHONY Come, no excuses, Jack;—why, your father, you rogue, was so before you:—the blood of the Absolutes was always impatient.—Ha! ha! ha! poor little Lydia!—why, you've frightened her, you dog, you have.

ABSOLUTE By all that's good, sir—

SIR ANTHONY Z——ds! say no more, I tell you.—Mrs. Malaprop shall make your peace.—You must make his peace, Mrs. Malaprop;—you must tell her 'tis Jack's way—tell her 'tis all our ways—it runs in the blood of our family!—Come, away, Jack—ha! ha! ha! Mrs. Malaprop—a young villain!   [*Pushes him out.*]

MRS. MALAPROP O! Sir Anthony!—O fie, Captain!

Exeunt severally.

SCENE THREE *The North Parade.*

Enter SIR LUCIUS O'TRIGGER.

SIR LUCIUS I wonder where this Capt. Absolute hides himself.—Upon my conscience!—these officers are always in one's way in love affairs:—I remember I might have married Lady Dorothy Carmine, if it had not been for a little rogue of a major, who ran away with her before she could get a sight of me!—And I wonder too what it is the ladies can see in them to be so fond of them—unless it be a touch of the old serpent[220] in 'em, that makes the little creatures be caught, like vipers[221] with a bit of red cloth.[222]—Hah!—isn't this the Captain coming?—faith it is!—There is a probability of succeeding about that fellow, that is mighty provoking!—Who the devil is he talking to? [*Steps aside.*]

Enter CAPTAIN ABSOLUTE.

ABSOLUTE To what fine purpose I have been plotting! a noble reward for all my schemes, upon my soul!—A little gypsy![223]—I did not think her romance could have made her so d—n'd absurd either—'Sdeath, I never was in a worse humour in my life!—I could cut my own throat, or any other person's, with the greatest pleasure in the world!

SIR LUCIUS Oh, faith! I'm in the luck of it—I never could have found him in a sweeter temper for my purpose—to be sure I'm just come in the nick! now to enter into conversation with him, and so quarrel genteelly.[224] [SIR LUCIUS *goes up to* ABSOLUTE.]——With regard to that matter, Captain, I must beg leave to differ in opinion with you.

ABSOLUTE Upon my word then, you must be a very subtle disputant:—because, sir, I happened just then to be giving no opinion at all.

SIR LUCIUS That's no reason.—For give me leave to tell you, a man may *think* an untruth as well as *speak* one.

ABSOLUTE Very true, sir, but if a man never utters his thoughts, I should think they might stand a chance of escaping controversy.

SIR LUCIUS Then, sir, you differ in opinion with me, which amounts to the same thing.

ABSOLUTE Hark'ee, Sir Lucius,—if I had not before known you to be a gentleman,

220 The tempter in the Garden of Eden: see Genesis iii.

221 Vipers waste their venom on the cloth, and can then be picked up without danger. 222 The military uniform, "redcoat." 223 Cheat. 224 In a gentlemanly way.

upon my soul, I should not have discovered it at this interview:—for what you can drive at, unless you mean to quarrel with me, I cannot conceive!

SIR LUCIUS   I humbly thank you, sir, for the quickness of your apprehension [*Bowing.*]—You have named the very thing I would be at.

ABSOLUTE   Very well, sir—I shall certainly not baulk your inclinations;—but I should be glad you would please to explain your motives.

SIR LUCIUS   Pray, sir, be easy—the quarrel is a very pretty quarrel as it stands—we should only spoil it, by trying to explain it.—However, your memory is very short —or you could not have forgot an affront you passed on me within this week.—So no more, but name your time and place.

ABSOLUTE   Well, sir, since you are so bent on it, the sooner the better;—let it be this evening—here, by the Spring-Gardens.[225] —We shall scarcely be interrupted.

SIR LUCIUS   Faith! that same interruption in affairs of this nature, shows very great ill-breeding.—I don't know what's the reason, but in England, if a thing of this kind gets wind, people make such a pother,[226] that a gentleman can never fight in peace and quietness.—However, if it's the same to you, Captain, I should take it as a particular kindness, if you'd let us meet in King's-Mead-Fields,[227] as a little business will call me there about six o'clock, and I may dispatch both matters at once.

ABSOLUTE   'Tis the same to me exactly.— A little after six, then, we will discuss this matter more seriously.

SIR LUCIUS   If you please, sir, there will be very pretty small-sword[228] light, tho' it won't do for a long shot.—So that matter's settled! and my mind's at ease!

225 A summer rendezvous for public breakfasts, teas, concerts, and fireworks. It lay on the Bathwick side of the Pulteney Bridge. 226 Commotion. 227 Sheridan himself had lived in Kingsmead Street. Open fields lay beyond it. 228 A light sword or rapier for thrusting only.

Exit SIR LUCIUS.

Enter FAULKLAND, *meeting* ABSOLUTE.

ABSOLUTE   Well met.—I was going to look for you.—O, Faulkland! all the dæmons of spite and disappointment have conspired against me! I'm so vexed, that if I had not the prospect of a resource in being knocked o' the head by and by, I should scarce have spirits to tell you the cause.

FAULKLAND   What can you mean?—Has Lydia changed her mind?—I should have thought her duty and inclination would now have pointed to the same object.

ABSOLUTE   Aye, just as the eyes do of a person who squints:—when her love-eye was fixed on me—t'other—her eye of duty, was finely obliqued:—but when duty bid her point that the same way— off t'other turned on a swivel, and secured its retreat with a frown!

FAULKLAND   But what's the resource you——

ABSOLUTE   O, to wind up the whole, a good-natured Irishman here has—[*mimicking* SIR LUCIUS]—begged leave to have the pleasure of cutting my throat—and I mean to indulge him—that's all.

FAULKLAND   Prithee, be serious.

ABSOLUTE   'Tis fact, upon my soul.—Sir Lucius O'Trigger—you know him by sight—for some affront, which I am sure I never intended, has obliged me to meet him this evening at six o'clock:—'tis on that account I wished to see you—you must go with me.

FAULKLAND   Nay, there must be some mistake, sure.—Sir Lucius shall explain himself—and I dare say matters may be accommodated:—but this evening did you say?—I wish it had been any other time.

ABSOLUTE   Why?—there will be light enough:—there will (as Sir Lucius says) "be very pretty small-sword light, though it won't do for a long shot."—Confound his long shots!

FAULKLAND   But I am myself a good deal ruffled, by a difference I have had with Julia—my vile tormenting temper has made me treat her so cruelly, that I shall not be myself till we are reconciled.

ABSOLUTE By heav'ns, Faulkland, you don't deserve her.

Enter SERVANT, *gives* FAULKLAND *a letter.*

FAULKLAND O Jack! this is from Julia.—I dread to open it.—I fear it may be to take a last leave—perhaps to bid me return her letters—and restore——O! how I suffer for my folly!

ABSOLUTE Here—let me see. [*Takes the letter and opens it.*] Aye, a final sentence indeed!—'tis all over with you, faith!

FAULKLAND Nay, Jack—don't keep me in suspense.

ABSOLUTE Hear then.—"*As I am convinced that my dear Faulkland's own reflections have already upbraided him for his last unkindness to me, I will not add a word on the subject.—I wish to speak with you as soon as possible.—Yours ever and truly, Julia.*"—There's stubbornness and resentment for you! [*Gives him the letter.*] Why, man, you don't seem one whit the happier at this.

FAULKLAND O, yes, I am—but—but——

ABSOLUTE Confound your *buts.*—You never hear anything that would make another man bless himself, but you immediately d——n it with a *but.*

FAULKLAND Now, Jack, as you are my friend, own honestly—don't you think there is something forward—something indelicate in this haste to forgive?—Women should never sue for reconciliation:—that should always come from us.—They should retain their coldness till *wooed* to kindness—and their *pardon,* like their *love,* should "not unsought be won."[229]

ABSOLUTE I have not patience to listen to you:—thou'rt incorrigible!—so say no more on the subject.—I must go to settle a few matters—let me see you before six—remember—at my lodgings.—A poor in-

dustrious devil like me, who have toiled, and drudged, and plotted to gain my ends, and am at last disappointed by other people's folly—may in pity be allowed to swear and grumble a little;—but a captious sceptic in love,—a slave to fretfulness and whim—who has no difficulties but of his own creating—is a subject more fit for ridicule than compassion!

Exit ABSOLUTE.

FAULKLAND I feel his reproaches!—yet I would not change this too exquisite nicety for the gross content with which *he* tramples on the thorns of love.—His engaging me in this duel, has started an idea in my head, which I will instantly pursue.—I'll use it as the touchstone[230] of Julia's sincerity and disinterestedness—if her love prove pure and sterling[231] ore—my name will rest on it with honour!—and once I've stamped it there, I lay aside my doubts for ever:—but if the dross of selfishness, the allay[232] of pride predominate—'twill be best to leave her as a toy for some less cautious fool to sigh for.

Exit FAULKLAND.

Act Five

SCENE ONE JULIA's *Dressing-room.*

JULIA *sola.*

JULIA How this message has alarmed me! What dreadful accident can he mean? why such charge to be alone?—O Faulkland!—how many unhappy moments!—how many tears have you cost me!

Enter FAULKLAND.

JULIA What means this?—why this caution, Faulkland?

FAULKLAND Alas! Julia, I am come to take a long farewell.

JULIA Heav'ns! what do you mean?

FAULKLAND You see before you a wretch,

---

229 From *Paradise Lost,* viii. 502–503:
Her virtue, and the conscience of her worth,
That would be wooed, and not unsought be won.

230 A black stone used to test the purity of gold or silver, but the word is also used of any criterion. 231 Of true worth. 232 Alloy.

whose life is forfeited.—Nay, start not!—the infirmity of my temper has drawn all this misery on me.—I left you fretful and passionate—an untoward accident drew me into a quarrel—the event is, that I must fly this kingdom instantly.—O Julia, had I been so fortunate as to have called you mine entirely, before this mischance had fallen on me, I should not so deeply dread my banishment!—

JULIA   My soul is oppressed with sorrow at the nature of your misfortune: had these adverse circumstances arisen from a less fatal cause, I should have felt strong comfort in the thought that I could now chase from your bosom every doubt of the warm sincerity of my love.—My heart has long known no other guardian—I now entrust my person to your honour—we will fly together.—When safe from pursuit, my father's will may be fulfilled—and I receive a legal claim to be the partner of your sorrows, and tenderest comforter. Then on the bosom of your wedded Julia, you may lull your keen regret to slumbering; while virtuous love, with a cherub's hand, shall smooth the brow of upbraiding thought, and pluck the thorn from compunction.

FAULKLAND   O Julia! I am bankrupt in gratitude! but the time is so pressing, it calls on you for so hasty a resolution. Would you not wish some hours to weigh the advantages you forego, and what little compensation poor Faulkland can make you beside his solitary love?

JULIA   I ask not a moment.—No, Faulkland, I have loved you for yourself: and if I now, more than ever, prize the solemn engagement which so long has pledged us to each other, it is because it leaves no room for hard aspersions on my fame, and puts the seal of duty to an act of love.——But let us not linger—Perhaps this delay——

FAULKLAND   'Twill be better I should not venture out again till dark.—Yet am I grieved to think what numberless distresses will press heavy on your gentle disposition!

JULIA   Perhaps your fortune may be forfeited by this unhappy act.—I know not whether 'tis so—but sure that alone can never make us unhappy.—The little I have will be sufficient to support us; and exile never should be splendid.

FAULKLAND   Aye, but in such an abject state of life, my wounded pride perhaps may increase the natural fretfulness of my temper, till I become a rude, morose companion, beyond your patience to endure. Perhaps the recollection of a deed my conscience cannot justify, may haunt me in such gloomy and unsocial fits, that I shall hate the tenderness that would relieve me, break from your arms, and quarrel with your fondness!

JULIA   If your thoughts should assume so unhappy a bent, you will the more want some mild and affectionate spirit to watch over and console you:—one who, by bearing *your* infirmities with gentleness and resignation, may teach you *so* to bear the evils of your fortune.

FAULKLAND   Julia, I have proved you to the quick! and with this useless device I throw away all my doubts. How shall I plead to be forgiven this last unworthy effect of my restless, unsatisfied disposition?

JULIA   Has no such disaster happened as you related?

FAULKLAND   I am ashamed to own that it was all pretended; yet in pity, Julia, do not kill me with resenting a fault which never can be repeated: but sealing, this once, my pardon, let me to-morrow, in the face of heaven, receive my future guide and monitress, and expiate my past folly, by years of tender adoration.

JULIA   Hold, Faulkland!—that you are free from a crime which I before feared to name, heaven knows how sincerely I rejoice!—These are tears of thankfulness for that! But that your cruel doubts should have urged you to an imposition that has wrung my heart, gives me now a pang, more keen than I can express!

FAULKLAND   By heav'ns! Julia——

JULIA   Yet hear me.—My father loved you,

Faulkland! and you preserved the life that tender parent gave me; in his presence I pledged my hand—joyfully pledged it—where before I had given my heart. When, soon after, I lost that parent, it seemed to me that Providence had, in Faulkland, shown me whither to transfer, without a pause, my grateful duty, as well as my affection: hence I have been content to bear from you what pride and delicacy would have forbid[233] me from another.—I will not upbraid you, by repeating how you have trifled with my sincerity.——

FAULKLAND I confess it all! yet hear——

JULIA After such a year of trial[234]—I might have flattered myself that I should not have been insulted with a new probation of my sincerity, as cruel as unnecessary! I now see it is not in your nature to be content, or confident in love. With this conviction—I never will be yours. While I had hopes that my persevering attention, and unreproaching kindness might in time reform your temper, I should have been happy to have gained a dearer influence over you; but I will not furnish you with a licensed power to keep alive an incorrigible fault, at the expense of one who never would contend with you.

FAULKLAND Nay, but Julia, by my soul and honour, if after this——

JULIA But one word more.—As my faith has once been given to you, I never will barter it with another.—I shall pray for your happiness with the truest sincerity; and the dearest blessing I can ask of heaven to send you, will be to charm you from that unhappy temper, which alone has prevented the performance of our solemn engagement.—All I request of *you* is, that you will yourself reflect upon this infirmity, and when you number up the many true delights it has deprived you of —let it not be your *least* regret, that it lost you the love of one—who would have followed you in beggary through the world!

FAULKLAND She's gone!—for ever!—There was an awful resolution in her manner, that riveted me to my place.—O fool!—dolt!—barbarian!—Curst as I am, with more imperfections than my fellow-wretches, kind Fortune sent a heaven-gifted cherub to my aid, and, like a ruffian, I have driven her from my side!—I must now haste to my appointment.—Well my mind is tuned for such a scene.—I shall wish only to become a principal in it, and reverse the tale my cursed folly put me upon forging here.—O love!—tormentor!—fiend! whose influence, like the moon's, acting on men of dull souls, makes idiots of them, but meeting subtler spirits, betrays their course, and urges sensibility to madness![235]

Exit.

Enter MAID *and* LYDIA.

MAID My mistress, ma'am, I know, was here just now—perhaps she is only in the next room.   *Exit* MAID.

LYDIA Heigh-ho!—Though he has used me so, this fellow runs strangely in my head. I believe one lecture from my grave cousin will make me recall him.

Enter JULIA.

LYDIA O Julia, I am come to you with such an appetite for consolation.—Lud! Child, what's the matter with you?—You have been crying!—I'll be hanged, if that Faulkland has not been tormenting you!

JULIA You mistake the cause of my uneasiness!—Something *has* flurried me a little.—Nothing that you can guess at.—[*Aside.*] I would not accuse Faulkland to a sister!

LYDIA Ah! whatever vexations you may have, I can assure you mine surpass them.—You know who Beverley proves to be?

JULIA I will now own to you, Lydia, that

233 Forbidden. 234 Trial.

235 "Lunatic" is derived from the Latin "luna," the moon. The idea is similar to that in *Midsummer Night's Dream*, V. i:
The lunatic, the lover, and the poet,
Are of imagination all compact.

Mr. Faulkland had before informed me of the whole affair. Had young Absolute been the person you took him for, I should not have accepted your confidence on the subject, without a serious endeavour to counteract your caprice.

LYDIA So, then, I see I have been deceived by everyone!—but I don't care—I'll never have him.

JULIA Nay, Lydia——

LYDIA Why, is it not provoking? when I thought we were coming to the prettiest distress imaginable, to find myself made a mere Smithfield bargain²³⁶ of at last.—There had I projected one of the most sentimental elopements!—so becoming a disguise!—so amiable a ladder of ropes!—Conscious²³⁷ moon—four horses—Scotch parson²³⁸—with such surprise to Mrs. Malaprop—and such paragraphs in the newspapers!—O, I shall die with disappointment!

JULIA I don't wonder at it!

LYDIA Now—sad reverse!—what have I to expect, but, after a deal of flimsy²³⁹ preparation, with a bishop's licence,²⁴⁰ and my aunt's blessing, to go simpering up to the altar; or perhaps be cried three times in a country-church, and have an unmannerly fat clerk ask the consent of every butcher in the parish to join John Absolute and Lydia Languish, *spinster!* O, that I should live to hear myself called spinster!

JULIA Melancholy, indeed!

LYDIA How mortifying, to remember the dear delicious shifts I used to be put to, to gain half a minute's conversation with this fellow!—How often have I stole forth, in the coldest night in January, and found him in the garden, stuck like a dripping statue!—There would he kneel to me in the snow, and sneeze, and cough so pathetically! he shivering with cold, and I with apprehension! and while the freezing blast numbed our joints, how warmly would he press me to pity his flame, and glow with mutual ardour!—Ah, Julia, that was something like being in love.

JULIA If I were in spirits, Lydia, I should chide you only by laughing heartily at you: but it suits more the situation of my mind, at present, earnestly to entreat you, not to let a man, who loves you with sincerity, suffer that unhappiness from your caprice, which I know too well caprice can inflict.

LYDIA O Lud!²⁴¹ what has brought my aunt here?

Enter MRS. MALAPROP, FAG, *and* DAVID.

MRS. MALAPROP So! so! here's fine work!—here's fine suicide, paracide,²⁴² and simulation²⁴³ going on in the fields! and Sir Anthony not to be found to prevent the antistrophe!²⁴⁴

JULIA For heaven's sake, madam, what's the meaning of this?

MRS. MALAPROP That gentleman can tell you—'twas he enveloped²⁴⁵ the affair to me.

LYDIA [*to* FAG] Do, sir, will you, inform us.

FAG Ma'am, I should hold myself very deficient in every requisite that forms the man of breeding, if I delayed a moment to give all the information in my power to a lady so deeply interested in the affair as you are.

LYDIA But quick! quick, sir!

FAG True, ma'am, as you say, one should be quick in divulging matters of this nature; for should we be tedious, perhaps while we are flourishing²⁴⁶ on the subject, two or three lives may be lost!

236 A marriage of interest in which money is the main consideration (Oxford English Dictionary). Smithfield was a London cattle-market. 237 Sympathetic, a meaning close to the Latin origin of the word. 238 Since minors could not be married in England without the consent of parents or guardians, impetuous couples eloped to Scotland where they merely had to signify their wish to marry before two witnesses. 239 Paltry. 240 Permission to marry in the church of a parish in which one of the parties resides. The alternative method—marriage by banns—is then described by Lydia.

241 A corruption of "Lord!" 242 Parricide, the murder of one's father or near relation. 243 Dissimulation. 244 Catastrophe. 245 Developed. 246 Speaking in a flowery way.

LYDIA O patience!—Do, ma'am, for heaven's sake! tell us what is the matter!

MRS. MALAPROP Why, murder's the matter! slaughter's the matter! killing's the matter!—but he can tell you the perpendiculars.[247]

LYDIA Then, prithee, sir, be brief.

FAG Why then, ma'am—as to murder—I cannot take upon me to say—and as to slaughter, or man-slaughter, that will be as the jury finds it.

LYDIA But who, sir—who are engaged in this?

FAG Faith, ma'am, one is a young gentleman whom I should be very sorry anything was to happen to—a very pretty behaved gentleman!—We have lived much together, and always on terms.

LYDIA But who is this? who! who! who!

FAG My master, ma'am—my master—I speak of my master.

LYDIA Heavens! What, Captain Absolute!

MRS. MALAPROP O, to be sure, you are frightened now!

JULIA But who are with him, sir?

FAG As to the rest, ma'am, this gentleman can inform you better than I.

JULIA [*to* DAVID] Do speak, friend.

DAVID Look'ee, my lady—by the Mass! there's mischief going on.—Folks don't use to meet for amusement with fire-arms, fire-locks, fire-engines, fire-screens, fire-office,[248] and the devil knows what other crackers beside!—This, my lady, I say, has an angry favour.[249]

JULIA But who is there beside Captain Absolute, friend?

DAVID My poor master—under favour, for mentioning him first.—You know me, my lady—I am David—and my master of course is, or *was,* Squire Acres.—Then comes Squire Faulkland.

JULIA Do, ma'am, let us instantly endeavour to prevent mischief.

MRS. MALAPROP O fie—it would be very inelegant in us:—we should only participate[250] things.

DAVID Ah! do, Mrs. Aunt, save a few lives. —They are desperately given, believe me. —Above all, there is that bloodthirsty Philistine,[251] Sir Lucius O'Trigger.

MRS. MALAPROP Sir Lucius O'Trigger!— O mercy! have they drawn poor little dear Sir Lucius into the scrape?—why, how you stand, girl! you have no more feeling than one of the Derbyshire putrefactions![252]

LYDIA What are we to do, madam?

MRS. MALAPROP Why, fly with the utmost felicity[253] to be sure, to prevent mischief— here, friend—you can show us the place?

FAG If you please, ma'am, I will conduct you.—David, do you look for Sir Anthony.   *Exit* DAVID.

MRS. MALAPROP Come, girls!—this gentleman will exhort[254] us.—Come, sir, you're our envoy[255]—lead the way, and we'll precede.[256]

FAG Not a step before the ladies for the world!

MRS. MALAPROP You're sure you know the spot?

FAG I think I can find it, ma'am; and one good thing is we shall hear the report of the pistols as we draw near, so we can't well miss them: never fear, ma'am, never fear.

Exit, he talking.

SCENE TWO *South Parade.*

Enter ABSOLUTE, *putting his sword under his great-coat.*

ABSOLUTE A sword seen in the streets of Bath[257] would raise as great an alarm as a

---

247 Particulars. 248 David is so alarmed that he reels off the names of everything connected with "fire" rather than with "fire-arms." The "fire-office" was the office of an insurance company dealing with fires. 249 Inflamed look, as of a wound.

250 Precipitate. 251 A harassing enemy. 252 Petrifactions. The "wonders of the Peak" were often described, and R. Brookes's *General Gazetteer* (10th ed., 1797) says of Pool's Hole, near Buxton, that it "contains many stalactitious concretions, and several curious representations both of art and nature, produced by the petrifying water continually dropping from the rock." 253 Velocity. 254 Escort. 255 Convoy. 256 Proceed. 257 Beau Nash had had both parties arrested whenever he had heard of a challenge to a duel at Bath.

mad-dog. How provoking this is in Faulk-land!—never punctual! I shall be obliged to go without him at last.—O, the devil! here's Sir Anthony!——how shall I escape him?

[*Muffles up his face, and takes a circle to go off.*]

Enter SIR ANTHONY.

SIR ANTHONY How one may be deceived at a little distance! Only that I see he don't know me, I could have sworn that was Jack!—Hey!—'Gad's life; it is.—Why, Jack—what are you afraid of?—hey!—sure I'm right.—Why, Jack—Jack Absolute!   [*Goes up to him.*]

ABSOLUTE Really, sir, you have the advantage of me:—I don't remember ever to have had the honour——my name is Saunderson, at your service.

SIR ANTHONY Sir, I beg your pardon—I took you—hey!—hey!—Why, z——ds! it is——Stay——[*Looks up to his face.*] So, so—your humble servant, Mr. Saunderson!—Why, you scoundrel, what tricks are you after now?

ABSOLUTE O! a joke, sir, a joke!—I came here on purpose to look for you, sir.

SIR ANTHONY You did! well, I am glad you were so lucky:—but what are you muffled up so for?—what's this for?—hey?

ABSOLUTE 'Tis cool, sir; isn't it?—rather chilly somehow:—but I shall be late—I have a particular engagement.

SIR ANTHONY Stay.—Why, I thought you were looking for me?—Pray, Jack, where is't you are going?

ABSOLUTE Going, sir!

SIR ANTHONY Aye—where are you going?

ABSOLUTE Where am I going?

SIR ANTHONY You unmannerly puppy!

ABSOLUTE I was going, sir, to—to—to—to Lydia—sir, to Lydia—to make matters up if I could;—and I was looking for you, sir, to—to——

SIR ANTHONY To go with you, I suppose.—Well, come along!

ABSOLUTE O! z——ds! no, sir, not for the world!—I wished to meet with you, sir,—to—to—to——You find it cool, I'm sure, sir—you'd better not stay out.

SIR ANTHONY Cool!—not at all.—Well, Jack—and what will you say to Lydia?

ABSOLUTE O, sir, beg her pardon, humour her—promise and vow:—but I detain you, sir—consider the cold air on your gout.

SIR ANTHONY O, not at all!—not at all!—I'm in no hurry.—Ah! Jack, you youngsters, when once you are wounded here—[*Putting his hand to* ABSOLUTE'*s breast.*] Hey! what the deuce have you got here?

ABSOLUTE Nothing, sir—nothing.

SIR ANTHONY What's this?—here's something d—d hard!

ABSOLUTE O, trinkets, sir! trinkets—a bauble for Lydia!

SIR ANTHONY Nay, let me see your taste. [*Pulls his coat open, the sword falls.*] Trinkets!—a bauble for Lydia!—z——ds! sirrah, you are not going to cut her throat, are you?

ABSOLUTE Ha! ha! ha!—I thought it would divert you, sir tho' I didn't mean to tell you till afterwards.

SIR ANTHONY You didn't?—Yes, this is a very diverting trinket, truly!

ABSOLUTE Sir, I'll explain to you.—You know, sir, Lydia is romantic—dev'lish romantic, and very absurd of course:—now, sir, I intend, if she refuses to forgive me—to unsheathe this sword—and swear—I'll fall upon its point, and expire at her feet!

SIR ANTHONY Fall upon a fiddle-stick's end!—why, I suppose it is the very thing that would please her.—Get along, you fool.—

ABSOLUTE Well, sir, you shall hear of my success—you shall hear.—'O Lydia!—forgive me, or this pointed steel'—says I.

SIR ANTHONY "O, booby! stab away and welcome"—says she.—Get along!—and d—n your trinkets!

Exit ABSOLUTE.

Enter DAVID *running.*

DAVID Stop him! stop him! Murder! thief! fire!—Stop fire! Stop fire!—O! Sir Anthony—call! call! bid 'm stop! Murder! Fire!

SIR ANTHONY Fire! murder! where?

DAVID Oons! he's out of sight! and I'm out of breath for my part! O, Sir Anthony, why didn't you stop him? why didn't you stop him?

SIR ANTHONY Z——ds! the fellow's mad!— Stop whom? stop Jack?

DAVID Aye, the Captain, Sir!—there's murder and slaughter.——

SIR ANTHONY Murder!

DAVID Aye, please you, Sir Anthony, there's all kinds of murder, all sorts of slaughter to be seen in the fields: there's fighting going on, sir—bloody sword-and-gun fighting!

SIR ANTHONY Who are going to fight, dunce?

DAVID Everybody that I know of, Sir Anthony:—everybody is going to fight, my poor master, Sir Lucius O'Trigger, your son, the Captain——

SIR ANTHONY O, the dog!—I see his tricks. —Do you know the place?

DAVID King's-Mead-Fields.

SIR ANTHONY You know the way?

DAVID Not an inch;—but I'll call the mayor — aldermen — constables — church-wardens—and beadles[258]—we can't be too many to part them.

SIR ANTHONY Come along—give me your shoulder![259] we'll get assistance as we go. —The lying villain!—Well, I shall be in such a frenzy—So—this was the history of his trinkets! I'll bauble him!

Exeunt.

SCENE THREE *King's-Mead-Fields.*

SIR LUCIUS *and* ACRES, *with pistols.*

ACRES By my valour! then, Sir Lucius, forty yards is a good distance.—Odds levels and aims!—I say it is a good distance.

SIR LUCIUS Is it for muskets or small field-

pieces?[260] upon my conscience, Mr. Acres, you must leave those things to me.—Stay now—I'll show you.—[*Measures paces along the stage.*] There now, that is a very pretty distance—a pretty gentleman's distance.

ACRES Z——ds! we might as well fight in a sentry-box!—I tell you, Sir Lucius, the farther he is off, the cooler I shall take my aim.

SIR LUCIUS Faith! then I suppose you would aim at him best of all if he was out of sight!

ACRES No, Sir Lucius—but I should think forty, or eight and thirty yards——

SIR LUCIUS Pho! pho! nonsense! Three or four feet between the mouths of your pistols is as good as a mile.

ACRES Odds bullets, no!—by my valour! there is no merit in killing him so near:— do, my dear Sir Lucius, let me bring him down at a long shot:—a long shot, Sir Lucius, if you love me!

SIR LUCIUS Well—the gentleman's friend and I must settle that.—But tell me now, Mr. Acres, in case of an accident, is there any little will or commission I could execute for you!

ACRES I am much obliged to you, Sir Lucius—but I don't understand——

SIR LUCIUS Why, you may think there's no being shot at without a little risk—and if an unlucky bullet should carry a quietus[261] with it—I say it will be no time then to be bothering you about family matters.

ACRES A quietus!

SIR LUCIUS For instance now—if that should be the case—would you choose to be pickled and sent home?—or would it be the same to you to lie here in the Abbey?[262]—I'm told there is very snug lying in the Abbey.

---

258 A parish official relieving the poor and keeping order in church. 259 Let me lean on you. Sir Anthony has the gout.

260 Movable artillery. 261 "Quietus est" meant, in medieval Latin, "he is quit (of his incumbrances)." Here, the sense is of a final discharge from life, as in Hamlet's "When he himself might his quietus make/With a bare bodkin" (III. i). 262 Beneath the floor of the Abbey Church at Bath. At this time it was nearly paved with memorial slabs.

ACRES   Pickled!—Snug lying in the Abbey! —Odds tremors! Sir Lucius, don't talk so!

SIR LUCIUS   I suppose, Mr. Acres, you never were engaged in an affair of this kind before?

ACRES   No, Sir Lucius, never before.

SIR LUCIUS   Ah! that's a pity!—there's nothing like being used to a thing.—Pray now, how would you receive the gentleman's shot?

ACRES   Odds files![263]—I've practised that—there, Sir Lucius—there [*Puts himself in an attitude.*]——a side-front, hey?—Odd! I'll make myself small enough:—I'll stand edgeways.

SIR LUCIUS   Now—you're quite out—for if you stand so when I take my aim—— [*Levelling at him.*]

ACRES   Z——ds! Sir Lucius—are you sure it is not cocked?

SIR LUCIUS   Never fear.

ACRES   But—but—you don't know—it may go off of its own head![264]

SIR LUCIUS   Pho! be easy.—Well, now if I hit you in the body, my bullet has a double chance—for if it misses a vital part on your right side—'twill be very hard if it don't succeed on the left!

ACRES   A vital part!

SIR LUCIUS   But, there—fix yourself so.— [*Placing him.*] Let him see the broad-side of your full front—there—now a ball or two may pass clean thro' your body, and never do any harm at all.

ACRES   Clean thro' me!—a ball or two clean thro' me!

SIR LUCIUS   Aye—may they—and it is much the genteelest attitude into the bargain.

ACRES   Look'ee! Sir Lucius—I'd just as lieve[265] be shot in an awkward posture as a genteel one—so, by my valour! I will stand edgeways.

SIR LUCIUS   [*looking at his watch*] Sure they don't mean to disappoint us.—Hah! —no, faith—I think I see them coming.

ACRES   Hey!—what!—coming!——

SIR LUCIUS   Aye.—Who are those yonder getting over the stile?

ACRES   There are two of them indeed!—well—let them come—hey, Sir Lucius! we —we—we—we—won't run.—

SIR LUCIUS   Run!

ACRES   No—I say—we *won't* run, by my valour!

SIR LUCIUS   What the devil's the matter with you?

ACRES   Nothing—nothing—my dear friend —my dear Sir Lucius—but—I—I—I don't feel quite so bold, somehow—as I did.

SIR LUCIUS   O fie!—consider your honour.

ACRES   Aye—true—my honour—Do, Sir Lucius, edge in a word or two every now and then about my honour.

SIR LUCIUS   [*looking*] Well, here they're coming.

ACRES   Sir Lucius—if I wa'n't with you, I should almost think I was afraid—if my valour should leave me!—Valour will come and go.

SIR LUCIUS   Then, pray, keep it fast, while you have it.

ACRES   Sir Lucius—I doubt[266] it is going— yes—my valour is certainly going!—it is sneaking off!—I feel it oozing out as it were at the palms of my hands!

SIR LUCIUS   Your honour—your honour.— Here they are.

ACRES   O mercy!—now—that I were safe at *Clod-Hall* or could be shot before I was aware!

Enter FAULKLAND *and* ABSOLUTE.

SIR LUCIUS   Gentlemen, your most obedient—hah!—what Captain Absolute!—So, I suppose, sir, you are come here, just like myself—to do a kind office, first for your friend—then to proceed to business on your own account.

ACRES   What, Jack!—my dear Jack!—my dear friend!

ABSOLUTE   Hark'ee, Bob, *Beverley's* at hand.

SIR LUCIUS   Well Mr. Acres—I don't blame your saluting the gentleman civilly.—So, Mr. Beverley [*to* FAULKLAND], if you'll

---

263 A file was a sword without edges used in fencing. 264 Accord. 265 More usually "lief": gladly.

266 Fear.

choose your weapons, the Captain and I will measure the ground.

FAULKLAND *My* weapons, sir!

ACRES Odds life! Sir Lucius, I'm not going to fight Mr. Faulkland; these are my particular friends.

SIR LUCIUS What, sir, did not you come here to fight Mr. Acres?

FAULKLAND Not, I, upon my word, sir.

SIR LUCIUS Well, now, that's mighty provoking! But I hope, Mr. Faulkland, as there are three of us come on purpose for the game—you won't be so cantankerous as to spoil the party by sitting out.

ABSOLUTE O pray, Faulkland, fight to oblige Sir Lucius.

FAULKLAND Nay, if Mr. Acres is so bent on the matter——

ACRES No, no, Mr. Faulkland—I'll bear my disappointment like a Christian.—Look'ee, Sir Lucius, there's no occasion at all for me to fight; and if it is the same to you, I'd as lieve let it alone.

SIR LUCIUS Observe me, Mr. Acres—I must not be trifled with. You have certainly challenged somebody—and you came here to fight him.—Now, if that gentleman is willing to represent him—I can't see, for my soul, why it isn't just the same thing.

ACRES Why no, Sir Lucius—I tell you, 'tis one Beverley I've challenged—a fellow, you see, that dare not show his face! If *he* were here, I'd make him give up his pretensions directly!—

ABSOLUTE Hold, Bob—let me set you right—there is no such man as *Beverley* in the case.—The person who assumed that name is before you; and as his pretensions are the same in both characters, he is ready to support them in whatever way you please.

SIR LUCIUS Well, this is lucky!—Now you have an opportunity——

ACRES What, quarrel with my dear friend Jack Absolute—not if he were fifty Beverleys! Z——ds! Sir Lucius, you would not have me be so unnatural.

SIR LUCIUS Upon my conscience, Mr. Acres, your valour has *oozed* away with a vengeance!

ACRES Not in the least! Odds backs[267] and abettors! I'll be your second with all my heart—and if you should get a *quietus*, you may command me entirely. I'll get you a *snug lying* in the *Abbey here;* or *pickle* you, and send you over to Blunderbuss-Hall, or anything of the kind with the greatest pleasure.

SIR LUCIUS Pho! pho! you are little better than a coward.

ACRES Mind, gentlemen, he calls me a *coward;* coward was the word, by my valour!

SIR LUCIUS Well, sir?

ACRES Look'ee, Sir Lucius, 'tisn't that I mind the word coward—*coward* may be said in joke. But if you had called me a *poltroon*,[268] odds daggers and balls!——

SIR LUCIUS Well, sir?

ACRES ——I should have thought you a very ill-bred man.

SIR LUCIUS Pho! you are beneath my notice.

ABSOLUTE Nay, Sir Lucius, you can't have a better second than my friend Acres.—He is a most *determined dog*—called in the country, *Fighting Bob.*—He generally *kills a man a week;* don't you, Bob?

ACRES Aye—at home!

SIR LUCIUS Well then, Captain, 'tis we must begin—so come out, my little counsellor[269] [*draws his sword*], and ask the gentleman, whether he will resign the lady, without forcing you to proceed against him.

ABSOLUTE Come on then, sir [*draws*]; since you won't let it be an amicable suit, here's *my reply.*

Enter SIR ANTHONY, DAVID, *and the* WOMEN.

DAVID Knock 'em all down, sweet Sir Anthony, knock down my master in par-

267 Supporters. Cf. Congreve's *The Old Bachelor,* II. 1: "Ah my Hector of Troy, welcome my bully, my back." 268 Completely without spirit or courage. 269 In its Irish sense of "barrister." This is a contemptuous reference to Acres as one fond of disputation rather than fighting.

ticular—and bind his hands over to their good behaviour!

SIR ANTHONY Put up, Jack, put up, or I shall be in a frenzy.—How came you in a duel, sir?

ABSOLUTE Faith, sir, that gentleman can tell you better than I; 'twas he called on me, and you know, sir, I serve his Majesty.[270]

SIR ANTHONY Here's a pretty fellow! I catch him going to cut a man's throat, and he tells me, he serves his Majesty!—Zounds! sirrah, then how durst you draw the King's sword against one of his subjects?

ABSOLUTE Sir, I tell you! That gentleman called me out, without explaining his reasons.

SIR ANTHONY Gad! sir, how came you to call my son out, without explaining your reasons?

SIR LUCIUS Your son, sir, insulted me in a manner which my honour[271] could not brook.

SIR ANTHONY Zounds! Jack, how durst you insult the gentleman in a manner which his honour could not brook?

MRS. MALAPROP Come, come, let's have no honour before ladies—Captain Absolute, come here—How could you intimidate us so?—Here's Lydia has been terrified to death for you.

ABSOLUTE For fear I should be killed, or escape, ma'am?

MRS. MALAPROP Nay, no delusions[272] to the past—Lydia is convinced;—speak, child.

SIR LUCIUS With your leave, ma'am, I must put in a word here—I believe I could interpret the young lady's silence—Now mark——

LYDIA What is it you mean, sir?

SIR LUCIUS Come, come, Delia, we must be serious now—this is no time for trifling.

LYDIA 'Tis true, sir; and your reproof bids me offer this gentleman my hand, and solicit the return of his affections.

ABSOLUTE O! my little angel, say you so? —Sir Lucius—I perceive there must be some mistake here.—With regard to the affront which you affirm I have given you—I can only say, that it could not have been intentional.—And as you must be convinced, that I should not fear to support a real injury—you shall now see that I am not ashamed to atone for an inadvertency.—I ask your pardon.—But for this lady, while honoured with her approbation, I will support my claim against any man whatever.

SIR ANTHONY Well said, Jack and I'll stand by you, my boy.

ACRES Mind, I give up all my claim—I make no pretensions to anything in the world—and if I can't get a wife without fighting for her, by my valour! I'll live a bachelor.

SIR LUCIUS Captain, give me your hand— an affront handsomely acknowledged becomes an obligation—and as for the lady —if she chooses to deny her own handwriting here——

[*Takes out letters.*]

MRS. MALAPROP O, he will dissolve[273] my mystery!—Sir Lucius, perhaps there's some mistake—perhaps, I can illuminate——

SIR LUCIUS Pray, old gentlewoman, don't interfere where you have no business.— Miss Languish, are you my Delia, or not?

LYDIA Indeed, Sir Lucius, I am not.

[LYDIA *and* ABSOLUTE *walk aside.*]

MRS. MALAPROP Sir Lucius O'Trigger—ungrateful as you are—I own the soft impeachment[274]—pardon my blushes, I am Delia.

SIR LUCIUS You Delia!—pho! pho! be easy.[275]

---

270 An army officer could not refuse a challenge. 271 Fighting to satisfy one's sense of honour. 272 Allusions.

273 Solve. 274 Gentle reproach. 275 Don't be sought after. The word is still used in this sense on the Stock Exchange.

MRS. MALAPROP Why, thou barbarous Vandyke[276]—those letters are mine.—When you are more sensible of my benignity—perhaps I may be brought to encourage your addresses.

SIR LUCIUS Mrs. Malaprop, I am extremely sensible of your condescension;[277] and whether you or Lucy have put this trick upon me, I am equally beholden to you.—And to show you I'm not ungrateful, Captain Absolute! since you have taken that lady from me, I'll give you my Delia into the bargain.

ABSOLUTE I am much obliged to you, Sir Lucius; but here's our friend, Fighting Bob, unprovided for.

SIR LUCIUS Hah! little Valour—here, will you make your fortune?

ACRES Odds wrinkles! No.—But give me your hand, Sir Lucius; forget and forgive; but if ever I give you a chance of *pickling* me again, say Bob Acres is a dunce, that's all.

SIR ANTHONY Come, Mrs. Malaprop, don't be cast down—you are in your bloom yet.

MRS. MALAPROP O Sir Anthony!—men are all barbarians——

[*All retire but* JULIA *and* FAULKLAND.]

JULIA [*aside*] He seems dejected and unhappy—not sullen.—There was some foundation, however, for the tale he told me.—O woman! how true should be your judgment, when your resolution is so weak!

FAULKLAND Julia—how can I sue for what I so little deserve? I dare not presume—yet Hope is the child of Penitence.

JULIA Oh! Faulkland, you have not been more faulty in your unkind treatment of me, than I am now in wanting inclination to resent it. As my heart honestly bids me place my weakness to the account of love, I should be ungenerous not to admit the same plea for yours.

FAULKLAND Now I shall be blest indeed!

[SIR ANTHONY *comes forward.*]

SIR ANTHONY What's going on here?—So you have been quarrelling too, I warrant.—Come, Julia, I never interfered before; but let me have a hand in the matter at last.—All the faults I have ever seen in my friend Faulkland, seemed to proceed from what he calls the *delicacy* and *warmth* of his affection for you.—There, marry him directly, Julia, you'll find he'll mend surprisingly!

[*The rest come forward.*]

SIR LUCIUS Come now, I hope there is no dissatisfied person, but what is content: for as I have been disappointed myself, it will be very hard if I have not the satisfaction of seeing other people succeed better——

ACRES You are right, Sir Lucius.—So, Jack, I wish you joy—Mr. Faulkland the same.—Ladies,—come now, to show you I'm neither vexed nor angry, odds tabors and pipes! I'll order the fiddles in half an hour, to the New Rooms[278]—and I insist on your all meeting me there.

SIR ANTHONY Gad! sir, I like your spirit; and at night we single[279] lads will drink a health to the young couples, and a husband to Mrs. Malaprop.

FAULKLAND Our partners are stolen from us, Jack—I hope to be congratulated by each other—*yours* for having checked in time, the errors of an ill-directed imagination, which might have betrayed an innocent heart; and *mine,* for having, by her gentleness and candour, reformed the unhappy temper of one who by it made wretched whom he loved most, and tortured the heart he ought to have adored.

ABSOLUTE Well, Jack, we have both tasted the bitters, as well as the sweets, of love—with this difference only, that *you* always

---

276 Vandal: the tribe of barbarians that plundered Rome in the fifth century. 277 Kindliness towards an inferior, but used here ironically.

278 See p. 362, n. 197. 279 Sir Anthony is a widower. The first edition of the play contains the line, "Sir Anthony, your wife, Lady Absolute, was fond of books" (II. i). Although Sheridan eliminated this from the third edition, I don't think he intended IV. ii. p. 365 to suggest that Jack Absolute was an illegitimate child.

prepared the bitter cup for yourself, while *I*——

LYDIA Was always obliged to *me* for it, hey! Mr. Modesty?——But come, no more of that—our happiness is now as unallayed as general.

JULIA Then let us study to preserve it so; and while Hope pictures to us a flattering scene of future bliss, let us deny its pencil those colours which are too bright to be lasting.—When hearts deserving happiness would unite their fortunes, Virtue would crown them with an unfading garland of modest, hurtless flowers; but ill-judging Passion will force the gaudier rose into the wreath, whose thorn offends them, when its leaves are dropped![280]

Exeunt omnes.

---

[280] The speech ends with two lines of blank verse.

The Wild Duck

Henrik Ibsen   translated by Rolf Fjelde

Introductory Comments

Rolf Fjelde   *Pratt Institute/Juilliard School of Music*

When Henrik Ibsen wrote his tragicomedy *The Wild Duck* in 1884, he was, at age fifty-six, at the peak of his creative powers. Following his usual method of composition, he slowly and painstakingly incubated the dramatic idea for what would become the fifth and most enigmatic of those twelve realistic plays of modern life pioneered by *Pillars of Society* (1877). Then, working rapidly, he completed the final text during a summer stay at Gossensass in the Austrian Alps, only four months after starting the first draft in Rome. In November of that same year the play was published simultaneously in Denmark and Norway, the first edition being sold out in less than a month.

By this date, Ibsen was fast becoming the most widely discussed, highly praised, and savagely denounced playwright in Europe. In a matter of time *The Wild Duck* was translated from the original Norwegian into English, French, German, Italian, and Russian. Performances were staged in most leading European cities, accompanied as always by heated debate over Ibsen's unsettling, elusive meanings and, at the time, still revolutionary dramatic technique. Nor did the play fail to stir parodists: in Berlin, for instance, playgoers could spice their diets with a burlesque entitled "the Midnight Sun of Hjalmar Knutson."

Parody, like imitation, is one of the ultimate tributes paid to greatness, and there is little doubt today that *The Wild Duck* ranks as one of the great works of the modern theatre. Like all of Ibsen's later plays, it is essentially a middle-class family drama, in sharp contrast to so many landmarks of the classic repertory preceding it (the tragedies of Marlowe and Shakespeare, for example) that concern themselves with the deaths of kings, queens, princes—the movers and shapers of empires. Here, the events of the action are, until the final moments, disarmingly commonplace and inconsequential: the impoverished, but basically compatible Ekdal family (consisting of the ineffectual dreamer Hjalmar, his stolid wife Gina, their adolescent daughter Hedwig, and Hjalmar's aging, defeated father) is intruded upon by a brooding, guilt-ridden loner, Gregers Werle, an idealist who sets out to rehabilitate them with all the officious zeal of an amateur social worker. In the name of truth he destroys, one by one, the props of illusion that sustain their common existence until, to his horror, he finds that his rescue mission has resulted in, not self-liberation, but the sacrificial death of the most vulnerable and generous-spirited member of the household.

The prosaic, if eventually poignant, events of the action are a collective reflection of Ibsen's lifelong struggle to bring drama in line with the defining tendencies of the modern era. The milieu of the play is middle class because, during the century of political revolutions initiated by the fall of the Bastille in 1789, western civilization had been transformed from an aristocratic to a predominantly democratic social order. Thus, in Act One, the court chamberlains, parasitical remnants of the old regime, now concentrate their flattering attention on the new mover and shaper of the times, the industrialist Haakon Werle. Similarly, the ostensible style of the play takes its naturalistic stamp from the influential theories of the French novelist Emile Zola, who argued that art in an age of science must dispassionately study documentable human beings with all the detailed precision of a medical case history. And indeed, *The Wild Duck* is typical of Ibsen's later works in that it contains no generalized stock parts; every character, whether large or small, is searchingly observed and meticulously recorded, offering a wealth of penetrating psychological insight to actors, audiences, and readers alike. Finally, the décor of the play subtly acknowledges the omnipresence of that technology that was permanently altering both the physical and the human landscape of the nineteenth century. Act Two presents us with the principal setting of the drama: a spacious, top-floor room once designed for an artist but now taken over as the place of business of a photographer, an operator of a machine. And that machine, the old-fashioned portrait camera on its tripod, stands throughout the last four acts as a visual metaphor counterposed against that other, hidden, equally suggestive symbol whose central importance is declared in the title.

Even though the political, industrial, and technological revolutions that gave birth to our problematic twentieth century are all indelibly recorded in Ibsen's drama, as if on a sensitive photographic plate, the richest range of understanding is opened up, not by tracing its historical content, but by exploring the implications of that symbolism. For one comes to see that the members of the Ekdal family are variously polarized between, and defined by, their affinities for the camera, producing its exact images of external reality in the studio downstage, and for the wild duck, presiding over its mysterious realm of fantasy within the loft upstage.

For example, the literal-minded Gina is the realist who runs the studio; she, not Hjalmar, appropriately turns out to be the actual photographer. By temperament, Hjalmar finds his natural role instead as a retoucher of photographic prints, just as, on his return from Werle's salon (representing the great world of money, position, and power), he salves his wounded ego with little touches of self-glorifying fantasy. From one perspective, then, that of objective reality, Gina appears admirably responsible, and Hjalmar contemptibly weak. But in the lifelike complexity of Ibsen's conception, there is no one uniform reality for all, no single sufficient perspective on truth. Hjalmar's fantasizing is linked to the domain of the wild duck within the loft, the same domain that sustains old Ekdal's nostalgic dreams of youthful prowess, as well as Hedwig's fancy that their shabby living quarters can be imaginatively conjured into "the depths of the sea." And since the wild duck is established as a creature of the forests, the marshes, the sea, and the sky, it could be equally maintained, from another perspective, that Hjalmar reveals an instinctive health in gravitating toward that fuller consciousness of primal forces for which modern man in his urban, industrialized, technological environment is starved; and that Gina, in succumbing in spirit to Werle's utilitarian business philosophy, even as she yielded to him in the flesh, proves herself, not admirable, but severely limited.

The Wild Duck is interlaced throughout with ambiguities such as these; they pervade not only its thematic concerns—spiritual versus physical blindness, ideals versus the doctrine of the vital lie, artificially imposed symbols versus valid, life-enchancing ones, to mention just a few—but also the mixed motives of every one of the characters. The play offers grounds for endless interpretation; and it would be easy to conclude that its creator was thereby serving notice on his less perceptive disciples, the Gregers-like Ibsenites, that life is too intricate for any formulizable solution, like the "true marriage" Nora, in *A Doll's House,* sets forth to find.

Yet for all its density of conflicting meanings, the action does have a ruling idea. One of the working notes for the first draft perhaps expresses it best: "Liberty consists of giving the individual the right to liberate himself, each according to his personal need." To extend the photographic metaphor, this is the positive into which Ibsen's negative picture of human self-delusion can be developed. If, as the play insists, the truth is always partial, then at least this part of the truth remains undisplaced; after nearly a century, its warning still stands for all those nations, groups, and individuals who presume to manage others' lives in lieu of confronting and realizing their own.

Henrik Ibsen (1828–1906) was born in the small Norwegian seaport of Skien. Eight years later his father, a prosperous merchant, declared bankruptcy. At fifteen Ibsen was apprenticed to a druggist in Grimsted, where an involvement with a servant girl produced an illegitimate child. Unable to enter the university, he turned to the theatre, holding positions as resident playwright and director at Bergen and Christiania (Oslo). His early works, chiefly romantic, nationalistic verse plays, culminated in *Brand* (1866), which made his Scandinavian reputation two years after he left the north for twenty-seven years of voluntary exile in Italy and Germany. Following *Peer Gynt* (1867), he wrote only prose plays, mainly on themes contemporary to the last quarter of the nineteenth century; these secured his standing as "the father of modern drama." Six years after a stroke terminated his writing career in 1900, Ibsen died in Oslo.

The Wild Duck

Henrik Ibsen
Translated by Rolf Fjelde

The Characters

HAAKON WERLE   *wholesale merchant and millowner*

GREGERS WERLE   *his son*

OLD EKDAL

HJALMAR EKDAL   *his son, a photographer*

GINA EKDAL   *Hjalmar's wife*

HEDVIG   *their daughter, aged fourteen*

MRS. SŒRBY   *housekeeper for the elder Werle*

RELLING   *a doctor*

MOLVIK   *a former divinity student*

GRAABERG   *a bookkeeper*

PETTERSEN   *manservant to the elder Werle*

JENSEN   *a hired waiter*

A FAT MAN

A BALD-HEADED MAN

A NEARSIGHTED MAN

SIX OTHER MEN   *dinner guests at Werle's*

OTHER HIRED SERVANTS

The first act takes place in WERLE's *house; the following four acts in* HJALMAR EKDAL's *studio.*

Act One

At WERLE's *house. A richly and comfortably furnished study, with bookcases and upholstered furniture, a writing table, with papers and reports, in the middle of the floor, and green-shaded lamps softly illuminating the room. In the rear wall, open folding doors with curtains drawn back disclose a large, fashionable room, brightly lit by lamps and candelabra. In the right foreground of the study, a small private door leads to the offices. In the left foreground, a fireplace filled with glowing coals, and further back a double door to the dining room.*

WERLE's *manservant,* PETTERSEN, *in livery, and* JENSEN, *a hired waiter, in black, are straightening up the study. In the larger room two or three other hired waiters are moving about, putting things in order and lighting more candles. In from the dining room come laughter and the hum of many voices in conversation; a knife clinks upon a glass; silence; a toast is made; cries of "Bravo," and the hum of conversation resumes.*

PETTERSEN (*lighting a lamp by the fireplace and putting on the shade*) Ah, you hear that, Jensen. Now the old boy's up on his feet, proposing a long toast to Mrs. Sœrby.

JENSEN (*moving an armchair forward*) Is it really true what people say, that there's something between them?

PETTERSEN Lord knows.

JENSEN I've heard he was a real goat in his day.

PETTERSEN Could be.

JENSEN But they say it's his son he's throwing this party for.

PETTERSEN Yes. His son came home yesterday.

JENSEN I never knew before that old Werle had any son.

PETTERSEN Oh yes, he's got a son. But he

spends all his time up at the works in Hoidal. He hasn't been in town all the years I've served in this house.

A HIRED WAITER (*in the door to the other room*) Say, Pettersen, there's an old guy here who——

PETTERSEN (*muttering*) What the hell—somebody coming now!

(*Old* EKDAL *appears from the right through the inner room. He is dressed in a shabby overcoat with a high collar, woolen gloves, and in his hand, a cane and a fur cap; under his arm is a bundle wrapped in brown paper. He has a dirty, reddish-brown wig and a little gray moustache.*)

PETTERSEN (*going toward him*) Good Lord, what do *you* want in here?

EKDAL (*at the door*) Just have to get into the office, Pettersen.

PETTERSEN The office closed an hour ago, and——

EKDAL Heard that one at the door, boy. But Graaberg's still in there. Be nice, Pettersen, and let me slip in that way. (*Pointing toward the private entrance.*) I've gone that way before.

PETTERSEN All right, go ahead, then. (*Opens the door.*) But don't forget now —take the other way out; we have guests.

EKDAL Got you—hmm! Thanks, Pettersen, good old pal! Thanks. (*To himself.*) Bonehead! (*He goes into the office;* PETTERSEN *shuts the door after him.*)

JENSEN Is *he* on the office staff too?

PETTERSEN No, he's just someone who does copying on the outside when it's needed. Still, in his time he was well up in the world, old Ekdal.

JENSEN Yes, he looks like he's been a little of everything.

PETTERSEN Oh yes. He was a lieutenant once, if you can imagine.

JENSEN Good Lord—him a lieutenant!

PETTERSEN So help me, he was. But then

391

he went into the lumber business or something. They say he must have pulled some kind of dirty deal on the old man once, for the two of them were running the Hoidal works together then. Oh, I know good old Ekdal, all right. We've drunk many a schnapps and bottle of beer together over at Eriksen's.

JENSEN   He can't have much money for standing drinks.

PETTERSEN   My Lord, Jensen, you can bet it's me that stands the drinks. I always say a person ought to act refined toward quality that's come down in life.

JENSEN   Did he go bankrupt, then?

PETTERSEN   No, worse than that. He was sent to jail.

JENSEN   To jail!

PETTERSEN   Or maybe it was the penitentiary. (*Laughter from the dining room.*) Hist! They're leaving the table.

(*The dining room door is opened by a pair of servants inside.* MRS. SŒRBY, *in conversation with two gentlemen, comes out. A moment later the rest of the guests follow, among them* WERLE. *Last of all come* HJALMAR EKDAL *and* GREGERS WERLE.)

MRS. SŒRBY (*to the servant, in passing*) Pettersen, will you have coffee served in the music room.

PETTERSEN   Yes, Mrs. Sœrby.

(*She and the two gentlemen go into the inner room and exit to the right.* PETTERSEN *and* JENSEN *leave in the same way.*)

A FAT GUEST (*to a balding man*) Phew! That dinner—that was a steep bit of work!

THE BALD-HEADED GUEST   Oh, with a little good will a man can do wonders in three hours.

THE FAT GUEST   Yes, but afterward, my dear fellow, afterward.

A THIRD GUEST   I hear we can sample coffee and liqueur in the music room.

THE FAT GUEST   Fine! Then perhaps Mrs. Sœrby will play us a piece.

THE BALD-HEADED GUEST (*in an undertone*) Just so Mrs. Sœrby doesn't play us to pieces.

THE FAT GUEST   Oh, now really, Berta wouldn't punish her old friends, would she? (*They laugh and enter the inner room.*)

WERLE (*in a low, depressed tone*)   I don't think anyone noticed it, Gregers.

GREGERS   What?

WERLE   Didn't you notice it either?

GREGERS   What should I have noticed?

WERLE   We were thirteen at the table.

GREGERS   Really? Were we thirteen?

WERLE (*with a glance at* HJALMAR EKDAL) Yes—our usual number is twelve. (*To the others.*) Be so kind, gentlemen.

(*He and those remaining, excepting* HJALMAR *and* GREGERS, *go out to the rear and right.*)

HJALMAR (*who has heard the conversation*)   You shouldn't have sent me the invitation, Gregers.

GREGERS   What! The party's supposed to be for *me*. And then I'm not supposed to have my best and only friend——

HJALMAR   But I don't think your father likes it. Ordinarily I never come to this house.

GREGERS   So I hear. But I had to see you and talk with you, for I'm sure to be leaving soon again. Yes, we two old classmates, we've certainly drifted a long way apart. You know, we haven't seen each other now in sixteen—seventeen years.

HJALMAR   Has it been so long?

GREGERS   Yes, all of that. Well, how have you been? You look well. You're almost becoming stout.

HJALMAR   Hm, stout is hardly the word, though I probably look more of a man than I did then.

GREGERS   Yes, you do. The outer man hasn't suffered.

HJALMAR (*in a gloomier tone*)   Ah, but the inner man! Believe me, he has a different look. You know how everything went to pieces for me and my family since you and I last saw each other.

GREGERS (*dropping his voice*) How's it going for your father now?

HJALMAR Oh, Gregers, let's not talk about that. My poor, unhappy father naturally lives at home with me. He's got no one else in the whole world to turn to. But this all is so terribly hard for me to talk about, you know. Tell me, instead, how you've found life up at the works.

GREGERS Marvelously solitary, that's what —with a good chance to mull over a great many things. Come on, let's be comfortable.

(*He sits in an armchair by the fire and urges* HJALMAR *down into another by its side.*)

HJALMAR (*emotionally*) In any case, I'm grateful that you asked me here, Gregers, because it proves you no longer have anything against me.

GREGERS (*astonished*) How could you think that I had anything against you?

HJALMAR In those first years you did.

GREGERS Which first years?

HJALMAR Right after that awful misfortune. And it was only natural you should. It was just by a hair that your own father escaped being dragged into this—oh, all this hideous business.

GREGERS And that's why I had it in for you? Whoever gave you that idea?

HJALMAR I know you did, Gregers; it was your father himself who told me.

GREGERS (*startled*) Father! I see. Hm—is that why I never heard from you—not a single word?

HJALMAR Yes.

GREGERS Not even when you went out and became a photographer.

HJALMAR Your father said it wasn't worth writing you—about anything.

GREGERS (*looking fixedly ahead*) No, no, maybe he was right there—But tell me, Hjalmar—do you find yourself reasonably content with things as they are?

HJALMAR (*with a small sigh*) Oh, I suppose I do. What else can I say? At first, you can imagine, it was all rather strange for me. They were such completely dif-

ferent expectations that I came into. But then everything was so different. That immense, shattering misfortune for Father —the shame and the scandal, Gregers——

GREGERS (*shaken*) Yes, yes. Of course.

HJALMAR I couldn't dream of going on with my studies; there wasn't a penny to spare. On the contrary, debts instead— mainly to your father, I think——

GREGERS Hm——

HJALMAR Anyway, I thought it was best to make a clean break—and cut all the old connections. It was your father especially who advised me to; and since he'd already been so helpful to me——

GREGERS He had?

HJALMAR Yes, you knew that, didn't you? Where could *I* get the money to learn photography and fit out a studio and establish myself? I can tell you, that all adds up.

GREGERS And all that Father paid for?

HJALMAR Yes, Gregers, didn't you know? I understood him to say that he'd written you about it.

GREGERS Not a word saying *he* was the one. Maybe he forgot. We've never exchanged anything but business letters. So that was Father, too—!

HJALMAR That's right. He never wanted people to know, but he was the one. And he was also the one who put me in a position to get married. Or perhaps— didn't you know that either?

GREGERS No, not at all. (*Takes him by the arm.*) But Hjalmar, I can't tell you how all this delights me—and disturbs me. Perhaps I've been unfair to my father —in certain ways. Yes, for all this does show good-heartedness, doesn't it? It's almost a kind of conscience——

HJALMAR Conscience?

GREGERS Yes, or whatever you want to call it. No, I can't tell you how glad I am to hear this about my father. So you're married, then, Hjalmar. That's further than I'll ever go. Well, I hope you're happy as a married man?

HJALMAR Oh, absolutely. She's as capable and fine a wife as any man could wish for. And she's not entirely without culture, either.

GREGERS (*a bit surprised*) No, I'm sure she's not.

HJALMAR No. Life is a teacher, you see. Associating with me every day—and then there are one or two gifted people who visit us regularly. I can tell you, you wouldn't recognize Gina now.

GREGERS Gina?

HJALMAR Yes, Gregers, had you forgotten her name is Gina?

GREGERS Whose name is Gina? I haven't the faintest idea——

HJALMAR But don't you remember, she was here in this very house a while—in service?

GREGERS (*looking at him*) You mean Gina Hansen—?

HJALMAR Yes, of course. Gina Hansen.

GREGERS Who was housekeeper for us that last year of Mother's illness?

HJALMAR Exactly. But my dear Gregers, I know for sure that your father wrote you about my marriage.

GREGERS (*who has gotten up*) Yes, of course he did. But not that—(*Walks about the floor.*) Yes, wait a minute—it may well be, now that I think of it. My father's letters are always so brief. (*Sits on chair arm.*) Listen, tell me, Hjalmar— this is interesting—how did you come to know Gina?—your wife, I mean.

HJALMAR Oh, it was all very simple. Gina didn't stay long here in the house; there was so much confusion—your mother's sickness and all. Gina couldn't stand it, so she just up and left. That was the year before your mother died—or maybe it was the same year.

GREGERS It was the same year. And I was up at the works at the time. But what then?

HJALMAR Well, then Gina lived at home with her mother, a Mrs. Hansen, a very capable, hardworking woman who ran a little restaurant. She also had a room for rent, a very pleasant, comfortable room.

GREGERS And you were lucky enough to find it?

HJALMAR Yes. Actually it was your father who suggested it to me. And it was there, you see—there that I really got to know Gina.

GREGERS And then your engagement followed?

HJALMAR Yes. Young people fall in love so easily—hm——

GREGERS (*getting up and pacing about a little*) Tell me—when you became engaged—was it *then* that my father got you to—I mean, was it then that you started in learning photography?

HJALMAR That's right. I wanted to get on and set up a home as soon as possible, and both your father and I decided that this photography idea was the most feasible one. And Gina thought so too. Yes, and you see, there was another inducement, a lucky break, in that Gina had already taken up retouching.

GREGERS That worked out wonderfully all around.

HJALMAR (*pleased, getting up*) Yes, isn't that so? Don't you think it's worked out wonderfully all around?

GREGERS Yes, I must say. My father has almost been a kind of providence to you.

HJALMAR (*with feeling*) He didn't abandon his old friend's son in a time of need. You see, he does have a heart.

MRS. SŒRBY (*entering with* WERLE *on her arm*) No more nonsense, my dear Mr. Werle. You mustn't stay in there any longer, staring at all those lights; it's doing you no good.

WERLE (*freeing his arm from hers and passing his hand over his eyes*) Yes, I guess you're right about that.

(PETTERSEN *and* JENSEN *enter with trays.*)

MRS. SŒRBY (*to the guests in the other room*) Gentlemen, please—if anyone wants a glass of punch, he must take the trouble to come in here.

THE FAT GUEST (*comes over to* MRS. SŒRBY) But really, is it true you've abolished our precious smoking privilege?

MRS. SŒRBY Yes. Here in Mr. Werle's sanctum, it's forbidden.

THE BALD-HEADED GUEST When did you pass these drastic amendments to the cigar laws, Mrs. Sœrby?

MRS. SŒRBY After the last dinner—when there were certain persons here who let themselves exceed all limits.

THE BALD-HEADED GUEST And my dear Berta, one isn't permitted to exceed the limits, even a little bit?

MRS. SŒRBY Not in any instance, Mr. Balle.

(*Most of the guests have gathered in the study; the waiters are proffering glasses of punch.*)

WERLE (*to* HJALMAR, *over by a table*) What is it you're poring over, Ekdal?

HJALMAR It's only an album, Mr. Werle.

THE BALD-HEADED GUEST (*who is wandering about*) Ah, photographs! Yes, of course, that's just the thing for you.

THE FAT GUEST (*seated in an armchair*) Haven't you brought along some of your own?

HJALMAR No, I haven't.

THE FAT GUEST You really should have. It's so good for the digestion to sit and look at pictures.

THE BALD-HEADED GUEST And then it always adds a morsel to the entertainment, you know.

A NEARSIGHTED GUEST And all contributions are gratefully received.

MRS. SŒRBY These gentlemen mean that if one's invited for dinner, one must also work for the food, Mr. Ekdal.

THE FAT GUEST Where the larder's superior, *that* is pure joy.

THE BALD-HEADED GUEST My Lord, it's all in the struggle for existence——

MRS. SŒRBY How right you are! (*They continue laughing and joking.*)

GREGERS (*quietly*) You should talk with them, Hjalmar.

HJALMAR (*with a shrug*) What could I talk about?

THE FAT GUEST Don't you think, Mr. Werle, that Tokay compares favorably as a healthful drink for the stomach?

WERLE (*by the fireplace*) The Tokay you had today I can vouch for in any case; it's one of the very, very finest years. But you recognized that well enough.

THE FAT GUEST Yes, it had a remarkably delicate flavor.

HJALMAR (*tentatively*) Is there some difference between the years?

THE FAT GUEST (*laughing*) Oh, that's rich!

WERLE (*smiling*) It certainly doesn't pay to offer you a noble wine.

THE BALD-HEADED GUEST Tokay wines are like photographs, Mr. Ekdal—sunshine is of the essence. Isn't that true?

HJALMAR Oh yes, light is very important.

MRS. SŒRBY Exactly the same as with court officials—who push for their place in the sun too, I hear.

THE BALD-HEADED GUEST Ouch! That was a tired quip.

THE NEARSIGHTED GUEST The lady's performing——

THE FAT GUEST And at our expense. (*Frowning.*) Mrs. Sœrby, Mrs. Sœrby!

MRS. SŒRBY Yes, but it certainly is true now that the years can vary enormously. The old vintages are the finest.

THE NEARSIGHTED GUEST Do you count me among the old ones?

MRS. SŒRBY Oh, far from it.

THE BALD-HEADED GUEST Ha, you see! But what about *me*, Mrs. Sœrby—?

THE FAT GUEST Yes, and me! What years would you put us among?

MRS. SŒRBY I would put you all among the sweet years, gentlemen. (*She sips a glass of punch; the guests laugh and banter with her.*)

WERLE Mrs. Sœrby always finds a way out —when she wants to. Pass your glasses, gentlemen. Pettersen, take care of them. Gregers, I think we'll have a glass together. (GREGERS *does not stir.*) Won't you join us, Ekdal? I had no chance to remember you at the table.

(GRAABERG, *the bookkeeper, peers out from the door to the offices.*)

GRAABERG Beg pardon, Mr. Werle, but I can't get out.

WERLE   What, are you locked in again?

GRAABERG   Yes, and Flakstad's left with the keys——

WERLE   Well, then, go through here.

GRAABERG   But there's someone else——

WERLE   All right, all right, both of you. Don't be shy.

(GRAABERG *and old* EKDAL *come out from the office.*)

WERLE (*involuntarily*)   Oh no!

(*The laughter and small talk die among the guests.* HJALMAR *starts at the sight of his father, sets down his glass, and turns away toward the fireplace.*)

EKDAL (*without looking up, but bowing slightly to each side and mumbling*)   Beg your pardon. It's the wrong way. Door locked—door locked. Beg pardon. (*He and* GRAABERG *exit in back to the right.*)

WERLE (*between his teeth*)   That damned Graaberg!

GREGERS (*with open mouth, staring at* HJALMAR)   But it couldn't have been—!

THE FAT GUEST   What's going on? Who was that?

GREGERS   Oh, no one. Only the bookkeeper and somebody else.

THE NEARSIGHTED GUEST (*to* HJALMAR)   Did *you* know him?

HJALMAR   I don't know—I didn't notice——

THE FAT GUEST (*getting up*)   What in thunder's wrong? (*He goes over to some others, who are talking.*)

MRS. SŒRBY (*whispering to the waiter*)   Slip something to him outside, something really fine.

PETTERSEN (*nodding*)   I'll see to it. (*He goes out.*)

GREGERS (*in a shocked undertone*)   Then it really was him!

HJALMAR   Yes.

GREGERS   And yet you stood here and denied you knew him!

HJALMAR (*whispering fiercely*)   But how could I—!

GREGERS   Be recognized by your father?

HJALMAR (*painfully*)   Oh, if you were in my place, then——

(*The hushed conversations among the guests now mount into a forced joviality.*)

THE BALD-HEADED GUEST (*approaching* HJALMAR *and* GREGERS *amiably*)   Ah ha! You over here, polishing up old memories from your student years? Well? Won't you smoke, Mr. Ekdal? Have a light? Oh, that's right, we're not supposed to——

HJALMAR   Thanks, I couldn't——

THE FAT GUEST   Haven't you got a neat little poem to recite for us, Mr. Ekdal? In times past you did that so nicely.

HJALMAR   I'm afraid I can't remember any.

THE FAT GUEST   Oh, that's a shame. Well, Balle, what can we find to do? (*The two men cross the floor into the other room and go out.*)

HJALMAR (*somberly*)   Gregers—I'm going! When a man's had a hammer blow from fate on his head—you understand. Say good night to your father for me.

GREGERS   Yes, of course. Are you going straight home?

HJALMAR   Yes, why?

GREGERS   Well, I may pay you a visit later.

HJALMAR   No, you mustn't. Not to my home. My house is a sad one, Gregers—especially after a brilliant occasion like this. We can always meet somewhere in town.

MRS. SŒRBY (*who has approached; in a low voice*)   Are you going, Ekdal?

HJALMAR   Yes.

MRS. SŒRBY   Greet Gina.

HJALMAR   Thank you.

MRS. SŒRBY   And tell her I'll stop by to see her one day soon.

HJALMAR   Yes. Thanks. (*To* GREGERS.) Stay here. I'd rather disappear without any fuss. (*He strolls around the floor, then into the other room and out to the right.*)

MRS. SŒRBY (*quietly to the waiter, who has returned*)   Well, did the old man get something to take home?

PETTERSEN   Sure. I slipped him a bottle of cognac.

MRS. SŒRBY   Oh, you could have found something better.

PETTERSEN   Not at all, Mrs. Sœrby. He knows nothing better than cognac.

THE FAT GUEST   (*in the doorway, holding a score of music*)   How about the two of us playing something, Mrs. Sœrby?

MRS. SŒRBY   All right. Let's.

(*The guests shout approval.* MRS. SŒRBY *and the others exit right, through the inner room.* GREGERS *remains standing by the fireplace.* WERLE *looks for something on the writing table, seeming to wish that* GREGERS *would leave; when he fails to stir,* WERLE *crosses toward the door.*)

GREGERS   Father, won't you wait a moment?

WERLE   (*pausing*)   What is it?

GREGERS   I must have a word with you.

WERLE   Can't it wait till we're alone?

GREGERS   No, it can't, because it just might occur that we never are alone.

WERLE   (*coming closer*)   What does *that* mean?

(*Distant piano music is heard from the music room during the following conversation.*)

GREGERS   How could anyone here let that family decay so pitifully?

WERLE   You're referring to the Ekdals, no doubt.

GREGERS   Yes, I mean the Ekdals. Lieutenant Ekdal was once so close to you.

WERLE   Yes, worse luck, he was all too close; and for that I've paid a price these many years. He's the one I can thank for putting something of a blot on my good name and reputation.

GREGERS   (*quietly*)   Was *he* really the only guilty one?

WERLE   Who else do you mean!

GREGERS   You and he were both in on buying that big stand of timber——

WERLE   But it was Ekdal, wasn't it, who made the survey of the sections—that incompetent survey? He was the one who carried out all the illegal logging on state property. In fact, he was in charge of the whole operation up there. I had no idea of what Lieutenant Ekdal was getting into.

GREGERS   Lieutenant Ekdal himself had no idea of what he was getting into.

WERLE   Very likely. But the fact remains that he was convicted and I was acquitted.

GREGERS   Yes, I'm aware that no proof was found.

WERLE   Acquittal is acquittal. Why do you rake up this ugly old story that's given me gray hair before my time? Is this what you've been brooding about all those years up there? I can assure you, Gregers —here in town the whole business has been forgotten long ago—as far as I'm concerned.

GREGERS   But that miserable Ekdal family!

WERLE   Seriously, what would you have me do for these people? When Ekdal was let out, he was a broken man, beyond any help. There are people in this world who plunge to the bottom when they've hardly been winged, and they never come up again. Take my word for it, Gregers; I've done everything I could, short of absolutely compromising myself and arousing all kinds of suspicion and gossip——

GREGERS   Suspicion—? So that's it.

WERLE   I've gotten Ekdal copying jobs from the office, and I pay him much, much more than his work is worth——

GREGERS   (*without loking at him*)   Hm. No doubt.

WERLE   You're laughing? Maybe you think what I'm saying isn't true? There's certainly nothing to show in my books; I don't record such payments.

GREGERS   (*with a cold smile*)   No. I'm sure that certain payments are best left unrecorded.

WERLE   (*surprised*)   What do you mean by *that*?

GREGERS   (*plucking up his courage*)   Did you record what it cost you to have Hjalmar Ekdal study photography?

WERLE   I? Why should I?

GREGERS   I know now it was you who paid

for that. And now I know, too, that it was you who set him up so comfortably in business.

WERLE Well, and I suppose this still means that I've done nothing for the Ekdals! I can assure you, those people have already cost me enough expense.

GREGERS Have you recorded any of the expenses?

WERLE Why do you ask that?

GREGERS Oh, there are reasons. Listen, tell me—the time when you developed such warmth for your old friend's son—wasn't that just when he was planning to marry?

WERLE How the devil—how, after so many years, do you expect me——?

GREGERS You wrote me a letter then—a business letter, naturally; and in a postscript it said, brief as could be, that Hjalmar Ekdal had gotten married to a Miss Hansen.

WERLE Yes, that's right; that was her name.

GREGERS But you never said that this Miss Hansen was Gina Hansen—our former housekeeper.

WERLE (*with a derisive, yet uneasy laugh*) No, it just never occurred to me that you'd be so very interested in our former housekeeper.

GREGERS I wasn't. But—(*Dropping his voice.*) there were others in the house who were quite interested in her.

WERLE What do you mean by that? (*Storming at him.*) You're not referring to me!

GREGERS (*quietly but firmly*) Yes, I'm referring to you.

WERLE And you dare—! You have the insolence—! How could he, that ungrateful dog, that—photographer; how could he have the gall to make such insinuations?

GREGERS Hjalmar hasn't breathed a word of it. I don't think he has the shadow of a doubt about all this.

WERLE Then where did you get it from? Who could have said such a thing?

GREGERS My poor, unhappy mother said it—the last time I saw her.

WERLE Your mother! Yes, I might have

guessed. She and you—you always stuck together. It was she who, right from the start, turned your mind against me.

GREGERS No. It was everything she had to suffer and endure until she broke down and died so miserably.

WERLE Oh, she had nothing to suffer and endure—no more, at least, than so many others. But you can't get anywhere with sick, high-strung people. I've certainly learned that. Now you're going around suspecting that sort of thing, digging up all manner of old rumors and slanders against your own father. Now listen, Gregers, I really think that at your age you could occupy yourself more usefully.

GREGERS Yes, all in due time.

WERLE Then your mind might be clearer than it seems to be now. What can it lead to, you up there at the works, slaving away year in and year out like a common clerk, never taking a penny over your month's salary. It's pure stupidity.

GREGERS Yes, if only I were so sure of that.

WERLE I understand you well enough. You want to be independent, without obligation to me. But here's the very opportunity for you to become independent, your own man in every way.

GREGERS So? And by what means—?

WERLE When I wrote you that it was essential you come to town now, immediately—hmm——

GREGERS Yes. What is it you really want of me? I've been waiting all day to find out.

WERLE I'm suggesting that you come into the firm as a partner.

GREGERS I! In your firm? As a partner?

WERLE Yes. It wouldn't mean we'd need to be together much. You could take over the offices here in town, and then I'd move up to the mill.

GREGERS You *would*?

WERLE Yes. You see, I can't take on work now the way I once could. I have to spare my eyes, Gregers; they're beginning to fail.

GREGERS They've always been weak.

WERLE Not like this. Besides—circumstances may make it desirable for me to live up there—at least for a while.

GREGERS   I never dreamed of anything like this.

WERLE   Listen, Gregers, there are so very many things that keep us apart, and yet, you know—we're father and son still. I think we should be able to reach some kind of understanding.

GREGERS   Just on the surface, is that what you mean?

WERLE   Well, at least that would be something. Think it over, Gregers. Don't you think it ought to be possible? Eh?

GREGERS   (*looking at him coldly*)   There's something behind all this.

WERLE   How so?

GREGERS   It might be that somehow you're using me.

WERLE   In a relationship as close as ours, one can always be of use to the other.

GREGERS   Yes, so they say.

WERLE   I'd like to have you home with me now for a while. I'm a lonely man, Gregers; I've always felt lonely—all my life through, but particularly now when the years are beginning to press me. I need to have someone around——

GREGERS   You have Mrs. Sœrby.

WERLE   Yes, I do—and she's become, you might say, almost indispensable. She's witty, even-tempered; she livens up the house—and that's what I need so badly.

GREGERS   Well, then, you've got everything the way you want it.

WERLE   Yes, but I'm afraid it can't go on. The world is quick to make inferences about a woman in her position. Yes, I was going to say, a man doesn't gain by it either.

GREGERS   Oh, when a man gives dinner parties like yours, he can certainly take a few risks.

WERLE   Yes, Gregers, but what about her? I'm afraid she won't put up with it much longer. And even if she did—even if, out of her feeling for me, she ignored the gossip and the backbiting and so on—do you still think, Gregers, you with your sharp sense of justice——

GREGERS   (*cutting him off*)   Tell me short and sweet just one thing. Are you planning to marry her?

WERLE   And if I *were* planning such a thing—what then?

GREGERS   Yes, that's what I'm asking. What then?

WERLE   Would you be so irreconcilably set against it?

GREGERS   No, not at all. Not in any way.

WERLE   Well, I really didn't know whether, perhaps out of regard for your dead mother's memory——

GREGERS   I am not high-strung.

WERLE   Well, you may or may not be, but in any case you've taken a great load off my mind. I'm really very happy that I can count on your support in this.

GREGERS   (*staring intently at him*)   Now I see how you want to use me.

WERLE   Use you! That's no way to talk!

GREGERS   Oh, let's not be squeamish in our choice of words. At least, not when it's man to man. (*He laughs brusquely.*) So that's it! That's why I—damn it all!—had to make my personal appearance in town. On account of Mrs. Sœrby, family life is in order in this house. Tableau of father with son! That's something new, all right!

WERLE   How dare you speak in that tone!

GREGERS   When has there ever been family life here? Never, as long as I can remember. But *now*, of course, there's need for a little of that. For who could deny what a fine impression it would make to hear that the son—on the wings of piety—came flying home to the aging father's wedding feast. What's left then of all the stories about what the poor dead woman suffered and endured? Not a scrap. Her own son ground them to dust.

WERLE   Gregers—I don't think there's a man in this world you hate as much as me.

GREGERS   I've seen you at too close quarters.

WERLE   You've seen me with your mother's eyes. (*Dropping his voice.*) But you should remember that those eyes were—clouded at times.

GREGERS (*faltering*) I know what you mean. But who bears the guilt for Mother's fatal weakness? You, and all those—! The last of them was that female that Hjalmar Ekdal was fixed up with when you had no more—ugh!

WERLE (*shrugs*) Word for word, as if I were hearing your mother.

GREGERS (*paying no attention to him*) . . . and there he sits right now, he with his great, guileless, childlike mind plunged in deception—living under the same roof with that creature, not knowing that what he calls his home is built on a lie. (*Coming a step closer.*) When I look back on all you've done, it's as if I looked out over a battlefield with broken human beings on every side.

WERLE I almost think the gulf is too great between us.

GREGERS (*bows stiffly*) So I've observed; therefore I'll take my hat and go.

WERLE You're going? Out of this house?

GREGERS Yes. Because now at last I can see a mission to live for.

WERLE What mission is that?

GREGERS You'd only laugh if you heard it.

WERLE A lonely man doesn't laugh so easily, Gregers.

GREGERS (*pointing toward the inner room*) Look—your gentleman friends are playing blindman's buff with Mrs. Sœrby. Good night and goodbye.

(*He goes out at the right rear. Laughter and joking from the company, which moves into view in the inner room.*)

WERLE (*muttering contemptuously after* GREGERS) Huh! Poor fool—and he says he's not high-strung!

Act Two

HJALMAR EKDAL's *studio. The room, which is fairly spacious, appears to be a loft. To the right is a sloping roof with great panes of glass, half hidden by a blue curtain. In the far right corner is the entrance; nearer on the same side, a door to the living room. Similarly, at the left there are two doors, and between these an iron stove. At the back is a wide double door, designed to slide back to the sides. The studio is simply but comfortably furnished and decorated. Between the right-hand doors, slightly away from the wall, stands a sofa beside a table and some chairs; on the table is a lighted lamp with a shade; by the stove an old armchair. Photographic apparatus and equipment of various sorts are set up here and there in the room. At the left of the double doors stands a bookcase containing a few books, small boxes and flasks of chemicals, various tools, implements, and other subjects. Photographs and such small articles as brushes, paper, and the like lie on the table.*

GINA EKDAL *sits on a chair by the table, sewing.* HEDVIG *sits on the sofa, hands shading her eyes, thumbs in her ears, reading a book.*

GINA (*having glanced over several times at* HEDVIG, *as if with anxiety*) Hedvig! (HEDVIG *does not hear.*)

GINA (*louder*) Hedvig!

HEDVIG (*removing her hands and looking up*) Yes, Mother?

GINA Hedvig dear, you mustn't sit and read anymore.

HEDVIG Oh, but Mother, can't I please read a little longer? Just a little!

GINA No, no—you must set the book down. Your father doesn't like it; he never reads in the evening.

HEDVIG (*closing the book*) No, Daddy's no great one for reading.

GINA (*lays her sewing aside and takes a pencil and a small notebook from the table*) Do you remember how much we spent for butter today?

HEDVIG It was one sixty-five.

GINA That's right. (*Making a note.*) It's awful how much butter gets used in this house. And then so much for smoked sausage, and for cheese—let me see— (*Making more notes.*) and so much for ham—hmm. (*Adds.*) Yes, that adds right up to——

HEDVIG   And then there's the beer.

GINA   Yes, of course. (*Makes another note.*) It mounts up—but it can't be helped.

HEDVIG   Oh, but you and I had no hot food for dinner, 'cause Daddy was out.

GINA   No, and that's to the good. What's more, I also took in eight crowns fifty for photographs.

HEDVIG   No! Was it that much?

GINA   Exactly eight crowns fifty.

(*Silence.* GINA *again picks up her sewing.* HEDVIG *takes paper and pencil and starts to draw, shading her eyes with her left hand.*)

HEDVIG   Isn't it something to think that Daddy's at a big dinner party at old Mr. Werle's?

GINA   You can't really say that he's at old Mr. Werle's. It was his son who sent him the invitation. (*After a pause.*) We have nothing to do with old Mr. Werle.

HEDVIG   I can hardly wait for Daddy to come home. He promised he'd ask Mrs. Sœrby about bringing me a treat.

GINA   Yes, you can bet there are lots of treats to be had in *that* house.

HEDVIG   (*again drawing*) Besides, I'm a little hungry, too.

(*Old* EKDAL, *with a bundle of papers under his arm and another bundle in his coat pocket, comes in through the hall door.*)

GINA   My, but you're late today, Grandfather.

EKDAL   They'd locked the office. Had to wait for Graaberg. And then I had to go through—uhh.

GINA   Did they give you something new to copy, Grandfather?

EKDAL   This whole pile. Just look.

GINA   That's fine.

HEDVIG   And you've got a bundle in your pocket, too.

EKDAL   Oh? Nonsense; that's nothing. (*Puts his cane away in the corner.*)

Here's work for a good spell, Gina, this here. (*Pulls one of the double doors slightly open.*) Shh! (*Peers into the room a moment, then carefully closes the door again.*) He, he! They're sound asleep, the lot of them. And she's bedded down in the basket all on her own. He, he!

HEDVIG   Are you sure she won't be cold in the basket, Grandpa?

EKDAL   What a thought! Cold? In all that straw? (*Goes toward the farther door on the left.*) I'll find some matches in here, eh?

GINA   The matches are on the bureau.

(EKDAL *goes into his room.*)

HEDVIG   It's wonderful that Grandpa got all that copying to do.

GINA   Yes, poor old Father; he'll earn himself a little pocket money.

HEDVIG   And he also won't be able to sit the whole morning down in that horrid Mrs. Eriksen's café.

GINA   That too, yes. (*A short silence.*)

HEDVIG   Do you think they're still at the dinner table?

GINA   Lord only knows; it may well be.

HEDVIG   Just think, all the lovely food Daddy's eaten! I'm sure he'll be happy and content when he comes. Don't you think so, Mother?

GINA   Of course. Imagine if we could tell him now that we'd rented out the room.

HEDVIG   But that's not necessary tonight.

GINA   Oh, it could well come in handy, you know. It's no good to us as it is.

HEDVIG   No, I mean it's not necessary because tonight Daddy's feeling good. It's better we have news about the room some other time.

GINA   (*looking over at her*) Are you glad when you have something nice to tell your father when he comes home at night?

HEDVIG   Yes, for things here are pleasanter then.

GINA   (*reflecting*) Well, there's something to that.

(*Old* EKDAL *comes in again and starts out through the nearer door to the left.*)

GINA (*half turning in her chair*) Does Grandfather want something from the kitchen?

EKDAL I do, yes. Don't stir. (*He goes out.*)

GINA He never fusses with the fire out there. (*After a moment.*) Hedvig, go see what he's doing.

(EKDAL *reenters with a small jug of steaming water.*)

HEDVIG Are you after hot water, Grandpa?

EKDAL Yes, I am. Need it for something. Have to write, and the ink is caked thick as porridge—hmm.

GINA But you ought to have supper first, Grandfather. It's all set and waiting in there.

EKDAL Never mind about the supper, Gina. Terribly busy, I tell you. I don't want anybody coming into my room—nobody. Hmm. (*He goes into his room.* GINA *and* HEDVIG *exchange glances.*)

GINA (*lowering her voice*) Where do you figure he's gotten money?

HEDVIG He must have got it from Graaberg.

GINA Not a chance. Graaberg always sends the pay to me.

HEDVIG Maybe he got a bottle somewhere on credit.

GINA Poor Grandpa, no one'll give him credit.

(HJALMAR EKDAL, *wearing an overcoat and a gray felt hat, enters from the right.*)

GINA (*dropping her sewing and getting up*) Ah, Hjalmar, here you are!

HEDVIG (*jumping up at the same time*) At last you're home, Daddy!

HJALMAR (*putting his hat down*) Yes, most of them were leaving.

HEDVIG So early?

HJALMAR Yes, it was only a dinner party. (*Starts to remove his overcoat.*)

GINA Let me help you.

HEDVIG Me too.

(*They take off his coat;* GINA *hangs it up on the rear wall.*)

HEDVIG Were there many there, Daddy?

HJALMAR Oh no, not many. We were some twelve, fourteen people at the table.

GINA And you got to talk with every one of them?

HJALMAR Oh yes, a little, though Gregers rather monopolized me.

GINA Is Gregers ugly as ever?

HJALMAR Well, he doesn't look any better. Isn't the old man home?

HEDVIG Yes, Grandpa's inside, writing.

HJALMAR Did he say anything?

GINA No, what should he say?

HJALMAR Didn't he mention anything of—I thought I heard that he'd been with Graaberg. I'll go in and have a word with him.

GINA No, no, don't bother.

HJALMAR Why not? Did he say he wouldn't see me?

GINA He doesn't want anyone in there this evening.

HEDVIG (*making signals*) Uh—uh!

GINA (*not noticing*) He's already been out here and gotten hot water.

HJALMAR Aha! Is he—?

GINA Yes, exactly.

HJALMAR Good Lord, my poor old white-haired father! Well, let him be, enjoying life's pleasures as he may.

(*Old* EKDAL *in a bathrobe, smoking a pipe, enters from his room.*)

EKDAL Home, eh? Thought it was your voice I heard.

HJALMAR I just arrived.

EKDAL You didn't see me at all, did you?

HJALMAR No, but they said you'd been through—so I thought I'd follow after.

EKDAL Hm, good of you, Hjalmar. Who were they, all those people?

HJALMAR Oh, different sorts. There was Flor—he's at the court—and Balle and Kaspersen and, uh—I forget his name, but people at court, all of them——

EKDAL (*nodding*) Listen to that, Gina! He travels only in the best circles.

GINA Yes, it's real elegant in that house now.

HEDVIG   Did the court people sing, Daddy? Or give readings?

HJALMAR   No, they just babbled away. Of course they wanted *me* to recite for them, but I couldn't see that.

EKDAL   You couldn't see that, eh?

GINA   That you could easily have done.

HJALMAR   Never. One mustn't be a doormat for every passing foot. (*Walking about the room.*) At least, that's not my way.

EKDAL   No, no, that's not for Hjalmar.

HJALMAR   I don't know why I should always provide the entertainment, when I'm out in society so rarely. Let the others make an effort. There those fellows go from one banquet to the next, eating and drinking day in and day out. So let them do their tricks in return for all the good food they get.

GINA   But you didn't say that there?

HJALMAR   (*humming*) Um—um—um—they were told a thing or two.

EKDAL   Right to the nobility!

HJALMAR   I don't see why not. (*Casually.*) Later we had a little quibble about Tokay.

EKDAL   Tokay, you mean? That's a fine wine, that.

HJALMAR   (*coming to a halt*) On occasion. But I must tell you that not all years are equally good. Everything depends strictly on how much sun the grapes have had.

GINA   Really? Oh, Hjalmar, you know everything.

EKDAL   And they could argue about that?

HJALMAR   They tried to. But then they were informed that it's exactly the same with court officials. Among them as well, all years are not equally fine—it was said.

GINA   The things you think of!

EKDAL   He—he! So you served that up to them, eh?

HJALMAR   Smack between the eyes they got it.

EKDAL   Hear, Gina! He laid that one smack between the eyes of the nobility.

GINA   Just think, smack between the eyes.

HJALMAR   That's right. But I don't want a lot of talk about this. One doesn't speak of such things. Everything really went off in the most friendly spirit, naturally. They're all pleasant, genial people. How could I hurt their feelings? Never!

EKDAL   But smack between the eyes——

HEDVIG   (*ingratiatingly*) How nice to see you in evening clothes, Daddy. You look so well in them.

HJALMAR   Yes, don't you think so? And this one here really fits very well. It's almost as if it were made for me. A bit snug under the arms, maybe—help me, Hedvig. (*Takes off the coat.*) I'd rather wear my jacket. What did you do with my jacket, Gina?

GINA   Here it is. (*Brings the jacket and helps him into it.*)

HJALMAR   There! Now don't forget to give Molvik his coat back first thing in the morning.

GINA   (*putting it away*) I'll take care of it.

HJALMAR   (*stretching*) Ah, but this feels much more comfortable. This kind of free and easy dress suits my whole personality better. Don't you think so, Hedvig?

HEDVIG   Yes, Daddy.

HJALMAR   And when I pull my necktie out into a pair of flowing ends—so! Look! What then?

HEDVIG   Yes, it goes so well with your moustache and your long, curly hair.

HJALMAR   Curly? I wouldn't say it's that. I'd call it wavy.

HEDVIG   Yes, but it *is* so curly.

HJALMAR   No—wavy.

HEDVIG   (*after a moment, tugs at his sleeve*) Daddy!

HJALMAR   What is it?

HEDVIG   Oh, you know what.

HJALMAR   No, I don't. Honestly.

HEDVIG   (*laughing fretfully*) Come on, Daddy, don't tease me any longer.

HJALMAR   But what is it, then?

HEDVIG   (*shaking him*) Silly! Out with it, Daddy. You know—all the treats you promised me.

HJALMAR   Oh—no! How did I ever forget that?

HEDVIG   No, you can't fool me. Shame on you! Where have you hidden it?

HJALMAR   So help me if I didn't forget. But wait a minute! I've got something else for you, Hedvig. (*Goes over and rummages in his coat pockets.*)

HEDVIG (*jumping and clapping her hands*) Oh, Mother, Mother!

GINA   You see, if you're only patient enough, then——

HJALMAR (*returning with a piece of paper*) See, here we have it.

HEDVIG   That? But that's just a piece of paper.

HJALMAR   It's the bill of fare, the complete bill of fare. Here it says "menu"; that means "bill of fare."

HEDVIG   Don't you have anything else?

HJALMAR   I forgot to bring anything else, I tell you. But take my word for it: it's bad business, this doting on sugar candy. Now, if you'll sit down at the table and read the menu aloud, I'll describe for you just how each dish tasted. How's that, Hedvig?

HEDVIG (*swallowing her tears*) Thanks. (*She sits, but does not read.* GINA *makes gestures at her, which* HJALMAR *notices.*)

HJALMAR (*pacing about the floor*) What incredible things a family breadwinner is asked to remember; and if he forgets even the tiniest detail—immediately he's met with sour faces. Well, he has to get used to that, too. (*Pauses at the stove beside* EKDAL.) Have you looked inside this evening, Father?

EKDAL   Oh, that you can be sure of. She's gone into the basket.

HJALMAR   No! Into the basket? Then she's begun to get used to it.

EKDAL   Yes. You see, it was just as I predicted. But now there are some little things to do——

HJALMAR   Some improvements, eh?

EKDAL   But they've got to be done, you know.

HJALMAR   All right, let's talk a bit about the improvements, Father. Come, we'll sit here on the sofa.

EKDAL   Very good. Umm—think I'll fill my pipe first. Needs cleaning, too. Hmm. (*He goes into his room.*)

GINA (*smiling at* HJALMAR) Clean his pipe!

HJALMAR   Ah, now, Gina, let him be. Poor shipwrecked old man. Yes, the improvements—it's best we get those off our hands tomorrow.

GINA   Tomorrow you won't have time, Hjalmar——

HEDVIG (*interrupting*) Oh yes, he will, Mother!

GINA   Remember those prints that need retouching. They've been called for so many times already.

HJALMAR   Oh yes, those prints again. They'll be finished in no time. Did any new orders come in?

GINA   No such luck. For tomorrow, I have nothing except those two portrait sittings you know about.

HJALMAR   Nothing else? Ah, well, if people won't even try, then naturally——

GINA   But what else can I do? I've put ads in the papers time and again.

HJALMAR   Yes, ads, ads—you see what a help they are. And of course nobody's been to look at the spare room either?

GINA   No, not yet.

HJALMAR   That was to be expected. If one doesn't keep wide awake—Gina, you've simply got to pull yourself together.

HEDVIG (*going to him*) Let me bring you your flute, Daddy.

HJALMAR   No, no flute. I want no pleasures in this world. (*Pacing about.*) Ah, yes, work—I'll be deep in work tomorrow; there'll be no lack of *that.* I'll sweat and slave as long as my strength holds out——

GINA   But Hjalmar dear, I didn't mean it that way.

HEDVIG   Can't I get you a bottle of beer, then?

HJALMAR   Absolutely not. There's nothing I need. (*Stopping.*) Beer? Did you say beer?

HEDVIG (*vivaciously*) Yes, Daddy, lovely cool beer.

HJALMAR Well—if you really insist, I suppose you could bring in a bottle.

GINA Yes, do that. Then we'll have it cozy.

(HEDVIG *runs toward the kitchen door.* HJALMAR *by the stove stops her, gazes at her, clasps her about the head and hugs her to him.*)

HJALMAR Hedvig! Hedvig!

HEDVIG (*with tears of joy*) Oh, my dearest Daddy!

HJALMAR No, don't call me that. There I sat, helping myself at a rich man's table, gorging myself with all good things—! I could at least have remembered——

GINA (*sitting at the table*) Oh, nonsense, Hjalmar.

HJALMAR Yes, I could! But you mustn't be too hard on me. You both know I love you anyway.

HEDVIG (*throwing her arms around him*) And we love you too, so much!

HJALMAR And if I should seem unreasonable at times, then—good Lord—remember that I am a man assailed by a host of cares. Ah, yes! (*Drying his eyes.*) No beer at a time like this. Bring me my flute. (HEDVIG *runs to the bookcase and fetches it.*) Thank you. There—so. With flute in hand, and you two close by me —ah!

(HEDVIG *sits at the table by* GINA, HJALMAR *walks back and forth, then forcefully begins to play a Bohemian folk dance, but in a slow elegiac tempo with sentimental intonation. After a moment he breaks off the melody and extends his left hand to* GINA.)

HJALMAR (*with feeling*) So what if we skimp and scrape along under this roof, Gina—it's still our home. And I'll say this: it's good to be here. (*He starts playing again; immediately there comes a knock on the hall door.*)

GINA (*getting up*) Shh, Hjalmar. I think someone's there.

HJALMAR (*returning the flute to the bookcase*) What, again! (GINA *goes over and opens the door.*)

GREGERS WERLE (*out in the hallway*) Excuse me——

GINA (*drawing back slightly*) Oh!

GREGERS But doesn't Mr. Ekdal, the photographer, live here?

GINA Yes, that's right.

HJALMAR (*going toward the door*) Gregers! Is it really you? Well, come right in.

GREGERS (*entering*) I said I was going to drop in on you.

HJALMAR But tonight? Have you left the party?

GREGERS Left both party and family home. Good evening, Mrs. Ekdal. I don't know whether you recognize me?

GINA Oh yes. Young Mr. Werle is not so hard to recognize.

GREGERS No. I look like my mother, and you remember her, no doubt.

HJALMAR Did you say you'd left your home?

GREGERS Yes, I've moved into a hotel.

HJALMAR I see. Well, now that you've come, take off your things and sit down.

GREGERS Thank you. (*Removes his overcoat. He is dressed now in a simple grey suit of somewhat rustic cut.*)

HJALMAR Here, on the sofa. Make yourself at home.

(GREGERS *sits on the sofa,* HJALMAR *on a chair at the table.*)

GREGERS (*looking around*) So this is where you work, then, Hjalmar. And you live here as well.

HJALMAR This is the studio, as you can see——

GINA There's more room in here, so we like it better.

HJALMAR We had a better place before; but this apartment has one great advantage: it has such wonderful adjoining rooms——

GINA And so we have a room on the other side of the hall that we can rent out.

GREGERS (*to* HJALMAR) Ah, then you have lodgers, too.

HJALMAR No, not yet. It's not that easy,

you know. One has to keep wide awake. (*To* HEDVIG.) But how about that beer?

(HEDVIG *nods and goes into the kitchen.*)

GREGERS   So that's your daughter, then?

HJALMAR   Yes, that's Hedvig.

GREGERS   An only child?

HJALMAR   She's the only one, yes. She's the greatest joy of our lives, and—(*Lowering his voice.*) also our deepest sorrow, Gregers.

GREGERS   What do you mean?

HJALMAR   Yes. You see, there's the gravest imminent danger of her losing her sight.

GREGERS   Going blind!

HJALMAR   Yes. So far only the first signs are present, and things may go well for a while. All the same, the doctor has warned us. It will come inevitably.

GREGERS   What a dreadful misfortune! How did this happen?

HJALMAR   (*sighing*)   Heredity, most likely.

GREGERS   (*startled*)   Heredity?

GINA   Hjalmar's mother also had bad eyes.

HJALMAR   Yes, so my father says. I don't remember her.

GREGERS   Poor child. And how is she taking it?

HJALMAR   Oh, you can well imagine, we haven't the heart to tell her. She suspects nothing. She's carefree, gay, and singing like a tiny bird, she's fluttering into life's eternal night. (*Overcome.*) Oh, it's a brutal blow for me, Gregers.

(HEDVIG *brings in beer and glasses on a tray, which she sets down on the table.*)

HJALMAR   (*stroking her head*)   Thanks. Thanks, Hedvig.

(HEDVIG *puts her arms around his neck and whispers in his ear.*)

HJALMAR   No. No bread and butter now. (*Looking over.*) Or maybe Gregers will have a piece?

GREGERS   (*making a gesture of refusal*) No. No, thanks.

HJALMAR   (*his tone still mournful*)   Well, you can bring in a little anyway. If you have a crust, that would be fine. And please, put enough butter on, too.

(HEDVIG *nods contentedly and returns to the kitchen.*)

GREGERS   (*after following her with his eyes*) In every other respect she looks so strong and healthy.

GINA   Yes, thank God, she's got nothing else wrong with her.

GREGERS   She'll certainly look like you when she grows up, Mrs. Ekdal. How old is she now?

GINA   Hedvig is almost fourteen exactly; her birthday's the day after tomorrow.

GREGERS   Rather tall for her age.

GINA   Yes, she's shot right up this past year.

GREGERS   Nothing like the growth of a child to show us how old we're getting. How long is it you've been married now?

GINA   We've been married now for—yes, near fifteen years.

GREGERS   No, truly! Has it been that long?

GINA   (*looking at him, becoming wary*) Yes, no doubt about it.

HJALMAR   That's right. Fifteen years, short a few months. (*Changing the subject.*) They must have been long years for you, Gregers, up there at the works.

GREGERS   They were long while I was living them—but now I scarcely know what became of the time.

(Old EKDAL *enters from his room, without his pipe, but with his old military cap on his head; his walk is a bit unsteady.*)

EKDAL   There, now, Hjalmar. Now we can settle down and talk about that—umm. What was it again?

HJALMAR   (*going toward him*)   Father, someone is here. Gregers Werle. I don't know if you remember him.

EKDAL   (*regarding* GREGERS, *who has gotten up*)   Werle? That's the son, isn't it? What does he want with me?

HJALMAR   Nothing; it's me he's come to see.

EKDAL   Well, then nothing's up, eh?

HJALMAR   No, of course not.

EKDAL   (*swinging his arms*)   It's not that

I'm scared of anything, you know, but——

GREGERS (*going over to him*)   I just want to greet you from your old hunting grounds, Lieutenant Ekdal.

EKDAL   Hunting grounds?

GREGERS   Yes, up there around the Hoidal works.

EKDAL   Oh, up there. Yes, I was well known there once.

GREGERS   In those days you were a tremendous hunter.

EKDAL   So I was. Still am, maybe. You're looking at my uniform. I ask nobody permission to wear it in here. As long as I don't walk in the streets with it—(HEDVIG *brings a plate of buttered bread, which she places on the table.*)

HJALMAR   Sit down, Father, and have a glass of beer. Help yourself, Gregers.

(EKDAL *stumbles, muttering, over to the sofa.* GREGERS *sits on the chair nearest him,* HJALMAR *on the other side of* GREGERS. GINA *sits near the table and sews;* HEDVIG *stands beside her father.*)

GREGERS   Do you remember, Lieutenant Ekdal, when Hjalmar and I would come up to visit you summers and at Christmas?

EKDAL   Did you? No, no, no, I don't recall. But I'll tell you something: I've been a first-rate hunter. Bear—I've shot them, too. Shot nine in all.

GREGERS (*looking sympathetically at him*) And now you hunt no more.

EKDAL   Oh, I wouldn't say *that,* boy. Get some hunting in now and then. Yes, but not that kind there. The woods, you see —the woods, the woods—(*Drinks.*) How do the woods look up there?

GREGERS   Not so fine as in your time. They've been cut into heavily.

EKDAL   Cut into? (*More quietly, as if in fear.*) It's a dangerous business, that. It catches up with you. The woods take revenge.

HJALMAR (*filling his glass*)   Here, a little more, Father.

GREGERS   How can a man like you—such an outdoorsman—live in the middle of a stuffy city, cooped up in these four walls?

EKDAL (*half laughs and glances at* HJALMAR)   Oh, it's not so bad here. Not bad at all.

GREGERS   But all those other things, the very roots of your soul—that cool, sweeping breeze, that free life of the moors and forests, among the animals and birds——?

EKDAL (*smiling*)   Hjalmar, should we show him?

HJALMAR (*quickly and a bit embarrassed*) No, no, Father, not tonight.

GREGERS   What's that he wants to show me?

HJALMAR   Oh, it's only a sort of—you can see it some other time.

GREGERS (*speaking again to* EKDAL)   Yes, my point was this, Lieutenant Ekdal, that now you might as well return with me to the works, for I'm sure to be leaving very soon. Without a doubt, you could get some copying to do up there; and here you've nothing in the world to stir your blood and make you happy.

EKDAL (*staring at him, astonished*)   I have nothing, nothing at all—!

GREGERS   Of course you have Hjalmar, but then again, he has his own. And a man like you, who's always felt himself so drawn to whatever is free and wild——

EKDAL (*striking the table*)   Hjalmar, now he's *got* to see it!

HJALMAR   But Father, is it worth it now? It's dark, you know——

EKDAL   Nonsense!   There's   moonlight. (*Getting up.*) I say he's got to see it. Let me by. Come and help me, Hjalmar!

HEDVIG   Oh yes, do that, Father!

HJALMAR (*getting up*)   Well—all right.

GREGERS (*to* GINA)   What's this all about?

GINA   Oh, you really mustn't expect anything special.

(EKDAL *and* HJALMAR *have gone to the back wall to push aside the two halves of the double door;* HEDVIG *helps her grandfather, while* GREGERS *remains standing by the sofa and* GINA *sits, imperturbably sewing. The doorway opens on an extensive, irregular loft room with many nooks and corners, and two separate chimney shafts ascending through it. Clear moonlight streams through skylights into certain parts of the large room; others lie in deep shadow.*)

EKDAL (*to* GREGERS) All the way over here, please.

GREGERS (*going over to them*) What *is* it, then?

EKDAL See for yourself—hmm.

HJALMAR (*somewhat self-conscious*) All this belongs to Father, you understand.

GREGERS (*peering in at the doorway*) So you keep poultry, Lieutenant Ekdal!

EKDAL I'll say we keep poultry! They're roosting now; but you just ought to see our poultry by daylight!

HEDVIG And then there's a——

EKDAL Shh, shh—don't say anything yet.

GREGERS And you've got pigeons too, I see.

EKDAL Oh yes, it might just be we've got some pigeons. They have their nesting boxes up there under the eaves; pigeons like to perch high, you know.

HJALMAR They're not ordinary pigeons, all of them.

EKDAL Ordinary! No, I should say not! We have tumblers, and we have a couple of pouters also. But look here! Can you see that hutch over there by the wall?

GREGERS Yes. What do you use that for?

EKDAL The rabbits sleep there at night, boy.

GREGERS Well, so you have rabbits too?

EKDAL Yes, what the devil do you think we have but rabbits! He asks if we have rabbits, Hjalmar! Hmm! But now listen, this is really something! This is it! Out of the way, Hedvig. Stand right here—that's it—and look straight down there. Do you see a basket there with straw in it?

GREGERS Yes, and there's a bird nesting in the basket.

EKDAL Hmm! "A bird"——

GREGERS Isn't it a duck?

EKDAL (*hurt*) Yes, of course it's a duck.

HJALMAR But what *kind* of duck?

HEDVIG It's not just any old duck—

EKDAL Shh!

GREGERS And it's no exotic breed, either.

EKDAL No, Mr.—Werle, it's not any exotic breed—because it's a wild duck.

GREGERS No, is it really? A wild duck?

EKDAL Oh yes, that's what it is. That "bird" as you said—that's a wild duck. That's our wild duck, boy.

HEDVIG *My* wild duck—I own it.

GREGERS And it can survive up here indoors? And do well?

EKDAL You've got to understand, she's got a trough of water to splash around in.

HJALMAR Fresh water every other day.

GINA (*turning to* HJALMAR) Hjalmar dear, it's freezing cold in here now.

EKDAL Hmm, let's close up, then. Doesn't pay to disturb their rest either. Lend a hand, Hedvig dear. (HJALMAR *and* HEDVIG *push the double doors together.*) Another time you can get a proper look at her. (*Sits in the armchair by the stove.*) Oh, they're most curious, the wild ducks, you know.

GREGERS But how did you capture it, Lieutenant Ekdal?

EKDAL Didn't capture it myself. There's a certain man here in town we can thank for it.

GREGERS (*starts slightly*) That man—it wouldn't be my father?

EKDAL Exactly right—your father. Hmm.

HJALMAR It was odd you were able to guess that, Gregers.

GREGERS Well, you said before that you owed Father for so many different things, so I thought here too——

GINA But we didn't get the duck from Mr. Werle himself——

EKDAL We might just as well thank Haakon Werle for her anyhow, Gina. (*To* GREGERS.) He was out in his boat—follow me?—and he shot for her, but he sees so bad now, your father, that—hm—he only winged her.

GREGERS I see. She took some shot in her body.

HJALMAR Yes, some one, two—three pieces.

HEDVIG She got it under the wing, and so she couldn't fly.

GREGERS Ah, so she dived right for the bottom, eh?

EKDAL (*sleepily, with a thick voice*) You can bet on that. They always do, the wild ducks—streak for the bottom, deep as they can get, boy—bite right into the weeds and sea moss—and all that devil's beard that grows down there. And then they never come up again.

GREGERS But Lieutenant Ekdal, *your* wild duck came up again.

EKDAL He had such a remarkably clever dog, your father. And that dog—he dove down and brought her up.

GREGERS (*turning to* HJALMAR) And then you got her here.

HJALMAR Not directly. First she went home to your father's, but there she didn't do well, so Pettersen got his orders to put an end to her——

EKDAL (*half asleep*) Hm—yes, Pettersen —that bonehead——

HJALMAR (*speaking more softly*) That's the way we got her, you see. Father knows Pettersen a bit and when he heard all this about the wild duck, he arranged to have her handed over to us.

GREGERS And now she's absolutely thriving in that attic room.

HJALMAR Yes, it's incredible. She's gotten fat. I think she's been in there so long, too, that she's forgotten her old wild life, and that's what it all comes down to.

GREGERS You're certainly right there, Hjalmar. Just don't let her ever catch sight of the sea and the sky—But I mustn't stay any longer, for I think your father's asleep.

HJALMAR Oh, don't bother about that.

GREGERS But incidentally—you said you had a room for rent, a free room?

HJALMAR Yes. Why? Do you know someone, perhaps—?

GREGERS Could I take that room?

HJALMAR You?

GINA No, not *you*, Mr. Werle——

GREGERS Could I take the room? If so, I'll move in first thing in the morning.

HJALMAR By all means, with the greatest pleasure——

GINA No, but Mr. Werle, it's not at all the room for *you*.

HJALMAR But Gina, how can you say that?

GINA Oh, the room isn't large enough, or light enough, and——

GREGERS That really doesn't matter, Mrs. Ekdal.

HJALMAR I think it's a very pleasant room, and it's not badly furnished, either.

GINA But remember those two who live right below.

GREGERS What two are those?

GINA Oh, one of them's been a private tutor——

HJALMAR That's Molvik, from the university.

GINA And then there's a doctor named Relling.

GREGERS Relling? I know him somewhat. He practiced a while up in Hoidal.

GINA They're a pretty wild pair, those fellows. They go out on the town evenings and then come home in the dead of night, and they're not always so——

GREGERS One gets used to that soon enough. I'm hoping things will go for me the same as with the wild duck——

GINA Well, I think you ought to sleep on it first, anyway.

GREGERS You're not very anxious to have me in the house, Mrs. Ekdal.

GINA Goodness, what makes you think that?

HJALMAR Yes, Gina, this is really peculiar of you. (*To* GREGERS.) But tell me, do you expect to stay here in town for a while?

GREGERS (*putting on his overcoat*) Yes, now I expect to stay on.

HJALMAR But not at home with your father? What do you plan to do with yourself?

GREGERS Yes, if I only knew that—then I'd be doing all right. But when one carries the cross of a name like Gregers— "Gregers"—and then "Werle" coming after—have you ever heard anything so disgusting?

HJALMAR Oh, I don't agree at all.

GREGERS Ugh! Phew! I feel I'd like to spit on any man with a name like that. But when you have to bear that cross of being Gregers—Werle in this world, as I do——

HJALMAR (*laughing*) If you weren't Gregers Werle, who would you want to be?

GREGERS If I could choose, above all else I'd like to be a clever dog.

GINA A dog!

HEDVIG (*involuntarily*) Oh no!

GREGERS Yes. A really fantastic, clever dog, the kind that goes to the bottom after wild ducks when they dive under and bite fast into the weeds down in the mire.

HJALMAR You know, Gregers—I can't follow a word you're saying.

GREGERS Never mind. There's really nothing very remarkable in it. But tomorrow morning, early, I'll be moving in. (*To* GINA.) I won't be any trouble to you; I do everything for myself. (*To* HJALMAR.) The rest we can talk over tomorrow. Good night, Mrs. Ekdal. (*Nods to* HEDVIG.) Good night.

GINA Good night, Mr. Werle.

HEDVIG Good night.

HJALMAR (*who has lit a lamp*) Just a minute. I'd better light your way; it's quite dark on the stairs.

(GREGERS *and* HJALMAR *go out through the hall.*)

GINA (*gazing into space, her sewing in her lap*) Wasn't that a queer business, his wanting to be a dog?

HEDVIG I'll tell you something, Mother— it seemed to me he meant something else by that.

GINA What else could he mean?

HEDVIG I don't know—but it was just as if he meant something else from what he said, all the time.

GINA Do you think so? It was strange, all right.

HJALMAR (*coming back*) The light was still lit. (*Putting out the lamp and setting it down.*) Ah, at last one can get a bite to eat. (*Beginning on the bread and butter.*) Well, now you see, Gina—if you simply keep wide awake, then——

GINA What do you mean, wide awake?

HJALMAR Well, it was lucky, then, that we got the room rented out for a while at last. And think—to a person like Gregers —a good old friend.

GINA Yes. I don't know what to say. I don't.

HEDVIG Oh, Mother, you'll see. It'll be fun.

HJALMAR You really are peculiar. Before you were so eager to rent, and now you don't like it.

GINA Yes, Hjalmar, if it could only have been somebody else. What do you think the old man will say?

HJALMAR Old Werle? This doesn't concern him.

GINA But you can sure bet that something has come up between them, since the son is moving out. You know how those two get along together.

HJALMAR Yes, that may well be, but——

GINA And now maybe the old man thinks it's you that's behind——

HJALMAR He can think that as much as he likes! Old Werle has done a tremendous amount for me. God knows, I'm aware of that. But even so, I can't make myself eternally dependent on him.

GINA But Hjalmar dear, that can have its effect on Grandfather. He may now lose that miserable little income he gets from Graaberg.

HJALMAR I could almost say, so much the better! Isn't it rather humiliating for a man like me to see his gray-haired father go around like an outcast? But now time is gathering to a ripeness, I think. (*Takes another piece of bread and butter.*) Just as sure as I've got a mission in life, I'm going to carry it out!

HEDVIG Oh yes, Daddy! Do!

GINA Shh! Don't wake him up.

HJALMAR (*more quietly*) I *will* carry it out, I tell you. There will come a day when—And that's why it's good we got the room rented out, for now I'm more independently fixed. Any man *must* be that, who's got a mission in life. (*Over by the armchair; emotionally.*) Poor old white-haired Father—lean on your Hjalmar. He has broad shoulders—powerful shoulders, in any case. One fine day you'll wake up and—(*To* GINA.) You do believe that, don't you?

GINA (*getting up*) Yes, of course I do. But first let's see about getting him to bed.

HJALMAR Yes, let's do that.

(*Gently they lift up the old man.*)

Act Three

HJALMAR EKDAL's *studio. It is morning. Daylight streams through the large window in the sloping roof; the curtain is drawn back.*

HJALMAR is sitting at the table, busy retouching a photograph; many other pictures lie in front of him. After a moment GINA, wearing a hat and coat, enters by the hall door; she has a covered basket on her arm.

HJALMAR Back so soon, Gina?

GINA Oh yes. Got to keep moving. (*She sets the basket on a chair and takes her coat off.*)

HJALMAR Did you look in on Gregers?

GINA Um-hm, I certainly did. Looks real nice in there. The moment he came, he got his room in beautiful shape.

HJALMAR Oh?

GINA Yes. He wanted to do everything himself, he said. So he starts building a fire in the stove, and the next thing he's closed down the damper so the whole room is full of smoke. Phew! What a stink, enough to——

HJALMAR Oh no!

GINA But that's not the best part! So then he wants to put it out, so he empties his whole water pitcher into the stove and now the floor's swimming in the worst muck.

HJALMAR That's a nuisance.

GINA I got the janitor's wife to come and scrub up after him, the pig; but it'll be unfit to live in till afternoon.

HJALMAR What's he doing with himself in the meantime?

GINA Thought he'd take a little walk, he said.

HJALMAR I was in to see him for a moment too—after you left.

GINA I heard that. You asked him for lunch.

HJALMAR Just the tiniest little midday snack, you understand. It's the very first day—we could hardly avoid it. You always have something in the house.

GINA I'll see what I can find.

HJALMAR But now don't make it too skimpy. Because Relling and Molvik are dropping in too, I think. I just met Relling on the stairs, you see, so of course I had to——

GINA Oh? Must we have those two also?

HJALMAR Good Lord, a couple of sandwiches more or less; what's the difference?

EKDAL (*opening his door and looking in*) Say, listen, Hjalmar—(*Noticing* GINA.) Oh, well.

GINA Is there something Grandfather wants?

EKDAL Oh no. Let it be. Hmm. (*Goes in again.*)

GINA (*picking up the basket*) Keep a sharp eye on him so he doesn't go out.

HJALMAR Oh yes, I'll do that. Listen, Gina, a little herring salad would be awfully good—because Relling and Molvik were out on a binge last night.

GINA Just so they don't come before I'm ready——

HJALMAR Not a chance. Take your time.

GINA That's fine, then—and meanwhile you can get a little work done.

HJALMAR Can't you see how I'm working! I'm working for all I'm worth!

GINA Because then you'll have *those* off

your hands, you know. (*She carries the basket out to the kitchen.* HJALMAR *sits for a while, tinting the photograph in a glum and listless manner.*)

EKDAL (*peeks in, peers about the studio, and whispers*) Are you busy, boy?

HJALMAR Of course. I'm sitting here struggling with these pictures——

EKDAL Oh well, don't bother. If you're so busy, then—Hm! (*He reenters his room, leaving the door ajar.*)

HJALMAR (*continues a moment in silence, then puts down the brush and goes over to the door*) Father, are *you* busy?

EKDAL (*grumbling from within*) When you're busy—I'm busy too. Huh!

HJALMAR Yes, of course. (*Returns to his work.*)

EKDAL (*a moment later, coming in again*) Hm. Well, now, Hjalmar, I'm really not *that* busy.

HJALMAR I thought you had copying to do.

EKDAL Oh, the devil! Can't he, Graaberg, wait a day or two? I'm sure it's no matter of life or death.

HJALMAR No, and you're no slave, either.

EKDAL And then there was that other business inside——

HJALMAR Yes, that's just it. Maybe you want to go in? Shall I open it up for you?

EKDAL Wouldn't be a bad idea, really?

HJALMAR (*getting up*) And then we'd have *that* off our hands.

EKDAL Yes, exactly. And it has to be ready first thing tomorrow. But it *is* tomorrow, isn't it?

HJALMAR It certainly is tomorrow.

(HJALMAR *and* EKDAL *each push back one of the double doors. Within, morning sunlight shines through the skylights. A few doves fly back and forth; others perch, cooing, on the rafters. Chickens cackle now and then from back in the loft.*)

HJALMAR There, now you can get in, Father.

EKDAL (*going in*) Aren't you coming along?

HJALMAR Well, you know what—I almost think—(*Sees* GINA *in the kitchen doorway.*) I? No, I haven't the time; I've got to work. But that means our new mechanism——

(*He pulls a cord; inside a curtain descends, its lower portion composed of a strip of old sailcloth, the upper part being a piece of worn-out fishnetting. By this means, the floor of the loft is rendered invisible.*)

HJALMAR (*returning to the table*) That's that. Now at last I can work in peace for a while.

GINA Is he in there, romping around again?

HJALMAR Isn't that better than having him run down to Mrs. Eriksen's? (*Sitting.*) Is there anything you want? You look so——

GINA I only wanted to ask, do you think we can set the lunch table in here?

HJALMAR Well, we haven't any portraits scheduled that early, have we?

GINA No. I don't expect anybody except that couple who want to be taken together.

HJALMAR Why the devil can't they be taken together some other day?

GINA Now, Hjalmar dear, I've got them booked for during your midday nap.

HJALMAR Well, that's fine, then. So we'll eat in here.

GINA All right. But there's no hurry about setting the table; you can certainly use it a while longer.

HJALMAR Oh, it's obvious I'm using the table as much as I can!

GINA Because then you'll be free later on, you know. (*She goes back into the kitchen. A short pause.*)

EKDAL (*at the door to the loft, behind the net*) Hjalmar!

HJALMAR Well?

EKDAL 'Fraid we'll have to move the water trough after all.

HJALMAR Yes, that's what I've been saying all along.

EKDAL Hm—hm—hm. (*Disappears from the doorway.*)

(HJALMAR *works a bit, glances toward the loft, and half rises.* HEDVIG *enters from the kitchen.*)

HJALMAR (*hurriedly sitting again*) What do you want?

HEDVIG I was just coming in to you, Father.

HJALMAR (*after a moment*) You seem to be kind of snooping around. Are you checking up, maybe?

HEDVIG No, not at all.

HJALMAR What's Mother doing out there now?

HEDVIG Oh, she's half through the herring salad. (*Going over to the table.*) Don't you have some little thing I could help you with, Daddy?

HJALMAR Oh no. It's better just to leave me alone with all this—so long as my strength holds out. Nothing to worry about, Hedvig—if only your father can keep his health——

HEDVIG Oh, Daddy, no. That's horrid; you mustn't talk like that. (*She wanders about a little, stops by the loft doorway, and looks in.*)

HJALMAR What's he trying to do now?

HEDVIG It must be a new pathway up to the water trough.

HJALMAR He can't possibly rig that up on his own! And I'm condemned to sit here—!

HEDVIG (*going to him*) Let *me* take the brush, Daddy. I know I can.

HJALMAR Oh, nonsense, you'll only ruin your eyes.

HEDVIG No such thing. Give me the brush.

HJALMAR (*getting up*) Well, it'll only be for a minute or two.

HEDVIG Pooh! How could that hurt me? (*Takes the brush.*) There now. (*Sitting.*) And here's one to go by.

HJALMAR But don't ruin your eyes! Hear me? I won't take the blame; you can take the blame yourself—you hear me?

HEDVIG (*at work retouching*) Yes, yes, sure I will.

HJALMAR You're wonderfully clever, Hedvig. Just for a couple of minutes now.

(*He slips around the edge of the curtain into the loft.* HEDVIG *sits at her work.* HJALMAR *and* EKDAL *are heard arguing inside.*)

HJALMAR (*appearing behind the net*) Hedvig, just hand me the pliers from the shelf. And the chisel, please. (*Turning over his shoulder.*) Yes, now you'll see, Father. Will you give me a chance to show you the way I mean! (HEDVIG *fetches the desired tools from the bookcase and passes them in to him.*) Ah, thanks. See, dear, it was a good thing I came. (*He vanishes from the doorway; sounds of carpentry and bantering are heard.* HEDVIG *remains, looking in at them. A moment later, a knock at the hall door; she fails to notice it.*)

GREGERS (*bareheaded, and without his overcoat, enters, hesitating slightly at the door*) Hm——

HEDVIG (*turning and going toward him*) Good morning. Please come in.

GREGERS Thanks. (*Looking at the loft.*) You seem to have workmen in the house.

HEDVIG No, that's only Father and Grandfather. I'll go tell them.

GREGERS No, no, don't bother. I'd rather wait a bit. (*He sits on the sofa.*)

HEDVIG It's so messy here—(*Starts to remove the photographs.*)

GREGERS Oh, they can stay. Are those some pictures that have to be finished?

HEDVIG Yes, it's a little job I'm helping Daddy with.

GREGERS Please don't let me disturb you.

HEDVIG All right. (*She gathers her materials around her and sets to work again;* GREGERS *meanwhile regards her in silence.*)

GREGERS Did the wild duck sleep well last night?

HEDVIG Yes, I'm sure she did, thanks.

GREGER (*turning toward the loft*) It looks so very different by daylight than it did by moonlight.

413

HEDVIG Yes, it can change so completely. In the morning it looks different from in the afternoon; and when it rains it's different from when it's clear.

GREGERS Have you noticed that?

HEDVIG Sure. You can't help it.

GREGERS And do you like it in there with the wild duck, too?

HEDVIG Yes, whenever I can be there——

GREGERS But of course you don't have much free time; you do go to school, don't you?

HEDVIG No, not anymore. Daddy's afraid I'll hurt my eyes.

GREGERS Oh. Then he tutors you himself.

HEDVIG Daddy's promised to, but he hasn't found time for that yet.

GREGERS But isn't there anyone else to help you a little?

HEDVIG Sure, there's Mr. Molvik, but he isn't always exactly, really—well——

GREGERS He gets drunk, eh?

HEDVIG He *certainly* does.

GREGERS Well, then you do have time to yourself. And inside—I'll bet in there it's just like a world of its own—am I right?

HEDVIG Oh, completely! And then there are so many wonderful things.

GREGERS Really?

HEDVIG Yes, big cupboards with books in them; and lots of the books have pictures.

GREGERS Ah!

HEDVIG And then there's an old cabinet with drawers and compartments, and a huge clock with figures that are supposed to come out. But the clock doesn't go anymore.

GREGERS Even time doesn't exist in there —with the wild duck.

HEDVIG Yes. And then there's an old watercolor set and things like that. And then all the books.

GREGERS And of course you read the books?

HEDVIG Oh yes, whenever I can. But they're mostly in English, and I don't understand that. But then I look at the pictures. There's one just enormous book called *Harryson's History of London;* it must be a hundred years old, and it's got

ever so many pictures in it. At the front there's a picture of Death with an hourglass and a girl. I think that's horrible. But then there are all the other pictures of churches and castles and streets and great ships sailing on the ocean.

GREGERS But tell me, where did all these rare things come from!

HEDVIG Oh, an old sea captain lived here once, and he brought them home. They called him "the flying Dutchman"—and that's the strangest thing, because he wasn't a Dutchman at all.

GREGERS No?

HEDVIG No. But then he didn't come back finally, and he left all these things behind.

GREGERS Listen, tell me—when you sit in there and look at pictures, don't you ever want to go out and see the real world all for yourself?

HEDVIG No, never! I'm going to stay at home always and help Daddy and Mother.

GREGERS You mean finishing photographs?

HEDVIG No, not just that. Most of all, I'd like to learn how to engrave pictures like those in the English books.

GREGERS Hm. What does your father say to that?

HEDVIG I don't think he likes it. Daddy's so funny about such things. Just think, he talks about me learning basketmaking and wickerwork! But I don't see anything in *that.*

GREGERS Oh no, I don't either.

HEDVIG But Daddy's right when he says that if I'd learned how to make baskets, I could have made the new basket for the wilk duck.

GREGERS You could have, yes—and that really was up to you.

HEDVIG Yes, because it's *my* wild duck.

GREGERS Yes, of course it is.

HEDVIG Uh-huh, I own it. But Daddy and Grandpa can borrow it as much as they want.

GREGERS Oh? What do they do with it?

HEDVIG Oh, they look after it and build things for it and so on.

GREGERS I can well imagine. The wild

duck rules supreme in there, doesn't she?

HEDVIG Yes, she does, and that's because she's a *real* wild bird. And then it's so sad for her; the poor thing has no one to turn to.

GREGERS No family, like the rabbits——

HEDVIG No. Even the chickens have all the others that they were baby chicks with, but she's so completely apart from any of her own. So you see, everything is so really mysterious about the wild duck. There's no one who knows her, and no one who knows where she's come from, either.

GREGERS And actually, she's been in the depths of the sea.

HEDVIG (*glances at him, suppresses a smile, and asks*) Why did you say "depths of the sea"?

GREGERS What else should I say?

HEDVIG You could have said "bottom of the sea"—or "the ocean's bottom"?

GREGERS But couldn't I just as well say "depths of the sea"?

HEDVIG Sure. But to me it sounds so strange when someone else says "depths of the sea."

GREGERS But why? Tell me why?

HEDVIG No, I won't. It's something so stupid.

GREGERS It couldn't be. Now tell me why you smiled.

HEDVIG That was because always, when all of a sudden—in a flash—I happen to think of that in there, it always seems to me that the whole room and everything in it is called "the depths of the sea"! But that's all so stupid.

GREGERS Don't you dare say that.

HEDVIG Oh yes, because it's only an attic.

GREGERS Are you so sure of that?

HEDVIG (*astonished*) That it's an attic!

GREGERS Yes. Do you know that for certain?

(HEDVIG, *speechless, stares at him open-mouthed.* GINA *enters from the kitchen with a tablecloth.*)

GREGERS (*getting up*) I'm afraid I've come too early for you.

GINA Oh, you can find yourself a spot; it's almost ready now. Clear the table, Hedvig.

(HEDVIG *puts away the materials; during the following dialogue, she and* GINA *set the table.* GREGERS *settles in the armchair and pages through an album.*)

GREGERS I hear you do retouching, Mrs. Ekdal.

GINA (*with a side-glance*) Um yes, I do that.

GREGERS That's really very lucky.

GINA Why "lucky"?

GREGERS With Hjalmar a photographer, I mean.

HEDVIG Mother does photography, too.

GINA Oh yes, I even got taught in *that* art.

GREGERS So we might say it's you who runs the business.

GINA Yes, when my husband hasn't the time himself——

GREGERS He finds himself so taken up with his old father, I suppose.

GINA Yes, and then it's no kind of thing for a man like Hjalmar to go taking portraits of your common average.

GREGERS I agree; but once he's chosen this line of work, then——

GINA Mr. Werle, you must realize that my husband is not just any old photographer.

GREGERS Well, naturally; but even so——

(*A shot is fired in the loft.*)

GREGERS (*jumping up*) What's that!

GINA Uff, now they're shooting again.

GREGERS They shoot, also?

HEDVIG They go hunting.

GREGERS What! (*Going to the loft doorway.*) Have you gone hunting, Hjalmar?

HJALMAR (*behind the net*) Are you here? I didn't realize; I was so occupied—(*To* HEDVIG.) And you, you didn't tell us. (*Comes into the studio.*)

GREGERS Do you go shooting in the loft?

HJALMAR (*producing a double-barreled pistol*) Oh, only with this here.

GINA Yes, some day you and Grandfather'll have an accident with that there gun.

HJALMAR (*annoyed*) I believe I've remarked that this type of firearm is called a pistol.

GINA I don't see that that makes it any better.

GREGERS So you've turned out a "hunter" as well, Hjalmar?

HJALMAR Just a little rabbit hunt, now and then. It's mainly for Father's sake, you understand.

GINA Men are so funny, really; they've always got to have their little diversities.

HJALMAR (*angrily*) That's right, yes—they always have to have their little diversions.

GINA Yes, that's just what I was saying.

HJALMAR Oh, well! (*To* GREGERS.) So that's it, and then we're very lucky in the way the loft is placed—nobody can hear us when we're shooting. (*Puts the pistol on the highest bookshelf.*) Don't touch the pistol, Hedvig! One barrel's still loaded, don't forget.

GREGERS (*peering through the netting*) You've got a hunting rifle too, I see.

HJALMAR Yes, that's Father's old rifle. It won't shoot anymore; something's gone wrong with the lock. But it's a lot of fun to have anyway, because we can take it all apart and clean it and grease it and put it together again—Of course, it's mostly Father who fools around with that sort of thing.

HEDVIG (*crossing to* GREGERS) Now you can really see the wild duck.

GREGERS I was just now looking at her. She seems to drag one wing a little.

HJALMAR Well, no wonder; she took a bad wound.

GREGERS And then she limps a little. Isn't that so?

HJALMAR Maybe just a tiny bit.

HEDVIG Yes, that was the foot the dog bit her in.

HJALMAR But she hasn't a thing wrong with her otherwise; and that's simply remarkable when you think that she's had

a charge of shot in her body and been held by the teeth of a dog——

GREGERS (*with a glance at* HEDVIG) And been in the depths of the sea—so long.

HEDVIG (*smiling*) Yes.

GINA (*arranging the table*) Oh, that sacred duck—haven't you made enough crucifixes out of her?

HJALMAR Hm. Are you nearly ready?

GINA Yes, right away. Hedvig, now you can come and help me.

(GINA *and* HEDVIG *exit into the kitchen.*)

HJALMAR (*in an undertone*) I don't think it's so good that you stand there, watching my father. He doesn't like it. (GREGERS *comes away from the loft doorway.*) And it's better, too, that I close up before the others come. (*Shooing away the menagerie with his hands.*) Hssh! Hssh! Go 'way now! (*With this he raises the curtain and draws the double doors together.*) I invented these contraptions myself. It's really great fun to have such things around to take care of and fix when they get out of whack. And besides, it's absolutely necessary, you know; Gina doesn't go for rabbits and chickens out here in the studio.

GREGERS Of course not. And I suppose it *is* your wife who manages here?

HJALMAR My general rule is to delegate the routine matters to her, and that leaves me free to retire to the living room to think over more important things.

GREGERS And what sort of things are these, Hjalmar?

HJALMAR I've been wondering why you haven't asked me that before. Or maybe you haven't heard about my invention.

GREGERS Invention? No.

HJALMAR Oh? Then you haven't? Well, no, up there in that waste and wilderness——

GREGERS Then you've really invented something!

HJALMAR Not completely invented it yet, but I'm getting very close. You must realize that when I decided to dedicate my life to photography, it wasn't my idea to spend time taking pictures of a lot of nobodies.

GREGERS Yes, that's what your wife was just now saying.

HJALMAR I swore that if I devoted my powers to the craft, I would then exalt it to such heights that it would become both an art and a science. That's when I decided on this amazing invention.

GREGERS And what does this invention consist of? What's its purpose?

HJALMAR Yes, Gregers, you mustn't ask for details like that yet. It takes time, you know. And you mustn't think it's vanity that's driving me, either. I'm certainly not working for myself. Oh no, it's my life's mission that stands before me day and night.

GREGERS What life's mission is that?

HJALMAR Remember the silver-haired old man?

GREGERS Your poor father. Yes, but actually what can you do for him?

HJALMAR I can raise his self-respect from the dead—by restoring the Ekdal name to dignity and honor.

GREGERS So that's your life's work.

HJALMAR Yes. I am going to rescue that shipwrecked man. That's just what he suffered—shipwreck—when the storm broke over him. When all those harrowing investigations took place, he wasn't himself anymore. That pistol, there—the one we use to shoot rabbits with—it's played a part in the tragedy of the Ekdals.

GREGERS Pistol! Oh?

HJALMAR When he was sentenced and facing prison, he had that pistol in his hand——

GREGERS You mean he—!

HJALMAR Yes. But he didn't dare. He was a coward. That shows how broken and degraded he'd become by then. Can you picture it? He, a soldier, a man who'd shot nine bears and was directly descended from two lieutenant colonels— I mean, one after the other, of course. Can you picture it, Gregers?

GREGERS Yes, I can picture it very well.

HJALMAR Well, I can't. And then that pistol intruded on our family history once again. When he was under lock and key, dressed like a common prisoner—oh, those were agonizing times for me, you can imagine. I kept the shades of both my windows drawn. When I looked out, I saw the sun shining the same as ever. I couldn't understand it. I saw the people going along the street, laughing and talking of trivial things. I couldn't understand it. I felt all creation should be standing still, like during an eclipse.

GREGERS I felt that way when my mother died.

HJALMAR During one of those times Hjalmar Ekdal put a pistol to his own breast.

GREGERS You were thinking of——

HJALMAR Yes.

GREGERS But you didn't shoot?

HJALMAR No. In that critical moment I won a victory over myself. I stayed alive. But you can bet it takes courage to choose life in those circumstances.

GREGERS Well, that depends on your point of view.

HJALMAR Oh, absolutely. But it was all for the best, because now I've nearly finished my invention; and then Dr. Relling thinks, just as I do, that they'll let Father wear his uniform again. That's the only reward I'm after.

GREGERS So it's really the uniform that he—?

HJALMAR Yes, that's what he really hungers and craves for. You've no idea how that makes my heart ache. Every time we throw a little family party—like my birthday, or Gina's, or whatever—then the old man comes in, wearing that uniform from his happier days. But if there's even a knock at the door, he goes scuttering back in his room fast as the old legs will carry him. You see, he doesn't dare show himself to strangers. What a heartrending spectacle for a son!

GREGERS   Approximately when do you think the invention will be finished?

HJALMAR   Oh, good Lord, don't hold me to a timetable. An invention, that's something you can hardly dictate to. It depends a great deal on inspiration, on a sudden insight—and it's nearly impossible to say in advance when that will occur.

GREGERS   But it *is* making progress?

HJALMAR   Of course it's making progress. Every single day I think about my invention. I'm brimming with it. Every afternoon, right after lunch, I lock myself in the living room where I can meditate in peace. But it's no use driving me; it simply won't work. Relling says so too.

GREGERS   And you don't think all those contraptions in the loft distract you and scatter your talents?

HJALMAR   No, no, no, on the contrary. You mustn't say that. I can't always go around here, brooding over the same nerve-racking problems. I need some diversion to fill in the time. You see, inspiration, the moment of insight—when that comes, nothing can stop it.

GREGERS   My dear Hjalmar, I suspect you've got a bit of the wild duck in you.

HJALMAR   Of the wild duck? What do you mean?

GREGERS   You've plunged to the bottom and clamped hold of the seaweed.

HJALMAR   I suppose you mean that near-fatal shot that brought down Father—and me as well?

GREGERS   Not quite that. I wouldn't say you're wounded; but you're wandering in a poisonous swamp, Hjalmar. You've got an insidious disease in your system, and so you've gone to the bottom to die in the dark.

HJALMAR   Me? Die in the dark! You know what, Gregers—you'll really have to stop that talk.

GREGERS   But never mind. I'm going to raise you up again. You know, I've found my mission in life, too. I found it yesterday.

HJALMAR   Yes, that may well be; but you can just leave me out of it. I can assure you that—apart from my quite understandable melancholy—I'm as well off as any man could wish to be.

GREGERS   And your thinking so is part of the sickness.

HJALMAR   Gregers, you're my old friend—please—don't talk any more about sickness and poison. I'm not used to that kind of conversation. In my house nobody talks to me about ugly things.

GREGERS   That's not hard to believe.

HJALMAR   Yes, because it isn't good for me. And there's no swamp air here, as you put it. In a poor photographer's house, life is cramped; I know that. My lot is a poor one—but, you know, I'm an inventor. And I'm the family breadwinner, too. *That's* what sustains me through all the pettiness. Ah, here they come with the lunch.

(GINA *and* HEDVIG *bring in bottles of beer, a decanter of brandy, glasses, and the like. At the same time,* RELLING *and* MOLVIK *enter from the hall. Neither wears a hat or overcoat;* MOLVIK *is dressed in black.*)

GINA (*setting things down on the table*) Well, the two of them—right on time.

RELLING   Molvik was positive he could smell that herring salad, and there was just no holding him back. 'Morning for the second time, Ekdal.

HJALMAR   Gregers, I'd like you to meet Mr. Molvik. And Dr.—ah, but don't you know Relling?

GREGERS   Yes, slightly.

RELLING   Well, Mr. Werle junior. Yes, we've had a few run-ins together up at the Hoidal works. You've just moved in, haven't you?

GREGERS   I moved in this morning.

RELLING   And Molvik and I live downstairs; so you're not very far from a doctor and a priest, if you ever have need of such.

GREGERS   Thanks; that could happen. After all, we had thirteen at the table last night.

HJALMAR Oh, don't start in on ugly subjects again!

RELLING You don't have to worry, Hjalmar; Lord knows this doesn't involve you.

HJALMAR I hope not, for my family's sake. But let's sit down and eat and drink and be merry.

GREGERS Shouldn't we wait for your father?

HJALMAR No, he'll have his lunch sent in to him later. Come now!

(*The men sit at the table, eating and drinking.* GINA *and* HEDVIG *go in and out, serving the food.*)

RELLING Last night Molvik was tight as a tick, Mrs. Ekdal.

GINA Oh? Last night again?

RELLING Didn't you hear him when I finally brought him home?

GINA No, can't say I did.

RELLING That's lucky—because Molvik was revolting last night.

GINA Is that so, Molvik?

MOLVIK Let's draw a veil over last night's activities. They have no bearing on my better self.

RELLING (*to* GREGERS) All of a sudden he's possessed by an impulse; and then I have to take him out on a bat. You see, Mr. Molvik is demonic.

GREGERS Demonic?

RELLING Molvik is demonic, yes.

GREGERS Hm.

RELLING And demonic natures aren't made to go through life on the straight and narrow; they've got to take detours every so often. Well—and you're still sticking it out there at that dark, hideous mill.

GREGERS I've stuck it out till now.

RELLING And did you ever get satisfaction on that "summons" you were going around with?

GREGERS Summons? (*Understanding him.*) Oh, that.

HJALMAR Were you serving summonses, Gregers?

GREGERS Nonsense.

RELLING Oh, but he was, definitely. He went around to all the cotters' cabins, presenting something he called "Summons to the Ideal."

GREGERS I was young then.

RELLING You're right, there. You were very young. And that summons to the ideal—it wasn't ever honored during my time up there.

GREGERS Nor later, either.

RELLING Well, I guess you've learned enough to cut down your expectations a bit.

GREGERS Never—when I meet a man who's a real man.

HJALMAR Yes, that seems quite reasonable to me. A little butter, Gina.

RELLING And then a piece of pork for Molvik.

MOLVIK Ugh, no pork!
(*There is a knock at the loft door.*)

HJALMAR Open it, Hedvig; Father wants to get out.

(HEDVIG *goes to open the door a little; old* EKDAL *enters with a fresh rabbit skin. He closes the door after him.*)

EKDAL Good morning, gentlemen. Good hunting today. Shot a big one.

HJALMAR And you went ahead and skinned it without waiting for me!

EKDAL Salted it, too. It's nice tender meat, this rabbit meat. And it's so sweet. Tastes like sugar. Enjoy your food, gentlemen!
(*He goes into his room.*)

MOLVIK (*getting up*) Pardon—I, I can't —got to go downstairs right——

RELLING Drink soda water, man!

MOLVIK (*rushing out the hall door*) Ugh —ugh!

RELLING (*to* HJALMAR) Let's empty a glass to the old hunter.

HJALMAR (*clinking glasses with him*) Yes, to the gallant sportsman on the brink of the grave.

RELLING To the old, gray-haired— (*Drinks.*) Tell me something, is it gray hair he's got, or is it white?

HJALMAR It's really a little of both. But as a matter of fact, he's scarcely got a hair on his head.

RELLING Well, fake hair will take you through life, good as any. You know, Ekdal, you're really a very lucky man. You have your high mission in life to fight for——

HJALMAR And I am fighting for it, too.

RELLING And then you've got this clever wife of yours, padding around in her slippers and waggling her hips and keeping you neat and cozy.

HJALMAR Yes, Gina—(*Nodding at her.*) You're a good companion for life's journey, you are.

GINA Oh, don't sit there deprecating me.

RELLING And what about your Hedvig, Ekdal?

HJALMAR (*stirred*) My child, yes! My child above all. Hedvig, come here to me. (*Caresses her head.*) What day is tomorrow, dear?

HEDVIG (*shaking him*) Oh, don't talk about it, Daddy!

HJALMAR It's like a knife turning in my heart when I think how bare it's all going to be, just the tiniest celebration out in the loft——

HEDVIG Oh, but that will be just wonderful!

RELLING And wait till that marvelous invention comes to the world, Hedvig!

HJALMAR Ah, yes—then you'll see! Hedvig, I've resolved to make your future secure. As long as you live, you'll live in style. I'll assure you of something, one way or another. That will be the poor inventor's sole reward.

HEDVIG (*whispering, with her arms around his neck*) Oh, you dear, dear Daddy!

RELLING (*to* GREGERS) Well, now, isn't it good for a change to be sitting around a well-spread table in a happy family circle?

HJALMAR Yes, I really prize these hours around the table.

GREGERS I, for my part, don't thrive in marsh gas.

RELLING Marsh gas?

HJALMAR Oh, don't start that rubbish again!

GINA Lord knows there isn't any marsh gas here, Mr. Werle; every blessed day I air the place out.

GREGERS (*leaving the table*) You can't air out the stench I mean.

HJALMAR Stench!

GINA What about that, Hjalmar!

RELLING Beg pardon—but it wouldn't be you who brought that stench in with you from the mines up there?

GREGERS It's just like you to call what I'm bringing into this house a stench.

RELLING (*crossing over to him*) Listen, Mr. Werle junior, I've got a strong suspicion that you're still going around with the uncut version of that "Summons to the Ideal" in your back pocket.

GREGERS I've got it written in my heart.

RELLING I don't care where the devil you've got it; I wouldn't advise you to play process-server here as long as I'm around.

GREGERS And what if I do anyway?

RELLING Then you'll go head first down the stairs, that's what.

HJALMAR (*getting up*) Come, now, Relling!

GREGERS Yes, just throw me out——

GINA (*coming between them*) You can't do that, Relling. But I'll tell you this, Mr. Werle—that you, who made all that mess with your stove, have no right to come to me talking about smells.

(*A knock at the hall door.*)

HEDVIG Mother, somebody's knocking.

HJALMAR Wouldn't you know, it's open house!

GINA I'll go—(*She crosses and opens the door, gives a start, shudders and shrinks back.*) Uff! Oh no!

(*Old* WERLE, *in a fur coat, steps into the room.*)

WERLE Excuse me, but I think my son is living in this house.

GINA (*catching her breath*) Yes.

HJALMAR (*coming closer*) If Mr. Werle will be so good as to——

WERLE Thanks, I'd just like to talk with my son.

GREGERS Yes, why not? Here I am.

WERLE I'd like to talk with you in your room.

GREGERS In my room—fine—(*Starts in.*)

GINA No. Good Lord, that's in no condition for——

WERLE Well, out in the hall, then. This is just between us.

HJALMAR You can talk here, Mr. Werle. Come into the living room, Relling.

(HJALMAR *and* RELLING *go out to the right;* GINA *takes* HEDVIG *with her into the kitchen.*)

GREGERS (*after a brief interval*) Well, now it's just the two of us.

WERLE You dropped a few remarks last night—And since you've now taken a room with the Ekdals, I must assume that you're planning something or other against me.

GREGERS I'm planning to open Hjalmar Ekdal's eyes. He's going to see his situation just as it is—that's all.

WERLE Is *that* the mission in life you talked about yesterday?

GREGERS Yes. You haven't left me any other.

WERLE Am I the one that spoiled your mind, Gregers?

GREGERS You've spoiled my entire life. I'm not thinking of all that with Mother. But you're the one I can thank for my going around, whipped and driven by this guilt-ridden conscience.

WERLE Ah, it's your conscience that's gone bad.

GREGERS I should have taken a stand against you when the trap was laid for Lieutenant Ekdal. I should have warned him, for I had a pretty good idea what was coming off.

WERLE Yes, you really should have spoken up then.

GREGERS I didn't dare; I was so cowed and frightened. I was unspeakably afraid of you—both then and for a long time after.

WERLE That fright seems to be over now.

GREGERS It is, luckily. The harm done to old Ekdal, both by me and—others, can never be undone; but Hjalmar I can free from all the lies and evasions that are smothering him here.

WERLE You believe you'd be doing him good by that?

GREGERS That's what I believe.

WERLE Maybe you think Ekdal's the kind of man who'll thank you for that friendly service?

GREGERS Yes! He *is* that kind of man.

WERLE Hmm—we'll see.

GREGERS And besides—if I'm ever to go on living, I'll have to find a cure for my sick conscience.

WERLE It'll never be sound. Your conscience has been sickly from childhood. It's an inheritance from your mother, Gregers—the only inheritance she left you.

GREGERS (*with a wry half-smile*) You've never been able to accept the fact, have you, that you calculated wrong when you thought she'd bring you a fortune?

WERLE Let's not get lost in irrelevancies. Then you're still intent on this goal of putting Ekdal on what you suppose is the right track?

GREGERS Yes, I'm intent on that.

WERLE Well, then I could have saved myself the walk up here. For there's no point in asking if you'll move back home with me?

GREGERS No.

WERLE And you won't come into the business either?

GREGERS No.

WERLE Very well. But since I'm now planning a second marriage, the estate, of course, will be divided between us.

GREGERS (*quickly*) No, I don't want that.

WERLE You don't want it?

GREGERS No, I wouldn't dare, for the sake of my conscience.

WERLE (*after a pause*) You going back to the works again?

GREGERS No. I consider that I've retired from your service.

WERLE But what are you going to do, then?

GREGERS Simply carry out my life's mission; nothing else.

WERLE Yes, but afterwards? What will you live on?

GREGERS I have some of my salary put aside.

WERLE Yes, that won't last long!

GREGERS I think it will last my time.

WERLE What do you mean by that?

GREGERS I'm not answering any more.

WERLE Good-bye then, Gregers.

GREGERS Good-bye.

(*Old* WERLE *goes out.*)

HJALMAR (*peering out*) Has he gone?

GREGERS Yes.

(HJALMAR *and* RELLING *come in.* GINA *and* HEDVIG *also return from the kitchen.*)

RELLING There's one lunch gone to the dogs.

GREGERS Put your things on, Hjalmar; you've got to take a long walk with me.

HJALMAR Yes, gladly. What did your father want? Was it anything to do with me?

GREGERS Just come. We have some things to talk over. I'll go and get my coat. (*He leaves by the hall door.*)

GINA You mustn't go out with him, Hjalmar.

RELLING No, don't go. Stay where you are.

HJALMAR (*getting his hat and overcoat*) But why? When a childhood friend feels a need to open his mind to me in private——

RELLING But damn it all! Can't you see the man's mad, crazy, out of his skull!

GINA Yes, that's the truth, if you'd listen. His mother, off and on, had those same conniption fits.

HJALMAR That's just why he needs a friend's watchful eye on him. (*To* GINA.) Be sure dinner's ready in plenty of time. See you later. (*Goes out the hall door.*)

RELLING It's really a shame that fellow didn't go straight to hell down one of the Hoidal mines.

GINA Mercy—why do you say that?

RELLING (*muttering*) Oh, I've got my reasons.

GINA Do you think Gregers Werle is really crazy?

RELLING No, worse luck. He's no crazier than most people. But he's got a disease in his system all the same.

GINA What is it that's wrong with him?

RELLING All right, I'll tell you, Mrs. Ekdal. He's suffering from an acute case of moralistic fever.

GINA Moralistic fever?

HEDVIG Is that a kind of disease?

RELLING Oh yes, it's a national disease, but it only breaks out now and then. (*Nodding to* GINA.) Thanks for lunch. (*He goes out through the hall door.*)

GINA (*walking restlessly around the room*) Ugh, that Gregers Werle—he was always a cold fish.

HEDVIG (*standing by the table, looking searchingly at her*) This is all so strange to me.

Act Four

HJALMAR EKDAL's *studio. A photograph has just been taken; a portrait camera covered with a cloth, a stand, a couple of chairs, a console table, among other things, stand well out in the room. Late afternoon light; it is near sunset; somewhat later it begins to grow dark.*

GINA *is standing in the hall doorway with a plate-holder and a wet photographic plate in her hand, talking with someone outside.*

GINA Yes, that's definite. When I promise something, I keep my word. On Monday the first dozen will be ready. Good-bye. Good-bye. (*Footsteps are heard descending the stairs.* GINA *closes the door, puts the plate into the holder, and slips both back into the covered camera.*)

HEDVIG (*coming in from the kitchen*) Are they gone?

GINA (*tidying up*) Yes, thank goodness, at last I'm rid of them.

HEDVIG But why do you suppose Daddy isn't home yet?

GINA Are you sure he's not below with Relling?

HEDVIG No, he's not there. I ran down the back stairs just now and asked.

GINA And his dinner's standing and getting cold, too.

HEDVIG Just imagine—Daddy's always sure to be on time for dinner.

GINA Oh, he'll be right along, you'll see.

HEDVIG Oh, I wish he would come! Everything's so funny around here.

GINA (*calling out*) There he is!

(HJALMAR *comes in by the hall door.*)

HEDVIG (*running toward him*) Daddy! Oh, we've waited ages for you!

GINA (*eyeing him*) You've been out pretty long, Hjalmar.

HJALMAR (*without looking at her*) I've been a while, yes. (*He takes off his overcoat.* GINA *and* HEDVIG *start to help him; he waves them away.*)

GINA Did you eat with Werle, maybe?

HJALMAR (*hanging his coat up*) No.

GINA (*going toward the kitchen*) I'll bring your dinner in, then.

HJALMAR No, the dinner can wait. I don't want to eat now.

HEDVIG (*coming closer*) Don't you feel well, Daddy?

HJALMAR Well? Oh yes, well enough. We had an exhausting walk, Gregers and I.

GINA You shouldn't do that, Hjalmar; you're not used to it.

HJALMAR Hm. There are a lot of things a man's got to get used to in this world. (*Walking about the room a bit.*) Did anyone come while I was out?

GINA No one but that engaged couple.

HJALMAR No new orders?

GINA No, not today.

HEDVIG You'll see, there'll be some tomorrow, Daddy.

HJALMAR I certainly hope so, because tomorrow I'm going to throw myself into my work—completely.

HEDVIG Tomorrow! But don't you remember what day tomorrow is?

HJALMAR Oh yes, that's right. Well, the day after tomorrow, then. From now on, I'm doing everything myself; I just want to be left alone with all the work.

GINA But Hjalmar, what's the point of that? It'll only make your life miserable. Let me handle the photographing, and then you'll be free to work on the invention.

HEDVIG And free for the wild duck, Daddy—and for all the chickens and rabbits——

HJALMAR Don't talk to me about that rubbish! Starting tomorrow I shall never again set foot in that loft.

HEDVIG Yes, but Daddy, you promised me tomorrow there'd be a celebration.

HJALMAR Hm, that's true. Well, the day after, then. That infernal wild duck—I'd almost like to wring its neck!

HEDVIG (*crying out*) The wild duck!

GINA What an idea!

HEDVIG (*shaking him*) Yes, but Daddy—it's my wild duck!

HJALMAR That's why I won't do it. I haven't the heart—for your sake, Hedvig, I haven't the heart. But deep inside me I feel I ought to. I shouldn't tolerate under my roof a creature that's been in that man's hands.

GINA My goodness, just because Grandfather got her from that worthless Pettersen——

HJALMAR (*pacing the floor*) There are certain claims—what should I call them—ideal claims, let's say—a kind of summons that a man can't put aside without damaging his soul.

HEDVIG (*following him*) But think—the wild duck—the poor wild duck!

HJALMAR (*stopping*) You heard me say I'd spare it—for your sake. It won't be hurt, not a hair on its—well, anyway, I'll spare it. After all, there are greater missions than that to take on. But, Hedvig, you ought to go out for your walk; the light's about right for your eyes.

HEDVIG No, I don't want to go out now.

HJALMAR Yes, go on. You seem to be blinking your eyes so. All these fumes in here aren't good for you; the air here under this roof is bad.

HEDVIG All right, then, I'll run down the back stairs and take a little walk. My coat and hat? Oh, they're in my room. Daddy —promise you won't hurt the wild duck while I'm out.

HJALMAR There won't be a feather ruffled on its head. (*Drawing her to him.*) You and I, Hedvig—we two! Now run along, dear.

(HEDVIG *nods to her parents and goes out through the kitchen.*)

HJALMAR (*walking around without looking up*) Gina.

GINA Yes?

HJALMAR From tomorrow on—or let's say the day after tomorrow—I'd prefer to keep the household accounts myself.

GINA You want to keep the household accounts, too?

HJALMAR Yes, or budget the income, in any case.

GINA Lord love us, there's nothing to that.

HJALMAR One wouldn't think so. It seems to me you can make our money stretch remarkably far. (*Stopping and looking at her.*) How *is* that?

GINA Hedvig and I, we don't need much.

HJALMAR Is it true that Father gets such good pay for the copying he does for Werle?

GINA I don't know how good it is. I don't know rates for such things.

HJALMAR Well, what does he get, just roughly? Tell me!

GINA It's never the same. I suppose it's roughly what he costs us, with a little pocket money thrown in.

HJALMAR What he costs us. That's something you've never told me before!

GINA No, I never could. You were always so happy thinking he got everything from you.

HJALMAR And instead it comes from Mr. Werle.

GINA Oh, but he's got plenty to spare, that one.

HJALMAR Let's have the lamp lit!

GINA (*lighting it*) And then we can't know if it really is the old man; it could well be Graaberg——

HJALMAR Why try to put me off with Graaberg?

GINA No, I don't know. I just thought——

HJALMAR Hm!

GINA You know it wasn't me that got Grandfather the copying. It was Berta, that time she came here.

HJALMAR Your voice sounds so shaky.

GINA (*putting the shade on the lamp*) It does?

HJALMAR And then your hands are trembling. Or aren't they?

GINA (*firmly*) Say it straight out, Hjalmar. What is it he's gone and said about me?

HJALMAR Is it true—can it possibly be that—that there was some kind of involvement between you and Mr. Werle while you were in service there?

GINA That's not true. Not then, there wasn't. Werle was after me, all right. And his wife thought there was something to it, and she made a big fuss and bother, and she roasted me coming and going, she did—so I quit.

HJALMAR But then what!

GINA Yes, so then I went home. And Mother—well, she wasn't all you took her to be, Hjalmar; she ran on telling me one thing and another, because Werle was a widower by then.

HJALMAR Yes. And then!

GINA Well, you might as well know it all. He didn't give up till he had his way.

HJALMAR (*with a clap of his hands*) And this is the mother of my child! How could you keep that hidden from me!

GINA Yes, I did the wrong thing; I really should have told you long ago.

HJALMAR Right at the start, you mean—so I could have known what sort you are.

GINA But would you have married me anyway?

HJALMAR How can you think that?

GINA No. But that's why I didn't dare say anything then. Because I'd come to be so terribly in love with you, as you know. And then how could I make myself utterly miserable——

HJALMAR (*walking about*) And this is my Hedvig's mother! And then to know that everything I see around me—(*Kicking at a table.*) my whole home—I owe to a favored predecessor. Ah, that charmer Werle!

GINA Do you regret the fourteen, fifteen years we've lived together?

HJALMAR (*stopping in front of her*) Tell me—don't you every day, every hour, regret this spider web of deception you've spun around me? Answer me that! Don't you really go around in a torment of remorse?

GINA Hjalmar dear, I've got so much to think about just with the housework and the day's routine——

HJALMAR Then you never turn a critical eye on your past!

GINA No. Good Lord, I'd almost forgotten that old affair.

HJALMAR Oh, this dull, unfeeling content! To me there's something outrageous about it. Just think—not one regret!

GINA But Hjalmar, tell me now—what would have happened to you if you hadn't found a wife like me?

HJALMAR Like you—!

GINA Yes, because I've always been a bit more hard-headed and resourceful than you. Well, of course I'm a couple of years older.

HJALMAR What would have happened to me?

GINA You were pretty bad off at the time you met me; you can't deny that.

HJALMAR "Pretty bad off" you call it. Oh, you have no idea what a man goes through when he's deep in misery and despair—especially a man of my fiery temperament.

GINA No, that may be. And I shouldn't say nothing about it, either, because you turned out such a good-hearted husband as soon as you got a house and home—and now we've made it so snug and cozy here, and pretty soon both Hedvig and I could begin spending a little on food and clothes.

HJALMAR In the swamp of deception, yes.

GINA Ugh, that disgusting creature, tracking his way through our house!

HJALMAR I also thought this home was a good place to be. That was a pipe dream. Now where can I find the buoyancy I need to carry my invention into reality? Maybe it'll die with me; and then it'll be your past, Gina, that killed it.

GINA (*close to tears*) No, you mustn't ever say such things, Hjalmar. All my days I've only wanted to do what's best for you!

HJALMAR I wonder—what happens now to the breadwinner's dream? When I lay in there on the sofa pondering my invention, I had a hunch it would drain my last bit of strength. I sensed that the day I took the patent in my hand—that would be the day of—departure. And it was my dream that then *you* would go on as the departed inventor's prosperous widow.

GINA (*drying her eyes*) No, don't say that, Hjalmar. Lord knows I never want to see the day I'm a widow.

HJALMAR Oh, what does it matter? Everything's over and done with now. Everything!

(GREGERS *cautiously opens the hall door and looks in.*)

GREGERS May I come in?

HJALMAR Yes, do.

GREGERS (*advancing with a beaming countenance, hands outstretched as if to take theirs*) Now, you dear people—! (*Looks from one to the other, then whispers to* HJALMAR.) But isn't it done, then?

HJALMAR (*resoundingly*) It's done.

425

GREGERS It is?

HJALMAR I've just known the bitterest hour of my life.

GREGERS But also the most exalted, I think.

HJALMAR Well, anyway, it's off our hands for the moment.

GINA God forgive you, Mr. Werle.

GREGERS (*with great surprise*) But I don't understand this.

HJALMAR What don't you understand?

GREGERS With this great rapport—the kind that forges a whole new way of life —a life, a companionship in truth with no more deception——

HJALMAR Yes, I know, I know all that.

GREGERS I was really positive that when I came through that door I'd be met by a transfigured light in both your faces. And what do I see instead but this gloomy, heavy, dismal——

GINA How true. (*She removes the lamp-shade.*)

GREGERS You don't want to understand me, Mrs. Ekdal. No, no, you'll need time —But you yourself, Hjalmar? You must have gained a sense of high purpose out of this great unburdening.

HJALMAR Yes, naturally. That is—more or less.

GREGERS Because there's nothing in the world that compares with showing mercy to a sinner and lifting her up in the arms of love.

HJALMAR Do you think a man can recover so easily from the bitter cup I've just emptied!

GREGERS Not an ordinary man, no. But a man like you—!

HJALMAR Good Lord, yes, I know that. But you mustn't be driving me, Gregers. You see, these things take time.

GREGERS You've *lots* of the wild duck in you, Hjalmar.

(RELLING *has entered through the hall door.*)

RELLING Aha! The wild duck's flying again, eh?

HJALMAR Yes, the wounded trophy of old Werle's hunt.

RELLING Old Werle? Is it him you're talking about?

HJALMAR Him and—all of us.

RELLING (*under his breath to* GREGERS) The devil take you!

HJALMAR What'd you say?

RELLING I merely expressed my heartfelt desire that this quack would cut out for home. If he stays here, he's just the man to ruin you both.

GREGERS They won't be ruined, Mr. Relling. Regarding Hjalmar, I'll say nothing. We know him. But she, too, surely, in the depths of her being, has something authentic, something sincere.

GINA (*near tears*) Well, if I *was* that, why didn't you leave me alone?

RELLING (*to* GREGERS) Would it be nosy to ask what you're really trying to do in this house?

GREGERS I want to establish a true marriage.

RELLING Then you don't think Ekdal's marriage is good enough as it is?

GREGERS It's about as good a marriage as most, unfortunately. But it isn't yet a *true* marriage.

HJALMAR You've never set your sights on the claim of the ideal, Relling.

RELLING Nonsense, sonny boy! Excuse me, Mr. Werle, but how many—in round numbers—how many "true marriages" have you seen in your time?

GREGERS I believe I've hardly seen a single one.

RELLING And I likewise.

GREGERS But I've seen innumerable marriages of the opposite kind. And I've had a chance to see at close range what such a marriage can destroy in two people.

HJALMAR A man's whole moral foundation can crumble under his feet; that's the dreadful thing.

RELLING Well, I've never really exactly been married, so I'm no judge of these things. But I do know this, that the child is part of the marriage too. And you've got to leave the child in peace.

HJALMAR Ah, Hedvig! My poor Hedvig!

RELLING Yes, you'll please see that Hedvig's left out of it. You're both grown people; you're free, God knows, to slop up your private lives all you want. But I tell you, you've got to be careful with Hedvig, or else you might do her some serious harm.

HJALMAR Harm!

RELLING Yes, or she could do harm to herself—and possibly others as well.

GINA But how can you know that, Relling?

HJALMAR There's no immediate threat to her eyes, is there?

RELLING This has nothing to do with her eyes. Hedvig's arrived at a difficult age. She's open to all kinds of erratic ideas.

GINA You know—she is at that! She's begun to fool around something awful with the fire in the kitchen stove. She calls it playing house afire. I'm often scared she *will* set the house on fire.

RELLING See what I mean? I knew it.

GREGERS (*to* RELLING) But how do you explain something like that?

RELLING (*brusquely*) Her voice is changing, junior.

HJALMAR As long as the child has *me!* As long as I'm above the sod.

(*A knock is heard at the door.*)

GINA Shh, Hjalmar, someone's in the hall. (*Calling out.*) Come on in!

(MRS. SŒRBY, *wearing street clothes, enters.*)

MRS. SŒRBY Good evening!

GINA (*going toward her*) Is it you, Berta!

MRS. SŒRBY Oh yes, it's me. But perhaps I came at an awkward time?

HJALMAR Oh, not at all; a messenger from *that* house——

MRS. SŒRBY (*to* GINA) As a matter of fact, I'd hoped that I wouldn't find your menfolk in at this hour, so I ran over just to have a word with you and say good-bye.

GINA Oh? Are you going away?

MRS. SŒRBY Yes, tomorrow, early—up to Hoidal. Mr. Werle left this afternoon.

(*Casually to* GREGERS.) He sends his regards.

GINA Just think!

HJALMAR So Mr. Werle has left? And you're following him?

MRS. SŒRBY Yes, what do you say to that, Ekdal?

HJALMAR I say watch out.

GREGERS Let me explain. My father is marrying Mrs. Sœrby.

HJALMAR He's marrying her!

GINA Oh, Berta, it's come at last!

RELLING (*his voice quavering slightly*) This really can't be true.

MRS. SŒRBY Yes, my dear Relling, it's completely true.

RELLING You want to marry again?

MRS. SŒRBY Yes, so it seems. Werle has gotten a special license, and we're going to have a very quiet wedding up at the works.

GREGERS So I ought to wish you happiness, like a good stepson.

MRS. SŒRBY Thank you, if you really mean it. I'm hoping it will bring us happiness, both Werle and me.

RELLING That's a reasonable hope. Mr. Werle never gets drunk—as far as *I* know; and he's certainly not given to beating up his wives the way the late horse doctor did.

MRS. SŒRBY Oh, now let Sœrby rest in peace. He did have some worthy traits, you know.

RELLING Old Werle's traits are worth rather more, I'll bet.

MRS. SŒRBY At least he hasn't wasted the best that's in him. Any man who does *that* has to take the consequences.

RELLING Tonight I'm going out with Molvik.

MRS. SŒRBY You shouldn't, Relling. Don't do it—for my sake.

RELLING What else is left? (*To* HJALMAR.) If you'd care to, you could come too.

GINA No, thanks. Hjalmar never goes dissipating.

HJALMAR (*in an angry undertone*) Can't you keep quiet!

RELLING Good-bye, Mrs.—Werle. (*He goes out the hall door.*)

GREGERS (*to* MRS. SŒRBY) It would seem that you and Dr. Relling know each other quite intimately.

MRS. SŒRBY Yes, we've known each other for many years. At one time something might have developed between us.

GREGERS It was certainly lucky for you that it didn't.

MRS. SŒRBY Yes, that's true enough. But I've always been wary of following my impulses. After all, a woman can't just throw herself away.

GREGERS Aren't you even a little bit afraid that I'll drop my father a hint about this old friendship?

MRS. SŒRBY You can be sure I've told him myself.

GREGERS Oh?

MRS. SŒRBY Your father knows every last scrap of gossip that holds any grain of truth about me. I told him all of those things; it was the first thing I did when he made his intentions clear.

GREGERS Then I think you're more frank than most people.

MRS. SŒRBY I've always been frank. In the long run, it's the best thing for us women to be.

HJALMAR What do you say to that, Gina?

GINA Oh, women are all so different. Some live one way and some live another.

MRS. SŒRBY Well, Gina, I do think it's wisest to handle things as I have. And Werle, for his part, hasn't held back anything either. Really, it's this that's brought us so close together. Now he can sit and talk to me as freely as a child. He's never had that chance before. He, a healthy, vigorous man, had to spend his whole youth and all his best years hearing nothing but sermons on his sins. And generally those sermons were aimed at the most imaginary failings—at least from what *I* could see.

GINA Yes, that's just as true as you say.

GREGERS If you women are going to explore this subject, I'd better leave.

MRS. SŒRBY You can just as well stay, for that matter; I won't say another word. But I did want you to understand that I haven't done anything sly or in any way underhanded. I suppose it looks like I've had quite a nice piece of luck, and that's true enough, up to a point. But, anyway, what I mean is that I'll not be taking any more than I give. One thing I'll never do is desert him. And I can be useful to him and care for him now better than anyone else after he's helpless.

HJALMAR After he's helpless?

GREGERS (*to* MRS. SŒRBY) All right, don't talk about that here.

MRS. SŒRBY No need to hide it any longer, much as he'd like to. He's going blind.

HJALMAR (*astounded*) He's going blind? But that's peculiar. Is he going blind too?

GINA Lots of people do.

MRS. SŒRBY And you can imagine what that means for a businessman. Well, I'll try to make my eyes do for his as well as I can. But I mustn't stay any longer; I've so much to take care of now. Oh yes, I was supposed to tell you this, Ekdal—that if there's anything Werle can do for you, please just get in touch with Graaberg.

GREGERS That offer Hjalmar Ekdal will certainly decline.

MRS. SŒRBY Come, now, I don't think that in the past he's——

GINA No, Berta, Hjalmar doesn't need to take anything from Mr. Werle now.

HJALMAR (*slowly and ponderously*) Would you greet your future husband from me and say that I intend very shortly to call on his bookkeeper, Graaberg——

GREGERS What! Is that what you want?

HJALMAR To call on his bookkeeper Graaberg, as I said, to request an itemized account of what I owe his employer. I shall repay this debt of honor—(*Laughs.*) That's a good name for it, "debt of honor"! But never mind. I shall repay every penny of it, with five percent interest.

GINA But Hjalmar dear, God knows we don't have the money for that.

HJALMAR Will you tell your husband-to-be that I'm working away relentlessly at my invention. Would you tell him that what keeps my spirits up through this grueling ordeal is the desire to be quit of a painful burden of debt. That's why I'm making my invention. The entire proceeds will be devoted to shedding my monetary ties with your imminent partner.

MRS. SŒRBY Something has really happened in this house.

HJALMAR Yes, it certainly has.

MRS. SŒRBY Well, good-bye, then. I still have a little more to talk about with you, Gina, but that can keep till another time. Good-bye.

(HJALMAR *and* GREGERS *silently nod;* GINA *accompanies* MRS. SŒRBY *to the door.*)

HJALMAR Not across the threshold, Gina!

(MRS. SŒRBY *leaves;* GINA *closes the door behind her.*)

HJALMAR There, now, Gregers—now I've got that pressing debt off my hands.

GREGERS You will soon, anyway.

HJALMAR I believe my attitude could be called correct.

GREGERS You're the man I always thought you were.

HJALMAR In certain circumstances it's impossible not to feel the summons of the ideal. As the family provider, you know, I've got to writhe and groan beneath it. Believe you me, it's really no joke for a man without means to try and pay off a long-standing debt over which the dust of oblivion, so to speak, had fallen. But it's got to be, all the same; my human self demands its rights.

GREGERS (*laying one hand on his shoulder*) Ah, Hjalmar—wasn't it a good thing I came?

HJALMAR Yes.

GREGERS Getting a clear picture of the whole situation—wasn't that a good thing?

HJALMAR (*a bit impatiently*) Of course it was good. But there's one thing that irks my sense of justice.

GREGERS What's that?

HJALMAR It's the fact that—oh, I don't know if I dare speak so freely about your father.

GREGERS Don't hold back on my account.

HJALMAR Well, uh—you see, I find something so irritating in the idea that I'm not the one, he's the one who's going to have the true marriage.

GREGERS How can you say such a thing!

HJALMAR But it's true. Your father and Mrs. Sœrby are entering a marriage based on complete trust, one that's wholehearted and open on both sides. They haven't bottled up any secrets from each other; there isn't any reticence between them; they've declared—if you'll permit me—a mutual forgiveness of sins.

GREGERS All right. So what?

HJALMAR Yes, but that's the whole thing, then. You said yourself that the reason for all these difficulties was the founding of a true marriage.

GREGERS But that marriage is a very different sort, Hjalmar. You certainly wouldn't compare either you or her with those two—well, you know what I mean.

HJALMAR Still, I can't get over the idea that there's something in all this that violates my sense of justice. It really seems as if there's no just order to the universe.

GINA Good Lord, Hjalmar, you mustn't say such things.

GREGERS Hm, let's not start on that question.

HJALMAR But then, on the other hand, I can definitely make out what seems to be the meticulous hand of fate. He's going blind.

GINA Oh, that's not for sure.

HJALMAR That is indisputable. Anyway, we oughtn't to doubt it, because it's precisely this fact that reveals the just retribution. Years back he abused the blind faith of a fellow human being——

GREGERS I'm afraid he's done that to many others.

HJALMAR And now a pitiless, mysterious something comes and claims the old man's eyes in return.

GINA What a horrible thing to say! It really frightens me.

HJALMAR It's useful sometimes to go down deep into the night side of existence.

(HEDVIG, *in her hat and coat, comes in, happy and breathless, through the hall door.*)

GINA Back so soon?

HEDVIG Yes, I got tired of walking, and it was just as well, 'cause then I met someone down at the door.

HJALMAR That must have been Mrs. Sœrby.

HEDVIG Yes.

HJALMAR (*pacing back and forth*) I hope that's the last time you'll see her.

(*Silence.* HEDVIG *glances timidly from one to the other, as if trying to read their feelings.*)

HEDVIG (*coaxingly, as she approaches*) Daddy.

HJALMAR Well—what is it, Hedvig?

HEDVIG Mrs. Sœrby brought along something for me.

HJALMAR (*stopping*) For you?

HEDVIG Yes. It's something meant for tomorrow.

GINA Berta's always brought some little gift for your birthday.

HJALMAR What is it?

HEDVIG No, you can't know that yet, because Mother has to bring it to me in bed first thing in the morning.

HJALMAR Oh, all this conspiracy that I'm left out of!

HEDVIG (*hurriedly*) Oh, you can see it all right. It's a big letter. (*She takes the letter out of her coat pocket.*)

HJALMAR A letter, too?

HEDVIG Well, it's only the letter. I guess the rest will come later. But just think—a letter! I've never gotten a real letter before. And on the outside there, it says "Miss." (*She reads.*) "Miss Hedvig Ekdal." Just think—that's me.

HJALMAR Let me see the letter.

HEDVIG (*handing it over*) See, there.

HJALMAR That's old Werle's writing.

GINA Are you positive, Hjalmar?

HJALMAR See for yourself.

GINA Oh, how would I know?

HJALMAR Hedvig, mind if I open the letter—and read it?

HEDVIG Sure. If you want to, go right ahead.

GINA No, not tonight, Hjalmar. It's meant for tomorrow.

HEDVIG (*softly*) Oh, won't you let him read it! It's got to be something good, and then Daddy'll be happy and things will be pleasant again.

HJALMAR May I open it, then?

HEDVIG Yes, please do, Daddy. It'll be fun to find out what it is.

HJALMAR Good. (*He opens the envelope, takes out a sheet of paper, and reads it through with growing bewilderment.*) Now what's this all about?

GINA But what does it say?

HEDVIG Oh yes, Daddy—tell us!

HJALMAR Be quiet. (*He reads it through once more, turns pale, then speaks with evident restraint.*) This is a deed of gift, Hedvig.

HEDVIG Honestly? What am I getting?

HJALMAR Read for yourself.

(HEDVIG *goes over to the lamp and reads for a moment.*)

HJALMAR (*clenching his fists, in almost a whisper*) The eyes! The eyes—and now that letter!

HEDVIG (*interrupting her reading*) Yes, but I think the gift is for Grandfather.

HJALMAR (*taking the letter from her*) Gina—do you understand this?

GINA I know nothing at all about it. Just tell me.

HJALMAR Mr. Werle writes Hedvig to say that her old grandfather needn't trouble himself any longer with copying work, but that henceforth he can draw one hundred crowns a month from the office——

GREGERS Aha!

HEDVIG One hundred crowns, Mother! I read that.

GINA That'll be nice for Grandfather.

HJALMAR One hundred crowns, as long as he needs it. That means till death, of course.

GINA Well, then he's provided for, poor dear.

HJALMAR But there's more. You didn't read far enough, Hedvig. Afterwards this gift passes over to you.

HEDVIG To me! All of it?

HJALMAR You're assured the same income for the rest of your life, he writes. Hear that, Gina?

GINA Yes, of course I heard.

HEDVIG Imagine me getting all that money! (*Shaking* HJALMAR.) Daddy, Daddy, aren't you glad?

HJALMAR (*disengaging himself*) Glad! (*Walking about the room.*) Ah, what vistas—what perspectives it offers me. Hedvig is the one, she's the one he remembers so bountifully.

GINA Of course, because it's Hedvig's birthday.

HEDVIG And anyway, you'll have it, Daddy. You know that I'll give all the money to you and Mother.

HJALMAR To Mother, yes! There we have it.

GREGERS Hjalmar, this is a trap that's been set for you.

HJALMAR You think it could be another trap?

GREGERS When he was here this morning, he said, "Hjalmar Ekdal is not the man you think he is."

HJALMAR Not the man—!

GREGERS "You'll find that out," he said.

HJALMAR Find out if I could be bought off for a price, eh—!

HEDVIG But Mother, what's this all about?

GINA Go and take your things off.

(HEDVIG, *close to tears, goes out the kitchen door.*)

GREGERS Yes, Hjalmar—now we'll see who's right, he or I.

HJALMAR (*slowing tearing the paper in half and putting both pieces on the table*) That is my answer.

GREGERS What I expected.

HJALMAR (*going over to* GINA, *who is standing by the stove, and speaking quietly*) And now no more pretenses. If that thing between you and him was all over when you—came to be so terribly in love with me, as you put it—then why did he give us the means to get married?

GINA Maybe he thought he could come and go here.

HJALMAR Is that all? Wasn't he afraid of a certain possibility?

GINA I don't know what you mean.

HJALMAR I want to know if—your child has the right to live under my roof.

GINA (*draws herself up, her eyes flashing*) And you can ask that?

HJALMAR Just answer me this: does Hedvig belong to me—or—? Well!

GINA (*regarding him with chill defiance*) I don't know.

HJALMAR (*with a slight quaver*) You don't know!

GINA How would *I* know that? A woman of my sort——

HJALMAR (*softly, turning from her*) Then I have nothing more to do in this house.

GREGERS You must think about this, Hjalmar.

HJALMAR (*putting on his overcoat*) There's nothing to think about for a man like me.

GREGERS Oh, there's so very much to think about. You three have got to stay together if you're ever going to win through to a self-sacrificial, forgiving spirit.

HJALMAR I don't want that. Never, never! My hat! (*Takes his hat.*) My home is down in ruins around me. (*Breaks into tears.*) Gregers, I have no child!

HEDVIG (*who has opened the kitchen door*) What are you saying! (*Running toward him.*) Daddy, Daddy!

GINA Now look!

HJALMAR Don't come near me, Hedvig! Keep away. I can't bear seeing you. Oh, the eyes! Good-bye. (*Starts for the door.*)

HEDVIG (*clinging fast to him and shrieking*) Oh no! Oh no! Don't leave me.

GINA (*crying out*) Look out for the child, Hjalmar. Look out for the child!

HJALMAR   I won't. I can't. I've got to get out—away from all this! (*He tears himself lose from* HEDVIG *and goes out through the hall door.*)

HEDVIG (*with desperate eyes*)   He's left us, Mother! He's left us! He'll never come back again!

GINA   Now don't cry, Hedvig. Daddy's coming back.

HEDVIG (*throws herself, sobbing, on the sofa*)   No, no, he'll never come home to us again.

GREGERS   Will you believe I've wanted everything for the best, Mrs. Ekdal?

GINA   Yes, I think I believe that—but God have mercy on you all the same.

HEDVIG (*lying on the sofa*)   I think I'll die from all this. What did I do to him? Mother, you've got to make him come home!

GINA   Yes, yes, yes, just be calm, and I'll step out and look for him. (*Putting on her coat.*) Maybe he's gone down to Relling's. But now don't you lie there, wailing away. Will you promise?

HEDVIG (*sobbing convulsively*)   Yes, I'll be all right—if only Daddy comes back.

GREGERS (*to* GINA, *about to leave*)   Wouldn't it be better, though, to let him fight through his painful battle first?

GINA   Oh, he can do that later. First of all, we've got to comfort the child. (*She goes out the hall door.*)

HEDVIG (*sitting up and drying her tears*)   Now you have to tell me what it's all about. Why does Daddy not want to see me anymore?

GREGERS   That's something you mustn't ask until you're big and grown-up.

HEDVIG (*catching her breath*)   But I can't go on being so horribly unhappy till I'm big and grown-up. I bet I know what it is. Perhaps I'm really not Daddy's child.

GREGERS (*disturbed*)   How could that ever be?

HEDVIG   Mother could have found me. And now maybe Daddy's found out. I've read about these things.

GREGERS   Well, but if that was the——

HEDVIG   Yes, I think he could love me even so. Or maybe more. The wild duck was sent us as a present too, and I'm terribly fond of it, all the same.

GREGERS (*divertingly*)   Of course, the wild duck, that's true. Let's talk a bit about the wild duck, Hedvig.

HEDVIG   The poor wild duck. He can't bear to see her again, either. Imagine, he wanted to wring her neck!

GREGERS   Oh, he certainly wouldn't do that.

HEDVIG   No, but that's what he said. And I think it was awful for Daddy to say, because each night I make a prayer for the wild duck and ask that she be delivered from death and everything evil.

GREGERS (*looking at her*)   Do you always say your prayers at night?

HEDVIG   Uh-huh.

GREGERS   Who taught you that?

HEDVIG   I taught myself, and that was once when Daddy was so sick and had leeches on his neck, and then he said he was in the jaws of death.

GREGERS   Oh yes?

HEDVIG   So I said a prayer for him when I went to bed. And I've kept it up ever since.

GREGERS   And now you pray for the wild duck, too?

HEDVIG   I thought it was best to put the wild duck in, because she was ailing so at the start.

GREGERS   Do you say morning prayers, too?

HEDVIG   No, not at all.

GREGERS   Why not morning prayers as well?

HEDVIG   In the morning it's light, and so there's nothing more to be afraid of.

GREGERS   And the wild duck you love so much—your father wants to wring her neck.

HEDVIG   No. He said it would be the best thing for him if he did, but for my sake he would spare her; and that was good of Daddy.

GREGERS (*coming closer*)   But what if you

now, of your own free will, sacrificed the wild duck for *his* sake.

HEDVIG (*springing up*) The wild duck!

GREGERS What if you, in a sacrificing spirit, gave up the dearest thing you own and know in the whole world?

HEDVIG Do you think that would help?

GREGERS Try it, Hedvig.

HEDVIG (*softly, with shining eyes*) Yes, I'll try it.

GREGERS And the strength of mind, do you think you have it?

HEDVIG I'll ask Grandpa to shoot the wild duck for me.

GREGERS Yes, do that. But not a word to your mother about all this!

HEDVIG Why not?

GREGERS She doesn't understand us.

HEDVIG The wild duck? I'll try it tomorrow, early.

(GINA *comes in through the hall door.*)

HEDVIG (*going toward her*) Did you find him, Mother?

GINA No. But I heard he'd looked in downstairs and gotten Relling along.

GREGERS Are you sure of that?

GINA Yes, I asked the janitor's wife. And Molvik was with them, she said.

GREGERS And this, right when his mind needs nothing so much as to wrestle in solitude—!

GINA (*taking off her coat*) Oh, men are strange ones, they are. God knows where Relling has led him! I ran over to Mrs. Eriksen's café, but they weren't there.

HEDVIG (*struggling with her tears*) Oh, what if he never comes back again!

GREGERS He *will* come back. I'll get a message to him tomorrow, and then you'll see just how quick he comes. Believe that, Hedvig, and sleep well. Good night. (*He goes out the hall door.*)

HEDVIG (*throwing herself, sobbing, into* GINA's *arms*) Mother, Mother!

GINA (*pats her on the back and sighs*) Ah, me, Relling was right. That's the way it goes when these crazy people come around, summoning up their ideals.

Act Five

HJALMAR EKDAL's *studio. A cold, gray morning light filters in; wet snow lies on the huge panes of the skylight.* GINA, *wearing a pinafore, comes in from the kitchen, carrying a feather duster and a cleaning cloth, and makes for the living room door. At the same moment* HEDVIG *rushes in from the hallway.*

GINA (*stopping*) Well?

HEDVIG You know, Mother, I'm pretty sure he's down at Relling's——

GINA There, you see!

HEDVIG 'Cause the janitor's wife said she heard Relling had two others with him when he came in last night.

GINA That's about what I thought.

HEDVIG But it's still no good if he won't come up to us.

GINA At least I can go down there and talk with him.

(EKDAL, *in dressing gown and slippers, smoking a pipe, appears in the doorway to his room.*)

EKDAL Say, Hjalmar—Isn't Hjalmar home?

GINA No, he's gone out, I guess.

EKDAL So early? In a raging blizzard like this? Oh, well, never mind; I'll take my morning walk alone, that's all.

(*He pulls the loft door ajar,* HEDVIG *helping him. He goes in; she closes up after him.*)

HEDVIG (*lowering her voice*) Just think, Mother, when Grandpa finds out that Daddy's leaving us.

GINA Go on, Grandpa won't hear anything of the kind. It was a real stroke of providence he wasn't here yesterday in all that racket.

HEDVIG Yes, but——

(GREGERS *comes in the hall entrance.*)

GREGERS Well? Had any reports on him?

GINA He should be down at Relling's, they tell me.

GREGERS With Relling! Did he really go out with those fellows?

GINA Apparently.

GREGERS Yes, but he who needed so much to be alone to pull himself together—!

GINA Yes, just as you say.

(RELLING *enters from the hall.*)

HEDVIG (*going toward him*) Is Daddy with you?

GINA (*simultaneously*) Is he there?

RELLING Yes, of course he is.

HEDVIG And you never told us!

RELLING Oh, I'm a beast. But first of all, I had that other beast to manage—you know, the demonic one, him—and then, next, I fell so sound asleep that——

GINA What's Hjalmar been saying today?

RELLING He's said absolutely nothing.

HEDVIG Hasn't he talked at all?

RELLING Not a blessed word.

GREGERS No, no, I can well understand that.

GINA But what's he doing, then?

RELLING He's laid out on the sofa, snoring.

GINA Oh? Yes, Hjalmar's great at snoring.

HEDVIG He's asleep? Can he sleep?

RELLING Well, so it seems.

GREGERS It's conceivable—when all that strife of spirit has torn him.

GINA And then he's never been used to roaming around the streets at night.

HEDVIG Maybe it's a good thing that he's getting some sleep, Mother.

GINA I think so too. But then it's just as well we don't rouse him too soon. Thanks a lot, Relling. Now I've got to clean and straighten up here a bit, and then—Come and help me, Hedvig.

(GINA *and* HEDVIG *disappear into the living room.*)

GREGERS (*turning to* RELLING) Have you an explanation for the spiritual upheaval taking place within Hjalmar Ekdal?

RELLING For the life of me, I can't remember any spiritual upheaval in him.

GREGERS What! At a time of crisis like this, when his life has been recast? How

can you believe that a rare individual like Hjalmar—?

RELLING Pah! Individual—him! If he's ever had a tendency toward anything so abnormal as what you call individuality, it was ripped up, root and vine, by the time he was grown, and that's a fact.

GREGERS That's rather surprising—with all the loving care he had as a child.

RELLING From those two warped, hysterical maiden aunts, you mean?

GREGERS I want to tell you they were women who never betrayed their highest ideals—yes, now of course you'll start mocking me again.

RELLING No, I'm hardly in a mood for that. Besides, I'm well informed here; he's regurgitated any amount of rhetoric about his "twin soul-mothers." I really don't believe he has much to thank them for. Ekdal's misfortune is that in his circle he's always been taken for a shining light——

GREGERS And isn't he, perhaps, exactly that? In his heart's core, I mean?

RELLING I've never noticed anything of the kind. His father thinks so—but that's nothing; the old lieutenant's been a fool all his life.

GREGERS He has, all his life, been a man with a childlike awareness; and that's something you just don't understand.

RELLING Oh, sure! But back when our dear, sweet Hjalmar became a student of sorts, right away he got taken up by his classmates as the great beacon of the future. Oh, he was good-looking, the lout —pink and white—just the way little moon-eyed girls like boys. And then he had that excitable manner and that heart-winning tremor in his voice, and he was so cute and clever at declaiming other people's poems and ideas——

GREGERS (*indignantly*) Is it Hjalmar Ekdal you're speaking of that way?

RELLING Yes, with your permission. That's an inside look at him, this idol you're groveling in front of.

GREGERS I really didn't think I was utterly blind.

RELLING Well, you're not far from it. Because you're a sick man, you are. You know that.

GREGERS There you're right.

RELLING Oh yes. Your case has complications. First there's this virulent moralistic fever; and then something worse—you keep going off in deliriums of hero worship; you always have to have something to admire that's outside of yourself.

GREGERS Yes, I certainly have to look for it outside myself.

RELLING But you're so woefully wrong about these great miraculous beings you think you see and hear around you. You've simply come back to a cotter's cabin with your summons to the ideal; there's nobody solvent here.

GREGERS If you've got no higher estimate of Hjalmar Ekdal than this, how can you ever enjoy seeing him day after day?

RELLING Good Lord, I *am* supposed to be some kind of doctor, I'm ashamed to say. Well, then I ought to look after the poor sick people I live with.

GREGERS Oh, come! Is Hjalmar Ekdal sick, too?

RELLING Most of the world is sick, I'm afraid.

GREGERS And what's your prescription for Hjalmar?

RELLING My standard one. I try to keep up the vital lie in him.

GREGERS The vital—lie? I don't think I heard——

RELLING Oh yes, I said the vital lie. The vital lie, don't you see—that's the animating principle of life.

GREGERS May I ask what kind of lie has infected Hjalmar?

RELLING No, thanks, I don't betray secrets like that to quacks. You'd just be able to damage him all the more for me. My method is tested, though. I've also used it on Molvik. I made him "demonic." That was my remedy for him.

GREGERS Then he isn't demonic?

RELLING What the devil does it mean to be demonic? That's just some hogwash I thought up to keep life going in him. If I

hadn't done that, the poor innocent mutt would have given in years ago to self-contempt and despair. And then take the old lieutenant! But he really discovered his own cure himself.

GREGERS Lieutenant Ekdal? How so?

RELLING Well, what do you think of this bear hunter going into a dark loft to stalk rabbits? There isn't a happier sportsman in the world than the old man when he's prowling around in that junkyard. Those four or five dried-out Christmas trees he's got—to him they're like all the green forests of Hoidal; the hens and the rooster—they're the game birds up in the fir tops; and the rabbits hopping across the floor—they're the bears that call up his youth again, out in the mountain air.

GREGERS Poor, unhappy old Ekdal, yes. He certainly had to pare down his early ideals.

RELLING While I remember it, Mr. Werle junior—don't use that exotic word *ideals*. Not when we've got a fine native word—*lies*.

GREGERS You're implying the two have something in common?

RELLING Yes, about like tetanus and lockjaw.

GREGERS Dr. Relling, I won't rest till I've gotten Hjalmar out of your clutches.

RELLING So much the worse for him. Deprive the average man of his vital lie, and you've robbed him of happiness as well. (*To* HEDVIG, *entering from the living room.*) Well, little wild-duck mother, now I'll go down and see if Papa's still lying and pondering his marvelous invention. (*He goes out the hall door.*)

GREGERS (*approaching* HEDVIG) I can see by your face that it's not fulfilled.

HEDVIG What? Oh, about the wild duck. No.

GREGERS Your courage failed you when the time came to act, I suppose.

HEDVIG No, it's not exactly that. But when I woke up this morning early and thought of what we talked about, then it seemed so strange to me.

GREGERS Strange?

HEDVIG Yes, I don't know—Last night, right at the time, there was something so beautiful about it, but after I'd slept and then thought it over, it didn't seem like so much.

GREGERS Ah, no, you couldn't grow up here without some taint in you.

HEDVIG I don't care about that; if only Daddy would come up, then——

GREGERS Oh, if only your eyes were really open to what makes life worth living—if only you had the true, joyful, courageous spirit of self-sacrifice, *then* you'd see him coming up to you. But I still have faith in you. (*He goes out the hall door.*)

(HEDVIG *wanders across the room, then starts into the kitchen. At that moment a knock comes on the loft door,* HEDVIG *goes over and opens it a space;* EKDAL *slips out, and she slides it shut again.*)

EKDAL Hm, a morning walk alone is no fun at all.

HEDVIG Don't you want to go hunting, Grandpa?

EKDAL The weather's no good for hunting. Awfully dark in there; you can hardly see ahead of you.

HEDVIG Don't you ever want to shoot at anything but rabbits?

EKDAL Aren't rabbits good enough, eh?

HEDVIG Yes, but the wild duck, say?

EKDAL Ha, ha! You're afraid I'll shoot the wild duck for you? Never in this world, dear. Never!

HEDVIG No, you couldn't do that. It must be hard to shoot wild ducks.

EKDAL Couldn't? I certainly could!

HEDVIG How would you go about it, Grandpa?—I don't mean with *my* wild duck, but with others.

EKDAL I'd be sure to shoot them in the breast, understand; that's the safest. And then they've got to be shot *against* the feathers, you see—not *with* the feathers.

HEDVIG They die then, Grandpa?

EKDAL Oh yes, they do indeed—if you shoot them right. Well, got to go in and clean up. Hm—you understand—hm. (*He goes into his room.*)

(HEDVIG *waits a moment, glances at the living room door, goes to the bookcase, stands on tiptoe, takes down the double-barreled pistol from the shelf and looks at it.* GINA, *with duster and cloth, comes in from the living room.* HEDVIG *hastily sets down the pistol, unnoticed.*)

GINA Don't mess with your father's things, Hedvig.

HEDVIG (*leaving the bookcase*) I was just straightening up a little.

GINA Go out in the kitchen instead and make sure the coffee's still hot; I'll take a tray along to him when I go down.

(HEDVIG *goes out;* GINA *begins to dust and clean up the studio. After a moment the hall door is cautiously opened, and* HJALMAR *peers in. He wears his overcoat, but no hat. He is unwashed, with tousled, unruly hair; his eyes are dull and inert.*)

GINA (*standing rooted with duster in hand, looking at him*) Don't tell me, Hjalmar —are you back after all?

HJALMAR (*steps in and answers in a thick voice*) I'm back—but only for one moment.

GINA Oh yes, I'm sure of that. But my goodness—what a sight you are!

HJALMAR Sight?

GINA And then your good winter coat! Well, it's done for.

HEDVIG (*at the kitchen door*) Mother, should I—(*Seeing* HJALMAR, *giving a squeal of delight, and running toward him.*) Oh, Daddy, Daddy!

HJALMAR (*turning from her and waving her off*) Get away! Get away! (*To* GINA.) Make her get away from me, will you!

GINA (*in an undertone*) Go in the living room, Hedvig.

(HEDVIG *silently goes out.*)

HJALMAR (*with a busy air, pulling out the table drawer*) I must have my books along. Where are my books?

GINA What books?

HJALMAR My scientific works, of course—the technical journals I use for my invention.

GINA (*looking over the bookshelves*) Are these them, the ones without covers?

HJALMAR Yes, exactly.

GINA (*putting a stack of booklets on the table*) Could I get Hedvig to cut the pages for you?

HJALMAR Nobody has to cut pages for me. (*A short silence.*)

GINA Then it's definite that you're moving out, Hjalmar?

HJALMAR (*rummaging among the books*) Yes, that would seem to me self-evident.

GINA I see.

HJALMAR How could I go on here and have my heart shattered every hour of the day!

GINA God forgive you for thinking so badly of me.

HJALMAR Show me proof——

GINA I think *you're* the one to show proof.

HJALMAR After your kind of past? There are certain claims—I'd like to call them ideal claims——

GINA But Grandfather? What'll happen to him, poor dear?

HJALMAR I know my duty; that helpless old soul leaves with me. I'm going downtown and make arrangements—hm—(*Hesitantly.*) Did anybody find my hat on the stairs?

GINA No. Have you lost your hat?

HJALMAR I had it on, naturally, when I came in last night; I'm positive of that. But today I couldn't find it.

GINA My Lord, where did you go with those two stumblebums?

HJALMAR Oh, don't bother me with petty questions. Do you think I'm in a mood to remember details?

GINA I just hope you didn't catch cold, Hjalmar. (*She goes out into the kitchen.*)

HJALMAR (*muttering to himself in exasperation, as he empties the table drawer*) You're a sneak, Relling! A barbarian, that's what! Oh, snake in the grass! If I could just get someone to strangle you! (*He puts some old letters to one side, discovers the torn deed of the day before, picks it up and examines the pieces. He hurriedly puts them down as* GINA *enters.*)

GINA (*setting a breakfast tray on the table*) Here's a drop of something hot, if you care for it. And there's some bread and butter and a little salt meat.

HJALMAR (*glancing at the tray*) Salt meat? Never under this roof! Of course I haven't enjoyed going without food for nearly twenty-four hours; but that doesn't matter—My notes! My unfinished memoirs! Where can I find my journal and my important papers? (*Opens the living room door, then draws back.*) There she is again!

GINA Well, goodness, the child has to be somewhere.

HJALMAR Come out. (*He stands aside, and* HEDVIG, *terrified, comes into the studio.*)

HJALMAR (*with his hand on the doorknob, says to* GINA) These last moments I'm spending in my former home, I'd like to be free from intruders—(*Goes into the living room.*)

HEDVIG (*rushing to her mother, her voice hushed and trembling*) Does he mean me?

GINA Stay in the kitchen, Hedvig. Or, no—go into your own room instead. (*Speaking to* HJALMAR *as she goes in to him.*) Just a minute, Hjalmar. Don't muss up the bureau like that; I know where everything is. (HEDVIG *stands for a moment as if frozen by fright and bewilderment, biting her lips to keep the tears back; then she clenches her fists convulsively.*)

HEDVIG (*softly*) The wild duck. (*She steals over and takes the pistol from the shelf, sets the loft door ajar, slips in and draws the door shut after her.* HJALMAR *and* GINA *start arguing in the living room.*)

HJALMAR (*reenters with some notebooks and old loose papers, which he lays on the table*) Oh, what good is that travel-

437

ing bag! I've got a thousand things to take with me.

GINA *(following with the traveling bag)* So leave everything else for the time being, and just take a shirt and a pair of shorts with you.

HJALMAR Phew! These agonizing preparations! *(Takes off his overcoat and throws it on the sofa.)*

GINA And there's your coffee getting cold, too.

HJALMAR Hm. *(Unthinkingly takes a sip and then another.)*

GINA The hardest thing for you will be to find another room like that, big enough for all the rabbits.

HJALMAR What! Do I have to take all the rabbits with me, too?

GINA Yes, Grandfather couldn't live without the rabbits, I'm sure.

HJALMAR He's simply got to get used to it. The joys of life *I* have to renounce are higher than rabbits.

GINA *(dusting the bookcase)* Should I put your flute in the traveling bag?

HJALMAR No. No flute for me. But give me the pistol!

GINA You want your pistol along?

HJALMAR Yes. My loaded pistol.

GINA *(looking for it)* It's gone. He must have taken it inside.

HJALMAR Is he in the loft?

GINA Of course he's in the loft.

HJALMAR Hm—lonely old man. *(He takes a piece of bread and butter, eats it, and finishes the cup of coffee.)*

GINA Now if we only hadn't rented the room, you could have moved in there.

HJALMAR I should stay on under the same roof as—! Never! Never!

GINA But couldn't you put up in the living room just for a day or two? You've got everything you need in there.

HJALMAR Never within these walls!

GINA Well, how about down with Relling and Molvik?

HJALMAR Don't mention those barbarians' names! I can almost lose my appetite just thinking about them. Oh no, I've got to go out in sleet and snow—tramp from house to house and seek shelter for Father and me.

GINA But you haven't any hat, Hjalmar! You've lost your hat.

HJALMAR Oh, those two vermin, wallowing in sin! The hat will have to be bought. *(Taking another piece of bread and butter.)* Someone's got to make arrangements. I certainly don't intend to risk my life. *(Looking for something on the tray.)*

GINA What are you looking for?

HJALMAR Butter.

GINA Butter's coming right up. *(Goes into the kitchen.)*

HJALMAR *(calling after her)* Oh, never mind; I can just as easily eat dry bread.

GINA *(bringing in a butter dish)* Look. It's fresh today.

(She passes him another cup of coffee. He sits on the sofa, spreads more butter on the bread, eats and drinks a moment in silence.)

HJALMAR Could I—without being annoyed by anybody—anybody at all—put up in the living room just for a day or two?

GINA Yes, of course you could, if you want to.

HJALMAR Because I can't see any possibility of getting all Father's things out in one trip.

GINA And then there's this, too, that you've first got to tell him you're not living with us any longer.

HJALMAR *(pushing the coffee cup away)* That too, yes. All these intricate affairs to unravel. I've got to clear my thinking; I need a breathing spell; I can't shoulder all these burdens in one day.

GINA No, and not when the weather's like it is out.

HJALMAR *(picking up* WERLE's *letter)* I see this letter's still kicking around.

GINA Yes, *I* haven't touched it.

HJALMAR This trash is nothing to me——

GINA Well, I'm not going to use it for anything.

HJALMAR All the same, there's no point in throwing it around helter-skelter. In

all the confusion of my moving, it could
easily——

GINA I'll take good care of it, Hjalmar.

HJALMAR First and foremost, the deed of
gift is Father's; it's really his affair
whether or not he wants to use it.

GINA (*sighing*) Yes, poor old Father——

HJALMAR Just for safety's sake—where
would I find some paste?

GINA (*going to the bookcase*) Here's the
pastepot.

HJALMAR And then a brush.

GINA Here's a brush, too. (*Bringing
both.*)

HJALMAR (*taking a pair of scissors*) A
strip of paper down the back, that's all.
(*Cutting and pasting.*) Far be it from me
to take liberties with another's property—
least of all, a penniless old man's. No, nor
with—the other person's. There, now. Let
it lie a while. And when it's dry, then
take it away. I don't want to set eyes on
that document again. Ever!

(GREGERS *enters from the hall.*)

GREGERS (*somewhat surprised*) What? Are
you sitting here, Hjalmar?

HJALMAR (*springing up*) I was overcome
by fatigue.

GREGERS Still, you've had breakfast, I see.

HJALMAR The body asserts its claims now
and then.

GREGERS What have you decided to do?

HJALMAR For a man like me there's only
one way open. I'm in the process of assembling my most important things. But
that takes time, don't you know.

GINA (*a bit impatient*) Should I get the
room ready for you, or should I pack your
bag?

HJALMAR (*after a vexed glance at* GREGERS)
Pack—and get the room ready!

GINA (*taking the traveling bag*) All right,
then I'll put in the shirt and the rest.
(*She goes into the living room, shutting
the door behind her.*)

GREGERS (*after a short silence*) I never
dreamed that things would end like this.
Is it really necessary for you to leave
house and home?

HJALMAR (*pacing restlessly about*) What
would you have me do? I wasn't made to
be unhappy, Gregers. I've got to have it
snug and secure and peaceful around me.

GREGERS But why can't you, then? Give it
a try. Now I'd say you have solid ground
to build on—so make a fresh start. And
don't forget you have your invention to
live for, too.

HJALMAR Oh, don't talk about the invention. That seems such a long way off.

GREGERS Oh?

HJALMAR Good Lord, yes. What would
you really have me invent? Other people
have invented so much already. It gets
more difficult every day——

GREGERS And you've put so much work in
it.

HJALMAR It was that dissolute Relling
who got me started.

GREGERS Relling?

HJALMAR Yes, he was the one who first
made me aware that I had a real talent
for inventing something in photography.

GREGERS Aha—that was Relling!

HJALMAR Oh, I was so blissfully happy as
a result. Not so much from the invention
itself, but because Hedvig believed in it
—believed in it with all the power and
force of a child's mind. Yes, in other
words, fool that I am, I've gone around
imagining that she believed in it.

GREGERS You can't really think that Hedvig could lie to you!

HJALMAR Now I can think anything. It's
Hedvig that ruins it all. She's managed
to blot the sun right out of my life.

GREGERS Hedvig! You mean Hedvig? How
could she ever do that?

HJALMAR (*without answering*) How inexpressibly I loved that child! How inexpressibly happy I was whenever I came
home to my poor rooms and she came flying to meet me with those sweet, fluttering eyes. I was so unspeakably fond of her
—and so I dreamed and deluded myself
into thinking that she, too, was fond of
me beyond words.

GREGERS Can you call *that* just a delusion?

HJALMAR How can I tell? I can't get anything out of Gina; and besides, she has no feeling at all for the ideal phase of these complications. But with you, Gregers, I feel impelled to open my mind. There's this horrible doubt—maybe Hedvig never really, truly has loved me.

GREGERS She may perhaps give you proof that she has. (*Listening.*) What's that? I thought I heard the wild duck cry.

HJALMAR The duck's quacking. Father's in the loft.

GREGERS Is he? (*His face radiates joy.*) I tell you, you may yet have proof that your poor, misjudged Hedvig loves you!

HJALMAR Oh, what proof could she give me? I don't dare hope to be reassured from that quarter.

GREGERS Hedvig's completely free of deceit.

HJALMAR Oh, Gregers, that's just what I can't be sure of. Who knows what Gina and this Mrs. Sœrby have whispered and gossiped about in all the times they've sat here? And Hedvig uses her ears, you know. Maybe the deed of gift wasn't such a surprise, after all. In fact, I seemed to get that impression.

GREGERS What is this spirit that's gotten into you?

HJALMAR I've had my eyes opened. Just wait—you'll see; the deed of gift is only the beginning. Mrs. Sœrby has always cared a lot for Hedvig, and now she has the power to do what she wants for the child. They can take her away from me any time they like.

GREGERS You're the last person in the world Hedvig would leave.

HJALMAR Don't be too sure of that. If they stand beckoning her with all they have—? Oh, I who've loved her so inexpressibly! I who'd find my highest joy in taking her tenderly by the hand and leading her as one leads a child terrified of the dark through a huge, empty room! I can feel it now with such gnawing certainty; the poor photographer up in this attic has never meant much to her. She's merely been clever to keep on a good footing with him till the right time came.

GREGERS You really don't believe that, Hjalmar.

HJALMAR The worst thing is precisely that I don't know what to believe—that I'll never know. But can you honestly doubt that it's just what I'm saying? (*With a bitter laugh.*) Oh, you trust too much in the power of ideals, my dear Gregers! Suppose the others come with their hands full of riches and call out to the child: Leave him. Life waits for you here with us——

GREGERS (*quickly*) Yes, then what?

HJALMAR If I asked her then: Hedvig, are you willing to give up life for me? (*Laughs derisively.*) Yes, thanks—you'd hear all right what answer I'd get!

(*A pistol shot is heard in the loft.*)

GREGERS (*with a shout of joy*) Hjalmar!

HJALMAR Hear that. He's got to go hunting as well.

GINA (*coming in*) Oh, Hjalmar, it sounds like Grandfather's shooting up the loft by himself.

HJALMAR I'll take a look——

GREGERS (*animated and exalted*) Wait now! Do you know what that was?

HJALMAR Of course I know.

GREGERS No, you don't know. But *I* do. That was the proof!

HJALMAR What proof?

GREGERS That was a child's sacrifice. She's had your father shoot the wild duck.

HJALMAR Shoot the wild duck!

GINA No, really—!

HJALMAR What for?

GREGERS She wanted to sacrifice to you the best thing she had in the world, because she thought then you'd have to love her again.

HJALMAR (*stirred, gently*) Ah, that child!

GINA Yes, the things she thinks of!

GREGERS She only wants your love again, Hjalmar; she felt she couldn't live without it.

GINA (*struggling with tears*) There you are, Hjalmar.

HJALMAR Gina, where's she gone?

GINA (*sniffling*) Poor thing. I guess she's out in the kitchen.

HJALMAR (*going over and flinging the kitchen door open*) Hedvig, come! Come here to me! (*Looking about.*) No, she's not there.

GINA Then she's in her own little room.

HJALMAR (*out of sight*) No, she's not there either. (*Coming back in.*) She may have gone out.

GINA Yes, you didn't want her around anywhere in the house.

HJALMAR Oh, if only she comes home soon—so I can just let her know—! Things will work out now, Gregers—for now I really believe we can start life over again.

GREGERS (*quietly*) I knew it; through the child everything rights itself.

(EKDAL *appears at the door to his room; he is in full uniform and is absorbed in buckling his sword.*)

HJALMAR (*astonished*) Father! Are you there?

GINA Were you out gunning in your room?

EKDAL (*approaching angrily*) So you've been hunting alone, eh, Hjalmar?

HJALMAR (*baffled and anxious*) Then it wasn't you who fired a shot in the loft?

EKDAL Me, shoot? Hm!

GREGERS (*shouting to* HJALMAR) She's shot the wild duck herself!

HJALMAR What is all this! (*Rushes to the loft doors, throws them open, looks in and cries:*) Hedvig!

GINA (*running to the door*) Lord, what now!

HJALMAR (*going in*) She's lying on the floor!

GREGERS Hedvig, on the floor! (*Follows* HJALMAR *in.*)

GINA (*simultaneously*) Hedvig! (*Going into the loft.*) No, no, no!

EKDAL Ha, ha! So she's a hunter, too.

(HJALMAR, GINA, *and* GREGERS *carry* HEDVIG *into the studio; her right hand hangs down and her fingers curve tightly about the pistol.*)

HJALMAR (*distraught*) The pistol's gone off. She's wounded herself. Call for help! Help!

GINA (*running into the hall and calling downstairs*) Relling! Relling! Dr. Relling, come up as quick as you can!

(HJALMAR *and* GREGERS *lay* HEDVIG *down on the sofa.*)

EKDAL (*hushed*) The woods take revenge.

HJALMAR (*on his knees by her*) She's just coming to now. She's coming to now—oh yes, yes.

GINA (*who has returned*) Where is she wounded? I can't see anything——

(RELLING *hurries in, and right after him,* MOLVIK, *who is without vest or tie, his dress coat open.*)

RELLING What's going on here?

GINA They say Hedvig shot herself.

HJALMAR Come here and help.

RELLING Shot herself! (*He shoves the table to one side and begins to examine her.*)

HJALMAR (*kneeling still, looking anxiously up at him*) It can't be serious? Huh, Relling? She's hardly bleeding. It can't be serious?

RELLING How did this happen?

HJALMAR Oh, how do I know——

GINA She wanted to shoot the wild duck.

RELLING The wild duck?

HJALMAR The pistol must have gone off.

RELLING Hm. I see.

EKDAL The woods take revenge. But I'm not scared, even so. (*He goes into the loft, shutting the door after him.*)

HJALMAR But Relling—why don't you say something?

RELLING The bullet's entered her breast.

HJALMAR Yes, but she's coming to!

RELLING You can see for yourself that Hedvig is dead.

GINA (*breaking into tears*) Oh, my child, my child!

GREGERS (*hoarsely*) In the depths of the sea——

HJALMAR (*jumping up*) No, no, she *must* live! Oh, in God's name, Relling—

just for a moment—just enough so I can tell her how inexpressibly I loved her all the time!

RELLING   It's reached the heart. Internal hemorrhage. She died on the spot.

HJALMAR   And I drove her from me like an animal! And she crept terrified into the loft and died out of love for me. (*Sobbing.*) Never to make it right again! Never to let her know—! (*Clenching his fists and crying to heaven.*) Oh, you up there—if you *do* exist. Why have you done this to me!

GINA   Hush, hush, you mustn't lash out like that. We just didn't deserve to keep her, I guess.

MOLVIK   The child isn't dead; she sleepeth.

RELLING   Rubbish!

HJALMAR   (*becoming calm, going over to the sofa to stand, arms folded, looking at* HEDVIG)   There she lies, so stiff and still.

RELLING   (*trying to remove the pistol*)   She holds it so tight, so tight.

GINA   No, no, Relling, don't break her fingers. Let the gun be.

HJALMAR   She should have it with her.

GINA   Yes, let her. But the child shouldn't lie displayed out here. She ought to go into her own little room, she should. Give me a hand, Hjalmar.

(HJALMAR *and* GINA *lift* HEDVIG *between them.*)

HJALMAR   (*as they carry her off*)   Oh, Gina, Gina, how can you bear it!

GINA   We must try to help each other. For now she belongs to us both, you know.

MOLVIK   (*outstretching his arms and mumbling*)   Praise be to God. Dust to dust, dust to dust——

RELLING   (*in a whisper*)   Shut up, you fool; you're drunk.

(HJALMAR *and* GINA *carry the body out through the kitchen door.* RELLING *closes it after them.* MOLVIK *steals out the hall door.*)

RELLING   (*going over to* GREGERS)   Nobody's ever going to sell me the idea that this was an accident.

GREGERS   (*who has stood in a convulsive fit of horror*)   Who can say how this awful thing happened?

RELLING   There are powder burns on her blouse. She must have held the pistol right at her breast and fired.

GREGERS   Hedvig did not die in vain. Did you notice how grief freed the greatness in him?

RELLING   The grief of death brings out greatness in almost everyone. But how long do you think this glory will last with *him*?

GREGERS   I should think it would last and grow all his life.

RELLING   In less than a year little Hedvig will be nothing more to him than a pretty theme for recitations.

GREGERS   You dare say that about Hjalmar Ekdal!

RELLING   We'll be lectured on this when the first grass shows on her grave. Then you can hear him spewing out phrases about "the child torn too soon from her father's heart," and you'll have your chance to watch him souse himself in conceit and self-pity. Wait and see.

GREGERS   If you're right, and I'm wrong, then life isn't worth living.

RELLING   Oh, life would be good in spite of all, if we only could have some peace from these damned shysters who come badgering us poor people with their "summons to the ideal."

GREGERS   (*staring straight ahead*)   In that case, I'm glad my destiny is what it is.

RELLING   Beg pardon—but what *is* your destiny?

GREGERS   (*about to leave*)   To be the thirteenth man at the table.

RELLING   Oh, the hell you say.

Hedda Gabler

Henrik Ibsen   translated by Michael Meyer

Introductory Comments

Sylvan Barnet   *Tufts University*
Morton Berman   *Boston University*
William Burto   *University of Lowell*

In the 1870s and 1880s Ibsen wrote the so-called "problem plays" in-cluding *A Doll's House, Ghosts,* and *An Enemy of the People* that for the next seventy-five years made his name familiar to the English-speaking world. A problem play, or "play of ideas," is concerned with some troublesome social institution, its author hoping to arouse the audience to do something about the problem (for example, to modify the divorce laws, to extend the ballot, to alter the tax structure). The more successful the play, the more it ensures its own death, for if the play helps people to change and to solve the problems, the play has no relevance to experience and becomes merely a thing of historical importance, a museum curio. But Ibsen's plays continue to live almost a century later; readers and viewers now see that Ibsen has something more to offer than thoughts on how to improve society.

In December 1890, a few weeks after he finished *Hedda Gabler,* Ibsen made the point that "it was not really my intention to deal in this play with so-called problems. What I principally wanted to do was to depict human beings, human emotions, and human destinies, upon a groundwork of certain of the social conditions and principles of the present day." We get some idea of what Ibsen meant by "the social conditions and principles of the present day" from another jotting he made while he was getting the play into shape: "Tesman represents propriety. Hedda represents a sense of weary dissatisfac-tion. Mrs. R. [i.e., Mrs. Elvsted] modern nervousness and hysteria. Brack the representative of middle-class society." This early summary does not, of course, correspond exactly to the finished play, but it gives us some idea of the direction Ibsen was taking. "Propriety," "weary dissatisfaction," "nervousness and hysteria," and even "middle-class society" are not problems that can be solved by legislation or by any other form of tinkering. The play, after all, is not about a society that foolishly restrains energetic women from putting their energy to use—though it is in part about the social conventions (especially aristocratic pride) that Hedda cannot abandon. The other jottings show even more clearly that Ibsen was concerned with unchanging experiences rather than with transitory problems. In one he states that "They aren't all created to be mothers." In another he says, "The demon in Hedda is that she wants to influence another human being, but once that has happened, she despises him."

Hedda wishes to influence someone, to shape a human destiny. Her own destiny, like everyone else's, has been partly shaped by the circumstances of her birth. She is the daughter of an aristocrat, General Gabler (in a letter Ibsen called attention to the fact that the play is entitled *Hedda Gabler,* and not, despite her marriage to George Tesman, *Hedda Tesman*). Her aristocratic background has given her leisure but no direction, energy but no channel for it, and we see her becoming increasingly desperate. Having married rashly, she now feels her identity is threatened. The point is obvious, but it is worth quoting Ibsen's own description, from a letter: "George Tesman, his old aunts, and the faithful servant Bertha together form a picture of complete unity. They think alike, they share the same memories and have the same outlook on life. To Hedda they appear like a strange and hostile power, aimed at her very being." Tesman is a bore, scarcely worth shaping, and the aunt and the maid are no challenge. Yet this family group frightens Hedda because she thinks it would lessen her identity if it absorbed her. Her distress at the thought of having a child is a further indication that, although she yearns to shape a human destiny, she does not want to become involved in any sort of relationship in which she herself may be shaped; that is, she evades responsibilities. Presumably, when she rejected Eilert Loevborg's advances she did so not only because she feared scandal, but also because she feared the relationship itself. Now she seeks to fulfill herself by controlling Loevborg's life to the point that, with "a crown of vine-leaves in his hair," he will kill himself "beautifully."

In Ibsen's world, as everywhere, people are drawn together and relationships are necessarily established. Miss Tesman's life, for example, is intertwined with the invalid Aunt Rina's, and when Rina dies, a replacement must be found: "Oh, there's always some poor invalid who needs care and attention." To Hedda's question, "Do you really want another cross like that to bear?" Miss Tesman replies, "Cross! God forgive you, child, it's been no cross for me." Similarly, Mrs. Elvsted and Loevborg require each other, and are shaped by each other as they shape each other, and Tesman is at his best when he is bringing to completion someone else's work. These people express themselves by taking on responsibilities. The play is built on a groundwork of "social conditions and principles" of nineteenth-century Norwegian life, but these conditions themselves, as Ibsen presents them, are rooted in elementary facts of life and are not outmoded institutions that needlessly create problems. (In *Peer Gynt* Ibsen earlier represented this matter of interrelationships with a brilliant image. Peer wishes "to be himself," but he finds he has no individuality when apart from others. He peels an onion, to get at the core, and finds that after all layers—relationships—are removed, there is nothing left.) Hedda seeks self-expression through power divorced from responsibility, which means that finally her power must be directed against herself. The attempt to have Loevborg do some "beautiful" deed in defiance of society fails because she cannot have full power over Loevborg unless she gives something of herself to him. When Loevborg is dead, and Tesman and Mrs. Elvsted are occupied with each other, and Hedda is at Judge Brack's mercy, Hedda releases her energy against herself by killing herself "beautifully." Judge Brack's final comment, "But, good God! People don't do such things!" is the sort of scandalized remark that Hedda had feared all her life, the voice of society, a society that does not know the depths of Hedda's anguish, a society that holds itself together by dull virtues, petty vices, and all sorts of dodges. But society does help men to survive, and to reject it is to annihilate oneself.

Henrik Ibsen (1828–1906) was born in the small Norwegian seaport of Skien. Eight years later his father, a prosperous merchant, declared bankruptcy. At fifteen Ibsen was apprenticed to a druggist in Grimsted, where an involvement with a servant girl produced an illegitimate child. Unable to enter the university, he turned to the theatre, holding positions as resident playwright and director at Bergen and Christiania (Oslo). His early works, chiefly romantic, nationalistic verse plays, culminated in *Brand* (1866), which made his Scandinavian reputation two years after he left the north for twenty-seven years of voluntary exile in Italy and Germany. Following *Peer Gynt* (1867), he wrote only prose plays, mainly on themes contemporary to the last quarter of the nineteenth century; these secured his standing as "the father of modern drama." Six years after a stroke terminated his writing career in 1900, Ibsen died in Oslo.

Hedda Gabler

Henrik Ibsen

Translated by Michael Meyer

Characters

GEORGE TESMAN *research graduate in cultural history*
HEDDA *his wife*
MISS JULIANA TESMAN *his aunt*
MRS. ELVSTED
JUDGE BRACK
EILERT LOEVBORG
BERTHA *a maid*

The action takes place in TESMAN's *villa in the fashionable quarter of town.*

Act One

A large drawing room, handsomely and tastefully furnished; decorated in dark colors. In the rear wall is a broad open doorway, with curtains drawn back to either side. It leads to a smaller room, decorated in the same style as the drawing room. In the right-hand wall of the drawing room, a folding door leads out to the hall. The opposite wall, on the left, contains french windows, also with curtains drawn back on either side. Through the glass we can see part of a verandah, and trees in autumn colors. Downstage stands an oval table, covered by a cloth and surrounded by chairs. Downstage right, against the wall, is a broad stove tiled with dark porcelain; in front of it stand a high-backed armchair, a cushioned footrest, and two footstools. Upstage right, in an alcove, is a corner sofa, with a small, round table. Downstage left, a little away from the wall, is another sofa. Upstage of the french windows, a piano. On either side of the open doorway in the rear wall stand what-nots holding ornaments of terra cotta and majolica. Against the rear wall of the smaller room can be seen a sofa, a table, and a couple of chairs. Above this sofa hangs the portrait of a handsome old man in general's uniform. Above the table a lamp hangs from the ceiling, with a shade of opalescent, milky glass. All round the drawing room bunches of flowers stand in vases and glasses. More bunches lie on the tables. The floors of both rooms are covered with thick carpets. Morning light. The sun shines in through the french windows.

[MISS JULIANA TESMAN, *wearing a hat and carrying a parasol, enters from the hall, followed by* BERTHA, *who is carrying a bunch of flowers wrapped in paper.* MISS TESMAN *is about sixty-five, of pleasant and kindly appearance. She is neatly but simply dressed in grey outdoor clothes.* BERTHA, *the maid, is rather simple and rustic-looking. She is getting on in years.*]

MISS TESMAN (*stops just inside the door, listens and says in a hushed voice*)   No, bless my soul! They're not up yet.

BERTHA (*also in hushed tones*)   What did I tell you, miss? The boat didn't get in till midnight. And when they did turn up—Jesus, miss, you should have seen all the things Madam made me unpack before she'd go to bed!

MISS TESMAN   Ah, well. Let them have a good lie in. But let's have some nice fresh air waiting for them when they do come down. [*Goes to the french windows and throws them wide open.*]

BERTHA (*bewildered at the table, the bunch of flowers in her hand*)   I'm blessed if there's a square inch left to put anything. I'll have to let it lie here, miss. [*Puts it on the piano.*]

MISS TESMAN   Well, Bertha dear, so now *Start* you have a new mistress. Heaven knows it nearly broke my heart to have to part with you.

BERTHA (*snivels*)   What about me, Miss Juju? How do you suppose I felt? After all the happy years I've spent with you and Miss Rena?

MISS TESMAN   We must accept it bravely, Bertha. It was the only way. George needs you to take care of him. He could never manage without you. You've looked after him ever since he was a tiny boy.

BERTHA   Oh, but, Miss Juju, I can't help thinking about Miss Rena, lying there all helpless, poor dear. And that new girl! She'll never learn the proper way to handle an invalid.

MISS TESMAN   Oh, I'll manage to train her. I'll do most of the work myself, you know. You needn't worry about my poor sister, Bertha dear.

451

BERTHA But Miss Juju, there's another thing. I'm frightened Madam may not find me suitable.

MISS TESMAN Oh, nonsense, Bertha. There may be one or two little things to begin with——

BERTHA She's a real lady. Wants everything just so.

MISS TESMAN But of course she does! General Gabler's daughter! Think of what she was accustomed to when the General was alive. You remember how we used to see her out riding with her father? In that long black skirt? With the feather in her hat?

BERTHA Oh, yes, miss. As if I could forget! But, Lord! I never dreamed I'd live to see a match between her and Master Georgie.

MISS TESMAN Neither did I. By the way, Bertha, from now on you must stop calling him Master Georgie. You must say: Dr. Tesman.

BERTHA Yes, Madam said something about that too. Last night—the moment they's set foot inside the door. Is it true, then, miss?

MISS TESMAN Indeed it is. Just imagine, Bertha, some foreigners have made him a doctor. It happened while they were away. I had no idea till he told me when they got off the boat.

BERTHA Well, I suppose there's no limit to what he won't become. He's that clever. I never thought he'd go in for hospital work, though.

MISS TESMAN No, he's not that kind of doctor. [*Nods impressively.*] In any case, you may soon have to address him by an even grander title.

BERTHA You don't say! What might that be, miss?

MISS TESMAN (*smiles*) Ah! If you only knew! [*Moved.*] Dear God, if only poor dear Joachim could rise out of his grave and see what his little son has grown into! [*Looks round.*] But Bertha, why have you done this? Taken the chintz covers off all the furniture!

BERTHA Madam said I was to. Can't stand chintz covers on chairs, she said.

MISS TESMAN But surely they're not going to use this room as a parlor?

BERTHA So I gathered, miss. From what Madam said. He didn't say anything. The Doctor.

[GEORGE TESMAN *comes into the rear room, from the right, humming, with an open, empty travelling bag in his hand. He is about thirty-three, of medium height and youthful appearance, rather plump, with an open, round, contented face, and fair hair and beard. He wears spectacles, and is dressed in comfortable, indoor clothes.*]

MISS TESMAN Good morning! Good morning, George!

TESMAN (*in open doorway*) Auntie Juju! Dear Auntie Juju! [*Comes forward and shakes her hand.*] You've come all the way out here! And so early! What?

MISS TESMAN Well, I had to make sure you'd settled in comfortably.

TESMAN But you can't have had a proper night's sleep.

MISS TESMAN Oh, never mind that.

TESMAN We were so sorry we couldn't give you a lift. But you saw how it was—Hedda had so much luggage—and she insisted on having it all with her.

MISS TESMAN Yes, I've never seen so much luggage.

BERTHA (*to* TESMAN) Shall I go and ask Madam if there's anything I can lend her a hand with?

TESMAN Er—thank you, Bertha; no, you needn't bother. She says if she wants you for anything she'll ring.

BERTHA (*over to right*) Oh. Very good.

TESMAN Oh, Bertha—take this bag, will you?

BERTHA (*takes it*) I'll put it in the attic. [*Goes out into the hall.*]

TESMAN Just fancy, Auntie Juju, I filled that whole bag with notes for my book. You know, it's really incredible what I've managed to find rooting through those archives. By Jove! Wonderful old things no one even knew existed——

MISS TESMAN I'm sure you didn't waste a

single moment of your honeymoon, George dear.

TESMAN   No, I think I can truthfully claim that. But, Auntie Juju, do take your hat off. Here. Let me untie it for you. What?

MISS TESMAN   (*as he does so*)   Oh dear, oh dear! It's just as if you were still living at home with us.

TESMAN   (*turns the hat in his hand and looks at it*)   I say! What a splendid new hat!

MISS TESMAN   I bought it for Hedda's sake.

TESMAN   For Hedda's sake? What?

MISS TESMAN   So that Hedda needn't be ashamed of me, in case we ever go for a walk together.

TESMAN   (*pats her cheek*)   You still think of everything, don't you, Auntie Juju? [*Puts the hat down on a chair by the table.*] Come on, let's sit down here on the sofa. And have a little chat while we wait for Hedda. [*They sit. She puts her parasol in the corner of the sofa.*]

MISS TESMAN   (*clasps both his hands and looks at him*)   Oh, George, it's so wonderful to have you back, and be able to see you with my own eyes again! Poor dear Joachim's own son!

TESMAN   What about me! It's wonderful for me to see you again, Auntie Juju. You've been a mother to me. And a father, too.

MISS TESMAN   You'll always keep a soft spot in your heart for your old aunties, won't you, George dear?

TESMAN   I suppose Auntie Rena's no better? What?

MISS TESMAN   Alas, no. I'm afraid she'll never get better, poor dear. She's lying there just as she has for all these years. Please God I may be allowed to keep her for a little longer. If I lost her I don't know what I'd do. Especially now I haven't you to look after.

TESMAN   (*pats her on the back*)   There, there, there!

MISS TESMAN   (*with a sudden change of mood*)   Oh but George, fancy you being a married man! And to think it's you who've won Hedda Gabler! The beautiful Hedda Gabler! Fancy! She was always so surrounded by admirers.

TESMAN   (*hums a little and smiles contentedly*)   Yes, I suppose there are quite a few people in this town who wouldn't mind being in my shoes. What?

MISS TESMAN   And what a honeymoon! Five months! Nearly six.

TESMAN   Well, I've done a lot of work, you know. All those archives to go through. And I've had to read lots of books.

MISS TESMAN   Yes, dear, of course. [*Lowers her voice confidentially.*] But tell me, George—haven't you any—any extra little piece of news to give me?

TESMAN   You mean, arising out of the honeymoon?

MISS TESMAN   Yes.

TESMAN   No, I don't think there's anything I didn't tell you in my letters. My doctorate, of course—but I told you about that last night, didn't I?

MISS TESMAN   Yes, yes, I didn't mean that kind of thing. I was just wondering—are you—are you expecting—?

TESMAN   Expecting what?

MISS TESMAN   Oh, come on George, I'm your old aunt!

TESMAN   Well actually—yes, I am expecting something.

MISS TESMAN   I knew it!

TESMAN   You'll be happy to hear that before very long I expect to become a professor.

MISS TESMAN   Professor?

TESMAN   I think I may say that the matter has been decided. But, Auntie Juju, you know about this.

MISS TESMAN   (*gives a little laugh*)   Yes, of course. I'd forgotten. [*Changes her tone.*] But we were talking about your honeymoon. It must have cost a dreadful amount of money, George?

TESMAN   Oh well, you know, that big research grant I got helped a good deal.

MISS TESMAN   But how on earth did you manage to make it do for two?

TESMAN   Well, to tell the truth it was a bit tricky. What?

MISS TESMAN Especially when one's travelling with a lady. A little bird tells me that makes things very much more expensive.

TESMAN Well, yes, of course it does make things a little more expensive. But Hedda has to do things in style, Auntie Juju. I mean, she has to. Anything less grand wouldn't have suited her.

MISS TESMAN No, no, I suppose not. A honeymoon abroad seems to be the vogue nowadays. But tell me, have you had time to look round the house?

TESMAN You bet. I've been up since the crack of dawn.

MISS TESMAN Well, what do you think of it?

TESMAN Splendid. Absolutely splendid. I'm only wondering what we're going to do with those two empty rooms between that little one and Hedda's bedroom.

MISS TESMAN (*laughs slyly*) Ah, George dear, I'm sure you'll manage to find some use for them—in time.

TESMAN Yes, of course, Auntie Juju, how stupid of me. You're thinking of my books. What?

MISS TESMAN Yes, yes, dear boy. I was thinking of your books.

TESMAN You know, I'm so happy for Hedda's sake that we've managed to get this house. Before we became engaged she often used to say this was the only house in town she felt she could really bear to live in. It used to belong to Mrs. Falk—you know, the Prime Minister's widow.

MISS TESMAN Fancy that! And what a stroke of luck it happened to come into the market. Just as you'd left on your honeymoon.

TESMAN Yes, Auntie Juju, we've certainly had all the luck with us. What?

MISS TESMAN But, George dear, the expense! It's going to make a dreadful hole in your pocket, all this.

TESMAN (*a little downcast*) Yes, I—I suppose it will, won't it?

MISS TESMAN Oh, George, really!

TESMAN How much do you think it'll cost? Roughly, I mean? What?

MISS TESMAN I can't possibly say till I see the bills.

TESMAN Well, luckily Judge Brack's managed to get it on very favorable terms. He wrote and told Hedda so.

MISS TESMAN Don't you worry, George dear. Anyway I've stood security for all the furniture and carpets.

TESMAN Security? But dear, sweet Auntie Juju, how could you possibly stand security?

MISS TESMAN I've arranged a mortgage on our annuity.

TESMAN (*jumps up*) What? On your annuity? And—Auntie Rena's?

MISS TESMAN Yes. Well, I couldn't think of any other way.

TESMAN (*stands in front of her*) Auntie Juju, have you gone completely out of your mind? That annuity's all you and Auntie Rena have.

MISS TESMAN All right, there's no need to get so excited about it. It's a pure formality, you know. Judge Brack told me so. He was so kind as to arrange it all for me. A pure formality; those were his very words.

TESMAN I dare say. All the same——

MISS TESMAN Anyway, you'll have a salary of your own now. And, good heavens, even if we did have to fork out a little—tighten our belts for a week or two—why, we'd be happy to do so for your sake.

TESMAN Oh, Auntie Juju! Will you never stop sacrificing yourself for me?

MISS TESMAN (*gets up and puts her hands on his shoulders*) What else have I to live for but to smooth your road a little, my dear boy? You've never had any mother or father to turn to. And now at last we've achieved our goal. I won't deny we've had our little difficulties now and then. But now, thank the good Lord, George dear, all your worries are past.

TESMAN Yes, it's wonderful really how everything's gone just right for me.

MISS TESMAN Yes! And the enemies who tried to bar your way have been struck down. They have been made to bite the dust. The man who was your most dangerous rival has had the mightiest fall. And now he's lying there in the pit he dug for himself, poor misguided creature.

TESMAN Have you heard any news of Eilert? Since I went away?

MISS TESMAN Only that he's said to have published a new book.

TESMAN What! Eilert Loevborg? You mean—just recently? What?

MISS TESMAN So they say. I don't imagine it can be of any value, do you? When your new book comes out, that'll be another story. What's it going to be about?

TESMAN The domestic industries of Brabant in the Middle Ages.

MISS TESMAN Oh George! The things you know about!

TESMAN Mind you, it may be some time before I actually get down to writing it. I've made these very extensive notes, and I've got to file and index them first.

MISS TESMAN Ah, yes! Making notes; filing and indexing; you've always been wonderful at that. Poor dear Joachim was just the same.

TESMAN I'm looking forward so much to getting down to that. Especially now I've a home of my own to work in.

MISS TESMAN And above all, now that you have the girl you set your heart on, George dear.

TESMAN (*embraces her*) Oh, yes, Auntie Juju, yes! Hedda's the loveliest thing of all! [*Looks towards the doorway.*] I think I hear her coming. What?

[HEDDA *enters the rear room from the left, and comes into the drawing room. She is a woman of twenty-nine. Distinguished, aristocratic face and figure. Her complexion is pale and opalescent. Her eyes are steel-grey, with an expression of cold, calm serenity. Her hair is of a handsome auburn color, but is not especially abundant. She is dressed in an elegant, somewhat loose-fitting morning gown.*]

MISS TESMAN (*goes to greet her*) Good morning, Hedda dear! Good morning!

HEDDA (*holds out her hand*) Good morning, dear Miss Tesman. What an early hour to call. So kind of you.

MISS TESMAN (*seems somewhat embarrassed*) And has the young bride slept well in her new home?

HEDDA Oh—thank you, yes. Passably well.

TESMAN (*laughs*) Passably. I say, Hedda, that's good! When I jumped out of bed, you were sleeping like a top.

HEDDA Yes. Fortunately. One has to accustom oneself to anything new, Miss Tesman. It takes time. [*Looks left.*] Oh, that maid's left the french windows open. This room's flooded with sun.

MISS TESMAN (*goes towards the windows*) Oh—let me close them.

HEDDA No, no, don't do that. Tesman dear, draw the curtains. This light's blinding me.

TESMAN (*at the windows*) Yes, yes, dear. There, Hedda, now you've got shade and fresh air.

HEDDA This room needs fresh air. All these flowers—But my dear Miss Tesman, won't you take a seat?

MISS TESMAN No, really not, thank you. I just wanted to make sure you have everything you need. I must see about getting back home. My poor dear sister will be waiting for me.

TESMAN Be sure to give her my love, won't you? Tell her I'll run over and see her later today.

MISS TESMAN Oh yes, I'll tell her that. Oh, George—[*Fumbles in the pocket of her skirt.*] I almost forgot. I've brought something for you.

TESMAN What's that, Auntie Juju? What?

MISS TESMAN (*pulls out a flat package wrapped in newspaper and gives it to him*) Open and see, dear boy.

TESMAN (*opens the package*) Good heavens! Auntie Juju, you've kept them! Hedda, this is really very touching. What?

HEDDA (*by the what-not on the right*) What is it, Tesman?

TESMAN My old shoes! My slippers, Hedda!

HEDDA Oh, them. I remember you kept

talking about them on our honeymoon.

TESMAN Yes, I missed them dreadfully. [*Goes over to her.*] Here, Hedda, take a look.

HEDDA (*goes away towards the stove*) Thanks, I won't bother.

TESMAN (*follows her*) Fancy, Hedda, Auntie Rena's embroidered them for me. Despite her being so ill. Oh, you can't imagine what memories they have for me.

HEDDA (*by the table*) Not for me.

MISS TESMAN No, Hedda's right there, George.

TESMAN Yes, but I thought since she's one of the family now——

HEDDA (*interrupts*) Tesman, we really can't go on keeping this maid.

MISS TESMAN Not keep Bertha?

TESMAN What makes you say that, dear? What?

HEDDA (*points*) Look at that! She's left her old hat lying on the chair.

TESMAN (*appalled, drops his slippers on the floor*) But, Hedda—!

HEDDA Suppose someone came in and saw it?

TESMAN But Hedda—that's Auntie Juju's hat.

HEDDA Oh?

MISS TESMAN (*picks up the hat*) Indeed it's mine. And it doesn't happen to be old, Hedda dear.

HEDDA I didn't look at it very closely, Miss Tesman.

MISS TESMAN (*trying on the hat*) As a matter of fact, it's the first time I've worn it. As the good Lord is my witness.

TESMAN It's very pretty, too. Really smart.

MISS TESMAN Oh, I'm afraid it's nothing much really. [*Looks round.*] My parasol? Ah, here it is. [*Takes it.*] This is mine, too. [*Murmurs.*] Not Bertha's.

TESMAN A new hat and a new parasol! I say, Hedda, fancy that!

HEDDA Very pretty and charming.

TESMAN Yes, isn't it? What? But Auntie Juju, take a good look at Hedda before you go. Isn't she pretty and charming?

MISS TESMAN Dear boy, there's nothing new in that. Hedda's been a beauty ever since the day she was born. [*Nods and goes right.*]

TESMAN (*follows her*) Yes, but have you noticed how strong and healthy she's looking? And how she's filled out since we went away?

MISS TESMAN (*stops and turns*) Filled out?

HEDDA (*walks across the room*) Oh, can't we forget it?

TESMAN Yes, Auntie Juju—you can't see it so clearly with that dress on. But I've good reason to know——

HEDDA (*by the french windows, impatiently*) You haven't good reason to know anything.

TESMAN It must have been the mountain air up there in the Tyrol——

HEDDA (*curtly, interrupts him*) I'm exactly the same as when I went away.

TESMAN You keep on saying so. But you're not. I'm right, aren't I, Auntie Juju?

MISS TESMAN (*has folded her hands and is gazing at her*) She's beautiful—beautiful. Hedda is beautiful. [*Goes over to* HEDDA, *takes her head between her hands, draws it down and kisses her hair.*] God bless and keep you, Hedda Tesman. For George's sake.

HEDDA (*frees herself politely*) Oh—let me go, please.

MISS TESMAN (*quietly, emotionally*) I shall come and see you both every day.

TESMAN Yes, Auntie Juju, please do. What?

MISS TESMAN Good-bye! Good-bye!

[*She goes out into the hall.* TESMAN *follows her. The door remains open.* TESMAN *is heard sending his love to* AUNT RENA *and thanking* MISS TESMAN *for his slippers. Meanwhile* HEDDA *walks up and down the room raising her arms and clenching her fists as though in desperation. Then she throws aside the curtains from the french windows and stands there, looking out. A few moments later,* TESMAN *returns and closes the door behind him.*]

TESMAN (*picks up his slippers from the floor*) What are you looking at, Hedda?

HEDDA (*calm and controlled again*) Only the leaves. They're so golden. And withered.

TESMAN (*wraps up the slippers and lays them on the table*) Well, we're in September now.

HEDDA (*restless again*) Yes. We're already into September.

TESMAN Auntie Juju was behaving rather oddly, I thought, didn't you? Almost as though she was in church or something. I wonder what came over her. Any idea?

HEDDA I hardly know her. Does she often act like that?

TESMAN Not to the extent she did today.

HEDDA (*goes away from the french windows*) Do you think she was hurt by what I said about the hat?

TESMAN Oh, I don't think so. A little at first, perhaps——

HEDDA But what a thing to do, throw her hat down in someone's drawing room. People don't do such things.

TESMAN I'm sure Auntie Juju doesn't do it very often.

HEDDA Oh well, I'll make it up with her.

TESMAN Oh Hedda, would you?

HEDDA When you see them this afternoon invite her to come out here this evening.

TESMAN You bet I will! I say, there's another thing which would please her enormously.

HEDDA Oh?

TESMAN If you could bring yourself to call her Auntie Juju. For my sake, Hedda? What?

HEDDA Oh no, really Tesman, you mustn't ask me to do that. I've told you so once before. I'll try to call her Aunt Juliana. That's as far as I'll go.

TESMAN (*after a moment*) I say, Hedda, is anything wrong? What?

HEDDA I'm just looking at my old piano. It doesn't really go with all this.

TESMAN As soon as I start getting my salary we'll see about changing it.

HEDDA No, no, don't let's change it. I don't want to part with it. We can move it into that little room and get another one to put in here.

TESMAN (*a little downcast*) Yes, we—might do that.

HEDDA (*picks up the bunch of flowers from the piano*) These flowers weren't here when we arrived last night.

TESMAN I expect Auntie Juju brought them.

HEDDA Here's a card. [*Takes it out and reads.*] "Will come back later today." Guess who it's from?

TESMAN No idea. Who? What?

HEDDA It says: "Mrs. Elvsted."

TESMAN No, really? Mrs. Elvsted! She used to be Miss Rysing, didn't she?

HEDDA Yes. She was the one with that irritating hair she was always showing off. I hear she used to be an old flame of yours.

TESMAN (*laughs*) That didn't last long. Anyway, that was before I got to know you, Hedda. By Jove, fancy her being in town!

HEDDA Strange she should call. I only knew her at school.

TESMAN Yes, I haven't seen her for—oh, heaven knows how long. I don't know how she manages to stick it out up there in the north. What?

HEDDA (*thinks for a moment, then says suddenly*) Tell me, Tesman, doesn't he live somewhere up in those parts? You know—Eilert Loevborg?

TESMAN Yes, that's right. So he does.

[BERTHA *enters from the hall.*]

BERTHA She's here again, madam. The lady who came and left the flowers. [*Points.*] The ones you're holding.

HEDDA Oh, is she? Well, show her in.

[BERTHA *opens the door for* MRS. ELVSTED *and goes out.* MRS. ELVSTED *is a delicately built woman with gentle, attractive features. Her eyes are light blue, large, and somewhat prominent, with a frightened, questioning expression. Her hair is extremely fair, almost flaxen, and is exceptionally wavy and abundant. She is two or three years younger than* HEDDA.

She is wearing a dark visiting dress, in good taste but not quite in the latest fashion.]

HEDDA (*goes cordially to greet her*) Dear Mrs. Elvsted, good morning. How delightful to see you again after all this time.

MRS. ELVSTED (*nervously, trying to control herself*) Yes, it's many years since we met.

TESMAN And since *we* met. What?

HEDDA Thank you for your lovely flowers.

MRS. ELVSTED Oh, please—I wanted to come yesterday afternoon. But they told me you were away——

TESMAN You've only just arrived in town, then? What?

MRS. ELVSTED I got here yesterday, around midday. Oh, I became almost desperate when I heard you weren't here.

HEDDA Desperate? Why?

TESMAN My dear Mrs. Rysing—Elvsted——

HEDDA There's nothing wrong, I hope?

MRS. ELVSTED Yes, there is. And I don't know anyone else here whom I can turn to.

HEDDA (*puts the flowers down on the table*) Come and sit with me on the sofa——

MRS. ELVSTED Oh, I feel too restless to sit down.

HEDDA You must. Come along, now. [*She pulls* MRS. ELVSTED *down on to the sofa and sits beside her.*]

TESMAN Well? Tell us, Mrs.—er——

HEDDA Has something happened at home?

MRS. ELVSTED Yes—that is, yes and no. Oh, I do hope you won't misunderstand me——

HEDDA Then you'd better tell us the whole story, Mrs. Elvsted.

TESMAN That's why you've come. What?

MRS. ELVSTED Yes—yes, it is. Well, then—in case you don't already know—Eilert Loevborg is in town.

HEDDA Loevborg here?

TESMAN Eilert back in town? By Jove, Hedda, did you hear that?

HEDDA Yes, of course I heard.

MRS. ELVSTED He's been here a week. A whole week! In this city. Alone. With all those dreadful people——

HEDDA But my dear Mrs. Elvsted, what concern is he of yours?

MRS. ELVSTED (*gives her a frightened look and says quickly*) He's been tutoring the children.

HEDDA Your children?

MRS. ELVSTED My husband's. I have none.

HEDDA Oh, you mean your stepchildren.

MRS. ELVSTED Yes.

TESMAN (*gropingly*) But was he sufficiently—I don't know how to put it—sufficiently regular in his habits to be suited to such a post? What?

MRS. ELVSTED For the past two to three years he has been living irreproachably.

TESMAN You don't say! By Jove, Hedda, hear that?

HEDDA I hear.

MRS. ELVSTED Quite irreproachably, I assure you. In every respect. All the same—in this big city—with money in his pockets—I'm so dreadfully frightened something may happen to him.

TESMAN But why didn't he stay up there with you and your husband?

MRS. ELVSTED Once his book had come out, he became restless.

TESMAN Oh, yes—Auntie Juju said he'd brought out a new book.

MRS. ELVSTED Yes, a big new book about the history of civilisation. A kind of general survey. It came out a fortnight ago. Everyone's been buying it and reading it—it's created a tremendous stir——

TESMAN Has it really? It must be something he's dug up, then.

MRS. ELVSTED You mean from the old days?

TESMAN Yes.

MRS. ELVSTED No, he's written it all since he came to live with us.

TESMAN Well, that's splendid news, Hedda. Fancy that!

MRS. ELVSTED Oh, yes! If only he can go on like this!

HEDDA Have you met him since you came here?

MRS. ELVSTED No, not yet. I had such dreadful difficulty finding his address. But this morning I managed to track him down at last.

HEDDA (*looks searchingly at her*) I must say I find it a little strange that your husband—hm——

MRS. ELVSTED (*starts nervously*) My husband! What do you mean?

HEDDA That he should send you all the way here on an errand of this kind. I'm surprised he didn't come himself to keep an eye on his friend.

MRS. ELVSTED Oh, no, no—my husband hasn't the time. Besides, I—er—wanted to do some shopping here.

HEDDA (*with a slight smile*) Ah. Well, that's different.

MRS. ELVSTED (*gets up quickly, restlessly*) Please, Mr. Tesman, I beg you—be kind to Eilert Loevborg if he comes here. I'm sure he will. I mean, you used to be such good friends in the old days. And you're both studying the same subject, as far as I can understand. You're in the same field, aren't you?

TESMAN Well, we used to be, anyway.

MRS. ELVSTED Yes—so I beg you earnestly, do please, please, keep an eye on him. Oh, Mr. Tesman, do promise me you will.

TESMAN I shall be only too happy to do so, Mrs. Rysing.

HEDDA Elvsted.

TESMAN I'll do everything for Eilert that lies in my power. You can rely on that.

MRS. ELVSTED Oh, how good and kind you are! [*Presses his hands.*] Thank you, thank you, thank you. [*Frightened.*] My husband's so fond of him, you see.

HEDDA (*gets up*) You'd better send him a note, Tesman. He may not come to you of his own accord.

TESMAN Yes, that'd probably be the best plan, Hedda. What?

HEDDA The sooner the better. Why not do it now?

MRS. ELVSTED (*pleadingly*) Oh yes, if only you would!

TESMAN I'll do it this very moment. Do you have his address, Mrs.—er—Elvsted?

MRS. ELVSTED Yes. [*Takes a small piece of paper from her pocket and gives it to him.*]

TESMAN Good, good. Right, well I'll go inside and—[*Looks round.*] Where are my slippers? Oh yes, here. [*Picks up the package and is about to go.*]

HEDDA Try to sound friendly. Make it a nice long letter.

TESMAN Right, I will.

MRS. ELVSTED Please don't say anything about my having seen you.

TESMAN Good heavens no, of course not. What? [*Goes out through the rear room to the right.*]

HEDDA (*goes over to* MRS. ELVSTED, *smiles, and says softly*) Well! Now we've killed two birds with one stone.

MRS. ELVSTED What do you mean?

HEDDA Didn't you realise I wanted to get him out of the room?

MRS. ELVSTED So that he could write the letter?

HEDDA And so that I could talk to you alone.

MRS. ELVSTED (*confused*) About this?

HEDDA Yes, about this.

MRS. ELVSTED (*in alarm*) But there's nothing more to tell, Mrs. Tesman. Really there isn't.

HEDDA Oh, yes there is. There's a lot more. I can see that. Come along, let's sit down and have a little chat. [*She pushes* MRS. ELVSTED *down into the armchair by the stove and seats herself on one of the footstools.*]

MRS. ELVSTED (*looks anxiously at her watch*) Really, Mrs. Tesman, I think I ought to be going now.

HEDDA There's no hurry. Well? How are things at home?

MRS. ELVSTED I'd rather not speak about that.

HEDDA But my dear, you can tell me. Good heavens, we were at school together.

MRS. ELVSTED Yes, but you were a year senior to me. Oh, I used to be terribly frightened of you in those days.

HEDDA Frightened of me?

MRS. ELVSTED Yes, terribly frightened. Whenever you met me on the staircase you used to pull my hair.

HEDDA No, did I?

MRS. ELVSTED Yes. And once you said you'd burn it all off.

HEDDA Oh, that was only in fun.

MRS. ELVSTED Yes, but I was so silly in those days. And then afterwards—I mean, we've drifted so far apart. Our backgrounds were so different.

HEDDA Well, now we must try to drift together again. Now listen. When we were at school we used to call each other by our Christian names——

MRS. ELVSTED No, I'm sure you're mistaken.

HEDDA I'm sure I'm not. I remember it quite clearly. Let's tell each other our secrets, as we used to in the old days. [*Moves closer on her footstool.*] There, now. [*Kisses her on the cheek.*] You must call me Hedda.

MRS. ELVSTED (*squeezes her hands and pats them*) Oh, you're so kind. I'm not used to people being so nice to me.

HEDDA Now, now, now. And I shall call you Tora, the way I used to.

MRS. ELVSTED My name is Thea.

HEDDA Yes, of course. Of course. I meant Thea. [*Looks at her sympathetically.*] So you're not used to kindness, Thea? In your own home?

MRS. ELVSTED Oh, if only I had a home! But I haven't. I've never had one.

HEDDA (*looks at her for a moment*) I thought that was it.

MRS. ELVSTED (*stares blankly and helplessly*) Yes—yes——yes.

HEDDA I can't remember exactly now, but didn't you first go to Mr. Elvsted as a housekeeper?

MRS. ELVSTED Governess, actually. But his wife—at the time, I mean—she was an invalid, and had to spend most of her time in bed. So I had to look after the house too.

HEDDA But in the end, you became mistress of the house.

MRS. ELVSTED (*sadly*) Yes, I did.

HEDDA Let me see. Roughly, how long ago was that?

MRS. ELVSTED When I got married, you mean?

HEDDA Yes.

MRS. ELVSTED About five years.

HEDDA Yes; it must be about that.

MRS. ELVSTED Oh, those five years! Especially the last two or three. Oh, Mrs. Tesman, if you only knew—!

HEDDA (*slaps her hand gently*) Mrs. Tesman? Oh, Thea!

MRS. ELVSTED I'm sorry, I'll try to remember. Yes—if you had any idea——

HEDDA (*casually*) Eilert Loevborg's been up there too, for about three years, hasn't he?

MRS. ELVSTED (*looks at her uncertainly*) Eilert Loevborg? Yes, he has.

HEDDA Did you know him before? When you were here?

MRS. ELVSTED No, not really. That is—I knew him by name, of course.

HEDDA But up there, he used to visit you?

MRS. ELVSTED Yes, he used to come and see us every day. To give the children lessons. I found I couldn't do that as well as manage the house.

HEDDA I'm sure you couldn't. And your husband—? I suppose being a magistrate he has to be away from home a good deal?

MRS. ELVSTED Yes. You see, Mrs.—you see, Hedda, he has to cover the whole district.

HEDDA (*leans against the arm of MRS. ELVSTED's chair*) Poor, pretty little Thea! Now you must tell me the whole story. From beginning to end.

MRS. ELVSTED Well—what do you want to know?

HEDDA What kind of man is your husband, Thea? I mean, as a person. Is he kind to you?

MRS. ELVSTED (*evasively*) I'm sure he does his best to be.

HEDDA I only wonder if he isn't too old for you. There's more than twenty years between you, isn't there?

MRS. ELVSTED (*irritably*) Yes, there's that too. Oh, there are so many things. We're different in every way. We've nothing in common. Nothing whatever.

HEDDA   But he loves you, surely? In his own way?

MRS. ELVSTED   Oh, I don't know. I think he just finds me useful. And then I don't cost much to keep. I'm cheap.

HEDDA   Now you're being stupid.

MRS. ELVSTED   (*shakes her head*)   It can't be any different. With him. He doesn't love anyone except himself. And perhaps the children—a little.

HEDDA   He must be fond of Eilert Loevborg, Thea.

MRS. ELVSTED   (*looks at her*)   Eilert Loevborg? What makes you think that?

HEDDA   Well, if he sends you all the way down here to look for him—[*Smiles almost imperceptibly.*] Besides, you said so yourself to Tesman.

MRS. ELVSTED   (*with a nervous twitch*) Did I? Oh yes, I suppose I did. [*Impulsively, but keeping her voice low.*] Well, I might as well tell you the whole story. It's bound to come out sooner or later.

HEDDA   But my dear Thea—?

MRS. ELVSTED   My husband had no idea I was coming here.

HEDDA   What? Your husband didn't know?

MRS. ELVSTED   No, of course not. As a matter of fact, he wasn't even there. He was away at the assizes. Oh, I couldn't stand it any longer, Hedda! I just couldn't. I'd be so dreadfully lonely up there now.

HEDDA   Go on.

MRS. ELVSTED   So I packed a few things. Secretly. And went.

HEDDA   Without telling anyone?

MRS. ELVSTED   Yes. I caught the train and came straight here.

HEDDA   But my dear Thea! How brave of you!

MRS. ELVSTED   (*gets up and walks across the room*)   Well, what else could I do?

HEDDA   But what do you suppose your husband will say when you get back?

MRS. ELVSTED   (*by the table, looks at her*) Back there? To him?

HEDDA   Yes. Surely—?

MRS. ELVSTED   I shall never go back to him.

HEDDA   (*gets up and goes closer*)   You mean you've left your home for good?

MRS. ELVSTED   Yes. I didn't see what else I could do.

HEDDA   But to do it so openly!

MRS. ELVSTED   Oh, it's no use trying to keep a thing like that secret.

HEDDA   But what do you suppose people will say?

MRS. ELVSTED   They can say what they like. [*Sits sadly, wearily on the sofa.*] I had to do it.

HEDDA   (*after a short silence*)   What do you intend to do now? How are you going to live?

MRS. ELVSTED   I don't know. I only know that I must live wherever Eilert Loevborg is. If I am to go on living.

HEDDA   (*moves a chair from the table, sits on it near* MRS. ELVSTED *and strokes her hands*)   Tell me, Thea, how did this—friendship between you and Eilert Loevborg begin?

MRS. ELVSTED   Oh, it came about gradually. I developed a kind of—power over him.

HEDDA   Oh?

MRS. ELVSTED   He gave up his old habits. Not because I asked him to. I'd never have dared to do that. I suppose he just noticed I didn't like that kind of thing. So he gave it up.

HEDDA   (*hides a smile*)   So you've made a new man of him. Clever little Thea!

MRS. ELVSTED   Yes—anyway, he says I have. And he's made a—sort of—real person of me. Taught me to think—and to understand all kinds of things.

HEDDA   Did he give you lessons too?

MRS. ELVSTED   Not exactly lessons. But he talked to me. About—oh, you've no idea—so many things! And then he let me work with him. Oh, it was wonderful. I was so happy to be allowed to help him.

HEDDA   Did he allow you to help him!

MRS. ELVSTED   Yes. Whenever he wrote anything we always—did it together.

HEDDA   Like good pals?

MRS. ELVSTED   (*eagerly*)   Pals! Yes—why, Hedda, that's exactly the word he used!

Oh, I ought to feel so happy. But I can't. I don't know if it will last.

HEDDA   You don't seem very sure of him.

MRS. ELVSTED   (*sadly*) Something stands between Eilert Loevborg and me. The shadow of another woman.

HEDDA   Who can that be?

MRS. ELVSTED   I don't know. Someone he used to be friendly with in—in the old days. Someone he's never been able to forget.

HEDDA   What has he told you about her?

MRS. ELVSTED   Oh, he only mentioned her once, casually.

HEDDA   Well! What did he say?

MRS. ELVSTED   He said when he left her she tried to shoot him with a pistol.

HEDDA   (*cold, controlled*) What non-sense. People don't do such things. The kind of people we know.

MRS. ELVSTED   No. I think it must have been that red-haired singer he used to——

HEDDA   Ah yes, very probably.

MRS. ELVSTED   I remember they used to say she always carried a loaded pistol.

HEDDA   Well then, it must be her.

MRS. ELVSTED   But Hedda, I hear she's come back, and is living here. Oh, I'm so desperate—!

HEDDA   (*glances towards the rear room*) Ssh! Tesman's coming. [*Gets up and whispers.*] Thea, we mustn't breathe a word about this to anyone.

MRS. ELVSTED   (*jumps up*) Oh, no, no! Please don't!

[GEORGE TESMAN *appears from the right in the rear room with a letter in his hand, and comes into the drawing room.*]

TESMAN   Well, here's my little epistle all signed and sealed.

HEDDA   Good. I think Mrs. Elvsted wants to go now. Wait a moment—I'll see you as far as the garden gate.

TESMAN   Er—Hedda, do you think Bertha could deal with this?

HEDDA   (*takes the letter*) I'll give her instructions.

[BERTHA *enters from the hall.*]

BERTHA   Judge Brack is here and asks if he may pay his respects to Madam and the Doctor.

HEDDA   Yes, ask him to be so good as to come in. And—wait a moment—drop this letter in the post box.

BERTHA   (*takes the letter*) Very good, madam.

[*She opens the door for* JUDGE BRACK, *and goes out.* JUDGE BRACK *is forty-five; rather short, but well-built, and elastic in his movements. He has a roundish face with an aristocratic profile. His hair, cut short, is still almost black, and is carefully barbered. Eyes lively and humorous. Thick eyebrows. His moustache is also thick, and is trimmed square at the ends. He is wearing outdoor clothes which are elegant but a little too youthful for him. He has a monocle in one eye; now and then he lets it drop.*]

BRACK   (*hat in hand, bows*) May one presume to call so early?

HEDDA   One may presume.

TESMAN   (*shakes his hand*) You're welcome here any time. Judge Brack—Mrs. Rysing. [HEDDA *sighs.*]

BRACK   (*bows*) Ah—charmed——

HEDDA   (*looks at him and laughs*) What fun to be able to see you by daylight for once, Judge.

BRACK   Do I look—different?

HEDDA   Yes. A little younger, I think.

BRACK   Obliged.

TESMAN   Well, what do you think of Hedda? What? Doesn't she look well? Hasn't she filled out—?

HEDDA   Oh, do stop it. You ought to be thanking Judge Brack for all the inconvenience he's put himself to——

BRACK   Nonsense, it was a pleasure——

HEDDA   You're a loyal friend. But my other friend is pining to get away. Au revoir, Judge. I won't be a minute.

[*Mutual salutations.* MRS. ELVSTED *and* HEDDA *go out through the hall.*]

BRACK   Well, is your wife satisfied with everything?

TESMAN   Yes, we can't thank you enough. That is—we may have to shift one or two things around, she tells me. And we're short of one or two little items we'll have to purchase.

BRACK   Oh? Really?

TESMAN   But you mustn't worry your head about that. Hedda says she'll get what's needed. I say, why don't we sit down? What?

BRACK   Thanks, just for a moment. [*Sits at the table.*] There's something I'd like to talk to you about, my dear Tesman.

TESMAN   Oh? Ah yes, of course. [*Sits.*] After the feast comes the reckoning. What?

BRACK   Oh, never mind about the financial side—there's no hurry about that. Though I could wish we'd arranged things a little less palatially.

TESMAN   Good heavens, that'd never have done. Think of Hedda, my dear chap. You know her. I couldn't possibly ask her to live like a suburban housewife.

BRACK   No, no—that's just the problem.

TESMAN   Anyway, it can't be long now before my nomination comes through.

BRACK   Well, you know, these things often take time.

TESMAN   Have you heard any more news? What?

BRACK   Nothing definite. [*Changing the subject.*] Oh, by the way, I have one piece of news for you.

TESMAN   What?

BRACK   Your old friend Eilert Loevborg is back in town.

TESMAN   I know that already.

BRACK   Oh? How did you hear that?

TESMAN   She told me. That lady who went out with Hedda.

BRACK   I see. What was her name? I didn't catch it.

TESMAN   Mrs. Elvsted.

BRACK   Oh, the magistrate's wife. Yes, Loevborg's been living up near them, hasn't he?

TESMAN   I'm delighted to hear he's become a decent human being again.

BRACK   Yes, so they say.

TESMAN   I gather he's published a new book, too. What?

BRACK   Indeed he has.

TESMAN   I hear it's created rather a stir.

BRACK   Quite an unusual stir.

TESMAN   I say, isn't that splendid news! He's such a gifted chap—and I was afraid he'd gone to the dogs for good.

BRACK   Most people thought he had.

TESMAN   But I can't think what he'll do now. How on earth will he manage to make ends meet? What?

[*As he speaks his last words,* HEDDA *enters from the hall.*]

HEDDA   (*to* BRACK, *laughs slightly scornfully*)   Tesman is always worrying about making ends meet.

TESMAN   We were talking about poor Eilert Loevborg, Hedda dear.

HEDDA   (*gives him a quick look*)   Oh, were you? [*Sits in the armchair by the stove and asks casually.*] Is he in trouble?

TESMAN   Well, he must have run through his inheritance long ago by now. And he can't write a new book every year. What? So I'm wondering what's going to become of him.

BRACK   I may be able to enlighten you there.

TESMAN   Oh?

BRACK   You mustn't forget he has relatives who wield a good deal of influence.

TESMAN   Relatives? Oh, they've quite washed their hands of him, I'm afraid.

BRACK   They used to regard him as the hope of the family.

TESMAN   Used to, yes. But he's put an end to that.

HEDDA   Who knows? [*With a little smile.*] I hear the Elvsteds have made a new man of him.

BRACK   And then this book he's just published——

TESMAN   Well, let's hope they find something for him. I've just written him a note. Oh, by the way, Hedda, I asked him to come over and see us this evening.

BRACK   But my dear chap, you're coming to me this evening. My bachelor party.

You promised me last night when I met you at the boat.

HEDDA   Had you forgotten, Tesman?

TESMAN   Good heavens, yes, I'd quite forgotten.

BRACK   Anyway, you can be quite sure he won't turn up here.

TESMAN   Why do you think that? What?

BRACK   (*a little unwillingly, gets up and rests his hands on the back of his chair*) My dear Tesman—and you, too, Mrs. Tesman—there's something I feel you ought to know.

TESMAN   Concerning Eilert?

BRACK   Concerning him and you.

TESMAN   Well, my dear Judge, tell us, please!

BRACK   You must be prepared for your nomination not to come through quite as quickly as you hope and expect.

TESMAN   (*jumps up uneasily*)   Is anything wrong? What?

BRACK   There's a possibility that the appointment may be decided by competition——

TESMAN   Competition! By Jove, Hedda, fancy that!

HEDDA   (*leans further back in her chair*) Ah! How interesting!

TESMAN   But who else—? I say, you don't mean—?

BRACK   Exactly. By competition with Eilert Loevborg.

TESMAN   (*clasps his hands in alarm*)   No, no, but this is inconceivable! It's absolutely impossible! What?

BRACK   Hm. We may find it'll happen, all the same.

TESMAN   No, but—Judge Brack, they couldn't be so inconsiderate towards me! [*Waves his arms.*] I mean, by Jove, I—I'm a married man! It was on the strength of this that Hedda and I *got* married! We ran up some pretty hefty debts. And borrowed money from Auntie Juju! I mean, good heavens, they practically promised me the appointment. What?

BRACK   Well, well, I'm sure you'll get it. But you'll have to go through a competition.

HEDDA   (*motionless in her armchair*) How exciting, Tesman. It'll be a kind of duel, by Jove.

TESMAN   My dear Hedda, how can you take it so lightly?

HEDDA   (*as before*)   I'm not. I can't wait to see who's going to win.

BRACK   In any case, Mrs. Tesman, it's best you should know how things stand. I mean before you commit yourself to these little items I hear you're threatening to purchase.

HEDDA   I can't allow this to alter my plans.

BRACK   Indeed? Well, that's your business. Good-bye. [*To* TESMAN.] I'll come and collect you on the way home from my afternoon walk.

TESMAN   Oh, yes, yes. I'm sorry, I'm all upside down just now.

HEDDA   (*lying in her chair, holds out her hand*)   Good-bye, Judge. See you this afternoon.

BRACK   Thank you. Good-bye, good-bye.

TESMAN   (*sees him to the door*)   Good-bye, my dear Judge. You will excuse me, won't you?

[JUDGE BRACK *goes out through the hall.*]

TESMAN   (*pacing up and down*)   Oh, Hedda! One oughtn't to go plunging off on wild adventures. What?

HEDDA   (*looks at him and smiles*)   Like you're doing?

TESMAN   Yes. I mean, there's no denying it, it was a pretty big adventure to go off and get married and set up house merely on expectation.

HEDDA   Perhaps you're right.

TESMAN   Well, anyway, we have our home, Hedda. By Jove, yes. The home we dreamed of. And set our hearts on. What?

HEDDA   (*gets up slowly, wearily*)   You agreed that we should enter society. And keep open house. That was the bargain.

TESMAN   Yes. Good heavens, I was looking forward to it all so much. To seeing you play hostess to a select circle! By Jove! What? Ah, well, for the time being we shall have to make do with each other's company, Hedda. Perhaps have Auntie

Juju in now and then. Oh dear, this wasn't at all what you had in mind——

HEDDA   I won't be able to have a liveried footman. For a start.

TESMAN   Oh no, we couldn't possibly afford a footman.

HEDDA   And that thoroughbred horse you promised me——

TESMAN   *(fearfully)* Thoroughbred horse!

HEDDA   I mustn't even think of that now.

TESMAN   Heaven forbid!

HEDDA   *(walks across the room)* Ah, well. I still have one thing left to amuse myself with.

TESMAN   *(joyfully)* Thank goodness for that. What's that, Hedda? What?

HEDDA   *(in the open doorway, looks at him with concealed scorn)* My pistols, George darling.

TESMAN   *(alarmed)* Pistols!

HEDDA   *(her eyes cold)* General Gabler's pistols. *[She goes into the rear room and disappears.]*

TESMAN   *(runs to the doorway and calls after her)* For heaven's sake, Hedda dear, don't touch those things. They're dangerous. Hedda—please—for my sake! What?

Act Two

The same as in Act One, except that the piano has been removed and an elegant little writing table, with a bookcase, stands in its place. By the sofa on the left a smaller table has been placed. Most of the flowers have been removed. MRS. ELVSTED's *bouquet stands on the larger table, downstage. It is afternoon.*

*[*HEDDA, *dressed to receive callers, is alone in the room. She is standing by the open french windows, loading a revolver. The pair to it is lying in an open pistol case on the writing table.]*

HEDDA   *(looks down into the garden and calls)* Good afternoon, Judge.

BRACK   *(in the distance, below)* Afternoon, Mrs. Tesman.

HEDDA   *(raises the pistol and takes aim)* I'm going to shoot you, Judge Brack.

BRACK   *(shouts from below)* No, no, no! Don't aim that thing at me!

HEDDA   This'll teach you to enter houses by the back door. *[Fires.]*

BRACK   *(below)* Have you gone completely out of your mind?

HEDDA   Oh dear! Did I hit you?

BRACK   *(still outside)* Stop playing these silly tricks.

HEDDA   All right, Judge. Come along in.

*[*JUDGE BRACK, *dressed for a bachelor party, enters through the french windows. He has a light overcoat on his arm.]*

BRACK   For God's sake! Haven't you stopped fooling around with those things yet? What are you trying to hit?

HEDDA   Oh, I was just shooting at the sky.

BRACK   *(takes the pistol gently from her hand)* By your leave, ma'am. *[Looks at it.]* Ah, yes—I know this old friend well. *[Looks around.]* Where's the case? Oh, yes. *[Puts the pistol in the case and closes it.]* That's enough of that little game for today.

HEDDA   Well, what on earth *am* I to do?

BRACK   You haven't had any visitors?

HEDDA   *(closes the french windows)* Not one. I suppose the best people are all still in the country.

BRACK   Your husband isn't home yet?

HEDDA   *(locks the pistol away in a drawer of the writing table)* No. The moment he'd finished eating he ran off to his aunties. He wasn't expecting you so early.

BRACK   Ah, why didn't I think of that? How stupid of me.

HEDDA   *(turns her head and looks at him)* Why stupid?

BRACK   I'd have come a little sooner.

HEDDA   *(walks across the room)* There'd have been no one to receive you. I've been in my room since lunch, dressing.

BRACK   You haven't a tiny crack in the door through which we might have negotiated?

HEDDA   You forgot to arrange one.

BRACK   Another stupidity.

HEDDA   Well, we'll have to sit down here.

And wait. Tesman won't be back for some time.

BRACK   Sad. Well, I'll be patient.

[HEDDA *sits on the corner of the sofa.* BRACK *puts his coat over the back of the nearest chair and seats himself, keeping his hat in his hand. Short pause. They look at each other.*]

HEDDA   Well?

BRACK   (*in the same tone of voice*)   Well?

HEDDA   I asked first.

BRACK   (*leans forward slightly*)   Yes, well, now we can enjoy a nice, cosy little chat —Mrs. Hedda.

HEDDA   (*leans further back in her chair*) It seems such ages since we had a talk. I don't count last night or this morning.

BRACK   You mean: *à deux?*

HEDDA   Mm—yes. That's roughly what I meant.

BRACK   I've been longing so much for you to come home.

HEDDA   So have I.

BRACK   You? Really, Mrs. Hedda? And I thought you were having such a wonderful honeymoon.

HEDDA   Oh, yes. Wonderful!

BRACK   But your husband wrote such ecstatic letters.

HEDDA   He! Oh, yes! He thinks life has nothing better to offer than rooting around in libraries and copying old pieces of parchment, or whatever it is he does.

BRACK   (*a little maliciously*)   Well, that *is* his life. Most of it, anyway.

HEDDA   Yes, I know. Well, it's all right for him. But for me! Oh no, my dear Judge. I've been bored to death.

BRACK   (*sympathetically*)   Do you mean that? Seriously?

HEDDA   Yes. Can you imagine? Six whole months without ever meeting a single person who was one of us, and to whom I could talk about the kind of things we talk about.

BRACK   Yes, I can understand. I'd miss that, too.

HEDDA   That wasn't the worst, though.

BRACK   What was?

HEDDA   Having to spend every minute of one's life with—with the same person.

BRACK   (*nods*)   Yes. What a thought! Morning; noon; and——

HEDDA   (*coldly*)   As I said: every minute of one's life.

BRACK   I stand corrected. But dear Tesman is such a clever fellow, I should have thought one ought to be able——

HEDDA   Tesman is only interested in one thing, my dear Judge. His special subject.

BRACK   True.

HEDDA   And people who are only interested in one thing don't make the most amusing company. Not for long, anyway.

BRACK   Not even when they happen to be the person one loves?

HEDDA   Oh, don't use that sickly, stupid word.

BRACK   (*starts*)   But. Mrs. Hedda—!

HEDDA   (*half laughing, half annoyed*) You just try it, Judge. Listening to the history of civilisation morning, noon and——

BRACK   (*corrects her*)   Every minute of one's life.

HEDDA   All right. Oh, and those domestic industries of Brabant in the Middle Ages! That really is beyond the limit.

BRACK   (*looks at her searchingly*)   But, tell me—if you feel like this why on earth did you—? Ha——

HEDDA   Why on earth did I marry George Tesman?

BRACK   If you like to put it that way.

HEDDA   Do you think it so very strange?

BRACK   Yes—and no, Mrs. Hedda.

HEDDA   I'd danced myself tired, Judge. I felt my time was up—[*Gives a slight shudder.*] No, I mustn't say that. Or even think it.

BRACK   You've no rational cause to think it.

HEDDA   Oh—cause, cause—[*Looks searchingly at him.*] After all, George Tesman— well, I mean, he's a very respectable man.

BRACK   Very respectable, sound as a rock. No denying that.

HEDDA   And there's nothing exactly ridiculous about him. Is there?

BRACK   Ridiculous? N-no, I wouldn't say that.

HEDDA   Mm. He's very clever at collecting material and all that, isn't he? I mean, he may go quite far in time.

BRACK   (*looks at her a little uncertainly*) I thought you believed, like everyone else, that he would become a very prominent man.

HEDDA   (*looks tired*)   Yes, I did. And when he came and begged me on his bended knees to be allowed to love and to cherish me, I didn't see why I shouldn't let him.

BRACK   No, well—if one looks at it like that——

HEDDA   It was more than my other admirers were prepared to do, Judge dear.

BRACK   (*laughs*)   Well, I can't answer for the others. As far as I myself am concerned, you know I've always had a considerable respect for the institution of marriage. As an institution.

HEDDA   (*lightly*)   Oh, I've never entertained any hopes of you.

BRACK   All I want is to have a circle of friends whom I can trust, whom I can help with advice or—or by any other means, and into whose houses I may come and go as a—trusted friend.

HEDDA   Of the husband?

BRACK   (*bows*)   Preferably, to be frank, of the wife. And of the husband too, of course. Yes, you know, this kind of—triangle is a delightful arrangement for all parties concerned.

HEDDA   Yes, I often longed for a third person while I was away. Oh, those hours we spent alone in railway compartments——

BRACK   Fortunately your honeymoon is now over.

HEDDA   (*shakes her head*)   There's a long, long way still to go. I've only reached a stop on the line.

BRACK   Why not jump out and stretch your legs a little, Mrs. Hedda?

HEDDA   I'm not the jumping sort.

BRACK   Aren't you?

HEDDA   No. There's always someone around who——

BRACK   (*laughs*)   Who looks at one's legs?

HEDDA   Yes. Exactly.

BRACK   Well, but surely——

HEDDA   (*with a gesture of rejection*)   I don't like it. I'd rather stay where I am. Sitting in the compartment. *À deux.*

BRACK   But suppose a third person were to step into the compartment?

HEDDA   That would be different.

BRACK   A trusted friend—someone who understood——

HEDDA   And was lively and amusing——

BRACK   And interested in—more subjects than one——

HEDDA   (*sighs audibly*)   Yes, that'd be a relief.

BRACK   (*hears the front door open and shut*)   The triangle is completed.

HEDDA   (*half under breath*)   And the train goes on.

[GEORGE TESMAN, *in grey walking dress with a soft felt hat, enters from the hall. He has a number of paper-covered books under his arm and in his pockets.*]

TESMAN   (*goes over to the table by the corner sofa*)   Phew! It's too hot to be lugging all this around. [*Puts the books down.*] I'm positively sweating, Hedda. Why, hullo, hullo! You here already, Judge? What? Bertha didn't tell me.

BRACK   (*gets up*)   I came in through the garden.

HEDDA   What are all those books you've got there?

TESMAN   (*stands glancing through them*)   Oh, some new publications dealing with my special subject. I had to buy them.

HEDDA   Your special subject?

BRACK   His special subject, Mrs. Tesman. [BRACK *and* HEDDA *exchange a smile.*]

HEDDA   Haven't you collected enough material on your special subject?

TESMAN   My dear Hedda, one can never have too much. One must keep abreast of what other people are writing.

HEDDA   Yes. Of course.

TESMAN   (*rooting among the books*)   Look

—I bought a copy of Eilert Loevborg's new book, too. [*Holds it out to her.*] Perhaps you'd like to have a look at it, Hedda? What?

HEDDA No, thank you. Er—yes, perhaps I will, later.

TESMAN I glanced through it on my way home.

BRACK What's your opinion—as a specialist on the subject?

TESMAN I'm amazed how sound and balanced it is. He never used to write like that. [*Gathers his books together.*] Well, I must get down to these at once. I can hardly wait to cut the pages. Oh, I've got to change, too. [*To* BRACK.] We don't have to be off just yet, do we? What?

BRACK Heavens, no. We've plenty of time yet.

TESMAN Good, I needn't hurry, then. [*Goes with his books, but stops and turns in the doorway.*] Oh, by the way, Hedda, Auntie Juju won't be coming to see you this evening.

HEDDA Won't she? Oh—the hat, I suppose.

TESMAN Good heavens, no. How could you think such a thing of Auntie Juju? Fancy—! No, Auntie Rena's very ill.

HEDDA She always is.

TESMAN Yes, but today she's been taken really bad.

HEDDA Oh, then it's quite understandable that the other one should want to stay with her. Well, I shall have to swallow my disappointment.

TESMAN You can't imagine how happy Auntie Juju was in spite of everything. At your looking so well after the honeymoon!

HEDDA (*half beneath her breath, as she rises*) Oh, these everlasting aunts!

TESMAN What?

HEDDA (*goes over to the french windows*) Nothing.

TESMAN Oh. All right. [*Goes into the rear room and out of sight.*]

BRACK What was that about the hat?

HEDDA Oh, something that happened with Miss Tesman this morning. She'd put her hat down on a chair. [*Looks at him and smiles.*] And I pretended to think it was the servant's.

BRACK (*shakes his head*) But my dear Mrs. Hedda, how could you do such a thing? To that poor old lady?

HEDDA (*nervously, walking across the room*) Sometimes a mood like that hits me. And I can't stop myself. [*Throws herself down in the armchair by the stove.*] Oh, I don't know how to explain it.

BRACK (*behind her chair*) You're not really happy. That's the answer.

HEDDA (*stares ahead of her*) Why on earth should I be happy? Can you give me a reason?

BRACK Yes. For one thing you've got the home you always wanted.

HEDDA (*looks at him*) You really believe that story?

BRACK You mean it isn't true?

HEDDA Oh, yes, it's partly true.

BRACK Well?

HEDDA It's true I got Tesman to see me home from parties last summer——

BRACK It was a pity my home lay in another direction.

HEDDA Yes. Your interests lay in another direction, too.

BRACK (*laughs*) That's naughty of you, Mrs. Hedda. But to return to you and Tesman——

HEDDA Well, we walked past this house one evening. And poor Tesman was fidgeting in his boots trying to find something to talk about. I felt sorry for the great scholar——

BRACK (*smiles incredulously*) Did you? Hm.

HEDDA Yes, honestly I did. Well, to help him out of his misery, I happened to say quite frivolously how much I'd love to live in this house.

BRACK Was that all?

HEDDA That evening, yes.

BRACK But—afterwards?

HEDDA Yes. My little frivolity had its consequences, my dear Judge.

BRACK Our little frivolities do. Much too often, unfortunately.

HEDDA Thank you. Well, it was our mutual admiration for the late Prime Minister's house that brought George Tesman and me together on common ground. So we got engaged, and we got married, and we went on our honeymoon, and—Ah well, Judge, I've—made my bed and I must lie in it, I was about to say.

BRACK How utterly fantastic! And you didn't really care in the least about the house?

HEDDA God knows I didn't.

BRACK Yes, but now that we've furnished it so beautifully for you?

HEDDA Ugh—all the rooms smell of lavender and dried roses. But perhaps Auntie Juju brought that in.

BRACK (*laughs*) More likely the Prime Minister's widow, rest her soul.

HEDDA Yes, it's got the odour of death about it. It reminds me of the flowers one has worn at a ball—the morning after. [*Clasps her hands behind her neck, leans back in the chair and looks up at him.*] Oh, my dear Judge, you've no idea how hideously bored I'm going to be out here.

BRACK Couldn't you find some kind of occupation, Mrs. Hedda? Like your husband?

HEDDA Occupation? That'd interest me?

BRACK Well—preferably.

HEDDA God knows what. I've often thought—[*Breaks off.*] No, that wouldn't work either.

BRACK Who knows? Tell me about it.

HEDDA I was thinking—if I could persuade Tesman to go into politics, for example.

BRACK (*laughs*) Tesman! No, honestly, I don't think he's quite cut out to be a politician.

HEDDA Perhaps not. But if I could persuade him to have a go at it?

BRACK What satisfaction would that give you? If he turned out to be no good? Why do you want to make him do that?

HEDDA Because I'm bored. [*After a moment.*] You feel there's absolutely no possibility of Tesman becoming Prime Minister, then?

BRACK Well, you know, Mrs. Hedda, for one thing he'd have to be pretty well off before he could become that.

HEDDA (*gets up impatiently*) There you are! [*Walks across the room.*] It's this wretched poverty that makes life so hateful. And ludicrous. Well, it is!

BRACK I don't think that's the real cause.

HEDDA What is, then?

BRACK Nothing really exciting has ever happened to you.

HEDDA Nothing serious, you mean?

BRACK Call it that if you like. But now perhaps it may.

HEDDA (*tosses her head*) Oh, you're thinking of this competition for that wretched professorship? That's Tesman's affair. I'm not going to waste my time worrying about that.

BRACK Very well, let's forget about that then. But suppose you were to find yourself faced with what people call—to use the conventional phrase—the most solemn of human responsibilities? [*Smiles.*] A new responsibility, little Mrs. Hedda.

HEDDA (*angrily*) Be quiet! Nothing like that's going to happen.

BRACK (*warily*) We'll talk about it again in a year's time. If not earlier.

HEDDA (*curtly*) I've no leanings in that direction, Judge. I don't want any—responsibilities.

BRACK But surely you must feel some inclination to make use of that—natural talent which every woman——

HEDDA (*over by the french windows*) Oh, be quiet, I say! I often think there's only one thing for which I have any natural talent.

BRACK (*goes closer*) And what is that, if I may be so bold as to ask?

HEDDA (*stands looking out*) For boring myself to death. Now you know. [*Turns, looks toward the rear room and laughs.*] Talking of boring, here comes the Professor.

BRACK (*quietly, warningly*) Now, now, now, Mrs. Hedda!

[GEORGE TESMAN, *in evening dress, with gloves and hat in his hand, enters through the rear room from the right.*]

TESMAN Hedda, hasn't any message come from Eilert? What?

HEDDA No.

TESMAN Ah, then we'll have him here presently. You wait and see.

BRACK You really think he'll come?

TESMAN Yes, I'm almost sure he will. What you were saying about him this morning is just gossip.

BRACK Oh?

TESMAN Yes. Auntie Juju said she didn't believe he'd ever dare to stand in my way again. Fancy that!

BRACK Then everything in the garden's lovely.

TESMAN (*puts his hat, with his gloves in it, on a chair, right*) Yes, but you really must let me wait for him as long as possible.

BRACK We've plenty of time. No one'll be turning up at my place before seven or half past.

TESMAN Ah, then we can keep Hedda company a little longer. And see if he turns up. What?

HEDDA (*picks up* BRACK's *coat and hat and carries them over to the corner sofa*) And if the worst comes to the worst, Mr. Loevborg can sit here and talk to me.

BRACK (*offering to take his things from her*) No, please. What do you mean by "if the worst comes to the worst"?

HEDDA If he doesn't want to go with you and Tesman.

TESMAN (*looks doubtfully at her*) I say, Hedda, do you think it'll be all right for him to stay here with you? What? Remember Auntie Juju isn't coming.

HEDDA Yes, but Mrs. Elvsted is. The three of us can have a cup of tea together.

TESMAN Ah, that'll be all right then.

BRACK (*smiles*) It's probably the safest solution as far as he's concerned.

HEDDA Why?

BRACK My dear Mrs. Tesman, you always say of my little bachelor parties that they should be attended only by men of the strongest principles.

HEDDA But Mr. Loevborg is a man of principle now. You know what they say about a reformed sinner——

[BERTHA *enters from the hall.*]

BERTHA Madam, there's a gentleman here who wants to see you——

HEDDA Ask him to come in.

TESMAN (*quietly*) I'm sure it's him. By Jove. Fancy that!

[EILERT LOEVBORG *enters from the hall. He is slim and lean, of the same age as* TESMAN, *but looks older and somewhat haggard. His hair and beard are of a blackish-brown; his face is long and pale, but with a couple of reddish patches on his cheekbones. He is dressed in an elegant and fairly new black suit, and carries black gloves and a top hat in his hand. He stops just inside the door and bows abruptly. He seems somewhat embarrassed.*]

TESMAN (*goes over and shakes his hand*) My dear Eilert! How grand to see you again after all these years!

EILERT LOEVBORG (*speaks softly*) It was good of you to write, George. [*Goes nearer to* HEDDA.] May I shake hands with you, too, Mrs. Tesman?

HEDDA (*accepts his hand*) Delighted to see you, Mr. Loevborg. [*With a gesture.*] I don't know if you two gentlemen——

LOEVBORG (*bows slightly*) Judge Brack, I believe.

BRACK (*also with a slight bow*) Correct. We—met some years ago——

TESMAN (*puts his hands on* LOEVBORG's *shoulders*) Now you're to treat this house just as though it were your own home, Eilert. Isn't that right, Hedda? I hear you've decided to settle here again? What?

LOEVBORG Yes. I have.

TESMAN Quite understandable. Oh, by the bye—I've just bought your new book. Though to tell the truth I haven't found time to read it yet.

LOEVBORG You needn't bother.

TESMAN   Oh? Why?

LOEVBORG   There's nothing much in it.

TESMAN   By Jove, fancy hearing that from you!

BRACK   But everyone's praising it.

LOEVBORG   That was exactly what I wanted to happen. So I only wrote what I knew everyone would agree with.

BRACK   Very sensible.

TESMAN   Yes, but my dear Eilert——

LOEVBORG   I want to try to re-establish myself. To begin again—from the beginning.

TESMAN   (*a little embarrassed*)   Yes, I—er—suppose you do. What?

LOEVBORG   (*smiles, puts down his hat and takes a package wrapped in paper from his coat pocket*)   But when this gets published—George Tesman—read it. This is my real book. The one in which I have spoken with my own voice.

TESMAN   Oh, really? What's it about?

LOEVBORG   It's the sequel.

TESMAN   Sequel? To what?

LOEVBORG   To the other book.

TESMAN   The one that's just come out?

LOEVBORG   Yes.

TESMAN   But my dear Eilert, that covers the subject right up to the present day.

LOEVBORG   It does. But this is about the future.

TESMAN   The future! But, I say, we don't know anything about that.

LOEVBORG   No. But there are one or two things that need to be said about it. [*Opens the package.*] Here, have a look.

TESMAN   Surely that's not your handwriting?

LOEVBORG   I dictated it. [*Turns the pages.*] It's in two parts. The first deals with the forces that will shape our civilisation. [*Turns further on towards the end.*] And the second indicates the direction in which that civilisation may develop.

TESMAN   Amazing! I'd never think of writing about anything like that.

HEDDA   (*by the french windows, drumming on the pane*)   No. You wouldn't.

LOEVBORG   (*puts the pages back into their cover and lays the package on the table*)   I brought it because I thought I might possibly read you a few pages this evening.

TESMAN   I say, what a kind idea! Oh, but this evening—? [*Glances at* BRACK.] I'm not quite sure whether——

LOEVBORG   Well, some other time, then. There's no hurry.

BRACK   The truth is, Mr. Loevborg, I'm giving a little dinner this evening. In Tesman's honor, you know.

LOEVBORG   (*looks round for his hat*)   Oh—then I mustn't——

BRACK   No wait a minute. Won't you do me the honor of joining us?

LOEVBORG   (*curtly, with decision*)   No I can't. Thank you so much.

BRACK   Oh, nonsense. Do—please. There'll only be a few of us. And I can promise you we shall have some good sport, as Mrs. Hed—as Mrs. Tesman puts it.

LOEVBORG   I've no doubt. Nevertheless——

BRACK   You could bring your manuscript along and read it to Tesman at my place. I could lend you a room.

TESMAN   By Jove, Eilert, that's an idea. What?

HEDDA   (*interposes*)   But Tesman, Mr. Loevborg doesn't want to go. I'm sure Mr. Loevborg would much rather sit here and have supper with me.

LOEVBORG   (*looks at her*)   With you, Mrs. Tesman?

HEDDA   And Mrs. Elvsted.

LOEVBORG   Oh. [*Casually.*] I ran into her this afternoon.

HEDDA   Did you? Well, she's coming here this evening. So you really must stay, Mr. Loevborg. Otherwise she'll have no one to see her home.

LOEVBORG   That's true. Well—thank you, Mrs. Tesman, I'll stay then.

HEDDA   I'll just tell the servant. [*She goes to the door which leads into the hall, and rings.* BERTHA *enters.* HEDDA *talks softly to her and points towards the rear room.* BERTHA *nods and goes out.*]

TESMAN   (*to* LOEVBORG, *as* HEDDA *does this*)   I say, Eilert. This new subject of yours—the—er—future—is that the one you're going to lecture about?

LOEVBORG   Yes.

TESMAN They told me down at the bookshop that you're going to hold a series of lectures here during the autumn.

LOEVBORG Yes, I am. I—hope you don't mind, Tesman.

TESMAN Good heavens, no! But—?

LOEVBORG I can quite understand it might queer your pitch a little.

TESMAN (*dejectedly*) Oh well, I can't expect you to put them off for my sake.

LOEVBORG I'll wait till your appointment's been announced.

TESMAN You'll wait! But—but—aren't you going to compete with me for the post? What?

LOEVBORG No. I only want to defeat you in the eyes of the world.

TESMAN Good heavens! Then Auntie Juju was right after all! Oh, I knew it, I knew it! Hear that, Hedda? Fancy! Eilert *doesn't* want to stand in our way.

HEDDA (*curtly*) Our? Leave me out of it, please. [*She goes towards the rear room, where* BERTHA *is setting a tray with decanters and glasses on the table.* HEDDA *nods approval, and comes back into the drawing room.* BERTHA *goes out.*]

TESMAN (*while this is happening*) Judge Brack, what do you think about all this? What?

BRACK Oh, I think honor and victory can be very splendid things——

TESMAN Of course they can. Still——

HEDDA (*looks at* TESMAN *with a cold smile*) You look as if you'd been hit by a thunderbolt.

TESMAN Yes, I feel rather like it.

BRACK There was a black cloud looming up, Mrs. Tesman. But it seems to have passed over.

HEDDA (*points towards the rear room*) Well, gentlemen, won't you go in and take a glass of cold punch?

BRACK (*glances at his watch*) A stirrup cup? Yes, why not?

TESMAN An admirable suggestion, Hedda. Admirable! Oh, I feel so relieved!

HEDDA Won't you have one, too, Mr. Loevborg?

LOEVBORG No, thank you. I'd rather not.

BRACK Great heavens, man, cold punch isn't poison. Take my word for it.

LOEVBORG Not for everyone, perhaps.

HEDDA I'll keep Mr. Loevborg company while you drink.

TESMAN Yes, Hedda dear, would you?

[*He and* BRACK *go into the rear room, sit down, drink punch, smoke cigarettes and talk cheerfully during the following scene.* EILERT LOEVBORG *remains standing by the stove.* HEDDA *goes to the writing table.*]

HEDDA (*raising her voice slightly*) I've some photographs I'd like to show you, if you'd care to see them. Tesman and I visited the Tyrol on our way home.

[*She comes back with an album, places it on the table by the sofa and sits in the upstage corner of the sofa.* EILERT LOEVBORG *comes towards her, stops and looks at her. Then he takes a chair and sits down on her left, with his back towards the rear room.*)

HEDDA (*opens the album*) You see these mountains, Mr. Loevborg? That's the Ortler group. Tesman has written the name underneath. You see: "The Ortler Group near Meran."

LOEVBORG, (*has not taken his eyes from her; says softly, slowly*) Hedda—Gabler!

HEDDA (*gives him a quick glance*) Ssh!

LOEVBORG (*repeats softly*) Hedda Gabler!

HEDDA (*looks at the album*) Yes, that used to be my name. When we first knew each other.

LOEVBORG And from now on—for the rest of my life—I must teach myself never to say: Hedda Gabler.

HEDDA (*still turning the pages*) Yes, you must. You'd better start getting into practice. The sooner the better.

LOEVBORG (*bitterly*) Hedda Gabler married? And to George Tesman?

HEDDA Yes. Well—that's life.

LOEVBORG Oh, Hedda, Hedda! How could you throw yourself away like that?

HEDDA (*looks sharply at him*) Stop it.

LOEVBORG What do you mean?

[TESMAN *comes in and goes towards the sofa.*]

HEDDA (*hears him coming and says casually*) And this, Mr. Loevborg, is the view from the Ampezzo valley. Look at those mountains. [*Glances affectionately up at* TESMAN.] What did you say those curious mountains were called, dear?

TESMAN Let me have a look. Oh, those are the Dolomites.

HEDDA Of course. Those are the Dolomites, Mr. Loevborg.

TESMAN Hedda, I just wanted to ask you, can't we bring some punch in here? A glass for you, anyway. What?

HEDDA Thank you, yes. And a biscuit or two, perhaps.

TESMAN You wouldn't like a cigarette?

HEDDA No.

TESMAN Right. [*He goes into the rear room and over to the right.* BRACK *is sitting there, glancing occasionally at* HEDDA *and* LOEVBORG.]

LOEVBORG (*softly, as before*) Answer me, Hedda. How could you do it?

HEDDA (*apparently absorbed in the album*) If you go on calling me Hedda I won't talk to you any more.

LOEVBORG Mayn't I even when we're alone?

HEDDA No. You can think it. But you mustn't say it.

LOEVBORG Oh, I see. Because you love George Tesman.

HEDDA (*glances at him and smiles*) Love? Don't be funny.

LOEVBORG You don't love him?

HEDDA I don't intend to be unfaithful to him. That's not what I want.

LOEVBORG Hedda—just tell me one thing——

HEDDA Ssh!

[TESMAN *enters from the rear room, carrying a tray.*]

TESMAN Here we are! Here come the goodies! [*Puts the tray down on the table.*]

HEDDA Why didn't you ask the servant to bring it in?

TESMAN (*fills the glasses*) I like waiting on you, Hedda.

HEDDA But you've filled both glasses. Mr. Loevborg doesn't want to drink.

TESMAN Yes, but Mrs. Elvsted'll be here soon.

HEDDA Oh yes, that's true. Mrs. Elvsted——

TESMAN Had you forgotten her? What?

HEDDA We're so absorbed with these photographs. [*Shows him one.*] You remember this little village?

TESMAN Oh, that one down by the Brenner Pass. We spent a night there——

HEDDA Yes, and met all those amusing people.

TESMAN Oh yes, it was there, wasn't it? By Jove, if only we could have had you with us, Eilert! Ah, well. [*Goes back into the other room and sits down with* BRACK.]

LOEVBORG Tell me one thing, Hedda.

HEDDA Yes?

LOEVBORG Didn't you love me either? Not—just a little?

HEDDA Well now, I wonder? No, I think we were just good pals—Really good pals who could tell each other anything. [*Smiles.*] You certainly poured your heart out to me.

LOEVBORG You begged me to.

HEDDA Looking back on it, there was something beautiful and fascinating—and brave—about the way we told each other everything. That secret friendship no one else knew about.

LOEVBORG Yes, Hedda, yes! Do you remember? How I used to come up to your father's house in the afternoon—and the General sat by the window and read his newspapers—with his back towards us——

HEDDA And we sat on the sofa in the corner——

LOEVBORG Always reading the same illustrated magazine——

HEDDA We hadn't any photograph album.

LOEVBORG Yes, Hedda. I regarded you as a kind of confessor. Told you things about myself which no one else knew about—then. Those days and nights of drinking and—Oh, Hedda, what power did you have to make me confess such things?

HEDDA Power? You think I had some power over you?

LOEVBORG Yes—I don't know how else to explain it. And all those—oblique questions you asked me——

HEDDA You knew what they meant.

LOEVBORG But that you could sit there and ask me such questions! So unashamedly——

HEDDA I thought you said they were oblique.

LOEVBORG Yes, but you asked them so unashamedly. That you could question me about—about that kind of thing!

HEDDA You answered willingly enough.

LOEVBORG Yes—that's what I can't understand—looking back on it. But tell me, Hedda—what you felt for me—wasn't that—love? When you asked me those questions and made me confess my sins to you, wasn't it because you wanted to wash me clean?

HEDDA No, not exactly.

LOEVBORG Why did you do it, then?

HEDDA Do you find it so incredible that a young girl, given the chance to do so without anyone knowing, should want to be allowed a glimpse into a forbidden world of whose existence she is supposed to be ignorant?

LOEVBORG So that was it?

HEDDA One reason. One reason—I think.

LOEVBORG You didn't love me, then. You just wanted—knowledge. But if that was so, why did you break it off?

HEDDA That was your fault.

LOEVBORG It was you who put an end to it.

HEDDA Yes, when I realised that our friendship was threatening to develop into something—something else. Shame on you, Eilert Loevborg! How could you abuse the trust of your dearest friend?

LOEVBORG (*clenches his fists*) Oh, why didn't you do it? Why didn't you shoot me dead? As you threatened to?

HEDDA I was afraid. Of the scandal.

LOEVBORG Yes, Hedda. You're a coward at heart.

HEDDA A dreadful coward. [*Changes her tone.*] Luckily for you. Well, now you've found consolation with the Elvsteds.

LOEVBORG I know what Thea's been telling you.

HEDDA I dare say you told her about us.

LOEVBORG Not a word. She's too silly to understand that kind of thing.

HEDDA Silly?

LOEVBORG She's silly about that kind of thing.

HEDDA And I am a coward. [*Leans closer to him, without looking him in the eyes, and says quietly.*] But let me tell you something. Something you don't know.

LOEVBORG (*tensely*) Yes?

HEDDA My failure to shoot you wasn't my worst act of cowardice that evening.

LOEVBORG (*looks at her for a moment, realises her meaning and whispers passionately*) Oh, Hedda! Hedda Gabler! Now I see what was behind those questions. Yes! It wasn't knowledge you wanted! It was life!

HEDDA (*flashes a look at him and says quietly*) Take care! Don't you delude yourself!

[*It has begun to grow dark.* BERTHA, *from outside, opens the door leading into the hall.*]

HEDDA (*closes the album with a snap and cries, smiling*) Ah, at last! Come in, Thea dear!

[MRS. ELVSTED *enters from the hall, in evening dress. The door is closed behind her.*]

HEDDA (*on the sofa, stretches out her arms towards her*) Thea darling, I thought you were never coming!

[MRS. ELVSTED *makes a slight bow to the gentlemen in the rear room as she passes the open doorway, and they to her. Then she goes to the table and holds out her hand to* HEDDA. EILERT LOEVBORG *has risen from his chair. He and* MRS. ELVSTED *nod silently to each other.*]

MRS. ELVSTED Perhaps I ought to go in and say a few words to your husband?

HEDDA Oh, there's no need. They're happy by themselves. They'll be going soon.

MRS. ELVSTED Going?

HEDDA Yes, they're off on a spree this evening.

MRS. ELVSTED (*quickly, to* LOEVBORG) You're not going with them?

LOEVBORG No.

HEDDA Mr. Loevborg is staying here with us.

MRS. ELVSTED (*takes a chair and is about to sit down beside him*) Oh, how nice it is to be here!

HEDDA No, Thea darling, not there. Come over here and sit beside me. I want to be in the middle.

MRS. ELVSTED Yes, just as you wish. [*She goes round the table and sits on the sofa, on* HEDDA's *right.* LOEVBORG *sits down again in his chair.*]

LOEVBORG (*after a short pause, to* HEDDA) Isn't she lovely to look at?

HEDDA (*strokes her hair gently*) Only to look at?

LOEVBORG Yes. We're just good pals. We trust each other implicitly. We can talk to each other quite unashamedly.

HEDDA No need to be oblique?

MRS. ELVSTED (*nestles close to* HEDDA *and says quietly*) Oh, Hedda, I'm so happy. Imagine—he says I've inspired him!

HEDDA (*looks at her with a smile*) Dear Thea! Does he really?

LOEVBORG She has the courage of her convictions, Mrs. Tesman.

MRS. ELVSTED I? Courage?

LOEVBORG Absolute courage. Where friendship is concerned.

HEDDA Yes. Courage. Yes. If only one had that——

LOEVBORG Yes?

HEDDA One might be able to live. In spite of everything. [*Changes her tone suddenly.*] Well, Thea darling, now you're going to drink a nice glass of cold punch.

MRS. ELVSTED No, thank you. I never drink anything like that.

HEDDA Oh. You, Mr. Loevborg?

LOEVBORG Thank you, I don't either.

MRS. ELVSTED No, he doesn't either.

HEDDA (*looks into his eyes*) But if I want you to?

LOEVBORG That doesn't make any difference.

HEDDA (*laughs*) Have I no power over you at all? Poor me!

LOEVBORG Not where this is concerned.

HEDDA Seriously, I think you should. For your own sake.

MRS. ELVSTED Hedda!

LOEVBORG Why?

HEDDA Or perhaps I should say for other people's sake.

LOEVBORG What do you mean?

HEDDA People might think you didn't feel absolutely and unashamedly sure of yourself. In your heart of hearts.

MRS. ELVSTED (*quietly*) Oh, Hedda, no!

LOEVBORG People can think what they like. For the present.

MRS. ELVSTED (*happily*) Yes, that's true.

HEDDA I saw it so clearly in Judge Brack a few minutes ago.

LOEVBORG Oh. What did you see?

HEDDA He smiled so scornfully when he saw you were afraid to go in there and drink with them.

LOEVBORG Afraid! I wanted to stay here and talk to you.

MRS. ELVSTED That was only natural, Hedda.

HEDDA But the Judge wasn't to know that. I saw him wink at Tesman when you showed you didn't dare to join their wretched little party.

LOEVBORG Didn't dare! Are you saying I didn't dare?

HEDDA I'm not saying so. But that was what Judge Brack thought.

LOEVBORG Well, let him.

HEDDA You're not going, then?

LOEVBORG I'm staying here with you and Thea.

MRS. ELVSTED Yes, Hedda, of course he is.

HEDDA (*smiles, and nods approvingly to* LOEVBORG) Firm as a rock! A man of principle! That's how a man should be!

[*Turns to* MRS. ELVSTED *and strokes her cheek.*] Didn't I tell you so this morning when you came here in such a panic——

LOEVBORG (*starts*) Panic?

MRS. ELVSTED (*frightened*) Hedda! But—Hedda!

HEDDA Well, now you can see for yourself. There's no earthly need for you to get scared to death just because—[*Stops.*] Well! Let's all three cheer up and enjoy ourselves.

LOEVBORG Mrs. Tesman, would you mind explaining to me what this is all about?

MRS. ELVSTED Oh, my God, my God, Hedda, what are you saying? What are you doing?

HEDDA Keep calm. That horrid Judge has his eye on you.

LOEVBORG Scared to death, were you? For my sake?

MRS. ELVSTED (*quietly, trembling*) Oh, Hedda! You've made me so unhappy!

LOEVBORG (*looks coldly at her for a moment. His face is distorted*) So that was how much you trusted me.

MRS. ELVSTED Eilert dear, please listen to me——

LOEVBORG (*takes one of the glasses of punch, raises it and says quietly, hoarsely*) Skoal, Thea! [*Empties the glass, puts it down and picks up one of the others.*]

MRS. ELVSTED (*quietly*) Hedda, Hedda! Why did you want this to happen?

HEDDA I—want it? Are you mad?

LOEVBORG Skoal to you too, Mrs. Tesman. Thanks for telling me the truth. Here's to the truth! [*Empties his glass and refills it.*]

HEDDA (*puts her hand on his arm*) Steady. That's enough for now. Don't forget the party.

MRS. ELVSTED No, no, no!

HEDDA Ssh! They're looking at you.

LOEVBORG (*puts down his glass*) Thea, tell me the truth——

MRS. ELVSTED Yes!

LOEVBORG Did you husband know you were following me?

MRS. ELVSTED Oh, Hedda!

LOEVBORG Did you and he have an agree-

ment that you should come here and keep an eye on me? Perhaps he gave you the idea? After all, he's a magistrate. I suppose he needed me back in his office. Or did he miss my companionship at the card table?

MRS. ELVSTED (*quietly, sobbing*) Eilert, Eilert!

LOEVBORG (*seizes a glass and is about to fill it*) Let's drink to him, too.

HEDDA No more now. Remember you're going to read your book to Tesman.

LOEVBORG (*calm again, puts down his glass*) That was silly of me, Thea. To take it like that, I mean. Don't be angry with me, my dear. You'll see—yes, and they'll see, too—that though I fell, I—I have raised myself up again. With your help, Thea.

MRS. ELVSTED (*happily*) Oh, thank God!

[BRACK *has meanwhile glanced at his watch. He and* TESMAN *get up and come into the drawing room.*]

BRACK (*takes his hat and overcoat*) Well, Mrs. Tesman, it's time for us to go.

HEDDA Yes, I suppose it must be.

LOEVBORG (*gets up*) Time for me too, Judge.

MRS. ELVSTED (*quietly, pleadingly*) Eilert, please don't!

HEDDA (*pinches her arm*) They can hear you.

MRS. ELVSTED (*gives a little cry*) Oh!

LOEVBORG (*to* BRACK) You were kind enough to ask me to join you.

BRACK Are you coming?

LOEVBORG If I may.

BRACK Delighted.

LOEVBORG (*puts the paper package in his pocket and says to* TESMAN) I'd like to show you one or two things before I send it off to the printer.

TESMAN I say, that'll be fun. Fancy—! Oh, but Hedda, how'll Mrs. Elvsted get home? What?

HEDDA Oh, we'll manage somehow.

LOEVBORG (*glances over towards the ladies*) Mrs. Elvsted? I shall come back and collect her, naturally. [*Goes closer.*] About ten o'clock, Mrs. Tesman? Will that suit you?

HEDDA Yes. That'll suit me admirably.

TESMAN Good, that's settled. But you mustn't expect me back so early, Hedda.

HEDDA Stay as long as you c—as long as you like, dear.

MRS. ELVSTED (*trying to hide her anxiety*) Well then, Mr. Loevborg, I'll wait here till you come.

LOEVBORG (*his hat in his hand*) Pray do, Mrs. Elvsted.

BRACK Well, gentlemen, now the party begins. I trust that, in the words of a certain fair lady, we shall enjoy good sport.

HEDDA What a pity the fair lady can't be there, invisible.

BRACK Why invisible?

HEDDA So as to be able to hear some of your uncensored witticisms, your honor.

BRACK (*laughs*) Oh, I shouldn't advise the fair lady to do that.

TESMAN (*laughs too*) I say, Hedda, that's good. By Jove! Fancy that!

BRACK Well, good night, ladies, good night!

LOEVBORG (*bows farewell*) About ten o'clock, then.

[BRACK, LOEVBORG, *and* TESMAN *go out through the hall. As they do so,* BERTHA *enters from the rear room with a lighted lamp. She puts it on the drawing-room table, then goes out the way she came.*]

MRS. ELVSTED (*has got up and is walking uneasily to and fro*) Oh Hedda, Hedda! How is all this going to end?

HEDDA At ten o'clock, then. He'll be here. I can see him. With a crown of vine-leaves in his hair. Burning and unashamed!

MRS. ELVSTED Oh, I do hope so!

HEDDA Can't you see? Then he'll be himself again! He'll be a free man for the rest of his days!

MRS. ELVSTED Please God you're right.

HEDDA That's how he'll come! [*Gets up and goes closer.*] You can doubt him as

much as you like. I believe in him! Now we'll see which of us——

MRS. ELVSTED You're after something, Hedda.

HEDDA Yes, I am. For once in my life I want to have the power to shape a man's destiny.

MRS. ELVSTED Haven't you that power already?

HEDDA No, I haven't. I've never had it.

MRS. ELVSTED What about your husband?

HEDDA Him! Oh, if you could only understand how poor I am. And you're allowed to be so rich, so rich! [*Clasps her passionately.*] I think I'll burn your hair off after all!

MRS. ELVSTED Let me go! Let me go! You frighten me, Hedda!

BERTHA (*in the open doorway*) I've laid tea in the dining room, madam.

HEDDA Good, we're coming.

MRS. ELVSTED No, no, no! I'd rather go home alone! Now—at once!

HEDDA Rubbish! First you're going to have some tea, you little idiot. And then —at ten o'clock—Eilert Loevborg will come. With a crown of vine-leaves in his hair!

[*She drags* MRS. ELVSTED *almost forcibly towards the open doorway.*]

Act Three

The same. The curtains are drawn across the open doorway, and also across the french windows. The lamp, half turned down, with a shade over it, is burning on the table. In the stove, the door of which is open, a fire has been burning, but it is now almost out.

[MRS. ELVSTED, *wrapped in a large shawl and with her feet resting on a footstool, is sitting near the stove, huddled in the armchair.* HEDDA *is lying asleep on the sofa, fully dressed, with a blanket over her.*]

MRS. ELVSTED (*after a pause, suddenly sits up in her chair and listens tensely. Then she sinks wearily back again and sighs*) Not back yet! Oh, God! Oh, God! Not back yet!

[BERTHA *tiptoes cautiously in from the hall. She has a letter in her hand.*]

MRS. ELVSTED (*turns and whispers*) What is it? Has someone come?

BERTHA (*quietly*) Yes, a servant's just called with this letter.

MRS. ELVSTED (*quickly, holding out her hand*) A letter! Give it to me!

BERTHA But it's for the Doctor, madam.

MRS. ELVSTED Oh. I see.

BERTHA Miss Tesman's maid brought it. I'll leave it here on the table.

MRS. ELVSTED Yes, do.

BERTHA (*puts down the letter*) I'd better put the lamp out. It's starting to smoke.

MRS. ELVSTED Yes, put it out. It'll soon be daylight.

BERTHA (*puts out the lamp*) It's daylight already, madam.

MRS. ELVSTED Yes. Broad day. And not home yet.

BERTHA Oh dear, I was afraid this would happen.

MRS. ELVSTED Were you?

BERTHA Yes. When I heard that a certain gentleman had returned to town, and saw him go off with them. I've heard all about him.

MRS. ELVSTED Don't talk so loud. You'll wake your mistress.

BERTHA (*looks at the sofa and sighs*) Yes. Let her go on sleeping, poor dear. Shall I put some more wood on the fire?

MRS. ELVSTED Thank you, don't bother on my account.

BERTHA Very good. [*Goes quietly out through the hall.*]

HEDDA (*wakes as the door closes and looks up*) What's that?

MRS. ELVSTED It was only the maid.

HEDDA (*looks round*) What am I doing here? Oh, now I remember. [*Sits up on the sofa, stretches herself and rubs her eyes.*] What time is it, Thea?

MRS. ELVSTED It's gone seven.

HEDDA When did Tesman get back?

MRS. ELVSTED He's not back yet.

HEDDA Not home yet?

MRS. ELVSTED (*gets up*) No one's come.

HEDDA And we sat up waiting for them till four o'clock.

MRS. ELVSTED How I waited for him!

HEDDA (*yawns and says with her hand in front of her mouth*) Oh, dear. We might have saved ourselves the trouble.

MRS. ELVSTED Did you manage to sleep?

HEDDA Oh, yes. Quite well, I think. Didn't you get any?

MRS. ELVSTED Not a wink, I couldn't, Hedda. I just couldn't.

HEDDA (*gets up and comes over to her*) Now, now, now. There's nothing to worry about. I know what's happened.

MRS. ELVSTED What? Please tell me.

HEDDA Well, obviously the party went on very late——

MRS. ELVSTED Oh dear, I suppose it must have. But——

HEDDA And Tesman didn't want to come home and wake us all up in the middle of the night. [*Laughs.*] Probably wasn't too keen to show his face either, after a spree like that.

MRS. ELVSTED But where could he have gone?

HEDDA I should think he's probably slept at his aunts'. They keep his old room for him.

MRS. ELVSTED No, he can't be with them. A letter came for him just now from Miss Tesman. It's over there.

HEDDA Oh? [*Looks at the envelope.*] Yes, it's Auntie Juju's handwriting. Well, he must still be at Judge Brack's then. And Eilert Loevborg is sitting there, reading to him. With a crown of vine-leaves in his hair.

MRS. ELVSTED Hedda, you're only saying that. You don't believe it.

HEDDA Thea, you really are a little fool.

MRS. ELVSTED Perhaps I am.

HEDDA You look tired to death.

MRS. ELVSTED Yes. I am tired to death.

HEDDA Go to my room and lie down for a little. Do as I say, now; don't argue.

MRS. ELVSTED No, no. I couldn't possibly sleep.

HEDDA   Of course you can.

MRS. ELVSTED   But your husband'll be home soon. And I must know at once——

HEDDA   I'll tell you when he comes.

MRS. ELVSTED   Promise me, Hedda?

HEDDA   Yes, don't worry. Go and get some sleep.

MRS. ELVSTED   Thank you. All right, I'll try.

[*She goes out through the rear room.* HEDDA *goes to the french windows and draws the curtains. Broad daylight floods into the room. She goes to the writing table, takes a small hand mirror from it and arranges her hair. Then she goes to the door leading into the hall and presses the bell. After a few moments,* BERTHA *enters.*]

BERTHA   Did you want anything, madam?

HEDDA   Yes, put some more wood on the fire. I'm freezing.

BERTHA   Bless you, I'll soon have this room warmed up. [*She rakes the embers together and puts a fresh piece of wood on them. Suddenly she stops and listens.*] There's someone at the front door, madam.

HEDDA   Well, go and open it. I'll see to the fire.

BERTHA   It'll burn up in a moment.

[*She goes out through the hall.* HEDDA *kneels on the footstool and puts more wood in the stove. After a few seconds,* GEORGE TESMAN *enters from the hall. He looks tired, and rather worried. He tiptoes towards the open doorway and is about to slip through the curtains.*]

HEDDA   (*at the stove, without looking up*) Good morning.

TESMAN   (*turns*) Hedda! [*Comes nearer.*] Good heavens, are you up already? What?

HEDDA   Yes, I got up very early this morning.

TESMAN   I was sure you'd still be sleeping. Fancy that!

HEDDA   Don't talk so loud. Mrs. Elvsted's asleep in my room.

TESMAN   Mrs. Elvsted? Has she stayed the night here?

HEDDA   Yes. No one came to escort her home.

TESMAN   Oh. No, I suppose not.

HEDDA   (*closes the door of the stove and gets up*) Well. Was it fun?

TESMAN   Have you been anxious about me? What?

HEDDA   Not in the least. I asked if you'd had fun.

TESMAN   Oh yes, rather! Well, I thought, for once in a while—The first part was the best; when Eilert read his book to me. We arrived over an hour too early—what about that, eh? By Jove! Brack had a lot of things to see to, so Eilert read to me.

HEDDA   (*sits at the right-hand side of the table*) Well? Tell me about it.

TESMAN   (*sits on a footstool by the stove*) Honestly, Hedda, you've no idea what a book that's going to be. It's really one of the most remarkable things that's ever been written. By Jove!

HEDDA   Oh, never mind about the book——

TESMAN   I'm going to make a confession to you, Hedda. When he'd finished reading a sort of beastly feeling came over me.

HEDDA   Beastly feeling?

TESMAN   I found myself envying Eilert for being able to write like that. Imagine that, Hedda!

HEDDA   Yes. I can imagine.

TESMAN   What a tragedy that with all those gifts he should be so incorrigible.

HEDDA   You mean he's less afraid of life than most men?

TESMAN   Good heavens, no. He just doesn't know the meaning of the word moderation.

HEDDA   What happened afterwards?

TESMAN   Well, looking back on it I suppose you might almost call it an orgy, Hedda.

HEDDA   Had he vine-leaves in his hair?

TESMAN   Vine-leaves? No, I didn't see any of them. He made a long, rambling oration in honor of the woman who'd inspired him to write this book. Yes, those were the words he used.

HEDDA Did he name her?

TESMAN No. But I suppose it must be Mrs. Elvsted. You wait and see!

HEDDA Where did you leave him?

TESMAN On the way home. We left in a bunch—the last of us, that is—and Brack came with us to get a little fresh air. Well, then, you see, we agreed we ought to see Eilert home. He'd had a drop too much.

HEDDA You don't say?

TESMAN But now comes the funny part, Hedda. Or I should really say the tragic part. Oh, I'm almost ashamed to tell you. For Eilert's sake, I mean——

HEDDA Why, what happened?

TESMAN Well, you see, as we were walking towards town I happened to drop behind for a minute. Only for a minute—er—you understand——

HEDDA Yes, yes—?

TESMAN Well then, when I ran on to catch them up, what do you think I found by the roadside. What?

HEDDA How on earth should I know?

TESMAN You mustn't tell anyone, Hedda. What? Promise me that—for Eilert's sake. [*Takes a package wrapped in paper from his coat pocket.*] Just fancy! I found this.

HEDDA Isn't this the one he brought here yesterday?

TESMAN Yes! The whole of that precious, irreplaceable manuscript! And he went and lost it! Didn't even notice! What about that? By Jove! Tragic.

HEDDA But why didn't you give it back to him?

TESMAN I didn't dare to, in the state he was in.

HEDDA Didn't you tell any of the others?

TESMAN Good heavens, no. I didn't want to do that. For Eilert's sake, you understand.

HEDDA Then no one else knows you have his manuscript?

TESMAN No. And no one must be allowed to know.

HEDDA Didn't it come up in the conversation later?

TESMAN I didn't get a chance to talk to him any more. As soon as we got into the outskirts of town, he and one or two of the others gave us the slip. Disappeared, by Jove!

HEDDA Oh? I suppose they took him home.

TESMAN Yes, I imagine that was the idea. Brack left us, too.

HEDDA And what have you been up to since then?

TESMAN Well, I and one or two of the others—awfully jolly chaps, they were—went back to where one of them lived, and had a cup of morning coffee. Morning-after coffee—what? Ah, well. I'll just lie down for a bit and give Eilert time to sleep it off, poor chap, then I'll run over and give this back to him.

HEDDA (*holds out her hand for the package*) No, don't do that. Not just yet. Let me read it first.

TESMAN Oh no, really, Hedda dear, honestly, I daren't do that.

HEDDA Daren't?

TESMAN No—imagine how desperate he'll be when he wakes up and finds his manuscript's missing. He hasn't any copy, you see. He told me so himself.

HEDDA Can't a thing like that be rewritten?

TESMAN Oh no, not possibly, I shouldn't think. I mean, the inspiration, you know——

HEDDA Oh, yes. I'd forgotten that. [*Casually.*] By the way, there's a letter for you.

TESMAN Is there? Fancy that!

HEDDA (*holds it out to him*) It came early this morning.

TESMAN I say, it's from Auntie Juju! What on earth can it be? [*Puts the package on the other footstool, opens the letter, reads it and jumps up.*] Oh, Hedda! She says poor Auntie Rena's dying.

HEDDA Well, we've been expecting that.

TESMAN She says if I want to see her I must go quickly. I'll run over at once.

HEDDA (*hides a smile*) Run?

TESMAN Hedda dear, I suppose you

wouldn't like to come with me? What about that, eh?

HEDDA (*gets up and says wearily and with repulsion*) No, no, don't ask me to do anything like that. I can't bear illness or death. I loathe anything ugly.

TESMAN Yes, yes. Of course. [*In a dither.*] My hat? My overcoat? Oh yes, in the hall. I do hope I won't get there too late, Hedda? What?

HEDDA You'll be all right if you run.

[BERTHA *enters from the hall.*]

BERTHA Judge Brack's outside and wants to know if he can come in.

TESMAN At this hour? No, I can't possibly receive him now.

HEDDA I can. [*To* BERTHA.] Ask his honor to come in. [BERTHA *goes.*]

HEDDA (*whispers quickly*) The manuscript, Tesman. [*She snatches it from the footstool.*]

TESMAN Yes, give it to me.

HEDDA No, I'll look after it for now.

[*She goes over to the writing table and puts it in the bookcase.* TESMAN *stands dithering, unable to get his gloves on.* JUDGE BRACK *enters from the hall.*]

HEDDA (*nods to him*) Well, you're an early bird.

BRACK Yes, aren't I? [*To* TESMAN.] Are you up and about, too?

TESMAN Yes, I've got to go and see my aunts. Poor Auntie Rena's dying.

BRACK Oh dear, is she? Then you mustn't let me detain you. At so tragic a——

TESMAN Yes, I really must run. Good-bye! Good-bye! [*Runs out through the hall.*]

HEDDA (*goes nearer*) You seem to have had excellent sport last night—Judge.

BRACK Indeed yes, Mrs. Hedda. I haven't even had time to take my clothes off.

HEDDA You haven't either?

BRACK As you see. What's Tesman told you about last night's escapades?

HEDDA Oh, only some boring story about having gone and drunk coffee somewhere.

BRACK Yes, I've heard about that coffee party. Eilert Loevborg wasn't with them, I gather?

HEDDA No, they took him home first.

BRACK Did Tesman go with him?

HEDDA No, one or two of the others, he said.

BRACK (*smiles*) George Tesman is a credulous man, Mrs. Hedda.

HEDDA God knows. But—has something happened?

BRACK Well, yes, I'm afraid it has.

HEDDA I see. Sit down and tell me.

[*She sits on the left of the table,* BRACK *at the long side of it, near her.*]

HEDDA Well?

BRACK I had a special reason for keeping track of my guests last night. Or perhaps I should say some of my guests.

HEDDA Including Eilert Loevberg?

BRACK I must confess—yes.

HEDDA You're beginning to make me curious.

BRACK Do you know where he and some of my other guests spent the latter half of last night, Mrs. Hedda?

HEDDA Tell me. If it won't shock me.

BRACK Oh, I don't think it'll shock you. They found themselves participating in an exceedingly animated *soirée*.

HEDDA Of a sporting character?

BRACK Of a highly sporting character.

HEDDA Tell me more.

BRACK Loevborg had received an invitation in advance—as had the others. I knew all about that. But he had refused. As you know, he's become a new man.

HEDDA Up at the Elvsteds', yes. But he went?

BRACK Well, you see, Mrs. Hedda, last night at my house, unhappily, the spirit moved him.

HEDDA Yes, I hear he became inspired.

BRACK Somewhat violently inspired. And as a result, I suppose, his thoughts strayed. We men, alas, don't always stick to our principles as firmly as we should.

HEDDA I'm sure you're an exception, Judge Brack. But go on about Loevborg.

BRACK Well, to cut a long story short, he

ended up in the establishment of a certain Mademoiselle Danielle.

HEDDA   Mademoiselle Danielle?

BRACK   She was holding the *soirée*. For a selected circle of friends and admirers.

HEDDA   Has she got red hair?

BRACK   She has.

HEDDA   A singer of some kind?

BRACK   Yes—among other accomplishments. She's also a celebrated huntress—of men, Mrs. Hedda. I'm sure you've heard about her. Eilert Loevborg used to be one of her most ardent patrons. In his salad days.

HEDDA   And how did all this end?

BRACK   Not entirely amicably, from all accounts. Mademoiselle Danielle began by receiving him with the utmost tenderness and ended by resorting to her fists.

HEDDA   Against Loevborg?

BRACK   Yes. He accused her, or her friends, of having robbed him. He claimed his pocketbook had been stolen. Among other things. In short, he seems to have made a bloodthirsty scene.

HEDDA   And what did this lead to?

BRACK   It led to a general free-for-all, in which both sexes participated. Fortunately, in the end the police arrived.

HEDDA   The police too?

BRACK   Yes. I'm afraid it may turn out to be rather an expensive joke for Master Eilert. Crazy fool!

HEDDA   Oh?

BRACK   Apparently he put up a very violent resistance. Hit one of the constables on the ear and tore his uniform. He had to accompany them to the police station.

HEDDA   Where did you learn all this?

BRACK   From the police.

HEDDA   (*to herself*)   So that's what happened. He didn't have a crown of vine-leaves in his hair.

BRACK   Vine-leaves, Mrs. Hedda?

HEDDA   (*in her normal voice again*)   But, tell me, Judge, why do you take such a close interest in Eilert Loevborg?

BRACK   For one thing it'll hardly be a matter of complete indifference to me if it's revealed in court that he came there straight from my house.

HEDDA   Will it come to court?

BRACK   Of course. Well, I don't regard that as particularly serious. Still, I thought it my duty, as a friend of the family, to give you and your husband a ful account of his nocturnal adventures.

HEDDA   Why?

BRACK   Because I've a shrewd suspicion that he's hoping to use you as a kind of screen.

HEDDA   What makes you think that?

BRACK   Oh, for heaven's sake, Mrs. Hedda, we're not blind. You wait and see. This Mrs. Elvsted won't be going back to her husband just yet.

HEDDA   Well, if there were anything between those two there are plenty of other places where they could meet.

BRACK   Not in anyone's home. From now on every respectable house will once again be closed to Eilert Loevborg.

HEDDA   And mine should be too, you mean?

BRACK   Yes. I confess I should find it more than irksome if this gentleman were to be granted unrestricted access to this house. If he were superfluously to intrude into——

HEDDA   The triangle?

BRACK   Precisely. For me it would be like losing a home.

HEDDA   (*looks at him and smiles*)   I see. You want to be the cock of the walk.

BRACK   (*nods slowly and lowers his voice*) Yes, that is my aim. And I shall fight for it with—every weapon at my disposal.

HEDDA   (*as her smile fades*)   You're a dangerous man, aren't you? When you really want something.

BRACK   You think so?

HEDDA   Yes, I'm beginning to think so. I'm deeply thankful you haven't any kind of hold over me.

BRACK   (*laughs equivocally*)   Well, well, Mrs. Hedda—perhaps you're right. If I had, who knows what I might not think up?

HEDDA Come, Judge Brack. That sounds almost like a threat.

BRACK (*gets up*) Heaven forbid! In the creation of a triangle—and its continuance—the question of compulsion should never arise.

HEDDA Exactly what I was thinking.

BRACK Well, I've said what I came to say. I must be getting back. Good-bye, Mrs. Hedda. [*Goes towards the french windows.*]

HEDDA (*gets up*) Are you going out through the garden?

BRACK Yes, it's shorter.

HEDDA Yes. And it's the back door, isn't it?

BRACK I've nothing against back doors. They can be quite intriguing—sometimes.

HEDDA When people fire pistols out of them, for example?

BRACK (*in the doorway, laughs*) Oh, people don't shoot tame cocks.

HEDDA (*laughs too*) I suppose not. When they've only got one.

[*They nod good-bye, laughing. He goes. She closes the french windows behind him, and stands for a moment, looking out pensively. Then she walks across the room and glances through the curtains in the open doorway. Goes to the writing table, takes* LOEVBORG'S *package from the bookcase and is about to leaf through the pages when* BERTHA *is heard remonstrating loudly in the hall.* HEDDA *turns and listens. She hastily puts the package back in the drawer, locks it and puts the key on the inkstand.* EILERT LOEVBORG, *with his overcoat on and his hat in his hand, throws the door open. He looks somewhat confused and excited.*]

LOEVBORG (*shouts as he enters*) I must come in, I tell you! Let me pass! [*He closes the door, turns, sees* HEDDA, *controls himself immediately and bows.*]

HEDDA (*at the writing table*) Well, Mr. Loevborg, this is rather a late hour to be collecting Thea.

LOEVBORG And an early hour to call on you. Please forgive me.

HEDDA How do you know she's still here?

LOEVBORG They told me at her lodgings that she has been out all night.

HEDDA (*goes to the table*) Did you notice anything about their behavior when they told you?

LOEVBORG (*looks at her, puzzled*) Notice anything?

HEDDA Did they sound as if they thought it—strange?

LOEVBORG (*suddenly understands*) Oh, I see what you mean. I'm dragging her down with me. No, as a matter of fact I didn't notice anything. I suppose Tesman isn't up yet?

HEDDA No, I don't think so.

LOEVBORG When did he get home?

HEDDA Very late.

LOEVBORG Did he tell you anything?

HEDDA Yes. I gather you had a merry party at Judge Brack's last night.

LOEVBORG He didn't tell you anything else?

HEDDA I don't think so. I was so terribly sleepy——

[MRS. ELVSTED *comes through the curtains in the open doorway.*]

MRS. ELVSTED (*runs towards him*) Oh, Eilert! At last!

LOEVBORG Yes—at last. And too late.

MRS. ELVSTED What is too late?

LOEVBORG Everything—now. I'm finished, Thea.

MRS. ELVSTED Oh, no, no! Don't say that!

LOEVBORG You'll say it yourself, when you've heard what I——

MRS. ELVSTED I don't want to hear anything!

HEDDA Perhaps you'd rather speak to her alone? I'd better go.

LOEVBORG No, stay.

MRS. ELVSTED But I don't want to hear anything, I tell you!

LOEVBORG It's not about last night.

MRS. ELVSTED Then what—?

LOEVBORG I want to tell you that from now on we must stop seeing each other.

MRS. ELVSTED   Stop seeing each other!

HEDDA (*involuntarily*)   I knew it!

LOEVBORG   I have no further use for you, Thea.

MRS. ELVSTED   You can stand there and say that! No further use for me! Surely I can go on helping you? We'll go on working together, won't we?

LOEVBORG   I don't intend to do any more work from now on.

MRS. ELVSTED (*desperately*)   Then what use have I for my life?

LOEVBORG   You must try to live as if you had never known me.

MRS. ELVSTED   But I can't!

LOEVBORG   Try to, Thea. Go back home——

MRS. ELVSTED   Never! I want to be wherever you are! I won't let myself be driven away like this! I want to stay here—and be with you when the book comes out.

HEDDA (*whispers*)   Ah, yes! The book!

LOEVBORG (*looks at her*)   Our book; Thea's and mine. It belongs to both of us.

MRS. ELVSTED   Oh yes! I feel that too! And I've a right to be with you when it comes into the world. I want to see people respect and honor you again. And the joy! The joy! I want to share it with you!

LOEVBORG   Thea—our book will never come into the world.

HEDDA   Ah!

MRS. ELVSTED   Not——?

LOEVBORG   It cannot. Ever.

MRS. ELVSTED   Eilert—what have you done with the manuscript? Where is it?

LOEVBORG   Oh Thea, please don't ask me that!

MRS. ELVSTED   Yes, yes—I must know. I've a right to know. Now!

LOEVBORG   The manuscript. I've torn it up.

MRS. ELVSTED (*screams*)   No, no!

HEDDA (*involuntarily*)   But that's not——!

LOEVBORG (*looks at her*)   Not true, you think?

HEDDA (*controls herself*)   Why—yes, of course it is, if you say so. It just sounded so incredible——

LOEVBORG   It's true, nevertheless.

MRS. ELVSTED   Oh, my God, my God, Hedda—he's destroyed his own book!

LOEVBORG   I have destroyed my life. Why not my life's work, too?

MRS. ELVSTED   And you—did this last night?

LOEVBORG   Yes, Thea. I tore it into a thousand pieces. And scattered them out across the fjord. It's good, clean, salt water. Let it carry them away; let them drift in the current and the wind. And in a little while, they will sink. Deeper and deeper. As I shall, Thea.

MRS. ELVSTED   Do you know, Eilert—this book—all my life I shall feel as though you'd killed a little child?

LOEVBORG   You're right. It is like killing a child.

MRS. ELVSTED   But how could you? It was my child, too!

HEDDA (*almost inaudibly*)   Oh—the child—!

MRS. ELVSTED (*breathes heavily*)   It's all over, then. Well—I'll go now, Hedda.

HEDDA   You're not leaving town?

MRS. ELVSTED   I don't know what I'm going to do. I can't see anything except—darkness. [*She goes out through the hall.*]

HEDDA (*waits a moment*)   Aren't you going to escort her home, Mr. Loevborg?

LOEVBORG   I? Through the streets? Do you want me to let people see her with me?

HEDDA   Of course I don't know what else may have happened last night. But is it so utterly beyond redress?

LOEVBORG   It isn't just last night. It'll go on happening. I know it. But the curse of it is, I don't want to live that kind of life. I don't want to start all that again. She's broken my courage. I can't spit in the eyes of the world any longer.

HEDDA (*as though to herself*)   That pretty little fool's been trying to shape a man's destiny. [*Looks at him.*] But how could you be so heartless towards her?

LOEVBORG   Don't call me heartless!

HEDDA   To go and destroy the one thing that's made her life worth living? You don't call that heartless?

LOEVBORG Do you want to know the truth, Hedda?

HEDDA The truth?

LOEVBORG Promise me first—give me your word—that you'll never let Thea know about this.

HEDDA I give you my word.

LOEVBORG Good. Well; what I told her just now was a lie.

HEDDA About the manuscript?

LOEVBORG Yes. I didn't tear it up. Or throw it in the fjord.

HEDDA You didn't? But where is it, then?

LOEVBORG I destroyed it, all the same. I destroyed it, Hedda!

HEDDA I don't understand.

LOEVBORG Thea said that what I had done was like killing a child.

HEDDA Yes. That's what she said.

LOEVBORG But to kill a child isn't the worst thing a father can do to it.

HEDDA What could be worse than that?

LOEVBORG Hedda—suppose a man came home one morning, after a night of debauchery, and said to the mother of his child: "Look here. I've been wandering round all night. I've been to—such-and-such a place and such-and-such a place. And I had our child with me. I took him to—these places. And I've lost him. Just —lost him. God knows where he is or whose hands he's fallen into."

HEDDA I see. But when all's said and done, this was only a book——

LOEVBORG Thea's heart and soul were in that book. It was her whole life.

HEDDA Yes. I understand.

LOEVBORG Well, then you must also understand that she and I cannot possibly ever see each other again.

HEDDA Where will you go?

LOEVBORG Nowhere. I just want to put an end to it all. As soon as possible.

HEDDA (*takes a step towards him*) Eilert Loevborg, listen to me. Do it—beautifully!

LOEVBORG Beautifully? [*Smiles.*] With a crown of vine-leaves in my hair? The way you used to dream of me—in the old days?

HEDDA No. I don't believe in that crown any longer. But—do it beautifully, all the same. Just this once. Good-bye. You must go now. And don't come back.

LOEVBORG Adieu, madam. Give my love to George Tesman. [*Turns to go.*]

HEDDA Wait. I want to give you a souvenir to take with you.

[*She goes over to the writing table, opens the drawer and the pistol-case, and comes back to* LOEVBORG *with one of the pistols.*]

LOEVBORG (*looks at her*) This? Is this the souvenir?

HEDDA (*nods slowly*) You recognise it? You looked down its barrel once.

LOEVBORG You should have used it then.

HEDDA Here! Use it now!

LOEVBORG (*puts the pistol in his breast pocket*) Thank you.

HEDDA Do it beautifully, Eilert Loevborg. Only promise me that!

LOEVBORG Good-bye, Hedda Gabler.

[*He goes out through the hall.* HEDDA *stands by the door for a moment, listening. Then she goes over to the writing table, takes out the package containing the manuscript, glances inside it, pulls some of the pages half out and looks at them. Then she takes it to the armchair by the stove and sits down with the package in her lap. After a moment, she opens the door of the stove; then she opens the packet.*]

HEDDA (*throws one of the pages into the stove and whispers to herself*) I'm burning your child, Thea! You with your beautiful wavy hair! [*She throws a few more pages into the stove.*] The child Eilert Loevborg gave you. [*Throws the rest of the manuscript in.*] I'm burning it! I'm burning your child!

Act Four

The same. It is evening. The drawing room is in darkness. The small room is illuminated by the hanging lamp over the table. The curtains are drawn across the french windows. [HEDDA, *dressed in black, is walking up and down in the darkened room. Then she goes into the small room and crosses to the left. A few chords are heard from the piano. She comes back into the drawing room.* BERTHA *comes through the small room from the right with a lighted lamp, which she places on the table in front of the corner sofa in the drawing room. Her eyes are red with crying, and she has black ribbons on her cap. She goes quietly out, right.* HEDDA *goes over to the french windows, draws the curtains slightly to one side and looks out into the darkness. A few moments later,* MISS TESMAN *enters from the hall. She is dressed in mourning, with a black hat and veil.* HEDDA *goes to meet her and holds out her hand.*]

MISS TESMAN   Well, Hedda, here I am in the weeds of sorrow. My poor sister has ended her struggles at last.

HEDDA   I've already heard. Tesman sent me a card.

MISS TESMAN   Yes, he promised me he would. But I thought, no, I must go and break the news of death to Hedda myself—here, in the house of life.

HEDDA   It's very kind of you.

MISS TESMAN   Ah, Rena shouldn't have chosen a time like this to pass away. This is no moment for Hedda's house to be a place of mourning.

HEDDA   (*changing the subject*)   She died peacefully, Miss Tesman?

MISS TESMAN   Oh, it was quite beautiful! The end came so calmly. And she was so happy at being able to see George once again. And say good-bye to him. Hasn't he come home yet?

HEDDA   No. He wrote that I mustn't expect him too soon. But please sit down.

MISS TESMAN   No, thank you, Hedda dear—bless you. I'd like to. But I've so little time. I must dress her and lay her out as well as I can. She shall go to her grave looking really beautiful.

HEDDA   Can't I help with anything?

MISS TESMAN   Why, you mustn't think of such a thing! Hedda Tesman mustn't let her hands be soiled by contact with death. Or her thoughts. Not at this time.

HEDDA   One can't always control one's thoughts.

MISS TESMAN   (*continues*)   Ah, well, that's life. Now we must start to sew poor Rena's shroud. There'll be sewing to be done in this house too before long, I shouldn't wonder. But not for a shroud, praise God.

[GEORGE TESMAN *enters from the hall.*]

HEDDA   You've come at last! Thank heavens!

TESMAN   Are you here, Auntie Juju? With Hedda? Fancy that!

MISS TESMAN   I was just on the point of leaving, dear boy. Well, have you done everything you promised me?

TESMAN   No, I'm afraid I forgot half of it. I'll have to run over again tomorrow. My head's in a complete whirl today. I can't collect my thoughts.

MISS TESMAN   But George dear, you mustn't take it like this.

TESMAN   Oh? Well—er—how should I?

MISS TESMAN   You must be happy in your grief. Happy for what's happened. As I am.

TESMAN   Oh, yes, yes. You're thinking of Aunt Rena.

HEDDA   It'll be lonely for you now, Miss Tesman.

MISS TESMAN   For the first few days, yes. But it won't last long, I hope. Poor dear Rena's little room isn't going to stay empty.

TESMAN   Oh? Whom are you going to move in there? What?

MISS TESMAN   Oh, there's always some poor invalid who needs care and attention.

HEDDA   Do you really want another cross like that to bear?

MISS TESMAN   Cross! God forgive you, child. It's been no cross for me.

HEDDA   But now—if a complete stranger comes to live with you—?

MISS TESMAN   Oh, one soon makes friends with invalids. And I need so much to have someone to live for. Like you, my dear. Well, I expect there'll soon be work in this house too for an old aunt, praise God!

HEDDA   Oh—please!

TESMAN   By Jove, yes! What a splendid time the three of us could have together if——

HEDDA   If?

TESMAN   (*uneasily*)   Oh, never mind. It'll all work out. Let's hope so—what?

MISS TESMAN   Yes, yes. Well, I'm sure you two would like to be alone. [*Smiles.*] Perhaps Hedda may have something to tell you, George. Good-bye. I must go home to Rena. [*Turns to the door.*] Dear God, how strange! Now Rena is with me and with poor dear Joachim.

TESMAN   Fancy that. Yes, Auntie Juju! What?

[MISS TESMAN *goes out through the hall.*]

HEDDA   (*follows* TESMAN *coldly and searchingly with her eyes*)   I really believe this death distresses you more than it does her.

TESMAN   Oh, it isn't just Auntie Rena. It's Eilert I'm so worried about.

HEDDA   (*quickly*)   Is there any news of him?

TESMAN   I ran over to see him this afternoon. I wanted to tell him his manuscript was in safe hands.

HEDDA   Oh? You didn't find him?

TESMAN   No. He wasn't at home. But later I met Mrs. Elvsted and she told me he'd been here early this morning.

HEDDA   Yes, just after you'd left.

TESMAN   It seems he said he'd torn the manuscript up. What?

HEDDA   Yes, he claimed to have done so.

TESMAN   You told him we had it, of course?

HEDDA   No. [*Quickly.*] Did you tell Mrs. Elvsted?

TESMAN   No, I didn't like to. But you ought to have told him. Think if he should go home and do something desperate! Give me the manuscript, Hedda. I'll run over to him with it right away. Where did you put it?

HEDDA   (*cold and motionless, leaning against the armchair*)   I haven't got it any longer.

TESMAN   Haven't got it? What on earth do you mean?

HEDDA   I've burned it.

TESMAN   (*starts, terrified*)   Burned it! Burned Eilert's manuscript!

HEDDA   Don't shout. The servant will hear you.

TESMAN   Burned it! But in heaven's name—! Oh, no, no, no! This is impossible!

HEDDA   Well, it's true.

TESMAN   But Hedda, do you realise what you've done? That's appropriating lost property! It's against the law! By Jove! You ask Judge Brack and see if I'm not right.

HEDDA   You'd be well advised not to talk about it to Judge Brack or anyone else.

TESMAN   But how could you go and do such a dreadful thing? What on earth put the idea into your head? What came over you? Answer me! What?

HEDDA   (*represses an almost imperceptible smile*)   I did it for your sake, George.

TESMAN   For my sake?

HEDDA   When you came home this morning and described how he'd read his book to you——

TESMAN   Yes, yes?

HEDDA   You admitted you were jealous of him.

TESMAN   But, good heavens, I didn't mean it literally!

HEDDA   No matter. I couldn't bear the thought that anyone else should push you into the background.

TESMAN   (*torn between doubt and joy*)   Hedda—is this true? But—but—but I never realized you loved me like that! Fancy——

HEDDA   Well, I suppose you'd better know. I'm going to have—[*Breaks off and says violently.*] No, no—you'd better ask your Auntie Juju. She'll tell you.

TESMAN Hedda! I think I understand what you mean. [*Clasps his hands.*] Good heavens, can it really be true! What?

HEDDA Don't shout. The servant will hear you.

TESMAN (*laughing with joy*) The servant! I say, that's good! The servant! Why, that's Bertha! I'll run out and tell her at once!

HEDDA (*clenches her hands in despair*) Oh, it's destroying me, all this—it's destroying me!

TESMAN I say, Hedda, what's up? What?

HEDDA (*cold, controlled*) Oh, it's all so —absurd—George.

TESMAN Absurd? That I'm so happy? But surely—? Ah, well—perhaps I won't say anything to Bertha.

HEDDA No, do. She might as well know too.

TESMAN No, no, I won't tell her yet. But Auntie Juju—I must let her know! And you—you called me George! For the first time! Fancy that! Oh, it'll make Auntie Juju so happy, all this! So very happy!

HEDDA Will she be happy when she hears I've burned Eilert Loevborg's manuscript —for your sake?

TESMAN No, I'd forgotten about that. Of course no one must be allowed to know about the manuscript. But that you're burning with love for me, Hedda, I must certainly let Auntie Juju know that. I say, I wonder if young wives often feel like that towards their husbands? What?

HEDDA You might ask Auntie Juju about that too.

TESMAN I will, as soon as I get the chance. [*Looks uneasy and thoughtful again.*] But I say, you know, that manuscript. Dreadful business. Poor Eilert!

[MRS. ELVSTED, *dressed as on her first visit, with hat and overcoat, enters from the hall.*]

MRS. ELVSTED (*greets them hastily and tremulously*) Oh, Hedda dear, do please forgive me for coming here again.

HEDDA Why, Thea, what's happened?

TESMAN Is it anything to do with Eilert Loevborg? What?

MRS. ELVSTED Yes—I'm so dreadfully afraid he may have met with an accident.

HEDDA (*grips her arm*) You think so?

TESMAN But, good heavens, Mrs. Elvsted, what makes you think that?

MRS. ELVSTED I heard them talking about him at the boarding-house, as I went in. Oh, there are the most terrible rumors being spread about him in town today.

TESMAN Fancy. Yes, I heard about them too. But I can testify that he went straight home to bed. Fancy that!

HEDDA Well—what did they say in the boarding-house?

MRS. ELVSTED Oh, I couldn't find out anything. Either they didn't know, or else— They stopped talking when they saw me. And I didn't dare to ask.

TESMAN (*fidgets uneasily*) We must hope —we must hope you misheard them, Mrs. Elvsted.

MRS. ELVSTED No, no, I'm sure it was he they were talking about. I heard them say something about a hospital—

TESMAN Hospital!

HEDDA Oh no, surely that's impossible!

MRS. ELVSTED Oh, I became so afraid. So I went up to his rooms and asked to see him.

HEDDA Do you think that was wise, Thea?

MRS. ELVSTED Well, what else could I do? I couldn't bear the uncertainty any longer.

TESMAN But *you* didn't manage to find him either? What?

MRS. ELVSTED No. And they had no idea where he was. They said he hadn't been home since yesterday afternoon.

TESMAN Since yesterday? Fancy that!

MRS. ELVSTED I'm sure he must have met with an accident.

TESMAN Hedda, I wonder if I ought to go into town and make one or two enquiries?

HEDDA No, no, don't you get mixed up in this.

[JUDGE BRACK *enters from the hall, hat in hand.* BERTHA, *who has opened the door for him, closes it. He looks serious and greets them silently.*]

TESMAN   Hullo, my dear Judge. Fancy seeing you!

BRACK   I had to come and talk to you.

TESMAN   I can see Auntie Juju's told you the news.

BRACK   Yes, I've heard about that too.

TESMAN   Tragic, isn't it?

BRACK   Well, my dear chap, that depends how you look at it.

TESMAN   (*looks uncertainly at him*)   Has something else happened?

BRACK   Yes.

HEDDA   Another tragedy?

BRACK   That also depends on how you look at it, Mrs. Tesman.

MRS. ELVSTED   Oh, it's something to do with Eilert Loevborg!

BRACK   (*looks at her for a moment*)   How did you guess? Perhaps you've heard already—?

MRS. ELVSTED   (*confused*)   No, no, not at all—I——

TESMAN   For heaven's sake, tell us!

BRACK   (*shrugs his shoulders*)   Well, I'm afraid they've taken him to the hospital. He's dying.

MRS. ELVSTED   (*screams*)   Oh God, God!

TESMAN   The hospital! Dying!

HEDDA   (*involuntarily*)   So quickly!

MRS. ELVSTED   (*weeping*)   Oh, Hedda! And we parted enemies!

HEDDA   (*whispers*)   Thea—Thea!

MRS. ELVSTED   (*ignoring her*)   I must see him! I must see him before he dies!

BRACK   It's no use, Mrs. Elvsted. No one's allowed to see him now.

MRS. ELVSTED   But what's happened to him? You must tell me!

TESMAN   He hasn't tried to do anything to himself? What?

HEDDA   Yes, he has. I'm sure of it.

TESMAN   Hedda, how can you—?

BRACK   (*who has not taken his eyes from her*)   I'm afraid you've guessed correctly, Mrs. Tesman.

MRS. ELVSTED   How dreadful!

TESMAN   Attempted suicide! Fancy that!

HEDDA   Shot himself!

BRACK   Right again, Mrs. Tesman.

MRS. ELVSTED   (*tries to compose herself*)   When did this happen, Judge Brack?

BRACK   This afternoon. Between three and four.

TESMAN   But, good heavens—where? What?

BRACK   (*a little hesitantly*)   Where? Why, my dear chap, in his rooms of course.

MRS. ELVSTED   No, that's impossible. I was there soon after six.

BRACK   Well, it must have been somewhere else, then. I don't know exactly. I only know that they found him. He'd shot himself—through the breast.

MRS. ELVSTED   Oh, how horrible! That he should end like that!

HEDDA   (*to* BRACK)   Through the breast, you said?

BRACK   That is what I said.

HEDDA   Not through the head?

BRACK   Through the breast, Mrs. Tesman.

HEDDA   The breast. Yes; yes. That's good, too.

BRACK   Why, Mrs. Tesman?

HEDDA   Oh—no, I didn't mean anything.

TESMAN   And the wound's dangerous, you say? What?

BRACK   Mortal. He's probably already dead.

MRS. ELVSTED   Yes, yes—I feel it! It's all over. All over. Oh Hedda—!

TESMAN   But, tell me, how did you manage to learn all this?

BRACK   (*curtly*)   From the police. I spoke to one of them.

HEDDA   (*loudly, clearly*)   At last! Oh, thank God!

TESMAN   (*appalled*)   For God's sake, Hedda, what are you saying?

HEDDA   I am saying there's beauty in what he has done.

BRACK   Hm—Mrs. Tesman——

TESMAN   Beauty! Oh, but I say!

MRS. ELVSTED   Hedda, how can you talk of beauty in connection with a thing like this?

HEDDA   Eilert Loevborg has settled his account with life. He's had the courage to do what—what he had to do.

MRS. ELVSTED No, that's not why it happened. He did it because he was mad.

TESMAN He did it because he was desperate.

HEDDA You're wrong! I know!

MRS. ELVSTED He must have been mad. The same as when he tore up the manuscript.

BRACK (*starts*) Manuscript? Did he tear it up?

MRS. ELVSTED Yes. Last night.

TESMAN (*whispers*) Oh, Hedda, we shall never be able to escape from this.

BRACK Hm. Strange.

TESMAN (*wanders round the room*) To think of Eilert dying like that. And not leaving behind him the thing that would have made his name endure.

MRS. ELVSTED If only it could be pieced together again!

TESMAN Yes, fancy! If only it could! I'd give anything——

MRS. ELVSTED Perhaps it can, Mr. Tesman.

TESMAN What do you mean?

MRS. ELVSTED (*searches in the pocket of her dress*) Look! I kept the notes he dictated it from.

HEDDA (*takes a step nearer*) Ah!

TESMAN You kept them, Mrs. Elvsted! What?

MRS. ELVSTED Yes, here they are. I brought them with me when I left home. They've been in my pocket ever since.

TESMAN Let me have a look.

MRS. ELVSTED (*hands him a wad of small sheets of paper*) They're in a terrible muddle. All mixed up.

TESMAN I say, just fancy if we can sort them out! Perhaps if we work on them together—?

MRS. ELVSTED Oh, yes! Let's try, anyway!

TESMAN We'll manage it. We must! I shall dedicate my life to this.

HEDDA *You*, George? Your life?

TESMAN Yes—well, all the time I can spare. My book'll have to wait. Hedda, you do understand? What? I owe it to Eilert's memory.

HEDDA Perhaps.

TESMAN Well, my dear Mrs. Elvsted, you and I'll have to pool our brains. No use crying over spilt milk, what? We must try to approach this matter calmly.

MRS. ELVSTED Yes, yes, Mr. Tesman. I'll do my best.

TESMAN Well, come over here and let's start looking at these notes right away. Where shall we sit? Here? No, the other room. You'll excuse us, won't you, Judge? Come along with me, Mrs. Elvsted.

MRS. ELVSTED Oh, God! If only we can manage to do it!

[TESMAN *and* MRS. ELVSTED *go into the rear room. He takes off his hat and overcoat. They sit at the table beneath the hanging lamp and absorb themselves in the notes.* HEDDA *walks across to the stove and sits in the armchair. After a moment,* BRACK *goes over to her.*]

HEDDA (*half aloud*) Oh, Judge! This act of Eilert Loevborg's—doesn't it give one a sense of release!

BRACK Release, Mrs. Hedda? Well, it's a release for him, of course——

HEDDA Oh, I don't mean him—I mean me! The release of knowing that someone can do something really brave! Something beautiful!

BRACK (*smiles*) Hm—my dear Mrs. Hedda——

HEDDA Oh, I know what you're going to say. You're a bourgeois at heart too, just like—ah, well!

BRACK (*looks at her*) Eilert Loevborg has meant more to you than you're willing to admit to yourself. Or am I wrong?

HEDDA I'm not answering questions like that from you. I only know that Eilert Loevborg has had the courage to live according to his own principles. And now, at last, he's done something big! Something beautiful! To have the courage and the will to rise from the feast of life so early!

BRACK It distresses me deeply, Mrs. Hedda, but I'm afraid I must rob you of that charming illusion.

HEDDA   Illusion?

BRACK   You wouldn't have been allowed to keep it for long, anyway.

HEDDA   What do you mean?

BRACK   He didn't shoot himself on purpose.

HEDDA   Not on purpose?

BRACK   No. It didn't happen quite the way I told you.

HEDDA   Have you been hiding something? What is it?

BRACK   In order to spare poor Mrs. Elvsted's feelings, I permitted myself one or two small—equivocations.

HEDDA   What?

BRACK   To begin with, he is already dead.

HEDDA   He died at the hospital?

BRACK   Yes. Without regaining consciousness.

HEDDA   What else haven't you told us?

BRACK   The incident didn't take place at his lodgings.

HEDDA   Well, that's utterly unimportant.

BRACK   Not utterly. The fact is, you see, that Eilert Loevborg was found shot in Mademoiselle Danielle's boudoir.

HEDDA   (*almost jumps up, but instead sinks back in her chair*)   That's impossible. He can't have been there today.

BRACK   He was there this afternoon. He went to ask for something he claimed they'd taken from him. Talked some crazy nonsense about a child which had got lost——

HEDDA   Oh! So that was the reason!

BRACK   I thought at first he might have been referring to his manuscript. But I hear he destroyed that himself. So he must have meant his pocketbook—I suppose.

HEDDA   Yes, I suppose so. So they found him there?

BRACK   Yes; there. With a discharged pistol in his breast pocket. The shot had wounded him mortally.

HEDDA   Yes. In the breast.

BRACK   No. In the—hm—stomach. The lower part——

HEDDA   (*looks at him with an expression of repulsion*)   That too! Oh, why does everything I touch become mean and ludicrous? It's like a curse!

BRACK   There's something else, Mrs. Hedda. It's rather disagreeable, too.

HEDDA   What?

BRACK   The pistol he had on him——

HEDDA   Yes? What about it?

BRACK   He must have stolen it.

HEDDA   (*jumps up*)   Stolen it! That isn't true! He didn't!

BRACK   It's the only explanation. He must have stolen it. Ssh!

[TESMAN *and* MRS. ELVSTED *have got up from the table in the rear room and come into the drawing-room.*]

TESMAN   (*his hands full of papers*)   Hedda, I can't see properly under that lamp. Think!

HEDDA   I am thinking.

TESMAN   Do you think we could possibly use your writing table for a little? What?

HEDDA   Yes, of course. [*Quickly.*] No, wait! Let me tidy it up first.

TESMAN   Oh, don't you trouble about that. There's plenty of room.

HEDDA   No, no, let me tidy it up first, I say. I'll take these in and put them on the piano. Here.

[*She pulls an object, covered with sheets of music, out from under the bookcase, puts some more sheets on top and carries it all into the rear room and away to the left.* TESMAN *puts his papers on the writing table and moves the lamp over from the corner table. He and* MRS. ELVSTED *sit down and begin working again.* HEDDA *comes back.*]

HEDDA   (*behind* MRS. ELVSTED's *chair, ruffles her hair gently*)   Well, my pretty Thea! And how is work progressing on Eilert Loevborg's memorial?

MRS. ELVSTED   (*looks up at her, dejectedly*)   Oh, it's going to be terribly difficult to get these into any order.

TESMAN   We've got to do it. We must! After all, putting other people's papers into order is rather my specialty, what?

[HEDDA *goes over to the stove and sits on one of the footstools.* BRACK *stands over her, leaning against the armchair.*]

HEDDA (*whispers*) What was that you were saying about the pistol?

BRACK (*softly*) I said he must have stolen it.

HEDDA Why do you think that?

BRACK Because any other explanation is unthinkable, Mrs. Hedda, or ought to be.

HEDDA I see.

BRACK (*looks at her for a moment*) Eilert Loevborg was here this morning. Wasn't he?

HEDDA Yes.

BRACK Were you alone with him?

HEDDA For a few moments.

BRACK You didn't leave the room while he was here?

HEDDA No.

BRACK Think again. Are you sure you didn't go out for a moment?

HEDDA Oh—yes, I might have gone into the hall. Just for a few seconds.

BRACK And where was your pistol-case during this time?

HEDDA I'd locked it in that——

BRACK Er—Mrs. Hedda?

HEDDA It was lying over there on my writing table.

BRACK Have you looked to see if both the pistols are still there?

HEDDA No.

BRACK You needn't bother. I saw the pistol Loevborg had when they found him. I recognised it at once. From yesterday. And other occasions.

HEDDA Have you got it?

BRACK No. The police have it.

HEDDA What will the police do with this pistol?

BRACK Try to trace the owner.

HEDDA Do you think they'll succeed?

BRACK (*leans down and whispers*) No, Hedda Gabler. Not as long as I hold my tongue.

HEDDA (*looks nervously at him*) And if you don't?

BRACK (*shrugs his shoulders*) You could always say he'd stolen it.

HEDDA I'd rather die!

BRACK (*smiles*) People say that. They never do it.

HEDDA (*not replying*) And suppose the pistol wasn't stolen? And they trace the owner? What then?

BRACK There'll be a scandal, Hedda.

HEDDA A scandal!

BRACK Yes, a scandal. The thing you're so frightened of. You'll have to appear in court. Together with Mademoiselle Danielle. She'll have to explain how it all happened. Was it an accident, or was it—homicide? Was he about to take the pistol from his pocket to threaten her? And did it go off? Or did she snatch the pistol from his hand, shoot him and then put it back in his pocket? She might quite easily have done it. She's a resourceful lady, is Mademoiselle Danielle.

HEDDA But I had nothing to do with this repulsive business.

BRACK No. But you'll have to answer one question. Why did you give Eilert Loevborg this pistol? And what conclusions will people draw when it is proved you did give it to him?

HEDDA (*bows her head*) That's true. I hadn't thought of that.

BRACK Well, luckily there's no danger as long as I hold my tongue.

HEDDA (*looks up at him*) In other words, I'm in your power, Judge. From now on, you've got your hold over me.

BRACK (*whispers, more slowly*) Hedda, my dearest—believe me—I will not abuse my position.

HEDDA Nevertheless, I'm in your power. Dependent on your will, and your demands. Not free. Still not free! [*Rises passionately.*] No. I couldn't bear that. No.

BRACK (*looks half-derisively at her*) Most people resign themselves to the inevitable, sooner or later.

HEDDA (*returns his gaze*) Possibly they do. [*She goes across to the writing table, represses an involuntary smile and says in*

TESMAN's *voice.*] Well, George. Think you'll be able to manage? What?

TESMAN Heaven knows, dear. This is going to take months and months.

HEDDA (*in the same tone as before*) Fancy that, by Jove! [*Runs her hands gently through* MRS. ELVSTED's *hair.*] Doesn't it feel strange, Thea? Here you are working away with Tesman just the way you used to work with Eilert Loevborg.

MRS. ELVSTED Oh—if only I can inspire your husband too!

HEDDA Oh, it'll come. In time.

TESMAN Yes—do you know, Hedda, I really think I'm beginning to feel a bit—well—that way. But you go back and talk to Judge Brack.

HEDDA Can't I be of use to you two in any way?

TESMAN No, none at all. [*Turns his head.*] You'll have to keep Hedda company from now on, Judge, and see she doesn't get bored. If you don't mind.

BRACK (*glances at* HEDDA) It'll be a pleasure.

HEDDA Thank you. But I'm tired this evening. I think I'll lie down on the sofa in there for a little while.

TESMAN Yes, dear—do. What?

[HEDDA *goes into the rear room and draws the curtains behind her. Short pause. Suddenly she begins to play a frenzied dance melody on the piano.*]

MRS. ELVSTED (*starts up from her chair*) Oh, what's that?

TESMAN (*runs to the doorway*) Hedda dear, please! Don't play dance music tonight! Think of Auntie Rena. And Eilert.

HEDDA (*puts her head out through the curtains*) And Auntie Juju. And all the rest of them. From now on I'll be quiet. [*Closes the curtains behind her.*]

TESMAN (*at the writing table*) It distresses her to watch us doing this. I say, Mrs. Elvsted, I've an idea. Why don't you move in with Auntie Juju? I'll run over each evening, and we can sit and work there. What?

MRS. ELVSTED Yes, that might be the best plan.

HEDDA (*from the rear room*) I can hear what you're saying, Tesman. But how shall I spend the evenings out here?

TESMAN (*looking through his papers*) Oh, I'm sure Judge Brack'll be kind enough to come over and keep you company. You won't mind my not being here, Judge?

BRACK (*in the armchair, calls gaily*) I'll be delighted, Mrs. Tesman. I'll be here every evening. We'll have great fun together, you and I.

HEDDA (*loud and clear*) Yes, that'll suit you, won't it, Judge? The only cock on the dunghill—!

[*A shot is heard from the rear room.* TESMAN, MRS. ELVSTED *and* JUDGE BRACK *start from their chairs.*]

TESMAN Oh, she's playing with those pistols again.

[*He pulls the curtains aside and runs in.* MRS. ELVSTED *follows him.* HEDDA *is lying dead on the sofa. Confusion and shouting.* BERTHA *enters in alarm from the right.*]

TESMAN (*screams to* BRACK) She's shot herself. Shot herself in the head! By Jove! Fancy that!

BRACK (*half paralysed in the armchair*) But, good God! People don't do such things!

Trelawny of the "Wells"

Arthur Wing Pinero

Introductory Comments

Jane W. Stedman   *Roosevelt University*

"I have always acted on the principle that everything matters," wrote Arthur Wing Pinero near the end of his life.* This assertion sums up the new concept of realistic drama that began with the "modern" comedies of Tom Robertson in the 1860s and culminated in late Victorian "problem" plays and in the social satire of George Bernard Shaw.

Trelawny of the "Wells" (first performed in the Court Theatre in 1898) is a "memory" play about this change in the theatre. Pinero himself began his career as a "utility," or small-parts, actor in a repertory company. He knew, and in *Trelawny* depicted, the family life of a dramatic company—with its affections and jealousies, its boarding-house community, its traditions of "splendid gypsies" such as the tragic actor Edmund Kean, and its intense theatricalism on and off stage.

The plays performed at Pinero's imaginary Bagnigge Wells Theatre (suggested by Sadler's Wells) were the standard fare on the mid-Victorian stage: Shakespeare; dramas such as Sheridan Knowles's *The Hunchback;* melodramas; and Christmas pantomimes or burlesques, such as H. J. Byron's *The Miller and His Men.* (Victorian burlesque meant a parodistic, punning musical, not a nude show.) To these were added farce and what was called "legitimate comedy," usually by Goldsmith or Sheridan. The actors who appeared in these plays intended to produce broad, exciting dramatic effects. Their larger-than-life gestures were grand and striking, partly because of the theories of acting then in vogue, and partly because the large size of important theatres made small movements imperceptible and subtle facial changes invisible. Because the auditorium was not darkened, the audience's attention was not automatically directed toward the lighted stage. The actor had to focus attention on himself by the force

* Letter to H. H. Fyfe, 17th May, 1930, in *The Collected Letters of Sir Arthur Pinero,* ed. J. P. Wearing (University of Minnesota Press; Minneapolis, 1974), p. 286.

of his performance if he were a serious actor or by the bustle of his action if he were a comedian. Augustus Colpoys, the low comic depicted in *Trelawny*, for instance, carried his typical stage performance into private life by "extravagant gestures of endearment," by pretending to wring tears from his handkerchief, by putting a pork pie on his head, and so on. Scenery was usually spectacular or negligible, although there was already a growing tradition at the best theatres of presenting Shakespeare's plays in their proper historical settings and costumes.

It remained for Tom Robertson (1829–1871) to bring this historicity to plays about contemporary life, and it is his entrance as a playwright into the world of theatre that Pinero dramatizes in *Trelawny*, with Robertson himself depicted in the character of Tom Wrench, a "utility actor" who wants to write dramas about people who talk in ordinary conversations, not speeches, and who live in rooms with doors and windows where they would be in real houses. To Robertson, who directed his own plays, every detail of production mattered, and he was fortunate in finding a theatre manageress and actress, Marie Wilton, who agreed with him. In *Trelawny*, Pinero turned Miss Wilton into Imogen Parrott, whose Pantheon Theatre recalls Miss Wilton's Prince of Wales's, where fashionable audiences sat in sky-blue seats (with antimacassars) to watch a new kind of play. Pinero's play ends with a rehearsal of Wrench's iconoclastic comedy *Life*, the one-word title of which recalls Robertson's own successes: *Society, Ours, Caste, School,* and others.

Robertson's (and Wrench's) plays were written for a new style of ensemble acting in small theatres—they were quietly performed, even under-acted if judged by earlier standards. For instance, in *Caste*, George, supposedly dead in battle, returns unexpectedly, not with a heroic speech, but bringing in the milk. In the longest-remembered scene of *Ours*, a girl makes a pudding on stage. The low-key atmosphere and the domestic realism of milk-cans, pudding basins, and tea tables earned Robertson's plays the epithet of "cup and saucer drama."

Such realistic settings and acting, depending on small, significant detail, were necessary for the development of the social protest and "problem" playwrights who followed Robertson and who included W. S. Gilbert, Henry Arthur Jones, Pinero himself, John Galsworthy, and George Bernard Shaw. Old-fashioned melodrama with its premise of virtue rewarded had been a good theatrical form for patriotism, for simple moral dilemmas, or for attacking the rich oppressors of the poor. But for plays dealing with social ethics or plays arguing social questions, a greater realism was needed. On the continent Henrik Ibsen was furnishing his *Doll's House* with great authenticity; in England, Tom Robertson's cup and saucer technique could serve both Pinero's most important problem play, *The Second Mrs. Tanqueray*

(St. James's Theatre, 1893), which attacked the sexual double standard, and *Trelawny of the "Wells"*, which deals with the social acceptability of the stage.

In fact, *Tanqueray* and *Trelawny* not only represent Pinero at his best in two different genres, but have more in common than met the eyes of audiences shocked by the first and charmed by the second. Both involve problems of social "outsiders," and both use the favorite Victorian theme of "masks and faces," or the difference between what people seem to be and what they are.

Paula Ray, the second Mrs. Tanqueray, has been the mistress successively of several fashionable gentlemen. She tries to become respectable by marrying, but is finally driven to suicide, her step-daughter exclaiming too late, "If I had only been merciful!" Although Shaw wrote *Mrs Warren's Profession* partly to show that Pinero did not understand the psychology of a "fallen woman," Pinero did show the rigid righteousness of society, and he attacked the sexual mores that did not penalize a man for leading "a man's life" but damned the woman with whom he led it. Under the mask of virtue, the "good" women in the play are harsh, uncharitable, and hypocritical; even Paula's virginal stepdaughter is willing to forgive her fiancé the sexual "sin" for which she rejects Paula.

The outsider in *Trelawny* is an actress, Rose Trelawny, and old-fashioned Victorian society is represented by Sir William Gower and his sister Trafalgar. To enter their family, Rose must give up acting and live with them in Cavendish Square until she is ladylike enough to marry Arthur Gower. Pinero evidently based this situation on an episode from real life. In the early 1880s, Miss Fortescue, who acted small roles for Gilbert and Sullivan, had become engaged to Lord Garmoyle, and had left the stage to "become a lady" at his strait-laced parents' insistence. (They made her sister give up acting too.) Lord Garmoyle soon jilted Miss Fortescue, and she sued him successfully for breach of promise.

Pinero turned these social antagonisms into plot complications. Each group of characters in his play sees first only the unattractive mask of the other group, a mask partly imposed, partly assumed. But each group finally sees the face behind the other's mask. Under Sir William's outward austere disapproval, there is justice, enthusiasm, and love—qualities that enable him to become the backer of Tom Wrench's play. Under Rose's outward unconventionality and staginess lie the delicacy of feeling and genuineness that enable her to act the lead in the new style of *Life*.

Pinero himself directed *Trelawny of the "Wells"*, as he did all his plays. He rehearsed for a month, and even then his passion for perfection was not quite satisfied, although his audiences were. Even in 1898, the costumes and settings of the 1860s had a nostalgic charm, as those of the 1920s have today. *Trelawny* ran for 135 performances.

By 1917 the *Times* was reviewing it as a classic, and a classic it has remained.

Arthur Wing Pinero (1855–1934) became a professional actor at nineteen and a playwright at twenty-two. In 1883 he married Myra Holme, an actress, and the next year he gave up acting to be a full-time dramatist and director of his own plays. From 1885 to 1893 he wrote very successful farces (among them are *The Magistrate, The Schoolmistress, Dandy Dick*), interspersed with such works as *Sweet Lavendar* (1888), a sentimental comedy, and *The Profligate* (1889), an early problem play.

Pinero's best-known drama was *The Second Mrs. Tanqueray* (1893); reviewers found its theme unpleasant but powerful, and it made Pinero the leading dramatist of the decade. His later problem plays included *The Notorious Mrs. Ebbsmith* (1895), *Iris* (1901), and in 1909, the year he was knighted, *Mid-Channel*. Pinero continued to write until his death, although critics increasingly considered him old-fashioned. His last well-known play was *The Enchanted Cottage* (1922).

Trelawny of the "Wells"   *Arthur W. Pinero*

The Persons of the Play

Theatrical Folk

TOM WRENCH

FERDINAND GADD

JAMES TELFER

AUGUSTUS COLPOYS   *of the Bagnigge-Wells Theatre*

ROSE TRELAWNY

AVONIA BUNN

MRS. TELFER   (*Miss Violet*)

IMOGEN PARROTT, *of the Royal Olympic Theatre*

O'DWYER, *prompter at the Pantheon Theatre*

MR. DENZIL

MR. MORTIMER   *of the Pantheon Theatre*

MR. HUNSTON

MISS BREWSTER

HALLKEEPER *at the Pantheon*

Non-Theatrical Folk

VICE-CHANCELLOR SIR WILLIAM GOWER, KT.

ARTHUR GOWER   *his grandchildren*

CLARA DE FŒNIX

MISS TRAFALGAR GOWER   *Sir William's sister*

CAPTAIN DE FŒNIX   *Clara's husband*

MRS. MOSSOP   *a landlady*

MR. ABLETT   *a grocer*

CHARLES   *a butler*

SARAH   *a maid*

THE FIRST ACT *at Mr. and Mrs.* TELFER's *Lodgings in No. 2, Brydon Crescent, Clerkenwell.* May.

THE SECOND ACT *at* SIR WILLIAM GOWER's, *in Cavendish Square.* June.

THE THIRD ACT *again in Brydon Crescent.* December.

THE FOURTH ACT *on the stage of the Pantheon Theatre.* A few days later.

PERIOD *somewhere in the early Sixties.*

Note.—BAGNIGGE-(locally pronounced Bagnidge) WELLS, formerly a popular mineral spring in *Islington, London,* situated not far from the better remembered SADLER's-WELLS. The gardens of BAGNIGGE-WELLS were at one time much resorted to; but, as a matter of fact, BAGNIGGE-WELLS, unlike SADLER's-WELLS, has never possessed a play-house. SADLER's-WELLS THEATRE, however, always familiarly known as the "WELLS," still exists. It was rebuilt in 1876–1877.

A Direction to the Stage Manager

The costumes and scenic decoration of this little play should follow, to the closest detail, the mode of the early Sixties, the period, in dress, of crinoline and the peg-top trouser; in furniture, of horsehair and mahogany, and the abominable "walnut-and-rep." No attempt should be made to modify such fashions in illustration, to render them less strange, even less grotesque, to the modern eye. On the contrary, there should be an endeavor to reproduce, perhaps to accentuate, any feature which may now seem particularly quaint and bizarre. Thus, lovely youth should be shown decked uncompromisingly as it was at the time indicated, at the risk (which the author believes to be a slight one) of pointing the chastening moral that, while beauty fades assuredly in its own time, it may appear to succeeding generations not to have been beauty at all.

Act One

The scene represents a sitting room on the first floor of a respectable lodging house. On the right are two sash-windows, having Venetian blinds and giving a view of houses on the other side of the street. The grate of the fireplace is hidden by an ornament composed of shavings and paper roses. Over the fireplace is a mirror: on each side there is a sideboard cupboard. On the left is a door, and a landing is seen outside. Between the windows stand a cottage piano and a piano stool. Above the sofa, on the left, stands a large black trunk, the lid bulging with its contents and displaying some soiled theatrical finery. On the front of the trunk, in faded lettering, appear the words "Miss Violet Sylvester, Theatre Royal, Drury Lane." Under the sofa there are two or three pairs of ladies' satin shoes, much the worse for wear, and on the sofa a white-satin bodice, yellow with age, a heap of dog-eared playbooks, and some other litter of a like character. On the top of the piano there is a wig-block, with a man's wig upon it, and in the corners of the room there stand some walking sticks and a few theatrical swords. In the center of the stage is a large circular table. There is a clean cover upon it, and on the top of the sideboard cupboards are knives and forks, plate, glass, cruet-stands, and some gaudy flowers in vases—all suggesting preparations for festivity. The woodwork of the room is grained, the ceiling plainly white-washed, and the wall paper is of a neutral tint and much faded. The pictures are engravings in maple frames, and a portrait or two, in oil, framed in gilt. The furniture, curtains, and carpet are worn, but everything is clean and well-kept.

The light is that of afternoon in early summer.

MRS. MOSSOP—*a portly, middle-aged Jewish lady, elaborately attired—is laying the tablecloth.* ABLETT *enters hastily, divesting himself of his coat as he does so. He is dressed in rusty black for "waiting."*

MRS. MOSSOP [*In a fluster.*] Oh, here you are, Mr. Ablett——!

ABLETT Good-day, Mrs. Mossop.

MRS. MOSSOP [*Bringing the cruet-stands.*] I declare I thought you'd forgotten me.

ABLETT [*Hanging his coat upon a curtain-knob, and turning up his shirt sleeves.*] I'd begun to fear I should never escape from the shop, ma'am. Jest as I was pre-parin' to clean myself, the 'ole universe seemed to cry aloud for pertaters. [*Relieving* MRS. MOSSOP *of the cruet-stands, and satisfying himself as to the contents of the various bottles.*] Now you take a seat, Mrs. Mossop. You 'ave but to say "Mr. Ablett, lay for so many," and the exact number shall be laid for.

MRS. MOSSOP [*Sinking into the armchair.*] I hope the affliction of short breath may be spared you, Ablett. Ten is the number.

ABLETT [*Whipping up the mustard energetically.*] Short-breathed you may be, ma'am, but not short-sighted. That gal of yours is no ordinary gal, but to 'ave set 'er to wait on ten persons would 'ave been to 'ave caught disaster. [*Bringing knives and forks, glass, etc., and glancing round the room as he does so.*] I am in Mr. and Mrs.

Telfer's setting-room, I believe, ma'am?

MRS. MOSSOP [*Surveying the apartment complacently.*] And what a handsomely proportioned room it is, to be sure!

ABLETT May I h'ask if I am to 'ave the honor of includin' my triflin' fee for this job in their weekly book?

MRS. MOSSOP No, Ablett—a separate bill, please. The Telfers kindly give the use of their apartment, to save the cost of holding the ceremony at the "Clown" Tavern; but share and share alike over the expenses is to be the order of the day.

ABLETT I thank you, ma'am. [*Rubbing up the knives with a napkin.*] You let fall the word "ceremony," ma'am——

MRS. MOSSOP Ah, Ablett, and a sad one—a farewell cold collation to Miss Tre-lawny.

ABLETT Lor' bless me! I 'eard a rumor——

MRS. MOSSOP A true rumor. She's taking her leave of us, the dear.

ABLETT This will be a blow to the "Wells," ma'am.

MRS. MOSSOP The best juvenile lady the "Wells" has known since Mr. Phillips's management.

ABLETT Report 'as it, a love affair, ma'am.

MRS. MOSSOP A love affair, indeed. And a poem into the bargain, Ablett, if poet was at hand to write it.

ABLETT Reelly, Mrs. Mossop! [*Polishing a tumbler.*] Is the beer to be bottled or draught, ma'am, on this occasion?

MRS. MOSSOP Draught for Miss Trelawny, invariably.

ABLETT Then draught it must be all round, out of compliment. Jest fancy! nevermore to 'ear customers speak of Trelawny of the "Wells," except as a pleasin' memory! A non-professional gentleman they give out, ma'am.

MRS. MOSSOP Yes.

ABLETT Name of Glover.

MRS. MOSSOP Gower. Grandson of Vice Chancellor Sir William Gower, Mr. Ablett.

ABLETT You don't say, ma'am!

MRS. MOSSOP No father nor mother, and

lives in Cavendish Square with the old judge and a great aunt.

ABLETT Then Miss Trelawny quits the Profession, ma'am, for good and all, I presoom?

MRS. MOSSOP Yes, Ablett, she's at the theaytre at this moment, distributing some of her little ornaments and fallals among the ballet. She played last night for the last time—the last time on any stage. [*Rising and going to the sideboard-cupboard.*] And without so much as a line in the bill to announce it. What a benefit she might have taken!

ABLETT I know one who was good for two box tickets, Mrs. Mossop.

MRS. MOSSOP [*Bringing the flowers to the table and arranging them, while* ABLETT *sets out the knives and forks.*] But no. "No fuss," said the Gower family, "no publicity. Withdraw quietly—" that was the Gower family's injunctions—"withdraw quietly, and have done with it."

ABLETT And when is the weddin' to be, ma'am?

MRS. MOSSOP It's not yet decided, Mr. Ablett. In point of fact, before the Gower family positively say Yes to the union, Miss Trelawny is to make her home in Cavendish Square for a short term— "short term" is the Gower family's own expression—in order to habituate herself to the West End. They're sending their carriage for her at two o'clock this afternoon, Mr. Ablett—their carriage and pair of bay horses.

ABLETT Well, I dessay a West End life has sooperior advantages over the Profession in some respecks, Mrs. Mossop.

MRS. MOSSOP When accompanied by wealth, Mr. Ablett. Here's Miss Trelawny but nineteen, and in a month-or-two's time she'll be ordering about her own powdered footman, and playing on her grand piano. How many actresses do *that*, I should like to know!

[TOM WRENCH'*s voice is heard.*]

TOM [*Outside the door.*] Rebecca! Rebecca, my loved one!

MRS. MOSSOP Oh, go along with you, Mr. Wrench!

[TOM *enters, with a pair of scissors in his hand. He is a shabbily-dressed ungraceful man of about thirty, with a clean-shaven face, curly hair, and eyes full of good-humor.*]

TOM My own, especial Rebecca!

MRS. MOSSOP Don't be a fool, Mr. Wrench! Now, I've no time to waste. I know you want something——

TOM Everything, adorable. But most desperately do I stand in need of a little skillful trimming at your fair hands.

MRS. MOSSOP [*Taking the scissors from him and clipping the frayed edges of his shirt-cuffs and collar.*] First it's patching a coat, and then it's binding an Inverness! Sometimes I wish that top room of mine was empty.

TOM And sometimes I wish my heart was empty, cruel Rebecca.

MRS. MOSSOP [*Giving him a thump.*] Now, I really will tell Mossop of you, when he comes home! I've often threatened it——

TOM [*To* ABLETT.] Whom do I see! No—it can't be—but yes—I believe I have the privilege of addressing Mr. Ablett, the eminent greengrocer, of Rosoman Street?

ABLETT [*Sulkily.*] Well, Mr. Wrench, and wot of it?

TOM You possess a cart, good Ablett, which may be hired by persons of character and responsibility. "By the hour or job"—so runs the legend. I will charter it, one of these Sundays, for a drive to Epping.

ABLETT I dunno so much about that, Mr. Wrench.

TOM Look to the springs, good Ablett, for this comely lady will be my companion.

MRS. MOSSOP Dooce take your impudence! Give me your other hand. Haven't you been to rehearsal this morning with the rest of 'em?

TOM I have, and have left my companions still toiling. My share in the interpretation of Sheridan Knowles's immortal work did not necessitate my remaining after the first act.

MRS. MOSSOP Another poor part, I suppose, Mr. Wrench?

TOM Another, and to-morrow yet another, and on Saturday two others—all equally, damnably rotten.

MRS. MOSSOP Ah, well, well! *somebody* must play the bad parts in this world, on and off the stage. There [*returning the scissors*], there's no more edge left to fray; we've come to the soft. [*He points the scissors at his breast.*] Ah! don't do that!

TOM You are right, sweet Mossop, I won't perish on an empty stomach. [*Taking her aside.*] But tell me, shall I disgrace the feast, eh? Is my appearance too scandalously seedy?

MRS. MOSSOP Not *it,* my dear.

TOM Miss Trelawny—do you think she'll regard me as a blot on the banquet? [*wistfully*] do you, Beccy?

MRS. MOSSOP She! la! don't distress yourself. She'll be too excited to notice *you.*

TOM H'm, yes! now I recollect, she has always been that. Thanks, Beccy.

[*A knock, at the front-door, is heard.* MRS. MOSSOP *hurries to the window down the stage.*]

MRS. MOSSOP Who's that? [*Opening the window and looking out.*] It's Miss Parrott! Miss Parrott's arrived!

TOM Jenny Parrott? Has Jenny condescended——?

MRS. MOSSOP *Jenny!* Where are your manners, Mr. Wrench?

TOM [*Grandiloquently.*] Miss Imogen Parrott, of the Olympic Theatre.

MRS. MOSSOP [*At the door, to* ABLETT.] Put your coat on, Ablett. We are not selling cabbages. [*She disappears and is heard speaking in the distance.*] Step up, Miss Parrott! Tell Miss Parrott to mind that mat, Sarah——!

TOM Be quick, Ablett, be quick! The *élite* is below! More dispatch, good Ablett!

ABLETT [*To* TOM, *spitefully, while struggling into his coat.*] Miss Trelawny's leavin' will make all the difference to the old "Wells." The season 'll terminate abrupt, and then the comp'ny 'll be h'out, Mr. Wrench—h'out, sir!

TOM [*Adjusting his necktie, at the mirror over the piano.*] Which will lighten the demand for the spongy turnip and the watery marrow, my poor Ablett.

ABLETT [*Under his breath.*] Presumpshus! [*He produces a pair of white cotton gloves, and having put one on makes a horrifying discovery.*] Two lefts! That's Mrs. Ablett all over!

[*During the rest of the act, he is continually in difficulties, through his efforts to wear one of the gloves upon his right hand.* MRS. MOSSOP *now re-enters, with* IMOGEN PARROTT. IMOGEN *is a pretty, light-hearted young woman, of about seven-and-twenty, daintily dressed.*]

MRS. MOSSOP [*To* IMOGEN.] There, it might be only yesterday you lodged in my house, to see you gliding up those stairs! And this the very room you shared with poor Miss Brooker!

IMOGEN [*Advancing to* TOM.] Well, Wrench, and how are you?

TOM [*Bringing her a chair, demonstratively dusting the seat of it with his pocket-handkerchief.*] Thank you, much the same as when you used to call me Tom.

IMOGEN Oh, but I have turned over a new leaf, you know, since I have been at the Olympic.

MRS. MOSSOP I am sure my chairs don't require dusting, Mr. Wrench.

TOM [*Placing the chair below the table, and blowing his nose with his handkerchief, with a flourish.*] My way of showing homage, Mossop.

MRS. MOSSOP Miss Parrott has sat on them often enough, when she was an honored member of the "Wells"—haven't you, Miss Parrott?

IMOGEN [*Sitting, with playful dignity.*] I suppose I must have done so. Don't remind me of it. I sit on nothing nowadays but down pillows covered with cloth of gold.

[MRS. MOSSOP *and* ABLETT *prepare to withdraw.*]

MRS. MOSSOP [*At the door, to* IMOGEN.] Ha, ha! ha! I could fancy I'm looking at Undine again—Undine, the Spirit of the Waters. She's not the least changed since she appeared as Undine—is she, Mr. Ablett?

ABLETT [*Joining* MRS. MOSSOP.] No—or as Prince Cammyralzyman in the pantomine. *I* never 'ope to see a pair o' prettier limbs——

MRS. MOSSOP [*Sharply.*] Now then!

[*She pushes him out; they disappear.*]

IMOGEN [*After a shiver at* ABLETT's *remark.*] In my present exalted station I don't hear much of what goes on at the "Wells," Wrench. Are your abilities still—still——

TOM Still unrecognized, still confined within the almost boundless and yet repressive limits of Utility—General Utility? [*Nodding.*] H'm, still.

IMOGEN Dear me! a thousand pities! I positively mean it.

TOM Thanks.

IMOGEN What do you think! You were mixed up in a funny dream I dreamt one night lately.

TOM [*Bowing.*] Highly complimented.

IMOGEN It was after a supper which rather —well, I'd had some strawberries sent me from Hertfordshire.

TOM Indigestion levels all ranks.

IMOGEN It was a nightmare. I found myself on the stage of the Olympic in that wig you—oh, gracious! You used to play your very serious little parts in it——

TOM The wig with the ringlets?

IMOGEN Ugh! yes.

TOM I wear it to-night, for the second time this week, in a part which is very serious—and very little.

IMOGEN Heavens! it *is* in existence then!

TOM And long will be, I hope. I've only three wigs, and this one accommodates itself to so many periods.

IMOGEN Oh, how it used to amuse the gallery-boys!

TOM They still enjoy it. If you looked in this evening at half-past-seven—I'm done at a quarter-to-eight—if you looked in at half-past-seven, you would hear the same glad, rapturous murmur in the gallery when the presence of that wig is discovered. Not that they fail to laugh at my other wigs, at every article of adornment I possess, in fact! Good God, Jenny——!

IMOGEN [*Wincing.*] Ssssh!

TOM Miss Parrott—if they gave up laughing at me now, I believe I—I believe I should—*miss* it. I believe I couldn't spout my few lines now in silence; my unaccompanied voice would sound so strange to me. Besides, I often think those gallery-boys are really fond of me, at heart. You can't laugh as they do—rock with laughter sometimes!—at what you dislike.

IMOGEN Of course not. *Of course* they like you, Wrench. You cheer them, make their lives happier——

TOM And to-night, by the bye, I also assume that beast of a felt hat—the gray hat with the broad brim, and the imitation wool feathers. You remember it?

IMOGEN Y-y-yes.

TOM I see you do. Well, that hat still persists in falling off, when I most wish it to stick on. It will tilt and tumble to-night—during one of Telfer's pet speeches; I feel it will.

IMOGEN Ha, ha, ha!

TOM And those yellow boots; I wear *them* to-night——

IMOGEN No!

TOM Yes!

IMOGEN Ho, ho, ho, ho!

TOM [*With forced hilarity.*] Ho, ho! ha, ha! And the spurs—the spurs that once tore your satin petticoat! You recollect——?

IMOGEN [*Her mirth suddenly checked.*] Recollect!

TOM You would see those spurs to-night, too, if you patronized us—*and* the red worsted tights. The worsted tights are a little thinner, a little more faded and discolored, a little more darned—Oh, yes, thank you, I am still, as you put it, still—still—still——

[*He walks away, going to the mantelpiece and turning his back upon her.*]

IMOGEN [*After a brief pause.*] I'm sure I didn't intend to hurt your feelings, Wrench.

TOM [*Turning, with some violence.*] You! you hurt my feelings! Nobody can hurt my feelings! I have no feelings——!

[ABLETT *re-enters, carrying three chairs of odd patterns.* TOM *seizes the chairs and places them about the table, noisily.*]

ABLETT Look here, Mr. Wrench! If I'm to be 'ampered in performin' my dooties——

TOM More chairs, Ablett! In my apartment, the chamber nearest heaven, you will find one with a loose leg. We will seat Mrs. Telfer upon that. She dislikes me, and she is, in every sense, a heavy woman.

ABLETT [*Moving toward the door—dropping his glove.*] My opinion, you are meanin' to 'arrass me, Mr. Wrench——

TOM [*Picking up the glove and throwing it to* ABLETT—*singing.*] "Take back thy glove, thou faithless fair!" Your glove, Ablett.

ABLETT Thank you, sir; it *is* my glove, and you are no gentleman.

[*He withdraws.*]

TOM True, Ablett—not even a Walking Gentleman.

IMOGEN Don't go on so, Wrench. What about your plays? Aren't you trying to write any plays just now?

TOM Trying! I am doing more than trying to write plays. I am writing plays. I have written plays.

IMOGEN Well?

TOM My cupboard upstairs is choked with 'em.

IMOGEN Won't anyone take a fancy——?

TOM Not a sufficiently violent fancy.

IMOGEN You know, the speeches were so short and had such ordinary words in them, in the plays you used to read to me—no big opportunity for the leading lady, Wrench.

TOM M' yes. I strive to make my people talk and behave like live people, don't I——?

IMOGEN I suppose you do.

TOM To fashion heroes out of actual, dull, every-day men—the sort of men you see smoking cheroots in the club windows in St. James's Street; and heroines from simple maidens in muslin frocks. Naturally, the managers won't stand that.

IMOGEN Why, of course not.

TOM If *they* did, the public wouldn't.

IMOGEN Is it likely?

TOM Is it likely? I wonder!

IMOGEN Wonder—what?

TOM Whether they would.

IMOGEN The public!

TOM The public. Jenny, I wonder about it sometimes so hard that that little bedroom of mine becomes a banqueting hall, and this lodging house a castle.

[*There is a loud and prolonged knocking at the front door.*]

IMOGEN Here they are, I suppose.

TOM [*Pulling himself together.*] Good Lord! Have I become disheveled?

IMOGEN Why, are you anxious to make an impression, even down to the last, Wrench?

TOM [*Angrily.*] Stop that!

IMOGEN It's no good your being sweet on her any longer, surely?

TOM [*Glaring at her.*] What cats you all are, you girls!

IMOGEN [*Holding up her hands.*] Oh! oh, dear! How vulgar—after the Olympic!

[ABLETT *returns, carrying three more chairs.*]

ABLETT [*Arranging these chairs on the left of the table.*] They're all 'ome! they're all 'ome! [TOM *places the four chairs belonging to the room at the table. To* IMOGEN.] She looks 'eavenly, Miss Trelawny does. I was jest takin' in the ale when she floated down the Crescent on her lover's arm. [*Wagging his head at* IMOGEN *admiringly.*] There, I don't know which of you two is the——

IMOGEN [*Haughtily.*] Man, keep your place!

ABLETT [*Hurt.*] H'as you please, miss—but you apperently forget I used to serve you with vegetables.

[*He takes up a position at the door as* TELFER *and* GADD *enter.* TELFER *is a thick-set, elderly man, with a worn, clean-shaven face and iron-gray hair "clubbed" in the theatrical fashion of the time. Sonorous, if somewhat husky, in speech, and elaborately dignified in bearing, he is at the same time a little uncertain about his H's.* GADD *is a flashily-dressed young man of seven-and-twenty, with brown hair arranged à la Byron and mustache of a deeper tone.*]

TELFER [*Advancing to* IMOGEN, *and kissing her paternally.*] Ha, my dear child! I heard you were 'ere. Kind of you to visit us. Welcome! I'll just put my 'at down——

[*He places his hat on the top of the piano, and proceeds to inspect the table.*]

GADD [*Coming to* IMOGEN, *in an elegant, languishing way.*] Imogen, my darling. [*Kissing her.*] Kiss Ferdy!

IMOGEN Well, Gadd, how goes it—I mean how are you?

GADD [*Earnestly.*] I'm hitting them hard this season, my darling. To-night, Sir Thomas Clifford. They're simply waiting for my Clifford.

IMOGEN But who on earth is your Julia?

GADD Ha! Mrs. Telfer *goes on* for it—a venerable stop-gap. Absurd, of course; but we daren't keep my Clifford from them any longer.

IMOGEN You'll miss Rose Trelawny in business pretty badly, I expect, Gadd?

GADD [*With a shrug of the shoulders.*] She was to have done Rosalind for my benefit. Miss Fitzhugh joins on Monday; I must pull *her* through it somehow. I would re-consider my bill, but they're waiting for my Orlando, waiting for it——

[COLPOYS *enters—an insignificant, wizen little fellow who is unable to forget that he is a low-comedian. He stands left, squinting hideously at* IMOGEN *and indulging in extravagant gestures of endearment, while she continues her conversation with* GADD.]

COLPOYS [*Failing to attract her attention.*] My love! my life!

IMOGEN [*Nodding to him indifferently.*] Good-afternoon, Augustus.

COLPOYS [*Ridiculously.*] She speaks! she hears me!

ABLETT [*Holding his glove before his mouth, convulsed with laughter.*] Ho, ho! oh, Mr. Colpoys! oh, reelly, sir! ho, dear!

GADD [*To* IMOGEN, *darkly.*] Colpoys is not nearly as funny as he was last year. Everybody's saying so. We want a low-comedian badly.

[*He retires, deposits his hat on the wig-block, and joins* TELFER *and* TOM.]

COLPOYS [*Staggering to* IMOGEN *and throwing his arms about her neck.*] Ah—h—h! after all these years!

IMOGEN [*Pushing him away.*] Do be careful of my things, Colpoys!

ABLETT [*Going out, blind with mirth.*] Ha, ha, ha! ho, ho!

[*He collides with* MRS. TELFER, *who is entering at this moment.* MRS. TELFER *is a tall, massive lady of middle age—a faded queen of tragedy.*]

ABLETT [*As he disappears.*] I'm sure I beg your pardon, Mrs. Telfer, ma'am.

MRS. TELFER Violent fellow! [*Advancing to* IMOGEN *and kissing her solemnly.*] How is it with you, Jenny Parrott?

IMOGEN Thank you, Mrs. Telfer, as well as can be. And you?

MRS. TELFER [*Waving away the inquiry.*] I am obliged to you for this response to my invitation. It struck me as fitting that at such a time you should return for a brief hour or two to the company of your old associates—— [*Becoming conscious of* COLPOYS, *behind her, making grimaces at* IMOGEN.] Eh—h—h? [*Turning to* COLPOYS *and surprising him.*] Oh—h—h! Yes, Augustus Colpoys, you are extremely humorous *off.*

COLPOYS [*Stung.*] Miss Sylvester—Mrs. Telfer!

MRS. TELFER *On* the stage, sir, you are enough to make a cat weep.

COLPOYS Madam! from one artist to another! well, I—! 'pon my soul! [*Retreating and talking under his breath.*] Popular favorite! draw more money than all the—old guys——

MRS. TELFER [*Following him.*] What do you say, sir! Do you mutter!

[*They explain mutually.* AVONIA BUNN *enters—an untidy, tawdrily-dressed young woman of about three-and-twenty, with the airs of a suburban soubrette.*]

AVONIA [*Embracing* IMOGEN.] Dear old girl!

IMOGEN Well, Avonia?

AVONIA This is jolly, seeing you again. My eye, what a rig-out! She'll be up directly. [*With a gulp.*] She's taking a last look-round at our room.

IMOGEN You've been crying, 'Vonia.

AVONIA No, I haven't. [*Breaking down.*] If I have I can't help it. Rose and I have chummed together—all this season—and part of last—and—it's a hateful profession! The moment you make a friend——! [*Looking toward the door.*] There! isn't she a dream? I dressed her——

[*She moves away, as* ROSE TRELAWNY *and* ARTHUR GOWER *enter.* ROSE *is nineteen, wears washed muslin, and looks divine. She has much of the extravagance of gesture, over-emphasis in speech, and freedom of manner engendered by the theatre, but is graceful and charming nevertheless.* ARTHUR *is a handsome, boyish young man—"all eyes" for* ROSE.]

ROSE [*Meeting* IMOGEN.] Dear Imogen!

IMOGEN [*Kissing her.*] Rose, dear!

ROSE To think of your journeying from the West to see me make my exit from Brydon Crescent! But you're a good sort; you always were. Do sit down and tell me—oh—! let me introduce Mr. Gower.

Mr. Arthur Gower—Miss Imogen Parrott. *The* Miss Parrott of the Olympic.

ARTHUR [*Reverentially.*] I know. I've seen Miss Parrott as Jupiter, and as—I forget the name—in the new comedy—— [IMOGEN *and* ROSE *sit, below the table.*]

ROSE He forgets everything but the parts *I* play, and the pieces *I* play in—poor child! don't you, Arthur?

ARTHUR [*Standing by* ROSE, *looking down upon her.*] Yes—no. Well, of course I do! How can I help it, Miss Parrott? Miss Parrott won't think the worse of me for that—will you, Miss Parrott?

MRS. TELFER I am going to remove my bonnet. Imogen Parrott——

IMOGEN Thank you, I'll keep my hat on, Mrs. Telfer—take care!

[MRS. TELFER, *in turning to go, encounters* ABLETT, *who is entering with two jugs of beer. Some of the beer is spilt.*]

ABLETT I beg your pardon, ma'am.

MRS. TELFER [*Examining her skirts.*] Ruffian! [*She departs.*]

ROSE [*To* ARTHUR.] Go and talk to the boys. I haven't seen Miss Parrott for ages.

[*In backing away from them,* ARTHUR *comes against* ABLETT.]

ABLETT I beg your pardon, sir.

ARTHUR I beg yours.

ABLETT [*Grasping* ARTHUR's *hand.*] Excuse the freedom, sir, if freedom you regard it as——

ARTHUR Eh——?

ABLETT You 'ave plucked the flower, sir; you 'ave stole our ch'icest blossom.

ARTHUR [*Trying to get away.*] Yes, yes, I know——

ABLETT Cherish it, Mr. Glover——!

ARTHUR I will, I will. Thank you——

[MRS. MOSSOP's *voice is heard calling "Ablett!"* ABLETT *releases* ARTHUR *and goes out.* ARTHUR *joins* COLPOYS *and* TOM.]

ROSE [*To* IMOGEN.] The carriage will be here in half an hour. I've so much to say to you. Imogen, the brilliant hits you've made! how lucky you have been!

IMOGEN *My* luck! what about *yours?*

ROSE Yes, isn't this a wonderful stroke of fortune for me! Fate, Jenny! that's what it is—Fate! Fate ordains that I shall be a well-to-do fashionable lady, instead of a popular but toiling actress. Mother often used to stare into my face, when I was little, and whisper, "Rosie, I wonder what is to be your—fate." Poor mother! I hope she *sees.*

IMOGEN Your Arthur seems nice.

ROSE Oh, he's a dear. Very young, of course—not much more than a year older than me—than I. But he'll grow manly in time, and have mustaches, and whiskers out to here, he says.

IMOGEN How did you——?

ROSE He saw me act Blanche in the *The Peddler of Marseilles,* and fell in love.

IMOGEN Do you prefer Blanche——?

ROSE To Celestine? Oh, yes. You see, I got leave to introduce a song—where Blanche is waiting for Raphael on the bridge. [*Singing, dramatically but in low tones.*] "Ever of thee I'm fondly dreaming——"

IMOGEN I know—— [*They sing together.*]

ROSE AND IMOGEN "Thy gentle voice my spirit can cheer."

ROSE It was singing that song that sealed my destiny, Arthur declares. At any rate, the next thing was he began sending bouquets and coming to the stage-door. Of course, I never spoke to him, never glanced at him. Poor mother brought me up in that way, not to speak to anybody, nor look.

IMOGEN Quite right.

ROSE I do hope she sees.

IMOGEN And then——?

ROSE Then Arthur managed to get acquainted with the Telfers, and Mrs. Telfer presented him to me. Mrs. Telfer has kept an eye on me all through. Not that it was necessary, brought up as I was—but she's a kind old soul.

IMOGEN And now you're going to live with his people for a time, aren't you?

ROSE Yes—on approval.

IMOGEN Ha, ha, ha! you don't mean that!

ROSE Well, in a way—just to reassure them, as they put it. The Gowers have such odd ideas about theatres, and actors and actresses.

IMOGEN Do you think you'll like the arrangement?

ROSE It'll only be for a little while. I fancy they're prepared to take to me, especially Miss Trafalgar Gower——

IMOGEN Trafalgar!

ROSE Sir William's sister; she was born Trafalgar year, and christened after it——

[MRS. MOSSOP *and* ABLETT *enter, carrying trays on which are a pile of plates and various dishes of cold food—a joint, a chicken and a tongue, a ham, a pigeon pie, etc. They proceed to set out the dishes upon the table.*]

IMOGEN [*Cheerfully.*] Well, God bless you, my dear. I'm afraid *I* couldn't give up the stage though, not for all the Arthurs——

ROSE Ah, your mother wasn't an actress.

IMOGEN No.

ROSE Mine was, and I remember her saying to me once, "Rose, if ever you have the chance, get out of it."

IMOGEN The Profession?

ROSE Yes. "Get out of it," mother said; "if ever a good man comes along, and offers to marry you and to take you off the stage, seize the chance—get out of it."

IMOGEN Your mother was never popular, was she?

ROSE Yes, indeed she was, most popular—till she grew oldish and lost her looks.

IMOGEN Oh, *that's* what she meant, then?

ROSE Yes, that's what she meant.

IMOGEN [*Shivering.*] Oh, lor', doesn't it make one feel depressed!

ROSE Poor mother! Well, I hope she sees.

MRS. MOSSOP Now, ladies and gentlemen, everything is prepared, and I do trust to your pleasure and satisfaction.

TELFER Ladies and gentlemen, I beg you to be seated. [*There is a general movement.*] Miss Trelawny will sit 'ere, on my right. On my left, my friend Mr. Gower will sit. Next to Miss Trelawny—who will sit beside Miss Trelawny?

GADD AND COLPOYS   I will.

AVONIA   No, do let me!

[GADD, COLPOYS, *and* AVONIA *gather round* ROSE *and wrangle for the vacant place.*]

ROSE [*Standing by her chair.*]   It must be a gentleman, 'Vonia. Now, if you two boys quarrel——!

GADD   Please don't push me, Colpoys!

COLPOYS   'Pon my soul, Gadd——!

ROSE   I know how to settle it. Tom Wrench——!

TOM [*Coming to her.*]   Yes?

[COLPOYS *and* GADD *move away, arguing.*]

IMOGEN [*Seating herself.*]   Mr. Gadd and Mr. Colpoys shall sit by me, one on each side.

[COLPOYS *sits on* IMOGEN's *right,* GADD *on her left,* AVONIA *sits between* TOM *and* GADD; MRS. MOSSOP *on the right of* COLPOYS. *Amid much chatter, the viands are carved by* MRS. MOSSOP, TELFER, *and* TOM. *Some plates of chicken, etc., are handed round by* ABLETT, *while others are passed about by those at the table.*]

GADD [*Quietly to* IMOGEN, *during a pause in the hubbub.*]   Telfer takes the chair, you observe. Why *he*—more than myself, for instance?

IMOGEN [*To* GADD.]   The Telfers have lent their room——

GADD   Their stuffy room! that's no excuse. I repeat, Telfer has thrust himself into this position.

IMOGEN   He's the oldest man present.

GADD   True. And he begins to age in his acting too. His H's! scarce as pearls!

IMOGEN   Yes, that's shocking. Now, at the Olympic, slip an H and you're damned for ever.

GADD   And he's losing all his teeth. To act with him, it makes the house seem half empty.

[ABLETT *is now going about pouring out the ale. Occasionally he drops his glove, misses it, and recovers it.*]

TELFER [*To* IMOGEN.]   Miss Parrott, my dear, follow the counsel of one who has sat at many a "good man's feast"—have a little 'am.

IMOGEN   Thanks, Mr. Telfer.

[MRS. TELFER *returns.*]

MRS. TELFER   Sitting down to table in my absence! [*To* TELFER.] How is this, James?

TELFER   We are pressed for time, Violet, my love.

ROSE   Very sorry, Mrs. Telfer.

MRS. TELFER [*Taking her place, between* ARTHUR *and* MRS. MOSSOP—*gloomily.*]   A strange proceeding.

ROSE   Rehearsal was over so late. [*To* TELFER.] You didn't get to the last act till a quarter-to-one, did you?

AVONIA [*Taking off her hat and flinging it across the table to* COLPOYS.]   Gus! catch! Put it on the sofa, there's a dear boy. [COLPOYS *perches the hat upon his head, and behaves in a ridiculous, mincing way.* ABLETT *is again convulsed with laughter. Some of the others are amused also, but more moderately.*] Take that off, Gus! Mr. Colpoys, you just take my hat off!

[COLPOYS *rises, imitating the manners of a woman, and deposits the hat on the sofa.*]

ABLETT   Ho, ho, ho! oh, don't Mr. Colpoys! oh, don't, sir!

[COLPOYS *returns to the table.*]

GADD [*Quietly to* IMOGEN.]   It makes me sick to watch Colpoys in private life. He'd stand on his head in the street, if he could get a ragged infant to laugh at him. [*Picking the leg of a fowl furiously.*] What I say is this. Why can't an actor, in private life, be simply a gentleman? [*Loudly and haughtily.*] More tongue here!

ABLETT [*Hurrying to him.*]   Yessir, certainly, sir. [*Again discomposed by some antic on the part of* COLPOYS.] Oh, don't, Mr. Colpoys! [*Going to* TELFER *with* GADD's *plate—speaking while* TELFER *carves a slice of tongue.*] I shan't easily forget this afternoon, Mr. Telfer. [*Exhausted.*] This 'll be something to tell Mrs. Ablett. Ho, ho! oh, dear, oh, dear!

[ABLETT, *averting his face from* COLPOYS, *brings back* GADD's *plate. By an unfortunate chance,* ABLETT's *glove has found its way to the plate and is handed to* GADD *by* ABLETT.]

GADD [*Picking up the glove in disgust.*] Merciful powers! what's this!

ABLETT [*Taking the glove.*] I beg your pardon, sir—my error, entirely.

[*A firm rat-tat-tat at the front door is heard. There is a general exclamation. At the same moment* SARAH, *a diminutive servant in a crinoline, appears in the doorway.*]

SARAH [*Breathlessly.*] The kerridge has just drove up!

[IMOGEN, GADD, COLPOYS, *and* AVONIA *go to the windows, open them, and look out.* MRS. MOSSOP *hurries away, pushing* SARAH *before her.*]

TELFER Dear me, dear me! before a single speech has been made.

AVONIA [*At the window.*] Rose, do look!

IMOGEN [*At the other window.*] Come here, Rose!

ROSE [*Shaking her head.*] Ha, ha! I'm in no hurry; I shall see it often enough. [*Turning to* TOM.] Well, the time has arrived. [*Laying down her knife and fork.*] Oh, I'm so sorry, now.

TOM [*Brusquely.*] Are you? I'm glad.

ROSE Glad! that *is* hateful of you, Tom Wrench!

ARTHUR [*Looking at his watch.*] The carriage is certainly two or three minutes before its time, Mr. Telfer.

TELFER Two or three——! The speeches, my dear sir, the speeches!

[MRS. MOSSOP *returns, panting.*]

MRS. MOSSOP The footman, a nice-looking young man with hazel eyes, says the carriage and pair can wait for a little bit. They must be back by three, to take their lady into the Park——

TELFER [*Rising.*] Ahem! Resume your seats, I beg. Ladies and gentlemen——

AVONIA Wait, wait! we're not ready!

[IMOGEN, GADD, COLPOYS, *and* AVONIA *return to their places.* MRS. MOSSOP *also sits again.* ABLETT *stands by the door.*]

TELFER [*Producing a paper from his breast-pocket.*] Ladies and gentlemen, I devoted some time this morning to the preparation of a list of toasts. I now 'old that list in my hand. The first toast——

[*He pauses, to assume a pair of spectacles.*]

GADD [*To* IMOGEN.] *He* arranges the toast-list! *he!*

IMOGEN [*To* GADD.] Hush!

TELFER The first toast that figures 'ere is, naturally, that of The Queen. [*Laying his hand on* ARTHUR's *shoulder.*] With my young friend's chariot at the door, his horses pawing restlessly and fretfully upon the stones, I am prevented from enlarging, from expatiating, upon the merits of this toast. Suffice it, both Mrs. Telfer and I have had the honor of acting before Her Majesty upon no less than two occasions.

GADD [*To* IMOGEN.] Tsch, tsch, tsch! an old story!

TELFER Ladies and gentlemen, I give you—[*to* COLPOYS]—the malt is with you, Mr. Colpoys.

COLPOYS [*Handing the ale to* TELFER.] Here you are, Telfer.

TELFER [*Filling his glass.*] I give you The Queen, coupling with that toast the name of Miss Violet Sylvester—Mrs. Telfer—formerly, as you are aware, of the Theatre Royal, Drury Lane. Miss Sylvester has so frequently and, if I may say so, so nobly impersonated the various queens of tragedy that I cannot but feel she is a fitting person to acknowledge our expression of loyalty. [*Raising his glass.*] The Queen! And Miss Violet Sylvester!

[*All rise, except* MRS. TELFER, *and drink the toast. After drinking* MRS. MOSSOP *passes her tumbler to* ABLETT.]

ABLETT The Queen! Miss Vi'lent Sylvester!

[*He drinks and returns the glass to* MRS. MOSSOP. *The company being reseated,* MRS. TELFER *rises. Her reception is a polite one.*]

MRS. TELFER [*Heavily.*] Ladies and gentlemen, I have played fourteen or fifteen queens in my time——

TELFER Thirteen, my love, to be exact; I was calculating this morning.

MRS. TELFER Very well, I have played thirteen of 'em. And, as parts, they are not worth a tinker's oath. I thank you for the favor with which you have received me.

[*She sits; the applause is heartier. During the demonstration* SARAH *appears in the doorway, with a kitchen chair.*]

ABLETT [*To* SARAH.] Wot's all this?

SARAH [*To* ABLETT.] Is the speeches on?

ABLETT H'on! yes, and you be h'off!

[*She places the chair against the open door and sits, full of determination. At intervals* ABLETT *vainly represents to her the impropriety of her proceeding.*]

TELFER [*Again rising.*] Ladies and gentlemen. Bumpers, I charge ye! The toast I 'ad next intended to propose was Our Immortal Bard, Shakspere, and I had meant, myself, to 'ave offered a few remarks in response——

GADD [*To* IMOGEN, *bitterly.*] Ha!

TELFER But with our friend's horses champing their bits, I am compelled—nay, forced—to postpone this toast to a later period of the day, and to give you now what we may justly designate the toast of the afternoon. Ladies and gentlemen, we are about to lose, to part with, one of our companions, a young comrade who came amongst us many months ago, who in fact joined the company of the "Wells" last February twelve-month, after a considerable experience in the provinces of this great country.

COLPOYS Hear, hear!

AVONIA [*Tearfully.*] Hear, hear! [*With a sob.*] I detested her at first.

COLPOYS Order!

IMOGEN Be quiet, 'Vonia!

TELFER Her late mother an actress, herself made familiar with the stage from childhood if not from infancy, Miss Rose Trelawny—for I will no longer conceal from you that it is to Miss Trelawny I refer—— [*Loud applause.*] Miss Trelawny is the stuff of which great actresses are made.

ALL Hear, hear!

ABLETT [*Softly.*] 'Ear, 'ear!

TELFER So much for the actress. Now for the young lady—nay, the woman, the gyirl. Rose is a good girl— [*Loud applause, to which* ABLETT *and* SARAH *contribute largely.* AVONIA *rises and impulsively embraces* ROSE. *She is recalled to her seat by a general remonstrance.*] A good girl——

MRS. TELFER [*Clutching a knife.*] Yes, and I should like to hear anybody, man or woman——!

TELFER She is a good girl, and will be long remembered by us as much for her private virtues as for the commanding authority of her genius. [*More applause, during which there is a sharp altercation between* ABLETT *and* SARAH.] And now, what has happened to "the expectancy and Rose of the fair state"?

IMOGEN Good, Telfer! good!

GADD [*To* IMOGEN.] Tsch, tsch! forced! forced!

TELFER I will tell you—[*impressively*]—a man has crossed her path.

ABLETT [*In a low voice.*] Shame!

MRS. MOSSOP [*Turning to him.*] Mr. Ablett!

TELFER A man—ah, but also a gentleman. [*Applause.*] A gentleman of probity, a gentleman of honor, and a gentleman of wealth and station. That gentleman, with the modesty of youth,—for I may tell you at once that 'e is not an old man,—comes to us and asks us to give him this gyirl to wife. And, friends, we have done so. A few preliminaries 'ave, I believe, still to be concluded between Mr. Gower and his family, and then the bond will be signed, the compact entered upon, the mutual

---

trust accepted. Riches this youthful pair will possess—but what is gold? May they be rich in each other's society, in each other's love! May they—I can wish them no greater joy—be as happy in their married life as my—my—as Miss Sylvester and I 'ave been in ours! [*Raising his glass.*] Miss Rose Trelawny—Mr. Arthur Gower! [*The toast is drunk by the company, upstanding. Three cheers are called for by* COLPOYS, *and given. Those who have risen then sit.*] Miss Trelawny.

ROSE [*Weeping.*] No, no, Mr. Telfer.

MRS. TELFER [*To* TELFER, *softly.*] Let her be for a minute, James.

TELFER Mr. Gower.

[ARTHUR *rises and is well received.*]

ARTHUR Ladies and gentlemen, I—I would I were endowed with Mr. Telfer's flow of—of—of splendid eloquence. But I am no orator, no speaker, and therefore cannot tell you how highly—how deeply I appreciate the—the compliment——

ABLETT You deserve it, Mr. Glover!

MRS. MOSSOP Hush!

ARTHUR All I can say is that I regard Miss Trelawny in the light of a—a solemn charge, and I—I trust that, if ever I have the pleasure of—of meeting any of you again, I shall be able to render a good—a—a—satisfactory—satisfactory——

TOM [*In an audible whisper.*] Account.

ARTHUR Account of the way—of the way—in which I—in which—— [*Loud applause.*] Before I bring these observations to a conclusion, let me assure you that it has been a great privilege to me to meet—to have been thrown with—a band of artists—whose talents—whose striking talents—whose talents——

TOM [*Kindly, behind his hand.*] Sit down.

ARTHUR [*Helplessly.*] Whose talents not only interest and instruct the—the more refined residents of this district, but whose talents——

IMOGEN [*Quietly to* COLPOYS.] Get him to sit down.

ARTHUR The fame of whose talents, I should say——

COLPOYS [*Quietly to* MRS. MOSSOP.] He's to sit down. Tell Mother Telfer.

ARTHUR The fame of whose talents has spread to—to regions——

MRS. MOSSOP [*Quietly to* MRS. TELFER.] They say he's to sit down.

ARTHUR To—to quarters of the town—to quarters——

MRS. TELFER [*To* ARTHUR.] Sit down!

ARTHUR Eh?

MRS. TELFER You finished long ago. Sit down.

ARTHUR Thank you. I'm exceedingly sorry. Great Heavens, how wretchedly I've done it!

[*He sits, burying his head in his hands. More applause.*]

TELFER Rose, my child.

[ROSE *starts to her feet. The rest rise with her, and cheer again, and wave handkerchiefs. She goes from one to the other, round the table, embracing and kissing and crying over them all excitedly.* SARAH *is kissed, but upon* ABLETT *is bestowed only a handshake, to his evident dissatisfaction.* IMOGEN *runs to the piano and strikes up the air of "Ever of Thee." When* ROSE *gets back to the place she mounts her chair, with the aid of* TOM *and* TELFER, *and faces them with flashing eyes. They pull the flowers out of the vases and throw them at her.*]

ROSE Mr. Telfer, Mrs. Telfer! My friends! Boys! Ladies and gentlemen! No, don't stop, Jenny! go on! [*Singing, her arms stretched out to them.*] "Ever of thee I'm fondly dreaming, Thy gentle voice——" You remember! the song I sang in *The Peddler of Marseilles*—which made Arthur fall in love with me! Well, I know I shall dream of *you*, of all of you, very often, as the song says. Don't believe [*wiping away her tears*], oh, don't believe that, because I shall have married a swell, you and the old "Wells"—the dear old "Wells"!—— [*Cheers.*]

ROSE You and the old "Wells" will have become nothing to me! No, many and many a night you will see me in the house, looking down at you from the Circle—me and my husband——

ARTHUR   Yes, yes, certainly!

ROSE   And if you send for me I'll come behind the curtain to you, and sit with you and talk of bygone times, these times that end to-day. And shall I tell you the moments which will be the happiest to me in my life, however happy I may be with Arthur? Why, whenever I find that I am recognized by people, and pointed out—people in the pit of a theatre, in the street, no matter where; and when I can fancy they're saying to each other, "Look! that was Miss Trelawny! you remember—Trelawny! Trelawny of the 'Wells!'"——

[*They cry "Trelawny!" and "Trelawny of the 'Wells!'" and again "Trelawny!" wildly. Then there is the sound of a sharp rat-tat at the front door.* IMOGEN *leaves the piano and looks out of the window.*]

IMOGEN [*To somebody below.*]   What is it?

A VOICE   Miss Trelawny, ma'am. We can't wait.

ROSE [*Weakly.*]   Oh, help me down——

[*They assist her, and gather round her.*]

Act Two

The scene represents a spacious drawing-room in a house in Cavendish Square. The walls are somber in tone, the ceiling dingy, the hangings, though rich, are faded, and altogether the appearance of the room is solemn, formal, and depressing. On the right are folding-doors admitting to a further drawing-room. Beyond these is a single door. The wall on the left is mainly occupied by three sash-windows. The wall facing the spectators is divided by two pilasters into three panels. On the center panel is a large mirror, reflecting the fireplace; on the right hangs a large oil painting—a portrait of Sir William Gower in his ju-dicial wig and robes. On the left hangs a companion picture—a portrait of Miss Gower. In the corners of the room there are marble columns supporting classical busts, and between the doors stands another marble column, upon which is an oil lamp. Against the lower window there are two chairs and a card-table. Behind a further table supporting a lamp stands a three-fold screen.

The lamps are lighted, but the curtains are not drawn, and outside the windows it is twilight.

[SIR WILLIAM GOWER *is seated, near a table, asleep, with a newspaper over his head, concealing his face.* MISS TRAFALGAR GOWER *is sitting at the further end of a couch, also asleep, and with a newspaper over her head. At the lower end of this couch sits* MRS. DE FŒNIX—CLARA—*a young lady of nineteen, with a "married" air. She is engaged upon some crochet work. On the other side of the room, near a table,* ROSE *is seated, wearing the look of a boredom which has reached the stony stage. On another couch* ARTHUR *sits, gazing at his boots, his hands in his pockets. On the right of this couch stands* CAPTAIN DE FŒNIX, *leaning against the wall, his mouth open, his head thrown back, and his eyes closed.* DE FŒNIX *is a young man of seven-and-twenty—an example of the heavily-whiskered "swell" of the period. Everybody is in dinner-dress. After a moment or two* ARTHUR *rises and tiptoes down to* ROSE. CLARA *raises a warning finger and says "Hush!" He nods to her, in assent.*]

ARTHUR [*On* ROSE'S *left—in a whisper.*] Quiet, isn't it?

ROSE [*To him, in a whisper.*]   Quiet! Arthur——! [*Clutching his arm.*] Oh, this dreadful half-hour after dinner, every, *every* evening!

ARTHUR [*Creeping across to the right of the table and sitting there.*]   Grandfather and Aunt Trafalgar must wake up soon. They're longer than usual to-night.

ROSE [*To him, across the table.*] Your sister Clara, over there, and Captain de Fœnix—when they were courting, did they have to go through this?

ARTHUR Yes.

ROSE And now that they are married, they still endure it!

ARTHUR Yes.

ROSE And we, when *we* are married, Arthur, shall *we*——?

ARTHUR Yes. I suppose so.

ROSE [*Passing her hand across her brow.*] Phe—ew!

[DE FŒNIX, *fast asleep, is now swaying, and in danger of toppling over.* CLARA *grasps the situation and rises.*]

CLARA [*In a guttural whisper.*] Ah, Frederick! no, no, no!

ROSE AND ARTHUR [*Turning in their chairs.*] Eh—what——? ah—h—h—h!

[*As* CLARA *reaches her husband, he lurches forward into her arms.*]

DE FŒNIX [*His eyes bolting.*] Oh! who——!

CLARA Frederick dear, wake!

DE FŒNIX [*Dazed.*] How did this occur?

CLARA You were tottering, and I caught you.

DE FŒNIX [*Collecting his senses.*] I we-member. I placed myself in an upwight position, dearwest, to pwevent myself dozing.

CLARA [*Sinking on to the couch.*] How you alarmed me!

[*Seeing that* ROSE *is laughing,* DE FŒNIX *comes down to her.*]

DE FŒNIX [*In a low voice.*] Might have been a very serwious accident, Miss Trelawny.

ROSE [*Seating herself on the footstool.*] Never mind! [*Pointing to the chair she has vacated.*] Sit down and talk. [*He glances at the old people and shakes his head.*] Oh, do, do, do! do sit down, and let us all have a jolly whisper. [*He sits.*] Thank you, Captain Fred. Go on! tell me something—anything; something about the military——

DE FŒNIX [*Again looking at the old people, then wagging his finger at* ROSE.] I know; you want to get me into a wow. [*Settling himself into his chair.*] Howwid girl!

ROSE [*Despairingly.*] Oh—h—h!

[*There is a brief pause, and then the sound of a street-organ, playing in the distance, is heard. The air is "Ever of Thee."*]

ROSE Hark! [*Excitedly.*] Hark!

CLARA, ARTHUR, AND DE FŒNIX Hush!

ROSE [*Heedlessly.*] The song I sang in *The Peddler—The Peddler of Marseilles!* the song that used to make you cry, Arthur——! [*They attempt vainly to hush her down, but she continues dramatically, in hoarse whispers.*] And then Raphael enters—comes on to the bridge. The music continues, softly. "Raphael, why have you kept me waiting? Man, do you wish to break my heart—[*thumping her breast*] a woman's hear—r—rt, Raphael?"

[SIR WILLIAM *and* MISS GOWER *suddenly whip off their newspapers and sit erect.* SIR WILLIAM *is a grim, bullet-headed old gentleman of about seventy;* MISS GOWER *a spare, prim lady, of gentle manners, verging upon sixty. They stare at each other for a moment, silently.*]

SIR WILLIAM What a hideous riot, Trafalgar!

MISS GOWER Rose, dear, I hope I have been mistaken—but through my sleep I fancied I could hear you shrieking at the top of your voice.

[SIR WILLIAM *gets on to his feet; all rise, except* ROSE, *who remains seated sullenly.*]

SIR WILLIAM Trafalgar, it is becoming impossible for you and me to obtain repose. [*Turning his head sharply.*] Ha! is not that a street-organ? [*To* MISS GOWER.] An organ?

MISS GOWER Undoubtedly. An organ in the Square, at this hour of the evening—singularly out of place!

SIR WILLIAM [*Looking round.*] Well, well, well, does no one stir?

ROSE [*Under her breath.*] Oh, don't stop it!

[CLARA *goes out quickly. With a great show of activity* ARTHUR *and* DE FŒNIX *hurry across the room and, when there, do nothing.*]

SIR WILLIAM [*Coming upon* ROSE *and peering down at her.*] What are ye upon the floor for, my dear? Have we no cheers? [*To* MISS GOWER—*producing his snuff-box.*] Do we lack cheers here, Trafalgar?

MISS GOWER [*Going to* ROSE.] My dear Rose! [*Raising her.*] Come, come, come, this is quite out of place! Young ladies do not crouch and huddle upon the ground —do they, William?

SIR WILLIAM [*Taking snuff.*] A moment ago I should have hazarded the opinion that they do not. [*Chuckling unpleasantly.*] He, he, he!

[CLARA *returns. The organ music ceases abruptly.*]

CLARA [*Coming to* SIR WILLIAM.] Charles was just running out to stop the organ when I reached the hall, grandpa.

SIR WILLIAM Ye'd surely no intention, Clara, of venturing, yourself, into the public street—the open Square——?

CLARA [*Faintly.*] I meant only to wave at the man from the door——

MISS GOWER Oh, Clara, that would hardly have been in place!

SIR WILLIAM [*Raising his hands.*] In mercy's name, Trafalgar, what *is* befalling my household?

MISS GOWER [*Bursting into tears.*] Oh, William——!

[ROSE *and* CLARA *creep away and join the others.* MISS GOWER *totters to* SIR WILLIAM *and drops her head upon his breast.*]

SIR WILLIAM Tut, tut, tut, tut!

MISS GOWER [*Between her sobs.*] I—I—I—I know what is in your mind.

SIR WILLIAM [*Drawing a long breath.*] Ah—h—h—h!

MISS GOWER Oh, my dear brother, be patient!

SIR WILLIAM Patient!

MISS GOWER Forgive me; I should have said hopeful. Be hopeful that I shall yet succeed in ameliorating the disturbing conditions which are affecting us so cruelly.

SIR WILLIAM Ye never will, Trafalgar; *I've* tried.

MISS GOWER Oh, do not despond already! I feel sure there are good ingredients in Rose's character. [*Clinging to him.*] In time, William, we shall shape her to be a fitting wife for our rash and unfortunate Arthur—— [*He shakes his head.*] In time, William, in time!

SIR WILLIAM [*Soothing her.*] Well, well, well! there, there, there! At least, my dear sister, I am perfectly aweer that I possess in you the woman above all others whose example should compel such a transformation.

MISS GOWER [*Throwing her arms about his neck.*] Oh, brother, what a compliment——!

SIR WILLIAM Tut, tut, tut! And now, before Charles sets the card-table, don't you think we had better—eh, Trafalgar?

MISS GOWER Yes, yes—our disagreeable duty; let us discharge it. [SIR WILLIAM *takes snuff.*] Rose, dear, be seated. [*To everybody.*] The Vice Chancellor has something to say to us. Let us all be seated.

[*There is consternation among the young people. All sit.*]

SIR WILLIAM [*Peering about him.*] Are ye seated?

EVERYBODY Yes.

SIR WILLIAM What I desire to say is this. When Miss Trelawny took up her residence here, it was thought proper, in the peculiar circumstances of the case, that you, Arthur—[*pointing a finger at* ARTHUR] you——

ARTHUR Yes, sir.

SIR WILLIAM That you should remove yourself to the establishment of your sister Clara and her husband in Holles Street, round the corner——

ARTHUR Yes, sir.

CLARA   Yes, grandpa.

DE FŒNIX   Certainly, Sir William.

SIR WILLIAM   Taking your food in this house, and spending other certain hours here, under the surveillance of your great-aunt Trafalgar.

MISS GOWER   Yes, William.

SIR WILLIAM   This was considered to be a decorous, and, toward Miss Trelawny, a highly respectful, course to pursue.

ARTHUR   Yes, sir.

MISS GOWER   Any other course would have been out of place.

SIR WILLIAM   And yet—[*again extending a finger at* ARTHUR] what is this that is reported to me?

ARTHUR   I don't know, sir.

SIR WILLIAM   I hear that ye have on several occasions, at night, after having quitted this house with Captain and Mrs. De Fœnix, been seen on the other side of the way, your back against the railings, gazing up at Miss Trelawny's window; and that you have remained in that position for a considerable space of time. Is this true, sir?

ROSE   [*Boldly.*]   Yes, Sir William.

SIR WILLIAM   I venture to put a question to my grandson, Miss Trelawny.

ARTHUR   Yes, sir, it is quite true.

SIR WILLIAM   Then, sir, let me acqueent you that these are not the manners, nor the practices, of a gentleman.

ARTHUR   No, sir?

SIR WILLIAM   No, sir, they are the manners, and the practices, of a troubadour.

MISS GOWER   A troubadour in Cavendish Square! quite out of place!

ARTHUR   I—I'm very sorry, sir; I—I never looked at it in that light.

SIR WILLIAM   [*Snuffing.*]   Ah—h—h—h! ho! pi—i—i—sh!

ARTHUR   But at the same time, sir, I dare say—of course I don't speak from precise knowledge—but I dare say there were a good many—a good many——

SIR WILLIAM   Good many—what sir?

ARTHUR   A good many very respectable troubadours, sir——

ROSE   [*Starting to her feet, heroically and defiantly.*]   And what I wish to say, Sir William, is this. I wish to avow, to declare before the world, that Arthur and I have had many lengthy interviews while he has been stationed against those railings over there; I murmuring to him softly from my bedroom window, he responding in tremulous whispers——

SIR WILLIAM   [*Struggling to his feet.*]   You—you tell me such things——! [*All rise.*]

MISS GOWER   The Square, in which we have resided for years——! Our neighbors——!

SIR WILLIAM   [*Shaking a trembling hand at* ARTHUR.]   The—the character of my house——!

ARTHUR   Again I am extremely sorry, sir—but these are the only confidential conversations Rose and I now enjoy.

SIR WILLIAM   [*Turning upon* CLARA *and* DE FŒNIX.]   And you, Captain de Fœnix—an officer and a gentleman! and you, Clara! this could scarcely have been without your cognizance, without, perhaps, your approval——!

[CHARLES, *in plush and powder and wearing luxuriant whiskers, enters, carrying two branch candlesticks with lighted candles.*]

CHARLES   The cawd-table, Sir William?

MISS GOWER   [*Agitatedly.*]   Yes, yes, by all means, Charles; the card-table, as usual. [*To* SIR WILLIAM.]   A rubber will comfort you, soothe you——

[CHARLES *carries the candlesticks to the card-table,* SIR WILLIAM *and* MISS GOWER *seat themselves upon a couch, she with her arm through his affectionately.* CLARA *and* DE FŒNIX *get behind the screen; their scared faces are seen occasionally over the top of it.* CHARLES *brings the card-table, opens it and arranges it, placing four chairs, which he collects from different parts of the room, round the table.* ROSE *and* ARTHUR *talk in rapid undertones.*]

ROSE   Infamous! infamous!

ARTHUR   Be calm, Rose, dear, be calm!

ROSE Tyrannical! diabolical! I cannot endure it.

[She throws herself into a chair. He stands behind her, apprehensively, endeavoring to calm her.]

ARTHUR [Over her shoulder.] They mean well, dearest——

ROSE [Hysterically.] Well! ha, ha, ha!

ARTHUR But they are rather old-fashioned people——

ROSE Old-fashioned! they belong to the time when men and women were put to the torture. I am being tortured—mentally tortured——

ARTHUR They have not many more years in this world——

ROSE Nor I, at this rate, many more months. They are killing me—like Agnes in *The Specter of St. Ives*. She expires, in the fourth act, as I shall die in Cavendish Square, painfully, of no recognized disorder——

ARTHUR And anything we can do to make them happy——

ROSE To make the Vice Chancellor happy! I won't try! I will not! he's a fiend, a vampire——!

ARTHUR Oh, hush!

ROSE [Snatching up SIR WILLIAM's snuff-box, which he has left upon the table.] His snuff-box! I wish I could poison his snuff, as Lucrezia Borgia would have done. *She* would have removed him within two hours of my arrival—I mean, her arrival. [Opening the snuff-box and mimicking SIR WILLIAM.] And here he sits and lectures me, and dictates to me! to Miss Trelawny! "I venture to put a question to my grandson, Miss Trelawny!" Ha, ha! [Taking a pinch of snuff, thoughtlessly but vigorously.] "Yah—h—h—h! pish! Have we no cheers? do we lack cheers here, Trafalgar?" [Suddenly.] Oh——!

ARTHUR What have you done?

ROSE [In suspense, replacing the snuff-box.] The snuff——!

ARTHUR Rose, dear!

ROSE [Putting her handkerchief to her nose, and rising.] Ah——!

[CHARLES, having prepared the card-table, and arranged the candlesticks upon it, has withdrawn. MISS GOWER and SIR WILLIAM now rise.]

MISS GOWER The table is prepared, William. Arthur, I assume you would prefer to sit and contemplate Rose——?

ARTHUR Thank you, aunt.

[ROSE sneezes violently, and is led away, helplessly, by ARTHUR.]

MISS GOWER [To ROSE.] Oh, my dear child! [Looking round.] Where are Frederick and Clara?

CLARA and DE FŒNIX [Appearing from behind the screen, shamefacedly.] Here.

[The intending players cut the pack and seat themselves. SIR WILLIAM sits facing CAPTAIN DE FŒNIX, MISS GOWER on the right of the table, and CLARA on the left.]

ARTHUR [While this is going on, to ROSE.] Are you in pain, dearest? Rose!

ROSE Agony!

ARTHUR Pinch your upper lip——

[She sneezes twice, loudly, and sinks back upon the couch.]

SIR WILLIAM [Testily.] Sssh! sssh! sssh! this is to be whist, I hope.

MISS GOWER Rose, Rose! young ladies do not sneeze quite so continuously. [DE FŒNIX is dealing.]

SIR WILLIAM [With gusto.] I will thank you, Captain de Fœnix, to exercise your intelligence this evening to its furthest limit.

DE FŒNIX I'll twy, sir.

SIR WILLIAM [Laughing unpleasantly.] He, he, he! last night, sir——

CLARA Poor Frederick had toothache last night, grandpa.

SIR WILLIAM [Tartly.] Whist is whist, Clara, and toothache is toothache. We will endeavor to keep the two things distinct, if you please. He, he!

MISS GOWER Your interruption was hardly in place, Clara, dear,—ah!

DE FŒNIX Hey! what——?

MISS GOWER A misdeal.

CLARA [*Faintly.*] Oh, Frederick!

SIR WILLIAM [*Partly rising.*] Captain de Fœnix!

DE FŒNIX I—I'm fwightfully gwieved, sir——

[*The cards are re-dealt by* MISS GOWER. ROSE *now gives way to a violent paroxysm of sneezing.* SIR WILLIAM *rises.*]

MISS GOWER William——!
              [*The players rise.*]

SIR WILLIAM [*To the players.*] Is this whist, may I ask?   [*They sit.*]

SIR WILLIAM [*Standing.*] Miss Trelawny——

ROSE [*Weakly.*] I—I think I had better—what d'ye call it?—withdraw for a few moments.

SIR WILLIAM [*Sitting again.*] Do so.

[ROSE *disappears.* ARTHUR *is leaving the room with her.*]

MISS GOWER [*Sharply.*] Arthur! where are you going?

ARTHUR [*Returning promptly.*] I beg your pardon, aunt.

MISS GOWER Really, Arthur——!

SIR WILLIAM [*Rapping upon the table.*] Tsch, tsch, tsch!

MISS GOWER Forgive me, William.
              [*They play.*]

SIR WILLIAM [*Intent upon his cards.*] My snuff-box, Arthur; be so obleeging as to search for it.

ARTHUR [*Brightly.*] I'll bring it to you, sir. It is on the——

SIR WILLIAM Keep your voice down, sir. We are playing—[*emphatically throwing down a card, as fourth player*] whist. Mine.

MISS GOWER [*Picking up the trick.*] No, William.

SIR WILLIAM [*Glaring.*] No!

MISS GOWER Clara played a trump.

DE FŒNIX Yes, sir, Clara played a trump—the seven——

SIR WILLIAM I will not trouble you, Captain de Fœnix, to echo Miss Gower's information.

DE FŒNIX Vevy sowwy, sir.

MISS GOWER [*Gently.*] It *was* a *little* out of place, Frederick.

SIR WILLIAM Sssh! whist. [ARTHUR *is now on* SIR WILLIAM's *right, with the snuff-box.*] Eh? what? [*Taking the snuff-box from* ARTHUR.] Oh, thank ye. Much obleeged, much obleeged.

[ARTHUR *walks away and picks up a book.* SIR WILLIAM *turns in his chair, watching* ARTHUR.]

MISS GOWER You to play, William. [*A pause.*] William, dear——?

[*She also turns, following the direction of his gaze. Laying down his cards,* SIR WILLIAM *leaves the card-table and goes over to* ARTHUR *slowly. Those at the card-table look on apprehensively.*]

SIR WILLIAM [*In a queer voice.*] Arthur.

ARTHUR [*Shutting his book.*] Excuse me, grandfather.

SIR WILLIAM Ye—ye're a troublesome young man, Arthur.

ARTHUR I—I don't mean to be one, sir.

SIR WILLIAM As your poor father was, before ye. And if you are fool enough to marry, and to beget children, doubtless your son will follow the same course. [*Taking snuff.*] Y—y—yes, but I shall be dead 'n' gone by that time, it's likely. Ah—h—h—h! pi—i—i—sh! I shall be sitting in the Court Above by that time—— [*From the adjoining room comes the sound of* ROSE's *voice singing "Ever of Thee" to the piano. There is great consternation at the card-table.* ARTHUR *is moving towards the folding-doors,* SIR WILLIAM *detains him.*] No, no, let her go on, I beg. Let her continue. [*Returning to the card-table, with deadly calmness.*] We will suspend our game while this young lady performs her operas.

MISS GOWER [*Rising and taking his arm.*] William——!

SIR WILLIAM [*In the same tone.*] I fear this is no longer a comfortable home for ye, Trafalgar; no longer the home for a gentlewoman. I apprehend that in these days my house approaches somewhat closely to a Pandemonium. [*Suddenly taking up the cards, in a fury, and flinging them across the room.*] And this is whist—whist——!

[CLARA *and* DE FŒNIX *rise and stand together.* ARTHUR *pushes open the upper part of the folding-doors.*]

ARTHUR   Rose! stop! Rose!

[*The song ceases and* ROSE *appears.*]

ROSE [*At the folding-doors.*]   Did anyone call?

ARTHUR   You have upset my grandfather.

MISS GOWER   Miss Trelawny, how—how dare you do anything so—so out of place?

ROSE   There's a piano in there, Miss Gower.

MISS GOWER   You are acquainted with the rule of this household—no music when the Vice Chancellor is within doors.

ROSE   But there are so many rules. One of them is that you may not sneeze.

MISS GOWER   Ha! you must never answer——

ROSE   No, that's another rule.

MISS GOWER   Oh, for shame!

ARTHUR   You see, aunt, Rose is young, and —and—you make no allowance for her, give her no chance——

MISS GOWER   Great Heaven! what is this you are charging me with?

ARTHUR   I don't think the "rules" of this house are fair to Rose! oh, I must say it— they are horribly unfair!

MISS GOWER [*Clinging to* SIR WILLIAM.] Brother!

SIR WILLIAM   Trafalgar! [*Putting her aside and advancing to* ARTHUR.] Oh, indeed, sir! and so you deliberately accuse your great-aunt of acting towards ye and Miss Trelawny *malâ fide*——

ARTHUR   Grandfather, what I intended to——

SIR WILLIAM   I will afford ye the opportunity of explaining what ye intended to convey, downstairs, at once, in the library.

[*A general shudder.*] Obleege me by following me, sir. [*To* CLARA *and* DE FŒNIX.] Captain de Fœnix, I see no prospect of any further social relaxation this evening. You and Clara will do me the favor of attending in the hall, in readiness to take this young man back to Holles Street. [*Giving his arm to* MISS GOWER.] My dear sister—— [*To* ARTHUR.] Now, sir.

[SIR WILLIAM *and* MISS GOWER *go out.* ARTHUR *comes to* ROSE *and kisses her.*]

ARTHUR   Good-night, dearest. Oh, goodnight! Oh, Rose——!

SIR WILLIAM [*Outside the door.*]   Mr. Arthur Gower!

ARTHUR   I am coming, sir——
       [*He goes out quickly.*]

DE FŒNIX [*Approaching* ROSE *and taking her hand sympathetically.*]   Haw——! I—weally—haw!——

ROSE   Yes, I know what you would say. Thank you, Captain Fred.

CLARA [*Embracing* ROSE.]   Never mind! we will continue to let Arthur out at night as usual. I am a married woman! [*joining* DE FŒNIX], and a married woman will turn, if you tread upon her often enough——!
       [DE FŒNIX *and* CLARA *depart.*]

ROSE [*Pacing the room, shaking her hands in the air desperately.*]   Oh—h—h! ah— h—h!

[*The upper part of the folding-doors opens, and* CHARLES *appears.*]

CHARLES [*Mysteriously.*]   Miss Rose——

ROSE   What——?

CHARLES [*Advancing.*]   I see Sir William h'and the rest descend the stairs. I 'ave been awaitin' the chawnce of 'andin' you this, Miss Rose.

[*He produces a dirty scrap of paper, wet and limp, with writing upon it, and gives it to her.*]

ROSE [*Handling it daintily.*]   Oh, it's damp!——

CHARLES Yes, miss; a little gentle shower 'ave been takin' place h'outside—'eat spots, cook says.

ROSE [*Reading.*] Ah! from some of my friends.

CHARLES [*Behind his hand.*] Perfesshunnal, Miss Rose?

ROSE [*Intent upon the note.*] Yes— yes——

CHARLES I was reprimandin' the organ, miss, when I observed them lollin' against the square railin's examinin' h'our premises, and they wentured for to beckon me. An egstremely h'affable party, miss. [*Hiding his face.*] Ho! one of them caused me to laff!

ROSE [*Excitedly.*] They want to speak to me—[*referring to the note*] to impart something to me of an important nature. Oh, Charles, I know not what to do!

CHARLES [*Languishingly.*] Whatever friends may loll against them railin's h'opposite, Miss Rose, you 'ave one true friend in this 'ouse—Chawles Gibbons——

ROSE Thank you, Charles. Mr. Briggs, the butler, is sleeping out to-night, isn't he?

CHARLES Yes, miss, he 'ave leave to sleep at his sister's. I 'appen to know he 'ave gone to Cremorne.

ROSE Then, when Sir William and Miss Gower have retired, do you think you could let me go forth; and wait at the front door while I run across and grant my friends a hurried interview?

CHARLES Suttingly, miss.

ROSE If it reached the ears of Sir William, or Miss Gower, you would lose your place, Charles!

CHARLES [*Haughtily.*] I'm aweer, miss; but Sir William was egstremely rood to me dooring dinner, over that mis'ap to the ontray—— [*A bell rings violently.*] S'william!

[*He goes out. The rain is heard pattering against the window panes.* ROSE *goes from one window to another, looking out. It is now almost black outside the windows.*]

ROSE [*Discovering her friends.*] Ah! yes, yes! ah—h—h—h! [*She snatches an antimacassar from a chair and jumping on to the couch, waves it frantically to those outside.*] The dears! the darlings! the faithful creatures——! [*Listening.*] Oh——!

[*She descends, in a hurry, and flings the antimacassar under the couch, as* MISS GOWER *enters. At the same moment there is a vivid flash of lightning.*]

MISS GOWER [*Startled.*] Oh, how dreadful! [*To* ROSE, *frigidly.*] The Vice Chancellor has *felt* the few words he has addressed to Arthur, and has retired for the night. [*There is a roll of thunder.* ROSE *alarmed,* MISS GOWER *clings to a chair.*] Mercy on us! Go to bed, child, directly. We will all go to our beds, hoping to awake to-morrow in a meeker and more submissive spirit. [*Kissing* ROSE *upon the brow.*] Good-night. [*Another flash of lightning.*] Oh——! Don't omit to say your prayers, Rose—and in a simple manner. I always fear that, from your peculiar training, you may declaim them. That is so out of place—oh——!

[*Another roll of thunder.* ROSE *goes across the room, meeting* CHARLES, *who enters carrying a lantern. They exchange significant glances, and she disappears.*]

CHARLES [*Coming to* MISS GOWER.] I am now at liberty to accompany you round the 'ouse, ma'am——

[*A flash of lightning.*]

MISS GOWER Ah——! [*Her hand to her heart.*] Thank you, Charles—but to-night I must ask you to see that everything is secure, alone. This storm—so very seasonable; but, from girlhood, I could never ——[*A roll of thunder.*] Oh, good-night!

[*She flutters away. The rain beats still more violently upon the window panes.*]

CHARLES [*Glancing at the window.*] Ph—e—e—w! Great 'evans!

[*He is dropping the curtains at the window when* ROSE *appears at the folding-doors.*]

ROSE [*In a whisper.*] Charles!

CHARLES Miss?

ROSE [*Coming into the room, distractedly.*] Miss Gower has gone to bed.

CHARLES Yes, miss—oh——!

[*A flash of lightning.*]

ROSE Oh! my friends! my poor friends!

CHARLES H'and Mr. Briggs at Cremorne! Reelly, I should 'ardly advise you to wenture h'out, miss——

ROSE Out! no! Oh, but get them in!

CHARLES In, Miss Rose! indoors!

ROSE Under cover—— [*A roll of thunder.*] Oh! [*Wringing her hands.*] They are my friends! is it a rule that I am never to see a friend, that I mayn't even give a friend shelter in a violent storm? [*To* CHARLES.] Are you the only one up?

CHARLES I b'lieve so, miss. Any'ow the wimming-servants is quite h'under my control.

ROSE Then tell my friends to be deathly quiet, and to creep—to tip-toe—— [*The rain strikes the window again. She picks up the lantern which* CHARLES *has deposited upon the floor, and gives it to him.*] Make haste! I'll draw the curtains —— [*He hurries out. She goes from window to window, dropping the curtains, talking to herself excitedly as she does so.*] My friends! my own friends! ah! I'm not to sneeze in this house! nor to sing! or breathe, next! wretches! oh, my! wretches! [*Blowing out the candles and removing the candlesticks to the table, singing, under her breath, wildly.*] "Ever of thee I'm fondly dreaming——" [*Mimicking* SIR WILLIAM *again.*] "What are ye upon the floor for, my dear? Have we no cheers? do we lack cheers here, Trafalgar——?"

[CHARLES *returns.*]

CHARLES [*To those who follow him.*] Hush! [*To* ROSE.] I discovered 'em clustered in the doorway——

[*There is a final peal of thunder as* AVONIA, GADD, COLPOYS, *and* TOM WRENCH

enter, somewhat diffidently. They are apparently soaked to their skins, and are altogether in a deplorable condition. AVONIA *alone has an umbrella, which she allows to drip upon the carpet, but her dress and petticoats are bedraggled, her finery limp, her hair lank and loose.*]

ROSE 'Vonia!

AVONIA [*Coming to her, and embracing her fervently.*] Oh, ducky, ducky, ducky! oh, but what a storm!

ROSE Hush! how wet you are! [*Shaking hands with* GADD] Ferdinand—[*crossing to* COLPOYS *and shaking hands with him*] Augustus—[*shaking hands with* TOM] Tom Wrench——

AVONIA [*To* CHARLES.] Be so kind as to put my umbrella on the landing, will you? Oh, thank you very much, I'm sure.

[CHARLES *withdraws with the umbrella.* GADD *and* COLPOYS *shake the rain from their hats on to the carpet and furniture.*]

TOM [*Quietly, to* ROSE.] It's a shame to come down on you in this way. But they would do it, and I thought I'd better stick to 'em.

GADD [*Who is a little flushed and unsteady.*] Ha! I shall remember this accursed evening.

AVONIA Oh, Ferdy——!

ROSE Hush! you must be quiet. Everybody has gone to bed, and I—I'm not sure I'm allowed to receive visitors——

AVONIA Oh!

GADD Then we are intruders?

ROSE I mean, such late visitors.

[COLPOYS *has taken off his coat, and is shaking it vigorously.*]

AVONIA Stop it, Augustus! ain't I wet enough? [*To* ROSE.] Yes, it is latish, but I so wanted to inform you—here—[*bringing* GADD *forward*] allow me to introduce —my husband.

ROSE Oh! no!

AVONIA [*Laughing merrily.*] Yes, ha, ha, ha!

ROSE Sssh, sssh, sssh!

AVONIA I forgot. [*To* GADD.] Oh, darling Ferdy, you're positively soaked! [*To* ROSE.] Do let him take his coat off, like Gussy——

GADD [*Jealously.*] 'Vonia, not so much of the Gussy!

AVONIA There you are, flying out again! as if Mr. Colpoys wasn't an old friend!

GADD Old friend or no old friend——

ROSE [*Diplomatically.*] Certainly, take your coat off, Ferdinand.

[GADD *joins* COLPOYS; *they spread out their coats upon the couch.*]

ROSE [*Feeling* TOM's *coat sleeve.*] And you?

TOM [*After glancing at the others—quietly.*] No, thank you.

AVONIA [*Sitting.*] Yes, dearie, Ferdy and I were married yesterday.

ROSE [*Sitting.*] Yesterday!

AVONIA Yesterday morning. We're on our honeymoon now. You know, the "Wells" shut a fortnight after you left us, and neither Ferdy nor me could fix anything, just for the present, elsewhere; and as we hadn't put by during the season—you know it never struck us to put by during the season—we thought we'd get married.

ROSE Oh, yes.

AVONIA You see, a man and his wife can live almost on what keeps one, rent *and* ceterer; and so, being deeply attached, as I tell you, we went off to church and did the deed. Oh, it will be such a save. [*Looking up at* GADD *coyly.*] Oh, Ferdy——!

GADD [*Laying his hand upon her head, dreamily.*] Yes, child, I confess I love you——

COLPOYS [*Behind* ROSE, *imitating* GADD.] Child, I confess I adore you.

TOM [*Taking* COLPOYS *by the arm and swinging him away from* ROSE.] Enough of that, Colpoys!

COLPOYS What!

ROSE [*Rising.*] Hush!

TOM [*Under his breath.*] If you've never learnt how to behave——

COLPOYS Don't you teach behavior, sir, to a gentleman who plays a superior line of business to yourself! [*Muttering.*] 'Pon my soul! rum start——!

AVONIA [*Going to* ROSE.] Of course I ought to have written to you, dear, properly, but you remember the weeks it takes me to write a letter—— [GADD *sits in the chair* AVONIA *has just quitted; she returns and seats herself upon his knee.*] And so I said to Ferdy, over tea, "Ferdy, let's spend a bit of our honeymoon in doing the West End thoroughly, and going and seeing where Rose Trelawny lives." And we thought it only nice and polite to invite Tom Wrench and Gussy——

GADD 'Vonia, much less of the Gussy!

AVONIA [*Kissing* GADD.] Jealous boy! [*Beaming.*] Oh, and we *have* done the West End thoroughly. There, I've never done the West End so thoroughly in my life! And when we got outside your house I couldn't resist. [*Her hand on* GADD's *shirt sleeve.*] Oh, gracious! I'm sure you'll catch your death, my darling——!

ROSE I think I can get him some wine. [*To* GADD.] Will you take some wine, Ferdinand?

[GADD *rises, nearly upsetting* AVONIA.]

AVONIA Ferdy!

GADD I thank you. [*With a wave of the hand.*] Anything, anything——

AVONIA [*To* ROSE.] Anything that goes with stout, dear.

ROSE [*At the door, turning to them.*] 'Vonia—boys—be very still.

AVONIA Trust *us!*

[ROSE *tiptoes out.* COLPOYS *is now at the card-table, cutting a pack of cards which remains there.*]

COLPOYS [*To* GADD.] Gadd, I'll see you for pennies.

GADD [*Loftily.*] Done, sir, with you!

[*They seat themselves at the table, and cut for coppers.* TOM *is walking about, surveying the room.*]

AVONIA [*Taking off her hat and wiping it with her handkerchief.*] Well, Thomas, what do you think of it?

TOM   *This* is the kind of chamber I want for the first act of my comedy——

AVONIA   Oh, lor', your head's continually running on your comedy. Half this blessed evening——

TOM   I tell you, I won't have doors stuck here, there, and everywhere; no, nor windows in all sorts of impossible places!

AVONIA   Oh, really! Well, when you do get your play accepted, mind you see that Mr. Manager gives you exactly what you ask for—won't you?

TOM   You needn't be satirical, if you *are* wet. Yes, I will! [*Pointing to the left.*] Windows on the one side [*pointing to the right*], doors on the other—just where they should be, architecturally. And locks on the doors, *real locks*, to work; and handles—to turn! [*Rubbing his hands together gleefully.*] Ha, ha! you wait! wait——!

[ROSE *re-enters, with a plate of biscuits in her hand, followed by* CHARLES, *who carries a decanter of sherry and some wineglasses.*]

ROSE   Here, Charles——

[CHARLES *places the decanter and the glasses on the table.*]

GADD [*Whose luck has been against him, throwing himself, sulkily, onto the couch.*] Bah! I'll risk no further stake.

COLPOYS   Just because you lose sevenpence in coppers you go on like this!

[CHARLES, *turning from the table, faces* COLPOYS.]

COLPOYS [*Tearing his hair, and glaring at* CHARLES *wildly.*] Ah—h—h, I am ruined! I have lost my all! my children are beggars——!

CHARLES   Ho, ho, ho! he, he, he!

ROSE   Hush, hush! [CHARLES *goes out laughing. To everybody.*] Sherry?

GADD [*Rising.*] Sherry!

[AVONIA, COLPOYS, *and* GADD *gather round the table, and help themselves to sherry and biscuits.*]

ROSE [*To* TOM.] Tom, won't you——?

TOM [*Watching* GADD *anxiously.*] No, thank you. The fact is, we—we have already partaken of refreshments, once or twice during the evening——

[COLPOYS *and* AVONIA, *each carrying a glass of wine and munching a biscuit, go to the couch, where they sit.*]

GADD [*Pouring out sherry—singing.*] "And let me the canakin clink, clink——"

ROSE [*Coming to him.*] Be quiet, Gadd!

COLPOYS [*Raising his glass.*] The Bride!

ROSE [*Turning, kissing her hand to* AVONIA.] Yes, yes—— [GADD *hands* ROSE *his glass; she puts her lips to it.*] The Bride!

[*She returns the glass to* GADD.]

GADD [*Sitting.*] My bride!

[TOM, *from behind the table, unperceived, takes the decanter and hides it under the table, then sits.* GADD, *missing the decanter, contents himself with the biscuits.*]

AVONIA   Well, Rose, my darling, we've been talking about nothing but ourselves. How are you getting along here?

ROSE   Getting along? oh, I—I don't fancy I'm getting along very well, thank you!

COLPOYS AND AVONIA   Not——!

GADD [*His mouth full of biscuit.*] Not——!

ROSE [*Sitting by the card-table.*] No, boys; no, 'Vonia. The truth is, it isn't as nice as you'd think it. I suppose the Profession had its drawbacks—mother used to say so—but [*raising her arms*] one could fly. Yes, in Brydon Crescent one was a dirty little London sparrow, perhaps; but here, in this grand square——! Oh, it's the story of the caged bird, over again.

AVONIA   A love-bird, though.

ROSE   Poor Arthur? yes, he's a dear. [*Rising.*] But the Gowers—the old Gowers! the Gowers! the Gowers!

[*She paces the room, beating her hands together. In her excitement, she ceases* to whisper, and gradually becomes loud and voluble. The others, following her lead, chatter noisily—excepting TOM, who sits, thoughtfully, looking before him.]

ROSE The ancient Gowers! the venerable Gowers!

AVONIA You mean, the grandfather——?

ROSE And the aunt—the great-aunt—the great bore of a great-aunt! The very mention of 'em makes something go "tap, tap, tap, tap" at the top of my head.

AVONIA Oh, I *am* sorry to hear this. Well, upon my word——!

ROSE Would you believe it? 'Vonia—boys—you'll never believe it! I mayn't walk out with Arthur alone, nor see him here alone. I mayn't sing; no, nor sneeze even——

AVONIA [*Shrilly.*] Not sing or sneeze!

COLPOYS [*Indignantly.*] Not sneeze!

ROSE No, nor sit on the floor—the *floor!*

AVONIA Why, when we shared rooms together, you were always on the floor!

GADD [*Producing a pipe, and knocking out the ashes on the heel of his boot.*] In Heaven's name, what kind of house can this be!

AVONIA I wouldn't stand it, would you, Ferdinand?

GADD [*Loading his pipe.*] Gad, no!

AVONIA [*To* COLPOYS.] Would you, Gus, dear?

GADD [*Under his breath.*] Here! not so much of the Gus dear——

AVONIA [*To* COLPOYS.] Would you?

COLPOYS No, I'm blessed if I would, my darling.

GADD [*His pipe in his mouth.*] Mr. Colpoys! less of the darling!

AVONIA [*Rising.*] Rose, don't you put up with it! [*Striking the top of the card-table vigorously.*] I say, don't you stand it! [*Embracing* ROSE.] You're an independent girl, dear; they came to you, these people; not you to them, remember.

ROSE [*Sitting on the couch.*] Oh, what can I do? I can't do anything.

AVONIA Can't you! [*Coming to* GADD.]

Ferdinand, advise her. You tell her how to——

GADD [*Who has risen.*] Miss Bunn—Mrs. Gadd, you have been all over Mr. Colpoys this evening, ever since we——

AVONIA [*Angrily, pushing him back into his chair.*] Oh, don't be a silly!

GADD Madam!

AVONIA [*Returning to* COLPOYS.] Gus, Ferdinand's foolish. Come and talk to Rose, and advise her, there's a dear boy——

[COLPOYS *rises; she takes his arm, to lead him to* ROSE. *At that moment* GADD *advances to* COLPOYS *and slaps his face violently.*]

COLPOYS Hey——!

GADD Miserable viper!

[*The two men close.* TOM *runs to separate them.* ROSE *rises with a cry of terror. There is a struggle and general uproar. The card-table is overturned, with a crash, and* AVONIA *utters a long and piercing shriek. Then the house-bells are heard ringing violently.*]

ROSE Oh——! [*The combatants part; all look scared. At the door, listening.*] They are moving—coming! Turn out the——!

[*She turns out the light at the table. The room is in half-light as* SIR WILLIAM *enters, cautiously, closely followed by* MISS GOWER. *They are both in dressing-gowns and slippers;* SIR WILLIAM *carries a thick stick and his bedroom candle.* ROSE *is standing by a chair;* GADD, AVONIA, COLPOYS, *and* TOM *are together.*]

SIR WILLIAM Miss Trelawny——!

MISS GOWER Rose——! [*Running behind the screen.*] Men!

SIR WILLIAM Who are these people?

ROSE [*Advancing a step or two.*] Some friends of mine who used to be at the "Wells" have called upon me, to inquire how I am getting on.

[ARTHUR *enters, quickly.*]

ARTHUR [*Looking round.*] Oh! Rose——!

SIR WILLIAM [*Turning upon him.*] Ah—h—h—h! How come you here?

ARTHUR I was outside the house. Charles let me in, knowing something was wrong.

SIR WILLIAM [*Peering into his face.*] Troubadouring——?

ARTHUR Troubadouring; yes, sir. [*To* ROSE.] Rose, what is this?

SIR WILLIAM [*Fiercely.*] No, sir, this is my affair. [*Placing his candlestick on the table.*] Stand aside! [*Raising his stick furiously.*] Stand aside!

[ARTHUR *moves to the right.*]

MISS GOWER [*Over the screen.*] William——

SIR WILLIAM Hey?

MISS GOWER Your ankles——

SIR WILLIAM [*Adjusting his dressing-gown.*] I beg your pardon. [*To* ARTHUR.] Yes, I can answer your question. [*Pointing his stick, first at* ROSE, *then at the group.*] Some friends of that young woman's connected with—the playhouse, have favored us with a visit, for the purpose of ascertaining how she is—getting on. [*Touching* GADD's *pipe, which is lying at his feet, with the end of his stick.*] A filthy tobacco-pipe. To whom does it belong? whose is it?

[ROSE *picks it up and passes it to* GADD, *bravely.*]

ROSE It belongs to one of my friends.

SIR WILLIAM [*Taking* GADD's *empty wine-glass and holding it to his nose.*] Phu, yes! In brief, a drunken debauch. [*To the group.*] So ye see, gentlemen—[*to* AVONIA] and you, madam; [*to* ARTHUR] and you, sir; you see, all of ye, [*sinking into a chair, and coughing from exhaustion*] exactly how Miss Trelawny is getting on.

MISS GOWER [*Over the screen.*] William——

SIR WILLIAM What is it?

MISS GOWER Your ankles——

SIR WILLIAM [*Leaping to his feet, in a frenzy.*] Bah!

MISS GOWER Oh, they seem so out of place!

SIR WILLIAM [*Flourishing his stick—to the group down left.*] Begone! a set of garish, dissolute gypsies! begone!

[GADD, AVONIA, COLPOYS, *and* WRENCH *gather, the men hastily putting on their coats, etc.*]

AVONIA Where's my umbrella?

GADD A hand with my coat here!

COLPOYS 'Pon my soul! London artists——!

AVONIA We don't want to remain where we're not heartily welcome, I can assure everybody.

SIR WILLIAM Open windows! let in the air!

AVONIA [*To* ROSE, *who is standing above the wreck of the card-table.*] Good-bye, my dear——

ROSE No, no, 'Vonia. Oh, don't leave me behind you!

ARTHUR Rose——!

ROSE Oh, I'm very sorry, Arthur. [*To* SIR WILLIAM.] Indeed, I am very sorry, Sir William. But you are right—gypsies—gypsies! [*To* ARTHUR.] Yes, Arthur, if you were a gypsy, as I am, as these friends o' mine are, we might be happy together. But I've seen enough of your life, my dear boy, to know that I'm no wife for you. I should only be wretched, and would make you wretched; and the end, when it arrived, as it very soon would, would be much as it is to-night——!

ARTHUR [*Distractedly.*] You'll let me see you, talk to you, to-morrow, Rose?

ROSE No, never!

SIR WILLIAM [*Sharply.*] You mean that?

ROSE [*Facing him.*] Oh, don't be afraid. I give you my word.

SIR WILLIAM [*Gripping her hand.*] Thank ye. Thank ye.

TOM [*Quietly to* ARTHUR.] Mr. Gower, come and see *me* to-morrow——
[*He moves away to the door.*]

ROSE [*Turning to* AVONIA, GADD, *and* COLPOYS.] I'm ready——

MISS GOWER [*Coming from behind the*

screen to the back of the couch.] Not to-night, child! not to-night! where will you go?

AVONIA [*Holding* ROSE.] To her old quarters in Brydon Crescent. Send her things after her, if you please.

MISS GOWER And then——?

ROSE Then back to the "Wells" again, Miss Gower! back to the "Wells"——!

Act Three

The scene represents an apartment on the second floor of MRS. MOSSOP's *house. The room is of a humbler character than that shown in the first act; but, though shabby, it is neat. On the right is a door, outside which is supposed to be the landing. In the wall at the back is another door, presumably admitting to a further chamber. Down left there is a fireplace, with a fire burning, and over the mantelpiece a mirror. In the left-hand corner of the room is a small bedstead with a tidily-made bed, which can be hidden by a pair of curtains of some common and faded material, hanging from a cord slung from wall to wall. At the foot of the bedstead stands a large theatrical dress-basket. On the wall, by the head of the bed, are some pegs upon which hang a skirt or two and other articles of attire. On the right, against the back wall, there is a chest of drawers, the top of which is used as a washstand. In front of this is a small screen, and close by there are some more pegs with things hanging upon them. On the right wall, above the sofa, is a hanging bookcase with a few books. A small circular table, with a somewhat shabby cover upon it, stands on the left. The walls are papered, the doors painted stone-color. An old felt carpet is on the floor. The light is that of morning. A fire is burning in the grate.*

[MRS. MOSSOP, *now dressed in a work-aday gown, has just finished making the bed. There is a knock at the center door.*]

AVONIA [*From the adjoining room.*] Rose!

MRS. MOSSOP [*Giving a final touch to the quilt.*] Eh?

AVONIA Is Miss Trelawny in her room?

MRS. MOSSOP No, Mrs. Gadd; she's at rehearsal.

AVONIA Oh——

[MRS. MOSSOP *draws the curtains, hiding the bed from view.* AVONIA *enters by the door on the right in a morning wrapper which has seen its best days. She carries a pair of curling-tongs, and her hair is evidently in process of being dressed in ringlets.*]

AVONIA Of course she is; I forgot. There's a call for *The Peddler of Marseilles.* Thank Gawd, *I'm* not in it. [*Singing.*] "I'm a great guerrilla chief, I'm a robber and a thief, I can either kill a foe or prig a pocket-handkerchief——"

MRS. MOSSOP [*Dusting the ornaments on the mantelpiece.*] Bless your heart, you're very gay this morning!

AVONIA It's the pantomime. I'm always stark mad as the pantomime approaches. I don't grudge letting the rest of the company have their fling at other times—but with the panto comes *my* turn. [*Throwing herself full length upon the sofa gleefully.*] Ha, ha, ha! the turn of Avonia Bunn! [*With a change of tone.*] I hope Miss Trelawny won't take a walk up to Highbury, or anywhere, after rehearsal. I want to borrow her gilt belt. My dress has arrived.

MRS. MOSSOP [*Much interested.*] No! has it?

AVONIA Yes, Mrs. Burroughs is coming down from the theatre at twelve-thirty to see me in it. [*Singing.* "Any kind of villainy cometh natural to me. So it endeth with a combat and a one, two, three——!"[1]

MRS. MOSSOP [*Surveying the room.*] Well,

---

1 These snatches of song are from *The Miller and His Men*, a burlesque mealy-drama, by Francis Talfourd and Henry J. Byron, produced at the Strand Theatre, April 9, 1860.

that's as cheerful as I can make things look, poor dear!

AVONIA [*Taking a look round, seriously.*] It's pretty bright—if it wasn't for the idea of Rose Trelawny having to economize!

MRS. MOSSOP Ah—h!

AVONIA [*Rising.*] That's what I can't swallow. [*Sticking her irons in the fire angrily.*] One room! and on the second floor! [*Turning to* MRS. MOSSOP.] Of course, Gadd and me are one-room people too—and on the same floor; but then Gadd is so popular *out* of the theatre, Mrs. Mossop—he's obliged to spend such a load of money at the "Clown"——

MRS. MOSSOP [*Who has been dusting the bookcase, coming to the table.*] Mrs. Gadd, dearie, I'm sure I'm not in the least inquisitive; no one could accuse me of it—but I should like to know just one thing.

AVONIA [*Testing her irons upon a sheet of paper which she takes from the table.*] What's that?

MRS. MOSSOP Why *have* they been and cut down Miss Trelawny's salary at the "Wells"?

AVONIA [*Hesitatingly.*] H'm, everybody's chattering about it; you could get to hear easily enough——

MRS. MOSSOP Oh, I dare say.

AVONIA So I don't mind—poor Rose! they tell her she can't act now, Mrs. Mossop.

MRS. MOSSOP Can't act!

AVONIA No, dear old girl, she's lost it; it's gone from her—the trick of it——

[TOM *enters by the door on the right, carrying a table-cover of a bright pattern.*]

TOM [*Coming upon* MRS. MOSSOP, *disconcerted.*] Oh——!

MRS. MOSSOP My first-floor table-cover!

TOM Y—y—yes. [*Exchanging the table-covers.*] I thought, as the Telfers have departed, and as their late sitting room is at present vacant, that Miss Trelawny might enjoy the benefit—hey?

MRS. MOSSOP [*Snatching up the old table-cover.*] Well, I never——!

[*She goes out.*]

AVONIA [*Curling her hair, at the mirror over the mantelpiece.*] I say, Tom, I wonder if I've done wrong——

TOM It all depends upon whether you've had the chance.

AVONIA I've told Mrs. Mossop the reason they've reduced Rose's salary.

TOM You needn't.

AVONIA She had only to ask any other member of the company——

TOM To have found one who could have kept silent!

AVONIA [*Remorsefully.*] Oh, I could burn myself!

TOM Besides, it isn't true.

AVONIA What——?

TOM That Rose Trelawny is no longer up to her work.

AVONIA [*Sadly.*] Oh, Tom!

TOM It isn't the fact, I say!

AVONIA Isn't it the fact that ever since Rose returned from Cavendish Square——?

TOM She has been reserved, subdued, ladylike——

AVONIA [*Shrilly.*] She was always ladylike!

TOM I'm aware of that!

AVONIA Well, then, what do you mean by——?

TOM [*In a rage, turning away.*] Oh——!

AVONIA [*Heating her irons again.*] The idea!

TOM [*Cooling down.*] She was always a ladylike *actress,* on the stage and off it, but now she has developed into a—[*at a loss*] into a——

AVONIA [*Scornfully.*] Ha!

TOM Into a ladylike human being. These fools at the "Wells"! Can't act, can't she! No, she can no longer *spout,* she can no longer *ladle,* the vapid trash, the—the—the turgid rodomontade——

AVONIA [*Doubtfully.*] You'd better be careful of your language, Wrench.

TOM [*With a twinkle in his eye—mopping his brow.*] You're a married woman, 'Vonia——

AVONIA [*Holding her irons to her cheek, modestly.*] I know, but still——

TOM Yes, deep down in the well of that girl's nature there has been lying a little, bright, clear pool of genuine refinement, girlish simplicity. And now the bucket has been lowered by love; experience has turned the handle; and up comes the crystal to the top, pure and sparkling. Why, her broken engagement to poor young Gower has really been the making of her! It has transformed her! Can't act, can't she! [*Drawing a long breath.*] How she would play Dora in my comedy!

AVONIA Ho, that comedy!

TOM How she would murmur those love-scenes!

AVONIA Murder——!

TOM [*Testily.*] Murmur. [*Partly to himself.*] Do you know, 'Vonia, I had Rose in my mind when I imagined Dora——?

AVONIA Ha, ha! you astonish me.

TOM [*Sitting.*] And Arthur Gower when I wrote the character of Gerald, Dora's lover. [*In a low voice.*] Gerald and Dora —Rose and Arthur—Gerald and Dora. [*Suddenly.*] 'Vonia——!

AVONIA [*Singeing her hair.*] Ah——! oh, lor'! what now?

TOM I wish you could keep a secret.

AVONIA Why, can't I?

TOM Haven't you just been gossiping with Mother Mossop?

AVONIA [*Behind his chair, breathlessly, her eyes bolting.*] A secret, Tom?

TOM [*Nodding.*] I should like to share it with you, because—you are fond of her too——

AVONIA Ah——!

TOM And because the possession of it is worrying me. But there, I can't trust you.

AVONIA Mr. Wrench!

TOM No, you're a warm-hearted woman, 'Vonia, but you're a sieve.

AVONIA [*Going down upon her knees beside him.*] I swear! By all my hopes, Tom Wrench, of hitting 'em as Prince Charming in the coming pantomime, I swear I will not divulge, leave alone tell a living soul, any secret you may intrust to me, or let me know of, concerning Rose Trelawny of the "Wells." Amen!

TOM [*In her ear.*] 'Vonia, *I know where Arthur Gower is.*

AVONIA *Is!* isn't he still in London?

TOM [*Producing a letter mysteriously.*] No. When Rose stuck to her refusal to see him—listen—mind, not a word——!

AVONIA By all my hopes——!

TOM [*Checking her.*] All right, all right! [*Reading.*] "Theatre Royal, Bristol. Friday——"

AVONIA Theatre Royal, Br——!

TOM Be quiet! [*Reading.*] "My dear Mr. Wrench. A whole week, and not a line from you to tell me how Miss Trelawny is. When you are silent I am sleepless at night and a haggard wretch during the day. Young Mr. Kirby, our Walking Gentleman, has been unwell, and the management has given me temporarily some of his business to play——"

AVONIA Arthur Gower——!

TOM Will you? [*Reading.*] "Last night I was allowed to appear as Careless in *The School for Scandal.* Miss Mason, the Lady Teazle, complimented me, but the men said I lacked vigor,"—the old cry!—"and so this morning I am greatly depressed. But I will still persevere, as long as you can assure me that no presuming fellow is paying attention to Miss Trelawny. Oh, how badly she treated me——!"

AVONIA [*Following the reading of the letter.*] "How badly she treated me——!"

TOM "I will never forgive her—only love her——"

AVONIA "Only love her——"

TOM "Only love her, and hope I may some day become a great actor, and, like herself, a gypsy. Yours very gratefully, Arthur Gordon."

AVONIA In the Profession!

TOM Bolted from Cavendish Square—went down to Bristol——

AVONIA How did he manage it all? [*TOM taps his breast proudly.*] But isn't Rose to be told? why shouldn't she be told?

TOM She has hurt the boy, stung him to the quick, and he's proud.

AVONIA But she loves him now that she

believes he has forgotten her. She only half loved him before. She loves him!

TOM   Serve her right.

AVONIA   Oh, Tom, is she never to know?

TOM [*Folding the letter carefully.*] Some day, when he begins to make strides.

AVONIA   Strides! he's nothing but General Utility at present?

TOM [*Putting the letter in his pocket.*] No.

AVONIA   And how long have you been that?

TOM   Ten years.

AVONIA [*With a little screech.*] Ah—h—h! she ought to be told!

TOM [*Seizing her wrist.*] Woman, you won't——!

AVONIA [*Raising her disengaged hand.*] By all my hopes of hitting 'em——!

TOM   All right, I believe you. [*Listening.*] Sssh!

[*They rise and separate, he moving to the fire, she to the right, as* ROSE *enters.* ROSE *is now a grave, dignified, somewhat dreamy young woman.*]

ROSE [*Looking from* TOM *to* AVONIA.] Ah——?

TOM AND AVONIA   Good-morning.

ROSE [*Kissing* AVONIA.] Visitors!

AVONIA   My fire's so black [*showing her irons*]; I thought you wouldn't mind——

ROSE [*Removing her gloves.*] Of course not. [*Seeing the table-cover.*] Oh——!

TOM   Mrs. Mossop asked me to bring that upstairs. It was in the Telfers' room, you know, and she fancied——

ROSE   How good of her! thanks, Tom. [*Taking off her hat and mantle.*] Poor Mr. and Mrs. Telfer! they still wander mournfully about the "Wells"; they can get nothing to do.

[*Carrying her hat and umbrella, she disappears through the curtains.*]

TOM [*To* AVONIA, *in a whisper, across the room.*] The Telfers——!

AVONIA   Eh?

TOM   She's been giving 'em money.

AVONIA   Yes.

TOM   Damn!

ROSE [*Reappearing.*] What are you saying about me?

AVONIA   I was wondering whether you'd lend me that belt you bought for Ophelia; to wear during the first two or three weeks of the pantomime——

ROSE   Certainly, 'Vonia, to wear throughout——

AVONIA [*Embracing her.*] No, it's too good; I'd rather fake one for the rest of the time. [*Looking into her face.*] What's the matter?

ROSE   I will make you a present of the belt, 'Vonia, if you will accept it. I bought it when I came back to the "Wells," thinking everything would go on as before. But—it's of no use; they tell me I cannot act effectively any longer——

TOM [*Indignantly.*] Effectively——!

ROSE   First, as you know, they reduce my salary——

TOM AND AVONIA [*With clenched hands.*] Yes!

ROSE   And now, this morning—[*sitting*] you can guess——

AVONIA [*Hoarsely.*] Got your notice?

ROSE   Yes.

TOM AND AVONIA   Oh—h—h!

ROSE [*After a little pause.*] Poor mother! I hope she doesn't see. [*Overwhelmed,* AVONIA *and* TOM *sit.*] I was running through Blanche, my old part in *The Peddler of Marseilles,* when Mr. Burroughs spoke to me. It is true I was doing it tamely, but—it is such nonsense.

TOM   Hear, hear!

ROSE   And then, that poor little song I used to sing on the bridge——

AVONIA [*Singing, softly.*] "Ever of thee I'm fondly dreaming——"

TOM AND AVONIA [*Singing.*] "Thy gentle voice my spirit can cheer."

ROSE   I told Mr. Burroughs I should cut it out. So ridiculously inappropriate!

TOM   And that—did it?

ROSE [*Smiling at him.*] That did it.

AVONIA [*Kneeling beside her, and embracing her tearfully.*] My ducky! oh, but there are other theatres besides the "Wells"——

ROSE   For me? only where the same trash is acted.

AVONIA   [*With a sob.*]   But a few months ago you l—l—liked your work.

ROSE   Yes [*dreamily*], and then I went to Cavendish Square, engaged to Arthur—— [TOM *rises and leans upon the mantelpiece, looking into the fire.*] How badly I behaved in Cavendish Square! how unlike a young lady! What if the old folks *were* overbearing and tyrannical, Arthur could be gentle with them. "They have not many more years in this world," he said—dear boy!—"and anything we can do to make them happy——" And what *did* I do? *There* was a chance for me—to be patient, and womanly; and I proved to them that I was nothing but—an actress.

AVONIA   [*Rising, hurt but still tearful.*]   It doesn't follow, because one is a——

ROSE   [*Rising.*]   Yes, 'Vonia, it does! We are only dolls, partly human, with mechanical limbs that *will* fall into stagey postures, and heads stuffed with sayings out of rubbishy plays. It isn't *the* world we live in, merely *a* world—such a queer little one! I was less than a month in Cavendish Square, and very few people came there; but they were *real* people— *real!* For a month I lost the smell of gas and oranges, and the hurry and noise, and the dirt and the slang, and the clownish joking, at the "Wells." I didn't realize at the time the change that was going on in me; I didn't realize it till I came back. And then, by degrees, I discovered what had happened—— [TOM *is now near her. She takes his hand and drops her head upon* AVONIA's *shoulder. Wearily.*] Oh, Tom! oh, 'Vonia—— [*From the next room comes the sound of the throwing about of heavy objects, and of* GADD's *voice uttering loud imprecations. Alarmed.*] Oh——!

AVONIA   [*Listening attentively.*]   Sounds like Ferdy. [*She goes to the center door. At the keyhole.*] Ferdy! aint you well, darling?

GADD   [*On the other side of the door.*]   Avonia!

AVONIA   I'm in Miss Trelawny's room.

GADD   Ah——?

AVONIA   [*To* ROSE *and* TOM.]   Now, what's put Ferdy out? [GADD *enters with a wild look.*] Ferdinand!

TOM   Anything wrong, Gadd?

GADD   Wrong! wrong! [*Sitting.*] What d'ye think?

AVONIA   Tell us!

GADD   I have been asked to appear in the pantomime.

AVONIA   [*Shocked.*]   Oh, Ferdy! you!

GADD   I, a serious actor, if ever there was one; a poetic actor——!

AVONIA   What part, Ferdy?

GADD   The insult, the bitter insult! the gross indignity!

AVONIA   What part, Ferdy?

GADD   I have not been seen in pantomime for years, not since I shook the dust of the T. R. Stockton from my feet.

AVONIA   Ferdy, what part?

GADD   I simply looked at Burroughs, when he preferred his request, and swept from the theatre.

AVONIA   What part, Ferdy?

GADD   A part, too, which is seen for a moment at the opening of the pantomime, and not again till its close.

AVONIA   Ferdy.

GADD   Eh?

AVONIA   What part?

GADD   A character called the Demon of Discontent.

[ROSE *turns away to the fireplace;* TOM *curls himself up on the sofa and is seen to shake with laughter.*]

AVONIA   [*Walking about indignantly.*]   Oh! [*Returning to* GADD.] Oh, it's a rotten part! Rose, dear, I assure you, as artist to artist, that part is absolutely rotten. [*To* GADD.] You won't play it, darling?

GADD   [*Rising.*]   Play it! I would see the "Wells" in ashes first.

AVONIA   We shall lose our engagements, Ferdy. I know Burroughs; we shall be out, both of us.

GADD   Of course we shall. D'ye think I have not counted the cost?

AVONIA [*Putting her hand in his.*] I don't mind, dear—for the sake of your position—[*struck by a sudden thought*] oh——!

GADD What——?

AVONIA There now—we haven't put by!

[*There is a knock at the door.*]

ROSE Who is that?

COLPOYS [*Outside the door.*] Is Gadd here, Miss Trelawny?

ROSE Yes.

COLPOYS I want to see him.

GADD Wrench, I'll trouble you. Ask Mr. Colpoys whether he approaches me as a friend, an acquaintance, or in his capacity of stage manager at the "Wells"—the tool of Burroughs.

[TOM *opens the door slightly.* GADD *and* AVONIA *join* ROSE *at the fireplace.*]

TOM [*At the door, solemnly.*] Colpoys, are you here as Gadd's bosom friend, or as a mere tool of Burroughs?

[*An inaudible colloquy follows between* TOM *and* COLPOYS. TOM'*s head is outside the door; his legs are seen to move convulsively, and the sound of suppressed laughter is heard.*]

GADD [*Turning.*] Well, well?

TOM [*Closing the door sharply, and facing* GADD *with great seriousness.*] He is here as the tool of Burroughs?

GADD I will receive him.

[TOM *admits* COLPOYS, *who carries a mean-looking "part," and a letter.*]

COLPOYS [*After formally bowing to the ladies.*] Oh, Gadd, Mr. Burroughs instructs me to offer you this part in the pantomime. [*Handing the part to* GADD.] Demon of Discontent.

[GADD *takes the part and flings it to the ground;* AVONIA *picks it up and reads it.*]

COLPOYS You refuse it?

GADD I do. [*With dignity.*] Acquaint Mr. Burroughs with my decision, and add that I hope his pantomime will prove an utterly mirthless one. May Boxing-night, to those unfortunate enough to find themselves in the theatre, long remain a dismal memory; and may succeeding audiences, scanty and dissatisfied——! [COLPOYS *presents* GADD *with the letter.* GADD *opens it and reads.*] I leave. [*Sitting.*] The Romeo, the Orlando, the Clifford—leaves!

AVONIA [*Coming to* GADD, *indicating some lines in the part.*] Ferdy, this aint so bad. [*Reading.*]
"I'm Discontent! from Orkney's isle to Dover
To make men's bile bile-over I endover——"

GADD 'Vonia! [*Taking the part from* AVONIA, *with mingled surprise and pleasure.*] Ho, ho! no, that's not bad. [*Reading.*]
"Tempers, though sweet, I whip up to a lather,
Make wives hate husbands, sons wish fathers farther."
'Vonia, there's something to lay hold of here! I'll think this over. [*Rising, addressing* COLPOYS.] Gus, I have thought this over. I play it.

[*They all gather round him, and congratulate him.* AVONIA *embraces and kisses him.*]

TOM AND COLPOYS That's right!

ROSE I'm very pleased, Ferdinand.

AVONIA [*Tearfully.*] Oh, Ferdy!

GADD [*In high spirits.*] Egad, I play it! Gus, I'll stroll back with you to the "Wells." [*Shaking hands with* ROSE.] Miss Trelawny——! [AVONIA *accompanies* COLPOYS *and* GADD *to the door, clinging to* GADD, *who is flourishing the part.*] 'Vonia, I see myself in this! [*Kissing her.*] Steak for dinner!

[GADD *and* COLPOYS *go out.* TOM *shrieks with laughter.*]

AVONIA [*Turning upon him, angrily and volubly.*] Yes, I heard you with Colpoys outside that door, if Gadd didn't. It's a pity, Mr. Wrench, you can't find something better to do——!

ROSE [*Pacifically.*] Hush, hush, 'Vonia! Tom, assist me with my basket; I'll give 'Vonia her belt——

[TOM *and* ROSE *go behind the curtains and presently emerge, carrying the dress-basket, which they deposit.*]

AVONIA [*Flouncing across the room.*] Making fun of Gadd! an artist to the roots of his hair! There's more talent in Gadd's little finger——!

ROSE [*Rummaging among the contents of the basket.*] 'Vonia, 'Vonia!

AVONIA And if Gadd *is* to play a demon in the pantomime, what do *you* figure as, Tom Wrench, among the half a dozen other things? Why, as part of a dragon! Yes, and *which end*——?

ROSE [*Quietly to* TOM.] Apologize to 'Vonia at once, Tom.

TOM [*Meekly.*] Mrs. Gadd, I beg your pardon.

AVONIA [*Coming to him and kissing him.*] Granted, Tom; but you should be a little more considerate——

ROSE [*Holding up the belt.*] Here——!

AVONIA [*Taking the belt ecstatically.*] Oh, isn't it lovely! Rose, you dear! you sweet thing! [*Singing a few bars of the Jewel song from Faust, then rushing at* ROSE *and embracing her.*] I'm going to try my dress on, to show Mrs. Burroughs. Come and help me into it. I'll unlock my door on my side—— [TOM *politely opens the door for her to pass out.*] Thank you, Tom— [*kissing him again*] only you should be more considerate toward Gadd——
[*She disappears.*]

TOM [*Calling after her.*] I will be; I will— [*Shutting the door.*] Ha, ha, ha!

ROSE [*Smiling.*] Hush! poor 'Vonia! [*Mending the fire.*] Excuse me, Tom— have you a fire upstairs, in your room, to-day?

TOM Er—n—not to-day—it's Saturday. I never have a fire on a Saturday.

ROSE [*Coming to him.*] Why not?

TOM [*Looking away from her.*] Don't know —creatures of habit——

ROSE [*Gently touching his coat-sleeve.*] Be-

cause if you would like to smoke your pipe by my fire while I'm with 'Vonia——

[*The key is heard to turn in the lock of the center door.*]

AVONIA [*From the next room.*] It's unlocked.

ROSE I'm coming.

[*She unbolts the door on her side, and goes into* AVONIA's *room, shutting the door behind her. The lid of the dress-basket is open, showing the contents; a pair of little satin shoes lie at the top.* TOM *takes up one of the shoes and presses it to his lips. There is a knock at the door. He returns the shoe to the basket, closes the lid, and walks away.*]

TOM Yes?

[*The door opens slightly and* IMOGEN *is heard.*]

IMOGEN [*Outside.*] Is that you, Wrench?

TOM Hullo!

[IMOGEN, *in out-of-door costume, enters breathlessly.*]

IMOGEN [*Closing the door—speaking rapidly and excitedly.*] Mossop said you were in Rose's room——

TOM [*Shaking hands with her.*] She'll be here in a few minutes.

IMOGEN It's you I want. Let me sit down.

TOM [*Going to the armchair.*] Here——

IMOGEN [*Sitting on the right of the table, panting.*] Not near the fire——

TOM What's up?

IMOGEN Oh, Wrench! p'r'aps my fortune's made!

TOM [*Quite calmly.*] Congratulate you, Jenny.

IMOGEN Do be quiet; don't make such a racket. You see, things haven't been going at all satisfactorily at the Olympic lately. There's Miss Puddifant——

TOM I know—no lady.

IMOGEN *How* do you know?

TOM Guessed.

IMOGEN Quite right; and a thousand other

annoyances. And at last I took it into my head to consult Mr. Clandon, who married an aunt of mine and lives at Streatham, and he'll lend me five hundred pounds.

TOM   What for?

IMOGEN   Towards taking a theatre.

TOM   [*Dubiously.*]   Five hundred——

IMOGEN   It's all he's good for, and he won't advance that unless I can get a further five, or eight, hundred from some other quarter.

TOM   What theatre!

IMOGEN   The Pantheon happens to be empty.

TOM   Yes; it's been that for the last twenty years.

IMOGEN   Don't throw wet blankets—I mean—[*referring to her tablets, which she carries in her muff*] I've got it all worked out in black and white. There's a deposit required on account of rent—two hundred pounds. Cleaning the theatre—[*looking at* TOM] what do *you* say?

TOM   Cleaning *that* theatre.

IMOGEN   I say, another two hundred.

TOM   That would remove the top-layer——

IMOGEN   Cost of producing the opening play, five hundred pounds. Balance for emergencies, three hundred. You generally have a balance for emergencies.

TOM   You generally have the emergencies, if not the balance?

IMOGEN   Now, the question is, will five hundred produce the play?

TOM   What play?

IMOGEN   Your play.

TOM   [*Quietly.*]   My——

IMOGEN   Your comedy.

TOM   [*Turning to the fire—in a low voice.*] Rubbish!

IMOGEN   Well, Mr. Clandon thinks it *isn't*. [*He faces her sharply.*] I gave it to him to read, and he—well, he's quite taken with it.

TOM   [*Walking about, his hands in his pockets, his head down, agitatedly.*] Clandon—Landon—what's his name——?

IMOGEN   Tony Clandon—Anthony Clandon——

TOM   [*Choking.*]   He's a—he's a——

IMOGEN   He's a hop-merchant.

TOM   No, he's not—[*sitting on the sofa, leaning his head on his hands*] he's a stunner.

IMOGEN   [*Rising.*]   So you grasp the position.   Theatre—manageress—author—play, found; and eight hundred pounds *wanted!*

TOM   [*Rising.*]   O Lord!

IMOGEN   Who's got it?

TOM   [*Wildly.*]   The Queen's got it! Miss Burdett-Coutts has got it!

IMOGEN   Don't be a fool, Wrench. Do you remember old Mr. Morfew, of Duncan Terrace? He used to take great interest in us all at the "Wells." *He* has money.

TOM   He has gout; we don't see him now.

IMOGEN   Gout! How lucky! That means he's at home. Will you run round to Duncan Terrace——?

TOM   [*Looking down at his clothes.*]   I!

IMOGEN   Nonsense, Wrench; we're not asking him to advance money on your clothes.

TOM   The clothes are the man, Jenny.

IMOGEN   And the woman——?

TOM   The face is the woman; there's the real inequality of the sexes.

IMOGEN   I'll go! Is my face good enough?

TOM   [*Enthusiastically.*]   I should say so!

IMOGEN   [*Taking his hands.*]   Ha, ha! It has been in my possession longer than you have had your oldest coat, Tom!

TOM   Make haste, Jenny!

IMOGEN   [*Running up to the door.*]   Oh, it will last till I get to Duncan Terrace. [*Turning.*] Tom, you may have to read your play to Mr. Morfew. Have you another copy? Uncle Clandon has mine.

TOM   [*Holding his head.*]   I think I have—I don't know——

IMOGEN   Look for it! Find it! If Morfew wants to hear it, we must strike while the iron's hot.

TOM   While the gold's hot!

IMOGEN AND TOM   Ha, ha, ha!

[MRS. MOSSOP *enters, showing some signs of excitement.*]

IMOGEN [*Pushing her aside.*] Oh, get out of the way, Mrs. Mossop——

[IMOGEN *departs.*]

MRS. MOSSOP Upon my——! [*To* TOM.] A visitor for Miss Trelawny! Where's Miss Trelawny?

TOM With Mrs. Gadd. Mossop!

MRS. MOSSOP Don't bother me now——

TOM Mossop! The apartments vacated by the Telfers! Dare to let 'em without giving me the preference.

MRS. MOSSOP You!

TOM [*Seizing her hands and swinging her round.*] I may be wealthy, sweet Rebecca! [*Embracing her.*] I may be rich and honored!

MRS. MOSSOP Oh, have done! [*Releasing herself.*] My lodgers do take such liberties——

TOM [*At the door, grandly.*] Beccy, half a scuttle of coal, to start with.

[*He goes out, leaving the door slightly open.*]

MRS. MOSSOP [*Knocking at the center door.*] Miss Trelawny, my dear! Miss Trelawny!

[*The door opens, a few inches.*]

ROSE [*Looking out.*] Why, what a clatter you and Mr. Wrench have been making——!

MRS. MOSSOP [*Beckoning her mysteriously.*] Come here, dear.

ROSE [*Closing the center door, and entering the room wonderingly.*] Eh?

MRS. MOSSOP [*In awe.*] Sir William Gower!

ROSE Sir William!

MRS. MOSSOP Don't be vexed with me. "I'll see if she's at home," I said. "Oh, yes, woman, Miss Trelawny's at home," said he, and hobbled straight in. I've shut him in the Telfers' room——

[*There are three distinct raps, with a stick, at the right-hand door.*]

ROSE AND MRS. MOSSOP Oh—h!

ROSE [*Faintly.*] Open it.

[MRS. MOSSOP *opens the door, and* SIR WILLIAM *enters. He is feebler, more decrepit, than when last seen. He wears a plaid about his shoulders and walks with the aid of a stick.*]

MRS. MOSSOP [*At the door.*] Ah, and a sweet thing Miss Trelawny is——!

SIR WILLIAM [*Turning to her.*] Are you a relative?

MRS. MOSSOP No, I am *not* a relative——!

SIR WILLIAM Go. [*She departs; he closes the door with the end of his stick. Facing* ROSE.] My mind is not commonly a wavering one, Miss Trelawny, but it has taken me some time—months—to decide upon calling on ye.

ROSE Won't you sit down?

SIR WILLIAM [*After a pause of hesitation, sitting upon the dress-basket.*] Ugh!

ROSE [*With quiet dignity.*] Have we no chairs? Do we lack chairs here, Sir William?

[*He gives her a quick, keen look, then rises and walks to the fire.*]

SIR WILLIAM [*Suddenly, bringing his stick down upon the table with violence.*] My grandson! my grandson! where is he?

ROSE Arthur——!

SIR WILLIAM I had but one.

ROSE Isn't he—in Cavendish Square——?

SIR WILLIAM Isn't he in Cavendish Square! no, he is not in Cavendish Square, as you know well.

ROSE Oh, I don't know——

SIR WILLIAM Tsch!

ROSE When did he leave you?

SIR WILLIAM Tsch!

ROSE When?

SIR WILLIAM He made his escape during the night, 22d of August last—[*pointing his finger at her*] as you know well.

ROSE Sir William, I assure you——

SIR WILLIAM Tsch! [*Taking off his gloves.*] How often does he write to ye?

ROSE He does not write to me. He did write day after day, two or three times a day, for about a week. That was in June,

535

when I came back here. [*With drooping head.*] He never writes now.

SIR WILLIAM Visits ye——?

ROSE No.

SIR WILLIAM Comes troubadouring——?

ROSE No, no, no. I have not seen him since that night. I refused to see him—— [*With a catch in her breath.*] Why, he may be——!

SIR WILLIAM [*Fumbling in his pocket.*] Ah, but he's not. He's alive [*producing a small packet of letters*]. Arthur's alive, [*advancing to her*] and full of his tricks still. His great-aunt Trafalgar receives a letter from him once a fortnight, posted in London——

ROSE [*Holding out her hand for the letters.*] Oh!

SIR WILLIAM [*Putting them behind his back.*] Hey!

ROSE [*Faintly.*] I thought you wished me to read them. [*He yields them to her grudgingly, she taking his hand and bending over it.*] Ah, thank you.

SIR WILLIAM [*Withdrawing his hand with a look of disrelish.*] What are ye doing, madam? what are ye doing?

[*He sits, producing his snuff-box; she sits, upon the basket, facing him, and opens the packet of letters.*]

ROSE [*Reading a letter.*] "To reassure you as to my well-being, I cause this to be posted in London by a friend——"

SIR WILLIAM [*Pointing a finger at her again, accusingly.*] A friend!

ROSE [*Looking up, with simple pride.*] He would never call me *that*. [*Reading.*] "I am in good bodily health, and as contented as a man can be who has lost the woman he loves, and will love till his dying day—" Ah——!

SIR WILLIAM Read no more! Return them to me! give them to me, ma'am! [*Rising, she restores the letters, meekly. He peers up into her face.*] What's come to ye? You are not so much of a vixen as you were.

ROSE [*Shaking her head.*] No.

SIR WILLIAM [*Suspiciously.*] Less of the devil——?

ROSE Sir William, I am sorry for having been a vixen, and for all my unruly conduct, in Cavendish Square. I humbly beg your, and Miss Gower's, forgiveness.

SIR WILLIAM [*Taking snuff, uncomfortably.*] Pi—i—i—sh! extraordinary change.

ROSE Aren't *you* changed, Sir William, now that you have lost him?

SIR WILLIAM I!

ROSE Don't you love him now, the more? [*His head droops a little, and his hands wander to the brooch which secures his plaid.*] Let me take your shawl from you. You would catch cold when you go out——

[*He allows her to remove the plaid, protesting during the process.*]

SIR WILLIAM I'll not trouble ye, ma'am. Much obleeged to ye, but I'll not trouble ye. [*Rising.*] I'll not trouble ye—— [*He walks away to the fireplace, and up the room. She folds the plaid and lays it upon the sofa. He looks round—speaking in an altered tone.*] My dear, gypsying doesn't seem to be such a good trade with ye, as it used to be by all accounts——

[*The center door opens and* AVONIA *enters boldly, in the dress of a burlesque princess, cotton-velvet shirt, edged with bullion trimming, a cap, white tights, ankle boots, etc.*]

AVONIA [*Unconsciously.*] How's this, Rose——?

SIR WILLIAM Ah—h—h—h!

ROSE Oh, go away, 'Vonia!

AVONIA Sir Gower! [*To* SIR WILLIAM.] Good-morning.
[*She withdraws.*]

SIR WILLIAM [*Pacing the room—again very violent.*] Yes! and these are the associates you would have tempted my boy—my grandson—to herd with! [*Flourishing his stick.*] Ah—h—h—h!

ROSE [*Sitting upon the basket—weakly.*] That young lady doesn't live in that attire. She is preparing for the pantomime——

SIR WILLIAM [*Standing over her.*] And

now he's gone; lured away, I suspect, by one of ye—[*pointing to the center door*] by one of these harridans!——

[AVONIA *reappears defiantly.*]

AVONIA Look here, Sir Gower——

ROSE [*Rising.*] Go, 'Vonia!

AVONIA [*To* SIR WILLIAM.] We've met before, if you remember, in Cavendish Square——

ROSE [*Sitting again, helplessly.*] Oh, Mrs. Gadd——!

SIR WILLIAM Mistress! a married lady!

AVONIA Yes, I spent some of my honeymoon at your house——

SIR WILLIAM What!

AVONIA Excuse my dress; it's all in the way of my business. Just one word about Rose.

ROSE Please, 'Vonia——!

AVONIA [*To* SIR WILLIAM, *who is glaring at her in horror.*] Now, there's nothing to stare at, Sir Gower. If you must look anywhere in particular, look at that poor thing. A nice predicament you've brought her to!

SIR WILLIAM Sir——! [*Correcting himself.*] Madam!

AVONIA You've brought her to beggary, amongst you. You've broken her heart; and, what's worse, you've made her genteel. She can't act, since she left your mansion; she can only mope about the stage with her eyes fixed like a person in a dream—dreaming of him, I suppose, and of what it is to be a lady. And first she's put upon half-salary; and then, to-day, she gets the sack—the entire sack, Sir Gower! So there's nothing left for her but to starve, or to make artificial flowers. Miss Trelawny I'm speaking of! [*Going to* ROSE, *and embracing her.*] Our Rose! our Trelawny! [*To* ROSE, *breaking down.*] Excuse me for interfering, ducky. [*Retiring, in tears.*] Good-day, Sir Gower.

[*She goes out.*]

SIR WILLIAM [*After a pause, to* ROSE.] Is this—the case?

ROSE [*Standing, and speaking in a low voice.*] Yes. As you have noticed, fortune has turned against me, rather.

SIR WILLIAM [*Penitently.*] I—I'm sorry, ma'am. I—I believe ye've kept your word to us concerning Arthur. I—I——

ROSE [*Not heeding him, looking before her, dreamily.*] My mother knew how fickle fortune could be to us gypsies. One of the greatest actors that ever lived warned her of that——

SIR WILLIAM Miss Gower will also feel extremely—extremely——

ROSE Kean once warned mother of that.

SIR WILLIAM [*In an altered tone.*] Kean? which Kean?

ROSE Edmund Kean. My mother acted with Edmund Kean when she was a girl.

SIR WILLIAM [*Approaching her slowly, speaking in a queer voice.*] With Kean? with Kean!

ROSE Yes.

SIR WILLIAM [*At her side, in a whisper.*] My dear, I—I've seen Edmund Kean.

ROSE Yes?

SIR WILLIAM A young man then, I was; quite different from the man I am now—impulsive, excitable. Kean! [*Drawing a deep breath.*] Ah, he was a *splendid* gypsy!

ROSE [*Looking down at the dress-basket.*] I've a little fillet in there that my mother wore as Cordelia to Kean's Lear——

SIR WILLIAM I may have seen your mother also. I was somewhat different in those days——

ROSE [*Kneeling at the basket and opening it.*] And the Order and chain, and the sword, he wore in Richard. He gave them to my father; I've always prized them. [*She drags to the surface a chain with an Order attached to it, and a sword-belt and sword—all very theatrical and tawdry—and a little gold fillet. She hands him the chain.*] That's the Order.

SIR WILLIAM [*Handling it tenderly.*] Kean! God bless me!

ROSE [*Holding up the fillet.*] My poor mother's fillet.

SIR WILLIAM [*Looking at it.*] I may have seen her. [*Thoughtfully.*] I was a young man then. [*Looking at* ROSE *steadily.*] Put it on, my dear.

Arthur W. Pinero *Act Three*

[*She goes to the mirror and puts on the fillet.*]

SIR WILLIAM [*Examining the Order.*] Lord bless us! how he stirred me! how he——!

[*He puts the chain over his shoulders.* ROSE *turns to him.*]

ROSE [*Advancing to him.*] There!

SIR WILLIAM [*Looking at her.*] Cordelia! Cordelia—with Kean!

ROSE [*Adjusting the chain upon him.*] This should hang so. [*Returning to the basket and taking up the sword-belt and sword.*] Look!

SIR WILLIAM [*Handling them.*] Kean! [*To her, in a whisper.*] I'll tell ye! I'll tell ye! when I saw him as Richard—I was young and a fool—I'll tell ye—he almost fired me with an ambition to—to—— [*Fumbling with the belt.*] How did he carry this?

ROSE [*Fastening the belt, with the sword, round him.*] In this way——

SIR WILLIAM Ah! [*He paces the stage, growling and muttering, and walking with a limp and one shoulder hunched. She watches him, seriously.*] Ah! he was a little man too! I remember him! as if it were last night! I remember—— [*Pausing and looking at her fixedly.*] My dear, your prospects in life have been injured by your unhappy acquaintanceship with my grandson.

ROSE [*Gazing into the fire.*] Poor Arthur's prospects in life—what of them?

SIR WILLIAM [*Testily.*] Tsch, tsch, tsch!

ROSE If I knew where he is——!

SIR WILLIAM Miss Trelawny, if you cannot act, you cannot earn your living.

ROSE How is he earning *his* living?

SIR WILLIAM And if you cannot earn your living, you must be provided for.

ROSE [*Turning to him.*] Provided for?

SIR WILLIAM Miss Gower was kind enough to bring me here in a cab. She and I will discuss plans for making provision for ye while driving home.

ROSE [*Advancing to him.*] Oh, I beg you will do no such thing, Sir William.

SIR WILLIAM Hey!

ROSE I could not accept any help from you or Miss Gower.

SIR WILLIAM You must! you shall!

ROSE I will not.

SIR WILLIAM [*Touching the Order and the sword.*] Ah!—yes, I—I'll buy these of ye, my dear.

ROSE Oh, no, no! not for hundreds of pounds! please take them off!

[*There is a hurried knocking at the door.*]

SIR WILLIAM [*Startled.*] Who's that? [*Struggling with the chain and belt.*] Remove these——!

[*The handle is heard to rattle.* SIR WILLIAM *disappears behind the curtains.* IMOGEN *opens the door and looks in.*]

IMOGEN [*Seeing only* ROSE, *and coming to her and embracing her.*] Rose darling, where is Tom Wrench?

ROSE He was here not long since——

IMOGEN [*Going to the door and calling, desperately.*] Tom! Tom Wrench! Mr. Wrench!

ROSE Is anything amiss?

IMOGEN [*Shrilly.*] Tom!

ROSE Imogen!

IMOGEN [*Returning to* ROSE.] Oh, my dear, forgive my agitation——!

[TOM *enters, buoyantly, flourishing the manuscript of his play.*]

TOM I've found it! at the bottom of a box—"deeper than did ever plummet sound——"! [*To* IMOGEN.] Eh? what's the matter?

IMOGEN Oh, Tom, old Mr. Morfew——!

TOM [*Blankly.*] Isn't he willing——?

IMOGEN [*With a gesture of despair.*] I don't know. He's dead.

TOM No!

IMOGEN Three weeks ago. Oh, what a chance he has missed!

[TOM *bangs his manuscript down upon the table savagely.*]

ROSE What is it, Tom? Imogen, what is it?

IMOGEN [*Pacing the room.*] I can think of no one else——

TOM   Done again!

IMOGEN   We shall lose it, of course——

ROSE   Lose what?

TOM   The opportunity—her opportunity, *my* opportunity, *your* opportunity, Rose.

ROSE   [*Coming to him.*]   My opportunity, Tom?

TOM   [*Pointing to the manuscript.*]   My play—my comedy—my youngest born! Jenny has a theatre—could have one—has five hundred towards it, put down by a man who believes in my comedy, God bless him!—the only fellow who has ever believed——?

ROSE   Oh, Tom! [*turning to* IMOGEN] oh, Imogen!

IMOGEN   My dear, five hundred! we want another five, at least.

ROSE   Another five!

IMOGEN   Or eight.

TOM   And you are to play the part of Dora. Isn't she, Jenny—I mean, wasn't she?

IMOGEN   Certainly. Just the sort of simple little Miss you *could* play now, Rose. And we thought that old Mr. Morfew would help us in the speculation. Speculation! it's a dead certainty!

TOM   *Dead* certainty? poor Morfew!

IMOGEN   And here we are, stuck fast——!

TOM   [*Sitting upon the dress-basket dejectedly.*]   And they'll expect me to rehearse that dragon to-morrow with enthusiasm.

ROSE   [*Putting her arm around his shoulder.*]   Never mind, Tom.

TOM   No, I won't—— [*Taking her hand.*] Oh, Rose——! [*Looking up at her.*] Oh, Dora——!

[SIR WILLIAM, *divested of his theatrical trappings, comes from behind the curtain.*]

IMOGEN   Oh——!

TOM   [*Rising.*]   Eh?

ROSE   [*Retreating.*]   Sir William Gower, Tom——

SIR WILLIAM   [*To* TOM.]   I had no wish to be disturbed, sir, and I withdrew [*bowing to* IMOGEN] when that lady entered the room. I have been a party, it appears, to a consultation upon a matter of business. [*To* TOM.] Do I understand, sir, that you have been defeated in some project which would have served the interests of Miss Trelawny.

TOM   Y—y—yes, sir.

SIR WILLIAM   Mr. Wicks——

TOM   Wrench——

SIR WILLIAM   Tsch! Sir, it would give me pleasure—it would give my grandson, Mr. Arthur Gower, pleasure—to be able to aid Miss Trelawny at the present moment.

TOM   S—s—sir William, w—w—would you like to hear my play——?

SIR WILLIAM   [*Sharply.*]   Hey! [*Looking round.*] Ho, ho!

TOM   My comedy?

SIR WILLIAM   [*Cunningly.*]   So ye think I might be induced to fill the office ye designed for the late Mr.—Mr.——

IMOGEN   Morfew.

SIR WILLIAM   Morfew, eh?

TOM   N—n—no, sir.

SIR WILLIAM   No! no!

IMOGEN   [*Shrilly.*]   Yes!

SIR WILLIAM   [*After a short pause, quietly.*]   Read your play, sir. [*Pointing to a chair at the table.*] Sit down. [*To* ROSE *and* IMOGEN.] Sit down.

[TOM *goes to the chair indicated.* MISS GOWER'S *voice is heard outside the door.*]

MISS GOWER   [*Outside.*]   William! [ROSE *opens the door;* MISS GOWER *enters.*] Oh, William, what has become of you? has anything dreadful happened?

SIR WILLIAM   Sit down, Trafalgar. This gentleman is about to read a comedy. A cheer! [*Testily.*] Are there no cheers here! [ROSE *brings a chair and places it for* MISS GOWER *beside* SIR WILLIAM'S *chair.*] Sit down.

MISS GOWER   [*Sitting, bewildered.*]   William, is all this—quite——?

SIR WILLIAM   [*Sitting.*]   Yes, Trafalgar, quite in place—quite in place——

[IMOGEN *sits.* ROSE *pulls the dress-basket round, as* COLPOYS *and* GADD *swagger in at the door,* COLPOYS *smoking a pipe,* GADD *a large cigar.*]

SIR WILLIAM [*To* TOM, *referring to* GADD *and* COLPOYS.] Friends of yours?

TOM Yes, Sir William.

SIR WILLIAM [*To* GADD *and* COLPOYS.] Sit down. [*Imperatively.*] Sit down and be silent.

[GADD *and* COLPOYS *seat themselves upon the sofa, like men in a dream.* ROSE *sits on the dress-basket.*]

AVONIA [*Opening the center door slightly —in an anxious voice.*] Rose——!

SIR WILLIAM Come in, ma'am, come in! [AVONIA *enters, coming to* ROSE. *A cloak is now attached to the shoulders of* AVONIA's *dress.*] Sit down, ma'am, and be silent!

[AVONIA *sits beside* ROSE, *next to* MISS GOWER.]

MISS GOWER [*In horror.*] Oh—h—h—h!

SIR WILLIAM [*Restraining her.*] Quite in place, Trafalgar; quite in place. [*To* TOM.] Now, sir!

TOM [*Opening his manuscript and reading.*] "Life, a comedy, by Thomas Wrench——"

Act Four

The scene represents the stage of a theatre with the proscenium arch, and the dark and empty auditorium in the distance. The curtain is raised. The stage extends a few feet beyond the line of the proscenium, and is terminated by a row of old-fashioned footlights with metal reflectors. On the left, from the proscenium arch runs a wall, in which is an open doorway supposed to admit to the Green-room. Right and left of the stage are the "P." and "O.P." and the first and second entrances, with wings running in grooves, according to the old fashion. Against the wall are some "flats." Just below the footlights is a T-light, burning gas, and below this the prompt-table. On the right of the prompt-table is a chair, and on the left another. Against the edge of the proscenium arch is another chair; and nearer, on the right, stands a large throne-chair, with a gilt frame and red velvet seat, now much dilapidated. In the "second entrance" there are a "property" stool, a table, and a chair, all of a similar style to the throne-chair and in like condition, and on the center, as if placed there for the purpose of rehearsal, are a small circular table and a chair. On this table is a work-basket containing a ball of wool and a pair of knitting-needles; and on the prompt-table there is a book. A faded and ragged green baize covers the floor of the stage.

The wings, and the flats and borders, suggest by their appearance a theatre fallen somewhat into decay. The light is a dismal one, but it is relieved by a shaft of sunlight entering through a window in the flies on the right.

[MRS. TELFER *is seated upon the throne-chair, in an attitude of dejection.* TELFER *enters from the Green-room.*]

TELFER [*Coming to her.*] Is that you, Violet?

MRS. TELFER Is the reading over?

TELFER Almost. My part is confined to the latter 'alf of the second act; so being close to the Green-room door [*with a sigh*], I stole away.

MRS. TELFER It affords you no opportunity, James?

TELFER [*Shaking his head.*] A mere fragment.

MRS. TELFER [*Rising.*] Well, but a few good speeches to a man of your stamp——

TELFER Yes, but this is so line-y. Violet; so very line-y. And what d'ye think the character is described as?

MRS. TELFER What?

TELFER "An old, stagey, out-of-date actor."

[*They stand looking at each other for a moment, silently.*]

MRS. TELFER [*Falteringly.*] Will you—be able—to get near it, James?

TELFER [*Looking away from her.*] I dare say——

MRS. TELFER [*Laying a hand upon his shoulder.*] That's all right, then.

TELFER And you—what have they called you for, if you're not in the play? They 'ave not dared to suggest understudy?

MRS. TELFER [*Playing with her fingers.*] They don't ask me to act at all, James.

TELFER Don't ask you——!

MRS. TELFER Miss Parrott offers me the position of Wardrobe-mistress.

TELFER Violet——!

MRS. TELFER Hush!

TELFER Let us both go home.

MRS. TELFER [*Restraining him.*] No, let us remain. We've been idle six months, and I can't bear to see you without your watch and all your comforts about you.

TELFER [*Pointing towards the Green-room.*] And so this new-fangled stuff, and these dandified people, are to push us, and such as us, from our stools!

MRS. TELFER Yes, James, just as some other new fashion will, in course of time, push *them* from their stools.

[*From the Green-room comes the sound of a slight clapping of hands, followed by a murmur of voices. The* TELFERS *move away.* IMOGEN, *elaborately dressed, enters from the Green-room and goes leisurely to the prompt-table. She is followed by* TOM, *manuscript in hand, smarter than usual in appearance; and he by* O'DWYER,—*an excitable Irishman of about forty, with an extravagant head of hair,—who carries a small bundle of "parts" in brown-paper covers.* TOM *and* O'DWYER *join* IMOGEN.]

O'DWYER. [*To* TOM.] Mr. Wrench, I congratulate ye; I have that honor, sir. Your piece will do, sir; it will take the town, mark me.

TOM Thank you, O'Dwyer.

IMOGEN Look at the sunshine! there's a good omen, at any rate.

O'DWYER Oh, sunshine's nothing. [*To* TOM.] But did ye observe the gloom on their faces whilst ye were readin'?

IMOGEN [*Anxiously.*] Yes, they did look glum.

O'DWYER Glum! it might have been a funeral! There's a healthy prognostication for ye, if ye loike! it's infallible.

[*A keen-faced gentleman and a lady enter, from the Green-room, and stroll across the stage to the right, where they lean against the wings and talk. Then two young gentlemen enter, and* ROSE *follows.*

Note.—The actors and the actress appearing for the first time in this act, as members of the Pantheon Company, are outwardly greatly superior to the GADDS, *the* TELFERS, *and* COLPOYS.]

ROSE [*Shaking hands with* TELFER.] Why didn't you sit near me, Mr. Telfer? [*Going to* MRS. TELFER.] Fancy our being together again, and at the West End! [*To* TELFER.] Do you like the play?

TELFER Like it! there's not a speech in it, my dear—not a real *speech;* nothing to dig your teeth into——

O'DWYER [*Allotting the parts, under the direction of* TOM *and* IMOGEN.] Mr. Mortimer! [*One of the young gentlemen advances and receives his part from* O'DWYER, *and retires, reading it.*] Mr. Denzil!

[*The keen-faced gentleman takes his part, then joins* IMOGEN *on her left and talks to her. The lady now has something to say to the solitary young gentleman.*]

TOM [*To* O'DWYER, *quietly, handing him a part.*] Miss Brewster.

O'DWYER [*Beckoning to the lady, who does not observe him, her back being towards him.*] Come here, my love.

TOM [*To* O'DWYER.] No, no, O'Dwyer—not your "love."

O'DWYER [*Perplexed.*] Not?

TOM No.

O'DWYER   No?

TOM   Why, you are meeting her this morning for the first time.

O'DWYER   That's true enough. [*Approaching the lady and handing her the part.*] Miss Brewster.

THE LADY   Much obliged.

O'DWYER [*Quietly to her.*]   It'll fit ye like a glove, darlin'.

[*The lady sits, conning her part.* O'DWYER *returns to the table.*]

TELFER [*To* ROSE.]   Your lover in the play? which of these young sparks plays your lover—Harold or Gerald——?

ROSE   Gerald. I don't know. There are some people not here to-day, I believe.

O'DWYER   Mr. Hunston!

[*The second young gentleman advances, receives his part, and joins the other young gentleman in the wings.*]

ROSE   Not that young man, I hope. Isn't he a little bandy?

TELFER   One of the finest Macduffs I ever fought with was bow-legged.

O'DWYER   Mr. Kelfer.

TOM [*To* O'DWYER.]   No, no—Telfer.

O'DWYER   Telfer.

[TELFER *draws himself erect, puts his hand in his breast, but otherwise remains stationary.*]

MRS. TELFER [*Anxiously.*]   That's you, James.

O'DWYER   Come on, Mr. Telfer! look alive, sir!

TOM [*To* O'DWYER.]   Sssh, sssh, sssh! don't, don't——! [TELFER *advances to the prompt-table, slowly. He receives his part from* O'DWYER. *To* TELFER, *awkwardly.*] I—I hope the little part of Poggs appeals to you, Mr. Telfer. Only a sketch, of course; but there was nothing else—quite—in your——

TELFER   Nothing? to whose share does the Earl fall?

TOM   Oh, Mr. Denzil plays Lord Parracourt.

TELFER   Denzil? I've never 'eard of 'im. Will you get to me to-day?

TOM   We—we expect to do so.

TELFER   Very well. [*Stiffly.*] Let me be called in the street.   [*He stalks away.*]

MRS. TELFER [*Relieved.*]   Thank Heaven! I was afraid James would break out.

ROSE [*To* MRS. TELFER.]   But you, dear Mrs. Telfer—you weren't at the reading —what are *you* cast for?

MRS. TELFER   I? [*Wiping away a tear.*] I am the Wardrobe-mistress of this theatre.

ROSE   You! [*Embracing her.*] Oh! oh!

MRS. TELFER [*Composing herself.*]   Miss Trelawny—Rose—my child, if we are set to scrub a floor—and we may come to that yet—let us make up our minds to scrub it legitimately—with dignity——

[*She disappears and is seen no more.*]

O'DWYER   Miss Trelawny! come here, my de——

TOM [*To* O'DWYER.]   Hush!

O'DWYER   Miss Trelawny!

[ROSE *receives her part from* O'DWYER *and, after a word or two with* TOM *and* IMOGEN, *joins the two young gentlemen who are in the "second entrance, left." The lady, who has been seated, now rises and crosses to the left, where she meets the keen-faced gentleman, who has finished his conversation with* IMOGEN.]

THE LADY [*To the keen-faced gentleman.*] I say, Mr. Denzil! who plays Gerald?

THE GENTLEMAN   Gerald?

THE LADY   The man I have my scene with in the third act—the hero——

THE GENTLEMAN   Oh, yes. Oh, a young gentleman from the country, I understand.

THE LADY   From the country!

THE GENTLEMAN   He is coming up by train this morning, Miss Parrott tells me; from Bath or somewhere——

THE LADY   Well, whoever he is, if he can't play that scene with me decently, my part's not worth rags.

TOM [*To* IMOGEN, *who is sitting at the prompt-table.*]   Er—h'm—shall we begin, Miss Parrott?

IMOGEN   Certainly, Mr. Wrench.

TOM   We'll begin, O'Dwyer.

[*The lady titters at some remark from the keen-faced gentleman.*]

O'DWYER   [*Coming down the stage, violently.*] Clear the stage there! I'll not have it! Upon my honor, this is the noisiest theatre I've ever set foot in!

[*The wings are cleared, the characters disappearing into the Green-room.*]

O'DWYER   I can't hear myself speak for all the riot and confusion!

TOM   [*To* O'DWYER.] My dear O'Dwyer, there is *no* riot, there is *no* confusion——

IMOGEN   [*To* O'DWYER.] Except the riot and confusion *you* are making.

TOM   You know, you're admirably earnest, O'Dwyer, but a little excitable.

O'DWYER   [*Calming himself.*] Oh, I beg your pardon, I'm sure. [*Emphatically.*] My system is, begin as you mean to go on.

IMOGEN   But we *don't* mean to go on like that.

TOM   Of course not; of course not. Now, let me see—[*pointing to the right center*] we shall want another chair here.

O'DWYER   Another chair?

TOM   A garden chair.

O'DWYER   [*Excitably.*] Another chair! Now, then, another chair! Properties! where are ye? de ye hear me callin'? must I raise my voice to ye——?

[*He rushes away.*]

IMOGEN   [*To* TOM.] Phew! where did you get *him* from?

TOM   [*Wiping his brow.*] Known Michael for years—most capable, invaluable fellow——

IMOGEN   [*Simply.*] I wish he was dead.

TOM   So do I.

[O'DWYER *returns, carrying a light chair.*]

TOM   Well, where's the property-man?

O'DWYER   [*Pleasantly.*] It's all right now. He's gone to dinner.

TOM   [*Placing the chair in position.*] Ah, then he'll be back some time during the afternoon. [*Looking about him.*] That will do. [*Taking up his manuscript.*] Call —haven't you engaged a call-boy yet, O'Dwyer?

O'DWYER   I have, sir, and the best in London.

IMOGEN   Where is he?

O'DWYER   He has sint an apology for his non-attindance.

IMOGEN   Oh——!

O'DWYER   A sad case, ma'am; he's buryin' his wife.

TOM   Wife!

IMOGEN   The call-boy?

TOM   What's his age?

O'DWYER   Ye see, he happens to be an elder brother of my own——

IMOGEN AND TOM   O Lord!

TOM   Never mind! let's get on! Call Miss —— [*Looking toward the right.*] Is that the Hall-Keeper?

[*A man, suggesting by his appearance that he is the Hall-Keeper, presents himself, with a card in his hand.*]

O'DWYER   [*Furiously.*] Now then! are we to be continually interrupted in this fashion? Have I, or have I not, given strict orders that nobody whatever——?

TOM   Hush, hush! see whose card it is; give me the card——

O'DWYER   [*Handing the card to* TOM.] Ah, I'll make rules here. In a week's time you'll not know this for the same theatre——

[TOM *has passed the card to* IMOGEN *without looking at it.*]

IMOGEN   [*Staring at it blankly.*] Oh——!

TOM   [*To her.*] Eh?

IMOGEN   Sir William!

TOM   Sir William!

IMOGEN   What can he want? what shall we do?

TOM   [*After referring to his watch—to the Hall-Keeper.*] Bring this gentleman on to the stage. [*The Hall-Keeper withdraws. To* O'DWYER.] Make yourself scarce for a few moments, O'Dwyer. Some private business——

O'DWYER All right. I've plenty to occupy me. I'll begin to frame those rules——

[*He disappears.*]

IMOGEN [*To* TOM.] Not here——

TOM [*To* IMOGEN.] The boy can't arrive for another twenty minutes. Besides, we must, sooner or later, accept responsibility for our act.

IMOGEN [*Leaning upon his arm.*] Heavens! I foretold this!

TOM [*Grimly.*] I know—"said so all along."

IMOGEN If he should withdraw his capital!

TOM [*With clenched hands.*] At least, that would enable me to write a melodrama.

IMOGEN Why?

TOM I should then understand the motives and the springs of Crime!

[*The Hall-Keeper reappears, showing the way to* SIR WILLIAM GOWER. SIR WILLIAM's *hat is drawn down over his eyes, and the rest of his face is almost entirely concealed by his plaid. The Hall-Keeper withdraws.*]

TOM [*Receiving* SIR WILLIAM.] How d'ye do, Sir William?

SIR WILLIAM [*Giving him two fingers—with a grunt.*] Ugh!

TOM These are odd surroundings for you to find yourself in—— [IMOGEN *comes forward.*] Miss Parrott——

SIR WILLIAM [*Advancing to her, giving her two fingers.*] Good-morning, ma'am.

IMOGEN This is perfectly delightful.

SIR WILLIAM What is?

IMOGEN [*Faintly.*] Your visit.

SIR WILLIAM Ugh! [*Weakly.*] Give me a cheer. [*Looking about him.*] Have ye no cheers here?

TOM Yes.

[TOM *places the throne-chair behind* SIR WILLIAM, *who sinks into it.*]

SIR WILLIAM Thank ye; much obleeged. [*To* IMOGEN.] Sit. [IMOGEN *hurriedly fetches the stool and seats herself beside the throne-chair.* SIR WILLIAM *produces his snuff-box.*] You are astonished at seeing me here, I dare say?

TOM Not at all.

SIR WILLIAM [*Glancing at* TOM.] Addressing the lady. [*To* IMOGEN.] You are surprised to see me?

IMOGEN Very.

SIR WILLIAM [*To* TOM.] Ah! [TOM *retreats, getting behind* SIR WILLIAM's *chair and looking down upon him.*] The truth is, I am beginning to regret my association with ye.

IMOGEN [*Her hand to her heart.*] Oh—h—h—h!

TOM [*Under his breath.*] Oh! [*Holding his first over* SIR WILLIAM's *head.*] Oh—h—h—h!

IMOGEN [*Piteously.*] You—you don't propose to withdraw your capital, Sir William?

SIR WILLIAM That would be a breach of faith, ma'am——

IMOGEN Ah!

TOM [*Walking about, jauntily.*] Ha!

IMOGEN [*Seizing* SIR WILLIAM's *hand.*] Friend!

SIR WILLIAM [*Withdrawing his hand sharply.*] I'll thank ye not to repeat that action, ma'am. But I—I have been slightly indisposed since I made your acqueentance in Clerkenwell; I find myself unable to sleep at night. [*To* TOM.] That comedy of yours—it buzzes continually in my head, sir.

TOM It was written with such an intention, Sir William—to buzz in people's heads.

SIR WILLIAM Ah, I'll take care ye don't read me another, Mr. Wicks; at any rate, another which contains a character resembling a member of my family—a *late* member of my family. I don't relish being reminded of late members of my family in this way, and being kept awake at night, thinking—turning over in my mind——

IMOGEN [*Soothingly.*] Of course not.

SIR WILLIAM [*Taking snuff.*] Pa—a—a—h! pi—i—i—sh! When I saw Kean, as Richard, he reminded me of no member of my family. Shakespeare knew better than that, Mr. Wicks. [*To* IMOGEN.] And therefore, ma'am, upon receiving your letter last night, acqueenting me with your intention to commence rehearsing your comedy—[*glancing at* TOM] *his* comedy——

IMOGEN [*Softly.*]   *Our* comedy——

SIR WILLIAM   Ugh—to-day at noon, I determined to present myself here and request to be allowed to—to——

TOM   To watch the rehearsal?

SIR WILLIAM   The rehearsal of those episodes in your comedy which remind me of a member of my family—a *late* member.

IMOGEN [*Constrainedly.*]   Oh, certainly——

TOM [*Firmly.*]   By all means.

SIR WILLIAM [*Rising, assisted by* TOM.]   I don't wish to be steered at by any of your —what d'ye call 'em?—your gypsy crew——

TOM   Ladies and Gentlemen of the Company, we call 'em.

SIR WILLIAM [*Tartly.*]   I don't care what ye call 'em. [TOM *restores the throne-chair to its former position.*] Put me into a curtained box, where I can hear, and see, and not be seen; and when I have heard and seen enough, I'll return home—and —and—obtain a little sleep; and to-morrow I shall be well enough to sit in Court again.

TOM [*Calling.*]   Mr. O'Dwyer——

[O'DWYER *appears;* TOM *speaks a word or two to him, and hands him the manuscript of the play.*]

IMOGEN [*To* SIR WILLIAM, *falteringly.*] And if you are pleased with what you see this morning, perhaps you will attend another——?

SIR WILLIAM [*Angrily.*]   Not I. After to-day I wash my hands of ye. What do plays and players do, coming into my head, disturbing my repose! [*More composedly, to* TOM, *who has returned to his side.*] Your comedy has merit, sir. You call it *Life.* There is a character in it—a young man —not unlike life, not unlike a late member of my family. Obleege me with your arm. [*To* IMOGEN.] Madam, I have arrived at the conclusion that Miss Trelawny belongs to a set of curious people who in other paths might have been useful members of society. But after to-day I've done with ye—done with ye—— [*To* TOM.] My box, sir—my box—

[TOM *leads* SIR WILLIAM *up the stage.*]

TOM [*To* O'DWYER.]   Begin rehearsal. Begin rehearsal! Call Miss Trelawny!

[TOM *and* SIR WILLIAM *disappear.*]

O'DWYER   Miss Trelawny! Miss Trelawny! [*Rushing to the left.*] Miss Trelawny! how long am I to stand here shoutin' myself hoarse——?   [ROSE *appears.*]

ROSE [*Gently.*]   Am I called?

O'DWYER [*Instantly calm.*]   You are, darlin'. [O'DWYER *takes his place at the prompt-table, book in hand.* IMOGEN *and* ROSE *stand together in the center. The other members of the company come from the Green-room and stand in the wings, watching the rehearsal.*] Now then! [*Reading from the manuscript.*] "At the opening of the play Peggy and Dora are discovered——" Who's Peggy? [*Excitedly.*] Where's Peggy? Am I to——?

IMOGEN   Here I am! here I am! I am Peggy.

O'DWYER [*Calm.*]   Of course ye are, lovey— ma'am, I should say——

IMOGEN   Yes, you should.

O'DWYER   "Peggy is seated upon the Right, Dora on the Left——" [ROSE *and* IMOGEN *seat themselves accordingly. In a difficulty.*] No—Peggy on the Left, Dora on the Right. [*Violently.*] This is the worst written scrip I've ever held in my hand—— [ROSE *and* IMOGEN *change places.*] So horribly scrawled over, and interlined, and—no—I was quite correct. Peggy is on the Right, and Dora is on the Left. [IMOGEN *and* ROSE *again change seats.* O'DWYER *reads from the manuscript.*] "Peggy is engaged in—in——" I can't decipher it. A scrip like this is a disgrace to any well-conducted theatre.

[*To* IMOGEN.] I don't know what you're
doin'. "Dora is—is——" [*To* ROSE.] You
are also doin' something or another. Now
then! When the curtain rises, you are discovered, both of ye, employed in the way
described—— [TOM *returns*.] Ah, here ye
are! [*Resigning the manuscript to* TOM,
and pointing out a passage.] I've got it
smooth as far as there.

TOM   Thank you.

O'DWYER [*Seating himself*.] You're welcome.

TOM [*To* ROSE *and* IMOGEN.]   Ah, you're
not in your right positions. Change
places, please.

[IMOGEN *and* ROSE *change seats once
more.* O'DWYER *rises and goes away*.]

O'DWYER [*Out of sight, violently*.]   A scrip
like that's a scandal! If there's a livin'
soul that can read bad handwriting, I am
that man! But of all the——!

TOM   Hush, hush! Mr. O'Dwyer!

O'DWYER [*Returning to his chair*.]   Here.

TOM [*Taking the book from the prompt-
table and handing it to* IMOGEN.]   You
are reading.

O'DWYER [*Sotto voce*.]   I thought so.

TOM [*To* ROSE.]   You are working.

O'DWYER   Working.

TOM [*Pointing to the basket on the table*.]
There are your needles and wool. [ROSE
*takes the wool and the needles out of the
basket.* TOM *takes the ball of wool from
her and places it in the center of the
stage*.] You have allowed the ball of wool
to roll from your lap on to the grass. You
will see the reason for that presently.

ROSE   I remember it, Mr. Wrench.

TOM   The curtain rises. [*To* IMOGEN.]
Miss Parrott——

IMOGEN [*Referring to her part*.]   What do
I say?

TOM   Nothing—you yawn.

IMOGEN [*Yawning, in a perfunctory way*.]
Oh—h!

TOM   As if you meant it, of course.

IMOGEN   Well, of course.

TOM   Your yawn must tell the audience

that you are a young lady who may be
driven by boredom to almost any extreme.

O'DWYER [*Jumping up*.]   This sort of
thing. [*Yawning extravagantly*.] He—oh!

TOM [*Irritably*.]   Thank you, O'Dwyer;
thank you.

O'DWYER [*Sitting again*.]   You're welcome.

TOM [*To* ROSE.]   You speak.

ROSE [*Reading from her part—retaining
the needles and the end of the wool*.]
"What are you reading, Miss Chaffinch?"

IMOGEN [*Reading from her part*.]   "A
novel."

ROSE   "And what is the name of it?"

IMOGEN   *"The Seasons."*

ROSE   "Why is it called that?"

IMOGEN   "Because all the people in it do
seasonable things."

ROSE   "For instance——?"

IMOGEN   "In the Spring, fall in love."

ROSE   "In the Summer?"

IMOGEN   "Become engaged. Delightful!"

ROSE   "Autumn?"

IMOGEN   "Marry. Heavenly!"

ROSE   "Winter?"

IMOGEN   "Quarrel. Ha, ha, ha!"

TOM [*To* IMOGEN.]   Close the book—with
a bang——

O'DWYER [*Bringing his hands together
sharply by way of suggestion*.]   Bang!

TOM [*Irritably*.]   Yes, yes, O'Dwyer. [*To*
IMOGEN.] Now rise——

O'DWYER   Up ye get!

TOM   And cross to Dora.

IMOGEN [*Going to* ROSE.]   "Miss Harrington, don't you wish occasionally that you
were engaged to be married?"

ROSE   "No."

IMOGEN   "Not on wet afternoons?"

ROSE   "I am perfectly satisfied with this
busy little life of mine, as your aunt's
Companion."

TOM [*To* IMOGEN.]   Walk about, discon-
tentedly.

IMOGEN [*Walking about*.]   "I've nothing
to do; let's tell each other our ages."

ROSE   "I am nineteen."

TOM [*To* IMOGEN.]   In a loud whisper——

IMOGEN "I am twenty-two."

O'DWYER [*Rising and going to* TOM.] Now, hadn't ye better make that *six-and-twenty*?

IMOGEN [*Joining them, with asperity.*] Why? Why?

TOM No, no, certainly not. Go on.

IMOGEN [*Angrily.*] Not till Mr. O'Dwyer retires into his corner.

TOM O'Dwyer—— [O'DWYER *takes his chair, and retires to the "prompt-corner," out of sight, with the air of martyrdom.* TOM *addresses* ROSE.] You speak.

ROSE "I shall think, and feel, the same when I am twenty-two, I am sure. I shall never wish to marry."

TOM [*To* IMOGEN.] Sit on the stump of the tree.

IMOGEN Where's that?

TOM [*Pointing to the stool down the stage.*] Where that stool is.

IMOGEN [*Sitting on the stool.*] "Miss Harrington, who is the Mr. Gerald Leigh who is expected down to-day?"

ROSE "Lord Parracourt's secretary."

IMOGEN "Old and poor!"

ROSE "Neither, I believe. He is the son of a college chum of Lord Parracourt's—so I heard his lordship tell Lady McArchie —and is destined for public life."

IMOGEN "Then he's young!"

ROSE "Extremely, I understand."

IMOGEN [*Jumping up, in obedience to a sign from* TOM.] "Oh, how can you be so spiteful!"

ROSE "I!"

IMOGEN "You mean he's too young!"

ROSE "Too young for what?"

IMOGEN "Too young for—oh, bother!"

TOM [*Looking towards the keen-faced gentleman.*] Mr. Denzil.

O'DWYER [*Putting his head round the corner.*] Mr. Denzil!

[*The keen-faced gentleman comes forward, reading his part, and meets* IMOGEN.]

THE GENTLEMAN [*Speaking in the tones of an old man.*] "Ah, Miss Peggy!"

TOM [*To* ROSE.] Rise, Miss Trelawny.

O'DWYER [*His head again appearing.*] Rise, darlin'!

[ROSE *rises.*]

THE GENTLEMAN [*To* IMOGEN.] "Your bravura has just arrived from London. Lady McArchie wishes you to try it over; and if I may add my entreaties——"

IMOGEN [*Taking his arm.*] "Delighted, Lord Parracourt. [*To* ROSE.] Miss Harrington, bring your work indoors and hear me squall. [*To* THE GENTLEMAN.] Why, you must have telegraphed to town!"

THE GENTLEMAN [*As they cross the stage.*] "Yes, but even telegraphy is too sluggish in executing your smallest command."

[IMOGEN *and the keen-faced gentleman go off on the left. He remains in the wings, she returns to the prompt-table.*]

ROSE "Why do Miss Chaffinch and her girl-friends talk of nothing, think of nothing apparently, but marriage? Ought a woman to make marriage the great object of life? can there be no other? I wonder——"

[*She goes off, the wool trailing after her, and disappears into the Green-room. The ball of wool remains in the center of the stage.*]

TOM [*Reading from his manuscript.*] "The piano is heard; and Peggy's voice singing. Gerald enters——"

IMOGEN [*Clutching* TOM's *arm.*] There——!

TOM Ah, yes, here is Mr. Gordon.

[ARTHUR *appears, in a traveling coat.* TOM *and* IMOGEN *hasten to him and shake hands with him vigorously.*]

TOM [*On* ARTHUR's *right.*] How are you?

IMOGEN [*On his left nervously.*] How are you?

ARTHUR [*Breathlessly.*] Miss Parrott! Mr. Wrench! forgive me if I am late; my cab horse galloped from the station——

TOM We have just reached your entrance. Have you read your part over?

ARTHUR Read it! [*Taking it from his pocket.*] I know every word of it! it has made my journey from Bristol like a flight through the air! Why, Mr. Wrench [*turning over the leaves of his part*], some of this is almost *me!*

TOM AND IMOGEN [*Nervously.*] Ha, ha, ha!

TOM Come! you enter! [*pointing to the right*] there! [*returning to the prompt-table with* IMOGEN] you stroll on, looking about you! Now, Mr. Gordon!

ARTHUR [*Advancing to the center of the stage, occasionally glancing at his part.*] "A pretty place. I am glad I left the carriage at the lodge and walked through the grounds."

[*There is an exclamation, proceeding from the auditorium, and the sound of the overturning of a chair.*]

IMOGEN Oh!

O'DWYER [*Appearing, looking into the auditorium.*] What's that? This is the noisiest theatre I've ever set foot in——!

TOM Don't heed it! [*To* ARTHUR.] Go on, Mr. Gordon.

ARTHUR "Somebody singing. A girl's voice. Lord Parracourt made no mention of anybody but his hostess—the dry, Scotch widow. [*Picking up the ball of wool.*] This is Lady McArchie's, I'll be bound. The very color suggests spectacles and iron-gray curls——"

TOM Dora returns. [*Calling.*] Dora!

O'DWYER Dora! where are ye?

THE GENTLEMAN [*Going to the Green-room door.*] Dora! Dora!

[ROSE *appears in the wings.*]

ROSE [*To* TOM.] I'm sorry.

TOM Go on, please!

[*There is another sound, nearer the stage, of the overturning of some object.*]

O'DWYER What——?

TOM Don't heed it!

ROSE [*Coming face to face with* ARTHUR.] Oh——!

ARTHUR Rose!

TOM Go on, Mr. Gordon!

ARTHUR [*To* ROSE, *holding out the ball of wool.*] "I beg your pardon—are you looking for this?"

ROSE "Yes, I—I—I——" [*Dropping her head upon his breast.*] Oh, Arthur!

[SIR WILLIAM *enters, and comes forward on* ARTHUR's *right.*]

SIR WILLIAM Arthur!

ARTHUR [*Turning to him.*] Grandfather!

O'DWYER [*Indignantly.*] Upon my soul——!

TOM Leave the stage, O'Dwyer!

[O'DWYER *vanishes.* IMOGEN *goes to those who are in the wings and talks to them; gradually they withdraw into the Greenroom.* ROSE *sinks on to the stool;* TOM *comes to her and stands beside her.*]

SIR WILLIAM What's this? what is it——?

ARTHUR [*Bewildered.*] Sir, I—I—you—and—and Rose—are the last persons I expected to meet here——

SIR WILLIAM Ah—h—h—h!

ARTHUR Perhaps you have both already learned, from Mr. Wrench or Miss Parrott, that I have—become—a gypsy, sir?

SIR WILLIAM Not I; [*pointing to* TOM *and* IMOGEN] these—these people have thought it decent to allow me to make the discovery for myself.

[*He sinks into the throne-chair.* TOM *goes to* SIR WILLIAM. ARTHUR *joins* IMOGEN; *they talk together rapidly and earnestly.*]

TOM [*To* SIR WILLIAM.] Sir William, the secret of your grandson's choice of a profession——

SIR WILLIAM [*Scornfully.*] Profession!

TOM Was one that I was pledged to keep as long as it was possible to do so. And pray remember that your attendance here this morning is entirely your own act. It was our intention——

SIR WILLIAM [*Struggling to his feet.*] Where is the door? the way to the door?

TOM And let me beg you to understand

this, Sir William—that Miss Trelawny was, till a moment ago, as ignorant as yourself of Mr. Arthur Gower's doings, of his movements, of his whereabouts. She would never have thrown herself in his way, in this manner. Whatever conspiracy——

SIR WILLIAM Conspiracy! the right word —conspiracy!

TOM Whatever conspiracy there has been is my own—to bring these two young people together again, to make them happy——

[ROSE *holds out her hand to* TOM; *he takes it. They are joined by* IMOGEN.]

SIR WILLIAM [*Looking about him.*] The door! the door!

ARTHUR [*Coming to* SIR WILLIAM.] Grandfather, may I, when rehearsal is over, venture to call in Cavendish Square——?

SIR WILLIAM Call——!

ARTHUR Just to see Aunt Trafalgar, sir? I hope Aunt Trafalgar is well, sir.

SIR WILLIAM [*With a slight change of tone.*] Your Great-aunt Trafalgar? Ugh, yes, I suppose she will consent to see ye——

ARTHUR Ah, sir——!

SIR WILLIAM But *I* shall be out; *I* shall not be within doors.

ARTHUR Then, if Aunt Trafalgar will receive me, sir, do you think I may be allowed to—to bring Miss Trelawny with me——?

SIR WILLIAM What! ha, I perceive you have already acquired the impudence of your vagabond class, sir; the brazen effrontery of a set of——!

ROSE [*Rising and facing him.*] Forgive him! forgive him! oh, Sir William, why may not Arthur become, some day, a *splendid* gypsy?

SIR WILLIAM Eh?

ROSE Like——

SIR WILLIAM [*Peering into her face.*] Like——?

ROSE Like——

TOM Yes, sir, a gypsy, though of a differ-

ent order from the old order which is departing—a gypsy of the new school!

SIR WILLIAM [*To* ROSE.] Well, Miss Gower is a weak, foolish lady; for aught I know she may allow this young man to—to— take ye——

IMOGEN I would accompany Rose, of course, Sir William.

SIR WILLIAM [*Tartly.*] Thank ye, ma'am. [*Turning.*] I'll go to my carriage.

ARTHUR Sir, if you have the carriage here, and if you would have the patience to sit out the rest of the rehearsal, we might return with you to Cavendish Square.

SIR WILLIAM [*Choking.*] Oh—h—h—h!

ARTHUR Grandfather, we are not rich people, and a cab to us——

SIR WILLIAM [*Exhausted.*] Arthur——!

TOM Sir William will return to his box! [*Going up the stage.*] O'Dwyer!

SIR WILLIAM [*Protesting weakly.*] No, sir! no!

[O'DWYER *appears.*]

TOM Mr. O'Dwyer, escort Sir William Gower to his box.

[ARTHUR *goes up the stage with* SIR WILLIAM, SIR WILLIAM *still uttering protests.* ROSE *and* IMOGEN *embrace.*]

O'DWYER [*Giving an arm to* SIR WILLIAM.] Lean on me, sir! heavily, sir——!

TOM Shall we proceed with the rehearsal, Sir William, or wait till you are seated?

SIR WILLIAM [*Violently.*] Wait! Confound ye, d'ye think I want to remain here all day!

[SIR WILLIAM *and* O'DWYER *disappear.*]

TOM [*Coming forward, with* ARTHUR *on his right—wildly.*] Go on with the rehearsal! Mr. Gordon and Miss Rose Trelawny! Miss Trelawny! [ROSE *goes to him.*] Trelawny—late of the "Wells"! Let us—let—— [*Gripping* ARTHUR'S *hand tightly, he bows his head upon* ROSE'S *shoulder.*] Oh, my dears——! let us—get on with the rehearsal——!

The Three Sisters

Anton Chekov   translated by Elisaveta Fen

Introductory Comments

Victor Erlich   *Yale University*

Anton Chekhov's *Three Sisters* was completed in 1900 and performed for the first time by the Moscow Art Theatre on January 31, 1901. Chekhov was then at the peak of his literary career. Russian art and society were about to enter a period of creative and political ferment. But the setting and atmosphere of this, Chekhov's next to last play, bear a strong imprint of a bleaker era, which was coming to an end. The spectacle of three sensitive and graceful young women and their gifted brother trapped in a provincial backwater town could be viewed as emblematic of the social stagnation of the 1880s, a decade dubbed "sour and flabby" by Chekhov. Yet the appeal of *Three Sisters* reaches far beyond the confines of time and place. Chekhov sounds here one of his most characteristic and most universal themes, that of the power of illusion as a mode of coping with a profoundly dispiriting reality.

The illusion shared by the three central figures, Olga, Masha, and Irena, is the myth of Moscow as the paradise lost, as the symbol of everything that is lacking in their dreary, uneventful existence. Moscow is the name of their desire to get away from it all, to find a magical solution to all life's problems. As the play progresses, it becomes increasingly obvious that the eagerly awaited move to the metropolis will never occur, that the obsessive refrain "to Moscow! to Moscow!" which dominates so much of the sisters' conversation and thoughts, is no more than an incantation, a pipe dream.

Another brand of escapism is revealed in the oft-repeated notion that "in two or three hundred years life on this earth will be beautiful beyond our dreams." This belief is professed insistently by Colonel Vershinin, the personable and voluble battery commander who falls in love with Masha. Some Russian critics notwithstanding, Vershinin's speechifying is too compulsive, and his rhetoric too extravagantly utopian and blatantly compensatory, to be interpreted as an expression of Chekhov's own views. Yet when he posits the urge to dream about "a life like that" as man's ineradicable emotional need,

Vershinin appears to have the author's sympathy, and, possibly, his assent.

If Vershinin's eulogies of a "marvelous" future sound at times like a parody of Chekhov's own faith in progress, in the portrayal of Baron Toozenbach, Irena's decent if unprepossessing-looking suitor, the great writer's sturdy respect for work becomes a high-minded fixation. Toozenbach's reaching out of the provincial sloth and empty military routine toward a socially useful life is genuine and creditable. But in a situation where talk looms considerably larger than action, even "work" can become a conversation piece, and discoursing about it at length a temporary substitute for actually working. Moreover, a socially conscious aristocrat, to whom "work" is essentially an exotic notion, is liable to romanticize what to most of us is a routine if not humdrum matter.

Other characters in the play seek to elude reality, not by means of myth-making but through outright denial. Fyodor Koolyghin, Masha's fatuous schoolmaster husband, continually proclaims his domestic happiness in the face of his wife's withering scorn. Andrey Prozorov, the promising brother, reduced to the status of a minor county official and manipulated by his scheming wife, pathetically protests a satisfaction with his life and work and reveals his true feelings only to those who, literally, cannot hear him.

The symbolism of the scene in which Andrey blurts out his gnawing sense of failure to the stone-deaf old messenger Ferapont is quintessentially Chekhovian. In *Three Sisters,* people tend to speak past each other rather than to each other; talk is as frequently a vehicle of self-expression or of inadvertent self-revelation as of purposive communication. Dialogue often is, or appears, disconnected. Rare moments of true emotional rapport do not require articulate speech: the love duet between Masha and Vershinin in Act Three consists of nonsense syllables. Some of the characters are given to muttering, humming, and echoing lines of famous poems or snatches from popular songs. Masha, perhaps the most colorful character in the play, is a good case in point. Her apparent inability to shake off the opening lines of Pushkin's poetic fairy tale *Ruslan and Ludmila* seems indicative of an inner turmoil that she can neither subdue nor convey directly. Disparate psychic themes, "private inner dramas" (in the words of Robert Corrigan), subtly and almost imperceptibly interweave without ever meshing.

As the viewer is alerted to small, at times almost subliminal, cues, he is also made aware of various background noises that keep obtruding upon the proceedings, such as a violin softly played offstage or the stirring music of the military band, first swelling up, then "becoming fainter and fainter." All these contribute to the atmosphere of the play, which in its apparent unselectiveness seeks to capture or emulate the dissonant music of experience.

Another essential facet of Chekhov's low-key dramatic technique is a dearth of external action, the absence of overt confrontations or grand gestures. The humanly significant is conveyed time and again through the medium of the ordinary, the unspectacular, the mundane. "Everything on stage," Chekhov once said, "should be as complex or as simple as it is in real life. People are having dinner, they are simply having dinner, and while they do, happiness is found and lives are broken."

Once again Masha Prozorov provides the prime example: she is about to walk out on her younger sister's birthday party; she is too restless and distraught to lend herself to the festivities. Yet Vershinin's arrival changes her frame of mind. Having listened intently to his impassioned tirade, she announces, "I'm staying to lunch"—an ostensibly trivial statement that in retrospect acquires the weight of a fateful decision.

Moments such as this are the stuff from which the action of *Three Sisters* is made as it moves inexorably toward its cheerless outcome: the Prozorov sisters are dispossessed and outwitted by their grasping, coarse-grained sister-in-law. Their overbred decency is no match for Natasha's animal cunning. Masha's romantic fling is over; Irena's more sober plans for a decent and productive if not a happy existence are shattered by a wanton act. Olga seems resigned to a life of provincial drudgery; Andrey's dreams of academic glory are a shambles.

Yet in the end the play refuses to succumb to unrelieved gloom. As the voices of the three sisters merge into a kind of lyrical fugue, the dominant note is one of resilience, tinged, almost incongruously, with wistful optimism. "We must go on living," Masha declaims defiantly. "I shall work, work, work!" pledges Irena. And Olga, strangely exhilarated by the rousing tune played offstage by the military band, summons her sisters to hope that their miseries and frustrations will not be in vain, that the future might somehow confer meaning and justification on what appears, on the face of it, senseless and futile. Is this a last-minute echo of Vershinin's utopian posturing, another comforting fiction? Perhaps. Yet it is also, I believe, a brave refusal to give up, to surrender to mere contingency, and a suggestion that loveliness and grace are no less real than are the vulgarity and greed that appear to carry the day; that, in the long run, no voice is wholly lost.

Anton Chekhov (1860–1904), the son of a small shopkeeper and the grandson of a serf, studied to become a doctor at the University of Moscow. Even before he received his medical degree in 1884 he had published short stories, chiefly in order to supplement his family's income, but also in the belief that his medical training assisted him in writing about people. In 1888 he was awarded the Pushkin Prize for his collection of stories entitled *In the Twilight*. His play

The Seagull (1896) was a failure when first produced, but when revived in 1898 by the Moscow Art Theatre became a huge success. Chekhov went on to write *Uncle Vanya* (1899), *Three Sisters* (1901), and perhaps his most famous play *The Cherry Orchard* (1904).

In 1901 he married the actress Olga Knipper, who played many of the roles in his plays. He died in Badenweiler, Germany at the height of his powers as a dramatist.

Three Sisters   *Anton Chekhov*

Characters

PROZOROV   *Andrey Serghyevich*

NATASHA   *[Natalia Ivanovna], his fiancée, afterwards his wife*

OLGA   *[Olga Serghyevna, Olia]*

MASHA   *[Maria Serghyevna]*   *his sisters*

IRENA   *[Irena Serghyevna]*

KOOLYGHIN   *Fiodor Ilyich, master at the High School for boys, husband of Masha*

VERSHININ   *Alexandr Ignatyevich, Lieutenant-Colonel, Battery Commander*

TOOZENBACH   *Nigolai Lvovich, Baron, Lieutenant in the Army*

SOLIONY   *Vassily Vassilich, Captain*

CHEBUTYKIN   *Ivan Romanych, Army Doctor*

FEDOTIK   *Aleksey Petrovich, Second Lieutenant*

RODÉ   *Vladimir Karlovich, Second Lieutenant*

FERAPONT   *[Ferapont Spiridonych], an old porter from the County Office*

ANFISA   *the Prozorovs' former nurse, an old woman of 80*

The action takes place in a county town.

Act One

[*A drawing-room in the Prozorovs' house; it is separated from a large ball-room[1] at the back by a row of columns. It is midday; there is cheerful sunshine outside. In the ballroom the table is being laid for lunch.* OLGA, *wearing the regulation dark-blue dress of a secondary school mistress, is correcting her pupils' work, standing or walking about as she does so.* MASHA, *in a black dress, is sitting reading a book, her hat on her lap.* IRENA, *in white, stands lost in thought.*]

OLGA It's exactly a year ago that Father died, isn't it? This very day, the fifth of May—your Saint's day, Irena. I remember it was very cold and it was snowing. I felt then as if I should never survive his death; and you had fainted and were lying quite still, as if you were dead. And now—a year's gone by, and we talk about it so easily. You're wearing white, and your face is positively radiant. . . . [*A clock strikes twelve.*] The clock struck twelve then, too. [*A pause.*] I remember when Father was being taken to the cemetery there was a military band, and a salute with rifle fire. That was because he was a general, in command of a brigade. And yet there weren't many people at the funeral. Of course, it was raining hard, raining and snowing.

IRENA Need we bring up all these memories?

[*Baron* TOOZENBACH, CHEBUTYKIN *and* SOLIONY *appear behind the columns by the table in the ballroom.*]

OLGA It's so warm to-day that we can keep the windows wide open, and yet there aren't any leaves showing on the birch trees. Father was made a brigadier eleven years ago, and then he left Moscow and took us with him. I remember so well how everything in Moscow was in blossom by now, everything was soaked in sunlight and warmth. Eleven years have gone by, yet I remember everything about it, as if we'd only left yesterday. Oh, Heavens! When I woke up this morning and saw this flood of sunshine, all this spring sunshine, I felt so moved and so happy! I felt such a longing to get back home to Moscow!

CHEBUTYKIN [*to* TOOZENBACH] The devil you have!

TOOZENBACH It's nonsense, I agree.

MASHA [*absorbed in her book, whistles a tune under her breath*].

OLGA Masha, do stop whistling! How can you? [*A pause.*] I suppose I must get this continual headache because I have to go to school every day and go on teaching right into the evening. I seem to have the thoughts of someone quite old. Honestly, I've been feeling as if my strength and youth were running out of me drop by drop, day after day. Day after day, all these four years that I've been working at the school. . . . I just have one longing and it seems to grow stronger and stronger. . . .

IRENA If only we could go back to Moscow! Sell the house, finish with our life here, and go back to Moscow.

OLGA Yes, Moscow! As soon as we possibly can.

[CHEBUTYKIN *and* TOOZENBACH *laugh.*]

IRENA I suppose Andrey will soon get a professorship. He isn't likely to go on living here. The only problem is our poor Masha.

OLGA Masha can come and stay the whole summer with us every year in Moscow.

MASHA [*whistles a tune under her breath*].

IRENA Everything will settle itself, with God's help. [*Looks through the window.*] What lovely weather it is to-day! Really,

1 A large room, sparsely furnished, used for receptions and dances in Russian houses.

557

I don't know why there's such joy in my heart. I remembered this morning that it was my Saint's day, and suddenly I felt so happy, and I thought of the time when we were children, and Mother was still alive. And then such wonderful thoughts came to me, such wonderful stirring thoughts!

OLGA You're so lovely to-day, you really do look most attractive. Masha looks pretty to-day, too. Andrey could be good-looking, but he's grown so stout. It doesn't suit him. As for me, I've just aged and grown a lot thinner. I suppose it's through getting so irritated with the girls at school. But to-day I'm at home, I'm free, and my headache's gone, and I feel much younger than I did yesterday. I'm only twenty-eight, after all. . . . I suppose everything that God wills must be right and good, but I can't help thinking sometimes that if I'd got married and stayed at home, it would have been a better thing for me. [*A pause.*] I would have been very fond of my husband.

TOOZENBACH [*to* SOLIONY] Really, you talk such a lot of nonsense, I'm tired of listening to you. [*Comes into the drawing-room.*] I forgot to tell you: Vershinin, our new battery commander, is going to call on you to-day. [*Sits down by the piano.*]

OLGA I'm very glad to hear it.

IRENA Is he old?

TOOZENBACH No, not particularly. Forty, forty-five at the most. [*Plays quietly.*] He seems a nice fellow. Certainly not a fool. His only weakness is that he talks too much.

IRENA Is he interesting?

TOOZENBACH He's all right, only he's got a wife, a mother-in-law and two little girls. What's more, she's his second wife. He calls on everybody and tells them that he's got a wife and two little girls. He'll tell you about it, too, I'm sure of that. His wife seems to be a bit soft in the head. She wears a long plait like a girl, she is always philosophizing and talking in high-flown language, and then she

often tries to commit suicide, apparently just to annoy her husband. I would have run away from a wife like that years ago, but he puts up with it, and just grumbles about it.

SOLIONY [*enters the drawing-room with* CHEBUTYKIN] Now I can only lift sixty pounds with one hand, but with two I can lift two hundred pounds, or even two hundred and forty. So I conclude from that that two men are not just twice as strong as one, but three times as strong, if not more.

CHEBUTYKIN [*reads the paper as he comes in*] Here's a recipe for falling hair . . . two ounces of naphthaline, half-a-bottle of methylated spirit . . . dissolve and apply once a day. . . . [*Writes it down in a notebook.*] Must make a note of it. [*To* SOLIONY.] Well, as I was trying to explain to you, you cork the bottle and pass a glass tube through the cork. Then you take a pinch of ordinary powdered alum, and . . .

IRENA Ivan Romanych, dear Ivan Romanych!

CHEBUTYKIN What is it, my child, what is it?

IRENA Tell me, why is it I'm so happy to-day? Just as if I were sailing along in a boat with big white sails, and above me the wide, blue sky, and in the sky great white birds floating around?

CHEBUTYKIN [*kisses both her hands, tenderly*] My little white bird!

IRENA You know, when I woke up this morning, and after I'd got up and washed, I suddenly felt as if everything in the world had become clear to me, and I knew the way I ought to live. I know it all now, my dear Ivan Romanych. Man must work by the sweat of his brow whatever his class, and that should make up the whole meaning and purpose of his life and happiness and contentment. Oh, how good it must be to be a workman, getting up with the sun and breaking stones by the roadside—or a shepherd—or a schoolmaster teaching the children—or an engine-driver on the railway. Good Heavens! it's better to be a mere ox or horse, and work, than the sort of young woman who wakes up at twelve, and drinks her coffee in bed, and then takes two hours dressing. . . . How dreadful! You know how you long for a cool drink in hot weather? Well, that's the way I long for work. And if I don't get up early from now on and really work, you can refuse to be friends with me any more, Ivan Romanych.

CHEBUTYKIN [*tenderly*] So I will, so I will. . . .

OLGA Father taught us to get up at seven o'clock and so Irena always wakes up at seven—but then she stays in bed till at least nine, thinking about something or other. And with such a serious expression on her face, too! [*Laughs.*]

IRENA You think it's strange when I look serious because you always think of me as a little girl. I'm twenty, you know!

TOOZENBACH All this longing for work. . . . Heavens! how well I can understand it! I've never done a stroke of work in my life. I was born in Petersburg, an unfriendly, idle city—born into a family where work and worries were simply unknown. I remember a valet pulling off my boots for me when I came home from the cadet school. . . . I grumbled at the way he did it, and my mother looked on in admiration. She was quite surprised when other people looked at me in any other way. I was so carefully protected from work! But I doubt whether they succeeded in protecting me for good and all—yes, I doubt it very much! The time's come: there's a terrific thunder-cloud advancing upon us, a mighty storm is coming to freshen us up! Yes, it's coming all right, it's quite near already, and it's going to blow away all this idleness and indifference, and prejudice against work, this rot of boredom that our society is suffering from. I'm going to work, and in twenty-five or thirty years' time every man and woman will be working. Every one of us!

CHEBUTYKIN I'm not going to work.

TOOZENBACH You don't count.

SOLIONY In twenty-five years' time you won't be alive, thank goodness. In a couple of years you'll die from a stroke—or I'll lose my temper with you and put a bullet in your head, my good fellow. [*Takes a scent bottle from his pocket and sprinkles the scent over his chest and hands.*]

CHEBUTYKIN [*laughs*] It's quite true that I never have done any work. Not a stroke since I left the university. I haven't even read a book, only newspapers. [*Takes another newspaper out of his pocket.*] For instance, here. . . . I know from the paper that there was a person called Dobroliubov, but what he wrote about I've not the faintest idea. . . . God alone knows. . . . [*Someone knocks on the floor from downstairs.*] There! They're calling me to come down: there's someone come to see me. I'll be back in a moment. . . . [*Goes out hurriedly, stroking his beard.*]

IRENA He's up to one of his little games.

TOOZENBACH Yes. He looked very solemn as he left. He's obviously going to give you a present.

IRENA I do dislike that sort of thing. . . .

OLGA Yes, isn't it dreadful? He's always doing something silly.

MASHA "A green oak grows by a curving shore, And round that oak hangs a golden chain" . . . [*Gets up as she sings under her breath.*]

OLGA You're sad to-day, Masha.

MASHA [*puts on her hat, singing*].

OLGA Where are you going?

MASHA Home.

IRENA What a strange thing to do.

TOOZENBACH What! Going away from your sister's party?

MASHA What does it matter? I'll be back this evening. Good-bye, my darling. [*Kisses* IRENA.] And once again—I wish you all the happiness in the world. In the old days when Father was alive we used to have thirty or forty officers at our parties. What gay parties we had! And to-day—what have we got to-day? A man and a half, and the place is as quiet as a tomb.

I'm going home. I'm depressed to-day, I'm sad, so don't listen to me. [*Laughs through her tears.*] We'll have a talk later, but good-bye for now, my dear. I'll go somewhere or other. . . .

IRENA [*displeased*] Really, you are a . . .

OLGA [*tearfully*] I understand you, Masha.

SOLIONY If a man starts philosophizing, you call that philosophy, or possibly just sophistry, but if a woman or a couple of women start philosophizing you call that . . . what would you call it, now? Ask me another!

MASHA What are you talking about? You are a disconcerting person!

SOLIONY Nothing.
"He had no time to say 'Oh, oh!'"
Before that bear had struck him low" . . .

[*A pause.*]

MASHA [*to* OLGA, *crossly*] Do stop snivelling!

[*Enter* ANFISA *and* FERAPONT, *the latter carrying a large cake.*]

ANFISA Come along, my dear, this way. Come in, your boots are quite clean. [*To* IRENA.] A cake from Protopopov, at the Council Office.

IRENA Thank you. Tell him I'm very grateful to him. [*Takes the cake.*]

FERAPONT What's that?

IRENA [*louder*] Tell him I sent my thanks.

OLGA Nanny, will you give him a piece of cake? Go along, Ferapont, they'll give you some cake.

FERAPONT What's that?

ANFISA Come along with me, Ferapont Spiridonych, my dear. Come along. [*Goes out with* FERAPONT.]

MASHA I don't like that Protopopov fellow, Mihail Potapych, or Ivanych, or whatever it is. It's best not to invite him here.

IRENA I haven't invited him.

MASHA Thank goodness.

[*Enter* CHEBUTYKIN, *followed by a soldier carrying a silver samovar. Murmurs of astonishment and displeasure.*]

OLGA [*covering her face with her hands*] A samovar! But this is dreadful! [*Goes through to the ballroom and stands by the table.*]

IRENA My dear Ivan Romanych, what are you thinking about?

TOOZENBACH [*laughs*] Didn't I tell you?

MASHA Ivan Romanych, you really ought to be ashamed of yourself!

CHEBUTYKIN My dear, sweet girls, I've no one in the world but you. You're dearer to me than anything in the world! I'm nearly sixty, I'm an old man, a lonely, utterly unimportant old man. The only thing that's worth anything in me is my love for you, and if it weren't for you, really I would have been dead long ago. [*To* IRENA.] My dear, my sweet little girl, haven't I known you since the very day you were born? Didn't I carry you about in my arms? . . . didn't I love your dear mother?

IRENA But why do you get such expensive presents?

CHEBUTYKIN [*tearfully and crossly*] Expensive presents! . . . Get along with you! [*To the orderly.*] Put the samovar over there. [*Mimics* IRENA.] Expensive presents!

[*The orderly takes the samovar to the ballroom.*]

ANFISA [*crosses the drawing-room*] My dears, there's a strange colonel just arrived. He's taken off his coat and he's coming up now. Irenushka, do be nice and polite to him, won't you? [*In the doorway.*] And it's high time we had lunch, too. . . . Oh, dear! [*Goes out.*]

TOOZENBACH It's Vershinin, I suppose.

[*Enter* VERSHININ.]

TOOZENBACH Lieutenant-Colonel Vershinin!

VERSHININ [*to* MASHA *and* IRENA] Allow me to introduce myself—Lieutenant-Colonel Vershinin. I'm so glad, so very glad to be here at last. How you've changed! Dear, dear, how you've changed!

IRENA Please, do sit down. We're very pleased to see you, I'm sure.

VERSHININ [*gayly*] I'm so glad to see you, so glad! But there were three of you, weren't there?—three sisters. I remember there were three little girls. I don't remember their faces, but I knew your father, Colonel Prozorov, and I remember he had three little girls. Oh, yes, I saw them myself. I remember them quite well. How time flies! Dear, dear, how it flies!

TOOZENBACH Alexandr Ignatyevich comes from Moscow.

IRENA From Moscow? You come from Moscow?

VERSHININ Yes, from Moscow. Your father was a battery commander there, and I was an officer in the same brigade. [*To* MASHA.] I seem to remember your face a little.

MASHA I don't remember you at all.

IRENA Olia, Olia! [*Calls towards the ballroom.*] Olia, do come!

[OLGA *enters from the ballroom.*]

IRENA It seems that Lieutenant-Colonel Vershinin comes from Moscow.

VERSHININ You must be Olga Serghyeevna, the eldest. And you are Maria. . . . And you are Irena, the youngest. . . .

OLGA You come from Moscow?

VERSHININ Yes. I studied in Moscow and entered the service there. I stayed there quite a long time, but then I was put in charge of a battery here—so I moved out here, you see. I don't really remember you, you know, I only remember that there were three sisters. I remember your father, though, I remember him very well. All I need to do is to close my eyes and I can see him standing there as if he were alive. I used to visit you in Moscow.

OLGA I thought I remembered everybody, and yet . . .

VERSHININ My Christian names are Alexandr Ignatyevich.

IRENA Alexandr Ignatyevich, and you come from Moscow! Well, what a surprise!

OLGA We're going to live there, you know.

IRENA We hope to be there by the autumn. It's our home town, we were born there. . . . In Staraya Basmannaya Street.

[*Both laugh happily.*]

MASHA Fancy meeting a fellow townsman so unexpectedly! [*Eagerly.*] I remember now. Do you remember, Olga, there was someone they used to call "the lovesick Major"? You were a Lieutenant then, weren't you, and you were in love with someone or other, and everyone used to tease you about it. They called you "Major" for some reason or other.

VERSHININ [*laughs*] That's it, that's it. . . . "The lovesick Major," that's what they called me.

MASHA In those days you only had a moustache. . . . Oh, dear, how much older you look! [*Tearfully.*] How much older!

VERSHININ Yes, I was still a young man in the days when they called me "the lovesick Major." I was in love then. It's different now.

OLGA But you haven't got a single grey hair! You've aged, yes, but you're certainly not an old man.

VERSHININ Nevertheless, I'm turned forty-two. Is it long since you left Moscow?

IRENA Eleven years. Now what are you crying for, Masha, you funny girl? . . . [*Tearfully.*] You'll make me cry, too.

MASHA I'm not crying. What was the street you lived in?

VERSHININ In the Staraya Basmannaya.

OLGA We did, too.

VERSHININ At one time I lived in the Niemietzkaya Street. I used to walk from there to the Krasny Barracks, and I remember there was such a gloomy bridge I had to cross. I used to hear the noise of the water rushing under it. I remember how lonely and sad I felt there. [*A pause.*] But what a magnificently wide river you have here! It's a marvellous river!

OLGA Yes, but this is a cold place. It's cold here, and there are too many mosquitoes.

VERSHININ Really? I should have said you had a really good healthy climate here, a real Russian climate. Forest, river . . . birch-trees, too. The dear, unpretentious birch-trees—I love them more than any of the other trees. It's nice living here. But there's one rather strange thing, the station is fifteen miles from the town. And no one knows why.

SOLIONY I know why it is. [*Everyone looks at him.*] Because if the station were nearer, it wouldn't be so far away, and as it is so far away, it can't be nearer. [*An awkward silence.*]

TOOZENBACH You like your little joke, Vassily Vassilich.

OLGA I'm sure I remember you now. I know I do.

VERSHININ I knew your mother.

CHEBUTYKIN She was a good woman, God bless her memory!

IRENA Mamma was buried in Moscow.

OLGA At the convent of Novo-Dievichye.

MASHA You know, I'm even beginning to forget what she looked like. I suppose people will lose all memory of us in just the same way. We'll be forgotten.

VERSHININ Yes, we shall all be forgotten. Such is our fate, and we can't do anything about it. And all the things that seem serious, important and full of meaning to us now will be forgotten one day—or anyway they won't seem important any more. [*A pause.*] It's strange to think that we're utterly unable to tell what will be regarded as great and important in the future and what will be thought of as just paltry and ridiculous. Didn't the great discoveries of Copernicus—or of Columbus, if you like—appear useless and unimportant to begin with?—whereas some rubbish, written up by an eccentric fool, was regarded as a revelation of great truth? It may well be that in time to come

the life we live to-day will seem strange and uncomfortable and stupid and not too clean, either, and perhaps even wicked. . . .

TOOZENBACH Who can tell? It's just as possible that future generations will think that we lived our lives on a very high plane and remember us with respect. After all, we no longer have tortures and public executions and invasions, though there's still a great deal of suffering!

SOLIONY [*in a high-pitched voice as if calling to chickens*] Cluck, cluck, cluck! There's nothing our good Baron loves as much as a nice bit of philosophizing.

TOOZENBACH Vassily Vassilich, will you kindly leave me alone? [*Moves to another chair.*] It's becoming tiresome.

SOLIONY [*as before*] Cluck, cluck, cluck! . . .

TOOZENBACH [*to* VERSHININ] The suffering that we see around us—and there's so much of it—itself proves that our society has at least achieved a level of morality which is higher. . . .

VERSHININ Yes, yes, of course.

CHEBUTYKIN You said just now, Baron, that our age will be called great; but people are small all the same. . . . [*Gets up.*] Look how small I am.

[*A violin is played off stage.*]

MASHA That's Andrey playing the violin; he's our brother, you know.

IRENA We've got quite a clever brother. . . . We're expecting him to be a professor. Papa was a military man, but Andrey chose an academic career.

OLGA We've been teasing him to-day. We think he's in love, just a little.

IRENA With a girl who lives down here. She'll be calling in to-day most likely.

MASHA The way she dresses herself is awful! It's not that her clothes are just ugly and old-fashioned, they're simply pathetic. She'll put on some weird-looking, bright yellow skirt with a crude sort of fringe affair, and then a red blouse to go with it. And her cheeks look as though they've been scrubbed, they're so shiny!

Andrey's not in love with her—I can't believe it; after all, he has got some taste. I think he's just playing the fool, just to annoy us. I heard yesterday that she's going to get married to Protopopov, the chairman of the local council. I thought it was an excellent idea. [*Calls through the side door.*] Andrey, come here, will you? Just for a moment, dear.

[*Enter* ANDREY.]

OLGA This is my brother, Andrey Serghyeevich.

VERSHININ Vershinin.

ANDREY Prozorov. [*Wipes the perspiration from his face.*] I believe you've been appointed battery commander here?

OLGA What do you think, dear? Alexandr Ignatyevich comes from Moscow.

ANDREY Do you, really? Congratulations! You'll get no peace from my sisters now.

VERSHININ I'm afraid your sisters must be getting tired of me already.

IRENA Just look, Andrey gave me this little picture frame to-day. [*Shows him the frame.*] He made it himself.

VERSHININ [*looks at the frame, not knowing what to say*] Yes, it's . . . it's very nice indeed. . . .

IRENA Do you see that little frame over the piano? He made that one, too.

[ANDREY *waves his hand impatiently and walks off.*]

OLGA He's awfully clever, and he plays the violin, and he makes all sorts of things, too. In fact, he's very gifted all round. Andrey, please, don't go. He's got such a bad habit—always going off like this. Come here!

[MASHA *and* IRENA *take him by the arms and lead him back, laughing.*]

MASHA Now just you come here!

ANDREY Do leave me alone, please do!

MASHA You are a silly! They used to call Alexandr Ignatyevich "the lovesick Major," and he didn't get annoyed.

VERSHININ Not in the least.

MASHA I feel like calling you a "lovesick fiddler."

IRENA Or a "lovesick professor."

OLGA He's fallen in love! Our Andriusha's in love!

IRENA [*clapping her hands*] Three cheers for Andriusha! Andriusha's in love!

CHEBUTYKIN [*comes up behind* ANDREY *and puts his arms round his waist*] "Nature created us for love alone." . . . [*Laughs loudly, still holding his paper in his hand.*]

ANDREY That's enough of it, that's enough. . . . [*Wipes his face.*] I couldn't get to sleep all night, and I'm not feeling too grand just now. I read till four o'clock, and then I went to bed, but nothing happened. I kept thinking about one thing and another . . . and it gets light so early; the sun just pours into my room. I'd like to translate a book from the English while I'm here during the summer.

VERSHININ You read English, then?

ANDREY Yes. My father—God bless his memory—used to simply wear us out with learning. It sounds silly, I know, but I must confess that since he died I've begun to grow stout, as if I'd been physically relieved of the strain. I've grown quite stout in a year. Yes, thanks to Father, my sisters and I know French and German and English, and Irena here knows Italian, too. But what an effort it all cost us!

MASHA Knowing three languages in a town like this is an unnecessary luxury. In fact, not even a luxury, but just a sort of useless encumbrance . . . it's rather like having a sixth finger on your hand. We know a lot of stuff that's just useless.

VERSHININ Really! [*Laughs.*] You know a lot of stuff that's useless! It seems to me that there's no place on earth, however dull and depressing it may be, where intelligence and education can be useless. Let us suppose that among the hundred thousand people in this town, all of them, no doubt, very backward and uncultured, there are just three people like yourselves. Obviously, you can't hope to triumph over all the mass of ignorance around you; as your life goes by, you'll have to keep giving in little by little until you get lost in the crowd, in the hundred thousand. Life will swallow you up, but you'll not quite disappear, you'll make some impression on it. After you've gone, perhaps six more people like you will turn up, then twelve, and so on, until in the end most people will have become like you. So in two or three hundred years life on this old earth of ours will have become marvellously beautiful. Man longs for a life like that, and if it isn't here yet, he must imagine it, wait for it, dream about it, prepare for it, he must know and see more than his father and his grandfather did. [*Laughs.*] And you're complaining because you know a lot of stuff that's useless.

MASHA [*takes off her hat*] I'll be staying to lunch.

IRENA [*with a sigh*] Really, someone should have written all that down.

[ANDREY *has left the room, unnoticed.*]

TOOZENBACH You say that in time to come life will be marvellously beautiful. That's probably true. But in order to share in it now, at a distance so to speak, we must prepare for it and work for it.

VERSHININ [*gets up*] Yes. . . . What a lot of flowers you've got here! [*Looks round.*] And what a marvellous house! I do envy you! All my life I seem to have been pigging it in small flats, with two chairs and a sofa and a stove which always smokes. It's the flowers that I've missed in my life, flowers like these! . . . [*Rubs his hands.*] Oh, well, never mind!

TOOZENBACH Yes, we must work. I suppose you're thinking I'm a sentimental German. But I assure you I'm not—I'm Russian. I don't speak a word of German. My father was brought up in the Greek Orthodox faith. [*A pause.*]

VERSHININ [*walks up and down the room*] You know, I often wonder what it would be like if you could start your life over again—deliberately, I mean, consciously.

. . . Suppose you could put aside the life you'd lived already, as though it was just a sort of rough draft, and then start another one like a fair copy. If that happened, I think the thing you'd want most of all would be not to repeat yourself. You'd try at least to create a new environment for yourself, a flat like this one, for instance, with some flowers and plenty of light. . . . I have a wife, you know, and two little girls; and my wife's not very well, and all that. . . . Well, if I had to start my life all over again, I wouldn't marry. . . . No, no!

[*Enter* KOOLYGHIN, *in the uniform of a teacher.*]

KOOLYGHIN [*approaches* IRENA] Congratulations, dear sister—from the bottom of my heart, congratulations on your Saint's day. I wish you good health and everything a girl of your age ought to have! And allow me to present you with this little book. . . . [*Hands her a book.*] It's the history of our school covering the whole fifty years of its existence. I wrote it myself. Quite a trifle, of course—I wrote it in my spare time when I had nothing better to do—but I hope you'll read it nevertheless. Good morning to you all! [*To* VERSHININ.] Allow me to introduce myself. Koolyghin's the name; I'm a master at the secondary school here. And a town councillor. [*To* IRENA.] You'll find a list in the book of all the pupils who have completed their studies at our school during the last fifty years. *Feci quod potui, faciant meliora potentes.* [*Kisses* MASHA.]

IRENA But you gave me this book last Easter!

KOOLYGHIN [*laughs*] Did I really? In that case, give it me back—or no, better give it to the Colonel. Please do take it, Colonel. Maybe you'll read it some time when you've nothing better to do.

VERSHININ Thank you very much. [*Prepares to leave.*] I'm so very glad to have made your acquaintance. . . .

OLGA You aren't going are you? . . . Really, you mustn't.

IRENA But you'll stay and have lunch with us! Please do.

OLGA Please do.

VERSHININ [*bows*] I see I've intruded on your Saint's day party. I didn't know. Forgive me for not offering you my congratulations. [*Goes into the ballroom with* OLGA.]

KOOLYGHIN To-day is Sunday, my friends, a day of rest; let us rest and enjoy it, each according to his age and position in life! We shall have to roll up the carpets and put them away till the winter. . . . We must remember to put some naphthaline on them, or Persian powder. . . . The Romans enjoyed good health because they knew how to work *and* how to rest. They had *mens sana in corpore sano.* Their life had a definite shape, a form. . . . The director of the school says that the most important thing about life is form. . . . A thing that loses its form is finished—that's just as true of our ordinary, everyday lives. [*Takes* MASHA *by the waist and laughs.*] Masha loves me. My wife loves me. Yes, and the curtains will have to be put away with the carpets, too. . . . I'm cheerful to-day, I'm in quite excellent spirits. . . . Masha, we're invited to the director's at four o'clock to-day. A country walk has been arranged for the teachers and their families.

MASHA I'm not going.

KOOLYGHIN [*distressed*] Masha, darling, why not?

MASHA I'll tell you later. . . . [*Crossly.*] All right, I'll come, only leave me alone now. . . . [*Walks off.*]

KOOLYGHIN And after the walk we shall all spend the evening at the director's house. In spite of weak health, that man is certainly sparing no pains to be sociable. A first-rate, thoroughly enlightened man! A most excellent person! After the conference yesterday he said to me: "I'm tired, Fiodor Ilyich. I'm tired!" [*Looks at the clock, then at his watch.*]

Your clock is seven minutes fast. Yes, "I'm tired," he said.

[*The sound of the violin is heard off stage.*]

OLGA Will you all come and sit down, please! Lunch is ready. There's a pie.

KOOLYGHIN Ah, Olga, my dear girl! Last night I worked up to eleven o'clock, and I felt tired, but to-day I'm quite happy. [*Goes to the table in the ballroom.*] My dear Olga!

CHEBUTYKIN [*puts the newspaper in his pocket and combs his beard*] A pie? Excellent!

MASHA [*sternly to* CHEBUTYKIN] Remember, you mustn't take anything to drink to-day. Do you hear? It's bad for you.

CHEBUTYKIN Never mind. I've got over that weakness long ago! I haven't done any heavy drinking for two years. [*Impatiently.*] Anyway, my dear, what does it matter?

MASHA All the same, don't you dare to drink anything. Mind you don't now! [*Crossly, but taking care that her husband does not hear.*] So now I've got to spend another of these damnably boring evenings at the director's!

TOOZENBACH I wouldn't go if I were you, and that's that.

CHEBUTYKIN Don't you go, my dear.

MASHA Don't go, indeed! Oh, what a damnable life! It's intolerable. . . . [*Goes into the ballroom.*]

CHEBUTYKIN [*follows her*] Well, well! . . .

SOLIONY [*as he passes* TOOZENBACH *on the way to the ballroom*] Cluck, cluck, cluck!

TOOZENBACH Do stop it, Vassily Vassilich. I've really had enough of it. . .

SOLIONY Cluck, cluck, cluck! . . .

KOOLYGHIN [*gaily*] Your health, Colonel! I'm a schoolmaster . . . and I'm quite one of the family here, as it were. I'm Masha's husband. She's got a sweet nature, such a very sweet nature!

VERSHININ I think I'll have a little of this dark vodka. [*Drinks.*] Your health! [*To* OLGA.] I do feel so happy with you people!

[*Only* IRENA *and* TOOZENBACH *remain in the drawing-room.*]

IRENA Masha's a bit out of humor today. You know, she got married when she was eighteen, and then her husband seemed the cleverest man in the world to her. It's different now. He's the kindest of men, but not the cleverest.

OLGA [*impatiently*] Andrey, will you please come?

ANDREY [*off stage*] Just coming. [*Enters and goes to the table.*]

TOOZENBACH What are you thinking about?

IRENA Oh, nothing special. You know, I don't like this man Soliony, I'm quite afraid of him. Whenever he opens his mouth he says something silly.

TOOZENBACH He's a strange fellow. I'm sorry for him, even though he irritates me In fact, I feel more sorry for him than irritated. I think he's shy. When he's alone with me, he can be quite sensible and friendly, but in company he's offensive and bullying. Don't go over there just yet, let them get settled down at the table. Let me stay beside you for a bit. Tell me what you're thinking about. [*A pause.*] You're twenty . . . and I'm not thirty yet myself. What years and years we still have ahead of us, a whole long succession of years, all full of my love for you! . . .

IRENA Don't talk to me about love, Nikolai Lvovich.

TOOZENBACH [*not listening*] Oh, I long so passionately for life, I long to work and strive so much, and all this longing is somehow mingled with my love for you, Irena. And just because you happen to be beautiful, life appears beautiful to me! What are you thinking about?

IRENA You say that life is beautiful. Maybe it is—but what if it only seems to be beautiful? Our lives, I mean the lives of us three sisters, haven't been beautiful up to now. The truth is that life has been stifling us, like weeds in a garden. I'm afraid I'm crying. . . . So unnecessary. . . . [*Quickly dries her eyes and smiles.*]

We must work, work! The reason we feel depressed and take such a gloomy view of life is that we've never known what it is to make a real effort. We're the children of parents who despised work. . . .

[*Enter* NATALIA IVANOVNA. *She is wearing a pink dress with a green belt.*]

NATASHA They've gone in to lunch already. . . . I'm late. . . . [*Glances at herself in a mirror, adjusts her dress.*] My hair seems to be all right. . . . [*Catches sight of* IRENA.] My dear Irena Serghyeevna, congratulations! [*Gives her a vigorous and prolonged kiss.*] You've got such a lot of visitors. . . . I feel quite shy. . . . How do you do, Baron?

OLGA [*enters the drawing-room*] Oh, there you are, Natalia Ivanovna! How are you, my dear?

[*They kiss each other.*]

NATASHA Congratulations! You've such a lot of people here, I feel dreadfully shy. . . .

OLGA It's all right, they're all old friends. [*Alarmed, dropping her voice.*] You've got a green belt on! My dear, that's surely a mistake!

NATASHA Why, is it a bad omen, or what?

OLGA No, but it just doesn't go with your dress . . . it looks so strange. . . .

NATASHA [*tearfully*] Really? But it isn't really green, you know, it's a sort of dull colour. . . . [*Follows* OLGA *to the ballroom.*]

[*All are now seated at the table; the drawing-room is empty.*]

KOOLYGHIN Irena, you know, I do wish you'd find yourself a good husband. In my view it's high time you got married.

CHEBUTYKIN You ought to get yourself a nice little husband, too, Natalia Ivanovna.

KOOLYGHIN Natalia Ivanovna already has a husband in view.

MASHA [*strikes her plate with her fork*] A glass of wine for me, please! Three cheers for our jolly old life! We keep our end up, we do!

KOOLYGHIN Masha, you won't get more than five out of ten for good conduct!

VERSHININ I say, this liqueur's very nice. What is it made of?

SOLIONY Black beetles!

IRENA Ugh! ugh! How disgusting!

OLGA We're having roast turkey for dinner to-night, and then apple tart. Thank goodness, I'll be here all day to-day . . . this evening, too. You must all come this evening.

VERSHININ May I come in the evening, too?

IRENA Yes, please do.

NATASHA They don't stand on ceremony here.

CHEBUTYKIN "Nature created us for love alone." . . . [*Laughs.*]

ANDREY [*crossly*] Will you stop it, please? Aren't you tired of it yet?

[FEDOTIK *and* RODÉ *come in with a large basket of flowers.*]

FEDOTIK Just look here, they're having lunch already!

RODÉ [*in a loud voice*] Having their lunch? So they are, they're having lunch already.

FEDOTIK Wait half a minute. [*Takes a snapshot.*] One! Just one minute more! . . . [*Takes another snapshot.*] Two! All over now.

[*They pick up the basket and go into the ballroom where they are greeted uproariously.*]

RODÉ [*loudly*] Congratulations, Irena Serghyeevna! I wish you all the best, everything you'd wish for yourself! Gorgeous weather to-day, absolutely marvellous. I've been out walking the whole morning with the boys. You do know that I teach gym at the high school, don't you? . . .

FEDOTIK You may move now, Irena Serghyeevna, that is, if you want to. [*Takes a snapshot.*] You do look attractive to-day. [*Takes a top out of his pocket.*] By the way, look at this top. It's got a wonderful hum.

IRENA What a sweet little thing!

MASHA "A green oak grows by a curving shore, And round that oak hangs a golden chain." . . . A green chain around that oak. . . . [*Peevishly.*] Why do I keep on saying that? Those lines have been worrying me all day long!

KOOLYGHIN Do you know, we're thirteen at table?

RODÉ [*loudly*] You don't really believe in these old superstitions, do you? [*Laughter.*]

KOOLYGHIN When thirteen people sit down to table, it means that some of them are in love. Is it you, by any chance, Ivan Romanych?

CHEBUTYKIN Oh, I'm just an old sinner. . . . But what I can't make out is why Natalia Ivanovna looks so embarrassed.

[*Loud laughter.* NATASHA *runs out into the drawing-room,* ANDREY *follows her.*]

ANDREY Please, Natasha, don't take any notice of them! Stop . . . wait a moment. . . . Please!

NATASHA I feel so ashamed. . . . I don't know what's the matter with me, and they're all laughing at me. It's awful of me to leave the table like that, but I couldn't help it. . . . I just couldn't. . . . [*Covers her face with her hands.*]

ANDREY My dear girl, please, please don't get upset. Honestly, they don't mean any harm, they're just teasing. My dear, sweet girl, they're really good-natured folks, they all are, and they're fond of us both. Come over to the window, they can't see us there. . . . [*Looks round.*]

NATASHA You see, I'm not used to being with a lot of people.

ANDREY Oh, how young you are, Natasha, how wonderfully, beautifully young! My dear, sweet girl, don't get so upset! Do believe me, believe me. . . . I'm so happy, so full of love, of joy. . . . No, they can't see us here! They can't see us! How did I come to love you, when was it? . . . I don't understand anything. My precious, my sweet, my innocent girl, please—I want you to marry me! I love you, I love you as I've never loved anybody. . . . [*Kisses her.*]

[*Enter two officers and, seeing* NATASHA *and* ANDREY *kissing, stand and stare in amazement.*]

Act Two

[*The scene is the same as in Act 1.*

It is eight o'clock in the evening. The faint sound of an accordion is heard coming from the street.

The stage is unlit. Enter NATALIA IVANOVNA *in a dressing-gown, carrying a candle. She crosses the stage and stops by the door leading to* ANDREY's *room.*]

NATASHA What are you doing, Andriusha? Reading? It's all right, I only wanted to know. . . . [*Goes to another door, opens it, looks inside and shuts it again.*] No one's left a light anywhere. . . .

ANDREY [*enters with a book in his hand*] What is it, Natasha?

NATASHA I was just going round to see if anyone had left a light anywhere. It's carnival week, and the servants are so excited about it . . . anything might happen! You've got to watch them. Last night about twelve o'clock I happened to go into the dining-room, and—would you believe it?—there was a candle alight on the table. I've not found out who lit it. [*Puts the candle down.*] What time is it?

ANDREY [*glances at his watch*] Quarter past eight.

NATASHA And Olga and Irena still out. They aren't back from work yet, poor things! Olga's still at some teachers' conference, and Irena's at the post office. [*Sighs.*] This morning I said to Irena: "Do take care of yourself, my dear." But she won't listen. Did you say it was a quarter past eight? I'm afraid Bobik is not at all well. Why does he get so cold? Yesterday he had a temperature, but to-day he feels

quite cold when you touch him. . . . I'm so afraid!

ANDREY It's all right, Natasha. The boy's well enough.

NATASHA Still, I think he ought to have a special diet. I'm so anxious about him. By the way, they tell me that some carnival party's supposed to be coming here soon after nine. I'd rather they didn't come, Andriusha.

ANDREY Well, I really don't know what I can do. They've been asked to come.

NATASHA This morning the dear little fellow woke up and looked at me, and then suddenly he smiled. He recognized me, you see. "Good morning, Bobik," I said, "good morning, darling precious!" And then he laughed. Babies understand everything, you know, they understand us perfectly well. Anyway, Andriusha, I'll tell the servants not to let that carnival party in.

ANDREY [*irresolutely*] Well . . . it's really for my sisters to decide, isn't it? It's their house, after all.

NATASHA Yes, it's their house as well. I'll tell them, too. . . . They're so kind. . . . [*Walks off.*] I've ordered sour milk for supper. The doctor says you ought to eat nothing but sour milk, or you'll never get any thinner. [*Stops.*] Bobik feels cold. I'm afraid his room is too cold for him. He ought to move into a warmer room, at least until the warm weather comes. Irena's room, for instance—that's just a perfect room for a baby: it's dry, and it gets the sun all day long. We must tell her: perhaps she'd share Olga's room for a bit. . . . In any case, she's never at home during the day, she only sleeps there. . . . [*A pause.*] Andriusha, why don't you say anything?

ANDREY I was just day-dreaming. . . . There's nothing to say, anyway. . . .

NATASHA Well. . . . What was it I was going to tell you? Oh, yes! Ferapont from the Council Office wants to see you about something.

ANDREY [*yawns*] Tell him to come up.

[NATASHA *goes out.* ANDREY, *bending over the candle which she has left behind, begins to read his book. Enter* FERAPONT *in an old shabby overcoat, his collar turned up, his ears muffled in a scarf.*]

ANDREY Hullo, old chap! What did you want to see me about?

FERAPONT The chairman's sent you the register and a letter or something. Here they are. [*Hands him the book and the letter.*]

ANDREY Thanks. That's all right. Incidentally, why have you come so late? It's gone eight already.

FERAPONT What's that?

ANDREY [*raising his voice*] I said, why have you come so late? It's gone eight already.

FERAPONT That's right. It was still daylight when I came first, but they wouldn't let me see you. The master's engaged, they said. Well, if you're engaged, you're engaged. I'm not in a hurry. [*Thinking that* ANDREY *has said something.*] What's that?

ANDREY Nothing. [*Turns over the pages of the register.*] To-morrow's Friday, there's no meeting, but I'll go to the office just the same . . . do some work. I'm so bored at home! . . . [*A pause.*] Yes, my dear old fellow, how things do change, what a fraud life is! So strange! To-day I picked up this book, just out of boredom, because I hadn't anything to do. It's a copy of some lectures I attended at the University. . . . Good Heavens! Just think —I'm secretary of the local council now, and Protopopov's chairman, and the most I can ever hope for is to become a member of the council myself! I—a member of the local council! I, who dream every night that I'm a professor in Moscow University, a famous academician, the pride of all Russia!

FERAPONT I'm sorry, I can't tell you. I don't hear very well.

ANDREY If you could hear properly I don't think I'd be talking to you like this. I must talk to someone, but my wife doesn't seem to understand me, and as for my sisters . . . I'm afraid of them for some reason or other, I'm afraid of them laughing at me and pulling my leg. . . . I don't drink and I don't like going to pubs, but my word! how I'd enjoy an hour or so at Tyestov's, or the Great Moscow Restaurant! Yes, my dear fellow, I would indeed!

FERAPONT The other day at the office a contractor was telling me about some business men who were eating pancakes in Moscow. One of them ate forty pancakes and died. It was either forty or fifty, I can't remember exactly.

ANDREY You can sit in some huge restaurant in Moscow without knowing anyone, and no one knowing you; yet somehow you don't feel that you don't belong there. . . . Whereas here you know everybody, and everybody knows you, and yet you don't feel you belong here, you feel you don't belong at all. . . . You're lonely and you feel a stranger.

FERAPONT What's that? [*A pause.*] It was the same man that told me—of course, he may have been lying—he said that there's an enormous rope stretched right across Moscow.

ANDREY Whatever for?

FERAPONT I'm sorry, I can't tell you. That's what he said.

ANDREY What nonsense! [*Reads the book.*] Have you ever been to Moscow?

FERAPONT [*after a pause*] No. It wasn't God's wish. [*A pause.*] Shall I go now?

ANDREY Yes, you may go. Good-bye. [FERAPONT *goes out.*] Good-bye. [*Reading.*] Come in the morning to take some letters. . . . You can go now. [*A pause.*] He's gone. [*A bell rings.*] Yes, that's how it is. . . . [*Stretches and slowly goes to his room.*]

[*Singing is heard off stage; a nurse is putting a baby to sleep. Enter* MASHA *and* VERSHININ. *While they talk together, a maid lights a lamp and candles in the ballroom.*]

MASHA I don't know. [*A pause.*] I don't know. Habit's very important, of course. For instance, after Father died, for a long time we couldn't get accustomed to the idea that we hadn't any orderlies to wait on us. But, habit apart, I think it's quite right what I was saying. Perhaps it's different in other places, but in this town the military certainly do seem to be the nicest and most generous and best-mannered people.

VERSHININ I'm thirsty. I could do with a nice glass of tea.

MASHA [*glances at her watch*] They'll bring it in presently. You see, they married me off when I was eighteen. I was afraid of my husband because he was a school-master, and I had only just left school myself. He seemed terribly learned then, very clever and important. Now it's quite different, unfortunately.

VERSHININ Yes. . . . I see. . . .

MASHA I don't say anything against my husband—I'm used to him now—but there are such a lot of vulgar and unpleasant and offensive people among the other civilians. Vulgarity upsets me, it makes me feel insulted, I actually suffer when I meet someone who lacks refinement and gentle manners, and courtesy. When I'm with the other teachers, my husband's friends, I just suffer.

VERSHININ Yes, of course. But I should have thought that in a town like this the civilians and the army people were equally uninteresting. There's nothing to choose between them. If you talk to any educated person here, civilian or military, he'll generally tell you that he's just worn out. It's either his wife, or his house, or his estate, or his horse, or something. . . . We Russians are capable of such elevated thoughts—then why do we have such low ideals in practical life? Why is it, why?

MASHA Why?

VERSHININ Yes, why does his wife wear him out, why do his children wear him out? And what about *him* wearing out his wife and children?

MASHA You're a bit low-spirited to-day, aren't you?

VERSHININ Perhaps. I haven't had any dinner to-day. I've had nothing to eat since morning. One of my daughters is a bit off colour, and when the children are ill, I get so worried. I feel utterly conscience-stricken at having given them a mother like theirs. Oh, if only you could have seen her this morning! What a despicable woman! We started quarrelling at seven o'clock, and at nine I just walked out and slammed the door. [*A pause.*] I never talk about these things in the ordinary way. It's a strange thing, but you're the only person I feel I dare complain to. [*Kisses her hand.*] Don't be angry with me. I've nobody, nobody but you. . . . [*A pause.*]

MASHA What a noise the wind's making in the stove! Just before Father died the wind howled in the chimney just like that.

VERSHININ Are you superstitious?

MASHA Yes.

VERSHININ How strange. [*Kisses her hand.*] You really are a wonderful creature, a marvellous creature! Wonderful, marvellous! It's quite dark here, but I can see your eyes shining.

MASHA [*moves to another chair*] There's more light over here.

VERSHININ I love you, I love you, I love you. . . . I love your eyes, I love your movements. . . . I dream about them. A wonderful, marvellous being!

MASHA [*laughing softly*] When you talk to me like that, somehow I can't help laughing, although I'm afraid at the same time. Don't say it again, please. [*Half-audibly.*] Well, no . . . go on. I don't mind. . . . [*Covers her face with her hands.*] I don't mind. . . . Someone's coming. . . . Let's talk about something else. . . .

[*Enter* IRENA *and* TOOZENBACH *through the ballroom.*]

TOOZENBACH I have a triple-barrelled name—Baron Toozenbach-Krone-Alschauer—but actually I'm a Russian. I was baptized in the Greek-Orthodox faith, just like yourself. I haven't really got any German characteristics, except maybe the obstinate patient way I keep on pestering you. Look how I bring you home every evening.

IRENA How tired I am!

TOOZENBACH And I'll go on fetching you from the post office and bringing you home every evening for the next twenty years—unless you send me away. . . . [*Noticing* MASHA *and* VERSHININ, *with pleasure.*] Oh, it's you! How are you?

IRENA Well, here I am, home at last! [*To* MASHA.] A woman came into the post office just before I left. She wanted to send a wire to her brother in Saratov to tell him her son had just died, but she couldn't remember the address. So we had to send the wire without an address, just to Saratov. She was crying and I was rude to her, for no reason at all. "I've no time to waste," I told her. So stupid of me. We're having the carnival crowd to-day, aren't we?

MASHA Yes.

IRENA [*sits down*] How nice it is to rest! I am tired!

TOOZENBACH [*smiling*] When you come back from work, you look so young, so pathetic, somehow. . . . [*A pause.*]

IRENA I'm tired. No, I don't like working at the post office, I don't like it at all.

MASHA You've got thinner. . . . [*Whistles.*] You look younger, too, and your face looks quite boyish.

TOOZENBACH It's the way she does her hair.

IRENA I must look for another job. This one doesn't suit me. It hasn't got what I always longed for and dreamed about. It's the sort of work you do without inspiration, without even thinking.

[*Someone knocks at the floor from below.*]

That's the Doctor knocking. [*To* TOOZENBACH.] Will you answer him, dear? . . . I can't. . . . I'm so tired.

TOOZENBACH [*knocks on the floor*].

IRENA He'll be up in a moment. We must do something about all this. Andrey and the Doctor went to the club last night and lost at cards again. They say Andrey lost two hundred roubles.

MASHA [*with indifference*] Well, what are we to do about it?

IRENA He lost a fortnight ago, and he lost in December, too. I wish to goodness he'd lose everything we've got, and soon, too, and then perhaps we'd move out of this place. Good Heavens, I dream of Moscow every night. Sometimes I feel as if I were going mad. [*Laughs.*] We're going to Moscow in June. How many months are there till June? . . . February, March, April, May . . . nearly half-a-year!

MASHA We must take care that Natasha doesn't get to know about him losing at cards.

IRENA I don't think she cares.

[*Enter* CHEBUTYKIN. *He has been resting on his bed since dinner and has only just got up. He combs his beard, then sits down at the table and takes out a newspaper.*]

MASHA There he is. Has he paid his rent yet?

IRENA [*laughs*] No. Not a penny for the last eight months. I suppose he's forgotten.

MASHA [*laughs*] How solemn he looks sitting there!

[*They all laugh. A pause.*]

IRENA Why don't you say something, Alexandr Ignatyevich?

VERSHININ I don't know. I'm just longing for some tea. I'd give my life for a glass of tea! I've had nothing to eat since morning. . . .

CHEBUTYKIN Irena Serghyeevna!

IRENA What is it?

CHEBUTYKIN Please come here. *Venez ici!*

[IRENA *goes over to him and sits down at the table.*] I can't do without you.

[IRENA *lays out the cards for a game of patience.*]

VERSHININ Well, if we can't have any tea, let's do a bit of philosophizing, anyway.

TOOZENBACH Yes, let's. What about?

VERSHININ What about? Well . . . let's try to imagine what life will be like after we're dead, say in two or three hundred years.

TOOZENBACH All right, then. . . . After we're dead, people will fly about in balloons, the cut of their coats will be different, the sixth sense will be discovered, and possibly even developed and used, for all I know. . . . But I believe, life itself will remain the same; it will still be difficult and full of mystery and full of happiness. And in a thousand years' time people will still be sighing and complaining: "How hard this business of living is!"—and yet they'll still be scared of death and unwilling to die, just as they are now.

VERSHININ [*after a moment's thought*] Well, you know . . . how shall I put it? I think everything in the world is bound to change gradually—in fact, it's changing before our very eyes. In two or three hundred years, or maybe in a thousand years—it doesn't matter how long exactly—life will be different. It will be happy. Of course, we shan't be able to enjoy that future life, but all the same, what we're living for now is to create it, we work and . . . yes, we suffer in order to create it. That's the goal of our life, and you might say that's the only happiness we shall ever achieve.

MASHA [*laughs quietly*].

TOOZENBACH Why are you laughing?

MASHA I don't know. I've been laughing all day to-day.

VERSHININ [*to* TOOZENBACH] I went to the same cadet school as you did but I never went on to the Military Academy. I read a great deal, of course, but I never know what books I ought to choose, and prob-

ably I read a lot of stuff that's not worth anything. But the longer I live the more I seem to long for knowledge. My hair's going grey and I'm getting on in years, and yet how little I know, how little! All the same, I think I do know one thing which is not only true but also most important. I'm sure of it. Oh, if only I could convince you that there's not going to be any happiness for our own generation, that there mustn't be and won't be. . . . We've just got to work and work. All the happiness is reserved for our descendants, our remote descendants. [*A pause.*] Anyway, if I'm not to be happy, then at least my children's children will be.

[FEDOTIK *and* RODÉ *enter the ballroom; they sit down and sing quietly, one of them playing on a guitar.*]

TOOZENBACH So you won't even allow us to dream of happiness! But what if I *am* happy?

VERSHININ You're not.

TOOZENBACH [*flinging up his hands and laughing*] We don't understand one another, that's obvious. How can I convince you?

MASHA [*laughs quietly*].

TOOZENBACH [*holds up a finger to her*] Show a finger to her and she'll laugh! [*To* VERSHININ.] And life will be just the same as ever not merely in a couple of hundred years' time, but in a million years. Life doesn't change, it always goes on the same; it follows its own laws, which don't concern us, which we can't discover anyway. Think of the birds that migrate in the autumn, the cranes, for instance: they just fly on and on. It doesn't matter what sort of thoughts they've got in their heads, great thoughts or little thoughts, they just fly on and on, not knowing where or why. And they'll go on flying no matter how many philosophers they happen to have flying with them. Let them philosophize as much as they like, as long as they go on flying.

MASHA Isn't there some meaning?

TOOZENBACH Meaning? . . . Look   out

there, it's snowing. What's the meaning of that? [*A pause.*]

MASHA I think a human being has got to have some faith, or at least he's got to seek faith. Otherwise his life will be empty, empty. . . . How can you live and not know why the cranes fly, why children are born, why the stars shine in the sky! . . . You must either know why you live, or else . . . nothing matters . . . everything's just wild grass. . . . [*A pause.*]

VERSHININ All the same, I'm sorry my youth's over.

MASHA "It's a bore to be alive in this world, friends," that's what Gogol says.

TOOZENBACH And I feel like saying: it's hopeless arguing with you, friends! I give you up.

CHEBUTYKIN [*reads out of the paper*] Balsac's marriage took place at Berdichev.[2]

IRENA [*sings softly to herself*].

CHEBUTYKIN Must write this down in my notebook. [*Writes.*] Balsac's marriage took place at Berdichev. [*Reads on.*]

IRENA [*playing patience, pensively*] Balsac's marriage took place at Berdichev.

TOOZENBACH Well, I've thrown in my hand. Did you know that I'd sent in my resignation, Maria Serghyeevna?

MASHA Yes, I heard about it. I don't see anything good in it, either. I don't like civilians.

TOOZENBACH Never mind. [*Gets up.*] What sort of a soldier do I make, anyway? I'm not even good-looking. Well, what does it matter? I'll work. I'd like to do such a hard day's work that when I came home in the evening I'd fall on my bed exhausted and go to sleep at once. [*Goes to the ballroom.*] I should think working men sleep well at nights!

FEDOTIK [*to* IRENA] I've got you some coloured crayons at Pyzhikov's, in Moscow Street. And this little penknife, too. . . .

IRENA You still treat me as if I were a little girl. I wish you'd remember I'm grown up now. [*Takes the crayons and the penknife, joyfully.*] They're awfully nice!

FEDOTIK Look, I bought a knife for myself, too. You see, it's got another blade here, and then another . . . this thing's for cleaning your ears, and these are nail-scissors, and this is for cleaning your nails. . . .

RODÉ [*in a loud voice*] Doctor, how old are you?

CHEBUTYKIN I? Thirty-two.

[*Laughter.*]

FEDOTIK I'll show you another kind of patience. [*Sets out the cards.*]

[*The samovar is brought in, and* ANFISA *attends to it. Shortly afterwards* NATASHA *comes in and begins to fuss around the table.*]

SOLIONY [*enters, bows to the company and sits down at the table*].

VERSHININ What a wind, though!

MASHA Yes. I'm tired of winter! I've almost forgotten what summer is like.

IRENA [*playing patience*] I'm going to go out. We'll get to Moscow!

FEDOTIK No, it's not going out. You see, the eight has to go on the two of spades. [*Laughs.*] That means you won't go to Moscow.

CHEBUTYKIN [*reads the paper*] Tzitzikar. Smallpox is raging. . . .

ANFISA [*goes up to* MASHA] Masha, the tea's ready, dear. [*To* VERSHININ.] Will you please come to the table, your Excellency? Forgive me, your name's slipped my memory. . . .

MASHA Bring it here, Nanny. I'm not coming over there.

IRENA Nanny!

ANFISA Comi-ing!

NATASHA [*to* SOLIONY] You know, even tiny babies understand what we say perfectly well! "Good morning, Bobik," I said to him only to-day, "Good morning, my precious!"—and then he looked at me

---

2 A town in Western Russia well known for its almost exclusively Jewish population.

in such a special sort of way. You may say it's only a mother's imagination, but it isn't, I do assure you. No, no! He really is an extraordinary child!

SOLIONY If that child were mine, I'd cook him up in a frying pan and eat him. [*Picks up his glass, goes into the drawing-room and sits down in a corner.*]

NATASHA [*covers her face with her hands*] What a rude, ill-mannered person!

MASHA People who don't even notice whether it's summer or winter are lucky! I think I'd be indifferent to the weather if I were living in Moscow.

VERSHININ I've just been reading the diary of some French cabinet minister—he wrote it in prison. He got sent to prison in connection with the Panama affair. He writes with such a passionate delight about the birds he can see through the prison window—the birds he never even noticed when he was a cabinet minister. Of course, now he's released he won't notice them any more. . . . And in the same way, you won't notice Moscow once you live there again. We're not happy and we can't be happy: we only want happiness.

TOOZENBACH [*picks up a box from the table*] I say, where are all the chocolates?

IRENA Soliony's eaten them.

TOOZENBACH All of them?

ANFISA [*serving* VERSHININ *with tea*] Here's a letter for you, Sir.

VERSHININ For me? [*Takes the letter.*] From my daughter. [*Reads it.*] Yes, of course. . . . Forgive me, Maria Serghye-evna, I'll just leave quietly. I won't have any tea. [*Gets up, agitated.*] Always the same thing. . . .

MASHA What is it? Secret?

VERSHININ [*in a low voice*] My wife's taken poison again. I must go. I'll get away without them seeing me. All this is so dreadfully unpleasant [*Kisses* MASHA's *hand.*] My dear, good, sweet girl. . . . I'll go out this way, quietly. . . . [*Goes out.*]

ANFISA Where's he off to? And I've just brought him some tea! What a queer fellow!

MASHA [*flaring up*] Leave me alone! Why do you keep worrying me? Why don't you leave me in peace? [*Goes to the table, cup in hand.*] I'm sick and tired of you, silly old woman!

ANFISA Why. . . . I didn't mean to offend you, dear.

ANDREY'S VOICE [*off stage*] Anfisa!

ANFISA [*mimics him*] Anfisa! Sitting there in his den! . . . [*Goes out.*]

MASHA [*by the table in the ballroom, crossly*] Do let me sit down somewhere! [*Jumbles up the cards laid out on the table.*] You take up the whole table with your cards! Why don't you get on with your tea?

IRENA How bad-tempered you are, Mashka!

MASHA Well, if I'm bad-tempered, don't talk to me, then. Don't touch me!

CHEBUTYKIN [*laughs*] Don't touch her! . . . Take care you don't touch her!

MASHA You may be sixty, but you're always gabbling some damn nonsense or other, just like a child. . . .

NATASHA [*sighs*] My dear Masha, need you use such expressions? You know, with your good looks you'd be thought so charming, even by the best people—yes, I honestly mean it—if only you wouldn't use these expressions of yours! Je vous prie, pardonnez moi, Marie, mais vous avez des manières un peu grossières.

TOOZENBACH [*with suppressed laughter*] Pass me . . . I say, will you please pass me. . . . Is that cognac over there, or what? . . .

NATASHA Il parait que mon Bobik déjà ne dort pas. . . . I think he's awake. He's not been too well to-day. I must go and see him . . . excuse me. [*Goes out.*]

IRENA I say, where has Alexandr Ignatye-vich gone to?

MASHA He's gone home. His wife's done something queer again.

TOOZENBACH [*goes over to* SOLIONY *with a decanter of cognac*] You always sit alone brooding over something or other—

though what it's all about nobody knows. Well, let's make it up. Let's have cognac together. [*They drink.*] I suppose I'll have to play the piano all night to-night—a lot of rubbishy tunes, of course. . . . Never mind!

SOLIONY Why did you say "let's make it up"? We haven't quarrelled.

TOOZENBACH You always give me the feeling that there's something wrong between us. You're a strange character, no doubt about it.

SOLIONY [*recites*] "I am strange, but who's not so? Don't be angry, Aleko!"

TOOZENBACH What's Aleko got to do with it? . . . [*A pause.*]

SOLIONY When I'm alone with somebody I'm all right, I'm just like other people. But in company, I get depressed and shy, and . . . I talk all sorts of nonsense. All the same, I'm a good deal more honest and well-intentioned than plenty of others. I can prove I am.

TOOZENBACH You often make me angry because you keep on pestering me when we're in company—but all the same, I do like you for some reason. . . . I'm going to get drunk to-night, whatever happens! Let's have another drink!

SOLIONY Yes, let's. [*A pause.*] I've never had anything against you personally, Baron. But my temperament's rather like Lermontov's. [*In a low voice.*] I even look a little like Lermontov, I've been told. . . . [*Takes a scent bottle from his pocket and sprinkles some scent on his hands.*]

TOOZENBACH I have sent in my resignation! Finished! I've been considering it for five years, and now I've made up my mind at last. I'm going to work.

SOLIONY [*recites*] "Don't be angry, Aleko. . . . Away, away with all your dreams!"

[*During the conversation* ANDREY *enters quietly with a book in his hand and sits down by the candle.*]

TOOZENBACH I'm going to work!

CHEBUTYKIN [*comes into the drawing-room with* IRENA] And the food they treated me to was the genuine Caucasian stuff:

onion soup, followed by chehartma—that's a meat dish, you know.

SOLIONY Chereshma isn't meat at all; it's a plant, something like an onion.

CHEBUTYKIN No-o, my dear friend. Chehartma isn't an onion, it's roast mutton.

SOLIONY I tell you chereshma is a kind of onion.

CHEBUTYKIN Well, why should I argue about it with you? You've never been to the Caucasus and you've never tasted chehartma.

SOLIONY I haven't tasted it because I can't stand the smell of it. Chereshma stinks just like garlic.

ANDREY [*imploringly*] Do stop it, friends! Please stop it!

TOOZENBACH When's the carnival crowd coming along?

IRENA They promised to be here by nine—that means any moment now.

TOOZENBACH [*embraces* ANDREY *and sings*] "Ah, my beautiful porch, my lovely new porch, my . . ."[3]

ANDREY [*dances and sings*] "My new porch all made of maple-wood. . . ."

CHEBUTYKIN [*dances*] "With fancy carving over the door. . . ."

[*Laughter.*]

TOOZENBACH [*kisses* ANDREY] Let's have a drink, the devil take it! Andriusha, let's drink to eternal friendship. I'll come with you when you go back to Moscow University.

SOLIONY Which university? There are two universities in Moscow.

ANDREY There's only one.

SOLIONY I tell you there are two.

ANDREY Never mind, make it three. The more the merrier.

SOLIONY There are two universities in Moscow.

[*Murmurs of protest and cries of "Hush!"*]

There are two universities in Moscow, an old one and a new one. But if you don't

---

3 A traditional Russian dance-song.

want to listen to what I'm saying, if my conversation irritates you, I can keep silent. In fact I can go to another room. . . . [*Goes out through one of the doors.*]

TOOZENBACH Bravo, bravo! [*Laughs.*] Let's get started, my friends, I'll play for you. What a funny creature that Soliony is! . . . [*Sits down at the piano and plays a waltz.*]

MASHA [*dances alone*] The Baron is drunk, the Baron is drunk, the Baron is drunk. . . .

[*Enter* NATASHA.]

NATASHA [*To* CHEBUTYKIN] Ivan Romanych! [*Speaks to him, then goes out quietly.* CHEBUTYKIN *touches* TOOZENBACH *on the shoulder and whispers to him.*]

IRENA What is it?

CHEBUTYKIN It's time we were going. Good-night.

IRENA But really. . . . What about the carnival party?

ANDREY [*embarrassed*] The carnival party's not coming. You see, my dear, Natasha says that Bobik isn't very well, and so . . . Anyway, I don't know . . . and I certainly don't care. . . .

IRENA [*shrugs her shoulders*] Bobik's not very well! . . .

MASHA Never mind, we'll keep our end up! If they turn us out, out we must go! [*To* IRENA.] It isn't Bobik who's not well, it's her. . . . There! . . . [*Taps her forehead with her finger.*] Petty little bourgeois housewife!

[ANDREY *goes to his room on the right.* CHEBUTYKIN *follows him. The guests say good-bye in the ballroom.*]

FEDOTIK What a pity! I'd been hoping to spend the evening here, but of course, if the baby's ill. . . . I'll bring him some toys to-morrow.

RODÉ [*in a loud voice*] I had a good long sleep after lunch to-day on purpose, I thought I'd be dancing all night. I mean to say, it's only just nine o'clock.

MASHA Let's go outside and talk it over. We can decide what to do then.

[*Voices are heard saying "Good-bye! God bless you!" and* TOOZENBACH *is heard laughing gaily. Everyone goes out.* ANFISA *and a maid clear the table and put out the lights. The nurse sings to the baby off stage. Enter* ANDREY, *wearing an overcoat and hat, followed by* CHEBUTYKIN. *They move quietly.*]

CHEBUTYKIN I've never found time to get married, somehow . . . partly because my life's just flashed past me like lightning, and partly because I was always madly in love with your mother and she was married. . . .

ANDREY One shouldn't marry. One shouldn't marry because it's so boring.

CHEBUTYKIN That may be so, but what about loneliness? You can philosophize as much as you like, dear boy, but loneliness is a dreadful thing. Although, really . . . well, it doesn't matter a damn, of course! . . .

ANDREY Let's get along quickly.

CHEBUTYKIN What's the hurry? There's plenty of time.

ANDREY I'm afraid my wife may try to stop me.

CHEBUTYKIN Ah!

ANDREY I won't play cards to-night, I'll just sit and watch. I'm not feeling too well. . . . What ought I to do for this breathlessness, Ivan Romanych?

CHEBUTYKIN Why ask me, dear boy? I can't remember—I simply don't know.

ANDREY Let's go through the kitchen.

[*They go out. A bell rings. The ring is repeated, then voices and laughter are heard.*]

IRENA [*coming in*] What's that?

ANFISA [*in a whisper*] The carnival party.

[*The bell rings again.*]

IRENA Tell them there's no one at home, Nanny. Apologize to them.

[ANFISA *goes out.* IRENA *walks up and down the room, lost in thought. She seems agitated. Enter* SOLIONY.]

SOLIONY [*puzzled*] There's no one here. . . . Where is everybody?

IRENA They've gone home.

SOLIONY How strange! Then you're alone here?

IRENA Yes, alone. [*A pause.*] Well . . . good-night.

SOLIONY I know I behaved tactlessly just now, I lost control of myself. But you're different from the others, you stand out high above them—you're pure, you can see where the truth lies. . . . You're the only person in the world who can possibly understand me. I love you. . . . I love you with a deep, infinite . . .

IRENA Do please go away. Good-night!

SOLIONY I can't live without you. [*Follows her.*] Oh, it's such a delight just to look at you! [*With tears.*] Oh, my happiness! Your glorious, marvellous, entrancing eyes—eyes like no other woman's I've ever seen. . . .

IRENA [*coldly*] Please stop it, Vassily Vassilich!

SOLIONY I've never spoken to you of my love before . . . it makes me feel as if I were living on a different planet. . . . [*Rubs his forehead.*] Never mind! I can't force you to love me, obviously. But I don't intend to have any rivals—successful rivals, I mean. . . . No, no! I swear to you by everything I hold sacred that if there's anyone else, I'll kill him. Oh, how wonderful you are!

[*Enter* NATASHA *carrying a candle.*]

NATASHA [*pokes her head into one room, then into another, but passes the door leading to her husband's room*] Andrey's reading in there. Better let him read. Forgive me, Vassily Vassilich, I didn't know you were here. I'm afraid I'm not properly dressed.

SOLIONY I don't care. Good-bye. [*Goes out.*]

NATASHA You must be tired, my poor dear girl. [*Kisses* IRENA.] You ought to go to bed earlier.

IRENA Is Bobik asleep?

NATASHA Yes, he's asleep. But he's not sleeping peacefully. By the way, my dear, I've been meaning to speak to you for some time but there's always been something . . . either you're not here, or I'm too busy. . . . You see, I think that Bobik's nursery is so cold and damp. . . . And your room is just ideal for a baby. Darling, do you think you could move into Olga's room?

IRENA [*not understanding her*] Where to?

[*The sound of bells is heard outside, as a "troika" is driven up to the house.*]

NATASHA You can share a room with Olia for the time being, and Bobik can have your room. He is such a darling! This morning I said to him: "Bobik, you're my very own! My very own!" And he just gazed at me with his dear little eyes. [*The door bell rings.*] That must be Olga. How late she is!

[*A maid comes up to* NATASHA *and whispers in her ear.*]

NATASHA Protopopov! What a funny fellow! Protopopov's come to ask me to go for a drive with him. In a troika! [*Laughs.*] Aren't these men strange creatures! . . .

[*The door bell rings again.*]

Someone's ringing. Shall I go for a short drive? Just for a quarter of an hour? [*To the maid.*] Tell him I'll be down in a minute. [*The door bell rings.*] That's the bell again. I suppose it's Olga. [*Goes out.*]

[*The maid runs out;* IRENA *sits lost in thought. Enter* KOOLYGHIN *and* OLGA, *followed by* VERSHININ.]

KOOLYGHIN Well! What's the meaning of this? You said you were going to have a party.

VERSHININ It's a strange thing. I left here about half an hour ago, and they were expecting a carnival party then.

IRENA They've all gone.

KOOLYGHIN Masha's gone, too? Where has

she gone to? And why is Protopopov waiting outside in a troika? Who's he waiting for?

IRENA   Please don't ask me questions. I'm tired.

KOOLYGHIN   You . . . spoilt child!

OLGA   The conference has only just ended. I'm quite worn out. The headmistress is ill and I'm deputizing for her. My head's aching, oh, my head, my head. . . . [*Sits down.*] Andrey lost two hundred roubles at cards last night. The whole town's talking about it. . . .

KOOLYGHIN   Yes, the conference exhausted me, too. [*Sits down.*]

VERSHININ   So now my wife's taken it into her head to try to frighten me. She tried to poison herself. However, everything's all right now, so I can relax, thank goodness. . . . So we've got to go away? Well, good-night to you, all the best. Fiodor Illych, would you care to come along with me somewhere or other? I can't stay at home to-night, I really can't. . . . Do come!

KOOLYGHIN   I'm tired. I don't think I'll come. [*Gets up.*] I'm tired. Has my wife gone home?

IRENA   I think so.

KOOLYGHIN   [*kisses* IRENA's *hand*] Good-night. We can rest to-morrow and the day after to-morrow, two whole days! Well, I wish you all the best. [*Going out.*] How I long for some tea! I reckoned on spending the evening in congenial company, but—*o, fallacem hominum spem!* Always use the accusative case in exclamations.

VERSHININ   Well, it looks as if I'll have to go somewhere by myself. [*Goes out with* KOOLYGHIN, *whistling.*]

OLGA   My head aches, oh, my head. . . . Andrey lost at cards . . . the whole town's talking. . . . I'll go and lie down. [*Going out.*] To-morrow I'm free. Heavens, what a joy! To-morrow I'm free, and the day after to-morrow I'm free. . . . My head's aching, oh, my poor head. . . .

IRENA   [*alone*] They've all gone. No one's left.

[*Someone is playing an accordion in the street. The nurse sings in the next room.*]

NATASHA   [*crosses the ballroom, wearing a fur coat and cap. She is followed by the maid.*] I'll be back in half an hour. I'm just going for a little drive. [*Goes out.*]

IRENA   [*alone, with intense longing*] Moscow! Moscow! Moscow!

Act Three

[*A bedroom now shared by* OLGA *and* IRENA. *There are two beds, one on the right; the other on the left, each screened off from the centre of the room. It is past two o'clock in the morning. Off stage the alarm is being sounded on account of a fire which has been raging for some time. The inmates of the house have not yet been to bed.* MASHA *is lying on a couch, dressed, as usual, in black.* OLGA *and* ANFISA *come in.*]

ANFISA   Now they're sitting down there, under the stairs. . . . I keep telling them to come upstairs, that they shouldn't sit down there, but they just cry. "We don't know where our Papa is," they say, "perhaps he's got burned in the fire." What an idea! And there are people in the yard, too . . . half-dressed. . . .

OLGA   [*takes a dress out of a wardrobe*] Take this grey frock, Nanny. . . . And this one. . . . This blouse, too. . . . And this skirt. Oh, Heavens! what is happening! Apparently the whole of the Kirsanovsky Street's been burnt down. . . . Take this . . . and this, too. . . . [*Throws the clothes into* ANFISA's *arms.*] The poor Vershinins had a fright. Their house only just escaped being burnt down. They'll have to spend the night here . . . we mustn't let them go home. Poor Fedotik's lost everything, he's got nothing left. . . .

ANFISA   I'd better call Ferapont, Oliushka, I can't carry all this.

OLGA   [*rings*] No one takes any notice

when I ring. [*Calls through the door.*] Is anyone there? Will someone come up, please!

[*A window, red with the glow of the fire, can be seen through the open door. The sound of a passing fire engine is heard.*]

How dreadful it all is! And how tired of it I am! [*Enter* FERAPONT.] Take this downstairs please. . . . The Kolotilin girls are sitting under the stairs . . . give it to them. And this, too. . . .

FERAPONT Very good, Madam. Moscow was burned down in 1812 just the same. Mercy on us! . . . Yes, the French were surprised all right.

OLGA Go along now, take this down.

FERAPONT Very good. [*Goes out.*]

OLGA Give it all away, Nanny, dear. We won't keep anything, give it all away. . . . I'm so tired, I can hardly keep on my feet. We mustn't let the Vershinins go home. The little girls can sleep in the drawing-room, and Alexandr Ignatyevich can share the downstairs room with the Baron. Fedotik can go in with the Baron, too, or maybe he'd better sleep in the ballroom. The doctor's gone and got drunk—you'd think he'd done it on purpose; he's so hopelessly drunk that we can't let anyone go into his room. Vershinin's wife will have to go into the drawing-room, too.

ANFISA [*wearily*] Don't send me away, Oliushka, darling! Don't send me away!

OLGA What nonsense you're talking, Nanny! No one's sending you away.

ANFISA [*leans her head against* OLGA's *breast*] My dearest girl! I do work, you know, I work as hard as I can. . . . I suppose now I'm getting weaker, I'll be told to go. But where can I go? Where? I'm eighty years old. I'm over eighty-one!

OLGA You sit down for a while, Nanny. . . . You're tired, you poor dear. . . . [*Makes her sit down.*] Just rest a bit. You've turned quite pale.

[*Enter* NATASHA.]

NATASHA They're saying we ought to start a subscription in aid of the victims of the fire. You know—form a society or something for the purpose. Well, why not? It's an excellent idea! In any case it's up to us to help the poor as best we can. Bobik and Sofochka are fast asleep as if nothing had happened. We've got such a crowd of people in the house; the place seems full of people whichever way you turn. There's 'flu about in the town. . . . I'm so afraid the children might catch it.

OLGA [*without listening to her*] You can't see the fire from this room; it's quiet in here.

NATASHA Yes. . . . I suppose my hair is all over the place. [*Stands in front of the mirror.*] They say I've got stouter, but it's not true! I'm not a bit stouter. Masha's asleep . . . she's tired, poor girl. . . . [*To* ANFISA, *coldly.*] How dare you sit down in my presence? Get up! Get out of here! [ANFISA *goes out. A pause.*] I can't understand why you keep that old woman in the house.

OLGA [*taken aback*] Forgive me for saying it, but I can't understand how you . . .

NATASHA She's quite useless here. She's just a peasant woman, her right place is in the country. You're spoiling her. I do like order in the home, I don't like having useless people about. [*Strokes* OLGA's *cheek.*] You're tired, my poor dear! Our headmistress is tired! You know, when my Sofochka grows up and goes to school, I'll be frightened of you.

OLGA I'm not going to be a headmistress.

NATASHA You'll be asked to, Olechka. It's settled.

OLGA I'll refuse. I couldn't do it. . . . I wouldn't be strong enough. [*Drinks water.*] You spoke so harshly to Nanny just now. . . . You must forgive me for saying so, but I just can't stand that sort of thing . . . it made me feel quite faint. . . .

NATASHA [*agitated*] Forgive me, Olia, forgive me. I didn't mean to upset you.

[MASHA *gets up, picks up a pillow and goes out in a huff.*]

OLGA Please try to understand me, dear. . . . It may be that we've been brought up in a peculiar way, but anyway I just can't bear it. When people are treated like that, it gets me down, I feel quite ill. . . . I simply get unnerved. . . .

NATASHA Forgive me, dear, forgive me! . . . [*Kisses her.*]

OLGA Any cruel or tactless remark, even the slightest discourtesy, upsets me. . . .

NATASHA It's quite true, I know I often say things which would be better left unsaid—but you must agree with me, dear, that she'd be better in the country somewhere.

OLGA She's been with us for thirty years.

NATASHA But she can't do any work now, can she? Either I don't understand you, or you don't want to understand me. She can't work, she just sleeps or sits about.

OLGA Well, let her sit about.

NATASHA [*in surprise*] What do you mean, let her sit about? Surely she is a servant! [*Tearfully.*] No, I don't understand you, Olia! I have a nurse for the children and a wet nurse and we share a maid and a cook. Whatever do we want this old woman for? What for?

[*The alarm is sounded again.*]

OLGA I've aged ten years to-night.

NATASHA We must sort things out, Olia. You're working at your school, and I'm working at home. You're teaching and I'm running the house. And when I say anything about the servants, I know what I'm talking about. . . . That old thief, that old witch must get out of this house to-morrow! . . . [*Stamps her feet.*] How dare you vex me so? How dare you? [*Recovering her self-control.*] Really, if you don't move downstairs, we'll always be quarrelling. This is quite dreadful!

[*Enter* KOOLYGHIN.]

KOOLYGHIN Where's Masha? It's time we went home. They say the fire's getting less fierce. [*Stretches.*] Only one block got burnt down, but to begin with it looked as if the whole town was going to be set on fire by that wind. [*Sits down.*] I'm so tired, Olechka, my dear. You know, I've often thought that if I hadn't married Masha, I'd have married you, Olechka. You're so kind. I'm worn out. [*Listens.*]

OLGA What is it?

KOOLYGHIN The doctor's got drunk just as if he'd done it on purpose. Hopelessly drunk. . . . As if he'd done it on purpose. [*Gets up.*] I think he's coming up here. . . . Can you hear him? Yes, he's coming up. [*Laughs.*] What a fellow, really! . . . I'm going to hide myself. [*Goes to the wardrobe and stands between it and the wall.*] What a scoundrel!

OLGA He's been off drinking for two years, and now suddenly he goes and gets drunk. . . . [*Walks with* NATASHA *towards the back of the room.*]

[CHEBUTYKIN *enters; walking firmly and soberly he crosses the room, stops, looks round, then goes to the wash-stand and begins to wash his hands.*]

CHEBUTYKIN [*glumly*] The devil take them all . . . all the lot of them! They think I can treat anything just because I'm a doctor, but I know positively nothing at all. I've forgotten everything I used to know. I remember nothing, positively nothing. . . . [OLGA *and* NATASHA *leave the room without his noticing.*] The devil take them! Last Wednesday I attended a woman at Zasyp. She died, and it's all my fault that she did die. Yes. . . . I used to know a thing or two twenty-five years ago, but now I don't remember anything. Not a thing! Perhaps I'm not a man at all, but I just imagine that I've got hands and feet and a head. Perhaps I don't exist at all, and I only imagine that I'm walking about and eating and sleeping. [*Weeps.*] Oh, if only I could simply stop existing! [*Stops crying, glumly.*] God knows. . . . The other day they were talking about Shakespeare and Voltaire at the club. . . . I haven't read either, never read a single line of either, but I tried to make out by my expression that I had. The others did the same. How petty it all is! How despicable! And then suddenly I thought of the woman I killed on Wednesday. It all came back to me, and I felt such a swine, so sick of myself that I went and got drunk. . . .

[*Enter* IRENA, VERSHININ *and* TOOZEN-BACH. TOOZENBACH *is wearing a fashion-able new civilian suit.*]

IRENA Let's sit down here for a while. No one will come in here.

VERSHININ The whole town would have been burnt down but for the soldiers. They're a fine lot of fellows! [*Rubs his hands with pleasure.*] Excellent fellows! Yes, they're a fine lot!

KOOLYGHIN [*approaches them*] What's the time?

TOOZENBACH It's gone three. It's beginning to get light.

IRENA Everyone's sitting in the ballroom and nobody thinks of leaving. That man Soliony there, too. . . . [*To* CHEBUTYKIN.] You ought to go to bed, Doctor.

CHEBUTYKIN I'm all right. . . . Thanks. . . . [*Combs his beard.*]

KOOLYGHIN [*laughs*] Half seas over, Ivan Romanych! [*Slaps him on the shoulder.*] You're a fine one! *In vino veritas*, as they used to say in Rome.

TOOZENBACH Everyone keeps asking me to arrange a concert in aid of the victims of the fire.

IRENA Well, who'd you get to perform in it?

TOOZENBACH It could be done if we wanted to. Maria Serghyeevna plays the piano wonderfully well, in my opinion.

KOOLYGHIN Yes, wonderfully well!

IRENA She's forgotten how to. She hasn't played for three years. . . . or maybe it's four.

TOOZENBACH Nobody understands music in this town, not a single person. But I do—I really do—and I assure you quite definitely that Maria Serghyeevna plays magnificently. She's almost a genius for it.

KOOLYGHIN You're right, Baron. I'm very fond of Masha. She's such a nice girl.

TOOZENBACH Fancy being able to play so exquisitely, and yet having nobody, no-body at all, to appreciate it!

KOOLYGHIN [*sighs*] Yes. . . . But would it be quite proper for her to play in a concert? [*A pause.*] I don't know anything about these matters, my friends. Perhaps it'll be perfectly all right. But you know, although our director is a good man, a very good man indeed, and most intelli-gent, I know that he does hold certain views. . . . Of course, this doesn't really concern him, but I'll have a word with him about it, all the same, if you like.

CHEBUTYKIN [*picks up a china clock and examines it*].

VERSHININ I've got my clothes in such a mess helping to put out the fire, I must look like nothing on earth. [*A pause.*] I believe they were saying yesterday that our brigade might be transferred to some-where a long way away. Some said it was to be Poland, and some said it was Cheeta, in Siberia.

TOOZENBACH I heard that, too. Well, the town will seem quite deserted.

IRENA We'll go away, too!

CHEBUTYKIN [*drops clock and breaks it*] Smashed to smithereens!

[*A pause. Everyone looks upset and em-barrassed.*]

KOOLYGHIN [*picks up the pieces.*] Fancy breaking such a valuable thing! Ah, Ivan Romanych, Ivan Romanych! You'll get a bad mark for that!

IRENA It was my mother's clock.

CHEBUTYKIN Well, supposing it was. If it was your mother's, then it was your mother's. Perhaps I didn't smash it. Per-haps it only appears that I did. Perhaps it only appears to us that we exist, whereas in reality we don't exist at all. I don't know anything, no one knows anything. [*Stops at the door.*] Why are you staring at me? Natasha's having a nice little affair with Protopopov, and you don't see it. You sit here seeing nothing, and meanwhile Natasha's having a nice little affair with Protopopov. . . . [*Sings.*] Would you like a date? . . . [*Goes out.*]

VERSHININ So. . . . [*Laughs.*] How odd it all is, really. [*A pause.*] When the fire started, I ran home as fast as I could. When I got near, I could see that our house was all right and out of danger, but the two little girls were standing there, in the doorway in their night clothes. Their mother wasn't there. People were rushing about, horses, dogs . . . and in the kiddies' faces I saw a frightened, anxious, appealing look, I don't know what! . . . My heart sank when I saw their faces. My God, I thought, what will these children have to go through in the course of their poor lives? And they may live a long time, too! I picked them up and ran back here with them, and all the time I was running, I was thinking the same thing: what will they have to go through? [*The alarm is sounded. A pause.*] When I got here, my wife was here already . . . angry, shouting!

[*Enter* MASHA *carrying a pillow; she sits down on the couch.*]

VERSHININ And when my little girls were standing in the doorway with nothing on but their night clothes, and the street was red with the glow of the fire and full of terrifying noises, it struck me that the same sort of thing used to happen years ago, when armies used to make sudden raids on towns, and plunder them and set them on fire. . . . Anyway, is there any essential difference between things as they were and as they are now? And before very long, say, in another two or three hundred years, people may be looking at our present life just as we look at the past now, with horror and scorn. Our own times may seem uncouth to them, boring and frightfully uncomfortable and strange. . . . Oh, what a great life it'll be then, what a life! [*Laughs.*] Forgive me, I'm philosophizing my head off again

. . . but may I go on, please? I'm bursting to philosophize just at the moment. I'm in the mood for it. [*A pause.*] You seem as if you've all gone to sleep. As I was saying: what a great life it will be in the future! Just try to imagine it. . . . At the present time there are only three people of your intellectual calibre in the whole of this town, but future generations will be more productive of people like you. They'll go on producing more and more of the same sort until at last the time will come when everything will be just as you'd wish it yourselves. People will live their lives in your way, and then even you may be outmoded, and a new lot will come along who will be even better than you are. . . . [*Laughs.*] I'm in quite a special mood to-day. I feel full of a tremendous urge to live. . . . [*Sings.*]

"To Love all ages are in fee,
The passion's good for you and me." . . .
[*Laughs.*]

MASHA [*sings*] Tara-tara-tara. . . .
VERSHININ Tum-tum. . . .
MASHA Tara-tara . . .
VERSHININ Tum-tum, tum-tum. . . .
[*Laughs.*]

[*Enter* FEDOTIK.]

FEDOTIK [*dancing about*] Burnt, burnt! Everything I've got burnt!

[*All laugh.*]

IRENA It's hardly a joking matter. Has everything really been burnt?
FEDOTIK [*laughs*] Everything, completely. I've got nothing left. My guitar's burnt, my photographs are burnt, all my letters are burnt. Even the little note-book I was going to give you has been burnt.

[*Enter* SOLIONY.]

IRENA No, please go away, Vassily Vassilich. You can't come in here.
SOLIONY Can't I? Why can the Baron come in here if I can't?
VERSHININ We really must go, all of us. What's the fire doing?
SOLIONY It's dying down, they say. Well,

I must say it's a peculiar thing that the Baron can come in here, and I can't.

[*Takes a scent bottle from his pocket and sprinkles himself with scent.*]

VERSHININ Tara-tara.

MASHA Tum-tum, tum-tum.

VERSHININ [*laughs, to* SOLIONY] Let's go to the ballroom.

SOLIONY Very well, we'll make a note of this. "I hardly need to make my moral yet more clear: That might be teasing geese, I fear!"[4] [*Looks at* TOOZENBACH.] Cluck, cluck, cluck! [*Goes out with* VERSHININ *and* FEDOTIK.]

IRENA That Soliony has smoked the room out. . . . [*Puzzled.*] The Baron's asleep. Baron! Baron!

TOOZENBACH [*waking out of his doze*] I must be tired. The brick-works. . . . No, I'm not talking in my sleep. I really do intend to go to the brick-works and start working there quite soon. I've had a talk with the manager. [*To* IRENA, *tenderly.*] You are so pale, so beautiful, so fascinating. . . . Your pallor seems to light up the darkness around you, as if it were luminous, somehow. . . . You're sad, you're dissatisfied with the life you have to live. . . . Oh, come away with me, let's go away and work together!

MASHA Nikolai Lvovich, I wish you'd go away.

TOOZENBACH [*laughs*] Oh, you're here, are you? I didn't see you [*Kisses* IRENA's hand.] Good-bye, I'm going. You know as I look at you now, I keep thinking of the day—it was a long time ago, your Saint's day—when you talked to us about the joy of work. . . . You were so gay and high-spirited then. . . . And what a happy life I saw ahead of me! Where is it all now? [*Kisses her hand.*] There are tears in your eyes. You should go to bed, it's beginning to get light . . . it's almost morning. . . . Oh, if only I could give my life for you!

4 From Krylov's fable *Geese* (translated by Bernard Pares).

MASHA Nikolai Lvovich, please go away! Really now. . . .

TOOZENBACH I'm going. [*Goes out.*]

MASHA [*lies down*] Are you asleep, Fiodor?

KOOLYGHIN Eh?

MASHA Why don't you go home?

KOOLYGHIN My darling Masha, my sweet, my precious Masha. . . .

IRENA She's tired. Let her rest a while, Fyedia.

KOOLYGHIN I'll go in a moment. My wife, my dear, good wife! . . . How I love you! . . . only you!

MASHA [*crossly*] *Amo, amas, amat, amamus, amatis, amant!*

KOOLYGHIN [*laughs*] Really, she's an amazing woman!—I've been married to you for seven years, but I feel as if we were only married yesterday. Yes, on my word of honour, I do! You really are amazing! Oh, I'm so happy, happy, happy!

MASHA And I'm so bored, bored, bored! [*Sits up.*] I can't get it out of my head. . . . It's simply disgusting. It's like having a nail driven into my head. No, I can't keep silent about it any more. It's about Andrey. . . . He's actually mortgaged this house to a bank, and his wife's got hold of all the money—and yet the house doesn't belong to him, it belongs to all four of us! Surely, he must realize that, if he's got any honesty.

KOOLYGHIN Why bring all this up, Masha? Why bother about it now? Andriusha owes money all round. . . . Leave him alone.

MASHA Anyway, it's disgusting. [*Lies down.*]

KOOLYGHIN Well, we aren't poor, Masha. I've got work, I teach at the county school, I give private lessons in my spare time. . . . I'm just a plain, honest man. . . . *Omnia mea mecum porto,* as they say.

MASHA I don't ask for anything, but I'm just disgusted by injustice. [*A pause.*] Why don't you go home, Fiodor?

KOOLYGHIN [*kisses her*] You're tired. Just rest here for a while. . . . I'll go home and wait for you. . . . Go to sleep. [*Goes to the door.*] I'm happy, happy, happy! [*Goes out.*]

IRENA   The truth is that Andrey is getting to be shallow-minded. He's ageing and since he's been living with that woman he's lost all the inspiration he used to have! Not long ago he was working for a professorship, and yet yesterday he boasted of having at last been elected a member of the County Council. Fancy him a member, with Protopopov as chairman! They say the whole town's laughing at him, he's the only one who doesn't know anything or see anything. And now, you see, everyone's at the fire, while he's just sitting in his room, not taking the slightest notice of it. Just playing his violin. [*Agitated.*] Oh, how dreadful it is, how dreadful, how dreadful! I can't bear it any longer, I can't, I really can't! . . .

[*Enter* OLGA. *She starts arranging things on her bedside table.*]

IRENA   [*sobs loudly*] You must turn me out of here! Turn me out; I can't stand it any more!

OLGA   [*alarmed*] What is it? What is it, darling?

IRENA   [*sobbing.*] Where. . . . Where has it all gone to? Where is it? Oh, God! I've forgotten. . . . I've forgotten everything . . . there's nothing but a muddle in my head. . . . I don't remember what the Italian for "window" is, or for "ceiling." . . . Every day I'm forgetting more and more, and life's slipping by, and it will never, never come back. . . . We shall never go to Moscow. . . . I can see that we shall never go. . . .

OLGA   Don't, my dear, don't. . . .

IRENA   [*trying to control herself*] Oh, I'm so miserable! . . . I can't work, I won't work! I've had enough of it, enough! . . . First I worked on the telegraph, now I'm in the County Council office, and I hate and despise everything they give me to do there. . . . I'm twenty-three years old, I've been working all this time, and I feel as if my brain's dried up. I know I've got thinner and uglier and older, and I find no kind of satisfaction in anything, none at all. And the time's passing . . . and I feel as if I'm moving away from any hope of a genuine, fine life, I'm moving further and further away and sinking into a kind of abyss. I feel in despair, and I don't know why I'm still alive, why I haven't killed myself. . . .

OLGA   Don't cry, my dear child, don't cry. . . . It hurts me.

IRENA   I'm not crying any more. That's enough of it. Look, I'm not crying now. Enough of it, enough! . . .

OLGA   Darling, let me tell you something. . . . I just want to speak as your sister, as your friend. . . . That is, if you want my advice. . . . Why don't you marry the Baron?

IRENA   [*weeps quietly*].

OLGA   After all, you do respect him, you think a lot of him. . . . It's true, he's not good-looking, but he's such a decent, clean-minded sort of man. . . . After all, one doesn't marry for love, but to fulfil a duty. At least, I think so, and I'd marry even if I weren't in love. I'd marry anyone that proposed to me, as long as he was a decent man. I'd even marry an old man.

IRENA   I've been waiting all this time, imagining that we'd be moving to Moscow, and I'd meet the man I'm meant for there. I've dreamt about him and I've loved him in my dreams. . . . But it's all turned out to be nonsense . . . nonsense. . . .

OLGA   [*embracing her*] My darling sweetheart, I understand everything perfectly. When the Baron resigned his commission and came to see us in his civilian clothes, I thought he looked so plain that I actually started to cry. . . . He asked me why I was crying. . . . How could I tell him? But, of course, if it were God's will that he should marry you, I'd feel perfectly happy about it. That's quite a different matter, quite different!

[NATASHA, *carrying a candle, comes out of the door on the right, crosses the stage and goes out through the door on the left without saying anything.*]

MASHA [*sits up*] She goes about looking as if she'd started the fire.

OLGA You're silly, Masha. You're the stupidest person in our family. Forgive me for saying so.

[*A pause.*]

MASHA My dear sisters, I've got something to confess to you. I must get some relief, I feel the need of it in my heart. I'll confess it to you two alone, and then never again, never to anybody! I'll tell you in a minute. [*In a low voice.*] It's a secret, but you'll have to know everything. I can't keep silent any more. [*A pause.*] I'm in love, in love. . . . I love that man. . . . You saw him here just now. . . . Well, what's the good? . . . I love Vershinin. . . .

OLGA [*goes behind her screen*] Don't say it. I don't want to hear it.

MASHA Well, what's to be done? [*Holding her head.*] I thought he was queer at first, then I started to pity him . . . then I began to love him . . . love everything about him—his voice, his talk, his misfortunes, his two little girls. . . .

OLGA Nevertheless, I don't want to hear it. You can say any nonsense you like, I'm not listening.

MASHA Oh, you're stupid, Olia! If I love him, well—that's my fate! That's my destiny. . . . He loves me, too. It's all rather frightening, isn't it? Not a good thing, is it? [*Takes* IRENA *by the hand and draws her to her.*] Oh, my dear! . . . How are we going to live through the rest of our lives? What's going to become of us? When you read a novel, everything in it seems so old and obvious, but when you fall in love yourself, you suddenly discover that you don't really know anything, and you've got to make your own decisions. . . . My dear sisters, my dear

sisters! . . . I've confessed it all to you, and now I'll keep quiet. . . . I'll be like that madman in the story by Gogol—silence . . . silence! . . .

[*Enter* ANDREY *followed by* FERAPONT.]

ANDREY [*crossly*] What do you want? I don't understand you.

FERAPONT [*stopping in the doorway, impatiently*] I've asked you about ten times already, Andrey Serghyevich.

ANDREY In the first place, you're not to call me Andrey Serghyevich—call me "Your Honour."

FERAPONT The firemen are asking Your Honour if they may drive through your garden to get to the river. They've been going a long way round all this time—it's a terrible business!

ANDREY All right. Tell them it's all right. [FERAPONT *goes out.*] They keep on plaguing me. Where's Olga? [OLGA *comes from behind the screen.*] I wanted to see you. Will you give me the key to the cupboard? I've lost mine. You know the key I mean, the small one you've got. . . .

[OLGA *silently hands him the key.* IRENA *goes behind the screen on her side of the room.*]

ANDREY What a terrific fire! It's going down though. That Ferapont annoyed me, the devil take him! Silly thing he made me say. . . . Telling him to call me "Your Honour"! . . . [*A pause.*] Why don't you say anything, Olia? [*A pause.*] It's about time you stopped this nonsense . . . sulking like this for no reason whatever. . . . You here, Masha? And Irena's here, too. That's excellent! We can talk it over then, frankly and once for all. What have you got against me? What is it?

OLGA Drop it now, Andriusha. Let's talk it over to-morrow. [*Agitated.*] What a dreadful night!

ANDREY [*in great embarrassment*] Don't get upset. I'm asking you quite calmly, what have you got against me? Tell me frankly.

VERSHININ'S VOICE [*off stage*] Tum-tum-tum!

MASHA [*in a loud voice, getting up*] Tara-tara-tara! [*To* OLGA.] Good-bye, Olia, God bless you! [*Goes behind the screen and kisses* IRENA.] Sleep well. . . . Good-bye, Andrey. I should leave them now, they're tired . . . talk it over to-morrow. . . . [*Goes out.*]

OLGA Really, Andriusha, let's leave it till to-morrow. . . . [*Goes behind the screen on her side of the room.*] It's time to go to bed.

ANDREY I only want to say one thing, then I'll go. In a moment. . . . First of all, you've got something against my wife, against Natasha. I've always been conscious of it from the day we got married. Natasha is a fine woman, she's honest and straightforward and high-principled. . . . That's my opinion. I love and respect my wife. You understand that I respect her, and I expect others to respect her, too. I repeat: she's an honest, high-principled woman, and all your grievances against her—if you don't mind my saying so—are just imagination, and nothing more. . . . [*A pause.*] Secondly, you seem to be annoyed with me for not making myself a professor, and not doing any academic work. But I'm working in the Council Office, I'm a member of the County Council, and I feel my service there is just as fine and valuable as any academic work I might do. I'm a member of the County Council, and if you want to know, I'm proud of it! [*A pause.*] Thirdly . . . there's something else I must tell you. . . . I know I mortgaged the house without asking your permission. . . . That was wrong, I admit it, and I ask you to forgive me. . . . I was driven to it by my debts. . . . I'm in debt for about thirty-five thousand roubles. I don't play cards any more, I've given it up long ago. . . . The only thing I can say to justify myself is that you girls get an annuity, while I don't

get anything . . . no income, I mean. . . . [*A pause.*]

KOOLYGHIN [*calling through the door*] Is Masha there? She's not there? [*Alarmed.*] Where can she be then? It's very strange. . . . [*Goes away.*]

ANDREY So you won't listen? Natasha is a good, honest woman, I tell you. [*Walks up and down the stage, then stops.*] When I married her, I thought we were going to be happy, I thought we should all be happy. . . . But . . . oh, my God! . . . [*Weeps.*] My dear sisters, my dear, good sisters, don't believe what I've been saying, don't believe it. . . . [*Goes out.*]

KOOLYGHIN [*through the door, agitated*] Where's Masha? Isn't Masha here? Extraordinary! [*Goes away.*]

[*The alarm is heard again. The stage is empty.*]

IRENA [*speaking from behind the screen*] Olia! Who's that knocking on the floor?

OLGA It's the doctor, Ivan Romanych. He's drunk.

IRENA It's been one thing after another all night. [*A pause.*] Olia! [*Peeps out from behind the screen.*] Have you heard? The troops are being moved from the district . . . they're being sent somewhere a long way off.

OLGA That's only a rumour.

IRENA We'll be left quite alone then. . . . Olia!

OLGA Well?

IRENA Olia, darling, I do respect the Baron. . . . I think a lot of him, he's a very good man. . . . I'll marry him, Olia, I'll agree to marry him, if only we can go to Moscow! Let's go, please do let's go! There's nowhere in all the world like Moscow. Let's go, Olia! Let's go!

Act Four

[*The old garden belonging to the Prozorovs' house. A river is seen at the end of a long avenue of fir-trees, and on the far bank of the river a forest. On the right of the stage there is a verandah with a table on which champagne bottles and glasses have been left. It is midday. From time to time people from the street pass through the garden to get to the river. Five or six soldiers march through quickly.*

CHEBUTYKIN, *radiating a mood of benevolence which does not leave him throughout the act, is sitting in a chair in the garden. He is wearing his army cap and is holding a walking stick, as if ready to be called away at any moment.* KOOLYGHIN, *with a decoration round his neck and with his moustache shaved off,* TOOZENBACH *and* IRENA *are standing on the verandah saying good-bye to* FEDOTIK *and* RODÉ, *who are coming down the steps. Both officers are in marching uniform.*]

TOOZENBACH [*embracing* FEDOTIK] You're a good fellow, Fedotik; we've been good friends! [*Embraces* RODÉ.] Once more, then. . . . Good-bye, my dear friends!

IRENA Au revoir!

FEDOTIK It's not "au revoir." It's good-bye. We shall never meet again!

KOOLYGHIN Who knows? [*Wipes his eyes, smiling.*] There! you've made me cry.

IRENA We'll meet some time.

FEDOTIK Perhaps in ten or fifteen years' time. But then we'll hardly know one another. . . . We shall just meet and say, "How are you?" coldly. . . . [*Takes a snapshot.*] Wait a moment. . . . Just one more, for the last time.

RODÉ [*embraces* TOOZENBACH] We're not likely to meet again. . . . [*Kisses* IRENA'*s hand.*] Thank you for everything . . . everything!

FEDOTIK [*annoyed*] Do just wait a second!

TOOZENBACH We'll meet again if we're fated to meet. Do write to us. Be sure to write.

RODÉ [*glancing round the garden*] Good-bye, trees! [*Shouts.*] Heigh-ho! [*A pause.*] Good-bye, echo!

KOOLYGHIN I wouldn't be surprised if you got married out there, in Poland. . . .

You'll get a Polish wife, and she'll put her arms round you and say: Kohane![5] [*Laughs.*]

FEDOTIK [*glances at his watch*] There's less than an hour to go. Soliony is the only one from our battery who's going down the river on the barge. All the others are marching with the division. Three batteries are leaving to-day by road and three more to-morrow—then the town will be quite peaceful.

TOOZENBACH Yes, and dreadfully dull, too.

RODÉ By the way, where's Maria Serghye-evna?

KOOLYGHIN She's somewhere in the garden.

FEDOTIK We must say good-bye to her.

RODÉ Good-bye. I really must go, or I'll burst into tears. [*Quickly embraces* TOOZENBACH *and* KOOLYGHIN, *kisses* IRENA'*s hand.*] Life's been very pleasant here. . . .

FEDOTIK [*to* KOOLYGHIN] Here's something for a souvenir for you—a note-book with a pencil. . . . We'll go down to the river through here. [*They go off, glancing back.*]

RODÉ [*shouts*] Heigh-ho!

KOOLYGHIN [*shouts*] Good-bye!

[*At the back of the stage* FEDOTIK *and* RODÉ *meet* MASHA, *and say good-bye to her; she goes off with them.*]

IRENA They've gone. . . . [*Sits down on the bottom step of the verandah.*]

CHEBUTYKIN They forgot to say good-bye to me.

IRENA Well, what about you?

CHEBUTYKIN That's true, I forgot, too. Never mind, I'll be seeing them again quite soon. I'll be leaving to-morrow. Yes . . . only one more day. And then, in a year's time I'll be retiring. I'll come back here and finish the rest of my life near you. There's just one more year to go and then I get my pension. . . . [*Puts a newspaper in his pocket and takes out an-*

5 A Polish word meaning "beloved."

other.] I'll come back here and lead a reformed life. I'll be a nice, quiet, well-behaved little man.

IRENA   Yes, it's really time you reformed, my dear friend. You ought to live a different sort of life, somehow.

CHEBUTYKIN   Yes. . . . I think so, too. [*Sings quietly.*] Tarara-boom-di-ay. . . . I'm sitting on a tomb-di-ay. . . .

KOOLYGHIN   Ivan Romanych is incorrigible! Incorrigible!

CHEBUTYKIN   Yes, you ought to have taken me in hand. You'd have reformed me!

IRENA   Fiodor's shaved his moustache off. I can't bear to look at him.

KOOLYGHIN   Why not?

CHEBUTYKIN   If I could just tell you what your face looks like now—but I daren't.

KOOLYGHIN   Well! Such are the conventions of life! *Modus vivendi,* you know. The director shaved his moustache off, so I shaved mine off when they gave me an inspectorship. No one likes it, but personally I'm quite indifferent. I'm content. Whether I've got a moustache or not, it's all the same to me. [*Sits down.*]

ANDREY [*passes across the back of the stage pushing a pram with a child asleep in it*].

IRENA   Ivan Romanych, my dear friend, I'm awfully worried about something. You were out in the town garden last night—tell me what happened there?

CHEBUTYKIN   What happened? Nothing. Just a trifling thing. [*Reads his paper.*] It doesn't matter anyway.

KOOLYGHIN   They say that Soliony and the Baron met in the town garden outside the theatre last night and . . .

TOOZENBACH   Don't please! What's the good? . . . [*Waves his hand at him deprecatingly and goes into the house.*]

KOOLYGHIN   It was outside the theatre. . . . Soliony started badgering the Baron, and he lost patience and said something that offended him.

CHEBUTYKIN   I don't know anything about it. It's all nonsense.

KOOLYGHIN   A school-master once wrote "nonsense" in Russian over a pupil's essay, and the pupil puzzled over it, think-

ing it was a Latin word. [*Laughs.*] Frightfully funny, you know! They say that Soliony's in love with Irena and that he got to hate the Baron more and more. . . . Well, that's understandable. Irena's a very nice girl. She's a bit like Masha, she tends to get wrapped up in her own thoughts. [*To* IRENA.] But your disposition is more easy-going than Masha's. And yet Masha has a very nice disposition, too. I love her, I love my Masha.

[*From the back of the stage comes a shout: "Heigh-ho!"*]

IRENA [*starts*]   Anything seems to startle me to-day. [*A pause.*] I've got everything ready, too. I'm sending my luggage off after lunch. The Baron and I are going to get married, to-morrow, and directly afterwards we're moving to the brickworks, and the day after to-morrow I'm starting work at the school. So our new life will begin, God willing! When I was sitting for my teacher's diploma, I suddenly started crying for sheer joy, with a sort of feeling of blessedness. . . . [*A pause.*] The carrier will be coming for my luggage in a minute. . . .

KOOLYGHIN   That's all very well, but somehow I can't feel that it's meant to be serious. All ideas and theories, but nothing really serious. Anyway, I wish you luck from the bottom of my heart.

CHEBUTYKIN [*moved*]   My dearest girl, my precious child! You've gone on so far ahead of me, I'll never catch you up now. I've got left behind like a bird which has grown too old and can't keep up with the rest of the flock. Fly away, my dears, fly away, and God be with you! [*A pause.*] It's a pity you've shaved your moustache off, Fiodor Illyich.

KOOLYGHIN   Don't keep on about it, please! [*Sighs.*] Well, the soldiers will be leaving to-day, and everything will go back to what it was before. Anyway, whatever they say, Masha is a good, loyal wife. Yes, I love her dearly and I'm thankful for what God has given me. Fate treats people so differently. For instance, there's an excise clerk here called Kozy-rev. He was at school with me and he was expelled in his fifth year because he just couldn't grasp the *ut consecutivum*. He's dreadfully hard up now, and in bad health, too, and whenever I meet him, I just say to him: "Hullo, *ut consecutivum!*" "Yes," he replies, "that's just the trouble —*consecutivum*" . . . and he starts coughing. Whereas I—I've been lucky all my life. I'm happy, I've actually been awarded the order of Saint Stanislav, second class—and now I'm teaching the children the same old *ut consecutivum*. Of course, I'm clever, cleverer than plenty of other people, but happiness does not consist of merely being clever. . . .

[In the house someone plays "The Maiden's Prayer."]

IRENA   To-morrow night I shan't have to listen to the "Maiden's Prayer." I shan't have to meet Protopopov. . . . *[A pause.]* By the way, he's in the sitting-room. He's come again.

KOOLYGHIN   Hasn't our headmistress arrived yet?

IRENA   No, we've sent for her. If you only knew how difficult it is for me to live here by myself, without Olia! She lives at the school now; she's the headmistress and she's busy the whole day. And I'm here alone, bored, with nothing to do, and I hate the very room I live in. So I've just made up my mind—if I'm really not going to be able to live in Moscow, that's that. It's my fate, that's all. Nothing can be done about it. It's God's will, everything that happens, and that's the truth. Nikolai Lvovich proposed to me. . . . Well, I thought it over, and I made up my mind. He's such a nice man, it's really extraordinary how nice he is. . . . And then suddenly I felt as though my soul had grown wings, I felt more cheerful and so relieved somehow that I wanted to work again. Just to start work! . . . Only something happened yesterday, and now I feel as though something mysterious is hanging over me. . . .

CHEBUTYKIN   Nonsense!

NATASHA   *[speaking through the window]* Our headmistress!

KOOLYGHIN   Our headmistress has arrived! Let's go indoors.

[Goes indoors with IRENA.]

CHEBUTYKIN   *[reads his paper and sings quietly to himself]* Tarara-boom-di-ay. . . . I'm sitting on a tomb-di-ay. . . .

[MASHA walks up to him; ANDREY passes across the back of the stage pushing the pram.]

MASHA   You look very comfortable sitting here. . . .

CHEBUTYKIN   Well, why not? Anything happening?

MASHA   *[sits down]*   No, nothing. *[A pause.]* Tell me something. Were you in love with my mother?

CHEBUTYKIN   Yes, very much in love.

MASHA   Did she love you?

CHEBUTYKIN   *[after a pause]*   I can't remember now.

MASHA   Is my man here? Our cook Marfa always used to call her policeman "my man." Is he here?

CHEBUTYKIN   Not yet.

MASHA   When you have to take your happiness in snatches, in little bits, as I do, and then lose it, as I've lost it, you gradually get hardened and bad-tempered. *[Points at her breast.]* Something's boiling over inside me, here. *[Looking at AN-DREY, who again crosses the stage with the pram.]* There's Andrey, our dear brother. . . . All our hopes are gone. It's the same as when thousands of people haul a huge bell up into a tower. Untold labour and money is spent on it, and then suddenly it falls and gets smashed. Suddenly, without rhyme or reason. It was the same with Andrey. . . .

ANDREY   When are they going to settle down in the house? They're making such a row.

CHEBUTYKIN   They will soon. *[Looks at his watch.]* This is an old-fashioned watch: it strikes. . . . *[Winds his watch which then strikes.*] The first, second and fifth batteries will be leaving punctually at one o'clock. [*A pause.*] And I shall leave to-morrow.

ANDREY   For good?

CHEBUTYKIN   I don't know. I may return in about a year. Although, God knows . . . it's all the same. . . .

[*The sounds of a harp and a violin are heard.*]

ANDREY   The town will seem quite empty. Life will be snuffed out like a candle. [*A pause.*] Something happened yesterday outside the theatre; everybody's talking about it. I'm the only one that doesn't seem to know about it.

CHEBUTYKIN   It was nothing. A lot of nonsense. Soliony started badgering the Baron, or something. The Baron lost his temper and insulted him, and in the end Soliony had to challenge him to a duel. [*Looks at his watch.*] I think it's time to go. . . . At half-past twelve, in the forest over there, on the other side of the river. . . . Bang-bang! [*Laughs.*] Soliony imagines he's like Lermontov. He actually writes poems. But, joking apart, this is his third duel.

MASHA   Whose third duel?

CHEBUTYKIN   Soliony's.

MASHA   What about the Baron?

CHEBUTYKIN   Well, what about him? [*A pause.*]

MASHA   My thoughts are all in a muddle. . . . But what I mean to say is that they shouldn't be allowed to fight. He might wound the Baron or even kill him.

CHEBUTYKIN   The Baron's a good enough fellow, but what does it really matter if there's one Baron more or less in the world? Well, let it be! It's all the same. [*The shouts of "Ah-oo!" and "Heigh-ho!" are heard from beyond the garden.*] That's Skvortsov, the second, shouting from the boat. He can wait.

ANDREY   I think it's simply immoral to fight a duel, or even to be present at one as a doctor.

CHEBUTYKIN   That's only how it seems.

. . . We don't exist, nothing exists, it only seems to us that we do. . . . And what difference does it make?

MASHA   Talk, talk, nothing but talk all day long! . . . [*Starts to go.*] Having to live in this awful climate with the snow threatening to fall at any moment, and then on the top of it having to listen to all this sort of talk. . . . [*Stops.*] I won't go into the house, I can't bear going in there. . . . Will you let me know when Vershinin comes? . . . [*Walks off along the avenue.*] Look, the birds are beginning to fly away already! [*Looks up.*] Swans or geese. . . . Dear birds, happy birds. . . . [*Goes off.*]

ANDREY   Our house will seem quite deserted. The officers will go, you'll go, my sister will get married, and I'll be left alone in the house.

CHEBUTYKIN   What about your wife?

[*Enter* FERAPONT *with some papers.*]

ANDREY   My wife is my wife. She's a good, decent sort of woman . . . she's really very kind, too, but there's something about her which pulls her down to the level of an animal . . . a sort of mean, blind, thick-skinned animal—anyway, not a human being. I'm telling you this as a friend, the only person I can talk openly to. I love Natasha, it's true. But at times she appears to me so utterly vulgar, that I feel quite bewildered by it, and then I can't understand why, for what reasons I love her—or, anyway, did love her.

CHEBUTYKIN [*gets up*]   Well, dear boy, I'm going away to-morrow and it may be we shall never see each other again. So I'll give you a bit of advice. Put on your hat, take a walking stick, and go away. . . . Go away, and don't ever look back. And the further you go, the better.

[SOLIONY *passes across the back of the stage accompanied by two officers. Seeing* CHEBUTYKIN, *he turns towards him, while the officers walk on.*]

SOLIONY   It's time, Doctor. Half past twelve already. [*Shakes hands with* ANDREY.]

CHEBUTYKIN   In a moment. Oh, I'm tired of you all. [*To* ANDREY.] Andriusha, if anyone asks for me, tell them I'll be back presently. [*Sighs.*] Oh-ho-ho!

SOLIONY   "He had no time to say 'Oh, oh!' Before that bear had struck him low.". . .

[*Walks off with him.*] What are you groaning about, old man?

CHEBUTYKIN   Oh, well!

SOLIONY   How do you feel?

CHEBUTYKIN   [*crossly*] Like a last year's bird's-nest.

SOLIONY   You needn't be so agitated about it, old boy. I shan't indulge in anything much, I'll just scorch his wings a little, like a woodcock's. [*Takes out a scent bottle and sprinkles scent over his hands.*] I've used up a whole bottle to-day, but my hands still smell. They smell like a corpse. [*A pause.*] Yes. . . . Do you remember that poem of Lermontov's?

"And he, rebellious, seeks a storm,
As if in storms there were tranquillity."

CHEBUTYKIN   Yes.

"He had no time to say 'Oh, oh!'
Before that bear had struck him low."

[*Goes out with* SOLIONY.]

[*Shouts of "Heigh-ho!" "Ah-oo!" are heard. Enter* ANDREY *and* FERAPONT.]

FERAPONT   Will you sign these papers, please?

ANDREY   [*with irritation*] Leave me alone! Leave me alone, for Heaven's sake. [*Goes off with the pram.*]

FERAPONT   Well, what am I supposed to do with the papers then? They are meant to be signed, aren't they? [*Goes to back of stage.*]

[*Enter* IRENA *and* TOOZENBACH, *the latter wearing a straw hat.* KOOLYGHIN *crosses the stage, calling: "Ah-oo! Masha! Ah-oo!"*]

TOOZENBACH   I think he's the only person in the whole town who's glad that the army is leaving.

IRENA   That's quite understandable, really. [*A pause.*] The town will look quite empty.

TOOZENBACH   My dear, I'll be back in a moment.

IRENA   Where are you going?

TOOZENBACH   I must slip back to the town, and then . . . I want to see some of my colleagues off.

IRENA   It's not true. . . . Nikolai, why are you so absent-minded to-day? [*A pause.*] What happened outside the theatre last night?

TOOZENBACH   [*with a movement of impatience*] I'll be back in an hour. . . . I'll be back with you again. [*Kisses her hands.*] My treasure! . . . [*Gazes into her eyes.*] It's five years since I first began to love you, and still I can't get used to it, and you seem more beautiful every day. What wonderful, lovely hair! What marvellous eyes! I'll take you away to-morrow. We'll work, we'll be rich, my dreams will come to life again. And you'll be happy! But—there's only one "but," only one—you don't love me!

IRENA   I can't help that! I'll be your wife, I'll be loyal and obedient to you, but I can't love you. . . . What's to be done? [*Weeps.*] I've never loved anyone in my life. Oh, I've had such dreams about being in love! I've been dreaming about it for ever so long, day and night . . . but somehow my soul seems like an expensive piano which someone has locked up and the key's got lost. [*A pause.*] Your eyes are so restless.

TOOZENBACH   I was awake all night. Not that there's anything to be afraid of in my life, nothing threatening. . . . Only the thought of that lost key torments me and keeps me awake. Say something to me. . . . [*A pause.*] Say something!

IRENA   What? What am I to say? What?

TOOZENBACH   Anything.

IRENA   Don't, my dear, don't. . . . [*A pause.*]

TOOZENBACH   Such trifles, such silly little things sometimes become so important suddenly, for no apparent reason! You laugh at them, just as you always have done, you still regard them as trifles, and yet you suddenly find they're in control, and you haven't the power to stop them. But don't let us talk about all that! Really, I feel quite elated. I feel as if I was seeing those fir-trees and maples and birches for the first time in my life. They all seem to be looking at me with a sort of inquisitive look and waiting for something. What beautiful trees—and how beautiful, when you think of it, life ought to be with trees like these! [*Shouts of "Ah-oo! Heigh-ho" are heard.*] I must go, it's time. . . . Look at that dead tree, it's all dried-up, but it's still swaying in the wind along with the others. And in the same way, it seems to me that, if I die, I shall still have a share in life somehow or other. Goodbye, my dear. . . . [*Kisses her hands.*] Your papers, the ones you gave me, are on my desk, under the calendar.

IRENA   I'm coming with you.

TOOZENBACH [*alarmed*]   No, no! [*Goes off quickly, then stops in the avenue.*] Irena!

IRENA   What?

TOOZENBACH [*not knowing what to say*]   I didn't have any coffee this morning. Will you tell them to get some ready for me? [*Goes off quickly.*]

[IRENA *stands, lost in thought, then goes to the back of the stage and sits down on a swing. Enter* ANDREY *with the pram;* FERAPONT *appears.*]

FERAPONT   Andrey Serghyeech, the papers aren't mine, you know, they're the office papers. I didn't make them up.

ANDREY   Oh, where has all my past life gone to?—the time when I was young and gay and clever, when I used to have fine dreams and great thoughts, and the present and the future were bright with hope? Why do we become so dull and commonplace and uninteresting almost before we've begun to live? Why do we get lazy, indifferent, useless, unhappy? . . . This town's been in existence for two hundred years; a hundred thousand people live in it, but there's not one who's any different from all the others! There's never been a scholar or an artist or a saint in this place, never a single man sufficiently outstanding to make you feel passionately that you wanted to emulate him. People here do nothing but eat, drink and sleep. . . . Then they die and some more take their places, and they eat, drink and sleep, too,—and just to introduce a bit of variety into their lives, so as to avoid getting completely stupid with boredom, they indulge in their disgusting gossip and vodka and gambling and law-suits. The wives deceive their husbands, and the husbands lie to their wives, and pretend they don't see anything and don't hear anything. . . . And all this overwhelming vulgarity and pettiness crushes the children and puts out any spark they might have in them, so that they, too, become miserable, half-dead creatures, just like one another and just like their parents! . . . [*To* FERAPONT, *crossly.*] What do you want?

FERAPONT   What? Here are the papers to sign.

ANDREY   What a nuisance you are!

FERAPONT [*hands him the papers*]   The porter at the finance department told me just now . . . he said last winter they had two hundred degrees of frost in Petersburg.

ANDREY   I hate the life I live at present, but oh! the sense of elation when I think of the future! Then I feel so light-hearted, such a sense of release! I seem to see light ahead, light and freedom. I see myself free, and my children, too,—free from idleness, free from *kvass*, free from eternal meals of goose and cabbage, free from after-dinner naps, free from all this degrading parasitism! . . .

FERAPONT   They say two thousand people were frozen to death. They say everyone was scared stiff. It was either in Petersburg or in Moscow, I can't remember exactly.

ANDREY [*with sudden emotion, tenderly*]

My dear sisters, my dear good sisters! [*Tearfully.*] Masha, my dear sister! . . .

NATASHA [*through the window*] Who's that talking so loudly there? Is that you, Andriusha? You'll wake Sofochka. *Il ne faut pas faire du bruit, la Sophie est dormie déjà. Vous êtes un ours.* [*Getting angry.*] If you want to talk, give the pram to someone else. Ferapont, take the pram from the master.

FERAPONT Yes, Madam. [*Takes the pram.*]

ANDREY [*shamefacedly*] I was talking quietly.

NATASHA [*in the window, caressing her small son*] Bobik! Naughty Bobik! Aren't you a naughty boy!

ANDREY [*glancing through the papers*] All right, I'll go through them and sign them if they need it. You can take them back to the office later. [*Goes into the house, reading the papers.*]

[FERAPONT *wheels the pram into the garden.*]

NATASHA [*in the window*] What's Mummy's name, Bobik? You darling! And who's that lady? Auntie Olia. Say: "Hullo, Auntie Olia."

[*Two street musicians, a man and a girl, enter and begin to play on a violin and a harp;* VERSHININ, OLGA *and* ANFISA *come out of the house and listen in silence for a few moments; then* IRENA *approaches them.*]

OLGA Our garden's like a public road; everybody goes through it. Nanny, give something to the musicians.

ANFISA [*giving them money*] Go along now, God bless you, good people! [*The musicians bow and go away.*] Poor, homeless folk! Whoever would go dragging round the streets playing tunes if he had enough to eat? [*To* IRENA.] How are you, Irenushka? [*Kisses her.*] Ah, my child, what a life I'm having! Such comfort! In a large flat at the school with Oliushka—and no rent to pay, either! The Lord's been kind to me in my old age. I've never had such a comfortable time in my life,

old sinner that I am! A big flat, and no rent to pay, and a whole room to myself, with my own bed. All free. Sometimes when I wake up in the night I begin to think, and then—Oh, Lord! Oh, Holy Mother of God!—there's no one happier in the world than me!

VERSHININ [*glances at his watch*] We shall be starting in a moment, Olga Serghyeevna. It's time I went. [*A pause.*] I wish you all the happiness in the world . . . everything. . . . Where's Maria Serghyeevna?

IRENA She's somewhere in the garden. I'll go and look for her.

VERSHININ That's kind of you. I really must hurry.

ANFISA I'll come and help to look for her. [*Calls out.*] Mashenka, ah-oo! [*Goes with* IRENA *towards the far end of the garden.*] Ah-oo! Ah-oo!

VERSHININ Everything comes to an end. Well, here we are—and now it's going to be "good-bye." [*Looks at his watch.*] The city gave us a sort of farewell lunch. There was champagne, and the mayor made a speech, and I ate and listened, but in spirit I was with you here. . . . [*Glances round the garden.*] I've grown so . . . so accustomed to you.

OLGA Shall we meet again some day, I wonder?

VERSHININ Most likely not! [*A pause.*] My wife and the two little girls will be staying on here for a month or two. Please, if anything happens, if they need anything. . . .

OLGA Yes, yes, of course. You needn't worry about that. [*A pause.*] To-morrow there won't be a single officer or soldier in the town. . . . All that will be just a memory, and, of course, a new life will begin for us here. . . . [*A pause.*] Nothing ever happens as we'd like it to. I didn't want to be a headmistress, and yet now I am one. It means we shan't be going to live in Moscow. . . .

VERSHININ Well. . . . Thank you for everything. Forgive me if ever I've done anything. . . . I've talked a lot too much, far too much. . . . Forgive me for that, don't think too unkindly of me.

OLGA [*wipes her eyes*] Now . . . why is Masha so long coming?

VERSHININ What else can I tell you now it's time to say "good-bye"? What shall I philosophize about now? . . . [*Laughs.*] Yes, life is difficult. It seems quite hopeless for a lot of us, just a kind of impasse. . . . And yet you must admit that it is gradually getting easier and brighter, and it's clear that the time isn't far off when the light will spread everywhere. [*Looks at his watch.*] Time, it's time for me to go. . . . In the old days the human race was always making war, its entire existence was taken up with campaigns, advances, retreats, victories. . . . But now all that's out of date, and in its place there's a huge vacuum, clamouring to be filled. Humanity is passionately seeking something to fill it with and, of course, it will find something some day. Oh! If only it would happen soon! [*A pause.*] If only we could educate the industrious people and make the educated people industrious. . . . [*Looks at his watch.*] I really must go. . . .

OLGA Here she comes!

[*Enter* MASHA.]

VERSHININ I've come to say good-bye. . . .

[OLGA *walks off and stands a little to one side so as not to interfere with their leave-taking.*]

MASHA [*looking into his face*] Good-bye! . . . [*A long kiss.*]

OLGA That'll do, that'll do.

MASHA [*sobs loudly*].

VERSHININ Write to me. . . . Don't forget me! Let me go . . . it's time. Olga Serghyeevna, please take her away . . . I must go . . . I'm late already. . . . [*Deeply moved, kisses* OLGA's *hands, then embraces* MASHA *once again and goes out quickly.*]

OLGA That'll do, Masha! Don't, my dear, don't. . . .

[*Enter* KOOLYGHIN.]

KOOLYGHIN [*embarrassed*] Never mind, let her cry, let her. . . . My dear Masha, my dear, sweet Masha. . . . You're my wife, and I'm happy in spite of everything. . . . I'm not complaining, I've no reproach to make—not a single one. . . . Olga here is my witness. . . . We'll start our life over again in the same old way, and you won't hear a word from me . . . not a hint. . . .

MASHA [*suppressing her sobs*] "A green oak grows by a curving shore, And round that oak hangs a golden chain." . . . "A golden chain round that oak." . . . Oh, I'm going mad. . . . By a curving shore . . . a green oak. . . .

OLGA Calm yourself, Masha, calm yourself. . . . Give her some water.

MASHA I'm not crying any more. . . .

KOOLYGHIN She's not crying any more . . . she's a good girl.

[*The hollow sound of a gun-shot is heard in the distance.*]

MASHA "A green oak grows by a curving shore, And round that oak hangs a golden chain." . . . A green cat . . . a green oak . . . I've got it all mixed up. . . . [*Drinks water.*] My life's messed up. . . . I don't want anything now. . . . I'll calm down in a moment. . . . It doesn't matter. . . . What *is* "the curving shore"? Why does it keep coming into my head all the time? My thoughts are all mixed up.

[*Enter* IRENA.]

OLGA Calm down, Masha. That's right . . . good girl! . . . Let's go indoors.

MASHA [*irritably*] I'm not going in there! [*Sobs, but immediately checks herself.*] I don't go into that house now, and I'm not going to. . . .

IRENA Let's sit down together for a moment, and not talk about anything. I'm going away to-morrow, you know. . . .

[*A pause.*]

KOOLYGHIN   Yesterday I took away a false beard and a moustache from a boy in the third form. I've got them here. [*Puts them on.*] Do I look like our German teacher? . . . [*Laughs.*] I do, don't I? The boys are funny.

MASHA   It's true, you do look like that German of yours.

OLGA [*laughs*]   Yes, he does.

[MASHA *cries.*]

IRENA   That's enough, Masha!

KOOLYGHIN   Very much like him, I think!

[*Enter* NATASHA.]

NATASHA [*to the maid*]   What? Oh, yes. Mr. Protopopov is going to keep an eye on Sofochka, and Andrey Serghyevich is going to take Bobik out in the pram. What a lot of work these children make! . . . [*To* IRENA.] Irena, you're really leaving to-morrow? What a pity! Do stay just another week, won't you? [*Catching sight of* KOOLYGHIN, *shrieks; he laughs and takes off the false beard and moustache.*] Get away with you! How you scared me! [*To* IRENA.] I've grown so accustomed to you being here. . . . You mustn't think it's going to be easy for me to be without you. I'll get Andrey and his old violin to move into your room: he can saw away at it as much as he likes there. And then we'll move Sofochka into his room. She's such a wonderful child, really! Such a lovely little girl! This morning she looked at me with such a sweet expression, and then she said: "Ma-mma!"

KOOLYGHIN   It's quite true, she is a beautiful child.

NATASHA   So to-morrow I'll be alone here. [*Sighs.*] I'll have this fir-tree avenue cut down first, then that maple tree over there. It looks so awful in the evenings. . . . [*To* IRENA.] My dear, that belt you're wearing doesn't suit you at all. Not at all in good taste. You want something brighter to go with that dress. . . . I'll tell them to put flowers all round here, lots of flowers, so that we get plenty of scent from them. . . . [*Sternly.*] Why is there a fork lying on this seat? [*Going into the house, to the maid.*] Why is that fork left on the seat there? [*Shouts.*] Don't answer me back!

KOOLYGHIN   There she goes again!

[*A band plays a military march off stage; all listen.*]

OLGA   They're going.

[*Enter* CHEBUTYKIN.]

MASHA   The soldiers are going. Well. . . . Happy journey to them! [*To her husband.*] We must go home. . . . Where's my hat and cape? . . .

KOOLYGHIN   I took them indoors. I'll bring them at once.

OLGA   Yes, we can go home now. It's time.

CHEBUTYKIN   Olga Serghyeevna!

OLGA   What is it? [*A pause.*] What?

CHEBUTYKIN   Nothing. . . . I don't know quite how to tell you. . . . [*Whispers into her ear.*]

OLGA [*frightened*]   It can't be true!

CHEBUTYKIN   Yes . . . a bad business. . . . I'm so tired . . . quite worn out. . . . I don't want to say another word. . . . [*With annoyance.*] Anyway, nothing matters! . . .

MASHA   What's happened?

OLGA [*puts her arms round* IRENA]   What a dreadful day! . . . I don't know how to tell you, dear. . . .

IRENA   What is it? Tell me quickly, what is it? For Heaven's sake! . . . [*Cries.*]

CHEBUTYKIN   The Baron's just been killed in a duel.

IRENA [*cries quietly*]   I knew it, I knew it. . . .

CHEBUTYKIN [*goes to the back of the stage and sits down*]   I'm tired. . . . [*Takes a newspaper out of his pocket.*] Let them cry for a bit. . . . [*Sings quietly to himself.*] Tarara-boom-di-ay, I'm sitting on a tomb-di-ay. . . . What difference does it make? . . .

[*The three sisters stand huddled together.*]

MASHA   Oh, listen to that band! They're leaving us . . . one of them's gone for good . . . for ever! We're left alone . . . to start our lives all over again. We must go on living . . . we must go on living. . . .

IRENA [*puts her head on* OLGA's *breast*] Some day people will know why such things happen, and what the purpose of all this suffering is. . . . Then there won't be any more riddles. . . . Meanwhile we must go on living . . . and working. Yes, we must just go on working! To-morrow I'll go away alone and teach in a school somewhere; I'll give my life to people who need it. . . . It's autumn now, winter will soon be here, and the snow will cover everything . . . but I'll go on working and working! . . .

OLGA [*puts her arms round both her sisters*] How cheerfully and jauntily that band's playing—really I feel as if I wanted to live! Merciful God! The years will pass, and we shall all be gone for good and quite forgotten. . . . Our faces and our voices will be forgotten and people won't even know that there were once three of us here. . . . But our sufferings may mean happiness for the people who come after us. . . . There'll be a time when peace and happiness reign in the world, and then we shall be remembered kindly and blessed. No, my dear sisters, life isn't finished for us yet! We're going to live! The band is playing so cheerfully and joyfully—maybe, if we wait a little longer, we shall find out why we live, why we suffer. . . . Oh, if we only knew, if only we knew!

[*The music grows fainter and fainter.* KOOLYGHIN, *smiling happily, brings out the hat and the cape.* ANDREY *enters; he is pushing the pram with* BOBIK *sitting in it.*]

CHEBUTYKIN [*sings quietly to himself*] Tarara-boom-di-ay. . . . I'm sitting on a tomb-di-ay. . . . [*Reads the paper.*] What does it matter? Nothing matters!

OLGA If only we knew, if only we knew! . . .

The Playboy of the Western World

John Millington Synge   edited by Ann Saddlemyer

Introductory Comments

Ann Saddlemyer   *University of Toronto*

When the poet William Butler Yeats first met John Millington Synge in Paris in 1896, he had no idea that they both would shortly be at the stormy center of a dramatic movement that, while dedicated to Ireland's "ancient idealism," came under frequent attack as being "anti-national, un-Irish, and immoral." Yet by 1904 the Irish National Theatre Society had moved into its permanent home, the Abbey Theatre, with Yeats, Synge, and Lady Gregory as artistic directors. Aided by his co-directors and a talented group of actors, Synge provided, in rapid succession, his one-act tragedy *Riders to the Sea* and two comedies, both of which roused a certain amount of indignation for being either non-Irish in subject matter or distasteful in treatment. Now, almost exactly ten years after that first meeting in Paris, Synge produced *The Playboy of the Western World,* which sparked disturbances lasting five days. The echoes of discontent reverberated down the years to emerge once again on the company's first American tour in 1911, when the players were hauled into court in Philadelphia and Lady Gregory's life was threatened in Chicago.

At a time when the downfall of the Irish statesman Charles Stewart Parnell was within easy recall and the notorious "stage Irishman" was still a figure of ridicule on the English stage, when there was still considerable prudery concerning clothing and sexual matters, and when Oscar Wilde's arrest just a few years previously had increased Irishmen's sensitivity concerning their country's good name, it is not surprising that a nationalist audience should object either on aesthetic or political grounds to the presentation, on the stage of their National Theatre, of a self-confessed parricide who is glorified as a hero and encouraged as a lover by an entire community in the west of Ireland. Lady Gregory saw the play as revealing the sad plight of a country debilitated through arranged marriages and enforced emigration until only the weak, the helpless, the unhealthy, remain—but even if this more tactful interpretation of the plot were accepted, *The Playboy* seemed a painfully public slander on a country so heroically celebrated in Yeats's and Lady Gregory's own play, *Kathleen ni Houlihan.*

But throughout the disturbances among the audiences and the press, Synge insisted that he wrote the play "directly, as a piece of life, without thinking, or caring to think, whether it was a comedy, tragedy, or extravaganza, or whether it would be held to have, or not to have, a purpose." Nor was he as concerned about the first-night violence as he was by certain weaknesses in the actors' performances and their inability to embody the subtleties of characterization. For Synge had devoted over two years and more than a thousand pages of painstaking rewriting to the intricate and richly textured design of *The Playboy,* making every possible effort to retain clarity and strength of line and plot while elaborating characterization and action through parallels and contrasts, crescendos and climaxes, "currents" of emotion and atmosphere. No wonder that the bewildered actors, loyal to their dramatist (although many, like Lady Gregory herself, disliked the play), succumbed in that first performance to exaggerations of realism rather than trusting to the carefully controlled fantasy of the text.

For the extravagance Synge depicts in his characters is carefully modulated by a deliberate balancing of moods and action until the audience is subtly drawn into a deliberately amoral world that banishes both priest and "polis." Once freed of moral and legal judgment, we are able to respond with the myth-making Mayoites to the excitement of a folk-hero in our midst, and to indulge in that "popular imagination that is fiery and magnificent, and tender" that Synge describes in his preface to the play. The power of the imagination, the liberation of Christy Mahon's spirit as he expands into the role of poet-hero cast by the Mayoites themselves, runs like a multicolored thread through the play. "Given the psychic state of the local," Synge insisted to a friend, "the story is probable." This small enclosed world, entered so timidly and cautiously first by Shawn and then by Christy, is one of deprivation and isolation, where heroes are few and familiar (even the lusty Widow Quin's belated husband has become a standard) and where only reminiscence, horseplay, and the occasional sup of poteen (illicitly distilled whiskey) brighten the darkness and silence of the unknown and threatening "big world" outside. The villagers are childlike in their response to "such poet's talking and bravery of heart"—notice their eager, inquisitive circling until Christy yields his story in appropriate heroic form; they do not recognize their part in the creation of this folk-hero even when the reality of murder is forced on them by a defiant Christy forced to "prove" his new-found self-respect. Nor, with the exception of Pegeen and the Widow, are they aware of the permanence of that creation or the violence of their own response.

When Synge was criticized for the brutality and violence in the play, he produced an argument he was later to develop more fully in the preface to his *Poems and Translations,* insisting that "the romantic note and a Rabelaisian note are working to a climax through a great part of the play, and that the Rabelaisian note, the 'gross' note, if you will, *must* have its climax no matter who may be shocked." Earthiness and lyricism must exist in equal proportions; the bitter belongs to the reality of life as much as the sweet; poetry must always "have its roots among the clay and the worms." The richer and more tender the imagination, the more fiery and extravagant the accompanying action is likely to be. In the play we see this deliberate paralleling most clearly in the treatment of Pegeen Mike, for the more Pegeen believes in the hero she has helped create, the greater is her loss when she dares not follow him "romancing through a romping lifetime from this hour to the dawning of the judgment day." And the greater is the need for her to show the pain of that loss by inflicting physical pain in turn as she burns Christy. It is not, in fact, until that moment that Christy is free to become the playboy in earnest; now he is no longer dependent on Pegeen's approval. And so Christy's triumph is Pegeen's heartbreak; in that final scene of rejection the various threads of bitter and sweet, violence and lyricism are drawn inextricably together.

But the world of fantasy and folk-myth Synge has created is not restricted to Pegeen and Christy. We first hear Old Mahon described in hyperbolic terms by his son (the deed must have a suitably heroic subject) ; Old Mahon too tastes the joyous moment of recognition and, as with Christy, "Is it me?" becomes "It is me!" In the two Mahons, the drunken antics and earthbound tales of the Mayoites are elevated to Dionysiac and truly grotesque proportions; with the final testing of courage, Christy's mask (and therefore his father's) becomes a reality, the playboy turns into the genuine player, the dreaming fool of the family becomes the proud poet-jester of Mayo. "Shut your yelling," he admonishes his attackers, "for if you're after making a mighty man of me this day by the power of a lie, you're setting me now to think if it's a poor thing to be lonesome, it's worse maybe go mixing with the fools of earth." His elevation isolates him further, and he and his "Da" enter a new world none other dare follow.

Among those left behind, the Widow Quin deserves special notice. For she too is carved of heroic stuff, even though her deed is too close to home to "win small glory with the boys itself." She too is set apart and in her isolation has a breadth of sympathy and realistic appraisal not granted her fellow villagers. Serving as an arch in the balance of tension between the "Rabelaisian" and the "romantic," she acts as foil to both Christy and Old Mahon in her lusty humor and materialism, as counterbalance to Pegeen and the village girls in her experience and longings. It is she who appropriately tags Christy "the walking playboy of the western world," with all the irony that complex title implies.

"In a good play every speech should be as fully flavored as a nut or apple," Synge wrote in his preface, acknowledging his debt to the language he heard spoken among the Irish country people. In *The Playboy* particularly he tests that flavor to the utmost, for here the language responds to sense and characterization, vigor and roughness of action leading to the violence and color of an imagery mingling pagan sentiment with religious overtones, whipping the mood of the play into ever-expanding spirals of excitement, tension, and surprise. This is a selective and artistically created speech pattern, but it is significant that only a handful of phrases are "invented"; for Synge believed that the most valuable drama is that sustained by the speech of the people. But the richness of the language in turn answers to the development of Christy as poet-hero, fulfilling the dual qualities of reality and joy Synge required in a work of art, and providing even further challenge to the making of the Playboy.

John Millington Synge (1871–1909) was born in Dublin, Ireland, and studied at Trinity College Dublin and the Royal Irish Academy of Music. After briefly studying music in Germany, he spent part of each year from 1895 to 1903 in Paris, writing and studying literature and languages. In 1905 he became co-director, with William Butler Yeats and Lady Gregory, of the Abbey Theatre. Frequent journeys to the west of Ireland resulted in his book *The Aran Islands* (1907) and in material for his one-act tragedy *Riders to the Sea* (1904) and for *The Playboy of the Western World* (1907). His other plays, *The Shadow of the Glen* (1903), *The Well of the Saints* (1905), *The Tinker's Wedding* (1908), *Deirdre of the Sorrows* (1909), and *When the Moon Has Set* (not published until 1968), as well as his slim volume *Poems and Translations* (1909), owe as much to County Wicklow, in the southeastern part of Ireland, where he spent most of his summers from childhood. Synge died of Hodgkin's disease shortly before he was to marry the Abbey actress Maire O'Neill, and with *Deirdre of the Sorrows* still not finished to his satisfaction.

The Playboy
of the Western World
John Millington Synge

CAST OF CHARACTERS

CHRISTOPHER MAHON

OLD MAHON *his father, a squatter*

MICHAEL JAMES FLAHERTY (*called* MICHAEL JAMES) *a publican*[1]

MARGARET FLAHERTY (*called* PEGEEN MIKE) *his daughter*

SHAWN KEOGH *her second cousin, a young farmer*

PHILLY O'CULLEN
JIMMY FARRELL
  small farmers

WIDOW QUIN

SARA TANSEY

SUSAN BRADY

HONOR BLAKE

NELLY MCLAUGHLIN
  village girls

A BELLMAN

SOME PEASANTS

1 **publican** owner or keeper of a public house where alcoholic beverages are sold.

Preface

SCENE   *The action takes place near a village, on a wild coast of Mayo. The first Act passes on a dark evening of autumn, the other two Acts on the following day.*

IN writing *The Playboy of the Western World,* as in my other plays, I have used one or two words only, that I have not heard among the country people of Ireland, or spoken in my own nursery before I could read the newspapers. A certain number of the phrases I employ I have heard also from herds and fishermen along the coast from Kerry to Mayo, or from beggar-women and ballad-singers nearer Dublin; and I am glad to acknowledge how much I owe to the folk-imagination of these fine people. Anyone who has lived in real intimacy with the Irish peasantry will know that the wildest sayings and ideas in this play are tame indeed compared with the fancies one may hear in any little hill-side cabin in Geesala, or Carraroe, or Dingle Bay. All art is a collaboration; and there is little doubt that in the happy ages of literature striking and beautiful phrases were as ready to the story-teller's or the play-wright's hand as the rich cloaks and dresses of his time. It is probable that when the Elizabethan dramatist took his ink-horn and sat down to his work he used many phrases that he had just heard, as he sat at dinner, from his mother or his children. In Ireland those of us who know the people have the same privilege. When I was writing *The Shadow of the Glen,* some years ago, I got more aid than any learning could have given me, from a chink in the floor of the old Wicklow house where I was staying, that let me hear what was being said by the servant girls in the kitchen. This matter, I think, is of importance, for in countries where the imagination of the people, and the language they use, is rich and living, it is possible for a writer to be rich and copious in his words, and at the same time to give the reality which is the root of all poetry, in a comprehensive and natural form. In the modern literature of towns, however, richness is found only in sonnets, or prose poems, or in one or two elaborate books that are far away from the profound and common interests of life. One has, on one side, Mallarmé and Huysmans producing this literature; and on the other Ibsen and Zola dealing with the reality of life in joyless and pallid words. On the stage one must have reality, and one must have joy, and that is why the intellectual modern drama has failed, and people have grown sick of the false joy of the musical comedy, that has been given them in place of the rich joy found only in what is superb and wild in reality. In a good play every speech should be as fully flavoured as a nut or apple, and such speeches cannot be written by anyone who works among people who have shut their lips on poetry. In Ireland, for a few years more, we have a popular imagination that is fiery and magnificent, and tender; so that those of us who wish to write start with a chance that is not given to writers in places where the springtime of the local life has been forgotten, and the harvest is a memory only, and the straw has been turned into bricks.

J. M. S.

January 21st, 1907.

Act One

Country public house or shebeen,² very rough and untidy. There is a sort of counter on the right with shelves, holding many bottles and jugs, just seen above it. Empty barrels stand near the counter. At back, a little to left of counter, there is a door into the open air; then, more to the left, there is a settle with shelves above it, with more jugs, and a table beneath a window. At the left there is a large open fire-place, with turf fire, and a small door into inner room. PEGEEN, *a wild-looking but fine girl of about twenty, is writing at table. She is dressed in the usual peasant dress.*

PEGEEN [*slowly, as she writes*] Six yards of stuff for to make a yellow gown. A pair of lace boots with lengthy heels on them and brassy eyes. A hat is suited for a wedding-day. A fine tooth comb. To be sent with three barrels of porter in Jimmy Farrell's creel cart³ on the evening of the coming Fair to Mister Michael James Flaherty. With the best compliments of this season: Margaret Flaherty.

SHAWN KEOGH [*a fat and fair young man comes in down right centre as she signs and looks round awkwardly, when he sees she is alone*] Where's himself?

PEGEEN [*without looking at him*] He's coming. [*She directs letter.*] To Mister Sheamus Mulroy, Wine and Spirit Dealer, Castlebar.

SHAWN [*uneasily*] I didn't see him on the road.

PEGEEN How would you see him [*licks

stamp and puts it on letter*] and it dark night this half an hour gone by?

SHAWN [*turning towards door again*] I stood a while outside wondering would I have a right to pass on or to walk in and see you, Pegeen Mike [*comes to the fire*], and I could hear the cows breathing, and sighing in the stillness of the air, and not a step moving any place from this gate to the bridge.

PEGEEN [*putting letter in envelope*] It's above at the cross-roads he is, meeting Philly O'Cullen and a couple more are going along with him to Kate Cassidy's wake.

SHAWN [*looking at her blankly*] And he's going that length in the dark night?

PEGEEN [*impatiently*] He is surely, and leaving me lonesome on the scruff of the hill. [*She gets up and puts envelope on dresser, then winds clock.*] Isn't it long the nights are now, Shawn Keogh, to be leaving a poor girl with her own self counting the hours to the dawn of day?

SHAWN [*with awkward humour*] If it is, when we're wedded in a short while you'll have no call to complain, for I've little will to be walking off to wakes or weddings in the darkness of the night.

PEGEEN [*with rather scornful good humour*] You're making mighty certain, Shaneen, that I'll wed you now.

SHAWN Aren't we after making a good bargain, the way we're only waiting these days on Father Reilly's dispensation from the bishops or the Court of Rome.

PEGEEN [*looking at him teasingly, washing up at dresser*] It's a wonder, Shaneen, the Holy Father'd be taking notice of the likes of you, for if I was him, I wouldn't bother with this place where you'll meet none but Red Linahan, has a squint in

---

2 **shebeen** wayside public house that sells poteen (pronounced potyeen), an illegally distilled liquor.
3 **creel cart** turf cart.

his eye, and Patcheen is lame in his heel, or the mad Mulrannies were driven from California and they lost in their wits. We're a queer lot these times to go troubling the Holy Father on his sacred seat.

SHAWN [*scandalized*] If we are, we're as good this place as another, maybe, and as good these times as we were for ever.

PEGEEN [*with scorn*] As good, is it? Where now will you meet the like of Daneen Sullivan knocked the eye from a peeler, or Marcus Quin, God rest him, got six months for maiming ewes, and he a great warrant to tell stories of holy Ireland till he'd have the old women shedding down tears about their feet. Where will you find the like of them, I'm saying?

SHAWN [*timidly*] If you don't, it's a good job, maybe, for [*with peculiar emphasis on the words*] Father Reilly has small conceit to have that kind walking around and talking to the girls.

PEGEEN [*impatiently, throwing water from basin out of the door*] Stop tormenting me with Father Reilly [*imitating his voice*], when I'm asking only what way I'll pass these twelve hours of dark, and not take my death with the fear. [*Looking out of door.*]

SHAWN [*timidly*] Would I fetch you the Widow Quin, maybe.

PEGEEN Is it the like of that murderer? You'll not, surely.

SHAWN [*going to her, soothingly*] Then I'm thinking himself will stop along with you when he sees you taking on, for it'll be a long night and with great darkness, and I'm after feeling a kind of fellow above in the furzy ditch, groaning wicked like a maddening dog, the way it's good cause you have, maybe, to be fearing now.

PEGEEN [*turning on him sharply*] What's that? Is it a man you seen?

SHAWN [*retreating*] I couldn't see him at all, but I heard him groaning out and breaking his heart. It should have been a young man from his words speaking.

PEGEEN [*going after him*] And you never went near to see was he hurted or what ailed him at all?

SHAWN I did not, Pegeen Mike. It was a dark lonesome place to be hearing the like of him.

PEGEEN Well, you're a daring fellow! And if they find his corpse stretched above in the dews of dawn, what'll you say then to the peelers[4] or the Justice of the Peace?

SHAWN [*thunderstruck*] I wasn't thinking of that. For the love of God, Pegeen Mike, don't let on I was speaking of him. Don't tell your father and the men is coming above, for if they heard that story they'd have great blabbing this night at the wake.

PEGEEN I'll maybe tell them, and I'll maybe not.

SHAWN They are coming at the door. Will you whisht, I'm saying.

PEGEEN Whisht yourself.

[*She goes behind counter.* MICHAEL JAMES, *fat jovial publican, comes in down right centre followed by* PHILLY O'CULLEN, *who is thin and mistrusting, and* JIMMY FARRELL, *who is fat and amorous, about forty-five.*]

MEN [*together*] God bless you. The blessing of God on this place.

PEGEEN God bless you kindly.

MICHAEL [*to men, who go to the counter right*] Sit down now, and take your rest. [*Crosses to* SHAWN *at the fire left.*] And how is it you are, Shawn Keogh? Are you coming over the sands to Kate Cassidy's wake?

SHAWN I am not, Michael James. I'm going home the short-cut to my bed.

PEGEEN [*speaking across from counter*] He's right too, and have you no shame, Michael James, to be quitting off for the whole night and leaving myself lonesome in the shop?

MICHAEL [*good-humouredly*] Isn't it the same whether I go for the whole night or a part only? and I'm thinking it's a queer daughter you are if you'd have me crossing backward through the Stooks of the Dead Women, with a drop taken.

4 **peelers** policemen.

PEGEEN [*angrily*] If I am a queer daughter, it's a queer father'd be leaving me lonesome these twelve hours of dark, and I piling the turf with the dogs barking, and the calves mooing, and my own teeth rattling with the fear.

JIMMY [*flatteringly*] What is there to hurt you and you a fine, hardy girl would knock the head of any two men in the place.

PEGEEN [*working herself up*] Isn't there the harvest boys with their tongues red for drink, and the ten tinkers is camped in the east glen, and the thousand militia —bad cess[5] to them!—walking idle through the land? There's lots surely to hurt me, and I won't stop alone in it, let himself do what he will.

MICHAEL If you're that afeard, let Shawn Keogh stop along with you. It's the will of God, I'm thinking, himself should be seeing to you now. [*They all turn on* SHAWN.]

SHAWN [*in horrified confusion*] I would and welcome, Michael James; but I'm afeard of Father Reilly, and what at all would the Holy Father and the Cardinals of Rome be saying if they heard I did the like of that?

MICHAEL [*with contempt*] God help you! Can't you sit in by the hearth with the light lit and herself beyond in the room? You'll do that surely, for I've heard tell there's a queer fellow above going mad or getting his death, maybe, in the gripe of the ditch, so she'd be safer this night with a person here.

SHAWN [*with plaintive despair*] I'm afeard of Father Reilly, I'm saying. Let you not be tempting me and we near married itself.

PHILLY [*with cold contempt*] Lock him in the west room. He'll stay then and have no sin to be telling to the priest.

MICHAEL [*to* SHAWN, *getting between him and the door*] Go up now.

SHAWN [*at the top of his voice*] Don't stop me, Michael James. Let me out of the door, I'm saying, for the love of the Almighty God. Let me out [*trying to dodge past him*]. Let me out of it and may God grant you His indulgence in the hour of need.

MICHAEL [*loudly*] Stop your noising and sit down by the hearth. [*Gives him a push and goes to counter laughing.*]

SHAWN [*turning back, wringing his hands*] Oh, Father Reilly and the saints of God, where will I hide myself today? Oh, St. Joseph and St. Patrick and St. Brigid and St. James, have mercy on me now! [*He turns round, sees door clear and makes a rush for it.*]

MICHAEL [*catching him by the coat-tail*] You'd be going, is it?

SHAWN [*screaming*] Leave me go, Michael James, leave me go, you old Pagan, leave me go or I'll get the curse of the priests on you, and of the scarlet-coated bishops of the courts of Rome. [*With a sudden movement he pulls himself out of his coat and disappears out of the door, leaving his coat in* MICHAEL's *hands.*]

MICHAEL [*turning round, and holding up coat*] Well, there's the coat of a Christian man. Oh, there's sainted glory this day in the lonesome west, and by the will of God I've got you a decent man, Pegeen, you'll have no call to be spying after if you've a score of young girls, maybe, weeding in your fields.

PEGEEN [*taking up the defence of her property*] What right have you to be making game of a poor fellow for minding the priest when it's your own fault is, not paying a penny pot-boy[6] to stand along with me and give me courage in the doing of my work? [*She snaps the coat away from him, and goes behind counter with it.*]

MICHAEL [*taken aback*] Where would I get a pot-boy? Would you have me send the bell-man[7] screaming in the streets of Castlebar?

SHAWN [*opening the door a chink and put-*

ting in his head, in a small voice] Michael James!

MICHAEL [*imitating him*]   What ails you?

SHAWN   The queer dying fellow's beyond looking over the ditch. He's come up, I'm thinking, stealing your hens. [*Looks over his shoulder.*] God help me, he's following me now [*he runs into room*], and if he's heard what I said, he'll be having my life and I going home lonesome in the darkness of the night.

[*For a perceptible moment they watch the door with curiosity. Someone coughs outside. Then* CHRISTY MAHON, *a slight young man, comes in, very tired and frightened and dirty.*]

CHRISTY [*in a small voice*]   God save all here!

MEN   God save you kindly.

CHRISTY [*going to counter*]   I'd trouble you for a glass of porter, woman of the house. [*He puts down coin.*]

PEGEEN [*serving him*]   You're one of the tinkers, young fellow, is beyond camped in the glen?

CHRISTY   I am not; but I'm destroyed walking.

MICHAEL [*patronizingly*]   Let you come up then to the fire. You're looking famished with the cold.

CHRISTY   God reward you. [*He takes up his glass, and goes a little way across to the left, then stops and looks about him.*] Is it often the polis[8] do be coming into this place, master of the house?

MICHAEL   If you'd come in better hours, you'd have seen "Licensed for the Sale of Beer and Spirits, to be consumed on the Premises," written in white letters above the door, and what would the polis want spying on me, and not a decent house within four miles, the way every living Christian is a bona fide saving one widow alone?

CHRISTY [*with relief*]   It's a safe house, so. [*He goes over to the fire, sighing and

moaning. Then he sits down putting his glass beside him and begins gnawing a turnip, too miserable to feel the others staring at him with curiosity.*]

MICHAEL [*going after him*]   Is it yourself is fearing the polis? You're wanting, maybe?

CHRISTY   There's many wanting.

MICHAEL   Many surely, with the broken harvest and the ended wars. [*He picks up some stockings etc. that are near the fire, and carries them away furtively.*] It should be larceny, I'm thinking?

CHRISTY [*dolefully*]   I had it in my mind it was a different word and a bigger.

PEGEEN   There's a queer lad! Were you never slapped in school, young fellow, that you don't know the name of your deed?

CHRISTY [*bashfully*]   I'm slow at learning, a middling scholar only.

MICHAEL   If you're a dunce itself, you'd have a right to know that larceny's robbing and stealing. Is it for the like of that you're wanting?

CHRISTY [*with a flash of family pride*]   And I the son of a strong farmer [*with a sudden qualm*], God rest his soul, could have bought up the whole of your old house a while since from the butt of his tail-pocket and not have missed the weight of it gone.

MICHAEL [*impressed*]   If it's not stealing, it's maybe something big.

CHRISTY [*flattered*]   Aye; it's maybe something big.

JIMMY   He's a wicked-looking young fellow. Maybe he followed after a young woman on a lonesome night.

CHRISTY [*shocked*]   Oh, the saints forbid, mister. I was all times a decent lad.

PHILLY [*turning on* JIMMY]   You're a silly man, Jimmy Farrell. He said his father was a farmer a while since, and there's himself now in a poor state. Maybe the land was grabbed from him, and he did what any decent man would do.

MICHAEL [*to* CHRISTY, *mysteriously*]   Was it bailiffs?

CHRISTY   The divil a one.

8 **polis** police.

MICHAEL   Agents?

CHRISTY   The divil a one.

MICHAEL   Landlords?

CHRISTY [*peevishly*]   Ah, not at all, I'm saying. You'd see the like of them stories on any little paper of a Munster town. But I'm not calling to mind any person, gentle, simple, judge or jury, did the like of me.

[*They all draw nearer with delighted curiosity.*]

PHILLY   Well that lad's a puzzle-the-world.

JIMMY   He'd beat Dan Davies' Circus or the holy missioners making sermons on the villainy of man. Try him again, Philly.

PHILLY   Did you strike golden guineas out of solder, young fellow, or shilling coins itself?

CHRISTY   I did not, mister, not sixpence nor a farthing coin.

JIMMY   Did you marry three wives maybe? I'm told there's a sprinkling have done that among the holy Luthers of the preaching North.

CHRISTY [*shyly*]   I never married with one, let alone with a couple or three.

PHILLY   Maybe he went fighting for the Boers, the like of the man beyond, was judged to be hanged, quartered, and drawn. Were you off east, young fellow, fighting bloody wars for Kruger and the freedom of the Boers?

CHRISTY   I never left my own parish till Tuesday was a week.

PEGEEN [*coming from counter*]   He's done nothing, so. [*To* CHRISTY.] If you didn't commit murder or a bad nasty thing, or false coining, or robbery, or butchery or the like of them, there isn't anything would be worth your troubling for to run from now. You did nothing at all.

CHRISTY [*his feelings hurt*]   That's an unkindly thing to be saying to a poor orphaned traveller, has a prison behind him, and hanging before, and hell's gap gaping below.

PEGEEN [*with a sign to the men to be quiet*]   You're only saying it. You did nothing at all. A soft lad the like of you wouldn't slit the wind-pipe of a screeching sow.

CHRISTY [*offended*]   You're not speaking the truth.

PEGEEN [*in mock rage*]   Not speaking the truth, is it? Would you have me knock the head of you with the butt of the broom?

CHRISTY [*twisting round on her with a sharp cry of horror*]   Don't strike me. . . . I killed my poor father, Tuesday was a week, for doing the like of that.

PEGEEN [*with blank amazement*]   Is it killed your father?

CHRISTY [*subsiding*]   With the help of God I did surely, and that the Holy Immaculate Mother may intercede for his soul.

PHILLY [*retreating with* JIMMY]   There's a daring fellow.

JIMMY   Oh, glory be to God!

MICHAEL [*with great respect*]   That was a hanging crime, mister honey. You should have had good reason for doing the like of that.

CHRISTY [*in a very reasonable tone*]   He was a dirty man, God forgive him, and he getting old and crusty, the way I couldn't put up with him at all.

PEGEEN   And you shot him dead?

CHRISTY [*shaking his head*]   I never used weapons. I've no licence, and I'm a law-fearing man.

MICHAEL   It was with a hilted knife maybe? I'm told, in the big world, it's bloody knives they use.

CHRISTY [*loudly, scandalized*]   Do you take me for a slaughter-boy?

PEGEEN   You never hanged him, the way Jimmy Farrell hanged his dog from the licence[9] and had it screeching and wriggling three hours at the butt of a string, and himself swearing it was a dead dog, and the peelers swearing it had life?

CHRISTY   I did not then. I just riz the loy[10] and let fall the edge of it on the ridge of his skull, and he went down at my feet

---

9 **from the licence** to avoid paying for a dog licence. 10 **loy** long, narrow spade.

like an empty sack, and never let a grunt or groan from him at all.

MICHAEL [*making a sign to* PEGEEN *to fill* CHRISTY's *glass*] And what way weren't you hanged, mister? Did you bury him then?

CHRISTY [*considering*] Aye. I buried him then. Wasn't I digging spuds in the field?

MICHAEL And the peelers never followed after you the eleven days that you're out?

CHRISTY [*shaking his head*] Never a one of them and I walking forward facing hog, dog, or divil on the highway of the road.

PHILLY [*nodding wisely*] It's only with a common week-day kind of a murderer them lads would be trusting their carcase, and that man should be a great terror when his temper's roused.

MICHAEL He should then. [*To* CHRISTY.] And where was it, mister honey, that you did the deed?

CHRISTY [*looking at him with suspicion*] Oh, a distant place, master of the house, a windy corner of high distant hills.

PHILLY [*nodding with approval*] He's a close man and he's right surely.

PEGEEN That'd be a lad with the sense of Solomon to have for a pot-boy, Michael James, if it's the truth you're seeking one at all.

PHILLY The peelers is fearing him, and if you'd that lad in the house there isn't one of them would come smelling around if the dogs itself were lapping poteen from the dung-pit of the yard.

JIMMY Bravery's a treasure in a lonesome place, and a lad would kill his father, I'm thinking, would face a foxy divil with a pitchpike on the flags of hell.

PEGEEN It's the truth they're saying, and if I'd that lad in the house, I wouldn't be fearing the loosèd khaki cut-throats, or the walking dead.

CHRISTY [*swelling with surprise and triumph*] Well, glory be to God!

MICHAEL [*with deference*] Would you think well to stop here and be pot-boy, mister honey, if we gave you good wages, and didn't destroy you with the weight of work?

SHAWN [*coming forward uneasily*] That'd be a queer kind to bring into a decent quiet household with the like of Pegeen Mike.

PEGEEN [*very sharply*] Will you whisht. Who's speaking to you?

SHAWN [*retreating*] A bloody-handed murderer the like of. . . .

PEGEEN [*snapping at him*] Whisht, I'm saying, we'll take no fooling from your like at all. [*To* CHRISTY *with a honeyed voice.*] And you, young fellow, you'd have a right to stop I'm thinking, for we'd do our all and utmost to content your needs.

CHRISTY [*overcome with wonder*] And I'd be safe this place from the searching law?

MICHAEL You would surely. If they're not fearing you itself, the peelers in this place is decent, droughty poor fellows, wouldn't touch a cur dog and not give warning in the dead of night.

PEGEEN [*very kindly and persuasively*] Let you stop a short while anyhow. Aren't you destroyed walking with your feet in bleeding blisters, and your whole skin needing washing like a Wicklow sheep.

CHRISTY [*loking round with satisfaction*] It's a nice room, and if it's not humbugging me you are, I'm thinking that I'll surely stay.

JIMMY [*jumps up*] Now, by the grace of God, herself will be safe this night, with a man killed his father holding danger from the door, and let you come on, Michael James, or they'll have the best stuff drunk at the wake.

MICHAEL [*going to the door with* MEN] And begging your pardon, mister, what name will we call you for we'd like to know.

CHRISTY Christopher Mahon.

MICHAEL Well, God bless you, Christy, and a good rest till we meet again when the sun'll be rising to the noon of day.

CHRISTY God bless you all.

MEN God bless you. [*They go out except* SHAWN *who lingers at door.*]

SHAWN [*to* PEGEEN] Are you wanting me

to stop along with you and keep you from harm?

PEGEEN [*gruffly*] Didn't you say you were fearing Father Reilly?

SHAWN There'd be no harm staying now, I'm thinking, and himself in it too.

PEGEEN You wouldn't stay when there was need for you, and let you step off nimble this time when there's none.

SHAWN Didn't I say it was Father Reilly. . . .

PEGEEN Go on then to Father Reilly [*in a jeering tone*], and let him put you in the holy brotherhoods and leave that lad to me.

SHAWN If I meet the Widow Quin. . . .

PEGEEN Go on, I'm saying, and don't be waking this place with your noise. [*She hustles him out and bolts door.*] That lad would wear the spirits from the saints of peace. [*Bustles about, then takes off her apron and pins it up in the window as a blind,* CHRISTY *watching her timidly. Then shes comes to him and speaks with bland good humour.*] Let you stretch out now by the fire, young fellow. You should be destroyed travelling.

CHRISTY [*shyly again, drawing off his boots*] I'm tired surely, walking wild eleven days and waking fearful in the night. [*He holds up one of his feet, feeling his blisters and looking at it with compassion.*]

PEGEEN [*standing beside him, watching him with delight*] You should have had great people in your family, I'm thinking, with the little small feet you have, and you with a kind of a quality name, the like of what you'd find on the great powers and potentates of France and Spain.

CHRISTY [*with pride*] We were great surely, with wide and windy acres of rich Munster land.

PEGEEN Wasn't I telling you, and you a fine, handsome young fellow with a noble brow.

CHRISTY [*with a flash of delighted surprise*] Is it me?

PEGEEN Aye. Did you never hear that

from the young girls where you come from in the west or south?

CHRISTY [*with venom*] I did not then. . . . Oh, they're bloody liars in the naked parish where I grew a man.

PEGEEN If they are itself, you've heard it these days, I'm thinking, and you walking the world telling out your story to young girls or old.

CHRISTY I've told my story no place till this night, Pegeen Mike, and it's foolish I was here, maybe, to be talking free, but you're decent people, I'm thinking, and yourself a kindly woman, the way I wasn't fearing you at all.

PEGEEN [*filling a sack with straw, right*] You've said the like of that, maybe, in every cot and cabin where you've met a young girl on your way.

CHRISTY [*going over to her, gradually raising his voice*] I've said it nowhere till this night, I'm telling you, for I've seen none the like of you the eleven days I am walking the world, looking over a low ditch or a high ditch on my north or south, into stony scattered fields, or scribes of bog, where you'd see young limber girls, and fine prancing women making laughter with the men.

PEGEEN [*nodding with approval*] If you weren't destroyed travelling you'd have as much talk and streeleen,[11] I'm thinking, as Owen Roe O'Sullivan or the poets of the Dingle Bay, and I've heard all times it's the poets are your like, fine fiery fellows with great rages when their temper's roused.

CHRISTY [*drawing a little nearer to her*] You've a power of rings, God bless you, and would there be any offence if I was asking are you single now?

PEGEEN What would I want wedding so young?

CHRISTY [*with relief*] We're alike, so.

PEGEEN [*putting sack on settle and beating it up*] I never killed my father. I'd be afeard to do that, except I was the like of

11 **streeleen** trail or stream of talk.

yourself with blind rages tearing me within, for I'm thinking you should have had great tussling when the end was come.

CHRISTY [*expanding with delight at the first confidential talk he has ever had with a woman*] We had not then. It was a hard woman was come over the hill, and if he was always a crusty kind, when he'd a hard woman setting him on, not the divil himself or his four fathers could put up with him at all.

PEGEEN [*with curiosity*] And isn't it a great wonder that one wasn't fearing you?

CHRISTY [*very confidentially*] Up to the day I killed my father, there wasn't a person in Ireland knew the kind I was, and I there drinking, waking, eating, sleeping, a quiet, simple poor fellow with no man giving me heed.

PEGEEN [*getting a quilt out of cupboard and putting it on the sack*] It was the girls were giving you heed maybe, and I'm thinking it's most conceit you'd have to be gaming with their like.

CHRISTY [*shaking his head, with simplicity*] Not the girls itself, and I won't tell you a lie. There wasn't anyone heeding me in that place saving only the dumb beasts of the field. [*He sits down at fire.*]

PEGEEN [*with disappointment*] And I thinking you should have been living the like of a king of Norway or the Eastern world. [*She comes and sits beside him after placing bread and mug of milk on the table.*]

CHRISTY [*laughing piteously*] The like of a king, is it! And I after toiling, moiling, digging, dodging from the dawn till dusk with never a sight of joy or sport saving only when I'd be abroad in the dark night poaching rabbits on hills, for I was a divil to poach, God forgive me [*very naïvely*], and I near got six months for going with a dung-fork and stabbing a fish.

PEGEEN And it's that you'd call sport is it, to be abroad in the darkness with yourself alone?

CHRISTY I did, God help me, and there I'd be as happy as the sunshine of St. Martin's Day, watching the light passing the north or the patches of fog, till I'd hear a rabbit starting to screech and I'd go running in the furze. Then when I'd my full share I'd come walking down where you'd see the ducks and geese stretched sleeping on the highway of the road, and before I'd pass the dunghill, I'd hear himself snoring out, a loud lonesome snore he'd be making all times, the while he was sleeping, and he a man'd be raging all times the while he was waking, like a gaudy officer you'd hear cursing and damning and swearing oaths.

PEGEEN Providence and Mercy, spare us all!

CHRISTY It's that you'd say surely if you seen him and he after drinking for weeks, rising up in the red dawn, or before it maybe, and going out into the yard as naked as an ash tree in the moon of May, and shying clods again the visage of the stars till he'd put the fear of death into the banbhs[12] and the screeching sows.

PEGEEN I'd be well-nigh afeard of that lad myself, I'm thinking. And there was no one in it but the two of you alone?

CHRISTY The divil a one, though he'd sons and daughters walking all great states and territories of the world, and not a one of them to this day would say their seven curses on him, and they rousing up to let a cough or sneeze, maybe, in the deadness of the night.

PEGEEN [*nodding her head*] Well, you should have been a queer lot. . . . I never cursed my father the like of that though I'm twenty and more years of age.

CHRISTY Then you'd have cursed mine, I'm telling you, and he a man never gave peace to any saving when he'd get two months or three, or be locked in the asylum for battering peelers or assaulting men [*with depression*], the way it was a

12 **banbhs** (pronounced bannuvs) young pigs.

bitter life he led me till I did up a Tuesday and halve his skull.

PEGEEN [*putting her hand on his shoulder*] Well, you'll have peace in this place, Christy Mahon, and none to trouble you, and it's near time a fine lad the like of you should have your good share of the earth.

CHRISTY It's time surely, and I a seemly fellow with great strength in me and bravery of. . . . [*Some one knocks.*]

CHRISTY [*clinging to* PEGEEN] Oh, glory! it's late for knocking, and this last while I'm in terror of the peelers, and the walking dead. . . . [*Knocking again.*]

PEGEEN Who's there?

VOICE [*outside*] Me.

PEGEEN Who's me?

VOICE The Widow Quin.

PEGEEN [*jumping up and giving him the bread and milk*] Go on now with your supper, and let on to be sleepy, for if she found you were such a warrant to talk, she'd be stringing gabble till the dawn of day.

[CHRISTY *takes bread and sits shyly with his back to the door.*]

PEGEEN [*opening door, with temper*] What ails you, or what is it you're wanting at this hour of the night?

WIDOW QUIN [*coming in a step and peering at* CHRISTY] I'm after meeting Shawn Keogh and Father Reilly below, who told me of your curiosity man, and they fearing by this time he was maybe roaring, romping on your hands with drink.

PEGEEN [*pointing to* CHRISTY] Look now, is he roaring, and he stretched out drowsy with his supper, and his mug of milk. Walk down and tell that to Father Reilly and to Shaneen Keogh.

WIDOW QUIN [*coming forward*] I'll not see them again, for I've their word to lead that lad forward for to lodge with me.

PEGEEN [*in blank amazement*] This night, is it?

WIDOW QUIN [*going over*] This night. "It isn't fitting," says the priesteen,[13] "to

have his likeness lodging with an orphaned girl." [*To* CHRISTY.] God save you, mister!

CHRISTY [*shyly*] God save you kindly.

WIDOW QUIN [*looking at him with half-amused curiosity*] Well, aren't you a little smiling fellow? It should have been great and bitter torments did rouse your spirits to a deed of blood.

CHRISTY [*doubtfully*] It should, maybe.

WIDOW QUIN It's more than "maybe" I'm saying, and it'd soften my heart to see you sitting so simple with your cup and cake, and you fitter to be saying your catechism than slaying your da.

PEGEEN [*at counter, washing glasses*] There's talking when any'd see he's fit to be holding his head high with the wonders of the world. Walk on from this, for I'll not have him tormented and he destroyed travelling since Tuesday was a week.

WIDOW QUIN [*peaceably*] We'll be walking surely when his supper's done, and you'll find we're great company, young fellow, when it's of the like of you and me you'd hear the penny poets singing in an August Fair.

CHRISTY [*innocently*] Did you kill your father?

PEGEEN [*contemptuously*] She did not. She hit himself with a worn pick, and the rusted poison did corrode his blood the way he never overed it and died after. That was a sneaky kind of murder did win small glory with the boys itself. [*She crosses to* CHRISTY'S *left.*]

WIDOW QUIN [*with good-humour*] If it didn't, maybe all knows a widow woman has buried her children and destroyed her man is a wiser comrade for a young lad than a girl the like of you who'd go helter-skeltering after any man would let you a wink upon the road.

PEGEEN [*breaking out into wild rage*] And you'll say that, Widow Quin, and you gasping with the rage you had racing the hill beyond to look on his face.

WIDOW QUIN [*laughing derisively*] Me, is it! Well, Father Reilly has cuteness to

13 **priesteen** priest (diminutive).

divide you now. [*She pulls* CHRISTY *up.*] There's great temptation in a man did slay his da, and we'd best be going, young fellow; so rise up and come with me.

PEGEEN [*seizing his arm*] He'll not stir. He's pot-boy in this place and I'll not have him stolen off and kidnabbed while himself's abroad.

WIDOW QUIN It'd be a crazy pot-boy'd lodge him in the shebeen where he works by day, so you'd have a right to come on, young fellow, till you see my little houseen, a perch off on the rising hill.

PEGEEN Wait till morning, Christy Mahon, wait till you lay eyes on her leaky thatch is growing more pasture for her buck goat than her square of fields, and she without a tramp itself to keep in order her place at all.

WIDOW QUIN When you see me contriving in my little gardens, Christy Mahon, you'll swear the Lord God formed me to be living lone and that there isn't my match in Mayo for thatching or mowing or shearing a sheep.

PEGEEN [*with noisy scorn*] It's true the Lord God formed you to contrive indeed! Doesn't the world know you reared a black ram at your own breast, so that the Lord Bishop of Connaught felt the elements of a Christian, and he eating it after in a kidney stew? Doesn't the world know you've been seen shaving the foxy skipper from France for a threepenny bit and a sop of grass tobacco would wring the liver from a mountain goat you'd meet lepping the hills?

WIDOW QUIN [*with amusement*] Do you hear her now, young fellow? Do you hear the way she'll be rating at your own self when a week is by?

PEGEEN [*to* CHRISTY] Don't heed her. Tell her to go on into her pigsty and not plague us here.

WIDOW QUIN I'm going; but he'll come with me.

PEGEEN [*shaking him*] Are you dumb, young fellow?

CHRISTY [*timidly to* WIDOW QUIN] God increase you; but I'm pot-boy in this place, and it's here I'd liefer stay.

PEGEEN [*triumphantly*] Now you've heard him, and go on from this.

WIDOW QUIN [*looking round the room*] It's lonesome this hour crossing the hill, and if he won't come along with me, I'd have a right maybe to stop this night with yourselves. Let me stretch out on the settle, Pegeen Mike, and himself can lie by the hearth.

PEGEEN [*short and fiercely*] Faith I won't. Quit off or I will send you now.

WIDOW QUIN [*gathering her shawl up*] Well, it's a terror to be aged a score! [*To* CHRISTY.] God bless you now, young fellow, and let you be wary, or there's right torment will await you here if you go romancing with her like, and she waiting only, as they bade me say, on a sheep-skin parchment to be wed with Shawn Keogh of Killakeen. [*She goes out.*]

CHRISTY [*going to* PEGEEN, *as she bolts door*] What's that she's after saying?

PEGEEN Lies and blather, you've no call to mind. Well isn't Shawn Keogh an impudent fellow to send up spying on me? Wait till I lay hands on him. Let him wait, I'm saying.

CHRISTY And you're not wedding him at all?

PEGEEN I wouldn't wed him if a bishop came walking for to join us here.

CHRISTY That God in glory may be thanked for that.

PEGEEN There's your bed now. I've put a quilt upon you I'm after quilting a while since with my own two hands, and you'd best stretch out now for your sleep, and may God give you a good rest till I call you in the morning when the cocks will crow.

CHRISTY [*as she goes to inner room*] May God and Mary and St. Patrick bless you and reward you for your kindly talk. [*She shuts the door behind her. He settles his bed slowly, feeling the quilt with immense satisfaction.*] Well it's a clean bed and soft with it, and it's great luck and company I've won me in the end of time

—two fine women fighting for the likes of me—, till I'm thinking this night wasn't I a foolish fellow not to kill my father in the years gone by.

Act Two

Scene as before. Brilliant morning light. CHRISTY, *looking bright and cheerful, is cleaning a girl's boot.*

CHRISTY [*to himself, counting jugs on dresser*] Half a hundred beyond. Ten there. A score that's above. Eighty jugs. Six cups and a broken one. Two plates. A power of glasses. Bottles, a school-master'd be hard set to count, and enough in them, I'm thinking, to drunken all the wealth and wisdom of the County Clare. [*He puts down the boot carefully.*] There's her boots now, nice and decent for her evening use, and isn't it grand brushes she has? [*He puts them down and goes by degrees to the looking-glass.*] Well, this'd be a fine place to be my whole life talking out with swearing Christians in place of my old dogs and cat, and I stalking around, smoking my pipe and drinking my fill, and never a day's work but drawing a cork an odd time, or wiping a glass, or rinsing out a shiny tumbler for a decent man. [*He takes the looking-glass from the wall and puts it on the back of a chair; then sits down in front of it and begins washing his face.*] Didn't I know rightly I was handsome, though it was the divil's own mirror we had beyond, would twist a squint across an angel's brow, and I'll be growing fine from this day, the way I'll have a soft lovely skin on me and won't be the like of the clumsy young fellows do be ploughing all times in the earth and dung. [*He starts.*] Is she coming again? [*He looks out.*] Stranger girls. God help me, where'll I hide myself away and my long neck naked to the world. [*He looks out.*] I'd best go to the room maybe till I'm dressed again.

[*He gathers up his coat and the looking-glass, and runs into the inner room. The door is pushed open, and* SUSAN BRADY *looks in, and knocks on door.*]

SUSAN There's nobody in it. [*Knocks again.*]

NELLY [*pushing her in and following her, with* HONOR BLAKE *and* SARA TANSEY] It'd be early for them both to be out walking the hill.

SUSAN I'm thinking Shawn Keogh was making game of us and there's no such man in it at all.

HONOR [*pointing to straw and quilt*] Look at that. He's been sleeping there in the night. Well, it'll be a hard case if he's gone off now, the way we'll never set our eyes on a man killed his father, and we after rising early and destroying ourselves running fast on the hill.

NELLY Are you thinking them's his boots?

SARA [*taking them up*] If they are, there should be his father's track on them. Did you never read in the papers the way murdered men do bleed and drip?

SUSAN Is that blood there, Sara Tansey?

SARA [*smelling it*] That's bog water, I'm thinking, but it's his own they are surely, for I never seen the like of them for whity mud, and red mud, and turf on them, and the fine sands of the sea. That man's been walking, I'm telling you. [*She goes down right, putting on one of his boots.*]

SUSAN [*going to window*] Maybe he's stolen off to Belmullet with the boots of Michael James, and you'd have a right so to follow after him, Sara Tansey, and you the one yoked the ass cart and drove ten miles to set your eyes on the man bit the yellow lady's nostril on the northern shore. [*She looks out.*]

SARA [*running to window, with one boot on*] Don't be talking, and we fooled today. [*Putting on other boot.*] There's a pair do fit me well, and I'll be keeping them for walking to the priest, when you'd be ashamed this place, going up winter and summer with nothing worth while to confess at all.

HONOR [*who has been listening at inner door*] Whisht! there's some one inside the room. [*She pushes door a chink open.*] It's a man.

[SARA *kicks off boots and puts them where they were. They all stand in a line looking through chink.*]

SARA I'll call him. Mister! Mister! [*He puts in his head.*] Is Pegeen within?

CHRISTY [*coming in as meek as a mouse, with the looking-glass held behind his back.*] She's above on the cnuceen,[14] seeking the nanny goats, the way she'd have a sup of goat's milk for to colour my tea.

SARA And asking your pardon, is it you's the man killed his father?

CHRISTY [*sidling toward the nail where the glass was hanging*] I am, God help me!

SARA [*taking eggs she has brought*] Then my thousand welcomes to you, and I've run up with a brace of duck's eggs for your food to-day. Pegeen's ducks is no use, but these are the real rich sort. Hold out your hand and you'll see it's no lie I'm telling you.

CHRISTY [*coming forward shyly, and holding out his left hand*] They're a great and weighty size.

SUSAN And I run up with a pat of butter, for it'd be a poor thing to have you eating your spuds dry, and you after running a great way since you did destroy your da.

CHRISTY Thank you kindly.

HONOR And I brought you a little cut of a cake, for you should have a thin stomach on you and you that length walking the world.

NELLY And I brought you a little laying pullet—boiled and all she is—was crushed at the fall of night by the curate's car. Feel the fat of that breast, Mister.

CHRISTY It's bursting, surely. [*He feels it with the back of his left hand, in which he holds the presents.*]

SARA Will you pinch it? Is your right hand too sacred for to use at all? [*She slips round behind him.*] It's a glass he

has. Well I never seen to this day, a man with a looking-glass held to his back. Them that kills their fathers is a vain lot surely.

[GIRLS *giggle.*]

CHRISTY [*smiling innocently and piling presents on glass*] I'm very thankful to you all to-day. . . .

WIDOW QUIN [*coming in quickly, at door*] Sara Tansey, Susan Brady, Honor Blake! What in glory has you here at this hour of day?

GIRLS [*giggling*] That's the man killed his father.

WIDOW QUIN [*coming to them*] I know well it's the man; and I'm after putting him down in the sports below for racing, lepping, pitching, and the Lord knows what.

SARA [*exuberantly*] That's right, Widow Quin. I'll bet my dowry that he'll lick the world.

WIDOW QUIN If you will, you'd have a right to have him fresh and nourished in place of nursing a feast. [*Taking presents.*] Are you fasting or fed, young fellow?

CHRISTY Fasting, if you please.

WIDOW QUIN [*loudly*] Well, you're the lot. Stir up now and give him his breakfast. [*To* CHRISTY.] Come here to me [*she puts him on bench beside her while the* GIRLS *make tea and get his breakfast*] and let you tell us your story before Pegeen will come, in place of grinning your ears off like the moon of May.

CHRISTY [*beginning to be pleased*] It's a long story you'd be destroyed listening.

WIDOW QUIN Don't be letting on to be shy, a fine, gamey, treacherous lad the like of you. Was it in your house beyond you cracked his skull?

CHRISTY [*shy, but flattered*] It was not. We were digging spuds in his cold, sloping, stony divil's patch of a field.

WIDOW QUIN And you went asking money of him, or making talk of getting a wife would drive him from his farm?

CHRISTY I did not, then; but there I was,

14 **cnuceen** (pronounced knuckeen) little hill.

digging and digging, and "You squinting idiot," says he, "let you walk down now and tell the priest you'll wed the Widow Casey in a score of days."

WIDOW QUIN And what kind was she?

CHRISTY [*with horror*] A walking terror from beyond the hills, and she two score and five years, and two hundredweights and five pounds in the weighing scales, with a limping leg on her, and a blinded eye, and she a woman of noted misbehaviour with the old and young. [*He begins gnawing a chicken leg.*]

GIRLS [*clustering round him, serving him*] Glory be!

WIDOW QUIN And what did he want driving you to wed with her? [*She takes a bit of the chicken.*]

CHRISTY [*eating with growing satisfaction*] He was letting on I was wanting a protector from the harshness of the world, and he without a thought the whole while but how he'd have her hut to live in and her gold to drink.

WIDOW QUIN There's maybe worse than a dry hearth and a widow woman and your glass at night. So you hit him then?

CHRISTY [*getting almost excited*] I did not. "I won't wed her," says I, "when all know she did suckle me for six weeks when I came into the world, and she a hag this day with a tongue on her has the crows and seabirds scattered, the way they wouldn't cast a shadow on her garden with the dread of her curse."

WIDOW QUIN [*teasingly*] That one should be right company!

SARA [*eagerly*] Don't mind her. Did you kill him then?

CHRISTY "She's too good for the like of you," says he, "and go on now or I'll flatten you out like a crawling beast has passed under a dray." "You will not if I can help it," says I. "Go on," says he, "or I'll have the divil making garters of your limbs to-night." "You will not if I can help it," says I. [*He sits bolt up, brandishing his mug.*]

SARA You were right surely.

CHRISTY [*impressively*] With that the sun came out between the cloud and the hill, and it shining green in my face. "God have mercy on your soul," says he, lifting a scythe; "or on your own," says I, raising the loy.

SUSAN That's a grand story.

HONOR He tells it lovely.

CHRISTY [*flattered and confident, waving bone*] He gave a drive with the scythe, and I gave a lep to the east. Then I turned around with my back to the north, and I hit a blow on the ridge of his skull, laid him stretched out, and he split to the knob of his gullet. [*He raises the chicken bone to his Adam's apple.*]

GIRLS [*together*] Well, you're a marvel! Oh, God bless you! You're the lad surely!

SUSAN I'm thinking the Lord God sent him this road to make a second husband to the Widow Quin, and she with a great yearning to be wedded though all dread her here. Lift him on her knee, Sara Tansey.

WIDOW QUIN Don't tease him.

SARA [*going over to dresser and counter very quickly, and getting two glasses and porter*] You're heroes surely, and let you drink a supeen[15] with your arms linked like the outlandish lovers in the sailor's song. [*She links their arms and gives them the glasses.*] There now. Drink a health to the wonders of the western world, the pirates, preachers, poteen-makers, with the jobbing jockies, parching peelers, and the juries fill their stomachs selling judgments of the English law. [*Brandishing the bottle.*]

WIDOW QUIN That's a right toast, Sara Tansey. Now Christy.

[*They drink with their arms linked, he drinking with his left hand, she with her right. As they are drinking, PEGEEN MIKE comes in with a milk can and stands aghast. They all spring away from CHRISTY. He goes down left. WIDOW QUIN remains seated.*]

PEGEEN [*angrily*] What is it you're wanting [*to SARA*]?

15 **supeen** little ship.

SARA [*twisting her apron*] An ounce of tobacco.

PEGEEN Have you tuppence?

SARA I've forgotten my purse.

PEGEEN Then you'd best be getting it and not be fooling us here. [*To the* WIDOW QUIN, *with more elaborate scorn.*] And what is it you're wanting, Widow Quin?

WIDOW QUIN [*insolently*] A penn'orth of starch.

PEGEEN [*breaking out*] And you without a white shift[16] or a shirt in your whole family since the drying of the flood. I've no starch for the like of you, and let you walk on now to Killamuck.

WIDOW QUIN [*turning to* CHRISTY, *as she goes out with the* GIRLS] Well, you're mighty huffy this day, Pegeen Mike, and you young fellow, let you not forget the sports and racing when the noon is by. [*They go out.*]

PEGEEN [*imperiously*] Fling out that rubbish and put them cups away. [CHRISTY *tidies away in great haste.*] Shove in the bench by the wall. [*He does so.*] And hang that glass on the nail. What disturbed it at all?

CHRISTY [*very meekly*] I was making myself decent only, and this a fine country for young lovely girls.

PEGEEN [*sharply*] Whisht your talking of girls. [*Goes to counter right.*]

CHRISTY Wouldn't any wish to be decent in a place. . . .

PEGEEN Whisht, I'm saying.

CHRISTY [*looks at her face for a moment with great misgivings, then as a last effort, takes up a loy, and goes towards her, with feigned assurance*] It was with a loy the like of that I killed my father.

PEGEEN [*still sharply*] You've told me that story six times since the dawn of day.

CHRISTY [*reproachfully*] It's a queer thing you wouldn't care to be hearing it and them girls after walking four miles to be listening to me now.

PEGEEN [*turning round astonished*] Four miles!

CHRISTY [*apologetically*] Didn't himself say there were only bona fides living in the place?

PEGEEN It's bona fides by the road they are, but that lot come over the river lepping the stones. It's not three perches when you go like that and I was down this morning looking on the papers the post-boy does have in his bag [*with meaning and emphasis*], for there was great news this day, Christopher Mahon. [*She goes into room left.*]

CHRISTY [*suspiciously*] Is it news of my murder?

PEGEEN [*inside*] Murder indeed!

CHRISTY [*loudly*] A murdered da?

PEGEEN [*coming in again and crossing right*] There was not, but a story filled half a page of the hanging of a man. Ah, that should be a fearful end, young fellow, and it worst of all for a man destroyed his da, for the like of him would get small mercies, and when it's dead he is, they'd put him in a narrow grave, with cheap sacking wrapping him round, and pour down quicklime on his head, the way you'd see a woman pouring any frish-frash[17] from a cup.

CHRISTY [*very miserably*] Oh, God help me. Are you thinking I'm safe? You were saying at the fall of night, I was shut of jeopardy and I here with yourselves.

PEGEEN [*severely*] You'll be shut of jeopardy no place if you go talking with a pack of wild girls the like of them, do be walking abroad with the peelers, talking whispers at the fall of night.

CHRISTY [*with terror*] And you're thinking they'd tell?

PEGEEN [*with mock sympathy*] Who knows, God help you.

CHRISTY [*loudly*] What joy would they have to bring hanging to the likes of me?

PEGEEN It's queer joys they have, and who knows the thing they'd do, if it'd make the green stones cry itself to think of you swaying and swiggling at the butt of a

16 **shift** undergarment, slip.

17 **frish-frash** Indian meal and raw cabbage boiled down as thin as gruel.

rope, and you with a fine, stout neck, God bless you! the way you'd be a half an hour, in great anguish, getting your death.

CHRISTY [*getting his boots and putting them on*] If there's that terror of them, it'd be best, maybe, I went on wandering like Esau or Cain and Abel on the sides of Neifin or the Erris Plain.

PEGEEN [*beginning to play with him*] It would, maybe, for I've heard the Circuit Judges this place is a heartless crew.

CHRISTY [*bitterly*] It's more than judges this place is a heartless crew. [*Looking up at her.*] And isn't it a poor thing to be starting again and I a lonesome fellow will be looking out on women and girls the way the needy fallen spirits do be looking on the Lord?

PEGEEN What call have you to be that lonesome when there's poor girls walking Mayo in their thousands now?

CHRISTY [*grimly*] It's well you know what call I have. It's well you know it's a lonesome thing to be passing small towns with the lights shining sideways when the night is down, or going in strange places with a dog nosing before you and a dog nosing behind, or drawn to the cities where you'd hear a voice kissing and talking deep love in every shadow of the ditch, and you passing on with an empty hungry stomach failing from your heart.

PEGEEN I'm thinking you're an odd man, Christy Mahon. The oddest walking fellow I ever set my eyes on to this hour to-day.

CHRISTY What would any be but odd men and they living lonesome in the world?

PEGEEN I'm not odd, and I'm my whole life with my father only.

CHRISTY [*with infinite admiration*] How would a lovely handsome woman the like of you be lonesome when all men should be thronging around to hear the sweetness of your voice, and the little infant children should be pestering your steps I'm thinking, and you walking the roads.

PEGEEN I'm hard set to know what way a

coaxing fellow the like of yourself should be lonesome either.

CHRISTY Coaxing!

PEGEEN Would you have me think a man never talked with the girls would have the words you've spoken to-day? It's only letting on you are to be lonesome, the way you'd get around me now.

CHRISTY I wish to God I was letting on; but I was lonesome all times and born lonesome, I'm thinking, as the moon of dawn. [*Going to door.*]

PEGEEN [*puzzled by his talk*] Well, it's a story I'm not understanding at all why you'd be worse than another, Christy Mahon, and you a fine lad with the great savagery to destroy your da.

CHRISTY It's little I'm understanding myself, saving only that my heart's scalded this day, and I going off stretching out the earth between us, the way I'll not be waking near you another dawn of the year till the two of us do arise to hope or judgment with the saints of God, and now I'd best be going with my wattle[18] in my hand, for hanging is a poor thing [*turning to go*], and it's little welcome only is left me in this house to-day.

PEGEEN [*sharply*] Christy! [*He turns round.*] Come here to me. [*He goes towards her.*] Lay down that switch and throw some sods on the fire. You're pot-boy in this place, and I'll not have you mitch off[19] from us now.

CHRISTY You were saying I'd be hanged if I stay.

PEGEEN [*quite kindly at last*] I'm after going down and reading the fearful crimes of Ireland for two weeks or three, and there wasn't a word of your murder. [*Getting up and going over to the counter.*] They've likely not found the body. You're safe so with ourselves.

CHRISTY [*astonished, slowly*] It's making game of me you were [*following her with fearful joy*], and I can stay so, working at your side, and I not lonesome from this mortal day.

18 **wattle** small stick. 19 **mitch off** play truant.

PEGEEN   What's to hinder you staying, except the widow woman or the young girls would inveigle you off?

CHRISTY [*with rapture*]   And I'll have your words from this day filling my ears, and that look is come upon you meeting my two eyes, and I watching you loafing around in the warm sun, or rinsing your ankles when the night is come.

PEGEEN [*kindly, but a little embarrassed*]   I'm thinking you'll be a loyal young lad to have working around, and if you vexed me a while since with your leaguing with the girls, I wouldn't give a thraneen[20] for a lad hadn't a mighty spirit in him and a gamey heart.

[SHAWN KEOGH *runs in carrying a cleeve*[21] *on his back, followed by the* WIDOW QUIN.]

SHAWN [*to* PEGEEN]   I was passing below and I seen your mountainy sheep eating cabbages in Jimmy's field. Run up or they'll be bursting surely.

PEGEEN   Oh, God mend them! [*She puts a shawl over her head and runs out.*]

CHRISTY [*looking from one to the other, still in high spirits*]   I'd best go to her aid maybe. I'm handy with ewes.

WIDOW QUIN [*closing the door*]   She can do that much, and there is Shaneen has long speeches for to tell you now. [*She sits down with an amused smile.*]

SHAWN [*taking something from his pocket and offering it to* CHRISTY]   Do you see that, Mister?

CHRISTY [*looking at it*]   The half of a ticket to the Western States!

SHAWN [*trembling with anxiety*]   I'll give it to you and my new hat [*pulling it out of hamper*]; and my breeches with the double seat [*pulling it out*]; and my new coat is woven from the blackest shearings for three miles around [*giving him the coat*]; I'll give you the whole of them and my blessing and the blessing of Father Reilly itself, maybe, if you'll quit from

this and leave us in the peace we had till last night at the fall of dark.

CHRISTY [*with a new arrogance*]   And for what is it you're wanting to get shut of me?

SHAWN [*looking to the* WIDOW *for help*]   I'm a poor scholar with middling faculties to coin a lie, so I'll tell you the truth, Christy Mahon. I'm wedding with Pegeen beyond, and I don't think well of having a clever fearless man the like of you dwelling in her house.

CHRISTY [*almost pugnaciously*]   And you'd be using bribery for to banish me?

SHAWN [*in an imploring voice*]   Let you not take it badly, mister honey, isn't beyond the best place for you where you'll have golden chains and shiny coats and you riding upon hunters with the ladies of the land. [*He makes an eager sign to the* WIDOW QUIN *to come to help him.*]

WIDOW QUIN [*coming over*]   It's true for him, and you'd best quit off and not have that poor girl setting her mind on you, for there's Shaneen thinks she wouldn't suit you though all is saying that she'll wed you now.

[CHRISTY *beams with delight.*]

SHAWN [*in terrified earnest*]   She wouldn't suit you, and she with the divil's own temper the way you'd be strangling one another in a score of days. [*He makes the movement of strangling with his hands.*] It's the like of me only that she's fit for, a quiet simple fellow wouldn't raise a hand upon her if she scratched itself.

WINDOW QUIN [*putting* SHAWN's *hat on* CHRISTY]   Fit them clothes on you anyhow, young fellow, and he'd maybe loan them to you for the sports. [*Pushing him towards inner door.*] Fit them on and you can give your answer when you have them tried.

CHRISTY [*beaming, delighted with the clothes*]   I will then, I'd like herself to see me in them tweeds and hat. [*He goes into room and shuts the door.*]

SHAWN [*in great anxiety*]   He'd like herself to see them! He'll not leave us,

<hr>

20 **thraneen** withered stalk of grass, i.e. a worthless thing. 21 **cleeve** basket.

WIDOW QUIN. He's a score of divils in him, the way it's well nigh certain he will wed Pegeen.

WIDOW QUIN [*jeeringly*] It's true all girls are fond of courage and do hate the like of you.

SHAWN [*walking about in desperation*] Oh, Widow Quin, what'll I be doing now? I'd inform again him, but he'd burst from Kilmainham and he'd be sure and certain to destroy me. If I wasn't so God-fearing, I'd near have courage to come behind him and run a pike into his side. Oh, it's a hard case to be an orphan and not to have your father that you're used to, and you'd easy kill and make yourself a hero in the sight of all. [*Coming up to her.*] Oh, Widow Quin, will you find me some contrivance when I've promised you a ewe?

WIDOW QUIN A ewe's a small thing, but what would you give me if I did wed him and did save you so?

SHAWN [*with astonishment*] You!

WIDOW QUIN Aye. Would you give me the red cow you have and the mountainy ram, and the right of way across your rye path, and a load of dung at Michaelmas, and turbary[22] upon the western hill?

SHAWN [*radiant with hope*] I would surely, and I'd give you the wedding-ring I have, and the loan of the new suit, the way you'd have him decent on the wedding-day. I'd give you two kids for your dinner and a gallon of poteen, and I'd call the piper on the long car to your wedding from Crossmolina or from Ballina. I'd give you . . .

WIDOW QUIN That'll do, so, and let you whisht, for he's coming now again.

[CHRISTY *comes in very natty in the new clothes.* WIDOW QUIN *goes to him admiringly.*]

WIDOW QUIN If you seen yourself now, I'm thinking you'd be too proud to speak to us at all, and it'd be a pity surely to have

your, like sailing from Mayo to the Western World.

CHRISTY [*as proud as a peacock*] I'm not going. If this is a poor place itself, I'll make myself contented to be lodging here.

[WIDOW QUIN *makes a sign to* SHAWN *to leave them.*]

SHAWN Well, I'm going measuring the race-course while the tide is low, so I'll leave you the garments and my blessing for the sports to-day. God bless you! [*He wriggles out.*]

WIDOW QUIN [*admiring* CHRISTY] Well you're mighty spruce, young fellow. Sit down now while you're quiet till you talk with me.

CHRISTY [*swaggering*] I'm going abroad on the hillside for to seek Pegeen.

WIDOW QUIN You'll have time and plenty for to seek Pegeen, and you heard me saying at the fall of night the two of us should be great company.

CHRISTY From this out I'll have no want of company when all sorts is bringing me their food and clothing [*he swaggers to the door, tightening his belt*], the way they'd set their eyes upon a gallant orphan cleft his father with one blow to the breeches belt. [*He opens door, then staggers back.*] Saints of glory! Holy angels from the throne of light!

WIDOW QUIN [*going over*] What ails you?

CHRISTY It's the walking spirit of my murdered da!

WIDOW QUIN [*looking out*] Is it that tramper?

CHRISTY [*wildly*] Where'll I hide my poor body from that ghost of hell?

[*The door is pushed open, and* OLD MAHON *appears on threshold.* CHRISTY *darts in behind door.*]

WIDOW QUIN [*in great amusement*] God save you, my poor man.

MAHON [*gruffly*] Did you see a young lad passing this way in the early morning or the fall of night?

WIDOW QUIN You're a queer kind to walk in not saluting at all.

MAHON Did you see the young lad?

---

22 **turbary** the right of cutting peat.

WIDOW QUIN [*stiffly*]   What kind was he?

MAHON   An ugly young streeler[23] with a murderous gob on him and a little switch in his hand. I met a tramper seen him coming this way at the fall of night.

WIDOW QUIN   There's harvest hundreds do be passing these days for the Sligo boat. For what is it you're wanting him, my poor man?

MAHON   I want to destroy him for breaking the head on me with the clout of a loy. [*He takes off a big hat, and shows his head in a mass of bandages and plaster, with some pride.*] It was he did that, and amn't I a great wonder to think I've traced him ten days with that rent in my crown?

WIDOW QUIN [*taking his head in both hands and examining it with extreme delight*]   That was a great blow. And who hit you? A robber maybe?

MAHON   It was my own son hit me, and he the divil a robber or anything else but a dirty, stuttering lout.

WIDOW QUIN [*letting go his skull and wiping her hands in her apron*]   You'd best be wary of a mortified scalp, I think they call it, lepping around with that wound in the splendour of the sun. It was a bad blow surely, and you should have vexed him fearful to make him strike that gash in his da.

MAHON   Is it me?

WIDOW QUIN [*amusing herself*]   Aye. And isn't it a great shame when the old and hardened do torment the young?

MAHON [*raging*]   Torment him is it? And I after holding out with the patience of a martyred saint, till there's nothing but destruction on me and I'm driven out in my old age with none to aid me?

WIDOW QUIN [*greatly amused*]   It's a sacred wonder the way that wickedness will spoil a man.

MAHON   My wickedness, is it? Amn't I after saying it is himself has me destroyed, and he a lier on walls, a talker of folly, a man you'd see stretched the half of the day in the brown ferns with his belly to the sun.

WIDOW QUIN   Not working at all?

MAHON   The divil a work, or if he did itself, you'd see him raising up a haystack like the stalk of a rush or driving our last cow till he broke her leg at the hip, and when he wasn't at that he'd be fooling over little birds he had—finches and felts[24]—or making mugs at his own self in the bit of a glass we had hung on the wall.

WIDOW QUIN [*looking at* CHRISTY]   What way was he so foolish? It was running wild after the girls maybe?

MAHON [*with a shout of derision*]   Running wild, is it? If he seen a red petticoat coming swinging over the hill, he'd be off to hide in the sticks, and you'd see him shooting out his sheep's eyes between the little twigs and leaves, and his two ears rising like a hare looking out through a gap. Girls indeed!

WIDOW QUIN   It was drink maybe?

MAHON   And he a poor fellow would get drunk on the smell of a pint! He'd a queer rotten stomach, I'm telling you, and when I gave him three pulls from my pipe a while since, he was taken with contortions till I had to send him in the ass cart to the females' nurse.

WIDOW QUIN [*clasping her hands*]   Well, I never till this day heard tell of a man the like of that.

MAHON   I'd take a mighty oath you didn't surely, and wasn't he the laughing joke of every female woman where four baronies meet, the way the girls would stop their wedding if they seen him coming the road to let a roar at him, and call him the looney of Mahon's.

WIDOW QUIN   I'd give the world and all to see the like of him. What kind was he?

MAHON   A small low fellow.

WIDOW QUIN   And dark?

MAHON   Dark and dirty.

WIDOW QUIN [*considering*]   I'm thinking I seen him.

---

23 **streeler** loiterer.

24 **felts** thrushes.

MAHON [*eagerly*] An ugly young black-guard?

WIDOW QUIN A hideous, fearful villain, and the spit of you.

MAHON What way is he fled?

WIDOW QUIN Gone over the hills to catch a coasting steamer to the north or south.

MAHON Could I pull up on him now?

WIDOW QUIN If you'll cross the sands below where the tide is out, you'll be in it as soon as himself, for he had to go round ten miles by the top of the bay. [*She points from the door.*] Strike down by the head beyond and then follow on the road-way to the north and east.

[MAHON *goes abruptly.*]

WIDOW QUIN [*shouting after him*] Let you give him a good vengeance when you come up with him, but don't put your-self in the power of the law, for it'd be a poor thing to see a judge in his black cap reading out his sentence on a civil war-rior the like of you. [*She swings the door to and looks at* CHRISTY, *who is cowering in terror, for a moment, then she bursts into a laugh.*] Well, you're the walking playboy of the western world, and that's the poor man you had divided to his breeches belt.

CHRISTY [*looking out; then, to her*] What'll Pegeen say when she hears that story? What'll she be saying to me now?

WIDOW QUIN She'll knock the head of you, I'm thinking, and drive you from the door. God help her to be taking you for a wonder, and you a little schemer mak-ing up a story you destroyed your da.

CHRISTY [*turning to the door, nearly speech-less with rage, half to himself*] To be letting on he was dead, and coming back to his life, and following me like an old weazel tracing a rat, and coming in here laying desolation between my own self and the fine women of Ireland, and he a kind of carcase that you'd fling upon the sea. . . .

WIDOW QUIN [*more soberly*] There's talk-ing for a man's one only son.

CHRISTY [*breaking out*] His one son, is it?

May I meet him with one tooth and it aching, and one eye to be seeing seven and seventy divils in the twists of the road, and one old timber leg on him to limp into the scalding grave. [*Looking out.*] There he is now crossing the strands, and that the Lord God would send a high wave to wash him from the world.

WIDOW QUIN [*scandalized*] Have you no shame? [*Putting her hand on his shoulder and turning him round.*] What ails you? Near crying, is it?

CHRISTY [*in despair and grief*] Amn't I after seeing the love-light of the star of knowledge shining from her brow, and hearing words would put you thinking on the holy Brigid speaking to the infant saints, and now she'll be turning again, and speaking hard words to me, like an old woman with a spavindy ass she'd have, urging on a hill.

WIDOW QUIN There's poetry talk for a girl you'd see itching and scratching, and she with a stale stink of poteen on her from selling in the shop.

CHRISTY [*impatiently*] It's her like is fitted to be handling merchandise in the heavens above, and what'll I be doing now, I ask you, and I a kind of wonder was jilted by the heavens when a day was by.

[*There is a distant noise of girls' voices.* WIDOW QUIN *looks from window and comes to him, hurriedly.*]

WIDOW QUIN You'll be doing like myself, I'm thinking, when I did destroy my man, for I'm above many's the day, odd times in great spirits, abroad in the sunshine, darning a stocking or stitching a shift, and odd times again looking out on the schooners, hookers, trawlers is sailing the sea, and I thinking on the gallant hairy fellows are drifting beyond, and myself long years living alone.

CHRISTY [*interested*] You're like me, so.

WIDOW QUIN I am your like, and it's for that I'm taking a fancy to you, and I with my little houseen above where there'd be myself to tend you, and none to ask were you a murderer or what at all.

CHRISTY   And what would I be doing if I left Pegeen?

WIDOW QUIN   I've nice jobs you could be doing, gathering shells to make a whitewash for our hut within, building up a little goose-house, or stretching a new skin on an old curagh[25] I have, and if my hut is far from all sides, it's there you'll meet the wisest old men, I tell you, at the corner of my wheel, and it's there yourself and me will have great times whispering and hugging . . .

VOICES [*outside, calling far away*]   Christy! Christy Mahon! Christy!

CHRISTY   Is it Pegeen Mike?

WIDOW QUIN   It's the young girls, I'm thinking, coming to bring you to the sports below, and what is it you'll have me to tell them now?

CHRISTY   Aid me for to win Pegeen. It's herself only that I'm seeking now. [WIDOW QUIN *gets up and goes to window.*] Aid me for to win her, and I'll be asking God to stretch a hand to you in the hour of death, and lead you short cuts through the Meadows of Ease, and up the floor of Heaven to the Footstool of the Virgin's Son.

WIDOW QUIN   There's praying!

VOICES [*nearer*]   Christy! Christy Mahon!

CHRISTY [*with agitation*]   They're coming. Will you swear to aid and save me for the love of Christ?

WIDOW QUIN [*looks at him for a moment*] If I aid you, will you swear to give me a right of way I want, and a mountainy ram, and a load of dung at Michaelmas, the time that you'll be master here?

CHRISTY   I will, by the elements and stars of night.

WIDOW QUIN   Then we'll not say a word of the old fellow, the way Pegeen won't know your story till the end of time.

CHRISTY   And if he chances to return again?

WIDOW QUIN   We'll swear he's a maniac and not your da. I could take an oath I seen him raving on the sands to-day.

25 **curagh** small canoe.

[GIRLS *run in.*]

SUSAN   Come on to the sports below. Pegeen says you're to come.

SARA TANSEY   The lepping's beginning, and we've a jockey's suit to fit upon you for the mule race on the sands below.

HONOR   Come on, will you.

CHRISTY   I will then if Pegeen's beyond.

SARA   She's in the boreen[26] making game of Shaneen Keogh.

CHRISTY   Then I'll be going to her now. [*He runs out, followed by the* GIRLS.]

WIDOW QUIN   Well, if the worst comes in the end of all, it'll be great game to see there's none to pity him but a widow woman, the like of me, has buried her children and destroyed her man. [*She goes out.*]

Act Three

Scene, as before. Later in the day. JIMMY *comes in, slightly drunk.*

JIMMY [*calls*]   Pegeen! [*Crosses to inner door.*] Pegeen Mike! [*Comes back again into the room.*] Pegeen! [PHILLY *comes in in the same state.*] [*To* PHILLY.] Did you see herself?

PHILLY   I did not; but I sent Shawn Keogh with the ass cart for to bear him home. [*Trying cupboards which are locked.*] Well, isn't he a nasty man to get into such staggers at a morning wake, and isn't herself the divil's daughter for locking, and she so fussy after that young gaffer, you might take your death with drought and none to heed you.

JIMMY   It's little wonder she'd be fussy, and he after bringing bankrupt ruin on the roulette man, and the trick-o'-the-loop man,[27] and breaking the nose of the cockshot-man,[28] and winning all in the sports below, racing, lepping, dancing,

26 **boreen** narrow lane between stone walls. 27 **trick-o'-the-loop man** man at a fair in charge of games in which spectator must guess center loop in a leather belt. 28 **cockshot-man** man at a fair whose blackened face is the target for wooden balls thrown by competitors.

and the Lord knows what! He's right luck, I'm telling you.

PHILLY If he has he'll be rightly hobbled yet, and he not able to say ten words without making a brag of the way he killed his father and the great blow he hit with the loy.

JIMMY A man can't hang by his own informing, and his father should be rotten by now.

[OLD MAHON *passes window slowly*.]

PHILLY Supposing a man's digging spuds in that field with a long spade, and supposing he flings up the two halves of that skull, what'll be said then in the papers and the courts of law?

JIMMY They'd say it was an old Dane, maybe, was drowned in the flood. [OLD MAHON *comes in and sits down near door listening*.] Did you never hear tell of the skulls they have in the city of Dublin, ranged out like blue jugs in a cabin of Connaught?

PHILLY And you believe that?

JIMMY [*pugnaciously*] Didn't a lad see them and he after coming from harvesting in the Liverpool boat? "They have them there," says he, "making a show of the great people there was one time walking the world. White skulls and black skulls and yellow skulls, and some with full teeth and some haven't only but one."

PHILLY It was no lie, maybe, for when I was a young lad, there was a graveyard beyond the house with the remnants of a man who had thighs as long as your arm. He was a horrid man, I'm telling you, and there was many a fine Sunday I'd put him together for fun, and he with shiny bones you wouldn't meet the like of these days in the cities of the world.

MAHON [*getting up*] You wouldn't is it? Lay your eyes on that skull, and tell me where and when there was another the like of it, is splintered only from the blow of a loy.

PHILLY Glory be to God! And who hit you at all?

MAHON [*triumphantly*] It was my own son hit me. Would you believe that?

JIMMY Well there's wonders hidden in the heart of man!

PHILLY [*suspiciously*] And what way was it done?

MAHON [*wandering about the room*] I'm after walking hundreds and long scores of miles, winning clean beds and the fill of my belly four times in the day, and I doing nothing but telling stories of that naked truth. [*He comes to them a little aggressively.*] Give me a supeen and I'll tell you now.

[WIDOW QUIN *comes in and stands aghast behind him. He is facing* JIMMY *and* PHILLY, *who are on the left.*]

JIMMY Ask herself beyond. She's the stuff hidden in her shawl.

WIDOW QUIN [*coming to* MAHON *quickly*] You here, is it? You didn't go far at all?

MAHON I seen the coasting steamer passing, and I got a drought upon me and a cramping leg, so I said, "The divil go along with him," and turned again. [*Looking under her shawl.*] And let you give me a supeen, for I'm destroyed travelling since Tuesday was a week.

WIDOW QUIN [*getting a glass, in a cajoling tone*] Sit down then by the fire and take your ease for a space. You've a right to be destroyed indeed, with your walking, and fighting, and facing the sun [*giving him poteen from a stone jar she has brought in*]. There now is a drink for you, and may it be to your happiness and length of life.

MAHON [*taking glass greedily, and sitting down by fire*] God increase you!

WIDOW QUIN [*taking* MEN *to the right stealthily*] Do you know what? That man's raving from his wound to-day, for I met him a while since telling a rambling tale of a tinker had him destroyed. Then he heard of Christy's deed, and he up and says it was his son had cracked his skull. Oh, isn't madness a fright, for he'll go killing someone yet and he thinking it's the man has struck him so!

JIMMY [*entirely convinced*] It's a fright surely. I knew a party was kicked in the head by a red mare, and he went killing horses a great while, till he eat the insides of a clock and died after.

PHILLY [*with suspicion*] Did he see Christy?

WIDOW QUIN He didn't. [*With a warning gesture.*] Let you not be putting him in mind of him, or you'll be likely summoned if there's murder done. [*Looking round at* MAHON.] Whisht! He's listening. Wait now till you hear me taking him easy and unravelling all. [*She goes to* MAHON.] And what way are you feeling, Mister? Are you in contentment now?

MAHON [*slightly emotional from his drink*] I'm poorly only, for it's a hard story the way I'm left to-day, when it was I did tend him from his hour of birth, and he a dunce never reached his second book, the way he'd come from school, many's the day, with his legs lamed under him, and he blackened with his beatings like a tinker's ass. It's a hard story, I'm saying, the way some do have their next and nighest raising up a hand of murder on them, and some is lonesome getting their death with lamentation in the dead of night.

WIDOW QUIN [*not knowing what to say*] To hear you talking so quiet, who'd know you were the same fellow we seen pass to-day?

MAHON I'm the same surely. The wrack and ruin of three score years; and it's a terror to live that length, I tell you, and to have your sons going to the dogs against you, and you wore out scolding them, and skelping[29] them, and God knows what.

PHILLY [*to* JIMMY] He's not raving. [*To* WIDOW QUIN.] Will you ask him what kind was his son?

WIDOW QUIN [*to* MAHON, *with a peculiar look*] Was your son that hit you a lad of one year and a score maybe, a great hand at racing and lepping and licking the world?

MAHON [*turning on her with a roar of rage*] Didn't you hear me say he was the fool of men, the way from this out he'll know the orphan's lot with old and young making game of him and they swearing, raging, kicking at him like a mangy cur.

[*A great burst of cheering outside, some way off.*]

MAHON [*putting his hands to his ears*] What in the name of God do they want roaring below?

WIDOW QUIN [*with the shade of a smile*] They're cheering a young lad, the champion playboy of the western world.

[*More cheering.*]

MAHON [*going to window*] It'd split my heart to hear them, and I with pulses in my brain-pan for a week gone by. Is it racing they are?

JIMMY [*looking from door*] It is then. They are mounting him for the mule race will be run upon the sands. That's the playboy on the winkered mule.[30]

MAHON [*puzzled*] That lad, is it? If you said it was a fool he was, I'd have laid a mighty oath he was the likeness of my wandering son. [PHILLY *nods at* JIMMY. MAHON, *uneasily, putting his hand to his head.*] Faith, I'm thinking I'll go walking for to view the race.

WIDOW QUIN [*stopping him, sharply*] You will not. You'd best take the road to Belmullet, and not be dilly-dallying in this place where there isn't a spot you could sleep.

PHILLY [*coming forward*] Don't mind her. Mount there on the bench and you'll have a view of the whole. They're hurrying before the tide will rise, and it'd be near over if you went down the pathway through the crags below.

MAHON [*mounts on bench,* WIDOW QUIN *beside him*]. That's a right view again the

---

29 **skelping** beating.

30 **winkered mule** mule with blinkers.

edge of the sea. They're coming now from the point. He's leading. Who is he at all?

WIDOW QUIN He's the champion of the world I tell you, and there isn't a hap'orth[31] isn't falling lucky to his hands to-day.

PHILLY [*looking out, interested in the race*] Look at that. They're pressing him now.

JIMMY He'll win it yet.

PHILLY Take your time, Jimmy Farrell. It's too soon to say.

WIDOW QUIN [*shouting*] Watch him taking the gate. There's riding.

JIMMY [*cheering*] More power to the young lad!

MAHON He's passing the third.

JIMMY He'll lick them yet.

WIDOW QUIN He'd lick them if he was running races with a score itself.

MAHON Look at the mule he has kicking the stars.

WIDOW QUIN There was a lep! [*Catching hold of* MAHON *in her excitement.*] He's fallen! He's mounted again! Faith, he's passing them all!

JIMMY Look at him skelping her!

PHILLY And the mountain girls hooshing him on!

JIMMY It's the last turn! The post's cleared for them now!

MAHON Look at the narrow place. He'll be into the bogs! [*With a yell.*] Good rider! He's through it again!

JIMMY He's neck and neck!

MAHON Good boy to him! Flames, but he's in!

[*Great cheering, in which all join.*]

MAHON [*with hesitation*] What's that? They're raising him up. They're coming this way. [*With a roar of rage and astonishment.*] It's Christy! by the stars of God! I'd know his way of spitting and he astride the moon. [*He jumps down and makes a run for the door, but* WIDOW QUIN *catches him and pulls him back.*]

WIDOW QUIN Stay quiet, will you. That's not your son. [*To* JIMMY.] Stop him, or you'll get a month for the abetting of manslaughter and be fined as well.

JIMMY I'll hold him.

MAHON [*struggling*] Let me out! Let me out the lot of you! till I have my vengeance on his head to-day.

WIDOW QUIN [*shaking him, vehemently*] That's not your son. That's a man is going to make a marriage with the daughter of this house, a place with fine trade, with a licence, and with poteen too.

MAHON [*amazed*] That man marrying a decent and a moneyed girl! Is it mad yous are? Is it in a crazy-house for females that I'm landed now?

WIDOW QUIN It's mad yourself is with the blow upon your head. That lad is the wonder of the western world.

MAHON I seen it's my son.

WIDOW QUIN You seen that you're mad. [*Cheering outside.*] Do you hear them cheering him in the zig-zags of the road? Aren't you after saying that your son's a fool, and how would they be cheering a true idiot born?

MAHON [*getting distressed*] It's maybe out of reason that man's himself. [*Cheering again.*] There's none surely will go cheering him. Oh, I'm raving with a madness that would fright the world. [*He sits down with his hand to his head.*] There was one time I seen ten scarlet divils letting on they'd cork my spirit in a gallon can; and one time I seen rats as big as badgers sucking the life blood from the butt of my lug;[32] but I never till this day confused that dribbling idiot with a likely man. I'm destroyed surely.

WIDOW QUIN And who'd wonder when it's your brain-pan that is gaping now?

MAHON Then the blight of the sacred drought upon myself and him, for I never went mad to this day, and I not three weeks with the Limerick girls drinking myself silly and parlatic[33] from the dusk to dawn. [*To* WIDOW QUIN, *suddenly.*] Is my visage astray?

---

31 **hap'orth** half-penny's worth.   32 **lug** ear. 33 **parlatic** paralytic from drink.

628

WIDOW QUIN It is then. You're a sniggering maniac, a child could see.

MAHON [*getting up more cheerfully*] Then I'd best be going to the Union beyond, and there'll be a welcome before me, I tell you [*with great pride*], and I a terrible and fearful case, the way that there I was one time screeching in a straitened waistcoat[34] with seven doctors writing out my sayings in a printed book. Would you believe that?

WIDOW QUIN If you're a wonder itself, you'd best be hasty, for them lads caught a maniac one time and pelted the poor creature till he ran out raving and foaming and was drowned in the sea.

MAHON [*with philosophy*] It's true mankind is the divil when your head's astray. Let me out now and I'll slip down the boreen and not see them so.

WIDOW QUIN [*showing him out*] That's it. Run to the right, and not a one will see.

[*He runs off.*]

PHILLY [*wisely*] You're at some gaming, Widow Quin; but I'll walk after him and give him his dinner and a time to rest, and I'll see then if he's raving or as sane as you.

WIDOW QUIN [*annoyed*] If you go near that lad, let you be wary of your head, I'm saying. Didn't you hear him telling he was crazed at times?

PHILLY I heard him telling a power; and I'm thinking we'll have right sport, before night will fall. [*He goes out.*]

JIMMY Well, Philly's a conceited and foolish man. How could that madman have his senses and his brain-pan slit? I'll go after them and see him turn on Philly now.

[*He goes;* WIDOW QUIN *hides poteen behind counter. Then hubbub outside.*]

VOICES There you are! Good jumper! Grand lepper! Darlint boy! He's the racer! Bear him on, will you!

[CHRISTY *comes in, in Jockey's dress, with* PEGEEN MIKE, SARA, *and other* GIRLS, *and* MEN.]

PEGEEN [*to* CROWD] Go on now and don't destroy him and he drenching with sweat. Go along, I'm saying, and have your tug-of-warring till he's dried his skin.

CROWD Here's his prizes! A bagpipes! A fiddle was played by a poet in the years gone by! A flat and three-thorned blackthorn[35] would lick the scholars out of Dublin town!

CHRISTY [*taking prizes from the* MEN] Thank you kindly, the lot of you. But you'd say it was little only I did this day if you'd seen me a while since striking my one single blow.

TOWN CRIER [*outside, ringing a bell*] Take notice, last event of this day! Tug-of-warring on the green below! Come on, the lot of you! Great achievements for all Mayo men!

PEGEEN Go on, and leave him for to rest and dry. Go on, I tell you, for he'll do no more. [*She hustles* CROWD *out*; WIDOW QUIN *following them.*]

MEN [*going*] Come on then. Good luck for the while!

PEGEEN [*radiantly, wiping his face with her shawl*] Well you're the lad, and you'll have great times from this out when you could win that wealth of prizes, and you sweating in the heat of noon!

CHRISTY [*looking at her with delight*] I'll have great times if I win the crowning prize I'm seeking now, and that's your promise that you'll wed me in a fortnight, when our banns is called.

PEGEEN [*backing away from him*] You've right daring to go ask me that, when all knows you'll be starting to some girl in your own townland, when your father's rotten in four months, or five.

CHRISTY [*indignantly*] Starting from you, is it! [*He follows her.*] I will not then, and when the airs is warming in four months

34 **straitened waistcoat** straightjacket.

35 **blackthorn** walking stick made from the stem of a black thorn shrub.

or five, it's then yourself and me should be pacing Neifin in the dews of night, the times sweet smells do be rising, and you'd see a little shiny new moon maybe sinking on the hills.

PEGEEN [*looking at him playfully*] And it's that kind of a poacher's love you'd make, Christy Mahon, on the sides of Neifin, when the night is down?

CHRISTY It's little you'll think if my love's a poacher's or an earl's itself when you'll feel my two hands stretched around you, and I squeezing kisses on your puckered lips till I'd feel a kind of pity for the Lord God is all ages sitting lonesome in his golden chair.

PEGEEN That'll be right fun, Christy Mahon, and any girl would walk her heart out before she'd meet a young man was your like for eloquence or talk at all.

CHRISTY [*encouraged*] Let you wait to hear me talking till we're astray in Erris when Good Friday's by, drinking a sup from a well, and making mighty kisses with our wetted mouths, or gaming in a gap of sunshine with yourself stretched back unto your necklace in the flowers of the earth.

PEGEEN [*in a lower voice, moved by his tone*] I'd be nice so, is it?

CHRISTY [*with rapture*] If the mitred bishops seen you that time, they'd be the like of the holy prophets, I'm thinking, do be straining the bars of Paradise to lay eyes on the Lady Helen of Troy, and she abroad pacing back and forward with a nosegay in her golden shawl.

PEGEEN [*with real tenderness*] And what is it I have, Christy Mahon, to make me fitting entertainment for the like of you that has such poet's talking, and such bravery of heart?

CHRISTY [*in a low voice*] Isn't there the light of seven heavens in your heart alone, the way you'll be an angel's lamp to me from this out, and I abroad in the darkness spearing salmons in the Owen or the Carrowmore.

PEGEEN If I was your wife, I'd be along with you those nights, Christy Mahon, the way you'd see I was a great hand at coaxing bailiffs, or coining funny nicknames for the stars of night.

CHRISTY You, is it! Taking your death in the hailstones or the fogs of dawn.

PEGEEN Yourself and me would shelter easy in a narrow bush, [*with a qualm of dread*] but we're only talking maybe, for this would be a poor thatched place to hold a fine lad is the like of you.

CHRISTY [*putting his arm round her*] If I wasn't a good Christian, it's on my naked knees I'd be saying my prayers and paters to every jackstraw you have roofing your head, and every stony pebble is paving the laneway to your door.

PEGEEN [*radiantly*] If that's the truth, I'll be burning candles from this out to the miracles of God have brought you from the south to-day, and I with my gowns bought ready the way that I can wed you, and not wait at all.

CHRISTY It's miracles and that's the truth. Me there toiling a long while, and walking a long while, not knowing at all I was drawing all times nearer to this holy day.

PEGEEN And myself a girl was tempted often to go sailing the seas till I'd marry a Jew-man with ten kegs of gold, and I not knowing at all there was the like of you drawing nearer like the stars of God.

CHRISTY And to think I'm long years hearing women talking that talk to all bloody fools, and this the first time I've heard the like of your voice talking sweetly for my own delight.

PEGEEN And to think it's me is talking sweetly, Christy Mahon, and I the fright of seven townlands for my biting tongue. Well the heart's a wonder, and I'm thinking there won't be our like in Mayo for gallant lovers from this hour to-day. [*Drunken singing is heard outside.*] There's my father coming from the wake, and when he's had his sleep we'll tell him, for he's peaceful then. [*They separate.*]

MICHAEL [*singing outside*]—

The jailor and the turnkey
  They quickly ran us down,
And brought us back as prisoners
  Once more to Cavan town.

[*He comes in supported by* SHAWN.]

There we lay bewailing
  All in a prison bound. . . .

[*He sees* CHRISTY. *Goes and shakes him drunkenly by the hand, while* PEGEEN *and* SHAWN *talk on the left.*]

MICHAEL [*to* CHRISTY] The blessing of God and the holy angels on your head, young fellow. I hear tell you're after winning all in the sports below; and wasn't it a shame I didn't bear you along with me to Kate Cassidy's wake, a fine, stout lad, the like of you, for you'd never see the match of it for flows of drink, the way when we sunk her bones at noonday in her narrow grave, there were five men, aye, and six men, stretched out retching speechless on the holy stones.

CHRISTY [*uneasily, watching* PEGEEN] Is that the truth?

MICHAEL It is then, and aren't you a louty schemer to go burying your poor father unbeknownst when you'd a right to throw him on the crupper of a Kerry mule and drive him westwards, like holy Joseph in the days gone by, the way we could have given him a decent burial and not have him rotting beyond and not a Christian drinking a smart drop to the glory of his soul.

CHRISTY [*gruffly*] It's well enough he's lying for the likes of him.

MICHAEL [*slapping him on the back*]. Well, aren't you a hardened slayer? It'll be a poor thing for the household man where you go sniffing for a female wife; and [*pointing to* SHAWN] look beyond at that shy and decent Christian I have chosen for my daughter's hand, and I after getting the gilded dispensation this day for to wed them now.

CHRISTY And you'll be wedding them this day, is it?

MICHAEL [*drawing himself up*] Aye. Are you thinking, if I'm drunk itself I'd leave my daughter living single with a little frisky rascal is the like of you?

PEGEEN [*breaking away from* SHAWN] Is it the truth the dispensation's come?

MICHAEL [*triumphantly*] Father Reilly's after reading it in gallous[36] Latin, and "It's come in the nick of time," says he; "so I'll wed them in a hurry, dreading that young gaffer who'd capsize the stars."

PEGEEN [*fiercely*] He's missed his nick of time, for it's that lad, Christy Mahon, that I'm wedding now.

MICHAEL [*loudly, with horror*] You'd be making him a son to me and he wet and crusted with his father's blood?

PEGEEN Aye. Wouldn't it be a bitter thing for a girl to go marrying the like of Shaneen, and he a middling kind of a scarecrow with no savagery or fine words in him at all?

MICHAEL [*gasping and sinking on a chair*] Oh, aren't you a heathen daughter to go shaking the fat of my heart, and I swamped and drownded with the weight of drink? Would you have them turning on me the way that I'd be roaring to the dawn of day with the wind upon my heart? Have you not a word to aid me, Shaneen? Are you not jealous at all?

SHAWN [*in great misery*] I'd be afeard to be jealous of a man did slay his da.

PEGEEN Well, it'd be a poor thing to go marrying your like. I'm seeing there's a world of peril for an orphan girl, and isn't it a great blessing I didn't wed you, before himself came walking from the west or south.

SHAWN It's a queer story you'd go picking a dirty tramp up from the highways of the world.

PEGEEN [*playfully*] And you think you're a likely beau to go straying along with, the shiny Sundays of the opening year, when it's sooner on a bullock's liver you'd put a poor girl thinking than on the lily or the rose.

36 **gallous** spirited.

SHAWN And have you no mind of my weight of passion, and the holy dispensation, and the drift of heifers I am giving, and the golden ring?

PEGEEN I'm thinking you're too fine for the like of me, Shawn Keogh of Killakeen, and let you go off till you'd find a radiant lady with droves of bullocks on the plains of Meath, and herself bedizened in the diamond jewelleries of Pharaoh's ma. That'd be your match, Shaneen. So God save you now! [*She retreats behind* CHRISTY.]

SHAWN Won't you hear me telling you. . . .

CHRISTY [*with ferocity*] Take yourself from this, young fellow, or I'll maybe add a murder to my deeds to-day.

MICHAEL [*springing up with a shriek*] Murder is it? Is it mad yous are? Would you go making murder in this place, and it piled with poteen for our drink to-night? Go on to the foreshore if it's fighting you want, where the rising tide will wash all traces from the memory of man. [*Pushing* SHAWN *towards* CHRISTY.]

SHAWN [*shaking himself free, and getting behind* MICHAEL] I'll not fight him, Michael James. I'd liefer live a bachelor simmering in passions to the end of time, than face a lepping savage the like of him has descended from the Lord knows where. Strike him yourself, Michael James, or you'll lose my drift of heifers and my blue bull from Sneem.

MICHAEL Is it me fight him, when it's father-slaying he's bred to now? [*Pushing* SHAWN.] Go on you fool and fight him now.

SHAWN [*coming forward a little*] Will I strike him with my hand?

MICHAEL Take the loy is on your western side.

SHAWN I'd be afeard of the gallows if I struck with that.

CHRISTY [*taking up the loy*] Then I'll make you face the gallows or quit off from this. [SHAWN *flies out of the door.*]

CHRISTY Well, fine weather be after him, [*going to* MICHAEL, *coaxingly*] and I'm thinking you wouldn't wish to have that quacking blackguard in your house at all. Let you give us your blessing and hear her swear her faith to me, for I'm mounted on the spring-tide of the stars of luck the way it'll be good for any to have me in the house.

PEGEEN [*at the other side of* MICHAEL] Bless us now, for I swear to God I'll wed him, and I'll not renege.

MICHAEL [*standing up in the centre, holding on to both of them*] It's the will of God, I'm thinking, that all should win an easy or a cruel end, and it's the will of God that all should rear up lengthy families for the nurture of the earth. What's a single man, I ask you, eating a bit in one house and drinking a sup in another, and he with no place of his own, like an old braying jackass strayed upon the rocks? [*To* CHRISTY.] It's many would be in dread to bring your like into their house for to end them maybe with a sudden end; but I'm a decent man of Ireland, and I'd liefer face the grave untimely and I seeing a score of grandsons growing up little gallant swearers by the name of God, than go peopling my bedside with puny weeds the like of what you'd breed, I'm thinking, out of Shaneen Keogh. [*He joins their hands.*] A daring fellow is the jewel of the world, and a man did split his father's middle with a single clout should have the bravery of ten, so may God and Mary and St. Patrick bless you, and increase you from this mortal day.

CHRISTY and PEGEEN Amen, O Lord!

[*Hubbub outside.* OLD MAHON *rushes in, followed by all the* CROWD *and* WIDOW QUIN. *He makes a rush at* CHRISTY, *knocks him down, and begins to beat him.*]

PEGEEN [*dragging back his arm*] Stop that, will you. Who are you at all?

MAHON His father, God forgive me!

PEGEEN [*drawing back*] Is it rose from the dead?

MAHON Do you think I look so easy quenched with the tap of a loy? [*Beats* CHRISTY *again.*]

PEGEEN [*glaring at* CHRISTY] And it's lies you told, letting on you had him slitted, and you nothing at all.

CHRISTY [*catching* MAHON's *stick*] He's not my father. He's a raving maniac would scare the world. [*Pointing to* WIDOW QUIN.] Herself knows it is true.

CROWD You're fooling Pegeen! The Widow Quin seen him this day and you likely knew! You're a liar!

CHRISTY [*dumbfounded*] It's himself was a liar, lying stretched out with an open head on him, letting on he was dead.

MAHON Weren't you off racing the hills before I got my breath with the start I had seeing you turn on me at all?

PEGEEN And to think of the coaxing glory we had given him, and he after doing nothing but hitting a soft blow and chasing northward in a sweat of fear. Quit off from this.

CHRISTY [*piteously*] You've seen my doings this day, and let you save me from the old man; for why would you be in such a scorch of haste to spur me to destruction now?

PEGEEN It's there your treachery is spurring me, till I'm hard set to think you're the one I'm after lacing in my heartstrings half-an-hour gone by. [*To* MAHON.] Take him on from this, for I think bad the world should see me raging for a Munster liar and the fool of men.

MAHON Rise up now to retribution, and come on with me.

CROWD [*jeeringly*] There's the playboy! There's the lad thought he'd rule the roost in Mayo. Slate[37] him now, Mister.

CHRISTY [*getting up in shy terror*] What is it drives you to torment me here, when I'd ask the thunders of the might of God to blast me if I ever did hurt to any saving only that one single blow.

MAHON [*loudly*] If you didn't, you're a poor good-for-nothing, and isn't it by the like of you the sins of the whole world are committed?

CHRISTY [*raising his hands*] In the name of the Almighty God. . . .

MAHON Leave troubling the Lord God. Would you have him sending down droughts, and fevers, and the old hen and the cholera morbus?

CHRISTY [*to* WIDOW QUIN] Will you come between us and protect me now?

WIDOW QUIN I've tried a lot, God help me! and my share is done.

CHRISTY [*looking round in desperation*] And I must go back into my torment is it, or run off like a vagabond straying through the Unions with the dusts of August making mudstains in the gullet of my throat, or the winds of March blowing on me till I'd take an oath I felt them making whistles of my ribs within.

SARA Ask Pegeen to aid you. Her like does often change.

CHRISTY I will not then, for there's torment in the splendour of her like and she a girl any moon of midnight would take pride to meet, facing southwards on the heaths of Keel. But what did I want crawling forward to scorch my understanding at her flaming brow?

PEGEEN [*to* MAHON, *vehemently, fearing she will break into tears*] Take him on from this or I'll set the young lads to destroy him here.

MAHON [*going to him, shaking his stick*] Come on now if you wouldn't have the company to see you skelped.

PEGEEN [*half laughing, through her tears*] That's it, now the world will see him pandied,[38] and he an ugly liar was playing off the hero and the fright of men!

CHRISTY [*to* MAHON, *very sharply*] Leave me go!

CROWD That's it. Now Christy. If them two set fighting, it will lick the world.

MAHON [*making a grab at* CHRISTY] Come here to me.

CHRISTY [*more threateningly*] Leave me go, I'm saying.

37 **Slate** thrash.

38 **pandied** struck on the palm of the hand.

MAHON I will maybe when your legs is limping, and your back is blue.

CROWD Keep it up, the two of you. I'll back the old one. Now the playboy.

CHRISTY [*in low and intense voice*] Shut your yelling, for if you're after making a mighty man of me this day by the power of a lie, you're setting me now to think if it's a poor thing to be lonesome, it's worse maybe go mixing with the fools of earth.

[MAHON *makes a movement towards him.*]

CHRISTY [*almost shouting*] Keep off . . . lest I do show a blow unto the lot of you would set the guardian angels winking in the clouds above. [*He swings round with a sudden rapid movement and picks up a loy.*]

CROWD [*half frightened, half amused*] He's going mad! Mind yourselves! Run from the idiot!

CHRISTY If I am an idiot, I'm after hearing my voice this day saying words would raise the topknot on a poet in a merchant's town. I've won your racing and your lepping and. . . .

MAHON Shut your gullet and come on with me.

CHRISTY I'm going but I'll stretch you first.

[*He runs at* OLD MAHON *with the loy, chases him out of the door, followed by* CROWD *and* WIDOW QUIN. *There is a great noise outside, then a yell, and dead silence for a moment.* CHRISTY *comes in, half dazed, and goes to fire.*]

WIDOW QUIN [*coming in, hurriedly, and going to him*] They're turning again you. Come on or you'll be hanged indeed.

CHRISTY I'm thinking from this out, Pegeen'll be giving me praises the same as in the hours gone by.

WIDOW QUIN [*impatiently*] Come by the back-door. I'd think bad to have you stifled on the gallows tree.

CHRISTY [*indignantly*] I will not then.

What good'd be my life-time if I left Pegeen?

WIDOW QUIN Come on and you'll be no worse than you were last night; and you with a double murder this time to be telling to the girls.

CHRISTY I'll not leave Pegeen Mike.

WIDOW QUIN [*impatiently*] Isn't there the match of her in every parish public, from Binghamstown unto the plain of Meath? Come on, I tell you, and I'll find you finer sweethearts at each waning moon.

CHRISTY It's Pegeen I'm seeking only, and what'd I care if you brought me a drift of chosen females, standing in their shifts itself maybe, from this place to the Eastern World.

SARA [*runs in, pulling off one of her petticoats*] They're going to hang him. [*Holding out petticoat and shawl.*] Fit these upon him and let him run off to the east.

WIDOW QUIN He's raving now; but we'll fit them on him and I'll take him in the ferry to the Achill boat.

CHRISTY [*struggling feebly*] Leave me go, will you, when I'm thinking of my luck to-day, for she will wed me surely and I a proven hero in the end of all. [*They try to fasten petticoat round him.*]

WIDOW QUIN Take his left hand and we'll pull him now. Come on, young fellow.

CHRISTY [*suddenly starting up*] You'll be taking me from her? You're jealous, is it, of her wedding me? Go on from this. [*He snatches up a stool, and threatens them with it.*]

WIDOW QUIN [*going*] It's in the mad-house they should put him not in jail at all. We'll go by the back-door to call the doctor and we'll save him so.

[*She goes out, with* SARA, *through inner room.* MEN *crowd in the doorway.* CHRISTY *sits down again by the fire.*]

MICHAEL [*in a terrified whisper*] Is the old lad killed surely?

PHILLY I'm after feeling the last gasps quitting his heart. [*They peer in at* CHRISTY.]

MICHAEL [*with a rope*] Look at the way he is. Twist a hangman's knot on it and slip it over his head while he's not minding at all.

PHILLY Let you take it, Shaneen. You're the soberest of all that's here.

SHAWN Is it me to go near him, and he the wickedest and worst with me? Let you take it, Pegeen Mike.

PEGEEN Come on, so. [*She goes forward with the others, and they drop the double hitch over his head.*]

CHRISTY What ails you?

SHAWN [*triumphantly, as they pull the rope tight on his arms*] Come on to the peelers till they stretch you now.

CHRISTY Me!

MICHAEL If we took pity on you, the Lord God would maybe bring us ruin from the law to-day, so you'd best come easy, for hanging is an easy and a speedy end.

CHRISTY I'll not stir. [*To* PEGEEN.] And what is it you'll say to me and I after doing it this time in the face of all?

PEGEEN I'll say a strange man is a marvel with his mighty talk; but what's a squabble in your back-yard and the blow of a loy, have taught me that there's a great gap between a gallous story and a dirty deed. [*To* MEN.] Take him on from this, or the lot of us will be likely put on trial for his deed to-day.

CHRISTY [*with horror in his voice*] And it's yourself will send me off to have a horny-fingered hangman hitching his bloody slip-knots at the butt of my ear?

MEN [*pulling rope*] Come on, will you?

[*He is pulled down on the floor.*]

CHRISTY [*twisting his legs round the table*] Cut the rope, Pegeen, and I'll quit the lot of you and live from this out like the madmen of Keel, eating muck and green weeds on the faces of the cliffs.

PEGEEN And leave us to hang, is it, for a saucy liar, the like of you? [*To* MEN.] Take him on out from this.

SHAWN Pull a twist on his neck, and squeeze him so.

PHILLY Twist yourself. Sure he cannot hurt you, if you keep your distance from his teeth alone.

SHAWN I'm afeard of him. [*To* PEGEEN.] Lift a lighted sod will you and scorch his leg.

PEGEEN [*blowing the fire with a bellows*] Leave go now young fellow or I'll scorch your shins.

CHRISTY You're blowing for to torture me? [*His voice rising and growing stronger.*] That's your kind, is it? Then let the lot of you be wary, for if I've to face the gallows I'll have a gay march down, I tell you, and shed the blood of some of you before I die.

SHAWN [*in terror*] Keep a good hold, Philly. Be wary for the love of God, for I'm thinking he would liefest wreak his pains on me.

CHRISTY [*almost gaily*] If I do lay my hands on you, it's the way you'll be at the fall of night hanging as a scarecrow for the fowls of hell. Ah, you'll have a gallous jaunt I'm saying, coaching out through Limbo with my father's ghost.

SHAWN [*to* PEGEEN] Make haste, will you. Oh, isn't he a holy terror, and isn't it true for Father Reilly that all drink's a curse that has the lot of you so shaky and uncertain now.

CHRISTY If I can wring a neck among you, I'll have a royal judgment looking on the trembling jury in the courts of law. And won't there be crying out in Mayo the day I'm stretched upon the rope with ladies in their silks and satins snivelling in their lacy kerchiefs, and they rhyming songs and ballads on the terror of my fate? [*He squirms round on the floor and bites* SHAWN's *leg.*]

SHAWN [*shrieking*] My leg's bit on me! He's the like of a mad dog, I'm thinking, the way that I will surely die.

CHRISTY [*delighted with himself*] You will then, the way you can shake out hell's flags of welcome for my coming in two weeks or three, for I'm thinking Satan hasn't many have killed their da in Kerry and in Mayo too.

[OLD MAHON *comes in behind on all fours and looks on unnoticed.*]

MEN [*to* PEGEEN] Bring the sod, will you.
PEGEEN [*coming over*] God help him so. [*Burns his leg.*]
CHRISTY [*kicking and screaming*] Oh, glory be to God!

[*He kicks loose from the table, and they all drag him towards the door.*]

JIMMY [*seeing* OLD MAHON] Will you look what's come in?

[*They all drop* CHRISTY *and run left.*]

CHRISTY [*scrambling on his knees face to face with* OLD MAHON] Are you coming to be killed a third time or what ails you now?
MAHON For what is it they have you tied?
CHRISTY They're taking me to the peelers to have me hanged for slaying you.
MICHAEL [*apologetically*] It is the will of God that all should guard their little cabins from the treachery of law and what would my daughter be doing if I was ruined or was hanged itself?
MAHON [*grimly, loosening* CHRISTY] It's little I care if you put a bag on her back and went picking cockles[39] till the hour of death; but my son and myself will be going our own way and we'll have great

times from this out telling stories of the villainy of Mayo and the fools is here. [*To* CHRISTY, *who is freed.*] Come on now.
CHRISTY Go with you, is it! I will then, like a gallant captain with his heathen slave. Go on now and I'll see you from this day stewing my oatmeal and washing my spuds, for I'm master of all fights from now. [*Pushing* MAHON.] Go on, I'm saying.
MAHON Is it me?
CHRISTY Not a word out of you. Go on from this.
MAHON [*walking out and looking back at* CHRISTY *over his shoulder*] Glory be to God! [*With a broad smile.*] I am crazy again! [*Goes.*]
CHRISTY Ten thousand blessings upon all that's here, for you've turned me a likely gaffer in the end of all, the way I'll go romancing through a romping lifetime from this hour to the dawning of the judgment day. [*He goes out.*]
MICHAEL By the will of God, we'll have peace now for our drinks. Will you draw the porter, Pegeen?
SHAWN [*going up to her*] It's a miracle Father Reilly can wed us in the end of all, and we'll have none to trouble us when his vicious bite is healed.
PEGEEN [*hitting him a box on the ear*] Quit my sight. [*Putting her shawl over her head and breaking out into wild lamentations.*] Oh my grief, I've lost him surely. I've lost the only playboy of the western world.

39 **cockles** weeds.

Mrs Warren's Profession

Bernard Shaw   edited by Dan H. Laurence

Introductory Comments

Dan H. Laurence *Literary Advisor
to the Estate of George Bernard Shaw*

Bernard Shaw was an avowed pedagogue. Like all the great writers of comedy from Aristophanes to Shakespeare, Molière, and Gilbert, he was a castigator of morals by ridicule. The function of comedy, he insisted, was nothing less than the repudiation of smug convention and desiccated dogma. The dramatist, Shaw believed, should be among other things "an elucidator of social conduct" and the theatre "a factory of thought."

When Shaw wrote *Mrs Warren's Profession* in 1894 he had already for ten years been ardently waving the Socialist banner, lecturing without recompense several times a week all over London and the provinces —on street corners and in parks, on the docks, in church halls and in workingmen's clubs—on the iniquities of the Victorian social system. At the same time he provided for his modest needs through ill-paid journalism, as a critic of music, art, and drama. He invaded the theatre in the 1890s convinced that it not only could provide him with a larger forum for his ideas and opinions, but would enable him to reach a hitherto inaccessible middle-class audience which had great need to sample his philosophy.

Mrs Warren's Profession, though styled a comedy ("all sincerely intellectual work," said Shaw, "is humorous"), was conceived as a sober polemic on economics, focusing attention on the uncomfortable truth that prostitution is not the product of "female depravity and male licentiousness" but, as Shaw stated in a preface in 1930, is a phenomenon produced "simply by underpaying, undervaluing, and overworking women so shamefully that the poorest of them are forced to resort to prostitution to keep body and soul together." There was added irony in the fact that a corruptive capitalistic system, while piously damning immorality, actually fostered socio-economic conditions that penalized virtue with privation and painful premature death, and lavishly rewarded vice (profiting from it, in the bargain, through rents and investments).

In labeling *Mrs Warren's Profession* (like the two plays that had preceded it) an "unpleasant play" Shaw brazenly broadcast his intention to oblige his audience to "go home thoroughly uncomfortable," for the word *unpleasant,* to the reticent Victorian, implied not merely a displeasing or dislikable subject, but an unsavory one, unfit to be uttered amongst decent people—particularly with ladies present. Shock was a prime weapon in Shaw's arsenal of rhetorical munitions. "Dramatic power," he indicated in the preface to *Plays Unpleasant* (1898), "is used to force the spectator to face unpleasant facts," and the conversion of an audience, he was convinced, was not possible without the impetus of an initial aggressive act of shock.

It was crucial that the play contain no conscious villain on whom audiences could fix blame and thus absolve themselves of complicity, for Shaw's message was that *all* members of society are culpable and must accordingly suffer their consciences to be smitten before leaving the theatre. Like Vivie Warren in Act Three the audience must "feel among the damned already."

The world of *Mrs Warren's Profession* is a terrifying world of grotesques, representing aristocracy, church, commerce, and art, all caught up in their hypocrisies, greed, lust, perverted sense of values, and superficialities. The conventions of this world demand unearned and undeserved parental respect and obedience by children. Its profit-motivated philosophy debauches the sacrament of marriage into mere sex relations for money. Its moral cant serves to mask a conviction that one can commit almost any depredation so long as one doesn't "fly openly in the face of society." Its platitudes of "love's young dream" and "the beauty and romance of life" reveal, as in Ibsen's *The Wild Duck,* a pitiful dependence on illusion. And it is doubly ironic that Kitty Warren, rebelling against its inequities and insensitivities, should survive by instinctively adopting the Victorian capitalist morality of doing what pays best, and then fall prey to the debilitating disease of conventionality, leading to the disenchantment and alienation of her admiring and sympathetic daughter.

Against the formidable array of Victorian pretensions boldly stands Vivie Warren, the one *vital* character in the play, a self-possessed realist, determined to follow and to fulfill the dictates of her own will. Vivie is, as Shaw said of her, "an absolutely new type in modern fiction." Isolated, defiantly alone, independent and unafraid, Vivie is quite prepared to renounce material comforts, family, even marriage if necessary, if the sacrifice will quicken the restoration of social integrity.

As a play *Mrs Warren's Profession* is a notable achievement, effectively balancing the conventions of Victorian melodrama with modern psychological insights, resulting in a sophisticated drama of clashing temperaments. Although it is an early work, Shaw already reveals an admirable skill and integrity as a theatrical craftsman. Ideologies never eclipse individualities. The melodramatics are tightly controlled, tempered by undercutting and deflation, as in the third-act climax with Frank and the gun. The tiny moments of babes-in-the-wood pathos, essential to reveal Vivie's desperate reaching out for affection and security, her last weakness, are never so prolonged as to grow sentimental or bathetic. The thesis elements are leavened with wit ("Lord help the world if everybody took to doing the right thing!"), and low-comedy stage business is unabashedly resorted to wherever it will effectively score a point, as in the opening scene when Vivie's brusque nature is displayed by her handshake and her refusal to permit Praed to wait upon her.

Shaw's characters are introduced rapidly, endowed with instant life by bold brush strokes. Then, as the play proceeds, we are gradually made aware of subtle, self-revealing nuances, as in the way Frank manipulates Mrs. Warren, "giving her shoulders the most delicate possible little caress with his fingers," thus providing an unconscious stimulus inciting her to flirtation. We note, too, Crofts's vulnerability to age, reflected both in his constant reference to his years and in his too youthful attire.

And all is accomplished with extraordinary economy. Try cutting the play and you will discover the fabric is so intricately and tightly woven that virtually not a single line is expendable. Every word has its purpose.

Three-quarters of a century ago *Mrs Warren's Profession* was banned from the London stage by Queen Victoria's censor; a leading critic accused Shaw of being unable to touch pitch without wallowing in it; the New York police raided the theatre after the first performance and arrested manager and cast; Shaw was denigrated as an "Irish smut dealer" and the play castigated as "the limit of stage indecency." Today's audiences, sexually emancipated and virtually unshockable, are now able to delve beneath the "unpleasant" surface of Shaw's play and to recognize its universal truth, that the best brought-up children (as Shaw himself has said in his "Maxims for Revolutionists") are those "who have seen their parents as they are. Hypocrisy is not the parent's first duty."

George Bernard Shaw (1856–1950) was born in Dublin, son of a ne'er-do-well grain merchant and a mother who dabbled in music and ignored her children. Self-sufficient from a tender age and largely self-educated, Shaw moved to London in 1876, wrote five unsuccessful novels, became a leader of the socialist Fabian Society, earned a reputation as an incisive critic of music and drama, and completed and produced his first play, *Widowers' Houses,* in 1892. He wrote more than fifty plays, including *Arms and the Man* (1894), *Candida* (1894), *Man and Superman* (1903), *Major Barbara* (1905), *Pygmalion* (1912), *Heartbreak House* (1917), *Back to Methuselah* (1920), *and Saint Joan* (1923). He was awarded the 1925 Nobel Prize for Literature, and gained international renown as a fearless advocate of reason and truth.

Mrs Warren's Profession   *Bernard Shaw*

PRAED

SIR GEORGE CROFTS

THE REVEREND SAMUEL GARDNER

FRANK GARDNER

VIVIE WARREN

MRS KITTY WARREN

Act One

Summer afternoon in a cottage garden on the eastern slope of a hill a little south of Haslemere in Surrey. Looking up the hill, the cottage is seen in the left hand corner of the garden, with its thatched roof and porch, and a large latticed window to the left of the porch. A paling completely shuts in the garden, except for a gate on the right. The common rises uphill beyond the paling to the sky line. Some folded canvas garden chairs are leaning against the side bench in the porch. A lady's bicycle is propped against the wall, under the window. A little to the right of the porch a hammock is slung from two posts. A big canvas umbrella, stuck in the ground, keeps the sun off the hammock, in which a young lady lies reading and making notes, her head towards the cottage and her feet towards the gate. In front of the hammock, and within reach of her hand, is a common kitchen chair, with a pile of serious-looking books and a supply of writing paper on it.

A gentleman walking on the common comes into sight from behind the cottage. He is hardly past middle age, with something of the artist about him, unconventionally but carefully dressed, and clean-shaven except for a moustache, with an eager susceptible face and very amiable and considerate manners. He has silky black hair, with waves of grey and white in it. His eyebrows are white, his moustache black. He seems not certain of his way. He looks over the paling; takes stock of the place; and sees the young lady.

THE GENTLEMAN [*taking off his hat*] I beg your pardon. Can you direct me to Hindhead View—Mrs Alison's?

THE YOUNG LADY [*glancing up from her book*] This is Mrs Alison's [*She resumes her work*].

THE GENTLEMAN Indeed! Perhaps—may I ask are you Miss Vivie Warren?

THE YOUNG LADY [*sharply, as she turns on her elbow to get a good look at him*] Yes.

THE GENTLEMAN [*daunted and conciliatory*] I'm afraid I appear intrusive. My name is Praed. [*Vivie at once throws her books upon the chair, and gets out of the hammock*]. Oh, pray don't let me disturb you.

VIVIE [*striding to the gate and opening it for him*] Come in, Mr Praed. [*He comes in*]. Glad to see you. [*She proffers her hand and takes his with a resolute and hearty grip. She is an attractive specimen of the sensible, able, highly-educated young middle-class Englishwoman. Age 22. Prompt, strong, confident, self-possessed. Plain business-like dress, but not dowdy. She wears a chatelaine at her belt, with a fountain pen and a paper knife among its pendants*].

PRAED Very kind of you indeed, Miss Warren. [*She shuts the gate with a vigorous slam. He passes in to the middle of the garden, exercising his fingers, which are slightly numbed by her greeting*]. Has your mother arrived?

VIVIE [*quickly, evidently scenting aggression*] Is she coming?

PRAED [*surprised*] Didn't you expect us?

VIVIE No.

PRAED Now, goodness me, I hope Ive not mistaken the day. That would be just like me, you know. Your mother arranged that she was to come down from London and that I was to come over from Horsham to be introduced to you.

VIVIE [*not at all pleased*] Did she? Hm! My mother has rather a trick of taking me by surprise—to see how I behave myself when she's away, I suppose. I fancy I shall take my mother very much by surprise one of these days, if she makes arrangements that concern me without consulting me beforehand. She hasnt come.

PRAED [*embarrassed*] I'm really very sorry.

VIVIE [*throwing off her displeasure*] It's not your fault, Mr Praed, is it? And I'm very glad youve come. You are the only one of my mother's friends I have ever asked her to bring to see me.

PRAED [*relieved and delighted*] Oh, now this is really very good of you, Miss Warren!

VIVIE Will you come indoors; or would you rather sit out here and talk?

PRAED It will be nicer out here, dont you think?

VIVIE Then I'll go and get you a chair. [*She goes to the porch for a garden chair*].

PRAED [*following her*] Oh, pray, pray! Allow me. [*He lays hands on the chair*].

VIVIE [*letting him take it*] Take care of your fingers: theyre rather dodgy things, those chairs. [*She goes across to the chair with the books on it; pitches them into the hammock; and brings the chair forward with one swing*].

PRAED [*who has just unfolded his chair*] Oh, now do let me take that hard chair. I like hard chairs.

VIVIE So do I. Sit down, Mr Praed. [*This invitation she gives with genial peremptoriness, his anxiety to please her clearly striking her as a sign of weakness of character on his part. But he does not immediately obey*].

PRAED By the way, though, hadnt we better go to the station to meet your mother?

VIVIE [*coolly*] Why? She knows the way.

PRAED [*disconcerted*] Er—I suppose she does [*he sits down*].

VIVIE Do you know, you are just like what I expected. I hope you are disposed to be friends with me.

PRAED [*again beaming*] Thank you, my d e a r Miss Warren: thank you. Dear me! I'm so glad your mother hasnt spoilt you!

VIVIE How?

PRAED Well, in making you too conventional. You know, my dear Miss Warren, I am a born anarchist. I hate authority. It spoils the relations between parent and child: even between mother and daughter. Now I was always afraid that your mother would strain her authority to make you very conventional. It's such a relief to find that she hasnt.

VIVIE Oh! have I been behaving unconventionally?

PRAED Oh no: oh dear no. At least not conventionally unconventionally, you understand. [*She nods and sits down. He goes on, with a cordial outburst*] But it was so charming of you to say that you were disposed to be friends with me! You modern young ladies are splendid: perfectly splendid!

VIVIE [*dubiously*] Eh? [*watching him with dawning disappointment as to the quality of his brains and character*].

PRAED When I was your age, young men and women were afraid of each other: there was no good fellowship. Nothing real. Only gallantry copied out of novels, and as vulgar and affected as it could be. Maidenly reserve! gentlemanly chivalry! always saying no when you meant yes! simple purgatory for shy and sincere souls.

VIVIE Yes, I imagine there must have been a frightful waste of time. Especially women's time.

PRAED Oh, waste of life, waste of everything. But things are improving. Do you know, I have been in a positive state of excitement about meeting you ever since your magnificent achievements at Cambridge: a thing unheard of in my day. It was perfectly splendid, your tieing with the third wrangler.[1] Just the right place,

1 There were distinctions of order for those candidates who obtained a place in the highest class of the mathematical examination (called the tripos)

you know. The first wrangler is always a dreamy, morbid fellow, in whom the thing is pushed to the length of a disease.

VIVIE   It doesnt pay. I wouldnt do it again for the same money.

PRAED [*aghast*]   The same money!

VIVIE   I did it for £50.

PRAED   Fifty pounds!

VIVIE   Yes. Fifty pounds. Perhaps you dont know how it was. Mrs Latham, my tutor at Newnham, told my mother that I could distinguish myself in the mathematical tripos if I went in for it in earnest. The papers were full just then of Phillipa Summers beating the senior wrangler. You remember about it, of course.

PRAED [*shakes his head energetically*]!!!

VIVIE   Well anyhow she did; and nothing would please my mother but that I should do the same thing. I said flatly it was not worth my while to face the grind since I was not going in for teaching; but I offered to try for fourth wrangler or thereabouts for £50. She closed with me at that, after a little grumbling; and I was better than my bargain. But I wouldnt do it again for that. £200 would have been nearer the mark.

PRAED [*much damped*]   Lord bless me! Thats a very practical way of looking at it.

VIVIE   Did you expect to find me an unpractical person?

PRAED   But surely it's practical to consider not only the work these honors cost, but also the culture they bring.

VIVIE   Culture! My dear Mr Praed: do you know what the mathematical tripos means? It means grind, grind, grind for six to eight hours a day at mathematics, and nothing but mathematics. I'm supposed to know something about science; but I know nothing except the mathematics it involves. I can make calculations for engineers, electricians, insurance companies, and so on; but I know next to nothing about engineering or electricity or insurance. I dont even know arithmetic well. Outside mathematics, lawn-tennis, eating, sleeping, cycling, and walking, I'm a more ignorant barbarian than any woman could possibly be who hadnt gone in for the tripos.

PRAED [*revolted*]   What a monstrous, wicked, rascally system! I knew it! I felt at once that it meant destroying all that makes womanhood beautiful.

VIVIE   I dont object to it on that score in the least. I shall turn it to very good account, I assure you.

PRAED   Pooh! In what way?

VIVIE   I shall set up in chambers in the City, and work at actuarial calculations and conveyancing. Under cover of that I shall do some law, with one eye on the Stock Exchange all the time. Ive come down here by myself to read law: not for a holiday, as my mother imagines. I hate holidays.

PRAED   You make my blood run cold. Are you to have no romance, no beauty in your life?

VIVIE   I dont care for either, I assure you.

PRAED   You cant mean that.

VIVIE   Oh yes I do. I like working and getting paid for it. When I'm tired of working, I like a comfortable chair, a cigar, a little whisky, and a novel with a good detective story in it.

PRAED [*rising in a frenzy of repudiation*] I dont believe it. I am an artist; and I cant believe it: I refuse to believe it. It's only that you havnt discovered yet what a wonderful world art can open up to you.

VIVIE   Yes I have. Last May I spent six weeks in London with Honoria Fraser. Mamma thought we were doing a round of sightseeing together; but I was really at Honoria's chambers in Chancery Lane every day, working away at actuarial calculations for her, and helping her as well as a greenhorn could. In the evenings we smoked and talked, and never dreamt of going out except for exercise. And I never enjoyed myself more in my life. I cleared all my expenses, and got initiated into the business without a fee into the bargain.

---

at Cambridge: "First" or "Senior Wrangler," "Second" or "Junior," "Third" or "Optime," etc.

PRAED But bless my heart and soul, Miss Warren, do you call that discovering art?

VIVIE Wait a bit. That wasnt the beginning. I went up to town on an invitation from some artistic people in Fitzjohn's Avenue: one of the girls was a Newnham chum. They took me to the National Gallery—

PRAED [*approving*] Ah!! [*He sits down, much relieved*].

VIVIE [*continuing*] —to the Opera—

PRAED [*still more pleased*] Good!

VIVIE —and to a concert where the band played all the evening: Beethoven and Wagner and so on. I wouldnt go through that experience again for anything you could offer me. I held out for civility's sake until the third day; and then I said, plump out, that I couldnt stand any more of it, and went off to Chancery Lane. Now you know the sort of perfectly splendid modern young lady I am. How do you think I shall get on with my mother?

PRAED [*startled*] Well, I hope—er—

VIVIE It's not so much what you hope as what you believe, that I want to know.

PRAED Well, frankly, I am afraid your mother will be a little disappointed. Not from any shortcoming on your part, you know: I dont mean that. But you are so different from her ideal.

VIVIE Her what?!

PRAED Her ideal.

VIVIE Do you mean her ideal of ME?

PRAED Yes.

VIVIE What on earth is it like?

PRAED Well, you must have observed, Miss Warren, that people who are dissatisfied with their own bringing-up generally think that the world would be all right if everybody were to be brought up quite differently. Now your mother's life has been—er—I suppose you know—

VIVIE Dont suppose anything, Mr Praed. I hardly know my mother. Since I was a child I have lived in England, at school or college, or with people paid to take charge of me. I have been boarded out all my life. My mother has lived in Brussels or Vienna and never let me go to her.

I only see her when she visits England for a few days. I dont complain: it's been very pleasant; for people have been very good to me; and there has always been plenty of money to make things smooth. But dont imagine I know anything about my mother. I know far less than you do.

PRAED [*very ill at ease*] In that case—[*He stops, quite at a loss. Then, with a forced attempt at gaiety*] But what nonsense we are talking! Of course you and your mother will get on capitally. [*He rises, and looks abroad at the view*]. What a charming little place you have here!

VIVIE [*unmoved*] Rather a violent change of subject, Mr Praed. Why wont my mother's life bear being talked about?

PRAED Oh, you really mustnt say that. Isnt it natural that I should have a certain delicacy in talking to my old friend's daughter about her behind her back? You and she will have plenty of opportunity of talking about it when she comes.

VIVIE No: she wont talk about it either. [*Rising*] However, I daresay you have good reasons for telling me nothing. Only, mind this, Mr Praed. I expect there will be a battle royal when my mother hears of my Chancery Lane project.

PRAED [*ruefully*] I'm afraid there will.

VIVIE Well, I shall win, because I want nothing but my fare to London to start there to-morrow earning my own living by devilling for Honoria. Besides, I have no mysteries to keep up; and it seems she has. I shall use that advantage over her if necessary.

PRAED [*greatly shocked*] Oh no! No, pray. Youd not do such a thing.

VIVIE Then tell me why not.

PRAED I really cannot. I appeal to your good feeling. [*She smiles at his sentimentality*]. Besides you may be too bold. Your mother is not to be trifled with when she's angry.

VIVIE You cant frighten me, Mr Praed. In that month at Chancery Lane I had opportunities of taking the measure of one or two women v e r y like my mother. You may back me to win. But if I hit harder in my ignorance than I need, remember that it is you who refuse to enlighten me. Now, let us drop the subject. [*She takes her chair and replaces it near the hammock with the same vigorous swing as before*].

PRAED [*taking a desperate resolution*] One word, Miss Warren. I had better tell you. It's very difficult; but—

MRS WARREN *and* SIR GEORGE CROFTS *arrive at the gate.* MRS WARREN *is between 40 and 50, formerly pretty, showily dressed in a brilliant hat and a gay blouse fitting tightly over her bust and flanked by fashionable sleeves. Rather spoilt and domineering, and decidedly vulgar, but, on the whole, a genial and fairly presentable old blackguard of a woman.*

CROFTS *is a tall powerfully-built man of about 50, fashionably dressed in the style of a young man. Nasal voice, reedier than might be expected from his strong frame. Clean-shaven bulldog jaws, large flat ears, and thick neck: gentlemanly combination of the most brutal types of city man, sporting man, and man about town.*

VIVIE Here they are. [*Coming to them as they enter the garden*] How do, mater? Mr Praed's been here this half hour waiting for you.

MRS WARREN Well, if youve been waiting, Praddy, it's your own fault: I thought youd have the gumption to know I was coming by the 3.10 train. Vivie: put your hat on, dear: youll get sunburnt. Oh, I forgot to introduce you. Sir George Crofts: my little Vivie.

CROFTS *advances to* VIVIE *with his most courtly manner. She nods, but makes no motion to shake hands.*

CROFTS May I shake hands with a young lady whom I have known by reputation very long as the daughter of one of my oldest friends?

VIVIE [*who has been looking him up and down sharply*] If you like. [*She takes his* tenderly proffered hand and gives it a squeeze that makes him open his eyes; then turns away, and says to her mother] Will you come in, or shall I get a couple more chairs? [*She goes into the porch for the chairs*].

MRS WARREN Well George, what do you think of her?

CROFTS [*ruefully*] She has a powerful fist. Did you shake hands with her, Praed?

PRAED Yes: it will pass off presently.

CROFTS I hope so. [VIVIE *reappears with two more chairs. He hurries to her assistance*]. Allow me.

MRS WARREN [*patronizingly*] Let Sir George help you with the chairs, dear.

VIVIE [*pitching them into his arms*] Here you are. [*She dusts her hands and turns to* MRS WARREN]. Youd like some tea, wouldnt you?

MRS WARREN [*sitting in* PRAED's *chair and fanning herself*] I'm dying for a drop to drink.

VIVIE I'll see about it. [*She goes into the cottage*].

SIR GEORGE *has by this time managed to unfold a chair and plant it beside* MRS WARREN, *on her left. He throws the other on the grass and sits down, looking dejected and rather foolish, with the handle of his stick in his mouth.* PRAED, *still very uneasy, fidgets about the garden on their right.*

MRS WARREN [*to* PRAED, *looking at* CROFTS] Just look at him, Praddy: he looks cheerful, dont he? He's been worrying my life out these three years to have that little girl of mine shewn to him; and now that Ive done it, he's quite out of countenance. [*Briskly*] Come! sit up, George; and take your stick out of your mouth. [CROFTS *sulkily obeys*].

PRAED I think, you know—if you dont mind my saying so—that we had better get out of the habit of thinking of her as a little girl. You see she has really distinguished herself; and I'm not sure, from what I have seen of her, that she is not older than any of us.

MRS WARREN [*greatly amused*] Only listen to him, George! Older than any of us! Well, she has been stuffing you nicely with her importance.

PRAED But young people are particularly sensitive about being treated in that way.

MRS WARREN Yes; and young people have to get all that nonsense taken out of them, and a good deal more besides. Dont you interfere, Praddy: I know how to treat my own child as well as you do. [PRAED, *with a grave shake of his head, walks up the garden with his hands behind his back.* MRS WARREN *pretends to laugh, but looks after him with perceptible concern. Then she whispers to* CROFTS] Whats the matter with him? What does he take it like that for?

CROFTS [*morosely*] Youre afraid of Praed.

MRS WARREN What! Me! Afraid of dear old Praddy! Why, a fly wouldnt be afraid of him.

CROFTS Y o u r e afraid of him.

MRS WARREN [*angry*] I'll trouble you to mind your own business, and not try any of your sulks on me. I'm not afraid of y o u, anyhow. If you cant make yourself agreeable, youd better go home. [*She gets up, and, turning her back on him, finds herself face to face with* PRAED]. Come, Praddy, I know it was only your tenderheartedness. Youre afraid I'll bully her.

PRAED My dear Kitty: you think I'm offended. Dont imagine that: pray dont. But you know I often notice things that escape you; and though you never take my advice, you sometimes admit afterwards that you ought to have taken it.

MRS WARREN Well, what do you notice now?

PRAED Only that Vivie is a grown woman. Pray, Kitty, treat her with every respect.

MRS WARREN [*with genuine amazement*] Respect! Treat my own daughter with respect! What next, pray!

VIVIE [*appearing at the cottage door and calling to* MRS WARREN] Mother: will you come to my room before tea?

MRS WARREN Yes, dearie. [*She laughs indulgently at* PRAED's *gravity, and pats*

him on the cheek as she passes him on her way to the porch*]. Dont be cross, Praddy. [*She follows* VIVIE *into the cottage*].

CROFTS [*furtively*] I say, Praed.

PRAED Yes.

CROFTS I want to ask you a rather particular question.

PRAED Certainly. [*He takes* MRS WARREN's *chair and sits close to* CROFTS].

CROFTS Thats right: they might hear us from the window. Look here: did Kitty ever tell you who that girl's father is?

PRAED Never.

CROFTS Have you any suspicion of who it might be?

PRAED None.

CROFTS [*not believing him*] I know, of course, that you perhaps might feel bound not to tell if she had said anything to you. But it's very awkward to be uncertain about it now that we shall be meeting the girl every day. We dont exactly know how we ought to feel towards her.

PRAED What difference can that make? We take her on her own merits. What does it matter who her father was?

CROFTS [*suspiciously*] Then you know who he was?

PRAED [*with a touch of temper*] I said no just now. Did you not hear me?

CROFTS Look here, Praed. I ask you as a particular favor. If you d o know [*movement of protest from* PRAED]—I only say, if you know, you might at least set my mind at rest about her. The fact is, I feel attracted.

PRAED [*sternly*] What do you mean?

CROFTS Oh, dont be alarmed: it's quite an innocent feeling. Thats what puzzles me about it. Why, for all I know, *I* might be her father.

PRAED You! Impossible!

CROFTS [*catching him up cunningly*] You know for certain that I'm not?

PRAED I know nothing about it, I tell you, any more than you. But really, Crofts— oh no, it's out of the question. Theres not the least resemblance.

CROFTS As to that, theres no resemblance between her and her mother that I can see. I suppose she's not y o u r daughter, is she?

PRAED [*rising indignantly*] Really, Crofts—!

CROFTS No offence, Praed. Quite allowable as between two men of the world.

PRAED [*recovering himself with an effort and speaking gently and gravely*] Now listen to me, my dear Crofts. [*He sits down again*]. I have nothing to do with that side of Mrs Warren's life, and never had. She has never spoken to me about it; and of course I have never spoken to her about it. Your delicacy will tell you that a handsome women needs s o m e friends who are not—well, not on that footing with her. The effect of her own beauty would become a torment to her if she could not escape from it occasionally. You are probably on much more confidential terms with Kitty than I am. Surely you can ask her the question yourself.

CROFTS I have asked her, often enough. But she's so determined to keep the child all to herself that she would deny that it ever had a father if she could. [*Rising*] I'm thoroughly uncomfortable about it, Praed.

PRAED [*rising also*] Well, as you are, at all events, old enough to be her father, I dont mind agreeing that we both regard Miss Vivie in a parental way, as a young girl whom we are bound to protect and help. What do you say?

CROFTS [*aggressively*] I'm no older than you, if you come to that.

PRAED Yes you are, my dear fellow: you were born old. I was born a boy: Ive never been able to feel the assurance of a grown-up man in my life. [*He folds his chair and carries it to the porch*].

MRS WARREN [*calling from within the cottage*] Prad-dee! George! Tea-ea-ea-ea!

CROFTS [*hastily*] She's calling us. [*He hurries in*].

PRAED *shakes his head bodingly, and is following* CROFTS *when he is hailed by a young gentleman who has just appeared*

on the common, and is making for the gate. He is pleasant, pretty, smartly dressed, cleverly good-for-nothing, not long turned 20, with a charming voice and agreeably disrespectful manners. He carries a light sporting magazine rifle.

THE YOUNG GENTLEMAN Hallo! Praed!

PRAED Why, Frank Gardner! [FRANK *comes in and shakes hands cordially*]. What on earth are you doing here?

FRANK Staying with my father.

PRAED The Roman father?

FRANK He's rector here. I'm living with my people this autumn for the sake of economy. Things came to a crisis in July: the Roman father had to pay my debts. He's stony broke in consequence; and so am I. What are you up to in these parts? Do you know the people here?

PRAED Yes: I'm spending the day with a Miss Warren.

FRANK [*enthusiastically*] What! Do you know Vivie? Isnt she a jolly girl? I'm teaching her to shoot with this [*putting down the rifle*]. I'm so glad she knows you: youre just the sort of fellow she ought to know. [*He smiles, and raises the charming voice almost to a singing tone as he exclaims*] It's e v e r so jolly to find you here, Praed.

PRAED I'm an old friend of her mother. Mrs Warren brought me over to make her daughter's acquaintance.

FRANK The mother! Is s h e here?

PRAED Yes: inside, at tea.

MRS WARREN [*calling from within*] Prad-dee-ee-ee-eee! The tea-cake'll be cold.

PRAED [*calling*] Yes, Mrs Warren. In a moment. Ive just met a friend here.

MRS WARREN A what?

PRAED [*louder*] A friend.

MRS WARREN Bring him in.

PRAED All right. [*To* FRANK] Will you accept the invitation?

FRANK [*incredulous, but immensely amused*] Is that Vivie's mother?

PRAED Yes.

FRANK By Jove! What a lark! Do you think she'll like me?

PRAED   Ive no doubt youll make yourself popular, as usual. Come in and try [*moving towards the house*].

FRANK   Stop a bit. [*Seriously*] I want to take you into my confidence.

PRAED   Pray dont. It's only some fresh folly, like the barmaid at Redhill.

FRANK   It's ever so much more serious than that. You say youve only just met Vivie for the first time?

PRAED   Yes.

FRANK   [*rhapsodically*] Then you can have no idea what a girl she is. Such character! Such sense! And her cleverness! Oh, my eye, Praed, but I can tell you she i s clever! And—need I add?—she loves me.

CROFTS   [*putting his head out of the window*] I say, Praed: what are you about? D o come along. [*He disappears*].

FRANK   Hallo! Sort of chap that would take a prize at a dog show, aint he? Who's he?

PRAED   Sir George Crofts, an old friend of Mrs Warren's. I think we had better come in.

On their way to the porch they are interrupted by a call from the gate. Turning, they see an elderly clergyman looking over it.

THE CLERGYMAN   [*calling*] Frank!

FRANK   Hallo! [*To* PRAED] The Roman father. [*To the clergyman*] Yes, gov'nor: all right: presently. [*To* PRAED] Look here, Praed: youd better go in to tea. I'll join you directly.

PRAED   Very good. [*He goes into the cottage*].

The clergyman remains outside the gate, with his hands on the top of it. The REV. SAMUEL GARDNER, *a beneficed clergyman of the Established Church, is over 50. Externally he is pretentious, booming, noisy, important. Really he is that obsolescent social phenomenon the fool of the family dumped on the Church by his father, the patron, clamorously asserting himself as father and clergyman without being able to command respect in either capacity.*

REV. S.   Well, sir. Who are your friends here, if I may ask?

FRANK   Oh, it's all right, gov'nor! Come in.

REV. S.   No sir; not until I know whose garden I am entering.

FRANK   It's all right. It's Miss Warren's.

REV. S.   I have not seen her at church since she came.

FRANK   Of course not: she's a third wrangler. Ever so intellectual. Took a higher degree than you did; so why should she go to hear you preach?

REV. S.   Dont be disrespectful, sir.

FRANK   Oh, it dont matter: nobody hears us. Come in. [*He opens the gate, unceremoniously pulling his father with it into the garden*]. I want to introduce you to her. Do you remember the advice you gave me last July, gov'nor?

REV. S.   [*severely*] Yes. I advised you to conquer your idleness and flippancy, and to work your way into an honorable profession and live on it and not upon me.

FRANK   No: thats what you thought of afterwards. What you actually said was that since I had neither brains nor money, I'd better turn my good looks to account by marrying somebody with both. Well, look here. Miss Warren has brains: you cant deny that.

REV. S.   Brains are not everything.

FRANK   No, of course not: theres the money—

REV. S.   [*interrupting him austerely*] I was not thinking of money, sir. I was speaking of higher things. Social position, for instance.

FRANK   I dont care a rap about that.

REV. S.   But I do, sir.

FRANK   Well, nobody wants y o u to marry her. Anyhow, she has what amounts to a high Cambridge degree; and she seems to have as much money as she wants.

REV. S.   [*sinking into a feeble vein of humor*] I greatly doubt whether she has as much money as y o u will want.

FRANK   Oh, come: I havnt been so very extravagant. I live ever so quietly; I dont drink; I dont bet much; and I never go regularly on the razzle-dazzle as you did when you were my age.

REV. S. [*booming hollowly*] Silence, sir.

FRANK Well, you told me yourself, when I was making ever such an ass of myself about the barmaid at Redhill, that you once offered a woman £50 for the letters you wrote to her when—

REV. S. [*terrified*] Sh-sh-sh, Frank, for Heaven's sake! [*He looks round apprehensively. Seeing no one within earshot he plucks up courage to boom again, but more subduedly*]. You are taking an ungentlemanly advantage of what I confided to you for your own good, to save you from an error you would have repented all your life long. Take warning by your father's follies, sir; and dont make them an excuse for your own.

FRANK Did you ever hear the story of the Duke of Wellington and his letters?

REV. S. No, sir; and I dont want to hear it.

FRANK The old Iron Duke didnt throw away £50: not he. He just wrote: "Dear Jenny: publish and be damned! Yours affectionately, Wellington." Thats what you should have done.

REV. S. [*piteously*] Frank, my boy: when I wrote those letters I put myself into that woman's power. When I told you about them I put myself, to some extent, I am sorry to say, in your power. She refused my money with these words, which I shall never forget. "Knowledge is power" she said; "and I never sell power." Thats more than twenty years ago; and she has never made use of her power or caused me a moment's uneasiness. You are behaving worse to me than she did, Frank.

FRANK Oh yes I dare say! Did you ever preach at her the way you preach at me every day?

REV. S. [*wounded almost to tears*] I leave you sir. You are incorrigible. [*He turns towards the gate*].

FRANK [*utterly unmoved*] Tell them I shant be home to tea, will you, gov'nor, like a good fellow? [*He moves towards the cottage door and is met by* PRAED *and* VIVIE *coming out*].

VIVIE [*to* FRANK] Is that your father, Frank? I do so want to meet him.

FRANK Certainly. [*Calling after his father*] Gov'nor. Youre wanted. [*The parson turns at the gate, fumbling nervously at his hat.* PRAED *crosses the garden to the opposite side, beaming in anticipation of civilities*]. My father: Miss Warren.

VIVIE [*going to the clergyman and shaking his hand*] Very glad to see you here, Mr Gardner. [*Calling to the cottage*] Mother: come along: youre wanted.

MRS WARREN *appears on the threshold, and is immediately transfixed recognizing the clergyman.*

VIVIE [*continuing*] Let me introduce—

MRS WARREN [*swooping on the* REVEREND SAMUEL] Why, it's Sam Gardner, gone into the Church! Well, I never! Dont you know us, Sam? This is George Crofts, as large as life and twice as natural. Dont you remember me?

REV. S. [*very red*] I really—er—

MRS WARREN Of course you do. Why, I have a whole album of your letters still: I came across them only the other day.

REV. S. [*miserably confused*] Miss Vavasour,[2] I believe.

MRS WARREN [*correcting him quickly in a loud whisper*] Tch! Nonsense! Mrs Warren: dont you see my daughter there?

Act Two

Inside the cottage after nightfall. Looking eastward from within instead of westward from without, the latticed window, with its curtains drawn, is now seen in the middle of the front wall of the cottage, with the porch door to the left of it. In the left-hand side wall is the door leading to the kitchen. Farther back against the same wall is a dresser with a candle and matches on it, and FRANK'S

---

2 Miss Vavasour was a name commonly used as a pseudonym by prostitutes.

rifle standing beside them, with the barrel resting in the plate-rack. In the centre a table stands with a lighted lamp on it. VIVIE's *books and writing materials are on a table to the right of the window, against the wall. The fireplace is on the right, with a settle: there is no fire. Two of the chairs are set right and left of the table.*

The cottage door opens, shewing a fine starlit night without; and MRS WARREN, *her shoulders wrapped in a shawl borrowed from* VIVIE, *enters, followed by* FRANK, *who throws his cap on the window seat. She has had enough of walking, and gives a gasp of relief as she unpins her hat; takes it off; sticks the pin through the crown; and puts it on the table.*

MRS WARREN   O Lord! I dont know which is the worst of the country, the walking or the sitting at home with nothing to do. I could do with a whisky and soda now very well, if only they had such a thing in this place.

FRANK   Perhaps Vivie's got some.

MRS WARREN   Nonsense! What would a young girl like her be doing with such things! Never mind: it dont matter. I wonder how she passes her time here! I'd a good deal rather be in Vienna.

FRANK   Let me take you there. [*He helps her to take off her shawl, gallantly giving her shoulders a very perceptible squeeze as he does so*].

MRS WARREN   Ah! would you? I'm beginning to think youre a chip of the old block.

FRANK   Like the gov'nor, eh? [*He hangs the shawl on the nearest chair, and sits down*].

MRS WARREN   Never you mind. What do you know about such things? Youre only a boy. [*She goes to the hearth, to be farther from temptation*].

FRANK   Do come to Vienna with me? It'd be ever such larks.

MRS WARREN   No, thank you. Vienna is no place for you—at least not until youre a little older. [*She nods at him to emphasize this piece of advice. He makes a mock-piteous face, belied by his laughing eyes. She looks at him; then comes back to him*]. Now, look here, little boy [*taking his face in her hands and turning it up to her*]: I know you through and through by your likeness to your father, better than you know yourself. Dont you go taking any silly ideas into your head about me. Do you hear?

FRANK [*gallantly wooing her with his voice*] Cant help it, my dear Mrs Warren: it runs in the family.

She pretends to box his ears; then looks at the pretty laughing upturned face for a moment, tempted. At last she kisses him, and immediately turns away, out of patience with herself.

MRS WARREN   There! I shouldnt have done that. I a m wicked. Never you mind, my dear: it's only a motherly kiss. Go and make love to Vivie.

FRANK   So I have.

MRS WARREN [*turning on him with a sharp note of alarm in her voice*]   What!

FRANK   Vivie and I are ever such chums.

MRS WARREN   What do you mean? Now see here: I wont have any young scamp tampering with my little girl. Do you hear? I wont have it.

FRANK [*quite unabashed*]   My dear Mrs Warren: dont you be alarmed. My intentions are honorable: ever so honorable; and your little girl is jolly well able to take care of herself. She dont need looking after half so much as her mother. She aint so handsome, you know.

MRS WARREN [*taken aback by his assurance*] Well, you h a v e got a nice healthy two inches thick of cheek all over you. I dont know where you got it. Not from your father, anyhow.

CROFTS [*in the garden*]   The gipsies, I suppose?

REV. S. [*replying*]   The broomsquires are far worse.

MRS WARREN [*to* FRANK] S-sh! Remember! youve had your warning.

CROFTS *and the* REVEREND SAMUEL *come in from the garden, the clergyman continuing his conversation as he enters.*

REV. S. The perjury at the Winchester assizes is deplorable.

MRS WARREN Well? What became of you two? And wheres Praddy and Vivie?

CROFTS [*putting his hat on the settle and his stick in the chimney corner*] They went up the hill. We went to the village. I wanted a drink. [*He sits down on the settle, putting his legs up along the seat*].

MRS WARREN Well, she oughtnt to go off like that without telling me. [*To* FRANK] Get your father a chair, Frank: where are your manners? [FRANK *springs up and gracefully offers his father his chair; then takes another from the wall and sits down at the table, in the middle, with his father on his right and* MRS WARREN *on his left*]. George: where are you going to stay tonight? You cant stay here. And whats Praddy going to do?

CROFTS Gardner'll put me up.

MRS WARREN Oh, no doubt youve taken care of yourself! But what about Praddy?

CROFTS Dont know. I suppose he can sleep at the inn.

MRS WARREN Havnt you room for him, Sam?

REV. S. Well—er—you see, as rector here, I am not free to do as I like. Er—what is Mr Praed's social position?

MRS WARREN Oh, he's all right: he's an architect. What an old stick-in-the-mud you are, Sam!

FRANK Yes, it's all right, gov'nor. He built that place down in Wales for the Duke. Caernarvon Castle they call it. You must have heard of it. [*He winks with lightning smartness at* MRS WARREN, *and regards his father blandly*].

REV. S. Oh, in that case, of course we shall only be too happy. I suppose he knows the Duke personally.

FRANK Oh, ever so intimately! We can stick him in Georgina's old room.

MRS WARREN Well, thats settled. Now if those two would only come in and let us have supper. Theyve no right to stay out after dark like this.

CROFTS [*aggressively*] What harm are they doing you?

MRS WARREN Well, harm or not, I dont like it.

FRANK Better not wait for them, Mrs Warren. Praed will stay out as long as possible. He has never known before what it is to stray over the heath on a summer night with my Vivie.

CROFTS [*sitting up in some consternation*] I say, you know! Come!

REV. S. [*rising, startled out of his professional manner into real force and sincerity*] Frank, once for all, it's out of the question. Mrs Warren will tell you that it's not to be thought of.

CROFTS Of course not.

FRANK [*with enchanting placidity*] Is that so, Mrs Warren?

MRS WARREN [*reflectively*] Well, Sam, I dont know. If the girl wants to get married, no good can come of keeping her unmarried.

REV. S. [*astounded*] But married to h i m! —your daughter to my son! Only think: it's impossible.

CROFTS Of course it's impossible. Dont be a fool, Kitty.

MRS WARREN [*nettled*] Why not? Isnt my daughter good enough for your son?

REV. S. But surely, my dear Mrs Warren, you know the reasons—

MRS WARREN [*defiantly*] I know no reasons. If you know any, you can tell them to the lad, or to the girl, or to your congregation, if you like.

REV. S. [*collapsing helplessly into his chair*] You know very well that I couldnt tell anyone the reasons. But my boy will believe me when I tell him there are reasons.

FRANK Quite right, Dad: he will. But has your boy's conduct ever been influenced by your reasons?

CROFTS You cant marry her; and thats all about it.

[*He gets up and stands on the hearth, with his back to the fireplace, frowning determinedly*].

MRS WARREN [*turning on him sharply*] What have you got to do with it, pray?

FRANK [*with his prettiest lyrical cadence*] Precisely what I was going to ask, myself, in my own graceful fashion.

CROFTS [*to* MRS WARREN] I suppose you dont want to marry the girl to a man younger than herself and without either a profession or twopence to keep her on. Ask Sam, if you dont believe me. [*To the parson*] How much more money are you going to give him?

REV. S. Not another penny. He has had his patrimony; and he spent the last of it in July. [MRS WARREN'*s face falls*].

CROFTS [*watching her*] There! I told you. [*He resumes his place on the settle and puts up his legs on the seat again, as if the matter were finally disposed of*].

FRANK [*plaintively*] This is ever so mercenary. Do you suppose Miss Warren's going to marry for money? If we love one another—

MRS WARREN Thank you. Your love's a pretty cheap commodity, my lad. If you have no means of keeping a wife, that settles it: you cant have Vivie.

FRANK [*much amused*] What do y o u say, gov'nor, eh?

REV. S. I agree with Mrs Warren.

FRANK And good old Crofts has already expressed his opinion.

CROFTS [*turning angrily on his elbow*] Look here: I want none of y o u r cheek.

FRANK [*pointedly*] I'm e v e r so sorry to surprise you, Crofts, but you allowed yourself the liberty of speaking to me like a father a moment ago. One father is enough, thank you.

CROFTS [*contemptuously*] Yah! [*He turns away again*].

FRANK [*rising*] Mrs Warren: I cannot give my Vivie up, even for your sake.

MRS WARREN [*muttering*] Young scamp!

FRANK [*continuing*] And as you no doubt intend to hold out other prospects to her,

I shall lose no time in placing my case before her. [*They stare at him; and he begins to declaim gracefully*]

He either fears his fate too much,
Or his deserts are small,
That dares not put it to the touch
To gain or lose it all.

The cottage door opens whilst he is reciting; and VIVIE *and* PRAED *come in. He breaks off.* PRAED *puts his hat on the dresser. There is an immediate improvement in the company's behavior.* CROFTS *takes down his legs from the settle and pulls himself together as* PRAED *joins him at the fireplace.* MRS WARREN *loses her ease of manner and takes refuge in querulousness.*

MRS WARREN Wherever have you been, Vivie?

VIVIE [*taking off her hat and throwing it carelessly on the table*] On the hill.

MRS WARREN Well, you shouldnt go off like that without letting me know. How could I tell what had become of you? And night coming on too!

VIVIE [*going to the door of the kitchen and opening it, ignoring her mother*] Now, about supper? [*All rise except* MRS WARREN]. We shall be rather crowded in here, I'm afraid.

MRS WARREN Did you hear what I said, Vivie?

VIVIE [*quietly*] Yes, mother. [*Reverting to the supper difficulty*] How many are we? [*Counting*] One, two, three, four, five, six. Well, two will have to wait until the rest are done: Mrs Alison has only plates and knives for four.

PRAED Oh, it doesn't matter about me. I—

VIVIE You have had a long walk and are hungry, Mr Praed: you shall have your supper at once. I can wait myself. I want one person to wait with me. Frank: are you hungry?

FRANK Not the least in the world. Completely off my peck, in fact.

MRS WARREN [*to* CROFTS]   Neither are you, George. You can wait.

CROFTS   Oh, hang it, I've eaten nothing since tea-time. Cant Sam do it?

FRANK   Would you starve my poor father?

REV. S. [*testily*]   Allow me to speak for myself, sir. I am perfectly willing to wait.

VIVIE [*decisively*]   Theres no need. Only two are wanted. [*She opens the door of the kitchen*]. Will you take my mother in, Mr Gardner. [*The parson takes* MRS WARREN; *and they pass into the kitchen.* PRAED *and* CROFTS *follow. All except* PRAED *clearly disapprove of the arrangement, but do not know how to resist it.* VIVIE *stands at the door looking in at them*]. Can you squeeze past to that corner, Mr Praed: it's rather a tight fit. Take care of your coat against the white-wash: thats right. Now, are you all comfortable?

PRAED [*within*]   Quite, thank you.

MRS WARREN [*within*]   Leave the door open, dearie. [VIVIE *frowns; but* FRANK *checks her with a gesture, and steals to the cottage door, which he softly sets wide open*]. Oh Lor, what a draught! Youd better shut it, dear.

VIVIE *shuts it with a slam, and then, noting with disgust that her mother's hat and shawl are lying about, takes them tidily to the window seat, whilst* FRANK *noiselessly shuts the cottage door.*

FRANK [*exulting*]   Aha! Got rid of em. Well, Vivvums: what do you think of my guvernor?

VIVIE [*preoccupied and serious*]   Ive hardly spoken to him. He doesn't strike me as being a particularly able person.

FRANK   Well, you know, the old man is not altogether such a fool as he looks. You see, he was shoved into the Church rather; and in trying to live up to it he makes a much bigger ass of himself than he really is. I dont dislike him as much as you might expect. He means well. How do you think youll get on with him?

VIVIE [*rather grimly*]   I dont think my future life will be much concerned with

him, or with any of that old circle of my mother's, except perhaps Praed. [*She sits down on the settle*]. What do you think of my mother?

FRANK   Really and truly?

VIVIE   Yes, really and truly.

FRANK   Well, she's ever so jolly. But she's rather a caution, isnt she? And Crofts! Oh, my eye, Crofts! [*He sits beside her*].

VIVIE   What a lot, Frank!

FRANK   What a crew!

VIVIE [*with intense contempt for them*]   If I thought that *I* was like that—that I was going to be a waster, shifting along from one meal to another with no purpose, and no character, and no grit in me, I'd open an artery and bleed to death without one moment's hesitation.

FRANK   Oh no, you wouldnt. Why should they take any grind when they can afford not to? I wish I had their luck. No: what I object to is their form. It isnt the thing: it's slovenly, ever so slovenly.

VIVIE   Do you think your form will be any better when youre as old as Crofts, if you dont work?

FRANK   Of course I do. Ever so much better. Vivvums mustnt lecture: her little boy's incorrigible. [*He attempts to take her face caressingly in his hands*].

VIVIE [*striking his hands down sharply*]   Off with you: Vivvums is not in a humor for petting her little boy this evening. [*She rises and comes forward to the other side of the room*].

FRANK [*following her*]   How unkind!

VIVIE [*stamping at him*]   Be serious. I'm serious.

FRANK   Good. Let us talk learnedly. Miss Warren: do you know that all the most advanced thinkers are agreed that half the diseases of modern civilization are due to starvation of the affections in the young. Now, I—

VIVIE [*cutting him short*]   You are very tiresome. [*She opens the inner door*]. Have you room for Frank there? He's complaining of starvation.

MRS WARREN [*within*]   Of course there is [*clatter of knives and glasses as she moves the things on the table*]. Here! theres room now beside me. Come along, Mr Frank.

FRANK Her little boy will be ever so even with his Vivvums for this. [*He passes into the kitchen*].

MRS WARREN [*within*] Here, Vivie: come on you too, child. You must be famished. [*She enters, followed by* CROFTS, *who holds the door open for* VIVIE *with marked deference. She goes out without looking at him; and he shuts the door after her*]. Why, George, you cant be done: youve eaten nothing. Is there anything wrong with you?

CROFTS Oh, all I wanted was a drink. [*He thrusts his hands in his pockets, and begins prowling about the room, restless and sulky*].

MRS WARREN Well, I like enough to eat. But a little of that cold beef and cheese and lettuce goes a long way. [*With a sigh of only half repletion she sits down lazily on the settle*].

CROFTS What do you go encouraging that young pup for?

MRS WARREN [*on the alert at once*] Now see here, George: what are you up to about that girl? Ive been watching your way of looking at her. Remember: I know you and what your looks mean.

CROFTS Theres no harm in looking at her, is there?

MRS WARREN I'd put you out and pack you back to London pretty soon if I saw any of your nonsense. My girl's little finger is more to me than your whole body and soul. [CROFTS *receives this with a sneering grin.* MRS WARREN, *flushing a little at her failure to impose on him in the character of a theatrically devoted mother, adds in a lower key*] Make your mind easy: the young pup has no more chance than you have.

CROFTS Maynt a man take an interest in a girl?

MRS WARREN Not a man like you.

CROFTS How old is she?

MRS WARREN Never you mind how old she is.

CROFTS Why do you make such a secret of it?

MRS WARREN Because I choose.

CROFTS Well, I'm not fifty yet; and my property is as good as ever it was—

MRS WARREN [*interrupting him*] Yes; because youre as stingy as youre vicious.

CROFTS [*continuing*] And a baronet isnt to be picked up every day. No other man in my position would put up with you for a mother-in-law. Why shouldnt she marry me?

MRS WARREN You!

CROFTS We three could live together quite comfortably. I'd die before her and leave her a bouncing widow with plenty of money. Why not? It's been growing in my mind all the time Ive been walking with that fool inside there.

MRS WARREN [*revolted*] Yes: it's the sort of thing that w o u l d grow in your mind.

He halts in his prowling; and the two look at one another, she steadfastly, with a sort of awe behind her contemptuous disgust: he stealthily, with a carnal gleam in his eye and a loose grin.

CROFTS [*suddenly becoming anxious and urgent as he sees no sign of sympathy in her*] Look here, Kitty: youre a sensible woman: you neednt put on any moral airs. I'll ask no more questions; and you need answer none. I'll settle the whole property on her; and if you want a cheque for yourself on the wedding day, you can name any figure you like—in reason.

MRS WARREN So it's come to that with you, George, like all the other worn-out old creatures!

CROFTS [*savagely*] Damn you!

Before she can retort the door of the kitchen is opened; and the voices of the others are heard returning. CROFTS, *unable to recover his presence of mind, hurries out of the cottage. The clergyman appears at the kitchen door.*

REV. S. [*looking round*] Where is Sir George?

MRS WARREN Gone out to have a pipe. [*The clergyman takes his hat from the table, and joins* MRS WARREN *at the fireside. Meanwhile* VIVIE *comes in, followed by* FRANK, *who collapses into the nearest chair with an air of extreme exhaustion.* MRS WARREN *looks round at* VIVIE *and says, with her affectation of maternal patronage even more forced than usual*] Well, dearie: have you had a good supper?

VIVIE You know what Mrs Alison's suppers are. [*She turns to* FRANK *and pets him*]. Poor Frank! was all the beef gone? did it get nothing but bread and cheese and ginger beer? [*Seriously, as if she had done quite enough trifling for one evening*] Her butter is really awful. I must get some down from the stores.

FRANK Do, in Heaven's name!

VIVIE *goes to the writing-table and makes a memorandum to order the butter.* PRAED *comes in from the kitchen, putting up his handkerchief, which he has been using as a napkin.*

REV. S. Frank, my boy: it is time for us to be thinking of home. Your mother does not know yet that we have visitors.

PRAED I'm afraid we're giving trouble.

FRANK [*rising*] Not the least in the world: my mother will be delighted to see you. She's a genuinely intellectual artistic woman; and she sees nobody here from one year's end to another except the gov'nor; so you can imagine how jolly dull it pans out for her. [*To his father*] Y o u r e not intellectual or artistic are you, pater? So take Praed home at once; and I'll stay here and entertain Mrs Warren. Youll pick up Crofts in the garden. He'll be excellent company for the bull-pup.

PRAED [*taking his hat from the dresser, and coming close to* FRANK] Come with us, Frank. Mrs Warren has not seen Miss Vivie for a long time; and we have prevented them from having a moment together yet.

FRANK [*quite softened, and looking at* PRAED *with romantic admiration*] Of course. I forgot. Ever so thanks for reminding me. Perfect gentleman, Praddy. Always were. My ideal through life. [*He rises to go, but pauses a moment between the two older men, and puts his hand on* PRAED's *shoulder*]. Ah, if you had only been my father instead of this unworthy old man! [*He puts his other hand on his father's shoulder*].

REV. S. [*blustering*] Silence, sir, silence: you are profane.

MRS WARREN [*laughing heartily*] You should keep him in better order, Sam. Goodnight. Here: take George his hat and stick with my compliments.

REV. S. [*taking them*] Goodnight. [*They shake hands. As he passes* VIVIE *he shakes hands with her also and bids her goodnight. Then, in booming command, to* FRANK] Come along, sir, at once. [*He goes out*].

MRS WARREN Byebye, Praddy.

PRAED Byebye, Kitty.

They shake hands affectionately and go out together, she accompanying him to the garden gate.

FRANK [*to* VIVIE] Kissums?

VIVIE [*fiercely*] No. I hate you. [*She takes a couple of books and some paper from the writing-table, and sits down with them at the middle table, at the end next the fireplace*].

FRANK [*grimacing*] Sorry. [*He goes for his cap and rifle.* MRS WARREN *returns. He takes her hand*] Good-night, d e a r Mrs Warren. [*He kisses her hand. She snatches it away, her lips tightening, and looks more than half disposed to box his ears. He laughs mischievously and runs off, clapping-to the door behind him*].

MRS WARREN [*resigning herself to an evening of boredom now that the men are gone*] Did you ever in your life hear anyone rattle on so? Isnt he a tease? [*She sits at the table*]. Now that I think of it, dearie, dont you go on encouraging him. I'm sure he's a regular good-for-nothing.

VIVIE [*rising to fetch more books*] I'm afraid so. Poor Frank! I shall have to get rid of him; but I shall feel sorry for him, though he's not worth it. That man Crofts does not seem to me to be good for much either: is he? [*She throws the books on the table rather roughly*].

MRS WARREN [*galled by* VIVIE's *indifference*] What do you know of men, child, to talk that way about them? Youll have to make up your mind to see a good deal of Sir George Crofts, as he's a friend of mine.

VIVIE [*quite unmoved*] Why? [*She sits down and opens a book*]. Do you expect that we shall be much together? You and I, I mean?

MRS WARREN [*staring at her*] Of course: until youre married. Youre not going back to college again.

VIVIE Do you think my way of life would suit you? I doubt it.

MRS WARREN Y o u r way of life! What do you mean?

VIVIE [*cutting a page of her book with the paper knife on her chatelaine*] Has it really never occurred to you, mother, that I have a way of life like other people?

MRS WARREN What nonsense is this youre trying to talk? Do you want to shew your independence, now that youre a great little person at school? Dont be a fool, child.

VIVIE [*indulgently*] Thats all you have to say on the subject, is it, mother?

MRS WARREN [*puzzled, then angry*] Dont you keep on asking me questions like that. [*Violently*] Hold your tongue. [VIVIE *works on, losing no time, and saying nothing*]. You and your way of life, indeed! What next? [*She looks at* VIVIE *again. No reply*]. Your way of life will be what I please, so it will. [*Another pause*]. Ive been noticing these airs in you ever since you got that tripos or whatever you call it. If you think I'm going to put up with them youre mistaken; and the sooner you find it out, the better. [*Muttering*] All I have to say on the subject, indeed! [*Again raising her voice angrily*] Do you know who youre speaking to, Miss?

VIVIE [*looking across at her without raising her head from her book*] No. Who are you? What are you?

MRS WARREN [*rising breathless*] You young imp!

VIVIE Everybody knows my reputation, my social standing, and the profession I intend to pursue. I know nothing about you. What is that way of life which you invite me to share with you and Sir George Crofts, pray?

MRS WARREN Take care. I shall do something I'll be sorry for after, and you too.

VIVIE [*putting aside her books with cool decision*] Well, let us drop the subject until you are better able to face it. [*Looking critically at her mother*] You want some good walks and a little lawn tennis to set you up. You are shockingly out of condition: you were not able to manage twenty yards uphill today without stopping to pant; and your wrists are mere rolls of fat. Look at mine. [*She holds out her wrists*].

MRS WARREN [*after looking at her helplessly, begins to whimper*] Vivie—

VIVIE [*springing up sharply*] Now pray dont begin to cry. Anything but that. I really cannot stand whimpering. I will go out of the room if you do.

MRS WARREN [*piteously*] Oh, my darling, how can you be so hard on me? Have I no rights over you as your mother?

VIVIE A r e you my mother?

MRS WARREN [*appalled*] A m I your mother! Oh, Vivie!

VIVIE Then where are our relatives? my father? our family friends? You claim the rights of a mother: the right to call me fool and child; to speak to me as no woman in authority over me at college dare speak to me; to dictate my way of life; and to force on me the acquaintance of a brute whom anyone can see to be the most vicious sort of London man about town. Before I give myself the trouble to resist such claims, I may as well find out whether they have any real existence.

MRS WARREN [*distracted, throwing herself on her knees*] Oh no, no. Stop, stop. I a m your mother: I swear it. Oh, you cant mean to turn on me—my own child! it's not natural. You believe me, dont you? Say you believe me.

VIVIE   Who was my father?

MRS WARREN   You dont know what youre asking. I cant tell you.

VIVIE [*determinedly*]   Oh yes you can, if you like. I have a right to know; and you know very well that I have that right. You can refuse to tell me, if you please; but if you do, you will see the last of me tomorrow morning.

MRS WARREN   Oh, it's too horrible to hear you talk like that. You wouldnt—you c o u l d n t leave me.

VIVIE [*ruthlessly*]   Yes, without a moment's hesitation, if you trifle with me about this. [*Shivering with disgust*] How can I feel sure that I may not have the contaminated blood of that brutal waster in my veins?

MRS WARREN   No, no. On my oath it's not he, nor any of the rest that you have ever met. I'm certain of that, at least.

VIVIE'*s eyes fasten sternly on her mother as the significance of this flashes on her.*

VIVIE [*slowly*]   You are certain of that, at least. Ah! You mean that that is all you are certain of. [*Thoughtfully*] I see. [MRS WARREN *buries her face in her hands*]. Don't do that, mother: you know you dont feel it a bit. [MRS WARREN *takes down her hands and looks up deplorably at* VIVIE, *who takes out her watch and says*] Well, that is enough for tonight. At what hour would you like breakfast? Is half-past eight too early for you?

MRS WARREN [*wildly*]   My God, what sort of woman are you?

VIVIE [*coolly*]   The sort the world is mostly made of, I should hope. Otherwise I don't understand how it gets its business done. Come [*taking her mother by the wrist, and pulling her up pretty resolutely*]: pull yourself together. Thats right.

MRS WARREN [*querulously*]   Youre very rough with me, Vivie.

VIVIE   Nonsense. What about bed? It's past ten.

MRS WARREN [*passionately*]   Whats the use of my going to bed? Do you think I could sleep?

VIVIE   Why not? I shall.

MRS WARREN   You! youve no heart. [*She suddenly breaks out vehemently in her natural tongue—the dialect of a woman of the people—with all her affectations of maternal authority and conventional manners gone, and an overwhelming inspiration of true conviction and scorn in her*] Oh, I wont bear it: I wont put up with the injustice of it. What right have you to set yourself up above me like this? You boast of what you are to me—to m e, who gave you the chance of being what you are. What chance had I! Shame on you for a bad daughter and a stuck-up prude!

VIVIE [*sitting down with a shrug, no longer confident; for her replies, which have sounded sensible and strong to her so far, now begin to ring rather woodenly and even priggishly against the new tone of her mother*]   Dont think for a moment I set myself above you in any way. You attacked me with the conventional authority of a mother: I defended myself with the conventional superiority of a respectable woman. Frankly, I am not going to stand any of your nonsense; and when you drop it I shall not expect you to stand any of mine. I shall always respect your right to your own opinions and your own way of life.

MRS WARREN   My own opinions and my own way of life! Listen to her talking! Do you think I was brought up like you? able to pick and choose my own way of life? Do you think I did what I did because I liked it, or thought it right, or wouldnt rather have gone to college and been a lady if I'd had the chance?

VIVIE   Everybody has some choice, mother. The poorest girl alive may not be able to choose between being Queen of England or Principal of Newnham; but she can choose between ragpicking and flower-selling, according to her taste. People are always blaming their circumstances for what they are. I dont believe in circumstances. The people who get on in this world are the people who get up and look for the circumstances they want, and, if they cant find them, make them.

MRS WARREN   Oh, it's easy to talk, very easy, isnt it? Here! would you like to know what m y circumstances were?

VIVIE   Yes: you had better tell me. Wont you sit down?

MRS WARREN   Oh, I'll sit down: dont you be afraid. [*She plants her chair farther forward with brazen energy, and sits down. Vivie is impressed in spite of herself*]. D'you know what your gran'mother was?

VIVIE   No.

MRS WARREN   No you dont. I do. She called herself a widow and had a fried-fish shop down by the Mint, and kept herself and four daughters out of it. Two of us were sisters: that was me and Liz; and we were both good-looking and well made. I suppose our father was a well-fed man: mother pretended he was a gentleman; but I dont know. The other two were only half sisters: undersized, ugly, starved looking, hard working, honest poor creatures: Liz and I would have half-murdered them if mother hadnt half-murdered u s to keep our hands off them. They were the respectable ones. Well, what did they get by their respectability? I'll tell you. One of them worked in a whitelead factory twelve hours a day for nine shillings a week until she died of lead poisoning. She only expected to get her hands a little paralyzed; but she died. The other was always held up to us as a model because she married a Government laborer in the Deptford victualling yard, and kept his room and the three children neat and tidy on eighteen shillings a week—until he took to drink. That was worth being respectable for, wasnt it?

VIVIE   [*now thoughtfully attentive*]   Did you and your sister think so?

MRS WARREN   Liz didnt, I can tell you: she had more spirit. We both went to a church school—that was part of the lady-like airs we gave ourselves to be superior to the children that knew nothing and went nowhere—and we stayed there until Liz went out one night and never came back. I know the school-mistress thought I'd soon follow her example; for the clergyman was always warning me that Lizzie'd end by jumping off Waterloo Bridge. Poor fool: that was all he knew about it! But I was more afraid of the whitelead factory than I was of the river; and so would you have been in my place. That clergyman got me a situation as a scullery maid in a temperance restaurant where they sent out for anything you liked. Then I was waitress; and then I went to the bar at Waterloo station: fourteen hours a day serving drinks and washing glasses for four shillings a week and my board. That was considered a great promotion for me. Well, one cold, wretched night, when I was so tired I could hardly keep myself awake, who should come up for a half of Scotch but Lizzie, in a long fur cloak, elegant and comfortable, with a lot of sovereigns in her purse.

VIVIE   [*grimly*]   My aunt Lizzie!

MRS WARREN   Yes; and a very good aunt to have, too. She's living down at Winchester now, close to the cathedral, one of the most respectable ladies there. Chaperones girls at the county ball, if you please. No river for Liz, thank you! You remind me of Liz a little: she was a first-rate business woman—saved money from the beginning—never let herself look too like what she was—never lost her head or threw away a chance. When she saw I'd grown up good-looking she said to me across the bar "What are you doing there, you little fool? wearing out your health and your appearance for other people's profit!" Liz was saving money then to take a house for herself in Brussels; and she thought we two could save faster than one. So she lent me some money and gave me a start; and I saved steadily and first paid her back, and then went into business with her as her partner. Why shouldnt I have done it? The house in Brussels was real high class: a much better place for a woman to be in than the factory where Anne Jane got poisoned. None of our girls were ever treated as I was treated in the scullery of that temperance place, or at the Waterloo bar, or at home. Would you have had me stay in them and become a worn out old drudge before I was forty?

VIVIE [*intensely interested by this time*] No; but why did you choose that business? Saving money and good management will succeed in any business.

MRS WARREN Yes, saving money. But where can a woman get the money to save in any other business? Could y o u save out of four shillings a week and keep yourself dressed as well? Not you. Of course, if youre a plain woman and cant earn anything more; or if you have a turn for music, or the stage, or newspaper-writing: thats different. But neither Liz nor I had any turn for such things: all we had was our appearance and our turn for pleasing men. Do you think we were such fools as to let other people trade in our good looks by employing us as shopgirls, or barmaids, or waitresses, when we could trade in them ourselves and get all the profits instead of starvation wages? Not likely.

VIVIE You were certainly quite justified—from the business point of view.

MRS WARREN Yes; or any other point of view. What is any respectable girl brought up to do but to catch some rich man's fancy and get the benefit of his money by marrying him?—as if a marriage ceremony could make any difference in the right or wrong of the thing! Oh! the hypocrisy of the world makes me sick! Liz and I had to work and save and calculate just like other people; elseways we should be as poor as any good-for-nothing drunken waster of a woman that thinks her luck will last for ever. [*With great energy*] I despise such people: theyve no

character; and if theres a thing I hate in a woman, it's want of character.

VIVIE Come now, mother: frankly! Isnt it part of what you call character in a woman that she should greatly dislike such a way of making money?

MRS WARREN Why, of course. Everybody dislikes having to work and make money; but they have to do it all the same. I'm sure Ive often pitied a poor girl, tired out and in low spirits, having to try to please some man that she doesnt care two straws for—some half-drunken fool that thinks he's making himself agreeable when he's teasing and worrying and disgusting a woman so that hardly any money could pay her for putting up with it. But she has to bear with disagreeables and take the rough with the smooth, just like a nurse in a hospital or anyone else. It's not work that any woman would do for pleasure, goodness knows; though to hear the pious people talk you would suppose it was a bed of roses.

VIVIE Still, you consider it worth while. It pays.

MRS WARREN Of course it's worth while to a poor girl, if she can resist temptation and is good-looking and well conducted and sensible. It's far better than any other employment open to her. I always thought that oughtnt to be. It c a n t be right, Vivie, that there shouldnt be better opportunities for women. I stick to that: it's wrong. But it's so, right or wrong; and a girl must make the best of it. But of course it's not worth while for a lady. If you took to it youd be a fool; but I should have been a fool if I'd taken to anything else.

VIVIE [*more and more deeply moved*] Mother: suppose we were both as poor as you were in those wretched old days, are you quite sure that you wouldnt advise me to try the Waterloo bar, or marry a laborer, or even go into the factory?

MRS WARREN [*indignantly*] Of course not. What sort of mother do you take me for! How could you keep your self-respect in such starvation and slavery? And whats a woman worth? whats life worth? without self-respect! Why am I independent and able to give my daughter a first-rate education, when other women that had just as good opportunities are in the gutter? Because I always knew how to respect myself and control myself. Why is Liz looked up to in a cathedral town? The same reason. Where would we be now if we'd minded the clergyman's foolishness? Scrubbing floors for one and sixpence a day and nothing to look forward to but the workhouse infirmary. Dont you be led astray by people who dont know the world, my girl. The only way for a woman to provide for herself decently is for her to be good to some man that can afford to be good to her. If she's in his own station of life, let her make him marry her; but if she's far beneath him she cant expect it: why should she? it wouldnt be for her own happiness. Ask any lady in London society that has daughters; and she'll tell you the same, except that I tell you straight and she'll tell you crooked. Thats all the difference.

VIVIE [*fascinated, gazing at her*] My dear mother: you are a wonderful woman: you are stronger than all England. And are you really and truly not one wee bit doubtful—or—or—ashamed?

MRS WARREN Well, of course, dearie, it's only good manners to be ashamed of it: it's expected from a woman. Women have to pretend to feel a great deal that they dont feel. Liz used to be angry with me for plumping out the truth about it. She used to say that when every woman could learn enough from what was going on in the world before her eyes, there was no need to talk about it to her. But then Liz was such a perfect lady! She had the true instinct of it; while I was always a bit of a vulgarian. I used to be so pleased when you sent me your photos to see that you were growing up like Liz: youve just her ladylike, determined way. But I cant stand saying one thing when everyone knows I mean another. Whats the use in such hypocrisy? If people arrange the world that way for women, theres no good pretending it's arranged the other way. No: I never was a bit ashamed really. I consider I had a right to be proud of how we managed everything so respectably, and never had a word against us, and how the girls were so well taken care of. Some of them did very well: one of them married an ambassador. But of course now I darent talk about such things: whatever would they think of us! [*She yawns*]. Oh dear! I do believe I'm getting sleepy after all. [*She stretches herself lazily, thoroughly relieved by her explosion, and placidly ready for her night's rest*].

VIVIE I believe it is I who will not be able to sleep now. [*She goes to the dresser and lights the candle. Then she extinguishes the lamp, darkening the room a good deal*]. Better let in some fresh air before locking up. [*She opens the cottage door, and finds that it is broad moonlight*]. What a beautiful night! Look! [*She draws aside the curtains of the window. The landscape is seen bathed in the radiance of the harvest moon rising over Blackdown*].

MRS WARREN [*with a perfunctory glance at the scene*] Yes, dear; but take care you dont catch your death of cold from the night air.

VIVIE [*contemptuously*] Nonsense.

MRS WARREN [*querulously*] Oh yes: everything I say is nonsense, according to you.

VIVIE [*turning to her quickly*] No: really that is not so, mother. You have got completely the better of me tonight, though I intended it to be the other way. Let us be good friends now.

MRS WARREN [*shaking her head a little ruefully*] So it h a s been the other way. But I suppose I must give in to it. I always got the worst of it from Liz; and now I suppose it'll be the same with you.

VIVIE Well, never mind. Come: goodnight, dear old mother. [*She takes her mother in her arms*].

MRS WARREN [*fondly*] I brought you up well, didnt I, dearie?

VIVIE You did.

MRS WARREN And youll be good to your poor old mother for it, wont you?

VIVIE I will, dear. [*Kissing her*] Goodnight.

MRS WARREN [*with unction*] Blessings on my own dearie darling! a mother's blessing!

She embraces her daughter protectingly, instinctively looking upward for divine sanction.

Act Three

In the Rectory garden next morning, with the sun shining from a cloudless sky. The garden wall has a five-barred wooden gate, wide enough to admit a carriage, in the middle. Beside the gate hangs a bell on a coiled spring, communicating with a pull outside. The carriage drive comes down the middle of the garden and then swerves to its left, where it ends in a little gravelled circus opposite the Rectory porch. Beyond the gate is seen the dusty high road, parallel with the wall, bounded on the farther side by a strip of turf and an unfenced pine wood. On the lawn, between the house and the drive, is a clipped yew tree, with a garden bench in its shade. On the opposite side the garden is shut in by a box hedge; and there is a sundial on the turf, with an iron chair near it. A little path leads off through the box hedge, behind the sundial.

FRANK, seated on the chair near the sundial, on which he has placed the morning papers, is reading The Standard. *His father comes from the house, red-eyed and shivery, and meets* FRANK's *eye with misgiving.*

FRANK [*looking at his watch*] Half-past eleven. Nice hour for a rector to come down to breakfast!

REV. S. Dont mock, Frank: dont mock. I am a little—er—[*Shivering*]—

FRANK Off color?

REV. S. [*repudiating the expression*] No, sir: u n w e l l this morning. Wheres your mother?

FRANK Dont be alarmed: she's not here. Gone to town by the 11.13 with Bessie. She left several messages for you. Do you feel equal to receiving them now, or shall I wait til youve breakfasted?

REV. S. I h a v e breakfasted, sir. I am surprised at your mother going to town when we have people staying with us. Theyll think it very strange.

FRANK Possibly she has considered that. At all events, if Crofts is going to stay here, and you are going to sit up every night with him until four, recalling the incidents of your fiery youth, it is clearly my mother's duty, as a prudent housekeeper, to go up to the stores and order a barrel of whisky and a few hundred siphons.

REV. S. I did not observe that Sir George drank excessively.

FRANK You were not in a condition to, gov'nor.

REV. S. Do you mean to say that I—?

FRANK [*calmly*] I never saw a beneficed clergyman less sober. The anecdotes you told about your past career were so awful that I really dont think Praed would have passed the night under your roof if it hadnt been for the way my mother and he took to one another.

REV. S. Nonsense, sir. I am Sir George Croft's host. I must talk to him about something; and he has only one subject. Where is Mr. Praed now?

FRANK He is driving my mother and Bessie to the station.

REV. S. Is Crofts up yet?

FRANK Oh, long ago. He hasnt turned a hair: he's in much better practice than you. Has kept it up ever since, probably. He's taken himself off somewhere to smoke.

FRANK *resumes his paper. The parson turns disconsolately towards the gate; then comes back irresolutely.*

REV. S. Er—Frank.

FRANK Yes.

REV. S. Do you think the Warrens will expect to be asked here after yesterday afternoon?

FRANK Theyve been asked already.

REV. S. [*appalled*] What!!!

FRANK Crofts informed us at breakfast that you told him to bring Mrs Warren and Vivie over here today, and to invite them to make this house their home. My mother then found she must go to town by the 11.13 train.

REV. S. [*with despairing vehemence*] I never gave any such invitation. I never thought of such a thing.

FRANK [*compassionately*] How do you know, gov'nor, what you said and thought last night?

PRAED [*coming in through the hedge*] Good morning.

REV. S. Good morning. I must apologize for not having met you at breakfast. I have a touch of—of—

FRANK Clergyman's sore throat, Praed. Fortunately not chronic.

PRAED [*changing the subject*] Well, I must say your house is in a charming spot here. Really most charming.

REV. S. Yes: it is indeed. Frank will take you for a walk, Mr Praed, if you like. I'll ask you to excuse me: I must take the opportunity to write my sermon while Mrs Gardner is away and you are all amusing yourselves. You wont mind, will you?

PRAED Certainly not. Dont stand on the slightest ceremony with me.

REV. S. Thank you. I'll—er—er—[*He stammers his way to the porch and vanishes into the house*].

PRAED Curious thing it must be writing a sermon every week.

FRANK Ever so curious, if he did it. He buys em. He's gone for some soda water.

PRAED My dear boy: I wish you would be more respectful to your father. You know you can be so nice when you like.

FRANK My dear Praddy: you forget that I have to live with the governor. When two people live together—it dont matter whether theyre father and son or husband and wife or brother and sister—they cant keep up the polite humbug thats so easy for ten minutes on an afternoon call. Now the governor, who unites to many admirable domestic qualities the irresoluteness of a sheep and the pompousness and aggressiveness of a jackass—

PRAED No, pray, pray, my dear Frank, remember! He is your father.

FRANK I give him due credit for that. [*Rising and flinging down his paper*] But just imagine his telling Crofts to bring the Warrens over here! He must have been ever so drunk. You know, my dear Praddy, my mother wouldnt stand Mrs Warren for a moment. Vivie mustnt come here until she's gone back to town.

PRAED But your mother doesnt know anything about Mrs Warren, does she? [*He picks up the paper and sits down to read it*].

FRANK I dont know. Her journey to town looks as if she did. Not that my mother would mind in the ordinary way: she has stuck like a brick to lots of women who had got into trouble. But they were all nice women. Thats what makes the real difference. Mrs Warren, no doubt, has her merits; but she's ever so rowdy; and my mother simply wouldnt put up with her. So—hallo! [*This exclamation is provoked by the reappearance of the clergyman, who comes out of the house in haste and dismay*].

REV. S. Frank: Mrs Warren and her daughter are coming across the heath with Crofts: I saw them from the study windows. What a m I to say about your mother?

FRANK Stick on your hat and go out and say how delighted you are to see them; and that Frank's in the garden; and that mother and Bessie have been called to the bedside of a sick relative, and were ever so sorry they couldnt stop; and that you hope Mrs Warren slept well; and—and—say any blessed thing except the truth, and leave the rest to Providence.

REV. S. But how are we to get rid of them afterwards?

FRANK Theres no time to think of that

now. Here! [*He bounds into the house*].

REV. S. He's so impetuous. I dont know what to do with him, Mr Praed.

FRANK [*returning with clerical felt hat, which he claps on his father's head*] Now: off with you. [*Rushing him through the gate*]. Praed and I'll wait here, to give the thing an unpremeditated air. [*The clergyman, dazed but obedient, hurries off*].

FRANK We must get the old girl back to town somehow, Praed. Come! Honestly, dear Praddy, do you like seeing them together?

PRAED Oh, why not?

FRANK [*his teeth on edge*] Dont it make your flesh creep ever so little? that wicked old devil, up to every villainy under the sun, I'll swear, and Vivie—ugh!

PRAED Hush, pray. Theyre coming.

The clergyman and CROFTS *are seen coming along the road, followed by* MRS WARREN *and* VIVIE *walking affectionately together.*

FRANK Look: she actually has her arm round the old woman's waist. It's her right arm: she began it. She's gone sentimental, by God! Ugh! ugh! Now do you feel the creeps? [*The clergyman opens the gate; and Mrs Warren and Vivie pass him and stand in the middle of the garden looking at the house. Frank, in an ecstasy of dissimulation, turns gaily to Mrs Warren, exclaiming*] Ever so delighted to see you, Mrs Warren. This quiet old rectory garden becomes you perfectly.

MRS WARREN Well, I never! Did you hear that, George? He says I look well in a quiet old rectory garden.

REV. S. [*still holding the gate for Crofts, who loafs through it, heavily bored*] You look well everywhere, Mrs Warren.

FRANK Bravo, gov'nor! Now look here: lets have a treat before lunch. First lets see the church. Everyone has to do that. It's a regular old thirteenth century church, you know: the gov'nor's ever so fond of it, because he got up a restoration fund and

had it completely rebuilt six years ago. Praed will be able to shew its points.

PRAED [*rising*] Certainly, if the restoration has left any to shew.

REV. S. [*mooning hospitably at them*] I shall be pleased, I'm sure, if Sir George and Mrs Warren really care about it.

MRS WARREN Oh, come along and get it over.

CROFTS [*turning back towards the gate*] Ive no objection.

REV. S. Not that way. We go through the fields, if you dont mind. Round here. [*He leads the way by the little path through the box hedge*].

CROFTS Oh, all right. [*He goes with the parson*].

PRAED *follows with* MRS WARREN, VIVIE *does not stir: she watches them until they have gone, with all the lines of purpose in her face marking it strongly.*

FRANK Aint you coming?

VIVIE No. I want to give you a warning, Frank. You were making fun of my mother just now when you said that about the rectory garden. That is barred in future. Please treat my mother with as much respect as you treat your own.

FRANK My dear Viv: she wouldnt appreciate it: the two cases require different treatment. But what on earth has happened to you? Last night we were perfectly agreed as to your mother and her set. This morning I find you attitudinizing sentimentally with your arm round your parent's waist.

VIVIE [*flushing*] Attitudinizing!

FRANK That was how it struck me. First time I ever saw you do a second-rate thing.

VIVIE [*controlling herself*] Yes, Frank: there has been a change; but I dont think it a change for the worse. Yesterday I was a little prig.

FRANK And today?

VIVIE [*wincing; then looking at him steadily*] Today I know my mother better than you do.

FRANK Heaven forbid!

VIVIE   What do you mean?

FRANK   Viv: theres a freemasonry among thoroughly immoral people that you know nothing of. Youve too much character. T h a t s the bond between your mother and me: thats why I know her better than youll ever know her.

VIVIE   You are wrong: you know nothing about her. If you knew the circumstances against which my mother had to struggle—

FRANK   [*adroitly finishing the sentence for her*]   I should know why she is what she is, shouldnt I? What difference would that make? Circumstances or no circumstances, Viv, you wont be able to stand your mother.

VIVIE   [*very angrily*]   Why not?

FRANK   Because she's an old wretch, Viv. If you ever put your arm round her waist in my presence again, I'll shoot myself there and then as a protest against an exhibition which revolts me.

VIVIE   Must I choose between dropping your acquaintance and dropping my mother's?

FRANK   [*gracefully*]   That would put the old lady at ever such a disadvantage. No, Viv: your infatuated little boy will have to stick to you in any case. But he's all the more anxious that you shouldnt make mistakes. It's no use, Viv: your mother's impossible. She may be a good sort; but she's a bad lot, a very bad lot.

VIVIE   [*hotly*]   Frank—! [*He stands his ground. She turns away and sits down on the bench under the yew tree, struggling to recover her self-command. Then she says*] Is she to be deserted by all the world because she's what you call a bad lot? Has she no right to live?

FRANK   No fear of that, Viv: s h e wont ever be deserted. [*He sits on the bench beside her*].

VIVIE   But I am to desert her, I suppose.

FRANK   [*babyishly, lulling her and making love to her with his voice*]   Mustnt go live with her. Little family group of mother and daughter wouldnt be a success. Spoil our little group.

VIVIE   [*falling under the spell*]   What little group?

FRANK   The babes in the wood: Vivie and little Frank. [*He nestles against her like a weary child*] Lets go and get covered up with leaves.

VIVIE   [*rhythmically, rocking him like a nurse*]   Fast asleep, hand in hand, under the trees.

FRANK   The wise little girl with her silly little boy.

VIVIE   The dear little boy with his dowdy little girl.

FRANK   Ever so peaceful, and relieved from the imbecility of the little boy's father and the questionableness of the little girl's—

VIVIE   [*smothering the word against her breast*]   Sh-sh-sh-sh! little girl wants to forget all about her mother. [*They are silent for some moments, rocking one another. Then Vivie wakes up with a shock, exclaiming*] What a pair of fools we are! Come: sit up. Gracious! your hair. [*She smoothes it*]. I wonder do all grown up people play in that childish way when nobody is looking. I never did it when I was a child.

FRANK   Neither did I. You are my first playmate. [*He catches her hand to kiss it, but checks himself to look round first. Very unexpectedly, he sees* CROFTS *emerging from the box hedge*]. Oh damn!

VIVIE   Why damn, dear?

FRANK   [*whispering*]   Sh! Here's this brute Crofts. [*He sits farther away from her with an unconcerned air*].

CROFTS   Could I have a few words with you, Miss Vivie?

VIVIE   Certainly.

CROFTS   [*to* FRANK]   Youll excuse me, Gardner. Theyre waiting for you in the church, if you dont mind.

FRANK   [*rising*]   Anything to oblige you, Crofts—except church. If you should happen to want me, Vivvums, ring the gate bell. [*He goes into the house with unruffled suavity*].

CROFTS   [*watching him with a crafty air as he disappears, and speaking to* VIVIE *with an assumption of being on privileged terms with her*] Pleasant young fellow that, Miss Vivie. Pity he has no money, isnt it?

VIVIE Do you think so?

CROFTS Well, whats he to do? No profession. No property. Whats he good for?

VIVIE I realize his disadvantages, Sir George.

CROFTS [*a little taken aback at being so precisely interpreted*] Oh, it's not that. But while we're in this world we're in it; and money's money. [VIVIE *does not answer*]. Nice day, isn't it?

VIVIE [*with scarcely veiled contempt for this effort at conversation*] Very.

CROFTS [*with brutal good humor, as if he liked her pluck*] Well, thats not what I came to say. [*Sitting down beside her*] Now listen, Miss Vivie. I'm quite aware that I'm not a young lady's man.

VIVIE Indeed, Sir George?

CROFTS No; and to tell you the honest truth I dont want to be either. But when I say a thing I mean it; when I feel a sentiment I feel it in earnest; and what I value I pay hard money for. Thats the sort of man I am.

VIVIE It does you great credit, I'm sure.

CROFTS Oh, I dont mean to praise myself. I have my faults, Heaven knows: no man is more sensible of that than I am. I know I'm not perfect: thats one of the advantages of being a middle-aged man; for I'm not a young man, and I know it. But my code is a simple one, and, I think, a good one. Honor between man and man; fidelity between man and woman; and no cant about this religion or that religion, but an honest belief that things are making for good on the whole.

VIVIE [*with biting irony*] "A power, not ourselves, that makes for righteousness," eh?

CROFTS [*taking her seriously*] Oh certainly. Not ourselves, of course. You understand what I mean. Well, now as to practical matters. You may have an idea that Ive flung my money about; but I havnt: I'm richer today than when I first came into the property. Ive used my knowledge of the world to invest my money in ways that other men have overlooked; and whatever else I may be, I'm a safe man from the money point of view.

VIVIE It's very kind of you to tell me all this.

CROFTS Oh well, come, Miss Vivie: you neednt pretend you dont see what I'm driving at. I want to settle down with a Lady Crofts. I suppose you think me very blunt, eh?

VIVIE Not at all: I am much obliged to you for being so definite and businesslike. I quite appreciate the offer: the money, the position, L a d y C r o f t s, and so on. But I think I will say no, if you dont mind. I'd rather not. [*She rises, and strolls across to the sundial to get out of his immediate neighborhood*].

CROFTS [*not at all discouraged, and taking advantage of the additional room left him on the seat to spread himself comfortably, as if a few preliminary refusals were part of the inevitable routine of courtship*] I'm in no hurry. It was only just to let you know in case young Gardner should try to trap you. Leave the question open.

VIVIE [*sharply*] My no is final. I wont go back from it.

CROFTS *is not impressed. He grins; leans forward with his elbows on his knees to prod with his stick at some unfortunate insect in the grass; and looks cunningly at her. She turns away impatiently.*

CROFTS I'm a good deal older than you. Twenty-five years: quarter of a century. I shant live for ever; and I'll take care that you shall be well off when I'm gone.

VIVIE I am proof against even that inducement, Sir George. Dont you think youd better take your answer? There is not the slightest chance of my altering it.

CROFTS [*rising, after a final slash at a daisy, and coming nearer to her*] Well, no matter. I could tell you some things that would change your mind fast enough; but I wont, because I'd rather win you by honest affection. I was a good friend to your mother: ask her whether I wasnt. She'd never have made the money that paid for your education if it hadnt been for my advice and help, not to mention the money I advanced her. There are not many men would have stood by her as I have. I put not less than £40,000 into it, from first to last.

VIVIE [*staring at him*] Do you mean to say you were my mother's business partner?

CROFTS Yes. Now just think of all the trouble and the explanations it would save if we were to keep the whole thing in the family, so to speak. Ask your mother whether she'd like to have to explain all her affairs to a perfect stranger.

VIVIE I see no difficulty, since I understand that the business is wound up, and the money invested.

CROFTS [*stopping short, amazed*] Wound up! Wind up a business thats paying 35 per cent in the worst years! Not likely. Who told you that?

VIVIE [*her color quite gone*] Do you mean that it is still—? [*She stops abruptly, and puts her hand on the sundial to support herself. Then she gets quickly to the iron chair and sits down*]. What business are you talking about?

CROFTS Well, the fact is it's not what would be considered exactly a high-class business in my set—the county set, you know—our set it will be if you think better of my offer. Not that theres any mystery about it: dont think that. Of course you know by your mother's being in it that it's perfectly straight and honest. Ive known her for many years; and I can say of her that she'd cut off her hands sooner than touch anything that was not what it ought to be. I'll tell you all about it if you like. I don't know whether youve found in travelling how hard it is to find a really comfortable private hotel.

VIVIE [*sickened, averting her face*] Yes: go on.

CROFTS Well, thats all it is. Your mother has a genius for managing such things. We've got two in Brussels, one in Ostend, one in Vienna, and two in Budapest. Of course there are others besides ourselves in it; but we hold most of the capital; and your mother's indispensable as managing director. Youve noticed, I daresay, that she travels a good deal. But you see you cant mention such things in society. Once let out the word hotel and everybody says you keep a public-house. You wouldnt like people to say that of your mother, would you? Thats why we're so reserved about it. By the way, youll keep it to yourself, wont you? Since it's been a secret so long, it had better remain so.

VIVIE And this is the business you invite me to join you in?

CROFTS Oh no. My wife shant be troubled with business. Youll not be in it more than youve always been.

VIVIE *I* always been! What do you mean?

CROFTS Only that youve always lived on it. It paid for your education and the dress you have on your back. Dont turn up your nose at business, Miss Vivie: where would your Newnhams and Girtons be without it?

VIVIE [*rising, almost beside herself*] Take care. I know what this business is.

CROFTS [*starting, with a suppressed oath*] Who told you?

VIVIE Your partner. My mother.

CROFTS [*black with rage*] The old—

VIVIE Just so.

He swallows the epithet and stands for a moment swearing and raging foully to himself. But he knows that his cue is to be sympathetic. He takes refuge in generous indignation.

CROFTS She ought to have had more consideration for you. *I'd* never have told you.

VIVIE I think you would probably have told me when we were married: it would have been a convenient weapon to break me in with.

CROFTS [*quite sincerely*] I never intended that. On my word as a gentleman I didnt.

VIVIE *wonders at him. Her sense of the irony of his protest cools and braces her. She replies with contemptuous self-possession.*

VIVIE It does not matter. I suppose you understand that when we leave here to-day our acquaintance ceases.

CROFTS Why? Is it for helping your mother?

VIVIE My mother was a very poor woman who had no reasonable choice but to do as she did. You were a rich gentleman; and you did the same for the sake of 35 per cent. You are a pretty common sort of scoundrel, I think. That is my opinion of you.

CROFTS [*after a stare: not at all displeased, and much more at his ease on these frank terms than on their former ceremonious ones*] Ha! ha! ha! ha! Go it, little missie, go it: it doesnt hurt me and it amuses you. Why the devil shouldnt I invest my money that way? I take the interest on my capital like other people: I hope you dont think I dirty my own hands with the work. Come! you wouldnt refuse the acquaintance of my mother's cousin the Duke of Belgravia because some of the rents he gets are earned in queer ways. You wouldnt cut the Archbishop of Canterbury, I suppose, because the Ecclesiastical Commissioners have a few publicans and sinners among their tenants. Do you remember your Crofts scholarship at Newnham? Well, that was founded by my brother the M.P. He gets his 22 per cent out of a factory with 600 girls in it, and not one of them getting wages enough to live on. How d'ye suppose they manage when they have no family to fall back on? Ask your mother. And do you expect me to turn my back on 35 per cent when all the rest are pocketing what they can, like sensible men? No such fool! If youre going to pick and choose your acquaintances on moral principles, youd better clear out of this country, unless you want to cut yourself out of all decent society.

VIVIE [*conscience stricken*] You might go on to point out that I myself never asked where the money I spent came from. I believe I am just as bad as you.

CROFTS [*greatly reassured*] Of course you are; and a very good thing too! What harm does it do after all? [*Rallying her jocularly*] So you dont think me such a scoundrel now you come to think it over. Eh?

VIVIE I have shared profits with you; and I admitted you just now to the familiarity of knowing what I think of you.

CROFTS [*with serious friendliness*] To be sure you did. You wont find me a bad sort: I dont go in for being superfine intellectually; but Ive plenty of honest human feeling; and the old Crofts breed comes out in a sort of instinctive hatred of anything low, in which I'm sure youll sympathize with me. Believe me, Miss Vivie, the world isnt such a bad place as the croakers make out. As long as you dont fly openly in the face of society, society doesnt ask any inconvenient questions; and it makes precious short work of the cads who do. There are no secrets better kept than the secrets everybody guesses. In the class of people I can introduce you to, no lady or gentleman would so far forget themselves as to discuss my business affairs or your mother's. No man can offer you a safer position.

VIVIE [*studying him curiously*] I suppose you really think youre getting on famously with me.

CROFTS Well, I hope I may flatter myself that you think better of me than you did at first.

VIVIE [*quietly*] I hardly find you worth thinking about at all now. When I think of the society that tolerates you, and the laws that protect you! when I think of how helpless nine out of ten young girls would be in the hands of you and my mother! the unmentionable woman and her capitalist bully—

CROFTS [*livid*] Damn you!

VIVIE   You need not. I feel among the damned already.

She raises the latch of the gate to open it and go out. He follows her and puts his hand heavily on the top bar to prevent its opening.

CROFTS [*panting with fury*]   Do you think I'll put up with this from you, you young devil?

VIVIE [*unmoved*]   Be quiet. Some one will answer the bell. [*Without flinching a step she strikes the bell with the back of her hand. It clangs harshly; and he starts back involuntarily. Almost immediately* FRANK *appears at the porch with his rifle*].

FRANK [*with cheerful politeness*]   Will you have the rifle, Viv; or shall I operate?

VIVIE   Frank: have you been listening?

FRANK [*coming down into the garden*]   Only for the bell, I assure you; so that you shouldn't have to wait. I think I shewed great insight into your character, Crofts.

CROFTS   For two pins I'd take that gun from you and break it across your head.

FRANK [*stalking him cautiously*]   Pray dont. I'm ever so careless in handling fire-arms. Sure to be a fatal accident, with a reprimand from the coroner's jury for my negligence.

VIVIE   Put the rifle away, Frank: it's quite unnecessary.

FRANK   Quite right, Viv. Much more sports-manlike to catch him in a trap. [CROFTS, *understanding the insult, makes a threatening movement*]. Crofts: there are fifteen cartridges in the magazine here; and I am a dead shot at the present distance and at an object of your size.

CROFTS   Oh, you neednt be afraid. I'm not going to touch you.

FRANK   Ever so magnanimous of you un-der the circumstances! Thank you!

CROFTS   I'll just tell you this before I go. It may interest you, since youre so fond of one another. Allow me, Mister Frank, to introduce you to your half-sister, the eldest daughter of the Reverend Samuel Gardner. Miss Vivie: your half-brother.

Good morning. [*He goes out through the gate and along the road*].

FRANK [*after a pause of stupefaction, rais-ing the rifle*]   Youll testify before the cor-oner that it's an accident, Viv. [*He takes aim at the retreating figure of* CROFTS. VIVIE *seizes the muzzle and pulls it round against her breast*].

VIVIE   Fire now. You may.

FRANK [*dropping his end of the rifle hast-ily*]   Stop! take care. [*She lets it go. It falls on the turf*] Oh, youve given your little boy such a turn. Suppose it had gone off! ugh! [*He sinks on the garden seat, overcome*].

VIVIE   Suppose it had: do you think it would not have been a relief to have some sharp physical pain tearing through me?

FRANK [*coaxingly*]   Take it ever so easy, dear Viv. Remember: even if the rifle scared that fellow into telling the truth for the first time in his life, that only makes us the babes in the wood in ear-nest. [*He holds out his arms to her*]. Come and be covered up with leaves again.

VIVIE [*with a cry of disgust*]   Ah, not that, not that. You make all my flesh creep.

FRANK   Why, whats the matter?

VIVIE   Goodbye. [*She makes for the gate*].

FRANK [*jumping up*]   Hallo! Stop! Viv! Viv! [*She turns in the gateway*] Where are you going to? Where shall we find you?

VIVIE   At Honoria Fraser's chambers, 67 Chancery Lane, for the rest of my life. [*She goes off quickly in the opposite di-rection to that taken by* CROFTS].

FRANK   But I say—wait—dash it! [*He runs after her*].

Act Four

Honoria Fraser's chambers in Chancery Lane. An office at the top of New Stone Buildings, with a plate-glass window, distempered walls, electric light, and a patent stove. Saturday afternoon. The chimneys of Lincoln's Inn and the west-ern sky beyond are seen through the window. There is a double writing-table in the middle of the room, with a cigar box, ash pans, and a portable electric reading lamp almost snowed up in heaps of papers and books. This table has knee holes and chairs right and left and is very untidy. The clerk's desk, closed and tidy, with its high stool, is against the wall, near a door communicating with the inner rooms. In the opposite wall is the door leading to the public corridor. Its upper panel is of opaque glass, lettered in black on the outside, FRASER AND WARREN. *A baize screen hides the corner between this door and the window.*

FRANK, *in a fashionable light-colored coaching suit, with his stick, gloves, and white hat in his hands, is pacing up and down the office. Somebody tries the door with a key.*

FRANK [*calling*] Come in. It's not locked.

VIVIE *comes in, in her hat and jacket. She stops and stares at him.*

VIVIE [*sternly*] What are you doing here?

FRANK Waiting to see you. Ive been here for hours. Is this the way you attend to your business? [*He puts his hat and stick on the table, and perches himself with a vault on the clerk's stool, looking at her with every appearance of being in a specially restless, teasing flippant mood*].

VIVIE Ive been away exactly twenty minutes for a cup of tea. [*She takes off her hat and jacket and hangs them up behind the screen*]. How did you get in?

FRANK The staff had not left when I arrived. He's gone to play cricket on Primrose Hill. Why dont you employ a woman, and give your sex a chance?

VIVIE What have you come for?

FRANK [*springing off the stool and coming close to her*] Viv: lets go and enjoy the Saturday half-holiday somewhere, like the staff. What do you say to Richmond, and then a music hall, and a jolly supper?

VIVIE Cant afford it. I shall put in another six hours work before I go to bed.

FRANK Cant afford it, cant we? Aha! Look here. [*He takes out a handful of sovereigns and makes them chink*]. Gold, Viv: gold!

VIVIE Where did you get it?

FRANK Gambling, Viv: gambling. Poker.

VIVIE Pah! It's meaner than stealing it. No: I'm not coming. [*She sits down to work at the table, with her back to the glass door, and begins turning over the papers*].

FRANK [*remonstrating piteously*] But, my dear Viv, I want to talk to you ever so seriously.

VIVIE Very well: sit down in Honoria's chair and talk here. I like ten minutes chat after tea. [*He murmurs*]. No use groaning: I'm inexorable. [*He takes the opposite seat disconsolately*]. Pass that cigar box, will you?

FRANK [*pushing the cigar box across*] Nasty womanly habit. Nice men dont do it any longer.

VIVIE Yes: they object to the smell in the office; and weve had to take to cigarets. See! [*She opens the box and takes out a cigaret, which she lights. She offers him one; but he shakes his head with a wry face. She settles herself comfortably in her chair, smoking*]. Go ahead.

FRANK Well, I want to know what youve done—what arrangements youve made.

VIVIE Everything was settled twenty minutes after I arrived here. Honoria has found the business too much for her this year; and she was on the point of sending for me and proposing a partnership when I walked in and told her I hadnt a farthing in the world. So I installed myself and packed her off for a fortnight's holiday. What happened at Haslemere when I left?

FRANK Nothing at all. I said youd gone to town on particular business.

VIVIE Well?

FRANK Well, either they were too flabbergasted to say anything, or else Crofts had prepared your mother. Anyhow, she didnt say anything; and Crofts didnt say anything; and Praddy only stared. After tea they got up and went; and Ive not seen them since.

VIVIE [*nodding placidly with one eye on a wreath of smoke*] Thats all right.

FRANK [*looking round disparagingly*] Do you intend to stick in this confounded place?

VIVIE [*blowing the wreath decisively away, and sitting straight up*] Yes. These two days have given me back all my strength and self-possession. I will never take a holiday again as long as I live.

FRANK [*with a very wry face*] Mps! You look quite happy. And as hard as nails.

VIVIE [*grimly*] Well for me that I am!

FRANK [*rising*] Look here, Viv: we must have an explanation. We parted the other day under a complete misunderstanding. [*He sits on the table, close to her*].

VIVIE [*putting away the cigaret*] Well: clear it up.

FRANK You remember what Crofts said?

VIVIE Yes.

FRANK That revelation was supposed to bring about a complete change in the nature of our feeling for one another. It placed us on the footing of brother and sister.

VIVIE Yes.

FRANK Have you ever had a brother?

VIVIE No.

FRANK Then you dont know what being brother and sister feels like? Now I have lots of sisters; and the fraternal feeling is quite familiar to me. I assure you my feeling for you is not the least in the world like it. The girls will go t h e i r way; I will go mine; and we shant care if we never see one another again. Thats brother and sister. But as to you, I cant be easy if I have to pass a week without seeing you. Thats not brother and sister. It's exactly what I felt an hour before Crofts made his revelation. In short, dear Viv, it's love's young dream.

VIVIE [*bitingly*] The same feeling, Frank, that brought your father to my mother's feet. Is that it?

FRANK [*so revolted that he slips off the table for a moment*] I very strongly object, Viv, to have my feelings compared to any which the Reverend Samuel is capable of harboring; and I object still more to a comparison of you to your mother. [*Resuming his perch*]. Besides, I dont believe the story. I have taxed my father with it, and obtained from him what I consider tantamount to a denial.

VIVIE What did he say?

FRANK He said he was sure there must be some mistake.

VIVIE Do you believe him?

FRANK I am prepared to take his word as against Crofts'.

VIVIE Does it make any difference? I mean in your imagination or conscience; for of course it makes no real difference.

FRANK [*shaking his head*] None whatever to me.

VIVIE Nor to me.

FRANK [*staring*] But this is ever so surprising! [*He goes back to his chair*]. I thought our whole relations were altered in your imagination and conscience, as you put it, the moment those words were out of that brute's muzzle.

VIVIE No: it was not that. I didnt believe him. I only wish I could.

FRANK Eh?

VIVIE I think brother and sister would be a very suitable relation for us.

FRANK You really mean that?

VIVIE Yes. It's the only relation I care for, even if we could afford any other. I mean that.

FRANK [*raising his eyebrows like one on whom a new light has dawned, and rising with quite an effusion of chivalrous sentiment*] My dear Viv: why didnt you say so before? I am ever so sorry for persecuting you. I understand, of course.

VIVIE [*puzzled*] Understand what?

FRANK Oh, I'm not a fool in the ordinary sense: only in the Scriptural sense of doing all the things the wise man declared to be folly, after trying them himself on the most extensive scale. I see I am no longer Vivvums's little boy. Dont be alarmed: I shall never call you Vivvums again—at least unless you get tired of your new little boy, whoever he may be.

VIVIE My new little boy!

FRANK [*with conviction*] Must be a new little boy. Always happens that way. No other way, in fact.

VIVIE None that you know of, fortunately for you.

Someone knocks at the door.

FRANK My curse upon yon caller, whoe'er he be!

VIVIE It's Praed. He's going to Italy and wants to say goodbye. I asked him to call this afternoon. Go and let him in.

FRANK We can continue our conversation after his departure for Italy. I'll stay him out. [*He goes to the door and opens it*]. How are you, Praddy? Delighted to see you. Come in.

PRAED, *dressed for travelling, comes in, in high spirits.*

PRAED How do you do, Miss Warren? [*She presses his hand cordially, though a certain sentimentality in his high spirits jars on her*]. I start in an hour from Holborn Viaduct. I wish I could persuade you to try Italy.

VIVIE What for?

PRAED Why, to saturate yourself with beauty and romance, of course.

VIVIE, *with a shudder, turns her chair to the table, as if the work waiting for her there were a support to her.* PRAED *sits opposite to her.* FRANK *places a chair near* VIVIE, *and drops lazily and carelessly into it, talking at her over his shoulder.*

FRANK No use, Praddy. Viv is a little Philistine. She is indifferent to my romance, and insensible to my beauty.

VIVIE Mr Praed: once for all, there is no beauty and no romance in life for me. Life is what it is; and I am prepared to take it as it is.

PRAED [*enthusiastically*] You will not say that if you come with me to Verona and on to Venice. You will cry with delight at living in such a beautiful world.

FRANK This is most eloquent, Praddy. Keep it up.

PRAED Oh, I assure you *I* have cried—I shall cry again, I hope—at fifty! At your age, Miss Warren, you would not need to go so far as Verona. Your spirits would absolutely fly up at the mere sight of Ostend. You would be charmed with the gaiety, the vivacity, the happy air of Brussels.

VIVIE [*springing up with an exclamation of loathing*] Agh!

PRAED [*rising*] Whats the matter?

FRANK [*rising*] Hallo, Viv!

VIVIE [*to* PRAED, *with deep reproach*] Can you find no better example of your beauty and romance than Brussels to talk to me about?

PRAED [*puzzled*] Of course it's very different from Verona. I dont suggest for a moment that—

VIVIE [*bitterly*] Probably the beauty and romance come to much the same in both places.

PRAED [*completely sobered and much concerned*] My dear Miss Warren: I—[*looking inquiringly at Frank*] Is anything the matter?

FRANK She thinks your enthusiasm frivolous, Praddy. She's had ever such a serious call.

VIVIE [*sharply*] Hold your tongue, Frank. Dont be silly.

FRANK [*sitting down*] Do you call this good manners, Praed?

PRAED [*anxious and considerate*] Shall I take him away, Miss Warren? I feel sure we have disturbed you at your work.

VIVIE Sit down: I'm not ready to go back to work yet. [PRAED *sits*]. You both think I have an attack of nerves. Not a bit of it. But there are two subjects I want dropped, if you dont mind. One of them [*to* FRANK] is love's young dream in any shape or form: the other [*to* PRAED] is the romance and beauty of life, especially Ostend and the gaiety of Brussels. You are welcome to any illusions you may have left on these subjects: I have none. If we three are to remain friends, I must be treated as a woman of business, permanently single [*to* FRANK] and permanently unromantic [*to* PRAED].

FRANK I also shall remain permanently

single until you change your mind. Praddy: change the subject. Be eloquent about something else.

PRAED [*diffidently*] I'm afraid theres nothing else in the world that I c a n talk about. The Gospel of Art is the only one I can preach. I know Miss Warren is a great devotee of the Gospel of Getting On; but we cant discuss that without hurting your feelings, Frank, since you are determined not to get on.

FRANK Oh, dont mind my feelings. Give me some improving advice by all means: it does me ever so much good. Have another try to make a successful man of me, Viv. Come: lets have it all: energy, thrift, foresight, self-respect, character. Dont you hate people who have no character, Viv?

VIVIE [*wincing*] Oh, stop, stop: let us have no more of that horrible cant. Mr Praed: if there are really only those two gospels in the world, we had better all kill ourselves; for the same taint is in both, through and through.

FRANK [*looking critically at her*] There is a touch of poetry about you today, Viv, which has hitherto been lacking.

PRAED [*remonstrating*] My dear Frank: arnt you a little unsympathetic?

VIVIE [*merciless to herself*] No: it's good for me. It keeps me from being sentimental.

FRANK [*bantering her*] Checks your strong natural propensity that way, dont it?

VIVIE [*almost hysterically*] Oh yes: go on: dont spare me. I was sentimental for one moment in my life—beautifully sentimental—by moonlight; and now—

FRANK [*quickly*] I say, Viv: take care. Dont give yourself away.

VIVIE Oh, do you think Mr Praed does not know all about my mother? [*Turning on* PRAED] You had better have told me that morning, Mr Praed. You are very old fashioned in your delicacies, after all.

PRAED Surely it is you who are a little old fashioned in your prejudices, Miss Warren. I feel bound to tell you, speaking as an artist, and believing that the most intimate human relationships are far beyond and above the scope of the law, that though I know that your mother is an unmarried woman, I do not respect her the less on that account. I respect her more.

FRANK [*airily*] Hear! Hear!

VIVIE [*staring at him*] Is that a l l you know?

PRAED Certainly that is all.

VIVIE Then you neither of you know anything. Your guesses are innocence itself compared to the truth.

PRAED [*rising, startled and indignant, and preserving his politeness with an effort*] I hope not. [*More emphatically*] I hope not, Miss Warren.

FRANK [*whistles*] Whew!

VIVIE You are not making it easy for me to tell you, Mr Praed.

PRAED [*his chivalry drooping before their conviction*] If there is anything worse—that is, anything else—are you sure you are right to tell us, Miss Warren?

VIVIE I am sure that if I had the courage I should spend the rest of my life in telling everybody—stamping and branding it into them until they all felt their part in its abomination as I feel mine. There is nothing I despise more than the wicked convention that protects these things by forbidding a woman to mention them. And yet I cant tell you. The two infamous words that describe what my mother is are ringing in my ears and struggling on my tongue; but I cant utter them: the shame of them is too horrible for me. [*She buries her face in her hands. The two men, astonished, stare at one another and then at her. She raises her head again desperately and snatches a sheet of paper and a pen*]. Here: let me draft you a prospectus.

FRANK Oh, she's mad. Do you hear, Viv? mad. Come! pull yourself together.

VIVIE You shall see. [*She writes*]. "Paid up capital: not less than £40,000 standing in the name of Sir George Crofts, Baronet, the chief shareholder. Premises at Brussels, Ostend, Vienna and Budapest. Managing director: Mrs Warren"; and now dont let us forget h e r qualifications: the two words. [*She writes the words and pushes the paper to them*]. There! Oh no: dont read it: dont! [*She snatches it back and tears it to pieces; then seizes her head in her hands and hides her face on the table*].

FRANK, *who has watched the writing over his shoulder, and opened his eyes very widely at it, takes a card from his pocket; scribbles the two words on it; and silently hands it to* PRAED, *who reads it with amazement, and hides it hastily in his pocket.*

FRANK [*whispering tenderly*] Viv, dear: thats all right. I read what you wrote: so did Praddy. We understand. And we remain, as this leaves us at present, yours ever so devotedly.

PRAED We do indeed, Miss Warren. I declare you are the most splendidly courageous woman I ever met.

This sentimental compliment braces VIVIE. *She throws it away from her with an impatient shake, and forces herself to stand up, though not without some support from the table.*

FRANK Dont stir, Viv, if you dont want to. Take it easy.

VIVIE Thank you. You can always depend on me for two things: not to cry and not to faint. [*She moves a few steps towards the door of the inner room, and stops close to* PRAED *to say*] I shall need much more courage than that when I tell my mother that we have come to the parting of the ways. Now I must go into the next room for a moment to make myself neat again, if you dont mind.

PRAED Shall we go away?

VIVIE No: I'll be back presently. Only for a moment. [*She goes into the other room,* PRAED *opening the door for her*].

PRAED What an amazing revelation! I'm extremely disappointed in Crofts: I am indeed.

FRANK I'm not in the least. I feel he's perfectly accounted for at last. But what a facer for me, Praddy! I cant marry her now.

PRAED [*sternly*] Frank! [*The two look at one another,* FRANK *unruffled,* PRAED *deeply indignant*]. Let me tell you, Gardner, that if you desert her now you will behave very despicably.

FRANK Good old Praddy! Ever chivalrous! But you mistake: it's not the moral aspect of the case: it's the money aspect. I really cant bring myself to touch the old woman's money now?

PRAED And was that what you were going to marry on?

FRANK What else? *I* havnt any money, nor the smallest turn for making it. If I married Viv now she would have to support me; and I should cost her more than I am worth.

PRAED But surely a clever bright fellow like you can make something by your own brains.

FRANK Oh yes, a little [*He takes out his money again*]. I made all that yesterday in an hour and a half. But I made it in a highly speculative business. No, dear Praddy: even if Bessie and Georgina marry millionaires and the governor dies after cutting them off with a shilling, I shall have only four hundred a year. And he wont die until he's three score and ten: he hasnt originality enough. I shall be on short allowance for the next twenty years. No short allowance for Viv, if I can help it. I withdraw gracefully and leave the field to the gilded youth of England. So thats settled. I shant worry her about it: I'll just send her a little note after we're gone. She'll understand.

PRAED [*grasping his hand*] Good fellow, Frank! I heartily beg your pardon. But must you never see her again?

FRANK Never see her again! Hang it all, be reasonable. I shall come along as often as possible, and be her brother. I can n o t understand the absurd consequences you romantic people expect from the most ordinary transactions. [*A knock at the door*]. I wonder who this is. Would you mind opening the door? If it's a client it will look more respectable than if I appeared.

PRAED Certainly. [*He goes to the door and opens it.* FRANK *sits down in* VIVIE's *chair to scribble a note*]. My dear Kitty: come in: come in.

MRS WARREN *comes in, looking apprehensively round for* VIVIE. *She has done her best to make herself matronly and dignified. The brilliant hat is replaced by a sober bonnet, and the gay blouse covered by a costly black silk mantle. She is pitiably anxious and ill at ease: evidently panic-stricken.*

MRS WARREN [*to* FRANK] What! Y o u r e here, are you?

FRANK [*turning in his chair from his writing, but not rising*] Here, and charmed to see you. You come like a breath of spring.

MRS WARREN Oh, get out with your nonsense. [*In a low voice*] Wheres Vivie?

FRANK *points expressively to the door of the inner room, but says nothing.*

MRS WARREN [*sitting down suddenly and almost beginning to cry*] Praddy: wont she see me, dont you think?

PRAED My dear Kitty: dont distress yourself. Why should she not?

MRS WARREN Oh, you never can see why not: youre too innocent. Mr Frank: did she say anything to you?

FRANK [*folding his note*] She m u s t see you, i f [*very expressively*] you wait til she comes in.

MRS WARREN [*frightened*] Why shouldnt I wait?

FRANK *looks quizzically at her; puts his note carefully on the inkbottle, so that* VIVIE *cannot fail to find it when next she dips her pen; then rises and devotes his attention entirely to her.*

FRANK My dear Mrs Warren: suppose you were a sparrow—ever so tiny and pretty a sparrow hopping in the roadway—and you saw a steam roller coming in your direction, would you wait for it?

MRS WARREN Oh, dont bother me with your sparrows. What did she run away from Haslemere like that for?

FRANK I'm afraid she'll tell you if you rashly await her return.

MRS WARREN Do you want me to go away?

FRANK No: I always want you to stay. But I a d v i s e you to go away.

MRS WARREN What! And never see her again!

FRANK Precisely.

MRS WARREN [*crying again*] Praddy: dont let him be cruel to me. [*She hastily checks her tears and wipes her eyes*]. She'll be so angry if she sees Ive been crying.

FRANK [*with a touch of real compassion in his airy tenderness*] You know that Praddy is the soul of kindness, Mrs Warren. Praddy: what do you say? Go or stay?

PRAED [*to* MRS WARREN] I really should be very sorry to cause you unnecessary pain; but I think perhaps you had better not wait. The fact is—[VIVIE *is heard at the inner door*].

FRANK Sh! Too late. She's coming.

MRS WARREN Dont tell her I was crying. [VIVIE *comes in. She stops gravely on seeing* MRS WARREN, *who greets her with hysterical cheerfulness*]. Well, dearie. So here you are at last.

VIVIE I am glad you have come: I want to speak to you. You said you were going, Frank, I think.

FRANK Yes. Will you come with me, Mrs Warren? What do you say to a trip to Richmond, and the theatre in the evening? There is safety in Richmond. No steam roller there.

VIVIE Nonsense, Frank. My mother will stay here.

MRS WARREN [*scared*] I dont know: perhaps I'd better go. We're disturbing you at your work.

VIVIE [*with quiet decision*] Mr Praed: please take Frank away. Sit down, mother. [MRS WARREN *obeys helplessly*].

PRAED Come, Frank. Goodbye, Miss Vivie.

VIVIE [*shaking hands*] Goodbye. A pleasant trip.

PRAED Thank you: thank you. I hope so.

FRANK [*to* MRS WARREN] Goodbye: youd ever so much better have taken my advice. [*He shakes hands with her. Then airily to* VIVIE] Byebye, Viv.

VIVIE Goodbye. [*He goes out gaily without shaking hands with her*].

PRAED [*sadly*] Goodbye, Kitty.

MRS WARREN [*snivelling*] —oobye!

PRAED *goes.* VIVIE, *composed and extremely grave, sits down in Honoria's chair, and waits for her mother to speak.* MRS WARREN, *dreading a pause, loses no time in beginning.*

MRS WARREN Well, Vivie, what did you go away like that for without saying a word to me? How could you do such a thing! And what have you done to poor George? I wanted him to come with me; but he shuffled out of it. I could see that he was quite afraid of you. Only fancy: he wanted me not to come. As if [*trembling*] I should be afraid of you, dearie. [VIVIE'S *gravity deepens*]. But of course I told him it was all settled and comfortable between us, and that we were on the best of terms. [*She breaks down*]. Vivie: whats the meaning of this? [*She produces a commercial envelope, and fumbles at the enclosure with trembling fingers*]. I got it from the bank this morning.

VIVIE It is my month's allowance. They sent it to me as usual the other day. I simply sent it back to be placed to your credit, and asked them to send you the lodgment receipt. In future I shall support myself.

MRS WARREN [*not daring to understand*] Wasnt it enough? Why didnt you tell me? [*With a cunning gleam in her eye*] I'll double it: I was intending to double it. Only let me know how much you want.

VIVIE You know very well that that has nothing to do with it. From this time I go my own way in my own business and among my own friends. And you will go yours. [*She rises*]. Goodbye.

MRS WARREN [*rising, appalled*] Goodbye?

VIVIE Yes: Goodbye. Come: dont let us make a useless scene: you understand perfectly well. Sir George Crofts has told me the whole business.

MRS WARREN [*angrily*] Silly old—[*She swallows an epithet, and turns white at the narrowness of her escape from uttering it*].

VIVIE Just so.

MRS WARREN He ought to have his tongue cut out. But I thought it was ended: you said you didnt mind.

VIVIE [*steadfastly*] Excuse me: I d o mind.

MRS WARREN But I explained—

VIVIE You explained how it came about. You did not tell me that it is still going on [*She sits*].

MRS WARREN, *silenced for a moment, looks forlornly at* VIVIE, *who waits, secretly hoping that the combat is over. But the cunning expression comes back into* MRS WARREN'S *face; and she bends across the table, sly and urgent, half whispering.*

MRS WARREN Vivie: do you know how rich I am?

VIVIE I have no doubt you are very rich.

MRS WARREN But you dont know all that that means: youre too young. It means a new dress every day; it means theatres and balls every night; it means having the pick of all the gentlemen in Europe at your feet; it means a lovely house and plenty of servants; it means the choicest of eating and drinking; it means everything you like, everything you want, everything you can think of. And what are you here? A mere drudge, toiling and moiling early and late for your bare living and two cheap dresses a year. Think over it. [*Soothingly*] Youre shocked, I know. I can enter into your feelings; and I think they do you credit; but trust me, nobody will blame you: you may take my word for that. I know what young girls are; and I know youll think better of it when youve turned it over in your mind.

VIVIE So thats how it's done, is it? You must have said all that to many a woman, mother, to have it so pat.

MRS WARREN [*passionately*] What harm

am I asking you to do? [VIVIE *turns away contemptuously*. MRS WARREN *continues desperately*] Vivie: listen to me: you dont understand: youve been taught wrong on purpose: you dont know what the world is really like.

VIVIE [*arrested*] Taught wrong on purpose! What do you mean?

MRS WARREN I mean that youre throwing away all your chances for nothing. You think that people are what they pretend to be: that the way you were taught at school and college to think right and proper is the way things really are. But it's not: it's all only a pretence, to keep the cowardly slavish common run of people quiet. Do you want to find that out, like other women, at forty, when youve thrown yourself away and lost your chances; or wont you take it in good time now from your own mother, that loves you and swears to you that it's truth: gospel truth? [*Urgently*] Vivie: the big people, the clever people, the managing people, all know it. They do as I do, and think what I think. I know plenty of them. I know them to speak to, to introduce you to, to make friends of for you. I dont mean anything wrong: thats what you dont understand: your head is full of ignorant ideas about me. What do the people that taught you know about life or about people like me? When did they ever meet me, or speak to me, or let anyone tell them about me? the fools! Would they ever have done anything for you if I hadnt paid them? Havnt I told you that I want you to be respectable? Havnt I brought you up to be respectable? And how can you keep it up without my money and my influence and Lizzie's friends? Cant you see that youre cutting your own throat as well as breaking my heart in turning your back on me?

VIVIE I recognize the Crofts philosophy of life, mother. I heard it all from him that day at the Gardners'.

MRS WARREN You think I want to force that played-out old sot on you! I dont, Vivie: on my oath I dont.

VIVIE It would not matter if you did: you would not succeed. [MRS WARREN *winces, deeply hurt by the implied indifference towards her affectionate intention*. VIVIE, *neither understanding this nor concerning herself about it, goes on calmly*] Mother: you dont at all know the sort of person I am. I dont object to Crofts more than to any other coarsely built man of his class. To tell you the truth, I rather admire him for being strong-minded enough to enjoy himself in his own way and make plenty of money instead of living the usual shooting, hunting, dining-out, tailoring, loafing life of his set merely because all the rest do it. And I'm perfectly aware that if I'd been in the same circumstances as my aunt Liz, I'd have done exactly what she did. I dont think I'm more prejudiced or straitlaced than you: I think I'm less. I'm certain I'm less sentimental. I know very well that fashionable morality is all a pretence, and that if I took your money and devoted the rest of my life to spending it fashionably, I might be as worthless and vicious as the silliest woman could possibly want to be without having a word said to me about it. But I dont want to be worthless. I shouldnt enjoy trotting about the park to advertize my dressmaker and carriage builder, or being bored at the opera to shew off a shopwindowful of diamonds.

MRS WARREN [*bewildered*] But—

VIVIE Wait a moment: Ive not done. Tell me why you continue your business now that you are independent of it. Your sister, you told me, has left all that behind her. Why dont you do the same?

MRS WARREN Oh, it's all very easy for Liz: she likes good society, and has the air of being a lady. Imagine me in a cathedral town! Why, the very rooks in the trees would find me out even if I could stand the dulness of it. I must have work and excitement, or I should go melancholy mad. And what else is there for me to do? The life suits me: I'm fit for it and not for anything else. If I didnt do it somebody else would; so I dont do any real harm by it. And then it brings in money; and I like making money. No: it's no use: I cant give it up—not for anybody. But what need you know about it? I'll never mention it. I'll keep Crofts away. I'll not trouble you much: you see I have to be constantly running about from one place to another. Youll be quit of me altogether when I die.

VIVIE   No: I am my mother's daughter. I am like you: I must have work, and must make more money than I spend. But my work is not your work, and my way not your way. We must part. It will not make much difference to us: instead of meeting one another for perhaps a few months in twenty years, we shall never meet: thats all.

MRS WARREN [*her voice stifled in tears*] Vivie: I meant to have been more with you: I did indeed.

VIVIE   It's no use, mother: I am not to be changed by a few cheap tears and entreaties any more than you are, I daresay.

MRS WARREN [*wildly*] Oh, you call a mother's tears cheap.

VIVIE   They cost you nothing; and you ask me to give you the peace and quietness of my whole life in exchange for them. What use would my company be to you if you could get it? What have we two in common that could make either of us happy together?

MRS WARREN [*lapsing recklessly into her dialect*] We're mother and daughter. I want my daughter. Ive a right to you. Who is to care for me when I'm old? Plenty of girls have taken to me like daughters and cried at leaving me; but I let them all go because I had you to look forward to. I kept myself lonely for you. Youve no right to turn on me now and refuse to do your duty as a daughter.

VIVIE [*jarred and antagonized by the echo of the slums in her mother's voice*] My duty as a daughter! I thought we should come to that presently. Now once for all, mother, you want a daughter and Frank wants a wife. I dont want a mother; and

I dont want a husband. I have spared neither Frank nor myself in sending him about his business. Do you think I will spare you?

MRS WARREN [*violently*] Oh, I know the sort you are: no mercy for yourself or anyone else. *I* know. My experience has done that for me anyhow: I can tell the pious, canting, hard, selfish woman when I meet her. Well, keep yourself to yourself: *I* dont want you. But listen to this. Do you know what I would do with you if you were a baby again? aye, as sure as there's a Heaven above us.

VIVIE   Strangle me, perhaps.

MRS WARREN   No: I'd bring you up to be a real daughter to me, and not what you are now, with your pride and your prejudices and the college education you stole from me: yes, stole: deny it if you can: what was it but stealing? I'd bring you up in my own house, I would.

VIVIE [*quietly*]   In one of your own houses.

MRS WARREN [*screaming*] Listen to her! listen to how she spits on her mother's grey hairs! Oh, may you live to have your own daughter tear and trample on you as you have trampled on me. And you will: you will. No woman ever had luck with a mother's curse on her.

VIVIE   I wish you wouldnt rant, mother. It only hardens me. Come: I suppose I am the only young woman you ever had in your power that you did good to. Dont spoil it all now.

MRS WARREN   Yes, Heaven forgive me, it's true; and you are the only one that ever turned on me. Oh, the injustice of it! the injustice! the injustice! I always wanted to be a good woman. I tried honest work; and I was slave-driven until I cursed the day I ever heard of honest work. I was a good mother; and because I made my daughter a good woman she turns me out as if I was a leper. Oh, if I only had my life to live over again! I'd talk to that lying clergyman in the school. From this time forth, so help me Heaven in my last hour, I'll do wrong and nothing but wrong. And I'll prosper on it.

VIVIE   Yes: it's better to choose your line and go through with it. If I had been you, mother, I might have done as you did; but I should not have lived one life and believed in another. You are a conventional woman at heart. That is why I am bidding you goodbye now. I am right, am I not?

MRS WARREN [*taken aback*] Right to throw away all my money?

VIVIE   No: right to get rid of you? I should be a fool not to! Isnt that so?

MRS WARREN [*sulkily*] Oh well, yes, if you come to that, I suppose you are. But Lord help the world if everybody took to doing the right thing! And now I'd better go than stay where I'm not wanted. [*She turns to the door*].

VIVIE [*kindly*] Wont you shake hands?

MRS WARREN [*after looking at her fiercely for a moment with a savage impulse to strike her*] No, thank you. Goodbye.

VIVIE [*matter-of-factly*] Goodbye. [MRS WARREN *goes out, slamming the door behind her. The strain on* VIVIE'S *face relaxes; her grave expression breaks up into one of joyous content; her breath goes out in a half sob, half laugh of intense relief. She goes buoyantly to her place at the writing-table; pushes the electric lamp out of the way; pulls over a great sheaf of papers; and is in the act of dipping her pen in the ink when she finds* FRANK'S *note. She opens it unconcernedly and reads it quickly, giving a little laugh at some quaint turn of expression in it*]. And goodbye, Frank. [*She tears the note up and tosses the pieces into the wastepaper basket without a second thought. Then she goes at her work with a plunge, and soon becomes absorbed in its figures*].